THE PSYCHOLOGY

THE CONTEXTS OF BEHAVIOR

PSYCHOLOGY

THE CONTEXTS OF BEHAVIOR

LARUE ALLEN
Michigan State University

JOHN W. SANTROCK
University of Texas, Dallas

WCB Brown &
Benchmark
PUBLISHERS

Madison, Wisconsin • Dubuque, Iowa • Indianapolis, Indiana
Melbourne, Australia • Oxford, England

Book Team

Editor *Michael Lange*
Developmental Editor *Sheralee Connors*
Production Editor *Debra DeBord*
Designer *Mark Elliot Christianson*
Art Editor *Rachel Imsland*
Photo Editor *Judi L. David*
Permissions Editor *Gail I. Wheatley*
Art Processor *Joyce E. Watters*

WCB Brown & Benchmark
PUBLISHERS
A Division of Wm. C. Brown Communications, Inc.

Vice President and General Manager *Thomas E. Doran*
Executive Managing Editor *Ed Bartell*
Executive Editor *Edgar J. Laube*
Director of Marketing *Kathy Law Laube*
National Sales Manager *Eric Ziegler*
Marketing Manager *Steven Yetter*
Advertising Manager *Jodi Rymer*
Managing Editor, Production *Colleen A. Yonda*
Manager of Visuals and Design *Faye M. Schilling*
Design Manager *Jac Tilton*
Art Manager *Janice Roerig*
Production Editorial Manager *Vickie Putman Caughron*
Publishing Services Manager *Karen J. Slaght*
Permissions/Records Manager *Connie Allendorf*

Wm. C. Brown Communications, Inc.

Chairman Emeritus *Wm. C. Brown*
Chairman and Chief Executive Officer *Mark C. Falb*
President and Chief Operating Officer *G. Franklin Lewis*
Corporate Vice President, Operations *Beverly Kolz*
Corporate Vice President, President of WCB Manufacturing *Roger Meyer*

Cover photo: Vincent van Gogh Foundation/Van Gogh Museum, Amsterdam

The credits section for this book begins on page 593 and is considered an extension of the copyright page.

BRIEF CONTENTS

CONTENTS

CHAPTER 4

States of Consciousness 101

CHAPTER 5

Learning 123

CHAPTER 6

Memory 151

CHAPTER 7

Thinking, Language, and Intelligence 177

CHAPTER

8

Child Development 215

CHAPTER

9

Adolescence, Adult Development, and Aging 257

CHAPTER

10

Gender and Sexuality 299

CHAPTER

11

Motivation and Emotion 335

CHAPTER

12

Personality 363

CHAPTER

13

Abnormal Psychology 395

CHAPTER

14

Therapies 423

CHAPTER 15

Stress and Health 453

CHAPTER 16

Social Psychology 489

PREFACE

The approach of this textbook is different from others. Throughout the book you will read about how the contexts in which we live influence the way we think, feel, and behave. Other authors have begun to include bits and pieces of contexts—culture, ethnicity, and gender—in introductory psychology textbooks. *Psychology: The Contexts of Behavior* goes far beyond these books by examining psychology with a sociocultural lens throughout its contents. For too long, psychology and introductory psychology texts were the province of a single culture—American—a single ethnic group—White American—a single sex—male—and a single social class—middle. Black Americans, Hispanic Americans, Asian Americans, Native Americans, people from other cultures, females, individuals from impoverished backgrounds, and other people from minority groups—both students and professors—have examined introductory psychology textbooks and have been unable to find discussions of many issues they confront in their everyday lives. Indeed, if you were to read the index of virtually every other introductory psychology text, you would find that "ethnicity" has no entries at all or, at most, a few.

Ethnicity, along with culture and gender, provides an important sociocultural lens for viewing human behavior. The sociocultural approach provides a critical perspective for analyzing and helping us understand who we are and how we can get along with people. Although we believe that introductory psychology textbooks are long overdue for a sociocultural overhaul, we also believe that, in its century-long existence, psychology has produced many theories and facts that should continue to be presented to students. Thus, psychology's basic theories and facts are presented just as in other introductory psychology texts, but where appropriate—in every chapter—how people think, feel, and behave is described, analyzed, and probed through a sociocultural lens.

There is an old saying, "Don't throw out the baby with the bathwater." We didn't throw out the baby—we kept the basic theories and facts in psychology that have withstood the test of time. However, we recognized that sometimes the baby is Black, sometimes Hispanic, sometimes Asian, sometimes Native American, sometimes female, sometimes from another country and culture, sometimes gay or lesbian, and sometimes poor—and that these differences are often important.

Author LaRue Allen has spent her entire career as a psychologist struggling to make theories and intervention more applicable to diverse cultural groups and to curtail the tendency to label as deficient groups for which prevailing theories don't seem to work. She believes that the psychology of Blacks, Latinos, Asians, gays, lesbians, and other minority groups should not be completely teased apart from the psychology of mainstream, homogenized human beings but, rather, examined in concert with them. Author John Santrock has spent almost 3 decades disseminating psychological knowledge to undergraduates and is committed to an understanding of behavior that recognizes the richness of diversity and the limitations of our knowledge. They are united in the belief that a field that calls itself "the study of human behavior" should embrace *all* humans under its umbrella.

How do we weave the sociocultural approach into psychology? At the beginning of the book—in chapter 1—and at the end of the book—in an Epilogue ("Critical Thinking About Sociocultural Issues")—we extensively discuss the role of sociocultural contexts in understanding behavior. Many chapters open with an easy-to-read, intriguing portrayal of a particular aspect of our sociocultural existence. For example, chapter 1 begins with the penetrating saga of Alice Walker, who picked up the pieces of a shattered life and turned poverty and trauma into a celebration of the human spirit. Every chapter includes a discussion of the sociocultural worlds in which we live and of how these worlds influence the way we think, feel, and act. For example, chapter 2 ("Biological Foundations and the Brain") has a discussion of biological *and* cultural evolution and an analysis of race; chapter 8 ("Child Development") contains sections on cultural, social, class, and ethnic variations among families, as well as social policy and children's development; chapter 10 ("Gender and Sexuality") has extensive information about gender and ethnicity, the feminist perspective, and cultural dimensions of sexuality; chapter 14 ("Therapies") addresses the roles of culture, ethnicity, and gender in therapy; and chapter 15 ("Stress and Health") includes many ideas about how poverty, ethnicity, and culture influence how we cope and how healthy we are. Also, boxed inserts called "Sociocultural Worlds" appear one or more times in every chapter. A brief sampling of the Sociocultural Worlds boxes reveals their special emphasis on culture, ethnicity, and gender: chapter 1 ("Women and Ethnic Minorities in

Psychology"); chapter 4 ("Sociocultural Influences on Alcohol Abuse"); chapter 9 ("Being Female, Ethnic, and Old"); chapter 10 ("Gender Roles in Egypt and China"); chapter 13 ("Hispanic Women and Mental Health"); and chapter 16 ("The Changing Forms of Prejudice"). As can readily be seen in this brief glimpse, the sociocultural dimensions of mind and behavior are extensively discussed and woven throughout the book.

The Research Base of *Psychology: The Contexts of Behavior*

Our text offers a blend of classic and contemporary research presented in a lively and entertaining manner. This balance exists in each chapter. For example, chapter 7 ("Thinking, Language, and Intelligence") examines both the early makers of intelligence tests and the contemporary theorists who are paving the way for new insights into intelligence. In keeping with the sociocultural theme of the text, the roles of culture and ethnicity in intelligence are highlighted, including John Berry's cultural adaptation model of intelligence.

Psychology: The Contexts of Behavior is also extremely up-to-date. Scientific knowledge is expanding on many frontiers—especially in understanding the contexts of behavior—and in each chapter we have attempted to capture the excitement of these new discoveries as well as the classic studies that are the foundation of the discipline. The currency of the research is reflected in the references included in the book—more than 275 come from 1991, 1992, 1993, or *in press* sources alone.

The Learning System in *Psychology: The Contexts of Behavior*

Psychology: The Contexts of Behavior incorporates an effective and challenging learning system. This text was designed to enhance student comprehension and encourage critical thinking, not only about sociocultural issues but about many areas of psychology. We want students to think, to analyze, and to understand the information we present. Topics are explored in sufficient depth to challenge students, and the complex nature of psychology is presented in such a way as to encourage critical thinking skills.

However, we wanted not only to encourage thinking skills but also to use textbook pedagogy effectively to help students learn. Thus, a carefully designed pedagogical framework has been built into *Psychology: The Contexts of Behavior*. An OUTLINE at the beginning of each chapter shows the overall organization of the material. Following the outline is an easy-to-read introduction designed to interest students in the chapter's contents. KEY TERMS appear in the text in **boldfaced** type, with their definition following immediately in *italics*. This provides students with a very clear understanding of important psychological concepts. The key terms also are listed with page references at the end of each chapter and defined in a page-referenced GLOSSARY at the end of the book.

Another important dimension of the learning system is the REVIEW sections that appear two to four times in each chapter. They are designed to activate students' memory and comprehension of the major topics or key ideas that have been discussed to that point. This allows students to get a handle on complex concepts and ideas and to understand how they are interrelated. Review sections provide a cognitive framework of the most important information in each of the chapter's sections.

The presentation of figures and tables has been carefully considered in *Psychology: The Contexts of Behavior*. Every chapter has a number of figures and tables that include both a description of important content information and photographs to illustrate the content. In many instances, these figures and tables represent summaries or reviews of important concepts. For example, in chapter 9, a visual figure summarizes Erikson's stages of development. The combination of summary descriptions and carefully selected photographs in the form of VISUAL FIGURES AND TABLES presented periodically within each chapter enhances students' retention and makes the book a more attractive one to study.

At the end of each chapter, a detailed SUMMARY in outline form provides a helpful review. An annotated list of SUGGESTED READINGS also appears at the end of each chapter. Finally, before students read the first chapter of *Psychology: The Contexts of Behavior*, they will come across a section, called "Your Study Skills," that provides helpful strategies for improving time use, memory, exam taking, and more. These elements should help students learn and, more important, understand the field of psychology.

Text Supplements

We've tried to combine a student-oriented textbook with an integrated ancillary package designed to meet the unique needs of instructors and students. Our goal has been to create a teaching package that is as enjoyable to teach with as it is to study from.

The *Instructor's Course Planner*, written by Steven A. Schneider of Pima Community College and a team of contributors, including Lisa Whitten of SUNY: College at Old Westbury, provides separate teaching units for each major topic in the textbook. Learning objectives, lecture suggestions, film suggestions, and much more information are provided, along with an array of suggested classroom activities and handouts. The *Instructor's Course Planner* is also available on disk for IBM, Apple, and Macintosh computers.

The *Test Item File*, by Eric Landrum of Boise State University, includes more than 2,000 multiple-choice items. Each item is keyed to the text and learning objectives and designated as factual, conceptual, or applied, using the first three levels of Benjamin Bloom's *Taxonomy of Educational Objectives*. Al Cohen, director of the Office of Testing and Evaluation Services at the University of Wisconsin–Madison, has provided valuable assistance in the development of this *Test Item File*. Dr. Cohen has worked directly with us to ensure that these questions are worded with precision and structured consistently.

The *Student Study Guide*, also by Steven A. Schneider, offers a guided review and a substantial number of practice questions among its many features.

TestPak 3.0 is an integrated computer program designed to print test masters; to permit on-line computerized testing; to help students review text material through an interactive self-testing, self-scoring quiz program; and to provide instructors with a gradebook program for classroom management. Test questions can be found in the *Test Item File*, or you can create your own. You can choose to use Testbank A for exam questions and Testbank B in conjunction with the quiz program. Printing the exam yourself requires access to a personal computer—an IBM that uses 5.25-inch or 3.5-inch diskettes, an Apple IIe or IIc, or a Macintosh. TestPak requires two disk drives and will work with any printer. Diskettes are available through your local Brown & Benchmark sales representative or by phoning Brown & Benchmark's Educational Services Department at 800–338–5371. The package you receive will contain complete instructions for making up an exam.

The *Brown & Benchmark Reference Disks,* created by Lester Sdorow of Beaver College, are available free to adopters. The disks include over 15,000 journal and book references arranged in files by introductory topics. The complete set of five disks is available in either IBM 5.25- or 3.5-inch size.

The *Brown & Benchmark Introductory Psychology Transparency or Slide Set* includes approximately 150 full-color acetates or slides specifically designed for classroom use. A second set of 38 additional full-color transparencies or slides based on the visuals in our textbook is also available to adopters.

The Critical Thinker, by Richard E. Mayer and Fiona M. Goodchild, both of the University of California, Santa Barbara, uses excerpts from introductory psychology textbooks to encourage critical thinking. This 80-page booklet is available free to adopters.

The *Instructor's Course Planning System* is a convenient and flexible housing unit for all of your print ancillaries. The *Course Planner* can be arranged by chapter in separate hanging file folders, along with an unbound copy of each text chapter, your own notes, the *Student Study Guide,* and the *Transparency Sets,* allowing you to keep all of your classroom materials organized and at your fingertips.

The *Brown & Benchmark Customized Reader* allows you to select over 100 journal or magazine articles from a menu provided by your sales representative. These readings will be custom-printed for your students and bound into an attractive 8½ × 11 book, giving you the opportunity to tailor-make your own student reader.

Our *Custom Publishing Service* will also allow you to have your own notes, handouts, or other classroom materials printed and bound for your course use very inexpensively. See your Brown & Benchmark representative for details.

A *Customized Transparency Program* is available to adopters of our text based on the number of textbooks ordered. Consult your Brown & Benchmark representative for ordering policies.

A large selection of videotapes is also available to adopters based on the number of textbooks ordered directly from Brown & Benchmark by your bookstore.

The *Brain/Anatomy Software Program,* a four-level SuperCard™ program, teaches the basic neuroanatomy of a primate brain. Students can browse through the brain, organize structures into systems, and request anatomical or functional information about any specific structure or system. One copy is available on adoption or it can be shrink-wrapped with our text for a small additional cost.

The Brain Modules on Videodisc, created by WNET New York, Antenne 2 TV/France, the Annenberg/CPB Foundation, and Professor Frank J. Vattano of Colorado State University, is based on the Peabody Award–winning series "The Brain." Thirty segments, averaging 6 minutes each, vividly illustrate an array of psychology topics. Consult your Brown & Benchmark sales representative for details on this or any other of our textbook supplements.

Acknowledgments

This book began to take form at the American Psychological Association's annual convention in New Orleans in 1989. Amid a multitude of sessions on culture, gender, and ethnicity, it became increasingly clear that the time was right to create a new introductory psychology textbook that focused on the diversity of human behavior as a central issue. After preliminary meetings in New Orleans, we established a Human Diversity Advisory Group of almost 100 psychologists from North America and abroad. These advisors have offered their time and expertise over the past 4 years as we have struggled with countless decisions about the specific coverage of topics and strategies for placing psychology "in context."

At the 1990 American Psychological Association Annual Convention in Boston, several members of our Advisory Group participated in discussion sessions focusing on an early draft of the manuscript. We would like to thank the following psychologists for their participation and helpful comments in those focus groups:

Yvonne Asamoah, CUNY: Hunter College
Robert T. Carter, Columbia University
George Cvetkovich, Western Washington University
John M. Davis, Southwest Texas State University
Martha Mednick, Howard University
John Moritsugu, Pacific Lutheran University
Michele Paludi, CUNY: Hunter College
Judy Rosenblith, Wheaton College
Selma Sapir, Bank Street College
Tod Sloan, University of Tulsa

Several members of the Center for Cross-Cultural Studies at Western Washington University have also been extremely helpful throughout the course of this textbook project. We thank them for their hospitality, advice, and encouragement of our efforts:

George Cvetkovich
Walter J. Lonner
Joseph E. Trimble

Three extraordinary psychologists played a special role as consultants and reviewers of our project. Their extensive and intensive critiques of the complete second draft have helped us communicate more clearly the intricacies of these issues. We wish to thank them sincerely for their time, their contributions, and their support:

Richard Brislin, East-West Center, University of Hawaii
Jeannette Ickovics, Yale University
Michele Paludi, CUNY: Hunter College

No textbook of this size or scope is possible without the efforts and scrutiny of a large group of thoughtful and conscientious reviewers. They, along with all those we have already mentioned, have played a crucial role in making this a much better book than we could have achieved on our own. Many thanks to the following:

Bruce Bain, University of Alberta, Edmonton
Robert Bell, Texarkana Community College
Deborah Best, Wake Forest University
Richard Brislin, East-West Center, University of Hawaii
Jagannath P. Das, University of Alberta
Larry Dohrn, San Antonio Community College

Pauline Ginsberg, Utica College of Syracuse University
Randall Gold, Cuesta College
Peter Gram, Pensacola Junior College
James Hart, Edison State Community College
Janet E. Helms, University of Maryland
Nils Hovik, Lehigh County Community College
Jeannette Ickovics, Yale University
Rick Kribs, Motlow State Community College
Stan Kuczaj, Southern Methodist University
V. K. Kumar, West Chester University
Ed Lawson, State University of New York, Fredonia
David Matsumoto, San Francisco State University
Steve Myers, Washburn University
Mary Ellen O'Connor, University of Tulsa
Michele Paludi, CUNY: Hunter College
Paul Pederson, Syracuse University
Retta Poe, Western Kentucky University
Marshall Segall, Syracuse University
Tod Sloan, University of Tulsa
Martha Spiker, University of Charleston
Joseph Trimble, Western Washington University
Cynthia Whissell, Laurentian University

Finally, we wish to express our continued gratitude to the Human Diversity Advisory Group that was created at the start of this project. They continue to serve us and the other authors of Brown & Benchmark by lending their expertise to our efforts to infuse psychology textbooks with the sociocultural perspective. We gratefully acknowledge the ongoing help of the following individuals:

John Adamopoulos, Indiana University at South Bend
Leonore Loeb Adler, Molloy College
Rhoda L. Agin, California State University, Hayward
Jeannette Altarriba, University of Massachusetts, Amherst
James Anderson, Indiana University of Pennsylvania
Bobbie M. Anthony, Chicago State University
Yvonne Asamoah, CUNY: Hunter College
Roya Ayman, Illinois Institute of Technology
Bruce Bain, University of Alberta, Edmonton
Deborah L. Best, Wake Forest University
Hector Betancourt, Loma Linda University
Richard Brislin, East-West Center, University of Hawaii
Phyllis A. Bronstein, University of Vermont
John E. Carr, University of Washington Medical Center
Robert T. Carter, Teachers' College, Columbia University
Felipe G. Castro, San Diego State University
S. Andrew Chen, Slippery Rock University
George Cvetkovich, Western Washington University
Jagannath P. Das, University of Alberta
John M. Davis, Southwest Texas State University
J. Peter Denny, University of Western Ontario
Geri Anne Dino, Frostburg State University
Juris Draguns, Pennsylvania State University
Nadya Fouad, University of Wisconsin, Milwaukee
William K. Gabrenya, Florida Institute of Technology
Peter Gamlin, Ontario Institute for Studies in Education
Uwe P. Gielen, St. Francis College
Pauline Ginsberg, Utica College of Syracuse University

Bernadette Gray-Little, The University of North Carolina
George M. Guthrie, Pennsylvania State University
Janet E. Helms, University of Maryland
Jeannette Ickovics, Yale University
Martha D. John, Marymount University
James M. Jones, University of Delaware
Prabha Khanna, Memphis State University
W. M. Klein, Princeton University
Stan Kuczaj, Southern Methodist University
V. K. Kumar, West Chester University
Teresa D. LaFromboise, University of Wisconsin
Hope Landrine, California State University, San Bernardino
Leonard M. Lansky, University of Cincinnati
Edwin D. Lawson, State University of New York, Fredonia
D. John Lee, Calvin College
Walter J. Lonner, Western Washington University
Chalsa Loo, University of Hawaii, Manoa
Gerardo Marin, University of San Francisco
Carol Markstrom-Adams, University of Guelph
David Matsumoto, San Francisco State University
Ogretta V. McNeil, College of the Holy Cross
Martha T. Mednick, Howard University
Anita M. Meehan, Kutztown University
Peter F. Merenda, The University of Rhode Island
John Moritsugu, Pacific Lutheran University
Ruth Munroe, Pitzer College
Linda J. Myers, The Ohio State University
Mary Ellen O'Connor, University of Tulsa
Virginia E. O'Leary, Indiana State University
Esteban Olmedo, California School of Professional Psychology
Harry Osser, Queen's University, Kingston
Amado M. Padilla, Stanford University
Anita Wan-ping Pak, Brock University
Michele Paludi, CUNY: Hunter College
Paul B. Pederson, Syracuse University
Anthony D. Pellegrini, University of Georgia
W. Clinton Pettus, Virginia State University
Retta E. Poe, Western Kentucky University
Pamela T. Reid, CUNY: Graduate School and University Center
Charles L. Richman, Wake Forest University
Ronald P. Rohner, University of Connecticut, Storrs
Judy F. Rosenblith, Wheaton College
Rosellen M. Rosich, University of Alaska, Anchorage
Selma Sapir, Bank Street College, Yonkers
B. Mark Schoenberg, Memorial University of Newfoundland
Marshall H. Segall, Syracuse University
Jack A. Shaffer, Humboldt State University
Laura Sidorowicz, Nassau Community College
Andrei Simic, University of Southern California
Carolyn H. Simmons, University of Colorado, Denver
Tod Sloan, University of Tulsa
Margaret Beale Spencer, Emory University
Mary L. Spencer, CAS, University of Guam
Harold Stevenson, University of Michigan
Michael Stevenson, Ball State University
Norman D. Sundberg, University of Oregon
Harold Takooshian, Fordham University

Irmgard M. Thiessen, Mount Royal College
Donald L. Tollefson, Canisius College
Judith Torney-Purta, University of Maryland
Harry C. Triandis, University of Illinois
Joseph E. Trimble, Western Washington University
Oliver C. S. Tzeng, Indiana University–Purdue University at
    Indianapolis
Susana P. Urbina, University of North Florida
Emmy E. Werner, University of California, Davis
Cynthia Whissell, Laurentian University
Lisa Whitten, SUNY–College at Old Westbury
Daniel E. Williams, Montclair State College
Julian Wohl, University of Toledo
Frankie Y. Wong, Texas A&M University
Joe Yamamoto, University of California, Los Angeles
Lucy Yu, Pennsylvania State University

In addition to the many consultants and psychologists who provided us with valuable reviews and feedback, the professionals at Brown & Benchmark established a supportive context for the development of this book. Michael Lange, Acquisitions Editor, played a special role in *Psychology: The Contexts of Behavior*. From the beginning of discussions about the project, he has been a staunch advocate of the need for books with a strong sociocultural focus. Both he and Sheralee Connors, Developmental Editor, have shepherded the book through its many phases with cheer, enthusiasm, and competence. Pam King, a writer with superb skills, also deserves special thanks. If the words of *Psychology: The Contexts of Behavior* seem sensible and enjoyable to read, Pam's voice has come through. Debra DeBord, Production Editor of considerable competence, copyedited the manuscript with care and spent long hours overseeing the production of the book—we sincerely appreciate her diligence. Mark Christianson, Designer, has a special skill in coming up with creative touches that make books enjoyable to look at and spend time with—we think he did his job well with *Psychology: The Contexts of Behavior*. Judi David went the extra mile in tracking down elusive and attractive photographs and Rachel Imsland and Joyce Watters professionally managed the art program. Gail Wheatley efficiently obtained permissions.

Special thanks go to Steven A. Schneider, who prepared the innovative *Instructor's Course Planner* and an outstanding *Student Study Guide*. The ICP provides a number of outstanding suggestions and exercises for including the sociocultural approach in teaching introductory psychology classes.

A final note of thanks goes to our spouses—David W. Britt and Mary Jo Santrock—for their continued support of our work and for the companionship they have provided. Author Allen also thanks Ebonya, a buddy like no other.

THE PSYCHOLOGY

THE CONTEXTS OF BEHAVIOR

CONSIDER THE FLOWERING OF A GARDEN,
THOUGH DIFFERING IN KIND, COLOR, FORM,
AND SHAPE, YET, INASMUCH AS THEY ARE
REFRESHED BY THE WATERS OF ONE SPRING,
REVIVED BY THE BREATH OF ONE WIND,
INVIGORATED BY THE RAYS OF ONE SUN, THIS
DIVERSITY INCREASETH THEIR CHARM, AND
ADDETH UNTO THEIR BEAUTY. HOW
UNPLEASING TO THE EYE IF ALL THE FLOWERS
AND THE PLANTS, THE LEAVES AND THE
BLOSSOMS, THE FRUITS, THE BRANCHES AND
THE TREES OF THAT GARDEN WERE ALL OF
THE SAME SHAPE AND COLOR! DIVERSITY OF
HUES, FORM, AND SHAPE ENRICHETH AND
ADORNETH THE GARDEN, AND HEIGHTENETH
THE EFFECT THEREOF.

Abdu'l-Baha

Further Reading About Study Skills

We have briefly focused on some important ideas that will help you perform better in the courses you are taking. Several books go into much greater detail. If you want to read more about improving your study skills, check your library for the following books.

Shaw, H. (1976). *30 ways to improve your grades*. New York: McGraw-Hill. This is a fun book with interesting chapters, such as "Taking Care of Your Body and Your Brain," "Learn to Listen While Listening to Learn," and "Put into Your Own Words What You Read and Hear." Twenty-seven other chapters provide valuable information about note taking, time management, thinking clearly, and many other aspects of study skill.

Walter, T., & Siebert, A. (1987). *Student success: How to succeed in college and still have time for your friends*. New York: Holt, Rinehart & Winston. This book covers the academic, social, and emotional aspects of meeting college's challenges; an extensive number of tips are provided that will help you study more effectively and still find enough time to enjoy yourself.

studying and arrange them in a meaningful pattern or outline. Then recite and repeat them until you can recall them when needed. Select, organize, and repeat—these are time-tested steps for helping you remember.

A number of memory tricks also can be helpful. One memory trick is to relate what you have read to your own life. You will be encouraged to do so throughout this book. You can also use a number of organized systems to improve your memory. One such system involves using the first letter of each word in an ordered series to form a new name or sentence. For example, in chapter 3, "Sensation and Perception," you will learn that the colors in the light spectrum are red, orange, yellow, green, blue, indigo, and violet. You can learn this order quickly by thinking of the name Roy G. Biv. Additional information about memory strategies appears in chapter 6, Memory.

Learning from This and Other Textbooks

This textbook has a number of built-in devices to improve your learning. You can read about many of these in the preface. One extraordinary technique that can make your reading more efficient is called the SQ3R method, and it was developed by Dr. Frances P. Robinson more than 40 years ago. S stands for Survey, Q represents Question, and 3R signifies Read, Recite, and Review.

To *survey*, glance over the headings in each chapter to find the main points that will be developed. The outline at the beginning of each chapter will help in this regard. This orientation will help you organize the ideas as you read them later.

To *question*, you may want to begin by turning each heading into a question. This will arouse your curiosity and should increase your comprehension. The question may help make important points stand out. Ask yourself questions as you read through the chapter. As you find information that answers your questions, underline or mark the material with a felt pen.

To accomplish the third step in the SQ3R method, you begin *reading* the book as you normally would. In the SQ3R method, though, your reading should be more efficient because you have already built a foundation for understanding the material by surveying and questioning.

The fourth step in the SQ3R method involves *reciting* information periodically as you go through a chapter. To help you use this strategy, reviews appear several times per chapter; they encourage you to recite what you have read in particular parts of the chapter. In many chapters, you will want to do this more than two or three times. Every several pages, you should stop, think about what you have just read, and briefly recite the main points.

After you have used the techniques suggested so far, you need to *review* the material you have read at least several times before you take a test. Do not think that, just because you have read a chapter, you will be able to recall all of its information. By reciting the information over and over and continuing to review the material, you will improve your test performance. At the end of each chapter in this book, you will find a summary outline that will help you in the review process.

The Classroom Lecture

What goes on in your classroom is just as important as what is in this textbook. You would not skip a chapter in this book if you knew it was assigned for a test, so it is not a good idea to skip a class just to reach

the allowable number of cuts or to cram for an exam. Some students feel that, because they go to class and listen passively to the lecture, they do not need to devote further time to it; however, by preparing for a lecture, using your learning skills during the lecture, and doing some follow-up work, you should be able to improve your performance on tests.

In preparing for a lecture, motivate yourself by telling yourself that it is important for you to stay alert, listen carefully to what is said, and take organized notes throughout the class period. During the lecture, record your notes in simple paragraph form. Strive to capture general ideas rather than minute details. Skip lines to show the end of one idea and the beginning of another. Use abbreviations to save time to listen more. Write legibly so that, when you review, you will know what you have written. It also is a wise idea to consolidate your notes during your first free time after the class. At that time, you may want to underline key ideas with a felt-tip pen, just as you would in this book, and, just before the next class period, go over the notes to further improve your ability to recall the information and to prepare yourself for what will be said.

How to Prepare for and Take Exams

In most cases, your grade in this course will depend on how well you do in 4 to 5 hours of exams spaced periodically throughout the semester or quarter. It is important to devote some time to thinking about how to prepare for and take exams.

All of your textbook reading should be completed several days before an exam. All of your classroom notes should be in order so you can review them easily. All term papers should be written and handed in. In the last few days before an exam, your mind should be free to concentrate on organizing and consolidating the information.

How can you arrive at this ideal state of affairs several days before an exam? Go back to the first day of class. If you have been following a routine of managing your time effectively, taking notes during every lecture, keeping up with textbook assignments, following the SQ3R method, and continuing to recite and review the material you have read and heard, you should be ready to summarize and consolidate what you have learned to prepare for the exam. You may want to develop a summary system, which would follow closely what you did for each chapter or lecture. Several days before the exam, you probably will have to review several chapters and a number of lectures. Try putting them together in an overall system the last day or so before the exam.

Should you cram for an exam? If you have not studied much until several days before the exam, you will probably have to do some cramming. However, be aware that cramming can never replace methodical, consistent study throughout the course.

To ensure success on an exam, you need to be physically and psychologically ready in addition to having the facts, ideas, and principles in your mind. First, you need to have enough rest; second, you need to feel confident. If you keep creating mountains of work for yourself, especially by not studying until the last minute, you will rob yourself of sleep, food, and exercise, probably leaving both your mind and your body in no shape to perform well on an exam. By following the advice given earlier about time management, concentration, memory techniques, the SQ3R method, the classroom lecture, and how to prepare for exams, you will feel confident going into the exam. You are less likely to panic and will have a positive attitude about taking the test.

| Time | | Time used | Activity-Description |
Start	End		
7:45	8:15	:30	Dress
8:15	8:40	:25	Breakfast
8:40	9:00	:20	Nothing
9:00	10:00	1:00	Psychology-Lecture
10:00	10:40	:40	Coffee-Talking
10:40	11:00	:20	Nothing
11:00	12:00	1:00	Economics-Lecture
12:00	12:45	:45	Lunch
12:45	2:00	1:15	Reading-Magazine
2:00	4:00	2:00	Biology-Lab
4:00	5:30	1:30	Recreation-Volleyball
5:30	6:00	:30	Nothing
6:00	7:00	1:00	Dinner
7:00	8:00	1:00	Nap
8:00	8:50	:50	Study-Statistics
8:50	9:20	:30	Break
9:20	10:00	:40	Study-Statistics
10:00	10:50	:50	Rap Session
10:50	11:30	:40	Study-Accounting
11:30	11:45	:15	Ready For Bed
11:45	7:45	8:00	Sleep

Paste on mirror 3 × 5 cards. Laws of economics; psychological terms; statistical formulas—study while brushing teeth, etc.

Look over textbook assignment and previous lecture notes to establish continuity for today's psychology lecture.

Break too long and too soon after breakfast. Should work on psychology notes just taken; also should look over economics assignment.

Should re-work the lecture notes on economics while still fresh in mind. Also, look over biology assignment to recall the objective of the coming lab.

Use this time for reading a magazine or newspaper.

Not a good idea. Better finish work, then get a good night's sleep.

Break—too long.

Good as a reward if basic work is done.

Insufficient time allotted, but better than no time.

While brushing teeth, study the 3 × 5 cards. Replace cards that have been mastered with new ones.

FIGURE P.1

Record of one day's activities and suggestions for better time management.

that is quiet when you study. If the library is the right place for you, then go there, especially if there are people in the dorm or at home who distract you. Noise is one of the main distractions to effective studying. For the most part, it is a good idea to turn off the stereo, radio, or television while you are studying.

So far we have talked about the physical aspects of the environment that may help or hinder your ability to concentrate on what you are studying. Psychological and personal situations may also interfere with your ability to concentrate. Daydreaming is one way to avoid hard work. Even though daydreaming may seem pleasant at the time we are doing it, we pay the consequences later, possibly with a poor grade on a test or in a course. Everyone has personal relationships that may intrude on study time. Force yourself to put personal relationships and problems out of your mind during the time you have set aside for studying. Tell yourself you will deal with them after you have finished studying.

If the problems seem overwhelming and you cannot avoid thinking about them, you may want to contact the student counsel-

ing service at your college or university. Most college and university counseling centers not only have counselors who help students with personal problems, but they often have study skills counselors who help students with such matters as time management and concentration.

Memory Techniques

At a certain point in this course and the other courses you are taking this semester, you will have to remember what you have heard in class and read in books. How can you remember more effectively?

First, make up your mind to remember. If you really want to improve your memory, you can, but you have to motivate yourself to improve it. Second, keep refreshing your memory. Almost everything tends to fade unless you periodically think about what it is you need to remember. Periodically rehearsing what you have heard in class or read in this book will help you store the information and retrieve it when you have a test. Third, organize, outline, or otherwise structure what you want to remember. Pick out the main points in the material you are

YOUR STUDY SKILLS

You have taken courses in history, math, English, and science, but have you taken a course in study skills? Have you ever seriously sat down and mapped out a time management program for yourself? Have you ever studied how to improve your memory, then tried the techniques to see if they work? Have you ever had an organized plan to "attack" a textbook? Before you begin reading the specific content of this book, take time to read this section on how to improve your study skills. You will be motivated to think about ways to manage your time, to improve your concentration, to memorize more effectively, and to function more efficiently in the classroom. You will learn skills to understand this and other books more clearly, and you will discover how to prepare for and take exams.

Managing Your Time

A student named Tom came to one of the authors' office about 2 weeks before the final exam in an introductory psychology course. He had a *D* average in the course and wanted to know what was causing him to get such a low grade. It turned out that he wasn't doing well in any of his classes, so we talked about his background. Eventually the conversation turned to his study techniques and what he could do to get better grades on his final exams. I asked Tom to put together a study schedule for the four final exams he was getting ready to take in 2 weeks. He planned to study a total of 4 hours for his psychology exam; only 1 of those hours was scheduled for the night before the exam, and no study time was allotted to the morning before the exam (the exam was in the late afternoon).

I told Tom that, although the psychology exam probably was not the most difficult one he would ever take in college, I thought the material would require more than 4 hours of study time if he wanted to improve his grade for the course. As we talked further, it became evident that Tom was a terrible manager of time. True, he had a part-time job in addition to the 12 credit hours he was taking, but, as we mapped out how he used his time during the day, Tom quickly became aware that he was wasting big chunks of it.

A week is made up of 168 hours. A typical college student sleeps 50 hours, attends classes 19 hours, eats 11 hours, and studies 20 hours per week. For Tom, we allotted 15 hours a week for his part-time job and 6 hours a week for transportation to and from school, work, and home. Subtracting the 20 hours of study time, Tom found that his main activities accounted for 101 of the week's 168 hours, suggesting that, even though he works, he still has 67 hours in which to find time for studying.

You may find it helpful to fill out a weekly schedule of your activities to see where your time goes. Figure P.1 on page xxiv provides an example of one student's daily time schedule, along with comments about how and where time could have been used more effectively. Some students are afraid that a schedule will make them too rigid; however, successful students usually follow organized schedules and manage their time efficiently. If you waste less time, you actually will have much more free time for personal activities, and, in managing your time effectively, you will feel a sense of control over your life. Try taking 5 minutes every morning to chart your plan for the day. Before you go to bed at night, review your day to see how well you met your schedule. After you have done this for several weeks, it should become routine.

Study Skills

Given that you manage your time efficiently, how can you effectively use the study time you have? First, you need to concentrate on *really* studying in the time set aside for that purpose. Second, you can use a number of memory techniques to help you recall information. Third, you can discover strategies for learning more effectively from textbooks, such as this one. Fourth, you can reduce your study time by functioning more effectively during class. Fifth, you can learn some important tips in preparing for and taking exams. Let's consider each of these.

Concentration

There are many distractions that keep you from studying or remembering what you have studied. Select your place of study carefully. Most individuals need a desk—a place where pens, paper, and a book can be placed. Use your desk *only* for studying. If you nap or daydream while you are at your desk, the desk can act as a cue for napping or daydreaming. Use your desk as a cue for studying. When you want to nap or daydream, go somewhere else. Be sure the area where you study is well lighted and does not have glare. Do your utmost to find a place whereas men usually manage the finances and material goods. Thus, women have better networks of friends, closer relationships with relatives, and experience in taking care of themselves psychologically. Older widows do better than younger widows, perhaps because the death of a partner is more expected for older women. For their part, widowers usually have more money than widows do, and they are much more likely to remarry (DiGiulio, 1989; Lopata, 1979).

For either widows or widowers, social support helps them adjust to the death of a spouse (Bass, Bowman, & Noelker, 1991; LaGrand, 1991; Sankar, 1991). Such programs as Widow-to-Widow, begun in the 1960s, provide support for newly widowed people. Its objective is to prevent the potentially negative effects of the loss. Volunteer widows reach out to other widows, introducing them to others who may have similar problems, leading group discussions, and organizing social activities. The program has been adopted by the American Association of Retired Persons and disseminated throughout the United States as the Widowed Person's Service. The model has since been adopted by numerous community organizations to provide support for those going through a difficult life transition that will confront the vast majority of us (Silverman, 1988).

By now you can appreciate that much development takes place in adolescence and adulthood, just as in infancy and childhood. In the next chapter, you will read about the nature of gender roles and sexuality, a discussion that includes information about how our gender roles develop and issues of sexuality at various points in the life cycle.

REVIEW

Social Development in Adulthood and Death and Dying

Special concerns in early and middle adulthood are careers and work, life-styles, theories of adult personality development, cohort effects, gender, culture, and the issue of continuity-discontinuity. Among the important aspects of careers and work are the increasing number of females in the workforce. Adults must choose the life-style they want to follow—single, married, or divorced, for example. One set of adult personality development theories proposes that adult development unfolds in stages (Erikson, Levinson). Other theories emphasize life events, social clocks, and cohort effects. The stage theorists have overexaggerated the prevalence of a midlife crisis. Critics say the adult stage theories have a male bias by emphasizing career choice and achievement. The stage theories do not adequately address women's concerns about relationships. The stage theories assume a normative sequence, but, as women's roles have become more varied and complex, determining what is normative is difficult. In many nonindustrialized societies, a woman's status often improves in middle age. In many cultures, the concept of middle age is not clear, although most cultures distinguish between young and old adults. There is both continuity and discontinuity in adult personality development. Everything we know about late adulthood suggests that an active older life is preferred to disengagement. Special concerns are ageism and the ethnic minority elderly. Cross-cultural comparisons reveal greater respect for the elderly in some cultures, such as Japan, than in the United States. Erikson believes that the final issue in the life cycle is integrity versus despair, which involves a life review.

Death may come at any point in the life cycle but in late adulthood we know it is near. Most societies have rituals that deal with death, although cultures vary in their orientation toward it. Kübler-Ross proposed five stages of coping with death. A special concern is the coping skills of widows and widowers.

Summary

I. Historical Beginnings and the Nature of Adolescence
G. Stanley Hall is the father of the scientific study of adolescence. In the early 1900s, he proposed the storm and stress view. Adolescence is a transition between childhood and adulthood that involves biological, cognitive, and social development. In most cultures, adolescence begins at approximately 10 to 13 years of age and ends at approximately 18 to 21 years of age. Adolescence is more appropriately viewed as a time of decision making and commitment than a time of rebellion, crisis, and pathology. Different portrayals of adolescence emerge, depending on the particular group of adolescents being described. Adults' idealized images and ambivalent messages may contribute to adolescent problems.

II. Physical Development in Adolescence
Puberty is a rapid change to maturation that usually occurs in early adolescence. It has arrived earlier in recent years. Hormone changes are prominent. Puberty occurs roughly 2 years later in boys than in girls, although its normal range is large. Early maturation generally favors

294 Chapter 9

Section Reviews

Two or three times in each chapter, we review what has been discussed so far in that chapter by outlining the information in prose form. This learning device helps you get a handle on material several times a chapter so you don't wait until the end of the chapter and have too much information to digest.

Chapter Summary

At the end of each chapter, a summary in outline form helps you review the main ideas of the entire chapter.

Key Terms

Listed at the end of each chapter are key terms that are defined throughout the chapter. They are listed with page references and are defined again in a page-referenced glossary at the end of the book.

Suggested Readings

A list of readings at the end of each chapter suggests references that can be used for further study of topics covered in the chapter.

Key Terms

gender 300
gender identity 300
gender role 300
androgen 300
estrogen 300
identification theory 302
social learning theory of gender 302
cognitive developmental theory of gender 303
gender schema 303
gender schema theory 303
gender role stereotypes 304
androgyny 308
gender role transcendence 309
human sexual response cycle 318
psychosexual disorders 321
psychosexual dysfunctions 321
incest 321
paraphilias 321
fetishism 321
transvestism 321
transsexualism 322
exhibitionism 322
voyeurism 322
sadism 322
masochism 322
pedophilia 322
rape 323
date, or acquaintance, rape 323
sexually transmitted diseases (STDs) 325
gonorrhea 325
syphilis 325
herpes 325
AIDS 326

Suggested Readings

Doyle, J., & Paludi, M. (1991). *Sex and gender: The human experience*. Dubuque, IA: Wm. C. Brown. In this up-to-date discussion, the authors examine a number of issues pertaining to gender. It includes chapters on how different power bases affect women's and men's relationships, psychological perspectives on gender, and anthropological perspectives on gender.

Greenberg, J. S., Bruess, C. E., Mullen, K. D., & Sands, D. W. (1989). *Sexuality* (2nd ed.). Dubuque, IA: Wm. C. Brown. This broad-based text covers many areas of sexuality. Separate chapters are devoted to such topics as sexual response and arousal, sexual diseases, fertility control, and sexual dysfunctions.

McWhirter, D. P., Reinisch, J. M., & Sanders, S. A. (1989). *Homosexuality/heterosexuality*. New York: Oxford University Press. Extensive information is presented about the biological, psychological, and social dimensions of homosexuality and heterosexuality.

Miller, J. B. (1986). *Toward a new psychology of women* (2nd ed.). Boston: Beacon. A leader in the feminist movement in psychology, Jean Baker Miller describes the male bias of society, females' connectionist strengths, and the future of women's roles.

332 Chapter 10

Understanding diversity within an ethnic, cultural, or gender group

Recognizing and respecting legitimate differences among ethnic, cultural, and gender groups

Searching for similarities among ethnic, cultural, and gender groups when differences have been incorrectly assumed

Reducing discrimination and prejudice

Comprehending that value conflicts are often important factors in understanding ethnic minority issues

Globalizing psychology and understanding American psychology's ethnocentrism

Recognizing that the behavior of every individual from every ethnic, cultural, and gender group is multiply determined

Considering different sides of sensitive ethnic, cultural, and gender issues

Using the fields of psychology to improve understanding of sociocultural issues and to promote the welfare of all human beings through education, teaching, research, and psychological prevention or intervention

FIGURE 1.4
Sociocultural issues.

Visual Summary Figures and Tables

Numerous figures and tables review and summarize important theories and ideas contained in the text.

Sociocultural Worlds

Psychology: The Contexts of Behavior gives special attention to our cultural, ethnic, and gender worlds. Each chapter has one or more boxed inserts that highlight the sociocultural dimensions of psychology.

Key Term Definitions

Key terms appear in boldfaced type, with their definitions immediately following in italic type. This provides you with a clear understanding of important concepts.

SOCIOCULTURAL WORLDS 1.1

The Changing Tapestry of American Culture

In 1989 one-fifth of all children and adolescents in the United States under the age of 17 were members of ethnic minority groups—Blacks, Hispanics, Native Americans (American Indians), and Asians. By the year 2000, one-third of all school-age children will fall into this category. This changing demographic tapestry promises national diversity, but it also carries the challenge of extending the American dream to people of all ethnic and minority groups (Buenker & Ratner, 1992). Historically ethnic minorities have found themselves at the bottom of the economic and social order. They have been disproportionately among the poor and the inadequately educated. Today, for instance, half of all Black children and one-third of all Hispanic children live in poverty, and the school dropout rate for minority youths is as high as 60 percent in some urban areas. Our social institutions can play an enormous part in helping correct these discrepancies. By becoming more sensitive to ethnic issues and by improving services to people of ethnic minority and low-income backgrounds, schools, colleges, social services, health and mental health agencies, and the courts can help bring minorities into the mainstream of American life (Fujino, 1991; Phelps & others, 1991).

An especially important fact for social planners to keep in mind is the tremendous diversity within each ethnic group. We're accustomed to thinking of American society as a melting pot of cultures—Anglo Americans, Black Americans, Hispanic Americans, Native Americans, Asian Americans, Italian Americans, Polish Americans, and so on. However, just as there are no cultural characteristics common across all American ethnic groups, there is no cultural characteristic common to all Black Americans or all Hispanic Americans, for instance.

Black Americans make up the largest ethnic minority group in the United States. Black Americans are distributed throughout the social class structure, although a disproportionate number are poor (Bell-Scott & Taylor, 1989).

Hispanic Americans also are a diverse group of individuals. Not all Hispanic Americans are Catholic. Many are, but some are not. Not all Hispanic Americans have a Mexican heritage. Many do, but others have cultural ties with South American countries, with Puerto Rico or other Caribbean countries, or with Spain (Marin & Marin, 1991; Pacheco & Valdez, 1989; Ramirez, 1990).

Native Americans, with 511 identifiable tribal units, also are an extremely diverse and complicated ethnic group (Trimble & Fleming, 1989). So are Asian Americans, with more than 30 distinct groups under this designation (Wong, 1982). Within each of these 511 identifiable Native American tribes and 30 distinct Asian American groups, there is considerable diversity and individual variation (Ho, 1992).

America has embraced many cultures, and, in the process, the cultures have often mixed their beliefs and identities. Some elements of the cultures of origin are retained, some are lost, and some are mixed with the American culture. As the number of ethnic minority groups continues to increase rapidly in the next decade, one of psychology's most important agenda items is to understand better the role that culture and ethnicity play in the way we think and act (Ickovics, 1991; Lange, 1991; Peterson, 1991; Russo, 1991; Thomas, 1991).

ethnicity is primarily a *sociocultural* term and race is primarily a *genetic, biological* term (Brislin, 1988). Race is a concept that has not been very beneficial in predicting behavior and mental processes (Jones, 1991). Race also is a concept that has led to considerable stereotyping of people and prejudice against them, and it does not adequately take into account the considerable diversity of a group of people, such as Blacks or Caucasians. Nonetheless, although race has some biological basis, it has taken on considerable social meaning as well and is a widely used label in society. More about the distinction between race and ethnicity appears in chapter 2, Biological Foundations and the Brain. More about the social meanings of race also appears in chapter 2, as well as in chapter 16, Social Psychology.

So far we have discussed two aspects of sociocultural influences—culture and ethnicity. A third important aspect is gender. Whereas *sex* refers to the biological dimension of being male or female (Sherif, 1982; Unger, 1990; Unger & Crawford, 1992), **gender** *refers to everything people learn about and think of their sex in different cultures.* Gender turns males and females into boys and girls, men and women. Few aspects of our existence are more central to our identity and to our social relationships than is our sex or gender. Our gender attitudes and behavior are changing, but how much? Is there a limit to how much society can determine what is appropriate behavior for males and for females? A special concern of many feminist writers and scholars is that much of psychology's history

Chapter Openings

Beginning each chapter is an imaginative, high-interest piece focusing on a topic related to the chapter's content.

One muggy morning in August 1966, a muscular young man hauled a footlocker to the top of the University of Texas' 27-story tower. Charles Joseph Whitman, described by those who knew him as friendly, intelligent, and ambitious, had filled the trunk with an arsenal of firearms before he made his way to the observation deck. At 11:45 A.M., the 25-year-old architectural engineering honor student and former Boy Scout leader began a 90-minute shooting rampage that left 14 people dead and 30 wounded. Earlier that day, Whitman had also shot his mother in the back of the head and had run a bayonet through his wife's heart to "save them from the embarrassment" of what he was going to do.

That same summer, Alice Walker, who would later win a Pulitzer Prize for her book *The Color Purple*, spent her days battling racism in Mississippi. She had recently won her first writing fellowship, but, rather than using the money to follow her dream of moving to Senegal, Africa, she put herself in the heart and heat of the civil rights movement. Walker grew up knowing the brutal effects of poverty and racism. Born in 1944, she was the eighth child of Georgia sharecroppers, who earned about $300 a year. When Walker was 8, her brother accidentally shot her in the left eye with a BB gun. By the time her parents got her to the hospital a week later (they had no car), she was blind in that eye and it had developed a disfiguring layer of scar tissue. Despite the counts against her, Walker went on to become an essayist, a poet, an award-winning novelist, a short-story writer, and a social activist, who, like her characters (especially the women), has overcome pain and anger to celebrate the human spirit. Walker writes about people who, as she puts it, "make it, who come out of nothing. People who triumph."

What leads one person, so full of promise, to commit brutal acts of violence and another to turn poverty and trauma into a rich literary harvest? How can we attempt to explain why one person can pick up the pieces of a life shattered by tragedy, such as a loved one's death, whereas another seems to come unhinged by life's minor hassles? Why is it some people are whirlwinds—involved in their work and with family and friends, with time left over for community organizations—whereas others hang out on the sidelines, mere spectators in life?

If you have ever wondered what makes people tick, you have asked yourself psychology's central question. In this book, you will explore the fascinating terrain of personality, motivation, the inner workings of the brain, and much, much more. You will learn about the methods psychologists use to explain human nature, as well as the progress psychology has made. In addition, you will see how cultural and ethnic background, gender, sexual orientation, economic circumstances, and other factors influence what people think and how they behave. However, psychology is still a young science and these are very complex issues; psychologists do not have all the answers.

Alice Walker won the Pulitzer Prize for her book *The Color Purple*. Like the characters in her book (especially the women), Walker overcame pain and anger to triumph and celebrate the human spirit.

Even so, psychology is uniquely qualified to help us make sense of our increasingly complex and challenging world. It isn't just your imagination; the world is getting tougher and tougher to keep up with. For example, one day's edition of the *New York Times* is packed with more information than a person who lived in the Middle Ages acquired during a lifetime, and gone are the days when the United States was an undisputed industrial giant. As the need to both import and export goods increases, so does global interdependence and the need to understand other cultures in order to develop good international relationships. We also live in a nation where the workforce is increasingly diverse. By the year 2000, for example, over 80 percent of the people entering the job market will be women and members of ethnic minority groups.

These shifts raise questions that are extremely important to the future of our society. Psychology can help us reduce conflict and meet the challenges that lie ahead by seeking answers to such questions as these: What social distance is appropriate between American and Latin American business

---

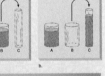
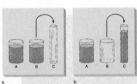

"I still don't have all the answers, but I'm beginning to ask the right questions."
Drawing by Lorenz; © 1989 The New Yorker Magazine, Inc.

As this point we have discussed four main characteristics of preoperational thought. A summary of these is presented in figure 8.14.

Concrete operational thought *is the term Piaget gave to the 7-to-11-year-old child's understanding of the world. At this stage of thought, children can use operations—they can mentally reverse the liquid from one beaker to another and understand that the volume is the same even though the beakers are different in height and width. Logical reasoning replaces intuitive thought as long as the principles are applied to concrete examples.* For instance, a concrete operational thinker cannot imagine the steps necessary to complete an algebraic equation, which is too abstract at this stage of children's development.

Earlier you read about a beaker task that was too difficult for a child who had not yet reached the stage of operational thought. Another well-known task used to demonstrate Piaget's concrete operational thought involves two equal amounts of clay (see figure 8.15). An experimenter shows a child two identical balls of clay and then rolls one ball into a long, thin shape. The other is retained in its original ball shape. The child is then asked if there is more clay in the ball or in the long, thin piece of clay. By the time children reach 7 to 8 years of age, most answer that the amount of clay is the same. To solve this problem correctly, children have to imagine that the clay ball is rolled out into a long, thin strip and then returned to its original round shape—imagination that involves a reversible mental action. Concrete operations allow the child to coordinate several characteristics rather than focusing on a single property of an object. In the clay example, the preoperational child is likely to focus on height or width. The child who has reached the stage of concrete operational thought coordinates information about both dimensions. Do children in all cultures acquire conservation skills at about the same age? To learn the answer to this question, turn to Sociocultural Worlds 8.2 on page 232.

FIGURE 8.13

Piaget's beaker test to assess operational thinking. The beaker test is a well-known Piagetian test to determine whether a child can think operationally—that is, can mentally reverse actions and show an understanding of the conservation of a substance. (a) Two identical beakers are presented to a child. Then the experimenter pours the liquid from B into C, which is taller and thinner than A or B. (b) The child is then asked if these beakers (A and C) have the same amount of liquid. A preoperational child says no. (c) When asked to point to the beaker that has more liquid, a preoperational child points to the tall, thin beaker.

Visual Figures and Tables

These include both a description of important information and photographs that illustrate the content.

This book contains a number of learning devices, each of which presents the field of psychology in a meaningful way. The learning devices in *Psychology: The Contexts of Behavior* will help you learn the material more effectively.

Chapter Outlines

Each chapter begins with an outline showing the organization of topics by heading levels. The outline gives you an overview of the arrangement and structure of the chapter, so you can plan your study time wisely.

STRESS AND HEALTH

CHAPTER 15

The Scope of Health Psychology
Stress
  The Body's Response to Stress
  Personality Factors in Stress
  Cognitive Factors in Stress
  Environmental Factors in Stress
  Sociocultural Factors in Stress
  Coping with Stress
Coping with Illness
  Recognizing, Interpreting, and
    Seeking Treatment for Symptoms
  The Patient's Role
  Compliance with Medical Advice and
    Treatment
Promoting Health
  Smoking
  Eating Problems
  Exercise
  Toward Healthier Lives
  Culture and Health
Women's Health Issues
Summary
Key Terms
Suggested Readings

Sociocultural Worlds 15.1
  The Acculturative Stress of Ethnic
    Minority Individuals
Sociocultural Worlds 15.2
  Ethnicity and Nutrition
Sociocultural Worlds 15.3
  Health Promotion in Black
    Americans, Hispanic Americans,
    Asian Americans, and Native
    Americans

WHAT IS PSYCHOLOGY?

CHAPTER 1

One muggy morning in August 1966, a muscular young man hauled a footlocker to the top of the University of Texas' 27-story tower. Charles Joseph Whitman, described by those who knew him as friendly, intelligent, and ambitious, had filled the trunk with an arsenal of firearms before he made his way to the observation deck. At 11:45 A.M., the 25-year-old architectural engineering honor student and former Boy Scout leader began a 90-minute shooting rampage that left 14 people dead and 30 wounded. Earlier that day, Whitman had also shot his mother in the back of the head and had run a bayonet through his wife's heart to "save them from the embarrassment" of what he was going to do.

That same summer, Alice Walker, who would later win a Pulitzer Prize for her book *The Color Purple*, spent her days battling racism in Mississippi. She had recently won her first writing fellowship, but, rather than using the money to follow her dream of moving to Senegal, Africa, she put herself in the heart and heat of the civil rights movement. Walker grew up knowing the brutal effects of poverty and racism. Born in 1944, she was the eighth child of Georgia sharecroppers, who earned about $300 a year. When Walker was 8, her brother accidentally shot her in the left eye with a BB gun. By the time her parents got her to the hospital a week later (they had no car), she was blind in that eye and it had developed a disfiguring layer of scar tissue. Despite the counts against her, Walker went on to become an essayist, a poet, an award-winning novelist, a short-story writer, and a social activist, who, like her characters (especially the women), has overcome pain and anger to celebrate the human spirit. Walker writes about people who, as she puts it, "make it, who come out of nothing. People who triumph."

What leads one person, so full of promise, to commit brutal acts of violence and another to turn poverty and trauma into a rich literary harvest? How can we attempt to explain why one person can pick up the pieces of a life shattered by tragedy, such as a loved one's death, whereas another seems to come unhinged by life's minor hassles? Why is it some people are whirlwinds—involved in their work and with family and friends, with time left over for community organizations—whereas others hang out on the sidelines, mere spectators in life?

If you have ever wondered what makes people tick, you have asked yourself psychology's central question. In this book, you will explore the fascinating terrain of personality, motivation, the inner workings of the brain, and much, much more. You will learn about the methods psychologists use to explain human nature, as well as the progress psychology has made. In addition, you will see how cultural and ethnic background, gender, sexual orientation, economic circumstances, and other factors influence what people think and how they behave. However, psychology is still a young science and these are very complex issues; psychologists do not have all the answers.

Alice Walker won the Pulitzer Prize for her book *The Color Purple*. Like the characters in her book (especially the women), Walker overcame pain and anger to triumph and celebrate the human spirit.

Even so, psychology is uniquely qualified to help us make sense of our increasingly complex and challenging world. It isn't just your imagination; the world is getting tougher and tougher to keep up with. For example, one day's edition of the *New York Times* is packed with more information than a person who lived in the Middle Ages acquired during a lifetime, and gone are the days when the United States was an undisputed industrial giant. As the need to both import and export goods increases, so does global interdependence and the need to understand other cultures in order to develop good international relationships. We also live in a nation where the workforce is increasingly diverse. By the year 2000, for example, over 80 percent of the people entering the job market will be women and members of ethnic minority groups.

These shifts raise questions that are extremely important to the future of our society. Psychology can help us reduce conflict and meet the challenges that lie ahead by seeking answers to such questions as these: What social distance is appropriate between American and Latin American business colleagues? Why do the Japanese have one of the lowest homicide rates in the world, despite the fact that their metropolitan areas are among the most crowded? Is intelligence the same concept in developing countries as it is in ours? Are women more often absent from work because they are less committed to their jobs, or is it their child-care responsibilities that produce the gender difference in absentee rates? Why does the United States have one of the highest teen pregnancy rates among the industrialized nations? As you can see, theories of behavior need to reflect the experience of all people, both within and across national boundaries.

Not only can psychology help us grapple with some of the largest issues we face, but it can also help guide us in our daily lives. For example, consider these findings, which have important implications:

- Stressful events place individuals at risk for psychological and physical problems. For example, both divorced and unhappily married people are more vulnerable to disease than are happily married people (Chase-Lansdale & Hetherington, 1990; Kiecolt-Glaser & others, 1987).
- Women are making strides in many areas relative to men, but researchers continue to find that men outperform women in some tests of math skill, including the Scholastic Aptitude Test (SAT) (Benbow, 1990; Feingold, 1988; Hyde, 1991; Jacklin, 1989).
- Moderate aerobic exercise not only improves most people's physical health but also improves their self-concept and reduces their anxiety (Moses & others, 1989; Paffenbarger & others, 1986; Sheridan & Radmacher, 1992).
- Although we on planet earth have much in common wherever and however we live, people also vary according to their cultural and ethnic backgrounds. For example, people in Eastern cultures (Japan and China) are more group-oriented, whereas people in Western cultures (United States and Canada) are more individual-oriented (Hofstede, 1980; Triandis, 1989). Hispanic American children use touch when interacting with each other more than Anglo American children do (Albert, 1988). Understanding true cultural variability does not undermine the value of equality; such knowledge reaffirms the cherished American value of diversity (Albert & Triandis, 1985; Triandis, 1991).

What Is Psychology?

These examples of psychological research—happiness in close relationships and its link to health, changing gender roles, the role of exercise in physical and psychological health, and ethnic and cultural influences on behavior—illustrate some of the many fascinating and varied aspects of behavior psychologists explore and seek to explain.

Psychology is not a cure-all for every knotty problem, and it doesn't tell us the meaning of life. It does, however, contribute enormously to our knowledge about why people are the way they are, why they think and act the way they do, and how they can cope more effectively with their lives. Psychologists are enthusiastic about psychology's potential to improve our lives as we approach the twenty-first century. It is an exciting time of discovery in the field of psychology.

Defining Psychology

To a degree, psychology's findings may strike you as being simple common sense, but studies often turn up the unexpected in human behavior. For example, it may seem obvious that couples who live together before marriage have a better chance of making the marriage last. After all, practice makes perfect. However, researchers have found a higher success rate for couples who legally marry initially rather than live together before marriage (Teachman & Polonko, 1990). As you can see, psychology doesn't accept assumptions about human nature at face value, however reasonable they sound. It is a rigorous discipline that tests assumptions. **Psychology** *is the scientific study of behavior and mental processes in contexts*. There are four aspects of this definition: behavior, mental processes, science, and contexts. Let's examine behavior first.

Behavior *is everything we do that can be directly observed*— two people *kissing*, a baby *crying*, a college student *riding* a motorcycle.

Mental processes *are trickier to define than behavior; they describe the thoughts, feelings, and motives that each of us experiences privately but that cannot be observed directly*. Although we cannot directly see thoughts and feelings, they are no less real. They include *thoughts* about kissing someone, a baby's *feelings* when its mother leaves the room, and a college student's *memory* of the motorcycle episode.

As a **science,** *psychology uses systematic methods to observe, describe, explain, and predict behavior*. Psychology's methods are not casual; they are carefully and precisely planned and conducted. They are often verified by checking to see if they describe the behavior of many different people. For example, researchers might construct a questionnaire on ethnic group relations and give it to 500 college students. They might spend considerable time devising the questions and determining the background of the individuals who are chosen to participate in the survey. After the psychologists analyze the data, they will also want to *explain* what they observe. Let's say the results from the survey indicate that college students are less tolerant of other ethnic groups than they were a decade ago. To find out why this is so, the researchers might ask if increased exposure to different groups generates confusion and misinterpretation because groups do not communicate well about their differences. Psychologists also want to *predict* behavior. The researchers might then try to predict the levels of college

Context is an important dimension of psychology. *Contexts* are settings, which are influenced by historical, economic, social, and cultural factors. Without reference to context, the racial tolerance of the college students shown here cannot be fully understood.

students' intolerance based on their liberal or conservative religious attitudes, or on their rural, suburban, or urban background.

The fourth key aspect of our definition of psychology is contexts. **Contexts** *refer to the historical, economic, social, and cultural factors that influence mental processes and behavior.* People do not act, or react, in a vacuum. Everything we think, say, or do is influenced by where we come from, whom we have spent time with, and what has happened to us. All human behavior occurs in a cultural context. These contexts—or settings—include homes, schools, churches, cities, neighborhoods, communities, university laboratories, the United States, China, Mexico, Egypt, and many others, each with important historical, economic, social, and cultural legacies.

Interest in contexts has fluctuated during psychology's history, often varying with the political and social climate of the times (Albert, 1988). In the late 1960s and early 1970s,

the United States had to cope with national discontent over an unpopular war, government corruption, and dwindling American influence and power in the world. It was a time of increasing social awareness reflected in the antiwar movement, the civil rights movement, and the women's movement. A parallel discontent arose in psychology, with many psychologists arguing that the field had become too narrow. One result of this upheaval was renewed interest in the contexts of behavior. Research began to focus on how people think and behave in real-world settings, such as schools, hospitals, and communities.

As our society continues to change, psychologists need to address new concerns in contexts, such as the dramatic increase in the ethnic minority population, increased interaction with cultures around the world, and women's roles in society. As you read this book, you will discover that it stresses the influence of contexts on behavior and mental processes. You may become more sensitive to how contexts shape behavior and mental processes. You might also learn to better understand yourself and the people in your life.

The Beginnings of Psychology

Ever since our ancestors first gathered around a fire to create and embellish myths, we've been trying to explain why things are the way they are. Myths attributed most events to the pleasure or displeasure of the gods: when a volcano erupted, the gods were angry; if two people fell in love, they were the target of Cupid's arrows. As we became more sophisticated, myth gave way to philosophy, the rational investigation of the underlying principles of being and knowledge.

The early Greek philosophers Socrates (469-399 B.C.) and Aristotle (384-322 B.C.) urged us to know ourselves, to use logic to make inferences about mind, and to systematically observe behavior. It was Aristotle who argued that an empirical approach, rather than dialogue, was the best route to knowledge. Direct observation remains an important dimension of psychology today.

Even before the early Greeks were developing ideas about mind and behavior, the Chinese philosopher Confucius (551-479 B.C.) expounded the principle of *jen*, which means to love all people. The Confucian tenet that benevolence and concern for others are the most important aspects of human behavior is still evident in many Asian cultures. Recent research shows that Asians often identify strongly with a group, whereas people who live in the United States and other parts of the West frequently have a strong sense of individualism (Kagitcibasi, 1988; Triandis, 1985).

For centuries philosophers loved to debate such questions as the following: How do we acquire knowledge? Does information come to us through our senses and our experiences with the environment, or is it inborn? Although such speculation fueled a great deal of intellectual passion, it didn't yield many concrete answers. It wasn't until the late nineteenth century, in Germany, that psychology emerged as a science.

Imagine that you are in Leipzig, Germany, in the year 1879. A bearded man with a wrinkled forehead and pensive expression is sitting in the room. His head turns toward a soft sound coming from the far side of the room. After several minutes, his head turns once again, this time toward a loud sound. The scenario is repeated with sounds of varying intensity. The man is Wilhelm Wundt, who is credited with developing the first scientific psychology laboratory. By exposing himself to environmental conditions that he systematically varied and then recording his reactions to different stimuli, Wundt investigated the elements, or "structures," of the mind (see figure 1.1).

To gain information about conscious experience, Wundt and many of the early psychologists used a research method known as "trained introspection." **Introspection** *is a process of*

FIGURE 1.1

The beginning of psychology as a science. Wilhelm Wundt established the first research laboratory in psychology at Germany's University of Leipzig in 1879. Wundt is the bearded gentleman in the middle.
Archives of the History of American Psychology, University of Akron.

turning inward in search of the mind's nature. Under controlled conditions, specially trained people carefully observed and analyzed their own mental experiences. Although the introspectionists thought they were studying immediate experience, they were actually involved in retrospection (remembering an experience). Since the act of introspection takes time, it changes the observer's experience; it modifies, or "contaminates," the observation.

William James, one of the first American psychologists, argued against analyzing consciousness into Wundt's "structures" (ideas, images, and feelings). Instead, James emphasized the dynamic nature of mental activity. His approach to psychology was influenced, in part, by Charles Darwin's (1859) theory of evolution. Darwin showed that entire species change over time. James wanted to know how thinking, emotion, and consciousness itself fulfill an organism's biological needs.

However, psychology's early emphasis on conscious experience lacked objectivity and investigated mental processes that were too vague. It soon went the way of the dinosaur, and the study of behavior took its place. Psychologists were more comfortable studying what they could observe directly rather than making inferences about what was going on in a person's mind. Behaviorists, such as John B. Watson, seeking to discover the *what* behind human nature rather than the *why*, dominated the field of psychology from the 1920s until the 1950s.

In another swing of the pendulum, psychologists are once again exploring the roots of consciousness. Many researchers believe that some of psychology's most fascinating phenomena will be discovered in the interior world of mental processes (Clark & Paivio, 1989; Neisser, 1991).

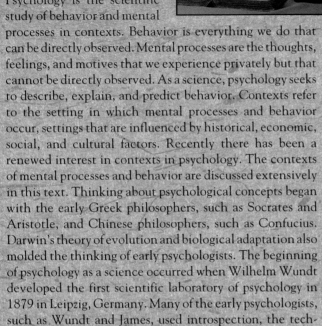

Defining Psychology and the Beginnings of Psychology

Psychology is the scientific study of behavior and mental processes in contexts. Behavior is everything we do that can be directly observed. Mental processes are the thoughts, feelings, and motives that we experience privately but that cannot be directly observed. As a science, psychology seeks to describe, explain, and predict behavior. Contexts refer to the setting in which mental processes and behavior occur, settings that are influenced by historical, economic, social, and cultural factors. Recently there has been a renewed interest in contexts in psychology. The contexts of mental processes and behavior are discussed extensively in this text. Thinking about psychological concepts began with the early Greek philosophers, such as Socrates and Aristotle, and Chinese philosophers, such as Confucius. Darwin's theory of evolution and biological adaptation also molded the thinking of early psychologists. The beginning of psychology as a science occurred when Wilhelm Wundt developed the first scientific laboratory of psychology in 1879 in Leipzig, Germany. Many of the early psychologists, such as Wundt and James, used introspection, the technique whereby specially trained individuals carefully observed and analyzed their own mental experiences.

Approaches to Behavior, Mental Processes, and Contexts

Whether psychologists study behavior and the external factors that influence behavior or the mental processes and internal factors that influence behavior depends on their approach. There are six important approaches to psychology: behavioral, psychoanalytic, humanistic, cognitive, neurobiological, and sociocultural. We will briefly describe each of these approaches in turn, but we will also discuss them in much greater detail in later chapters.

Because the abstract principles of psychological approaches can be difficult to remember—almost like swimming upstream against an onrushing current—we'll apply each approach to something most of us have done in our lives, dating. Meet Ron and Angela, freshmen at the same campus. They're bright, attractive, and outgoing. We'll see how each psychological approach explains what draws them to one another.

The Behavioral Approach

The **behavioral approach** *emphasizes the scientific study of observable behavioral responses and their environmental determinants.* According to behaviorists, the only appropriate subject matter for psychological investigation is observable, measurable behavior. What we *do* is the ultimate test of who we are, and our behavior is determined by the rewards, or punishments, we experience. We behave in a well-mannered fashion for our parents because of the controls they place on us, and we work hard at our jobs because of the money we receive for our effort. We don't do these things, say behaviorists, because of an inborn motivation to be competent people. We do them because of the environmental conditions we have experienced and continue to experience (Skinner, 1938).

What can the behavioral approach tell us about dating? The behavioral approach tells us not to look inside a person for clues about dating behavior. Inner motives and feelings about another person cannot be directly observed, so they will be of no help in understanding dating. The behaviorists say we should be sensitive to what goes on before and after a date, searching for the rewards people experience. Ron might ask Angela out because of her engaging smile or because she's beautiful. If Ron receives a lot of attention for being with Angela, he might ask her out again, even if his date with her is just so-so. Being seen with Angela also increases Ron's status in the group, which provides a further reward.

The Psychoanalytic Approach

The **psychoanalytic approach** *emphasizes the unconscious aspects of the mind, conflict between biological instincts and society's demands, and early family experiences.* Stemming from the ideas of Sigmund Freud (1856-1939), the psychoanalytic approach stresses that unlearned biological instincts, especially sexual and aggressive impulses, influence the way people think, feel, and act. These instincts, buried deep within the unconscious mind, are often at odds with society's demands. Society's job is to keep these instincts in check. For example, in Freud's view, a child who once ran wildly through a neighbor's flower garden but who grows up to be a successful surgeon or comedian has learned to channel her aggressive instincts in positive ways. Although Freud saw much of psychological development as instinctually based, he argued that our early relationships with our parents are the chief environmental contributions that shape our personality.

What can the psychoanalytic approach tell us about dating? Above all, the psychoanalytic approach tells us we will have a difficult time understanding our own dating behavior. The reasons we behave in a given way are pushed deep within our unconscious mind and are primarily sexual. Sex is an unlearned human instinct that dominates our dating behavior. Society's job, which conflicts with our inner sexual motivation, is to keep this instinct in check. Our dating behavior can also be traced to our experiences with our parents during our childhood. Initially Ron may have dated Angela because something about her appearance or behavior unconsciously reminded him of his early relationship with his mother.

The Humanistic Approach

The **humanistic approach** *emphasizes a person's capacity for personal growth, freedom to choose one's own destiny, and positive qualities.* Humanistic psychologists criticize the behavioral approach, stressing that people have the ability to control their lives rather than be manipulated by the environment (Maslow, 1971; Rogers, 1961). They also criticize the psychoanalytic approach, stressing that people are not driven by unconscious sexual and aggressive impulses. Humanists believe we have the ability to live by higher human values, such as altruism, aesthetics, and free will. They also think we have a tremendous potential for conscious self-understanding and we can help others achieve this self-understanding by being warm, nurturant, and supportive.

What can the humanistic approach tell us about dating? Humanistic psychologists do not believe that dating is based on sexual instinct. Rather, it is a natural tendency of human beings to be loving toward each other. Humanistic psychologists believe that each of us has the potential to be a loving person if only we would recognize it. According to the humanists, Ron asks Angela out because he is trusting, warm, and open to loving her.

The Cognitive Approach

The **cognitive approach** *emphasizes the mental processes involved in knowing.* Cognition *comes from the Latin, meaning "to know."* Cognitive psychologists want to know such things as how we direct our attention, perceive, remember, think, and solve problems. For example, cognitive psychologists want to know how we solve algebraic equations, why we remember some things only for a short while and others for a lifetime, and how we can use mental imagery to plan for the future. A cognitive psychologist views the mind as an active and aware problem-solving system (Anderson, 1990; Simon, 1990). This positive view of human nature agrees with the humanistic view and contrasts with the pessimistic psychoanalytic view.

What can the cognitive approach tell us about dating? According to cognitive psychologists, our conscious thoughts are the key to understanding dating. Memories and images of people we want to date, or have dated, influence our behavior. As you read these words, you can stop and think about your most memorable dates, including some you probably want to forget. You can think about your current dating or marital situation or project what it will be like in the future: Is he loyal to me? What will the future of our relationship be like? Is she getting tired of me? Ron asks Angela out on a date because he's thought about the engaging conversations they've had after class, and he decides he'd like to get to know her better.

The Neurobiological Approach

The **neurobiological approach** *emphasizes that the brain and nervous system play central roles in understanding behavior, thought, and emotion.* Rather than study only thoughts, as cognitive psychologists do, neurobiologists believe that thoughts have a physical basis in the brain (Squire, 1992). Electrical impulses zoom throughout the brain's cells, and chemical substances are released as we think, feel, and act. Our remarkable capabilities as human beings would not be possible without our brains. The human brain and nervous system is the most complex, intricate, and elegant system imaginable.

What can the neurobiological approach tell us about dating? The neurobiological approach reminds us that underlying our thoughts, emotions, and behaviors in a dating situation is a physical brain, a nervous system, and hormones. Have you ever thought about how your brain changes when you are attracted to someone? When your heart pitter-patters, we sometimes say "the chemistry is right." Attraction may literally involve the brain's chemistry. When your feelings for someone increase, the chemistry of the brain changes. In this manner, dating behavior is wired into the circuitry of the brain. Dating behavior also may be influenced by the chemical messengers in the body known as hormones. For example, pheromones, or subtle "sex perfumes," act as sexual attractants. In the neurobiological view, Ron and Angela are drawn to one another because their brains trigger chemical come-hithers.

The Sociocultural Approach

The **sociocultural approach** *emphasizes that culture, ethnicity, and gender are essential to understanding behavior, thought, and emotion.* **Culture** *refers to the behavior patterns, beliefs, and other products of a particular group of people, such as the values, work patterns, music, dress, diet, and ceremonies that are passed on from generation to generation.* A cultural group can be as large and complex as the United States, or it can be as small as an African hunter-gatherer tribe, but, whatever its size, the group's culture influences the identity, learning, and social behavior of its members (Berry & others, 1992; Brislin, 1990, 1991; Cole, 1992; Hamilton, 1992; Lonner, 1980, 1988; Triandis, 1980, 1991; Whiting, 1989).

Ethnicity (*the word* ethnic *comes from the Greek word for "nation") is based on cultural heritage, nationality characteristics, race, religion, and language. Ethnicity involves descent from common ancestors, usually in a specifiable part of the world. Ethnicity is central to the development of an* **ethnic identity,** *which is a sense of membership based on the shared language, religion, customs, values, history, and race of an ethnic group. Ethnic identity involves the relative importance of one's ethnicity in comparison with the other aspects of the self that contribute to one's identity.* Without distinguishing between ethnicity and ethnic identity, we fail to understand the nature of people who have an ethnicity (they are Polish American, for example) but who do not identify with

Culture refers to the behavior patterns, beliefs, and all other products of a particular group of people that are passed on from generation to generation. This Bororo nomad of Niger in west central Africa is washing a friend's back at a well, a custom that has been passed down through the generations in their culture.

or have feelings about this fact. Consider a college student who identifies herself as a fifth-generation Texan and is proud of it—this is her ethnic identity; she doesn't know much about her ancestors from Europe and is not very interested in her European descent (her ethnicity). Given the descent of individuals from common ancestors, people often make inferences about someone's ethnicity based on physical features believed to be typical of an ethnic group. For example, one of the downed American flyers in the Persian Gulf War had features that would be considered "Arab." He was treated worse than the other prisoners of war, who had non-Arab features. This reminds us that ethnicity is a category that an individual may use toward people, even if they don't want to be categorized that way, they feel the inferences are wrong and unfair, and so on (Brislin, 1987). To read further about ethnicity, turn to Sociocultural Worlds 1.1, where we will discuss the increasing ethnic diversity in the United States.

Recently some individuals have voiced dissatisfaction with the use of the term *minority* within the phrase *ethnic minority group*. Some individuals have also raised objections about using the term *Blacks* or *Black Americans*, preferring instead the term *African Americans* to emphasize their ancestry. What is the nature of such dissatisfaction and objections? The term *minority* has traditionally been associated with inferiority and deficits. Further, the concept of minority implies that there is a majority. Indeed, it can be argued that there really is no majority in the United States because Whites are actually composed of many different ethnic groups, and Whites are not a majority in the world. The term *ethnic minority* is used intentionally in this text. Rather than implying that ethnic minority groups should be viewed as inferior or deficient, this text will convey the impact that minority status has had on many ethnic groups. The circumstances of each ethnic group are not solely a function of its own culture. Rather, many ethnic groups have experienced considerable discrimination and prejudice. For example, patterns of alcohol abuse among Native Americans cannot be fully understood unless the exploitation that has accompanied Native Americans' history is considered (Sue, 1990).

You might be wondering why this text uses the term *ethnicity* rather than *race* to describe the sociocultural heritage of a group of people, such as Native Americans, Black Americans, Hispanic Americans, or Asian Americans. That is because

The Changing Tapestry of American Culture

I n 1989 one-fifth of all children and adolescents in the United States under the age of 17 were members of ethnic minority groups—Blacks, Hispanics, Native Americans (American Indians), and Asians. By the year 2000, one-third of all school-age children will fall into this category. This changing demographic tapestry promises national diversity, but it also carries the challenge of extending the American dream to people of all ethnic and minority groups (Buenker & Ratner, 1992). Historically ethnic minorities have found themselves at the bottom of the economic and social order. They have been disproportionately among the poor and the inadequately educated. Today, for instance, half of all Black children and one-third of all Hispanic children live in poverty, and the school dropout rate for minority youths is as high as 60 percent in some urban areas. Our social institutions can play an enormous part in helping correct these discrepancies. By becoming more sensitive to ethnic issues and by improving services to people of ethnic minority and low-income backgrounds, schools, colleges, social services, health and mental health agencies, and the courts can help bring minorities into the mainstream of American life (Fujino, 1991; Phelps & others, 1991).

An especially important fact for social planners to keep in mind is the tremendous diversity within each ethnic group. We're accustomed to thinking of American society as a melting pot of cultures—Anglo Americans, Black Americans, Hispanic Americans, Native Americans, Asian Americans, Italian Americans, Polish Americans, and so on. However, just as there are no cultural characteristics common *across* all American ethnic groups, there is no cultural characteristic common to all Black Americans or all Hispanic Americans, for instance.

Black Americans make up the largest ethnic minority group in the United States. Black Americans are distributed throughout the social class structure, although a disproportionate number are poor (Bell-Scott & Taylor, 1989).

Hispanic Americans also are a diverse group of individuals. Not all Hispanic Americans are Catholic. Many are, but some are not. Not all Hispanic Americans have a Mexican heritage. Many do, but others have cultural ties with South American countries, with Puerto Rico or other Caribbean countries, or with Spain (Marín & Marín, 1991; Pacheco & Valdez, 1989; Ramirez, 1990).

Native Americans, with 511 identifiable tribal units, also are an extremely diverse and complicated ethnic group (Trimble & Fleming, 1989). So are Asian Americans, with more than 30 distinct groups under this designation (Wong, 1982). Within each of these 511 identifiable Native American tribes and 30 distinct Asian American groups, there is considerable diversity and individual variation (Ho, 1992).

America has embraced many cultures, and, in the process, the cultures have often mixed their beliefs and identities. Some elements of the cultures of origin are retained, some are lost, and some are mixed with the American culture. As the number of ethnic minority groups continues to increase rapidly in the next decade, one of psychology's most important agenda items is to understand better the role that culture and ethnicity play in the way we think and act (Ickovics, 1991; Lange, 1991; Peterson, 1991; Russo, 1991; Thomas, 1991).

ethnicity is primarily a *sociocultural* term and race is primarily a *genetic, biological* term (Brislin, 1988). Race is a concept that has not been very beneficial in predicting behavior and mental processes (Jones, 1991). Race also is a concept that has led to considerable stereotyping of people and prejudice against them, and it does not adequately take into account the considerable diversity of a group of people, such as Blacks or Caucasians. Nonetheless, although race has some biological basis, it has taken on considerable social meaning as well and is a widely used label in society. More about the distinction between race and ethnicity appears in chapter 2, Biological Foundations and the Brain. More about the social meanings of race also appears in chapter 2, as well as in chapter 16, Social Psychology.

So far we have discussed two aspects of sociocultural influences—culture and ethnicity. A third important aspect is gender. Whereas *sex* refers to the biological dimension of being male or female (Sherif, 1982; Unger, 1990; Unger & Crawford, 1992), **gender** *refers to everything people learn about and think of their sex in different cultures.* Gender turns males and females into boys and girls, men and women. Few aspects of our existence are more central to our identity and to our social relationships than is our sex or gender. Our gender attitudes and behavior are changing, but how much? Is there a limit to how much society can determine what is appropriate behavior for males and for females? A special concern of many feminist writers and scholars is that much of psychology's history

Psychologist Rhoda Unger (shown here talking with college students) urges psychologists to use the word *sex* only when referring to biological mechanisms (such as sex chromosomes or sexual anatomy) and to use the word *gender* only when describing the social, cultural, and psychological aspects of being male or female. Like Unger, psychologist Carolyn Sherif noted some of the problems the word *sex* has brought to the study of gender. Sherif argued that the term *sex roles* uncritically couples a biological concept (sex) with a sociocultural, psychological concept (gender). Sherif stressed that, through this coupling, many myths about sex may be smuggled into the concept of sociocultural aspects of male and female roles, causing confusion and possible stereotyping (Doyle & Paludi, 1991).

In Xinjiang, China, a woman prepares for horseback courtship. Her suitor must chase her, kiss her, and evade her riding crop—all on the gallop. A new marriage law took effect in China in 1981. The law sets a minimum age for marriage—22 years for males, 20 years for females. Late marriage and late childbirth are critical aspects of China's effort to control population growth (Engel, 1984).

portrays human behavior with a "male dominant theme" (DeFour & Paludi, in press; Denmark, 1991; Denmark & Paludi, in press; Paludi, 1992).

What can the sociocultural approach tell us about dating? The sociocultural approach tells us that dating behavior may vary according to one's ethnic, cultural, and gender background. For example, some cultural and ethnic groups have extremely conservative beliefs about dating, especially for women. The age at which young people first date varies from culture to culture. Cultures also differ in the value they place on dating as a precursor to marriage and the importance of sexuality in dating. Ron may not be able to go out on a car date with Angela until she is 18 because of her parents' cultural beliefs.

Our introductory discussion of the six main approaches to psychology has been necessarily brief. For a glimpse of some of the most important pioneers in the various areas of psychol-ogy, turn to figure 1.2. Most of these people and their views will be discussed in much greater detail at appropriate places later in the book.

All of these approaches to psychology are, in a sense, correct. They are all valid ways of looking at human behavior, just as blueprints, floor plans, and photographs are all valid ways of looking at a house. Some approaches are better for some purposes. A floor plan, for instance, is more useful than a photograph for deciding how much lumber to buy, just as the neurobiological approach is probably more useful than the cognitive approach for understanding epilepsy. However, no single approach is "right" or "wrong." (For a summary of psychology's six main approaches, see figure 1.3.)

Sociocultural Issues

The sociocultural approach is psychology's newest lens for examining behavior and mental processes. As the future brings increasing contact between people from quite different cultural backgrounds, the sociocultural approach is especially well

Wilhelm Wundt
(1832–1920)

William James
(1842–1910)

Alfred Binet
(1857–1911)

Ivan Pavlov
(1849–1936)

Ruth Howard
(1900–)

B. F. Skinner
(1904–1990)

Erik Erikson
(1902–)

Abraham Maslow
(1908–1970)

Carl Rogers
(1902–1987)

Albert Bandura
(1925–)

Sandra Bem
(1944–)

Eleanor Maccoby
(1917–)

1879: Wilhelm Wundt develops the first psychology laboratory at the University of Leipzig.

1890: William James publishes *Principles of Psychology*, which promotes functionalism.

1891: Mary Calkins establishes a laboratory for psychology at Wellesley.

1892: E. B. Titchener popularizes structuralism in the United States.

1900: Sigmund Freud publishes *Interpretation of Dreams*, reflecting his psychoanalytic view.

1905: Alfred Binet (with Theodore Simon) develops the first intelligence test to assess French schoolchildren.

1906: The Russian Ivan Pavlov publishes the results of his learning experiments with dogs.

1908: Margaret Washburn becomes the first woman to receive a Ph.D. in psychology.

1913: John Watson publishes his volume on behaviorism, promoting the importance of environmental influences.

1934: Ruth Howard becomes the first Black woman to receive a Ph.D. in psychology.

1938: B. F. Skinner publishes *The Behavior of Organisms*, expanding the view of behaviorism.

1939: Mamie Phipps Clark and Kenneth Clark conduct research on Black children's self-conceptions and identity. Later, in 1971, Kenneth Clark becomes the first Black president of the American Psychological Association.

1945: Karen Horney criticizes Freud's psychoanalytic theory as male-biased and presents her sociocultural approach.

1950: Erik Erikson publishes *Childhood and Society*, a psychoanalytic revision of Freud's views.

1954: Abraham Maslow presents the humanistic view, emphasizing the positive potential of the individual.

1954: Gordon Allport writes his now classic book, *The Nature of Prejudice*.

1958: Herbert Simon presents his information-processing view.

1961: Carl Rogers publishes *On Becoming a Person*, highlighting the humanistic approach.

1961: Albert Bandura presents ideas about social learning theory, emphasizing the importance of imitation.

1964: Roger Sperry publishes his split-brain research, showing the importance of the brain in behavior.

1969: John Berry, a Canadian psychologist, presents his ideas on the importance of cross-cultural research in psychology.

1974: Sandra Bem and Janet Spence develop tests to assess androgyny and promote the competence of females; Eleanor Maccoby (with Carol Jacklin) calls attention to the importance of sex and gender in understanding behavior and analyzing gender similarities and differences.

1977: Judith Rodin (with Ellen Langer) conducts research showing the powerful influence of perceived control over one's environment on behavior.

Mary Calkins
(1863–1930)

Sigmund Freud
(1856–1939)

Margaret
Washburn
(1871–1939)

John B. Watson
(1878–1958)

Mamie Clark
(1917–)

Karen Horney
(1885–1952)

Gordon Allport
(1897–1967)

Herbert Simon
(1916–)

Roger Sperry
(1913–)

John Berry
(1939–)

Judith Rodin
(1944–)

FIGURE 1.2

Important pioneers and theorists in psychology's history.

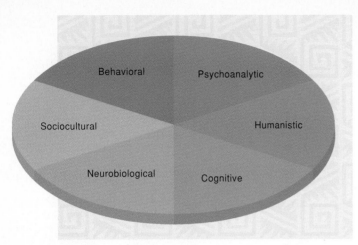

FIGURE 1.3

Psychology's approaches.

equipped to make psychology a relevant discipline in the twenty-first century. Schools and neighborhoods can no longer be the fortresses of one privileged group, whose agenda is to exclude those whose skin color or customs are different from its own. Increasingly immigrants, refugees, and ethnic minority members are refusing to become part of a homogeneous melting pot and, instead, are requesting that the nation's schools, employers, and governments honor many of their cultural customs. However, our institutions cannot accommodate every aspect of every culture; consequently, children often learn attitudes in school that challenge traditional authority patterns at home (Brislin, 1990). These are a few of the sociocultural issues that must be addressed if psychology is to become meaningful to culturally diverse people. Let's examine some others.

Understanding Diversity Within an Ethnic, Cultural, or Gender Group

An especially important fact is that there is diversity within every ethnic, cultural, and gender group (Kavanaugh & Kennedy, 1992). This point was strongly made in Sociocultural Worlds 1.1, where you saw how no cultural characteristic is common to all or nearly all members of a particular ethnic group—such as Black Americans—unless, as in the case of Black Americans, it is the experiences of being Black and the beliefs that develop from that experience. Diversity also characterizes the members of any cultural group, such as Germans, Italians, and Indonesians. Diversity also characterizes females and males. For example, some females excel at math, but others do not; likewise, some males excel at math, but others do not. Some females have highly connected friendships, others are lonely, and the same is true for males. Diversity and individual differences exist in every ethnic, cultural, and gender group. Failure to recognize this strong diversity and individual variation results in the stereotyping of ethnic, cultural, and gender groups.

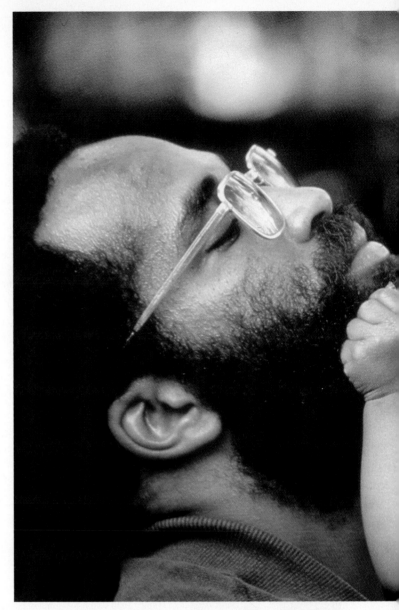

Diversity characterizes the members of any ethnic group. Black Americans have a higher divorce rate than White Americans—almost one-half of all Black children live in a single-parent family. However, as shown here, not all Black children grow up in father-absent families. Failure to recognize the strong diversity in any ethnic group results in stereotyping.

Recognizing and Respecting Legitimate Differences Among Ethnic, Cultural, and Gender Groups

Ours is a diverse, multicultural world, teeming with different languages, family structures, and customs. A cascade of historical, economic, and social experiences have produced these differences among ethnic, cultural, and gender groups (Albert, 1988; Triandis, 1990, 1991). We need to recognize

Harry Triandis (above left) has been a pioneer in the field of cross-cultural psychology. He is past-president of the International Association of Cross-Cultural Psychology and has conducted insightful analyses of the individualistic and collectivistic dimensions of cultures.

thought of as a deficit. Too often these differences have been seized on by segments of society seeking to justify their own biases and to exploit, oppress, or humiliate people from ethnic minority backgrounds (Jones, 1991). Historically being female has also meant exposure to a world of restrictions, barriers, and unfair treatment. Many psychologists now seek to discover the psychological assets of females and the strengths of ethnic groups. This new trend is long overdue.

Searching for Similarities Among Ethnic, Cultural, and Gender Groups When Differences Have Incorrectly Been Assumed

Almost every aspect of American society created by middle-class White males bears the imprint of a middle-class White male bias. Psychology is no exception. As a result, females and members of ethnic minorities have had inadequate opportunities to contribute their ideas and values to society and psychology. In addition, incorrect assumptions about the differences between White Americans and ethnic minority Americans, as well as between women and men, proliferate and take on a power all their own. As ethnic minorities and women begin to have a stronger voice in society, similarities will emerge. Recognizing legitimate similarities among people, regardless of ethnicity or gender, will help break down the stereotypes that lead to prejudice.

and respect these differences in order to facilitate communication and cooperation in our increasingly interdependent world. Although others' behavior may be different from ours, we can develop empathy and better understand them by taking their perspective and thinking about what life would be like if we were in their shoes. We can then begin to celebrate the richness that comes with diversity and to appreciate the common ground we share with people whose ethnicity, cultural heritage, or gender differs from ours.

Although this sounds reasonable to many of us now, for too long the dominant White culture disparaged ethnic minority differences. Virtually any difference—from the way people looked to the kind of music they listened to—was

Stanley Sue, shown lecturing to Asian Americans, has been an important advocate of increased research on ethnic minority issues in psychology. Sue has conducted extensive research on the role of ethnicity in abnormal behavior and psychotherapy. He also has provided considerable insight into ethnic minority issues.

Reducing Discrimination and Prejudice

In a recent Gallup poll, Americans said they believe that the United States is tolerant of ethnic differences and that overt racism is basically unacceptable (*Asian Week*, 1990). However, many ethnic minority members experience persistent forms of discrimination and prejudice in many domains of life—in the media, in interpersonal interactions, and in daily conversations (Edelman, 1992; Sue, 1990, 1991; White & Parham, 1990). As we will discuss later, in the chapter on social psychology (chapter 16), prejudice and racism today are often expressed in more subtle and indirect ways than they once were (Sears & others, 1988). Although important progress has been made in civil rights through such programs as affirmative action, there is much that still needs to be accomplished.

Discrimination, of course, is not confined to ethnic minority groups. Through much of our culture's history, women have faced almost insurmountable odds when they have strived to be heard. As Charlotte Whitton (1990), former mayor of Ottawa, Canada, recently commented, "Whatever women do, they must do twice as well as men to be thought half as good." Coping with the challenge of living in a male-dominated world has not been easy for many women, although their efforts to revolutionize society into a world where women and men are treated equally have met with some success, the revolution is far from complete.

Value Conflicts: Underlying Factors in Ethnic Minority Issues

Most ethnic minorities want to participate fully in society, but they don't necessarily agree on how to accomplish that goal. People are often caught between the conflicting values of assimilation and cultural pluralism (Sue, 1989, 1990, 1991).

Assimilation *refers to the absorption of an ethnic minority group into the dominant group, which often means the loss of some or all of the behaviors and values of the ethnic minority group.* Those who advocate assimilation usually exhort ethnic minority groups to become more American. By contrast, **pluralism** *refers to the coexistence of distinct ethnic and cultural groups in the same society.* Those who advocate pluralism usually promote cultural differences, urging that those differences be maintained and appreciated. Because the mainstream way of life was considered superior for so many years, assimilation was thought to be the best course for American society. Although assimilation still has many supporters, many people now believe that pluralism is the best approach.

Value conflicts have been a source of considerable controversy. According to Sue, without properly identifying the assumptions and effects of the conflicting values of assimilation and pluralism, it is difficult to resolve ethnic minority issues.

Globalizing Psychology and Understanding American Psychology's Ethnocentrism

For the most part, American psychology has been ethnocentric, emphasizing American values, especially those of middle-class White males. Of course, it is not just individuals in the United States who are ethnocentric; people in all societies are ethnocentric. One example of American psychology's **ethnocentrism**—*the tendency to favor one's own group over other groups*—is American individualism. As mentioned earlier, many of the world's cultures—Japanese, Chinese, Indian, and Mexican, for example—are group-oriented.

Although people from different cultures may vary in how strongly they identify with their group, some attitudes appear to be constant from culture to culture. For example, American social psychologist Donald Campbell and his colleagues (Brewer & Campbell, 1976; Campbell & LeVine, 1968) found that people in all cultures have a tendency to do the following:

- Believe that what happens in their culture is "natural" and "correct" and what happens in other cultures is "unnatural" and "incorrect"
- Perceive their cultural customs as universally valid; that is, what is good for them is good for everyone
- Behave in ways that favor their cultural group
- Feel proud of their cultural group
- Feel hostile toward other cultural groups

In fact, many cultures define the word *human* in terms of their own characteristics. The ancient Greeks distinguished between those who spoke Greek and those whose language sounded like "barber," a repetitive chatter; they called those who did not speak Greek *barbarians*. Similarly the ancient Chinese labeled themselves "the central kingdom." In many languages, the word *human* is the same as the name of the tribe, suggesting that people from foreign cultures are not perceived as fully human (Triandis, 1990).

Global interdependence is no longer a matter of preference or choice. It is an inescapable reality. We are not just citizens of the United States or Canada. We are citizens of the world, a world that through modern communication and transport has become increasingly intertwined. By improving our understanding of the behavior and values of cultures around the world, we can interact more effectively with each other and make this a more hospitable, peaceful planet (Brislin, 1981, 1991; Sloan, 1990; Solantus, 1992).

Recognizing That the Behavior of Every Individual from Every Ethnic, Cultural, and Gender Group Is Multiply Determined

When we think about what causes a person's behavior, we tend to think in terms of a single cause. Human behavior is not that simple, however. Consider Tom, a 16-year-old Native American high school dropout. It's possible he quit school because his family doesn't adequately appreciate the importance of education, but, even if that were true, it's likely that other factors are involved. It's also possible, for example, that Tom comes from a low-income family that he helps support. The school Tom attended may have a poor history of helping Native Americans adapt to school; perhaps it has no multicultural programs and no Native Americans in the school administration. It may also be that the town in which Tom lives devotes few resources to youth programs. Undoubtedly there are more factors that contributed to Tom's dropping out of school. Because behavior is the result of many factors, it is said to be multiply determined.

Considering Different Sides of Sensitive Ethnic, Cultural, and Gender Issues

Seeing things from multiple points of view is as crucial to understanding ethnic, cultural, and gender issues as it is to understanding one person's behavior. If we do not seek alternative explanations and interpretations of problems and issues, our conclusions may be based on our own expectations, prejudices, and stereotypes.

Consider, for instance, Stanley Sue's (1990) commentary about an 11-year-old Japanese American child named John. John's grades were slightly above average, but he was excessively quiet and shy. John's teacher noticed that he was extremely anxious when he had to speak in front of the class, and eventually the teacher referred John to the school psychologist, who administered some standard psychological tests. Based on the test results, the school psychologist concluded that John was emotionally disturbed. When informed, John's parents were shocked. They perceived him as quiet and well behaved but able to relate to them and to his friends in an appropriate manner. Because of the school psychologist's concerns, John's parents took him to see a therapist who knew more about Japanese culture. The therapist examined the test results, saw John for several sessions, and concluded that John was not emotionally disturbed; his behavior was simply appropriate for his cultural background. John's case illustrates a controversy between cultural universal-

ity and cultural specificity. The school psychologist assumed that the tests he gave John were culturally universal. However, the therapist recognized that the test's standards had not been developed for Japanese Americans and, therefore, might not be as relevant to John's behavior. By not considering the possible cultural specificity of John's behavior and interpreting his behavior only in a culturally universal fashion, the school psychologist made an erroneous judgment about John's behavior.

Using the Field of Psychology to Improve Understanding of Sociocultural Issues and to Promote the Welfare of All Human Beings Through Education, Teaching, Research, and Psychological Prevention or Intervention

Psychologists' understanding of sociocultural issues is improving, but there are still many gaps. Psychology must devote increased effort toward expanding our knowledge of ethnicity, culture, and gender. For example, we need to know more about how to help people integrate diverse socialization experiences and adapt to changing environments, especially when those situations present competing demands (Jones, 1991). Many cultural groups in the United States—Hispanics and Asians, for example—socialize their youths to put family first, in contrast to the mainstream cultural emphasis on putting oneself first. In school, on the job, even in social interactions, people who put family first have to learn how to honor their background without losing face with teachers, employers, or peers who hold the keys to success in the mainstream culture.

To promote better coping skills for people from different ethnic and cultural groups, we need to know more about the psychological treatments that are most effective (Sue, 1991, in press). We also need to know more about the similarities and differences between females and males and especially the social and psychological factors that explain these similarities and differences (Hyde, 1991). Ethnicity, culture, and gender should be increasingly included in the curricula of all levels of education, from preschool through graduate school. Through much of the history of psychology, (1) research on ethnicity, culture, and gender has been either scant or skewed to reflect poorly on women and minorities (Graham, 1992) and (2) in colleges and universities, the record for recruiting minority students and hiring minority faculty members has been poor (Barnard & Lentz, 1992; Stricker & others, 1990). The 1990s offer an outstanding opportunity for psychologists to make important contributions to our understanding of sociocultural issues.

A summary of the sociocultural issues we have just discussed appears in figure 1.4. We'll continue to discuss these issues throughout the book. At the end, an epilogue restates, elaborates, and provides a number of examples with a special focus on how to think critically about sociocultural issues.

As we discussed the nature of psychology, we stressed the role of science. Next we'll discuss how researchers put science to work in psychology. Just how do psychologists know what they know?

Understanding diversity within an ethnic, cultural, or gender group

Recognizing and respecting legitimate differences among ethnic, cultural, and gender groups

Searching for similarities among ethnic, cultural, and gender groups when differences have been incorrectly assumed

Reducing discrimination and prejudice

Comprehending that value conflicts are often important factors in understanding ethnic minority issues

Globalizing psychology and understanding American psychology's ethnocentrism

Recognizing that the behavior of every individual from every ethnic, cultural, and gender group is multiply determined

Considering different sides of sensitive ethnic, cultural, and gender issues

Using the fields of psychology to improve understanding of sociocultural issues and to promote the welfare of all human beings through education, teaching, research, and psychological prevention or intervention

FIGURE 1.4

Sociocultural issues.

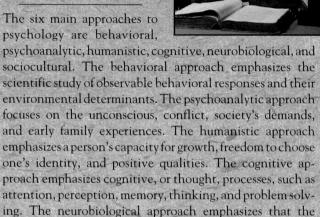

Approaches to Psychology and Sociocultural Issues

The six main approaches to psychology are behavioral, psychoanalytic, humanistic, cognitive, neurobiological, and sociocultural. The behavioral approach emphasizes the scientific study of observable behavioral responses and their environmental determinants. The psychoanalytic approach focuses on the unconscious, conflict, society's demands, and early family experiences. The humanistic approach emphasizes a person's capacity for growth, freedom to choose one's identity, and positive qualities. The cognitive approach emphasizes cognitive, or thought, processes, such as attention, perception, memory, thinking, and problem-solving. The neurobiological approach emphasizes that the brain and nervous system play central roles in understanding behavior, thought, and emotion. The sociocultural approach emphasizes that culture, ethnicity, and gender are key dimensions of understanding behavior, thought, and emotion.

If psychology is to be a relevant discipline in the twenty-first century, increased attention needs to be given to sociocultural issues. These issues include diversity within, and differences and similarities among ethnic, cultural, and gender groups; reducing discrimination and prejudice; understanding the importance of value conflicts; globalizing psychology and reducing ethnocentrism; multiple determination of behavior; considering both sides of issues; and the role of psychology in improving the understanding of sociocultural issues and promoting the welfare of all human beings.

The Science Base of Psychology

Some people have difficulty thinking of psychology as a science in the same way that physics, chemistry, and biology are sciences. Can a discipline that studies why people are attracted to each other, how they reason about moral values, and how ethnicity affects identity be equated with disciplines that examine gravity, the molecular structure of a compound, or the flow of blood in the circulatory system?

Science is not defined by *what* it investigates but by *how* it investigates. Whether you investigate photosynthesis, butterflies, Saturn's moons, or the reasons people bite their nails, it is the way you investigate that makes the approach scientific or not.

To be a scientist is to be skeptical. When we think about ourselves and our world, we can speculate about mind and behavior: people don't change; love is blind; happiness is the key to success; people are maladjusted because society makes them that way; communication with spirits is possible. Such statements spark a psychologist's curiosity *and* skepticism. Psychology seeks to sort fact from fantasy by critically questioning the nature of mind and behavior. Shortly you will read about the role of theory and the scientific method in psychology. The scientific method is a tool that leads psychologists to be skeptical about pseudosciences, such as astrology, which appear to be, or are presented as, "scientific" but which are not.

Theory and the Scientific Method

A **theory** *is a coherent set of ideas that helps explain data and make predictions. A theory has hypotheses, assumptions that can be tested to determine their accuracy.* For example, a theory about depression explains our observations of depressed people and explains why they get depressed. We might predict that people will get depressed because they fail to focus on their strengths and dwell on their weaknesses. This prediction directs our observations by telling us to look for exaggerations of weaknesses and underestimations of strengths and skills.

The **scientific method** *is an approach used to discover accurate information about mind and behavior; it includes the following steps: identify and analyze the problem, collect data, draw conclusions, and revise theories.* We often generate hypotheses as we identify and analyze problems, and then again as we draw conclusions and revise theories. Let's apply the scientific method to the investigation of depression. For example, you decide you want to help people overcome depression. You have *identified a problem,* which does not seem to be a difficult task. As part of this first step, however, you need to go beyond a general description of the problem by isolating, analyzing, narrowing, and focusing on what you hope to investigate. What specific strategies do you want to use to reduce depression? Do you want to look at only one strategy or several strategies? What aspect of depression do you want to study— its biological characteristics, cognitive characteristics, or behavioral characteristics? Peter Lewinsohn and his colleagues (1984), for example, chose to study the behavioral and cognitive characteristics of depression. They analyzed depression's many components and chose to focus on whether people's lives could be improved by taking a course on coping with depression. One of the course's components involved teaching depressed people to control their negative thoughts. In this first step of the scientific method, the researchers identified and analyzed a problem.

The next step in the scientific method involves *collecting information (data).* Psychologists observe behavior and draw inferences about thoughts and emotions. In their investigation of depression, Lewinsohn and his colleagues observed how effectively people who completed the course on coping with depression monitored their moods and engaged in productive work.

Once psychologists have collected data, they *use statistical (mathematical) procedures* to understand the meaning of the quantitative data (information about statistical procedures appears in the appendix at the end of this book). Psychologists then *draw conclusions*. In an investigation of depression, statistics help a researcher determine whether the observations reflect real differences in how people cope with depression or whether they are due to chance or random fluctuations in the data. After psychologists analyze data, they compare their findings with what others have discovered about the same issue or problem.

The final step in the scientific method is *revising theory*. Psychologists have developed a number of theories about why we become depressed and how we can cope with depression. Data collected by Lewinsohn and his associates forced psychologists to reexamine existing theories of depression to see if they still held up (theories of depression are discussed in chapter 13). Over the years, some psychological theories were discarded, others revised. Wundt's theory of introspection was discarded, whereas behaviorism and psychoanalytic theory were substantially revised. The cognitive, neurobiological, and sociocultural approaches are undergoing revision as the scientific method is applied to the questions they raise. Figure 1.5 summarizes the main steps in the scientific method and provides an example of each.

Collecting Information—Measures

Systematic information is collected in a variety of ways. For example, we can watch behavior in the laboratory or in a more natural setting, such as on a street corner. We can question people using interviews and surveys, develop and administer standardized tests, conduct case studies, examine behavior cross-culturally, or carry out physiological research or research with animals. To help you understand how psychologists use these methods, we will apply each method to the study of aggression.

Observation

Sherlock Holmes chided Watson, "You see but you do not observe." We look at things all the time, but casually watching a friend cross the campus is not scientific observation. Unless you are a trained observer and practice your skills regularly, you may not know what to look for, you may not remember what you saw, what you are looking for may change from one moment to the next, and you may not communicate your observations effectively.

For observations to be effective, we have to know what we are looking for, whom we are observing, when and where we will observe, how the observations will be made, and in what form they will be recorded. That is, we need to observe in a *systematic* way. Consider aggression. Do we want to study verbal or physical aggression, or both? How will we know it when we see it? If one

man punches another in the arm, will we mark that down as aggression? If both men are laughing and one punches the other in the arm, will we still count the punch as aggression? Do we want to study men, women, children, or all of the above? Do we want to evaluate them in a university laboratory, at work, at play, in their homes, or at all of these locations? Do we want to audiotape or videotape their behavior, or both? A common way to record observations is to write them down, using shorthand or symbols; however, psychologists increasingly use tape recorders, video cameras, special coding sheets, and one-way mirrors to make observations more efficient.

When we observe, we often need to *control* certain factors that determine behavior but are not the focus of our inquiry. For this reason, much psychological research is conducted in a **laboratory,** *a controlled setting with many of the complex factors of the "real world" removed.* For example, Albert Bandura (1965) had an adult repeatedly hit a plastic, inflated doll about 3 feet tall. Bandura wondered to what extent the children would copy the adult's behavior. After the children saw the adult attack the Bobo doll, they also aggressively hit the inflated toy. By conducting his experiment in a laboratory with adults the children did not know, Bandura had complete control over when the children witnessed aggression, how much aggression they saw, and what form the aggression took. Bandura could not have conducted his experiment as effectively if other factors, such as parents, siblings, friends, television, and a familiar room, had been present.

Laboratory research has some drawbacks, however. First, it is almost impossible to conduct research without the participants knowing they are being studied. Second, the laboratory setting is *unnatural* and, therefore, can cause the participants to behave unnaturally. Research participants usually show less aggressive behavior in a laboratory than in a more familiar or natural setting, such as in a park or at home. They also show less aggression when they are aware they are being observed than when they are unaware they are being observed. Third, people who are willing to go to a university laboratory are unlikely to represent groups from diverse cultural backgrounds. Those who are unfamiliar with university settings, and with the idea of "helping science," may be intimidated by the setting. Fourth, some aspects of mind and behavior are difficult if not impossible to examine in the laboratory. For example, certain types of stress are difficult (and unethical) to study in the laboratory. Alcohol, for instance, consistently increases aggression in an individual when provoked. In 1985 at a soccer game in Brussels, Belgium, a riot broke out. The English fans, intoxicated by alcohol, aroused by the competition, and taunted by the Italian fans, attacked the Italians. As the Italians retreated, they were crushed against a wall—the death toll was 38. Recreating the circumstances in a laboratory that even remotely resemble the Brussels soccer game is impossible and unethical.

Although laboratory research is a valuable tool for psychologists, naturalistic observation provides insight that cannot be achieved in the laboratory. In **naturalistic observation,**

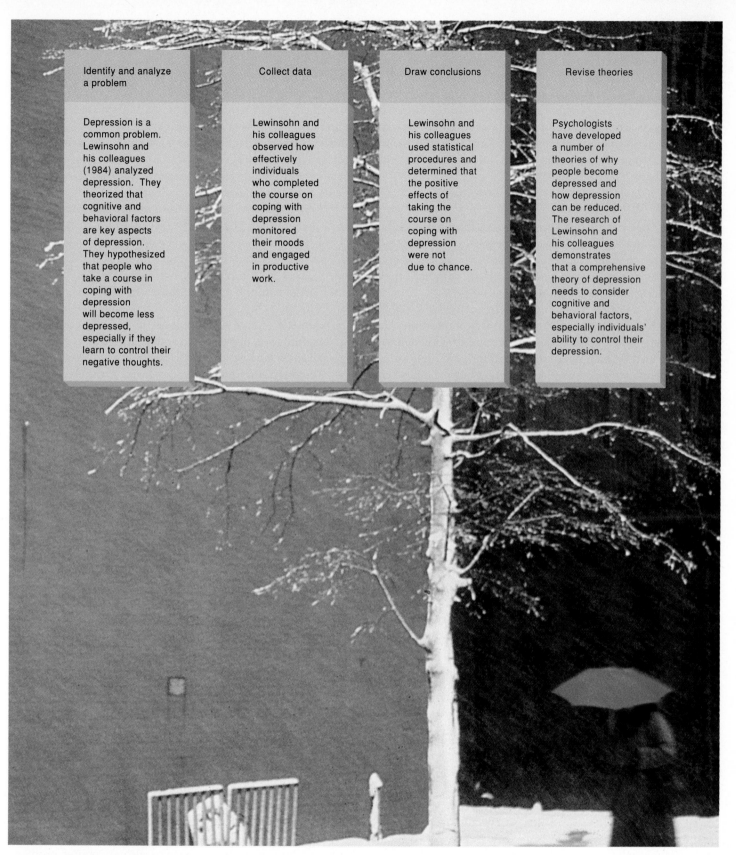

Identify and analyze a problem	Collect data	Draw conclusions	Revise theories
Depression is a common problem. Lewinsohn and his colleagues (1984) analyzed depression. They theorized that cognitive and behavioral factors are key aspects of depression. They hypothesized that people who take a course in coping with depression will become less depressed, especially if they learn to control their negative thoughts.	Lewinsohn and his colleagues observed how effectively individuals who completed the course on coping with depression monitored their moods and engaged in productive work.	Lewinsohn and his colleagues used statistical procedures and determined that the positive effects of taking the course on coping with depression were not due to chance.	Psychologists have developed a number of theories of why people become depressed and how depression can be reduced. The research of Lewinsohn and his colleagues demonstrates that a comprehensive theory of depression needs to consider cognitive and behavioral factors, especially individuals' ability to control their depression.

FIGURE 1.5

Steps in the scientific method and an application to depression.

psychologists observe behavior in real-world settings and make no effort to manipulate or control the situation. Psychologists conduct naturalistic observations at soccer games, day-care centers, college dormitories, rest rooms, corporations, shopping malls, restaurants, dances, and other places where people live and frequent. In contrast to Bandura's observations of aggression in a laboratory, psychologists using naturalistic methods observe the aggression of children in nursery schools, of marital partners at home, and of people at sporting events and political protests (Bronfenbrenner, 1989; Patterson, 1991).

Interviews and Questionnaires

Sometimes the best and quickest way to get information from people is to ask them for it. Psychologists use interviews and questionnaires to find out about a person's experiences and attitudes. Most interviews occur face-to-face, although they can take place over the telephone.

Interviews range from highly unstructured to highly structured. Examples of unstructured interview questions are the following: How aggressive do you see yourself? How aggressive is your child? Examples of structured interview questions include the following: In the past week, how often did you yell at your spouse? How often in the past year was your child involved in fights at school? Structure is imposed by the questions themselves, or the interviewer can categorize answers by asking respondents to choose from several options. For example, in the question about level of aggressiveness, you might be asked to choose from "highly aggressive," "moderately aggressive," "moderately unaggressive," and "highly unaggressive." In the question about how often you yelled at your spouse in the past week, you might be asked to choose "0," "1-2," "3-5," "6-10," or "more than 10 times."

An experienced interviewer knows how to put respondents at ease and how to encourage them to open up. A competent interviewer is sensitive to the way people respond to questions and often probes for more information. A person may respond with fuzzy statements to questions about the nature of marital conflict—for example, "Well, I don't know whether we have a lot of conflict or not." A skilled interviewer pushes for more specific, concrete answers, possibly asking, "If you had it to do over, would you get married?" or "Tell me the worst things you and your husband said to each other in the past week." Using these strategies forces researchers to be involved with, rather than detached from, the people they interview and yields a better understanding of mind and behavior (Gregory, 1992).

Interviews also have shortcomings. Perhaps the most critical is known as "social desirability," in which participants tell interviewers what they think is most socially acceptable or desirable rather than what they truly think or feel. When asked about her marital conflict, Jane may not want to disclose that arguments have been painfully tense in the past month. Sam, her husband, may not want to divulge his extramarital affair when asked about his sexual relationships. Skilled interviewing techniques and questions to help eliminate such defenses are critical in obtaining accurate information.

Psychologists also question people using questionnaires or surveys. A **questionnaire** *is similar to a highly structured interview except that respondents read the questions and mark their answers on paper rather than responding verbally to the interviewer.* One major advantage of surveys and questionnaires is that they can be given to a large number of people easily. Good surveys have concrete, specific, and unambiguous questions, and they assess the authenticity of the replies.

Sometimes psychologists want information about a small set of people, such as all Black graduates of a particular high school in the past 5 years or all college students from your campus who participated in a nuclear arms protest. At other times, we want to know something about a large population of people, such as all people in the United States. In each instance, it is important that the people surveyed represent the group to be described. This important task is accomplished by surveying a random sample of subjects. In a **random sample,** *every member of a population or group has an equal chance of being selected.*

Random samples are important because, in most instances, psychologists cannot survey everyone they are trying to describe—for example, all people in the United States. The National Crime Survey is an example of a random sample survey (U.S. Department of Justice, 1983). If we were to ask people from a high-crime area of Miami, Florida, if they had been a victim of crime and use this information to project the frequency of crime in the United States, projections would be inflated. Although certain pockets of Miami do have extremely high crime rates, the recent National Crime Survey, giving each household in the United States an equal chance of being surveyed, indicated that crime is high across the country—close to one-third of the households surveyed were victimized by violence or theft.

How do researchers obtain a random sample of subjects? In such cases as the National Crime Survey, methods ensure that those sampled are representative of the proportion of Anglo American, Black American, Hispanic American, Asian American, Native American, low-income, middle-income, high-income, rural, and urban individuals in the United States. A national random sample of 5,000 subjects, for example, has fewer Blacks than Whites, fewer high-income than low-income persons, and fewer rural than urban subjects.

Appropriate sampling methods are not always followed, however. Newspapers and magazines often conduct surveys of their readership. Those who participate by mailing or calling in their opinions probably feel more strongly about the issue in question than those who do not respond. Issues such as whether or not drunk driving laws should be tougher or whether or not premarital sex is morally wrong are likely to galvanize those with strong feelings into action. Surveys also encounter problems similar to interviews—people don't necessarily tell the truth, and the willingness to answer questions varies among groups.

Case Studies

A **case study** *is an in-depth look at one individual; it is used mainly by clinical psychologists when the unique aspects of an individual's life cannot be duplicated for study, either for practical or ethical reasons.* A case study provides information about one person's fears, hopes, fantasies, traumatic experiences, upbringing, family relationships, health, or anything else that helps the psychologist understand the person's mind and behavior.

Traumatic experiences have produced some fascinating case studies in psychology. Consider the following. A 26-year-old school teacher met a woman with whom he fell intensely in love. Several months after their love affair began, the school teacher became depressed, drank heavily, and talked about suicide. The suicidal ideas progressed to images of murder and suicide. His actions became bizarre. On one occasion, he punctured the tires of his beloved's car. On another he stood on the side of the road where she passed frequently in her car and extended his hand in his pocket so she would think he was holding a gun. His relationship with the woman vacillated between love and hate. Only 8 months after meeting her, the teacher shot her while he was a passenger in the car she was driving. Soon after the act, he ran to a telephone booth to call his priest. The woman died (Revitch & Schlesinger, 1978). This case reveals how depressive moods and bizarre thinking can precede violent acts, such as murder. Other vivid case studies appear throughout this text, among them a woman with three personalities, each of which is unaware of the others, and a modern-day wild child named Genie, who lived in near isolation during her childhood.

Although case histories provide dramatic, in-depth portrayals of people's lives, we need to exercise caution when generalizing from this information. The subject of a case study is unique, with a genetic makeup and experiences no one else shares. In addition, case studies involve judgments of unknown reliability. Psychologists who conduct case studies rarely check to see if other psychologists agree with their observations.

Standardized Tests

Standardized tests *require people to answer a series of written and oral questions. They have two distinct features. First, psychologists usually total an individual's score to yield a single score, or a set of scores, that reflects something about the individual. Second, psychologists compare the individual's score to the scores of a large group of similar people to determine how the individual responded relative to others.* Scores are often described in percentiles. For example, perhaps you scored in the 92nd percentile on the SAT. This measure tells you how much higher or lower you scored than the large group of individuals who previously took the test. Among the most widely used standardized tests in psychology are the Stanford-Binet intelligence test and the Minnesota Multiphasic Personality Inventory (MMPI).

To continue our look at how psychologists use various methods to evaluate aggression, consider the MMPI, which includes a scale to assess an individual's delinquency and antisocial tendencies. The items on this scale ask you to respond whether or not you are rebellious, are impulsive, and have trouble with authority figures. The 26-year-old teacher who murdered his girlfriend likely would have scored high on a number of the MMPI scales, including one designed to measure how strange our thoughts and ideas are.

The main advantage of standardized tests is that they provide information about *individual differences* among people. However, information obtained from standardized tests does not always predict behavior in nontest situations. Standardized tests are based on the belief that a person's behavior is consistent and stable. Although personality and intelligence, two of the primary targets of standardized tests, have some stability, they can vary with the situation. For example, a person may perform poorly on a standard intelligence test in an office setting but may display a much higher level of intelligence at home, where he or she is less anxious. This criticism is especially relevant for members of minority groups, some of whom have been inappropriately classified as mentally retarded on the basis of their scores on standardized intelligence tests. Cross-cultural psychologists caution that, although many psychological tests work reasonably well in Western cultures, they may not always be appropriate in cultures in which they were not developed (Lonner, 1990). For example, people in other cultures simply may not have had as much exposure to the information in the test questions. More about intelligence tests, including sociocultural issues in their use, appears in chapter 8, and more about personality tests is presented in chapter 12. Next we will examine cross-cultural research strategies and research with ethnic minority groups.

Cross-Cultural Research and Research with Ethnic Minority Groups

Researchers who are unfamiliar with the cultural and ethnic groups they are studying must take extra precautions to shed any biases they bring with them from their own culture. For example, they must make sure they construct measures that are meaningful for each of the cultural or ethnic minority groups being studied (Berry, 1980; Berry & others, in press).

In conducting research on cultural and ethnic minority issues, investigators distinguish between the emic approach and the etic approach. In the **emic approach,** *the goal is to describe behavior in one culture or ethnic group in terms that are meaningful and important to the people in that culture or ethnic group, without regard to other cultures or ethnic groups.* In the **etic approach,** *the goal is to describe behavior so that generalizations can be made across cultures.* That is, the emic approach is culture specific; the etic approach is culture universal. If researchers construct a questionnaire in an emic fashion, their concern is only that the questions are meaningful to the particular culture or ethnic

Systematic observations in natural settings provide valuable information about behavior across cultures. For example, in one investigation, observations in different cultures revealed that American children often engage in less work and more play than children in many other cultures (Whiting & Whiting, 1975). However, conducting cross-cultural research using such methods as systematic observation in natural settings is difficult and requires attention to a number of methodological issues (Berry & others, in press; Longabaugh, 1980).

group being studied. If, however, the researchers construct a questionnaire in an etic fashion, they want to include questions that reflect concepts familiar to all cultures involved (Atkinson, Morten, & Sue, 1989; Berry, 1969, 1990).

How might the emic and etic approaches be reflected in the study of family processes? In the emic approach, the researchers might choose to focus only on middle-class White families, without regard for whether the information obtained in the study can be generalized or is appropriate for ethnic minority groups. In a subsequent study, the researchers may decide to adopt an etic approach by studying not only middle-class White families, but also lower-income White families, Black American families, Hispanic American families, and Asian American families. In studying ethnic minority families, the researchers would likely discover that the extended family is more frequently a support system in ethnic minority families than in White American families. If so, the emic approach would reveal a different pattern of family interaction than would the etic approach, documenting that research with middle-class White families cannot always be generalized to all ethnic groups.

Cross-cultural psychologist Joseph Trimble (1989, 1991) is especially concerned about researchers' tendency to use *ethnic gloss* when they select and describe ethnic groups. By ethnic gloss, Trimble means using an ethnic label, such as Black, Hispanic, Asian, or Native American, in a superficial way that makes an ethnic group seem more homogeneous than it actually is. For example, the following is an unsuitable description of a research sample, according to Trimble: "The subjects included 28 Blacks, 22 Hispanics, and 24 Whites." An acceptable description of each of the groups requires much more detail about the participants' country of origin, socioeconomic status, language, and ethnic self-identification, such as this: "The 22 subjects were Mexican Americans from low-income neighborhoods in the southwestern area of Los Angeles. Twelve spoke Spanish in the home, while 10 spoke English; 11 were born in the United States, 11 were born in Mexico; 16 described themselves as Mexican, 3 as Chicano, 2 as American, and 1 as Latino." Trimble believes that ethnic gloss can cause researchers to obtain samples of ethnic groups and cultures that are not representative of their ethnic and cultural diversity, leading to overgeneralizations and stereotypes.

Let's go back to the study of aggression. Cross-cultural psychologists have found that aggression is universal, appearing in every culture. In this sense, it is an etic behavior; however, the expression of aggression may be culture specific, so aggression is also an emic behavior (Segall & others, 1990). For example, the !Kung of southern Africa actively dissuade one another from behaving aggressively, whereas the Yanomamo Indians of South America promote aggression. Yanomamo youths are told that adult status cannot be achieved unless they are capable of killing, fighting, and pummeling others (see figure 1.6).

Physiological Research and Research with Animals

Two additional methods that psychologists use to gather data are physiological research and research with animals. Research on the biological basis of behavior and technological advances continue to produce remarkable insights about mind and behavior. For example, researchers have found that the electrical stimulation of certain areas of the brain turn docile, mild-mannered people into hostile, vicious attackers, and higher concentrations of some hormones have been associated with anger in adolescents (Herbert, 1989; Susman & Dorn, 1991).

Since much physiological research cannot be carried out with humans, psychologists sometimes use animals. Animal studies permit researchers to control their subjects' genetic background, diet, experiences during infancy, and many other

a.   b.

FIGURE 1.6

Cultural influences on aggression. (a) The peaceful !Kung of Southern Africa discourage any kind of aggression; the !Kung are called the "harmless people." (b) Hardly harmless, the violent Yanomamo are called the "fierce people." Yanomamo youths are told that manhood cannot be achieved unless they are capable of killing, fighting, and pummeling others.

factors (Catania, 1990). In studying humans, psychologists treat these factors as random variation, or "noise," that may interfere with accurate results. In addition, animal researchers can investigate the effects of treatments (brain implants, for example) that would be unethical with humans. Moreover, it is possible to track the entire life cycle of some animals over a relatively short period of time. Laboratory mice, for instance, have a life span of approximately 1 year.

With regard to aggression, researchers know that castration turns ferocious bulls into docile oxen by acting on the male hormone system. After a number of breedings of aggressive mice, researchers have created mice that are ferocious (Manning, 1989). Do these findings with animals apply to humans? Hormones and genes do influence human aggression, but the influence is less powerful than in animals. Because humans differ from animals in many ways, one disadvantage of research with animals is that the results may not apply to humans.

Strategies for Setting Up Research Studies

Does listening to rock music deaden a person's hearing? Is overeating influenced by one's state of mind? Is high blood pressure due to stress? To answer such questions, psychologists not only choose a measure or measures, they also decide whether to use a correlational or an experimental research strategy.

Correlational Strategy

In the **correlational strategy,** *the goal is to describe the strength of the relation between two or more events or characteristics. This is a useful strategy because the more strongly events are correlated (related, or associated) the more effectively we can predict one from the other.* For example, consider one of our major national health problems, high blood pressure. If we find that high blood pressure is strongly associated with an inability to manage stress, then we can use the inability to manage stress to predict high blood pressure.

Often the next step is to conclude from such evidence that one event causes the other. Following this line of reasoning, we would erroneously conclude that the inability to manage stress causes high blood pressure. Why is this reasoning faulty? Why doesn't a strong correlation between two events mean that one event causes the other? A strong correlation could mean that the inability to manage stress causes high blood pressure; on the other hand, it could mean that high blood pressure causes an inability to manage stress. A third possibility also exists: although strongly correlated, the inability to manage stress and high blood pressure might not cause each other at all. It's possible that a third factor, such as a genetic tendency, poor nutrition, or a lack of exercise, underlies their association (see figure 1.7).

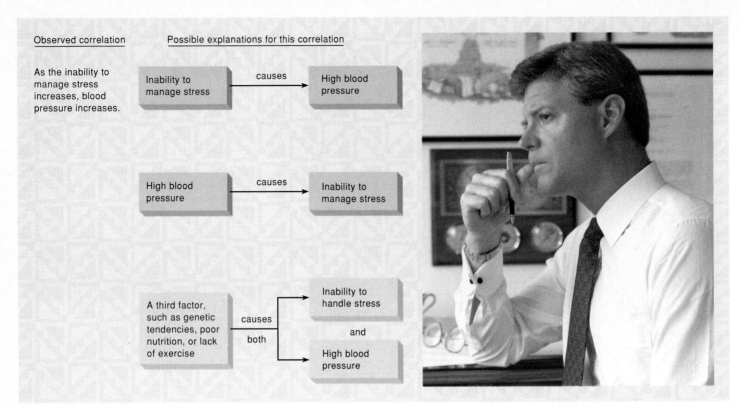

Observed correlation | Possible explanations for this correlation

As the inability to manage stress increases, blood pressure increases.

Inability to manage stress — causes → High blood pressure

High blood pressure — causes → Inability to manage stress

A third factor, such as genetic tendencies, poor nutrition, or lack of exercise — causes both → Inability to handle stress and High blood pressure

FIGURE 1.7

Possible explanations of correlational data. An observed correlation between two events cannot be used to conclude that one event causes a second event. Other possibilities are that the second event causes the first event or that a third, unknown event causes the correlation between the first two events.

To ensure that your understanding of correlation is clear, let's look at another example. Suppose that people who make a lot of money have higher self-esteem than those who make less money. We could mistakenly interpret this to mean that making a lot of money causes us to have high self-esteem. What are the two other interpretations we need to consider? It could be that developing high self-esteem causes us to make a lot of money, or that a third factor, such as education, social upbringing, or genetic tendencies, causes the correlation between making a lot of money and high self-esteem. Throughout this text, you will read about numerous studies that were based on a correlational strategy. Keep in mind how easy it is to assume causality when two events or characteristics are merely correlated.

Experimental Strategy

Whereas the correlational strategy allows us to say only that two events are related, the **experimental strategy** *allows us to precisely determine behavior's causes.* Psychologists accomplish this task by performing an **experiment,** *which is a carefully regulated procedure in which one or more of the factors believed to influence the behavior being studied are manipulated and all others are held constant.* If the behavior under study changes when a factor is manipulated, the manipulated factor has caused the behavior to change. Experiments are used to establish cause and effect between events, something correlational studies cannot do. *Cause* is the event being manipulated and *effect* is the behavior that changes because of the manipulation. Remember that, in testing correlation, nothing is manipulated; in an experiment, the researcher actively changes an event to see the effect on behavior.

The following example illustrates the nature of an experiment. Let's say we want to find out if marijuana impairs alertness and increases confidence (Saslow, 1982). Since marijuana is not legally available, we obtain permission from the appropriate authorities to use the drug in an experiment. We decide that, to conduct our experiment, we need one group of participants who will smoke marijuana and one group who will not. We randomly assign the participants to these two groups. **Random assignment** *occurs when psychologists assign subjects to experimental and control conditions by chance, thus reducing the likelihood that the results of the experiment will be due to preexisting differences between the two groups.* For example, random assignment greatly reduces the probability that the two groups will differ on such factors as prior use of marijuana, health problems, intelligence, alertness, social class, and age.

In our example, the participants who smoke the marijuana are called the **experimental group**—*that is, the group whose experience is manipulated.* Those who do not smoke marijuana make up the **control group**—*that is, a comparison group treated in every way like the experimental group except for the manipulated factor. The control group serves as a baseline against which the effects found in the manipulated condition can be compared.*

After the participants in the experimental group have smoked the marijuana, the behaviors of the two groups are compared. We choose to study how fast the subjects will react when asked to make a simple hand movement in response to a flash of light. We also decide to ask them later how well they thought they performed this task. When we analyze the results, we find that the subjects who smoked the marijuana were slower in reacting to the flash of light but actually thought they did better than those who did not smoke marijuana. We then conclude that smoking marijuana decreases alertness but increases confidence.

The **independent variable** is *the manipulated, influential, experimental factor in an experiment. The label* independent *is used because this variable can be changed independently of other factors.* In the marijuana experiment, the amount of marijuana smoked is the independent variable. The experimenter manipulates how much marijuana the subjects use independently of all other factors. The **dependent variable** *is the factor that is measured in an experiment; it may change as the independent variable is manipulated. The label* dependent *is used because this variable depends on what happens to the subjects in the experiment.* In the marijuana experiment, the dependent variable is represented by two measures: a task that measures reaction time to determine alertness and a question to evaluate confidence. The subjects' responses on these measures depend on the influence of the independent variable (whether or not marijuana was smoked). An illustration of the nature of the experimental strategy, applied to the marijuana study, is shown in figure 1.8.

Remember that the correlational study of the relation between stress and blood pressure gave us little indication of whether stress influences blood pressure, or vice versa. A third factor may have caused the correlation. The following example of an experimental study of stress management and high blood pressure allows us to make conclusions about *causality* (Irvine & others, 1986). Thirty-two men and women with high blood pressure were randomly assigned to either a group trained in relaxation and stress management (experimental group) or a group who received no training (control group). The independent variable consisted of 10 weekly 1-hour sessions that included educational information about the nature of stress and how to manage it, as well as extensive training in learning to relax and control stress in everyday life. The blood pressure of both groups was assessed before the training program and 3 months after it was completed. At the 3-month follow-up, nurses who were unaware of which group the subjects had been in

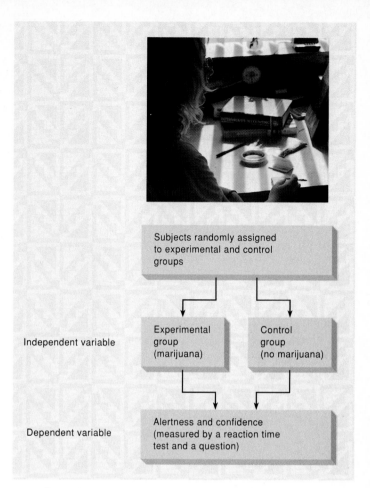

FIGURE 1.8

Experimental strategy in psychology: its nature and an example of the effects of marijuana on alertness and confidence.

measured their blood pressure. The results indicated that the relaxation and stress management program (the independent variable) was effective in reducing high blood pressure.

It might seem that we should always choose an experimental strategy over a correlational strategy, since the experimental strategy gives us a better sense of the influence of one variable over another. However, there are three instances when a correlational strategy might be preferred: (1) when the focus of the investigation is so new (as when AIDS first appeared) that we have little knowledge of which variables to manipulate, (2) when it is impossible to manipulate the variables (such as the factors involved in suicide), and (3) when it is unethical to manipulate the variables (for example, determining the association between illness and exposure to dangerous chemicals).

Now that we have considered the basic ways that psychologists conduct research, it is also important to examine how psychological research can become less sexist and ethical considerations in psychological research.

Reducing Sexism in Research

Traditional science is supposed to be objective, unbiased. However, there is a growing consensus that science in general, and psychology in particular, are not (Doyle & Paludi, 1991). A special concern is that the vast majority of psychological research has been male oriented and male dominated. Some researchers believe that sciences, such as psychology, need to be challenged to examine the world in a new way, one that incorporates women's perspectives and respects their ethnicity, sexual orientation, age, and socioeconomic status (Denmark & others, 1988; McHugh, Koeske, & Frieze, 1986; Paludi, 1992; Quina, 1986).

Gender bias can influence any stage of the research process and should be guarded against from the time a study is designed until conclusions about the data are written (Denmark & others, 1988; Gannon & others, 1992). For example, researchers who study contraceptives but use only female subjects reflect the assumption and stereotypes about who should be responsible for birth control. Studies of this type often have titles, such as "perceptions of contraceptive use," that imply that the study has a broader scope than is warranted. The use of more precise titles and concluding statements are needed to clarify who was in the sample and, therefore, to whom the study results apply (Denmark & others, 1988).

Florence Denmark (shown here talking with a group of students) has developed a number of guidelines for nonsexist research. Denmark and others believe that psychology needs to be challenged to examine the world in a new way, one that incorporates girls' and women's perspectives.

Ethics in Psychological Research

When Anne and Pete, two 19-year-old college students, agreed to participate in an investigation of dating couples, they did not consider the possibility that the questionnaire they completed would stimulate them to think about issues that might lead to conflict in their relationship, and possibly end it. One year after the study was conducted, 9 of 10 participants said they had discussed their answers with their dating partner (Rubin & Mitchell, 1976). In most instances, the discussions helped strengthen the relationships, but, in some cases, the participants used the questionnaire as a springboard to discuss problems or concerns previously hidden. One participant said, "The study definitely played a role in ending my relationship with Larry." In this case, the couple had held different views about how long they expected to be together. She was thinking of a short-term dating relationship only, whereas he was thinking in terms of a lifetime. Their answers to the questions brought disparity in their views to the surface and eventually led Larry to find someone who was more interested in marrying him.

Ethics Guidelines of the American Psychological Association

At first glance, you would not imagine that a questionnaire on dating relationships would have any substantial impact on those who participate in such research. However, increasingly psychologists are recognizing that considerable caution must be taken to ensure the well-being of the participants in a psychological study. Today colleges and universities have review boards that evaluate the ethical nature of the research conducted at their institutions. Proposed research plans must pass the scrutiny of a research ethics committee before the research can be initiated. In addition, the American Psychological Association (APA) has developed ethics guidelines for its members.

The code of ethics adopted by the APA instructs psychologists to protect their research subjects from mental and physical harm. The best interest of the subjects needs to be kept foremost in the researcher's mind. All subjects must give their informed consent to participate in research, which requires that subjects know what their participation will involve and any risks that might develop. For example, dating research subjects should be told beforehand that a questionnaire may stimulate thought about issues in their relationship that they haven't considered. Subjects also should be informed that, in some instances, a discussion of the issues raised can improve their dating relationship, whereas, in other cases, it can worsen the relationship or end it. Even after giving their informed consent, subjects retain the right to withdraw from a study at any time.

Deception is an ethical issue that psychologists have debated extensively. In some circumstances, telling subjects beforehand what the research study is about substantially alters their behavior and destroys the investigator's data. For example, a psychologist wants to know whether a bystander will report a theft. A mock theft is staged, and the psychologist observes which bystanders report it. Had the psychologist informed the bystanders beforehand that the study intended to discover the percentage of bystanders who will report a theft, the intent of the study would have been lost. In all cases of deception, psychologists must ensure that the deception will not harm the subjects and must tell the subjects the complete nature of the study (called debriefing) as soon as possible after the study is completed.

Researchers who conduct studies in communities and with various ethnic and cultural groups have ethical responsibilities to large groups of people. As researchers, psychologists have a responsibility to respect local morals and customs. They also should be honest with the community, ethnic, and cultural groups about the nature of the research agenda, especially if the research plans violate local sensibilities. As guests in another's setting, psychologists need to avoid the temptation to dispense wisdom and should resist trying to change situations they were not invited to change. As ethical professionals, psychologists have an obligation to write research findings in a nonjudgmental way that does not unfairly portray any particular group. They also should share such findings with interested representatives of the community, cultural, or ethnic group (Levine & Perkins, 1987).

How Ethical Is Research with Animals?

The annual meeting of the American Psychological Association has been the frequent target of animal welfare and animal rights activists over the past decade. They often chant slogans, such as PSYCHOLOGISTS ARE KILLING OUR ANIMALS and STOP THE PAIN AND ABUSE.

For generations, some psychologists have used animals in their research, research that has provided a better understanding of, and solutions for, many human problems. Neal Miller (1985), a leading figure in contemporary psychology who has made important discoveries about the effects of biofeedback on health, listed the following areas in which animal research has benefited humans:

• Psychotherapy and behavioral medicine
• Rehabilitation of neuromuscular disorders
• Understanding and alleviating the effects of stress and pain

Psychologists show concern about the ethical standards for conducting research with animals. Psychologists must carefully evaluate the benefits of their animal research for humankind.

• Discovery and testing of drugs to treat anxiety and severe mental illness
• Knowledge about drug addiction and relapse
• Treatments to help premature infants gain weight so they can leave the hospital sooner
• Knowledge about memory used to alleviate deficits of memory in old age

How widespread is animal research in psychology? Only about 5 percent of all APA members use animals in their research. Rats and mice are by far the most widely used, accounting for 90 percent of all psychological research with animals.

How widespread is abuse to animals in psychological research? According to animal welfare and rights activists, it is extensive (Dawkins, 1990). It is true that researchers sometimes use procedures that would be unethical with humans, but they are guided by a stringent set of standards that addresses such matters as the housing, feeding, and psychological well-being of animals. Researchers are required to weigh the potential benefit of their research against the possible harm to the animal and to avoid inflicting unnecessary pain. Animal abuse is not as common as animal activists groups charge. However, stringent ethical guidelines must be followed when animals or humans are the subjects in psychological research (Driscoll & Bateson, 1988).

REVIEW

The Scientific Basis of Psychology

Theories are general beliefs that help us explain what we observe and make predictions. A good theory has hypotheses, which are assumptions that can be tested to determine their accuracy. The scientific method is a series of procedures (identifying and analyzing a problem, collecting data, drawing conclusions, and revising theory) to obtain accurate information.

Systematic observation is a key ingredient in psychological research; it includes laboratory and naturalistic observations. Interviews and questionnaires (or surveys) assess people's perceptions and attitudes, although people sometimes lie or give socially desirable responses. Representative sampling is crucial to a good survey. A case study provides an in-depth look at an individual. Caution in generalizing to others from a case study is warranted. Standardized tests are designed to assess an individual's characteristics relative to those of a large group of similar individuals. Cross-cultural research and research with ethnic minorities require certain strategies; one consideration is whether to follow an emic or an etic approach. Physiological research and research with animals focus on the biological dimensions of organisms. Although greater control over conditions can be achieved with animals, generalization from animals to humans may be problematic.

The correlational strategy describes how strongly two or more events or characteristics are related. It does not allow causal statements. The experimental strategy involves the manipulation of influential factors—the independent variables—and the measurement of their effect on the dependent variables. Subjects are assigned randomly to experimental and control groups in many studies. The experimental strategy can reveal the causes of behavior and tell us how one event influences another.

The vast majority of psychological research has been male oriented and male dominated. Some researchers believe that psychology needs to be challenged to examine the world in a new way, one that incorporates girls' and women's perspectives. Recommendations have been made for conducting nonsexist research. Researchers must ensure the well-being of subjects in psychological studies. The risk of mental and physical harm must be reduced, informed consent should occur, and deception should be used with caution. Controversy currently surrounds the use of animals in psychological research, although abuse is not as extensive as some activists charge.

Psychology's Many Areas of Specialization

Psychologists don't spend all of their time in a laboratory, white-smocked with clipboard in hand, observing rats and crunching numbers. Some psychologists spend their days seeing people with problems; others teach at universities and conduct research. Still others work in business and industry, designing more efficient criteria for hiring. In short, psychology is a field with many areas of specialization.

Careers in Psychology

You may already be wondering whether or not to major in psychology. Studying psychology as an undergraduate can give you a sound preparation for what lies ahead by helping you understand, predict, and control the events in your own life. You'll also gain a solid academic background that will enable you to enter various careers and go on to graduate programs, not just in psychology but in other areas as well, such as business and law (Woods & Wilkinson, 1987). A bachelor's degree in psychology will not automatically lead to fame and fortune, but it is a highly marketable degree for a wide range of jobs, including parent educator, drug abuse counselor, mental health aide, teacher for mentally retarded children, and staff member at a crisis hotline center. An undergraduate degree in psychology also provides excellent training for many jobs in business, especially in the areas of sales, personnel, or training. If you choose a career in psychology, you can greatly expand your opportunities (and income) by obtaining a graduate degree, although a master's or doctoral degree is not absolutely necessary. Also, because there are so few ethnic minority psychologists, job opportunities are increasingly available to qualified applicants. Where do psychologists work? Only slightly more than one-third are teachers, researchers, or counselors at colleges or universities. Most psychologists—almost half, in fact—work in clinical and private practice settings (see figure 1.9).

Areas of Specialization in Psychology

If you go to graduate school, you will be required to specialize in a particular area of psychology. Following is a list of some of the specializations: clinical and counseling; community; experimental and physiological; developmental, social, and personality; school and educational; industrial and organizational; cross-cultural; and women's psychology. Sometimes the categories are not mutually exclusive. For example, some social psychologists are also experimental psychologists.

Clinical and counseling psychology *is the most widely practiced specialization in psychology; clinical and counseling psychologists diagnose and treat people with psychological problems. The*

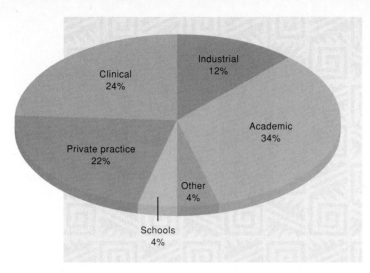

FIGURE 1.9

Settings in which psychologists work.

work of clinical psychologists often does not differ from that of counseling psychologists, although a counseling psychologist sometimes deals with people who have less serious problems. In many instances, counseling psychologists work with students, advising them about personal problems and career planning.

Clinical psychologists are different from psychiatrists. Typically a clinical psychologist has a doctoral degree in psychology, which requires 3 to 4 years of graduate work, plus 1 year of internship in a mental health facility. **Psychiatry** *is a branch of medicine practiced by physicians with a doctor of medicine (M.D.) degree, who subsequently specialize in abnormal behavior and psychotherapy.* Clinical psychologists and psychiatrists both are interested in improving the lives of people with mental health problems. One important distinction is that psychiatrists can prescribe drugs, whereas clinical psychologists cannot.

Community psychology *focuses on providing accessible care for people with psychological problems. Community-based mental health centers are one means of providing such services as outreach programs to people in need, especially those who traditionally have been underserved by mental health professionals.* Community psychologists view human behavior in terms of adaptation to resources and to one's situation. They work to create communities that are more supportive of residents by pinpointing needs, by providing needed services, and by teaching people how to gain access to resources already available. Finally, community psychologists are also concerned about prevention. They try to prevent mental health problems by identifying high-risk groups and then intervening to provide appropriate services and by stimulating new opportunities in the community.

Experimental and physiological psychology *are areas that often involve pure research. Although psychologists in other areas conduct experiments,* virtually all experimental and physiological psychologists follow precise, careful experimental strategies. These psychologists are more likely to work with animals, although many do not. Experimental psychologists explore the mental terrain of memory, sensation and perception, motivation, and emotion. Physiological psychologists investigate a range of topics—from the role of the brain in behavior to the influence of drugs on hormones. The neurobiological approach to psychology is closely aligned with physiological psychology.

Developmental psychology *is concerned with how we become who we are from birth to death.* In particular, developmental psychologists focus on the biological and environmental factors that contribute to human development. For many years, the major emphasis was on child development. However, an increasing number of today's developmental psychologists show a strong interest in adult development and aging. Their inquiries range across the biological, cognitive, and social domains of life.

Social psychology *deals with people's social interactions, relationships, perceptions, and attitudes.* Social psychologists believe we can better understand mind and behavior if we know something about how people function in groups.

Personality psychology *focuses on the relatively enduring traits and characteristics of individuals.* Personality psychologists study such topics as self-concept, aggression, moral development, gender roles, and inner or outer directedness.

School and educational psychology *is concerned with children's learning and adjustment in school.* School psychologists counsel children and parents when children have problems in school. They often give children psychological tests to assess personality and intelligence. Most educational psychologists, like other academic psychologists, also teach and conduct research.

Industrial/organizational psychology *deals with the workplace, focusing on both the workers and the organizations that employ them.* Industrial/organizational psychologists are concerned with training employees, improving working conditions, and developing criteria for selecting employees. For example, an organizational psychologist might recommend that a company adopt a new management structure that would increase communication between managers and staff. The background of industrial and organizational psychologists often includes training in social psychology.

Cross-cultural psychology *examines the role of culture in understanding behavior, thought, and emotion. Cross-cultural psychologists compare the nature of psychological processes in different cultures, with a special interest in whether or not psychological phenomena are universal or culture specific.* The International Association for Cross-Cultural Psychology promotes research on cross-cultural comparisons and awareness of culture's role in psychology.

The **psychology of women** *emphasizes the importance of promoting the research and study of women, integrating this information about women with current psychological knowledge and* beliefs, and applying the information to society and its institutions (Russo, 1984). The Division of the Psychology of Women in the American Psychological Association was formed in 1973. Information about the history and careers of women psychologists, as well as ethnic minority psychologists, appears in Sociocultural Worlds 1.2.

In the second half of this chapter, we have discussed the science base of psychology and psychology's many areas of specialization. In this first chapter, we also briefly examined the area of psychology known as neurobiology and physiological psychology. In chapter 2, we will explore it further, revealing a cascade of fascinating events that underlie our thoughts, emotions, and actions. These events often take place in the 100 billion nerve cells that neuroscientists sometimes refer to as the "three-pound universe," the brain.

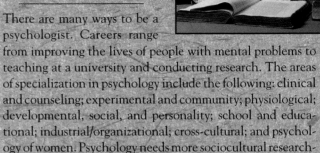

REVIEW

Psychology's Many Areas of Specialization

There are many ways to be a psychologist. Careers range from improving the lives of people with mental problems to teaching at a university and conducting research. The areas of specialization in psychology include the following: clinical and counseling; experimental and community; physiological; developmental, social, and personality; school and educational; industrial/organizational; cross-cultural; and psychology of women. Psychology needs more sociocultural researchers, as well as more ethnic minority individuals, in all areas.

Summary

I. Defining Psychology and the Beginnings of Psychology

Psychology is the scientific study of behavior and mental processes in contexts. Behavior is everything we do that can be directly observed. Mental processes are the thoughts, feelings, and motives that we experience privately but that cannot be directly observed. As a science, psychology seeks to describe, explain, and predict behavior. Contexts are the settings in which mental processes and behavior occur, settings that are influenced by historical, economic, social, and cultural factors. Recently there has been a renewed interest in contexts in psychology. The contexts of mental processes and behavior are discussed extensively in this text. Thinking about psychological concepts began with the early Greek philosophers, such as Socrates and Aristotle, and Chinese philosophers, such as Confucius. The beginning of psychology as a science occurred when Wilhelm Wundt developed the first scientific laboratory of psychology in 1879 in Leipzig, Germany. Many of the early psychologists, such as Wundt and James, used introspection, the technique whereby specially trained individuals carefully observe and analyze their own mental experiences.

II. Approaches to Behavior, Mental Processes, and Contexts

The behavioral approach emphasizes the scientific study of observable behavioral responses and their environmental determinants. The psychoanalytic approach focuses on the unconscious, conflict, and early family experiences. The humanistic approach emphasizes a person's capacity for growth, freedom to choose an identity, and positive qualities. The cognitive approach emphasizes cognitive, or thought, processes, such as attention, perception, memory, thinking, and problem solving. The neurobiological approach emphasizes that the brain and nervous system play central roles in understanding behavior, thought, and emotion. The sociocultural approach emphasizes that culture, ethnicity, and gender are key dimensions of understanding behavior, thought, and emotion.

III. Sociocultural Issues

If psychology is to be a relevant discipline in the twenty-first century, increased attention needs to be given to sociocultural issues. These issues include diversity, differences, and similarities among ethnic, cultural, and gender groups; reducing discrimination and prejudice; understanding the importance of value conflicts; globalizing psychology and reducing

ethnocentrism; multiple determination of behavior; considering both sides of issues; and the role of psychology in improving understanding of sociocultural issues and promoting the welfare of all human beings.

IV. Theory and the Scientific Method

Theories are general beliefs that help us explain what we observe and make predictions. A good theory has hypotheses, which are assumptions that can be tested to determine their accuracy. The scientific method is a series of procedures (identifying and analyzing a problem, collecting data, drawing conclusions, and revising theory) used to obtain accurate information.

V. Collecting Information About Mind and Behavior

Systematic observation is a key ingredient in psychological research; it includes laboratory and naturalistic observations. Interviews and questionnaires (or surveys) assess people's perceptions and attitudes, although people sometimes lie or give socially desirable responses. Representative sampling is crucial to a good survey. A case study provides an in-depth look at an individual. Caution in generalizing to others from a case study is warranted. Standardized tests are designed to assess an individual's characteristics relative to those

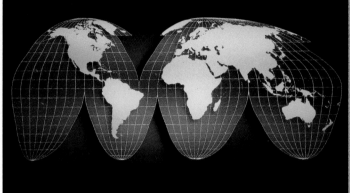

SOCIOCULTURAL WORLDS 1.2

Women and Ethnic Minorities in Psychology

Until recently psychology, like so many professions, kept women out (Kimmel, 1992). During its first 75 years, few women broke through to psychology's inner sanctum. In fact, the first American woman to complete requirements for a doctorate in psychology, Christine Ladd-Franklin, was denied the degree in 1892 simply because she was a woman. Mary Calkins' history is another example of the barriers women faced. In 1891 she introduced psychology into Wellesley College's curriculum and established its first psychology laboratory. In 1892 she returned to Harvard for additional training. By 1894 Mary Calkins had developed a technique for investigating memory and had completed the requirements for a doctoral degree. Her Harvard psychology professors enthusiastically recommended that she be awarded the degree, but the administration refused because Calkins was a woman (Furumoto, 1989).

The first woman actually to be awarded a doctorate in psychology was Margaret Washburn in 1894. By 1906 about 1 in every 10 psychologists was a woman. Today the number of men and women receiving a doctorate in psychology is approximately equal (Furumoto & Scarborough, 1986).

Similarly, discrimination has barred many individuals from ethnic minority groups from entering the field of psychology. The first Black American to become a professor of psychology was Gilbert Jones, who obtained his doctorate at the University of Jena in Germany in 1909. Ethnic minority women, especially, faced overwhelming odds. It wasn't until 1934 that a Black woman, Ruth Howard at the University of Minnesota, finally received a doctorate in psychology. Over a period of about 50 years, the 10 universities with the most prestigious programs in psychology granted several thousand doctoral degrees, yet by 1969 these universities had awarded only 8 doctoral degrees to Black students (Albee, 1988). Few Hispanics have been awarded doctoral degrees—recent surveys indicate that less than 2 percent of all psychologists are Hispanic (Cervantes, 1987). George Sanchez is one of the few. His pioneering research demonstrated that intelligence tests are culturally biased against ethnic minority children. There are also very few Native American psychologists (McShane, 1987).

Over the past 25 years, the women's movement and the civil rights movement helped put the rights and needs of women and ethnic minorities on politicians' agendas and led to social change (Bronstein & Quina, 1988). Similarly psychologists, especially those belonging to these groups, were spurred to reexamine psychology's basic premises and to question its relevance to their own experiences and concerns. This reexamination sparked new inquiry into populations that previously had been omitted from psychological research and the mainstream theories of psychology. Such journals as *Psychology of Women Quarterly*, *Sex Roles*, the *Hispanic Journal of Behavioral Science*, and the *Journal of Black Psychology* address the growing interest in gender and ethnic minority issues.

In recognizing the dearth of ethnic minority psychologists, the American Psychological Association has formed the Committee on Ethnic Minority Affairs to ensure that the concerns of its ethnic group members are heard. The Association of Black Psychologists directly involves its members in issues that are important to the Black community (Jones, 1987). The Asian American Psychological Association identifies resources, develops ideas for education and training, and fosters scientific research on issues of importance to the Asian American community (Suinn, 1987).

of a large group of similar individuals. Cross-cultural research and research with ethnic minorities require certain strategies; one consideration is whether to follow an emic or an etic approach. Physiological research and research with animals focus on the biological dimensions of the organism. Although greater control over conditions can be achieved with animals, generalization from animals to humans may be problematic.

VI. Strategies for Setting Up Research Studies

The correlational strategy describes how strongly two or more events or characteristics are related. It does not allow causal statements. The experimental strategy involves the manipulation of influential factors—the independent variables—and the measurement of their effect on the dependent variables. Subjects are assigned randomly to experimental and control

groups in many studies. The experimental strategy can reveal the causes of behavior and tell us how one event influences another.

VII. Reducing Sexism in Research; Ethics

The vast majority of psychological research has been male oriented and male dominated. Some researchers believe that psychology needs to be challenged to examine the world in a new way, one that incorporates girls' and women's perspectives. Recommendations have been made for conducting nonsexist research. Researchers must ensure the well-being of subjects in psychological studies. The risk of mental and physical harm must be reduced, informed consent should occur, and deception should be used with caution. Controversy currently surrounds the use of animals in psychological research, although abuse is not as extensive as some activists charge.

VIII. Psychology's Many Areas of Specialization

There are many ways to be a psychologist. Careers range from improving the lives of people with mental problems to teaching at a university and conducting research. The areas of specialization in psychology include clinical and counseling; experimental and community; physiological; developmental, social, and personality; school and educational; industrial/organizational; cross-cultural; and psychology of women. Psychology needs more sociocultural researchers, as well as more ethnic minority individuals, in all areas.

Key Terms

psychology 5
behavior 5
mental processes 5
science 5
contexts 6
introspection 7
behavioral approach 8
psychoanalytic approach 8
humanistic approach 9
cognitive approach 9
neurobiological approach 9
sociocultural approach 9
culture 9
ethnicity 9
ethnic identity 9
gender 11

assimilation 16
pluralism 16
ethnocentrism 16
theory 19
scientific method 19
laboratory 20
naturalistic observation 20
questionnaire 22
random sample 22
case study 23
standardized tests 23
emic approach 23
etic approach 23
correlational strategy 25
experimental strategy 26
experiment 26
random assignment 26

experimental group 27
control group 27
independent variable 27
dependent variable 27
clinical and counseling psychology 30
psychiatry 31
community psychology 31
experimental and physiological psychology 31
developmental psychology 31
social psychology 31
personality psychology 31
school and educational psychology 31
industrial/organizational psychology 31
cross-cultural psychology 31
psychology of women 31

Suggested Readings

Agnew, N. Mck., & Pyke, S. W. (1987). *The science game* (4th ed.). Englewood Cliffs, NJ: Prentice-Hall. This popular book covers a number of important ideas about research methods in an entertaining and informative way.

Bronstein, P. A., & Quina, K. (Eds.). (1988). *Teaching a psychology of people: Resources for gender and sociocultural awareness.* Washington, DC: American Psychological Association. This important resource book includes a number of chapters devoted to cultural, ethnic, and gender issues. A special emphasis is given to how gender balance and ethnic diversity can be achieved in psychology.

Watson, R. I. (1986). *The great psychologists: Aristotle to Freud.* Philadelphia: Lippincott. A fascinating look at early psychologists' views on mind and behavior is provided.

Woods, P. J., & Wilkinson, C. S. (1987). *Is psychology the major for you?* Washington, DC: American Psychological Association. This book is must reading for any student interested in a career in psychology. It shows how a degree in psychology can be valuable in preparing for many diverse careers, including human services, management, and marketing. It also includes separate chapters on women in psychology, Native Americans and Alaska natives, Asian Americans, Blacks, Hispanics, and the reentry of men and women into psychology. The book provides the addresses of various organizations and associations in psychology, including those involved in ethnic psychology and women's studies. Some of these organizations, including the American Psychological Association, have student memberships.

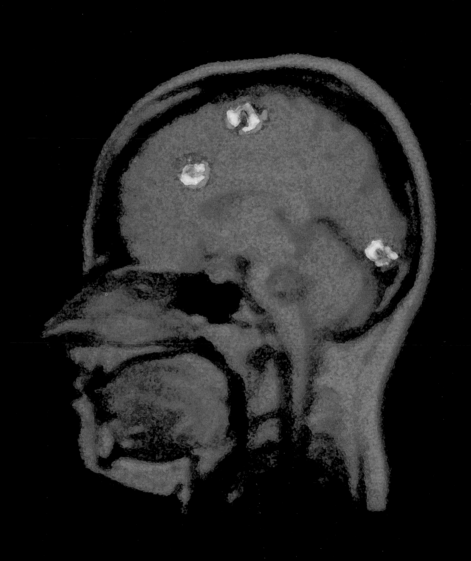

BIOLOGICAL FOUNDATIONS
AND THE BRAIN

CHAPTER 2

Jim Springer and Jim Lewis are identical twins. They were separated at the age of 4 weeks and didn't see one another again until they were 39 years old. Even so, they share uncanny similarities that read more like fiction than fact. For example, they have both worked as a part-time deputy sheriff, have vacationed in Florida, have driven Chevrolets, have had dogs named Toy, and have married and divorced women named Betty. In addition, one twin named his son James Allan, and the other named his son James Alan. Both like math but not spelling, and both enjoy carpentry and mechanical drawing. They have chewed their fingernails down to the nubs and have almost identical drinking and smoking habits. Both have had hemorrhoids, put on 10 pounds at about the same time, and first suffered headaches at the age of 18. They also have similar sleep patterns.

Jim and Jim have some differences as well. One wears his hair over his forehead, whereas the other wears it slicked back with sideburns. One expresses himself better verbally; the other is more proficient in writing. For the most part, however, they are more alike than different.

The Jim and Jim twins were part of the Minnesota Study of Twins Reared Apart, directed by Thomas Bouchard and his colleagues. The researchers brought identical (genetically identical because they come from the same egg) and fraternal (genetically dissimilar because they come from two eggs) twins from all over the world to Minneapolis to investigate the psychological aspects of the twins' lives. For example, the twins were interviewed and asked more than 15,000 questions about their family and childhood environment, personal interests, vocational orientation, values, and aesthetic judgments. Detailed medical histories were obtained, including information about their smoking, diet, and exercise habits. The researchers also took chest X rays and gave heart stress tests and EEGs (brain wave tests). The twins were also given a number of personality, ability, and intelligence tests (Bouchard & others, 1981; McGue & Bouchard, 1989).

Critics of the Minnesota twins study point out that some of the separated twins had been together several months prior to their adoption, that some twins had been reunited prior to their testing (in some cases a number of years earlier), that adoption agencies often place twins in similar homes, and that even strangers who spend several hours together and start comparing their lives are likely to come up with coincidental similarities (Adler, 1991). Still, even in the face of such criticism, the Minnesota study demonstrates the interest scientists have shown in the genetic basis of behavior.

The bizarre similarities between the Jim and Jim twins raise questions about the role genes play in human behavior and the biological foundations of our existence. How are characteristics transmitted from one generation to the next, for instance? How did the human species come to be? What gives us our extraordinary ability to adapt to our world? These questions focus on genetics, evolution, and the brain, this chapter's main topics.

The Jim twins: how coincidental? Springer, left, and Lewis were unaware of each other for 40 years.

FIGURE 2.1

The remarkable substance known as DNA. Notice that a DNA molecule is shaped like a spiral staircase. Genes are short segments of the DNA molecule. The horizontal bars that look like the rungs of a ladder play a key role in locating the identity of a gene.

Genetics, the Evolutionary Perspective, Sociobiology, and Nature and Nurture

In the words of twentieth-century French essayist Antoine de Saint-Exupéry, "The seed of the cedar will become cedar, the seed of the bramble can only become bramble." An English proverb says, "That which comes of a cat will catch mice." Why does the bramble only become bramble? Why does the cat catch mice? No matter what the species, there must be a mechanism used to pass the message of inheritance from one generation to the next. That mechanism is genetics.

Genetics

You began life as a single cell, a fertilized human egg, weighing about one-twenty-millionth of an ounce. From this single cell, you developed into a human being made of trillions of cells. The nucleus of each human cell contains 46 **chromosomes,** *which are threadlike structures that come in 23 pairs, one member of each pair coming from each parent.* Chromosomes contain the remarkable genetic substance **deoxyribonucleic acid, or DNA,** *a complex molecule that contains genetic information.* DNA's double helix shape looks like a circular staircase (see figure 2.1). **Genes,** *the units of hereditary information, are short segments of the DNA "staircase." Genes act as a blueprint for cells to reproduce themselves and manufacture the proteins that maintain life.* Chromosomes, DNA, and genes can be mysterious. To help you turn mystery into understanding, see figure 2.2.

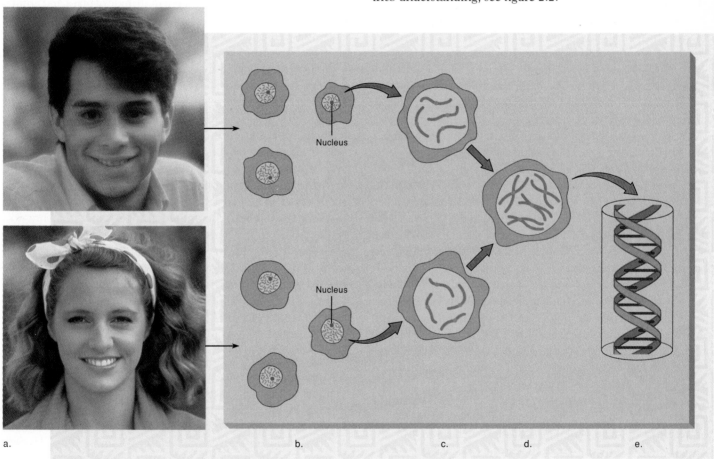

Nucleus

Nucleus

a.   b.   c.   d.   e.

FIGURE 2.2

Facts about chromosomes, DNA, and genes. (a) The body contains billions of cells that are organized into tissue and organs. (b) Each cell contains a central structure, the nucleus, which controls reproduction. (c) Chromosomes reside in the nucleus of each cell. The male's sperm and the female's egg are specialized reproductive cells that contain chromosomes. (d) At conception the offspring receives matching chromo-somes from the mother's egg and the father's sperm. (e) The chromosomes contain DNA, a chemical substance. Genes are short segments of the DNA molecule. They are the units of hereditary information that act as a blueprint for cells to reproduce themselves and manufacture the proteins that sustain life. The rungs in the DNA ladder are an important location of genes.

Although we have a long way to go before we unravel all the mysteries about the way genes work, some aspects of heritability are well understood. Every person has two genes for each characteristic governed by heredity. When genes combine to determine our characteristics, some genes are dominant over others. According to the **dominant-recessive genes principle,** *if one gene of a pair is dominant and one is recessive (goes back or recedes), the dominant gene exerts its effect, overriding the potential influence of the recessive gene. A recessive gene exerts its influence only if both genes of a pair are recessive.* If you inherit a recessive gene from only one parent, you may never know you carry the gene. In the world of dominant-recessive genes, brown eyes, far-sightedness, and dimples rule over blue eyes, near-sightedness, and freckles. If you inherit a recessive gene for a trait from both of your parents, you will show the trait. That's why two brown-eyed parents can have a blue-eyed child. In each parent, the genes that govern eye color include a dominant gene for brown eyes and a recessive gene for blue eyes. Since dominant genes override recessive genes, the parents have brown eyes; however, both may pass on their recessive genes for blue eyes. With no dominant gene to override them, the recessive genes make the child's eyes blue.

Long before people wondered how brown-eyed parents could possibly bear a blue-eyed child, they wondered what determined a child's sex. Aristotle believed that, as the father's sexual excitement increased, so did the odds of producing a son. He was wrong, of course, but it was not until the 1920s that researchers confirmed the existence of human sex chromosomes, the genetic material that determines sex. As already mentioned, humans normally have 46 chromosomes arranged in pairs. The 23rd pair may have two X-shaped chromosomes to produce a female, or it may have both an X-shaped and a Y-shaped chromosome to produce a male. The 23rd pair of chromosomes also carries some sex-linked characteristics, such as color blindness or hairy ear rims, both of which are more common in men.

Most genetic transmission is more complex than these rather simple examples. Few psychological characteristics are the result of a single gene pair. Most are determined by the combination of different genes. Each of us has at least 50,000 genes in our chromosomes. When the 50,000 genes from one parent combine at conception with the 50,000 genes of the other parent, the number of possible combinations—in the trillions—is staggering. No wonder scientists are struck by the complexity of genetic transmission.

The Evolutionary Perspective

Humans are relative newcomers to Earth. If we consider evolution in terms of a calendar year, humans arrived on the planet late in December (Sagan, 1980). Despite our brief existence, we have established ourselves as the most successful and dominant species. As our earliest ancestors left the steamy forests to form hunting societies on the grassy savannas, their thinking and behavior changed. How did these changes in thinking and behavior come about?

Over time, entire species may change through **natural selection,** *the evolutionary process that favors individuals within a species that are best adapted to survive and reproduce in a particular environment.* Also known as "the survival of the fittest," natural selection lies at the heart of Charles Darwin's theory of evolution. Darwin, a nineteenth-century naturalist, sailed to South America to study a multitude of plant and animal species in their natural surroundings. He observed that most organisms reproduce at rates that should result in overpopulation, yet somehow populations remain nearly constant.

Darwin reasoned that each new generation must engage in an intense, constant struggle for food, water, and other resources. In the course of this struggle, many of the young would die. Those who survive would be those who had better adapted to their environment. The survivors would reproduce and, in turn, pass on some of their characteristics to the next generation. Over the course of many generations, the organisms with the characteristics needed for survival (speed and sharp claws in predators or thick fur in Arctic animals, for instance) would make up an increasingly larger percentage of the population. Over many, many generations, this process could modify the entire population. If environmental conditions were to change, however, other characteristics might be needed and would move the process in a different direction. Darwin (1859) published his observations and thoughts in *On the Origin of Species.*

Sociobiology

Sociobiology *is a contemporary evolutionary view in psychology that emphasizes the power of genes in determining behavior and explains complex social interactions that natural selection cannot. It states that all behavior is motivated by the desire to contribute one's genetic heritage to the greatest number of descendants.* That is, sociobiologists believe that an organism is motivated by a desire to dominate the gene pool (Wilson, 1975).

Even complex social behaviors, such as altruism, aggression, and socialization, have been explained as the urge to propagate our own genes. Take altruism, for example. Parents are likely to risk their own lives to save their children from a blazing fire. Although the parents may die, their children's genes survive, increasing the probability that their genes will dominate the gene pool. Similarly, males have been said to be more aggressive than females because the males' former role as a hunter required them to be aggressive if they were to be successful.

Drawing by Ziegler; © 1985 The New Yorker Magazine, Inc.

Since evolution's imperative, according to sociobiologists, is to spread our genes, men and women have evolved different strategies for doing so. Sperm is abundant; men produce billions in a lifetime. However, women have a limited number of eggs, only about 400 in a lifetime. Men have the potential, then, to produce many more offspring than do women. To ensure that they spread their genes, it is to a male's advantage to impregnate as many females as possible. Given that women have few eggs and gestation takes a long time, it is to a woman's advantage to choose a mate who will protect her. This, say some sociobiologists, explains why women tend to be monogamous and men do not.

Sociobiologists point to animal models to support their theories. For example, the males of most species initiate sexual behavior more frequently than females. In some species, such as seals, cattle, and elephants, the male maintains a large harem of females to inseminate and protect. Some human societies incorporate this reproductive strategy into their culture (Hinde, 1984). Sociobiologists also contend that the universality of certain behaviors, such as incest taboos and religious laws, are proof that such behaviors are genetic.

Sociobiology is controversial (Hinde, 1992; Lerner & von Eye, 1992). Critics argue that sociobiology does not adequately consider human adaptability and experience and that it reduces human beings to mere automatons caught in the thrall of their genes. They point out that sociobiologists explain things only after the fact, with no evidence of predictive ability, which would characterize a good theory. Male aggression is said to be a sociobiological imperative, but only after sociobiologists have seen that males do indeed behave more aggressively than females. Much of the evidence to support sociobiology is based on animal research. Critics assert that findings from animal research cannot always be generalized to humans. Further, some critics see sociobiology as little more than a justification to discriminate against women and minorities under a scientific umbrella, using genetic determinism as an excuse for ignoring the social injustice and discrimination that contribute to inequality (Doyle & Paludi, 1991; Paludi, 1992).

Nature and Nurture

Although genes play a role in human behavior, they alone do not determine who we are. Genes exist within the context of a complex environment and are necessary for an organism to exist. Biologists who study even the simplest animals agree it is virtually impossible to separate the effects of an animal's genes from the effects of its environment (Mader, 1991). **Environment** *refers to all of the surrounding conditions and influences that affect the development of living things.* Environment includes the food we eat, the air we breathe, and the many different physical and social contexts we experience—the cities and towns we live in; our relationships with our parents, peers, and teachers; and our continuing interactions at work, at home, and at play. The term **nurture** *is often used to describe an organism's environmental experiences.* The term **nature** *is often used to describe an organism's*

biological inheritance. The interaction of nature *and* nurture, genes *and* environment, influences every aspect of mind and behavior to a degree. Neither factor operates alone (Loehlin, 1992; Plomin, 1991; Plomin, DeFries, & McClearn, 1990; Scarr, 1991; Wachs, 1992).

To illustrate how both genes and the environment mold human behavior, let's consider shyness. Imagine we could identify the precise genetic combination that predisposes a person to become either outgoing or shy. Even with that information, we couldn't predict how shy a person might become because shyness is also shaped by life's experiences. Parents, for example, may support and nurture a shy child in a way that encourages the child to feel comfortable in social situations. On the other hand, an initially outgoing child may experience a traumatic event and become shy and withdrawn in response. More information about the environment's role in human behavior appears in Sociocultural Worlds 2.1, where we will discuss how the human species is a culture-making species.

Race and Ethnicity

In keeping with the sociocultural theme in this text, let's examine race and see how it has taken on elaborate, often unfortunate, social meanings. **Race** *originated as a biological concept. It refers to a system for classifying plants and animals into subcategories according to specific physical and structural characteristics.* Race is one of the most misused and misunderstood words in the English language (Atkinson, Morten, & Sue, 1989; Clark, 1991; Essed, 1992; Mays, 1991; Root, 1992). Loosely, it has come to mean everything from a person's religion to skin color.

The three main classifications of the human race are Mongoloid, or Asian; Caucasoid, or European; and Negroid, or African. Skin color, head shape, facial features, stature, and the color and texture of body hair are the physical characteristics most widely used to determine race.

These racial classifications presumably were created to define and clarify the differences among groups of people; however, they have not been very useful. Today many people define races as groups that are socially constructed on the basis of physical differences because race is a social construction and no longer a biological fact (Van den Berghe, 1978). For example, some groups, such as Native Americans, Australians, and Polynesians, do not fit into any of the three main racial categories. Also, obvious differences *within* groups are not adequately accounted for. Arabs, Hindus, and Europeans, for instance, are physically different, yet they are all called Caucasians. Although there are some physical characteristics that distinguish "racial" groups, there are, in fact, more similarities than differences.

Too often we are socialized to accept as facts many myths and stereotypes about people whose skin color, facial features, and hair texture differ from ours. For example, some people still believe that Asians are inscrutable, Jews are acquisitive, and Hispanics are lazy. What people believe about race has profound

The Human Species Is a Culture-Making Species

More than 99 percent of all humans now live in a different kind of environment from that in which the species evolved. By creating cultures, humans have, in effect, built, shaped, and carved out their own environments.

Unlike all other animal species, which evolve in blind response to random changes in their environment, humans have considerable control over their own evolution. We change primarily through *cultural evolution*. For example, we've made astonishing accomplishments in the past 10,000 years or so, ever since we developed language. Biological (Darwinian) evolution continues in our species, but its rate, compared with cultural evolution, is so slow that its impact seems almost negligible. There is no evidence, for example, that brain size or structure has changed since *Homo sapiens* appeared on the fossil record about 50,000 years ago.

As humans evolved, we acquired knowledge and passed it on from generation to generation. This knowledge, which originally instructed us how to hunt, make tools, and communicate, became our **culture.** The accumulation of knowledge has gathered speed—

from a slow swell to a meteoric rise. Hunter-gatherer tribes, characteristic of early human society, changed over thousands of years into small agricultural communities. With people rooted in one place, cities grew and flourished. Life within those cities remained relatively unchanged for generations. Then industrialization put a dizzying speed on cultural change. Now technological advances in communication and transportation—computers, FAX machines, the SST—transform everyday life at a staggering pace.

Whatever one generation learns, it can pass to the next through writing, word of mouth, ritual, tradition, and a host of other methods humans have developed to assure their culture's continuity (Gould, 1981). By creating cultures, humans have built, shaped, and carved out their own environments. The human species is no longer primarily at nature's mercy. Rather, humans are capable of changing their environment to fit their needs (McCandless & Trotter, 1977).

social consequences. Until recently, for instance, Black Americans were denied access to schools, hospitals, churches, and other social institutions attended by Whites.

Although scientists are supposed to be a fair-minded lot, some also have used racial distinctions to further their own biases. Some even claim that one racial group has a biological inheritance that gives it an adaptive advantage over other racial groups. Nineteenth-century biologist Louis Agassiz, for example, asserted that God had created Blacks and Whites as separate species. Also, in Nazi Germany, where science and death made their grisliest alliance, Jews and other "undesirables" were attributed with whatever characteristics were necessary to reinforce the conclusion that "survival of the fittest" demanded their elimination.

Unfortunately, racism cloaked in science still finds champions. Recently psychologist Philipe Rushton (1985, 1988)

argued that evolution accounts for racial differences in sexual practices, fertility, intelligence, and criminality. Using these traits, he ranks Asians as superior, followed by Caucasians and people of African descent. Asians, Rushton claims, are the most intelligent, most sexually restrained, most altruistic, and least criminal of the races. Rushton ascribes a similar order to social classes: those who are impoverished resemble Blacks; those who earn high incomes resemble Asians and Whites. Rushton's theory, according to his critics, is full of "familiar vulgar stereotypes" (Weizmann & others, 1990). His notions are stitched together with frequent misinterpretations and overgeneralizations about racial differences and evolutionary history, and the data are tailored to fit his bias. Regrettably, even flimsy theories such as Rushton's provide whole cloth for anyone intent on justifying racism.

Race is primarily a biological concept, whereas ethnicity is primarily a sociocultural concept. Race is used in society much more than many psychologists recommend. Thus, in society, race has taken on a strong social meaning that goes far beyond its biological basis.

Remember that, although race is primarily a *biological* concept, ethnicity is primarily a *sociocultural* concept (Brislin, 1987; Jackson, 1991; Jones, 1991). In chapter 1, you read that cultural heritage, national characteristics, religion, language, *and* race constitute *ethnicity*. Race is just one component. However, the term *race* is often mistakenly used to refer to ethnicity. Jews, for example, are thought of as a race. Most are Caucasian, but they are too diverse to group into one racial subcategory. They also share too many anatomical similarities with other Caucasians to separate them as a distinct race (Thompson & Hughes, 1958). If we think of ethnicity predominately in terms of social and cultural heritage, then Jews constitute an ethnic group.

Although we distinguish between race and ethnicity in this book, society usually does not. Race is used in a much broader way than many sociocultural psychologists recommend (Brislin, 1987). Social psychologist James Jones (1990) points out that thinking in racial terms has become embedded in cultures as an important factor in human interactions. For example, people often consider what race they will associate with when they decide on such things as where to live, who will make a suitable spouse, where to go to school, and what kind of job they want. Similarly, people often use race to judge whether or not another person is intelligent, competent, responsible, or socially acceptable. Children tend to adopt their parents' attitudes about race as they grow up, often perpetuating stereotypes and prejudice. Much more about the social meanings of race and the nature of racism appears in chapter 16, Social Psychology.

At this point, we have discussed some important ideas about genetics, evolution, sociobiology, and the interplay of genetics and the environment (nature-nurture) to shape human behavior. As was mentioned earlier, cultural evolution—our ability to impart vast amounts of knowledge from one generation to the next—sets us apart from other organisms. However, nowhere is our uniqueness more apparent than in the human brain, which we will discuss next.

REVIEW

Genetics, the Evolutionary Perspective, Sociobiology, and Nature and Nurture

The nucleus of each human cell contains 46 chromosomes, which are composed of DNA. Genes are short segments of DNA and act as blueprints for cells to reproduce and manufacture proteins that maintain life. Most genetic transmission involves combinations of genes. Sociobiologists argue that all behavior is motivated by the drive to dominate the gene pool. Critics say sociobiology ignores the environmental determinants of behavior and is biased against females. Every behavior is, to a degree, the product of both genetic heritage and environment. As a culture-making species, humans are no longer at the mercy of the environment. Race is primarily a biological concept; ethnicity is primarily a sociocultural concept. The term *race* has been misunderstood and abused.

The Brain and Nervous System

The nervous system's central command, the brain, controls all your thoughts and movements. It weighs about 3 pounds and is slightly larger than a grapefruit. With a crinkled outer layer, it looks like an oversized, shelled walnut. Inside, the brain resembles undercooked custard or a ripe avocado. Nerve cells, or **neurons,** *are the basic units of the nervous system.* Highly organized, the nervous system is continuously processing information about everything we do—whether we are taking out the garbage, spotting a loved one from across a crowded room, or preparing a speech. Let's explore what the brain and nervous system are like.

Elegant Organization

The purpose of the nervous system is to pass messages back and forth among cells. The nervous system is divided into two parts: the central nervous system and the peripheral nervous system. The **central nervous system (CNS)** *is made up of the brain and spinal cord. More than 99 percent of all neurons in the body are located in the CNS.* The **peripheral nervous system** *is a network of nerves that connects the brain and spinal cord to other parts of the body. The peripheral nervous system takes information to and from the brain and spinal cord and carries out the command of the CNS to execute various muscular and glandular activities.* Figure 2.3 displays the hierarchical organization of the nervous system's major divisions.

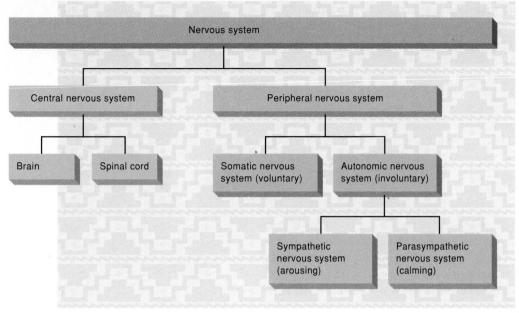

FIGURE 2.3

Major divisions of the human nervous system.

The two major divisions of the peripheral nervous system are the *somatic nervous system* and *autonomic nervous system*. The **somatic nervous system** *consists of sensory nerves, which convey information from the skin and muscles to the CNS about such matters as pain and temperature, and motor nerves, which inform muscles when to act*. The **autonomic nervous system** *takes messages to and from the body's internal organs, monitoring such processes as breathing, heart rate, and digestion*. It also is divided into two parts, the **sympathetic nervous system,** *the division of the autonomic nervous system that arouses the body*, and the **parasympathetic nervous system,** *the division of the autonomic nervous system that calms the body*. More information about the autonomic nervous system appears toward the end of this chapter.

To get a better feel for how the human nervous system works, imagine that you are preparing to give a speech in a class. As you go over your notes one last time, your peripheral nervous system carries information about the notes to your central nervous system. Your central nervous system processes the marks on the paper, interpreting the words as you memorize key points and plan ways to keep the audience interested. After studying the notes several minutes longer, you scribble a joke midway through them. Your peripheral nervous system is at work again, conveying the information that enables you to make the marks on the paper from your brain to the muscles in your arm and hand. The information transmitted from your eyes to your brain and from your brain to your hand is being handled by the somatic nervous system. Since this is your first speech in a while, you've got the jitters. As you think about getting up in front of the class, your stomach feels queasy and your heart begins to thump. This is the sympathetic division of the autonomic nervous system functioning as you become aroused. You regain your confidence after reminding yourself that you know the speech. As you relax, the parasympathetic division of the autonomic nervous system is working.

Neurons

So far, we have discussed the nervous system's major divisions. However, there is much more to the intriguing story of how the nervous system processes information. Let's go inside the huge nervous system and find out more about the cells, chemicals, and electrical impulses that are the nuts and bolts of this operation.

Neuron Pathways

Information flows to the brain, within the brain, and out of the brain along specialized nerve cells known as *afferent nerves, interneurons,* and *efferent nerves*. **Afferent nerves,** *or sensory nerves, carry information to the brain*. Afferent *comes from the Latin word meaning "bring to."* **Efferent nerves,** *or motor nerves, carry the brain's output*. *The word* efferent *is derived from the Latin word meaning "bring forth."* To see how afferent and efferent nerves work, let's consider a well-known reflex, the knee jerk. When your knee jerks in response to a tap just below your kneecap, afferent cells transmit information directly to efferent cells; the information processing is quick and simple.

The information involving the knee jerk is processed at the spinal cord and does not require the brain's participation. More complex information processing is accomplished by passing the information through systems of **interneurons,** *central nervous system neurons that go between sensory input and motor output. Interneurons make up most of the brain.* For example, as you read the notes for your speech, the afferent input from your eye is transmitted to your brain, then is passed through many interneuron systems, which translate (process) the patterns of black and white into neural codes for letters, words, associations, and meanings. Some of the information is stored in the interneuron systems for future associations, and, if you read aloud, some is output as efferent messages to your lips and tongue.

Structure of the Neuron

As indicated earlier, *neuron* is a neuroscientist's label for nerve cell. Neurons handle information processing in the nervous system at the cellular level. There are about 100 billion neurons in the human brain. The average neuron is as complex as a small computer, with as many as 15,000 physical connections with other cells. At times the brain may be "lit up" with as many as a quadrillion connections.

The three basic parts of the neuron are the cell body, the dendrites, and the axon (see figure 2.4). The neuron's **cell body** *contains the nucleus, which directs the manufacture of the substances the neuron uses for its growth and maintenance.* Most neurons are created very early in life and will not be replaced if they are destroyed. Interestingly, though, some types of neurons continue to multiply in adults, and most are capable of changing their shape, size, and connections throughout the life span (Levitan & Kaczmarek, 1991).

The **dendrite** *is the receiving part of the neuron, serving the important function of collecting information and orienting it toward the cell body.* Most nerve cells have a number of dendrites radiating from the cell body of the neuron, but there is only one axon. The **axon** *is the part of the neuron that carries information away from the cell body to other cells.* The axon is much thinner and longer than a dendrite and looks like an ultrathin cylindrical tube. The axon of a single neuron may extend all the way from the top of the brain to the base of the spinal cord, a distance of over 3 feet. A **myelin sheath,** *a layer of fat cells, encases most axons. Not only does the myelin sheath insulate the nerve cell, it also helps the nerve impulse travel faster.* The myelin sheath developed as the brain evolved and became larger, making it necessary for information to travel over long distances in the nervous system. This is similar to the appearance of freeways and turnpikes as cities grew. The newly developed roadways keep the fast-moving long-distance traffic from getting tangled up with slow-moving traffic.

The Nerve Impulse

Neurons send information down the axon as brief impulses, or waves, of electricity. Perhaps in a movie you have seen a telegraph operator sending a series of single clicks down a telegraph wire to the next station. That is what neurons do. To transmit information to other neurons, they send a series of single electrical clicks down their axons. By changing the rate

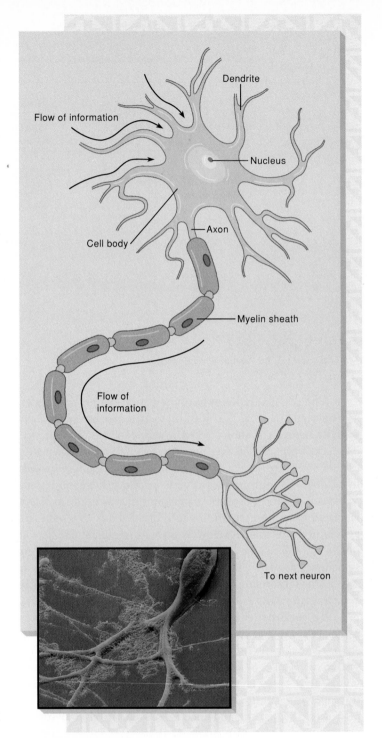

FIGURE 2.4

The neuron. The cell body receives information from the dendrites of other neurons. Information leaves the cell body and travels to other neurons, muscles, or glands through the axon. A myelin sheath covers most axons and speeds information transmission. As it ends, the axon branches out. Shown in the insert is a photograph of a neuron. Notice the branching dendrites at the bottom and the cell body at the top right.

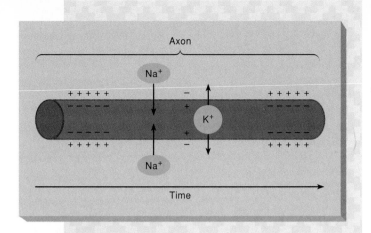

FIGURE 2.5

Movement of sodium and potassium ions down the axon and the action potential. Electrical/chemical changes in the neuron produce an action potential. The sodium and potassium ions are shown moving down the axon. As the nerve impulse moves down the axon, electrical stimulation of the membrane makes it more permeable to sodium ions (Na^+). Sodium rushes into the axon, carrying an electrical charge, and that charge causes the next group of gates on the axon to flip open briefly. So it goes, all the way down the axon. After the sodium gates close, potassium ions (K^+) flow out of the cell.

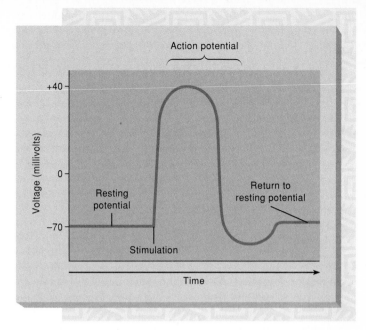

FIGURE 2.6

Action potential. The action potential is shown on this graph in terms of its electrical voltage. The action potential is the positive charge in the cell generated by the influx of sodium (Na^+) ions. In the example shown here, the wave of electrical charge reaches about 40 millivolts. After the sodium gates close, potassium ions (K^+) flow out of the cell and bring the voltage back to its resting potential.

and timing of the clicks, neurons can vary the nature of the message they send. As you reach to turn this page, hundreds of such clicks stream down the axons in your arm to tell your muscles when to flex and how vigorously.

To understand how a neuron, which is a living cell, creates and sends electrical signals, we need to examine this cell and the fluids in which it floats. A neuron is a balloonlike bag filled with one kind of fluid and surrounded by a slightly different kind of fluid. A piece of this balloonlike bag is stretched and pulled to form a long, hollow tube, which is the axon. The axon tube is very thin; a few dozen in a bundle would be about the thickness of a human hair.

To see how this fluid-filled "balloon" creates electrical signals, we must look at two things: the particles that float in the fluids and the actual wall of the cell, the membrane. The important particles in the fluids are the elements sodium, chloride (which we get from common table salt—sodium chloride), and potassium. **Ions** *are electrically charged particles. The neuron creates electrical signals by moving these charged ions back and forth through its membrane; the waves of electricity that are created sweep along the membrane.*

How does the neuron move these ions? The membrane, the wall of the neuron, is covered with hundreds of thousands of small doors, or gates, that open and close to let the ions pass in or out to the cell. Normally, when resting, or not sending information, the membrane gates for sodium are closed and

those for potassium and chloride are partly open. Therefore, the membrane is in what is called a semipermeable state, and the ions separate; sodium is kept outside, lots of potassium ends up inside, and most of the chloride goes outside. Because the ions are separated, a charge is present along the membrane of the cell (figure 2.5 shows movement of the sodium and potassium ions). **Resting potential** *is the stable, negative charge of an inactive neuron.* That potential is about one-fourteenth of a volt, so fourteen neurons could make a one-volt battery; an electric eel's 8,400 cells could generate 600 volts.

When a neuron gets enough excitatory input to cause it to send a message, the sodium gates at the base of the axon open briefly, then shut again. While those gates are open, sodium rushes into the axon, carrying an electrical charge, and that charge causes the next group of gates on the axon to flip open briefly. So it goes, all the way down the axon, like a long row of cabinet doors opening and closing in sequence. After the sodium gates close, potassium ions flow out of the cell and bring the membrane charge back to the resting condition. **Action potential** *is the brief wave of electrical charge that sweeps down the axon* (see figure 2.6).

The wave of electrical charge that sweeps down the axon abides by the **all-or-none principle,** *which means that, once the electrical impulse reaches a certain level of intensity, it fires and moves all the way down the axon, remaining at the same strength* *throughout its travel.* The electrical impulse traveling down an axon is much like a fuse on a firecracker. It doesn't matter whether a match or blowtorch is used to light the fuse; as long as a certain minimal intensity is reached, the spark travels quickly and at the same level of strength down the fuse until it reaches the firecracker (see figure 2.7).

Synapses and Neurotransmitters

What happens once the neural impulse reaches the end of the axon? Neurons do not touch each other directly; nevertheless, they manage to communicate. The story of the connection between one neuron and another is one of the most intriguing and highly researched areas of contemporary neuroscience.

Synapses *are tiny gaps between neurons. Most synapses are between the axon of one neuron and the dendrites or cell body of another neuron.* How does information get across this gap to the next neuron? The end of an axon branches out into a number of fibers, which end in structures called synaptic knobs. Neurotransmitters are found in the tiny synaptic vesicles (chambers) located in the synaptic knobs. **Neurotransmitters** *are chemical substances that carry information across the synaptic gap to the next neuron.* The molecules of these chemical substances wait for a nerve impulse to come down through the axon. Once the nerve impulse reaches the synaptic knobs, the electrical signal causes these miniature, springlike molecules to contract, pulling the vesicles out to the edge of the synaptic knobs. At the edge, the vesicles burst open, and the neurotransmitter molecules spew forth into the gap between the two neurons. In the synaptic gap, the neurotransmitter molecules bump about in random motion, and some land on receptor sites in the next neuron, where they open a "door," and electrical signals begin to sweep through the next neuron. Think of a synapse as a river that cuts a section of railroad track in two. When the train gets to the river via the tracks on one side of it, it crosses the water by ferry and rolls on to the second section of track to continue its journey. Similarly, a message in the brain is "ferried" across the synapse by a neurotransmitter, which pours out of the end of the cell just as the message approaches the synapse. Synapses and neurotransmitters can be just as mysterious as genes and DNA. To help turn more mystery into understanding, turn to figure 2.8.

More than 50 neurotransmitters, each with a unique chemical makeup, have been discovered, and the list probably will grow to 100 or more in the near future (Barnard & Darlison, 1989). Interestingly, most creatures that have been studied, from snails to whales, use the same type of neurotransmitter molecules that our own brains use. Many animal venoms, such as that of the black widow, actually are neurotransmitterlike substances that disturb neurotransmission.

What are some of these neurotransmitters and how are they related to our behavior? **GABA,** *which stands for the imposing chemical name gamma aminobutyric acid, is a neurotransmitter that inhibits the firing of neurons.* It is found throughout the brain

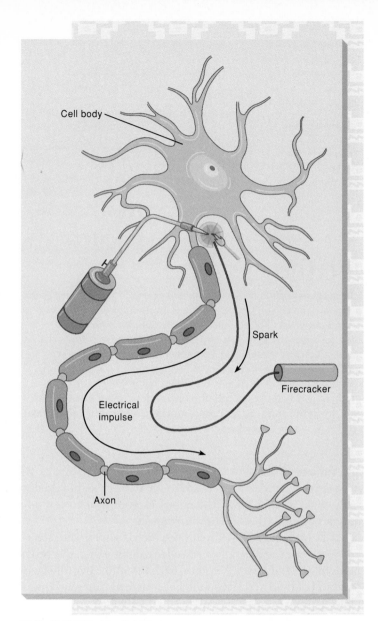

FIGURE 2.7

All-or-none principle. The all-or-none principle can be compared to a fuse and a firecracker. Regardless of whether it is lit by a blowtorch or a match, once a certain level of intensity is reached, the fuse lights and then the spark travels at the same level of strength until it reaches the firecracker. So it is with an electrical impulse firing and traveling the entire length of an axon.

and spinal cord and is believed to be the neurotransmitter in as many as one-third of the brain's synaptic connections. GABA is so important in the brain because it keeps many neurons from firing. This inhibition helps control the precision of the signal being carried from one neuron to the next. The degeneration of GABA may be responsible for Huntington's chorea, a deadly disease that includes a loss of muscle control. Without GABA's

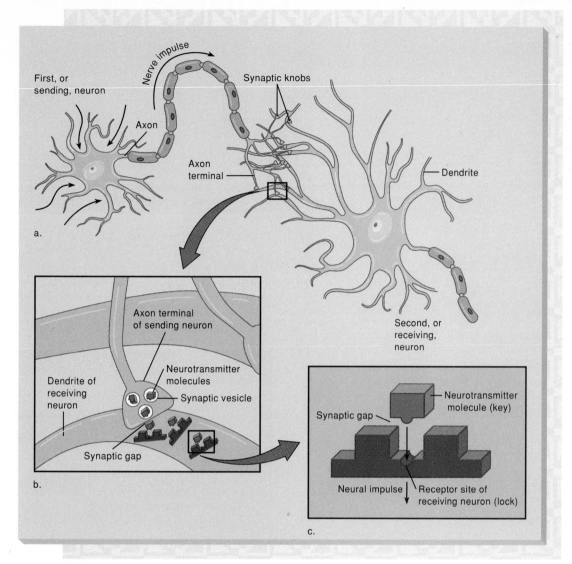

FIGURE 2.8

How synapses and neurotransmitters work. (a) When an axon reaches its destination, it branches out into a number of fibers that end in synaptic knobs. There is a tiny gap between these synaptic knobs at the tip of the axon terminal and the next neuron. (b) When it reaches the synaptic knob, the neural impulse releases tiny chemical molecules that are stored in synaptic vesicles in the knobs. These chemical substances are called neurotransmitters. They bump around in the synaptic gap between the sending and receiving neurons. Some of them land on receptor sites in the next neuron, where the neural impulse continues its travel. (c) Neurotransmitter molecules fit like small keys in equally small locks, once they reach the receptor site in the receiving neuron. The key in the lock opens the "door," and the neural impulse begins its travel through the second neuron.

inhibiting influence, nerve impulses become imprecise and muscles lose their coordination. GABA may also be involved in modulating anxiety (Sullivan & others, 1989; Zorumski & Isenberg, 1991).

Acetylcholine (ACh) *is a neurotransmitter that produces contractions of skeletal muscles by acting on motor nerves* (see figure 2.9). Whereas GABA inhibits neurons from firing, in most instances ACh excites neurons and stimulates them to fire. The venom of the black widow causes ACh to gush through the synapses between the spinal cord and skeletal muscles, producing violent spasms. The drug curare, found on the tips of some South American Indians' poisoned darts, blocks some receptors for ACh. This paralyzes skeletal muscles.

Norepinephrine *is a neurotransmitter that usually inhibits the firing of neurons in the brain and spinal cord but excites the heart muscles, intestines, and urogenital tract.* Too little norepinephrine is associated with depression and too much is linked to highly agitated, manic states. Figure 2.10 provides a look at

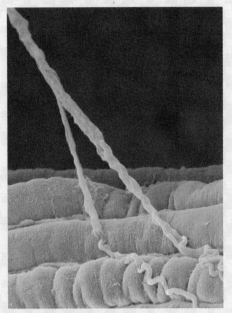

FIGURE 2.9

Nerves, acetylcholine, and muscles. The nerve impulse, conducted down a nerve fiber that ends in skeletal muscle, releases a small amount of the chemical acetylcholine. The action of acetylcholine at the motor end-plate initiates the chemical changes that cause the muscle to contract. The photo shows a number of nerve fibers leading to and crossing several striated muscle cells.

FIGURE 2.10

The neurotransmitter norepinephrine. Norepinephrine causes neurons in the human brain to glow bright yellowish green. Too little norepinephrine in the brain's neurons is associated with depression, too much with manic, agitated behavior.

what norepinephrine-containing cells in the brain look like. **Dopamine** *is a neurotransmitter that is related to mental health— too much dopamine in the brain's synapses is associated with the severe disturbance called schizophrenia, in which an individual loses contact with reality.* More about the role of neurotransmitters in mental health and how drugs can be used to control their action appears in chapters 13 and 14. **Serotonin** *is a neurotransmitter that is involved in the regulation of sleep and, like norepinephrine, seems to play a role in depression as well* (Marek & Seiden, 1991).

As early as the fourth century B.C., the Greeks used the wild poppy to induce euphoria. However, it wasn't until more than 2,000 years later that the magical formula behind opium's addictive action was discovered. In the early 1970s, scientists found that opium plugs into a sophisticated system of natural opiates lying deep within the brain's pathways (Pert & Snyder, 1973). The system is involved in shielding the body from pain and elevating feelings of pleasure. A long-distance runner, a woman giving childbirth, and a person in shock after a car wreck all have elevated levels of **endorphins,** *natural opiates that are neurotransmitters. Endorphins are involved in pleasure and the control of pain.*

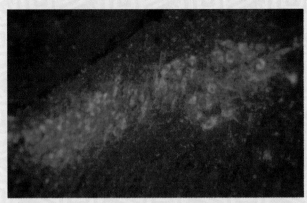

REVIEW

The Brain and Nervous System

The central nervous system consists of the brain and spinal cord; it contains more than 99 percent of all neurons. The peripheral nervous system is a network of nerves that connects the brain and spinal cord to other parts of the body. Two major divisions are the somatic nervous system and the autonomic nervous system. The autonomic nervous system is subdivided into the sympathetic and parasympathetic systems.

Afferent nerves (sensory nerves) carry input to the brain; efferent nerves (motor nerves) carry output away from the brain; interneurons do most of the information processing within the brain. The three basic parts of the neuron are the cell body, dendrite, and axon. The myelin sheath speeds information transmission. Neurons send information in the form of brief impulses, or waves, of electricity. These waves are called the action potential; they operate according to the all-or-none principle.

The gaps between neurons are called synapses. The neural impulse reaches the axon terminal and stimulates the release of neurotransmitters from tiny vesicles. These carry information to the next neuron, which fits like a key in a lock. Important neurotransmitters are GABA, acetylcholine, norepinephrine, serotonin, and endorphins.

Brain Structure and Function

Most of the information we have covered about the brain has been about one or two cells. Earlier you learned that about 99 percent of all neurons in the nervous system are located in the brain and the spinal cord; however, neurons do not simply float in the brain. Connected in precise ways, they constitute the various structures of the brain.

As a human embryo develops inside the womb, the nervous system begins as a long, hollow tube on the embryo's back. At 3 weeks or so after conception, the brain forms into a large mass of neurons and loses its tubular appearance. The elongated tube changes shape and develops into three major divisions: the hindbrain, which is the portion of the brain adjacent to the spinal cord; the midbrain, which is above the hindbrain; and the forebrain, which is at the highest region of the brain (see figure 2.11)

Hindbrain

The **hindbrain,** *located at the skull's rear, is the lowest portion of the brain. The three main parts of the hindbrain are the medulla, cerebellum, and pons* (figure 2.12 shows the location of these brain structures as well as some of the forebrain's main structures). The **medulla** *begins where the spinal cord enters the skull. It helps control breathing and regulates a portion of the reflexes that allow us to maintain an upright posture.* The **cerebellum** *extends from the rear of the hindbrain and is located just above the medulla. It consists of two rounded structures thought to play important roles in motor control.* Leg and arm movements are coordinated at the cerebellum, for example. When we play golf, practice the piano, or perfect our moves on the dance floor, the cerebellum is hard at work. If a higher portion of the brain commands us to write the number 7, it is the cerebellum that integrates the muscular activities required to do so. If the cerebellum becomes damaged, our movements become uncoordinated and jerky. The **pons** *is a bridge in the hindbrain that contains several clusters of fibers involved in sleep and arousal.*

Midbrain

The **midbrain,** *located between the hindbrain and forebrain, is an area where many nerve fiber systems ascend and descend to connect the higher and lower portions of the brain. In particular, the midbrain relays information between the brain and the eyes and ears.* The ability to attend to an object visually, for example, is linked to one bundle of neurons in the midbrain. Parkinson's disease, a deterioration of movement that produces rigidity and tremors in the elderly, damages a section near the bottom of the midbrain.

It is not the hindbrain or midbrain that separates humans from animals, however; it is the forebrain. In humans the forebrain has become enlarged and specialized.

"Runner's high" may be due to an elevation of endorphins, a type of neurotransmitter in the brain that is involved in shielding the body from pain and increasing pleasurable feelings.

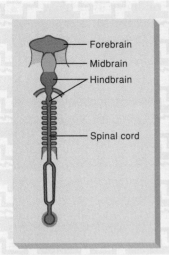

FIGURE 2.11

Embryological development of the nervous system. In the photograph on the right, you can see the primitive, tubular appearance of the nervous system at 6 weeks in the human embryo. The drawing shows the major brain regions and spinal cord as they appear early in the development of a human embryo.

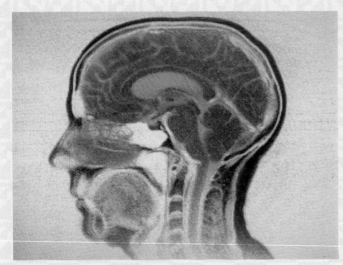

a.

FIGURE 2.12

Structure and regions in the human brain. (a) This image of a cross-section of the brain includes some of the brain's most important structures, which we will discuss shortly. As these structures are discussed, you might want to refer to this figure to obtain a visual image of what the structures look like. (b) This drawing reproduces some of the brain's main structures from the image of the brain shown in (a) and describes some of their main functions. (Midbrain structures are not shown here but will be discussed later in the chapter.)

Forebrain

You try to understand what all of these terms and parts of the brain mean. You talk with friends and plan a party for this weekend. You remember it has been 6 months since you went to the dentist. You are confident you will do well on the next exam in this course. All of these experiences and millions more would not be possible without the **forebrain,** *the highest region of the human brain. Among its most important structures are the thalamus, hypothalamus, and neocortex, each of which we will discuss in turn.*

The **thalamus** *sits at the top of the brain stem in the central core of the brain. It serves as a very important relay station, functioning much like a telephone switchboard.* Whereas one area of the thalamus orients information from the sense receptors (hearing, seeing, and so on), another region is involved in sleep and wakefulness (see figure 2.12 for the location of the thalamus).

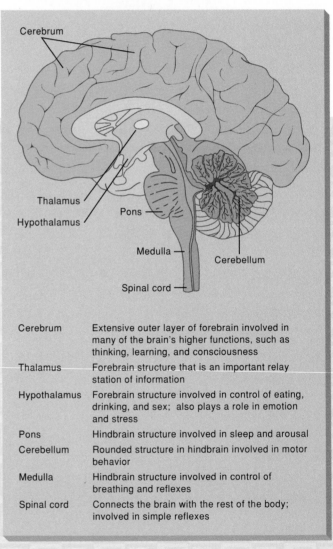

Cerebrum	Extensive outer layer of forebrain involved in many of the brain's higher functions, such as thinking, learning, and consciousness
Thalamus	Forebrain structure that is an important relay station of information
Hypothalamus	Forebrain structure involved in control of eating, drinking, and sex; also plays a role in emotion and stress
Pons	Hindbrain structure involved in sleep and arousal
Cerebellum	Rounded structure in hindbrain involved in motor behavior
Medulla	Hindbrain structure involved in control of breathing and reflexes
Spinal cord	Connects the brain with the rest of the body; involved in simple reflexes

b.

The **hypothalamus,** *much smaller than the thalamus and about the size of a kidney bean, is located just below the thalamus. The hypothalamus monitors three enjoyable activities—eating, drinking, and sex; it helps direct the endocrine system through the pituitary gland; and it is involved in emotion, stress, and reward.* Perhaps the best way to describe the hypothalamus is in terms of a regulator. It is sensitive to changes in the blood and neural input, and it responds by influencing the secretion of hormones and neural outputs. For example, if the temperature of circulating blood near the hypothalamus is increased by just 1 or 2 degrees, certain cells in the hypothalamus increase their rate of firing. As a result, a chain of events is set into motion. Circulation in the skin and sweat glands increases immediately to release perspiration from the body. The cooled blood circulating to the hypothalamus slows down the activity of some of the neurons there, stopping the process when the temperature is right—37.1 degrees C. These temperature-sensitive neurons function like a finely tuned thermostat to restore the body to a balanced state.

The hypothalamus acts as an essential coordinator of the central nervous system. It is also involved in emotional states and plays an important role in handling stress. The hypothalamus acts on the pituitary gland, located just below it, to integrate sensory signals, such as hunger, aggression, and pleasure. When certain areas of the hypothalamus are electrically stimulated, feelings of pleasure result.

In a classic experiment, James Olds and Peter Milner (1954) implanted an electrode in the hypothalamus of a rat's brain. When the rat ran to a corner of an enclosed area, its hypothalamus received a mild electric shock. The researchers thought the rat would steer clear of the corner to avoid the shock. Much to their surprise, the rat kept returning. Olds and Milner believed they had discovered a pleasure center in the hypothalamus.

In similar experiments, Olds (1958) later found that rats would press bars until they dropped from exhaustion just to feel pleasure. Figure 2.13 shows one rat that pressed a bar more than 2,000 times an hour for 24 hours to receive the pleasurable stimulus to its hypothalamus. Today researchers agree that the hypothalamus is one of the links between the brain and pleasure, but they know that other areas of the brain also are important (Kornetsky, 1986).

Recently an area adjacent to the hypothalamus has been linked with the intense pleasure and craving triggered by cocaine use. This finding has important implications for treating drug addiction. Researchers hope eventually to develop drugs that mimic or block an addictive drug's effects on the brain. There also is increasing evidence that the pleasure or reward a drug induces outweighs the fear of pain or suffering that withdrawal produces (Restak, 1988; Wise & Rompre, 1989). The Olds and Milner experiments illustrate this: when the rats pressed the bar, the pleasure they received overrode the pain from the electric shock. Similarly, when cocaine users talk about the drug, they highlight its ability to heighten pleasure in a variety of activities, including eating and sex. They tend to overlook the discomfort that comes as the drug's effects wear off. The story of addiction is complex; it is not like a bout of pneumonia that goes away with antibiotics. Much more about drug addiction appears in chapter 4.

The **neocortex** *is the most recently evolved part of the brain. Covering the rest of the brain almost like a cap, it is the largest part of the brain and makes up about 80 percent of its volume.* It's the brain region that people think of when they hear the term "grey matter." Let's look at the neocortex in more detail.

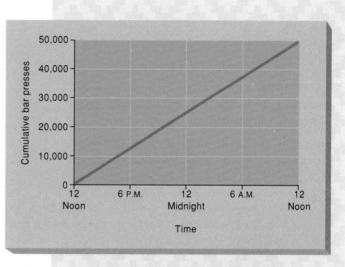

FIGURE 2.13

Results of the experiment by Olds (1958) on the role of the hypothalamus in pleasure. The graphed results for one rat show that it pressed the bar more than 2,000 times an hour for a period of 24 hours to receive the stimulus to its hypothalamus. One of the rats in Olds and Milner's experiments is shown pressing the bar to receive stimulation to its hypothalamus.

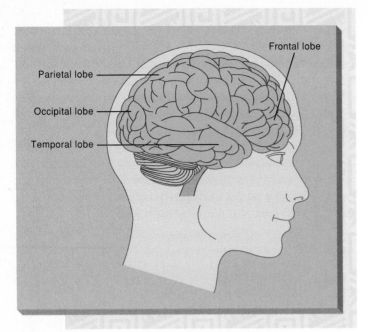

FIGURE 2.14

The brain's four lobes. Shown here are the locations of the brain's four lobes: occipital, temporal, frontal, and parietal.

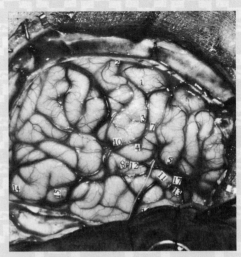

FIGURE 2.15

The exposed cortex of one of Penfield's patients. The numbers identify the locations that Penfield stimulated with a very thin electric probe. When he stimulated the area marked by number 11, for example, the patient opened his mouth, sneezed, and began chewing.

Exploring the Neocortex

The wrinkled surface of the neocortex is divided into halves, called hemispheres. Each hemisphere is divided into four lobes—occipital, temporal, frontal, and parietal—each conveniently named for the main skull bone that covers it (see figure 2.14). These landmarks help us map the surface of the brain, but the lobes are not strictly functional regions. Nonetheless, they are often used in somewhat loose ways to describe the brain's functions. For example, the **occipital lobe,** *the portion of the neocortex at the back of the head, is involved in vision;* the **temporal lobe,** *the portion of the neocortex just above the ears, is involved in hearing;* the **frontal lobe,** *the portion of the neocortex behind the forehead, is involved in the control of voluntary muscles and in intelligence;* and the **parietal lobe,** *the portion of the neocortex at the top of the head and toward the rear, is involved in body sensations.*

In the same way that each neocortex lobe is associated with different processes, regions within each lobe have different jobs. Scientists have determined this primarily through topographic mapping. Wilder Penfield (1947), a neurosurgeon at the Montreal Neurological Institute, pioneered mapping the brain. He worked with a number of patients who had very serious forms of epilepsy. Although Penfield sometimes surgically removed portions of the epileptic patients' brains to reduce their symptoms, he was concerned that such surgery might impair some of the patients' ability to function normally. Penfield's solution was to map the neocortex during surgery. Penfield gave the patients a local anesthetic so they would remain awake during the operation. As he stimulated certain sensory and motor areas of the brain, different parts of the patient's body moved (see figure 2.15). For both sensory and motor areas, there is a point-to-point relation between a body part and a location on the neocortex (see figure 2.16). The face and hands have proportionally more space on the neocortex than other body parts because they are capable of finer perceptions and movements.

Our ability to perceive the world in an accurate and orderly way depends on this point-to-point mapping of sensory input onto the neocortex's surface. When something touches your lip, for example, your brain registers "lip." That's because the nerve pathways from your lips project to a specific part of the neocortex designated to receive only signals from your lips. This arrangement is analogous to the private "hot line" that connects Washington and Moscow. If the red phone rings in the President's office in Washington, the call must be from Moscow, because Moscow is the only city that is connected to the other end of the line. In the sensory cortex, every small region has its own neural hot line bringing in information directly from the corresponding part of the sensory field. In our telephone analogy, it would be as if the President (the neocortex) had hundreds of telephones, each one connected directly to the capital city of a different country. Whichever phone was ringing would indicate which country (sensory field) had a message to convey.

Occasionally these neural hot lines get tangled or connected the wrong way. One familiar example of this is the Siamese cat. Many Siamese cats have a genetic defect that causes the pathways from the eyes to connect to the wrong parts of

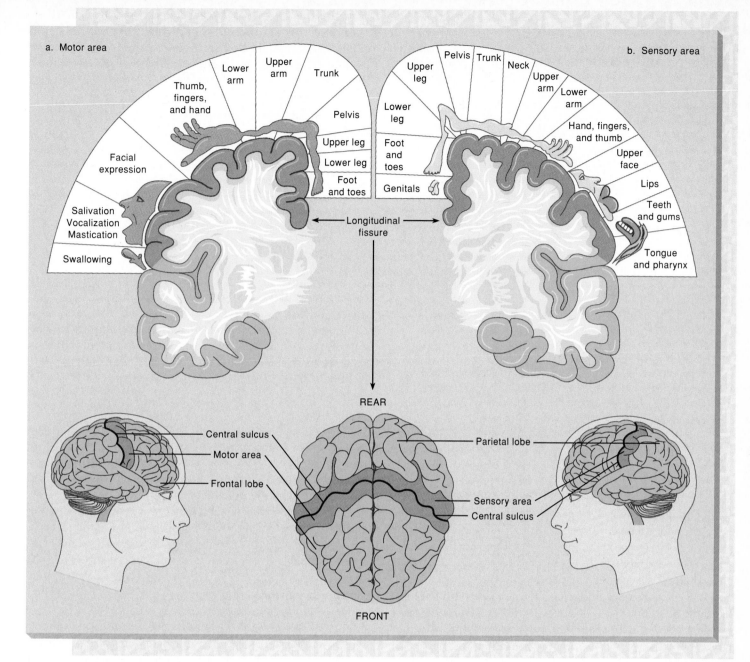

FIGURE 2.16

Locations of the motor and sensory areas on the neocortex. This figure shows (a) the motor areas involved with the control of voluntary muscles and (b) the sensory areas involved with cutaneous and certain other senses. The body is disproportionately represented on the parietal and frontal lobes, with the hands and face receiving the most representation. Organization is inverse—functions represented at the top of the parietal lobe occur in the lower regions of the body, for example.

the visual cortex. The result is that, in an effort to get the visual image to straighten out on their visual cortex, these cats spend their lives looking cross-eyed.

So far our description of the neocortex has focused on sensory and motor areas, but more than 75 percent of the neocortex is made up of areas called the association cortex (see figure 2.17). The **association cortex** (*or association areas*) *is involved in our highest intellectual functions, such as problem solving and thinking.* The neurons in the association cortex communicate with each other and with neurons in the motor cortex. By observing brain-damaged people and using topographic mapping techniques, scientists have found that the association

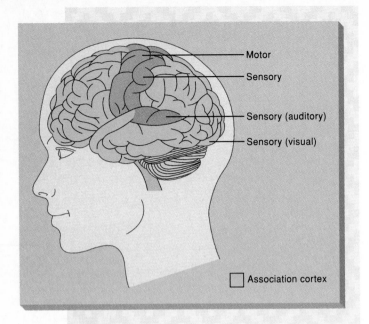

FIGURE 2.17

Association cortex. The very large areas of the cerebral cortex, called the association cortex or association areas, do not respond when electrically stimulated, unlike the motor and sensory areas. Neurons in the association cortex communicate with neurons in other areas of the association cortex and with sensory and motor areas. Neuroscientists believe that the association areas are involved in thinking and problem solving.

cortex is involved in linguistic and perceptual processes. Interestingly, damage to a specific part of the association cortex does not necessarily lead to a specific loss of function. With the exception of language areas, which *are* localized, loss of function seems to depend more on the extent of damage to the association areas than to the specific location of the damage. The largest portion of the association cortex is located in the frontal lobe, beneath the forehead. An individual whose frontal lobes have been damaged does not lose sensory or motor control but may become "a different person," leading researchers to believe that the frontal lobes are linked with personality. This area may be most directly related to thinking and problem solving. Early experiments suggested that the frontal lobe is the center of intelligence, but more recent research indicates that damage to the frontal lobes may not result in a loss of intelligence. The ability to make plans, think creatively, and make decisions are other mental processes associated with the frontal lobe.

Split-Brain Research and the Cerebral Hemispheres

For many years, scientists speculated that the **corpus callosum,** *a large bundle of axons that connects the brain's two hemispheres,* had something to do with relaying information between the two sides. Roger Sperry and Ronald Myers confirmed this in experiments in which they cut the corpus callosum in cats. They also severed certain nerve endings leading from the eyes to the brain. After the operations, Sperry and Myers trained the cats to solve a series of visual problems with one eye blindfolded. After each cat learned the task, with only one eye uncovered, its other eye was covered and the animal was tested again. The split-brain cat behaved as if it had never learned the task. It seems that the memory was stored only in the left hemisphere, which could no longer directly communicate with the right hemisphere.

Further evidence of the corpus callosum's function has come from experiments with patients who have severe, even life-threatening, forms of epilepsy. Epilepsy is caused by electrical brain storms that flash uncontrollably across the corpus callosum. One of the most famous cases is that of "W. J." Neurosurgeons severed the corpus callosum of this epileptic patient in a final attempt to reduce his unbearable seizures. Sperry (1968) examined W. J. and found that the corpus callosum functions the same in humans as in animals— cutting the corpus callosum seems to leave patients with two separate minds that learn and operate independently. The right hemisphere receives information only from the left side of the body, and the left hemisphere receives information only from the right side of the body. When you hold an object in your left hand, for example, only the right hemisphere of your brain detects the object. When you hold an object in your right hand, only the left hemisphere of your brain detects the object (see figure 2.18). In a normal corpus callosum, both hemispheres receive this information.

The most extensive and consistent research findings on the brain's hemispheres involve language. The left hemisphere controls the ability to use language, whereas the right hemisphere is unable to translate sensations into words. The split-brain patients in Sperry's experiments, such as W. J., could verbally describe sensations that were received by the left hemisphere—that is, a stimulus in the right visual field (Sperry, 1974; Sperry & Gazzaniga, 1967), but they could not verbally describe sensations that were received by the right hemisphere—a stimulus in the left visual field. Because the corpus callosum was severed, the information could not be communicated from one hemisphere to the other. More recent investigations of split-brain patients document that language is rarely processed in the right hemisphere (Gazzaniga, 1983, 1986).

There has been lots of speculation over the past few years about the brain's hemispheric specialization, the notion being that the hemispheres function in different ways and that some psychological processes are restricted to one hemisphere. In fact, Americans commonly use the terms *left-brained* and *right-brained* to describe which hemisphere is dominant. You've probably seen James Garner on TV advertising beef. "Ya heard about the left-brain/right-brain stuff? The logical left brain understands nutrition," Garner explains, "but the right brain just

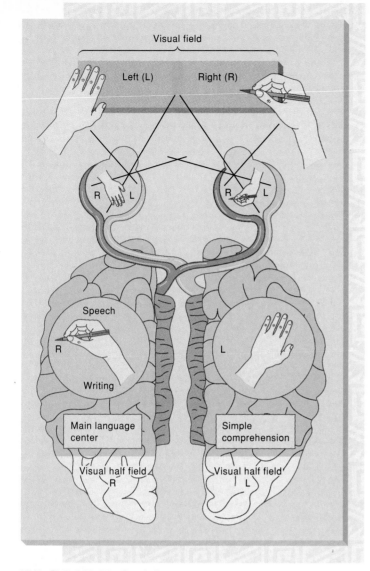

FIGURE 2.18

Visual information in the split brain. In a split-brain patient, information from the visual field's left side projects only to the right hemisphere. Information from the visual field's right side projects only to the left hemisphere. Because of these projections, stimuli can be presented to only one of a split-brain patient's hemispheres.

Jerre Levy has conducted extensive research on the nature of hemispheric function in the brain.

knows it's good." Garner's pitch, and that of others in the media and popular books, is that the left hemisphere is rational, logical, and Western, whereas the brain's right hemisphere is creative, intuitive, and Eastern.

Everyone seems to accept this, everyone, that is, except the scientists who have researched left and right hemisphere functions. To them, the concept of the brain as split into tidy halves—one the source of creativity, the other the source of logical thinking—is simplistic (Dolnick, 1988). Jerre Levy, a neuroscientist at the University of Chicago, points out that no complex function—making music, creating art, reading, and so

on—can be assigned to one hemisphere. Complex thinking in normal people involves communication between both sides of the brain (Efron, in press).

How did the left-brain/right-brain myth get started? It actually had its origin in Sperry's classic studies of split-brain patients. Remember that Sperry examined people whose corpus callosum had been severed and found that after surgery the two sides of the brain learned and operated independently. As his findings made their way into the media, the complexity of Sperry's research was lost and his findings became oversimplified. Media reports indicated that, when a writer works on a novel, the left hemisphere is busy while the right is silent. In creating an oil painting, the right brain is working while the left is quiet. People appeared either right-brained (artistic) or left-brained (logical). An example of the either/or oversimplification of the brain's left and right hemispheres is shown in the drawing of how the brain divides its work (see figure 2.19).

Roger Sperry discovered that the left hemisphere is superior in the kind of logic used to prove geometric theorems, but, in the logic of everyday life, our problems involve integrating information and drawing conclusions. In these instances, the right brain's functions are crucial. In virtually all activities, there is an interplay between the brain's hemispheres (Hellige, 1990; Patterson, Vargha-Khadem, & Polkey, 1989). For example, in reading, the left hemisphere comprehends syntax and grammar, which the right does not. However, the right brain is better at understanding a story's intonation and emotion. The same is true for music and art. Pop psychology assigns both to the right brain. In some musical skills, such as recognizing chords, the right hemisphere is better. In others, such as distinguishing which of two sounds is heard first, the left hemisphere takes over. Enjoying or creating music requires the use of both hemispheres.

Another offshoot of the left-brain/right-brain hoopla is speculation that more right-brain activities and exercises should be incorporated into our nation's schools (Edwards, 1979). In schools that rely heavily on rote learning to instruct students, children probably would benefit from exercises in intuitive

FIGURE 2.19

Stereotyped myths about left-brain, right-brain.

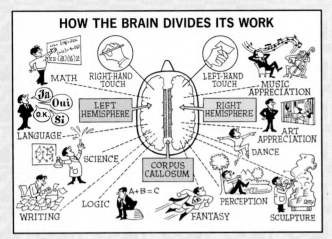

HOW THE BRAIN DIVIDES ITS WORK

MATH · RIGHT-HAND TOUCH · LEFT-HAND TOUCH · MUSIC APPRECIATION · LEFT HEMISPHERE · RIGHT HEMISPHERE · LANGUAGE · ART APPRECIATION · SCIENCE · DANCE · CORPUS CALLOSUM · WRITING · LOGIC · A+B=C · FANTASY · PERCEPTION · SCULPTURE

Is left-brain, right-brain specialization all-or-none, as this drawing implies? No.
© Roy Doty, *Newsweek*.

Popular visions of right-brain, left-brain specialization suggest that Andy Warhol's and Aretha Franklin's right brains are responsible for their artistic and music talents, and that Guion Stewart Bluford's and Albert Einstein's left brains are responsible for their gifts. Is this popular vision overdramatized? Yes, extensively.

thought and holistic thinking, but this deficiency in school curricula has *nothing at all* to do with left-brain/right-brain specialization.

There is so much more to understanding brain function and organization than to characterize people as right- or left-brained. After all, we are trying to understand the most complex piece of matter in the known universe. As we will see next, scientists have been ingenious at developing techniques to learn more about this astonishing organ.

REVIEW

Brain Structure and Function

A neural tube develops into the hindbrain (lowest level), midbrain (middle level), and forebrain (highest level). The main structures of the hindbrain are the medulla, cerebellum, and pons. The midbrain is an area where many fiber systems ascend or descend. Among the forebrain's most important structures are the thalamus, hypothalamus, and neocortex. Each is specialized to process certain kinds of information. The neocortex is a vast sheet of neural tissue.

The wrinkled surface of the cortex is divided into two hemispheres (left and right) and four lobes (frontal, parietal, temporal, and occipital). Topographic mapping has helped scientists determine the neocortex's role in different behaviors. The neocortex consists of sensory, motor, and association areas. Pioneered by Sperry, split-brain research involves severing the corpus callosum. This led to the conclusion that language is primarily a left-hemisphere function. In normal people, the hemispheres work together to process information. A number of myths have developed that exaggerate left-brain/right-brain functions.

Techniques to Study the Brain

Neuroscientists no longer have to perform surgery on living patients or cadavers to study the brain. Sophisticated techniques—such as using high-powered microscopes, the electroencephalograph, single-unit recordings, CAT scan, PET scan, and nuclear magnetic resonance (NMR)—allow researchers to peer into the brain while it's at work. We will consider each of these techniques in turn.

High-powered microscopes are widely used in neuroscience research. Neurons are stained with the salts of various heavy metals, such as silver and lead. These stains coat only

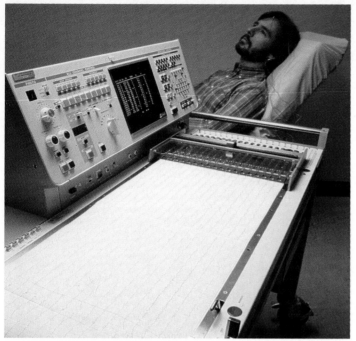

FIGURE 2.20

An individual shown during an EEG recording. The electroencephalogram (EEG) is widely used in sleep research. Its use led to some major breakthroughs in understanding sleep by showing how the brain's electrical activity changes during sleep.

a small portion of any group of neurons, and they allow neuroscientists to view and study every part of a neuron in microscopic detail.

Also widely used, the **electroencephalograph** *records the electrical activity of the brain. Electrodes placed on an individual's scalp record brain-wave activity, which is reproduced on a chart known as an electroencephalogram (or EEG)* (see figure 2.20). This device has been used to assess brain damage, epilepsy, and other problems. In chapter 4, we will see how the EEG has been helpful in charting sleeping and waking patterns.

Not every recording of brain activity is made with electrodes. In single-unit recording—a portrayal of a single neuron's electrical activity—a thin wire or needle is inserted in or near an individual neuron. The wire or needle transmits the neuron's electrical activity to an amplifier.

For years X rays have been used to determine damage inside or outside our bodies, both in the brain and in other locations. However, a single X ray of the brain is hard to interpret because it shows the three-dimensional nature of the brain's interior in a two-dimensional image. **Computer-assisted axial tomography, or CAT scan,** *is a three-dimensional imaging technique obtained by passing X rays through the head; then a computer assembles the individual pictures into a composite image.* The CAT scan provides valuable information about the location of damage due to a stroke, language disorder, or loss of memory.

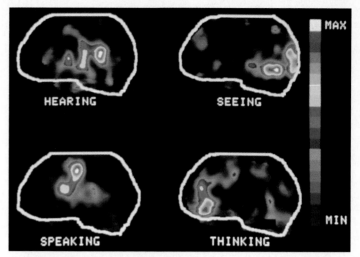

FIGURE 2.21

This PET scan of the left hemisphere of the brain contrasts the areas used in various aspects of language activity: hearing, seeing, speaking, and thinking.

Positron-emission tomography, or PET scan, *measures the amount of specially treated glucose in various areas of the brain, then sends this information to a computer.* Because glucose levels vary with the levels of activity throughout the brain, tracing the amounts of glucose generates a picture of activity level in the brain. Several PET scans of a person's brain activity while she was hearing, seeing, speaking, and thinking are shown in figure 2.21.

Another technique used to study the brain is **nuclear magnetic resonance (NMR),** *sometimes called magnetic resonance imaging (MRI), which involves placing a magnetic field around a person's body and using radio waves to construct images of brain tissues and biochemical activity.* It provides very clear pictures of the brain's interior, it does not require the brain to be injected with a substance, and it does not pose a problem of radiation overexposure. A photograph of NMR is shown in figure 2.22.

At this point, we have discussed many aspects of the brain and techniques for studying it. One more important aspect of the body's biological makeup deserves further attention—the endocrine system.

The Endocrine System— Glandular Information Processing

Recall that the autonomic nervous system involves connections with internal organs, regulating such processes as respiration, heart rate, and digestion. The autonomic nervous system acts on the endocrine glands to produce a number of important physiological reactions to strong emotions, such as rage and fear.

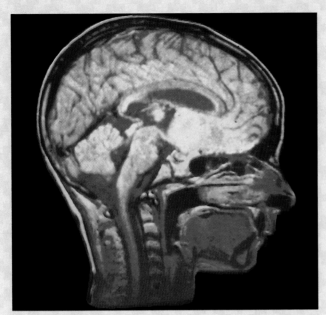

FIGURE 2.22

Nuclear magnetic resonance (NMR) involves placing a magnetic field around the individual's body and using radio waves to produce images of brain tissues and biochemical activity. As shown here, NMR gives a vivid picture of the brain's interior.

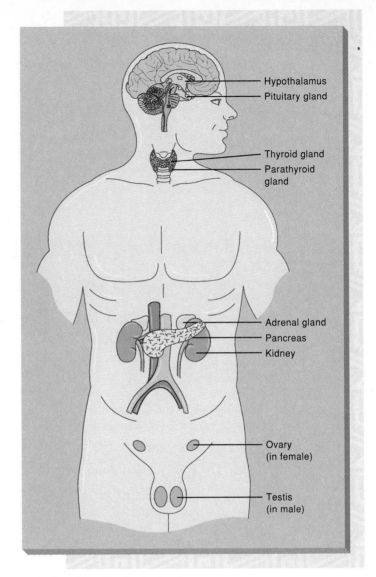

FIGURE 2.23

The major endocrine glands. The pituitary gland releases hormones that regulate the hormone secretions of the other glands. The pituitary gland is itself regulated by the hypothalamus.

The **endocrine glands** *are glands that release their chemical products directly into the bloodstream.* **Hormones** *are chemical messengers manufactured by the endocrine glands.* The bloodstream conveys hormones to all parts of the body, and the membrane of every cell has receptors for one or more hormones.

The endocrine glands consist of the hypothalamus and the pituitary gland at the base of the brain, the thyroid and parathyroid glands at the front of the neck, the adrenal glands just above the kidneys, the pancreas in the abdomen, the ovaries in the female's pelvis, and the testes in the male's scrotum (see figure 2.23). Other hormones are produced as well, including several that control digestion in the gastrointestinal tract. In much the same way that the brain's control of muscular activity is constantly monitored and altered to suit the information received by the brain, the action of the endocrine glands is continuously monitored and changed by the nervous, hormonal, and chemical information sent to them.

The **pituitary gland** *is an important endocrine gland that sits at the base of the skull and is about the size of a pea; the pituitary gland controls growth and regulates other glands.* The anterior (front) part of the pituitary is known as the master gland because most of its hormones direct the activity of target glands elsewhere in the body. For example, follicle-stimulat-

ing hormone (FSH) produced by the pituitary monitors the level of sex hormones in the ovaries of females and the testes of males. Although most pituitary hormones influence specific organs, growth hormone (GH) acts on all tissues to produce growth during childhood and adolescence. Dwarfs have too little of this hormone, giants too much.

The **adrenal glands** *play an important role in our moods, our energy level, and our ability to cope with stress. Each adrenal gland secretes epinephrin (also called adrenaline) and norepinephrine (also called noradrenaline).* Although most hormones travel rather slowly, epinephrine and norepinephrine do their work quickly. Epinephrine helps a person get ready for an emergency by acting on the smooth muscles, heart, stomach, intestines, and sweat glands. Epinephrine also stimulates neurons in the midbrain, which in turn arouses the sympathetic nervous system; this system subsequently excites the adrenal glands to produce more epinephrine. Norepinephrine also alerts the individual for emergency situations by interacting with the pituitary and the liver. You may remember that norepinephrine also functions as a neurotransmitter when released by neurons. In the case of the adrenal glands, norepinephrine is released as a hormone. In both instances, norepinephrine conveys information—in the first instance to neurons, in the second to glands.

In the next chapter, you will learn more about the brain and the endocrine system as we investigate the nature of sensation and perception by examining such fascinating questions as how we see, hear, smell, touch, and feel pain.

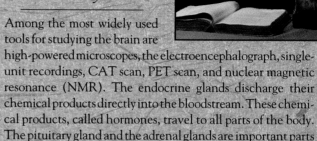

REVIEW

Techniques to Study the Brain and the Endocrine System

Among the most widely used tools for studying the brain are high-powered microscopes, the electroencephalograph, single-unit recordings, CAT scan, PET scan, and nuclear magnetic resonance (NMR). The endocrine glands discharge their chemical products directly into the bloodstream. These chemical products, called hormones, travel to all parts of the body. The pituitary gland and the adrenal glands are important parts of the endocrine system.

Summary

I. Evolution
Charles Darwin proposed the theory of evolution. Its main principle is natural selection, which states that genetic diversity occurs in each species. In this diversity, some organisms have characteristics that help them adapt to their environment. These beneficial characteristics are likely to be perpetuated.

II. Genetics, Sociobiology, and Nature/ Nurture
The nucleus of each human cell contains 46 chromosomes, which are composed of DNA. Genes, the unit of hereditary information, are short segments of DNA. The genes act as a blueprint for cells to reproduce themselves and manufacture proteins that maintain life. Most genetic information involves a combination of genes. Sociobiology argues that all behavior is motivated by the impulse to dominate the gene pool. Critics say sociobiology ignores the environmental determinants of behavior and is biased against women. Scientists believe that both genes and environment are necessary for an organism to exist; every behavior is, to a degree, the interaction of genes and environment. Today the vast majority of human beings do not live in the same environment in which the species evolved. The human species is a culture-making species. Race is a biologi-

cal concept; ethnicity is a sociocultural concept. The concept of race is misunderstood and abused.

III. The Elegant Organization of the Nervous System
The central nervous system consists of the brain and spinal cord, which contain more than 99 percent of all neurons. The peripheral nervous system is a network of nerves that connects the brain and spinal cord to other parts of the body. Two major divisions are the somatic nervous system and the autonomic nervous system. The autonomic nervous system is subdivided into the sympathetic and parasympathetic systems.

IV. Neurons
The pathways of neurons include afferent nerves (sensory nerves), which carry information to the brain, efferent neurons (motor nerves), which carry information away from the brain, and interneurons, which do most of the information processing in the brain itself. *Neuron* is the neuroscientist's label for nerve cell. The three basic parts of the neuron are the cell body, dendrites (which carry information to the cell body), and the axon (which carries information away from the cell body). Most axons are covered with a myelin sheath, which speeds information transmission. Neurons send information down the axon in the

form of brief impulses, or waves, of electricity. These waves are called the action potential. This impulse operates according to the all-or-none principle. The gaps between the neurons are called synapses. The neural impulse comes down the axon and reaches the axon terminal, where it stimulates the release of neurotransmitters from tiny vesicles. The neurotransmitters carry information across the synapse to the next neuron, where it fits like a key into a lock. Among the neurotransmitters that play important roles in mind and behavior are GABA, acetylcholine, norepinephrine, serotonin, and endorphins.

V. Embryological Development and Levels in the Brain
During embryological development, the neural tube changes shape and develops into three major divisions—hindbrain (lowest level), midbrain (middle level), and forebrain (highest level). The main structures of the hindbrain are the medulla, cerebellum, and pons. The midbrain is an area where many fiber systems ascend and descend. Among the forebrain's main structures are the thalamus, hypothalamus, and neocortex. Each is specialized to perform certain information-processing jobs. The neocortex is a vast sheet of neural tissue.

VI. Exploring the Neocortex

The wrinkled surface of the neocortex is divided into two hemispheres (left and right), each containing four lobes (occipital, temporal, frontal, and parietal). Topographic mapping has helped scientists determine the neocortex's role in various behaviors. The neocortex consists of sensory areas, motor areas, and association areas. Sperry pioneered split-brain research, which involves severing the corpus callosum. This research led to the conclusion that language is mainly a left-hemisphere function. In normal people, the hemispheres work together to process information. A number of myths have developed that exaggerate left-brain/right-brain functions.

VII. Techniques to Study the Brain

Among the most widely practiced techniques are using high-powered microscopes, the electroencephalograph, single-unit recordings, CAT scan, PET scan, and nuclear magnetic resonance (NMR).

VIII. The Endocrine System

The endocrine system discharges its chemical products directly into the bloodstream. These chemical products, called hormones, travel to all parts of the body. The pituitary gland and adrenal glands are important parts of the endocrine system.

Key Terms

chromosomes 39
deoxyribonucleic acid (DNA) 39
genes 39
dominant-recessive genes principle 40
natural selection 40
sociobiology 40
environment 41
nurture 41
nature 41
race 41
neurons 44
central nervous system (CNS) 44
peripheral nervous system 44
somatic nervous system 45
autonomic nervous system 45
sympathetic nervous system 45
parasympathetic nervous system 45
afferent nerves 45
efferent nerves 45
interneurons 46
cell body 46

dendrite 46
axon 46
myelin sheath 46
ions 47
resting potential 47
action potential 47
all-or-none principle 47
synapses 48
neurotransmitters 48
GABA 48
acetylcholine (ACh) 49
norepinephrine 49
dopamine 50
serotonin 50
endorphins 50
hindbrain 51
medulla 51
cerebellum 51
pons 51
midbrain 51

forebrain 52
thalamus 52
hypothalamus 53
neocortex 53
occipital lobe 54
temporal lobe 54
frontal lobe 54
parietal lobe 54
association cortex 55
corpus callosum 56
electroencephalograph 59
computer-assisted axial tomography
    (CAT scan) 59
positron-emission tomography
    (PET scan) 59
nuclear magnetic resonance (NMR) 59
endocrine glands 60
hormones 60
pituitary gland 60
adrenal glands 60

Suggested Readings

Bloom, F. E., Lazerson, A., & Hofstader, L. (1988). *Brain, mind, and behavior* (2nd ed.). New York: W.H. Freeman. This book is part of a multimedia teaching package involving the Public Broadcasting System's eight-part series "The Brain." The beauty of the brain is captured in both photographs and well-written essays on its many facets.

Gould, S. J. (1981). *The mismeasure of man.* New York: W.W. Norton. Gould is one of the best contemporary scientist-writers. In this book, he provides fascinating insights into the nature of biological and cultural evolution.

Nilsson, L. (1973). *Behold man.* Boston: Little, Brown. Incredible photographs taken through high-powered microscopes take you inside the human brain to see what its structures and neurons look like.

Watson, J. D. (1968). *The double helix.* New York: New American Library. This book presents a personal account of the research leading up to one of the most provocative discoveries of the twentieth century—the DNA molecule. The book reads like a mystery novel and illustrates the exciting discovery process in science.

SENSATION AND PERCEPTION

CHAPTER 3

Heat is everywhere now. I can't ignore it anymore. The air is like a furnace blast, so hot that my eyes under the goggles feel cool compared to the rest of my face. My hands are cool but the gloves have big black spots from perspiration on the back surrounded by white streaks of dried salt. . . . On the horizon appears an image of buildings, shimmering slightly. . . . I think about ice water and air conditioning (Pirsig, 1974).

The desert's intense heat makes the motorcyclist acutely aware of his abilities to sense his surroundings and his body. Just as with the motorcyclist in Pirsig's book, our lives depend on our ability to sense the world we move through and on the accuracy of our sensations to guide our movements. We move away from threatening stimuli—extreme heat or the sight, sounds, or smells of a predator—and toward food, comfort, and protection (Bloom, Lazerson, & Hofstadter, 1985).

Each of us has a number of sensory and perceptual systems to detect, process, and interpret what we experience in our environment. Sensing and perceiving involve a complex and sophisticated visual system; an auditory system that is an elaborate engineering marvel compacted into a space the size of a small cookie; and other processes that inform us about soft caresses and excruciating pain, sweet and sour tastes, and floral and peppermint odors. Before we tackle each of the senses in greater detail, we need to know more about the nature of sensation and perception.

What Are Sensation and Perception?

How do you know that grass is green, that a smell is sweet, that a sound is a sigh, and that the lights around a shoreline are dim? You know these things because of your *senses*. All outside information comes into us through our senses. Without vision, hearing, touch, taste, smell, and other senses, your brain would be isolated from the world: you would live in a dark silence—a tasteless, colorless, feelingless void.

Sensation *is the process of detecting and encoding stimulus energy in the world.* Stimuli emit physical energy—light, sound, and heat, for example. The sense organs detect this energy and then transform it into a code that can be transmitted to the brain. The first step in sensing the world is the work of receptor cells, which respond to certain forms of energy. The retina of the eye is sensitive to light, and special cells in the ear are sensitive to sound, for example. This physical energy is transformed into electrical impulses; the information carried by these electrical impulses travels through nerve fibers that connect the sense organs to the central nervous system. Once in the brain, the information about the external world travels to the appropriate area of the cerebral cortex. (Recall from chapter 2, for example,

that visual information travels to the occipital lobes at the back of the head, whereas auditory information goes to the temporal lobes just above the ears.)

Perception *is the process of organizing and interpreting sensory information to give it meaning.* The retinas of our eyes record a fast-moving silver object in the sky, but they do not "see" a passenger jet; our eardrum vibrates in a particular way, but it does not "hear" a Beethoven symphony. Organizing and interpreting what is sensed—that is, seeing and hearing meaningful patterns in sensory information—is perception.

In our everyday lives, the two processes of sensation and perception are virtually inseparable. When the brain receives sensory information, for example, it automatically interprets the information. Because of this, most contemporary psychologists refer to sensation and perception as a unified information-processing system.

Detecting the Sensory World

A radar operator's task is to detect blips on a radar screen and decide whether they signify hostile or friendly aircraft. How bright do the blips have to be for the radar operator to see them? Similarly, how do psychologists study our abilities to take in the stimulation in our environment? What are some of the factors that affect how we detect these stimuli?

Thresholds

Could you detect the wing of a fly falling on your cheek from a distance of one centimeter? Could you tell the difference between a drink sweetened with one spoon of sugar and one sweetened with two spoons?

Absolute Threshold

A basic problem in any sensory system is its ability to detect varying degrees of energy in the environment. This energy can take the form of light, sound, chemical, or mechanical stimulation. How much of a stimulus is necessary for you to see, hear, taste, smell, or feel something? The **absolute threshold** *is the minimum amount of energy an individual can detect 50 percent of the time.* Below the absolute threshold, you cannot detect that a stimulus is present; when the threshold is reached, you can detect the stimulus.

An experiment with a wristwatch or clock will help you understand the principle of absolute threshold. Find a wristwatch or clock that ticks; put it on a table and walk far enough across the room so that you no longer hear the ticking. Then gradually move toward the wristwatch or clock. At a certain point, you will begin to hear the ticking. Hold your position and notice that occasionally the ticking fades and you may have to move forward to reach the threshold; at other times, it may become loud and you can move backward (Coren & Ward, 1989). In this experiment, the absolute threshold was not always

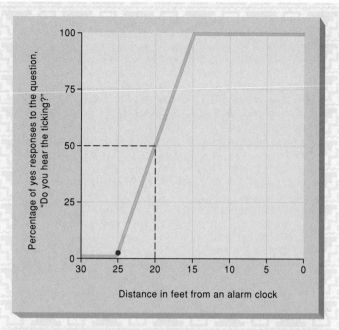

FIGURE 3.1

Determining the absolute threshold. Absolute threshold is the stimulus value a person detects 50 percent of the time. Here the individual's absolute threshold for detecting the ticking of a clock is 20 feet. People have different absolute thresholds. Another individual tested with the ticking clock might have an absolute threshold of 22 feet, for example.

what you thought. If the experiment was conducted a number of times, several distances would have been recorded as the absolute threshold. For example, the first time you tried the experiment, you may have heard the ticking at 25 feet from the clock, but you probably didn't hear it every time at 25 feet. Maybe you heard it ticking at 25 feet 38 percent of the time. You might have heard the ticking at 20 feet 50 percent of the time or at 15 feet 65 percent of the time. Because of this variability, psychologists arbitrarily define absolute threshold as the stimulus value that a person detects 50 percent of the time.

People have different absolute thresholds. Figure 3.1 shows one person's absolute threshold for detecting a clock's ticking sound. Using the same clock, another person might have an absolute threshold of 26 feet, another 22 feet, and yet another 17 feet. To learn about the approximate absolute thresholds of five senses, see table 3.1.

Under ideal circumstances, our senses have very low absolute thresholds. For example, you might have been surprised to learn in table 3.1 that the human eye can see a candle flame at 30 miles on a dark, clear night. However, our environment seldom gives us ideal conditions to detect stimuli. If the night is cloudy and the air is polluted, for example, you would have to be much closer to see the flicker of a candle flame, and other lights on the horizon—car or house lights—would hinder your ability to detect the candle's flame. **Noise** *is the term given to irrelevant and competing stimuli.* For example, someone speaks to you from the door of the room in which you are sitting. You may fail to respond because your roommate is talking on the phone and a CD player is blaring out your favorite song. We usually think of noise as being auditory, but, as a psychological term, noise also involves other senses. Pollution, cloudiness, car lights, and house lights are forms of *visual noise* that hamper your ability to see a candle flame from a great distance.

Subliminal Perception

We have discussed sensations that are above a person's threshold of awareness; however, what about the possibility that we experience the sensory world at levels below our conscious detection? **Subliminal perception** *is the perception of stimuli below the threshold of awareness.* Is this type of perception possible? Some years ago, *Life* magazine reported that 45,000 unknowing movie viewers were exposed to very brief flashes of the words *Drink Coca-Cola* while they were watching movie screens. The article stated that Coke sales soared more than 50 percent because of the subliminal messages (Brean, 1958). Scientists have shown that sensory information too faint to be recognized consciously may be picked up by sensory receptors and transmitted to the brain at a level beneath conscious awareness (Fowler & others, 1981).

Advertisers are still interested in knowing whether or not they can coax us to buy their products by embedding subliminal messages in their advertisements. The belief that subliminal messages have been slipped into rock music has stirred considerable controversy. Some rock groups allegedly have inserted Satanic messages played backwards into their records and tapes. According to this theory, when the record is played normally (forward), the messages cannot be consciously perceived, but they influence our behavior in a subliminal way. Among the backward messages *supposedly* embedded in songs include the following:

- A song by Styx about cocaine says, "Satan, move in our voices."
- "A Child Is Coming" by Jefferson Starship has the words *son of Satan.*
- "I love you, said the Devil" is said in a Rolling Stones song.
- Mötley Crüe's "Shout at the Devil" album has the phrase "Backward mask where are you, oh. Lost in error, Satan."

Researchers have been unable to find any evidence whatsoever that these and other Satanic messages exist or, if they do, that they can influence our behavior (McIver, 1988). Even if we were to play a very clearly recorded message backwards, no one would be able to tell what it said.

What can we make of the claims of the subliminal persuasion enthusiasts and the research conducted by experimental psychologists? First, weak sensory stimuli can be registered by sensory receptors and possibly be encoded in the brain at a level below conscious awareness. Second, no evidence supports the claims of advertisers and rock music critics that such sensory registry and neural encoding have any substantial impact on our thoughts and behavior. Rather, we are influenced by the sounds and sights we are consciously aware of and can attend to efficiently.

Difference Threshold

In addition to studying the amount of stimulation required for a stimulus to be detected, psychologists investigate the degree of

Mötley Crüe's "Shout at the Devil" album has been one of the targets of groups who believe that backward messages are embedded in songs. The protestors say that this album has the phrase, "Backward mask where are you, oh. Lost in error, Satan." However, researchers have been unable to find any evidence whatsoever that these and other Satanic messages exist or, if they do, that they can influence behavior.

difference that must exist between two stimuli before this difference is detected. This **difference threshold,** *or just noticeable difference (jnd), is the smallest difference in stimulation required to discriminate one stimulus from another 50 percent of the time.* An artist might detect the difference between two similar shades of color. A tailor might determine a difference in the texture of two fabrics by feeling them. How different must the colors and textures be for these people to determine the difference? Just as the absolute threshold is determined by a 50 percent detection rate, the difference threshold is the point at which a person detects two stimuli as different 50 percent of the time.

An important aspect of difference thresholds is that the threshold increases with the magnitude of the stimulus. You may notice when your roommate turns up the volume on the stereo by even a small amount when the music is playing softly, but if he turns the volume up an equal amount when the music is playing very loudly, you may not notice. More than 150 years ago, E. H. Weber, a German psychologist, noticed that, regardless of their magnitude, two stimuli must differ by a constant proportion to be detected. **Weber's law** *states that the difference threshold is a constant percentage rather than a constant amount.* Weber's law generally holds true. For example, we add 1 candle to 60 candles and notice a difference in the brightness of the candles; we add 1 candle to 120 candles and do not notice a difference. We discover, though, that adding 2 candles to 120 candles does produce a difference in brightness. Adding 2 candles to 120 candles is the same proportionately as adding 1 candle to 60 candles. The exact proportion also varies with the stimulus involved. For example, a change in a tone's pitch of .3 percent can be detected, but a 20 percent change in taste and a 25 percent change in smell are required for a person to detect a difference.

Sensory Adaptation

Naked except for capes that hang to their knees, two Ona Indians wade in freezing water as they use a bow and arrow to kill fish for their dinner. Darwin encountered the Ona Indians when he rounded Cape Horn on the southern tip of South America. At night they slept naked on the wet, virtually frozen ground. The ability of these Indians to endure the freezing temperatures, wearing little or no clothing, reflects the principle of **sensory adaptation,** *weakened sensitivity to prolonged stimulation*. You have experienced sensory adaptation countless times in your life—adapting to the temperature of a shower, to the water in a swimming pool, to the taste of jalapenos, to loud sounds of rock music, or to the rank smell of a locker room. Over time we become less responsive and less sensitive to these sensory experiences; this is due to sensory adaptation.

At this point, you should have a basic understanding of sensation and perception, the thresholds of sensory awareness, and sensory adaptation. Now we will turn our attention to each of the senses in more detail. We will begin with the sense we know the most about—vision.

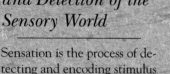

REVIEW

The Nature of Sensation and Perception and Detection of the Sensory World

Sensation is the process of detecting and encoding stimulus energy in the environment. Perception is the process of organizing and interpreting sensed information to give it meaning. The absolute threshold is the minimum stimulus intensity an individual can detect 50 percent of the time. Noise is irrelevant and competing stimuli. Subliminal perception is the perception of stimuli below the threshold of awareness; this is a controversial topic. The difference threshold is also called the just noticeable difference (jnd), the smallest amount of stimulation required to discriminate one stimulus from another 50 percent of the time. Weber's law states that, regardless of magnitude, two stimuli must differ by a constant percentage for the difference to be detected. Sensory adaptation is weakened sensitivity to prolonged stimulation.

Vision

We see a world of shapes and sizes, some stationary, others moving, some in black and white, others in color. *How* do we see this way? What is the machinery that enables us to experience this marvelous landscape?

The Visual Stimulus and the Eye

Light *is a form of electromagnetic energy that can be described in terms of wavelengths*. Waves of light are much like the waves formed when a pebble is tossed into a lake. The **wavelength** *is the distance from the peak of one wave to the peak of the next*. Visible light's wavelengths range from about 400 to 700 nanometers (a nanometer is one-billionth of a meter and is abbreviated nm). The difference between visible light and other forms of electromagnetic energy is its wavelength. Outside the range of visible light are longer radio and infrared radiation waves, and shorter ultraviolet and X rays (see figure 3.2). These other wavelengths can bombard us, but we do not see them. Why do we see only the narrow band of the electromagnetic spectrum between 400 and 700 nanometers? The most likely answer is that our visual system evolved in the sun's light. Thus, our visual system is able to perceive the spectrum of energy emitted by the sun. By the time sunlight reaches the earth's surface, it is strongest in the 400 to 700 nanometer range.

This narrow band of the electromagnetic spectrum strikes our eyes, which have a number of structures to handle the incoming light. By looking closely at your eyes in a mirror, you notice three parts—the sclera, iris, and pupil (figure 3.3 shows the main structures of the eye). The **sclera** *is the white part of the eye, which helps maintain the shape of the eye and protect it from injury*. The **iris** *is a ring of muscles, which range in color from light blue to dark brown*. The **pupil,** *which appears black, is the opening in the center of the iris; its primary function is to reduce glare in high illumination*. The **cornea** *is a clear membrane just in front of the iris that bends light rays as they enter the eye*. The **lens** *is the part of the eye that changes shape to bring objects into focus*. The **retina** *is the light-sensitive surface in the back of the eye. It consists of light receptors called rods and cones and various kinds of neurons*, which you will read about shortly. The **fovea** *is a minute area in the center of the retina where the optic nerve leaves the eye on its way to the brain. Because no light receptors are present on this blind spot, we cannot see anything that reaches only this point on the retina*. To experience your blind spot, turn to figure 3.4 and follow the directions.

Because the retina is so important to vision, we need to study its makeup more closely. **Rods** *are receptors in the retina that are sensitive to black, white, and gray; they especially function in night vision*. **Cones** *are receptors in the retina that are sensitive to color; they especially function in daytime vision*. The rods and cones in the retina are specialized nerve cells that break light into neural impulses by means of a photochemical reaction. The breakdown of the chemicals produces a neural impulse that is first transmit-

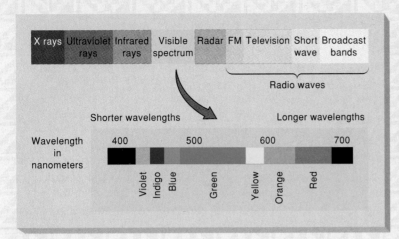

b.

c.

FIGURE 3.2

The electromagnetic spectrum and visible light. (a) Visible light is only a narrow band in the electromagnetic spectrum. Visible light's wavelengths range from about 400 to 700 nanometers; X rays are much shorter and radio waves are much longer. (b) Most ultraviolet rays are absorbed by the ozone in the earth's upper atmosphere. The small fraction that reaches the earth is the ingredient in sunlight that tans the skin (and can cause skin cancer). (c) The electromagnetic radiation just beyond red in the spectrum (infrared) is felt as heat by receptors in the skin.

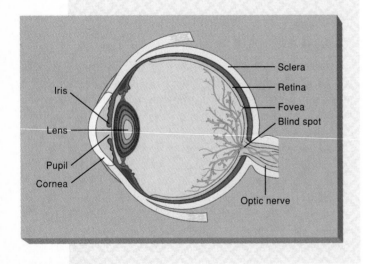

FIGURE 3.3

Main structures of the eye.

FIGURE 3.4

The eye's blind spot. There is a normal blind spot in your eye, a small area where the optic nerve leads to the brain. To find your blind spot, hold this book at arm's length, cover your left eye, and stare at the red pepper with your right eye. Move the book slowly toward you until the yellow pepper disappears. To find the blind spot in your left eye, cover your right eye, concentrate on the yellow pepper, and adjust the distance of the book until the red pepper disappears.

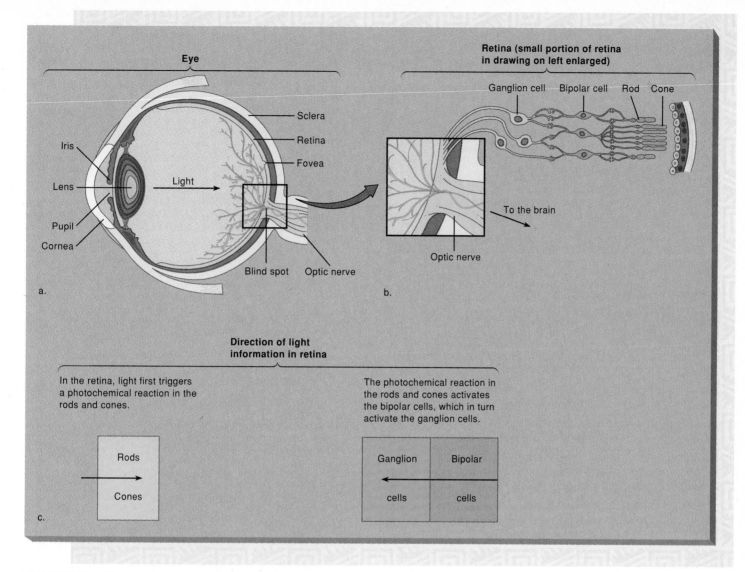

FIGURE 3.5

Transmission of light information through the eye. (a) Light passes through the cornea, pupil, and lens and then falls on the retina, a light-sensitive surface. (b) In the retina, light first triggers a photochemical reaction in the rods and cones. The photochemical reaction of the rods and cones activates the bipolar cells, which in turn activate the ganglion cells. (c) The drawing at the bottom shows the direction of light information in the retina. The ganglion cells intersect to become the optic nerve, which carries information to the brain.

ted to the *bipolar cells* and then moves to the *ganglion cells* (see figure 3.5). The nerve impulse then passes along the axon of the ganglion cells, which make up the optic nerve.

Rods and cones are involved in different aspects of vision. Rods, which are long and cylindrical, are very sensitive to light. Thus, they function well under low illumination; as you might anticipate, they are hard at work at night. Rods, however, are not sensitive to color. For this reason, we have difficulty seeing color at night. Cones, which are shorter and fatter than rods, detect color but only under good illumination. Rods and cones are concentrated in different parts of the retina; rods are found almost everywhere except the fovea, whereas cones are concentrated at the fovea. Because we know that rods are used in poorly lit conditions and that the fovea has no rods, we can conclude that vision is poor for objects registered on the fovea at night. A summary of some of the main characteristics of rods and cones is presented in table 3.2.

So far we have studied the importance of light and the structures of the eye. The journey of vision now leads us to the brain and how it processes visual information.

TABLE 3.2
Characteristics of Rods and Cones

Characteristics	Rods	Cones
Type of vision	Black and white	Color
Light conditions	Dimly lighted	Well lighted
Shape	Thin and long	Short and fat
Distribution	Not on fovea	On fovea

From Eye to Brain and Neural Visual Processing

The **optic nerve** *leads out of the eye toward the brain, carrying information about light.* The **optic chiasm** *is the point at which approximately two-thirds of the fibers that make up the optic nerve cross over the midline of the brain.* Before reaching the optic chiasm, stimuli in the left visual field are registered in the right half of the retina in both eyes, and stimuli in the right visual field are registered in the left half of the retina in both eyes. Optic nerves from the right half of each retina converge at the optic chiasm. From there visual information moves to the right side of the occipital lobe in the back of the brain. Optic nerves from the left half of each retina also converge at the optic chiasm; then information is conveyed to the left side of the occipital lobe. What all of these crossings mean is that what we see in the left side of our visual field ends up in the right side of our brain, and what we see in the right visual field ends up in the left side of our brain (see figure 3.6).

The visual cortex in the occipital lobe combines information from both eyes and is responsible for higher levels of visual processing. David Hubel and Torsten Wiesel (1965) won a Nobel Prize for their discovery that some neurons detect different features of the visual field. By recording the activity of a *single* neuron in a cat while it looked at patterns that varied in size, shape, color, and movement, the researchers found that the visual cortex has neurons that are individually sensitive to different types of lines and angles. For example, one neuron might show a sudden burst of activity when stimulated by lines of a particular angle; another neuron might fire only when moving stimuli appear; yet another neuron might be stimulated when the object in the visual field has a combination of angles, sizes, and shapes.

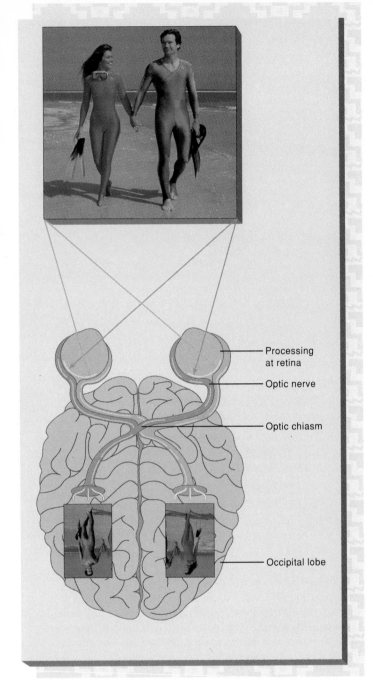

Processing at retina
Optic nerve
Optic chiasm
Occipital lobe

FIGURE 3.6

Visual pathways to and through the brain. Light from each side of the visual field falls on the opposite side of each eye's retina. Visual information then travels along the optic nerve to the optic chiasm, where most of the visual information crosses over to the other side of the brain. From there visual information goes to the occipital lobe at the rear of the brain. What all of the crossings mean is that what we see in the left side of our visual field (in this figure, the woman) ends up in the right side of our brain, and what we see in the right visual field (the man) ends up on the left side of our brain.

Color Vision

We spend a lot of time thinking about color—the color of the car we want to buy, the color we are going to paint the walls of our room, the color of the clothes we wear. We can change our hair color or even the color of our eyes to make us look more attractive.

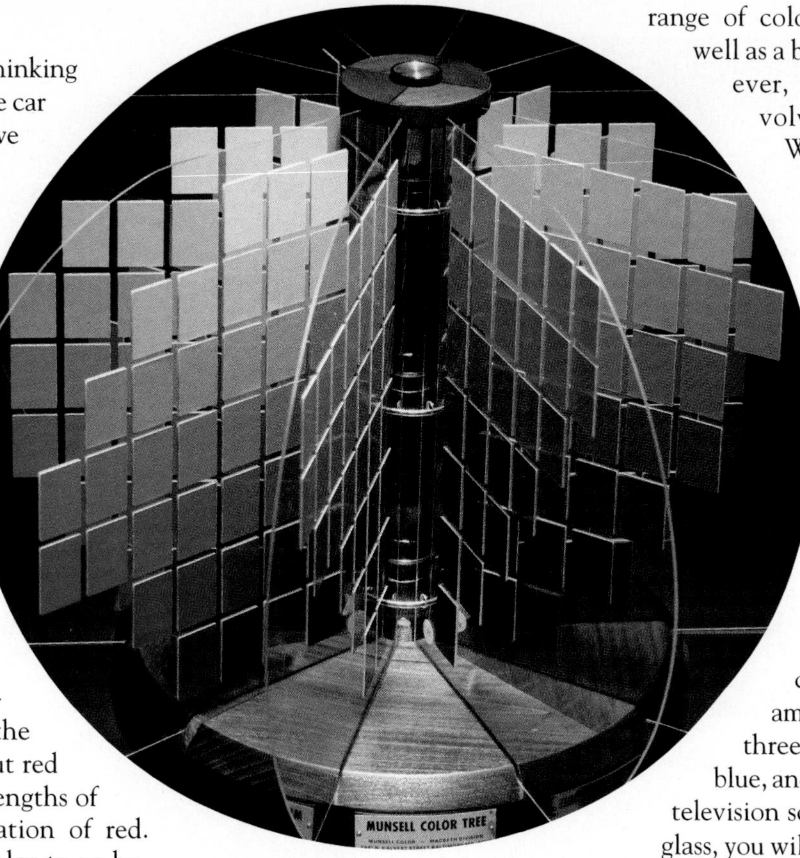

What Is Color?

As was mentioned before, the human eye registers light wavelengths between 400 and 700 nm (as you saw in figure 3.2). Light waves themselves have no color. The sensations of color reside in the visual system of the observer, so, if we talk about red light, we refer to the wavelengths of light that evoke the sensation of red. Objects appear a certain color to us because they reflect specific wavelengths of light to our eyes. These wavelengths are split apart into a spectrum of colors when the light passes through a prism, as in the formation of a rainbow. We can remember the colors of the light spectrum by thinking of an imaginary man named ROY G. BIV, for the colors red, orange, yellow, green, blue, indigo, and violet.

If you go into a paint store and ask for some red paint, the salesperson will probably ask you what kind of red paint you want—dark or light, pinkish or more crimson, pastel or deep, and so on. A color's **hue** *is based on its intensity,* a color's **saturation** *on its purity,* and a color's **brightness** *on its intensity.* As shown in figure 3.2, the longest wavelengths seen by the human eye (about 700 nm) appear as red; the shortest (about 400 nm) appear as violet. Hue is what we commonly think of color to be. To understand a color's saturation, turn to figure 3.7. The purity of a color is determined by the amount of white light added to a single wavelength of color. Colors that are very pure have no white light—they are located on the outside of the color tree. As we move toward the color tree's interior, notice how the saturation of the color changes. The closer we get to the tree's center, the more white light has been added to the single wavelength of a particular color. That is, the deep colors at the edge fade into the more pastel colors toward the center. When saturation is added to hue, we see a much larger

FIGURE 3.7

A color tree showing color's three dimensions: hue, saturation, and brightness.

range of colors—pink and crimson, as well as a basic red, for example. However, another dimension is involved in color—brightness. White has the most brightness, black the least.

When we mix colors, we get different results depending on whether we mix light or pigments (see figure 3.8). An **additive mixture** *of color refers to mixing beams of light from different parts of the color spectrum.* Through additive mixing, we can produce virtually the entire color circle by using any three widely spaced colors. Television is an example of additive mixing—only three colors are involved—red, blue, and green. If you look at a color television screen through a magnifying glass, you will notice that a yellow patch of light is actually a combination of tiny red and green dots. Look at the other patches of color on a television screen with a magnifying glass to observe their composition.

In contrast, a **subtractive mixture** *of color refers to mixing pigments rather than beams of light.* An artist's painting is an example of subtractive mixing. When blue and yellow are mixed on the television screen, a gray or white hue appears, but, when an artist mixes a dab of blue paint with a dab of yellow paint, the color green is produced. In a subtractive color mixture, each pigment absorbs (subtracts) some of the light falling on it and reflects the rest of the light. When two pigments are mixed, only the light that is not absorbed or subtracted from either one emerges (Wasserman, 1978).

Theories of Color Vision

For centuries scientists have puzzled over how the human eye sees the infinite variety of color in the world. Though we can discriminate among 319 colors, no one believes that we have 319 kinds of cones in our retinas (Bartley, 1969). Instead, even the earliest theorists assumed that our retinas respond to a few primary colors and then relay the information to the brain, where it is synthesized into the many different hues we perceive. However, early theorists disagreed about which colors the retina was selecting. Two main theories were proposed, and each turned out to be right (Boynton, 1989).

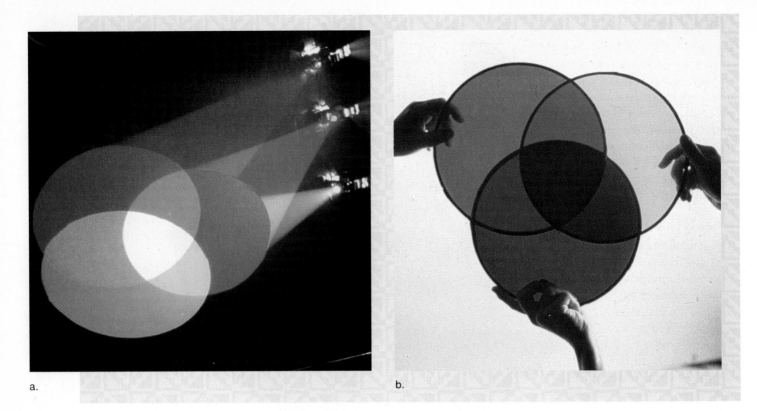

a.

b.

FIGURE 3.8

Comparing the mixing of light with the mixing of pigments. (a) Additive color mixtures occur when lights are mixed. For example, red and green lights when combined yield yellow. The three colors together give white. (b) Subtractive color mixtures occur when pigments are mixed or light is shown through colored filters placed over one another. Most of the time, a mixture of blue-green and yellow produces green, and a mixture of complementary colors produces black.

The first theory was based on what you just learned—that mixing red, blue, and green light produces all of the colors we perceive. Thomas Young and Hermann von Helmholtz considered that fact and made the reasonable suggestion that the retina responds only to the amount of red, blue, and green light coming from the stimulus, letting the brain remix them to produce the actual color. This is called the **Young-Helmholtz trichromatic theory,** *the theory of color vision which states that the retina's cones are sensitive to one of three colors—red, green, or blue.* Individual cones respond either to red, blue, and green, just as Young and Helmholtz thought. In an investigation related to trichromatic theory, geneticists discovered the three individual genes in the human chromosome that direct cones to produce the three pigments that make them sensitive to red, blue, or green light (Nathans, Thomas & Hogness, 1986).

Trichromatic theory finds further convincing support in the study of defective color vision. The term *color-blind* is somewhat misleading because it suggests that a person who is color-blind cannot see color at all. Complete color blindness is rare; most people who are color-blind, the vast majority of whom are males, can see some colors but not others. The nature of their color blindness depends on whether the red-, green-, or blue-responding cones are inoperative. For example, in the most common form of color blindness, the green cone system malfunctions. Green is indistinguishable from certain combinations of blue and red. Two examples of tests given to evaluate color blindness are shown in figure 3.9.

German physiologist Ewald Hering was not completely satisfied with the trichromatic theory of color vision. Hering observed that, when most people are given a large number of color samples, they pick out four colors (red, green, blue, and yellow) rather than the three colors of trichromatic theory (red, green, and blue). Hering also observed that trichromatic theory could not adequately explain **afterimages**—*sensations that remain after a stimulus is removed.* Visual afterimages are common and they involve complementary colors. If you look at red long enough, eventually a green afterimage will appear; if you look at yellow long enough, eventually a blue afterimage will appear. (To experience an afterimage, see figure 3.10.) Such information led Hering to propose that the visual system treats colors as complementary pairs—red-green and blue-yellow. Hering's view is called **opponent-process theory,** *which states that cells in the*

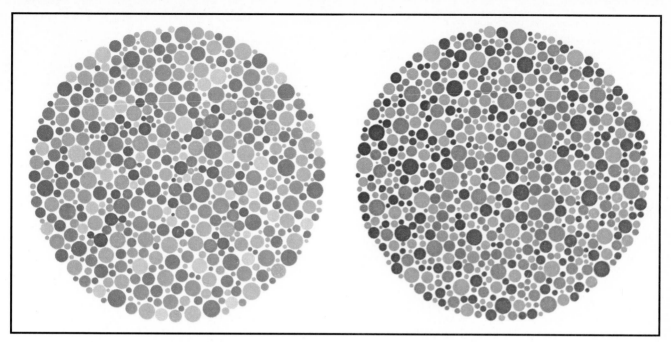

FIGURE 3.9

Examples of stimuli used to test for color blindness. In the left circle, people with normal vision see the number 16, but people with red-green color blindness do not. In the right circle, people with normal vision detect the number 8, but those with red-green color blindness see one number or none. A complete color blindness assessment involves the use of 15 stimuli.

The above has been reproduced from *Ishihara's Tests for Colour Blindness* published by Kanehara & Co., Ltd., Tokyo, Japan, but tests for color blindness cannot be conducted with this material. For accurate testing, the original plates should be used.

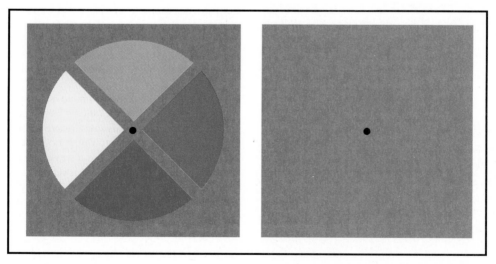

FIGURE 3.10

Negative afterimage—complementary colors. If you gaze steadily at the dot in the colored panel on the left for a few moments, then shift your gaze to the gray box on the right, you will see the original hues change into their complementary colors. The blue appears as yellow, the red as green, the green as red, and the yellow as blue. This pairing of colors has to do with the fact that color receptors in the eye are apparently sensitive as pairs; when one color is turned off (when you stop staring at the panel), the other color in the receptor is briefly "turned on." The afterimage effect is especially noticeable when you spend time painting walls or objects in bright colors.

retina respond to red-green and blue-yellow colors—*with a given cell, for example, being excited by red and inhibited by green and another cell excited by yellow and inhibited by blue*. Researchers have found that the opponent-process theory effectively explains afterimages (Hurvich & Jameson, 1969; Jameson & Hurvich, 1989).

Our tour of the visual system has been an extensive one—you have read about the light spectrum, the structures of the eye, neural visual processing, and the marvels of color vision. Next, you will study the second-most researched sensory system, our hearing.

The Auditory System

Just as light provides us with information about the environment, so does sound. Think about what life would be like without music, the rushing sound of ocean waves, or the gentle voice of someone you love.

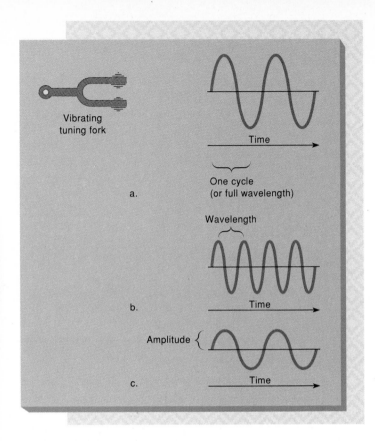

FIGURE 3.11

Frequency and amplitude of sound waves. (a) A tuning fork is an instrument with two prongs that produces a tone when struck. You may have seen one in a music classroom or science laboratory. The vibrations of the tuning fork cause air molecules to vibrate like a musical instrument, producing a sound wave pattern like the one shown. (b) Wavelength determines the frequency of the sound wave, which is the number of cycles, or full wavelengths, that can pass through a point in a given time. In the tuning fork example, two cycles (full wavelengths) have occurred in the time frame shown. In the sound waves shown here, four cycles have occurred in this time frame, so this sound wave has a higher frequency than the sound wave with the tuning fork; hence, it has a higher pitch. (c) The amplitude of the sound wave is the change in pressure created by the sound wave and is reflected in the sound wave's height. This sound wave has a smaller amplitude than the sound wave shown with the tuning fork; thus, it does not sound as loud.

The Nature of Sound and How We Experience It

At a rock concert, you may have felt the throbbing pulse of loud sounds or sensed that the air around you was vibrating. Bass instruments are especially effective at creating mechanical pulsations, even causing the floor or a seat to vibrate on occasion. When a bass instrument is played loudly, we can sense air molecules being pushed forward in waves from the speaker.

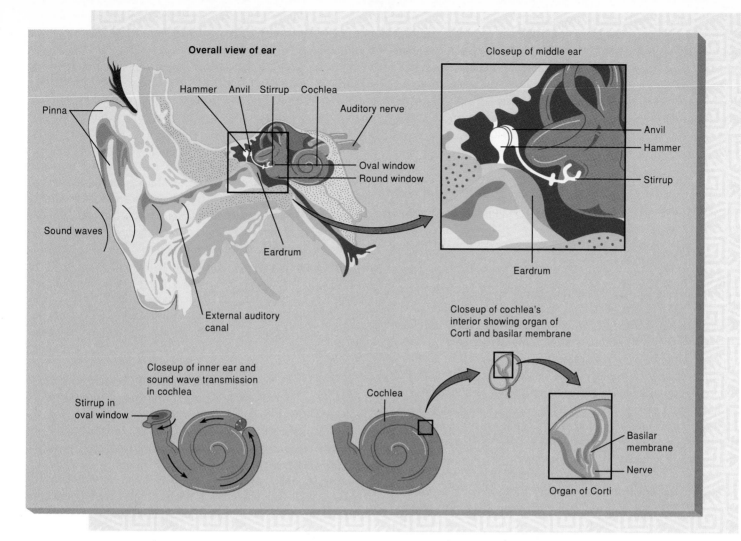

FIGURE 3.12

Major structures of the human ear and the transmission of sound waves. Sound waves are funneled through the external auditory canal to the eardrum in the middle ear. Three bony structures in the middle ear—hammer, anvil, and stirrup—concentrate sound waves so they can be further processed in the inner ear. The stirrup relays the eardrum's vibrations through the oval window to the cochlea, a snaillike, fluid-filled structure, where sound waves are further processed before the auditory information moves on to the auditory nerve to be transmitted to the brain. The organ of Corti runs the entire length of the cochlea and contains the basilar membrane at its base. The movement of sound waves in the cochlear fluid causes the basilar membrane to vibrate and its hair cells to bend. The vibrating hair cells stimulate nearby nerve cells, which join to form the auditory nerve.

Sound, *or sound waves, refer to vibrations in the air that are processed by our auditory (hearing) system.* Remember that light waves are much like the waves formed when a pebble is tossed into a lake—concentric circles move outward from where the pebble entered the water. Sound waves are similar. They vary in wavelength, which determines the **frequency** *of the sound wave— the number of cycles (or full wavelengths) that pass through a point in a given time* (see figure 3.11). **Pitch** *is the ear's detection of the sound wave's frequency. High-frequency sounds are high-pitched; low-frequency sounds are low-pitched.* A soprano voice sounds high-pitched; a bass voice sounds low-pitched. Sound waves not only vary in frequency, but also in **amplitude,** *which is the change in pressure created by sound waves.* As shown in figure 3.12, the height of the sound wave reflects its amplitude. The sound wave's amplitude is measured in **decibels (dB),** *the amount of pressure produced by a sound wave relative to a standard; the typical standard is the weakest sound the human ear can detect.* Thus, zero would be the softest noise detectable by humans. Noise rated at 80 decibels or higher, if heard for prolonged periods of time, can cause permanent hearing loss. A quiet library is about 40 decibels, a car horn about 90 decibels, a rock band at close range 120 decibels, and a rocket launching 180 decibels.

So far we have been describing a single sound wave with just one frequency. Most sounds, including those of speech and music, are complex sounds. **Complexity** *refers to the numerous frequencies of sound blending together, which is sensed as the sound's timbre.* The numerous blends result in our experience of various **timbres,** *or tone colors, which we experience as different qualities of sound.* Timbre is what makes one human voice sound different from another and what makes an oboe sound different from a flute.

Structures and Functions of the Ear

What happens to sound waves once they reach your ear? How do various structures of the ear transform sound waves of compressed air so they can be understood by the brain as sound?

The ear is divided into the outer ear, middle ear, and inner ear (the major structures of the ear are shown in figure 3.12). The **outer ear** *is made up of the pinna and external auditory canal.* The pinna is the outer part of the ear (elephants have very large ones), which helps us localize sounds by making the sound different in front of us than behind us. The sound waves are then funneled through the external auditory canal to the middle ear.

The **middle ear** *has four main structures: eardrum, hammer, anvil, and stirrup.* The eardrum is the first structure that sound touches in the middle ear. The eardrum vibrates in response to a sound, and the sound then touches three bony structures: the hammer, anvil, and stirrup. The middle ear structures translate the sound waves in air into sound waves in water (lymph) so they can be processed further in the inner ear.

The main parts of the **inner ear** *are the oval window, the cochlea, and the organ of Corti, located in the cochlea.* The stirrup is connected to the oval window, which transmits the waves to the **cochlea,** *a snail-shaped, fluid-filled structure that contains the receptors for hearing.* The organ of Corti runs the entire length of the cochlea. It contains the ear's sensory receptors, which change the energy of the sound waves into nerve impulses that can be processed by the brain. Hairlike sensory receptors in the organ of Corti are stimulated by vibrations of the *basilar membrane.* These receptors generate nerve impulses, which vary with the frequency and extent of the membrane's vibrations.

One of the auditory system's mysteries is how the inner ear registers the frequency of sound. Three theories have been proposed to explain this mystery: place theory, frequency theory, and volley theory. **Place theory** *is a theory of hearing which states that each frequency produces vibrations at a particular spot on the basilar membrane.* Georg von Bekesy won a Nobel Prize in 1961 for his research on the basilar membrane. Von Bekesy (1960) studied the effects of vibration on the oval window of human cadavers. Through a microscope, he saw that this stimulation produced a traveling wave. High-frequency vibrations create traveling waves that stimulate the area of the basilar membrane next to the oval window; low-frequency vibrations stimulate other areas of the membrane closer to the tip of the cochlea.

Place theory adequately explains high-frequency sounds but fares poorly with low-frequency sounds. A low-frequency sound does not stimulate a particular spot on the basilar membrane; rather, it transforms the entire basilar membrane. Because humans can hear low-frequency sounds, another factor must account for the perception of sound. **Frequency theory** *states that perception of sound is due to how often the auditory nerve fires.* Frequency theory argues that the basilar membrane does indeed vibrate as a whole at lower frequencies.

Volley theory *modifies and expands frequency theory to account for high-frequency sounds. A single neuron has a maximum firing capacity of about 1,000 times per second. Because of this limitation, frequency theory cannot be applied to tone frequencies above 1,000 times per second. Volley theory argues that these high-frequency tones can be accounted for by a team of neurons, with each neuron on the team firing at a different time.* The term *volley* is used because the neurons fire in a sequence of rhythmic volleys at higher frequencies. The alternation in neural firing makes possible frequencies above 1,000 times per second. Thus, frequency theory better explains low-pitched sounds, such as a dog's growl or a motorcycle's roar, whereas place theory and volley theory better explain high-pitched sounds, such as an ambulance's siren or a whistler's tune. Sound pitches in the middle ranges involve a combination of theories.

Now that we have discussed the visual and auditory systems in some detail, we will turn to a number of other sensory systems—the skin senses, the chemical senses, the kinesthetic senses, and the vestibular sense. As you can tell from this list, humans have more than the traditional five senses of sight, hearing, touch, taste, and smell.

The Skin Senses

Many of us think of our skin as a canvas rather than a sense. We color it with cosmetics, dyes, and tattoos. We modify it with face lifts, hair transplants, and fake fingernails. However, the skin is actually our largest sensory system, draping over the body, with receptors for touch, temperature, and pain.

Touch

With a rubber band, lightly touch the following parts of your body: the bottom of your foot, your leg, your nose, and your forefinger. You should be able to sense that these different parts of your body do not have the same sensitivity to touch. The body's most sensitive areas are in the head region (nose and upper lip, for example), and the least sensitive areas are in the foot region (sole of the foot, for example) (Weinstein, 1968). Women are more sensitive to touch over most of their body than men are.

Temperature

Do you feel too hot or too cold right now, or do you feel about right? Our bodies have a regulatory system that keeps the body's temperature at about 98.6° F, and the skin plays an important role in this regulatory system. Some years ago, it was found that we have separate locations on our skin that sense warmth and cold (Dallenbach, 1927). The forehead is especially sensitive to heat, the arm is less sensitive, and the calf is the least sensitive.

Pain

For all living things, avoiding harm is critical for a strategy of survival, and pain is part of that strategy. Pain is information that warns us, protects us, and instructs us about what is harmful in the world. The importance of pain for humans is clearly illustrated by 7-year-old Sarah, who was born with an insensitivity to pain. She constantly hurts herself but does not realize it. A wound on her knee is protected from further harm by a cast on her leg. Her arm is bandaged to heal a bruise on her elbow. Sarah has something wrong with the nerve pathways that normally transmit signals to the brain that it interprets as pain.

Aside from a few people like Sarah, we all experience pain. Even so, we can never be sure whether another person is experiencing pain. You may infer from her expression or behavior that your friend is in pain, but you cannot directly experience her pain.

Many stimuli can cause pain. Intense stimulation of any one of our senses can produce pain—too much light, very loud sounds, extreme temperatures, strong pressure on the skin, for example. However, like other perceptions, our perception of pain reflects our subjective judgments. Among other factors, our expectations, moods, and body's makeup influence how we perceive pain. If we expect something to hurt us, we are more likely to perceive pain, and, if our body has a weak spot, we are more likely to experience pain there. **Pain threshold** *is the stimulation level at which pain is first perceived.* Because our perception of pain reflects subjective judgments, pain thresholds vary considerably from one person to another, from one point in time to another, and from one cultural group to another. Information about cultural and ethnic reactions to pain appears in Sociocultural Worlds 3.1.

How is pain transmitted to the brain? Consider the situation when you miss a nail with a hammer and smash your thumb—it almost hurts just to think about it. The pain message begins with the release of chemicals usually found in or near the nerve endings in the skin (among these are chemicals known as substance P and bradykinin). These chemicals sensitize the nerve endings and help transmit the pain message from your thumb to your brain. The pain signal is converted into a series of electrochemical impulses that travel through the peripheral nervous system to the central nervous system and up the spinal cord. From there the pain signal becomes a cascade of chemical messages as it relays through the brain to the thalamus. Then, the pain message is routed to the cerebral cortex, where the pain's intensity and specific location is identified. It is also in the cerebral cortex that the pain is symbolically interpreted. In the case of martyrs and patriots, the pain may even be welcome (Restak, 1988). In our case of slamming our thumb with a hammer, it is undoubtedly not welcome.

Further understanding of how we experience pain involves a closer look at the spinal cord. Ronald Melzack and Patrick Wall (1965, 1983) pointed out that the nervous system can process only a limited amount of sensory information of any kind—pain, touch, or anything else—at a given moment. They discovered that, when too much information moves through the nervous system, certain neural cells in the spinal column stop the signal. **Gate-control theory** *is Melzack and Wall's theory that the spinal column contains a neural "gate" that can be opened (allowing the perception of pain) or closed (blocking the perception of pain).* In the case of the throbbing thumb you hammered, you quickly grab a bunch of ice cubes and press them against your thumb. The pain lessens. According to gate-control theory (see figure 3.13 on page 81), the ice sent signals to the spinal cord and slammed the gate in the face of competing pain signals. The brain also, in turn, can send information down the spinal cord and influence whether a gate is open or closed. In this way, emotions, attitudes, hypnosis, and neurotransmitters can influence how much pain we sense. The gate in gate-control theory is not a physical gate that opens and shuts; rather, the gate is the inhibition of neural impulses.

When the spinal cord receives a strong peripheral signal, such as the prick of an acupuncture needle, it, too, can turn on the interneuron and close the gate (see figure 3.14 on page 82). **Acupuncture** *is a technique in which thin needles are inserted at specific points in the body to relieve specific symptoms* (see figure 3.14). Interestingly, the point of stimulation may be some distance from the symptom being treated. For example, when acupuncture is used as an anesthetic in abdominal surgery, four acupuncture needles are placed in the pinna of each ear. Although acupuncture is still considered somewhat unorthodox in the United States, the technique is used widely in China in dentistry and occasionally in abdominal surgery. How does acupuncture reduce the sensation of pain? The gate-control mechanisms may be partly responsible, and neurotransmitters, such as endorphins (see chapter 2), may also play a role.

Our ability to interpret a specific sensation as pain hinges on complex neurochemical reactions. Researchers are investigating this cascade of events, not only to understand better the mechanism of pain but also to find ways to reduce human suffering.

Cultural and Ethnic Reactions to Pain

In a remote village, a cart slowly wends its way along a dusty road. A man swings from a pole in the cart; ropes from two large steel hooks embedded in the man's back attach him to the pole. The man is not being punished or tortured; he is blessing the children and crops in a centuries-old ritual practiced in certain parts of India. His role is an honor. The man does not seem to be suffering; instead, he appears to be in a state of exaltation. What's more, his wounds heal rapidly after the hooks are removed, even with little medical treatment.

How does the man unflinchingly withstand such pain? Experiences such as these have been described as hypnotic, inducing an altered state of consciousness (which we will discuss extensively in chapter 4). Aside from culturally variant religious roles, studies of several ethnic and cultural groups have shown differences in how people in more usual states of mind react to pain. In one investigation, Jewish patients tended to postpone taking an analgesic until after the determination of their diagnosis and future prognosis, whereas Italian patients were more likely to request immediate pain relief (Weisenberg, 1982).

Another example of cultural differences regarding pain is how Haitian Americans react to both familiar and unfamiliar symptoms. Any symptom that resembles an illness a relative died from, for instance, is a red flag for Haitian Americans to seek medical attention immediately. Conversely, they are likely to dismiss any sign of illness if there is no family history of that particular symptom. For example, Joseph, a Haitian American teacher from Port-au-Prince who migrated to New York, had no family history of diabetes; his diabetic condition remained undiagnosed until he fell into a coma and was hospitalized (Laguerre, 1981).

Stoicism may also have cultural roots. Both Navaho and Chinese American patients have been described as "stoic." Navahos and Chinese Americans may be reluctant to breach the barriers between their culture and Western medical practices. This reluctance may keep them from seeking medical assistance and may increase their psychological tolerance of pain. Their impassive demeanor may be learned; as they observe how others react, they adopt the culturally appropriate response to pain. Verbal expressions of pain may also be learned. If you were Navaho or Chinese, for example, you may give out a 50 or 60 decibel moan after pounding your thumb with a hammer, but a 90 decibel shriek may be a typical response if you're from a middle-class White background.

Social class may be another factor that influences a person's ideas about illness and wellness. People from poor neighborhoods may not have access to adequate health care through an HMO or good health insurance. As a result, they may use a higher threshold to define unbearable pain. For example, a person who must take a day off from work without pay, find a physician or clinic, and pay immediately for medical services may wait until a symptom becomes severe before seeking treatment.

Although cross-cultural research on the perception of pain may yield some intriguing findings, several caveats are warranted. First, even when differences among groups are found, as in the comparison between Jewish and Italian patients, there are differences within groups as well. Not all of the Italian patients in the study moaned, groaned, and wanted immediate medication—many did, but some did not. Second, many studies on the cultural and ethnic reactions to pain are based on findings from a small number of people who are not always carefully selected to be truly comparable on all dimensions except the one difference the researcher is studying. Third, researchers in this area have not attended to the effects of mixing cultures. For instance, are Italians who live in the Little Italy section of an urban area more likely to show a desire for early medication than Italians who live in more integrated areas?

The Chemical Senses

In the spring of 1985, a group of chemists practically turned American society upside down simply by shifting a few carbon, hydrogen, and oxygen atoms, or so it seemed when the Coca-Cola Company changed the formula for Coke. The uproar forced the company to bring back the original flavor that summer— even after spending millions of dollars advertising the virtues of the new Coke. The chemists at the Coca-Cola Company were dealing with one of the chemical senses—the gustatory (taste) sense. The other chemical sense, the olfactory sense, involves smell. Both taste and smell differ from other senses—seeing, hearing, and the skin senses, for example—because they react to *chemicals*, whereas the other senses react to *energy*.

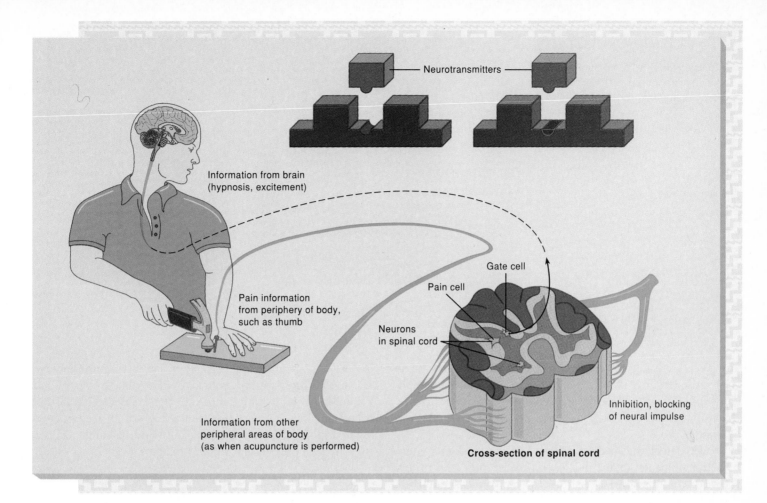

Neurotransmitters

Information from brain
(hypnosis, excitement)

Pain information
from periphery of body,
such as thumb

Neurons
in spinal cord

Information from other
peripheral areas of body
(as when acupuncture is performed)

Gate cell

Pain cell

Inhibition, blocking
of neural impulse

Cross-section of spinal cord

FIGURE 3.13

Gate-control theory of pain. In the case of hitting your thumb with a hammer, pain signals initially go through the spinal cord and then to the brain. Gate-control theory states that pain information can be blocked in the spinal cord. Pain pathways from the periphery of the body (thumb, foot, etc.) make a synaptic connection in the spinal cord and then ascend to the brain. Interneurons can inhibit transmission through these pathways, as shown in the drawing on the right. When a strong peripheral stimulus (as applied during acupuncture) comes into the spinal cord, this can turn on the interneuron and close the gate in the pain pathway. Also, when a signal comes down from the brain (during hypnosis or the excitement of athletic competition), it, too, can turn on the interneuron and close the gate. The gate is not a physical structure that actually opens and shuts; rather, the gate is the inhibition of neural impulses. Neurotransmitters (the tiny circles in the synapse between the pain cell and the gate cell) are involved in gate control, but much is yet to be known about their identity.

Taste

It's not the prettiest sight you've ever seen, but try this anyway. Take a drink of milk and allow it to coat your tongue. Then go to a mirror, stick out your tongue, and look carefully at its surface. You should be able to see rounded bumps above the surface of your tongue (Matlin, 1983). Those bumps, called **papillae,** *contain your taste buds, the receptors for taste.* About 10,000 of these taste buds are located on your tongue, around your mouth, and even in your throat.

Taste buds respond to four main qualities: sweet, bitter, salty, and sour. Though all areas of the tongue can detect each of the four tastes, different regions of the tongue are more sensitive to one taste than to another. The tip of the tongue is the most sensitive to sweet; the rear of the tongue is the most sensitive to bitter; just behind the area for sweet is the most sensitive area for salty; and just behind that is the most sensitive area for sour.

Smell

Smell is an important but mysterious sense. We take the time to see a sunset or a play, to hear a symphony or a rock concert, and to feel the tension leave our muscles during a massage.

FIGURE 3.14

Acupuncture. (a) A woman is being treated for pain by an acupuncturist. (b) Acupuncture points are carefully noted on this nineteenth-century Japanese papier-mâché figure. In their adaptation of the Chinese methodology, the Japanese identified 660 points.

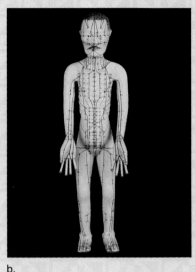

a.

b.

However, have you ever thought of taking the time to indulge your sense of smell (Matlin, 1988)? Probably not, but smell can kindle pleasure or trigger discomfort—when we inhale the aroma of a fresh flower or when we encounter a skunk, for example.

We detect the scent of a fresh flower or a skunk when airborne molecules of an odor reach tiny receptor cells in the roof of the nasal cavity (see figure 3.15). The **olfactory epithelium,** *located at the top of the nasal cavity, is the sheet of receptor cells for smell.* These receptor sites are covered with millions of minute, hairlike antennae that project through mucus in the nasal cavity and make contact with air on its way to the throat and lungs. Ordinarily only a small part of the air you inhale passes the smell receptors. That is why we sometimes have to sniff deeply to get the full odor of an interesting or alarming smell—the bouquet of a fine wine or the odor of escaping gas, for example. Doing so changes the normal flow of air so that more air, with its odorous molecules, contacts the receptors.

You just read about how taste can be classified into four main categories: sweet, sour, salty, and bitter. Are there agreed-upon main categories of odors too? Some researchers argue that there are seven primary odors—floral, peppermint, ethereal (as in the gas ether), musky, camphoraceous (such as mothballs), pungent, and putrid (Amoore, 1970). However, the consensus is that olfactory researchers have yet to demonstrate that different categories of smell have distinct chemical makeups and receptor sites on the olfactory epithelium.

How good are you at recognizing smells? Without practice, most people do a rather poor job of identifying odors; however, the human olfactory sense can be improved. Per-fumers, as perfume testers are called, can distinguish between 100 and 200 fragrances. If you have or have had a dog, though, you probably know that canines have a keener sense of smell than humans. One reason is that a dog's smell receptors are located along the main airflow route and its smell-receptor sites are 100 times larger than a human's.

The Kinesthetic and Vestibular Senses

You know the difference between walking and running and between lying down and sitting up, and you know when you are upside down on a loop-to-loop ride at an amusement park. How do you know these things? Your body has two kinds of senses that provide information to your brain about your movement and orientation in space: **kinesthetic senses** *provide information about movement, posture, and orientation,* and the **vestibular sense** *provides information about balance and movement.*

No specific organ contains the kinesthetic senses. Instead, these senses are located in the cells of our muscles, joints, and tendons. For example, you decide to strengthen your body. You begin a weight-lifting regimen and are at the point where you can bench press 150 pounds. You decide to really go for it and put the key in the Nautilus machine at 200 pounds. After several deep breaths, you thrust the 200 pounds upward; it quickly falls back to the bar holding the rest of the weights. Your body's ability to sense that it was not ready to press the 200 pounds was due to your kinesthetic senses.

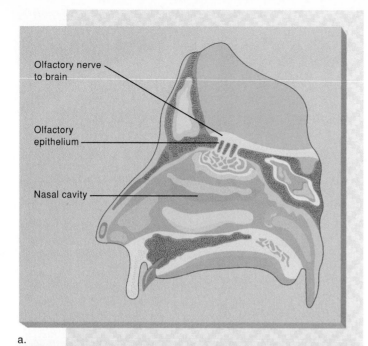

a.

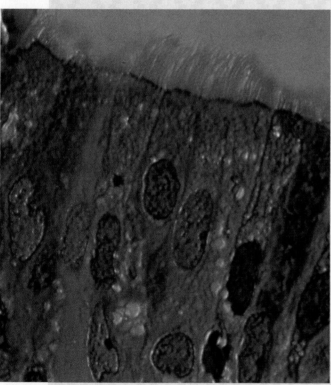

b.

FIGURE 3.15

The olfactory sense. (a) Airborne molecules of an odor reach tiny receptor cells in the roof of our nasal cavity. The receptor cells form a mucous-covered membrane called the olfactory epithelium. Then the olfactory nerve carries information about the odor to the brain for further processing. (b) Shown here is a microphotograph of the olfactory epithelium with the minute hairlike antennae at the bottom.

However, it doesn't take 200 pounds of weights to set off your kinesthetic senses. Move your hand forward and touch this page. Wiggle your toes. Smile. Frown.

The vestibular sense tells you whether your body is tilted, moving, slowing down, or speeding up. It works in concert with the kinesthetic senses to coordinate your proprioceptive feedback, which is the information about the position of your limbs and body parts in relation to other body parts. The **semicircular canals,** *located in the inner ear, contain sensory receptors that detect body motion, such as tilting the head or body* (see figure 3.16). These canals consist of three circular tubes that lie in three planes of the body—left-right, up-down, and front-back. The tubes provide feedback to the brain when the body or head tilts in one of these three directions.

Because the semicircular canals and the vestibular sense inform us about our equilibrium, this sense is sometimes called the *equilibratory sense.* The most accepted view of why we are able to maintain our equilibrium and orientation is that the brain is constantly receiving information about the body's motion and position from three sources: the inner ear, the eyes, and other sensors in various parts of the body. Information from these sources is fed into the brain, which compares

Reprinted with special permission of King Features Syndicate Inc.

b.

FIGURE 3.16

The semicircular canals and vestibular sense. (a) This is a photograph of the semicircular canals located in the ear. The semicircular canals play an important role in the vestibular sense. The three canals are roughly perpendicular to each other in three planes of space. Any angle of head rotation is registered by hair cells in one or more semicircular canals in both ears. (b) The semicircular canals provide feedback to this gymnast's brain as her body and head tilt in different directions.

it with stored information about motion and position. There are occasions when we might wish our equilibratory sense were not so sensitive. When motion sickness occurs, these various sources send contradictory messages. For example, passengers on a ship's deck can see the rail of the ship rising and falling as they watch the waves. The roll of the deck makes them feel like they are riding a roller coaster. The brain is not accustomed to all of this contradictory information. Over time, though, the brain recognizes that stored information is no longer relevant to the current discordant input. Two to three days usually is long enough to adjust to sensory conflict, but it can take longer.

REVIEW

The Auditory System, the Skin Senses, the Chemical Senses, and the Kinesthetic and Vestibular Senses

Sound waves vary in frequency, amplitude, and complexity; the perceptions are pitch, loudness, and timbre, respectively. The ear comprises the outer ear, the middle ear, and the inner ear. The basilar membrane, located inside the cochlea in the inner ear, is where vibrations are changed into nerve impulses. There are three main theories of hearing. Place theory emphasizes a particular place on the basilar membrane; frequency theory stresses the frequency of auditory nerve firing; and volley theory is a modification and expansion of frequency theory to handle high-frequency sounds. Frequency theory is better for explaining lower-frequency sounds, volley and place theories for higher-frequency sounds.

Skin contains three important senses: touch, temperature (warmth, cold), and pain. Pain has the important adaptive function of informing us when something is wrong on our body. No theory of pain is completely accepted. Gate-control theory has been given considerable weight.

The chemical senses—taste, smell—differ from other senses because they react to chemicals rather than energy. The kinesthetic senses provide information about movement, posture, and orientation; the vestibular sense provides information about balance and movement.

Perception

Earlier in this chapter, you learned that perception is the brain's process of organizing and interpreting sensory information to give it meaning. When perception goes to work, sensory receptors have received energy from stimuli in the external world and sensory organs have processed and transformed the information so it can be transmitted to the brain. Perception is a creation of the brain; it is based on input extracted from sensory organs, such as the eye, ear, and nose. However, perception goes beyond this input. The brain uses information previously extracted as a basis for making educated guesses, or interpretations, about the state of the outside world. Usually the interpretations are correct and useful. For example, on the basis of a change in color or texture, we can conclude that a dog is on the rug. On the basis of a continuous increase in size, we can conclude that a train is coming toward us. Sometimes, though, the interpretations or inferences are wrong; the result is an illusion—we see something that is not there. Our exploration of perceptual worlds evaluates the following questions: How do we perceive shape, depth, motion, and constancy? What are perceptual illusions and why do we see these illusions? Is perception innate or learned? What is extrasensory perception? Is it real?

Shape Perception

Think about the world you see and its shapes—buildings against the sky, boats on the horizon, letters on this page. We see these shapes because they are marked off from the rest of what we see by **contour,** *a location at which a sudden change of brightness occurs.* Think about the letters on this page again. As you look at the page, you see letters, which are shapes, in a field or background, the white page. The **figure-ground relationship** *is the principle by which we organize the perceptual field into stimuli that stand out (figure) and those that are leftover (ground).* Some figure-ground relationships, though, are highly ambiguous, and it is difficult to tell what is figure and what is ground. A well-known ambiguous figure-ground relationship is shown in figure 3.17. As you look at the figure, your perception is likely to shift between seeing two faces or a single goblet. Another example of figure-ground ambiguity is found in the work of artist M. C. Escher, which keeps us from favoring one figure over another seemingly because spatial location and depth cues are not provided (see figure 3.18).

One group of psychologists has been especially intrigued by how we perceive shapes in our world—the Gestalt psychologists. **Gestalt psychology** *is an approach which states that people naturally organize their perceptions according to certain patterns; Gestalt is a German word that means "configuration" or "form." One of Gestalt psychology's main principles is that perception of the whole is not equal to the sum of its parts.* For example, when you watch a movie, the motion you see in the film cannot be found in the film itself; if you examine the film, you see only separate

FIGURE 3.17

Reversible figure-ground pattern. Either a goblet or a pair of silhouetted faces in profile can be seen.

FIGURE 3.18

Sophisticated use of figure-ground relationship in Escher's woodcut Relativity *(1938).*
© 1988 M. C. Escher. c/o Corson Art—Baarn—Holland

frames per second. When you watch the film, you perceive a whole that is very different from the individual pictures that are its parts. Figure 3.19 also illustrates this fundamental principle of Gestalt psychology.

The figure-ground relationship just described is another Gestalt principle. Three other Gestalt principles are closure, proximity, and similarity. The principle of *closure* states that, when individuals see a disconnected or incomplete figure, they fill in the spaces and see it as a complete figure (see figure 3.20*a*). The principle of *proximity* states that, when individuals see objects close to each other, they tend to group them together (see figure 3.20*b*). The principle of *similarity* states that, the more similar objects are, the more likely we are to group them together (see figure 3.20*c*). By turning to figure 3.21, you can observe some of the basic principles of Gestalt psychology in a famous artist's work.

Depth Perception

The images of the world we see appear on our retinas in two-dimensional form, yet we see a three-dimensional world. **Depth perception** *is the ability to perceive objects three-dimensionally.* Look at the setting you are in. You don't see it as flat. You see some objects farther away, some closer. Some objects overlap. The scene you are looking at and the objects in it have depth. How do we see depth? We use binocular cues. **Binocular cues** *are depth cues that are based on both eyes working together.* **Monocular cues** *are depth cues based on each eye working independently.*

FIGURE 3.19

Example of the Gestalt principle that the whole does not equal the sum of the parts. In A Kindly Man of Fearful Aspect *by Kuniyoshi Ichiyusai, the configuration of the whole is clearly qualitatively different than the sum of its parts.*

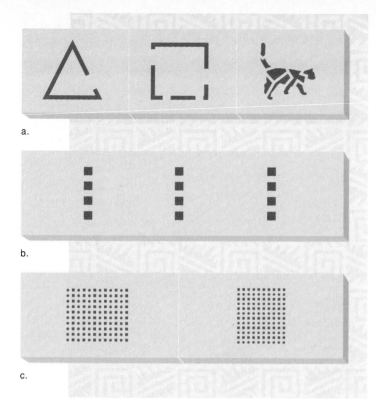

a.

b.

c.

FIGURE 3.20

Gestalt principles of closure, proximity, and similarity. (a) Closure: when we see disconnected or incomplete figures, we fill in the spaces and see them as complete figures. (b) Proximity: when we see objects that are near each other, they tend to be seen as a unit. You are likely to perceive the grouping as 3 columns of 4 squares, not 1 set of 12 squares. (c) Similarity: when we see objects that are similar to each other, they tend to be seen as a unit. In this display, you are likely to see vertical columns of circles and squares in the left box but horizontal rows of circles and squares in the right box.

Located several inches apart above your nose, your two eyes see the world from slightly different locations. **Retinal or binocular disparity** *is the perception in which an individual sees a single scene, even though the images on the eyes are slightly different.* The brain blends the two sets of overlapping information it receives from the retinas into a single image that gives the proper impression of depth and distance. Retinal disparity is one binocular cue that helps us see depth. **Convergence** *is a binocular cue for depth perception in which the eyes turn more inward as an object gets closer. When the eyes converge or diverge, information is sent to the brain, which interprets the information about the inward (object is closer) or outward (object is farther away) eye movement.* To experience convergence, hold your finger at arm's length and then slowly move it to a point between your eyes. As you move your finger closer, you have to turn your eyes inward to follow it.

FIGURE 3.21

Gestalt principles of closure, proximity, and similarity in Picasso's The Nude Woman, *1910.* Look at the painting and think about some of the Gestalt principles of perception that are incorporated. The nude is an incomplete figure. You have to fill in the spaces to make it a complete figure (principle of closure). Both the principles of proximity and similarity cause you to see the two objects toward the bottom of the painting as feet.
The National Gallery of Art

FIGURE 3.22

An artist's use of the monocular cue of linear perspective. Famous landscape artist J. M. W. Turner used linear perspective to give the perception of depth to his painting *Rain, Steam, and Speed*.

People with vision in only one eye do not have binocular cues for depth perception available to them, but they still see a world of depth. They can still see depth because of monocular cues that can be perceived by one eye only. Following are four monocular cues:

1. Linear perspective. The farther an object is from the viewer, the less space it takes up in the visual field. As an object recedes in the distance, parallel lines in the object converge.
2. Texture gradient. Texture becomes denser the farther away it is from the viewer.
3. Relative size. Objects farther away create a smaller retinal image than those nearby.
4. Interposition. An object that partially conceals or overlaps another object is perceived as closer.

Depth perception is especially intriguing to artists. Their challenge is to depict the three-dimensional world on a two-dimensional canvas. As shown in figure 3.22, artists often use monocular cues to give the feeling of depth to their paintings. Indeed, monocular cues have become so widely used by artists that they have also been call *pictorial cues*.

Perceptual Constancy

Retinal images are constantly changing as we experience our world. Even though the stimuli that fall on the retinas of our eyes change as we move closer to or farther away from objects, or as we look at objects from different orientations and in light or dark settings, we perceive objects as unchanging. We experience three types of perceptual constancies: size constancy, shape constancy, and brightness constancy. **Size con-**

FIGURE 3.23

Size constancy. Even though our retinal image of the hot air balloons changes, we still perceive the different balloons as being approximately the same size. This illustrates the principle of size constancy.

stancy *is the recognition that an object is the same size even though the retinal image of the object changes* (see figure 3.23). **Shape constancy** *is the recognition that an object remains the same even though its orientation to us changes.* Look around the room in which you are reading this book. You probably see objects of various shapes—chairs and tables, for example. If you walk around the room, you will see these objects from different sides and angles. Even though the retinal image of the object changes as you walk, you still perceive the objects as being the same shape (see figure 3.24). **Brightness constancy** *is the recognition that an object retains the same degree of brightness even though different amounts of light fall on it.* For example, regardless of whether you are reading this book indoors or outdoors, the white pages and the black print do not look any different to you in terms of their whiteness or blackness.

FIGURE 3.24

Shape constancy. The various projected images from an opening door are quite different, yet a rectangular door is perceived.

How are we able to resolve the discrepancy between a retinal image of an object and its actual size, shape, and brightness? Experience is important. For example, no matter how far away you are from your car, you know how large it is. Not only is familiarity important in size constancy, but so are binocular and monocular distance cues. Even if we have never previously seen an object, these cues provide us with information about an object's size. Many visual illusions are influenced by our perception of size constancy.

Illusions

A **visual illusion** *occurs when two objects produce exactly the same retinal image but are perceived as different images*. Illusions are incorrect, but they are not abnormal. They can provide insight into how our perceptual processes work. More than 200 types of illusions have been discovered; we will study five.

One of the most famous is the Müller-Lyer illusion, shown in figure 3.25. The two lines are exactly the same length, although *b* looks longer than *a*. Another illusion is the horizontal-vertical illusion (see figure 3.26), in which the vertical line looks longer than the horizontal line, even though the two are equal. The Ponzo illusion is another line illusion in which the top line looks much longer than the bottom line (see figure 3.27).

Why do these line illusions trick us? One reason is that we mistakenly use certain cues for maintaining size constancy. For example, in the Ponzo illusion, we see the upper line as being farther away (remember that objects higher in a picture are perceived as being farther away). The Müller-Lyer illusion, though, is not as easily explained. We may make our judgments about the lines by comparing incorrect parts of the figures. For example, when people were shown the Müller-Lyer illusion with the wings painted a different color than the horizontal lines, the illusion was greatly reduced (Coren & Girus, 1972). Shortly we also will discuss how cultural experiences influence an individual's perception of the Müller-Lyer illusion.

Another well-known illusion is the moon illusion (see figure 3.28). The moon is 2,000 miles in diameter and 289,000 miles away. Since both the moon's size and its distance from us are beyond our own experience, we have difficulty judging how far away it really is. When the moon is high in the sky, directly above us, little information is present to help us judge its distance—no texture gradients or stereoscopic cues exist, for example. However, when the moon is on the horizon, we can judge its distance in relation to familiar objects—trees and buildings, for example—which makes it appear farther away. The result is that we estimate the size of the moon as much larger when it is on the horizon than when it is overhead (Hershenson, 1989).

The devil's tuning fork is another fascinating illusion. Look at figure 3.29 for about 30 seconds, then close the book. Now try to draw the tuning fork. You undoubtedly found this a difficult, if not impossible, task. Why? Since the figure's depth cues are ambiguous, you had problems interpreting it correctly.

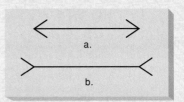

FIGURE 3.25

Müller-Lyer illusion. The two lines are exactly the same length, although (b) looks longer than (a).

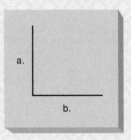

FIGURE 3.26

The horizontal-vertical illusion. The vertical line looks longer than the horizontal line, but they are the same length.

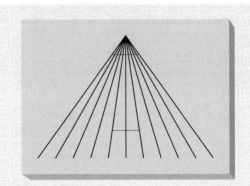

FIGURE 3.27

Ponzo illusion. The top line looks much longer than the bottom line, but they are equal in length.

Is Perception Innate or Learned?

One long-standing question in psychology is whether or not perception is innate (inborn, unlearned) or learned. Researchers have tried to unravel this nature-nurture question on depth perception in a number of ways: experiments with infants, studies of individuals who recover from blindness, and cross-cultural studies about how people perceive their world.

a. b.

FIGURE 3.28

The moon illusion. The moon illusion is that when the moon is on the horizon (a), it looks much larger than when it is high in the sky, directly above us (b). Why does the moon look so much larger on the horizon?

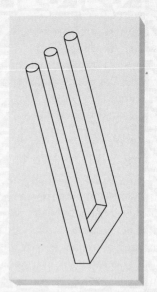

FIGURE 3.29

Devil's tuning fork.

The Visual Cliff

An experiment by Eleanor Gibson and Richard Walk (1960) indicates that, by at least 6 months of age, infants have an understanding of depth. Gibson and Walk constructed a miniature cliff with a shallow side and a drop-off that was covered by firm glass (see figure 3.30). This structure is known as a *visual cliff.* Infants old enough to crawl (6 months and older) were placed on the shallow side. The infants stayed in place rather than venture out onto the glass-covered drop-off, indicating that they perceived depth. However, infants at 6 months are old enough to have encountered many situations where they could have *learned* to perceive depth, so the visual cliff experiment failed to provide convincing evidence that depth perception is innate. Whether or not infants younger than 6 months perceive depth is controversial.

Other studies have shown that, during the first month of life, human infants turn away to avoid objects that move directly toward them but do not turn away when objects move toward them at angles that would not collide with them (Ball & Tronick, 1971). Also, animals with little visual experience—including day-old goats and just-hatched chicks—respond just as 6-month-old infants do; they remain on the visual cliff's shallow side and do not venture out onto the glass-covered drop-off. These studies suggest that some of the ability to perceive depth is innate.

Recovery from Blindness

In further attempts to determine whether or not depth perception is innate, psychologists have also studied people who were born blind, or became blind shortly after birth, and

FIGURE 3.30

Visual cliff. The visual cliff was developed by Eleanor Gibson and Richard Walk (1960). The infant shown here hesitates as he moves onto the glass-covered drop-off, the deep side of the visual cliff. In the study, even when coaxed by their mothers, the infants were still reluctant to venture out onto the deep drop-off, indicating they could perceive depth.

whose sight later was restored by medical procedures. If the ability to interpret sensory information is innate, such people should be able to see their world clearly after they recover from the operation. Consider S. B., blind since birth, who had a successful corneal transplant at the age of 52 (Gregory, 1978). Soon after S. B.'s bandages were removed, he was able to recognize common objects, identify the letters of the alphabet, and tell time from a clock. However, S. B. had some perceptual deficiencies. Although his eyes functioned effectively, S. B. had difficulty perceiving objects he had not previously touched (see figure 3.31).

The findings for formerly blind persons also do not answer the question of whether perception is innate or learned. Some people recognize objects soon after their bandages are removed; others require weeks of training before they recognize such simple shapes as a triangle. Neural connections, such as those between the eyes and the brain, can deteriorate from disuse, so a person whose sight has been restored after a lifetime of blindness may have an impaired ability to perceive visual information. Further, previously blind adults, unlike infants, have already experienced the world through their nonvisual senses, such as touch and hearing, and those perceptual systems may continue to contribute to their perception after they regain their vision.

Culture and Perception

Whereas our biological inheritance equips us with some elegant perceptual capabilities, our experiences also contribute to how we perceive the world. Some cross-cultural psychologists have proposed that the demands of various cultures lead to a greater emphasis on certain senses (Wober, 1966). For example, hunters who have to stalk small game animals may develop their kinesthetic senses more than office workers in highly industrialized nations.

Cross-cultural psychologists have been especially interested in how people from different cultures perceive visual illusions (Segall & others, 1990). The **carpentered-world hypothesis** *states that people who live in cultures in which straight lines, right angles, and rectangles predominate (rooms and buildings are usually rectangular, for example, and many objects have right-angled corners, such as city streets) learn to interpret nonrectangular figures as rectangular, to perceive the figures in perspective, and to interpret them as two-dimensional representations of three-dimensional objects.* This tendency enhances the Müller-Lyer illusion (see figure 3.25) and makes people from carpentered environments more susceptible to it than people from noncarpentered environments. For example, the Zulu in isolated regions of southeastern Africa live in a world of open spaces and curves. Their huts are round with round doors, and they even plow their fields in curved, rather than straight, furrows. According to the carpentered-world hypothesis, the

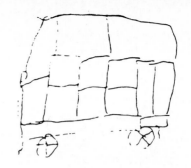

FIGURE 3.31

S. B.'s drawings of a bus after his recovery from blindness. S. B. drew the bus at the top 48 days after a corneal transplant restored his vision, and he drew the bus at the bottom a year after the operation. Both drawings reflect more detail for the parts of the bus S. B. used or touched while he was blind than the parts he did not use or touch. In the bottom drawing, notice the absence of the front of the bus, which S. B. never touched.

Zulu would not be very susceptible to the Müller-Lyer illusion. Cross-cultural psychologists have found this to be the case (Segall, Campbell, & Herskovits, 1963).

Another example in which culture shapes perception is found in the pygmies who live in the dense rain forests of the African Congo. Because of the thick vegetation, the pygmies rarely see objects at long distances. Anthropologist Colin Turnbull (1961) observed that, when the pygmies traveled to the African plains and saw buffalo on the horizon, they thought the animals were tiny insects and not huge buffalo. The pygmies' lack of experience with distant objects probably accounts for their inability to perceive size constancy. More information about cultural influences on perception is presented in Sociocultural Worlds 3.2, where you will read about the role of experience with three-dimensional objects.

The Zulu live in isolated regions of southeastern Africa in a world of open spaces and curves. Their huts are round with round doors, and they even plow their fields in curved, rather than straight, furrows. Supporting the carpentered-world hypothesis, the Zulu are not very susceptible to the Müller-Lyer illusion.

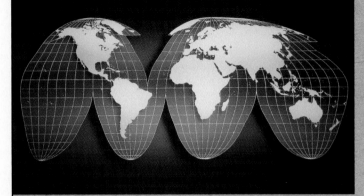

FIGURE 3.A

Drawing used to assess the perception of pictorial cues for depth in different cultures.

Adapted from "Pictorial Perception and Culture" by Jean B. Dergowski.
Copyright © by Scientific American, Inc. All rights reserved.

Perceiving Three-Dimensionality in Two-Dimensional Drawings in Different Cultures

Y ou probably had difficulty drawing the Devil's tuning fork in figure 3.29. The world you live in bombards you with visual representations of three-dimensional objects in two-dimensional form—such as billboards, travel posters, and artwork in magazines. Your eyes are constantly taking in information in a two-dimensional format, which your brain then perceives as three-dimensional, so, even though the tuning fork had ambiguous depth cues, your brain interpreted it as a three-dimensional object. Africans who have no formal education easily reproduce the Devil's tuning fork. Why? Because they don't interpret the form as three-dimensional. We see a "Devil's tuning fork"; they simply see a pattern of flat lines they can easily reproduce.

Researchers have also investigated people from isolated tribes to determine if they have difficulty perceiving depth in two-dimensional drawings or photographs (Deregowski, 1980; Hudson, 1960). For example, look at figure 3.A, a drawing used to test the ability to respond to pictorial depth cues. A person

responding to pictorial depth would say that the hunter is trying to spear the antelope (which would appear nearer to the hunter than to the elephant). Conversely, a person responding only to the two-dimensional cues would say that the hunter is trying to spear the elephant, which is actually closer to the spear's tip in the picture. This interpretation would indicate that the observer had not responded to the depth cues (such as the fact that the antelope partially conceals the hill, meaning it is closer to the hunter) that place the elephant at a greater distance from the hunter.

In Hudson's examination of cultures, although education and intellectual endowment were related to depth perception in Western cultures, this was not the case with the African Bantu tribe. Hudson hypothesized that it was exposure to pictures at a preschool age that influenced performance, since the Bantu live in environments that do not include many pictorial materials. Perception, as with most complex human abilities, is influenced by several factors in both Western and non-Western cultures. No matter how smart you are or how much you have achieved in school spelling and arithmetic, if you have not seen many pictures, it is unlikely that you would immediately be able to perceive depth cues.

It seems that both nature and nurture are responsible for the way we perceive the world. One view of how the two influences interact to shape perception is that all people, regardless of culture, have the same perceptual processes and the same potential for perceptual development, but cultural factors determine what is learned and at what age (Kagitcibasi & Berry, 1989; Irvine & Berry, 1988). So far we have discussed perception in terms of shape, depth, constancy, illusion, and whether or not perception is innate or learned. However, we will also briefly discuss another, curious realm of perceptual phenomena—extrasensory perception.

Extrasensory Perception

Our eyes, ears, mouth, nose, and skin provide us with sensory information about the external world. Our perceptions are based on our interpretation of this sensory information. Some people, though, claim they can perceive the world through something other than normal sensory pathways. Literally, **extrasensory perception (ESP)** *is perception that occurs outside of the use of known sensory process.* The majority of psychologists do not believe in ESP; however, a small number of psychologists do investigate it (Persinger & Krippner, in press).

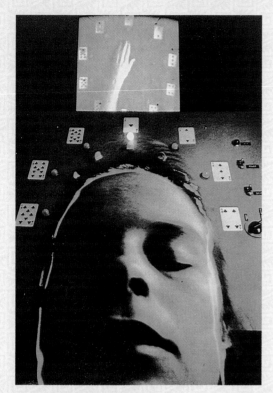

FIGURE 3.32

An experimental situation involving an attempt to demonstrate telepathy. At the top (blue insert), a person in one room tries to "send" a message through thought to a person (the subject) in another room. The sender selects a card and then attempts to relay the information mentally to the subject. The subject then selects a card, and it is compared to the one previously chosen by the sender to see if the cards match. If the mind-to-mind communication occurs beyond chance, then it would be argued that telepathy has taken place.

Extrasensory experiences fall into three main categories. The first is **telepathy,** *which involves the transfer of thought from one person to another.* For example, this skill is supposedly possessed by people who can "read" another person's mind. If two people are playing cards and one person can tell what cards the other person picks up, telepathy is taking place (see figure 3.32). **Precognition** *involves "knowing" events before they happen.* For example, a fortune teller might claim to see into the future and tell you what will happen to you in the coming year. **Clairvoyance** *involves the ability to perceive remote events that are not in sight.* For example, a person at a movie theater "sees" a burglar breaking into his house at that moment. **Psychokinesis,** *closely associated with ESP, is the mind-over-matter phenomenon of being able to move objects without touching them, such as mentally getting a chair to rise off the floor or shattering a glass merely by concentrating on doing so.*

One of the most famous claims of ESP involved Uri Geller, a psychic who supposedly performed mind-boggling feats. Observers saw Geller correctly predict the number on a die rolled in a closed box eight out of eight times, reproduce drawings that were hidden in sealed envelopes, bend forks without touching them, and start broken watches. Although he had worked as a magician, Geller claimed his supernatural powers were created by energy sent from another universe. Careful investigation of Geller's feats revealed they were nothing more than a magician's tricks. For example, in the case of the die, Geller was allowed to shake the box and open it himself, giving him an opportunity to manipulate the die (Randi, 1980).

Through their astonishing stage performances, many psychics are very convincing. They seemingly are able to levitate tables, communicate with spirits, and read an audience member's mind. Many psychics, such as Uri Geller, are also magicians, who have the ability to perform sleight-of-hand maneuvers and dramatic manipulations that go unnoticed by most human eyes. One magician's personal goal, though, is to expose the hoaxes of such psychics. James Randi (1980) has investigated a number of psychics' claims and publicized their failures (see figure 3.33).

Not only have magicians, such as Randi, investigated some psychics' claims, but scientists have also examined ESP in experimental contexts. Some ESP enthusiasts believe that the phenomenon is more likely to occur when a subject is totally relaxed and deprived of sensory input. In this kind of ESP experiment, the subject lies down, and half a Ping-Pong ball is affixed over each eye with cotton and tape. An experimenter watches through a one-way mirror from an adjacent room, listening to and recording the subject's statements. At an agreed-upon time, someone from another location concentrates on the message to be sent mind-to-mind.

Carl Sargent (1987) has used this procedure in a number of telepathy experiments and reported a great deal of success. In one experiment, Sargent had a "sender" mentally transmit an image of one of four pictures selected from 1 of 27 randomly selected sets of four pictures. Immediately afterward, the experimenter and the subject examined a duplicate set of four pictures and together judged and ranked their degree of correspondence with the subject's recorded impression. Experimental psychologist Susan Blackmore (1987) was skeptical about Sargent's success in ESP experiments, so she visited his laboratory at Cambridge University in England and observed a number of his telepathy sessions. With the subject shown four pictures, the success rate expected by chance was 25 percent (one of four pictures). In the experimental sessions Blackmore observed, the subjects' hit rate was 50 percent, far exceeding chance.

Sargent supposedly invokes a number of elaborate procedures to protect randomization, experimenter bias, unbiased selection by the subject, and so on. Blackmore was still skeptical, finding some disturbing flaws in the way Sargent's experiments were conducted. In some sessions, he randomized the pictures

FIGURE 3.33

Magician James Randi. Randi has a standing offer of $10,000 to anyone whose psychic claims can withstand his analysis. No one has yet claimed Randi's $10,000 prize.

himself, putting himself where he could manipulate the order of the pictures. In other sessions, he came in while the subject was judging the pictures and "pushed" the subject toward the picture that had been "transmitted by the sender."

No one has been able to replicate the high hit rates in Sargent's experiments. Proponents of ESP, such as Sargent, claim they have demonstrated the existence of ESP, but critics, such as Blackmore, demand to see or experience the same phenomena themselves. Replication is one of the hallmarks of scientific investigation, yet replication has been a major thorn in the side of ESP researchers. ESP phenomena have not been reproducible when rigorous experimental standards have been applied (Alcock, 1989; Hines, 1988; Hines & Dennison, 1989).

In the next chapter, we will explore many other aspects of our awareness, both of the external world and the internal world. Sleep, dreams, altered states of consciousness, and the influence of drugs on mental processes and behavior await you in chapter 4.

REVIEW

Perception

Shape is perceived because it is marked off by contour. An important aspect is figure-ground relationship. Gestalt psychologists have developed a number of principles of perceptual organization, a fundamental one being that the whole is not equal to the sum of its parts. Depth perception is our ability to perceive objects as three-dimensional. To see a world of depth, we use binocular cues, such as retinal disparity and convergence, and monocular cues (also called pictorial cues), such as linear perspective, texture gradient, relative size, and interposition. Perceptual constancy includes size, shape, and brightness. Experience with objects and with distance cues helps us see objects as unchanging.

Illusions occur when two objects produce exactly the same retinal image but are perceived as different images. Among the more than 200 visual illusions are the Müller-Lyer illusion and the moon illusion. Perceptual constancies and cultural experiences are among the factors responsible for illusions.

Is perception innate or learned? Experiments using the visual cliff with young infants and animals indicate that some of the ability to perceive depth is innate. Investigations of formerly blind adults are inconclusive with regard to whether perception is innate or learned. Our experiences contribute to how we perceive the world. People in different cultures do not always perceive the world in the same way. The carpentered-world hypothesis and varying abilities to respond to depth cues in two-dimensional drawings across cultures reveal how experiences influence perception.

Extrasensory perception is perception that does not occur through normal sensory channels. Three main forms are telepathy, precognition, and clairvoyance. Psychokinesis is a closely related phenomenon. The claims of ESP enthusiasts have not held up to scientific scrutiny.

Summary

I. What Are Sensation and Perception?
Sensation is the process of detection and encoding stimulus energy in the environment. Perception is the process of organizing and interpreting the information sensed to give it meaning.

II. Detecting the Sensory World
Absolute threshold is the minimum amount of stimulus an individual can detect.

Psychologists have determined that the absolute threshold is the stimulus value detected 50 percent of the time. Noise refers to the presence of irrelevant and competing stimuli; motivation also influences our ability to detect the presence of stimuli. Subliminal perception is the perception of stimuli below the threshold of awareness; this is a controversial topic. The difference

threshold is the smallest amount of stimulation required to discriminate one stimulus from another. When this is done 50 percent of the time, it is called a just noticeable difference. Weber's law states that, regardless of their magnitude, two stimuli must differ by a constant proportion to be detected. Sensory adaptation is a weakened response to stimulus energy.

III. The Visual Stimulus and the Eye

Light is a form of electromagnetic energy that can be described in terms of wavelengths. The receptors in the human eye are sensitive to wavelengths between 400 and 700 nm. The key external parts of the eye are the sclera, iris, pupil, and cornea. The lens focuses light rays on the retina, the light-sensitive mechanism in the eye. Chemicals in the retina break down chromatic light into neural impulses to the brain. Because of crossovers of nerve fibers, what we see in the left visual field is registered in the right side of the brain and vice versa. Visual information reaches the occipital lobe of the brain, where it is stored and further integrated. Hubel and Wiesel discovered that some neurons in the visual cortex detect different features of our visual world, such as line angle and size.

IV. Color Vision

Objects appear colored because they reflect only certain wavelengths of light between 400 and 700 nm. Three important properties of colors are hue, saturation, and brightness. When mixing color, we get different results depending on whether we mix light or pigments: light involves an additive mixture, pigments a subtractive mixture. Scientists have found support for two theories of color vision. The Young-Helmholtz theory states that the retina's cones are sensitive to one of three colors—red, blue, or green. The Young-Helmholtz theory explains color blindness but not afterimages. The opponent-process theory can explain afterimages. It states that information is coded into pairs of opposite colors—blue-yellow and red-green.

V. The Auditory System

Sound waves, vibration changes in the air, vary in frequency, amplitude, and complexity; the perception of these three dimensions of sound are pitch, loudness, and timbre, respectively. The ear is made up of the outer ear, middle ear, and inner ear. The basilar membrane, located inside the cochlea in the inner ear, is where vibrations are changed into neural impulses. Three theories of hearing explain auditory processing in the cochlea: place theory, frequency theory, and volley theory.

VI. The Skin Senses

The skin contains three important senses: touch, temperature (warmth, cold), and pain. Pain has the important adaptive function of informing us when something is wrong in our body. No theory of pain is completely accepted; gate-control theory has been given considerable attention.

VII. The Chemical, Kinesthetic, and Vestibular Senses

The chemical senses are taste and smell. These senses differ from other senses because they react to chemicals rather than energy. The kinesthetic senses provide information about movement, posture, and orientation. The vestibular sense provides information about balance and movement.

VIII. Shape Perception, Depth Perception, and Perceptual Constancy

One important reason we see a world of shapes is because of contour. An important aspect of shape perception is figure-ground relationship. Gestalt psychologists developed a number of principles of perceptual organization, a fundamental one being that the whole is not equal to the sum of its parts. Depth perception is our ability to perceive objects three-dimensionally. To see a world of depth, we use binocular cues, such as retinal disparity and convergence, and monocular cues (pictorial cues), such as linear perspective, texture gradient, relative size, and interposition. Perceptual constancy involves size constancy, shape constancy, and brightness constancy. Experience with objects and distance cues helps us see objects as unchanging.

IX. Illusions

A visual illusion occurs when two objects produce exactly the same retinal image but are perceived as different images. Among the more than 200 visual illusions are the M¥üller-Lyer illusion and the moon illusion. Perceptual constancies and cultural experiences are among the factors thought to be responsible for illusions.

X. Is Perception Innate or Learned?

Experiments using the visual cliff with young infants and animals indicate that some of the ability to perceive depth is innate. Studies of formerly blind adults are inconclusive with regard to whether perception is innate or learned. Our experiences contribute to how we perceive the world. People in different cultures do not always perceive the world in the same way. The carpentered-world hypothesis and varying abilities to respond to depth cues in two-dimensional drawings across cultures reveal how experiences influence perception.

XI. Extrasensory Perception

Extrasensory perception is perception that does not occur through normal sensory channels. Three main forms are telepathy, precognition, and clairvoyance. Psychokinesis is a closely related phenomenon. The claims of ESP enthusiasts have not held up to scientific scrutiny.

Key Terms

Suggested Readings

Frisby, J. P. (1980). *Seeing: Illusion, brain, and mind*. New York: Oxford University Press. This fascinating book on illusions not only presents many different illusions but attempts to show how computer scientists are trying to develop simulations of the visual process.

Hines, T. (1988). *Pseudoscience and the paranormal*. Buffalo, NY: Prometheus. An excellent examination of ESP, this book is especially good at teaching us how to critically evaluate ESP and other types of paranormal phenomena. It includes chapters on such topics as astrology, UFOs, faith healing, and psychics.

Keller, H. (1970). *Story of my life*. New York: Airmont. This fascinating story of Helen Keller's life as a blind person provides insight into blind people's perception of the world and how they use other senses.

Matlin, M. W. (1988). *Perception*. Needham Heights, MA: Allyn & Bacon. For a more detailed look at some of this chapter's topics, spend some time with this textbook on perception. Individual chapters include color, distance, motion, time, and constancy and illusion.

Segall, M. H. (1979). *Cross-cultural psychology: Human behavior in global perspective*. Monterey, CA: Wadsworth. Segall's research has made important contributions to our understanding of cultural influences on perception. An entire chapter is devoted to how culture affects our perception of visual illusions.

WHAT IS CONSCIOUSNESS?

CHAPTER 4

It was August 1985, and Colin Kemp, a 33-year-old salesman in Caterham, England, went to sleep as usual. About 2 hours later, he was confronted by two Japanese soldiers in his bedroom. They started to chase him. One soldier had a knife; the other a gun. Kemp ran away from them as fast as he could, but he wasn't fast enough. Kemp wrestled with the knife-wielding soldier. The other soldier aimed his gun at Kemp's head. Kemp tripped him, gripped his neck, and began choking him, but he slipped away. He turned, aimed the gun at Kemp, and fired. Kemp awoke in a state of panic, sweat pouring down his head. In a frenzy of terror, he turned to his wife, who was lying next to him in bed. She was dead. Kemp had strangled her, not a Japanese soldier.

A trial was held 9 months later. Kemp said he was asleep when he killed his wife, pleading not guilty to the murder charge because he intended to kill a Japanese soldier, not his wife. Psychiatrists testified on Kemp's behalf, instructing the jury that Kemp was having a night terror at the time he killed his wife. A **night terror** *is characterized by sudden arousal from sleep and intense fear, usually accompanied by a number of physiological reactions, such as rapid heart rate and breathing, loud screams, heavy perspiration, and physical movement.* In most instances, individuals have little or no memory of what happens during a night terror.

Kemp experienced night terrors on two occasions prior to the fatal event. Both times he was being chased during his sleep. In one of the night terrors, he punched at his wife. She awakened and asked what was happening. The second time, he kicked her in the back. Strangling someone to death is a much more elaborate and sustained activity than kicking an individual in the back. Is it possible that an action like Kemp's—strangling someone to death—could actually take place during sleep? The jury apparently thought so, because they acquitted Kemp. His act was viewed as an *automatic* one. That is, although Kemp was capable of the action, the jury concluded he was not *conscious* of what he was doing (Restak, 1988).

Most of us take for granted this nightly sojourn into the realm of sleep; however, Kemp's experiences make us wonder about the nature of sleep and states of consciousness. What is consciousness? What are sleep and dreams really like? In this chapter, we'll explore those questions, as well as the fascinating subjects of hypnosis and how psychoactive drugs alter states of consciousness.

What Is Consciousness?

Consciousness *is awareness, of both external and internal stimuli or events.* External events include what you attend to as you go through your day—the comment your best friend makes about your new hair style, the car in front of you that swerves to miss a dog, the music you are listening to on your cassette player, for example. Internal events include your awareness of your sensations—your headache has returned, you're breathing too fast, your stomach's rumbling—as well as your thoughts and feelings—you're having trouble in biology this semester, you're anxious about the exam next week, you're happy Marsha is going with you to the game tonight.

The contents of our awareness may change from one moment to the next, since information can move rapidly in and out of consciousness. Many years ago, William James (1890) described the mind as a **stream of consciousness**—*a continuous flow of changing sensations, images, thoughts, and feelings.* Your mind races from one topic to the next—from thinking about the person who is approaching you, to how well you feel, to what you are going to do tomorrow, to where you are going for lunch.

Whereas William James was interested in charting the shifting nature of our stream of consciousness, Sigmund Freud (1900/1953) believed that most of our thoughts are unconscious. **Unconscious thought** *is Freud's concept of a reservoir of unacceptable wishes, feelings, and thoughts that are beyond conscious awareness.* Unconscious thought in the Freudian sense has nothing to do with being unconscious after being knocked out by a blow on the head in a boxing match, being anesthetized, or falling into a coma.

According to Freud, unconscious thoughts are too laden with sexual and aggressive meaning for consciousness to admit them. For example, a young man who is nervous around women breaks into a cold sweat as a woman approaches him. He is unconscious that his fear of women springs from the cold, punitive way his mother treated him when he was a child. Freud believed that one of psychotherapy's main goals is to bring unconscious thoughts into conscious awareness so they can be addressed and dealt with.

Freud accurately recognized the complexity of consciousness. It is not simply a matter of being aware or unaware. Consciousness comes in different forms and levels. Sometimes consciousness is highly focused and alert; at other times it is more passive (Baars, 1989). Even sleep, once thought to be completely passive and unconscious, is now known to have active and at least minimally conscious properties.

Controlled processes *represent the most alert state of consciousness in which individuals actively focus their effort toward a goal.* Controlled processes require focused attention and interfere with other ongoing activities. Consider Anne, who is learning how to use her new personal computer. She is completely absorbed in reading the tutorial manual that accompanies the computer—she doesn't hear her roommate humming to herself or the song on the radio. This state of focused awareness is what is meant by controlled processes.

Once Anne learns how to use the software, maneuvers on the computer keyboard become almost automatic; that is, she doesn't have to concentrate so hard on how to perform each of the steps required to get the computer to do something. Two weeks ago she had to stop and concentrate on which keys to press to move a paragraph from one page to another. Now her fingers fly across the computer keyboard when she needs to move a block of material. This kind of consciousness involves automatic processes. **Automatic processes** *are a form of consciousness that requires minimal attention and does not interfere with other ongoing activities*. Automatic processes require less conscious effort than controlled processes. Remember that a jury acquitted Colin Kemp because they reasoned that he acted automatically rather than consciously. When we are awake, our automatic behaviors should be thought of as lower in awareness than controlled processes, rather than not conscious at all. Since Anne pushed the right keys at the right time on her computer keyboard, she apparently was aware of what she was doing at a certain level.

Daydreaming *is another form of consciousness that involves a low level of conscious effort*. Daydreaming lies somewhere between active consciousness and dreaming while we are asleep. It is a little like dreaming when we are awake. Daydreams usually start spontaneously when what we are doing requires less than our full attention. Mind wandering is probably the most obvious type of daydreaming. We regularly take brief side trips into our own private kingdoms of imagery and memory even as we read, listen, or work. When we daydream, we drift off into a world of fantasy. We imagine ourselves on dates, at parties, on television, at faraway places, at another time in our lives. Sometimes our daydreams are about ordinary, everyday events, such as paying the rent, getting our hair done, or dealing with someone at work. This semiautomatic thought flow can be useful. As you daydream while you shave, iron a pair of pants, or walk to the store, you may be making plans or solving a problem. Daydreams can remind us of important things ahead. Daydreaming keeps our minds active while helping us to cope, to create, and to fantasize (Klinger, 1987).

When we sleep and dream, our level of awareness is lower than when we daydream, but remember that we no longer think of being asleep as the complete absence of consciousness. Sleep and dreams, though, are at very low levels of consciousness. How is sleep different from being in a coma? Sleep differs from being in a coma in that it is periodic, natural, and reversible.

The states of consciousness we have described so far are normal, everyday occurrences in our lives. An **altered state of consciousness** *occurs when a person is in a mental state that noticeably differs from normal awareness. Drugs, meditation, traumas, fatigue, hypnosis, and sensory deprivation produce altered states of consciousness*. Whether a state of consciousness is described as normal or altered depends on how the word *normal* is defined.

"MY PROBLEM HAS ALWAYS BEEN AN OVERABUNDANCE OF ALPHA WAVES"

© 1990 by Sidney Harris.

Someone who drinks a caffeinated soda to increase alertness, for instance, is considered to be in a normal state of consciousness. However, someone who takes a drug that induces hallucinations, such as LSD, is considered to be in an altered state of consciousness. In Sociocultural Worlds 4.1, we will discuss the role that altered states of consciousness played in the origin of some of the world's great religions.

As you can see, our states of consciousness are many, varied, and complex. A summary of some of the main forms of consciousness and their level of awareness-unawareness is presented in figure 4.1 on page 106. Now we will turn our attention to the fascinating world of sleep and dreams.

Sleep and Dreams

Each night something lures us from work, from play, and from our loved ones into a solitary state. It is sleep, which claims about one-third of the time in our lives, more than any other pursuit. This alluring realm of mental escapades we enter each night has intrigued philosophers and scientists for centuries. Those who investigated sleep were primarily interested in its role as a springboard for dreams. We no longer regard sleep as the complete absence of consciousness. Now we know that sleep involves much more.

Kinds of Sleep

Although sleeping and dreaming occur at an even lower level of awareness than daydreaming, the brain is not inactive. The invention of the electroencephalograph (described in chapter 2) led to some major breakthroughs in understanding sleep by revealing how the brain's electrical activity changes during sleep. **Alpha waves** *make up the EEG pattern of individuals who are in a relaxed or drowsy state*. Figure 4.2 shows the EEG pattern for alpha waves and for the various stages of sleep.

As we fall asleep, slow brain waves replace the rapid brain waves of the waking state. These slow brain waves characterize Stage 1 sleep, which is a light sleep that lasts up to 10 minutes (see figure 4.2 on page 107). Then we enter Stage 2 sleep. **Sleep spindles,** *brief bursts of higher-frequency waves, periodically occur during Stage 2 sleep*. Stage 2 sleep lasts up to about 20 minutes. Stage 3, which lasts up to 40 minutes, involves progressively more muscle relaxation and slower brain waves. Stage 4 sleep is also called deep sleep. **Delta waves** *are large, slow EEG waves that last up to 30 minutes in Stage 4 sleep*. A sleeper who awakens during this stage often appears confused. It is in this deep state of sleep that sleepwalking, sleeptalking, and bedwetting are most likely to occur.

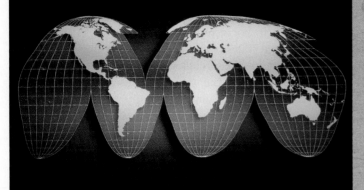

SOCIOCULTURAL WORLDS 4.1

Altered States of Consciousness and the World's Religions

- Yemenite Jews in a Jerusalem synagogue—wrapped in their prayer shawls, barefoot, sitting cross-legged, and swaying back and forth—recite the Torah.
- Dai Jo and Lai San, Zen monks, sitting cross-legged and immovable from 3 A.M. to 11 P.M., explore the Buddha-nature at the center of their beings.
- Coptic Christians in Cairo, Egypt, emit an eerie and spine-tingling cry of spiritual fervor.
- Muslims in Pakistan fast from dawn to dusk for an entire month because one of the five pillars of Islamic faith is that fasting bends minds into spiritual nourishment and brings people closer to God.

Most of the world's great religions began in a moment of revelation, an ecstatic moment infused with such mystery, power, and beauty it forever altered the founding prophet's consciousness (Weil, 1972). God called Abraham, bidding him to leave his Mesopotamian homeland and seek a promised land known as Canaan. There he founded a people, the Jews, who were to be locked forever in a special relationship with the creator of heaven and earth. In the Christian religion, death could not vanquish Jesus in 29 A.D.; following his death, Jesus appeared in a revelation to Paul, who then became a believer in Christ's resurrection and traveled widely to preach Christianity. In the late sixth century B.C., Siddhartha Gautama (Buddha) experienced a transcending revelation, which told him that it was his responsibility to preach the secrets of an enlightened life. The Buddhist path to enlightenment involves meditating—turning inward to discover that within one's self is the origin of the world, the end of the world, and the way to all goals. In the Islamic religion, Mohammed saw a vision and heard a voice in the year 610 that would alter his life; God's angel Gabriel came to Mohammed and said, "Mohammed, thou art a messenger of God."

Today billions of people around the world guide their lives by the tenets of Judaism, Christianity, Islam, and Buddhism.

b.

Regardless of whether you believe in the teachings of one or more of the world's religions, your understanding of mind and behavior is enhanced by knowing the religions' beliefs about the altered states of consciousness that led to the founding of the religions and the impact of those beliefs on their members' pursuits of similar states.

Among the roles of altered states of consciousness in the world's religions are (a) Zen monks who explore the Buddha-nature at the center of their beings and (b) Moslems in Pakistan who fast from dawn to dusk for an entire month because one of the five pillars of Islamic faith is that fasting bends minds into spiritual nourishment and brings people closer to God.

Controlled processes	High level of awareness, focused attention required.		This student is using controlled processes that require focused concentration.
Automatic processes	Awareness but minimal attention required.		This woman is an experienced computer operator. Her maneuvers with the keyboard are automatic, requiring minimal awareness.
Daydreaming	Low level of awareness and conscious effort, somewhere between active consciousness and dreaming while asleep.		Our daydreams often start spontaneously when what we are doing requires less than our full attention.
Altered states of consciousness	A mental state noticeably different from normal awareness. Produced by drugs, trauma, fatigue, hypnosis, and sensory deprivation.		Shown here is a woman being hypnotized.
Sleep and dreams	No longer thought of as the absence of consciousness, but they are at very low levels of consciousness.	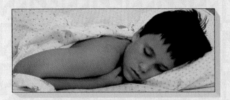	All of us dream while we sleep, but some of us dream more than others.
Unconscious mind (Freudian)	Reservoir of unacceptable wishes, feelings, and memories, often with sexual and aggressive overtones, that are too painful to be admitted to consciousness.		The woman shown lying on the couch is undergoing therapy to reveal her unconscious thoughts.
Unconscious (non-Freudian)	Being knocked unconscious by a blow or when we are anesthetized. Deep prolonged unconciousness characterizes individuals who go into a coma as the result of injury, disease, or poison.		Unconsciousness can result from an injury, such as a blow to the head.

Note: The different states of consciousness displayed in this chart are not ordered on a continuum of awareness-unawareness.

FIGURE 4.1

Forms of consciousness and levels of awareness-unawareness.

EEG pattern	Characteristics
Alpha waves	Alpha waves occur when we are relaxed or become drowsy. They are slower than when we are in a focused, alert state but faster than those in the sleep stages 1–4.
Stage 1	Light sleep, lasts up to 10 minutes.
Stage 2 (Sleep spindle)	Characterized by occasional appearance of sleep spindles. Lasts up to 20 minutes.
Stage 3	Progressively more muscle relaxation and slower brain waves. Lasts up to 40 minutes.
Stage 4 (Delta waves)	Deep sleep, a time when the sleeper is difficult to rouse. Large, slow brain waves called delta waves occur.
REM stage	Instead of reentering Stage 1 sleep, the individual now enters REM sleep, in which the EEG pattern shows waves similar to those of relaxed wakefulness. Most dreaming occurs in this stage. Lasts for about 10 minutes in first sleep cycle of the night, up to an hour in the last.

Time

FIGURE 4.2

EEG recordings of brain activity during stages of wakefulness and sleep.

After about 70 minutes of sleep, much of which is spent in Stages 3 and 4, the sleeper moves restlessly and drifts up through the sleep stages toward wakefulness. Instead of reentering Stage 1, however, the person enters a form of sleep called "rapid eye movement," or REM, sleep. **REM sleep** *is a periodic stage of sleep during which dreaming occurs.* During REM sleep, the EEG pattern shows fast waves similar to those of relaxed wakefulness. During REM sleep, the eyeballs move up and down and from left to right (Siegel, 1989) (see figure 4.3).

A person who is awakened during REM sleep is more likely to report having dreamed than at any other stage. Even people who claim they rarely dream frequently report dreaming when they are awakened during REM sleep (McCarley, 1989). The longer the period of REM sleep, the more likely a person will

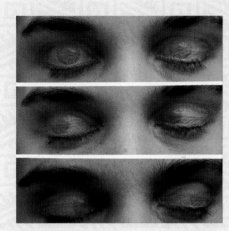

FIGURE 4.3

REM sleep. During REM sleep, our eyes move rapidly as if we were observing the images we see moving in our dreams.

report dreaming. Dreams do occur during slow-wave or non-REM sleep, but the frequency of dreams in the other stages is relatively low (Webb, 1978).

So far we have described a normal cycle of sleep, which consists of four stages plus REM sleep. There are several important points to remember about the nature of these cycles (see figure 4.4). One of these cycles lasts about 90 minutes and recurs several times during the night. The amount of deep sleep (Stage 4) is much greater in the first half of a night's sleep than in the second half. The majority of REM sleep takes place during the latter part of a night's sleep, when the REM period becomes progressively longer. The night's first REM period might last for only 10 minutes, the final REM period for as long as an hour.

Sleep and Circadian Rhythms

We are unaware of most of our body's rhythms—for example, the rise and fall of hormones in the bloodstream, accelerated and decelerated cycles of brain activity, highs and lows in body temperature (Monk, 1989). Some rhythms are *circadian,* from the Latin words *circa* meaning "about" and *dies* meaning "day." A **circadian rhythm** *is a daily behavioral or physiological cycle; an example is the 24-hour sleep/wake cycle.*

The natural circadian rhythm of most animals, including humans, is 25 to 26 hours, but our internal clocks easily adapt to the 24-hour rhythms (light, sounds, warmth) of the turning earth. When we are isolated from environmental cues, our sleep/wake cycles continue to be rather constant but slightly longer than 24 hours. For example, in 1972 French scientist Michel Siffre isolated himself in Midnight Cave near Del Rio, Texas, for 6 months (see figure 4.5). What were Siffre's days and nights like when he was completely isolated from clocks, calendars, the moon, the sun, and all the normal markers of time? Siffre's

(1975) days closely resembled a 24-hour cycle, but they were slightly longer and more varied toward the end of his 6-month stay in the cave.

Our circadian rhythm may become desynchronized when we take a cross-country or transoceanic flight (Dement, 1976; Dinges, 1989; Mistleberger & Rusak, 1989). If you fly from Los Angeles to New York and then go to bed at 11 P.M. Eastern Standard Time, you may have trouble falling asleep because your body is still on West Coast time. Even if you sleep for 8 hours that night, you may find it hard to wake up at 7 A.M. (which would be 4 A.M. in Los Angeles).

Why Do We Sleep?

There are two theories about why we sleep—repair theory and ecological theory. **Repair theory** *states that sleep restores, replenishes, and rebuilds our brains and bodies, which somehow are worn out or used up by the day's waking activities.* This idea fits with the feeling of being "worn out" before we sleep and "restored" when we wake. Aristotle proposed a repair theory of sleep centuries ago, and most experts today believe in a version of repair.

How much sleep do we need each night? Some of us can get by on an average of 5 to 6 hours of sleep; others may need 9 to 10 hours to function effectively. The idea that each of us needs 8 hours of sleep each night is a myth.

How long can people go without sleep and still function in their world? The effects of profound sleep loss have been difficult to study because preventing a person from sleeping causes stress. After 2 or 3 days without sleep, people tend to become irritable, lose concentration, and show other signs of stress (Webb, 1978). As people become more motivated to sleep, they may snatch bits of sleep while standing up. However, people who are highly motivated and able to cope with the stress can function surprisingly well after as many as 8 to 10 days without sleep (Dement, 1976).

Ecological theory *is a relatively recent view of why we sleep. This evolution-based approach argues that the main purpose of sleep is to prevent animals from wasting their energy and harming themselves during the parts of the day or night to which they have not adapted.* For example, it was not adaptive for our ancestors to fumble around in the dark, risking accidents or attack by large predators, such as lions and tigers, so, like chimpanzees that slept safely in treetops, our ancestors presumably hid and slept through the night.

Both repair theory and ecological theory have some merit. Perhaps sleep was originally most important for keeping us out of trouble but has since evolved to allow for certain repair processes.

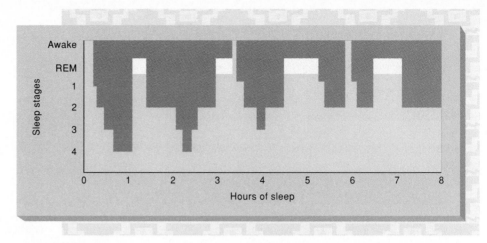

FIGURE 4.4

Normal sleep patterns of young adults. Notice the reduction of slow-wave sleep, especially Stage 4 sleep, during the latter part of the night, and notice the increase of REM sleep in the latter part of the night.

FIGURE 4.5

Michel Siffre, in Midnight Cave near Del Rio, Texas. Because Siffre could not see or sense the sun rising and setting in the cave, he began to live by biological cycles instead of by days. When Siffre wanted to go to sleep, he called the support crew outside and told them to turn off the lights in the cave. When he woke up, he called the support crew and asked them to turn on the cave's lights. Siffre's days closely resembled a 24-hour pattern through most of the 6 months in the cave, but toward the end they were slightly longer and more varied. In the last month of his cave stay, his days averaged about 28 hours.

Neural Basis of Sleep

For many years, researchers thought sleep occurred in the absence of enough sensory stimulation to keep the brain awake. Without stimuli, the brain was believed to just slow down, producing sleep. However, researchers realized that sleep comes and goes without any obvious change in the amount of environmental stimulation. Theorists suggested we might have an internal "activating system" in the reticular formation that keeps the brain activated, or awake, all day. According to this theory, fatigue of the so-called activating system, or an accumulation of "sleep toxin" that chemically depresses the activating system, induces sleep (Monnier & Hosli, 1965).

The contemporary view of sleep is radically different. As you have learned, the brain does not stop during sleep but instead carries out complex processes that produce both REM and non-REM sleep behaviors. In fact, when sleep is examined at the cellular level, many neurons fire faster than in a waking state (Jones, 1989).

The puzzle is not completely solved, but some of the major pieces of the brain's machinery involved in sleep have been identified. Non-REM sleep, for example, requires the participation of neurons in both the forebrain and medulla. REM sleep is a period of especially intense brain activity, also requiring the cooperation of a number of brain systems (Hobson, 1992; Hobson, Lydic, & Baghdoyan, 1986).

So far we have discussed normal aspects of sleep. Next we'll see that sleep is not always predictable; there are many ways sleep can go awry.

Sleep Disorders

Most people go to bed, fall asleep, and have a restful night. However, some people have fitful nights and want to sleep much of the day. Others sleepwalk, sleeptalk, have nightmares or night terrors, or have breathing problems while they sleep.

Insomnia

Insomnia *is a common sleep problem; put simply, it is the inability to sleep.* Insomnia may involve a problem in falling asleep, waking up during the night, or waking up too early. As many as one in five Americans has insomnia (Zorick, 1989). It is more common among women, older adults, thin people, depressed or stressed people, and people who are poor (Aldrich, 1989).

We spend large sums of money, especially on drugs, trying to sleep better. Many sleep experts now believe that physicians have been too quick to prescribe sedatives for insomniacs (Nicholson, Bradley, & Pasco, 1989). Sedatives reduce the amount of time a person spends in Stage 4 and REM sleep and may disrupt the restfulness of sleep. There is a danger of overdose and, over time, sedatives lose their effectiveness, requiring ever greater dosages to achieve the same effect (Syvalahti, 1985). Sedatives and nonprescription sleeping pills should be used with caution and only for short-term sleep problems.

What can you do if you spend too many sleepless nights tossing and turning in bed? Rather than turning to sleeping pills, a risk-free alternative is the chemical compound *tryptophan*, which is found in milk and milk products. Although it's not a sure-fire cure for insomnia, it does seem to help some people sleep better. Next time you have trouble falling asleep, a glass of milk may do the trick.

Caffeine and nicotine may be the culprits in some cases of insomnia. Experts recommend decreasing their use if you are having sleep problems (Zarcone, 1989). Avoid large quantities of alcohol before going to bed. Drinking before going to bed may initially help you fall asleep, but after the sedative effects wear off you probably will have difficulty staying asleep. Other suggested remedies for insomniacs include adopting a regular schedule so that you go to sleep and wake up at approximately the same time each day; doing something relaxing before you go to bed, such as listening to soft music; avoiding discussion of highly stressful issues, such as money or dating problems; and adopting a regular exercise program (but don't exercise just before going to bed; it increases your energy and alertness).

Sleepwalking and Sleeptalking

Somnambulism *is the formal term for sleepwalking; it occurs during the deepest stages of sleep.* For many years, experts believed that somnambulists were acting out their dreams. However, somnambulism occurs during Stages 3 and 4 of sleep, the time when a person usually does not dream. Although some adults sleepwalk, sleepwalking is most common in children. Most children outgrow the problem without having to seek professional help. Except for the danger of accidents while wandering about in the dark, there is nothing abnormal about sleepwalking. It is safe to awaken sleepwalkers, and it's probably a good idea, since they might harm themselves as they roam through the night.

Another quirky night behavior is sleeptalking. Most sleeptalkers are young adults, but sleeptalkers come in all ages. If you were to interrogate a sleeptalker, could you find out what he did last Thursday night? Probably not. Although he may speak to you and make fairly coherent statements, the sleeptalker is soundly asleep. Most likely, the sleeptalker will mumble a response to your question, but don't count on its accuracy.

Nightmares and Night Terrors

A **nightmare** *is a frightening dream that awakens the sleeper from REM sleep.* A nightmare's content invariably involves some danger—the dreamer is chased, robbed, raped, murdered, or thrown off a cliff. Nightmares are common. Most of us have had them, especially when we were children. Even most adults experience a nightmare occasionally. Nightmares are usually so vivid that we can remember them if someone awakens us, although they account for only a small portion of our dream world (Hartmann, 1989).

Recall from the opening of the chapter that night terrors are characterized by sudden arousal from sleep and intense fear, usually accompanied by a number of physiological reactions, such as rapid heart rate and breathing, loud screams, heavy perspiration, and physical movement. Night terrors are less common than nightmares, and the person usually has little or no recall of an accompanying dream. Also unlike nightmares, night terrors occur in slow-wave, non-REM sleep.

Narcolepsy

Narcolepsy *is the overpowering urge to fall asleep.* The urge is so strong that the person may fall asleep while talking or standing up. Narcoleptics immediately enter REM sleep rather than moving through the first four sleep stages (Guilleminault, 1989). Researchers suspect it is an inherited disorder, since narcolepsy runs in families.

Sleep Apnea

Sleep apnea *is a sleep disorder in which individuals stop breathing while they are asleep because their windpipe fails to open or brain processes involved in respiration fail to work properly.* They wake up periodically during the night so they can breathe better, although they are not usually aware of their awakened state. During the day, these people may feel sleepy because they were deprived of sleep at night. This disorder is most common among infants and people over the age of 65 (White, 1989).

In our tour of sleep, we have seen that dreams usually occur during REM sleep. Let's now explore the fascinating world of dreams in greater detail.

Dreams

Ever since the dawn of language, dreams have been imbued with historical, personal, and religious significance (Dement, 1976). As early as 5000 B.C., Babylonians recorded and interpreted their dreams on clay tablets. Egyptians built temples in honor of Serapis, the god of dreams. People occasionally slept there, hoping Serapis would make their dreams more enjoyable. Dreams are described at length in more than 70 passages in the Bible, and in many primitive cultures dreams are an extension of reality. For example, there is an account of an African chief who dreamed that he had visited England. On awakening, he ordered a wardrobe of European clothes. As he walked through the village in his new wardrobe, he was congratulated for having made the trip. Similarly Cherokee Indians who dreamed of being bitten by a snake were treated for the snake bite.

Today we still try to figure out what dreams mean. Much of the interest stems from psychoanalysts who have probed the unconscious mind to understand the symbolic content of dreams. Although there is concrete information regarding sleep stages, there is very little scientific data to explain why we dream or what dreams mean.

Interpretation of Dreams

Many of us dismiss the nightly excursion into the world of dreams as a second-rate mental activity, unworthy of our rational selves. By focusing only on the less mysterious waking world, we deny ourselves the opportunity of chance encounters with distant friends, remote places, dead relatives, gods, and demons.

In Freud's (1900/1953) theory, the reason we dream is *wish fulfillment*. After analyzing clients' dreams in therapy, Freud concluded that dreams are unconscious attempts to fulfill needs, especially those involving sex and aggression, that cannot be expressed or that go ungratified during waking hours. For example, people who are sexually inhibited while awake would likely have dreams with erotic content; those who have strong aggressive tendencies and hold in anger while awake would likely have dreams filled with violence and hostility. Freud also stressed that dreams often contain memories of infancy and childhood experiences, and especially of events associated with parents. He also said our dreams frequently contain information from the day or two preceding the dream. In his view, many of our dreams consist of combinations of these distant, early experiences with our parents and more recent daily events. He emphasized that the task of dream interpretation is complicated because we successfully disguise our wish fulfillment in dreams.

Freud believed that, in disguising our wish fulfillment, our dreams create a great deal of symbolism. Do you dream about elongated objects—sticks, tree trunks, umbrellas, neckties, and snakes? If so, Freud would have said you are dreaming about male genitals. Do you dream about small boxes, ovens, cavities, ships, and rooms? Freud would have claimed your dreams were about female genitals. Freud thought that, once a therapist understood a client's symbolism, the nature of a dream could then be interpreted.

Whether or not dreams are an arena for us to play out ungratified needs, they are a mental realm where we can solve problems and think creatively. Scottish author Robert Louis Stevenson (1850-1894), for example, claimed he got the idea for *Dr. Jekyll and Mr. Hyde* in a dream. Elias Howe, attempting to invent a machine that sewed, reportedly dreamed he was captured by savages carrying spears with holes in their tips. On waking, Howe realized he should place the hole for the thread at the end of the needle, not the middle. Dreams may spark such gifts of inspiration because they weave together, in unique and creative ways, current experiences with the past.

Rosalind Cartwright (1978, 1989) studied the role of dreaming in problem solving. Participants in her study were awakened just after they had completed a period of REM sleep and then were questioned about their dreams. The first dream of the night, it turns out, often reflects a realistic view of a problem. The second dream usually deals with a similar experience in the recent past. Frequently the third dream goes back to an earlier point in the dreamer's life. The next several dreams often take place in the future. It is at this point, Cartwright says, that problem solving begins. However, many sleepers never get this far in a night's dreaming, and others just keep repeating the problem.

The **activation-synthesis view** *states that dreams have no inherent meaning. Rather, they reflect the brain's efforts to make sense out of or find meaning in the neural activity that takes place during REM sleep. In this view, the brain's activity involves a great deal of random activity during REM sleep, and dreams are an attempt to synthesize this chaos* (Hobson & McCarley, 1977; McCarley, 1989).

Dreams and Culture

Although dreams are a private world, reflecting our unique hopes, fears, and circumstances, they also reflect the world around us. For example, Americans may dream about being naked in front of strangers and feeling deeply embarrassed about their predicament, but it's unlikely that someone from an African culture who wears little or no clothing would have such a dream. Similarly, few urban Americans dream of being chased by cows, but this is a common nightmare for the inhabitants of Ghana in western Africa (Barnouw, 1963).

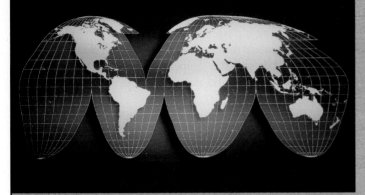

The Role of Dreams in the Senoi Tribe of Malaysia

The Senoi, numbering between 20,000 and 30,000, are an easygoing and nonviolent people who inhabit the jungle highlands of West Malaysia in Southeast Asia. They hunt small game with blowpipes, gather fruit and berries, and fish with traps and baskets when they are not tending their fields. They are said to be among the happiest and healthiest people in the world. Their happiness and health have been attributed to their ability to control their dreams and to use dreams as an integral part of their culture.

According to Kilton Stewart (1953, 1972), who studied the Senoi culture in the 1930s, Senoi life is a veritable dream clinic. Not only do the Senoi share and interpret their dreams, more importantly, they shape and control them. They dream the dreams they desire, free of fearful chases and frightening falls and full of sensuality and creativity. Senoi parents discuss their children's dreams every day at breakfast. They ask their children what they dreamed, praise them for dreaming, and talk about the dreams' significance.

When a Senoi child recounted a dream about falling, Stewart reported that the parent answered, "That is a wonderful dream, one of the best dreams a person can have. Where did you fall to, and what did you discover?" According to Stewart, the adult further encouraged the child by saying, "Everything you do in a dream has a purpose, beyond your understanding while you are asleep. You must relax and enjoy yourself when you fall in a dream. Falling is the quickest way to get in contact with the powers of the spirit world, the powers laid open to you through your dreams." Stewart claimed that instructions such as these brought about changes in the child's dreams.

Recently Stewart's claims have been questioned by anthropologists who spent considerable time observing the Senoi culture throughout the 1960s and 1970s (Denton, 1988; Domhoff, 1985). In keeping with Stewart's conclusions, the anthropologists found that dreams are far more important in the Senoi culture than in any Western culture. Dreams are essential for contacting the supernatural world and play a role in Senoi healing ceremonies. However, the anthropologists found that dreams do not dominate the Senoi culture the way Stewart described, and they also could find no evidence that the Senoi conduct morning dream clinics with their children. In fact, there was no evidence that parents instruct their children about dreaming in any way. In addition, the anthropologists found that violent acts did occur and that the Senoi were not as healthy as Stewart had claimed.

According to his critics, Stewart was a well-meaning charmer and storyteller, but he was not a careful, data-gathering scientist. He misunderstood how dreams are used in the Senoi culture and he let his imagination work overtime. The saga of Stewart reminds us of one of science's most important caveats, mentioned in chapter 1: be skeptical of anything that claims access to wondrous powers and supernatural forces.

In one study, the dreams of Mexican American and Anglo American college students were analyzed for images of death, such as cadavers and graveyards (Roll, Hinton, & Glazer, 1974). Predictably, the theme of death figured considerably greater in the dreams of Mexican American students than in Anglo American students' dreams. One explanation for the difference is that the Mexican American students probably had more experience in caring for sick or dying relatives at home.

Although dreams are used in psychotherapy to gain insight and self-awareness, they do not play much of a role in our everyday lives. Some cultures, however, regard dreams as supernatural visions that guide personal behavior. Sociocultural Worlds 4.2 describes the role of dreams in a remote Malaysian culture.

More About Dreams

The world of dreams raises some intriguing questions: Do we dream in color? Do animals dream? Why can't we remember all of our dreams? Can we influence what we dream about?

Some people say they dream only in black-and-white, but virtually everyone's dreams contain color. However, we often forget the color by the time we awaken and recall the dream. Some people claim that certain colors have fixed meanings in their dreams—white for purity, red for passion, green for vitality, black for evil or death, for example. However, no evidence has been found to support this belief. Red may stand for passion in one dream, danger in another, and anger in yet another dream.

It is impossible to say for certain whether or not animals dream; we know they have periods of REM sleep, so it is possible that they do. However, dogs' twitching and howling during sleep, for instance, should not be taken as evidence that they are dreaming.

Everyone dreams, but some of us remember our dreams better than others. It's not surprising we don't remember all our dreams, since dreaming occurs at such a low level of consciousness. Psychoanalytic theory suggests we forget most of our dreams because they are threatening, but there is no evidence to support this belief. We remember our dreams best when we are awakened during or just after a dream. Similarly the dreams we have just before we awaken are the ones we are most likely to remember. People whose sleep cycles have long periods between their last REM stage and awakening are more likely to report they don't dream at all or rarely remember their dreams.

Can we banish evil, fly high and fast, or create a happy ending for our dreams at will? According to Stanford researcher Stephen LaBerge (1985, 1988, 1992), in the landscape of "lucid dreams," you can actually learn to take control of your dreams. **Lucid dreams** *are a class of dreams in which a person "wakes up" mentally but remains in the sensory landscape of the dream world.* During a lucid dream, the sleeper is consciously aware that the dream is taking place and can gain some control over dream content.

LaBerge describes a number of techniques to increase lucid dreaming. If you awaken from a dream in the middle of the night, immediately return to the dream in your imagination. Then envision yourself recognizing the dream. Tell yourself that the next time you dream you want to recognize that you are dreaming. If your intention is strong and clear enough, when you return to sleep you may discover that you are in a lucid dream. Next we will turn our attention to hypnosis and altered states of consciousness.

REVIEW

Consciousness, Sleep, and Dreams

Consciousness is awareness of both external and internal stimuli and events. Consciousness is a rich, complex landscape of the mind, consisting of processes at varying levels of awareness. Among the many forms of consciousness are controlled processes, automatic processes, daydreaming, altered states of consciousness, sleep and dreams, unconscious thought (Freudian), and unconsciousness (non-Freudian, such as in an anesthetized state).

Important dimensions of sleep include the kinds of sleep, circadian rhythms, why we sleep, the neural basis of sleep, and sleep disorders. Various kinds of sleep can be measured by an electroencephalograph (EEG), which measures the brain's electrical activity. Alpha waves occur when we are in a relaxed state. The transition from waking to sleep is called a hypnagogic state. When we sleep, we move from light sleep in Stage 1 to deep sleep in Stage 4 (delta waves). Then we go directly into REM sleep, where dreams occur. Each night we go through a number of these sleep cycles.

A circadian rhythm refers to cycles that are about 24 hours long. The human sleep/wake cycle is an important circadian rhythm. This cycle can become desynchronized. In some experiments, people have isolated themselves in caves for months; these people continue to have an approximate 24-hour cycle, although at times the cycle is slightly longer. There is no set amount of sleep we need each night.

We sleep mainly for two reasons—for restoration and repair (repair theory) and to keep us from wasting energy and harming ourselves during the times of the day or night to which we are not adapted (ecological theory). Early views of sleep emphasized the role of environmental stimulation and subsequently an internal activating system in the reticular formation. The contemporary view is radically different: the brain is actively engaged in producing sleep behaviors and different neurotransmitters are involved. Among the most prominent sleep disorders are insomnia, sleepwalking and sleeptalking, nightmares and night terrors, narcolepsy, and sleep apnea.

Understanding dreams requires knowledge of how dreams are interpreted, the role of culture in dreams, whether we dream in color, whether animals dream, why we can't remember all of our dreams, and whether we can influence what we dream about. Freud's psychoanalytic view states that dreams are wish fulfillment of unmet needs in our waking state. Freud believed that dreams often involve a combination of daily residue and early childhood experiences. He stressed that dreams have rich symbolic content. A second view of dreams states that dreams are thinking activities and attempts to solve problems. A third view, the activation-synthesis view, states that dreams are the brain's way of trying to make sense out of neural activity during REM sleep. The content of dreams is often influenced by cultural experiences. Dreams play a more salient role in many cultures other than Western cultures. We usually dream in color but don't remember. We don't know whether or not animals dream, but they may, since they experience REM sleep. Some people can influence their dreams through lucid dreams.

Hypnosis

A young cancer patient is about to undergo a painful bone marrow transplant procedure. A doctor directs the boy's attention, asking him to breathe with him and listen carefully. The boy becomes absorbed in a pleasant fantasy—he is riding a motorcycle over a huge pizza, dodging anchovies and maneuvering around chunks of mozzarella. Minutes later the procedure is over. The boy is relaxed and feels good about his self-control (Long, 1986). The doctor successfully used hypnosis as a technique to help the young cancer patient control pain.

Hypnosis *is a psychological state of altered attention and awareness in which the individual is unusually receptive to suggestions.* Hypnosis has been used since the beginning of recorded history. It has been associated with religious ceremonies, magic, the supernatural, and many erroneous theories. Today hypnosis is recognized as a legitimate process in psychology and medicine, although much is yet to be learned about how it works.

In the eighteenth century, Austrian physician Anton Mesmer cured his patients by passing magnets over their bodies. Mesmer said the problems were cured by "animal magnetism," an intangible force that passes from therapist to patient. In reality, the cures were due to a form of hypnotic suggestion. Mesmer's claims were investigated by a committee appointed by the French Academy of Science. The committee agreed that Mesmer's treatment was effective. However, they disputed his theoretical claims about animal magnetism and prohibited him from practicing in Paris. Mesmer's theory of animal magnetism was called mesmerism, and even today we use the term *mesmerized* to mean hypnotized or enthralled.

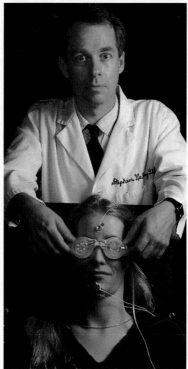

One of Stephen LaBerge's strategies for studying lucid dreaming is to ask volunteers to wear a sleep mask with sensors that turn on a red flashing light when REM sleep appears. The drowsy individual detects the flashing red light, then usually goes back to sleep after the light is turned off. The red light alerts dreamers that they were dreaming.

Features of the Hypnotic State

There are four steps used to induce hypnosis. First, distractions are minimized and the person to be hypnotized is made comfortable. Second, the subject is told to concentrate on something specific, such as an imagined scene or the ticking of a watch. Third, the subject is told what to expect in the hypnotic state (for example, relaxation or a pleasant floating sensation). Fourth, the hypnotist suggests certain events or feelings he or she knows will occur or observes occurring (for instance, "your eyes are getting tired"). When the suggested effects occur, the subject interprets them as being caused by the hypnotist's suggestions and accepts them as an indication that something is happening. This increases the subject's expectations that the hypnotism will make things happen in the future and makes the subject even more suggestible.

An important characteristic of the hypnotic state is the subject's suggestibility. When individuals are hypnotized, they readily accept and respond to ideas offered by the hypnotist. **Posthypnotic suggestion** *is a suggestion, made by the hypnotist while the subject is in a hypnotic state, that the subject carries out after emerging from the hypnotic state.* **Posthypnotic amnesia,** *induced by the hypnotist's suggestion, is the subject's inability to remember what took place during hypnosis.*

Individual Differences in Hypnosis

Do you think you could be hypnotized? What about your friends—are they more likely or less likely to be influenced by hypnosis than you are? For as long as hypnosis has been studied, about 200 years, it has been known that some people are more easily hypnotized than others. In fact, about 10 to 20 percent of the population are very susceptible to hypnosis, 10 percent or less cannot be hypnotized at all, and the remainder fall somewhere in between (Hilgard, 1965). There is no simple way to tell whether you can be hypnotized, but if you have the capacity to immerse yourself in imaginative activities—listening to a favorite piece of music or reading a novel, for example—you are a likely candidate. People susceptible to hypnosis become completely absorbed in what they are doing, removing the boundaries between themselves and what they are experiencing in their environment (Piccione, Hilgard, & Zimbardo, 1989; Plotnick, Payne, & O'Grady, 1991).

Theories of Hypnosis

Ever since Anton Mesmer proposed his theory of "animal magnetism," psychologists have been trying to figure out why hypnosis works. Contemporary theorists are divided as to whether hypnosis produces a special cognitive process or is simply a form of learned social behavior.

In the **special process theory,** *hypnotic behavior is different from nonhypnotic behavior. Hypnotic responses elicited by suggestions are involuntary, rather than voluntary, reactions. Dissociations in cognitive systems take place and amnesic barriers are formed.* The **hidden observer** *is the term used by Ernest Hilgard to describe how*

"You certainly may not try to hypnotize me."

Drawing by Frascino; © 1983 The New Yorker Magazine, Inc.

part of a hypnotized individual's mind is completely unaware of what is happening. The individual remains a passive, or hidden, observer until called on to comment. Hilgard (1977) discovered this double train of thought in hypnosis during a class demonstration with a blind student. Hilgard, the hypnotist, induced deafness in the blind student and demonstrated that the subject was completely unresponsive to what was going on around him. A student asked whether the subject really was as unresponsive as he seemed. Hilgard, being a flexible teacher, asked the subject if there was a part of him that could hear. If so, he was told to raise a finger. Surprisingly, the finger rose. Hilgard asked the subject to report from the part that was listening and made his finger rise; at the same time, he told the subject that he would not be able to hear what this part of himself said. The second part of the individual's awareness had heard all that went on and reported it. Further inquiry by Hilgard revealed that approximately half of a group of highly hypnotizable subjects had a hidden observer but were unaware of it until they went through a procedure similar to the blind individual's.

A conflicting perspective, the **nonstate view,** *says that hypnotic behavior is similar to other forms of social behavior and can be explained without resorting to special processes. According to this perspective, hypnotic behavior is purposeful, goal-directed action that is best understood by the way subjects interpret their situation and how they try to present themselves* (Barber & Wilson, 1977; Coe, 1989; Spanos & others, 1992). The nonstate view recognizes that "good" hypnotic subjects often act as if they have lost control over their behavior, but these aspects of behavior are interpreted as voluntary rather than automatic.

Applications of Hypnosis

Hypnosis is widely used in psychotherapy, medicine and dentistry, criminal investigation, and sports. Hypnosis has been used in psychotherapy to treat alcoholism, somnambulism, suicidal tendencies, overeating, and smoking. One of hypnosis's least effective, yet most often used, applications is to help people stop overeating and quit smoking. Hypnotists direct their patients to stop these behaviors, but dramatic results rarely are achieved

unless the patient is already highly motivated to change. The most effective use of hypnosis is as an adjunct to various forms of psychotherapy, which we will discuss in chapter 14.

In our discussion of hypnosis, we have seen that, in the special process view, hypnosis alters a person's state of consciousness. Next, we will see that ever since the dawn of human history people have used drugs to alter consciousness, to "get high."

REVIEW

Hypnosis

Hypnosis is a psychological state of altered attention in which the subject is unusually receptive to suggestion. The history of hypnosis began with Austrian physician Anton Mesmer and his belief in animal magnetism; a present view is the hidden-observer view. Regardless of how hypnosis is induced, it includes these features: the subject is made comfortable and distracting stimuli are reduced; the individual is told to concentrate on something that takes him or her away from the immediate environment; and suggestions are made about what the subject is expected to experience in the hypnotic state. About 10 to 20 percent of the population are highly susceptible to hypnosis, about 10 percent cannot be hypnotized at all, and the remainder fall in between.

There are two broad, competing theories about hypnosis. In the special process view, hypnotic behavior is qualitatively different from normal behavior. It is involuntary and dissociation between cognitive systems and amnesic barriers is believed to be involved. Hilgard's hidden observer theory is an important perspective. The alternative, nonstate view, argues that hypnotic behavior is similar to other forms of social behavior and can be explained without special processes. From this perspective, goal-directed action is purposeful and understood by the way subjects interpret their role and how they try to present themselves. Hypnosis has been widely applied, with mixed results, to a variety of circumstances, including psychotherapy, medicine and dentistry, criminal investigation, and sports.

Psychoactive Drugs

When Sigmund Freud began to experiment with cocaine he was looking for possible medical applications, perhaps as a painkiller in eye surgery. He soon found that the drug induced ecstasy. He even wrote to his fiancée and told her how just a small dose of cocaine produced lofty, wonderful sensations. As it grew apparent that some people became psychologically addicted to cocaine and several died from overdoses, Freud quit using the drug. Cocaine is one of many drugs taken to alter consciousness.

Uses of Psychoactive Drugs

Psychoactive drugs *act on the nervous system to alter state of consciousness, modify perceptions, and change moods.* Ever since the ancients first sat, entranced, in front of communal fires, humans have searched for substances that produce pleasurable sensations and alter their state of consciousness. Among the substances that alter consciousness are alcohol, hemp and cactus plants, mushrooms, poppies, and tobacco, an herb that has been smoked and sniffed for more than 400 centuries.

Human beings are attracted to psychoactive substances because they help us adapt to an ever-changing environment. Smoking, drinking, and taking drugs reduce tension and frustration, relieve boredom and fatigue, and in some cases help us escape from the harsh realities of the world. Psychoactive drugs provide us with pleasure by giving us inner peace, joy, relaxation, kaleidoscopic perceptions, surges of exhilaration, and prolonged heightened sensation. They may be useful in helping us get along in our world. For example, amphetamines may keep us awake all night so we can study for an exam. We may also take drugs because we are curious about their effects, in some cases because of sensational accounts in the media. We may wonder if the drugs described can provide us with unique, profound experiences. We also take drugs for social reasons, hoping they will make us feel more at ease and happier in our interactions and relationships with others.

These adolescents are at an anti-drug rally in Pasadena, California. The number one substance abuse problem among adolescents is alcohol abuse.

However, the use of psychoactive drugs for such personal gratification and temporary adaptation carries a high price tag: drug dependence, personal and social disorganization, and a predisposition to serious and sometimes fatal diseases. What was initially intended as enjoyment and adaptation can eventually turn into sorrow and maladaptation. For example, drinking may initially help people relax and forget about their worries; however, then they may begin to drink more and more, until the drinking becomes an addiction that destroys relationships and careers and leads to physical and psychological damage, including permanent liver damage and major depression (Avis, 1990; George, 1990; Harris & Buck, 1991).

As a person continues to take a psychoactive drug, the body develops a **tolerance,** *which means that a greater amount of the drug is needed to produce the same effect.* The first time someone takes 5 mg of Valium, for example, the drug will make them feel very relaxed. However, after taking the pill every day for 6 months, 10 mg may be needed to achieve the same calming effect.

Addiction *is physical dependence on a drug.* **Withdrawal** *is undesirable intense pain and the craving of an addictive drug.* **Psychological dependence** *is the need to take a drug to cope with problems and stresses.* In both physical addiction and psychological dependence, the psychoactive drug plays a powerful role in the user's life.

Psychoactive drugs come in three main forms: depressants, stimulants, and hallucinogens, each of which we will consider in turn.

Depressants

Depressants *are psychoactive drugs that slow down the central nervous system, body functions, and behaviors.* Medically, depressants have been used to reduce anxiety and induce sleep. Among the most widely used depressants are alcohol, barbiturates, tranquilizers, and opiates.

Alcohol

We do not always think of alcohol as a drug, but it is an extremely potent one. Alcohol acts on the body primarily as a depressant and slows down the brain's activities. This may seem surprising, since people who normally tend to be inhibited may begin to talk, dance, or socialize after a couple of drinks. People "loosen up" after one or two drinks because the areas in the brain involved in controlling inhibition and judgment *slow down.* As people drink more, their inhibitions become reduced even further and their judgments increasingly become impaired. Activities requiring skill, such as driving, and intellectual functioning become impaired as more alcohol is consumed. Eventually the drinker becomes drowsy and falls asleep. With extreme intoxication, a person may even lapse into a coma and die. Each of these effects varies with how the person's body metabolizes alcohol, the person's body weight, the amount of alcohol consumed, and whether previous drinking has led to tolerance.

Alcohol is the most widely used drug in our society; more than 13 million people define themselves as alcoholics. Alcoholism is the third leading killer in the United States. Each year approximately 25,000 people are killed and 1.5 million are injured by drunk drivers. More than 60 percent of homicides involve the use of alcohol by either the offender or the victim, and 65 percent of aggressive sexual acts against women involve the use of alcohol by the offender. Alcohol costs the United States more than $40 billion each year in health costs, lost productivity, accidents, and crimes.

Alcohol is the substance most abused by adolescents. According to national surveys taken every year since 1975, of more than 16,000 high school seniors, from one-third to two-fifths have consumed five or more drinks in a row in the past two-week interval. Such heavy drinking is even more common among college students, especially males (Johnston, O'Malley, & Bachman, 1991, 1992). Studies reveal that individuals who abuse one drug, such as alcohol, run the risk of abusing other drugs as well. As a result, researchers are concerned that an entire generation of adolescents who drink heavily now may go on to abuse other drugs (Blount & Dembo, 1984).

Psychologists try to determine "risk factors" for alcohol abuse—red flags that describe certain people who may be predisposed to drinking problems. Such risk factors enable psychologists to identify groups of people who are most likely to need help. With regard to substance abuse, at-risk groups include young women with small children, women with alcoholic husbands, and women employed in stressful occupations. Also at risk are the children of alcoholic families and those with other troubled backgrounds, as well as youths from certain ethnic backgrounds, especially Native Americans, Blacks, and Hispanics. The role of sociocultural factors in determining risk for alcohol abuse is discussed in Sociocultural Worlds 4.3.

Barbiturates and Tranquilizers

Barbiturates, *such as Nembutal and Seconal, are depressant drugs that induce sleep or reduce anxiety.* **Tranquilizers,** *such as Valium and Xanax, are depressant drugs that reduce anxiety and induce relaxation.* Both barbiturates and tranquilizers can be habit forming. They can also produce symptoms of withdrawal when a person stops taking them. Tranquilizers are among the most widely used drugs in the United States today.

Opiates

Opiates, *which consist of opium and its derivatives, depress the central nervous system's activity.* Many drugs have been produced from the opium poppy, among them morphine and heroin (which is converted to morphine when it enters the brain). For several hours after taking an opiate, a person feels euphoric, is relieved of pain, and has an increased appetite for food and sex. The opiates are among the most physically addictive drugs (Marlatt & others,

"JUST TELL ME WHERE YOU KIDS GET THE IDEA TO TAKE SO MANY DRUGS."
© 1990 by Sidney Harris.

1989), however, leading to craving and painful withdrawal when the drug becomes unavailable. The neurotransmitters most dramatically affected by the opiates are the endorphins. When the drug is taken away, the brain has an insufficient amount of endorphins, which accounts for the excruciating pain of withdrawal. Recently another hazardous consequence of opiate addiction has surfaced: AIDS. Most heroin addicts inject the drug intravenously. When they share needles with other addicts, blood from the needles may be passed on. When this blood comes from someone with AIDS, the virus can spread from the infected user to the uninfected user.

Stimulants

Whereas depressants slow down central nervous system activity, **stimulants** *are psychoactive drugs that increase the central nervous system's activity.* The most widely used stimulants are caffeine, nicotine, amphetamines, and cocaine. Stimulants increase heart rate, breathing, and temperature and decrease appetite. Stimulants increase energy, decrease feelings of fatigue, lift mood, and boost self-confidence. After the effects of the stimulant wear off, though, the user may become tired, irritable, and depressed and may experience headaches. As with depressants, stimulants can be physically addictive.

Amphetamines *are stimulants that are widely prescribed, often in the form of diet pills.* They are also called pep pills and uppers. Cocaine comes from the coca plant, native to Bolivia and Peru. For centuries Bolivians and Peruvians chewed on the plant to increase their stamina. Today cocaine is either snorted or injected in the form of crystals or powder. The effect is a rush of euphoria, which eventually wears off, followed by depression, lethargy, insomnia, and irritability. Cocaine can even trigger a heart attack, stroke, or brain seizure. University of Maryland basketball star Len Bias died from a cocaine-induced heart attack.

How many people use cocaine? According to a national survey by the National Institute on Drug Abuse (1989), the number of people who said they had used cocaine within the month declined from 5,800,000 in 1985 to 2,900,000 in 1988. Unfortunately, the number of people who used cocaine once a week or more rose from 647,000 to 862,000 in 1988, and the number of daily, or almost daily, cocaine users increased from 246,000 to 292,000 in 1988. Emergency room admissions related to the potent, smokable form of cocaine known as crack soared from 549 cases in 1985 to 15,306 in 1988.

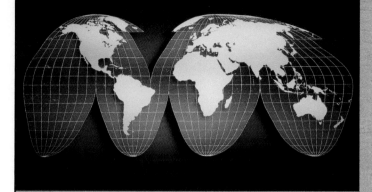

SOCIOCULTURAL WORLDS 4.3

Sociocultural Influences on Alcohol Abuse

Cultural attitudes about drinking are related to alcohol abuse. For example, Muslims and Mormons, whose religious views prohibit drinking alcohol, as well as Orthodox Jews, who traditionally have limited drinking alcohol for religious purposes, have low incidences of alcoholism. In contrast, alcoholism is high among Europeans, who make up less than 15 percent of the world's population but consume approximately half the alcohol. The French have the highest rate of alcoholism in the world—approximately 15 percent are alcoholics, and 30 percent have impaired health as a result of alcohol consumption.

However, culture alone does not necessarily determine who will or will not have drinking problems. Recently American Jews have dispelled the stereotype that Jews are immune to alcoholism. More and more Jews are joining Alcoholics Anonymous and are seeking help for alcohol-related problems (Heath, 1987). The rate of alcohol abuse among women has also increased in recent years (Nathan, 1985).

How can these undesirable changes in drinking patterns be explained? Stress may be an important factor. For Jews, the stress includes the loosening of family ties, the weakening of religious commitment, and the pressure to conform to social norms of drinking at business and social functions. For women, the stress likely involves changes in gender roles. More women have taken on career responsibilities but still have to perform their usual household duties.

Anxiety and stress may also help explain the increase in alcohol abuse in other ethnic and cultural subgroups. People who must make the transition from one cultural tradition to another often experience conflict and alienation. These stresses may lead to excessive drinking. For example, the Agringados in southern Texas, who face the challenge of shifting from the Latin to the Anglo culture, have a high incidence of alcohol abuse (Madsen, 1964). Higher rates of cirrhosis of the liver also have been found among Hopi Indians who moved into cities than among those who remained on the reservation (Kunitz & others, 1971). Alcoholism occurs in significant numbers among the Tarahumara Indians of northern Mexico only when they come into frequent contact with other cultures, such as through intermarriage with *mestizos* (persons with mixed Indian and European ancestry) (West, 1972). Another study has shown that most of the Muslims who violate the religious prohibition against drinking live in a predominately Christian neighborhood and are not active in their mosques (Midgely, 1971).

Strategies to help people navigate the stressful transition between cultures also help reduce alcohol abuse. Some of the more promising strategies include education programs that encourage the whole community to support those members at risk for alcohol abuse; economic development programs for Native Americans, who have an especially high rate of alcoholism (Watts & Lewis, 1988); and training programs to teach alternative ways of coping with stress (Lorion & Allen, 1989).

a.   b.   c.

Three cultures in which there is a low incidence of alcohol abuse are the (a) Muslim, (b) Mormon, and (c) Orthodox Jewish cultures.

Treating cocaine addiction has not been very successful—more than 50 percent of all cocaine abusers return to the drug 6 months after treatment.

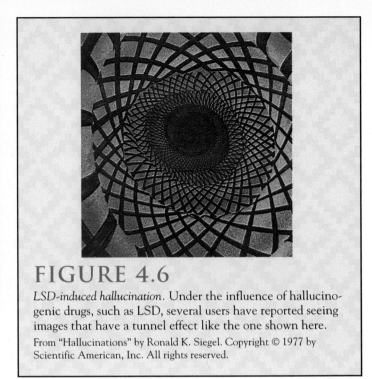

FIGURE 4.6

LSD-induced hallucination. Under the influence of hallucinogenic drugs, such as LSD, several users have reported seeing images that have a tunnel effect like the one shown here.

Treating cocaine addiction has been relatively unsuccessful. Cocaine's addictive powers are so strong that, 6 months after treatment, more than 50 percent of cocaine abusers return to the drug. Researchers believe that the best approach to reducing cocaine addiction is through prevention programs.

Hallucinogens

Hallucinogens *are psychoactive drugs that modify a person's perceptual experiences and produce visual images that are not real. Hallucinogens are called* psychedelic *drugs, which means mind altering.* LSD is a powerful hallucinogen, marijuana a milder one.

LSD

LSD, *lysergic acid diethylamide, is a hallucinogen that, even in low doses, produces striking perceptual changes.* Objects change their shape and glow. Colors become kaleidoscopic. Fabulous images unfold as users close their eyes. Designs swirl, colors shimmer, bizarre scenes appear. Sometimes the images are pleasurable; sometimes they are grotesque. Figure 4.6 shows one type of perceptual experience that a number of LSD users have reported. LSD can influence the user's perception of time as well. Time often seems to slow down, so that brief glances at objects are experienced as deep, penetrating, and lengthy examinations, and minutes may be experienced as hours or days. LSD's effects on the body may include dizziness, nausea, and tremors; emotional and cognitive effects may include rapid mood swings or impaired attention and memory. LSD's popularity in the late 1960s and early 1970s dropped after its unpredictable effects became well publicized. Today the use of LSD continues to be very low (Johnston, Bachman, & O'Malley, 1991).

Marijuana

Marijuana *is a milder hallucinogen than LSD. It comes from the hemp plant,* Cannabis sativa, *which originated in central Asia but is now grown in most parts of the world.* Marijuana is made of the hemp plant's dry leaves; its dried resin is known as hashish. The active ingredient in marijuana is THC, the chemical delta-9-tetrahydrocannabinol. This ingredient does not resemble the chemicals of other psychoactive drugs, and for the most part the brain processes affected by marijuana remain uncharted.

Because marijuana is metabolized slowly, its effects may be felt over the course of several days. The physical effects of marijuana include increases in pulse rate and blood pressure, reddening of the eyes, coughing, and dryness of the mouth. The drug's psychological effects include a mixture of excitatory, depressive, and hallucinatory characteristics, making it a difficult drug to classify. Marijuana can trigger spontaneous unrelated ideas, distorted perceptions of time and place, increased sensitivity to sounds and colors, and erratic verbal behavior. It also can impair attention and memory. When it's used daily in heavy amounts, marijuana also can impair the human reproductive system and may be involved in some birth defects. Marijuana use declined during the 1980s (Johnston, Bachman, & O'Malley, 1989).

This concludes our discussion of drugs and the chapter on states of consciousness. In the next chapter, we will turn our attention to learning.

REVIEW

Psychoactive Drugs

Psychoactive drugs act on the central nervous system to alter state of consciousness, modify perceptions, and change mood. Psychoactive substances have been used since the beginning of recorded history for pleasure, utility, curiosity, and social reasons. Tolerance for a psychoactive drug develops when a greater amount of the drug is needed to produce the same effect. Withdrawal refers to the undesirable effects of intense pain and a craving for the drug when its use is discontinued. Withdrawal takes place because the user's body has developed a physical dependency on the drug, which is called addiction. People who use drugs to help them cope with problems and stress can also become psychologically dependent.

Depressants slow down the central nervous system's activity; they include alcohol, tranquilizers, barbiturates, and opiates (narcotics). Stimulants increase central nervous system activity. The most widely used stimulants are caffeine, nicotine, amphetamines, and cocaine. Hallucinogens modify a person's perceptual experiences and produce hallucinations. LSD is a powerful hallucinogen; marijuana is a milder hallucinogen.

Summary

I. What Is Consciousness?

Consciousness is awareness of both external and internal stimuli and events. Consciousness is a rich, complex landscape of the mind, consisting of processes at varying levels of awareness. Among the many forms of consciousness are controlled processes, automatic processes, daydreaming, altered states of consciousness, sleep and dreams, unconscious thought (Freudian), and unconsciousness (non-Freudian, such as in an anesthetized state).

II. The Brain's Electrical Activity and Sleep Stages

An EEG measures the brain's electrical activity. Alpha waves occur when we are in a relaxed state. The transition from waking to sleep is called a hypnagogic state. When we sleep, we move from light sleep in Stage 1 to deep sleep in Stage 4 (delta waves). Then we go directly into REM sleep, where dreams occur. Each night we go through a number of these sleep cycles.

III. Sleep and Circadian Rhythms

A circadian rhythm refers to cycles that are about 24 hours long. The human sleep/wake cycle is an important circadian rhythm. This cycle can become desynchronized. In some experiments, people have isolated themselves in caves for months; these people continue to have an approximate 24-hour cycle, although at times the cycle is slightly longer. There is no set amount of sleep we need each night.

IV. Why We Sleep, the Neural Basis of Sleep, and Sleep Disorders

We sleep mainly for two reasons—for restoration and repair (repair theory) and to keep us from wasting energy and harming ourselves during those times of the day or night to which we are not adapted (ecological theory). Early views of sleep emphasized the role of environmental stimulation and subsequently an internal "activating system" in the reticular formation. The contemporary view is radically different: the brain is actively engaged in producing sleep behaviors and various neurotransmitters are involved. Among the most prominent sleep disorders are insomnia, sleepwalking and sleeptalking, nightmares and night terrors, narcolepsy, and sleep apnea.

V. Dreams

Freud's psychoanalytic view states that dreams are wish fulfillment of needs that are unmet in our waking state. Freud believed that dreams often involve a combination of daily residue and early childhood experiences. He stressed that dreams have rich, symbolic content. A second view of dreams states that dreams are thinking activities and attempts to solve problems. A third view, the activation-synthesis view, states that dreams are the brain's way of trying to make sense out of neural activity during REM sleep. The content of dreams is often influenced by cultural experiences. Dreams play a more salient role in many primitive cultures than in Western cultures. We usually dream in color but don't remember. We don't know whether or not animals dream, but they may, since they experience REM sleep. Some people can influence their dreams through lucid dreams.

VI. Hypnosis: Nature, History, and Features of Induction

Hypnosis is a psychological state of altered attention in which the subject is unusually receptive to suggestion. The history of hypnosis began with Austrian physician Anton Mesmer and his belief in animal magnetism; a present view is the hidden-observer view. Regardless of how hypnosis is induced, it includes these features: the subject is made comfortable and distracting stimuli are reduced; the individual is told to concentrate on something that takes him or her away from the immediate environment; and suggestions are made about what the subject is expected to experience in the hypnotic state. About 10 to 20 percent of the population are highly susceptible to hypnosis, about 10 percent cannot be hypnotized at all, and the remainder fall in between.

VII. Hypnosis: Theories and Applications

There are two broad, competing theories about hypnosis. In the special-process view, hypnotic behavior is qualitatively different from normal behavior. It is involuntary and dissociation between cognitive systems and amnesic barriers is believed to be involved. Hilgard's hidden-observer theory is an important perspective. The alternative, the nonstate view, argues that hypnotic behavior is similar to other forms of social behavior and can be explained without special processes. From this perspective, goal-directed action is purposeful and understood by the way subjects interpret their role and how they try to present themselves. Hypnosis has been widely applied with mixed results to a variety of circumstances, which include psychotherapy, medicine and dentistry, criminal investigations, and sports.

VIII. Psychoactive Drugs: Their Nature, Tolerance, Withdrawal, Addiction, and Psychological Dependence

Psychoactive drugs act on the central nervous system to alter state of consciousness, modify perceptions, and change mood. Psychoactive substances have been used since the beginning of recorded history for pleasure, utility, curiosity, and social reasons. When tolerance for a psychoactive drug develops, a greater amount of the drug is needed to produce the same effect. Withdrawal refers to the undesirable effects of intense pain and craving for the drug when its use is discontinued. Withdrawal takes place because the user's body has developed a physical dependency on the drug, which is called addiction. People who use drugs to help them cope with problems and stress can also become psychologically dependent.

IX. Depressants, Stimulants, and Hallucinogens

Depressants slow down the central nervous system's activity; they include alcohol, tranquilizers, barbiturates, and opiates (narcotics). Stimulants increase central nervous system activity. The most widely used stimulants are caffeine, nicotine, amphetamines, and cocaine. Hallucinogens modify a person's perceptual experiences and produce hallucinations. LSD is a powerful hallucinogen; marijuana is a milder hallucinogen.

Key Terms

night terror 102
consciousness 102
stream of consciousness 102
unconscious thought (Freudian) 102
controlled processes 102
automatic processes 103
daydreaming 103
altered state of consciousness 103
alpha waves 103
sleep spindles 103
delta waves 103
REM sleep 107
circadian rhythm 107
repair theory 108

ecological theory 108
insomnia 109
somnambulism 109
nightmare 109
narcolepsy 109
sleep apnea 109
activation-synthesis view 110
lucid dreams 112
hypnosis 113
posthypnotic suggestion 113
posthypnotic amnesia 113
special process theory 113
hidden observer 113
nonstate view 114

psychoactive drugs 115
tolerance 115
addiction 115
withdrawal 115
psychological dependence 115
depressants 115
barbiturates 116
tranquilizers 116
opiates 116
stimulants 116
amphetamines 116
hallucinogens 118
LSD 118
marijuana 118

Suggested Readings

Carroll, C. R. (1989). *Drugs in modern society.* Dubuque, IA: Wm. C. Brown. Current, accurate, and documented information about drugs is provided.

Dement, W. C. (1976). *Some must watch while some must sleep.* New York: Doubleday. This easy-to-read paperback includes fascinating information about our world of sleep and dreams.

International Journal of Addiction. This journal has many articles about the nature of drug use in various cultures, including a recent article by Joseph Trimble on ethnic gloss in drug abuse research.

LaBerge, S. P. (1985). *Lucid dreaming.* Los Angeles: Tarcher. If you want to see if you can increase your lucid dreaming, this is the book to read. Easy-to-follow instructions by sleep and dream expert Stephen LaBerge are provided.

Zilbergeld, B., Edelstein, M. G., & Araoz, D. L. (1986). *Hypnosis: Questions and answers?* New York: W. W. Norton. A number of experts answer questions about a wide range of topics pertaining to hypnosis.

LEARNING

CHAPTER

5

uch of what we do results from what we have *learned.* If you had grown up in another part of the world, you would speak a different language, would like different foods and clothing, and would behave in ways characteristic of that culture. Why? Because your *learning* experiences in that culture would have been different.

One way we learn is by watching what other people do and say. This kind of learning is called *observational learning.* Observational learning has changed drastically in the twentieth century because of the introduction and pervasive use of television, which has touched virtually every American's life. Television has been called a lot of names, not all of them good—the one-eyed monster and the boob tube, for example. Television has also been accused of interfering with children's learning; critics say television lures children from schoolwork and books and makes them passive learners. Rarely does television require active responses from its audience.

Television can contribute to children's learning, however. For example, television can introduce children to worlds that are different from the one in which they live. *Sesame Street* was designed to improve children's cognitive and social skills. Almost half of America's 2-to-5-year-olds watch it regularly (Liebert & Sprafkin, 1988). Highly successful at teaching children, *Sesame Street* uses fast-paced action, sound effects, music, and humorous characters to grab the attention of its young audience. With their eyes glued to the screen, young children learn basic academic skills, such as letter and number recognition. Studies have shown that regular *Sesame Street* viewers from low-income families, when they enter first grade, are rated by their teachers as better prepared for school than their light-viewing counterparts (Bogatz & Ball, 1972).

When *Sesame Street* first appeared in 1969, the creators of the show had no idea that this "street" would lead to locations as distant as Kuwait, Israel, Latin America, and the Philippines. Since *Sesame Street* first aired in the United States, the show has been televised in 84 countries. Thirteen foreign-language versions of the show have been produced. *Plaza Sesamo* is shown in 17 South and Central American countries, as well as Puerto Rico. Learning about the diversity of cultures and life-styles in South America is emphasized. *Rechov Sumsum* is shown in Israel; it especially encourages children to learn how people from different ethnic and religious backgrounds can live in harmony. *Sesamstraat* is

Don Pimpon of Spain's *Barrio Sesamo* is a shaggy old codger who has traveled extensively and entertains with stories of his adventures. *Barrio Sesamo* helps young children in Spain learn social and cognitive skills.

shown in the Netherlands; children learn about the concept of school, and a 7-foot-tall blue bird named Pino is always eager to learn. Let's now explore the concept of learning in more detail.

What Is Learning?

In learning how to use a computer, you might make some mistakes along the way, but at a certain point you will get the knack of how to use it. You will change from someone who could not operate a computer to one who can. Learning anything new involves change. Usually once you have learned to use a computer, the skill does not leave. Once you learn how to drive a car, you do not have to go through the process again later. Learning also involves a relatively permanent influence on behavior. You learned how to use a computer through experience with the machine. Through experience you also learned that you have to study to do well on a test, that when you go to a concert there usually is a warm-up act, and that a field goal in football scores three points. Putting these pieces together, we arrive at a definition of **learning,** *a relatively permanent change in behavior that occurs through experience.*

Psychologists explain our many experiences with a few basic learning processes. We respond to things that happen to us, we act and then experience the consequences of our behavior, and we observe what others say and do. These three aspects of experience form the three types of learning we will study in this chapter—classical conditioning (responding), operant conditioning (acting), and observational learning (observing). As we study the nature of learning, you will discover that early approaches investigated the way experience and behavior are connected without referring to cognitive, or mental, processes. In recent years, cognitive processes have assumed a more important role in learning (Leahey & Harris, 1989). We will discuss cognitive approaches to learning later in the chapter, but first we will examine the most fundamental type of learning, classical conditioning.

Classical Conditioning

It is a nice spring day. A father takes his baby out for a walk. The baby reaches over to touch a pink flower and is stung by a bumblebee sitting on the petals. The next day, the baby's mother brings home some pink flowers. She removes a flower from the arrangement and takes it over for her baby to smell. The baby cries loudly as soon as she sees the pink

If a bee stings this young girl while she is holding a pink flower, how would classical conditioning explain her panic at the sight of pink flowers in the future?

Pavlov set aside his work on digestion and devoted his time to studying the association of various stimuli with food. He wanted to know *why* the dog salivated to various sights and sounds before eating the meat powder. Pavlov observed that the dog's behavior included both learned and unlearned components. The unlearned part of classical conditioning is based on the fact that some stimuli automatically produce certain responses apart from any prior learning; in other words, the responses are inborn, or innate. **Reflexes** *are automatic stimulus-response connections*. They include salivation in response to food, nausea in response to bad food, shivering in response to low temperature, coughing in response to the throat being clogged, pupil constriction in response to light, and withdrawal in response to blows or burns. An **unconditioned stimulus (UCS)** *is a stimulus that produces a response without prior learning*; food was the UCS in Pavlov's experiments. An **unconditioned response (UCR)** *is an unlearned response that is automatically associated with the UCS*. In Pavlov's experiments, the saliva that flowed from the dog's mouth in response to the food was the UCR. In the case of the baby and the flower, the baby's learning and experience did not cause her to cry when the bee stung her. Her crying was unlearned and occurred automatically. The bee's sting was the UCS and the crying was the UCR.

In classical conditioning, the **conditioned stimulus (CS)** *is a previously neutral stimulus that eventually elicits the conditioned response after being paired with the unconditioned stimulus*. The **conditioned response (CR)** *is the learned response to the conditioned stimulus that occurs after CS-UCS pairing* (Pavlov, 1927). In studying a dog's response to various stimuli associated with meat powder, Pavlov rang a bell before giving meat powder to the dog. Until then, ringing the bell did not have a particular effect on the dog, except perhaps to wake the dog from a nap. The bell was a neutral stimulus. However, the dog began to associate the sound of the bell with the food and salivated when it heard the bell. The bell became a conditioned (learned) stimulus (CS) and the salivation a conditioned response (CR). Before conditioning (or learning), the bell and the food were not related. After their association, the conditioned stimulus (the bell) produced a conditioned response (salivation). For the unhappy baby, the flower was the baby's bell or CS, with crying the CR after the sting (UCS) and the flower (CS) were paired. Figure 5.1 shows Pavlov's laboratory setting for studying classical conditioning and Pavlov demonstrating the procedure of classical conditioning. A summary of how classical conditioning works is shown in figure 5.2.

The interval between the CS and UCS is one of the most important aspects of classical conditioning. It is important because it defines the degree of association, or *contiguity*, of the stimuli. Conditioned responses develop when the interval between the CS and UCS is very short, as in a matter of seconds. In many instances, optimal spacing is a fraction of a second (Kimble, 1961).

flower. The baby's panic at the sight of the pink flower illustrates the learning process of **classical conditioning,** *in which a neutral stimulus acquires the ability to produce a response originally produced by another stimulus*.

How Classical Conditioning Works

In the early 1900s, Russian physiologist Ivan Pavlov investigated the way the body digests food. As part of his experiments, he routinely placed meat powder in a dog's mouth, causing the dog to salivate. Pavlov began to notice that the meat powder was not the only stimulus that caused the dog to salivate. The dog also salivated in response to a number of stimuli associated with the food, such as the sight of the food dish, the sight of the individual who brought the food into the room, and the sound of the door closing when the food arrived. Pavlov recognized that the dog's association of these sights and sounds with the food was an important type of learning that came to be called classical conditioning.

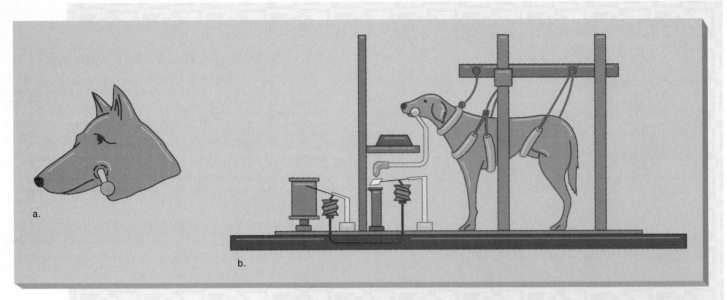

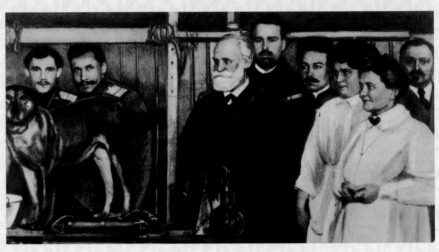

FIGURE 5.1

Pavlov's experimentation. (a) Surgical preparation for studying the salivary reflex: when the dog salivated, the saliva collected in a glass funnel attached to the dog's cheek. This way the strength of the salivary response could be measured precisely. (b) Shown here is Pavlov's experimental apparatus used to examine classical conditioning. (c) Pavlov (the white-bearded gentleman in the center) is shown demonstrating the nature of classical conditioning to students at the Military Medical Academy in the Soviet Union.

Generalization, Discrimination, and Extinction

After a time, Pavlov found that the dog also responded by salivating to other sounds, such as a whistle. The more bell-like the noise, the stronger the dog's response. The baby not only cried at the sight of pink flowers but also at the sight of red or orange flowers. **Generalization** *in classical conditioning is the tendency of a stimulus similar to the original conditioned stimulus to produce a response that is similar to the conditioned response.*

Stimulus generalization is not always beneficial; for example, a cat who generalizes from a minnow to a piranha has a major problem. Therefore, it is important to discriminate between stimuli. **Discrimination** *in classical conditioning is the process of learning to respond to certain stimuli and not to others.* To produce discrimination, Pavlov gave food to the dog only after ringing the bell and not after any other sounds. In this way, the dog learned to distinguish between the bell and other sounds. Also, the baby did not cry at the sight of blue flowers, thus discriminating between them and pink flowers.

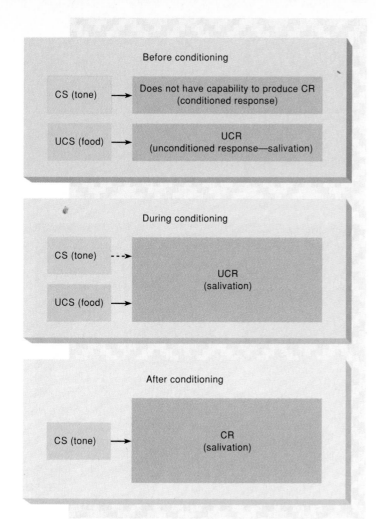

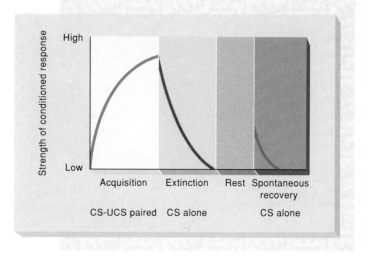

FIGURE 5.2

Classical conditioning procedure. At the start of conditioning, the UCS will evoke the UCR, but the CS does not have this capacity. During conditioning, the CS and UCS are paired so that the CS comes to elicit the response. The key learning ingredient is the association of the UCS and CS.

Pavlov rang the bell repeatedly in a single session and did not give the dog any food. Eventually the dog stopped salivating. This result is **extinction,** *which in classical conditioning is the weakening of the CS's tendency to elicit the CR as a result of unreinforced presentations of the CS.* Over time the baby encountered many pink flowers and was not stung by a bee. Consequently her fear of pink flowers subsided and eventually disappeared.

Extinction is not always the end of the conditioned response. The day after Pavlov extinguished the conditioned salivation at the sound of a bell, he took the dog to the laboratory and rang the bell, still not giving the dog any meat powder. The dog salivated, indicating that an extinguished response can spontaneously recur. **Spontaneous recovery** *is the process in classical conditioning by which a conditioned response*

FIGURE 5.3

The strength of a conditioned response during acquisition, extinction, and spontaneous recovery. During acquisition the conditioned stimulus and unconditioned stimulus are paired. As seen in the graph, when this occurs, the strength of the conditioned response increases. During extinction the conditioned stimulus is presented alone, and, as can be seen, this results in a decrease of the conditioned response. After a rest period, spontaneous recovery appears, although the strength of the conditioned response is not nearly as great at this point as it was after a number of CS-UCS pairings. When the CS is presented alone again after spontaneous recovery, the response is extinguished rapidly.

can recur without further conditioning. In the case of the baby, even though she saw many pink flowers after her first painful encounter and was not "stung" by them, she showed some signs of fear from time to time. Figure 5.3 shows the sequence of extinction and spontaneous recovery. Spontaneous recovery can occur several times; however, as long as the conditioned stimulus is presented alone, spontaneous recovery becomes weaker and eventually ceases to occur.

Classical Conditioning in Humans

Since Pavlov's experiments, individuals have been conditioned to respond to the sound of a buzzer, a glimpse of light, or the touch of a hand. Classical conditioning has a great deal of survival value (Kimmel, 1989; Turkkan, 1989). Because of classical conditioning, we jerk our hands away before they are burned by fire, and we move out of the way of a rapidly approaching truck before it hits us. Classical conditioning is at work in words that serve as important signals. Walk into an abandoned house with a friend and yell, "Snake!" Your friend probably will bolt out the door. Describe a peaceful, tranquil scene—an abandoned beach with waves lapping onto the sand—and a harried executive may relax as if she were actually lying on the beach.

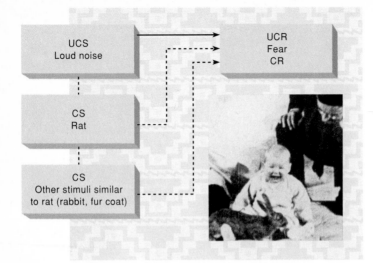

FIGURE 5.4

Little Albert's generalized fear. In 1920, 9-month-old little Albert was conditioned to fear a white rat by pairing the rat with a loud noise. When little Albert was subsequently placed with other stimuli similar to the white rat, such as the rabbit shown here with little Albert, he was afraid of them too. This illustrates the principle of stimulus generalization in classical conditioning.
Photo courtesy of Professor Benjamin Harris, University of Wisconsin.

Phobias *are irrational fears.* Classical conditioning provides an explanation of these and other fears. Behaviorist John Watson conducted an investigation to demonstrate classical conditioning's role in phobias. A little boy named Albert was shown a white laboratory rat to see if he was afraid of it. He was not. As Albert played with the rat, a loud noise was sounded behind his head. As you might imagine, the noise caused little Albert to cry. After only seven pairings of the loud noise with the white rat, Albert began to fear the rat even when the noise was not sounded. Albert's fear was generalized to a rabbit, a dog, and a sealskin coat (see figure 5.4). Today we could not ethically conduct such an experiment. Especially noteworthy is the fact that Watson and his associate (Watson & Raynor, 1920) did not remove Albert's fear of rats, so presumably this phobia remained with him after the experiment. Many of our fears—fear of the dentist from a painful experience, fear of driving from being in an automobile accident, and fear of dogs from being bitten, for example—can be learned through classical conditioning.

If we can produce fears by classical conditioning, we should be able to eliminate them. **Counterconditioning** *is a classical conditioning procedure for weakening a CR by associating the stimuli to a new response incompatible with the CR.* Though Watson did not eliminate little Albert's fear of white rats, an associate of Watson's, Mary Cover Jones (1924), did eliminate the fears of a 3-year-old boy named Peter. Peter had many of the same fears as Albert; however, Peter's fears were not produced by Jones. Among Peter's fears were white rats, fur

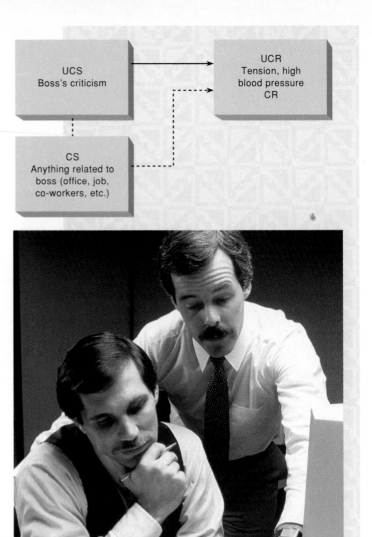

FIGURE 5.5

Classical conditioning: boss's criticism and high blood pressure.

coats, frogs, fish, and mechanical toys. To eliminate these fears, a rabbit was brought into Peter's view but kept far enough away that it would not upset him. At the same time the rabbit was brought into view, Peter was fed crackers and milk. On each successive day, the rabbit was moved closer to Peter as he ate crackers and milk. Eventually Peter reached the point where he could eat the food with one hand and pet the rabbit with the other.

Some of the behaviors we associate with health problems or mental disturbances can involve classical conditioning. Certain physical complaints—asthma, headaches, ulcers, and high blood pressure, for example—may be partly the products of classical conditioning. We usually say that such health problems are caused by stress, but often certain stimuli, such as a boss's critical attitude or a wife's threat of divorce, are conditioned stimuli for physiological responses. Over time the frequent presence of the physiological responses may produce a health problem or disorder. A boss's persistent criticism may cause an employee to develop muscle tension, headaches, or high blood pressure. Anything associated with the boss, such as work itself, can then trigger stress in the employee (see figure 5.5).

Classical conditioning is not restricted to unpleasant emotions. Among the things in our lives that produce pleasure because they have become conditioned might be the sight of a rainbow, a sunny day, or a favorite song. If you have had a positive romantic experience, the location where that experience took place can become a conditioned stimulus. This is the result of the pairing of a place (CS) with an event (UCS). Sometimes, though, classical conditioning involves an experience that is both pleasant and deviant from the norm. Consider a fetishist who becomes sexually aroused by the sight and touch of certain clothing, such as undergarments or shoes. The fetish may have developed when the fetish object (undergarment, shoe) was associated with sexual arousal, especially when the individual was young. The fetish object becomes a conditioned stimulus that can produce sexual arousal by itself (Chance, 1979).

Evaluation of Classical Conditioning

Pavlov described learning in terms of classical conditioning. Although classical conditioning helps us learn about our environment, we learn about our world in other ways too. Classical conditioning describes an organism as *responding* to the environment, a view that fails to capture the active nature of the organism and its influence on the environment. Next we will study a major form of learning that places more emphasis on the organism's *activity* in the environment—operant conditioning.

Operant Conditioning

Classical conditioning excels at explaining how neutral stimuli become associated with unlearned, involuntary responses, but it does not do so well in explaining voluntary behaviors, such as studying hard for a test, playing slot machines in Las Vegas, or teaching a pigeon to play Ping-Pong. Operant conditioning is usually better than classical conditioning at explaining *voluntary* behavior. The concept of operant conditioning was developed by the American psychologist B. F. Skinner (1938). **Operant conditioning (instrumental conditioning)** *is a form of learning in which the consequences of a behavior produce changes in the probabil-*

REVIEW
The Nature of Learning and Classical Conditioning

Learning is a relatively permanent change in behavior due to experiences. How we respond to the environment (classical conditioning), how we act in the environment (operant conditioning), and how we observe the environment (observational learning) are the most important ways in which we experience. Early approaches emphasized connections between environment and behavior; many contemporary approaches stress that cognitive factors mediate environment-behavior connections.

Pavlov discovered that an organism learns the association between an unconditioned stimulus (UCS) and a conditioned stimulus (CS). The UCS automatically produces the UCR (unconditioned response). After conditioning (CS-UCS pairing), the CS elicits the CR (conditioned response) by itself. Generalization, discrimination, and extinction also are involved. Classical conditioning has survival value for humans, as when we develop fear of hazardous conditions. Irrational fears often are explained by classical conditioning. Counterconditioning has been used to eliminate fears. Classical conditioning is important in explaining the way learning occurs in animals. It is not the only way we learn and misses the active nature of organisms in the environment.

ity of the behavior's occurrence. In operant conditioning, an organism acts, or *operates,* on the environment to produce a change in the probability of the behavior's occurrence; Skinner chose the term *operant* to describe the organism. The consequences are *contingent,* or dependent, on the organism's behavior. For example, a simple operant might press a lever that leads to the delivery of food; the delivery of food is contingent on pressing the lever.

We have mentioned one difference between classical and operant conditioning—classical conditioning is better at explaining involuntary responding, whereas operant conditioning is better at explaining voluntary responding. A second difference is that the stimuli that govern behavior in classical conditioning precede the behavior; the stimuli that govern behavior in operant conditioning *follow* the behavior. For example, if we teach a dog a trick, such as learning to roll over and play dead, in classical conditioning we would present the conditioned stimulus, such as the sound of a bell paired with meat (UCS), before the dog performed the trick. In operant conditioning, we would present the rewarding stimulus (meat or a pat on the head, for example) *after* the dog performed the trick.

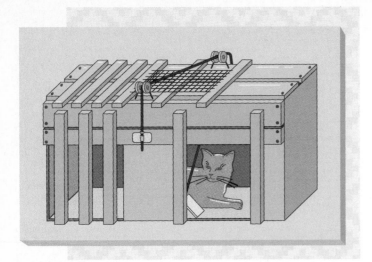

FIGURE 5.6

Thorndike puzzle box. This box is typical of the puzzle boxes Thorndike used in his experiments with cats to study the law of effect. Stepping on the treadle released the door bolt. A weight attached to the door then pulled the door open and allowed the cat to escape.

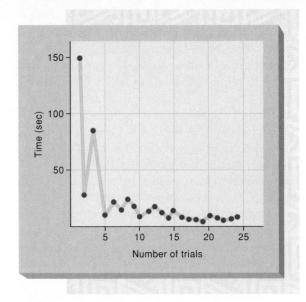

FIGURE 5.7

Learning curve of one cat's escape time. This learning curve shows the time required by one cat to escape from the puzzle box on 24 separate trials. Notice how the cat learned to escape much more quickly after about 5 trials.

Thorndike's Law of Effect

At about the same time Ivan Pavlov was conducting classical conditioning experiments with salivating dogs, American psychologist E. L. Thorndike was studying cats in puzzle boxes (see figure 5.6). Thorndike put a hungry cat inside a box and a piece of fish outside. To escape from the box, the cat had to learn how to open the latch inside the box. At first the cat made a number of ineffective responses. It clawed and bit at the bars or thrust its paw through the openings. Eventually the cat accidentally stepped on the treadle that released the door bolt. When the cat returned to the box, it went through the same random activity until it stepped on the treadle once more. On subsequent trials, the cat made fewer and fewer random movements until it learned to claw the treadle immediately to open the door (see figure 5.7). The **law of effect,** *developed by Thorndike, states that behaviors followed by positive outcomes are strengthened, whereas behaviors followed by negative outcomes are weakened.*

Drawing by Bernard Schoenbaum; © 1987 The New Yorker Magazine, Inc.

The key question for Thorndike was how the correct stimulus-response bond strengthens and eventually dominates incorrect stimulus-response bonds. According to Thorndike, the correct S-R association strengthens and the incorrect association weakens because of the *consequences* of the organism's actions. Thorndike's view is called *S-R theory* because the organism's behavior is due to a connection between a stimulus and a response. As we will see next, Skinner's operant conditioning approach expanded Thorndike's basic ideas.

Skinner's Operant Conditioning

Earlier you learned that Skinner describes operant conditioning as a form of learning in which the consequences of behavior lead to changes in the probability of that behavior's occurrence. The consequences—rewards or punishments—are contingent on the organism's behavior. **Reinforcement (reward)** *is a consequence that increases the probability a behavior will occur.* In contrast, **punishment** *is a conse-*

FIGURE 5.8

Positive reinforcement. In positive reinforcement, the frequency of a response increases because it is followed by a pleasant stimulus. For example, in this stimulus situation, a male's flattering comments to a female have positive consequences, increasing the male's chances of getting to know the female better.

FIGURE 5.9

Negative reinforcement. In negative reinforcement, the frequency of a response increases because the response either removes an unpleasant stimulus or lets the individual avoid the stimulus. For example, taking an aspirin removes or lessens pain.

quence that decreases the probability a behavior will occur. For example, if someone you meet smiles at you and the two of you continue talking for some time, the smile has reinforced your talking. However, if someone you meet frowns at you and you quickly leave the situation, then the frown has punished your talking with the individual.

Reinforcement can be complex. Usually we think of reinforcement as positive, but it can be positive or negative. In **positive reinforcement,** *the frequency of a response increases because it is followed by a pleasant stimulus,* as in our example of the smile increasing talking. Similarly, complimenting someone you are attracted to may make that person more receptive to your advances and increase the probability you will get to know the person better (see figure 5.8). The same principle of positive reinforcement is at work when an animal trainer teaches a dog to "shake hands" by giving it a piece of food when it lifts its paw. Conversely, in **negative reinforcement,** *the frequency of a response increases because the response either removes an unpleasant stimulus or lets an individual avoid the stimulus.* For example, your

father nags at you to clean the garage. He keeps nagging. Finally you get tired of the nagging and clean the garage. Your response (cleaning the garage) removed the unpleasant stimulus (nagging). Torture works the same way. An interrogator might say, "Tell me what I want to know and I will stop dripping water on your forehead." Taking aspirin is the same process: taking aspirin is reinforced when this behavior is followed by a reduction of pain (see figure 5.9).

Another way to remember the distinction between positive and negative reinforcement is to understand that, in positive reinforcement, something is added, or obtained; in negative reinforcement, something is subtracted, avoided, or escaped. For example, if you receive a sweater as a graduation present, something has been added to increase your achievement behavior. However, consider the situation in which your parents criticize you for not studying hard enough. As you study harder, they stop criticizing you—something has been subtracted, in this case their criticism.

Negative reinforcement and punishment are easily confused because they both involve aversive or unpleasant stimuli, such as an electric shock or a slap in the face. To keep them straight, remember that negative reinforcement increases the probability a response will occur, whereas punishment decreases the probability a response will occur. When an alcoholic consumes liquor to alleviate uncomfortable withdrawal symptoms,

TABLE 5.1
Positive Reinforcement, Negative Reinforcement, and Punishment

Process	Type of stimulus	Effect on response
Positive reinforcement	Pleasant	Increases
Negative reinforcement	Aversive	Increases
Punishment	Aversive	Decreases

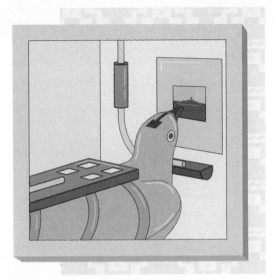

FIGURE 5.10

Skinner's pigeon-guided missile. Skinner wanted to shake up the kamikaze by using pigeons' tracking behavior. A gold electrode covered the tip of the pigeons' beaks. Contact with the screen on which the image of the target was projected sent a signal informing the missile's control mechanism of the target's location. A few grains of food occasionally given to the pigeons maintained their tracking behavior.

the probability of future alcohol use is increased. The reduction of the withdrawal symptoms is a negative reinforcer for drinking. However, if an inebriated alcoholic is seriously injured in a car wreck in which his drinking was a factor and he subsequently stops drinking, then punishment is involved because a behavior—drinking—was decreased. Table 5.1 provides an overview of the distinctions among positive reinforcement, negative reinforcement, and punishment.

Now that you know the basic concepts of operant conditioning, several additional points will help you understand how behaviorists study operant conditioning. One of Skinner's basic beliefs was that the mechanisms of learning are the same for all species. This belief led him to an extensive study of animals in the hope that the basic mechanisms of learning could be understood with organisms more simple than humans.

For example, during World War II, Skinner constructed a rather strange project—a pigeon-guided missile. A pigeon in the warhead of a missile operated the flaps on the missile and guided it home by pecking at an image of a target. How could this possibly work? When the missile was in flight, the pigeon pecked the moving image on a screen. This produced corrective signals to keep the missile on its course. The pigeons did their job well in trial runs, but top Navy officials could not accept pigeons piloting their missiles in a war. Skinner, however, congratulated himself on the degree of control he was able to exercise over the pigeons (see figure 5.10).

Following the pigeon experiment, Skinner (1948) wrote *Walden Two,* a novel in which he presented his ideas about building a scientifically managed society. Skinner envisioned a utopian society that could be engineered through behavioral control. Skinner viewed existing societies as poorly managed because people believe in such myths as free will. He pointed out that humans are no more free than pigeons; denying that our behavior is controlled by environmental forces is to ignore science and reality, he argued. In the long run, Skinner

believed we would be much happier when we recognized such truths, especially his concept that we could live a prosperous life under the control of positive reinforcement.

Skinner and other behaviorists have made every effort to study organisms under precisely controlled conditions so that the connection between the operant and the specific consequences could be examined in minute detail. One of the ways in which Skinner achieved such control was his development in the 1930s of the Skinner box (see figure 5.11). A device in the box delivered food pellets into a tray at random. After a rat became accustomed to the box, Skinner installed a lever and observed the rat's behavior. As the hungry rat explored the box, it occasionally pressed the lever and a food pellet was dispensed. Soon after, the rat learned that the consequences of pressing the lever were positive—it would be fed. Further control was achieved by soundproofing the box to ensure that the experimenter was the only influence on the organism. In many experiments, the responses were mechanically recorded by a cumulative recorder, and the food (the stimulus) was dispensed automatically. Such precautions were designed to avoid human error.

Some Principles of Operant Conditioning

As Skinner searched for a more precise analysis of behavior and its controlling conditions, he developed a number of concepts. Among the questions to which he sought answers were these: When is the most efficient time for consequences to be experi-

FIGURE 5.11

Operant conditioning in a behavioral laboratory. Shown here is a rat being conditioned in a Skinner box. Notice the elaborate machinery used to deliver food pellets as reinforcers and to keep track of the rat's behavior.

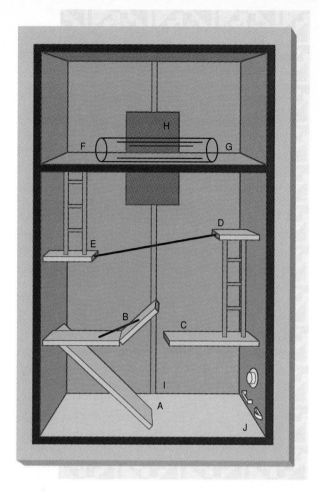

FIGURE 5.12

An example of chaining. Starting at A, the rat climbs the ramp to B, crosses the drawbridge to C, climbs the ladder to D, crosses the tightrope to E, climbs the ladder to F, crawls through the tunnel to G, enters the elevator at H, descends to I, presses the lever at J, and then receives food.

enced? How can you shorten the learning process if it takes a long time for a behavior to occur before it can be rewarded? Are there distinctions between reinforcements that acquire their value through experience and those that are biologically based? How does operant conditioning proceed when we are not reinforced every time we make a response? How can behavior be eliminated, generalized, and discriminated? We will explore each of these questions in turn.

Time Interval

As with classical conditioning, learning is more efficient in operant conditioning when the interval is more likely on the order of seconds rather than minutes or hours. An especially important distinction to remember is that learning is more efficient under *immediate* rather than delayed consequences.

Shaping and Chaining

When a behavior takes time to occur, the learning process in operant conditioning may be shortened if an *approximation* of the desired behavior is rewarded. **Shaping** *is the process of rewarding approximations of desired behavior.* In one situation, parents used shaping to toilet train their 2-year-old son. The parents knew all too well that the child's grunting sound signaled he was about to fill his diaper. In the first week, they gave him candy if the boy

made the sound within 20 feet of the bathroom. The second week he was given candy only if he grunted within 10 feet of the bathroom, the third week only if he was in the bathroom, and the fourth week he had to use the toilet to get the candy. It worked (Fischer & Gochros, 1975).

Chaining *is an operant conditioning technique used to teach a complex sequence, or chain, of behaviors. The procedure begins by shaping the final response in the sequence, then working backward until a chain of behaviors is learned.* For example, after the final response is learned, the next-to-last response is reinforced, and so on. Both shaping and chaining are used extensively by animal trainers to teach complex or unusual sequences of behavior. A dolphin who does three back flips, throws a ball through a hoop, places a hat on its head, and finally applauds itself has been trained through a combination of shaping and chaining. Figure 5.12 shows a sequence of behaviors a rat learned through the process of chaining.

Primary and Secondary Reinforcement

Positive reinforcement can be classified as primary reinforcement or secondary reinforcement, which focuses on a distinction between inborn (unlearned) and learned aspects of behavior. **Primary reinforcement** *involves the use of reinforcers that are innately satisfying; that is, they do not take any learning on an organism's part to make them pleasurable.* Food, water, and sexual satisfaction are primary reinforcers.

Secondary reinforcement *acquires its positive value through experience; secondary reinforcers are learned, or conditional, reinforcers.* Hundreds of secondary reinforcers characterize our lives. For example, secondary reinforcers include such social situations as getting praise and making eye contact. One popular story in psychology focuses on the use of eye contact as a secondary reinforcer to shape the behavior of a famous university professor, an expert on operant conditioning. Some students decided to train the professor to lecture from one corner of the classroom. They used eye contact as a reinforcer and began reinforcing successive approximations of the desired response. Each time the professor moved toward the appropriate corner, the students looked at him. If he moved in another direction, they looked away. By gradually rewarding successive approximations to the desired response, the students were able to get the professor to deliver his lecture from one corner of the classroom. The well-known operant conditioning expert denies that this shaping ever took place. Whether it did or not, the story provides an excellent example of how secondary reinforcers can be used to shape behavior in real-life circumstances (Chance, 1979).

Another example may also help you understand the importance of secondary reinforcement in our everyday lives. When a student is given $25 for an A on her report card, the $25 is a secondary reinforcer. It is not innate, and it increases the likelihood the student will work to get another A in the future. Money is often referred to as a *token reinforcer.* When an object can be exchanged for another reinforcer, the object may have reinforcing value itself, so it is called a token reinforcer. Gift certificates and poker chips are token reinforcers.

Schedules of Reinforcement

In most of life's experiences, we are not reinforced every time we make a response. A golfer does not win every tournament she enters; a chess whiz does not win every match he plays; a student is not patted on the back each time she solves a problem. **Partial reinforcement** *(intermittent reinforcement) simply means that responses are not reinforced each time they occur.* **Schedules of reinforcement** *are timetables that determine when a response will be reinforced.* Four schedules of reinforcement are fixed-ratio, variable-ratio, fixed-interval, and variable-interval.

A **fixed-ratio schedule** *reinforces a behavior after a set number of responses.* For example, if you are playing the slot machines in Atlantic City and they are on a fixed-ratio schedule, you might get $5 back every 20 times you put money in the

machine. It wouldn't take long to figure out that, if you watched someone else play the machine 18 or 19 times, not get any money back, and then walk away, you should step up, insert your coin, and collect $5.

Consequently, slot machines are on a **variable-ratio schedule,** *a timetable in which responses are rewarded an average number of times, but on an unpredictable basis.* For example, a slot machine might pay off every twentieth time, but, unlike the fixed-ratio schedule, the gambler does not know when this payoff will be. The slot machine might pay off twice in a row and then not again until after 58 coins have been inserted, which averages out to a reward for every 20 responses, but when the reward is given is unpredictable.

The remaining two reinforcement schedules are determined by *time elapsed* since the last behavior was rewarded. A **fixed-interval schedule** *reinforces the first appropriate response after a fixed amount of time has elapsed.* For example, you might get a reward the first time you put money in a slot machine after every 10-minute period has elapsed. A **variable-interval schedule** *reinforces a response after a variable amount of time has elapsed.* On this schedule, the slot machines might reward you after 10 minutes, then after 2 minutes, then after 18 minutes, and so forth.

Which of these schedules is the most effective? The closer a schedule is to continuous reinforcement, the faster an individual learns. However, once behavior is learned, the intermittent schedules can be effective in maintaining behavior. As shown in figure 5.13, the rate of behavior varies from one schedule to the next (Skinner, 1961). The fixed-ratio schedule produces a high rate of behavior, with a pause occurring between the reinforcer and the behavior. This type of schedule is used widely in our lives. For example, if an individual is paid $100 for every 10 lawns he mows, then he is on a fixed-ratio schedule. The variable-ratio schedule also elicits a high rate of behavior, and the pause after the reinforcement is eliminated. This schedule usually elicits the highest response rate of all four schedules.

The interval schedules produce behavior at a lower rate than the ratio schedules. The fixed-interval schedule stimulates a low rate of behavior at the start of an interval and a somewhat faster rate toward the end. This happens because the organism apparently recognizes that the behavior early in the interval will not be rewarded but that later behavior will be rewarded. A scallop-shaped curve characterizes the behavior pattern of an organism on a fixed-interval schedule. The variable-interval schedule produces a slow, consistent rate of behavior.

Extinction, Generalization, and Discrimination

Remember from our discussion of classical conditioning that extinction is the weakening of the CS's tendency to elicit the CR by unreinforced presentations of the CS. **Extinction** *in operant conditioning is a decrease in the tendency to perform the response.* Spontaneous recovery also characterizes the operant form of extinction. For example, a factory worker gets a monthly bonus

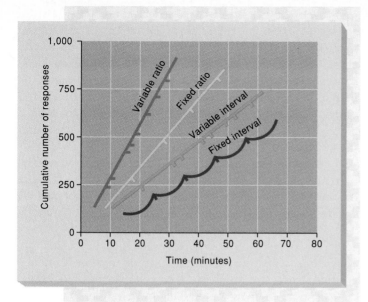

FIGURE 5.13

Performance curves produced by four schedules of reinforcement. The steeper the slope of the curve, the faster the response. Each pause indicated by a hash mark indicates the point at which reinforcement was given. Notice that the fixed interval schedule reveals a scalloped effect rather than a straight line because the organism stops responding for a while after each reinforcement but quickly responds as the next reinforcement approaches.

Adapted from "Teaching Machines" by B. F. Skinner. Copyright © 1961 by Scientific American, Inc. All rights reserved.

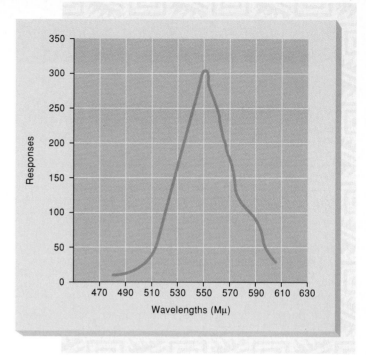

FIGURE 5.14

Stimulus generalization. In the experiment by Guttman and Kalish (1956), pigeons initially pecked a disc of a particular color (in this graph, a color with a wavelength of 550 Mμ) after they had been reinforced for this wavelength. Subsequently, when the pigeons were presented discs of colors with varying wavelengths, they were more likely to peck discs that were similar to the original disc.

Source: N. Guttman and H. I. Kalish, "Discriminability and Stimulus Generalization," *Journal of Experimental Psychology* 51:81. Copyright © 1956 American Psychological Association.

for producing more than her quota. Then, as a part of economic tightening, the company decides it can no longer afford the bonuses. When bonuses were given, the worker's productivity was above quota every month; once the bonuses were stopped, performance decreased.

In classical conditioning, generalization is the tendency of a stimulus similar to the conditioned stimulus to produce a response similar to the conditioned response. **Generalization** *in operant conditioning means giving the same response to similar stimuli.* For example, in one study, pigeons were reinforced for pecking at a disc of a particular color (Guttman & Kalish, 1956). Stimulus generalization was tested by presenting the pigeons with discs of varying colors. As shown in figure 5.14, the pigeons were most likely to peck at the disc closest in color to the original. An example of stimulus generalization in everyday life that is familiar to many parents involves an infant learning to say "doggie" to a hairy, four-legged creature with floppy ears and a friendly bark (Martin & Pear, 1988). Later the infant sees a different kind of dog and says, "doggie." This is an example of stimulus generalization because a previously reinforced response ("doggie") appeared in the presence of a new stimulus (a new kind of dog). Later the infant sees a horse and says, "doggie." This

is another example of stimulus generalization, even though the infant's labeling is incorrect, which indicates that not all instances of stimulus generalization are favorable and illustrates why discriminations need to be taught.

In classical conditioning, discrimination is the process of learning to respond to certain stimuli and not to others. **Discrimination** *in operant conditioning is the process of responding in the presence of another stimulus that is not reinforced.* For example, you might look at two street signs, both made of metal, both the same color, and both with words on them. However, one sign says "Enter at your own risk" and the other reads "Please walk this way." The words serve as discriminative stimuli because the sign that says "Please walk this way" indicates that you will be rewarded for doing so, whereas the sign that says "Enter at your own risk" suggests that the consequences may not be positive. **Discriminative stimuli** *signal that a response will be reinforced.* Discrimination is one of the techniques used to teach animals to perform tricks. When Kent Burgess (1968) wanted to teach a killer whale tricks, he used a whistle as the discriminative stimulus (S^D). Whenever the whistle sounded, the killer whale

FIGURE 5.15

Teaching behavior to a killer whale. When spouting water was followed by a whistle, it reinforced spouting and provided the signal for approaching the feeding platform to receive the reinforcing stimulus (S^R) of food (Chance, 1979).

got fed. Burgess blew the whistle immediately after a correct response and the killer whale approached the feeding platform, where it was fed. Using this tactic, Burgess taught the killer whale to spout water, leap in the air, and so on (see figure 5.15).

Applications of Operant Conditioning

A preschool child repeatedly throws his glasses and breaks them. A high school student and her parents have intense arguments. A college student is deeply depressed. An elderly woman is incontinent. Operant conditioning procedures have helped such people adapt more successfully to their environment and cope more effectively with their problems.

Behavior modification *is the application of operant conditioning principles to changing human behavior; its main goal is to replace unacceptable responses with acceptable, adaptive ones.* Consequences for behavior are established to ensure that acceptable actions are reinforced and unacceptable ones are not. Advocates of behavior modification believe that many emotional and behavioral problems are caused by inadequate (or inappropriate) response consequences. A child who throws down his glasses and breaks them may be receiving too much attention from his teacher and peers for his behavior; they unwittingly reinforce an unacceptable behavior. In this instance, the parents and teachers would be instructed to divert their attention from the destructive behavior and transfer it to a more constructive behavior, such as working quietly or playing cooperatively with peers (Harris, Wolf, & Baer, 1964).

Consider another circumstance in which behavior modification can help people solve problems. Barbara and her parents were on a collision course. Things got so bad that her parents decided to see a clinical psychologist. The psychologist, who had a behavioral orientation, talked with each family member, trying to get them to pinpoint the problem. The psychologist convinced the family to sign a behavioral contract that spelled out what everyone needed to do to reduce the conflict. Barbara agreed to (1) be home before 11 P.M. on weeknights, (2) look for a parttime job so she could begin to pay for some of her activities, and (3) refrain from calling her parents insulting names. Her parents agreed to (1) talk to Barbara in a low tone of voice rather than yell if they were angry; (2) refrain from criticizing teenagers, especially Barbara's friends; and (3) give Barbara a small sum of money each week for gas, makeup, and socializing, but only until she found a job.

Also consider Sam, a 19-year-old college student, who has been deeply depressed lately. His girlfriend broke off their relationship of 2 years, and his grades have been dropping. He decides to go to a psychologist who has a behavioral orientation. The psychologist enrolls him in the Coping with Depression course developed by Peter Lewinsohn and his colleagues (1987). Sam learns to monitor his daily moods and increase his ratio of positive to negative life events. The psychologist trains Sam to develop more efficient coping skills and gets Sam to agree to a behavioral contract, just as the psychologist did with Barbara and her parents.

Mary is an elderly woman who lives in a nursing home. In recent months, she has become incontinent and is increasingly dependent on the staff for help with her daily activities. The behavioral treatment designed for Mary's problem involves teaching her to monitor her behavior and schedule going to the toilet. She is also required to do pelvic exercises. The program for decreasing Mary's dependence requires that the nursing home staff attend more to her independent behavior when it occurs and remove attention from dependent behavior whenever possible. Such strategies with the elderly have been effective in reducing problems with incontinence and dependence (Burgio & Burgio, 1986).

Behavior modification is also used to teach couples to communicate more effectively, to encourage fathers to engage in more competent caregiving with their infants, to train autistic children's interpersonal skills, to help individuals lose weight, and to reduce individuals' fear of social situations (Craighead & Blum, 1989; Heimberg, 1989).

Another effective use of behavior modification is to improve a person's self-control. Chances are each of us could stand to change something about our lives. What would you like to change? What would you like to be able to control more effectively in your life? To answer these questions, you first have to specify your problem in a concrete way. This is easy for Bob—he wants to lose 30 pounds. Stated even more precisely, he wants to consume about 1,000 fewer calories per day than he uses to give him a weight loss of about 2 pounds per week. Some problems are more difficult to specify, such as "wasting time," "having a bad attitude toward school," "having a poor relationship with _____," or "being too nervous and worrying a lot." These types of problems have been called "fuzzies" because of their vague, abstract nature (Mager, 1972). It is important to "unfuzzify" these abstract problems and make

a.

b.

c.

d.

Behavioral strategies for improving self-control have been effectively applied to college students' (a) smoking, (b) eating, (c) studying, and (d) relationships. For ways to tailor a self-control program to your specific needs, you might want to contact the counseling center at your college or university.

them more specific and concrete. You can make your problems more precise by writing out your goal and by listing the things that would give you clear evidence you have reached your goal.

A second important step in a self-control program is to make a *commitment* to change (Martin & Pear, 1988). Both a commitment to change and a knowledge of change techniques have been shown to help college students become more effective self-managers of their smoking, eating, studying, and relationship problems. Building a commitment to change requires you to do things that increase the likelihood you will stick to your project. First, tell others about your commitment to change—they will remind you to stick to your program. Second, rearrange your environment to provide frequent reminders of your goal, making sure the reminders are associated with the positive benefits of reaching your goal. Third, put a lot of time and energy into planning your project. Make a list of statements about your projects, such as "I've put a lot of time into this project; I certainly am not going to waste all of this effort now." Fourth, because you will invariably face temptations to backslide or quit your project, plan ahead for ways you can deal with temptation, tailoring these plans to your specific problem.

A third major step in developing a self-control program is to collect data about your behavior. This is especially important in decreasing such excessive behaviors as overeating and frequent smoking. One of the reasons for tracking your behavior is that it provides a reference point for evaluating your progress. When recording the frequency of a problem during initial observations, you should examine the immediate consequences that could be maintaining the problem (Martin & Pear, 1988). Consider Bob's situation. When first asked why he eats so much, Bob said, "Because I like the taste, and eating makes me feel comfortable." However, when Bob began evaluating the circumstances in which he usually snacks, he noticed that, most of the time, when he eats, his behavior is reinforced:

a candy bar and then he meets his girlfriend; potato chips and then his favorite basketball star scores another basket; a beer and then his fraternity brothers laugh at his jokes. Bob eats while getting ready to meet his girlfriend, while watching television, while socializing with his fraternity brothers, and in many other social situations, during which he comes into contact with a variety of reinforcing events in the environment. No wonder Bob has trouble with his weight.

A fourth important step in improving your self-control is to design a program. There are many strategies you can follow. Virtually every self-control program incorporates self-instruction or self-talk (Meichenbaum, 1986). Consider the self-instruction program followed by a Canadian psychologist to improve his running (Martin & Pear, 1988). During the winter, he started an exercise program that consisted of running 2 miles (14 laps) at a university's indoor track. He often found that, after 9 or 10 laps, fatiguing thoughts set in and he talked himself out of completing the last few laps, saying, "I've done pretty well today by running 9 laps." He decided to start a self-reinforcement program to increase his antifatigue thoughts in the last few laps of his running regimen. Specifically, during the tenth to fourteenth laps, he came up with an antifatigue thought and followed it with a pleasurable one. The antifatigue thought he chose was a TV commercial for fitness that claimed that the average 60-year-old Swede is in the same physical condition as the average 30-year-old Canadian (the claim is actually false, but this is not important to this example). Each time the psychologist got to a certain place on the track, he thought about a healthy Swede jogging smoothly along the track. At the next turn, he thought about something enjoyable, such as going to the beach or a party where others complimented him on his healthy appearance. After practicing this sequence of thoughts for about 2 weeks as he ran, he was able to eliminate his fatiguing thoughts and complete his 2-mile runs.

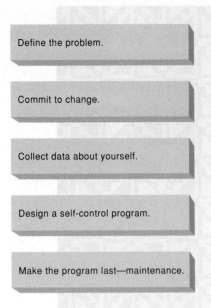

Define the problem.

Commit to change.

Collect data about yourself.

Design a self-control program.

Make the program last—maintenance.

FIGURE 5.16

Five important steps in developing a program of self-control.

A fifth important step in improving your self-control is to make it last. One strategy is to establish specific dates for post-checks and to plan a course of action if your post-checks are not favorable. For instance, if your self-control program involves weight reduction, you might want to weigh yourself once a week. If your weight increases to a certain level, then you immediately go back on your self-control program. Another strategy is to establish a buddy system by finding a friend or someone with a similar problem. The two of you set mutual maintenance goals. Once a month, get together and check each other's behavior. If your goals have been maintained, get together and celebrate. Figure 5.16 summarizes the main steps in the self-control program just described.

For other ideas on how to establish an effective self-control program tailored to your specific needs, you might want to contact the counseling center at your college or university. A good book on behavior modification or self-control also can be helpful: one is described in the suggested readings at the end of the chapter (Martin & Pear, 1988); another is by Brian Yates (1985).

Observational Learning

Would it make sense to teach a 15-year-old boy how to drive by either classical conditioning or operant conditioning procedures? Driving a car is a voluntary behavior, so classical conditioning doesn't really apply. In terms of operant conditioning, we would ask him to drive down the road and then reward his positive behaviors. Not many of us would want to be

on the road, though, when some of his disastrous mistakes occur. Albert Bandura (1971, 1986, 1989) believes that, if we were to learn only in such a trial-and-error fashion, it would be exceedingly tedious and at times hazardous. Instead, many of our complex behaviors are the result of exposure to competent

FIGURE 5.17

Bandura's experiment on imitation and aggression. In the top frame, an adult model aggressively attacks a Bobo doll. In the bottom frame, the preschool-aged girl who has observed the adult model's aggressive actions follows suit.

models who display appropriate behavior in solving problems and coping with their world. **Observational learning**, *also called imitation or modeling, is learning that occurs when a person observes and imitates someone's behavior.* The capacity to learn behavior patterns by observation eliminates tedious trial-and-error learning. In many instances, observational learning takes less time than operant conditioning.

The following experiment by Bandura (1965) illustrates how observational learning can occur by watching a model who is neither reinforced nor punished. The only requirement for learning is that the individual be connected in time and space with the model. The experiment also illustrates an important distinction between learning and performance.

An equal number of boys and girls of nursery school age watched one of three films in which someone beat up an adult-sized plastic toy called a Bobo doll (see figure 5.17). In the first film, the aggressor was rewarded with candy, soft drinks, and praise for aggressive behavior; in the second film, the aggressor was criticized and spanked for the aggressive behavior; and in the third film, there were no consequences to the aggressor for the behavior. Subsequently each child was left alone in a room filled with toys, including a Bobo doll. The child's

behavior was observed through a one-way mirror. As shown in figure 5.18, children who watched the film in which the aggressive behavior was reinforced or went unpunished imitated the behavior more than the children who saw aggressive behavior punished. As might be expected, boys were more aggressive than girls. The important point about these results is that observational learning occurred just as extensively when modeled aggressive behavior was not reinforced as when it was reinforced.

A second important point focuses on the distinction between *learning* and *performance*. Just because an organism does not perform a response does not mean that it did not learn the response. In Bandura's study, when children were rewarded (in the form of stickers or fruit juice) for imitating the model, differences in the imitative behavior among the children in the three conditions were eliminated. In this experiment, all of the children learned about the model's behavior, but some children did not perform the behavior until reinforcement was presented. Bandura believes that, when an individual observes behavior but makes no observable response, the individual still may have acquired the modeled response in cognitive form.

Since his early experiments, Bandura (1986, 1989) has focused on some of the processes that influence an observer's behavior following exposure to a model. One of these is attention. Before a person can reproduce a model's actions, she must attend to what the model is doing or saying. You may not hear what a friend says if the stereo is blaring or you might miss the teacher's analysis of a problem if you are admiring someone sitting in the next row. Attention to the model is influenced by a host of characteristics. For example, warm, powerful, atypical people command more attention than do cold, weak, typical people.

Retention is considered next. To reproduce a model's actions, you must code the information and keep it in memory so that it can be retrieved. A simple verbal description or a vivid image of what the model did assists retention. Memory is such an important cognitive process that most of the next chapter is devoted to it.

Another process involved in observational learning is motor reproduction. A person may attend to a model and code in memory what he has seen, but because of limitations in motor development he may not be able to reproduce the model's action. A 13-year-old may see Monica Seles hit a great two-handed backhand or Michael Jordan do a reverse two-handed dunk but be unable to reproduce the pro's actions.

A final process in Bandura's conception of observational learning involves reinforcement or incentive conditions. On many occasions, we attend to what a model says or does, retain the information in memory, and possess the motor capabilities to perform the action, but we fail to repeat the behavior because of inadequate reinforcement. This was demonstrated in Bandura's study (1965) when the children who had seen a

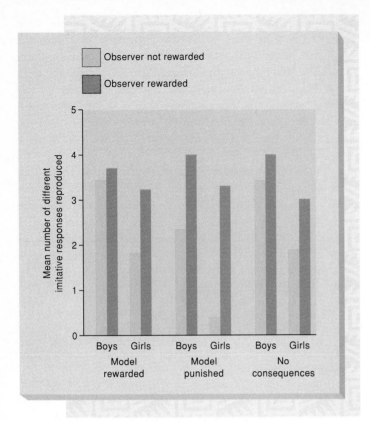

FIGURE 5.18

Results of Bandura's experiment on observational learning and aggression. Children who watched an aggressor be reinforced or experience no consequences for aggressive behavior imitated the aggressive behavior more than children who watched the aggressor be punished. Boys were more aggressive than girls. When children were offered rewards for imitating the aggressive model's behavior, even those children who had seen the model punished demonstrated they had learned the model's behavior by behaving aggressively.

model punished for aggression reproduced the model's aggression only when they were offered an incentive to do so. A summary of Bandura's model of observational learning is shown in figure 5.19.

At the beginning of this chapter, we discussed the powerful role of television in children's lives and how observational learning is the basic way people learn information from television. To find out about the types of models children observe on television and in schools, turn to Sociocultural Worlds 5.1.

Bandura views observational learning as an information-processing activity. As a person observes, information about the world is transformed into cognitive representations that serve as guides for action. As we will see next, interest in the cognitive factors of learning has increased dramatically in recent years.

Cognitive Factors in Learning

When we learn, we often cognitively represent or transform our experiences. In our excursion through learning, we have had little to say about these cognitive processes, except in our description of observational learning. In the operant conditioning view of Skinner and the classical conditioning view of Pavlov, no room is given to the possibility that cognitive factors, such as memory, thinking, planning, or expectations, might be important in the learning process. Skinnerians point out that they do not deny the existence of thinking processes, but since they cannot be observed they may interfere with the discovery of important environmental conditions that govern behavior.

Many contemporary psychologists, including behavioral revisionists who recognize that cognition should not have been ignored in classical and operant conditioning, believe that learning involves much more than stimulus-response connections. The **S-O-R model** *is a model of learning that gives some*

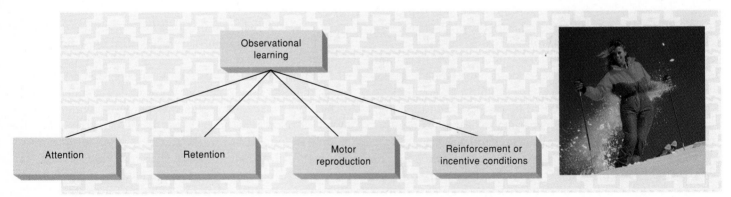

FIGURE 5.19

Bandura's model of observational learning. Bandura argues that observational learning consists of four main processes: attention, retention, motor reproduction, and reinforcement or incentive conditions. Consider a circumstance involving learning to ski. You need to attend to the instructor's words and demonstrations. You need to remember what the instructor did and her tips for avoiding disasters. You also need the motor abilities to reproduce what the instructor has shown you, and praise from the instructor after you have completed a few moves on the slopes should improve your motivation to continue skiing.

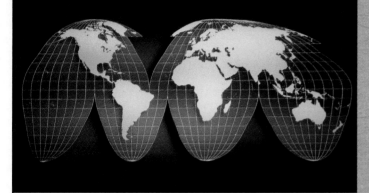

SOCIOCULTURAL WORLDS 5.1

Ethnicity, Observational Learning, Television, and Mentoring

Ethnic minorities have historically been underrepresented and misrepresented on television (Pouissant, 1972). Blacks, Asians, Hispanics, and Native Americans have been presented as less positive and less dignified than White characters (Condry, 1989). One study looked at portrayals of ethnic minorities during children's heavy viewing hours (weekdays 4–6 P.M. and 7–11 P.M.) (Williams & Condry, 1989). The percentage of White characters far exceeded the actual percentage of Whites in the United States; the percentage of Black, Asian, and Hispanic characters fell short of their true representations. Hispanic characters were especially underrepresented—only .6 percent of the characters were Hispanic, although the Hispanic population was actually 6.4 percent of the total U.S. population in 1989. When portrayed on television, ethnic minorities tended to hold lower-status jobs and were more likely than Whites to be cast as criminals or victims.

It is important for children from ethnic minority groups to be exposed to competent role models with whom they can identify and from whom they can learn, not just on television but in school and other realms of society as well. A number of educators believe that the exposure of children and adolescents to competent role models is one way to reduce the high school dropout problem. One way this is being accomplished is through *mentoring*, which occurs when an older, more experienced person helps a younger person in a one-to-one relationship that goes beyond the formal obligations of a teaching or supervisory role. Mentors, who are competent and caring, offer young people important role models. As such, mentors provide young

A special concern is that children and adolescents from ethnic minority groups be exposed to competent role models with whom they can identify and from whom they can learn. One way this is being accomplished is through mentoring.

people with a concrete image of who a younger person can become and lend guidance and support to enable the younger person to become whoever he or she chooses to be.

In the Each One/Reach One Program in Milwaukee, Wisconsin, Black professional women are recruited and trained to serve as role models. Paired with an adolescent, they spend a minimum of 10 hours a month together, visiting each other's homes and attending cultural events. The adolescent may also visit the professional at work. Because the program hopes to expose not only the girl but her whole family to an alternative lifestyle, the mother and siblings of the adolescent are included whenever possible. One study of mentoring, an adopt-a-student program in Atlanta, Georgia, paired 200 underachieving juniors and seniors with mentors from the business community, who helped students plan their futures and counseled them about achieving goals. The participating students were much more likely to be employed or to continue their education than similar students who did not take part (Anson, 1988; William T. Grant Foundation Commission, 1988).

importance to cognitive factors. S stands for stimulus, O for organism, and R for response. The O sometimes is referred to as the black box because the mental activities of the organism cannot be seen and, therefore, must be inferred.

Bandura (1986, 1989) described another model of learning that involves behavior, person, and environment. As shown in figure 5.20, behavior, personal and cognitive factors, and environmental influences interact. Behavior influences cognition and vice versa; a person's cognitive activities influence the environment; environmental experiences change the person's thought; and so on.

Let's consider how Bandura's model might work in the case of a college student's achievement behavior. As the student studies diligently and gets good grades, her behavior produces positive thoughts about her abilities. As part of her effort to make good grades, she plans and develops a number of strategies to make her studying more efficient. In these ways, her behavior has influenced her thought, and her thought has influenced her behavior. At the beginning of the semester, her college made a special effort to involve students in a study skills program. She decided to join. Her success, along with that of other students who attended the program, has led the college to expand the program next semester. In these ways, environment influenced behavior, and behavior changed the environment. The expectations of the college administrators that the study skills program would work made it possible in the first place. The program's success has spurred expectations that this type of program could work in other colleges. In these ways, cognition changed environment, and the environment changed cognition. Expectations are an important variable in Bandura's model. How might expectations be further involved in understanding learning?

Expectations and Cognitive Maps

E. C. Tolman says that, when classical and operant conditioning occur, the organism acquires certain expectations. In classical conditioning, a young boy fears a rabbit because he expects it to hurt him. In operant conditioning, a woman works hard all week because she expects to be paid on Friday.

In 1946 Tolman and his colleagues conducted a classic experiment to demonstrate the power of expectations in learning. Initially rats ran on an elevated maze (see figure 5.21a). The rats started at A and then ran across the circular table at B, through an alley at CD, then along the path to the food box at G. H represents a light that illuminated the path from F to G. This maze was replaced by one with several false runways (see figure 5.21b). The rats ran down what had been the correct path before but found that it was blocked. Which of the remaining paths would the rats choose? We might anticipate that they would choose paths 9 and 10 because those were nearest the path that led to success. Instead, the rats explored several paths, running along one for a short distance, returning to the table, then trying out another one, and so on. Eventually

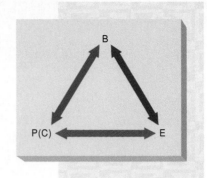

FIGURE 5.20

Bandura's model of reciprocal influences of behavior—B, personal and cognitive factors—P(C), and environment—E. The arrows reflect how relations between these factors are reciprocal rather than unidirectional. Examples of personal factors include intelligence, skills, and self-control.

From Albert Bandura, *SOCIAL FOUNDATIONS OF THOUGHT AND ACTION: A Social Cognitive Theory,* © 1986 p. 24. Adapted by permission of Prentice-Hall, Englewood Cliffs, New Jersey.

the rats ran along one path all the way to the end. This path was number 6, not 9 or 10. Path 6 ran to a point about 4 inches short of where the food box had been located previously. According to Tolman, the rats had not only learned how to run the original maze, but they also had learned to expect food on reaching a specific place.

In his paper "Cognitive Maps in Rats and Men," Tolman (1948) articulated his belief that organisms select information from the environment and construct a cognitive map of their experiences. A **cognitive map** *is an organism's mental representation of the structure of physical space.* In Tolman's maze experiment just described, the rats had developed a mental awareness of physical space and the elements in it. The rats used this cognitive map to find where the food was located. Tolman's idea of cognitive maps is alive and well today. When we move around in our environment, we develop a cognitive map of where things are located, both on small and large scales. We have a cognitive map of where rooms are located in our house or apartment, and we have a cognitive map of where we are located in the United States, for example. A popular tradition is to draw a cognitive map reflecting our perception of the city or state in which we live relative to the rest of the United States. In Texas, for example, the state of Texas is usually drawn about three-fourths the size of the entire United States. In Manhattan, "The City" is often drawn about nine-tenths the size of the United States. Of course, such cognitive maps deliberately distort the physical world, reflecting the perceivers' egocentric interest in their city or state.

Tolman was not the only psychologist who was dissatisfied with the S-R view of learning. Gestalt psychologist Wolfgang Kohler thought that the cognitive process of insight learning was also an important form of learning.

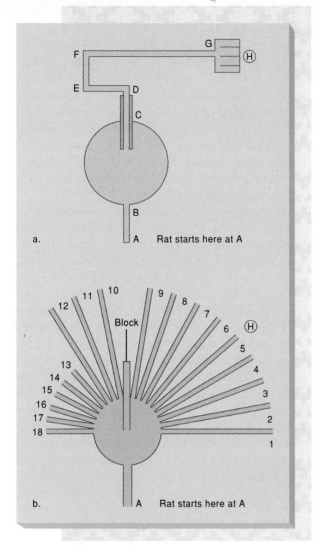

FIGURE 5.22

Kohler's box problem involving insight learning. Sultan, one of Kohler's brightest chimps, is faced with the problem of reaching a cluster of bananas overhead. Suddenly he solves the problem by stacking boxes on top of one another to reach the bananas. Kohler called this type of problem solving insight learning.

FIGURE 5.21

Tolman's experiment on expectations in learning. In Tolman's classic experiment on the role of expectations in learning, initially rats ran on this elevated maze from A through G, with H representing a light that illuminated the path from F to G. After the rats ran the maze in (a), they were placed in the maze shown in (b). What path did the rats follow in (b)? Why?

THE FAR SIDE cartoon by Gary Larson is reprinted by permission of Chronicle Features, San Francisco, CA.

Insight Learning

During World War I, Wolfgang Kohler, a German psychologist, spent 4 months in the Canary Islands, observing the behavior of apes. While there he conducted two fascinating experiments. One is called the "stick" problem, the other the "box" problem. Though these two experiments are basically the same, the solutions to the problems are different. In both situations, an ape discovers that it cannot reach an alluring piece of fruit, either because the fruit is too high or it is outside of the ape's cage and beyond its reach. To solve the stick problem, the ape has to insert

a small stick inside a larger stick to reach the fruit. To master the box problem, the ape must stack several boxes to reach the fruit (see figure 5.22).

According to Kohler (1925), solving these problems does not involve trial and error or mere connections between stimuli and responses. Rather, when the ape realizes that its customary actions are not going to get the fruit, it sits for a period of time and appears to ponder how to solve the problem. Then it quickly gets up, as if it had a sudden flash of insight, piles the boxes on top of one another, and gets the fruit. **Insight learning** *is a form of problem solving in which an organism develops a sudden insight into or understanding of a problem's solution.*

REVIEW

*Observational
Learning and
Cognitive Factors in
Learning*

Observational learning occurs when an individual observes someone else's behavior. Observational learning is also called imitation or modeling. It is important to distinguish between what is learned and whether it is performed. Bandura believes that observational learning involves attention, retention, motor reproduction, and reinforcement or incentive conditions.

Many psychologists recognize the importance of studying how cognitive factors mediate environment-behavior connections. The S-O-R model reflects this, as does Bandura's contemporary model, which emphasizes reciprocal connections between behavior, person (cognition), and environment. Tolman reinterpreted classical and operant conditioning in terms of expectations. We construct cognitive maps of our experiences that guide our behavior; psychologists still study the nature of cognitive maps. Kohler, like Tolman, was dissatisfied with the S-R view of learning. He believed that organisms reflect and suddenly gain insight into how a problem should be solved.

Biological and Cultural Factors in Learning

Albert Einstein had many talents. He combined enormous creativity with great analytic ability to develop some of this century's most important insights about the nature of matter and the universe. Genes obviously provided Einstein extraordinary intellectual skills to think and reason on a very high plane, but cultural factors also contributed to Einstein's genius. Einstein received an excellent, rigorous European education, and later in the United States he experienced the freedom and support believed to be important in creative exploration. It is unlikely that Einstein would have been able to fully develop his intellectual skills and make such brilliant insights if he had grown up in the more primitive cultures of his time or even in a Third World country today. Both biological *and* cultural factors contribute to learning.

Biological Factors

We can't breathe under water, fish can't play Ping-Pong, and cows can't solve math problems. The structure of an organism's body permits certain kinds of learning and inhibits others. For example, chimpanzees cannot learn to speak English because they lack the necessary vocal equipment. Some of us cannot solve difficult calculus problems; others of us can; and the differences do not all seem to be the result of experiences.

Some animals learn readily in one situation but have difficulty learning in slightly different circumstances. The difficulty might not result from an aspect of the learning situation but from the predisposition of the organism (Seligman, 1970). **Preparedness** *is the species-specific biological predisposition to learn in certain ways but not in others.* For example, cats can escape from a cage by pulling a string to open the door or by pushing the door, but, if they have to lick, their escape ability is greatly reduced. In most situations, humans are prepared to walk and talk.

Another example of biological influences on learning is **instinctive drift,** *the tendency of animals to revert to instinctive behavior that interferes with learning.* Consider the situation of two students of B. F. Skinner, Keller and Marion Breland (1961), who used operant conditioning to train animals to perform at fairs, at conventions, and in television commercials. They used Skinner's techniques of shaping, chaining, and discrimination to teach pigs to cart large wooden nickels to a piggy bank and deposit them. They also trained raccoons to pick up a coin and place it in a metal tray. Although the pigs, raccoons, and other animals, such as chickens, performed well at most of the tasks (raccoons became adept basketball players, for example—see figure 5.23), some of the animals began acting strangely. Instead of picking up the large wooden nickel and carrying it to the piggy bank, the pigs dropped the nickel on the ground, shoved it with their snouts, tossed it in the air, and then repeated these actions. The raccoons began to hold onto their coin rather than drop it into the metal container. When two coins were introduced, the raccoons rubbed them together in a miserly fashion. Somehow these behaviors overwhelmed the strength of the reinforcement that was given. Why were the pigs and raccoons misbehaving? The pigs were rooting, an instinct used to uncover edible roots. The raccoons engaged in an instinctive food-washing response. Their instinctive drift interfered with their learning.

Cultural Factors

In traditional views of learning, such concepts as culture and ethnicity have been given little or no attention. The behavioral orientation that dominated American psychology for much of the twentieth century focuses on the contexts of learning, but the organisms in those contexts have often been animals. When humans have been the subjects, there has been no interest in the cultural context. Esteemed psychologist Robert Guthrie (1976) once wrote a book entitled *Even the Rat Was White*—a comment on psychology's heavy reliance on animal research and the failure to consider cultural and ethnic factors in behavioral research.

How does culture influence learning? Most psychologists agree that the principles of classical conditioning, operant conditioning, and observational learning are universal

FIGURE 5.23

Instinctive drift. This raccoon's skill in using its hands made it an excellent basketball player, but, because of instinctive drift, the raccoon had a much more difficult time taking money to the bank.

and are powerful learning processes in every culture. However, culture can influence the *degree* to which these learning processes are used, and it often determines the *content* of learning. For example, punishment is a universal learning process, but, as we will see next, its use and type show considerable sociocultural variation.

When behaviorism was dominant in the United States between 1910 and 1930, childrearing experts regarded an infant as capable of being shaped into almost any child. Desirable social behavior could be achieved if the child's antisocial behaviors were always punished and never indulged and if positive behaviors were carefully conditioned and rewarded in a highly controlled and structured childrearing regime. Behaviorist John Watson (1928) authored a publication, "Psychological Care of the Infant and Child," which was the official government booklet for parents. This booklet advocated never letting children suck their thumb and, if necessary, restraining the child by tying her hands to the crib at night and painting her fingers with foul-tasting liquids. Parents were advised to let infants "cry themselves out" rather than reinforce this unacceptable behavior by picking them up to rock and soothe them.

However, from the 1930s to 1960s, a more permissive attitude prevailed and parents were advised to be concerned with the feelings and capacities of the child. Since the 1960s, there has been a continued emphasis on the role of parental love in children's socialization, but experts now advise parents to play a less permissive and more active role in shaping children's behavior. Experts stress that parents should set limits and make authoritative decisions in areas where the child is not capable of reasonable judgment. However, they should listen and adapt to the child's point of view and should explain their restrictions and discipline, but they should not discipline the child in a hostile, punitive manner.

Most childrearing experts in the United States today do not advocate the physical punishment of children, but the United States does not have a law that prohibits parents from spanking their children. In 1979 Sweden passed a law forbidding parents from using physical punishment, including spanking and slapping, when disciplining their children (Ziegert, 1983). Physical punishment of children is treated as a punishable offense, just like any other attack on a person. The law is especially designed to curb child abuse. Sweden is the only industrial country in the world to pass such a law.

The United States probably could not pass this type of law. Many Americans would view such a law as totalitarian, and the law would likely stimulate protest from civil libertarians and others. An important factor in Sweden's "antispanking" law is its attitude toward rule of law. The United States enforces laws through punishment, but Sweden takes a softer approach, encouraging respect for law through education designed to change attitudes and behavior. When people, often teachers or doctors, suspect that a parent has spanked a child, they often will report the incident because they know that the state will try to provide the parent with emotional and educational support rather than assessing a fine or sending the parent to jail. Accompanying the antispanking law was a parenting guide—*Can One Manage to Raise Children Without Spanking or Slapping?*—that was widely available at day-care centers, preschool programs, physicians' offices, and other similar locations. The publication includes advice about why physical punishment is not a good strategy for disciplining children, along with specific information about better ways to handle children's problems.

The content of learning is also influenced by culture (Cole & Cole, 1989; Cushner, 1990). We cannot learn about something we do not experience. A 4-year-old who grows up among the Bushmen of the Kalahari desert is unlikely to learn about taking baths or pouring water from one glass into another. Similarly a child growing up in Chicago is unlikely to be skilled at tracking animals or finding water-bearing roots in the desert. Learning usually requires practice, and certain behaviors are practiced much more often in some cultures than in others. In Bali many children are skilled dancers by the age of 6, whereas Norwegian children are much more likely to be good skiers and skaters by that age. Children growing up in a Mexican village famous for its pottery may work with clay day after day, whereas children in a nearby village famous for its woven rugs and sweaters rarely become experts at making clay pots (Price-Williams, Gordon, & Ramirez, 1969). More about a culture's role in learning is presented in Sociocultural Worlds 5.2, where you will read about cultural influences on the learning of mathematics.

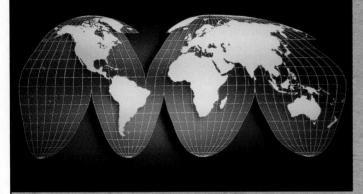

Learning Math in New Guinea, Brazil, Japan, China, and the United States

C hildren's math learning depends not only on their innate ability to handle abstractions and adult efforts to teach math concepts, but also on the adults' own knowledge about numbers, which in turn depends on culture's heritage (Cole & Cole, 1989). Children growing up among the Oksapmin of New Guinea seem to have the same ability to grasp basic number concepts as children growing up in Tokyo or Los Angeles. However, the counting system used in the Oksapmin culture—counting by body parts—does not support the more sophisticated development of algebraic thinking (Saxe, 1981). The Oksapmin use 29 body parts in their system of counting (see figure 5.A). In America it is not unusual for children to use their fingers to keep track of numbers early in their math learning, but because of American schooling they go far beyond Oksapmin children in learning math.

Although schooling often helps with learning math, in some cultures children who do not attend school learn math as part of their everyday experience. For example, whereas most Brazilian children attend school, Brazilian market children do not, yet they learn remarkable math skills in the context of everyday buying and selling. However, when presented with the same math problems in a schoollike format, they have difficulty (Carraher & Carraher, 1981). In another example, many high school students in the United States can solve certain physics problems, which they consider elementary, that baffled the brilliant Greek philosopher Aristotle in ancient times. In each of these instances, culture has shaped the course of learning.

Harold Stevenson and his colleagues compared the nature of math learning in the United States, Japan, and China. In one study, they examined the math accomplishments of 240 first-graders and 240 fifth-graders (Stevenson, Stigler, & Lee, 1986). As shown in figure 5.B, the Japanese children clearly outscored the American children on the math test in both the first and fifth grades. By the fifth grade, the highest average score of any of the American classrooms fell below the worst score of the Japanese classrooms.

Why are there such dramatic differences between American and Japanese children's math learning? Curriculum does not seem to be a factor. Neither does the educational background of the children's parents. Neither does intelligence. The American children sampled actually scored slightly higher than the Japanese children on various components of an intelligence test, such as perceptual speed, vocabulary, and general information. Did the Japanese teachers have more experience? Apparently this was not the case, since there were no differences in educational degrees and years of teaching between the Japanese and American teachers.

An important factor was the amount of time spent in school and math classes. The Japanese school year consists of 240 days of instruction and each school week is 5.5 days long. The American school year consists of 178 days of instruction and each school week is 5 days long. In the fifth grade, Japanese children are in school an average of 37.3 hours per week, American children only 30.4 hours. Observations in the children's classrooms revealed that the Japanese teachers spend far more time teaching math than do American teachers. Approximately one-fourth of total classroom time in the first grade is spent in math instruction in Japan, only about one-tenth in the United States. Observations also indicated that the Japanese children attend more efficiently to what the teacher is saying than American children do. Japanese children also spend far more time doing homework than American children—on weekends, 66 minutes versus 18 minutes.

In another study, it was found that Chinese children are assigned more homework and spend more time on homework than Japanese children, who, in turn, are assigned more homework and spend more time on homework than American children (Chen & Stevenson, 1989). Chinese children have more positive attitudes about homework than Japanese children, who in turn have more positive attitudes about homework than American children.

The conclusion is that learning requires time and practice. Cultures vary extensively in the amount of time and practice devoted to schooling and to math learning. When the amount of either time or practice is reduced, learning is impaired.

FIGURE 5.A

The counting system of the Oksapmin of New Guinea. The arithmetic counting of the Oksapmin of New Guinea is based on 29 numbers that correspond to a sequence of body parts.

FIGURE 5.B

Average mathematics achievement by Japanese and American children. Notice that Japanese children outscored American children on the math test in both the first and fifth grades.

Country	Boys	Girls
Grade 1		
Japan	20.7	19.5
United States	16.6	17.6
Grade 5		
Japan	53.0	53.5
United States	45.0	43.8

In this chapter, we have seen that learning is a pervasive aspect of life and has a great deal of adaptive significance for organisms. We have studied many forms of learning and have seen how cognitive, biological, and cultural factors influence learning. In the next chapter, we will become absorbed more deeply in the world of cognition as we explore the nature of memory.

REVIEW

Biological and Cultural Factors in Learning

Biological factors restrict what an organism can learn from experience. These constraints include physical characteristics, preparedness, and instinctive drift. Although most psychologists would agree that the principles of classical conditioning, operant conditioning, and observational learning are universal, cultural customs can influence the degree to which these learning processes are used, and culture often determines the content of learning.

Summary

I. What Is Learning?
Learning is a relatively permanent change in behavior due to experience. Psychologists have explained our many experiences with a few basic learning processes. Among the most important experiences are how we respond to the environment (classical conditioning), how we act in the environment (operant conditioning), and how we observe the environment (observational learning). Early approaches emphasized connections between environment and behavior; many contemporary approaches stress that cognitive factors mediate environment-behavior connections.

II. Classical Conditioning: Its Nature
Pavlov discovered the principle of classical conditioning, in which an organism learns the association between an unconditioned stimulus (UCS) and a conditioned stimulus (CS). The UCS automatically produces the UCR (unconditioned response). After conditioning (CS-UCS pairing), the CS alone elicits the CR (conditioned response). Generalization, discrimination, and extinction are involved in classical conditioning.

III. Classical Conditioning in Humans and Evaluation of Classical Conditioning
Classical conditioning has survival value for humans, such as when we develop a fear of hazardous conditions. Irrational fears are explained by classical conditioning. Counterconditioning is used to alleviate fears. Classical conditioning is very important in explaining the way learning in animals occurs. Although classical conditioning explains some aspects of human learning, it is not the only way we learn. Classical conditioning misses the active nature of the organism in the environment.

IV. Operant Conditioning: Its Nature
E. L. Thorndike's law of effect states that behaviors followed by a positive outcome are strengthened, whereas those followed by a negative outcome are weakened. Thorndike's theory is referred to as S-R theory. Skinner says that an organism operates in the environment to produce change that will lead to a reward. Operant conditioning is a form of learning in which the consequences of a behavior lead to changes in the probability of its occurrence.

V. Operant Processes and Comparison with Classical Conditioning
Reinforcement increases the probability a behavior will occur. In positive reinforcement, the frequency of a response increases because it is followed by a pleasant stimulus. In negative reinforcement, the frequency of a response increases because it either removes an unpleasant stimulus or allows the organism to avoid the stimulus. Punishment decreases the probability that a behavior will occur. Operant conditioning focuses on what happens after a response is made; classical conditioning emphasizes what occurs before a response is made. The key connection in classical conditioning is between two stimuli; it is between the organism's response and its consequences. Operant conditioning mainly involves voluntary behavior, classical conditioning involuntary behavior.

VI. Principles of Operant Conditioning
Operant conditioning involves the principles of time interval, shaping and chaining, primary and secondary reinforcement, schedules of reinforcement, extinction, generalization, and discrimination.

VII. Applications of Operant Conditioning
Behavior modification uses learning principles to change maladaptive or abnormal behavior. Behavior modification based on operant conditioning focuses on changing behavior and following it with reinforcement. Behavior modification is used widely to reduce maladaptive behavior.

VIII. Observational Learning
Observational learning, also called imitation or modeling, occurs when an

individual learns from someone else's behavior. An important distinction must be made between what is learned and what is performed. Bandura believes that observational learning involves attention, retention, motor reproduction, and reinforcement or incentive conditions.

IX. Cognitive Factors in Learning
Psychologists recognize the importance of studying how cognitive factors mediate environment-behavior connections. The S-O-R model reflects this cognitive interest, as does Bandura's contemporary model, which emphasizes reciprocal connections between behavior, person (cognition), and environment.

X. Some Cognitive Factors in Learning
Tolman reinterpreted classical and operant conditioning in terms of expectations. He argued that we construct cognitive maps of our experiences that guide our behavior: psychologists still study the nature of cognitive maps. Kohler, like Tolman, was dissatisfied with the S-R view of learning. He believed that organisms reflect on a problem-solving situation and then suddenly gain insight into how the problem should be solved.

XI. Biological and Cultural Factors in Learning
Biological factors restrict what an organism can learn from experience. These constraints include physical characteristics, preparedness, and instinctive drift. Although most psychologists would agree that the principles of classical conditioning, operant conditioning, and observational learning are universal, cultural customs can influence the degree to which these learning processes are used, and culture often determines the content of learning.

Key Terms

learning   124
classical conditioning   125
reflexes   125
unconditioned stimulus (UCS)   125
unconditioned response (UCR)   125
conditioned stimulus (CS)   125
conditioned response (CR)   125
generalization (classical conditioning)   126
discrimination (classical conditioning)   126
extinction (classical conditioning)   127
spontaneous recovery (classical conditioning)   127
phobias   128
counterconditioning   128

operant conditioning (instrumental conditioning)   129
law of effect   130
reinforcement (reward)   130
punishment   130
positive reinforcement   131
negative reinforcement   131
shaping   133
chaining   133
primary reinforcement   134
secondary reinforcement   134
partial reinforcement   134
schedules of reinforcement   134
fixed-ratio schedule   134

variable-ratio schedule   134
fixed-interval schedule   134
variable-interval schedule   134
extinction (operant conditioning)   134
generalization (operant conditioning)   135
discrimination (operant conditioning)   135
discriminative stimuli   135
behavior modification   136
observational learning   139
S-O-R model   140
cognitive map   142
insight learning   143
preparedness   144
instinctive drift   144

Suggested Readings

Axelrod, S., & Apsche, J. (Eds.). (1983). *The effects of punishment on human behavior.* New York: Academic Press. This is an authoritative volume on how punishment can be used effectively to control behavior. Considerable detail about reducing the negative side effects of punishment and a full consideration of the ethical issues involved in the use of punishment are included.

Bandura, A. (1986). *Social foundations of thought and action.* Englewood Cliffs, NJ: Prentice-Hall. This book presents Bandura's cognitive view of learning, including the importance of considering reciprocal connections between behavior, environment, and cognition. An extensive discussion of observational learning is included.

Martin, G., & Pear, J. (1988). *Behavior modification: What it is and how to do it* (3rd ed.). Englewood Cliffs, NJ: Prentice-Hall. This excellent overview of behavior modification is an easy-to-read book for individuals who want to know how to apply behavior modification to their everyday lives. It includes extensive information on how to improve self-control.

Skinner, B. F. (1948). *Walden two.* New York: Macmillan. Skinner once entertained the possibility of a career as a writer. In this interesting and provocative book, he outlines his ideas on how a more complete understanding of the principles of instrumental conditioning can lead to a happier life. Critics argue that his approach is far too manipulative.

CHAPTER 6

There are few moments when we are not steeped in memory. Memory can quietly stir, or spin off, with each step we take, each thought we think, each word we utter. Memory is the skein of private images that weaves the past into the present. It anchors the self in continuity. Memory is, to a large extent, what makes us unique.

Consider the unfortunate case of M. K., a high school teacher who at the age of 43 was stricken with an acute episode of encephalitis. Within hours the viral agent robbed him of most of the memories he had formed during the previous 5 years. Worse still, he was rendered incapable of forming new memories. Since his illness began, M. K. has learned a few names and a few major events, and he can get around the hospital. However, he is doomed to an existence in which every moment vanishes behind him as soon as he lives it. M. K.'s tragic circumstance conveys the emptiness of a life without memory.

In contrast, consider the wealth of images stored in the mind of the narrator in a monumental work by Marcel Proust (1928). In the first of its seven volumes, *Remembrance of Things Past*, the narrator sips a spoonful of tea in which a crumb of cake is soaked and immediately experiences a flood of memories:

> The taste was that of the little crumb of "madeleine" which on Sunday mornings at Combray . . . my Aunt Leonie used to give me. . . . Immediately the old grey house upon the street rose up like the scenery of a theatre . . . and just as the Japanese amuse themselves by filling a porcelain bowl with water and steeping in it little crumbs of paper which . . . stretch and bend, take on color and distinctive shapes, so in that moment all the flowers in our garden . . . , and the water lilies on the Vivonne and the good folk of the village and their little dwellings and the parish church and the whole of Combray and of its surroundings, taking their proper shapes and growing solid, sprang into being, town and gardens alike, from my cup of tea. (p. 65)

Proust was an invalid who rarely ventured from his bedroom, yet both he and his characters enjoyed lives filled with vivid imagery born out of his powerful ability to create and store memories, then retrieve them, either at will or when prompted by a cue from the past.

What Is Memory?

Memory *is the retention of information over time. Psychologists study how information is initially placed, or* encoded *into memory, how it is retained, or* stored, *after being encoded, and how it is found, or* retrieved, *for a certain purpose later.* Sometimes information is retained for an instant, sometimes for a life-

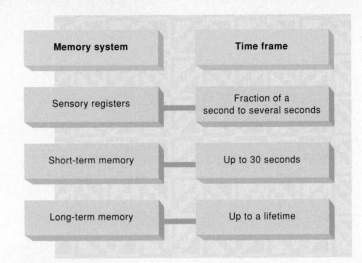

FIGURE 6.1

Memory systems.

time. Memory is involved when you look up a telephone number and dial it a few seconds later, when you recall—or fail to recall—the name of a friend from high school, and when you study for an exam. Think how barren your life would be without memory. If you had no memory, you would know nothing of what happened to you 2 seconds ago, let alone 20 minutes or 10 years ago. You would have no sense of self because you could see no connections between what is happening now and what happened in the past. Although you might have feelings, they would be meaningless without the ability to contemplate them later.

Memory is complex, consisting of not one, but several systems that operate simultaneously and interact in many ways. In this chapter, we will examine these systems, which vary in two important ways: the length of time memory lasts and the type of information remembered. After learning about various memory systems, we will turn to memory's main processes, paying special attention to how information is encoded into memory and how we retrieve it later. Then we will study the way memories are stored in the brain, the role of culture in memory, and some strategies for improving memory.

Memory Systems

Some information we remember only for a second, some for half a minute, and other information for minutes, hours, years, even a lifetime. Many psychologists believe that these three time frames involve three memory systems. Sensory registers involve time frames from a fraction of a second to several seconds, short-term memory involves time frames up to 30 seconds, and long-term memory involves time frames up to a lifetime (see figure 6.1).

FIGURE 6.2

Auditory and visual sensory registers. If you hear this bird's call while walking through the woods, your auditory sensory registers hold the information for several seconds. If you see the bird, your visual sensory registers hold the information for only about one-quarter of a second.

Type of sensory register	
Auditory	Visual
Up to several seconds	About 1/4 second

Sensory Registers

Sensory registers *are the initial part of the memory system in which information from the world is retained in its original sensory form for only an instant, not much longer than the brief time it is exposed to the visual, auditory, and other senses.* If the information is not processed further, it does not reach short-term or long-term memory.

Think about all the sights and sounds you encounter as you walk to class on a typical morning. Literally thousands of stimuli come into your fields of vision and hearing—cracks in the sidewalk, chirping birds, a noisy motorcycle, the blue sky, faces of hundreds of people. You do not process *all* of these stimuli, but you process a number of them. In general you process many more stimuli at the sensory level than you consciously notice. The sensory registers retain this information from your senses, including a large portion of what you think you ignore. However, the sensory registers do not retain the information very long. **Echoic memory** (*from the word* echo) *is the name given to the auditory sensory registers in which information is retained up to several seconds.* **Iconic memory** (*from the word* icon, *which means image*) *is the name given to the visual sensory registers, in which information is retained only for about one-quarter of a second* (see figure 6.2).

FIGURE 6.3

Sperling's sensory registers experiment. This array of stimuli is similar to those flashed for about 1/20th of a second to subjects in Sperling's experiment.

Though the workings of the sensory registers are difficult for us to detect, several common experiences reveal their existence. Consider the "What-did-you-say-Oh-never-mind" phenomenon that can occur when you are reading. You are engrossed in a book when someone walks into the room and asks you a question. You notice they are speaking, but, since your attention is focused on your book, you do not comprehend the message. You experience the *sound* but not the *sense*. Looking up, you ask, "What did you say?" Before the person can answer, though, you somehow just "know." Then you say, "Oh, never mind," and respond to the question because you now understand. The sensory features of the spoken message made it to your sensory registers, but initially they made it no further. Looking up, you switched your attention, retrieving the information from the sensory registers and sending it further for higher-level analysis (comprehension).

The "What-did-you-say-Oh-never-mind" phenomenon involves echoic memory. The first scientific research on sensory memory, however, focused on iconic memory. In George Sperling's (1960) classic study, subjects were presented with patterns of stimuli such as those in figure 6.3. As you look at the letters you have no trouble recognizing them. However, Sperling flashed the letters on a screen for only very brief intervals, about 1/20th of a second. After a pattern was flashed on the screen, the subjects could report only four or five letters. With such short exposure, reporting all nine letters was impossible.

However, some of the participants in Sperling's study reported feeling that, for an instant, they could *see* all nine letters within a briefly flashed pattern, but they ran into trouble when they tried to *name* all the letters they had initially seen. One hypothesis to explain this experience is that all nine letters were initially processed as far as the visual sensory register. This is why all nine letters were seen. However, forgetting was so rapid that the subjects could name only a handful of letters before they were lost from the register. Sperling decided to test this hypothesis. He reasoned that, if all nine letters were actually processed in the sensory register, they should all be available for a brief time. To test this possibility, Sperling sounded a low, medium, or high tone just after a pattern of letters was shown. The subjects were told that the tone was a signal to report only the letters from the bottom, middle, or top row, respectively. Under these conditions, the subjects performed much better, suggesting a brief memory for most or all of the letters.

Short-Term Memory

Short-term memory *is a limited-capacity memory system in which information is retained for as long as 30 seconds unless the information is rehearsed, in which case it can be retained longer.* Compared to sensory registers, short-term memory is more limited in capacity but is longer in duration. Its limited capacity was examined by George Miller (1956) in a classic paper with a catchy title, "The Magical Number Seven, Plus or Minus Two." Miller pointed out that on many tasks individuals are limited in how much information they can keep track of without external aids. Usually the limit is in the range of seven, plus or minus two, items. The most widely cited example of the seven, plus or minus two, phenomenon involves **memory span,** *which is the number of digits an individual can report back in order after a single presentation.* Most college students can handle lists of eight or nine digits without making any errors. Longer lists, however, pose problems because they exceed short-term memory capacity. If you rely on simple short-term memory to retain longer lists of items, you probably will make errors.

There are many examples where short-term memory seems to hold much more than five or six units. For instance, consider a simple list of words: *hot, city, book, time, forget, tomorrow,* and *smile.* Try to hold these words in memory for a moment; then write them down. If you recall all seven words, you have succeeded in holding 34 letters in your short-term memory. Does this make you a genius with outrageous short-term memory skills, or does it disprove the idea of limited capacity? The answer is neither. **Chunking** *is the grouping, or packing, of information into higher-order units that can be remembered as single units. Chunking expands short-term memory by making large amounts of information more manageable.* In demonstrating short-term memory for 34 letters, you chunked the letters into seven meaningful words. Since your short-term memory can handle seven chunks, you were successful in remembering 34 letters. Although short-term memory has limited capacity, chunking lets you make the most of it.

Maintenance rehearsal *is the conscious repetition of information that increases the length of time it stays in short-term memory* (Craik & Lockhart, 1972). To understand what is meant by maintenance rehearsal, imagine you are looking up a telephone number. If you can reach for the telephone immediately after finding out the number, you will probably have no trouble dialing the number, because the combined

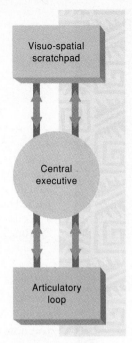

FIGURE 6.4

A model of working memory. In the model, the two slave systems—visuo-spatial scratchpad and articulatory loop—help the executive do its job. The visuo-spatial scratchpad involves our spatial imagery skills, the articulatory loop our language skills (Baddeley, 1986, 1990).

action of looking up the number and dialing it can take place in the 30-second time frame of your short-term memory. However, what if the telephone is not right by the phone book? Perhaps the phone book is in the kitchen and you want to talk privately on the extension in the den. You will probably *rehearse* the number as you walk from the kitchen to the den. Most of us experience a kind of inner voice that repeats the number until we finally dial it. If someone or something interrupts our maintenance rehearsal, we may lose the information from short-term memory.

Short-term memory without maintenance rehearsal lasts half a minute or less, but, if rehearsal is not interrupted, information can be retained indefinitely. Our rehearsal is often verbal—giving the impression of an inner voice—but it can also be visual or spatial—giving the impression of a private inner eye. One way to use your visualization skills is to maintain the appearance of an object or a scene for a time after you have viewed it. People who are unusually good at this task are said to have *eidetic imagery*, or a photographic memory. All of us can do this to a degree, but a small number of people are so good at maintaining an image that they literally "see" the page of a textbook while they are trying to remember information during a test.

Rehearsal is one important aspect, but there is much more to understanding short-term memory. Recently much of the research interest in short-term memory has focused on *what else* short-term memory can do. As the evidence mounts, it is becoming increasingly clear that short-term memory does a great deal, much more than just giving us brief memories. **Working memory** *is the concept currently used to describe short-term memory as a place for mental work. Working memory is a kind of mental workbench that allows us to manipulate and assemble information when making decisions, solving problems, and comprehending written and spoken language* (Klatzky, 1984). Although the terms *working memory* and *short-term memory* are interchangeable, working memory is now being used more often by memory researchers.

One model of working memory is shown in figure 6.4 (Baddeley, 1986, 1990, 1992; Baddeley & others, in press). In this model, working memory consists of a general "executive" and two "slave" systems that help the executive do its job. One of the slave systems is the articulatory loop, which is specialized to process language information. This is where maintenance rehearsal occurs. The other slave system is the visuo-spatial scratchpad, which underlines some of our spatial imagery skills, such as visualizing an object or a scene. We will soon see that such visualization has powerful effects when we learn new information.

To gain a better grasp of the working memory system, imagine that a friend is giving you directions to a party, telling you to head north on Central Expressway, turn right at Renner, turn left at Shiloh, and then turn left again on Leon Drive. Having nothing to write on, you might try to hold this information in memory through maintenance rehearsal. This would involve your articulatory loop. However, an additional strategy is to picture the route using your visuo-spatial scratchpad. In using this tactic, you notice that the route follows a zig-zag pattern going generally northeast until the last turn, which goes west. Although you still want to remember the sequence of street names, you no longer have to worry about the left and right turns—your memory has captured this information. The articulatory loop and the visuo-spatial scratchpad often work in concert like this to help us process information more efficiently.

Long-Term Memory

Long-term memory *is the relatively permanent memory system that holds huge amounts of information for a long period of time.* In one study, people remembered the names and faces of their high school classmates with considerable accuracy for at least 25 years (Bahrick, Bahrick, & Wittlinger, 1975). The storehouse of long-term memory is staggering. John von Neumann, a distinguished computer scientist, put its size at 2.8×10^{20} (280 quintillion) bits, which in practical terms means that our storage capacity is virtually unlimited. Von Neumann assumed we never forget anything, but, even considering that we do forget things, we can hold several billion times more information than a large computer. Even more impressive is the efficiency with which we retrieve information. It usually takes only a moment to search through this vast storehouse to find the information we want. Who discovered America? What was the name of your first date? When were you born? Who developed the first psychology laboratory? You can probably answer these questions instantly.

Long-term memory is also categorized by the two kinds of knowledge retained. One is called **declarative memory,** *the conscious recollection of information, such as specific facts or events, and, at least in humans, information that can be verbally communicated. Declarative memory is called* "knowing that." Examples of declarative memory include recounting the events of a movie you have seen and describing a basic principle of psychology to someone. The other category of long-term memory is called **procedural memory,** *which is knowledge of skills and cognitive operations, of how to do something. Procedural memory cannot be consciously recollected, at least not in the form of specific events or facts, which makes such memory difficult if not impossible to communicate verbally. Procedural memory is called* "knowing how." Examples of procedural memory include the skills of playing tennis, riding a bicycle, and typing. To further illustrate the distinction

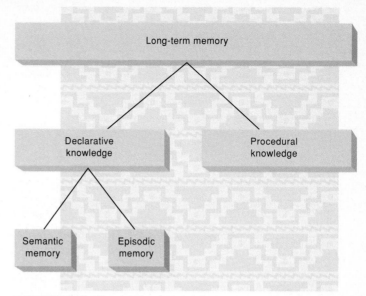

FIGURE 6.5

Declarative and procedural knowledge and semantic and episodic memory. One way of analyzing long-term memory is to divide it into declarative knowledge (or memory), which is the memory of specific facts, and procedural knowledge (or memory), which is the memory of skills and cognitive operations. Declarative knowledge can be subdivided into semantic memory, which is an individual's world knowledge, and episodic memory, which is the memory of events the individual has experienced.

between declarative and procedural memory, imagine you're at Wimbledon: Steffi Graf moves gracefully for a wide forehand, finishes her follow-through, skips quickly back to the center of the court, pushes off for a short ball, and volleys the ball for a winner. If we were to ask her about this rapid sequence of movements, she probably would have difficulty explaining each move. In contrast, if we were to ask her to name her toughest opponent, she might quickly respond, "Martina." In the first instance, she was unable to describe verbally exactly what she had done. In the second instance, she had no problem answering the question.

Declarative knowledge has been studied more extensively than procedural knowledge. Researchers propose that it is not based on a single memory system but, rather, on two separate systems. Endel Tulving (1972) has argued for a distinction between two types of declarative memory: episodic and semantic (see figure 6.5). **Episodic memory** *is a declarative memory system that involves the retention of information about the where and when of life's happenings*—what it was like when your younger brother or sister was born, what happened to you on your first date, what you were doing when you heard that Magic Johnson had tested positive for the AIDS virus, and what you had for breakfast this morning (Craik, 1989). **Semantic memory** *is a declarative memory system that describes a person's world knowledge. It includes a person's fields of expertise (knowledge of chess for a skilled chess*

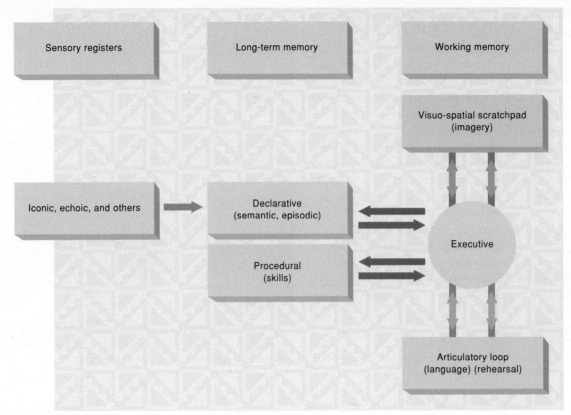

FIGURE 6.6

Interaction among sensory registers, long-term memory, and working memory. Information from the world enters the sensory registers and then activates declarative knowledge in long-term memory. Activated declarative knowledge enters short-term (working) memory (see the left-to-right arrow from long-term memory to working memory) and receives further processing by the executive and two slave systems—the articulatory loop (language) and visuo-

spatial scratchpad (imagery). This additional processing in working memory can cause changes in long-term declarative knowledge (right-to-left arrow from working memory to long-term memory). In addition, information in working memory can trigger the use of procedural knowledge, which adds more information to working memory (see the arrows between procedural and working memory).

player, for example); general academic knowledge of the sort learned in school (knowledge of geometry, for example); and everyday knowledge about meanings of words, famous individuals, important places, and common things (who Nelson Mandela and Mahatma Gandhi are, for example). The critical point about semantic memory knowledge is that it appears to be independent of the individual's personal identity with the past. You can access a fact—for example, Lima is the capital of Peru—and not have the foggiest notion of when and where you learned it.

Several examples help clarify the distinction between episodic and semantic memory. In a certain type of amnesic state, a person might forget her identity, her name, her family, her career, and all other personal information about herself, yet she can talk and demonstrate general knowledge about the world. In this case, episodic memory is impaired; semantic memory is functioning. Consider also the experience of finding yourself in a dangerous situation and having your life "flash before your eyes." What would flash before your eyes are your episodic memories—it seems doubtful you would review your knowledge of geometry or great chess moves at that point.

Interaction Among Memory Systems

The **working memory model** *is the most widely accepted explanation of how sensory registers, short-term memory, and long-term memory interact. In the working memory model, long-term memory comes before short-term memory (working memory), and short-term memory uses long-term memory in a variety of flexible ways (rehearsal, imagery, and so on)* (see figure 6.6). To get a better feel for the working memory model, consider your situation now—of reading this textbook for your introductory psychology class. Information flows into your sensory registers, activating knowledge of visual features, word sounds, and word meanings in declarative memory. Some of this activated knowledge reaches working memory, where the articulatory loop and visuo-spatial scratchpad can be brought into play to help comprehension. For example, in tackling a tough section of this book, you might find yourself proceeding very slowly through a sentence, using maintenance rehearsal (in the articulatory loop) to hold on to the first words while you take in words that follow. Alternately, when studying a book with rich spatial content (such as one on architecture or astronomy), you might visualize the meaning of the sentences you are reading using the visuo-spatial scratchpad. The comprehension you achieve through such working memory processes results in new learning, which is represented in figure 6.6 by the arrow from working memory back to the declarative portion of long-term memory.

The important role of procedural memory is also illustrated in such tasks as reading (Carpenter & Just, 1981). Activated knowledge in the working memory system can trigger small units of procedural knowledge, often called "procedures." These pro-

cedures detect information in working memory and replace it with new knowledge (see the arrows between working memory and procedural knowledge in figure 6.6). Some of these procedures apply to language rules. For example, if you had just read the words, *Susan, hit,* and *John,* and representations of these words were placed in working memory, a procedure might add the semantic knowledge that *Susan* was an agent, *hit* was an action, and *John* was an object of the action. If the words had been *Susan, was, hit, by, John,* another procedure might add that *John* was the agent and *Susan* was the object.

REVIEW

Memory Systems

Memory is the retention of information over time. Psychologists study how information is encoded into memory, how it is stored, and how it is retrieved. Memory's time frames include sensory registers, short-term memory, and long-term memory. Sensory registers retain information only for a brief time, often for only a fraction of a second; short-term memory retains information up to 30 seconds; long-term memory retains information up to a lifetime.

Sensory registers, which retain information for only a brief instant, include visual sensory registers (iconic memory) that retain information for about one-quarter of a second, and auditory sensory registers (echoic memory) that retain information for several seconds. Compared to sensory registers, short-term memory is limited in capacity but lasts a relatively longer

time, up to about 30 seconds. According to George Miller, the limitation is seven, plus or minus two, bits of information. Chunking can expand short-term memory. The contemporary view of short-term memory describes it in terms of working memory.

Long-term memory is huge in capacity and very long in duration. Long-term memory consists of declarative memory (what is consciously recollected) and procedural memory (what is not consciously remembered, at least not in the form of specific facts or events). Declarative memory (or knowledge) consists of semantic memory, which has to do with the where and when of events, and episodic memory, which is essentially world knowledge. Many of our memories include both types of information. A common example of procedural memory is our skills, such as golf or typing.

The working memory model is the most widely accepted contemporary model of memory. It emphasizes that long-term memory precedes short-term memory.

Memory Processes

Psychologists who study memory are especially interested in **memory processes,** *the encoding of new information into memory and the retrieval of information that was previously stored.*

Encoding

Encoding *is the transformation and/or transfer of information into a memory system.* Information can be encoded into sensory memory and short-term (working) memory, but here our main focus is on encoding information into long-term memory. Encoding has much in common with learning. When you are listening to a lecture, watching a movie, listening to music, or talking to a friend, you are encoding information into long-term memory. It is unlikely, though, that you are encoding all the information you receive. Psychologists are interested not only in how much encoding takes place, but also in the types of processes involved

and their operating principles. Among the processes believed to be extremely important in encoding are attention, automatic and effortful processing, depth of processing and elaboration of information, imagery, and organization, each of which we will consider in turn.

Attention

"Pay attention" is a phrase we hear all the time. What is attention? When you take an exam, you attend to it. This implies that you have the ability to focus your mental effort on certain stimuli (the test questions) while excluding other stimuli. Thus, an important aspect of attention is *selectivity.* **Selective attention** *is the focusing of attention on a narrow band of information.* Sometimes we have difficulty ignoring information that is irrelevant to our interests or goals (Posner & Rothbart, 1989; Sperling, 1989). For example, if a television set or stereo is blaring while you are studying, you may have trouble concentrating.

The more you elaborate about an event, the better your memory of the event will be. For example, if you encode information about how large the crowd is, the people with you, the songs you hear, their performers, and how much money is raised, you probably will remember a concert—such as the Kurd Aid Benefit—more vividly.

Not only is attention selective, but it also is *shiftable*. If a professor asks you to pay attention to a certain question and you do so, your behavior indicates that you can shift the focus of your mental effort from one stimulus to another. If the telephone rings while you are studying, you shift your attention from studying to the telephone. An external stimulus is not necessary to elicit an attention shift. At this moment, you can shift your attention from one topic to another virtually at will. You might think about the last time you ate at a Chinese restaurant, then think about the last time you ate at an Italian restaurant, then think about your favorite restaurant.

As we have seen, attention is concentrated and focused mental effort, a focus that is both selective and shifting. Effort plays an important role in the two ways of encoding information—automatic and effortful processing.

Automatic and Effortful Processing

Research on attention sparked an interest in the role of effort in encoding information. Encoding processes differ in how much effort they require. For example, imagine you are driving down the street and chatting with a friend. You're fine as long as the driving is easy and the conversation involves an everyday topic, such as gossip about a mutual acquaintance. However, what if the streets are icy or the conversation turns serious and you find yourself in an intense argument? Something probably has to give, either the driving or the talking. If two or more activities are somewhat difficult, it is almost impossible to perform them simultaneously without overloading the focus of attention. In explaining this potential for overload, many cognitive psychologists state that, in attention, a kind of mental energy is focused for doing mental work. They believe that the amount of this energy is limited; thus, overload occurs. This mental energy is defined as *capacity*, *cognitive resources*, or simply *effort*. Psychologists make a distinction between effortful processing and automatic processing. **Effortful processing** *requires capacity or resources to encode information in memory.* **Automatic processing** *does not require capacity, resources, or effort to encode information in memory.* Automatic processing occurs regardless of how people focus their attention (Hasher & Zacks, 1979).

Information about spatial aspects of the environment or the frequency of events can be encoded automatically. For example, "a baseball field is diamond-shaped" and "she came to

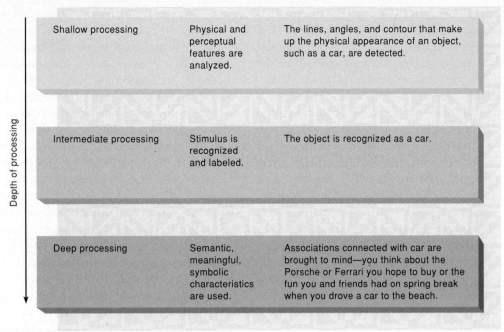

FIGURE 6.7

Levels of processing. In the levels of processing theory, memory is conceptualized as being on a continuum from shallow to deep; in this theory, deeper processing produces better memory.

the chess match twice this week" are encoded automatically. However, such activities as organization, rehearsal, visualization, and elaboration require more effort to encode. A number of studies have shown that this allocation of capacity, or effort, is related to improved memory (Ellis, Thomas, & Rodriguez, 1984; O'Brien & Myers, 1985).

Where do effortful processes take place within our memory systems? Return to figure 6.6 and take another look at the portion labeled "working memory." Effortful processing takes place mainly in working memory. Now we will consider some of the most important effortful processes—depth of processing and elaboration, mental imagery, and organization.

Depth of Processing and Elaboration

Following the discovery that maintenance rehearsal was not an efficient way to improve long-term memory, Fergus Craik and Robert Lockhart (1972) developed a new model of memory. **Levels of processing** *is Craik and Lockhart's theory that memory is on a continuum from shallow to deep; in this theory, deeper processing produces better memory.* The sensory, or physical, features of stimuli are analyzed first at a *shallow* level. This might involve detecting the lines, angles, and contours of a printed word's letters or a spoken word's frequency, duration, and loudness. At an *intermediate* level of processing, the stimulus is recognized and given a label. For example, a four-legged barking object is identified as a dog. Then, at the *deepest* level, information is processed semantically, in terms of its meaning. For example, if you see the word *boat,* at the shallow level you might notice the shapes of the

letters, at the intermediate level you might think of characteristics of the word (such as it rhymes with *coat*), and at the deepest level you might think about the kind of boat you would like to own and the last time you went fishing. Figure 6.7 depicts the levels of processing theory of memory. A number of studies have shown that people's memories improve when they make semantic associations to stimuli, as opposed to attending just to their physical aspects. In other words, you're more likely to remember something when you process information at a deep, rather than a shallow, level (Hyde & Jenkins, 1969; Parkin, 1984).

However, cognitive psychologists recognize that there is more to a good memory than depth. Within deep, semantic processing, psychologists discovered that, the more extensive the processing, the better the memory (Craik & Tulving, 1975). **Elaboration** *is the term used to describe the extensiveness of processing at any given depth in memory.* For instance, rather than memorizing the definition of *memory,* you would do better to learn the "concept" of memory by coming up with examples of how information enters your mind, how it is stored, and how you can retrieve it. Thinking of examples is a good way to understand a concept. Self-reference is another effective way to elaborate information. For example, if the word *win* is on a list of words to remember, you might think of the last time you won a bicycle race, or, to remember the word *cook*, you might imagine the last time you cooked dinner. In general, deep elaboration—elaborate processing of meaningful information—is an excellent way to remember (Schacter & McGlynn, 1989).

One reason that elaboration produces good memory is that it adds to the *distinctiveness* of the "memory codes" (Ellis, 1987). To remember a piece of information, such as a name, an experience, or a fact about geography, you need to search for the code that contains this information among the mass of codes contained in your long-term memory. The search process is easier if the memory code is somehow unique. The situation is not unlike searching for a friend at a crowded airport. If your friend is 6 feet tall and has flaming red hair, it is relatively easy to find him in a crowd. Similarly, highly distinctive memory codes can be more easily differentiated. Also, as encoding becomes more elaborate, more information is stored. As more information is stored, the more likely it is that this highly distinctive code will be easy to differentiate from other memory codes. For example, if you witness a bank robbery and observe that the getaway car is a red 1987 or 1988 Pontiac with tinted windows and spinners on the wheels, your memory of the car is more distinctive than that of the person who notices only that the getaway car is red.

Imagery

How many windows are in your apartment or house? If you live in a dorm room with only one or two windows, this question may be too easy. If so, how many windows are in your parents' apartment or house? Few of us have ever memorized this information, but many of us believe we can come up with a good answer, especially if we use imagery to "reconstruct" each room. We take a mental walk through the house, counting windows as we go.

For many years, behaviorists ignored the role of imagery in memory because it was believed to be too mentalistic. However, the studies of Allan Paivio (1971, 1986) document how imagery can improve memory. Paivio argued that memory is stored in two ways: as a verbal code or as an image code. For example, a picture can be remembered by a label (verbal code) or a mental image. Paivio thought that the image code, which is highly detailed and distinctive, produces better memory. Although imagery is widely accepted as an important aspect of memory, there is controversy over whether we have separate codes for words and images (Pylyshyn, 1973). More about imagery appears later in the chapter, when we will discuss strategies for improving memory. For now, just keep in mind that, if you need to remember a list of things, forming mental images will help you.

Organization

Recall the 12 months of the year as quickly as you can. How long did it take you? What was the order of your recall? The answers to these questions probably are "4 to 6 seconds" and "chronological order" (January, February, March, etc.). Now try to remember the months in alphabetical order. Did you make any errors? How long did it take you? There is a clear distinction between recalling the months naturally and alphabetically. This demonstration makes it easy to see that your memory for the months of the year is organized. Indeed, one of memory's most distinctive features is its organization.

An important feature of memory's organization is that sometimes it is hierarchical. A *hierarchy* is a system in which items are organized from general classes to more specific classes. An example of a hierarchy for the general category of minerals is shown in figure 6.8. In an experiment using conceptual hierarchies of words, such as those in figure 6.8, Gordon Bower and his colleagues (1969) showed the importance of organization in memory. Subjects who were presented the words in hierarchies remembered the words much better than those who were given the words in random groupings. Other investigations have revealed that, if people are simply encouraged to organize material, their memory of the material improves, even if no warning is given that memory will be tested (Mandler, 1980).

We have seen that semantic elaboration, organization, and imagery are effective ways to encode information for long-term memory storage but that maintenance rehearsal is not. Now we will turn our attention to the ways we can retrieve information from memory storage.

REVIEW

Encoding

Encoding is the transformation and/or transfer of information into a memory system. Information can be encoded into sensory memory and short-term memory, but the main focus is on encoding information into long-term memory. Among the important aspects of encoding are attention, automatic and effortful processing, depth of processing and elaboration, imagery, and organization.

Attention is the ability to focus on certain stimuli. Attention is both selective (the ability to focus and concentrate on a narrow band of information) and shifting. Automatic processes do not require capacity or resources; conversely, effortful processes require capacity or resources. Effortful processing includes depth of processing and elaboration, imagery, and organization. Craik and Lockhart developed the levels of processing view of memory, which stresses that memory is on a continuum from shallow to deep. In this view, deeper processing produces better memory. Elaboration refers to the extensiveness of processing at any depth and it leads to improved memory, making encoding more distinctive. Imagery involves sensations without an external stimulus present. Paivio argued that we have two separate verbal and imaginal codes, but this is controversial. Imagery often improves memory. One of the most pervasive aspects of memory is organization, which involves grouping or combining items. Information is often organized hierarchically.

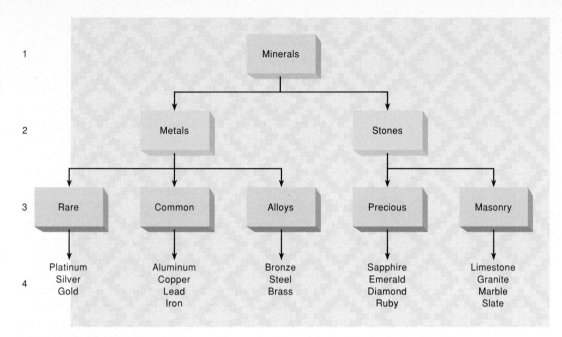

FIGURE 6.8

Example of a hierarchical organization.

FRANK & ERNEST reprinted by permission of NEA, Inc.

Retrieval and Forgetting

Have you ever forgotten where you parked your car, your mother's birthday, or the time you were supposed to meet a friend to study? Have you ever sat in class, taking an exam, unable to remember the answer to a question? Psychologists have developed a number of theories about how we retrieve information and why we forget it.

Retrieval from Long-Term Memory

To retrieve something from our mental "data bank," we search our store of memory to find the relevant information. Just as with encoding, this search can be virtually automatic or it can require effort. For example, if someone asks you what your mother's first name is, the answer immediately springs to your lips; that is, retrieval is automatic. However, if someone asks you the name of your first-grade teacher, it may take some time to dredge up the answer; that is, retrieval requires more effort. As appropriate information is found, it is pulled together to guide and direct a person's verbal and motor responses.

One glitch in retrieving information that we're all familiar with is the **tip-of-the-tongue phenomenon (TOT state).** *It is a type of effortful retrieval that occurs when people are confident they know something but just can't quite seem to pull it out of memory.* In one study on the TOT state, participants were shown photographs of famous people and asked to say their names (Yarmey, 1973). The researcher found that people tend to use two strategies to try to retrieve the name of a person they think they know. One strategy is to pinpoint the person's profession. For example, one participant in the study correctly identified a famous person as an artist but the artist's name, Picasso, remained elusive. Another retrieval strategy was to repeat letters or syllables—such as Monetti, Mona, Magett, Spaghetti, and Bogette in the attempt to identify Liza Minelli. The tip-of-the-tongue phenomenon suggests that, without good retrieval cues, information encoded in memory may be difficult to find.

Understanding how retrieval works also requires knowledge of the **serial position effect,** *which states that recall is superior for the items at the beginning and at the end of a list.* If someone gave you the directions "left on Mockingbird, right on Central, right on Stemmons, left on Balboa, and right on Parkside," you probably would remember "left on Mockingbird" and "right on Parkside" more easily than the turns and streets in the middle. The **primacy effect** *refers to superior recall for items at the beginning of a list.* The **recency effect** *refers to superior recall for items at the end of a list.* Together with the relatively low recall of items from the middle of the list, this pattern makes up the serial position effect. (See figure 6.9 for a typical serial position effect that shows a weaker primacy effect and a stronger recency effect.)

How can primacy and recency effects be explained? The first few items in the list are easily remembered because they are rehearsed more often than later items (Atkinson & Shiffrin, 1968). Short-term memory is relatively empty when the first few

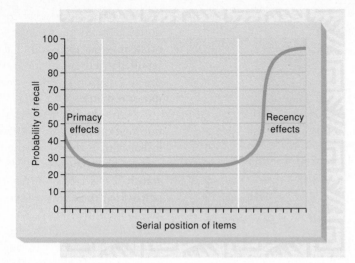

FIGURE 6.9

The serial position effect. When a person is asked to memorize a list of words, the words memorized last usually are recalled best, those at the beginning next best, and those in the middle least efficiently.

items enter, so there is little competition for rehearsal time, and, since they get more rehearsal, they stay in short-term memory longer and are more likely to be transferred to long-term memory. In contrast, many items from the middle of the list drop out of short-term memory before being transferred. The last several items are remembered for a different reason. At the time they are recalled, they are still in short-term memory.

Two other factors involved in retrieval are (1) the nature of the cues that can prompt your memory and (2) the retrieval task you set for yourself. If effective cues for what you are trying to remember do not seem to be available, you need to create them, a process that takes place in working memory. For example, if you have a "block" about remembering a new friend's name, you might go through the alphabet, generating names that begin with each letter. If you manage to stumble across the right name, you'll probably recognize it.

Although cues help, your success in retrieving information also depends on the task you set for yourself. For instance, if you're simply trying to decide if something seems familiar, retrieval is probably a snap. Let's say you see a short, dark-haired woman walking toward you. You quickly decide she's someone who lives in the next dorm; however, remembering her name or a precise detail, such as when you met her, can be harder (Brown, Deffenbacher, & Sturgill, 1977). Such findings have implications for police investigations: a witness might be certain she has previously seen a face, yet she might have a hard time deciding if it was at the scene of the crime or in a mugshot.

The two factors just discussed—the presence or absence of good cues and the retrieval task required—are involved in an important memory distinction: recall versus recognition memory. **Recall** *is a memory measure in which an individual must retrieve*

previously learned information, as on an essay test. **Recognition** *is a memory measure in which the individual only has to identify (recognize) learned items, as on multiple-choice tests.* Most college students prefer multiple-choice tests because they're easier than essay tests or fill-in-the blank tests. Recall tests, such as fill-in-the-blank tests, have poor retrieval cues. You are told to try to recall a certain class of information ("Discuss the factors that caused World War II."). In multiple-choice (recognition) tests, you merely judge whether a stimulus is familiar or not (does it match something you experienced in the past?).

You have probably heard people say they are terrible at remembering names but they "never forget a face." If you have made that claim yourself, try to *recall* a face. It's not easy. Police officers know that witnesses can be terrible at describing a suspect, so they often bring in an artist to reconstruct a suspect's face. If you think you are better at remembering faces than names, it is probably because you are better at recognition than at recall.

When faced with a recall task—a professor gives a lengthy essay exam, for example—researchers have found that a person's memory improves when retrieval cues correspond to the situation in which the information was encoded (Eich, 1989, 1990). For example, you'll probably recall information more easily when you take a test in the same room in which you heard the lecture and took notes—that is, where the information was originally encoded. The strongest evidence for this conclusion is based on a study in which scuba divers learned information both on land and under water (Godden & Baddeley, 1975). They were then asked to recall the information. The scuba divers' recall was much better when the encoding and retrieval locations were constant (both on land or both under water) (see figure 6.10). Although changing from on land to under water or vice versa adversely affects one's memory, less dramatic changes in environmental context, such as moving to a new room to take an exam, show weaker effects.

Cue-dependent forgetting *is a form of forgetting information because of failure to use effective retrieval cues.* Cue-dependent forgetting can explain why we sometimes fail to retrieve a needed fact on an exam even when we "know" that piece of information. These failures to retrieve what is stored in memory occur because we do not use the right cues. For example, you might forget the point of Sperling's experiment, described on page 153, if you are using "short-term memory" as a cue instead of "sensory registers."

Interference and Decay

The principle of cue-dependent forgetting is consistent with a previously developed view of forgetting—**interference theory,** *which states that we forget, not because memories are actually lost from storage, but because other information gets in the way of what we want to remember.* There are two kinds of interference: proactive and retroactive.

Proactive interference *occurs when material that was learned earlier disrupts the recall of material learned later.* Remember that *pro* means "forward in time." For example, suppose you had a

FIGURE 6.10

Experiment by Godden and Baddeley on encoding and retrieval cues. Divers recalled information better when encoding and retrieval locations were constant (both on land, both under water).

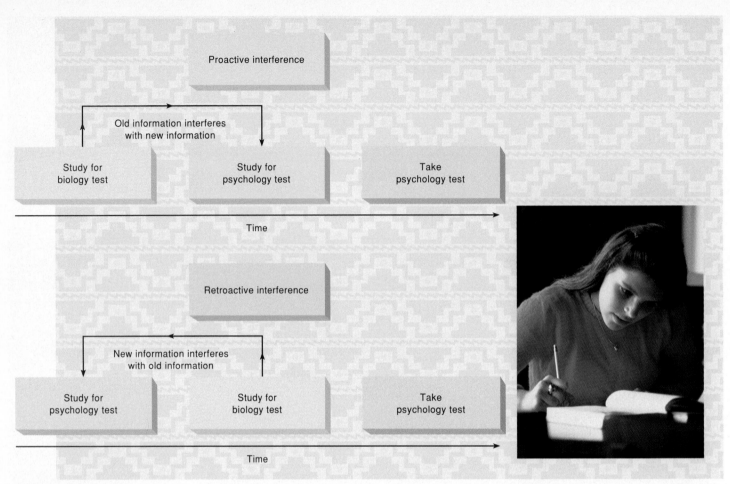

FIGURE 6.11

Proactive and retroactive interference. Pro means forward, so in proactive interference old information has a forward influence by getting in the way of new material learned. *Retro* means backward, so in retroactive interference new information has a backward influence by getting in the way of material learned earlier.

good friend 10 years ago named Mary, and last night you met someone at a party named Marie. You might find yourself calling your new friend Mary because the old information ("Mary") interferes with the retrieval of new information ("Marie"). **Retroactive interference** *occurs when material learned later disrupts retrieval of information learned earlier.* Remember that *retro* means "backward in time." Suppose you have become friends with Marie (and finally have gotten her name straight). If you find yourself sending a letter to your old friend Mary, you might address it to "Marie," because the new information ("Marie") interferes with the old information ("Mary") (see figure 6.11).

Proactive and retroactive interference *both* can be explained by cue-dependent forgetting. The reason that "Mary" interferes with "Marie" and "Marie" interferes with "Mary" might be that the cue you are using to remember does not distinguish between the two memories. For example, if the cue you are using is "my good friend," it might evoke both names. This could result in retrieving the wrong name or in a kind of

blocking in which each name interferes with the other and neither comes to mind. Memory researchers have shown that retrieval cues (such as "friend" in our example) can become overloaded; when that happens, we are likely to forget.

Although interference is involved in forgetting, it is not the whole story. **Decay theory** *states that, when something new is learned, a neurochemical "memory trace" is formed, but over time this trace tends to disintegrate.* Decay theory suggests that the passage of time always increases forgetting. However, there is one circumstance in which older memories can be stronger than more recent ones. Older memories are sometimes more resistant to shocks or physical assaults on the brain than are recent memories.

Consider the case of H. M. At the age of 10, H. M. underwent surgery to stop his epileptic seizures and emerged with his intelligence and most of his mental abilities intact, but the part of his brain that was responsible for laying down new memories was damaged beyond repair. **Amnesia** *is the loss of* *memory.* Although some types of amnesia clear up over time, H. M.'s amnesia endured. In the years following surgery, H. M.'s memory showed no improvement. The amnesia suffered by H. M. was anterograde. **Anterograde amnesia** *is a memory disorder that affects the retention of new information or events. What was learned before the onset of the condition is not affected.* For example, H. M. could identify his friends, recall their names, and even tell stories about them—but only if he had known them before surgery. Anyone H. M. met after surgery remained a virtual stranger, even if they spent thousands of hours with him. The vast majority of H. M.'s experiences were never encoded in long-term memory. Oddly enough, H. M.'s short-term memory remained unchanged, and, as indicated earlier, his overall intelligence, which was above average, remained intact.

Contrary to all logic, even though anterograde amnesiacs cannot remember new information, recent evidence illustrates that they can manage to learn new skills (Glisky & Schacter, 1987). One especially intriguing case involves a patient with

severe amnesia who acquired the necessary skills to perform a complex data entry job. Just like any normal person, with time she became more adept at her job, but it was as though each day was her first day because she could never remember having learned her job. This finding supports the distinction between declarative knowledge (for information or knowing that) and procedural knowledge (for skill or knowing how).

Amnesia also occurs in a form known as **retrograde amnesia,** *which involves memory loss for a segment of the past but not for new events.* It is much more common than anterograde amnesia and frequently occurs when the brain is assaulted by a physical blow or an electrical shock. For example, a football player might receive a head injury and suffer retrograde amnesia. The key difference between retrograde and anterograde amnesia is that, in retrograde amnesia, the forgotten information is *old* (prior to the event that caused the amnesia) and the person's ability to acquire new memories is not affected.

REVIEW

Retrieval and Forgetting

Retrieval involves getting information out of long-term memory. The search can be automatic or effortful. An interesting aspect is the tip-of-the-tongue phenomenon (TOT state), which occurs when we just can't quite pull something out of memory. The implication of TOT is that, without good retrieval cues, stored information is difficult to find. The serial position effect influences retrieval—retrieval is superior for items at the beginning of a list (primacy effect) and at the end of a list (recency effect). One key factor that makes retrieval effortful is the absence of effective cues. A second factor is the nature of the retrieval task, which, along with the presence or absence of retrieval cues, distinguishes recall from recognition memory. Failure to use

effective retrieval cues is one reason we forget, a phenomenon known as cue-dependent forgetting.

The principle of cue-dependent forgetting is consistent with a previously developed view of forgetting—interference theory, the belief that we forget, not because memories are actually lost from storage, but because other information gets in the way of what we want to remember. Proactive interference occurs when material that was learned earlier disrupts the recall of material learned later. Retroactive interference occurs when material learned later disrupts the retrieval of information learned earlier. Decay theory argues that, when something new is learned, a memory trace is formed, but as time passes this trace begins to disintegrate.

Amnesia involves extreme memory deficits. There are two forms of amnesia. Anterograde amnesia is a memory disorder that affects the retention of new information and events. Retrograde amnesia is a memory disorder that involves memory loss for a segment of the past but not for new events.

The Representation of Knowledge in Memory

Although we have talked about time frames of memory, and about the processes of encoding and retrieval, we have not yet tackled the question of how knowledge is represented in memory. Two approaches have addressed this issue: network theories and schema theories.

Network Theories

One of the first network theories claimed that our memories consist of a complex network of nodes that stand for labels or concepts (see figure 6.12). The network was assumed to be hierarchically arranged, with more concrete concepts (canary, for example) nestled under more abstract concepts (bird). More recently cognitive psychologists realized that such hierarchical networks are too neat and regular to fit the way human cognition

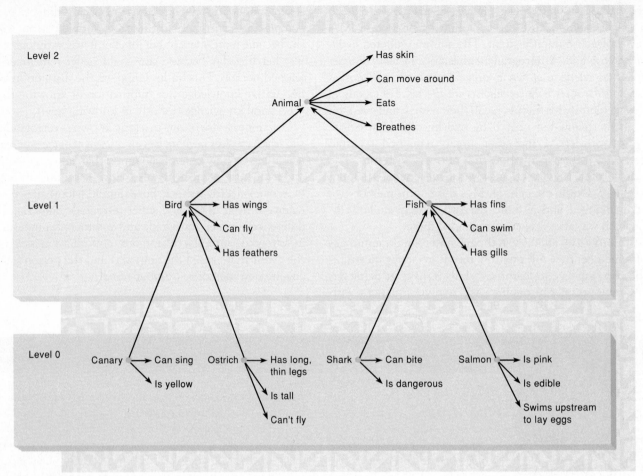

FIGURE 6.12

Hierarchical organization of memory with nodes at three levels in the hierarchy.

actually works (Shanks, 1991). For example, people take longer to answer the true-or-false statement "An ostrich is a bird" than they do the statement "A canary is a bird." Memory researchers now envision the network as more irregular and distorted: a *typical* bird, such as a canary, is closer to the node, or center, of the category "bird" than is an ostrich, an *atypical* bird. An example of the revised model is shown in figure 6.13; this model allows for the typicality of information while retaining the original notion of node and network.

We add new material to this network by placing it in the middle of the appropriate region. We gradually tie in new material—by meaningful connections—to the appropriate nodes in the surrounding network. That is why, if you cram for a test, you will not remember the information over the long term. The new material is not knit into the long-term web. In contrast, discussing the material or incorporating it into a research paper interweaves it with other knowledge you have. These multiple connections increase the probability you can retrieve the information many months or even years later.

Schema Theories

Long-term memory has been compared to a library. Your memory stores information just as a library stores books. You retrieve information in a fashion similar to the process you use to locate and check out a book. However, the process of retrieving information from long-term memory is not as precise as the library analogy suggests. When we search through our long-term memory storehouse, we don't always find *exactly* the "book" we want, or we might find the book we want but discover that only several pages are intact. We have to *reconstruct* the rest.

When we reconstruct information, we fit it into information that already exists in our mind. A **schema** *is information—concepts, events, and knowledge—that already exists in a person's mind.* Schemas from prior encounters with the environment influence the way we code, make inferences about, and retrieve information. Unlike network theories, which assume that retrieval involves specific facts, schema theory claims that long-term memory search is not very exact. We seldom find precisely

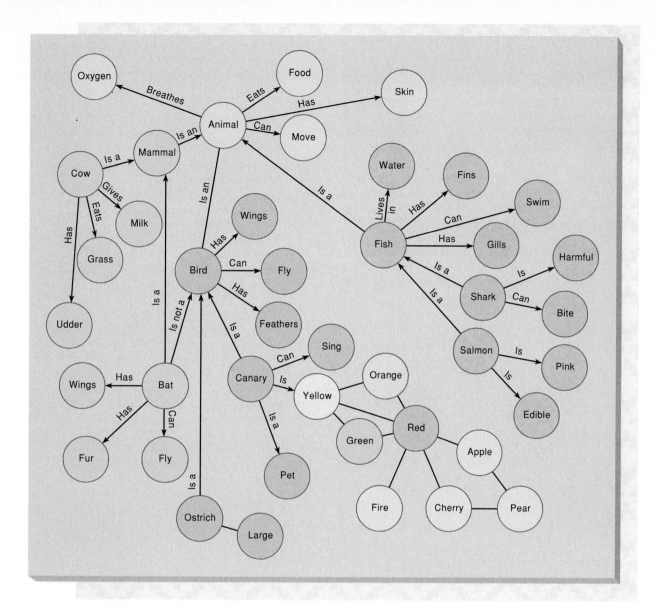

FIGURE 6.13

Revision of the hierarchical network view of how information is organized in long-term memory.

what we want, or at least not all of what we want. Hence, we have to reconstruct the rest. Our schemas support this reconstruction process, helping us fill in the gaps between our fragmented memories.

The schema theory of memory began with Sir Frederick Bartlett's (1932) studies of how people remember stories. Bartlett was concerned about how a person's background determines what he or she encodes and remembers about stories. Bartlett chose stories that sounded strange and were difficult to understand. He reasoned that a person's background, which is encoded in schemas, would reveal itself in the person's reconstruction (modification and distortion) of the story's content. For example, one of Bartlett's stories was called "War of the Ghosts," an English translation of a Native American folktale. The story contained events that were completely foreign to the experiences of the middle-class British research participants. Summarized, the story goes like this: an Indian joins a war party that turns out to consist entirely of ghosts. They go off to fight some other Indians and the main character gets hit but feels no pain. He returns to his people, describes his adventure, and goes to sleep. However, in the morning he dies as something black comes out of his mouth.

Eyewitness Testimony

At times, one person's memories can take on national importance. This was true for John Dean in the Watergate cover-up in the early 1970s. It is in the legal arena, especially, that one person's memory of events given as testimony can be crucial in determining a defendant's, or a nation's, future. Much of the interest in eyewitness testimony has focused on distortion, bias, and inaccuracy in memory (Brigham, 1989; Fisher & Quigley, 1989; Loftus, 1979; Willis & Wrightsman, 1989).

Memory fades over time. That's why the amount of time that has passed between an incident and a person's recollection of it is a critical factor in eyewitness testimony. In one study, people were able to identify pictures with 100 percent accuracy after a 2-hour time lapse. However, 4 months later they achieved an accuracy of only 57 percent; chance alone accounts for 50 percent accuracy (Shepard, 1967).

Unlike a videotape, memory can be altered by new information. In one study, students were shown a film of an automobile accident (Loftus, 1975). Some of the students were asked how fast the white sports car was going when it passed a barn. Other students were asked the same question without any mention of a barn. In fact, there was no barn in the film. However, 17 percent of the students who heard the question that included the barn mentioned it in their answer; only 3 percent of those whose question did not include the barn mentioned that they saw it. New information, then, can add or even replace existing information in memory.

Studies have shown that people of one ethnic group are less likely to recognize individual differences among people of another ethnic group. Hispanic eyewitnesses, for example, may have trouble distinguishing among several Asian suspects. This makes identifying individuals from a police lineup or photographs an unreliable tool. In one investigation, clerks in small stores were asked to identify photographs of customers who had shopped there 2 hours earlier (Brigham & others, 1982). Only 33 percent of the customers were correctly identified. In another experiment, a mugging was shown on a television news program. Immediately after, a lineup of six suspects was broadcast and viewers were asked to phone in and identify which of the six individuals they thought committed the robbery. Of the 2,000 callers, more than 1,800 identified the wrong person. In addition, even though the robber was White, one-third of the viewers identified a Black or Hispanic suspect as the criminal.

Identification of individuals from police lineups or photographs is not always reliable. People from one ethnic group often have difficulty recognizing differences among people of another ethnic group.

What interested Bartlett was how differently the participants might reconstruct this and other stories from the original versions. The British participants used both their general schemas for daily experiences and their schemas for adventurous ghost stories in particular to reconstruct "War of the Ghosts." The participants recalled familiar details from the story that "fit into" their schemas; however, the participants extensively distorted the details that departed from their schemas. For example, the "something black" that came out of the Indian's mouth became "blood" in one reconstruction and "condensed air" in another.

There has been a flurry of interest in reconstructive memory, especially in the way people recall stories, give eyewitness testimony, remember their past, and recall conversations (Cohen, 1989; Klein, Loftus, & Burton, 1989; Ross, 1989). To learn more about the nature of reconstructive memory in eyewitness testimony, turn to Sociocultural Worlds 6.1.

We have schemas not only for stories but also for scenes or spatial layouts (a beach or bathroom), as well as for common events (going to a restaurant, playing football, or writing a term paper). The term **script** *is given to a schema for an event* (Schank

Name: Restaurant

Props: Tables   Bill
         Menu   Money
         Food   Tip

Entry conditions: Customer is hungry.
                   Customer has money.

Roles: Customer   Cashier
         Waiter   Owner
         Cook

Results: Customer has less money.
           Owner has more money.
           Customer is not hungry.

Scene 1: *Entering*
           Customer enters restaurant.
           Customer looks for table.
           Customer decides where to sit.
           Customer goes to table.
           Customer sits down.

Scene 2: *Ordering*
           Customer picks up menu.
           Customer looks at menu.
           Customer decides on food.
           Customer signals waitress.
           Waitress comes to table.
           Customer orders food.
           Waitress goes to cook.
           Waitress gives food order to cook.
           Cook prepares food.

Scene 3: *Eating*
           Cook gives food to waitress.
           Waitress takes food to customer.
           Customer eats food.

Scene 4: *Exiting*
           Waitress writes bill.
           Waitress goes over to customer.
           Waitress gives bill to customer.
           Customer gives tip to waitress.
           Customer goes to cashier.
           Customer gives money to cashier.
           Customer leaves restaurant.

FIGURE 6.14

Simplified version of Schank and Abelson's script for a restaurant. Think about how your organized knowledge of these activities occurring in a restaurant influences your encoding of, inferences about, and retrieval of information.

& Abelson, 1977). An example of a restaurant script is shown in figure 6.14. Notice that this script has information about physical features, people, and typical occurrences. This kind of information is helpful when people need to figure out what is happening around them. For example, if you are enjoying your afterdinner coffee in a restaurant and a man in a tuxedo comes over and puts a piece of paper on the table, your script tells you that the man probably is a waiter who has just given you the check.

The Neurobiological Basis of Memory

Karl Lashley (1950) spent a lifetime looking for the location in the brain where memories are stored. Lashley trained rats to discover the correct pathway in a maze. He then cut out a portion of the animal's brain to impair its memory of the maze. After experimenting with thousands of rats, Lashley found that the loss of various cortical areas did not affect the rat's ability to remember the path through the maze. Lashley eventually concluded that memories are not stored in a specific location in the brain.

In the past several decades, researchers have been trying to unravel the mysteries of the biological basis of memory. As they probe the brain and monitor single neurons for clues, they ask questions such as these: Is memory highly localized? Does a specific neuron remember anything or is there a memory trace through many interconnected neurons? How do the cells and circuits of the brain change to accommodate and store the new information that we get from experience?

Many neuroscientists believe that memory is located in discrete sets or circuits of neurons. Brain researcher Larry Squire (1987, 1990), for example, says that most memories are probably clustered in groups of about 1,000 neurons. He points out that

"Why? You cross the road because it's in the script—that's why!"

Drawing by Bernard Schoenbaum;
© 1988 The New Yorker Magazine, Inc.

memory is distributed throughout the brain in the sense that no specific memory center exists. Many parts of the brain and nervous system participate in the memory of a particular event, yet memory is localized in the sense that a limited number of brain systems and pathways are involved and they probably contribute in different ways (Lynch, 1990; McGaugh, Weinberger, & Lynch, 1990).

Single neurons are at work in memory. Researchers who measure the electrical activity of single cells have found, for example, that some respond to faces, others to eye or hair color. However, for you to recognize someone, individual neurons that provide information about hair color, size, and other characteristics must act together.

Ironically, some of the answers to the complex questions about the neural mechanics of memory come from studies on a very simple experimental animal—sea slugs. Eric Kandel and James Schwartz (1982) chose this large snail-without-a-shell because of the simple architecture of its nervous system, which consists of only about 10,000 neurons. A sea slug can hardly be called a quick learner or an animal with a good memory, but it is equipped with a reliable reflex. When anything touches the gill on its back, a sea slug quickly withdraws it. First the researchers habituated the sea slug to having its gill prodded. After a while, it ignored the prod and stopped withdrawing its gill. Next the researchers applied an electric shock to its tail when they touched the gill. After many rounds of the shock-accompanied prod, the sea slug violently withdrew its gill at the slightest touch. The researchers found that the sea slug remembered this message for hours, even weeks.

More important than the discovery that sea slugs have memories was the finding that memory seems to be written in chemicals. Shocking a sea slug's gill releases the neurotransmitter serotonin at the synapses, and this chemical release basically provides a reminder that the gill was shocked. This memory informs the nerve cell to send out chemical commands to retract the gill the next time it is touched. If nature builds complexity out of simplicity, then the mechanism used by a sea slug may work in the human brain as well. Chemicals, then, may be the ink with which memories are written.

As neuroscientists increasingly reveal the cellular basis of memory, might we reach a point where the psychological study of memory becomes unimportant? That's unlikely. First, we are far from working out all the complexities of the neurochemical underpinnings of human memory. Second, even if we are successful in unraveling the neurochemical mystery, each person's private kingdom of memories will remain unique.

Cultural Factors in Memory

A culture sensitizes its members to certain objects and events in the environment, which in turn can influence the nature of memory (Harris, Schoen, & Hensley, 1992). Remember from our discussion of schema theory that Sir Frederick Bartlett believed that a person's background, which is encoded in schemas, is revealed in the way the person reconstructs a story. This effect of background on memory has been called the **culture specificity hypothesis,** *which states that cultural experiences determine what is socially relevant in a person's life and, therefore, what the person is most likely to remember.* Bartlett reported this social relevance for the Swazi (a tribe in southeastern Africa). A cowhand in this agrarian culture remembered, a year after the events, identifying marks and prices from cow sales in which he had been only peripherally involved.

We might hypothesize that culture specificity explains why basketball fans can rattle off NBA statistics long after nonfans have heard more than they care to. In an experiment conducted among the Tumbuka tribe in Zambia, researchers investigated the culture specificity of time (Deregowski, 1970). The investigator reasoned that memory for time concepts would be greater among groups for whom time was culturally valued. He selected two contrasting groups: students living in town, whose daily experiences usually meant adhering to strict time schedules, and people living in a rural village, whose lives did not depend on clocks. The subjects were given a short story containing eight numerical details, four of which dealt with time. After the participants heard the story, they were asked questions designed to elicit how much numerical information they had retained. Predictably the rural inhabitants recalled less information relating to time than did the students, but they recalled just as many nontemporal numerical details. Research such as this suggests that cultural experiences influence *what* we remember.

In another study, two dimensions of memory and cultural contexts were studied: structural features of memory—such as echoic memory and short-term memory, which develop early in life—and control processes—such as retrieval strategies, which are more likely to be influenced by cultural and environmental experiences, such as schooling (Wagner, 1980). The participants were males from 7 years of age through adulthood who lived in the northwest African country of Morocco. The groups were from rural or urban areas and were either educated or illiterate. Their short-term memory for seven drawings was assessed. The researcher found that all the groups of Moroccans

Cultural Literacy

In his provocative book, *Cultural Literacy*, University of Virginia English Professor E. D. Hirsch (1987) argued that every literate adult should learn certain things in school to function well in contemporary society. To get a feel for the kinds of information Hirsch regarded as important, look at the following terms and see if you can identify the significance of each one:

1066
Zurich
mainspring
golden fleece
burgher
golden rule
nicotine
probate court

These words were randomly selected from a glossary of several thousand that Hirsch believes should define every literate person's "memory knowledge." The glossary includes terms drawn from history, literature, government, science, math, art, geography, and other areas of knowledge.

Simply, the following are Hirsch's bold claims.

1. To be a full participant in our modern democratic culture, it is necessary to be literate.
2. Adult literacy is built on a broad and wide-ranging base of knowledge.
3. This knowledge is *schematic*. It doesn't have to be detailed or complete. For example, it's sufficient to know that nicotine is an ingredient in cigarettes or that Zurich is a city in Switzerland.
4. American schools used to make students commit more schematic knowledge to memory. The curriculum had substance and factual content. Recently it has slipped into faddish concerns, such as critical thinking, process, and developmental curricula.
5. We need to overhaul the American educational curriculum, beginning during the earliest years of elementary school, to incorporate more memorization of facts, specifically of the sort outlined in Hirsch's glossary.
6. To guarantee that recommendation 5 is taken seriously, school systems should immediately begin creating tests to determine whether the base of children's knowledge is improving.

What do you think of Hirsch's ideas? Do they make sense to you? Do you accept his arguments? If you haven't already done so, you might want to read his book and think about it further. Few educators could, or would want to, argue against the notion that a broad base of knowledge is important. A child's general knowledge is an important factor in learning and probably is related to success as an adult in our literate culture. However, Hirsch's approach raises several questions: Should we be content with the kind of "shallow" knowledge that would be encouraged by a test like Hirsch's? Should everyone be expected to be a Renaissance collector and memorizer of information? More important, how will we solve the perpetually thorny issue of who defines what is on the test and what constitutes contemporary cultural literacy? Shouldn't we also be concerned about improving children's memory skills, not just their memory knowledge?

---

tended to remember the last (most recent) drawing. The recency effect is a structural dimension of memory (see the serial position effect in figure 6.9). However, the tendency to remember the first drawing (the primacy effect) was much more pronounced among the educated Moroccans and, to a lesser extent, among the uneducated urban Moroccans. The primacy effect is more strongly influenced by the control process of rehearsal. This study showed that the cultural factors of education and urbanization influence an important aspect of memory, the primacy effect.

Because we do not have comparable information from students in diverse schools within a single culture, we cannot say precisely what it is about education that influences memory skills. Schools train students to use specialized memory strategies—such as committing large amounts of information to memory in a short time and using logical organization and categories to remember information—that have few analogies in societies without formal schooling.

In some cultures, children are required to memorize huge amounts of information. For example, in Iran children must memorize large blocks of cultural and religious texts. Iranians are often surprised at how little Americans seem to know. Some educational reformists in the United States are also concerned about Americans' general lack of cultural literacy. To read more about this issue, turn to Sociocultural Worlds 6.2.

In sum, being able to remember is a universal requirement of cultures around the world, but specific forms of remembering, as well as the amount and type of memory knowledge, are not always universal. Most forms of memory studied by psychologists have been those associated with formal schooling in a middle-class cultural setting.

Mnemonics and Memory Strategies

In the fifth century B.C., Greek poet Simonides attended a banquet. After he left, the building collapsed, crushing the guests and maiming them beyond recognition. Simonides was able to identify the bodies by using a memory technique. He generated vivid images of each person and mentally pictured where they had sat at the banquet table. Specific techniques such as this, many of which involve imagery, have been used to improve memory. **Mnemonics** *is the term used to describe the techniques designed to make memory more efficient.*

Imagery

The technique for remembering used by Simonides is called the method of loci. It is a visual imagery technique you can apply to memory problems of your own. Suppose you have a list of chores to do. To ensure that you remember them all, first associate a concrete object with each chore. A trip to the store becomes a dollar bill, a telephone call to a friend becomes a telephone, clean-up duty becomes a broom, and so on. Then produce an image of each "object" so you can imagine it in a particular location in a familiar building, such as your house. You might imagine the dollar bill in the kitchen, the telephone in the dining room, and so on. The vividness of the image and the unusual placement virtually guarantee recollection. It also helps if you mentally move through the house in a logical way as you "place" the images.

A second strategy using imagery is the peg method, in which a set of mental pegs, such as numbers, have items attached to them. For instance, you might begin by thinking about the following: "One is a bun, two is a shoe, three is a tree," and so forth up to as many as 10 to 20 numbers. Once you can readily reproduce these rhymes, you can use them as mental pegs. For example, if you were required to remember a list of items in a specific order—such as the directions to someone's house—you would use the following mental pegs: One-bun-left on Market, two-shoe-right on Sandstone, three-tree-right on Balboa, and so on. Then develop an image for each direction: I left the bun at the market; my right shoe got caught in the sand and stone; there's a tree right on Balboa. When you have to retrieve the directions, you select the appropriate cue word, such as *bun* or *shoe*, and this should conjure the compound image with the correct response. Researchers have been encouraged by the effectiveness of such strategies in improving memory (McDaniel & Pressly, 1987).

Systematic Memory and Study Strategies

Such techniques as the method of loci and the peg method can be used to improve memory, but strategies that incorporate an understanding of how we remember are especially helpful. One such strategy, ARESIDORI, is a simple mnemonic code for (1) Attention, (2) Rehearsal, (3) Elaboration, (4) Semantic processing, (5) Imagery, (6) Distinctiveness, (7) Organization, (8) Retrieval, (9) Interest (Ellis, 1987). Most of the components of ARESIDORI have been discussed in this chapter and are basic to memory. Note that number 9, interest, essentially refers to motivation. It is helpful to determine which of the principles of ARESIDORI you already use effectively and which you could use more often in order to improve your study habits.

Many approaches to study exist and many of them include some basic principles of memory. The most widely used system is SQ3R (Robinson, 1961), discussed in the Study Skills section at the beginning of this text. S stands for survey, Q for question, and *3R* for read, recite, review. To use this system in the next chapter, you might do the following. To survey, glance over the headings to find the main points of the chapter (the chapter outline helps in this regard). To question, turn each heading into a question, and continue to ask yourself questions throughout the chapter. To accomplish the 3R part of the system, start reading the chapter as you normally would, recite information periodically as you go through the chapter, and then review the material you have read several times before you take a test. The in-chapter reviews and summary will help you with the review process.

In this chapter, we have focused extensively on one of cognition's most important components—memory. In the next chapter, we will explore other aspects of cognition, giving special attention to how we think and how we use language.

REVIEW

The Representation of Knowledge in Memory, Neurobiological and Cultural Factors in Memory, and Mnemonics and Memory Strategies

Two theories of how knowledge is represented in memory are network and schema. Early network theories stressed that memories consist of a complex network of nodes that are hierarchically arranged. More recent network theories stress the role of meaningful nodes in the surrounding network. The concept of schema refers to information we have about various concepts, events, and knowledge. Schema theory claims that long-term memory is not very exact and that we reconstruct our past. Schemas for events are called scripts.

In the study of the neurobiological basis of memory, a major issue is the extent to which memory is localized or distributed. Single neurons are involved in memory, but some neuroscientists believe that most memories are stored in circuits of about 1,000 neurons. There is no specific memory center in the brain; many parts of the brain participate in the memory of an event.

A culture sensitizes its members to certain objects and events in the environment, and these cultural experiences can influence the nature of memory. Bartlett's schema theory and Hirsch's ideas about cultural literacy reflect the role of culture in memory.

Mnemonics are techniques that improve memory. Many of these involve imagery, including the method of loci and the peg method. Systems based on a number of aspects of our knowledge about memory have been developed, including ARESIDORI and SQ3R, to improve memory.

Summary

I. What Is Memory?

Memory is the retention of information over time. Psychologists study how information is encoded into memory, how it is stored, and how it is retrieved.

II. Memory's Systems

Memory's time frames involve sensory registers, short-term memory, and long-term memory. Sensory registers retain information for only an instant, often just a fraction of a second; short-term memory retains information for up to 30 seconds; long-term memory retains information for as long as a lifetime. Visual sensory registers (iconic memory) retain information for about one-quarter of a second, auditory sensory registers (echoic memory) for several seconds.

III. Short-Term Memory

Compared to sensory registers, short-term memory is limited in capacity but has relatively long duration, up to about 30 seconds. According to George Miller, the limitation is about seven, plus or minus two, bits of information. Chunking can expand short-term memory. The contemporary view of short-term memory describes it in terms of working memory.

IV. Long-Term Memory

Long-term memory is huge in capacity and very long in duration. Long-term memory consists of declarative memory, what is consciously recollected, and procedural memory, what is not consciously remembered, at least not in the form of specific facts or events. Declarative memory (or knowledge) consists of episodic memory, events in your past you personally experienced, and semantic memory, which is essentially world knowledge. Many of our memories include both of these types of information. Common examples of procedural memory are the skills to play golf or repair a toaster.

V. Relations Among Memories

The working model of memory is the most widely accepted contemporary model of memory; it emphasizes that long-term memory precedes working memory.

VI. Encoding

Encoding is the transformation and/or transfer of information into a memory system. Information can be encoded into sensory memory and short-term (working) memory, but the main focus is on encoding information into long-term memory.

Attention, automatic versus effortful processing, depth of processing and elaboration, imagery, and organization are factors in encoding. Attention is the ability to focus on certain stimuli. Attention is both selective and shifting. Automatic processes do not require capacity or resources; effortful processes do. Effortful processing includes depth of processing and elaboration, imagery, and organization. Craik and Lockhart developed the levels of processing view of memory, which stresses that memory is on a continuum from shallow to deep. In this view, deeper processing produces better memory. Elaboration refers to the extensiveness of processing at any given depth. Elaboration makes encoding more distinctive. Imagery refers to sensations without an external stimulus present. Paivio argues that we have separate verbal image codes, but this is controversial. Organization is one of the most pervasive aspects of memory; it involves grouping or combining items. Often information is organized hierarchically. Encoding usually is improved with selective attention, effortful processing, deep processing and elaboration, imagery, and organization.

VII. Retrieval from Long-Term Memory

The search for information from long-term memory can be automatic or effortful. An interesting aspect is the tip-of-the-tongue phenomenon (TOT state), which occurs when we just can't quite pull something out of memory. The implication of TOT is that, without good retrieval cues, information stored in memory is difficult to find. The serial position effect describes the tendency to remember items at the beginning of a list (primacy effect) and at the end of a list (recency effect). One key factor that makes retrieval effortful is the absence of effective cues. A second factor is the nature of the retrieval task, which, along with the presence or absence of retrieval cues, distinguishes recall from recognition memory. Failure to use effective retrieval cues is one reason we forget, a phenomenon known as cue-dependent forgetting.

VIII. Interference, Decay, and Amnesia

The principle of cue-dependent forgetting is consistent with an earlier view of forgetting—interference theory, the belief that we forget not because memories are actually lost from storage but because other information gets in the way of what we want to remember. Proactive interference is when material that was learned earlier disrupts the recall of material learned later. Decay theory argues that, when something new is learned, a memory trace is formed, but as time passes this trace tends to disintegrate. Amnesia refers to extreme memory deficits and comes in two forms. Anterograde amnesia is a memory disorder that affects the retention of new information and events. Retrograde amnesia is a memory disorder that involves memory loss for a segment of the past but not for new events.

IX. Representation of Knowledge in Memory

Two theories have been proposed: network and schema. Early network theories stressed that memories consist of a complex network of nodes that are hierarchically arranged. More recent network theories stress the role of meaningful nodes in the surrounding network. The concept of schema refers to information we have about various concepts, events, and knowledge. Schema theory claims that long-term memory is not very exact and that we construct our past.

X. The Neurobiological Basis of Memory

A major issue in the neurobiological basis of memory is the extent to which memory is localized or distributed. Single neurons are involved in memory, but some neuroscientists believe that most memories are stored in circuits of about 1,000 neurons. There is no specific memory center in the brain; many parts of the brain participate in the memory for an event.

XI. Cultural Factors in Memory

A culture sensitizes its members to certain objects and events in the environment, and these cultural experiences can influence the nature of memory. Bartlett's schema theory, research on schooling and memory, and Hirsch's ideas on cultural literacy reflect the role of culture in memory.

XII. Mnemonics and Memory Strategies

Mnemonics are techniques that improve memory. Many of these involve imagery, including the method of loci and the peg method. Systems based on a number of aspects of our knowledge of memory have been developed, including ARESIDORI and SQ3R.

Key Terms

memory 152
sensory registers 153
echoic memory 153
iconic memory 153
short-term memory 154
memory span 154
chunking 154
maintenance rehearsal 154
working memory 154
long-term memory 155
declarative memory 155
procedural memory 155
episodic memory 155
semantic memory 155

working memory model 156
memory processes 157
encoding 157
selective attention 157
effortful processing 158
automatic processing 158
levels of processing 159
elaboration 159
tip-of-the-tongue phenomenon
   (TOT state) 161
serial position effect 161
primacy effect 161
recency effect 161
recall 162

recognition 162
cue-dependent forgetting 162
interference theory 162
proactive interference 162
retroactive interference 164
decay theory 164
amnesia 164
anterograde amnesia 165
retrograde amnesia 165
schema 166
script 168
culture specificity hypothesis 170
mnemonics 172

Suggested Readings

Baddeley, A. D. (1990). *Human memory: Theory and practice*. Boston: Allyn & Bacon. Baddeley is one of the most influential thinkers in contemporary memory research. In this book, he describes the working memory model emphasized in this chapter.

Best, J. B. (1989). *Cognitive psychology* (2nd ed.). St. Paul, MN: West. This text on cognitive psychology explores many of the topics in this chapter in greater detail. Included are chapters on imagery, organization, encoding, storing, and retrieving.

Hunt, M. (1982). *The universe within*. New York: Simon & Schuster. Hunt traveled to many universities and talked to top scholars in the cognitive area. This book represents his distillation of their ideas. The outcome is a well-written, accurate overview of the current state of knowledge on cognition. It includes many intriguing comments about the relation between the human mind and computers.

McDaniel, M. A., & Pressly, M. (1987). *Imagery and related mnemonic processes*. New York: Springer-Verlag. This book provides a number of excellent strategies, especially those involving imagery, for improving memory.

Neisser, U. (1982). *Memory observed*. San Francisco: W. H. Freeman. Neisser, one of the leading figures in cognition, has stressed for many years that context is important in the study of cognition. This book consists of a series of articles, by many individuals, that focus on memory in natural settings and includes a series of chapters on eidetic memory.

THINKING, LANGUAGE, AND INTELLIGENCE

CHAPTER 7

It's a beautiful thing, the destruction of words. . . . If you have a word like "good," what need is there for a word like "bad"? "Ungood" will do just as well. . . . It was B.B.'s [Big Brother's] idea originally, of course. . . . Do you know that Newspeak is the only language in the world whose vocabulary gets smaller every year? . . . Don't you see that the whole aim of Newspeak is to narrow the range of thought? In the end we shall make thoughtcrime literally impossible, because there will be no words in which to express it. . . . Every year fewer and fewer words, and the range of consciousness always a little smaller. . . .

So says a colleague at the Ministry of Truth to Winston Smith in George Orwell's novel *Nineteen Eighty-Four*, published in 1949. The novel is about the life of an intelligent man who lives under absolute totalitarian control. The government regulates every facet of life and, above all, corrupts language in its pursuit of power. The purpose of Newspeak is not only to provide a means of expressing "appropriate" thoughts, but to make all other modes of thought impossible.

Although the year 1984 is long gone and the English language is still overflowingly rich, some of Orwell's predictions have an eerily familiar ring. In recent years, politicians have illegally funded mercenaries, called "freedom fighters," to overthrow the Nicaraguan government, have referred to nuclear warheads as "peacemakers," and have forbidden federally funded clinics to counsel pregnant women about the option of abortion.

Later in the chapter, we will discuss much more about whether or not language shapes thought. The chapter's main topics are thought, language, and intelligence. We will begin by examining the nature of cognition and the cognitive revolution in psychology.

The Nature of Cognition and the Cognitive Revolution in Psychology

The term **cognition** *refers to the mental processes—perception, memory, thought, and language—that together produce knowledge. The study of cognition deals with how information enters the mind, how it is transformed and stored in memory, and how it is retrieved to perform mental activity, such as forming a new concept, reasoning through an argument, or solving a difficult problem.* We studied perception in chapter 3 and memory in chapter 6. In this chapter, we will focus extensively on thinking, language, and intelligence.

Theories of thinking and language did not always have a cognitive slant. In the 1920s and 1930s, the dominant views of thinking and language were behavioral; they downplayed the idea of internal cognitive processes and knowledge, emphasizing instead the effects of environment on behavior. Although a variety of factors stimulated the growth of cognitive psychology, perhaps the most important was the development of computers (Hunt, 1989; Johnson-Laird, 1989). The first modern computer, developed by John von Neumann in the late 1940s, showed that inanimate machines can perform logical operations. This indicated that some mental operations might be modeled by computers, possibly telling us something about the way cognition works. Cognitive psychologists often use the analogy of a computer to help explain the relation between cognition and the brain. The physical brain is described as a computer's hardware and cognition as its software (see figure 7.1).

Although the development of computers played an important role in psychology's cognitive revolution, it is important to realize that inanimate computers and human brains function quite differently in some respects (Restak, 1988). For example, each brain cell, or neuron, is alive and can be altered in its functioning by events in its biological environment; computer chips cannot change. Most computers also operate in a serial manner, performing one operation at a time at very high speed. In contrast, brains include many subsystems that operate simultaneously, and often slowly when compared to a computer. Finally, hundreds or even thousands of neurons in the brain work together—communicating back and forth in highly complicated ways—in networks. Nothing like these networks exists in most computers.

These differences between computers and brains mean that computers can do some things that humans cannot, and humans can do some things that computers cannot. Computers can calculate numbers much faster and more accurately than humans could ever hope to. Computers are also better than humans at routing air traffic, predicting weather, and detecting whether certain disputed literary works were written by certain authors. However, there are some important things humans can do that computers cannot. A machine can learn and improve on its own program, but it does not have the means to develop a new goal. Computers also cannot simulate the mind's nonlogical, intuitive, and unconscious nature. Also, the human mind is aware of itself; computers are not. Indeed, no computer is likely to approach the richness of human consciousness. In short, the brain's extraordinary pathways probably produce thinking that cannot be mimicked by computers.

Thinking

Information in memory is manipulated and transformed through thinking. We can think about the concrete, such as boats and beaches, and the abstract, such as freedom and independence. We can think about the past—life in the 1940s, 1960s, and 1980s—and the future—life in the year 2000. We can think about reality—how to do better on the next test in this course— and fantasy—what it would be like to meet Catherine the Great

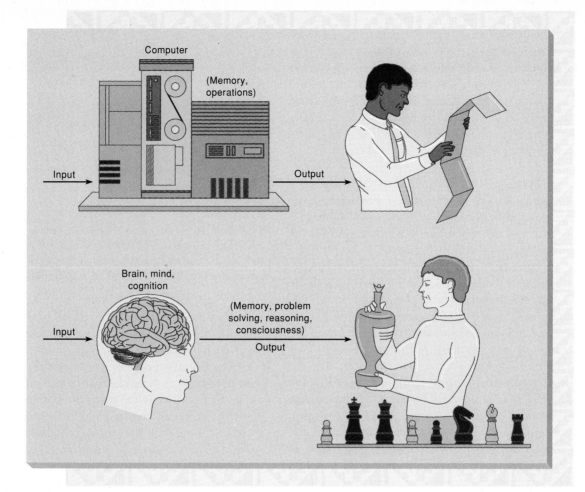

FIGURE 7.1

Computers and cognition: an analogy. The physical brain is described as analogous to a computer's hardware; cognition is described as analogous to a computer's software.

or land a spacecraft on Jupiter. When we think, we often use concepts. What characterizes these basic units of thinking and how are they formed?

Concept Formation

We have a special ability for categorizing things. We know that apples and oranges are fruits but they have different tastes and colors. We know that Porsches and Yugos are both automobiles, but we also know that they differ in cost, speed, and prestige. How do we know that apples and oranges are fruits and that Porsches and Yugos are automobiles despite their differences? The answer lies in our ability to ignore their different forms and group them on the basis of their features. For example, all Porsches and Yugos have four wheels and a steering wheel and provide transportation. In other words, we have a concept of what an automobile is. A **concept** *is a category used to group objects, events, and characteristics on the basis of common properties.*

Drawing by Koren; © 1986 The New Yorker Magazine, Inc.

Why are concepts important? Without concepts, each object and event in our world would be unique. Any kind of generalization would be impossible. Concepts allow us to relate experiences and objects. Weimaraners, cocker spaniels, and labrador retrievers are all called sporting dogs by the American Kennel Club. Without the concept of sporting dogs, we would be unable to compare these dogs.

Concepts grease the wheels of memory, making it more efficient. When we group objects to form a concept, we remember the characteristics of the concept rather than each object or experience. When one stockbroker tells another stockbroker that the Dow Jones Industrial Average went up today, the second broker knows that IBM, Exxon, and General Motors, whose stocks contribute to the average, had a good chance of increasing in value. By using the concept of the Dow Jones Industrial Average, communication is more efficient and probably jogs memory as well.

Concepts also keep us from "reinventing the wheel" each time we come across a piece of information. For example, we don't have to relearn what the Dow Jones Industrial Average is each time we pick up a newspaper. We already know what the concept means. Concepts also provide clues about how to react to an object or experience. For example, if we see a bowl of pretzels, our concept of food lets us know it is okay to eat them. Concepts allow us to associate classes of objects or events. Some classes of objects are associated in structured patterns. For example, the Indigo Girls won a Grammy Award; Grammies are given for achievements in the music recording industry. Music recording is a performing art.

Because concepts are so critical to our ability to make sense of the world around us, researchers have spent a lot of time studying the process of concept formation. In studying concept formation, psychologists have investigated an individual's ability to discover a rule for why some objects fall within a concept whereas others do not (Keil, 1989). These rules are based on features or combinations of features. For example, a rule for a concept might be "all stimuli that are triangles (but not circles or squares)," "all stimuli that are circles," "all stimuli that are colored red," or "stimuli that are both circles and red" ("all that are circles and red").

To get a better sense of cognition, let's examine more closely how an experiment on concept formation might proceed. Figure 7.2 displays a number of cards shown to a person in a typical concept formation study (Moates & Schumacher, 1980). The shapes (square, circle, or triangle), sizes (small or large), and position (left, middle, or right) of the figures on the cards vary. The experimenter arbitrarily chooses a concept, such as "large circles," and asks the subjects to discover it. They are shown an example of the concept (such as card 3) and asked to choose other cards until they discover the nature of the concept. After each choice, subjects are told whether or not the chosen card is an example of the concept.

An important process in concept formation is to develop hypotheses about what defines the concept and to test these hypotheses in new examples. Suppose you are an avid tennis player but feel you are losing too many matches because your serve is weak. Despite hours of practice, your serve just isn't getting any better. Your problem might be that you have only a vague concept of what a "killer" serve is really like. In order to get

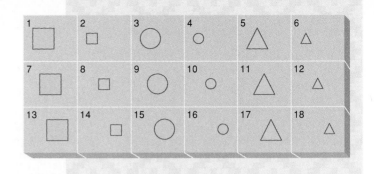

FIGURE 7.2

Typical concept formation task. This array of cards might be presented to a number of subjects. The experimenter arbitrarily chooses the correct concept, such as "large circles," and then the subject tries to discover the rule that defines the concept.

a feel for the concept and to see how the best players serve, you head for the tennis courts. Based on your observations, you develop a hypothesis about the mechanics of an excellent serve. For example, after hours of watching the "weekend pros" ace their opponents, you decide that the ball must be tossed high so the server has to stretch to reach it and that the server needs to swing the racket as a baseball pitcher throws a ball. You might want to scrutinize the serves of more skilled players to see if they confirm your hypothesis. You'll also want to test the hypothesis in your own game to see if the two aspects of the hypothesis—that good servers toss the ball high and swing the racket as a baseball player throws a ball—improve your serve.

Even though your concept formation is on track and your tennis serve improves, chances are you'll still be somewhat dissatisfied. With a difficult concept (such as the mechanics of a good serve), you may need an expert—a professional tennis coach—to help you. The pro's concept is likely to include many more features than the ones you discovered, as well as complex rules related to those features. For example, the pro might tell you that tossing the ball high helps, but it works much better if you rotate the grip on your racket counterclockwise. In general, concepts with more features and more complicated rules are more difficult to learn. Part of being an expert in any field is grasping the complicated rules of difficult concepts.

In any type of cognitive testing, it's important to keep in mind that culture affects concept formation. Around the world, people perform better when asked questions that are consistent with their cultural experiences (Berry & others, in press; Lonner, 1990; Segall & others, 1990).

Although psychologists have learned much about concept formation, some believe that most of the research has been too artificial. Eleanor Rosch (1973) argues that real-life concepts are less precise than those used in many psychological experiments, such as the earlier example of "large circles." Real-life concepts,

The large football player shown studying in the library does not completely fit our prototype of a football player—his size does, but his academic orientation does not.

she says, often have "fuzzy boundaries"; that is, it often is unclear exactly which features are critical to a concept. Consider the concept of "cup." A little thought might suggest five properties of cups: they (1) are concrete objects, (2) are concave, (3) can hold liquids and solids, (4) have handles, and (5) can be used to drink hot liquids. However, what about the cups in Chinese restaurants that do not have handles? What about the poor-quality paper cups that conduct too much heat to be used for hot drinks? Although such objects lack certain "critical features" of cups, we still call them cups.

Rosch also contends that our everyday concepts have "internal structure"; that is, some members of concepts are better examples of the concept than others. Think of your concept of a football player: perhaps very muscular, big, and stressed out by the pressure of combining athletics and academics. Football players who match this description are said to be prototypical—they fit our prototype of a football player. However, some football players are large and do well in academic pursuits; others are skinny and fail every subject. They are not prototypical, but they are still football players. Thus, the internal structure of a concept simply means that the members of a concept are not all treated equally.

Problem Solving

It would be impossible to solve problems without using concepts. Think about driving, something most of us do every day. Signs and traffic signals every few blocks tell us to stop, yield, or proceed apace. Usually we don't think of these signs and signals as solutions to problems, but they are (Bransford & Stein, 1984). Most of the symbols that keep traffic moving so smoothly are the brainchild of William Eno, the "father of traffic safety." Eno, born in New York City in 1858, became concerned about the horrendous traffic jams in the city. The horsedrawn vehicles were making street traffic dangerous. Eno published a paper about the urgency of street traffic reform. His concept proposed solutions to the problem—stop signs, one-way streets, and pedestrian safety islands—ideas that affect our behavior today.

What is problem solving? **Problem solving** *is an attempt to find an appropriate way of attaining a goal when the goal is not readily available.* We face many problems in the course of our everyday lives—trying to figure out why our car won't start, planning how to get enough money to buy a stereo, working a jigsaw puzzle, or estimating our chances of winning at blackjack. Whatever the problem is, we want to come up with the best and fastest solution possible. John Bransford and Barry Stein developed an effective method of problem solving with a catchy title, the IDEAL problem solver (1984). IDEAL stands for (*I*) identify the problem, (*D*) define and represent the problem, (*E*) explore possible strategies, (*A*) act on the strategies, and (*L*) look back and evaluate the effects of your activities. Let's run through this problem-solving strategy step by step.

Identifying Problems

Before a problem can be solved, it first needs to be recognized and identified. Consider the problem two brothers faced. Ladislao and George Biro were proofreaders who spent a lot of their time correcting spelling mistakes and typographical errors in the days before computers. Even though fountain pens were messy, they recorded the errors they found in ink because pencil marks faded. The Biro brothers recognized they had a problem, so they came up with a solution—they invented the ballpoint pen. Their original company is now part of a corporation known as Bic.

The next time you receive a mail-order catalog, sit down and peruse it. Depending on the catalog, you'll find everything from continuous-feed pet food bowls to inflatable bathtub pillows. Most of the gadgets are good examples of clever solutions to common problems (see figure 7.3 on page 183). The first step the inventors of these objects took was to identify a problem.

Defining Problems

The second step is to define the problem as carefully as possible. For example, a doctor recognizes her patient's symptoms as high blood pressure. The doctor knows that different sources, or definitions, of the problem call for different treatments. Both

In the nineteenth century, New York City began to experience traffic jams. The horse-drawn vehicles were making street traffic dangerous. How did William Eno solve this problem?

hardening of the arteries and everyday stress can produce high blood pressure; however, hardening of the arteries may require surgery, whereas reducing stress may require a change in lifestyle.

Defining the problem may sound simple. Sometimes it is, as in the case of studying before a big test or fixing a leaky faucet. However, many of life's most interesting problems are ill-defined. How can you write a book that will become a bestseller? What does it take before you can call yourself a success? What is happiness?

Exploring Alternative Approaches

The next step is to explore alternative strategies for solving the problem. To do this, analyze how you are reacting to the problem and then consider the options or strategies you might use. You might try dividing a problem into subproblems, attacking it piece by piece, or you might work a problem backward. Imagine that you need to meet someone for lunch across town and you don't want to be late. If you want to arrive at noon and know that it takes 30 minutes of travel time, the problem can easily be worked backward in time (noon − 30 minutes = 11:30 departure). Working backward is a good strategy when the goal is clear but the original intention is not.

Two strategies for problem solving are using algorithms and heuristics. **Algorithms** *are procedures that guarantee an answer to a problem.* When you solve a multiplication problem, you are using an algorithm—you learned this algorithm as part of your schooling. When you follow the directions for putting together a lawn chair, you are using an algorithm. In contrast to algorithms, **heuristics** *are rules of thumb that can suggest a solution to a problem but do not ensure that it will work.* Let's say you're heading to a friend's house and you've never been there before. You are driving around in an unfamiliar part of town and after a while you realize you're lost. If you know your destination is north, you might use the heuristic of turning onto a road that heads in that direction. This procedure might work, but it also might fail—the road might end or turn off to the east.

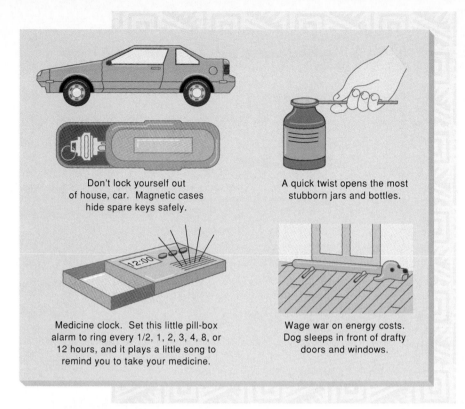

FIGURE 7.3

Inventions designed to solve some common problems.

Image labels:

Don't lock yourself out of house, car. Magnetic cases hide spare keys safely.

A quick twist opens the most stubborn jars and bottles.

Medicine clock. Set this little pill-box alarm to ring every 1/2, 1, 2, 3, 4, 8, or 12 hours, and it plays a little song to remind you to take your medicine.

Wage war on energy costs. Dog sleeps in front of drafty doors and windows.

Although we can solve some problems by using algorithms, we are usually forced to rely on heuristics. Working backward and dividing into subproblems are both heuristics. They do not guarantee a problem will be solved, but they often help.

Each of us occasionally gets into the mental rut of solving problems by using a particular strategy. A **learning set** *is the tendency to solve problems with the same strategy.* Learning sets often serve us efficiently. Without them, we would waste time looking for the solution to a problem we already know. You may have encountered a problem with learning sets in your college classes. Let's say several of your professors base their exams primarily on lecture materials. You pore over your lecture notes and ace the exams, so you follow the same strategy for your psychology class and spend very little time studying the textbook. When you see the first exam in this class, you learn that the strategy is inappropriate—this exam has a number of questions based only on the text.

The following puzzle is often used to demonstrate the concept of a learning set. It's called the nine dot problem. Take out a piece of paper and copy the arrangement of the dots:

Without lifting your pencil, connect the dots using only four straight lines. Most people have difficulty—and lots just give up on—finding a solution to the nine dot problem. Part of the difficulty is that we have a learning set that tells us to think of the nine dot configuration as a square. We consider the outer dots as the boundary and do not extend the lines beyond them, yet the solution to the nine dot problem, shown at the end of the chapter, requires going outside the square.

If you've ever used a shoe to hammer a nail, you've overcome what's called "functional fixedness" to solve a problem. The concept of **functional fixedness,** *the inability to solve a problem because it is viewed only in terms of its usual function,* is similar to the concept of learning set. If the problem to be solved involves usual functions, then it can easily be solved, but, if the problem involves something new and different, solving the problem will be trickier. An example of functional fixedness involves pliers (Maier, 1931). The problem is to figure out how to tie two strings together that are hanging from a ceiling (see figure 7.4). If you hold one and then move toward the other, you cannot reach the second one. It seems as though you're stuck, but there is a pair of pliers on a table. Can you solve the problem?

The solution is to use the pliers as a weight and tie them to the end of one string (see figure 7.5). Swing this string back and forth like a pendulum. Then let go of the "weight" and grasp the stationary string. Finally, reach out and grab the swinging string. Your past experience with pliers makes this a difficult problem to solve. To solve the problem, you need to find a unique use for the pliers, in this case as a weight to create a pendulum.

Acting on a Plan and Looking at the Effects

We can't know if we have correctly identified a problem, defined it, and explored strategies for solving it until we act on them to see if they really work. These final two steps (acting on and looking at the effects of a strategy) are closely related. Figure 7.6 illustrates the importance of acting on the strategies and looking at the effects. This item was invented to solve the problem of following a recipe in a cookbook while your hands are busy chopping vegetables and measuring spices. Let's say you invented this apparatus. You probably would want to try it out to see if it works. As you use it, you would soon see that there's a problem—the cookbook is not protected from spilled or splat-

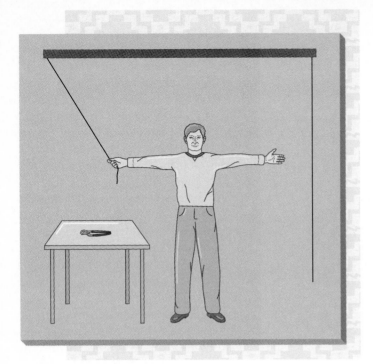

FIGURE 7.4

Maier string problem. How can you tie the two strings together if you cannot reach them both at the same time?

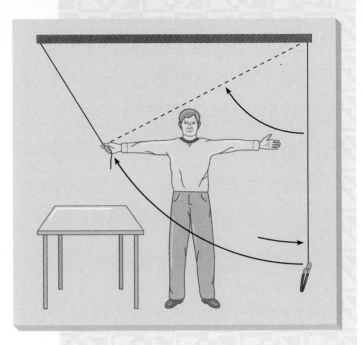

FIGURE 7.5

Solution to the Maier string problem. Use the pliers as a weight to create a pendulum motion that brings the second string closer.

tered food. Looking at these effects, you might revise the apparatus to look like the holder shown in figure 7.7. Without acting on your plan and evaluating the effects, you might not have improved your invention.

A summary of the steps in the IDEAL problem solver is shown in figure 7.8.

Reasoning

"Elementary, my dear Watson," Sherlock Holmes, the master detective, would say to his baffled companion. Holmes would then go on to explain how he had solved a particularly difficult case. No matter how tough the problem, Holmes always came up with the right solution. Dr. Watson would listen in amazement at how Holmes had spotted all the clues and made sense of them, whereas he had either missed them or misinterpreted them. Holmes' adventures, written by Sir Arthur Conan Doyle, all involve intricate problems that Holmes solves with amazing powers of reasoning.

What exactly is reasoning? **Reasoning** *is the mental activity of transforming information to reach conclusions* (Galotti, 1989). Examples of this transformation of information to reach conclusions are found in inductive reasoning and deductive reasoning, as well as other forms of reasoning we will discuss.

FIGURE 7.6

Book holder.

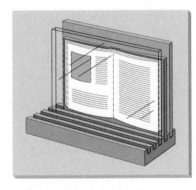

FIGURE 7.7

Book holder that guards against stains.

Inductive Versus Deductive Reasoning

Inductive reasoning *is reasoning from the specific to the general—that is, drawing conclusions about all members of a category based on observing only some of the members.* Any time a psychologist studies a small number of individuals (say, 20 college freshmen) and draws conclusions about a larger number of individuals (say, all college students), inductive reasoning is taking place.

In contrast, **deductive reasoning** *is reasoning from the general to the specific. Deductive reasoning involves working with*

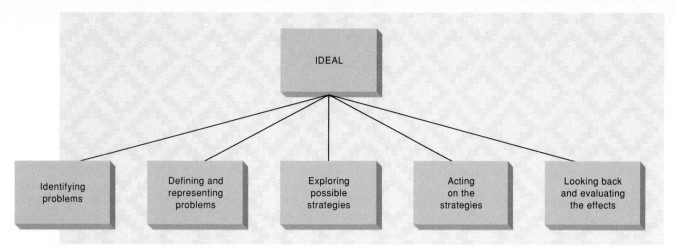

FIGURE 7.8

IDEAL problem solver. According to Bransford and Stein's model of the IDEAL problem solver, problem solving can be divided into five steps.

abstract statements, usually called "premises," and deriving an implication. When a psychologist makes a prediction from a theory, deductive reasoning is taking place.

Working out any complex problem often requires both inductive and deductive reasoning. For example, a psychologist might use her theory of how children develop to predict that 6-year-olds will succeed in a task but 4-year-olds will fail. To test this prediction, the psychologist conducts an experiment on a sample of 20 4-year-olds. Making a prediction is an example of deductive reasoning, but conducting a study and applying the findings to children in general is an example of inductive reasoning.

Formal Reasoning Tasks

Four kinds of formal reasoning tasks have been studied more than any others: one is the inductive task of making analogies; three others are the deductive tasks of ordering ideas, judging relations between conditions, and understanding syllogisms. We will consider each in turn.

An **analogy** *is a type of formal reasoning that is always made up of four parts, and the relation between the first two parts is the same as the relation between the last two.* Consider the following example. Beethoven is to music as Picasso is to _____. To answer correctly (fill in the word *art*), you must make an induction. You must induce the relation between "Beethoven" and "music" (the former created the latter) and apply this to "Picasso" (what did Picasso create?). When you took the SAT or ACT test, you probably were asked to supply the correct word in analogies.

Analogies can be very helpful in solving problems, especially when they are visually represented (Bransford & others, 1989; Vosniadou & Ortony, 1989). Benjamin Franklin no-

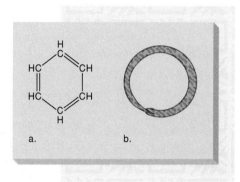

FIGURE 7.9

Use of analogy in problem solving. The benzene ring (a) is one of the most important structures in organic chemistry. It was discovered by Wilhelm Kekulé after he imagined how its structure might be analogous to a snake biting its tail (b).

ticed that a pointed object drew a stronger spark than a blunt object when both were in the vicinity of an electrified body. Originally he believed that this was an unimportant observation. It was not until he recognized that clouds did not draw a strong spark in the vicinity of an electrified body that he realized that pointed rods of iron could be used to protect buildings and ships from lightning. The pointed rod attracted the lightning, thus deflecting it from buildings and ships. Wilhelm Kekulé discovered the ringlike structure of the benzene molecule in organic chemistry only after he visualized its structure using the analogy of a snake biting its tail (see figure 7.9). In many ways, analogies make the strange familiar and the familiar strange.

Deductive reasoning can also facilitate problem solving. Perhaps the simplest form of deduction involves the ordering of ideas, such as the problem that follows:

If you like Jean better than Julie,
and you like Jane less than Julie,
whom do you like the least?

A second deductive reasoning task involves judging relationships between conditions, which requires processing if/then statements. For example, is the following reasoning valid?

If it's raining, the streets are wet.
The streets are wet.
Therefore, it is raining.

The reasoning is not valid. The streets could be wet for a variety of reasons—it may have snowed, someone may have washed her car, or a fire hydrant may have been opened. The fact that the streets are wet will not support the inference of rain.

A **syllogism** *is a deductive reasoning task that consists of a major premise, a minor premise, and a conclusion.* A premise is a general assumption. This kind of problem invariably involves a reference to quantity, such as some, all, or none. Consider the following statements:

All elephants are fond of dry martinis.
All those who are fond of dry martinis are bankers.
Therefore, all elephants are bankers.

The first sentence about elephants is the major premise and the second sentence about bankers is the minor premise. Though it may seem a little ridiculous, the conclusion—that all elephants are bankers—is technically correct because, in this kind of reasoning, it is assumed that all of the premises are correct (Matlin, 1983).

How Logical Is Everyday Reasoning?

The Greeks sometimes referred to humans as featherless bipeds. However, they also gave us another lofty distinction: rational beings. How rational are we? If we look at ourselves objectively, we can come up with countless examples of failures in rational thinking. Many people do not do very well on formal reasoning problems, such as analogies and syllogisms. In our everyday lives, we are not as systematic and logical as formal logicians.

What are some of the differences between formal reasoning and everyday reasoning? The differences are sufficient to make some theorists wonder if the two kinds of reasoning have any relation to each other at all. Consider the reasoning involved in deciding where to go to college or deciding whether to marry someone. There is no clear set of premises with which to begin your reasoning. It often is unclear exactly what information you should use even to start reasoning at all. The problem you face also is not self-contained. Your decision about marriage might influence your decision about where to go to school and even the career you pursue. Also, although some of your friends might offer strong opinions, their opinions are likely to disagree—there is no one correct answer to most everyday reasoning dilemmas that you face. Similarly a textbook on logic is of doubtful use in teaching you the best methods that will ensure the best answers to your everyday reasoning problems. It may not even be clear when you have solved or completed work on this problem about getting married. Three years after marriage, you may begin to wonder if this was, after all, the appropriate decision. Finally, everyday reasoning tasks are too important to you personally for you to simply work on them "for their own sake." Your work on these problems is directed at your larger life goals. In all of these ways, everyday reasoning differs from formal reasoning as examined by logicians and from formal reasoning studied in laboratories by psychologists.

Although there are fundamental differences between formal reasoning and the reasoning we use everyday to get along in the world, there are many circumstances when it helps to have the power of reasoning on our side (Gardner, 1985). In almost every scientific investigation, reasoning is used to set up the basic hypothesis to be studied and to understand the findings. When we perform analytical and computational tasks, such as working out a family budget or filing an income tax report, we use reasoning. When we play chess, bridge, or even ticktacktoe, we reason. When we are a juror, plaintiff, or defendant, we reason about the law. When we talk, plead, or argue with another or grapple with some of life's knotty problems, much of our reasoning consists of logical inferences—whether valid or not—from what we already know or think we know. In short, our reasoning is both rational and irrational, not always perfect, but usually functional.

REVIEW

Thinking

Cognition involves knowledge and the processes that use this knowledge. Cognition consists of how information enters the mind, is transformed and stored in memories, and is subsequently retrieved to perform an activity, such as forming a concept, solving a problem, or engaging in reasoning. The cognitive revolution in psychology has occurred in the past half century. The computer has played an important role, stimulating the model of the mind as an information-processing system.

A concept is used to group objects, events, or characteristics. Concepts help us generalize, improve our memory, keep us from constantly needing to learn, have informational value, and improve our association skills. Psychologists have often investigated a person's ability to detect why an object is included in a particular concept. Developing hypotheses about concepts is important in thinking. Natural concepts have fuzzy boundaries

Our next topic, language, like thinking, is an important dimension of our cognitive world. Language helps us think, make inferences, tackle tough decisions, and solve problems. Thinking influences language too. For example, because of the ways we think, we choose certain words to name objects. Let's now examine the nature of language.

Language

In 1799 a nude boy was observed running through the woods in France. The boy was captured when he was approximately 11 years old, and it was believed he had lived in the wild for at least 6 years. He was called the Wild Boy of Aveyron (Lane, 1976). When the boy was found, he made no effort to communicate. Even after a number of years, he never learned to communicate effectively. The Wild Boy of Aveyron raises an important issue in language—what are the biological, environmental, and cultural underpinnings of language? Later in the chapter, we will describe a modern-day wild child named Genie, who will shed some light on this issue. The contributions of biology, environment, and culture figure prominently in our discussion of language.

What Is Language?

Language is the human ability to communicate in a spoken and written language that sets us completely apart from all other animals. Our language allows us to describe past events in detail and to plan for the future in carefully considered

© Bob Thaves. Reprinted by permission.

steps. Language gives us the opportunity to pass along knowledge from generation to generation and to create a rich cultural heritage.

Every culture depends on language. Human languages number in the thousands, differing so much on the surface that many of us despair of learning even more than one. However, all human languages have some common characteristics. **Language** *is a system of symbols used to communicate with others. In humans, language is characterized by organizational rules and infinite generativity.* **Infinite generativity** *is a person's ability to produce an endless number of meaningful sentences using a finite set of words and rules*, which makes language a highly creative enterprise. Studies on the structure and mechanics of language include phonology, morphology, syntax, and semantics, each of which we will now discuss.

Language is made up of basic sounds, or phonemes. In the English language, there are approximately 36 phonemes. **Phonology** *is the study of language's sound system.* Phonological rules ensure that certain sound sequences occur (for example, *sp*, *ba*, or *ar*) and others do not (for example, *zx* or *qp*). A good example of a phoneme in the English language is /k/, the sound represented by the letter *k* in the word *ski* and the letter *c* in the word *cat*. Although the /k/ sound is slightly different in these two words, the variation is not distinguished, and the /k/ sound is described as a single phoneme. In some languages, such as Arabic, this kind of variation represents separate phonemes.

Morphology *refers to the rules for combining morphemes, the smallest string of sounds that gives meaning to what we say and hear.* Every word in the English language is made up of one or more morphemes. Some words consist of a single morpheme (for example, *help*), whereas others are made up of more than one morpheme (for example, *helper*, which has two morphemes, *help* + *er*, with the morpheme *er* meaning "one who," in this case "one who helps"). However, not all morphemes are words (for example, *pre-*, *-tion*, and *-ing*). Just as the rules that govern phonemes ensure that certain sound sequences occur, the rules that govern morphemes ensure that certain strings of sounds occur in particular sequences. For example, we would not reorder *helper* to *erhelp*.

Syntax *involves the way words are combined to form acceptable phrases and sentences.* If someone says to you, "Bob slugged Tom," and "Bob was slugged by Tom," you know who did the slugging and who was slugged in each case because you share the same syntactic understanding of sentence structure. You also understand that the sentence "You didn't stay, did you?" is a grammatical sentence but that "You didn't stay, didn't you?" is unacceptable and ambiguous.

Semantics *refers to the meaning of words and sentences.* Every word has a set of semantic features. *Girl* and *woman*, for example, share the same semantic features as the words *female* and *human* but differ in regard to age. Words have semantic restrictions on how they can be used in sentences. The sentence "The bicycle talked the boy into buying a candy bar" is syntactically correct but semantically incorrect. The sentence violates our semantic knowledge—bicycles do not talk.

Biological and Cultural Evolution

Is the ability to generate rules for language and then use them to create an infinite number of words learned and influenced by the environment and cultural factors, or is it the product of biological factors and biological evolution? Estimates vary as to how long ago humans acquired language—from about 20,000 to 70,000 years ago. In evolutionary time, then, language is a very recent acquisition. A number of experts believe that biological evolution shaped humans into linguistic creatures (Chomsky, 1957; Maratsos, 1989; Miller, 1981; Studdert-Kennedy, 1991). The brain, nervous system, and vocal apparatus of our predecessors changed over hundreds of thousands of years. Physically equipped to do so, *Homo sapiens* went beyond grunting and shrieking to develop abstract speech. However, both biological and cultural evolution explain the development of language.

Anthropologists speculate about the social conditions that led to the development of language. Social forces may have pushed humans to develop abstract reasoning and to create an efficient system for communicating with others (Crick, 1977). For example, early humans probably developed complex plans and strategies for hunting. If hunters could verbally signal one another about changes in strategies for hunting big game, the hunt was much more likely to be successful. Language gave humans an enormous edge over other animals and increased the humans' chances of survival. Questions about the role of language in human evolution have also led psychologists to think about the possibility that animals have language.

Do Animals Have Language?

Many animal species have complex and ingenious ways to signal danger and to communicate about basic needs, such as food and sex. For example, in one species of firefly, the females have learned to imitate the flashing signal of another species to lure the aliens into their territory. Then they eat the aliens. However, is this language in the human sense? What about higher animals, such as apes? Is ape language similar to human language? Can we teach language to them?

Some researchers believe that apes can learn language. One simian celebrity in this field is a chimp named Washoe, who was adopted when she was about 10 months old (Gardner & Gardner, 1971). Since apes do not have the vocal apparatus to speak, the researchers tried to teach Washoe American Sign Language, which is one of the sign languages of the deaf. Washoe used sign language during everyday activities, such as meals, play, and car rides. In 2 years, Washoe learned 38 signs and, by the age of 5, she had a vocabulary of 160 signs. Washoe learned how to put signs together in novel ways, such as "you drink" and "you me tickle." A number of other efforts to teach language to chimps have had similar results (Premack, 1986).

The debate about chimpanzees' ability to use language focuses on two key issues. Can apes understand the meaning of symbols—that is, can they comprehend that one thing stands for another—and can apes learn syntax—that is, can they learn the mechanics and rules that give human language its creative productivity? The first of these issues may have been settled recently by Duane Rumbaugh and Sue Savage-Rumbaugh (1990). The researchers found strong evidence that two chimps named Sherman and Austin can understand symbols (see figure 7.10). For example, if Sherman or Austin is sitting in a room and a symbol for an object is displayed on a screen, the chimp goes into another room, finds the object, and brings it back. If the object is not there, the chimp comes back empty-handed (Cowley, 1988). Austin can play a game in which one chimp points to a symbol for food (candy), the other chimp selects the food from a tray, then they both eat it. These observations are clear evidence that chimps can understand symbols (Rumbaugh & others, 1991; Savage-Rumbaugh, 1991).

Although there still is no strong evidence that chimps can learn syntax, perhaps other animals can. Ron Schusterman has worked with a sea lion named Rocky, teaching him to follow such commands as "ball fetch" and "disc ball fetch." The first command means that Rocky should take a disc to a ball in his tank. The second command means that Rocky should take the ball to the disc. Although Rocky and other sea lions make some errors in decoding these complex commands, they perform much better than chance, indicating they have learned rules that link the ordering of symbols to abstract meanings. Such rules are either syntax or something close to it.

FIGURE 7.10

Sue Savage-Rumbaugh with a chimp in front of a board with languagelike symbols. The Rumbaughs (Sue and Duane) of the Yerkes Primate Center and Georgia State University have studied the basic question of whether chimps understand symbols. Their research evidence suggests chimps can understand symbols.

The debate over whether or not animals can use language to express thoughts is far from resolved. Researchers agree that animals can communicate with each other and that some can be trained to manipulate languagelike symbols. However, although such accomplishments may be remarkable, they fall far short of human language, with its infinite number of novel phrases to convey the richness and subtleties of meaning that are the foundation of human relationships.

Is There a Critical Period for Learning Language?

Former Secretary of State Henry Kissinger's heavy German accent illustrates the theory that there is a critical period for learning language. According to this theory, people who emigrate after the age of 12 will probably speak the new country's language with a foreign accent the rest of their lives, but, if people emigrate as young children, the accent goes away as the new language is learned (Asher & Garcia, 1969). Acquiring an accent is less related to how long you have lived somewhere than to the age at which you moved there. For example, if you move to a certain part of New York City before you turn 12 you'll probably "tawk" like a native. Apparently, puberty marks the close of a critical period for acquiring the phonological rules of various languages and dialects.

The stunted language development of a modern "wild child" also supports the idea of a critical period for language acquisition (see figure 7.11). In 1970 a California social worker made a routine visit to the home of a partially blind woman who had applied for public assistance. The social worker discovered that the woman and her husband had kept their 13-year-old daughter Genie locked away from the world. Kept in almost total isolation during childhood, Genie could not speak or stand erect. During the day, she was left to sit naked

FIGURE 7.11

An artist's drawing of Genie, a modern-day wild child.
Illustration by Roger Burkhart.

on a child's potty seat, restrained by a harness her father had made—she could move only her hands and feet. At night she was placed in a kind of straitjacket and caged in a crib with wire mesh sides and a cover. Whenever Genie made a noise, her father beat her. He never communicated with her in words but growled and barked at her instead.

Genie spent a number of years in extensive rehabilitation programs, such as speech and physical therapy (Curtiss, 1977). She eventually learned to walk with a jerky motion and to use the toilet. Genie also learned to recognize many words and to speak in rudimentary sentences. At first she spoke in one-word utterances. Later she was able to string together two-word combinations, such as "big teeth," "little marble," and "two hand." Consistent with the language development of most children, three-word combinations followed—for example, "small two cup." Unlike normal children, however, Genie did not learn how to ask questions and she doesn't understand grammar. Genie is not able to distinguish between

pronouns or passive and active verbs. Four years after she began stringing words together, her speech still sounded like a garbled telegram. As an adult she speaks in short, mangled sentences, such as "father hit leg," "big wood," and "Genie hurt."

Children who are abandoned, abused, and not exposed to language for years, such as Genie and the Wild Boy of Aveyron, rarely learn to speak normally. Such tragic evidence supports the critical period hypothesis in language development.

Environmental Influences on Language Learning

We do not learn language in a social vacuum. Most children are imbued with language at a very early age (Furrow & Moore, 1991; Snow, 1989a). Children's earliest exposures to language are usually through their parents. Roger Brown (1973) wondered how parents might help their children learn language. He was especially interested in whether parents reinforce their children for speaking in grammatical ways, as behavioral theories would predict. After spending many hours observing parents and their young children, he found that parents sometimes smile and praise their children for correct sentences, but they also reinforce many ungrammatical sentences. Brown concluded that learning grammar is not based on reinforcement.

What are some of the ways that environment contributes to language development? Imitation is one important candidate. A child who is slow to develop her language ability can be helped if her parents speak to her carefully in grammatically correct sentences. Recent evidence also suggests that parents provide more corrective feedback for children's ungrammatical utterances than Brown originally thought (Bohannon & Stanowicz, 1988; Penner, 1987). Even so, a number of experts believe that imitation and reinforcement *facilitate* language but are not absolutely *necessary* for language acquisition.

One intriguing environmental factor that contributes to a young child's language acquisition is called **motherese**, *the way parents and other adults often talk to babies in a higher-than-normal frequency, in a greater-than-normal pitch, and in simple*

In every culture, individuals are bathed in language from a very early age.

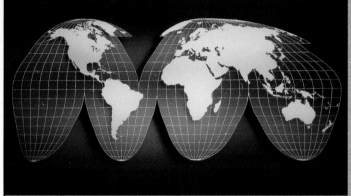

The Rich Language Tradition of Black Americans

Many Black Americans have a rich language tradition that is varied, cognitively demanding, and well suited to many real-life situations. How has this tradition recently been abandoned?

Shirley Heath (1989) recently examined the language traditions of Black Americans from low-income backgrounds. She traced some aspects of Black English to the time of slavery. Heath also examined how those speech patterns have carried over into Black English today. She found that agricultural areas in the southern United States have an especially rich oral tradition.

Specifically she found that adults do not simplify or edit their talk for children, in essence challenging the children to be highly active listeners. Also, adults ask only "real questions" of children—that is, questions for which the adult does not already know the answer. Adults also engage in a type of teasing with children, encouraging them to use their wits in communication. For example, a grandmother might pretend that she wants to take a child's hat and then starts a lively exchange in which the child must understand many subtleties of argument, mood, and humor—does Grandma really want my hat? Is she mad at me? Is she making a joke? Can I persuade her to give it back to me? Finally, there is an appreciation of wit and flexibility in how language is used, as well as an acknowledgement of individual differences—one person might be respected for recounting stories, another for negotiating and peace-making skills.

Heath argues that the language tradition she describes is richly varied, cognitively demanding, and well suited to many real-life situations. She says that the oral and literary traditions among poor Blacks in the cities are well suited for many job situations. Years ago many inner-city jobs required only that a person follow directions in order to perform repetitive tasks. Today many positions require continuous interactions involving considerable flexibility in language, such as the ability to persuade co-workers or to express dissatisfaction, in a subtle way, for example.

Despite its utility in many job situations, the rich language tradition possessed by low-income Black Americans does not meet with the educational priorities of our nation's schools. Too often schools stress rote memorization, minimizing group interaction and discouraging individual variations in communicative style. Also, the language tradition of Black culture is rapidly dying in the face of current life among poor Blacks, where the structure of low-income, frequently single-parent families often provides little verbal stimulation for children. In sum, the rich language tradition of many Black Americans is too often being squashed in the classroom and neglected at home, despite its utility in many real-world circumstances.

words and sentences. Although no one talks to another adult in that sing-song way, most people automatically shift into motherese as soon as they start talking to a baby—usually without being aware they're doing so. We speak in motherese, it seems, to capture the infant's attention and maintain communication (Snow, 1989b).

Motherese was documented as early as the first century B.C., and it's virtually universal (Ferguson, 1977). However, the particular format motherese takes varies somewhat from culture to culture. For example, a study of American English and Spanish speakers in Texas showed that English speakers favor altering the volume and pitch of speech, or altering the sounds of words, such as shortening vowels or consonants. In contrast, Spanish speakers tend to substitute and repeat words, strategies designed to promote interaction between the speaker and the child (Blount, 1982). Sociocultural Worlds 7.1 describes how language is used in Black culture to engage children in intellectually challenging ways.

How Language Develops

Even before babies say their first words, at the age of 10 to 13 months, they babble. Babbling—endlessly repeating sounds and syllables, such as "goo-goo" and "ga-ga"—begins at about the age of 3 to 6 months and is determined by biological readiness, not reinforcement or the ability to hear (Locke & others, 1991). Even deaf babies babble for a time (Lenneberg, Rebelsky, & Nichols, 1965). Babbling probably allows the baby to exercise its vocal chords and helps develop articulation.

A child's first words name important people (*dada*), familiar animals (*kitty*), vehicles (*car*), toys (*ball*), food (*milk*), body parts (*eye*), clothes (*hat*), household items (*clock*), or greetings (*bye*). These were babies' first words 50 years ago and they are babies' first words today (Clark, 1983). The **holophrase hypothesis** *is the concept that a single word is used to imply a complete sentence; it is characteristic of an infant's first words.* For example, the demand "Milk!" may mean, "I'm hungry and want to eat *now*."

By the time children reach the age of 18 to 24 months, they usually utter two-word statements. They quickly grasp the importance of expressing concepts and the role that language plays in communicating with others. To convey meaning in two-word statements, children rely heavily on gesture, tone, and context. The wealth of meaning children can communicate with two words includes the following:

Identification: See doggie.
Location: Book there.
Repetition: More milk.
Nonexistence: Allgone thing.
Negation: Not wolf.
Possession: My candy.
Attribution: Big car.
Agent-action: Mama walk.
Action-direct-object: Hit you.
Action-indirect-object: Give Papa.
Action-instrument: Cut knife.
Question: Where ball? (Slobin, 1972)

These examples are from children all over the world, who first learned to speak English, German, Russian, Finnish, Turkish, or Samoan. Although these two-word sentences omit many parts of speech, they are remarkably succinct in conveying many messages. In fact, in every language, a child's first combination of words has this economical quality. **Telegraphic speech** *is the use of short and precise words to communicate; it is characteristic of young children's two- or three-word combinations.* When we send a telegram, for example, we try to be short and precise, excluding any unnecessary words. As a result, articles, auxiliary verbs, and other connectives usually are omitted. However, telegraphic speech is not limited to two-word phrases. "Mommy give ice cream" and "Mommy give Susie ice cream" also are examples of telegraphic speech. As children leave the two-word stage, they move rather quickly into three-, four-, and five-word combinations.

As we have just seen, language unfolds in a sequence. At every point in development, a child's linguistic interaction with parents and others obeys certain principles (Brown, 1988; Conti-Ramsden & Snow, 1991; Maratsos, 1991). Not only is this development strongly influenced by the child's biological wiring, but the language environment is more complex than behaviorists, such as Skinner, imagined. As we take a final look at this remarkable concept called language, we will consider its ties with culture and cognition.

Language, Culture, and Cognition

Take a moment and reflect on the following questions. Did the culture in which you grew up influence your language? What role does language play in academic achievement? Would the range of thought diminish if language were cut down to the bone, as Smith's colleague at the Ministry of Truth predicted at the beginning of this chapter?

Linguist Benjamin Whorf argued that language actually determines the way we think. Whorf's (1956) **linguistic relativity hypothesis** *states that language determines the structure of thinking and shapes our basic ideas.* The Inuit in Alaska, for instance, have a dozen or more words to describe the various textures, colors, and physical states of snow, the Hopi Indians have no words for past and future, and Arabs have 6,000 words for camels.

Our cultural experiences for a particular concept shape a catalog of names that can be either rich or poor. For example, if the "camel" part of your mental library of names is the product of years of experience with camels, you probably "see" and "think" about this desert animal in finer gradations than does someone who has no experience with camels. In this way, language acts like a window that filters the amount and nature of information passed on for further processing.

Critics of Whorf's theory say that words merely reflect, rather than cause, the way we think. The Inuits' adaptability and livelihood in Alaska depend on their capacity to recognize various conditions of snow and ice. The professional football player's vocabulary also

Our cultural experiences for a particular concept shape a catalog of names that can be either rich or poor. Consider how different your mental library of names for *camel* might be if you had extensive experience with camels in a desert world and how different your mental library of names for *snow* might be if you lived in an arctic world of ice and cold.

contains a number of unique words—for example, a player might know 30 terms for a defensive alignment and 7 terms for rushing the passer. However, even though you don't know the words for the different types of snow or defensive alignments in football, you may still be able to perceive these differences.

Rosch (1973) found just that. She studied the effect of language on color perception among the Dani in New Guinea. The Dani have only two words for color—one that approximates white and one that approximates black. If the linguistic relativity hypothesis were correct, the Dani would lack the ability to tell the difference among such colors as green, blue, red, yellow, and purple. However, Rosch found that the Dani perceive colors just as we perceive them. As we know from chapter 3, color perception is biologically determined by receptors in the retinas in the eyes. Even though Whorf's linguistic relativity hypothesis missed the mark, researchers agree that, although language does not determine thought, it can influence it.

What are the arguments for and against bilingual education?

Language's Role in Achievement and School

A hot debate in many local school districts, especially in Florida, Texas, California, New Mexico, and Arizona, is how best to educate children whose first language is not English (Beals & DeTemple, 1991; Dickinson & Moreton, 1991). Today educators realize that such children have a difficult time in English-speaking classes. As bilingual education researchers Kenji Hakuta and Eugene Garcia (1989) point out, the ultimate goal of mainstreaming students into English-speaking classrooms is widely shared, but the question of how to achieve this goal has both parents and educators up in arms.

One camp favors native-language instruction. According to proponents of this approach, mainstreaming should be deferred until a child has mastered his or her native language. They argue that developing competence in fundamental skills, such as reading and writing in the student's native tongue, provides a basic foundation for learning all academic subjects, such as math and science, as well as English.

In contrast, opponents of this strategy argue that the first step toward mainstreaming nonnative speakers should be to teach them English. Once the children are fluent in English, they are ready to go into standard classrooms. If these children find themselves behind in subjects, catching up should be relatively easy if they have mastered English. The approach advocated by the all-English theory is that classes should be taught in English—simplified if necessary—from the start. This English-only approach to education can be coupled with English-as-a-second-language instruction to speed the children's progress.

Unfortunately, even after 20 years of debate and research, psychologists still have little wisdom to offer on the subject. Although there have been many studies on bilingual education, the methods have often been weak and the outcomes inconclusive. One persistent problem is that too many studies have focused on only one measure, such as a child's competence in English. These studies have overlooked how well the children are doing in other subjects, such as math and science. In addition, these studies have not considered such critical factors as how well the children are coping with school and developing positive social relationships.

Even so, research has shed light on at least one aspect of the bilingual education debate. At one time, bilingualism was believed to be detrimental. Educators reasoned that a child's first language would interfere with learning a second language. However, research has shown that children *can* learn a second language without being hampered by their first (McLaughlin, 1987). What's more, children who are proficient in one language tend to learn a second language much more easily (Cummins, 1983). It is also clear that children who speak nonstandard English, such as children with inner-city backgrounds, are likely to have a more difficult time acquiring academic skills than their middle-class counterparts.

Our thinking and language skills set us apart from other life forms on this planet. Through our thinking and language, we have mastered our world and adapted effectively to its challenges. We will continue our investigation of thinking and language as we explore individual differences in mental functioning by studying the nature of intelligence.

Intelligence

The primary components of intelligence are close to the mental processes we have already discussed in this chapter—thinking and language. The difference between how we discussed thinking and language and how we will discuss intelligence lies in the concept of individual differences in assessment. **Individual differences** *are the consistent, stable ways people are different from each other.* We can talk about individual differences in personality (which we will do in chapter 12) or in any other domain of psychology, but it is in the area of intelligence that psychologists give the most attention to individual differences. For example, an intelligence test informs you if you can logically reason better than most others who have taken the test. Before we discuss intelligence tests, though, we need to examine what intelligence is and how tests are constructed.

What Is Intelligence?

Intelligence is one of our most highly prized possessions, yet it's a concept that even the most intelligent people have failed to agree on. Unlike such characteristics as height, weight, and age, intelligence cannot be directly measured. It's a bit like size, which is a more abstract notion than height or weight. We can only estimate size from a set of empirical measures of height and weight. Similarly, we can only estimate a person's intelligence. We cannot peel back a scalp and observe intellectual processes in action. The only way we can study these processes is indirectly, by evaluating a person's intelligent acts (Kail & Pellegrino, 1985). For the most part, psychologists rely on intelligence tests to provide an estimate of these mental abilities.

Many psychologists and lay people equate intelligence with verbal ability and problem-solving skills. Others prefer to define it as a person's ability to learn from and adapt to the experiences of everyday life. Let's combine the two and settle on the following definition of **intelligence**: *verbal ability, problem-solving skills, and the ability to learn from and adapt to the experiences of everyday life* (see figure 7.12).

Although we have just defined general intelligence, keep in mind that the way intelligence is expressed in behavior may vary from culture to culture (Lonner, 1990). For example, in most Western cultures, people are considered intelligent if they are both smart (have considerable knowledge and can solve verbal problems) and fast (can process information quickly). On the other hand, in the Buganda culture in Uganda, people who are wise, slow in thought, and say the socially correct thing are considered intelligent (Wober, 1974).

How Tests Are Constructed and Evaluated

The first evidence of formal tests comes from China. In 2200 B.C. the emperor Ta Yu conducted a series of three oral "competency tests" for government officials; based on the results, they were either promoted or fired (Sax, 1989). Numerous variations on those early exams have been causing anxiety for employees and students ever since.

Any good test must meet three criteria—it must be reliable, it must be valid, and it must be standardized. With a reliable test, scores should not fluctuate significantly as a result of chance

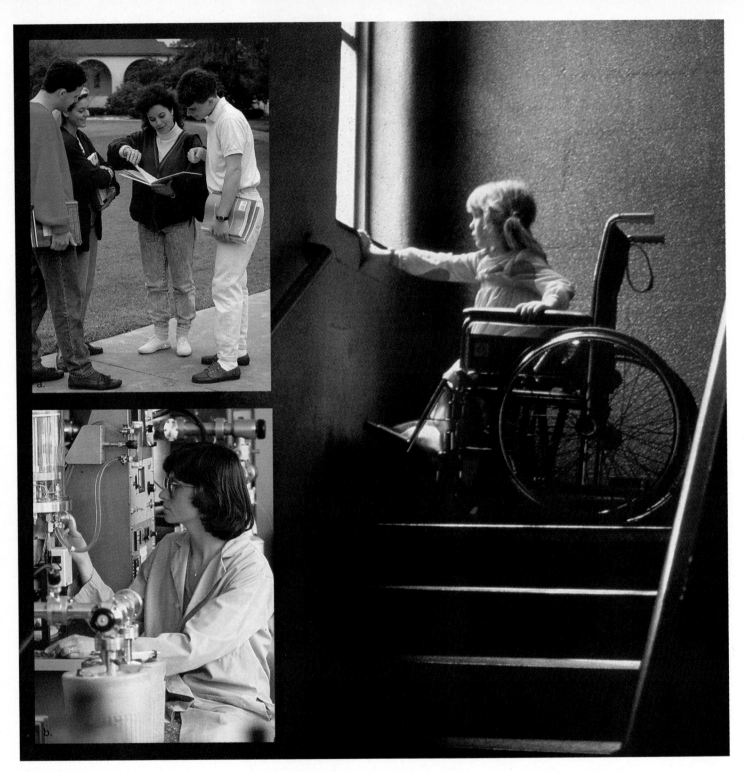

FIGURE 7.12

Defining intelligence. Intelligence is an abstract concept that has been defined in various ways. The three most commonly agreed-upon aspects of intelligence are the following: (a) verbal ability as reflected in the verbal skills of these college students faced with the task of writing a paper for tomorrow morning's class; (b) problem-solving skills, as reflected in this scientist's search for an AIDS cure; and (c) the ability to learn from and adapt to experiences of everyday life, as reflected in this handicapped child's adaptation to her inability to walk.

factors, such as how much sleep the test taker got the night before, who the examiner is, or the temperature in the testing room. **Reliability** *is how consistently a person performs on a test.* One method of assessing reliability is **test-retest reliability,** *which involves giving the same person the same test on two different occasions.* For example, a reliable test would be one on which the same college students who score high one day also score high 6 months later. One drawback of test-retest reliability is that people sometimes do better the second time they take the test because they are familiar with it.

Another way that consistency can be deceptive is that a test may or may not measure the attribute we seek. For example, let's say we want to measure intelligence but the test design is flawed and we actually measure something else, such as anxiety. The test might consistently measure how anxious the subjects are and, thus, have high reliability but fail to measure intelligence. **Validity** *is the extent to which a test measures what it is intended to measure.* Two important forms of validity are content and criterion validity.

Content validity *refers to a test's ability to give a broad picture of what is to be measured.* For example, if your instructor for this class plans a comprehensive final exam, it will probably cover topics from each of the chapters rather than just two or three chapters. If an intelligence test purports to measure both verbal ability and problem-solving ability, the test should include a liberal sampling of each. The test would not have high content validity if it asked you to define several vocabulary items (one measure of verbal ability) and did not require you to use reason in solving a number of problems.

Criterion validity *refers to a test's ability to predict other measures, or criteria, of an attribute.* For example, rather than relying solely on the results of one intelligence test to assess a person's intelligence, a psychologist might also ask that person's employer how he or she performs at work. The employer's perceptions would be another criterion for assessing intelligence. Using more than one measure—such as administering a different intelligence test, soliciting an employer's perception of intelligence, and observing a person's problem-solving ability—is a good strategy for establishing criterion validity.

Good tests are not only reliable and valid, but they also are standardized. **Standardization** *involves developing uniform procedures for administering and scoring a test, and it also involves developing norms for the test.* Uniform testing procedures require that the testing environment be as similar as possible for everyone who takes the test. For example, the test directions and the amount of time allowed to complete the test should be uniform. **Norms** *are established standards of performance for a test. This is accomplished by giving the test to a large group of people who represent the target population. This allows the researcher to determine the distribution of test scores. Norms inform us which scores are considered high, low, or average.* For example, a score of 120 on an intelligence test has little meaning alone. The score takes on meaning when we compare it with other scores. If only 20 percent of the standardized group scores above 120, then we can interpret that score as high, rather than average or low. Many tests of intelligence are designed for people from diverse groups. So that the tests will be applicable to such different groups, many tests have norms—that is, established standards of performance for people of different ages.

Although there has been some effort to standardize intelligence tests for Blacks and Hispanics, little has been done to standardize tests for people from other ethnic minorities. Psychologists need to ensure that the tests are standardized for a person's particular ethnic group and to put the test results in an appropriate cultural context (Sue, 1990). Otherwise they must use caution interpreting the test's results.

The Measurement and Nature of Intelligence

Robert J. Sternberg recalls being terrified of taking IQ tests as a child. He literally froze, he says, when the time came to take such tests. Even as an adult, Sternberg stings with humiliation when he recalls being in sixth grade and taking an IQ test with the fifth graders. Sternberg finally overcame his anxieties about IQ tests and not only performed much better on them, but at age 13 he even devised his own IQ test and began assessing his classmates—until the school psychologist found out and scolded him. In fact, Sternberg became so fascinated with the topic that he's made it a lifelong pursuit. Sternberg's theory of intelligence, which we will discuss later in the chapter, has received considerable attention recently. We will begin at the beginning, with the first intelligence test, in our discussion of measuring intelligence and its nature.

The Binet Tests

In 1904 the French Ministry of Education asked psychologist Alfred Binet to devise a method of identifying children who were unable to learn in school. School officials wanted to reduce overcrowding by placing those who did not benefit from regular classroom teaching into special schools. Binet and his student Theophile Simon developed an intelligence test to meet this request. The test is referred to as the 1905 Scale and consisted of 30 questions ranging from the ability to touch one's nose or ear when asked to the ability to draw designs from memory and define abstract concepts.

Binet developed the concept of **mental age (MA),** *which is an individual's level of mental development relative to others.* Binet reasoned that a mentally retarded child would perform like a normal child of a younger age. He developed averages for intelligence by testing 50 normal children from 3 to 11 years of age. Children who were thought to be mentally retarded also

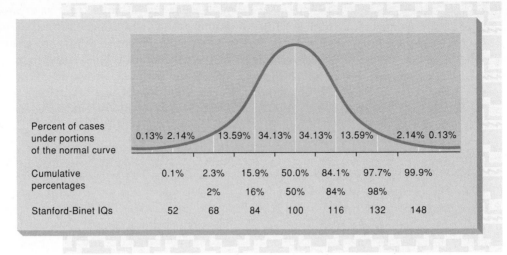

Percent of cases under portions of the normal curve	0.13%	2.14%	13.59%	34.13%	34.13%	13.59%	2.14%	0.13%
Cumulative percentages	0.1%	2.3%	15.9%	50.0%	84.1%	97.7%	99.9%	
		2%	16%	50%	84%	98%		
Stanford-Binet IQs	52	68	84	100	116	132	148	

FIGURE 7.13

The normal curve and Stanford-Binet IQ scores. The distribution of IQ scores approximates a normal curve. Most of the population falls in the middle range of scores. Notice that extremely high and extremely low scores are very rare. Slightly more than two-thirds of the scores fall between 84 and 116. Only about 1 in 50 individuals has an IQ of more than 132 and only about 1 in 50 individuals has an IQ of less than 68.

were tested. Their scores were then compared with the scores of normal children the same chronological age. Average mental-age scores (MA) correspond to chronological age (CA), which is age from birth. A bright child has an MA above CA; a dull child has an MA below CA.

The term **intelligence quotient (IQ)** *was devised in 1912 by William Stern. IQ consists of a person's mental age divided by chronological age, multiplied by 100:*

$$IQ = MA/CA \times 100$$

If mental age is the same as chronological age, then the person's IQ is 100; if mental age is above chronological age, then IQ is more than 100; if mental age is below chronological age, then IQ is less than 100. Scores noticeably above 100 are considered above average, and scores noticeably below 100 are considered below average. For example, a 6-year-old child with a mental age of 8 would have an IQ of 133, whereas a 6-year-old child with a mental age of 5 would have an IQ of 83.

The Binet test has been revised many times to incorporate advances in the understanding of intelligence and intelligence testing. These revisions are called the Stanford-Binet tests (Stanford University is where the revisions were done). Many of the revisions were carried out by Lewis Terman, who applied Stern's IQ concept to the test, developed extensive norms, and provided detailed, clear instructions for each problem on the test.

In an extensive effort to standardize the Stanford-Binet test, it has been given to thousands of children and adults of different ages, selected at random from various parts of the United States. By administering the test to large numbers of people and recording the results, researchers have found that intelligence measured by the Stanford-Binet approximates a normal distribution (see figure 7.13). A **normal distribution** *is symmetrical, with a majority of cases falling in the middle of the possible range of scores and few scores appearing toward the extremes of the range.*

The Wechsler Scales

Besides the Stanford-Binet, the other widely used intelligence tests are the Wechsler scales, developed by David Wechsler. They include the Wechsler Adult Intelligence Scale-Revised (WAIS-R); the Wechsler Intelligence Scale for Children-Revised (WISC-R), to test children between the ages of 6 and 16; and the Wechsler Preschool and Primary Scale of Intelligence (WPPSI), to test children from the ages of 4 to 6 1/2 (Wechsler, 1949, 1955, 1967, 1974, 1981).

Not only do the Wechsler scales provide an overall IQ score, but the items are grouped according to 11 subscales, 6 of which are verbal and 5 nonverbal. This allows an examiner to obtain separate verbal and nonverbal IQ scores and to see quickly the areas of mental performance in which a tested individual is below average, average, or above average. The inclusion of a number of nonverbal subscales makes the Wechsler test more representative of verbal and nonverbal intelligence; the Stanford-Binet test includes some nonverbal items but not as many as the Wechsler scales. Several of the Wechsler subscales are shown in figure 7.14.

Verbal subtests

Similarities

An individual must think logically and abstractly to answer a number of questions about how things might be similar.

For example, "In what ways are boats and trains the same?"

Comprehension

This subtest is designed to measure an individual's judgment and common sense.

For example, "Why do individuals buy automobile insurance?"

Performance subtests

Picture arrangement

A series of pictures out of sequence is shown to an individual, who is asked to place them in their proper order to tell an appropriate story. This subtest evaluates how individuals integrate information to make it logical and meaningful.

For example, "The pictures below need to be placed in an appropriate order to tell a story."

Block design

An individual must assemble a set of multicolored blocks to match designs that the examiner shows. Visual-motor coordination, perceptual organization, and the ability to visualize spatially are assessed.

For example, "Use the four blocks on the left to make the pattern at the right."

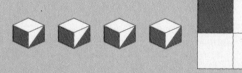

Remember that the Wechsler includes 11 subscales, 6 verbal and 5 nonverbal. Four of the subscales are shown here.

FIGURE 7.14

Sample subtests of the Wechsler Adult Intelligence Scale-Revised. Remember that the Wechsler includes 11 subscales, 6 verbal and 5 nonverbal. Four of the subscales are shown here.

Does Intelligence Have a Single Nature?

Is it more appropriate to think of intelligence as a general term that can peg people in terms of how "smart" or "dumb" they are, or is it a number of specific abilities? Long before Wechsler analyzed intelligence in terms of general and specific abilities (giving an individual an overall IQ but also providing information about specific subcomponents of intelligence), Charles Spearman (1927) proposed that intelligence has two factors. **Two-factor theory** *is Spearman's theory that individuals have both general intelligence, which he called g, and a number of specific intelligences, which he called s.* Spearman believed that these two factors accounted for a person's performance on an intelligence test.

However, some researchers abandoned the idea of a general intelligence and searched for specific factors only. **Multiple-factor theory** *is L. L. Thurstone's (1938) theory that intelligence consists of seven primary mental abilities: verbal comprehension, number ability, word fluency, spatial visualization, associative memory, reasoning, and perceptual speed.*

Sternberg (1986, 1988) believes that intelligence has three factors. **Triarchic theory** *is Sternberg's theory that intelligence consists of componential intelligence, experiential intelligence, and contextual intelligence.* Consider Ann, who scores high on traditional intelligence tests, such as the Stanford-Binet, and is a star analytical thinker. Consider Juan, who does not have the best test scores but has an insightful and creative mind. Consider also Art, a street-smart person who has learned to deal in practical ways with his world, although his scores on traditional IQ tests are low.

Sternberg calls Ann's analytical thinking and abstract reasoning componential intelligence; it is the closest to what we call intelligence in this chapter and what is commonly measured by intelligence tests. Juan's insightful and creative thinking is called experiential

a.

b.

c.

FIGURE 7.15

Sternberg's triarchic model of intelligence.
(a) Componential intelligence is the closest to what is commonly measured on intelligence tests and is reflected in the ability to process information as we read. (b) Photographer Mieke Maas showed experiential intelligence in creating this unique image of a printed circuit board inside an individual's head. Experiential intelligence involves creativity and insight.
(c) Contextual intelligence refers to practical knowledge, especially "street smarts."

intelligence by Sternberg. Art's street smarts and practical knowledge are called contextual intelligence by Sternberg (see figure 7.15).

In Sternberg's view of componential intelligence, the basic unit in intelligence is a component, simply defined as a basic unit of information processing. Sternberg believes that such components include the ability to acquire or store information, to retain or retrieve information, to transfer information, to plan, to make decisions, to solve problems, and to translate thoughts into performance. Notice the similarity of these components to the description of memory in chapter 6 and the description of thinking earlier in this chapter.

The second part of Sternberg's model focuses on experience. According to Sternberg, intellectual people have the ability to solve new problems quickly, but they also learn how to solve familiar problems in an automatic, rote way so their minds are free to handle other problems that require insight and creativity.

The third part of the model involves practical intelligence—such as how to get out of trouble, how to replace a fuse, and how to get along with people. Sternberg describes this practical, or contextual, intelligence as all of the important information about getting along in the real world that we are not taught in school. He believes that contextual intelligence is sometimes more important than "book knowledge."

The Heredity-Environment Controversy

Arthur Jensen (1969) sparked lively and at times hostile debate when he stated his theory that intelligence is primarily inherited and that environment and culture play only a minimal role in intelligence. In one of his most provocative statements, Jensen claimed that genetics account for clear-cut differences in the average intelligence among races, nationalities, and social classes. When Jensen published an article in the *Harvard Educational Review* stating that lower intelligence probably is the reason that Blacks do not perform as well in school as Whites, he was called naive and racist. He received hate mail by the bushel and police had to escort him to his classes at the University of California at Berkeley.

Jensen reviewed the research on intelligence, much of which involved comparisons of identical and fraternal twins. Remember that identical twins have exactly the same genetic makeup. If intelligence is genetically determined, Jensen reasoned, identical twins' IQs should be similar. Fraternal twins and ordinary siblings are less similar genetically, so their IQs should be less similar. Jensen found support for his argument. The studies on intelligence in identical twins that Jensen examined showed an average correlation between their IQs of .82, a very high positive association. Investigations of fraternal twins, however, produced an average correlation of .50, a moderately high positive correlation. Note the substantial difference of .32. To show that genetic factors are more important than environmental factors, Jensen compared the intelligence of identical twins reared together with that of those reared apart. The correlation for those reared together was .89 and for those reared apart it was .78, a difference of .11. Jensen argued that, if environmental factors are more important than genetic factors, siblings reared apart, who experience different environments, should have IQs that differ more than .11. Jensen places heredity's influence on intelligence at about 80 percent.

Today most researchers agree that genetics do not determine intelligence to the extent Jensen envisioned. Their estimates fall more in the 50/50 range—50 percent genetic makeup, 50 percent environmental factors (Plomin, 1989; Plomin, DeFries, & McClearn, in press). For most people, this means that modifying their environment can change their IQ scores considerably (Weinberg, 1989). It also means that programs designed to enrich a person's environment can have a considerable impact, improving school achievement and the acquisition of skills needed for employability. Although genetic endowment may always influence a person's intellectual ability, the environmental influences and opportunities we provide children and adults make a difference (Brody, 1992).

Keep in mind, though, that environmental influences are complex. Growing up with "all the advantages," for example, does not necessarily guarantee success. Children from wealthy families may have easy access to excellent schools, books, travel, and tutoring, but they may take such opportunities for granted and fail to develop the motivation to learn and achieve. In the same way, being "poor" or "disadvantaged" does not automatically equal "doomed."

Some years ago, one of the authors of this book knocked on the door of a house in a low-income area of a large city. The father came to the door and invited the author into the living room. Even though it was getting dark outside, no lights were on inside

the house. The father excused himself, then returned with a light bulb, which he screwed into a lamp socket. He said he could barely pay his monthly mortgage and the electric company had threatened to turn off the electricity, so he was carefully monitoring how much electricity his family used. There were seven children in the family, ranging in age from 2 to 16 years old. Neither parent had completed high school. The father worked as a bricklayer when he could find a job, and the mother ironed clothes in a laundry. The parents wanted their children to pursue education and to have more opportunities in life than they had had. The children from the inner-city family were exposed to both positive and negative influences. On the one hand, they were growing up in an intact family in which education was encouraged, and their parents provided a model of the work ethic. On the other hand, they were being shortchanged by society and had few opportunities to develop their intellectual abilities.

Researchers increasingly are interested in manipulating the early environment of children who are at risk for impoverished intelligence. The emphasis is on prevention rather than remediation (Garwood & others, 1989; Heinicke, Beckwith, & Thompson, 1988). Many low-income parents have difficulty providing an intellectually stimulating environment for their children. Programs that educate parents to be more sensitive caregivers and that train them to be better teachers, as well as support services such as Head Start, can make a difference in a child's intellectual development (Ramey, 1989).

Culture and Ethnicity

Are there cultural and ethnic differences in intelligence? How does adaptation affect the role culture plays in understanding intelligence? Are standard intelligence tests biased? If so, can we develop tests that are fair?

Cultural and Ethnic Comparisons

In the United States, children from Black and Hispanic families score below children from White families on standardized intelligence tests. On the average, Black American school children score 10 to 15 points lower on standardized intelligence tests than White American school children (Anastasi, 1988). We are talking about average scores, though. Estimates also indicate that 15 to 25 percent of all Black school children score higher than half of all White school children, and many Whites score lower than most Blacks. This is because the distributions of the scores for Blacks and Whites overlap.

Although the greatest interest has been in Black-White comparisons, studies on intelligence suggest some differences among Jewish, Chinese, Black, and Puerto Rican children (Lesser, Fifer, & Clark, 1965). Jewish children score higher on verbal abilities, lower on numerical and spatial abilities; Chinese children score higher on numerical and spatial abilities, lower on

a. b. c. d.

(a) Jewish, (b) Chinese, (c) African American, and (d) Puerto Rican children: what are some of the strengths and weaknesses in the intelligence of these children from different ethnic and cultural backgrounds?

verbal abilities; Black children score higher on verbal abilities, lower on reasoning and numerical abilities; Puerto Rican children score higher on spatial and reasoning abilities, lower on verbal abilities.

How extensively are ethnic differences in intelligence influenced by heredity and environment? There is no evidence to support a genetic interpretation. For example, as Black Americans have gained social, economic, and educational opportunities, the gap between Black and White children on standardized intelligence tests has begun to narrow, and when children from disadvantaged Black families are adopted into more advantaged middle-class families their scores on intelligence tests more closely resemble national averages for middle-class than for lower-class children (Scarr, 1989; Scarr & Weinberg, 1976).

Culture, Intelligence, and Adaptation

People adapt to their environment, and what's appropriate in one environment may not be appropriate in another. As mentioned earlier in the chapter, intelligence is expressed differently in different cultures (Berry & Bennett, 1992; Berry & others, 1992; Irvine & Berry, 1988; Kagitcibasi & Berry, 1989; Sternberg, 1988). In one study, the researcher asked members of the Kpelle in Liberia (located on the western coast of Africa) to sort 20 objects (Glick, 1975). Rather than sort the objects into the "appropriate" categories the researcher had predicted, the Kpelle sorted the objects into functional groups—such as a knife with an apple and a potato with a hoe. Surprised by the answers, the researcher asked the Kpelle to explain their reasoning. The Kpelle responded that that was the way a wise person would group things. When the researcher asked how a fool would classify the objects, the Kpelle answered that four neat piles of food in one category, four tools in another category, and so on

was the fool's way. The Kpelle were not lacking in intelligence; the researcher lacked an understanding of the Kpelle culture. The Kpelle sorted the items in ways that were adaptive for their culture.

Another example of human adaptability involves spatial ability. One study showed that people who live in hunter-gatherer societies score higher on spatial ability tests than do people from industrialized societies (Berry, 1971). People who must hunt to eat depend on their spatial skills for survival.

Few of us will ever have first-hand experience with hunter-gatherer societies, but many of us know people who are adaptable, savvy, and successful yet do not score correspondingly high on intelligence tests. Canadian cross-cultural psychologist John Berry (1983) has an explanation for this gap between intelligence exhibited in one's own culture and intelligence displayed in a formal testing situation. He describes people as being embedded in four levels of environmental contexts. Level one, the ecological context, is an individual's natural habitat. Level two, the experiential context, is the pattern of recurring experiences from which the individual regularly learns. Level three, the performance context, is the limited set of circumstances in which the individual's natural behavior is observed. Level four, the experimental context, is the set of environmental circumstances under which test scores are actually generated (Berry's model is presented in figure 7.16).

When the experimental context differs considerably from the ecological or experiential context, Berry says, the individuals being tested are at a disadvantage. Presumably, the greater the difference, the greater the disadvantage. However, relations among contexts change. If an individual has been given the same test previously, some of the gap between the experiential and experimental contexts closes, resulting in higher test scores.

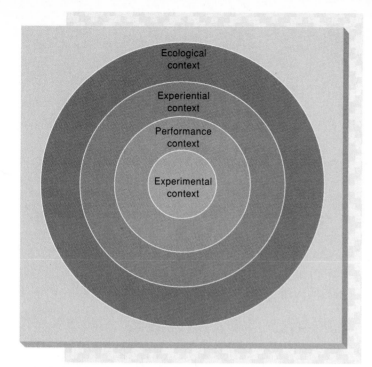

FIGURE 7.16

Berry's model of the contexts of intelligence. In this model of the intelligence, there is much more to consider than the actual context in which a test is being administered (the experimental context). In addition, it is also important to consider three other contextual levels—the performance context, experiential context, and ecological context.

Cultural Bias and Culture-Fair Tests

Many of the early intelligence tests were culturally biased, favoring people from urban rather than rural environments, middle-class rather than lower-class people, and Whites rather than Blacks (Miller-Jones, 1989). For example, a question on an early test asked what should be done if you find a 3-year-old child in the street. The correct answer was "call the police"; however, children from inner-city families who perceive the police as adversaries are unlikely to choose this answer. Similarly, children from rural areas might not choose this answer if there is no police force nearby. Such questions clearly do not measure the knowledge necessary to adapt to one's environment or to be "intelligent" in an inner-city neighborhood or in rural America (Scarr, 1984). Also, members of minority groups often do not speak English or may speak nonstandard English. Consequently, they may be at a disadvantage in trying to understand verbal questions framed in standard English, even if the content of the test is appropriate (Gibbs & Huang, 1989).

Cultures also vary in the way they define intelligence (Rogoff, 1990). Most European Americans, for example, think of intelligence in terms of technical skills, but people in Kenya

consider responsible participation in family and social life an integral part of intelligence. Similarly, an intelligent person in Uganda is someone who knows what to do and then follows through with appropriate action. Intelligence to the Iatmul people of Papua, New Guinea, involves the ability to remember the names of 10,000 to 20,000 clans, and the islanders in the widely dispersed Caroline Islands incorporate the talent of navigating by the stars into their definition of intelligence (see figure 7.17).

Cultural bias is dramatically underscored by such tests as the one shown in table 7.1 on page 205. This test was developed to reduce the cultural disadvantage Black children face. More information about cultural bias in intelligence testing appears in Sociocultural Worlds 7.2 on page 206, where you will read about a widely publicized case in which a 6-year-old Black boy was classified as mentally retarded.

Another example of possible cultural bias in intelligence tests can be seen in the life of Gregory Ochoa. When Gregory was a high school student, he and his classmates took an IQ test. When Gregory looked at the test questions, he understood only a few words, since he did not speak English very well and spoke Spanish at home. Several weeks later, Gregory was placed in a special class for mentally retarded students. Many of the students in the class, it turns out, had last names such as Ramirez and Gonzales. Gregory lost interest in school, dropped out, and eventually joined the Navy. In the Navy, Gregory took high school courses and earned enough credits to attend college later. He graduated from San Jose City College as an honor student, continued his education, and became a professor of social work at the University of Washington in Seattle.

As a result of such cases, researchers have tried to develop tests that accurately reflect a person's intelligence. **Culture-fair tests** *are intelligence tests that attempt to reduce cultural bias.* Two types of culture-fair tests have been devised. The first includes questions that are familiar to people from all socioeconomic and ethnic backgrounds. For example, a child might be asked how a bird and a dog are different, on the assumption that virtually all children are familiar with birds and dogs. The second type of culture-fair test removes all verbal questions. Figure 7.18 on page 207 shows a sample question from the Raven Progressive Matrices Test. Even though such tests as the Raven Progressive Matrices are designed to be culture-fair, people with more education still score higher than those with less education.

One test that takes into account the socioeconomic background of children is the SOMPA, which stands for System of Multicultural Pluralistic Assessment (Mercer & Lewis, 1978). This test can be given to children from 5 to 11 years of age and was especially designed for children from low-income families. Instead of relying on a single test, SOMPA is based on information from four areas of a child's life:

a.

FIGURE 7.17

Iatmul and Caroline Islander intelligence. (a) The intelligence of the Iatmul people of Papua, New Guinea, involves the ability to remember the names of many clans. (b) The Caroline Islands number 680 in the Pacific Ocean east of the Philippines. The intelligence of their inhabitants includes the ability to navigate by the stars.

b.

TABLE 7.1
The Chitling Intelligence Test

1. A "gas head" is a person who has a
   a. fast-moving car
   b. stable of "lace"
   c. "process"
   d. habit of stealing cars
   e. long jail record for arson

2. "Bo Diddley" is a
   a. game for children
   b. down-home cheap wine
   c. down-home singer
   d. new dance
   e. Moejoe call

3. If a pimp is uptight with a woman who gets state aid, what does he mean when he talks about "Mother's day"?
   a. second Sunday in May
   b. third Sunday in June
   c. first of every month
   d. none of these
   e. first and fifteenth of every month

4. A "handkerchief head" is
   a. a cool cat
   b. a porter
   c. an Uncle Tom
   d. a hoddi
   e. a preacher

5. If a man is called a "blood," then he is a
   a. fighter
   b. Mexican-American
   c. Negro
   d. hungry hemophile
   e. red man, or Indian

6. Cheap chitlings (not the kind you purchase at a frozen-food counter) will taste rubbery unless they are cooked long enough. How soon can you quit cooking them to eat and enjoy them?
   a. 45 minutes
   b. 2 hours
   c. 24 hours
   d. 1 week (on a low flame)
   e. 1 hour

Answers: 1. c 2. c 3. e 4. c 5. c 6. c

Source: Adrian Dove, 1968.

Larry P., Intelligent but Not on Intelligence Tests

L arry P. is Black and poor. When he was 6 years old, he was placed in a class for the "educable mentally retarded" (EMR), which to school psychologists means that Larry learns much more slowly than average children. The primary reason Larry was placed in the EMR class was his very low score of 64 on an intelligence test.

Is there a possibility that the intelligence test Larry was given is culturally biased? Psychologists still debate this issue. The controversy has been the target of a major class action suit challenging the use of standardized IQ tests to place Black elementary school students in EMR classes. The initial lawsuit, filed on behalf of Larry P., claimed that the IQ test he took underestimated his true learning ability. The lawyers for Larry P. argued that IQ tests place too much emphasis on verbal skills and

fail to account for the background of Black children. Therefore, it was argued, Larry was incorrectly labeled mentally retarded and may forever be saddled with that stigma.

As part of the lengthy court battle involving Larry P., six Black EMR students were independently retested by members of the Bay Area Association of Black Psychologists in California. The psychologists made sure they established good rapport with the students and made special efforts to overcome the students' defeatism and distraction. For example, items were rewarded in terms more consistent with the children's social background, and recognition was given to nonstandard answers that showed a logical, intelligent approach to problems. This testing approach produced scores of 79 to 104—17 to 38 points higher than the scores the students received when initially tested by school psychologists. In every case, the retest scores were above the ceiling for placement in an EMR class.

In Larry's case, the judge ruled that IQ tests are biased and that their use discriminates against Blacks and other ethnic minorities. IQ tests cannot be used now in California to place children in EMR classes. During the Larry P. trial, it was revealed that 66 percent of the elementary school students in EMR classes in San Francisco were Black, whereas Blacks make up only 28.5 percent of the San Francisco school population.

What was the state's argument for using intelligence tests as one criterion for placing children in EMR classes? At one point, the state suggested that, because Blacks tend to be poor and poor pregnant women tend to suffer from inadequate nutrition, it is possible that the brain development of many Black children has been retarded by their mothers' poor prenatal diet. The state also argued that Blacks are genetically inferior to Whites in intelligence.

The decision in favor of Larry P. was upheld by a three-judge appeals panel in 1984. However, in another court case, *Pase v. Hannon* in Illinois, a judge was unconvinced by the same arguments and ruled that IQ tests are not culturally biased.

(1) verbal and nonverbal intelligence, assessed by the WISC-R; (2) social and economic background, obtained through a 1-hour parent interview; (3) social adjustment to school, determined through a questionnaire that parents complete; and (4) physical health, assessed by a medical examination.

The Kaufman Assessment Battery for Children (K-ABC) has been trumpeted as an improvement over other culture-fair tests (Kaufman & Kaufman, 1983). The test is based on a more representative sample, which includes a greater number of minority and handicapped children. The intelligence portion focuses less on language than the Stanford-Binet does, and the K-ABC includes an achievement section, with subtests for arithmetic and reading. However, the K-ABC, like other

culture-fair tests, has its detractors. Based on the three main criteria for evaluating tests, the K-ABC fares well on reliability and standardization, but not as well on validity (Sax, 1989).

Most researchers agree that traditional intelligence tests are probably culturally biased. However, efforts to develop culture-fair tests so far have yielded unsatisfactory results.

The Use and Misuse of Intelligence Tests

Psychological tests are tools. Like all tools, their effectiveness depends on the knowledge, skill, and integrity of the user. A hammer can be used to build a beautiful kitchen cabinet or it can be used as a weapon of assault. Like a hammer, psychological tests can be used for positive purposes or they can be badly abused. It

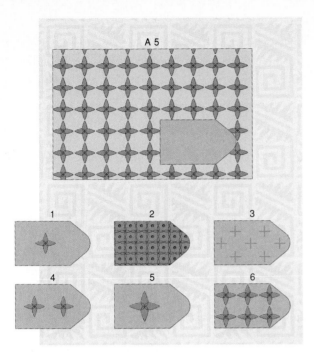

FIGURE 7.18

Sample item from the Raven Progressive Matrices Test. Individuals are presented with a matrix arrangement of symbols, such as the one at the top of this figure and must then complete the matrix by selecting the appropriate missing symbol from a group of symbols.

Figure A5 from the Raven STANDARD PROGRESSIVE MATRICES. Copyright © J. C. Raven Limited. Reprinted by permission.

is important for both the test constructor and the test examiner to be familiar with the current state of scientific knowledge about intelligence and intelligence tests (Anastasi, 1988; Reynolds & Kamphaus, 1990).

Even though they have limitations, tests of intelligence are among psychology's most widely used tools. To be effective, though, intelligence tests must be viewed realistically. They should not be thought of as unchanging indicators of intelligence. They should be used in conjunction with other information about an individual, not relied on as the sole indicator of intelligence. For example, an intelligence test should not solely determine whether a child is placed in a special education or gifted class. The child's developmental history, medical background, performance in school, social competencies, and family experiences should be taken into account too.

The single number provided by many IQ tests can easily lead to stereotypes and expectations about an individual. Many people do not know how to interpret the results of intelligence tests, and sweeping generalizations are too often made on the basis of an IQ score. For example, imagine that you are a teacher in the teacher's lounge the day after school

has started in the fall. You mention a student—Johnny Jones—and a fellow teacher remarks that she had Johnny in class last year; she comments that he was a real dunce and points out that his IQ is 78. You cannot help but remember this information, and it may lead to thoughts that Johnny Jones is not very bright so it is useless to spend much time teaching him. In this way, IQ scores are misused and stereotypes are formed (Rosenthal & Jacobsen, 1968).

Ability tests can help a teacher divide children into homogeneous groups who function at roughly the same level in math or reading so they can be taught the same concepts together. However, when children are placed in tracks, such as "advanced," "intermediate," and "low," extreme caution needs to be taken. Periodic assessment of the groups is needed, especially with the "low" group. Ability tests measure *current* performance, and maturational changes or enriched environmental experiences may advance a child's intelligence, requiring that she be moved to a higher group.

Despite their limitations, when used judiciously by a competent examiner, intelligence tests provide valuable information about individuals. There are not many alternatives to these tests. Subjective judgments about individuals simply reintroduce the bias the tests were designed to eliminate.

The Extremes of Intelligence: Mental Retardation and Giftedness

Intelligence tests have been used to discover indications of mental retardation or intellectual giftedness, the extremes of intelligence. At times intelligence tests have been misused for this purpose. Keep in mind the theme that an intelligence test should not be used as the sole indicator of mental retardation or giftedness as we explore the nature of these intellectual extremes.

Mental Retardation

The most distinctive feature of mental retardation is inadequate intellectual functioning. Long before formal tests were developed to assess intelligence, the mentally retarded were identified by a lack of age-appropriate skills in learning and caring for themselves. Once intelligence tests were developed, numbers were assigned to indicate degree of mental retardation. It is not unusual to find two retarded people with the same low IQ, one of whom is married, employed, and involved in the community and the other requiring constant supervision in an institution. These differences in social competence led psychologists to include deficits in adaptive behavior in their definition of mental retardation. **Mental retardation** *is a condition of limited mental ability in which an individual has a low IQ, usually below 70 on a traditional intelligence test, and has difficulty adapting to everyday life.* About 5 million Americans fit this definition of mental retardation.

There are several classifications of mental retardation. About 89 percent of the mentally retarded fall into the mild category, with IQs of 55 to 70. About 6 percent are classified as moderately retarded, with IQs of 40 to 54; these people can attain a second-grade level of skills and may be able to support themselves as adults through some types of labor. About 3.5 percent of the mentally retarded are in the severe category, with IQs of 25 to 39; these individuals learn to talk and engage in very simple tasks but require extensive supervision. Less than 1 percent have IQs below 25; they fall into the profoundly mentally retarded classification and are in constant need of supervision.

Mental retardation can have an organic cause, or it can be social and cultural in origin. **Organic retardation** *is mental retardation caused by a genetic disorder or by brain damage; organic refers to the tissues or organs of the body, so there is some physical damage in organic retardation.* Down syndrome, one form of mental retardation, occurs when an extra chromosome is present in an individual's genetic makeup (see figure 7.19). It is not known why the extra chromosome is present, but it may involve the health or age of the female ovum or male sperm. Most people who suffer from organic retardation have IQs that range between 0 and 50.

Cultural-familial retardation *is a mental deficit in which no evidence of organic brain damage can be found; individuals' IQs range from 50 to 70.* Psychologists suspect that such mental deficits result from the normal variation that distributes people along the range of intelligence scores above 50, combined with growing up in a below-average intellectual environment (Hodapp, Burack, & Zigler, in press). As children those who are familially retarded can be detected in schools, where they often fail, need tangible rewards (candy rather than praise), and are highly sensitive to what others—both peers and adults—want from them. However, as adults the familially retarded are usually invisible, perhaps because adult settings don't tax their cognitive skills as sorely. It may also be that the familially retarded increase their intelligence as they move toward adulthood (Sattler, 1988).

Giftedness

There have always been people whose abilities and accomplishments outshine others'—the whiz kid in class, the star athlete, the natural musician. People who are **gifted** *have above-average intelligence (an IQ of 120 or higher) and/or superior talent for something.* When it comes to programs for the gifted, most school systems select children who have intellectual superiority and academic aptitude. Children who are talented in the visual and performing arts (arts, drama, dance), athletics, or other special aptitudes tend to be overlooked.

Until recently giftedness and emotional distress were thought to go hand in hand. English novelist Virginia Woolf suffered from severe depression, for example, and eventually committed suicide. Sir Isaac Newton, Vincent van Gogh, Ann Sexton, Socrates, and Sylvia Plath all had emotional problems.

FIGURE 7.19

A Down syndrome child. What causes a child to develop Down syndrome? In what major classification of mental retardation does the condition fall?

However, these are the exception rather than the rule; in general, no relation between giftedness and mental disturbance has been found. A number of recent studies support the conclusion that gifted people tend to be more mature and have fewer emotional problems than others (Janos & Robinson, 1985).

Lewis Terman (1925) has followed the lives of approximately 1,500 children whose Stanford-Binet IQs averaged 150 into adulthood; the study will not be complete until the year 2010. Terman has found that this remarkable group is an accomplished lot: of the 800 males, 78 have obtained doctorates (they include two past presidents of the American Psychological

Association), 48 have earned M.D.s, and 85 have been granted law degrees. Most of these figures are 10 to 30 times greater than those found among the 800 men of the same age chosen randomly as a comparison group. These findings challenge the commonly held belief that the intellectually gifted are emotionally disturbed or socially maladjusted.

Creativity

Most of us would like to be both gifted and creative. Why was Thomas Edison able to invent so many things? Was he simply more intelligent than most people? Did he spend long hours toiling away in private? Surprisingly, when Edison was a young boy, his teacher told him he was too dumb to learn anything. Other famous people whose creative genius went unnoticed when they were young include Walt Disney, who was fired from a newspaper job because he did not have any good ideas; Enrico Caruso, whose music teacher told him that his voice was terrible; and Winston Churchill, who failed 1 year of secondary school.

Disney, Edison, Caruso, and Churchill were intelligent and creative men; however, experts on creativity believe that intelligence is not the same as creativity (Winner, 1989). One common distinction is between **convergent thinking,** *which produces one correct answer and is characteristic of the kind of thinking on standardized intelligence tests* and **divergent thinking,** *which produces many answers to the same question and is more characteristic of creativity* (Guilford, 1967). For example, the following is a typical problem on an intelligence test that requires convergent thinking: "How many quarters will you get in return for 60 dimes?" The following question, though, has many possible answers: "What image comes to mind when you hear the phrase 'sitting alone in a dark room'?" (Barron, 1989). Such responses as "the sound of a violin with no strings" and "patience" are considered creative answers. Conversely, common answers, such as "a person in a crowd" or "insomnia" are not very creative.

Creativity *is the ability to think about something in novel and unusual ways and to come up with unique solutions to problems.* When creative people, such as artists and scientists, are asked what enables them to solve problems in novel ways, they say that the ability to find affinities between seemingly unrelated elements plays a key role. They also say they have the time and independence in an enjoyable setting to entertain a wide range of possible solutions to a problem. How strongly is creativity related to intelligence? Although most creative people are quite intelligent, the reverse is not necessarily true. Many highly intelligent people (as measured by IQ tests) are not very creative.

Some experts remain skeptical that we will ever fully understand the creative process. Others believe that a psychology of creativity is in reach. Most experts do agree that the concept of creativity as spontaneously bubbling up from a

Creativity involves thinking about something in novel and unusual ways and coming up with unique solutions to problems. Creativity is enhanced when individuals have the time and independence to entertain a wide range of possible solutions in an enjoyable setting.

magical well is a myth. Momentary flashes of insight, accompanied by images, make up only a small part of the creative process. At the heart of creativity lie ability and sustained effort. As Edison supposedly put it, "Genius is one-tenth inspiration and nine-tenths perspiration."

In this chapter, we have discussed many facets of thinking, language, and intelligence, including some ideas about how children's language develops and the nature of children's intelligence. In the next chapter, we will turn our attention exclusively to how we develop as human beings.

REVIEW

Intelligence

Intelligence is verbal ability, problem-solving skills, and the ability to learn from and adapt to the experiences of everyday life. In the study of intelligence, extensive attention is given to individual differences and the assessment of intelligence. The way intelligence is expressed in behavior may vary from one culture to another. Three important criteria for tests are reliability, validity, and standardization. Reliability is how consistently an individual performs on a test; one type is test-retest reliability. Validity is the extent to which a test measures what it is intended to measure. Two kinds of validity are content and criterion. Standardization involves uniform procedures for administering and scoring a test, as well as norms.

Binet developed the first intelligence test, known as the 1905 Scale. He developed the concept of mental age, whereas Stern developed the concept of IQ. The Binet has been standardized and revised a number of times. The many revisions are called the Stanford-Binet tests. The test approximates a normal distribution. Besides the Stanford-Binet, the most widely used intelligence tests are the Wechsler scales. They include the WAIS-R, WISC-R, and WPPSI. These tests provide an overall IQ, verbal and performance IQs, and information about 11 subtests. Psychologists debate whether intelligence is a general ability or a number of specific abilities.

Spearman's two-factor theory and Thurstone's multiple-factor theory state that a number of specific factors are involved. Sternberg's triarchic theory states that intelligence consists of three factors: componential, experiential, and contextual.

In the late 1960s, Jensen argued that intelligence is approximately 80 percent hereditary and that genetic differences exist in the average intelligence of ethnic groups and social classes. Intelligence is influenced by heredity, but not as strongly as Jensen believed. The environments we provide children and adults make a difference. There are cultural and ethnic differences on intelligence tests, but the evidence suggests they are not genetically based. In recent decades, the gap between Blacks and Whites on intelligence test scores has diminished as Blacks have experienced more socioeconomic opportunities. To understand intelligence within a given culture, the adaptive requirements of the culture must be known. Early intelligence tests favored White, middle-class, urban individuals. Current tests try to reduce this bias. Culture-fair tests are an alternative to traditional tests; most psychologists believe they cannot completely replace the traditional tests.

A mentally retarded individual has a low IQ, usually below 70 on a traditional IQ test, and has difficulty adapting to everyday life. There are several classifications of mental retardation. The two main types of retardation are organic and cultural-familial. A gifted individual has above-average intelligence (an IQ of 120 or more) and/or superior talent for something. Creativity is the ability to think about something in a novel and unusual way and to come up with unique solutions to problems.

Summary

I. The Nature of Cognition and the Cognitive Revolution

Cognition involves knowledge and the mental processes that transform information into knowledge. Cognitive psychologists study how information enters the mind, is transformed and stored in memories, and is subsequently retrieved to perform an activity, such as forming a concept, solving a problem, or engaging in reasoning. The cognitive revolution has occurred in the past half century. Computers have played an important role, stimulating the model of the mind as an information-processing system.

II. Concept Formation

A concept is used to group objects, events, or characteristics. Concepts help us generalize, improve our memory, keep us from constantly relearning, and improve our association skills. Psychologists have often investigated individuals' ability to detect when an object is included in a particular concept. Developing hypotheses about concepts is important in thinking. Natural concepts have fuzzy boundaries (unclear which features are critical to the concept) and internal structure (some members are better examples than others).

III. Problem Solving

Problem solving is an attempt to find an appropriate way of attaining a goal that is not readily available. Bransford and Stein described a valuable model, IDEAL, to illustrate the steps in problem solving: *I* = identifying problems, *D* = defining problems, *E* = exploring alternative approaches, *A* = acting on a plan, and *L* = looking at the effects. Algorithms, heuristics, learning sets, and functional fixedness are involved in exploring alternative approaches.

IV. Reasoning

Reasoning is the mental activity of transforming information to reach a conclusion. Inductive reasoning is reasoning from the specific to the general; deductive reasoning is reasoning from the general to the specific. Four types of formal reasoning tasks have been studied more than others: one is an inductive task (analogies); three are deductive tasks (ordering of ideas, judging relations between conditions, and syllogisms). Much of our everyday reasoning does not follow formal logic, but it often helps to have the power of logic on our side.

V. The Nature of Language and Evolution

Language involves a system of symbols we use to communicate with each other. The system is characterized by infinite generativity and by rules. The rules include phonology, morphology, syntax, and semantics. The fact that biological evolution shaped humans into linguistic creatures is undeniable. Cultural evolution spurred early humans, with their newly evolved language capacity, to generate a way of communicating.

VI. Do Animals Have Language? Is There a Critical Period for Learning Language?

Animals clearly can communicate, and chimpanzees can be taught to use symbols. Whether animals have all of the properties of human language is debated. The experiences of Genie and other children suggest that the early years of childhood are a critical time for learning language. If exposure to language does not occur before puberty, life-long deficits in grammar occur.

VII. Environmental Influences and Language Development

Reinforcement and imitation probably play a facilitative rather than a necessary role in language. An intriguing aspect of early language learning is the use of motherese. One-word utterances occur at about 10 to 13 months; the holophrase hypothesis is applied to this. By 18 to 24 months, most infants use two-word utterances. Language at this point is called telegraphic speech.

VIII. Language, Culture, and Cognition

Whorf's linguistic relativity hypothesis states that language determines the structure of thinking. Thoughts and ideas are associated with words, and different languages promote different ways of thinking. Language influences thought, but it does not determine it. One critical variable in understanding language's role in achievement and school is whether a child speaks the language in which the classes are taught and, if so, how well. Debate flourishes about the best way to teach children whose native language is not English in our nation's schools. Black Americans have a rich language tradition that is often ignored by schools.

IX. What Is Intelligence? How Are Tests Constructed?

Intelligence is verbal ability, problem-solving skills, and the ability to learn from and adapt to the experiences of everyday life. In the study of intelligence, extensive attention is given to individual differences and the assessment of intelligence. The behavioral indicators of intelligence can vary across cultures. Reliability, validity, and standardization are three key aspects of intelligence tests.

X. The Measurement and Nature of Intelligence

Binet developed the first intelligence test, known as the 1905 Scale. He developed the concept of mental age, whereas Stern developed the concept of IQ. The Binet has been standardized and revised a number of times. The many revisions are called the Stanford-Binet tests. The test approximates a normal distribution. Besides the Stanford-Binet, the most widely used intelligence tests are the Wechsler scales. They include the WAIS-R, WISC-R, and WPPSI. These tests provide an overall IQ, verbal and performance IQs, and information about 11 subtests. Psychologists debate whether intelligence is a general ability or a number of specific abilities. Spearman's two-factor theory and Thurstone's multiple-factor theory state that a number of specific factors are involved. Sternberg's contemporary triarchic theory states that intelligence consists of three factors: componential, experiential, and contextual.

XI. The Heredity-Environment Controversy and Culture and Ethnicity

In the late 1960s, Jensen argued that intelligence is approximately 80 percent hereditary and that genetic differences exist in the average intelligence of ethnic groups and social classes. Intelligence is influenced by heredity, but not as strongly as Jensen believed. The environments we provide children and adults make a difference. Ethnic differences in intelligence exist, but the evidence suggests they are not genetically based. In recent decades, as Blacks have experienced more opportunities, the Black-White gap has diminished. Early intelligence tests favored White, middle-class, urban individuals. Current tests try to reduce this bias. Culture-fair tests are an alternative to traditional tests; most psychologists believe they cannot completely replace the traditional tests.

XII. The Use and Misuse of Intelligence Tests

Despite limitations, when used by a judicious examiner, tests can be valuable tools for determining differences in intelligence. The tests should always be used with other information about the individual. IQ scores can produce some unfortunate stereotypes and expectations. Ability tests can help divide children into homogeneous groups, although periodic testing should always be done. Intelligence or a high IQ is not necessarily the ultimate human value.

XIII. The Extremes of Intelligence

A mentally retarded individual has a low IQ, usually below 70 on a traditional IQ test, and has difficulty adapting to everyday life. Classifications of mental retardation have been made. The two main causes of retardation are organic and cultural-familial. A gifted individual has above-average intelligence (an IQ of 120 or more) and/or superior talent for something. Creativity involves thinking about something in novel and unusual ways and coming up with unique solutions to problems. Creativity is enhanced when individuals have the time and independence to entertain a wide range of possible solutions in an enjoyable setting.

Key Terms

cognition 178
concept 179
problem solving 181
algorithms 182
heuristics 182
learning set 183
functional fixedness 183
reasoning 184
inductive reasoning 184
deductive reasoning 184
analogy 185
syllogism 186
language 187
infinite generativity 187
phonology 187

morphology 187
syntax 188
semantics 188
motherese 190
holophrase hypothesis 192
telegraphic speech 192
linguistic relativity hypothesis 192
individual differences 195
intelligence 195
reliability 197
test-retest reliability 197
validity 197
content validity 197
criterion validity 197
standardization 197

norms 197
mental age (MA) 197
intelligence quotient (IQ) 198
normal distribution 198
two-factor theory 200
multiple-factor theory 200
triarchic theory 200
culture-fair tests 203
mental retardation 207
organic retardation 208
cultural-familial retardation 208
gifted 208
convergent thinking 209
divergent thinking 209
creativity 209

Suggested Readings

Anastasi, A. (1988). *Psychological testing* (6th ed.). New York: Macmillan. This widely used text on psychological testing provides extensive information about test construction, test evaluation, and the nature of intelligence testing.

Baron, J. B., & Sternberg, R. J. (1987). *Teaching thinking skills*. New York: W. H. Freeman. Twelve eminent psychologists, educators, and philosophers contribute information about the latest approaches to teaching thinking skills. Descriptions of promising training programs are provided.

Bransford, J. D., & Stein, B. S. (1984). *The ideal problem solver*. New York: W. H. Freeman. Bransford and Stein present their model of problem solving, called the IDEAL Problem Solver. This book includes hundreds of fascinating problems, along with a number of tips on how to solve problems more effectively.

Curtiss, S. (1977). *Genie*. New York: Academic Press. Susan Curtiss tells the remarkable story of Genie, a modern-day wild child, and her ordeal of trying to acquire language.

Gardner, H., & Perkins, D. (Eds.). (1989). *Art, mind, and education*. Ithaca, NY: The University of Illinois Press. Extensive, valuable information is provided about enhancing the creative thinking of children.

Hakuta, K., & Garcia, E. E. (1989). Bilingualism and education. *American Psychologist, 44,* 374-379. The concept of bilingualism as applied to individual children and to educational programs is discussed, and the history of research on bilingual children and bilingual education in the United States is reviewed.

Solution to Nine-Dot Problem

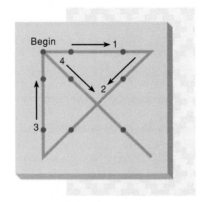

CHILD DEVELOPMENT

CHAPTER

I t is both the best of times and the worst of times for today's children. Their world possesses powers and perspectives inconceivable 50 years ago: computers; longer life expectancies; and the entire planet accessible through television, satellites, and air travel. So much knowledge, though, can be chaotic, even dangerous. School curricula have been adapted to teach new topics—AIDS, suicide, drug and alcohol abuse, incest. Children want to trust, but the world has become untrustworthy. The adult world's hazards—its sometimes fatal temptations—descend upon children so early that their ideals become tarnished. Crack cocaine is far more addictive and deadly than marijuana, the drug of an earlier generation. Strange fragments of violence and sex come flashing out of the television set and lodge in the minds of children. The messages are powerful and contradictory. Rock videos suggest orgiastic sex. Public health officials counsel safe sex. Oprah Winfrey and Phil Donahue conduct seminars on exotic drugs, transsexual surgery, and serial murders. Television pours a bizarre version of reality into children's imaginations. In New York City, two 5-year-olds argue about whether there is a Santa Claus and what Liberace died of. In New Orleans, a first grader shaves chalk and passes it around the classroom, pretending it is cocaine (Morrow, 1988).

At times the challenges young people face can seem overwhelming. How are they going to navigate safely through such treacherous waters? We're still a long way off from explaining—in grand or simple statements—all the enigmas of how children get to be the way they are. Why do some children, for instance, manage to overcome grinding poverty or physical abuse and turn into well-adjusted adolescents who embrace life? Conversely, why do some children who "have it all" turn to drugs and run their lives aground? Psychology has some clues about why children develop the way they do and what we can and cannot do to shape who they become. Our exploration of childhood begins by examining the question of what development is, then winds its way through the natural course of every child's development.

What Is Development?

Each of us—from Leonardo Da Vinci, Joan of Arc, and Martin Luther King, Jr., to you—unfolded as a human being in some predictable ways. We all start as infants, become children, mature into adults, and grow old, yet we are unique. No one else in the world, for example, has the same set of fingerprints as you. Researchers who study child development are intrigued by children's universal characteristics, as well as by their idiosyncracies.

When we speak of a child's **development,** we mean *a pattern of movement or change that begins at conception and continues throughout the life cycle. Most development involves growth, although it also consists of decay (as in death). The pattern of change is complex because it is the product of several processes—biological, cognitive, and social.*

Biological processes *involve changes in an individual's physical nature.* Genes inherited from parents, the development of the brain, height and weight gains, motor skills, and the hormonal changes of puberty all reflect the role of biological processes in development.

Cognitive processes *involve changes in an individual's thought, intelligence, and language.* Watching a colorful mobile swinging above a crib, putting together a two-word sentence, memorizing a poem, solving a math problem, and imagining what it would be like to be a movie star all reflect the role of cognitive processes in children's development.

Social processes *involve changes in an individual's relationships with other people, changes in emotions, and changes in personality.* An infant's smile in response to her mother's touch, a young boy's aggressive attack on a playmate, a girl's development of assertiveness, and an adolescent's joy at the senior prom all reflect the role of social processes in children's development.

Maturation and Experience

In addition to biological, cognitive, and social processes, human development is shaped by the interplay between maturation and experience. **Maturation** *is the orderly sequence of changes dictated by the genetic code.* We all grow rapidly in infancy and less so in early childhood, experience a rush of sexual hormones in puberty after a lull in childhood, reach the peak of our physical strength in late adolescence and early adulthood, and then decline. Psychologists who emphasize the role of maturation argue that, despite the vast range of environments humans inhabit, the genetic code determines a common path for human growth and development. They do, however, acknowledge that psychologically barren or hostile environments can depress development.

In contrast, other psychologists emphasize the importance of experience in shaping human development. Our individual experiences spring from our environment, whether biological (such as nutrition, medical care, and physical accidents) or social (such as family, peers, and culture).

The debate about whether development is influenced primarily by maturation or by experience is yet another version of the nature-nurture controversy, discussed in chapter 2.

Continuity and Discontinuity

Think for a moment about who you are. Did you become this person gradually, like the slow, cumulative growth of a seedling into a giant oak, or did you experience sudden, distinct changes in your development, the way a caterpillar changes into a butterfly (see figure 8.1)? For the most part, developmental psychologists who emphasize experience have described devel-

FIGURE 8.1

Continuity and discontinuity in development. Is development more like a seedling gradually growing into a giant oak or a caterpillar suddenly becoming a butterfly?

opment as a gradual, continuous process; those who emphasize maturation have described development as a series of distinct stages (Bornstein & Krasnegor, 1989).

Continuity of development *is the view that development involves gradual, cumulative change from conception to death.* A child's utterance of its first word, although seemingly an abrupt, discrete event, is actually the result of weeks and months of growth and practice. Similarly, although the onset of puberty may seem to erupt overnight, it is actually a gradual process that occurs over several years.

Discontinuity of development *is the view that development involves distinct stages in the life span. Each of us is described as passing through a sequence of stages in which change is qualitatively rather than quantitatively different.* As a caterpillar changes to a butterfly, it does not just become *more* caterpillar—it changes into a

Marian Wright Edelman, president of the Children's Defense Fund, is shown here with a young child. She has been a tireless advocate of children's rights and has worked extensively to improve our nation's social policy for children.

different kind of organism; its development is discontinuous. For example, a child who earlier could think only in concrete terms becomes capable of thinking abstractly about the world. This is a qualitative, discontinuous change in development, not a quantitative, continuous change.

Social Policy and Children's Development

Social policy *is a national government's course of action designed to influence the welfare of its citizens.* When more than 25 percent of all children and more than half of all ethnic minority children are being raised in poverty, when between 40 and 50 percent of all children born in a particular era can expect to spend at least 5 years in a single-parent home, when children and young adolescents are giving birth, and when the spectre and spread of AIDS are present, our nation needs revised social policy related to children (Horowitz & O'Brien, 1989; Scales, 1992; Wilcox & Naimark, 1991). Both table 8.1, which vividly portrays one day in the lives of children in the United States, and Sociocultural Worlds 8.1, which provides some rather stunning comparisons of American children with children in other countries, underscore the need for improved social policy for children.

Among the groups that have worked to improve the lives of the world's children are UNICEF in New York and the Children's Defense Fund in Washington, DC. Marian Wright Edelman (1987, 1992), president of the Children's Defense

TABLE 8.1

One Day in the Lives of Children in the United States

17,051	women get pregnant.
2,795	of them are teenagers.
1,106	teenagers have abortions.
372	teenagers miscarry.
1,295	teenagers give birth.
689	babies are born to women who have had inadequate prenatal care.
719	babies are born at low birthweight (less than 5 pounds 8 ounces).
129	babies are born at very low birthweight (less than 3 pounds 5 ounces).
67	babies die before 1 month of life.
105	babies die before their first birthday.
27	children die from poverty.
10	children die from guns.
30	children are wounded by guns.
6	teenagers commit suicide.
135,000	children bring a gun to school.
7,742	teens become sexually active.
623	teenagers get syphilis or gonorrhea.
211	children are arrested for drug abuse.
437	children are arrested for drinking or drunken driving.
1,512	teenagers drop out of school.
1,849	children are abused or neglected.
3,288	children run away from home.
1,629	children are in adult jails.
2,556	children are born out of wedlock.
2,989	see their parents divorced.
34,285	people lose jobs.

Source: Children's Defense Fund, 1990.

SOCIOCULTURAL WORLDS 8.1

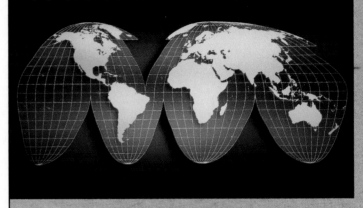

Caring for Children: Cross-Cultural Comparisons

According to a recent report by the Children's Defense Fund (1990), the United States does not fare well in caring for children when compared with other nations. In this report, the Children's Defense Fund gave the United States an A for capacity to care for children but an F for performance on many key markers of children's well-being. Consider the following cross-cultural comparisons:

In the United States, 1-year-olds have lower immunization rates against polio than 1-year-olds in 14 other countries. Polio immunization rates for non-White infants in the United States rank behind 48 other countries, including Albania, Colombia, and Jamaica.

The United States overall infant mortality rate lags behind 18 other countries. Our non-White infant mortality rate ranks 13th, compared to other nations' overall rates. A Black American child born in inner-city Boston has less of a chance of surviving the first year of life than a child born in Panama, North or South Korea, or Uruguay.

In a study of eight industrialized nations (the United States, Switzerland, Sweden, Norway, West Germany, Canada, England, and Australia), the United States had the highest poverty rate.

The United States has the highest adolescent pregnancy rate of any industrialized Western nation.

The United States and South Africa are the only industrialized countries that do not provide universal health coverage to families, child care, and parental leave when a child is born.

American school children know less geography than school children in Iran, less math than school children in Japan, and less science information than school children in Spain.

a.

b.

(a) A Black American child born in inner-city Boston has less of a chance of surviving the first year of life than a child born in Korea. (b) American school children know less science information than school children in Spain.

The United States invests a smaller portion of its gross national product (GNP) in child health than 18 other industrialized nations. It invests a smaller portion of its GNP in education than 6 other industrialized countries.

In sum, the United States needs to devote more attention to caring for its children. Too many American children from every socioeconomic and ethnic group are neglected and are not given the opportunity to reach their full potential.

Fund, has been a tireless advocate of children's rights and has been instrumental in calling attention to the needs of children. Edward Zigler (1991) has also worked extensively as a champion of children's rights, initially to urge government funding of Project Head Start and to improve the lives of handicapped children, and more recently to encourage the formation of a national policy on day care. Child developmentalists can play an important role in social policy related to children by helping develop more positive public opinion regarding comprehensive welfare legislation, by contributing to and promoting research that will benefit children's welfare, and by providing legislators with information that will influence their support of comprehensive child welfare legislation (Garwood & others, 1989).

Prenatal Development and Birth

Within a matter of hours after fertilization, a human egg divides, becomes a system of cells, and continues this mapping of cells at an astonishing rate until, in a mere 9 months, there is a squalling bundle of energy that has its grandmother's nose, its father's eyes, and its mother's abundant hair.

The Course of Prenatal Development

Conception *occurs when a single sperm cell from the male penetrates the female's ovum (egg). This process is also called fertilization.* A **zygote** *is a fertilized egg.* It receives one-half of its chromosomes from the mother, the other half from the father. The zygote begins as a single cell. The **germinal period** *takes place in the first 2 weeks after conception.* After 1 week and many cell divisions, the zygote is made up of 100 to 150 cells. At the end of 2 weeks, the mass of cells attaches to the uterine wall.

During the **embryonic period,** *which takes place from 2 to 8 weeks after conception,* some remarkable developments unfold (see figure 8.2). Before most women even know they are pregnant, the rate of cell differentiation intensifies, support systems for the cells form, and organs appear. In the third week, the neural tube that eventually becomes the spinal cord is forming. At about 21 days, eyes begin to appear, and by 24 days, the cells of the heart begin to differentiate. During the fourth week, arm and leg buds emerge. At 5 to 8 weeks, arms and legs become more differentiated, the face starts to form, and the intestinal tract appears. All of this is happening in an organism that, by 8 weeks, weighs only one-thirtieth of an ounce and is just over 1 inch long (see figure 8.3).

The **fetal period** *begins 2 months after conception and lasts, on average, for 7 months.* Growth and development continue their dramatic course, and organs mature to the point where life can be sustained outside the womb. At 4 months after conception, the fetus is about 6 inches long and weighs 4 to 7 ounces.

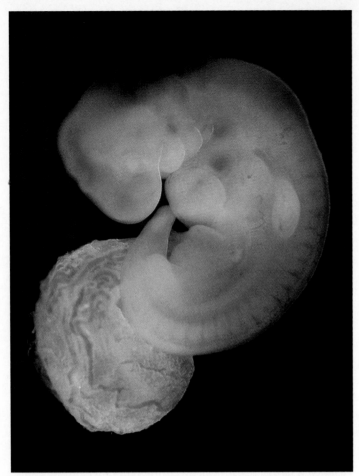

FIGURE 8.2

Embryo at 4 weeks. At about 4 weeks, an embryo is about .2 inch in length. The head, eyes, and ears begin to show. The head and neck are half the body length; the shoulders will be located where the whitish arm buds are attached.

Prenatal reflexes become more apparent, and the mother feels the fetus move for the first time (see figure 8.4). At 6 months after conception, the eyes and eyelids are completely formed, a fine layer of hair covers the fetus, the grasping reflex appears, and irregular breathing begins. By 7 to 9 months, the fetus is much longer and weighs considerably more. In addition, the functioning of various organs steps up.

As these massive changes take place during prenatal development, some pregnant women tiptoe about in the belief that everything they do has a direct effect on the unborn child. Others behave more casually, assuming their experiences have little impact. The truth lies somewhere between these extremes. Although it floats in a comfortable, well-protected environment, the fetus is not totally immune to the larger environment surrounding the mother (Kopp & Kaler, 1989).

A **teratogen,** *which comes from the Greek word tera, meaning "monster," is any agent that causes a birth defect.* Rarely do specific teratogens, such as drugs, link up with specific birth defects, such

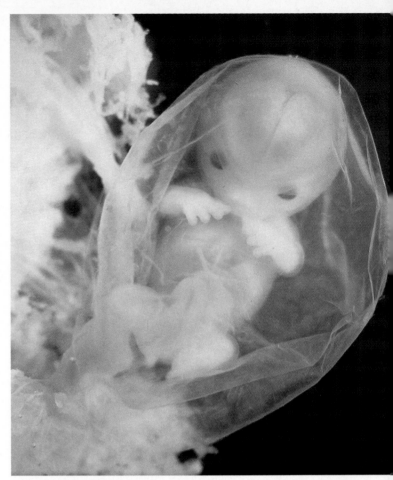

FIGURE 8.3

Embryo at 8 weeks. At 8 weeks and 4 centimeters (1.6 inches), the developing individual is no longer an embryo, but a fetus. Everything that will be found in the fully developed human being has now been formed. The fetal stage is a period of growth and perfection of detail. The heart has been beating for a month, and the muscles have just begun their first exercises. Two of the mother-to-be's menstrual periods have now been skipped. Ideally, at about this time, the mother-to-be goes to a doctor or clinic for prenatal care.

as leg malformation. One example is the drug *thalidomide*. During the late 1950s, several hundred women took thalidomide early in pregnancy to prevent morning sickness and insomnia. Tragically, babies born to these mothers had arms and legs that had not developed beyond stumps. Heavy drinking by pregnant women can also have a devastating effect on offspring (Abel, 1984; Coles, Platzman, & Smith, 1991). **Fetal alcohol syndrome (FAS)** *is a cluster of characteristics that describes children born to mothers who are heavy drinkers. It includes a small head (called microencephaly), as well as defective limbs, face, and heart. Most of these children are also of below average intelligence* (see figure 8.5). Recently concern has increased about the well-being of the fetus when pregnant women drink even small amounts of alcohol. In

FIGURE 8.4

Fetus at 4¹/₂ months. At 4¹/₂ months, the fetus is about 18 cm (just over 7 inches). When the thumb comes close to the mouth, the head may turn, and lips and tongue begin their sucking motions—a reflex for survival.

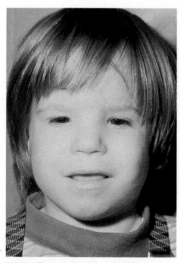

FIGURE 8.5

Fetal alcohol syndrome. This child has fetal alcohol syndrome. Notice the wide-set eyes, flat bones, and thin upper lip. This child also is mentally retarded.

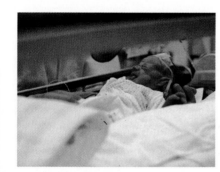

FIGURE 8.6

Cocaine baby. Shown here is a baby born addicted to cocaine because its mother was a cocaine addict. Researchers have found that the offspring of women who use cocaine during pregnancy often have hypertension and heart damage. Many of these infants face a childhood full of medical problems.

one study, infants whose mothers drank moderately during pregnancy (for example, one to two drinks a day) were less attentive and alert, with the effects still present at 4 years of age (Streissguth & others, 1984). Cocaine and its newest form, crack, can also harm the developing fetus (Beckwith & Howard, 1991; Dixon, 1991). When taken by pregnant women, crack can cause infant hypertension and damage to the offspring's heart (see figure 8.6). Table 8.2 on page 222 lists a number of drugs, their effects on the fetus and offspring, and safe or unsafe use of the drug.

Birth and the Newborn

The newborn is on a threshold between two worlds. In the womb, the fetus exists in a dark, free-floating, low-gravity environment at a relatively warm, constant temperature. At birth the newborn must quickly adapt to light, gravity, cold—a buzzing array of changing stimuli.

Whereas a full-term infant has grown in the womb for the full 38 to 42 weeks between conception and delivery, a **preterm infant** *(also called a premature infant) is an infant born prior to 38 weeks after conception.* Preterm infants are more likely than full-term infants to suffer distress during the birth process and to experience medical difficulties, such as breathing problems, in the days following birth (Crisafi & Driscoll, 1991). Some long-term developmental difficulties may occur as well, although there is no evidence that preterm infants have more difficulty in school than full-term infants (Kopp, 1987; Kopp & Kaler, 1989). Socioeconomic background is associated with the preterm infant's development. Simply put, the wealthier the premature infant's family, the better is its chance for a physically and intellectually healthy life (Kleinman, 1992). The Children's Defense Fund found that Black children, many of whom come from poor families, are twice as likely to be born prematurely, have low birthweight, and have mothers who received late or no prenatal care, and their mothers are three times as likely to die in childbirth (Edelman, 1987).

Children's Physical Development

At no other time in a person's life will there be so many changes occurring so fast as during the first few years. During infancy we change from virtually immobile, helpless beings to insatiably curious, talking creatures who toddle as fast as our legs can carry us.

TABLE 8.2
Drug Use During Pregnancy

Drug	Effects on fetus and offspring	Safe use of the drug
Alcohol	Small amounts increase the risk of spontaneous abortion. Moderate amounts (one to two drinks a day) are associated with poor attention in infancy. Heavy drinking can lead to fetal alcohol syndrome. Some experts believe that even low to moderate amounts, especially in the first 3 months of pregnancy, increase the risk of FAS.	Use should be avoided.
Nicotine	Heavy smoking is associated with low-birthweight babies, which means the baby may have more health problems. Smoking may be especially harmful in the second half of pregnancy.	Use should be avoided.
Tranquilizers	Taken during the first 3 months of pregnancy, may cause cleft palate or other congenital malformations.	Avoid if you might become pregnant and during early pregnancy. Use only under doctor's supervision.
Barbiturates	Mothers who have taken large doses may have babies who are addicted. Babies may have tremors, restlessness, and irritability.	Use only under doctor's supervision.
Amphetamines	May cause birth defects.	Use only under doctor's supervision.
Cocaine	May cause drug dependency and withdrawal symptoms at birth, as well as physical and mental problems, especially if used in the first 3 months of pregnancy. Higher risk of hypertension and heart problems. Possible developmental retardation and learning difficulties.	Use should be avoided.
Marijuana	May cause a variety of birth defects. Associated with low birthweight and height.	Use should be avoided.

Source: National Institute on Drug Use (modified).

Infancy

An old French proverb says, "A baby is an angel whose wings decrease as its legs increase." Learning to walk, though, is only one of infancy's physical milestones. We will find out how infants respond to their world, what an infant's nutritional needs are, and whether or not a newborn can see and hear.

Reflexes

A newborn is not an empty-headed organism. It comes into the world already equipped with several genetically "wired" reflexes. For example, a newborn has no fear of water, naturally holding its breath and contracting its throat to keep water out. Some of the reflexes we possess as newborns persist throughout our lives—coughing, blinking, and yawning, for example. Others disappear in the months following birth as higher brain functions mature and we develop voluntary control over many behaviors. One of the most dramatic reflexes of a newborn is the Moro reflex (see figure 8.7). When a newborn is roughly handled, hears a

loud noise, sees a bright light, or feels a sudden change of position, it becomes startled, arches its back, and throws back its head. At the same time, the newborn flings its arms and legs out and then rapidly closes them to the center of its body as if falling. The Moro reflex disappears by 3 to 4 months of age.

An infant's physical development in the first 2 years of life is dramatic. At birth a newborn (neonate) has a gigantic head (relative to the rest of the body), which flops around uncontrollably. In the span of 12 months, the infant becomes capable of sitting anywhere, standing, stooping, climbing, and often walking. During the second year, growth decelerates, but rapid increases in such activities as running and climbing take place (White, 1988).

Rates of infant motor development vary among some ethnic groups, largely for environmental reasons (Super, 1981). In many Black African cultures, infants have precocious motor skills. Black African infants ride on their caregivers' hips or backs—which strengthens the muscles used for sitting and walking—much more often than Anglo American infants. In

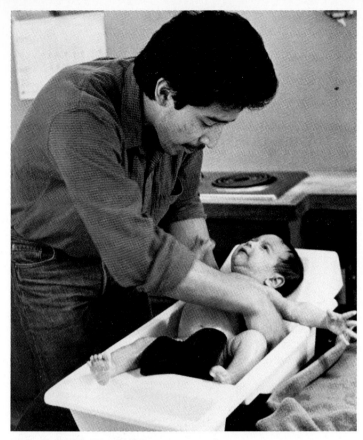

FIGURE 8.7

The Moro reflex. A father bathing his 10-week-old son stimulates the Moro reflex.

In many Black African cultures, infants have precocious motor skills.

addition, Black African infants are actually taught to sit and to walk, so they tend to reach these motor milestones much sooner than infants from other cultures.

Perception

William James (1890) described a newborn's world as "a great, blooming, buzzing confusion." A century later, we know James was wrong. A newborn's ability to perceive visual information is far more advanced than previously thought. We now know that newborns can see; they're just terribly near-sighted, registering at about 20/600 on the well-known Snellen chart used by optometrists. By 6 months of age, this improves to 20/100. Since newborns cannot tell us if they can see, researchers have had to devise experiments to test their vision. One way is to move a large object toward newborns, then observe if they turn their head away, as if to avoid a collision. Newborns do turn away from an oncoming object, indicating they can see.

We also know that infants can hear. In fact, the fetus responds to sounds 2 weeks before birth (Spence & DeCasper, 1982). Shortly after birth, infants also can smell, taste, touch, and sense pain.

The Brain

An infant's brain develops dramatically. Remember that you began as a single cell, and just 9 months later your brain and nervous system alone contained 10 to 20 billion neurons. This means that, at a point during prenatal development, neurons were reproducing at a rate of 25,000 per minute. You are born with all the neurons you will ever have in your life. At birth and during early infancy the networks connecting neurons are sparse. In figure 8.8, you can see the substantial increase in dendritic growth, which allows greater communication between neurons, from birth to 2 years of age.

Nutrition

Babies need adequate nutrition if they are to grow into healthy adults. The importance of this factor cannot be overstated (Pipes, 1988). Infants depend on human milk or "formula" for the first 4 to 6 months. One debate that has raged for years is the "breast or bottle" issue. Those who favor breast-feeding assert that it provides clean, digestible milk and helps immunize newborns from diseases (see figure 8.9). Breast-fed babies also

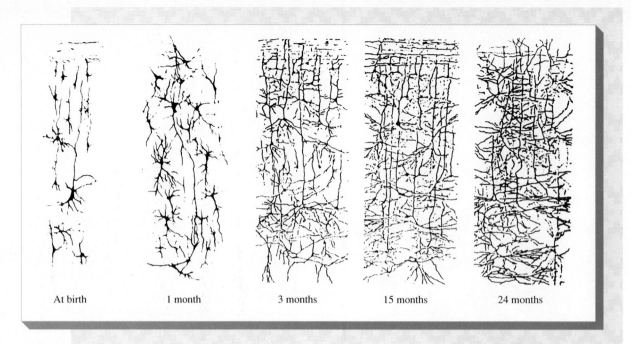

At birth · 1 month · 3 months · 15 months · 24 months

FIGURE 8.8

Increased dendritic branching from birth to 2 years of age. The branching of dendrites spreads dramatically during the course of life's first 2 years, allowing for more extensive connections among neurons. Notice how many more connections exist between dendrites at 2 years of age than at birth. Some developmentalists and neuroscientists believe the increased dendritic spreading plays an important role in the infant's advances in information processing.

gain weight more rapidly than bottle-fed babies. Only about one-half of all mothers nurse their newborns and even fewer continue to nurse after several months.

This may be, in part, because many mothers who work outside the home find it impossible to breast-feed their infants. Proponents of bottle-feeding argue that there is no long-term evidence of physiological or psychological harm to American infants when they are bottle-fed (Caldwell, 1964; Ferguson, Harwood, & Shannon, 1987; Forsyth, Leventhal, & McCarthy, 1985). Even so, the American Academy of Pediatrics, the majority of physicians and nurses, and two leading publications for parents—the *Infant Care* manual and *Parents* magazine—endorse breast-feeding for its physiological and psychological benefits over bottle-feeding (Young, 1990). In addition, experts agree that breast-feeding is the preferred practice in developing countries where poverty and inadequate nutrition are common. Although the issue of breast- versus bottle-feeding continues to be hotly debated, the growing consensus is that breast-feeding is better for a baby's health (Lozoff, 1989; Worthington-Roberts, 1988).

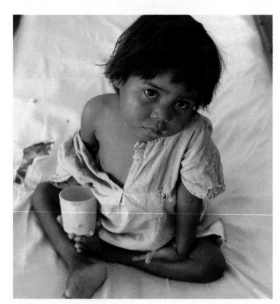

FIGURE 8.9

Malnutrition in impoverished countries. Malnutrition is common among children in many parts of the world (Grant, 1989). In an infant's first year of life, severe protein-calorie deficiency can lead to a wasting away of the infant's body tissues. One of the main causes of this wasting away is early weaning from breast milk to inadequate nutrients, such as unsuitable and unsanitary cow's milk formula. In many third world countries, mothers used to breast-feed their infants for at least 2 years. To become more modern, they stopped breast-feeding much earlier and replaced it with bottle-feeding. In impoverished countries, such as Afghanistan, Haiti, Ghana, and Chile, comparisons of bottle-fed and breast-fed infants reveal a death rate that is at times 500 percent higher for bottle-fed infants.

In our health-conscious society, a surprising problem has recently surfaced: some parents are almost starving their babies by feeding them the low-fat, low-calorie diets intended for adults who watch their weight. Diets designed for adult weight-loss and the prevention of heart disease may actually retard an infant's growth and development. Fat is very important for babies. Nature's food—the mother's breast milk—is high in fat and calories. No child under the age of 2 should be given skim milk. In one study, seven babies 7 to 22 months of age were unwittingly undernourished by their health-conscious parents (Lifshitz & others, 1987). Several of the parents had been fat themselves and were determined that their child was not going to go through life overweight.

Childhood

By their third birthday, children are full of new tricks, such as climbing, skipping, and jumping. They are beginning to be able to make their body do what they want it to do, giving them a greater sense of self-control.

Catching, throwing, kicking, balancing, rolling, cutting, stacking, snapping, pushing, dancing, and swimming—preschool children perform these physical feats and many, many more. As poet Dylan Thomas put it, "All the sun long they were running." The growth rate slows down in early childhood. Otherwise, we would be a species of giants. The growth and development of the brain underlie a young child's improvement in motor skills, reflected in such activities as the ability to hold a pencil and make increasingly efficient marks with it. A child's brain is closer to full growth than is the rest of its body, attaining 75 percent of the brain's adult weight by the age of 3 and 90 percent by age 5 (Schuster & Ashburn, 1986).

In middle and late childhood, motor development is much smoother and more coordinated than in early childhood. Whereas a preschool child can zip, cut, latch, and dance, an elementary school child can zip, cut, latch, and dance more efficiently and with more flair. Physical activities are essential for children to refine their developing skills. Child development experts in the United States believe that children should be *active*, rather than passive, and should be able to plan and select many of their own activities (Katz & Chard, 1989). An ideal elementary school, for example, would include the following: a gym and a safe, elaborate outdoor play area, where students can participate in a variety of games and sports; a classroom with a fully equipped publishing center, com-

Child development experts believe that children should be active, not passive. Physical activities are essential for children to refine their developing skills.

plete with materials for writing, typing, illustrating, and binding student-made books; and a science area with animals and plants for observation and books to study. Children also need to "just play." Education experts recognize that spontaneous play provides additional opportunities for children to learn.

Schools that offer children many opportunities to engage in a wide range of self-initiated activities, such as the ideal school just described, greatly enhance their students' physical and cognitive development.

Children's Cognitive Development

Matthew is 1 year old. He has seen over 1,000 flash cards, each containing a picture of objects—shells, flowers, insects, flags, countries, or words, for example. His mother, Billie, has made close to 10,000 such cards for Matthew and his 4-year-old brother Mark. Billie is following the regimen recommended by Glenn Doman, director of the Philadelphia Institute for Human Potential. Using Doman's methods, Billie expects Matthew to be reading and mastering simple math problems by the age of 2. She is also teaching Matthew Japanese.

Although some parents may believe that such strategies give their child an academic edge in a competitive world, many developmental psychologists believe that Doman's institute is a money-making scheme and that something is fundamentally wrong with his methods. They argue that intense tutoring stifles curiosity, creativity, and the ability to learn, and it keeps children from discovering the world on their own.

Famous Swiss developmental psychologist Jean Piaget was so often asked by American audiences "What should we do to foster a child's cognitive development?" that he called it the American question. As we will see next, Piaget's theory suggests that Doman's approach is not the best way to help children learn about their world.

Piaget's Theory

Piaget (1896-1980) stressed that children do not just passively receive information from their environment; they actively construct their own cognitive world. Two processes underlie a child's mental construction of the world—organization and adaptation. To make sense of our world, we organize our experiences. For example, we separate important ideas from less important ones. We connect one idea to another. However, not only do we organize our observations and experiences, but we also *adapt* our thinking to include those new ideas. Piaget (1960) believed we adapt in two ways: assimilation and accommodation.

Assimilation *occurs when individuals incorporate new information into their existing knowledge.* **Accommodation** *occurs when individuals adjust to new information.* Imagine that a 5-year-old girl is given a hammer and some nails and asked to hang a picture on the wall. She has never used a hammer, but from experience and observation she realizes that a hammer is an object to be held, that to hit the nail she must swing the hammer by the handle, and that she probably will need to swing it a number of times. Recognizing each of these things, she fits her behavior into information she already has (assimilation). However, the hammer is heavy, so she holds it near the top. She swings too hard and the nail bends, so she adjusts the pressure of her strikes. These adjustments reveal her ability to alter slightly her conception of the world (accommodation).

Jean Piaget, the famous Swiss developmental psychologist, changed the way we think about the development of children's minds. For Piaget, a child's mental development is a continuous creation of increasingly complex forms.

TABLE 8.3
Piaget's Stages of Cognitive Development

Stage	Description	Age range
Sensorimotor	An infant progresses from reflexive, instinctual action at birth to the beginning of symbolic thought. The infant constructs an understanding of the world by coordinating sensory experiences with physical actions.	Birth to 2 years
Preoperational	The child begins to represent the world with words and images; these words and images reflect increased symbolic thinking and go beyond the connection of sensory information and physical action.	2 to 7 years
Concrete operational	The child can now reason logically about concrete events and classify objects into different sets.	7 to 11 years
Formal operational	The adolescent reasons in more abstract and logical ways. Thought is more idealistic.	11 to 15 years

Piaget thought that even young infants are capable of assimilation and accommodation. Newborns reflexively suck everything that touches their lips (assimilation), but after several months they come to a new understanding of their world. Some objects, such as fingers and the mother's breast, can be sucked but others, such as fuzzy blankets, should not (accommodation).

Piaget also believed that we go through four stages in understanding the world. Each of the stages is age related and consists of distinct ways of thinking. Remember, it is the *different* way of understanding the world that makes one stage more advanced than another; knowing *more* information does not make a child's thinking more advanced, in Piaget's view. This is what Piaget meant when he said that a child's cognition is *qualitatively* different in one stage compared to another. A brief overview of Piaget's four stages of cognitive development is shown in table 8.3. We will discuss preoperational and concrete operational thought later in this chapter and formal operational thought, which characterizes adolescents, in the next chapter. For now, let's find out more about an infant's cognitive world.

Sensorimotor Thought

Sensorimotor thought *is Piaget's name for the stage of development that lasts from birth to about 2 years of age, corresponding to the period of infancy. An infant constructs an understanding of the world by coordinating sensory experiences (such as seeing and hearing) with physical (motor) actions*—hence the term *sensorimotor*. At the beginning of this stage, a newborn engages with its environment with little more than reflexive patterns; at the end of the stage, however, the 2-year-old has complex sensorimotor patterns and is beginning to use primitive symbols in thinking.

We live in a world of objects. Imagine yourself as a 5-month-old infant and how you might experience the world. You are in a playpen filled with toys. One of the toys, a monkey, falls out of your grasp and rolls behind a larger toy, a hippopotamus. Would you know the monkey is behind the hippopotamus, or would you think it is completely gone? Piaget believed that "out of sight" literally was "out of mind" for young infants; at 5 months of age, then, you would not have reached for the monkey when it fell behind the hippopotamus. By 8 months of age, though, an infant begins to understand that out of sight is not out of mind; at this age you probably would have reached behind the hippopotamus to search for the monkey, coordinating your senses with your movements.

Object permanence *is Piaget's term for one of an infant's most important accomplishments: understanding that objects and events continue to exist even when they cannot directly be seen, heard, or touched.* The most common way to study object permanence is to show an infant an interesting toy and then cover the toy with a

a.

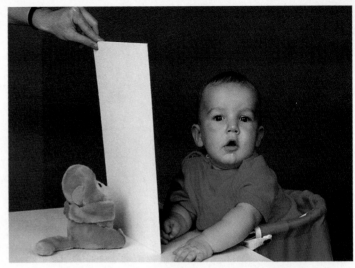

b.

FIGURE 8.10

Object permanence. Piaget thought that object permanence was one of infancy's landmark cognitive accomplishments. For this 5-month-old boy, out of sight is literally out of mind. The infant looks at the toy monkey (a), but when his view of the toy is blocked (b) he does not search for it. Eventually (by 8 to 9 months of age for most infants), he will search for hidden toys, demonstrating object permanence.

sheet or blanket. If infants understand that the toy still exists, they try to uncover it (see figure 8.10). Object permanence continues to develop throughout the sensorimotor period. For example, when infants initially understand that objects exist even when out of sight, they look for them only briefly. By the end of the sensorimotor period, infants engage in a more prolonged and sophisticated search for hidden objects (Flavell, 1985).

Object permanence is also important in an infant's social world. Infants develop a sense that people are permanent, just as they come to understand that toys are permanent. Five-month-old infants do not sense that caregivers exist beyond moment-to-moment encounters, but they do by 8 months of age. Infants' cognitive accomplishments, then, not only tell us how infants understand a world of blocks, toys, and playpens but also how they construct a world of relationships with people. A summary of the main characteristics of sensorimotor thought is presented in figure 8.11.

Preoperational and Concrete Operational Thought

Possibly because young children are not very concerned about reality, their drawings are fanciful and inventive. Suns are blue, skies are yellow, and cars float on clouds in their symbolic, imaginative world. One 3½-year-old looked at a scribble he had just drawn and described it as a pelican kissing a seal (see figure 8.12a). The symbolism is simple but strong, like the abstractions found in some modern art. As Picasso commented, "I used to draw like Raphael but it has taken me a lifetime to draw like young children." In the elementary school years, a child's drawings become more realistic, neat, and precise (see figure 8.12b). Suns are yellow, skies are blue, and cars travel on roads (Winner, 1986).

Preschool children represent their world with words, images, and drawings. Symbolic thoughts go beyond simple connections of sensorimotor information and physical action. Although preschool children can symbolically represent the world, they still cannot perform operations. **Operations,** *in Piaget's theory, describe mental representations that are reversible*. Preschool children have difficulty understanding that reversing an action brings about the original conditions from which the action began. This sounds rather complicated; however, the following two examples will help you understand Piaget's concept of reversibility. A preschool child may know that 4 + 2 = 6 but not understand that the reverse is true, 6 − 2 = 4. Let's say a preschooler walks to her friend's house each day but always gets a ride home. If you were to ask her to walk home one day, she would probably reply that she doesn't know the way, since she has never walked home before. **Preoperational thought** *is the term Piaget gave to a 2-to-7-year-old child's understanding of the world. Children at this stage of reasoning cannot understand such logical operations as the reversibility of mental representations.*

A well-known test of whether a child can think "operationally" is to present a child with two identical beakers, A and B, filled with liquid to the same height (see figure 8.13 on page 230). Next to them is a third beaker, C. Beaker C is tall and thin, whereas beakers A and B are wide and short. The liquid is poured from B into C, and the child is asked whether the amounts in A

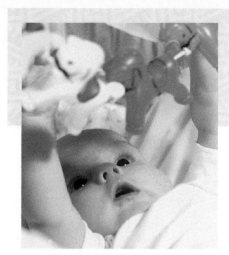

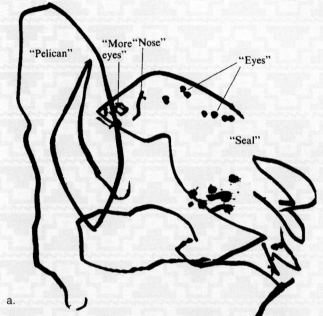

| Ability to organize and coordinate sensations with physical movements | Is nonsymbolic through most of its duration | Consists of six substages of cognitive development | Object permanence develops |

FIGURE 8.11

Piaget's description of the main characteristics of sensorimotor thought.

a.

A 3½-year-old's symbolic drawing. Halfway into this drawing, the 3½-year-old artist said it was "a pelican kissing a seal."

and C are the same. A 4-year-old child invariably says that the amount of liquid in the tall, thin beaker (C) is greater than that in the short, fat beaker (A). Eight-year-old children consistently say the amounts are the same. The 4-year-old child, a preoperational thinker, cannot mentally reverse the pouring action; that is, she cannot imagine the liquid going back from container C to container B. Piaget said that children like this 4-year-old have not grasped the concept of **conservation,** *the principle that a substance's quantity stays the same even though its shape changes.*

In the preoperational stage, a child's thought is also egocentric. By egocentrism, Piaget meant the inability to distinguish between one's own perspective and someone else's. The following telephone conversation between 4-year-old Mark, who is at home, and his father, who is at work, illustrates Mark's egocentric thought:

Father: Mark, is Mommy there?
Mark: (silently nods)
Father: Mark, may I speak to Mommy?
Mark: (nods again silently)

Piaget also called preoperational thought *intuitive,* because, when he asked children why they knew something, they often did not give logical answers but offered personal insights or guesses instead. However, as Piaget observed, young children seem sure they know something, even though they do not use logical reasoning to arrive at the answer. Young children also have an insatiable desire to know their world, and they ask a trillion questions:

"Who was the mother when everybody was the baby?"
"Why do leaves fall?"
"Why does the sun shine?"

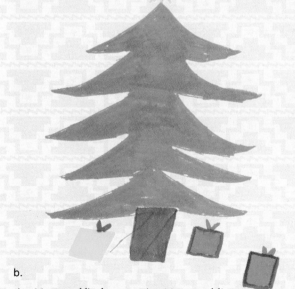

b.

An 11-year-old's drawing. An 11-year-old's drawing is neater and more realistic but also less inventive.

FIGURE 8.12

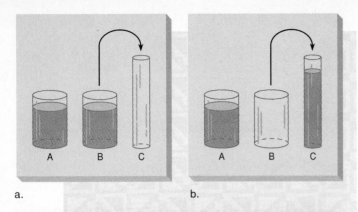

a.

b.

c.

"I still don't have all the answers, but I'm beginning to ask the right questions."
Drawing by Lorenz; © 1989 The New Yorker Magazine, Inc.

FIGURE 8.13

Piaget's beaker test to assess operational thinking. The beaker test is a well-known Piagetian test to determine whether a child can think operationally—that is, can mentally reverse actions and show an understanding of the conservation of a substance. (a) Two identical beakers are presented to a child. Then the experimenter pours the liquid from B into C, which is taller and thinner than A or B. (b) The child is then asked if these beakers (A and C) have the same amount of liquid. A preoperational child says no. (c) When asked to point to the beaker that has more liquid, a preoperational child points to the tall, thin beaker.

At this point, we have discussed four main characteristics of preoperational thought. A summary of these is presented in figure 8.14.

Concrete operational thought *is the term Piaget gave to the 7-to-11-year-old child's understanding of the world. At this stage of thought, children can use operations—they can mentally reverse the liquid from one beaker to another and understand that the volume is the same even though the beakers are different in height and width. Logical reasoning replaces intuitive thought as long as the principles are applied to concrete examples.* For instance, a concrete operational thinker cannot imagine the steps necessary to complete an algebraic equation, which is too abstract at this stage of children's development.

Earlier you read about a beaker task that was too difficult for a child who had not yet reached the stage of operational thought. Another well-known task used to demonstrate Piaget's concrete operational thought involves two equal amounts of clay (see figure 8.15). An experimenter shows a child two identical balls of clay and then rolls one ball into a long, thin shape. The other is retained in its original ball shape. The child is then asked if there is more clay in the ball or in the long, thin piece of clay. By the time children reach 7 to 8 years of age, most answer that the amount of clay is the same. To solve this problem correctly, children have to imagine that the clay ball is rolled out into a long, thin strip and then returned to its original round shape—imagination that involves a reversible mental action. Concrete operations allow the child to coordinate several characteristics rather than focusing on a single property of an object. In the clay example, the preoperational child is likely to focus on height *or* width. The child who has reached the stage of concrete operational thought coordinates information about both dimensions. Do children in all cultures acquire conservation skills at about the same age? To learn the answer to this question, turn to Sociocultural Worlds 8.2 on page 232.

All of the concrete operations Piaget identified focus on the way children think about the properties of objects. One important skill at this stage of reasoning is the ability to classify, or divide, things into different sets or subsets and to consider their interrelations. One way to see if children possess this ability is to see if they can understand a family tree of four generations (see figure 8.16) (Furth & Wachs, 1975). This family tree suggests that the grandfather (A) has three sons (B, C, and D), each of whom has two sons (E through J), and that one of these sons (J) has three sons (K, L, and M). A child who comprehends the classification system can move up and down a level (vertically), across a level (horizontally), and up and down and across a level (obliquely) within the system. A child who grasps concrete operational thought understands that person J can, at the same time, be father, brother, and grandson, for example. A preoperational child cannot perform this classification and says that a father cannot fulfill these other roles.

We have discussed four main characteristics of concrete operational thought. A summary of these characteristics is presented in figure 8.17. In the next chapter, we will discuss Piaget's fourth stage, formal operational thought—the way, he believed, adolescents think.

Evaluating Piaget

Piaget was a genius at observing children, and his insights are often surprisingly easy to verify. Piaget showed us some important things to look for in cognitive development, such as object permanence in infancy, egocentrism in early childhood, and operational thought in middle and late childhood. He also told us how we must make experiences fit our cognitive framework yet simultaneously adapt our understanding to new experiences.

Piaget's views, however, have been criticized and modified (Beilin, 1989; Case, 1991; Gelman, 1991).

| More symbolic than sensorimotor thought | Inability to engage in operations; can't mentally reverse actions; lacks conservation skills | Egocentric (inability to distinguish between own perspective and someone else's) | Intuitive rather than logical |

FIGURE 8.14

Characteristics of preoperational thought.

Type of conservation	Initial presentation	Manipulation	Preoperational child's answer	Concrete operational child's answer
Matter	Two identical balls of clay are shown to the child. The child agrees that they are equal.	The experimenter changes the shape of one of the balls and asks the child whether they still contain equal amounts of clay.	"No, the longer one has more."	"Yes, the same amount."

FIGURE 8.15

Preoperational and concrete operational children's views on the conservation of matter.

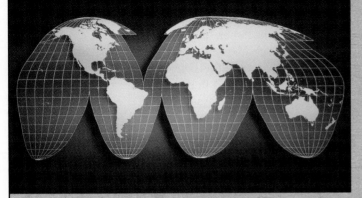

Conservation Skills Around the World

Psychologist Patricia Greenfield (1966) conducted a series of studies among Wolof children in the West African nation of Senegal to see if Piaget's theory of concrete operational thought is universal. Using Piaget's beaker tasks, she found that only 50 percent of the 10-to-13-year-olds understood the principle of conservation. Comparable studies among cultures in central Australia, New Guinea (an island north of Australia), the Amazon jungle region of Brazil, and rural Sardinia (an island off the coast of Italy) yielded strikingly similar results (Dasen, 1977). These findings suggested that adults in some cultures do not reach the stage of concrete operational thought. However, if this were so, such adults would be severely handicapped in everyday life. Like preschool children, they would be unable to think through the implications of their actions and would be unable to coordinate various kinds of information about objects. They also would be incapable of going beyond an egocentric perspective to understand another person's point of view.

Some researchers believe that the failure to find concrete operational thought in various cultures is due to inadequate communication between the experimenter and the children. For example, in one study of two cultural groups from Cape Breton, Nova Scotia—one English-speaking European, the other Micmac Indian—no difference in conservation abilities appeared between the groups of 10-to-11-year-olds when they were interviewed in their native languages (Nyiti, 1982). The Micmac children all spoke their ancestral tongue at home but had also spoken English since the first grade. However, when the Micmac children were interviewed in English, they understood the concept of conservation only half as well as the English-speaking children of European descent. This study illustrates the importance of communication between the experimenter and the research participants in cross-cultural studies.

Researchers have also investigated whether or not a child's ability to use the concept of conservation can improve if the child comes from a culture in which conservation is not widely prac-

The age at which individuals acquire conservation skills is related to the extent to which the culture provides practice relevant to the concept of conservation. The children shown here live in Nepal, and they have extensive experience as potters. They gain an understanding of the concept of conservation of quantity earlier than children the same age who do not have experience manipulating a material like clay.

ticed. In one study, rural aboriginal Australian children performed some exercises similar to Piaget's beaker task (Dasen, Ngini, & Lavalée, 1979). This "training" improved their performance on the beaker task. Even so, their grasp of the conservation concept lagged behind children from the Australian city of Canberra by approximately 3 years. These findings suggest that the aboriginal culture does not provide practice that is relevant to the conservation concept.

In sum, the age at which individuals acquire conservation skills appears to be associated with the degree to which their culture provides relevant practice. However, such cross-cultural differences tend to disappear when the studies are conducted by experimenters who are familiar with the language of the people being studied or when the participants receive special training (Cole & Cole, 1989).

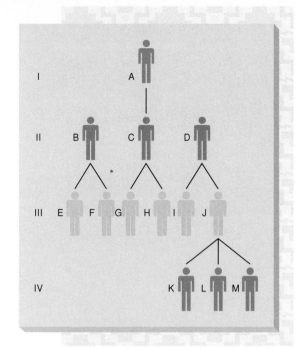

FIGURE 8.16

Classification: an important ability in concrete operational thought. A family tree of four generations (I to IV): the preoperational child has trouble classifying the members of the four generations; the concrete operational child can classify the members vertically, horizontally, and obliquely (up and down and across).

The stages of cognitive development are not as neatly packaged as Piaget envisioned. For example, children do not always learn to classify objects at the same time they learn to reverse mental operations. Some cognitive skills appear earlier than Piaget believed; for example, infants may be capable of symbolic thought earlier than Piaget believed. Other cognitive skills, such as developing hypotheses and deducing solutions to problems, may appear later than Piaget thought. Also, as we will see next, one view suggests that culture and social interaction play more important roles in cognitive development than Piaget envisioned.

Vygotsky's Theory

Children grow up in environments that can nurture their cognitive development—or allow it to wither on the vine. Lev Vygotsky (1896-1934), a Russian psychologist, recognized this important point about children's minds more than half a century ago. Vygotsky's ideas are receiving increased attention as we move toward the close of the twentieth century (Belmont, 1989; Rogoff, in press; Rogoff & Morelli, 1989).

One of Vygotsky's (1962) most important concepts is the **zone of proximal development (ZPD),** *which refers to tasks too*

FIGURE 8.17

Characteristics of concrete operational thought.

difficult for children to master alone but that can be mastered with the guidance and assistance of adults or more skilled children. Thus, the lower limit of the ZPD is the level of problem solving reached by a child working independently. The upper limit is the level of additional responsibility the child can accept with the assistance of an able instructor (see figure 8.18). Vygotsky's emphasis on the ZPD underscored his belief in the importance of social influences on cognitive development. The practical teaching involved in ZPD begins toward the zone's upper limit, where the child is able to reach the goal only through close collaboration with an instructor. With continued instruction and practice, the child depends less and less on explanations, hints, and demonstrations until she masters the skills necessary to perform the task alone. Once the goal is achieved, it may become the foundation for a new ZPD.

Many researchers who work in the field of culture and development find themselves comfortable with Vygotsky's theory, which focuses on sociocultural contexts (Pellegrini & others, 1990; Rogoff & Morelli, 1989). Vygotsky emphasized how the development of higher mental processes, such as reasoning, involve learning to use the inventions of society, such as language and mathematical systems. He also stressed the importance of teachers and role models in children's mental development. Vygotsky's emphasis on the importance of social interaction and culture in children's cognitive development contrasts with Piaget's description of the child as a solitary little scientist.

American developmental psychologist Barbara Rogoff (1990) also believes that social interaction and culture play important roles in children's cognitive development. She argues that a child's cognitive development should involve an "apprenticeship" with companions who will strengthen the child's written and oral language skills, math skills, and memory strategies to preserve information over time. In mastering these skills, a child would use all sorts of tools—everything from notches on sticks to calculators and computers.

Piaget once observed that children's cognitive development is a continuous creation of increasingly complex forms. As we will see next, this observation applies to children's social development as well.

REVIEW

Children's Cognitive Development

Piaget, a famous Swiss psychologist, developed an important theory of children's minds. A child constructs an understanding of the world through organization and adaptation. Adaptation consists of assimilation and accommodation. Piaget identified four stages of cognitive development: sensorimotor, preoperational, concrete operational, and formal operational. Sensorimotor thought lasts from birth to about 2 years of age and involves the coordination of sensorimotor action. Object permanence is an important accomplishment in the sensorimotor stage. A key aspect of cognitive development is being able to perform operations, mental representations that are reversible. The preoperational child (2 to 7 years) cannot do this. Preoperational thought is more symbolic than sensorimotor thought, it lacks conservation skills, it is egocentric, and it is intuitive rather than logical. A concrete operational child (7 to 11 years) can engage in operations, shows conservation skills, reasons logically but only in concrete circumstances, does not think abstractly, and has classification skills. Piaget was a genius at observing children, and he changed the way we view a child's understanding of the world. However, his views have not gone unchallenged.

In Vygotsky's view, cognitive skills develop through social interaction embedded in a cultural backdrop. Vygotsky emphasized the importance of the zone of proximal development (ZPD), which refers to tasks too difficult for children to master alone but that can be mastered with the guidance and assistance of adults or more highly skilled children. Vygotsky's view is receiving increased attention.

Upper limit — Level of additional responsibility child can accept with assistance of an able instructor

Zone of proximal development (ZPD)

Lower limit — Tasks too difficult for children to master alone; level of problem solving reached on these tasks by child working alone

FIGURE 8.18

Vygotsky's zone of proximal development. Vygotsky's zone of proximal development has a lower limit and an upper limit. Tasks in the ZPD are too difficult for the child to perform alone. They require assistance from an adult or a skilled child. As children experience the verbal instruction or demonstration, they organize the information in their existing mental structures so they can eventually perform the skill or task alone.

Children's Social Development

As children grow and develop, they socialize and are socialized by others—parents, siblings, peers, and teachers. Their small world widens as they discover new refuges and new challenges. We will examine Erikson's masterpiece on how we develop socially; it is a grand perspective of our complex journey through life.

Erikson's Theory of Social Development

Erik Erikson (1902–) spent his childhood and adolescence in Europe. After working as a psychoanalyst under Freud's direction, Erikson came to the United States in 1933. He became a U.S. citizen and taught at Harvard University.

Erikson recognized Freud's contributions to our understanding of human development, but he broke rank with some of Freud's basic tenets. In contrast to Freud's psychosexual stages, for instance, Erikson (1950, 1968) argues that we develop in *psychosocial stages*. In addition, Freud believed that our basic personality is shaped in the first 5 years of life, but Erikson emphasizes developmental change throughout the life span. The **epigenetic principle** *is Erikson's term for the process that guides development through the life cycle. The epigenetic principle states that human beings unfold according to a blueprint, with each stage of* *development coming at a predictable time.* In Erikson's view, everyone must pass through eight stages of development on the way to maturity and wisdom. The first four of these stages occur in childhood (see figure 8.19), the last four in adolescence and adulthood (these last four stages will be discussed in chapter 9). Each stage is precipitated by a "crisis" that requires a person to grapple with a unique developmental task. According to Erikson, this crisis is not a catastrophe but a turning point of increased vulnerability and enhanced potential. The more successfully a person resolves the crises, the more complete a human being he or she will become.

Trust versus mistrust, *which occurs during an infant's first year, is Erikson's first psychosocial stage. Trust is built when an infant's basic needs— such as comfort, food, and warmth—are met.* Trust in infancy sets the stage for a life-long expectation that the world will be a good and pleasant place to live.

Erikson's second stage of development, **autonomy versus shame and doubt,** *occurs from approximately 1 to 3 years of age. After developing trust, infants begin to discover that their behavior is their own. They start to assert their sense of independence, or autonomy; they realize their will. If infants are overly restrained or punished too harshly, they are likely to develop a sense of shame and doubt.*

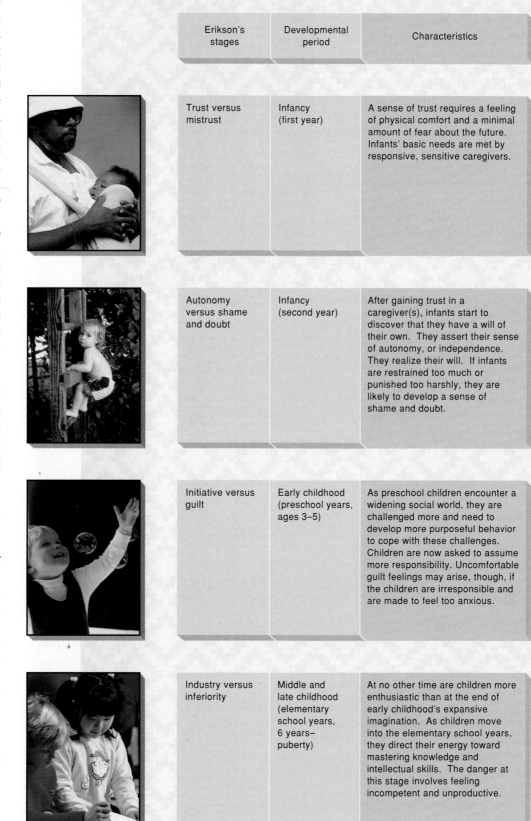

Erikson's stages	Developmental period	Characteristics
Trust versus mistrust	Infancy (first year)	A sense of trust requires a feeling of physical comfort and a minimal amount of fear about the future. Infants' basic needs are met by responsive, sensitive caregivers.
Autonomy versus shame and doubt	Infancy (second year)	After gaining trust in a caregiver(s), infants start to discover that they have a will of their own. They assert their sense of autonomy, or independence. They realize their will. If infants are restrained too much or punished too harshly, they are likely to develop a sense of shame and doubt.
Initiative versus guilt	Early childhood (preschool years, ages 3–5)	As preschool children encounter a widening social world, they are challenged more and need to develop more purposeful behavior to cope with these challenges. Children are now asked to assume more responsibility. Uncomfortable guilt feelings may arise, though, if the children are irresponsible and are made to feel too anxious.
Industry versus inferiority	Middle and late childhood (elementary school years, 6 years–puberty)	At no other time are children more enthusiastic than at the end of early childhood's expansive imagination. As children move into the elementary school years, they direct their energy toward mastering knowledge and intellectual skills. The danger at this stage involves feeling incompetent and unproductive.

FIGURE 8.19

Erikson's stages of childhood.

Initiative versus guilt, *Erikson's third stage of development, occurs during the preschool years.* As preschool children encounter a widening social world, they are challenged more than they were as infants. Active, purposeful behavior is needed to cope with these challenges. Children are asked to assume responsibility for their body, their behavior, their toys, and their pets. Developing a sense of responsibility increases initiative. Uncomfortable guilt feelings may arise, though, if the child is irresponsible and is made to feel too anxious. Erikson has a positive outlook on this stage. He believes most guilt is quickly compensated for by a sense of accomplishment.

Sometime during the elementary school years, children go through Erikson's fourth developmental stage, **industry versus inferiority.** *Children's initiative brings them into contact with a wealth of new experiences. As they move into middle and late childhood, they direct their energy toward mastering knowledge and intellectual skills.* With their expansive imaginations, children at this stage are eager to learn. The danger in the elementary school years is a sense of inferiority—feeling incompetent and inadequate. Erikson believes that teachers have a responsibility to help children develop a sense of competence and achievement. They should "mildly but firmly coerce children into the adventure of finding out that one can learn to accomplish things which one would never have thought of by oneself" (Erikson, 1968, p. 127).

Attachment

Erikson (1968) believes that caregivers' responsive and sensitive behavior toward infants during their first year provides an important foundation for later development. So do a number of contemporary developmental psychologists who study the process of "attachment" during infancy. Attachment usually refers to a strong relationship between two people, in which each person does a number of things to continue the relationship. Many types of people are attached: relatives, lovers, a teacher and student. In the language of developmental psychology, **attachment** *is primarily the close emotional bond between an infant and its caregiver.*

Theories about infant attachment abound. Freud believed that an infant becomes attached to the person or object that provides oral satisfaction. For most infants, this is the mother, since she is most likely to feed the infant. However, researchers

FIGURE 8.20

Wire and cloth monkeys in Harlow and Zimmerman's study. In the classic Harlow and Zimmerman study, infant monkeys, even though fed from the wire "mother," clung to the cloth "mother." This study demonstrated that feeding is not the critical factor in attachment but that contact comfort is an important factor.

have questioned the importance of feeding in attachment. In a classic study, Harry Harlow and Robert Zimmerman (1959) evaluated whether feeding or contact comfort was more important to infant attachment. The researchers separated infant monkeys from their mothers at birth and placed them in cages, where they had access to two artificial "mothers." As shown in figure 8.20, one of the mothers was made of wire, the other of cloth. Half of the infant monkeys were fed by the wire mother, half by the cloth mother. The infant monkeys nestled close to the cloth mother and spent little time on the wire one, even when it was the wire mother that gave milk. This study clearly demonstrated that contact comfort, not feeding, is the crucial element in the attachment process.

The importance of contact over feeding has also been demonstrated among humans. Hausa infants in Nigeria, for example, have several caregivers, but they show the strongest attachment to the person with whom they have the most physical contact, not the person who feeds them (Super, 1980).

In another classic study, Konrad Lorenz (1965) examined attachment behavior in geese. Lorenz separated the eggs laid by one goose into two groups. He returned one group to the goose to be hatched; the other group was hatched in an incubator. The goslings in the first group performed as predicted; they followed their mother as soon as they hatched. However, those in the second group, which first saw Lorenz after hatching, followed him everywhere as if he were their mother. Lorenz marked the goslings and then placed both groups under a box. Mother goose and "mother" Lorenz stood aside as the box was lifted. Each group of goslings went directly to its "mother" (see figure 8.21). Lorenz called this process **imprinting,** *the tendency of an infant animal to form an attachment to the first moving object it sees and/or hears.*

For goslings the critical period for imprinting is the first 36 hours after birth. There appears to be a longer, more flexible critical period for attachment in human infants. Many developmental psychologists believe that human attachment to a caregiver during the *first year* provides an important foundation for later development. This view has been especially emphasized in recent years by John Bowlby (1969, 1988) and Mary Ainsworth (1988). Bowlby believes that an infant and its mother instinctively form an attachment. He believes that a newborn is innately equipped to elicit its mother's attachment behavior; it cries, clings, smiles, and coos. Later the infant crawls, walks, and

FIGURE 8.21

Imprinting. Konrad Lorenz, a pioneering student of animal behavior, is followed through the water by three imprinted greylag geese. Lorenz described imprinting as rapid, innate learning within a critical period that involves attachment to the first moving object seen. For goslings the critical period is the first 36 hours after birth.

follows the mother. The infant's goal is to keep the mother nearby. Research on attachment supports Bowlby's view that the infant's attachment to its caregiver intensifies at about 6 to 7 months (Ainsworth, 1967; Schaffer & Emerson, 1964).

Some babies seem to have a more positive attachment experience than others. Ainsworth (1979, 1988) believes that the difference depends on how sensitive a caregiver is to an infant's signals. Ainsworth says that, in **secure attachment,** *infants use the caregiver, usually the mother, as a secure base from which to explore the environment.* Infants who are securely attached are more likely to have mothers who are more sensitive, accepting, and expressive of affection toward them than those who are insecurely attached (Baruch, 1991; Egeland & Farber, 1984; Waters, 1991).

A securely attached infant moves freely away from its mother but also keeps tabs on her location by periodically glancing at her. The infant responds positively to being picked up by others and, when put back down, happily moves away to play. In contrast, an insecurely attached infant avoids its mother or is ambivalent toward her. Such an infant fears strangers and is upset by minor, everyday separations.

As mentioned previously, many researchers, such as Ainsworth and Bowlby, believe that secure attachment during an infant's first year provides an important foundation for psychological development later in life. Research by Alan Sroufe (1985, in press) documents this connection. For example, in one study, researchers found that infants who are securely attached to their mothers are less frustrated and happier at 2 years of age than are their insecurely attached counterparts (Matas, Arend, & Sroufe, 1978).

Other researchers have failed to confirm consistently that secure attachment is the key to social competence (Lewis & others, 1984). Some developmentalists believe that too much importance is attributed to the attachment bond in infancy. For example, Jerome Kagan (1988, 1989) believes that infants are highly resilient and adaptive. He argues that infants are evolutionarily equipped to stay on a positive developmental path, even in the face of wide parenting variations. Kagan also stresses that temperament (biologically based personality traits, such as being inhibited versus outgoing) and genetic characteristics play more important roles in a child's competence than attachment theorists acknowledge. For example, a child may have inherited a low tolerance for stress. This, rather than an insecure attachment bond, may be responsible for the child's inability to get along with peers.

Another criticism of attachment theory is that it ignores the diversity of socializing agents and contexts that exist in an infant's world (Thompson, 1991). In some cultures, infants show attachments to many people. Among the Hausa, mentioned earlier in our discussion of contact and feeding, both grandmothers and siblings provide a significant amount of care to infants (Super, 1980). Infants in agricultural societies tend to form attachments to older siblings who are assigned a major responsibility for younger siblings' care. The attachments formed by infants in group care in Israeli kibbutzim provide another challenge to the singular attachment thesis.

Researchers recognize the importance of competent, nurturant caregivers in an infant's development—at issue, though, is whether or not secure attachment, especially to a single caregiver, is critical. As we will see next, infants and young children are increasingly being cared for in many arrangements outside of the home during much of their day.

Day Care

In the 1950s, an average of less than one out of five mothers with infants and young children worked outside the home. In 1989 almost three out of five such mothers had joined the workforce, and by 1995 that figure is expected to jump to two out of three. More than 10 million children under the age of 5 have mothers who work. Day care has clearly become a basic need for most American families.

Day-care arrangements vary extensively (Caldwell, 1991; Phillips, 1989). Many centers provide care for large groups of children and have elaborate facilities. Some are commercial operations; others are nonprofit centers run by churches, civic groups, or employers. Home care, sometimes provided by child-care professionals but more often by mothers who want to supplement the family income, is another option.

Just as the arrangements for day care vary enormously, so does the quality of the care. Following are two examples that illustrate the ease or anxiety that parents can face when they entrust the care of their children to others. Each weekday at 6 A.M., Ellen Smith drops off her 4-year-old daughter, Tanya, at the Brookhaven College day-care center in Dallas. She goes to work, confident that Tanya is having a great time in a safe and nurturant environment. When Ellen returns from work in the afternoon, Tanya is happy to be going home with her mom but also looks forward to returning to her friends the next day. Ellen reports that her daughter, who has been at the Brookhaven day-care center for 3 years, is adventurous and socially at ease with peers and adults alike. Ellen believes that day care has been a wonderful environment for Tanya. In Los Angeles, however, day care has been a series of problems for Barbara Jones. After 2 years of unpleasant experiences with sitters, day-care centers, and

In the Hausa culture, older siblings provide a significant amount of caregiving to their younger siblings. In such cultures, younger siblings often form strong attachments to older siblings.

day-care homes, Barbara quit her job as a successful real estate agent to stay home and take care of her 2½-year-old daughter, Gretchen. Caught in the conflict between her work and family roles, Barbara, who was unable to find good substitute care in day-care homes, resolved the conflict in favor of her family obligations. When Gretchen was in a day-care center, she said that she felt her daughter was being treated like a piece of merchandise—dropped off and picked up.

Recently, some experts have argued that the quality of day care most children receive in the United States is poor. Developmental psychologist Jay Belsky (1989) believes that, not only is the quality of day care generally poor, but, more important, this translates into negative developmental outcomes for children. Belsky concludes that extensive day-care experience in the first 12 months of life—as typically experienced in the United

What constitutes quality child care? The following recommendations were made by the National Association for the Education of Young Children (1988). They are based on a consensus arrived at by experts in early childhood education and child development. It is especially important for parents to meet the adults who will care for their children—they are responsible for every aspect of the program's operation.

1. *The Adult Caregivers*
   - The adults should enjoy and understand how infants and young children grow.
   - There should be enough adults to work with a group and to care for the individual needs of children. There should be no more than four infants for each adult caregiver, no more than eight 2-to-3-year-old children for each caregiver, and no more than ten 4-to-5-year-old children for each adult caregiver.
   - They observe and record each child's progress and development.

2. *The Program Activities and Equipment*
   - The environment fosters the growth and development of young children working and playing together.
   - A good center provides appropriate and sufficient equipment and play materials and makes them readily available.
   - Infants and children are helped to increase their language skills and to expand their understanding of the world.

3. *Relation of Staff to Families and the Community*
   - A good program considers and supports the needs of the entire family. Parents should be welcome to observe, discuss policies, make suggestions, and work in the activities of the center.
   - The staff members in a good center are aware of and contribute to community resources. The staff should share information about community recreational and learning opportunities with families.

4. *The Facility and Program Should Be Designed to Meet the Varied Demands of Infants and Young Children, Their Families, and the Staff*
   - The health of children, staff, and parents is protected and promoted. The staff should be alert to the health of each child.
   - The facility should be safe for children and adults.
   - The environment should be spacious to accommodate a variety of activities and equipment. There should be a minimum of 35 square feet of usable playroom floor space indoors per child and 75 square feet of play space outdoors per child.

FIGURE 8.22

What is high-quality day care?

States—is associated with insecure attachment, as well as increased aggression, noncompliance, and social withdrawal in the preschool and elementary school years. One recent investigation supported Belsky's beliefs (Vandell & Corasaniti, 1988). In this study, children who went into full-time day care (more than 30 hours per week) as infants were less compliant, had poorer peer relations, had poorer work habits in school, and received lower grades in school than children who began full-time day care later.

Belsky's conclusions about day care are controversial. Other respected researchers have arrived at a different conclusion; their review of the research on day care suggests no ill effects (Clarke-Stewart, 1989; Scarr, 1984; Scarr, Lande, & McCartney, 1989). For example, Sandra Scarr (1984) stresses that young children are resilient and can thrive in a variety of life circumstances, including day care. They develop well, she says, in many kinds of caregiving situations, as long as the care is good.

What can we conclude? Does day care have adverse effects on children's development? Parents must be very careful, of course, about the quality of day care they select for their children and infants, especially those 1 year of age or less. However, even Belsky agrees that day care itself is not the culprit; he acknowledges that no evidence exists to show that children in high-quality day care are at risk in any way.

One example of high-quality child care is the program developed by Jerome Kagan and his colleagues (1978) at Harvard University. Their day-care center included a pediatrician, a nonteaching director, and an infant-teacher ratio of three to one. Teachers' aides assisted at the center. The teachers and the aides were trained to smile frequently, to talk with the infants, and to provide them with a safe environment that included many stimulating toys. More information about what to look for in high-quality day care is presented in figure 8.22.

Unfortunately, few day-care centers like the one at Harvard University exist. High-quality child care carries with it a high price tag, one that few parents can afford to pay (Hofferth & Phillips, 1991). Despite the lobbying efforts of a number of child development experts, the child-care bills currently being intro-

From the *Notebook of a Printer*, "The frightening part about heredity and environment is that we parents provide both": developmental psychologists have been especially interested in pinning down the aspects of parenting that contribute to children's social competence. Diana Baumrind believes that a cluster of characteristics she calls *authoritative parenting* is the best parenting strategy. What does authoritative parenting involve?

duced in Congress do not adequately address the quality of child care or the low pay of child-care workers (DeAngelis, 1990; Zigler, 1991).

Parent-Child Relationships

Although many children spend a great deal of time in child-care situations away from the home, parents are still the main caregivers for the vast majority of the world's children. Parents have always wondered what is the best way to rear their children. "Spare the rod and spoil the child." "Children are to be seen and not heard." There was a time when parents took those adages seriously. However, our attitudes toward children—and parenting techniques—have changed. In this section, we'll discuss various

parenting styles; the role of culture, social class, and ethnicity in parenting; and changes in the role fathers play, as well as changes within the structure of the American family itself.

Parenting Styles

Diana Baumrind (1971, 1989, in press) believes that parents interact with their children in one of three basic ways. She classifies these parenting styles as authoritarian, authoritative, and permissive.

Authoritarian parenting *is a restrictive, punitive style that exhorts a child to follow the parent's directions and to respect work and effort. An authoritarian parent firmly limits and controls the child, allowing little verbal exchange. Authoritarian parenting is associated with children's social incompetence. In a difference of opinion*

"Are you going to believe me, your own flesh and blood, or some stranger you married?"

Reprinted by permission of Jerry Marcus.

about how to do something, for example, an authoritarian parent might say, "You do it my way or else. There will be no discussion!" Children of authoritarian parents often are anxious about social comparison, they fail to initiate activity, and they have poor communication skills.

Authoritative parenting *encourages children to be independent but still places limits and controls on their behavior. Parents allow extensive verbal give-and-take and are warm and nurturant toward the child. Authoritative parenting is associated with children's social competence.* An authoritative parent might put his arm around the child in a comforting way and say, "You know you should not have done that; let's talk about how you can handle the situation better next time." Children whose parents are authoritative tend to be socially competent, self-reliant, and socially responsible.

Permissive parenting comes in two forms: permissive-indifferent and permissive-indulgent (Maccoby & Martin, 1983). Parents who use a **permissive-indifferent** *style are very removed from their child's life; this style is associated with children's social incompetence, especially a lack of self-control.* This parent cannot give an affirmative answer to the question, "It is 10 P.M. Do you know where your child is?" Children have a strong need for their parents to care about them; children whose parents are permissive-indifferent may develop the sense that other aspects of the parents' lives are more important than they are. Children whose parents are permissive-indifferent tend to show poor self-control and do not handle independence well.

Parents who use a **permissive-indulgent** *style are highly involved with their children but place few demands or controls on them. Permissive-indulgent parenting is associated with children's social*

incompetence, *especially a lack of self-control.* Such parents let their children do what they want, with the result that children never learn to control their own behavior and always expect to get their way. Some parents deliberately rear their children this way because they believe the combination of warm involvement with few restraints will produce a creative, confident child. One boy whose parents deliberately reared him in a permissive-indulgent manner moved his parents out of their bedroom suite and took it over for himself. He is almost 18 years old and still has not learned to control his behavior; when he can't get something he wants, he throws temper tantrums. As you might expect, he is not very popular with his peers. Children whose parents are permissive-indulgent never learn respect for others and have difficulty controlling their behavior.

There is more to understanding parent-child relations than parenting style (Hooper & Hooper, 1992; Roopnarine & Carter, 1992). For many years, the socialization of children was viewed as a straightforward, one-way matter of indoctrination—telling small children about the use of spoons and potties, the importance of saying "thank you," and not killing their baby brother. The basic philosophy was that children had to be trained to fit into the social world, so their behavior had to be shaped into that of a mature adult. However, young children are not like inanimate blobs of clay sculptors form into polished statues. **Reciprocal socialization** *is the process by which children socialize parents, just as parents socialize children.* For example, the interaction of mothers and their infants is symbolized by a dance or dialogue in which successive actions of the partners are closely coordinated, as when one partner imitates the other or when there is mutual smiling.

As developmental psychologists probe the nature of reciprocal socialization, they are impressed with the importance of synchrony in parent-child relationships. **Synchrony** *refers to the carefully coordinated interaction between parent and child in which, often unknowingly, they are attuned to each other's behavior.* The turn-taking that takes place in a number of enjoyable parent-infant games reflects the reciprocal, synchronous nature of some parent-child relationships.

As is true of a great deal of human behavior, synchronous interactions are also shaped by cultural values. Japanese mothers, for example, spend more time than American mothers soothing and lulling their infants. Japanese mothers want to have quiet, contented babies, a reflection of Japanese cultural values about appropriate adult demeanor. In contrast, many American mothers engage their babies in high-energy games and chatter. They want their infants to develop into assertive, autonomous, expressive individuals, a reflection of American cultural values (Bronstein, 1988; Super & Harkness, 1982).

Another factor that shapes the parent-child relationship is the child's developmental status. A competent parent does not interact with a 10-year-old child in the same way as with a 2-year-old child (Maccoby, 1980; Santrock, 1993a). Parents usually discipline a toddler by physical manipulation—by carrying the child away from mischievous activity, by placing fragile objects out of reach, or sometimes by spanking the child. As the child grows older, parents turn to reasoning, lecturing, and giving or withholding privileges. Parents also spend less time with older children and monitor their activities more indirectly.

In discussing parent-child relationships, we have focused primarily on parents rather than mothers and fathers separately. In recent years, psychologists have become especially interested in the father's role.

The Father's Role

The father's role has undergone major changes over time (Bronstein, 1988; Lamb, 1986). Earlier in our history, fathers bore the primary responsibility for teaching children morals and providing religious guidance. Fathers also have been the main breadwinners and disciplinarians and have always, in one way or another, provided a gender role model. In the 1970s, however, fathers began to take a more nurturant, active role in their children's day-to-day lives.

As a result of this change, researchers began to take a fresh look at the dynamics between fathers and their children. Researchers have found that fathers can respond sensitively to an infant's signals to be touched and fed (Cowan, 1988). What's more, infants and children often prefer to play with fathers more than with mothers. This may be because most fathers play actively with their kids—wrestling, tossing balls, and "rough-housing"—more than mothers do. Perhaps some kids prefer to play with their fathers simply because they're not around as much as their mothers, making play seem all the more special. However, in stressful circumstances, such as a skinned knee or hurt feelings, young children tend to turn to their mothers first for comfort.

Fathers spend more time with their children now than they did a decade ago, but they still fall far short of mothers. Even when both parents work full-time, fathers tend to interact one-on-one with their children only about one-third as much as mothers. Also, mothers still carry the responsibility for everyday matters—such as making sure the child gets to school on time, eats nutritious meals, and goes to the dentist (Lamb, 1986).

Researchers have wondered if parent-infant interactions are different in families who adopt nontraditional gender roles. In one such study, Michael Lamb and his colleagues (1982) looked at the dynamics in Swedish families in which the fathers were the primary caregivers of firstborn 8-month-old infants and

The father's role in China has been slow to change, but it is changing. Traditionally in China, the father has been expected to be strict, the mother kind. The father is characterized as a stern disciplinarian; the child is expected to fear the father. The notion of the strict father has ancient roots. The Chinese character for father (*fu*) evolved from a primitive character representing a hand holding a cane, which symbolizes authority. However, the twentieth century has witnessed a decline in the father's authority. Younger fathers are more inclined to allow children to express their opinions and be more independent. Influenced to a degree by the increased employment of mothers, Chinese fathers are becoming more involved in caring for their children. In some instances, intergenerational tension has developed between fathers and sons, as younger generations behave in less traditional ways (Ho, 1987).

the mothers worked full-time. Despite this reversal in gender roles, the researchers found that the mothers were more likely than the fathers to coo at, talk to, cuddle, and soothe their infants. These parents dealt with their babies along the lines of American fathers and mothers who follow traditional gender roles. Even though fathers assumed the primary caregiving role, it did not substantially alter the way they interacted with their infants. These findings may be due to biological reasons or to deeply ingrained socialization patterns.

Cultural, Social Class, and Ethnic Variations Among Families

In the broadest sense, good parents everywhere seem to share a common approach to child-rearing. One study examined the behavior of parents in 186 cultures around the world and found that most parents use a warm and controlling style, one that is neither permissive nor restrictive, in dealing with their children (Rohner & Rohner, 1981). Good parents seem to know instinctively that children do best when they are guided by love and at least some moderate parental control.

a.

b.

c.

The role of the extended family has been especially strong in (a) Chinese American families, (b) Black American families, and (c) Hispanic American families. Sometimes these families stretch out in a score of relatives, who can help the members cope with adversity.

Despite such commonalities, researchers have also found telling differences in parenting across social classes and cultures. For example, there is wide variation in some childrearing practices among social classes in the United States and most Western cultures. Working-class and low-income parents, for instance, often place a high value on "external characteristics," such as obedience and neatness. Middle-class families, on the other hand, seem to prize "internal characteristics," such as self-control and the ability to delay gratification. Middle-class parents also are more likely to explain things, to use reasoning to accompany their discipline, to ask their children questions, and to praise them. In contrast, parents in low-income and working-class households are more likely to discipline their children with physical punishment and to criticize their children (Heath, 1983; Kohn, 1977).

Ethnic minority families differ from White American families in their size, structure, and composition, their reliance on kinship networks, and their levels of income and education (Spencer & Dornbusch, 1990). Large and extended families are more common among ethnic minority groups than among White Americans (Wilson, 1989; Wilson & others, 1991). For example, more than 30 percent of Hispanic American families consist of five or more individuals (Keefe & Padilla, 1987). Black American and Hispanic American children interact more with grandparents, aunts, uncles, cousins, and more distant relatives than do White American children.

Single-parent families are more common among Black Americans and Hispanic Americans than among White Americans (Marín & Marín, 1991; Rogler, Cortes, & Malgady, 1991). In comparison with two-parent households, single parents often have more limited resources of time, money, and energy. This shortage of resources may prompt them to encourage early autonomy among their children and adolescents (Spencer & Dornbusch, 1990). Also, ethnic minority parents are less well educated and engage in less joint decision making than do White American parents, and ethnic minority children are more likely to come from low-income families than are White American children (Committee for Economic Development, 1987; McLoyd, in press). Although impoverished families often raise competent children, poor parents may have a diminished capacity for supportive and involved parenting (McLoyd, in press).

Some aspects of home life can help protect ethnic minority children from social patterns of injustice (Spencer & Dornbush, 1990). The community and family can filter out destructive racist messages, parents can provide alternate frames of reference than those presented by the majority, and parents can also provide competent role models and encouragement (Jones, 1990). The extended family system in many ethnic minority families also provides an important buffer against stress.

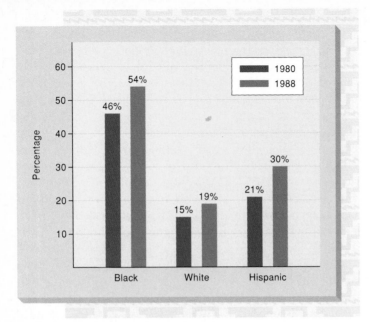

FIGURE 8.23

Percentage of children under 18 living with one parent in 1980 and 1988. The percentage of children under 18 living with one parent increased from 20 percent in 1980 to 24 percent in 1988. This figure reveals the breakdown of single parents in Black, White, and Hispanic families. Note the substantially higher percentage of Black single-parent families.

Many Native Americans value autonomy and, thus, encourage their children to become independent at an early age (LaFromboise & Low, 1989). Conversely, Puerto Rican parents living in the United States are more likely to promote nonassertive and compliant behavior in their children (Inclan & Herron, 1989). Japanese American families value the family over the individual, stress duty and obligation over love, and encourage social conformity. Mainstream American families, however, emphasize the individual, promote social control through love and punishment, and praise independent behavior (Nagata, 1989). In addition, Black parents are less likely than White parents to socialize their children along strict gender lines. Black parents are also more likely to share child care and decision making about childrearing and to value a child's social competence over an ability to deal with objects (Allen & Majidi-Ahi, 1989). As we will see next, the changing tapestry of American families includes not only an increasing mix of ethnic backgrounds, but also an increasing mix of family structures.

The Changing Tapestry of American Families

More and more children are growing up in single-parent families. In fact, less than 19 percent of the children in the United States live in a two-parent family in which only one parent, usually the father, is the breadwinner. As shown in figure 8.23, a substantial increase in the number of children under 18 who lived in a single-parent family occurred between 1980 and 1988. In addition, the percentage of single-parent families is higher for Blacks than for White or Hispanic families. If current trends continue, by the year 2000 one in every four children will also have lived a portion of their lives in a stepparent family.

As a result of these trends, researchers have been concerned about the effects on children. The contemporary approach to research advocates evaluating the strengths and weaknesses of children prior to divorce, the nature of events surrounding the divorce itself, and postdivorce family functioning. Investigators are finding that the availability and use of support systems (babysitters, relatives, day care); an ongoing, positive relationship between the custodial parent and the ex-spouse; authoritative parenting; financial stability; and children's competencies at the time of a divorce are related to the children's adjustment (Barber & Eccles, 1992; Hetherington, 1989, 1991; Hetherington & Clingempeel, in press; Hetherington, Hagan, & Anderson, 1989; Santrock & Warshak, 1986; Wallerstein, 1989).

As mentioned earlier, 10 million children under the age of 5 have mothers who work outside of the home. A young child whose mother works because she chooses to and is able to arrange reasonable child care without a great deal of stress is just as well adjusted as the child of a nonemployed mother (Zigler & Frank, 1988). In fact, having an employed mother has been shown to have some benefits for the child. For example, both sons and daughters of employed mothers view men and women less stereotypically and are more likely to approve of their mother's employment (Hoffman, 1988). When mothers work because of personal choice, daughters view both parents with increased admiration, and, in the long run, college women whose mothers work in traditionally male occupations are more likely to aspire to nontraditional occupations (Heyns, 1982). By contrast, sons from poor families often view fathers more negatively when their mothers work. Research with ethnic minority families, although sparse, has consistently shown that a working mother is a positive contribution to her child's achievement—unless the child is poorly supervised (Heyns, 1982).

Good child care after school and during school vacations is a conundrum for many families. Children who have no supervision are at greater risk for getting into trouble. In one study, 90 percent of the juvenile delinquents in Montgomery County, Maryland, were latchkey children—so-called because after school they return to an empty house and carry a key to let themselves in (Long & Long, 1984). Some researchers caution against generalizing about the effects of being a latchkey kid (Belle & Burr, 1992; Belle & others, 1991; Steinberg, 1988). In one investigation, parents who structured their latchkey children's after-school hours with clubs, school activities, and neighborhood cooperatives and who were authoritative rather than authoritarian or permissive had children who were less likely to follow negative peer influences (Steinberg, 1986).

REVIEW

Erikson's Theory of Social Development, Attachment, and Families

Erikson's theory emphasizes development throughout the human life span. Erikson says that individuals go through eight psychosocial stages, guided by the epigenetic principle. Erikson's four childhood stages are trust vs. mistrust (first year), autonomy vs. shame and doubt (second year), initiative vs. guilt (3–5 years), and industry vs. inferiority (6 years-puberty).

Attachment is a close bond between an infant and caregiver(s). A number of attachment theories exist. Feeding does not seem to be critical in attachment, but contact comfort, familiarity, and the caregiver's sensitivity and responsiveness are. Many developmental psychologists, especially Bowlby and Ainsworth, believe that attachment in the first year provides an important foundation for later development. Ainsworth argues that secure attachment is critical for competent social development; others do not. Day care has become a basic need for many American families. The type and quality of day care vary enormously. Belsky argues that day care in the first year of life is detrimental to social development; others, such as Scarr, disagree.

Baumrind's parenting strategies—authoritarian, authoritative, and permissive—are widely used classifications. Socially competent children are more likely to have authoritative parents. However, the socialization of children is a reciprocal process; children also socialize parents. Over time the father's role has changed from moral teacher to breadwinner to gender role model to active, nurturant caregiver. Fathers have increased their interaction with their children, but they still lag far behind mothers, even when mothers are employed. Fathers can act sensitively to infants' signals, but some do not. Infants usually prefer their mothers in stressful circumstances. Even in families in which the father is the primary caregiver, mothers and fathers often behave along traditional gender lines.

Although there are cross-cultural variations in families, authoritative parenting is the most common childrearing style around the world. Working-class and low-income parents place a higher value on "external characteristics," middle-class parents a higher value on "internal characteristics." However, there are variations in any social class, especially among ethnic groups. Chinese American, Black American, and Mexican families all have a strong tradition of the extended family. Children are increasingly growing up in single-parent and stepparent families. In studying the effects of divorce on children, researchers examine a complex set of factors. The mother's employment and latchkey experiences are not uniformly negative experiences for children.

Peers and Play

If you think back to your childhood, some of the first memories that spring to mind may be of the times you spent hanging out with friends. You learned all sorts of things from your peers about the world outside your family. All children do. By talking to a friend, a child may learn that another child's parents argue all the time, make him go to bed early, or give him an allowance. Many children get their first information (much of it wrong) about sex from friends. Children frequently compare themselves with their peers: are they better than, about the same as, or worse than their peers at skateboarding, math, or making friends?

Most children want to have friends and be popular (Rawlins, 1992). Children who are happy and enthusiastic, show concern for others, and have good conversational skills tend to be popular and make friends easily (Hartup, 1983; Parker & Gottman, 1989). In fact, peer relations have been found to be important predictors of children's adjustment and future competence. For example, children who are rejected by their peers tend to have more problems than children who are popular (Asher & Parker, in press; Parker & Asher, 1987; Price & Dodge, in press).

It is largely through play that children forge the bonds of friendship. The word *play* is a conspicuous part of children's conversations: "What can we play now?" "Let's play hide-and-seek." "Let's play outside." Most young children spend a good deal of their day playing. Children learn to cooperate with their peers, set and follow rules, work off frustrations, and explore the world around them through play (Goldstein, 1989). By the age of 5 or 6, however, children in most societies face an important transition—they can no longer spend their day at play; they must devote most of their day to school.

Schools

Children spend many years as members of a small society that exerts tremendous influence on who they will become—school. In addition to teaching children to write and read, schools help shape the fundamental aspects of a child's personality, such as a sense of identity, standards of right and wrong, and the way in which social systems outside the family function. In this section, we will explore a number of issues, such as what the best education for young children might be, the transition to elementary school, and the influence of social class and ethnicity on schooling.

The Education of Young Children

In a kindergarten class at the Greenbrook School in South Brunswick, New Jersey, 23 5- and 6-year-olds eagerly pick up geometric puzzles, playing cards, and counting equipment from the shelves lining the room. At one round table, some young children fit together brightly colored shapes. One girl forms a hexagon out of triangles. Other children gather around her to count how many parts are needed to make the whole. After about half an hour, the children prepare for story time. They put away their counting equipment and sit in a circle around one young girl, who holds up a giant book about a character named Mrs. Whishywashy, who insists on giving farm animals a bath. The children recite the whimsical lines, clearly enjoying one of their favorite stories. The hallway outside the kindergarten is lined with the children's drawings depicting their interpretation of the book. After the first reading, volunteers act out various parts of the story. There is not one bored face in the room (Kantrowitz & Wingert, 1989).

This is not reading, writing, and arithmetic the way most of us remember it. A growing number of educators and psychologists believe that preschool and young elementary school children learn best through active, hands-on teaching methods, such as games and dramatic play. They know that children develop at varying rates and that schools need to allow for these individual differences. They also believe that schools should focus on improving children's social development as well as their cognitive development. Educators refer to this type of schooling as **developmentally appropriate practice,** *an approach to teaching based on knowledge of the typical development of children within an age span (age appropriateness), as well as the uniqueness of the child (individual appropriateness). Developmentally appropriate practice takes a concrete, hands-on approach to teaching.* In contrast, teaching large groups of young children through abstract, paper-and-pencil activities is believed to be developmentally inappropriate (Burts, Charlesworth, & Fleege, 1991; Charlesworth & others, in press).

One of the most comprehensive documents on developmentally appropriate practice was put together by the National Association for the Education of Young Children (NAEYC)

a.

b.

(a) Is the play of today's children different from the play of children in collective village life, as shown in *Children's Games* by Pieter Breughel? (b) American children's play once took place in the rural fields and city streets. Today play is often confined to backyards, basements, playrooms, and bedrooms. The content of children's play today is often derived from video games, television dramas, and Saturday morning cartoons.

(Bredekamp, 1987). Many of the foremost experts in the field of early childhood education contributed to this document. A brief overview of the NAEYC's recommendations in just two of many areas is presented in figure 8.24.

One of the concerns of Americans is that our school children fare poorly when their achievement tests scores in math and science are compared with the test scores of school children from many other industrialized nations, especially such Asian nations as Japan and China (McKnight & others, 1987). Many

Component	Appropriate practice	Inappropriate practice
Curriculum goals	Experiences are provided in all developmental areas—physical, cognitive, social, and emotional.	Experiences are narrowly focused on cognitive development without recognition that all areas of the child's development are interrelated.
	Individual differences are expected, accepted, and used to design appropriate activities.	Children are only evaluated against group norms and all are expected to perform the same tasks and achieve the same narrowly defined skills.
	Interactions and activities are designed to develop children's self-esteem and positive feelings toward learning.	Children's worth is measured by how well they conform to rigid expectations and perform on standardized tests.
Teaching strategies	Teachers prepare the environment for children to learn through active exploration and interaction with adults, other children, and materials.	Teachers use highly structured, teacher-directed lessons almost exclusively.
	Children select many of their own activities from among a variety the teacher prepares.	The teacher directs all activity, deciding what children will do and when.
	Children are expected to be mentally and physically active.	Children are expected to sit down, be quiet, and listen, or do paper-and-pencil tasks for long periods of time. A major portion of time is spent passively sitting, watching, and listening.

FIGURE 8.24

Developmentally appropriate and inappropriate practice in early childhood education: NAEYC recommendations.

Americans attribute the differences in achievement scores to a rigid system that sets young children in a lockstep from cradle to college. In fact, the early years of Japanese schooling are anything but a boot camp. To read further about the nature of early childhood education in Japan, turn to Sociocultural Worlds 8.3.

Project Head Start

For many years, children from poor families did not receive any education before they entered the first grade. In the 1960s, "compensatory education" was created to try to break the cycle of poverty and poor education for young children in the United States. **Project Head Start** *is a compensatory education program designed to provide children from low-income families with an opportunity to acquire the skills and experiences needed to succeed in school.* Recent evaluations of Project Head Start reaffirm its positive influence on both the cognitive and social skills of disadvantaged young children (Haskins, 1989; Kagan, 1988).

Such programs as Project Head Start reap benefits that last over the long haul as well. Irving Lazar, Richard Darlington, and their colleagues (1982) found that children between the ages of

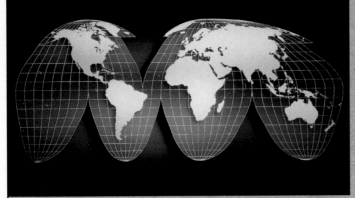

Early Childhood Education in Japan

In the midst of low academic achievement by children in the United States, many Americans are turning to Japan, a country of high academic achievement and economic success, for possible answers. However, the answers provided by Japanese preschools are not the ones Americans expected to find. In most Japanese preschools, surprisingly little emphasis is put on academic instruction. In one recent investigation, 300 Japanese and 210 American preschool teachers, child development specialists, and parents were asked about various aspects of early childhood education (Tobin, Wu, & Davidson, 1989). Only 2 percent of the Japanese respondents listed "to give children a good start academically" as one of their top three reasons for a society to have preschools. In contrast, over half the American respondents chose this as one of their top three choices. To prepare children for successful careers in first grade and beyond, Japanese schools do not teach reading, writing, and mathematics but rather skills, such as persistence, concentration, and the ability to function as a member of a group. The vast majority of young Japanese children are taught to read at home by their parents.

In the recent comparison of Japanese and American preschool education, 91 percent of Japanese respondents chose providing children with a group experience as one of their top three reasons for a society to have preschools (Tobin, Wu, & Davidson, 1989). Sixty-two percent of the more individually oriented Americans listed group experience as one of their top three choices. An emphasis on the importance of the group seen in Japanese early childhood education continues into elementary school education.

Lessons in living and working together grow naturally out of the Japanese culture. In many Japanese kindergartens, children wear the same uniforms, including caps, which are of different colors to indicate the classrooms to which they belong. They have identical sets of equipment, kept in identical drawers and shelves. This is not intended to turn the young children into robots, as

In Japan, learning how to cooperate and participating in group experiences are viewed as extremely important reasons for the existence of early childhood education.

some Americans have observed, but to impress on them that other people, just like themselves, have needs and desires that are equally important (Hendry, 1986).

Like in America, there is diversity in Japanese early childhood education. Some Japanese kindergartens have specific aims, such as early musical training or the practice of Montessori aims (Hendry, 1986). In large cities, some kindergartens are attached to universities that have elementary and secondary schools. Some Japanese parents believe that, if their young children attend a university-based program, it will increase the children's chances of eventually being admitted to top-rated schools and universities. Several more progressive programs have introduced free play as an antidote for the heavy intellectualizing in some Japanese kindergartens.

These preschool children are attending a Head Start program, a national effort to provide children from low-income families the opportunity to experience an enriched environment.

9 and 19 who have been involved in such preschool programs fare better in school, score higher on standard intelligence and achievement tests, and are more likely to feel good about themselves because of school accomplishments. In addition, children who participated in model preschool programs had lower rates of being placed into special education, being held back a grade, dropping out of school, becoming delinquents, or using welfare programs. Program parents were more satisfied with their children's school performance and had higher aspirations for them than did parents of youth who were not in the program.

In dollars and cents, taxpayers receive about $1.50 in return on every dollar by the time Project Head Start participants reach the age of 20 (Haskins, 1989). "Bottomline" benefits include savings on public school education (such as special-education services), tax payments on additional earnings, reduced welfare payments, and savings in juvenile justice system costs. Predicted benefits over a lifetime are much greater to the

taxpayer, a return of $5.73 on every dollar invested. In short, such programs as Project Head Start have been a rousing success (Haskins, 1989; Kagan, 1988).

The Transition to Elementary School

For most children, entering the first grade signals a change from being a "little kid" to being "in school." Children take on a new role (being a student), develop relationships with new adults and peers, and develop new standards by which to judge themselves. School provides children with a rich source of new ideas to shape their sense of self.

Children of all ages learn in an *integrated* fashion (NAEYC, 1988). For example, children sharpen their reading and writing skills when they work on social studies projects; they learn mathematical concepts through music and physical education (Katz & Chard, 1989; Van Deusen-Henkel & Argondizza, 1987), yet elementary teachers, pressed to "cover the curriculum" within the school year, frequently adhere to tight schedules that allocate only discrete segments of time for each subject. This approach ignores the fact that children don't care if an assignment sticks to one topic or spills over into another, as long as the project engages them.

Hands-on education is one of the best ways to engage kids in learning. One group of young children, for example, decided to do a project about a school bus. They wrote to the district superintendent and arranged to have a bus parked at their school for a few days. They explored and scrutinized the bus, discovered the functions of its parts, and discussed traffic rules. Then they built their own bus out of cardboard (Katz & Chard, 1989). The project was a lot of work; the children had to do a great deal of writing, problem solving, and even some arithmetic, but it was fun. When the parents went to "open house," the teacher was ready with reports on how each child was doing. However, the first thing the parents wanted to see was the bus, because their children had been talking about it for weeks. Many education experts believe that all children deserve this kind of concrete, hands-on education.

Social Class and Ethnicity in Schools

Sometimes it seems as though the major function of schools has been to train children to contribute to a middle-class, White society. The standard bearers of education—principals, school board members, and politicians who vote on school funding—tend to be from middle-class or elite, White backgrounds.

Critics argue that schools have done a poor job of educating children from low-income and ethnic minority backgrounds (Glasser, 1990; Huang & Gibbs, 1989). In *Dark Ghetto*, Kenneth Clark (1965) described differences between the ways children in lower-class schools and children in middle-class schools are treated. According to Clark, teachers in middle-class schools spend more time actually teaching students, and they spend more than twice as much time evaluating students' work. He also observed that teachers in middle-class schools make more positive than negative comments to students, whereas teachers in low-income schools make three times as many negative comments to students. The following passage from Clark's book vividly describes a school in a large urban slum:

> It is 2 P.M., the beginning of sixth-period class, and Warren Benson, a young teacher, looks around the room. Eight students are present out of thirty. "Where is everybody?" he demands. "They don't like your class," a girl volunteers. Three girls saunter in. Cora, who is playing a cassette recorder, bumps over to her desk in time with the music. She lowers the volume. "Don't mark us down late," she shouts, "We was right here." . . . Here you find students whose families live in poverty, students who can't read, students with drug problems, students wanting to drop out. . . .

American anthropologist John Ogbu (1974, 1986, 1989) proposed a controversial view that ethnic minority children are placed in a position of subordination and exploitation in the American educational system. He believes that ethnic minority children, especially Black and Hispanic Americans, have inferior educational opportunities, are exposed to teachers and administrators who have low academic expectations for them, and encounter negative stereotypes about ethnic minority groups. Ogbu states that ethnic minority opposition to the middle-class, White educational system stems from a lack of trust because of years of discrimination and oppression. Says Ogbu, it makes little sense to do well academically if occupational opportunities are often closed to ethnic minority youth.

Completing high school, or even college, does not always bring the same job opportunities for many ethnic minority youths as for White youths (Entwisle, 1990). In terms of earnings and employment rates, Black American high school graduates do not do as well as their White counterparts. Giving up in school because of a perceived lack of reward involving inadequate job opportunities characterizes many Hispanic American youths as well.

According to American educational psychologist Margaret Beale Spencer and sociologist Sanford Dornbusch (1990), a form of institutional racism prevails in many American schools. That is, well-meaning teachers, acting out of misguided liberalism, often fail to challenge ethnic minority students. Knowing the handicaps these children face, some teachers accept a low level of performance from them, substituting warmth and affection for academic challenge and high standards of performance. Ethnic minority students, like their White counterparts, learn best when teachers combine warmth with challenging standards.

One person who is trying to do something about the poor quality of education for inner-city children is psychiatrist James Comer (1988). He has devised an intervention model that is based on a simple principle: everyone with a stake in a school should have a say in how it's run. Comer's model calls for forming a school governance team, made up of the principal, psychologists, and even cafeteria workers. The team develops a comprehensive plan for operating the school, including a calendar of academic and social events that encourages parents to come to school as often as possible. Comer is convinced that a strong family orientation is a key to educational success, so he tries to create a familylike environment in schools and also to make parents feel comfortable in coming to their children's school. Among the reasons for Comer's concern about the lack of parental involvement in Black American and Hispanic American children's education is the high rate of single-parent families in these ethnic minority groups. A special concern is that 70 percent of the Black American and Hispanic American single-parent families headed by mothers are in poverty (McLoyd, in press). Poor

James Comer (left) is shown with some of the inner-city Black American children who attend a school that became a better learning environment because of Comer's intervention. Comer is convinced that a strong, familylike atmosphere is a key to improving the quality of inner-city schools.

school performance among many ethnic minority children is related to this pattern of single-parenting and poverty (Dornbusch & others, 1985; Spencer & Dornbusch, 1990).

Cooperative learning *is an approach to teaching in which children from various ethnic backgrounds or ability levels are assigned to groups. Each member works on problems at his or her skill level and pace but is also encouraged to perform as part of a group.* All children in a group are encouraged to monitor the other members' activities and to offer assistance when appropriate. Educational psychologist Robert Slavin (1987, 1989) believes that cooperative learning is one way to foster acceptance among ethnic groups. He found that barriers between students from different ethnic backgrounds break down when the students have to pool their efforts and cooperate to achieve the group's goals.

Children: The Future of Society

As the twenty-first century approaches, the well-being of children is one of America's foremost concerns. Children are the future of any society. Those who do not reach their potential, who are destined to make fewer contributions to society than society needs, and who do not take their place as productive adults diminish the power of that society's future (Horowitz & O'Brien, 1989).

The United States currently lags behind many other countries in developing adequate policies for children and families (Edelman, 1987, 1992). For instance, the United States is the only industrialized country in the world that does not have a policy guaranteeing women paid leave for childbirth and the care of young infants. In the United States, many employed mothers must use their own sick leave time or take leave without pay in the weeks before and after the baby's birth. By contrast, many European countries give one parent 6 to 12 months leave, and they usually allow parents to stay home when a child is ill in the early years of the child's life.

Some government-sponsored programs do provide support for children and families in the United States. However, most of these programs are directed at only the neediest families—income assistance, medical care, food programs, job training, and day care, for example. Most of these programs have come into being in a piecemeal fashion over many years. Also, most are crisis-oriented interventions, with few aimed at preventing family problems before they occur, and funding for these various government programs to support families has been inconsistent. To an extent, the American tradition of individualism, self-sufficiency, and family privacy has made government decision makers unwilling to become involved in family matters, except when extreme problems surface. As child development expert Edward Zigler (1989) commented, it is difficult to find any overarching or consistent goals for the support of children and families in America.

Development does not end with childhood. We also develop as adolescents and adults, which we will discuss in the next chapter.

REVIEW

Peers, Play, Schools, and Children's Well-Being

Peers and play are important dimensions of children's development. Psychologists study the factors that contribute to peer popularity and friendship. Play takes up a major portion of many young children's days and serves many functions.

Developmentally appropriate practice, especially advocated in the education of young children, is based on knowledge of the typical development of children within an age span (age appropriateness) and the uniqueness of the child (individual appropriateness). Developmentally appropriate practice contrasts with developmentally inappropriate practice, which ignores the concrete, hands-on approach to learning. Project Head Start is a compensatory education program designed to provide children from low-income families the opportunity to acquire the skills and experiences important for success in school. Recent evaluations continue to document Head Start's positive influence on disadvantaged children. The curriculum in elementary schools should be integrated. Many educators and psychologists believe that children should be taught through concrete, hands-on experience in the early elementary school years.

Schools have a stronger middle-class than lower-class orientation. Not only do many lower-class children have problems in school, so do children from ethnic minorities. Ogbu proposed a controversial view that ethnic minority children are placed in a position of subordination and exploitation in the American educational system. Some experts believe that a form of institutional racism exists in some schools because teachers fail to academically challenge ethnic minority children. Efforts are being made to reduce ethnic bias in schools, among them cooperative learning.

Children are the future of any society. Unfortunately, the United States lags behind many other countries in developing adequate policies for children and families. Consistent goals that foster the well-being of children and families need to be implemented.

Summary

I. What Is Development?

Development is a pattern of movement or change that occurs throughout the life span. Development involves an interplay of biological, cognitive, and social processes. Development is influenced by the interaction of maturation and experience. The debate over the role of maturation and experience is another version of the nature-nurture controversy. Development also may be described as either continuous (gradual, cumulative change) or discontinuous (an abrupt sequence of stages). Social policy is a national government's course of action designed to influence the welfare of its citizens. Improved social policy related to children is needed to help all children reach their potential.

II. Prenatal Development and Birth

Conception occurs when a sperm unites with an ovum. The fertilized egg is the zygote. The first 2 weeks after conception is the germinal period, 2 to 8 weeks is the embryonic period, and 2 to 9 months is the fetal period. Teratogens are agents that cause birth defects. Drugs and maternal diseases are examples of teratogens. Birth marks a dramatic transition for the fetus. Special interest focuses on preterm infants. Social class and ethnic differences affect a preterm infant's development.

III. Children's Physical Development

An infant comes into the world equipped with a number of reflexes. At birth, infants can see, but their vision is about 20/600. Shortly after birth, infants also can hear, smell, touch, taste, and feel pain. Brain development is dramatic during both prenatal development and the first 2 years of life. Nutrition is important for infant growth. Breast-feeding is healthier than bottle-feeding, but the merits of breast-feeding over bottle-feeding continue to be debated. Physical development slows during the childhood years, although motor development becomes smoother and more coordinated.

IV. Piaget's Approach

Piaget, a famous Swiss psychologist, developed an important theory about children's minds. A child constructs an understanding of the world through organization and adaptation. Adaptation is made up of assimilation and accommodation. Piaget identified four stages of cognitive development: sensorimotor, preoperational, concrete operational, and formal operational.

V. Piaget's Childhood Stages

Sensorimotor thought lasts from birth to about 2 years of age and involves the coordination of sensorimotor action. Object permanence is an important accomplishment in the sensorimotor stage. A key aspect of cognitive development is the ability to perform operations, mental representations that are reversible. A preoperational child (2-7 years) cannot do this. Preoperational thought is more symbolic than sensorimotor but lacks conservation skills, is egocentric, and is intuitive rather than logical. A concrete operational child (7-11 years) can engage in operations, shows conservation skills, reasons logically but only in concrete circumstances, does not think abstractly, and has classification skills. Piaget was a genius at observing children, and he changed the way we view a child's understanding of the world. However, his views have not gone unchallenged.

VI. Vygotsky's Theory

In Vygotsky's view, cognitive skills develop through social interaction. Vygotsky emphasized the importance of the zone of proximal development (ZPD), which refers to tasks too difficult for children to master alone but that can be mastered with the guidance and assistance of adults or more highly skilled children. Vygotsky's view is receiving increased attention.

VII. Erikson's Theory

Erikson's theory emphasizes development throughout the human life span. Erikson says that individuals go through eight psychosocial stages, guided by the epigenetic principle. Erikson's four childhood stages are trust vs. mistrust (first year), autonomy vs. shame and doubt (1-3 years), initiative vs. guilt (3-5 years), and industry vs. inferiority (6 years-puberty).

VIII. Attachment and Day Care

Attachment is a close bond between an infant and caregiver(s). A number of attachment theories exist. Feeding is not critical in attachment, but contact comfort, familiarity, and the caregiver's sensitivity and responsiveness are. Many developmental psychologists, especially Bowlby and Ainsworth, believe that attachment in the first year provides an important foundation for later development. Ainsworth thinks that secure attachment is critical for competent social development; others do not. Day care has become a basic need for many American families. The type and quality of day care vary enormously. Belsky argues that day care in the first year of life is detrimental to social development; others, such as Scarr, disagree.

IX. Parent-Child Relationships

Baumrind's parenting strategies—authoritarian, authoritative, and permissive—are widely used classifications. Socially competent children are more likely to have authoritative parents. However, the socialization of children is a reciprocal process; children also socialize parents. Over time the father's role has changed from moral teacher to breadwinner to gender role model to active, nurturant caregiver. Fathers have increased their interaction with their children, but they still lag far behind mothers, even when mothers are employed. Fathers can act sensitively to infants' signals, but some do not. Infants usually prefer their mother in stressful circumstances. Even in families in which the father is the primary caregiver, mothers and fathers often behave along traditional gender lines.

X. Cultural, Social Class, and Ethnic Variations and the Changing Tapestry of American Families

Although there are cross-cultural variations in families, authoritative parenting is the most common childrearing style around the world. Working-class and low-income parents place a higher value on "external characteristics," middle-class parents a higher value on "internal characteristics." However, there are variations in any social class, especially among ethnic groups. Chinese American, Black American, and Mexican families all have a strong tradition of the extended family. Children are increasingly growing up in single-parent and stepparent families. In studying the effects of divorce on children, researchers examine a complex set of factors. The mother's employment and latchkey experiences are not uniformly negative circumstances for children.

XI. Peers and Play

Peers and play are important dimensions of children's development. Psychologists study the factors that contribute to peer popularity and friendship. Play takes up a major portion of many young children's days and serves many functions.

XII. Schools

Developmentally appropriate practice, especially advocated in the education of young children, is based on knowledge of the typical development of children within an age span (age appropriateness) and the uniqueness of the child (individual appropriateness). Developmentally appropriate practice contrasts with developmentally inappropriate practice, which ignores the concrete, hands-on approach to learning. Project Head Start is a compensatory education program designed to provide children from low-income families the opportunity to acquire the skills and experiences important for success in school. Recent evaluations continue to document Head Start's positive influence on disadvantaged children. The curriculum in elementary schools should be integrated. Many educators and psychologists believe that children should be taught through concrete, hands-on experience in the early elementary school years. Schools have a stronger middle-class than lower-class orientation. Not only do many lower-class children have problems in school, but so do children from ethnic minorities. Ogbu proposed a controversial view that ethnic minority children are placed in a position of subordination and exploitation in the American educational system. Some experts believe that a form of institutional racism exists in some schools because teachers fail to academically challenge ethnic minority children. Efforts are being made to reduce ethnic bias in schools, among them cooperative learning.

XIII. Children: The Future of Society

Children are the future of any society. Unfortunately, the United States lags behind many other countries in developing adequate policies for children and families. Consistent goals that foster the well-being of children and families need to be implemented.

Key Terms

development 216
biological processes 216
cognitive processes 216
social processes 216
maturation 216
continuity of development 217
discontinuity of development 217
social policy 217
conception 219
zygote 219
germinal period 219
embryonic period 219
fetal period 219
teratogen 220

fetal alcohol syndrome (FAS) 220
preterm infant 221
assimilation 226
accommodation 226
sensorimotor thought 227
object permanence 227
operations 228
preoperational thought 228
conservation 229
concrete operational thought 230
zone of proximal development (ZPD) 233
epigenetic principle 234
trust versus mistrust 235
autonomy versus shame and doubt 235

initiative versus guilt 236
industry versus inferiority 236
attachment 236
imprinting 236
secure attachment 237
authoritarian parenting 240
authoritative parenting 241
permissive-indifferent 241
permissive-indulgent 241
reciprocal socialization 241
synchrony 241
developmentally appropriate practice 246
Project Head Start 247
cooperative learning 251

Suggested Readings

American Psychologist. (1989). *44.* This special issue of *American Psychologist* focuses entirely on children and their development. It includes more than 40 articles by experts on the frontiers of current research, health, and development; on children and social change; on culture and American children; and on children and social policy.

Bjorklund, D. F. (1989). *Children's thinking.* Monterey, CA: Brooks/Cole. This recent overview of children's cognitive development includes chapters on Piaget's theory, perceptual development, and children's information processing.

Gibbs, J. T., & Huang, L. N. (Eds.). (1989). *Children of color.* San Francisco: Jossey-Bass. An excellent overview of the lives of ethnic minority children, this book includes guidelines for their special problems and separate chapters on many ethnic groups.

Santrock, J. W. (1993). *Children* (3rd ed.). Dubuque, IA: Wm. C. Brown. This broad overview of children's development includes detailed information about physical development, cognitive development, and social development. Special attention is given to children's cultural worlds.

Whiting, B. B., & Edwards, C. P. (1988). *Children of different worlds.* Cambridge, MA: Harvard University Press. This book describes the work of the Whitings that compares children's development in six cultures: India, Okinawa, the Philippines, Mexico, Kenya, and the United States. It provides a feel for how researchers conduct cross-cultural work on childrearing.

ADOLESCENCE, ADULT DEVELOPMENT, AND AGING

If I could save time in a bottle
the first thing that I'd like to do
is save every day till eternity passes away
just to spend them with you . . .
If I had a box just for wishes
and dreams that never came true,
the box would be empty except for
the memory of how they were answered by you.
But there never seems to be enough time to do
the things you want to do once you find them.
Looked around enough to know that you're the one
I want to go through time with. (Jim Croce, *Time in a Bottle*)

im Croce's song *Time in a Bottle* reflects a perspective on time that unfolds as we move into the adult years. As young adults, love and intimacy are central to our lives. We begin to look back at where we have been. In adolescence, we rarely looked back and analyzed our lives. Adolescents look toward a boundless future and live in the immediacy of the here and now. Since they perceive their future as virtually limitless, adolescents feel they can attempt almost anything.

As middle-aged adults, we do more looking back, reflecting on what we have done with the time we have had, and we look more toward the future, considering how much time remains to accomplish what we wish to do with our lives. In late adulthood, we look back and review our lives, adding up the pluses and minuses of our many experiences, integrating them into a sense of who we are and what our lives have been about. No one has captured time in a bottle, but, as we go through our adult years, time consumes more of our thinking and we develop hypotheses about how to use it more effectively.

Adolescence

Twentieth-century poet and essayist Roger Allen remarked, "In case you are worried about what's going to become of the younger generation, it's going to grow up and start worrying about the younger generation." Virtually every society has worried about its younger generation, but it was not until the beginning of the twentieth century that the scientific study of adolescence began.

Historical Beginnings and the Nature of Adolescence

Adolescence *is the transition from childhood to adulthood, which involves physical, cognitive, and social changes. In most cultures, adolescence begins at approximately 10 to 13 years of age and ends at approximately 18 to 21 years.* In 1904 psychologist G. Stanley Hall wrote the first scientific book on the nature of adolescence. Hall referred to the teen years as a period of "storm and stress." The

Adults often have short memories about their adolescence. With a little effort, though, most adults can remember behavior that stretched, or even broke, the patience of their elders. Acting out and boundary testing are time-honored methods that move adolescents toward identities of their own. Adolescence should not be viewed as a time of crisis, rebellion, pathology, and deviation. Far more accurate is a vision of adolescence as a time of evaluation, a time of decision making, and a time of commitment as adolescents seek to find out who they are and carve out a place for themselves in the world.

storm and stress view *is G. Stanley Hall's concept that adolescence is a turbulent time charged with conflict and mood swings.* Thoughts, feelings, and actions oscillate between conceit and humility, good and temptation, happiness and sadness. An adolescent may be nasty to a peer one moment and kind the next moment. At one time the adolescent may want to be alone but seconds later seek companionship.

Anthropologist Margaret Mead (1928) studied adolescents in the Samoan Islands in the South Pacific. She observed that Samoan adolescents make a smooth, gradual

image of adolescents as stressed and disturbed, from "Sixteen Candles" and "The Breakfast Club" in the 1980s to "Boyz in the Hood" in the 1990s.

Adults probably forget their own adolescence. With a little effort, though, most adults can recall things they did that stretched—even broke—the patience of their own parents. In matters of taste and manners, young people of every generation have seemed radical, unnerving, and different to adults—in how they look, how they behave, and the music they enjoy. However, it is an enormous error to confuse adolescent enthusiasm for trying on new identities and for enjoying moderate amounts of outrageous behavior with hostility toward parental and societal standards. Acting out and boundary testing are time-honored ways in which adolescents move toward accepting, rather than rejecting, parental values (Santrock, 1993b).

It does little good, and can do considerable disservice, to think of adolescence as a time of rebellion, crisis, pathology, and deviation. It's far more accurate to view adolescence as a time of evaluation, decision making, and commitment as young people carve out their place in the world. How competent they will become often depends on their access to a range of legitimate opportunities and long-term support from adults who deeply care about them (William T. Grant Foundation Committee, 1988).

As we move toward the close of the twentieth century, experts on adolescence are trying to dispel the myth that adolescents are a sorry lot (Brooks-Gunn, 1992; Offer & Church, 1991). That stereotype is usually based on a small group of highly visible adolescents. A study by Daniel Offer and his colleagues (1988) showed that the vast majority of adolescents are competent human beings who are not experiencing deep emotional turmoil. They sampled the self-images of adolescents around the world—the United States, Australia, Bangladesh, Hungary, Israel, Japan, Taiwan, Turkey, and Germany—and found that three out of four had a positive self-image. The adolescents were moving toward adulthood in generally healthy ways—happy most of the time, enjoying life, valuing work and school, having positive feelings about their family and friends, expressing confidence in their sexual selves, and believing they have the ability to cope with life's stresses—not exactly in the throes of storm and stress.

At the same time, adolescents have not experienced an improvement in health over the past 30 years, largely as a result of a new group of dangers called the "new morbidity" (Roghmann, 1981). These include such problems as accidents, suicide, homicide, substance abuse, sexual diseases (including AIDS), delinquency, and emotional difficulties (Ahlstrom & others, 1992; Dryfoos, 1992).

Poverty exacerbates the problems of adolescence. In 1988, 16.3 percent of all adolescents were poor, with ethnic minorities vastly overrepresented in this figure: 38 percent of all Black teenagers and 32.2 percent of all Hispanics, compared to 11.6 percent of all White teenagers lived in poverty (Aber & others,

transition from childhood to adulthood, rather than experiencing the storm and stress Hall envisioned in all cultures. Mead argued that, in a culture which allows children to observe sexual activity, engage in sex play, do important work, be assertive, and know precisely what adult roles will encompass, adolescence is relatively free of stress. A recent, controversial critique of Mead's work, however, suggested that Samoan adolescents experience considerably more stress than Mead believed (Freeman, 1983), leaving the cultural prescription for stress-free adolescents still debated.

During most of the twentieth century, American adolescents have been described as abnormal and deviant. In addition to Hall, Freud described adolescents as sexually driven and conflicted, and some media portrayals of adolescents—"Rebel Without a Cause" in the late 1950s, "Easy Rider" in the 1960s—portrayed adolescents as rebellious, conflicted, faddish, delinquent, and self-centered. Consider also the current

From *Penguin Dreams and Stranger Things* by Berke Breathed.
Copyright © 1985 Little, Brown and Company.

1992; Allen & Mitchell, in press; Block, 1992). Poverty increases the chance that an adolescent will fall prey to the physical, emotional, and social problems of the new morbidity.

Our discussion underscores an important point about adolescents: they do not make up a homogeneous group. The majority of adolescents negotiate the lengthy path to adult maturity successfully, but a large group does not. Ethnic, cultural, gender, socioeconomic, age, and life-style differences influence the actual life trajectory of every adolescent. Different portrayals of adolescence emerge. As we will see, some of the problems faced by today's adolescents involve adults' idealized images of what adolescents should be and society's ambivalent messages to adolescents.

Our society seems to be uncertain about what adolescence should be or should not be. The following examples illustrate how adults' idealized images of adolescents and society's ambivalent messages to adolescents may contribute to adolescent problems (Feldman & Elliott, 1990):

Many adults treasure the independence of youth yet insist that adolescents do not have the maturity to make autonomous, competent decisions about their lives. Some of the ambiguity in messages about adult status and maturity that society communicates to adolescents appears in the form of laws dictating that they cannot drive until they are 16, vote until they are 18, or drink until age 21, yet in some states 14-year-olds now have the legal right to choose the parent with whom they want to live after a parental divorce and to override parental wishes about such medical matters as abortion and psychiatric care.

Society's sexual messages to adolescents are especially ambiguous. Adolescents are somehow supposed to be sexually naive but become sexually knowledgeable. The message to many adolescents is this: you can experiment with sex and "sow your wild oats" but be sure to maintain high standards of maturity and safety. Adolescents must negotiate this formidable task in a society that cannot agree on how much and what kind of explicit sex education adolescents should be given. This same society sanctions alluring messages about the power and attractiveness of sexuality in the media.

Laws prohibit adolescents from using alcohol, tobacco, or other drugs and adults decry the high level of drug use by adolescents, yet many of the same adults who stereotype and criticize adolescents for their drug use are themselves drug abusers and heavy cigarette smokers.

Society promotes education and the development of knowledge as essential to success as an adult, yet adolescents frequently observe the rewards society doles out to individuals who develop their athletic skills and business acumen. As adolescents interact with adults who do not value the process of learning, adolescents may attach more importance to simply attaining a diploma than to the process of getting one.

The complex relationships among physical, cognitive, and social development that influence rates of health and emotional problems make it important for us to understand these aspects of adolescent development. Let's examine physical development first.

Physical Development

Imagine a toddler displaying all the features of puberty—a 3-year-old girl with fully developed breasts or a boy just slightly older with a deep male voice. We would see this by the year 2250 if the age of puberty were to continue to decrease at its present pace. Menarche (first menstruation) has declined from 14.2 years of age in 1900 to about 12.45 years today. Age of menarche has been declining an average of about 4 months a decade for the

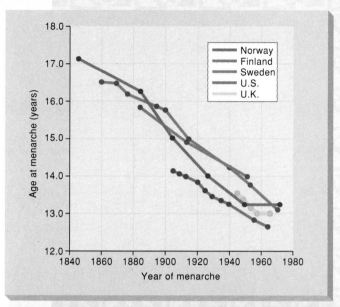

FIGURE 9.1

Median ages at menarche in selected northern European countries and the United States from 1845 to 1969. Notice the steep decline in the age at which girls experienced menarche in five different countries. Recently the age at which girls experience menarche has been leveling off.

past century (see figure 9.1). We are unlikely, though, to see pubescent toddlers in the future because what happened in the last century is special. That something special is the acquisition of a higher level of nutrition and health (Brooks-Gunn, 1991). A lower age of menarche is associated with higher standards of living (Petersen, 1979).

Menarche is one event that characterizes puberty, but there are others as well. **Puberty** *is a period of rapid skeletal and sexual maturation that occurs mainly in early adolescence.* However, it is not a single, sudden event. We know when a young person is going through puberty, but pinpointing its beginning and its end is difficult. Except for menarche, which occurs rather late in puberty, no single marker heralds puberty. For boys, the first whisker or first wet dream could mark its appearance, but both may go unnoticed.

Hormonal changes characterize pubertal development (Rabin & Chrousos, 1991). Remember from chapter 2 that hormones are powerful chemical substances secreted by the endocrine glands and carried through the body in the bloodstream. The concentrations of certain hormones increase dramatically during puberty. **Testosterone** *is a hormone associated with the development of genitals, an increase in height, and a change in voice in boys.* **Estradiol** *is a hormone associated with breast, uterine, and skeletal development in girls.* In one study, testosterone levels only doubled in the girls but increased 18-fold in the boys during puberty; similarly, estradiol doubled in the boys but increased 8-fold in the girls (Nottelmann & others, 1987). These hormonal and body changes occur, on the average, about 2 years earlier in girls ($10\frac{1}{2}$ years) than in boys ($12\frac{1}{2}$ years) (see figure 9.2).

Some children enter puberty early, others late, and those who are "off schedule" one way or the other often think of themselves as "different." Some years ago, in the California Longitudinal Study, the early-maturing boys perceived themselves more positively and had more successful peer relations than their late-maturing counterparts (Jones, 1965). The findings for the early-maturing girls were similar but not as strong. When the late-maturing boys were studied in their thirties, however, they had developed a stronger sense of identity than the early-maturing boys (Peskin, 1967). This may have occurred because the late-maturing boys had more time to explore life's options or because the early-maturing boys continued to focus on their advantageous physical status instead of career development and achievement.

More recent research confirms, though, that at least during adolescence it is advantageous to be an early-maturing rather than a late-maturing boy (Simmons & Blyth, 1987). More recent findings for girls suggest that early maturation is a mixed blessing: these girls experience more problems in school but also more independence and popularity with boys. Grade level also makes a difference. In the sixth grade, the early-maturing girls were more satisfied with their figures than the late-maturing

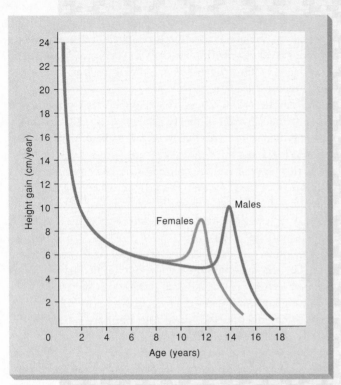

FIGURE 9.2

Pubertal growth spurt. On the average, the growth spurt that characterizes pubertal change occurs 2 years earlier for girls (10½) than for boys (12½).

girls, but by the 10th grade the late-maturing girls were more satisfied (see figure 9.3). The explanation is that, by late adolescence, early-maturing girls tend to be shorter and stockier, late-maturing girls taller and thinner; late-maturing girls in late adolescence have bodies that more closely resemble today's media ideal of feminine beauty—tall and thin.

Some researchers now question whether the effects of puberty are as strong as once believed (Lerner, Petersen, & Brooks-Gunn, 1991; Montemayor, Adams, & Gulotta, 1990). Puberty affects some adolescents more strongly than others, and

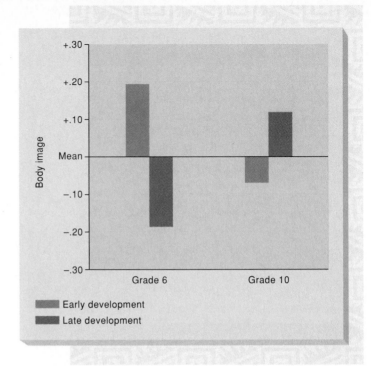

FIGURE 9.3

Early- and late-maturing adolescent girls' perceptions of body image in early and late adolescence.

some behaviors more strongly than others. Body image, interest in dating, and sexual behavior are clearly affected by pubertal change. If we were to look at overall development and adjustment in the human life cycle, pubertal variations (such as early and late maturation) would appear less dramatic than is commonly thought. In thinking about puberty's effects, keep in mind that an adolescent's world involves cognitive and social changes, as well as physical changes. As with all periods of development, these processes work in concert to produce who we are in adolescence. Now we will turn our attention to the cognitive changes that occur in adolescence.

Cognitive Development

Aristotle remarked that adolescents think they know everything and are quite sure about it. We will examine this egocentrism of adolescence shortly, but first let's see what Piaget had to say about cognitive development in adolescence. **Formal operational thought** *is Piaget's name for the fourth stage of cognitive development, which appears between 11 and 15 years of age. Formal operational thought is abstract, idealistic, and logical.* Unlike an elementary school child, an adolescent is no longer limited to actual concrete experience as the anchor of thought. Adolescents can conceive make-believe situations, hypothetical possibilities, or purely abstract propositions.

Abstract	Idealistic	Logical
Adolescents think more abstractly than children. Formal operational thinkers can solve abstract algebraic equations, for example.	Adolescents often think about what is possible. They think about ideal characteristics of themselves, others, and the world.	Adolescents begin to think more like scientists, devising plans to solve problems and systematically testing solutions. Piaget called this type of logical thinking hypothetical-deductive reasoning.

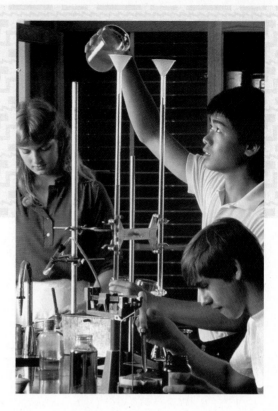

FIGURE 9.4

Characteristics of formal operational thought. Adolescents begin to think more as scientists think, devising plans to solve problems and systematically testing solutions. Piaget gave this type of thinking the imposing name of hypothetical-deductive reasoning.

Thought also becomes more idealistic. Adolescents often compare themselves and others to ideal standards, and they think about what an ideal world would be like, wondering if they couldn't carve out a better world than the one the adult generation has handed to them.

At the same time that adolescents think more abstractly and idealistically, they also think more logically. Adolescents begin to think more as a scientist thinks, devising plans to solve problems and systematically testing solutions. This type of problem solving has an imposing name. **Hypothetical-deductive reasoning** *is Piaget's name for adolescents' cognitive ability to develop hypotheses, or best guesses, about ways to solve problems, such as an algebraic equation. They then systematically deduce, or conclude, which is the best path to follow to solve the equation.* By contrast, children are more likely to solve problems in a trial-and-error fashion. Figure 9.4 summarizes the main features of formal operational thought.

Some of Piaget's ideas on formal operational thought are currently being challenged (Byrnes, 1988a; Keating, in press; Lapsley, 1989; Overton & Byrnes, 1991). There is much more individual variation in formal operational thought than Piaget envisioned. Only about one in three young adolescents is a formal operational thinker. Not only do many American adults never become formal operational thinkers, but many adults in other cultures don't either. Consider the following conversation between a researcher and an illiterate Kpelle farmer in the West African country of Liberia (Scribner, 1977):

Researcher: All Kpelle men are rice farmers. Mr. Smith is not a rice farmer. Is he a Kpelle man?

Kpelle farmer: I don't know the man. I have not laid eyes on the man myself.

Members of the Kpelle culture who had gone through formal schooling were able to deal with the abstract example and answered the researcher in a formal operational way.

As many as half of all adults never reach the stage of formal thinking (Muuss, 1988). It's difficult to assess formal operational thinking in nonliterate adults of other cultures because the usual tests for this kind of thinking are all from the math and science curriculum of Western schools, making them inappropriate for use in other cultures, and perhaps for many adults in the United States. Adults in other cultures do demonstrate formal thinking when queried about situations with which they are more familiar, however (Jahoda, 1980). As with concrete operational thought, cultural experiences influence whether individuals reach a Piagetian stage of thought. Education in the logic of science and mathematics is an important cultural experience that promotes the development of formal operational thinking.

Adolescent thought, especially in early adolescence, is also egocentric. **Adolescent egocentrism** *involves the belief that others are as preoccupied with the adolescent as she herself is, the belief that one is unique, and the belief that one is indestructible* (Elkind, 1978). Attention-getting behavior, so common in adolescence, reflects egocentrism and the desire to be onstage, noticed, and visible. Imagine an eighth-grade boy who feels as if all eyes are riveted on his tiny facial blemish. Imagine also the sense of uniqueness felt by the following adolescent girl: "My mother has no idea about how much pain I'm going through. She has never been hurt like I have. Why did Bob break up with me?" Also imagine the sense of indestructibility of two adolescent males drag racing down a city street. This sense of indestructibility may lead to drug use and suicide attempts.

So far we have discussed a number of physical and cognitive changes in adolescence. Next, we will study the equally impressive social changes in adolescence.

The colorful attire of this skateboarder reflects adolescent egocentrism. Attention-getting behavior indicates the desire to be onstage and noticed. The risk-taking behavior of skateboarding, as well as racing cars, taking drugs, and many other behaviors, reflects adolescents' sense of indestructibility. Joseph Conrad commented, "I remember my youth and the feeling that never came back anymore—the feeling that I could last forever, outlast the sea, the earth, and all men."

REVIEW

The Nature of Adolescence, Physical Development, and Cognitive Development

G. Stanley Hall is the father of the scientific study of adolescence. In the early 1900s, he proposed the storm and stress view. Adolescence is a transition between childhood and adulthood that involves biological, cognitive, and social development. In most cultures, adolescence begins at approximately 10 to 13 years of age and ends at approximately 18 to 21 years of age. Adolescence is more appropriately viewed as a time of decision making and commitment rather than a time of rebellion, crisis, and disturbance. Different portrayals of adolescence emerge. Adults' idealized images and ambivalent messages may contribute to adolescent problems.

Puberty is a rapid change in maturation that occurs during early adolescence. Its onset has begun earlier in recent years. Hormonal changes are prominent. Puberty occurs roughly 2 years earlier for girls than boys, although its normal range is large. Early maturation generally favors boys and often has mixed effects for girls. Some experts believe that puberty's effects are overstated.

Piaget stated that formal operational thought begins between 11 and 15 years of age. Formal operational thought is abstract and idealistic but includes planning and logical analysis. Some of Piaget's ideas on formal operational thought are being challenged. Egocentrism also characterizes adolescent thought.

Social Development

Mark Twain, reflecting on his youth, commented, "When I was a boy of 14 my father was so ignorant I could hardly stand to have the man around. But when I got to be 21, I was astonished how much he learnt in seven years." Let's explore the world of parent-adolescent relationships that Twain spoke about.

Parent-Adolescent Relationships

There are many myths about parent-adolescent relationships, including: (1) adolescents detach themselves from parents and move into an isolated world of peers and (2) throughout adolescence, parent-adolescent relationships are intense, filled with conflict, and highly stressful.

Adolescents do not simply move away from parental influence into a decision-making world all their own. As adolescents move toward becoming more autonomous, it is healthy for them to continue to be attached to their parents. Just as they did in infancy and childhood, parents continue to provide an important support system that helps an adolescent explore a wider, more complex social world full of uncertainties, challenges, and stresses (Hill & Holmbeck, 1986; Santrock, 1993b). Although adolescents show a strong desire to spend more time with their peers, they do not necessarily isolate themselves. In one investigation, adolescents who were securely attached to their parents were also securely attached to their peers; those who were insecurely attached to their parents were also insecurely attached to their peers (Armsden & Greenberg, 1984). Of course, there are times when adolescents reject this closeness, connection, and attachment as they pursue a more autonomous life. For the most part, however, an adolescent's worlds of parents and peers are coordinated and connected, not uncoordinated and disconnected. For example, parents' choices of neighborhoods, churches, schools, and their own friends influence the pool from which their adolescents select possible friends (Cooper & Ayers-Lopez, 1985).

Adolescence is a period of development when individuals push for autonomy, but the development of mature autonomy is a lengthy process, taking place over 10 to 15 years. As adolescents pursue a more autonomous life, many parents perceive them as changing from compliant children to noncompliant adolescents. Parents tend to adopt one of two strategies to handle the noncompliance: they either clamp down and put more pressure on the adolescents to conform to parental standards, or they become more permissive and let the adolescents do as they please. Neither is a wise overall strategy; rather, a more flexible, adaptive approach is called for. At the onset of adolescence, the average boy or girl does not have the knowledge to make appropriate decisions in all areas of life. As adolescents push for autonomy, a wise parent relinquishes control in areas where adolescents can make mature decisions. A wise parent also calmly communicates with an adolescent and tries to help the adolescent make reasonable decisions in areas where he or she shows less mature behavior (Santrock, 1993b).

Conflict with parents does increase in adolescence, but it does not reach the tumultuous proportions described by G. Stanley Hall, and it is not uniformly intense throughout adolescence (Steinberg, 1989, 1991). Rather, much of the conflict involves the everyday events of family life, such as keeping a bedroom clean, dressing neatly, getting home by a certain hour, not talking on the phone so long, and so on. Such conflicts with parents are more common in early adolescence, especially during the apex of pubertal change, than in late adolescence, and the conflicts usually do not involve major dilemmas, such as drugs and delinquency (Montemayor & Flannery, 1991; Montemayor & Hanson, 1985). The everyday negotiations and conflicts that characterize parent-adolescent relationships can even serve a positive developmental function (Blos, 1989; Cooper & Grotevant, 1989). These minor disputes and negotiations facilitate an adolescent's transition from being dependent on parents to being more autonomous. For example, in one investigation, the adolescents who disagreed with their parents also explored identity issues more actively than the adolescents who consistently agreed with their parents (Cooper & others, 1982).

In sum, the old model of parent-adolescent relationships suggested that, as adolescents mature, they detach themselves from parents and move into a world of autonomy apart from parents. The old model also suggested that parent-adolescent conflict is intense and stressful throughout adolescence. The new model emphasizes that parents serve as important attachment figures and support systems as adolescents explore a wider, more complex social world (Cooper & others, 1992; Hughes, Power, & Francis, 1992). The new model also emphasizes that, in the majority of families, parent-adolescent conflict is moderate rather than severe and that everyday negotiations and minor disputes can serve the positive developmental function of helping adolescents make the transition from childhood dependency to adult independence (see figure 9.5).

The developmental trajectories of both parents and adolescents are changing (Parke, 1988). In the past 2 decades, the timing of parenthood has undergone some dramatic shifts. Parenthood is taking place earlier for some, later for others. On the one hand, there has been a substantial increase in the number of adolescent pregnancies, and on the other there has been a simultaneous increase in the number of women who postpone childbearing until their thirties or forties. When childbearing is delayed, education usually has been completed and career development is well established. Researchers have found that older fathers are warmer and communicate better with their children. However, they are less likely to place demands on them and enforce rules (MacDonald, 1987).

Peers

Imagine you are back in junior or senior high school: friends, cliques, parties, and clubs probably come to mind. During adolescence, especially early adolescence, we conform more than we did in childhood. Conformity to peers, especially to their antisocial standards, often peaks around the eighth or ninth grade, a time when teenagers might join a peer in stealing hubcaps from a car, drawing graffiti on a wall, or harassing a teacher (Berndt, 1979; Berndt & Perry, 1990).

Old model		New model	
Autonomy, detachment from parents; parent and peer worlds are isolated	Intense, stressful conflict throughout adolescence; parent-adolescent relationships are filled with storm and stress on virtually a daily basis	Attachment and autonomy; parents are important support systems and attachment figures; adolescent-parent and adolescent-peer worlds have some important connections	Moderate parent-adolescent conflict common and can serve a positive developmental function; conflict greater in early adolescence, especially during the apex of puberty

FIGURE 9.5

Old and new models of parent-adolescent relationships.

© 1982, Washington Post Writers Group. Reprinted with permission.

Adolescent peer relations take place in diverse settings—at school, in the neighborhood, and in the community. Ethnic minority adolescents often have two sets of peer relationships, one at school, the other in the community. Community peers are more likely to be from their own ethnic group in their immediate neighborhood. Sometimes, they go to the same church and participate in activities together, such as Black History Week, Chinese New Year, or the Cinco de Mayo Festival. As a result, researchers should focus their questions on relationships both at school and in the community when they ask about adolescents' peers and friends. Ethnic-minority-group adolescents who are social isolates at school may be very popular in their more segregated community (Gibbs & Huang, 1989). Next, we will examine the school's role in adolescent development in much greater detail.

Schools

School is an important cultural setting in any society. What are the functions of secondary schools? What makes a good middle school? What is the nature of school dropouts and how can we reduce their numbers? We will consider each of these questions in turn.

As we enter the last decade of the twentieth century, the back-to-basics movement has gained momentum, with proponents arguing that the main function of schools should be rigorous training in intellectual skills through such subjects as English, math, and science (Kearns, 1988). Advocates of the back-to-basics movement point to the excessive fluff in secondary school curricula and to the extensive time students spend in extracurricular activities. They argue that schools should be in the business of imparting knowledge to adolescents and should not be so concerned about adolescents' social and emotional lives. Some critics of the fluff in secondary schools argue that the school day should be longer and that the school year should be extended into the summer months.

Should the main—and perhaps only—major goal of schooling for adolescents be the development of an intellectually mature individual, or should schools also focus on an

Peers play a powerful role in adolescent development. When adolescents are asked what they do with peers, one of the most frequent answers is "just hang around, talking, having a good time."

The transition from elementary to middle or junior high school occurs at the same time a number of other changes are taking place in development. Biological, cognitive, and social changes converge with this schooling transition to make it a time of considerable adaptation.

adolescent's social and emotional maturity? Should schools be comprehensive, providing a multifaceted curriculum that includes many electives and alternative subjects to basic core courses? These are provocative questions, and they continue to be heatedly debated in educational and community circles (Bloome, 1989; Duke & Canady, 1991; Goodlad, 1983; MacIver & others, 1992; Sizer, 1984).

Most American secondary schools are divided into middle school, or junior high, and high school. The emergence of junior high schools in the 1920s and 1930s was justified on the basis of physical, cognitive, and social changes in early adolescence and the need for more schools in response to a growing school population. Middle schools (usually grades 6 through 8, coinciding with puberty's earlier arrival) have become more popular in recent years. What makes a successful middle school? Joan Lipsitz (1984) and her colleagues searched the nation for the best middle schools. Based on the recommendations of education experts and observations in schools in various parts of the United States, four middle schools were chosen for their outstanding ability to educate young adolescents. The most striking feature of the best schools was their willingness and ability to adapt all school practices to the individual differences in their students' physical, cognitive, and social development. For example, two

middle schools expended considerable energy on a complex school organization so that small groups of students worked with small groups of teachers, who could vary the tone and pace of the school day depending on students' needs. Another middle school developed an advisory system so that each student had daily contact with an adult who was willing to listen, explain, comfort, and prod the teenager. Such school policies reflect thoughtfulness and personal concern about students who have compelling developmental needs.

Another characteristic of the effective middle schools was that, early in their existence—the first year in three of the schools and the second year in the fourth school—they emphasized the importance of creating an environment that was positive for the adolescents' social and emotional development. This goal was established not only because such environments contribute to academic excellence, but also because social and emotional development are valued as important in themselves in adolescents' schooling.

Recognizing that the vast majority of middle schools do not approach the level of excellence described by Lipsitz, the Carnegie Corporation (1989) issued an extremely negative evaluation of our nation's middle schools. The report, "Turning

Points: Preparing American Youth for the 21st Century," concluded that most young adolescents attend massive, impersonal schools, learn from seemingly irrelevant curricula, trust few adults in school, and lack access to health care and counseling. The Carnegie report recommended the following:

- Divide large schools into units of 200 to 500 students so students can get to know each other and their teachers better.
- Give teachers and administrators more creative power and hire teachers who specialize in working with young adolescents.
- Involve parents and community leaders in middle schools.
- Teach a core academic program aimed at producing students who are literate; understand the sciences; and have a sense of health, ethics, and citizenship.
- Boost students' health and fitness with more in-school programs, and help students who need public health care to get it.

In summary, middle schools need a major overhaul if they are to be effective in educating young adolescents for the twenty-first century.

Dropouts are a serious educational and societal problem. By leaving high school before graduating, many dropouts take with them educational deficiencies that severely curtail their economic and social well-being throughout their adult lives (Rumberger, 1987). We will study the scope of the problem, the causes of dropping out, and ways to reduce dropout rates.

Although dropping out of high school often has negative consequences for young people, the picture is not entirely bleak (William T. Grant Foundation Commission on Work, Family, and Citizenship, 1988). Over the past 40 years, the number of adolescents who have not finished high school has decreased considerably. In 1940 more than 60 percent of all 25-to-29-year-olds had not completed high school. By 1986 this proportion had dropped to less than 14 percent. From 1973 to 1983, the annual dropout rate nationwide fell by almost 20 percent, from 6.3 to 5.2 percent.

Despite the decline in overall high school dropout rates, the higher dropout rate of minority group and low-income students, especially in large cities, remains a major concern (Carrasquillo, 1991; Eccles, 1991; McCall, 1991). Although the dropout rates of most minority group students have been declining, they remain substantially above those of White students. Hispanics made up a disproportionate percentage of high school dropouts in 1986. More than one-third of Hispanic students, about 17 percent of Black students and 13.5 percent of White students had dropped out (William T. Grant Foundation, 1989). Dropout rates are staggeringly high for Native Americans: fewer than 10 percent graduate from high school (LaFromboise & Low, 1989). In some inner-city areas, the dropout rate for ethnic minority students is especially high, reaching more than 50 percent in Chicago, for example (Hahn, 1987).

Students drop out of school for many reasons (Bachman, 1991). In one study, almost 50 percent of the dropouts cited school-related reasons for leaving school, such as simply not liking school or being expelled or suspended (Rumberger, 1983). Twenty percent of the dropouts (but 40 percent of the Hispanic students) cited economic reasons for leaving school. One-third of the female students dropped out for personal reasons, such as pregnancy or marriage.

To help reduce the dropout rate, community institutions, especially schools, need to break down the barriers between work and school. Many young people leave school long before reaching the level of a professional career, often left to their own devices to search for work. They need more assistance than they are now receiving. The following are among the approaches worth considering (William T. Grant Foundation, 1988):

- Monitored work experiences, through cooperative education, apprenticeships, internships, preemployment training, and youth-operated enterprises
- Community and neighborhood services, including voluntary service and youth-guided services
- Redirected vocational education, the principal thrust of which should not be preparation for specific jobs but acquisition of basic skills needed for a wide range of jobs
- Guarantees of continuing education, employment, or training, especially in conjunction with mentor programs
- Career information and counseling to expose young people to job opportunities and career options as well as to successful role models
- School volunteer programs, not only for tutoring but to provide access to adult friends and mentors

Our discussion so far has taken us through families, peers, and school—three of the most important social contexts in adolescent development. Experiences in these social settings influence one of the most dramatic changes in an adolescent's life—identity development.

Identity Development

Identity versus identity confusion *is the fifth of Erik Erikson's (1968) stages of human development, occurring primarily during the adolescent years. The development of identity involves finding out who we are, what we are all about, and where we are headed in life.* Seeking an identity is about trying on one face after another, looking for one's own.

During adolescence, individuals enter what Erikson calls a "psychological moratorium"—a gap between the security of childhood and the autonomy of adulthood. In their search for

"Do you have *any* idea who I am?"
Drawing by Koren; © 1988 The New Yorker Magazine, Inc.

identity, adolescents experiment with various roles. Those who successfully explore a number of alternatives emerge with a new sense of self that is both refreshing and acceptable; those who do not successfully resolve the identity crisis are confused, suffering what Erikson calls identity confusion. This confusion takes one of two courses: individuals either withdraw, isolating themselves from peers and family, or lose themselves in the crowd. Adolescents want to decide freely for themselves such matters as what careers they will pursue, whether they will go to college, and whether they will marry. In other words, they want to free themselves from the shackles of their parents and other adults and make their own choices. At the same time, many adolescents have a deep fear of making the wrong decision and of failing. However, as adolescents pursue their identity and their thoughts become more abstract and logical, they reason in more sophisticated ways. They are better able to judge what is morally right and wrong and become capable decision makers (Suls, 1989; Waterman & Archer, in press).

Black American psychologists Janet Helms (1985, 1990) and William Cross (1972), as well as Asian American psychologists Derald Wing Sue and David Sue (1972), believe that a number of stages are involved in the development of an ethnic identity, whether for minorities or Whites. Helms amended Cross' four-stage model of minority identity development to include the following: preencounter, encounter, immersion/emersion, and internalization/commitment, each of which we will consider in turn.

Stage 1: Preencounter. In this first step, ethnic minority individuals prefer dominant cultural values to those of their own culture. Their role models, life-styles, and value systems are adopted from the dominant group, whereas the physical and/or cultural characteristics that single them out as ethnic minority individuals are a source of pain. These characteristics are either disdained or repressed. For example, Black Americans may perceive their own physical features as undesirable and their Black cultural values and ways a handicap to success in the White American society.

Stage 2: Encounter. Although moving to the encounter stage is usually a gradual process, movement may be propelled by an event that causes individuals to realize they will never be members of mainstream White America. This might be a monumental event, such as the assassination of Martin Luther King, Jr., or more personal "identity shattering" events that are the trigger. In the encounter stage, ethnic minority individuals begin to break through their denial. Hispanic Americans who feel ashamed of their cultural upbringing may have conversations with Hispanic Americans who are proud of their cultural heritage. At this stage, ethnic minority individuals become aware that not all cultural values of the dominant group are beneficial to them. This stage is characterized by conflicting attitudes about the self, minority group culture, and the dominant culture. The person wants to identify with the minority group but does not know how to develop this identity. The recognition that an identity must be developed and not found leads into the third stage, immersion/emersion.

Stage 3: Immersion/emersion. At the beginning of this stage, ethnic minority individuals completely endorse minority views and reject the dominant society. The individual becomes strongly motivated to eliminate oppression of his or her ethnic minority group. Movement into this stage is likely to occur because (1) individuals begin to resolve some of the conflicts of the previous stage and develop a better understanding of societal forces, such as racism, oppression, and discrimination and (2) individuals begin to ask themselves, "Why should I feel ashamed of who and what I am?" The answer at this point is likely to evoke both guilt and anger—the guilt of "selling out" in the past, which is viewed as contributing to the ethnic minority group's oppression, and anger at having been oppressed and "brainwashed" by the dominant group. In the second phase of this stage, individuals experience feelings of discontent and discomfort with their rigid views of the previous stage and develop notions of greater individual autonomy. Emersion allows them to vent the anger that characterizes the beginning of this stage, through rap groups, explorations of their own culture, discussions of racial/ethnic issues, and so on. Education and opportunities to expel hostile feelings allow individuals' emotions to level off, so that they can think more flexibly. It is no longer necessary to reject everything from the dominant culture and accept everything from one's own culture. People now have the autonomy to decide for themselves what the strengths and weaknesses of their culture are, and which parts of the culture will become a part of their own identity.

Stage 4: Internalization/commitment. The main theme of this stage of ethnic minority identity development is that individuals experience a sense of fulfillment regarding the integration of their personal and cultural identities. They have resolved the conflicts and discomforts they experienced in the immersion/emersion stage, and they achieve greater control and flexibility. They also more objectively evaluate the cultural values of other ethnic minority individuals and groups, as well as those of the dominant group. At this stage, individuals want to eliminate all forms of oppression. The commitment in this stage refers to the behavioral manifestation of the newly realized identity. The individual takes actions, large or small, to realize the desire to eliminate oppression, whether by engaging in large-scale political or social activism or by performing everyday activities in ways consistent with one's ethnic identity.

Helms (1990) has proposed a model of White racial identity, in which White individuals move from a state of naivete about racial matters to a sophisticated state of biculturalism or racial transcendence. Helms' theory assumes that consciousness of racial identity in both minority and majority individuals increases our understanding of success or failure in cross-racial and cross-ethnic interactions. The five stages in this model parallel the process in the minority identity model, with the following progression:

Stage 1: Contact—obliviousness to racial/cultural issues. White persons in this stage rarely think of themselves in racial terms.

Stage 2: Disintegration—awareness of the social implications of race on a personal level. The person is caught between the privileges of the White culture and the humane desire to treat Blacks fairly.

Stage 3: Reintegration—idealization of things White and denigration of things Black. Anger is common at this stage, as with the immersion phase of immersion/emersion in the minority ethnic identity model.

Stage 4: Pseudo-independence—internalization of an understanding of the privileges of Whiteness and the ability to recognize a personal responsibility to combat racism.

Stage 5: Autonomy—bicultural or racially transcendent world view. The individual in this stage has internalized a positive, nonracist White identity, feels a kinship with people regardless of race, and seeks to abolish racial oppression.

Although the identity development models include distinct stages, the boundaries between the stages are not always abrupt and clearly defined. In many instances, one stage blends into the next. Also, not all individuals experience the entire range of these stages in their lifetime. Some individuals born and raised in a family functioning at Stage 4 on the White racial identity scale may never experience Stage 1.

For ethnic minority individuals, adolescence is often a special juncture in their development (Spencer, 1991; Spencer & Dornbusch, 1990). Although children are aware of some ethnic and cultural differences, most ethnic minority individuals first consciously confront their ethnicity in adolescence. In contrast to children, adolescents have the ability to interpret ethnic and cultural information, to reflect on the past, and to speculate about the future (Harter, 1990a,b). As they mature cognitively, ethnic minority adolescents become acutely aware of the evaluations of their ethnic group by the majority White culture (Comer, 1988; Ogbu, 1989). As one researcher commented, a young Black American child may learn that Black is beautiful but conclude as an adolescent that White is powerful (Semaj, 1985).

Ethnic minority youths' awareness of negative appraisals, conflicting values, and restricted occupational opportunities can influence life choices and plans for the future (Spencer & Dornbusch, 1990). As one ethnic minority youth stated, "The future seems shut off, closed. Why dream? You can't reach your dreams. Why set goals? At least if you don't set any goals, you don't fail."

For many ethnic minority youths, a lack of successful ethnic minority role models with whom to identify is a special concern (Jackson & others, 1991). The problem is especially acute for inner-city ethnic minority youths. Because of the lack of adult ethnic minority role models, some ethnic minority youths may conform to middle-class White values and identify with successful White role models. However, for many adolescents, their ethnicity and skin color constrain their acceptance by the White culture. Thus, many ethnic minority adolescents have a difficult task: negotiating two value systems—that of their own ethnic group and that of the White society. Some adolescents reject the mainstream, foregoing the rewards controlled by White Americans; others adopt the values and standards of the majority White culture; still others take the difficult path of biculturality (Phinney, Chavira, & Williamson, 1992; Phinney, Espinoza, & Onwughalu, 1992).

In one recent investigation, ethnic identity exploration was higher among ethnic minority than White American college students (Phinney & Alipuria, 1990). In this same investigation, ethnic minority college students who had thought about and resolved issues involving their ethnicity had higher self-esteem than their ethnic minority counterparts, who had not. In another investigation, the ethnic identity development of Asian American, Black American, Hispanic American, and White

American 10th-grade students in Los Angeles was studied (Phinney, 1989). Adolescents from each of the three ethnic minority groups faced a similar need to deal with their ethnic-group identification in a predominately White American culture. In some instances, the adolescents from the three ethnic minority groups perceived different issues to be important in their resolution of ethnic identity. For Asian American adolescents, pressures to achieve academically and concerns about quotas that make it difficult to get into good colleges were salient issues. Many Black American adolescent females discussed their realization that White American standards of beauty (especially hair and skin color) did not apply to them; Black American adolescent males were concerned with possible job discrimination and the need to distinguish themselves from a negative societal image of Black male adolescents. For Hispanic American adolescents, prejudice was a recurrent theme, as was conflicting values between their Hispanic cultural heritage and the majority culture. To read further about identity development in ethnic minority youths, turn to Sociocultural Worlds 9.1, where we will discuss the identity development of Native American adolescents.

Finding out who you are, what you are all about, and where you are going—the search for identity—is an important developmental task for every human being. As we will see next, another important developmental task involves developing a system of moral standards.

Moral Development

In Europe a woman was near death from a rare form of cancer. There was one drug that the doctors thought might save her: a form of radium that a druggist in the same town had recently discovered. The drug was expensive to make, but the druggist was charging 10 times what the drug cost him to make. He paid $200 for the radium and charged $2,000 for a small dose of the drug. The sick woman's husband, Heinz, went to everyone he knew to borrow the money, but he could get together only $1,000. He told the druggist that his wife was dying and asked him to sell it cheaper or let him pay later. However, the druggist said, "No. I discovered the drug, and I am going to make money from it." Desperate, Heinz broke into the man's store to steal the drug for his wife (Kohlberg, 1969, p. 379).

This story is one of 11 devised by Lawrence Kohlberg (1976, 1986) to investigate the nature of moral thought. After reading the story, interviewees answer a series of questions about the moral dilemma. Should Heinz have done that? Was it right or wrong? Why? Is it a husband's duty to steal the drug for his wife if he can get it in no other way? Would a good husband do it? Did the druggist have the right to charge that much when there was no law setting a limit on the price? Why?

Based on the answers that individuals have given to questions about this and other moral dilemmas, Kohlberg believes that three levels of moral development exist, each of which is characterized by two stages. A key concept in understanding moral development, especially Kohlberg's theory, is **internalization,** *the developmental change from behavior that is externally controlled to behavior that is controlled by internal, self-generated standards and principles.*

1. The **preconventional level** *is Kohlberg's lowest level of moral thinking, in which an individual shows no internalization of moral values—moral thinking is based on punishments (Stage 1) or rewards (Stage 2) that come from the external world.* In regard to the story about Heinz and the druggist, at Stage 1 an individual might say that Heinz should not steal the drug because it is a big crime; at Stage 2, an individual might say he shouldn't steal the drug because the druggist needs to make a profit.

2. The **conventional level** *is Kohlberg's second level of moral thinking, in which an individual has an intermediate level of internalization. The individual abides by certain standards (internal), but they are the standards of others (external), such as the standards of parents (Stage 3) or the laws of society (Stage 4).* At Stage 3, an individual might say that Heinz should steal the drug for his wife because that is what a good husband would do; at Stage 4, an individual might say that it is natural to want to save his wife but that it is always wrong to steal.

3. The **postconventional level** *is Kohlberg's highest level of moral thinking; moral development is completely internalized and not based on others' standards. An individual recognizes alternative moral courses, explores the options, and then develops a personal moral code. The code is among the principles generally accepted by the community (Stage 5) or it is more individualized (Stage 6).* At Stage 5, an individual might say that the law was not set up for these circumstances so Heinz can steal the drug; it is not really right, but he is justified in doing it. At Stage 6, the individual is faced with the decision of whether to consider the other people who need the drug just as badly as Heinz's wife. Heinz should consider the value of all lives involved.

Kohlberg believed that these levels and stages occur in a sequence and are age-related. Some evidence for Kohlberg's theory has been found, although few people reach Stages 5 and 6 (Colby & others, 1983). Kohlberg stated that moral development occurs through maturation of thought, the mutual give-and-take of peer relations, and opportunities for role taking. Parent-child relationships do not contribute to moral thought in Kohlberg's view because they are too dominated by parents' moral values, with little opportunity for the youths to experiment with alternative moral choices.

Kohlberg's provocative view continues to generate considerable research on moral development, but critics challenge his theory (Kurtines & Gewirtz, 1991). One criticism of Kohlberg's

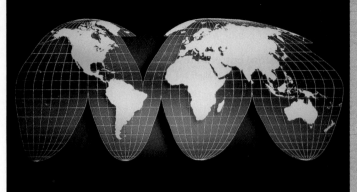

The Native American adolescent's quest for identity involves a cultural meshing of tribal customs and the technological, educational demands of modern society.

The Development of Identity in Native American Adolescents

S ubstandard living conditions, poverty, and chronic unemployment place many Native American youths at risk for school failure and poor health, which can contribute to problems in developing a positive identity (LaFromboise & Low, 1989). A special concern is the negative image of Native Americans that has been perpetuated for centuries in the majority White American culture. To consider further the development of identity in Native American youth, we will examine the experiences of a 12-year-old Hopi Indian boy.

The Hopi Indians are a quiet, thoughtful people who go to great lengths not to offend anyone. In a pueblo north of Albuquerque, a 12-year-old boy speaks: "I've been living in Albuquerque for a year. The Anglos I've met, they're different. I don't know why. In school, I drew a picture of my father's horse. One of the other kids wouldn't believe that it was ours. He said, 'You don't really own that horse.' I said, 'It's a horse my father rides, and I feed it every morning.' He said, 'How come?' I said, 'My uncle and my father are good riders, and I'm pretty good.' He said, 'I can ride a horse better than you, and I'd rather be a pilot.' I told him I never thought of being a pilot."

The Hopi boy continues, "Anglo kids, they won't let you get away with anything. Tell them something, and fast as lightning and loud as thunder, they'll say, 'I'm better than you, so there!' My father says it's always been like that."

The Indian adolescent is not really angry or envious of the White adolescent. Maybe he is in awe of his future power; maybe he fears it, and the White adolescent can't keep from wondering somehow that he has missed out on something and may end up "losing" (Coles, 1986).

The following words of another American Indian vividly capture some important ingredients of a Hopi adolescent's interest in a peaceful identity:

Rivers flow.   A small pebble
The sea sings.   On a giant shore;
Oceans roar.   Who am I
Tides rise.   To ask who I am?
Who am I?   Isn't it enough to be?

Carol Gilligan is shown with some of the students she has interviewed about the importance of relationships in a female's development. According to Gilligan, the sense of relationships and connectedness is at the heart of female development.

view is that moral reasons are often a shelter for immoral behavior. When bank embezzlers and presidents are asked about their moral reasoning, they may be at an advanced level, even at Kohlberg's postconventional level, but when their behavior is examined it may be filled with cheating, lying, and stealing. The cheaters, liars, and thieves may know what is right and what is wrong but still do what is wrong.

A second major criticism of Kohlberg's view is that it does not adequately reflect relationships and concerns for others. The **justice perspective** *is a theory of moral development that focuses on the rights of the individual; individuals independently make moral decisions.* Kohlberg's theory is a justice perspective. By contrast, the **care perspective** *is Carol Gilligan's theory of moral development, which sees people in terms of their connectedness with others and focuses on interpersonal communication, relationships with others, and concern for others.* According to Gilligan (1982), Kohlberg greatly underplayed the care perspective in moral development. She believes that this may have happened because he was a male, most of his research was with males rather than females, and he used male responses as a model for his theory.

Recently Gilligan conducted extensive interviews with girls from 6 to 18 years of age (Brown & Gilligan, 1990; Gilligan, 1990, 1992; Gilligan, Brown, & Rogers, 1990). She and her colleagues found that girls consistently reveal reported, detailed knowledge about human relationships, based on listening and watching what happens between people. According to Gilligan, girls have the ability to sensitively pick up different rhythms in relationships and are often able to follow the pathways of feelings.

Gilligan also believes that girls reach a critical juncture in their development when they reach adolescence. Gilligan says that, at the beginning of adolescence, at about 11 to 12 years of age, girls become aware that their intense interest in intimacy is not prized by the male-dominated culture, even though society values females as caring and altruistic. The dilemma, says Gilligan, is that girls are presented with a choice that makes them appear either selfish (if they become independent and self-sufficient) or selfless (if they remain responsive to others). Gilligan states that, as young adolescent girls experience this dilemma, they increasingly "silence" their distinctive voice. They become less confident and more tentative in offering their opinions, which often persists into adulthood. Some researchers believe that this self-doubt and ambivalence too often translates into depression and eating disorders among adolescent girls.

Some critics argue that Gilligan and her colleagues overemphasize differences between genders. One of those critics is developmentalist Eleanor Maccoby, who says that Gilligan exaggerates the differences in intimacy and connectedness between males and females. Other critics fault Gilligan's research strategy, which rarely includes a comparison group of boys and rarely includes statistical analysis. Instead, Gilligan conducts extensive interviews with girls and then provides excerpts from the girls' narratives to buttress her ideas. Other critics fear that Gilligan's findings reinforce stereotypes—females as nurturing and sacrificing, for example—that might undermine females' struggle for equality. These critics say that Gilligan's different voice should perhaps be called "the voice of the victim."

In reply, revisionists, such as Gilligan, say that their work provides a way to liberate females and transform a society that has far too long discriminated against females. They also say that, if females' approach to life is acknowledged as authentic, they will no longer have to act like males. The revisionists state that females' sensitivity in relationships is a special gift in our culture. Influenced by Gilligan's and other feminists' thinking, some schools are beginning to incorporate the feminine voice into their curriculum. For example, at the Emma Willard School in Troy, New York, the entire curriculum has been revamped to emphasize cooperation rather than competition and to encourage girls to analyze and express ideas from their own perspective rather than responding in stereotyped or conformist ways.

A third criticism of Kohlberg's view is that it is culturally biased (Bronstein & Paludi, 1988; Miller & Bersoff, in press). One review of research on moral development in 27 countries found that moral reasoning appears to be more culture specific than Kohlberg envisioned and that Kohlberg's scoring system does not recognize higher-level moral reasoning in certain cultural groups (Snarey, 1987). Kohlberg did not recognize

such values as communal equity and collective happiness in Israel, the unity and sacredness of all life forms in India, or the relation of an individual to the community in New Guinea as examples of higher-level moral reasoning. Kohlberg's system would not score these values at the highest level of moral reasoning because they do not emphasize an individual's rights and abstract principles of justice. In summary, moral reasoning is shaped more by the values and beliefs of a culture than Kohlberg acknowledged.

The Cultural Worlds of Adolescents

Aunts, uncles, and cousins from all over came to celebrate Josh Maisel's bar mitzvah. That morning Josh entered the temple as a child. According to his faith, he emerged as a man. Josh's bar mitzvah represents one of the few American **rites of passage—** *a ceremony or ritual that marks an individual's transition from one status to another.*

Rites of passage, such as those found in some cultures, mark a clear distinction between childhood and adulthood. Their absence in many industrialized cultures tends to leave many young people unsure whether or not they have reached adult status. Perhaps high school graduation ceremonies come closest to being a rite of passage for adolescents in today's industrialized world (Fasick, 1988). Even so, many high school graduates continue to live with their parents, are economically dependent on them, and are undecided about their career and life-style.

Another rite of passage, the initiation of sexual intercourse, occurs earlier each decade (Kilpatrick, 1992). Approximately 5 million adolescent females and 7 million adolescent males are sexually active. Twenty percent of all 15-year-olds report having experienced sexual intercourse; by age 16, that proportion increases to 33 percent, and by the age of 17 it reaches over 40 percent. Overall, 60 percent of all female and 70 percent of all male adolescents report having had sexual intercourse.

As a result of early sexuality, the rate of adolescent pregnancy has soared. For example, 14-year-old girls become pregnant at the rate of more than 5 per 1,000, and the rate for young women between the ages of 15 and 17 has jumped to 62 per 1,000. What's more, one of every eight births to young women under the age of 18 is not a first birth (Rickel & Allen, 1987).

The long-range consequences of teenage births are bleak. Young mothers tend to drop out of school. With little education, their job opportunities are limited. In addition, there are significant increases in maternal mortality and nonfatal maternal complication rates—especially among young, poor, and Black adolescents. The offspring of adolescent mothers also are adversely affected. For example, they often have low birthweights and other medical and psychological complications (Alan Guttmacher Institute, 1981; Rickel & Allen, 1987).

a.

(a) High school graduation is one of the few candidates for rites of passage in the lives of American youth. (b) In many primitive societies, rites of passage are more prevalent than in industrialized countries, such as the United States. Shown here is a Nigerian girl painted for a coming of age festival dance called "OBITUN."

In addition to the lives put on hold or potentials never reached, teen pregnancies represent significant costs to society. Many of these young women and their children may need social service supports, such as Aid to Families with Dependent Children, Medicaid, or educational and job-training programs. The best use of tax dollars, say many experts, is to prevent adolescent pregnancies in the first place (Stevens-Simon & McAnarney, 1992).

As Jean Erskine Stewart put it, "In no order of things is adolescence the time of simple life." Although many of today's adolescents are privileged, wielding unprecedented economic power, they simultaneously move through what seems like an endless preparation for life. Each generation of adolescents is the fragile cable by which the best and worst of their parents' generation is transmitted to the present. In the end, there are only two lasting gifts adults can leave youth—one being roots, the other wings.

b.

Adolescent Social Development

The old model of parent-adolescent relationships emphasized autonomy and detachment from parents, as well as intense, stressful conflict throughout adolescence. The new model emphasizes both attachment and autonomy, with parents acting as important support systems and attachment figures for adolescents; the new model also emphasizes that moderate, rather than severe, conflict is common and that it can serve a positive developmental function. Conflict with parents is greater in early adolescence, especially during the apex of puberty, than in late adolescence. The developmental trajectories of parent-adolescent relationships are changing. Adolescents spend increased time with peers. Conformity to antisocial behavior peaks at about the eighth or ninth grade. A special concern is the peer relations of ethnic minority adolescents.

The function of secondary schools continues to be debated. Some maintain that the function should be to promote intellectual development; others argue for a much more comprehensive scope. Successful schools take individual differences in development seriously, show a deep concern for what is known about early adolescence, and emphasize social and emotional development as much as intellectual development. Dropping out of school has been a serious problem for decades. Many dropouts have educational deficiencies that curtail their economic and social well-being for much of their adult lives. Some progress has been made; dropout rates for most ethnic minority groups have declined in recent decades, although dropout rates for inner-city, low-income minorities are still precariously high. Students drop out of school for school-related, economic, and personal reasons. To reduce the dropout rate, community institutions, especially schools, need to break down the barrier between work and school.

Erikson believes that identity versus identity confusion, the fifth stage of the human life cycle, characterizes adolescence. Adolescents enter a psychological moratorium between childhood dependency and adult independence, seeking to discover who they are and where they are going in life. Erikson shows a special concern for the role of culture and ethnicity in identity development. Adolescence is often a special juncture in the identity development of ethnic minority adolescents because, for the first time, they consciously confront their ethnic identity. Helms adapted Cross' model of minority identity development to include four stages: preencounter, encounter, immersion/emersion, and internalization/commitment. Helms also proposed a model of White racial identity. Kohlberg proposed three levels (each with two stages) of moral development that vary in the degree to which moral development is internalized—preconventional, conventional, and postconventional. Among his critics is Gilligan, who believes he underrepresented the care perspective.

Rites of passage are ceremonies that mark an individual's transition from one status to another, especially from childhood to adulthood. In some primitive cultures, rites of passage are well defined. In contemporary America, rites of passage are ill defined. The dropout rate for ethnic minority adolescents is disproportionately high. Many American adolescents are experiencing one rite of passage, sexual intercourse, earlier than adolescents in the past. One untoward consequence is adolescent pregnancy.

Adult Development and Aging

Just as the years from conception to adulthood are characterized by certain stages, so, too, are the adult years. **Early adulthood** *begins in the late teens or early twenties and ends in the late thirties to early forties. It is a time when individuals establish personal and economic independence, intensely pursuing a career, and seek intimacy with one or more individuals.* **Middle adulthood** *begins at about 35 to 45 years of age and ends at 55 to 65 years of age. It is a time of expanding personal and social involvement, increased responsibility, adjustment to physical decline, and career satisfaction.* **Late adulthood** *begins around the age of 60 to 70 and ends when an individual dies. It is a time of adjustment to decreased strength and health, retirement, reduced income, and new social roles.*

Notice that approximate age bands identify the periods of adult development and that the age bands overlap. Psychologists are more certain about the periods of childhood than adulthood—most of us would agree that a 1-year-old child is in the period of infancy and that a 4-year-old child is in the period of early childhood. However, the periods of adulthood are much broader; there is less agreement on whether or not a 41-year-old is in middle adulthood. Not only are the criteria and age bands for adult periods less clear-cut than for childhood, but as prominent life-span theorist Bernice Neugarten (1986) argues, we are rapidly becoming an age-irrelevant society. She points out that we are already familiar with the 28-year-old mayor, the 30-year-old college president, the 35-year-old grandmother, and the 65-year-old father of a preschooler.

Neugarten believes that most adult themes appear and reappear throughout the adult years. Issues of intimacy and freedom that haunt a couple throughout a relationship in early adulthood may be just as salient in late adulthood. The pressure of time, reformulating goals, and coping with success and failure are not the exclusive properties of adults at any particular age. Keeping in mind that the age bands of adult periods are fuzzy, let's now see what physical, cognitive, and social changes take place during the adult years.

Physical Development in Adulthood

What is the nature of physical change as we go through the adult years? First, we will consider physical changes in early and middle adulthood and, second, physical changes in late adulthood.

Early and Middle Adulthood

Athletes keep getting better. They run faster, jump higher, lift more weight. Despite steady improvement, the age at which athletes are at their best has stayed virtually the same. Richard Schultz and Christine Curnow (1988) analyzed records from track and field, swimming, baseball, and golf to learn at what age athletes truly hit their stride. They found that most athletes reach their peak performance under the age of 30, often between the ages of 19 and 26. Athletes who specialize in the strength and speed events peak relatively early, golf stars around the age of 31. In recent years, though, the "biological window" of peak performance has widened, even in the strength and speed events. Weight training, once unthinkable for women, has become standard procedure for such star athletes as Florence Griffith Joyner. At age 28, her ability to lift 320 pounds helped build the strength behind her explosive start and leg drive that won world records in the 100 and 200 meters in the 1988 Olympics.

Not only do we reach our peak performance during early adulthood, but we also are the healthiest then. Few young adults have chronic health problems, and they have fewer colds and respiratory problems than they had as children. However, young adults rarely recognize that bad eating habits, heavy drinking, and smoking in early adulthood can impair their health as they age. Despite warnings on packages and in advertisements that cigarettes are hazardous to health, individuals actually increase their use of cigarettes as they enter early adulthood (Bachman, O'Malley, & Johnston, 1978; Johnston, Bachman, & O'Malley, 1989). They also increase their use of alcohol, marijuana, am-

Weight lifting has helped some athletes gain their peak performance at an older age than was possible in the past. In the 1988 Olympics, Florence Griffith Joyner broke world records in the 100-meter and 200-meter races at the age of 28. In previous Olympics, dating back to 1896, the average age of Olympic champion female sprinters was 22.

phetamines, barbiturates, and hallucinogens.

As we enter middle adulthood, we are more acutely concerned about our health status. We experience a general decline in physical fitness throughout middle adulthood and some deterioration in health. The three greatest health concerns at this age are heart disease, cancer, and weight. Cancer related to smoking often surfaces for the first time in middle adulthood (Ferrini, 1989).

The *Harvard Medical School Newsletter* reports that about 20 million Americans are on a "serious" diet at any particular moment. Being overweight is a critical health problem, especially in middle adulthood. For individuals who are 30 percent or more overweight, the probability of dying in middle adulthood increases by 40 percent. Obesity also increases the probability an individual will suffer other ailments, including hypertension and digestive disorders.

Because our culture stresses a youthful appearance, physical deterioration—graying hair, wrinkling skin, and a sagging body—in middle adulthood is difficult to handle. Many middle-aged adults dye their hair and join weight reduction programs; some even undergo cosmetic surgery to look young. In one study, the middle-aged women focused more attention on their facial attractiveness than did the older or younger women. The middle-aged women also perceived that the signs of aging had a more detrimental effect on their appearance (Novak, 1977).

Late Adulthood and Aging

In the words of twentieth-century Italian poet Salvatore Quasimodo, "Each of us stands alone at the heart of the earth pierced through by a ray of sunlight: And suddenly it is evening." Although we may be in the evening of our lives in late adulthood, we are not meant to live out passively our remaining years.

An Active Older Life. Everything we know about older adults suggests that, the more active they are, the healthier and happier they are. John Pianfetti, age 70, and Madge Sharples, age 65, recently completed the New York Marathon. Older adults don't have to run marathons to be healthy and happy; even moderate exercise benefits their health. One investigation over an 11-year period of more than 13,000 men and women at the Aerobics Institute in Dallas, Texas, found that the sedentary participants were more than twice as likely to die during that period than those who were moderately fit (Blair, 1989).

FIGURE 9.6

The experimental setup in Bloor and White's study of exercise and health. Hogs, such as the one shown here, were trained to run approximately 100 miles per week. Then the experimenters narrowed the arteries that supplied blood to the hogs' hearts. The jogging hogs' hearts developed alternative pathways for the blood supply, whereas a group of nonjogging hogs were less likely to recover.

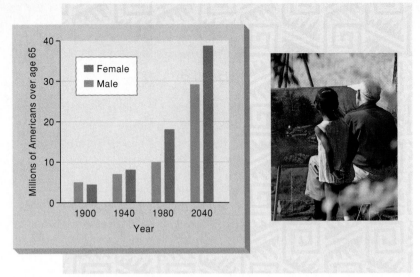

FIGURE 9.7

Millions of Americans over age 65 in 1900, 1940, 1980, and projected for the year 2040.

Jogging hogs have even shown the dramatic effects of exercise on health. Colin Bloor and Frank White (1983) trained a group of hogs to run approximately 100 miles per week. Then they narrowed the arteries that supplied blood to the hogs' hearts. The hearts of these jogging hogs developed extensive alternate pathways for the blood supply and 42 percent of the threatened heart tissue was salvaged, compared to only 17 percent in a control group of hogs (see figure 9.6).

Exercise is an excellent way to maintain health in late adulthood and possibly increase our longevity. Many strategies have been tried throughout history. Just how long can we live, and what influences our longevity?

Longevity. We are no longer a youthful society. The concept of a late adulthood period is a recent one. Until the twentieth century, most people died before age 65. In 1900 only 1 American in 25 was over 65. Today the figure is 1 in 9. By the middle of the twenty-first century, 1 in 4 Americans will be 65 years of age or older (see figure 9.7).

The life span has remained virtually unchanged since the beginning of recorded history. What has changed is life expectancy, the number of people expected to reach what seems to be an unbudging end point. Even though improvements in medicine, nutrition, exercise, and life-style have given us, on the average, 22 additional years of life since 1900, few of us will live to be 100. In Sociocultural Worlds 9.2, you will read about three areas of the world purported to have large numbers of inhabitants who live to be more than 100 years old.

Biological Theories of Aging. Even if we are remarkably healthy through our adult years, we begin to age at a certain point. What are the biological explanations of aging?

Virtually all biological theories of aging and life span assign an important role to genes. Research demonstrates that the body's cells can divide only a limited number of times; cells from embryonic tissue can divide about 50 times, for example (Hayflick, 1977). Cells extracted from older adults divide fewer times than those taken from younger adults. Although the cells of elderly people still have dividing capability, we rarely live to the end of our life-span potential. Based on the rate at which human cells divide, biologists place the upper limit of the human life cycle at 115 to 120 years.

The Course of Physical Development in Late Adulthood. In old age, arteries become more resistant to the flow of blood and heart output—about 5 quarts a minute at age 50—drops about 1 percent a year thereafter. With blood vessels more resistant, heart rate and blood pressure rise, both of which are related to heart disease. Even in a healthy older person, blood pressure that was 100/75 at age 25 will probably be 160/90 at age 70.

As we age in late adulthood, the probability that we will have a disease or become seriously ill increases. For example, a majority of individuals who are alive at age 80 have some

Selakh Butka, who says he is 113 years old, is shown with his wife, who says she is 101. The Butkas live in the Republic of Georgia in Russia, where reports of unusual longevity have surfaced. Why are scientists skeptical about their ages?

Eighty-seven-year-old José Maria Roa is from the Vilcabamba region of Ecuador, which also is renowned for the longevity of its inhabitants.

Aging in Russia, Ecuador, and Kashmir

Imagine that you are 120 years old. Would you still be able to write your name? Could you think clearly? What would your body look like? Would you be able to walk or run? Could you still have sex? Would you want to? Would your eyes and ears still function? Could you work?

Has anyone ever lived to be 120 years old? In three areas of the world, not just a single person but many people reportedly have lived more than 130 years. These areas are the Republic of Georgia in Russia, the Vilcabamba valley in Ecuador, and the province of Hunza in Kashmir (in northern India). Three people over 100 years old (centenarians) per 100,000 people is considered normal, but, in the Russian region where the Abkhasian people live, approximately 400 centenarians per 100,000 people have been reported. Some of the Abkhasians are said to be 120 to 170 years old (Benet, 1976).

There is reason to believe that some of these claims are false, however (Medvedev, 1974). There is no sound documentation of anyone living more than approximately 115 to 120 years. In the case of the Abkhasians, birth registrations, as well as other documents, such as marriage certificates and military registrations, are not available. In most instances, the ages of the Abkhasians have been based on the individuals' recall of important historical events and interviews with other members of the village (Benet, 1976). In the Russian villages where people have been reported to live long lives, the elderly experience unparalleled esteem and honor. Centenarians are often given special positions in the community, such as the leader of social celebrations; thus, there is a strong motivation to give one's age as older than one really is. One individual who claimed to be 130 years of age was found to have used his father's birth certificate during World War I to escape army duty. Later it was discovered that he was only 78 years old (Hayflick, 1975).

---

physical impairment. Alzheimer's disease is of special concern. **Alzheimer's disease** *is a degenerative, irreversible brain disorder that impairs memory and social behavior.* More than 2 million people over the age of 65 have Alzheimer's disease.

Cognitive Development in Adulthood

We have seen that, the further we go through the late adulthood years, the more likely it is we will be physically impaired. Controversy continues about whether our cognitive abilities, such as memory and intelligence, decline as we become older. We will examine this controversy shortly, but first we will tackle the question of whether there are cognitive changes that take place earlier in adulthood.

Early and Middle Adulthood

Piaget believed that an adult and an adolescent think in the same way; however, some developmental psychologists believe it is not until adulthood that individuals consolidate their formal operational thinking. That is, they may begin to plan and hypothesize about problems as adolescents, but as adults they become more systematic in approaching problems. Although some adults are more proficient at developing hypotheses and deducing solutions to problems than adolescents, many adults do not think in formal operational ways at all (Keating, in press).

Some psychologists believe that the absolute nature of adolescent logic and youth's buoyant optimism diminish in early adulthood (Labouvie-Vief, 1986). They argue that competent young adults are less caught up in idealism than they were in childhood, and they tend to think logically and to adapt to life as circumstances demand. Less clear is whether our mental skills, especially memory, decline with age.

Memory appears to decline more often when long-term rather than short-term memory is involved. For example, middle-aged individuals can remember a phone number they heard 30 seconds ago, but they probably won't remember the number as efficiently the next day. Memory is also more likely to decline when organization and imagery are not used. In addition, memory tends to decline when the information to be recalled is recently acquired or when the information is not used often. For example, middle-aged adults probably won't remember the rules to a new card game after only a lesson or two, and they are unlikely to know the new fall television schedule after its first week. Finally, memory tends to decline if recall rather than recognition is required. Middle-aged individuals can more efficiently select a phone number they heard yesterday if they are shown a list of phone numbers (recognition) rather than simply recalling the number off the top of their head. Memory in middle adulthood also declines if the individual's health is poor (Rybash, Roodin, & Santrock, 1991).

Late Adulthood

At age 70, Dr. John Rock developed the birth-control pill. At age 89, Arthur Rubinstein gave one of his best performances at New York's Carnegie Hall. From 85 to 90 years of age, Pablo Picasso completed three sets of drawings, and at age 76 Anna Mary Robertson Moses took up painting. As Grandma Moses, she became internationally famous and staged 15 one-woman shows throughout Europe. Are the feats of Grandma Moses and others rare exceptions? As Aeschylus said in the fifth century B.C., "It is always in season for the old to learn."

Intelligence test maker David Wechsler (1972) concluded that intellectual decline is simply part of the general aging process we all go through. The issue seems more complex, however. Although it is true that older adults do not score as high on intelligence tests as young adults do, this is probably because older adults just don't think as fast as young adults. When we consider general knowledge and wisdom, however, older adults often outperform younger adults (Baltes & Baltes, in press; Perlmutter, in press; Wilkinson & Allison, 1989).

Social Development in Adulthood

As both Sigmund Freud and Russian novelist Leo Tolstoy observed, adulthood is a time for work and a time for love. For some of us, though, finding our place in society and committing ourselves to a stable relationship take longer than we would have imagined.

REVIEW

Physical and Cognitive Development in Adulthood

The peak of our physical skills and health usually comes in early adulthood, a time when it is easy to develop bad health habits. In middle adulthood, most individuals experience a decline in physical fitness, and they start to take an interest in health as they notice signs that their health begins to deteriorate. Everything we know about older adults suggests that, the more physically active they are, the healthier and happier they are, and they live longer. Life expectancy has increased dramatically, but the life span has remained virtually stable for centuries. Longevity is influenced by such factors as heredity, family, health, education, personality, and life-style. Virtually all biological theories of aging assign an important role to genes. Based on the rate at which cells divide, biologists place the upper limit on the human life cycle at 115 to 120 years. As we grow old, our chances of becoming seriously ill increase. Alzheimer's disease is a degenerative brain disorder that impairs memory and social behavior.

Some psychologists argue that cognition is more pragmatic in early adulthood. Cognitive skills are strong in early adulthood. In middle adulthood, memory may decline, although such strategies as organization can reduce the decline. Whether or not intelligence actually declines in late adulthood is unclear. Remember that we have many forms of intelligence and the overall question of intellectual decline is a global one. As we age, some of our mental skills slow down, but wisdom often increases.

Early and Middle Adulthood

Among the changes in social development during early and middle adulthood are those involving careers and work, lifestyles, marriage, and other life events.

Careers and Work. At age 21, Thomas Smith graduated from college and accepted a job as a science teacher at a high school in Boston. At age 26, Sally Caruthers graduated from medical school and took a job as an intern at a hospital in Los Angeles. At age 20, Barbara Breck finished her training at a vocational school and went to work as a computer programmer for an engineering firm in Chicago. Earning a living, choosing an occupation, establishing a career, and developing a career— these are important themes of adulthood.

By the end of adolescence or the beginning of early adulthood, most people have an occupation. A few people seem to have known what they wanted to be ever since they were children, but for many people "getting there" may seem more like a time of foundering, ambiguity, and stress. Career counselors widely recommend exploring a variety of career options.

Among the most important social changes in the past few decades is the increased number of women in the workforce. Women have made great strides into careers that were once male bastions. For example, slightly more than half of all law students are women. However, some experts believe that many women restrict their career choices to nurturant, traditionally feminine occupations, such as nursing and teaching, overlooking other fields, such as mathematics and engineering (Diamond, 1988).

In today's economic climate, one wage is often no longer adequate to support a family. When married women with children decide to become paid employees, it is important for men and women to share the roles and responsibilities of both work and family life (Gustafson & Magnusson, 1991; Steil & Weltman, 1991). Fortunately, despite some role strain, multiple roles are healthy for both women and men. That is, the more roles (such as spouse, parent, worker) women and men have, the higher are their levels of psychological well-being and physical health (Crosby, 1991).

A popular notion about midlife is that it is a time when people carefully examine their career, evaluate what they have accomplished, and seriously consider a change. However, only about 10 percent of Americans change careers in midlife, and only some do so because they seek greater fulfillment; others do so because they get laid off or fired.

Marriage. Until about 1930, the goal of having a stable marriage was accepted as a legitimate end point of adult development. In the past 50 years, however, we have seen the emergence of the desire for personal fulfillment—both inside and outside a marriage—as a force that can compete with marriage's stability. The changing norm of male-female equality in marriage has produced relationships that are more fragile and intense than they were earlier in the twentieth century. More adults are remaining single longer in the 1990s, and the average duration of a marriage in the United States is just over 9 years. The divorce rate, which increased astronomically in the 1970s, has finally begun to slow down, although it still remains alarmingly high. Even with adults remaining single for longer and divorce a frequent occurrence, Americans still show a strong predilection for marriage—the proportion of women who never marry has remained at about 7 percent throughout the twentieth century, for example (Hernandez, 1988).

The age at which men and women marry, their expectations about what the marriage will be like, and how the marriage unfolds are aspects of marriage that vary both over time within a given culture and across cultures. For example, you might remember from chapter 1 that a marriage law that sets a minimum age for marriage—22 years for males, 20 years for females—took effect in China in 1981. Late marriage and late childbirth are critical to China's efforts to control population growth. More information about the nature of marriage in different cultures appears in Sociocultural Worlds 9.3.

Americans often have idealistic expectations of marriage, which helps explain our nation's high divorce rate and dissatisfaction in marriage. We expect our spouse to be simultaneously a lover, a friend, a confidant, a counselor, a career person, and a parent. Many myths about marriage contribute to these unrealistic expectations. Jeffrey Larson (1988) developed a marriage quiz to measure college students' knowledge about marriage and compared their responses with what social scientists know about marriage in the research literature. The college students responded incorrectly to almost half of the questions. Female students missed fewer items than male students, and students with a less romantic perception of marriage missed fewer items than more romantic students. See table 9.1 on page 283 to take the marriage quiz yourself.

As growing numbers of women pursue careers, they are faced with questions involving career and family (Anderson & Leslie, 1991; Gustafson & Magnusson, 1991; Spade & Reese, 1991; Steil & Weltman, 1991). Should they delay marriage and childbearing and establish their career first, or should they combine their career, marriage, and childbearing in their twenties? Some females continue to embrace the domestic patterns of an earlier historical period. They have married, borne children, and committed themselves to full-time mothering. These "traditional" women have worked outside the home only intermittently, if at all, and have subordinated the work role to the family role. Many other women, though, have veered from this time-honored path. They have postponed motherhood, or in some cases chosen not to have children. They have developed committed, permanent ties to the workplace that resemble the pattern once reserved only for men. When they have had children, they have strived to combine a career and motherhood. Although there have always been "career" women, their numbers are growing at an unprecedented rate.

Dual-career marriages can have both advantages and disadvantages (Thompson & Walker, 1989). One of the main advantages is financial. One of every three wives earns 30 to 50 percent of the family's total income, which helps explain why most first-time home buyers are dual-career couples. Other than financial benefits, dual-career marriages can contribute to a more equal relationship between husband and wife and enhanced feelings of self-esteem for women. Among the possible disadvantages of dual-career marriages are added time and energy demands, conflict between work and family roles, competitive rivalry between husband and wife, and, if the family includes children, concerns of whether the children's needs are being met adequately.

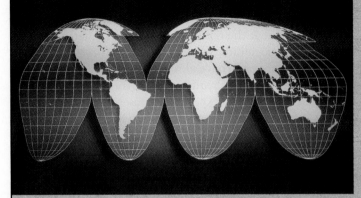

Marriage Around the World

The traits that people look for in a marriage partner vary around the world. In one recent large-scale study of 9,474 adults from 37 cultures on six continents and five islands, people varied the most on how much they valued chastity—desiring a marital partner with no previous experience in sexual intercourse (Buss & others, 1990). Chastity was the most important factor in marital selection in China, India, Indonesia, Iran, Taiwan, and the Palestinian Arab culture. Adults from Ireland and Japan placed moderate importance on chastity. In contrast, adults in Sweden, Finland, Norway, the Netherlands, and Germany generally said that chastity was not important in selecting a marital partner.

In this study, domesticity was also valued in some cultures and not in others. Adults from the Zulu culture in South Africa, Estonia, and Colombia placed a high value on housekeeping skills in their marital preference. By contrast, adults in the United States, Canada, and all Western European countries except Spain said that housekeeping was not an important trait in their partner.

Religion plays an important role in marital preferences in many cultures. For example, Islam stresses the honor of the male and the purity of the female. It also emphasizes the woman's role in childbearing, childrearing, educating children, and instilling the Islamic faith in their children.

International comparisons of marriage also reveal that individuals in Scandinavian countries marry late, whereas their counterparts in Eastern Europe marry early (Bianchi & Spani, 1986). In Denmark in the 1980s, for example, almost 80 percent of the women and 90 percent of the men aged 20 to 24 had never been married. In Hungary less than 40 percent of the women and 70 percent of the men the same age had never been married. In Scandinavian countries, cohabitation is popular among young adults; however, most Scandinavians eventually marry—in the 1980s, only 5 percent of the women and 11 percent of the men in their early forties had never been married by their early forties. Some countries, such as Hungary, encourage early marriage and childbearing to offset current and future population losses. Like Scandinavian countries, Japan has a high proportion of unmarried young people, but, rather than cohabiting as the Scandinavians do, unmarried Japanese young adults live at home longer with their parents before marrying.

a.   b.   c.

(a) In Scandinavian countries, cohabitation is popular; only a small percentage of 20-to-24-year-olds are married. (b) Many Soviet-influenced countries encourage early marriage and childbearing to offset current and future population issues. (c) The Islam religion stresses the honor of the male and the purity of the female.

TABLE 9.1
The Marriage Quiz

On a sheet of paper, number from 1 to 15. Answer each of the following items true or false. After completing the quiz, turn to the end of this chapter for the correct answers.

1. A husband's marital satisfaction is usually lower if his wife is employed full time than if she is a full-time homemaker.

2. Today most young, single, never-married people will eventually get married.

3. In most marriages, having a child improves marital satisfaction for both spouses.

4. The best single predictor of overall marital satisfaction is the quality of a couple's sex life.

5. The divorce rate in America increased from 1960 to 1980.

6. A greater percentage of wives are in the work force today than in 1970.

7. Marital satisfaction for a wife is usually lower if she is employed full time than if she is a full-time homemaker.

8. If my spouse loves me, he/she should instinctively know what I want and need to be happy.

9. In a marriage in which the wife is employed full time, the husband usually assumes an equal share of the housekeeping.

10. For most couples, marital satisfaction gradually increases from the first year of marriage through the childbearing years, the teen years, the empty nest period, and retirement.

11. No matter how I behave, my spouse should love me simply because he/she *is* my spouse.

12. One of the most frequent marital problems is poor communication.

13. Husbands usually make more life-style adjustments in marriage than wives.

14. Couples who cohabited before marriage usually report greater marital satisfaction than couples who did not.

15. I can change my spouse by pointing out his/her inadequacies, errors, etc.

From J. Larson, "The Marriage Quiz: College Students' Beliefs in Selected Myths About Marriage" in *Family Relations* 37:4. Copyrighted 1988 by the National Council on Family Relations, 3989 Central Ave., N.E., Suite 550, Minneapolis, MN 55421. Reprinted by permission.

Many men, especially those with low earnings, have a difficult time accepting their wives' employment. For example, in one investigation, married men who opposed their wives' employment were more depressed when their own earnings were low rather than high (Ulbrich, 1988). These men apparently experience a double insult to themselves as providers. Many husbands whose wives work report that they would like to have a wife who is a full-time homemaker. For example, in one study, although husbands appreciated their wives' earnings, they felt they had lost the services of a full-time homemaker—someone who is there when they get home, someone who cooks all their meals, and someone who irons all their clothes (Ratcliff & Bogdan, 1988). Some husbands, of course, encourage their wives' employment, or support their decision to pursue a career. In one investigation of high-achieving women, many of their husbands took pride in their wives' accomplishments and did not feel competitive with them (Epstein, 1987).

Gender, Intimacy, and Family Work. The experiences and implications of marriage for a wife may differ from those for her husband (Thompson & Walker, 1989). This is especially true in the expression of intimacy and in family work. In one study, only one-third of the married Black women said they would go to their husbands first for support if they had a serious problem, such as being depressed or anxious (Brown & Gary, 1985), and only one-third of these women named their husbands as one of the three people closest to them. More of the men than the women viewed their spouses as best friends (Rubin, 1984).

Wives consistently disclose more to their partners than husbands do (Peplau & Gordon 1985). Women also tend to express more tenderness, fear, and sadness than their partners. Many women complain that their husbands do not care about their emotional lives and do not express their own feelings and thoughts, whereas men feel that they are open or they do not understand what their wives want from them (Rubin, 1984). Men often say that, no matter how much they talk, it is not enough for their wives; women say they want more warmth and openness from their husbands. For example, women are more likely than men to give their partners a spontaneous kiss or hug when something positive happens (Blumstein & Schwartz, 1983). Overall, women are more expressive and affectionate than men in marriage, and this difference bothers many women.

Not only are there gender differences in terms of marital intimacy, but there also are strong gender differences in family work (Thompson & Walker, 1989). Most women and men agree that women should be responsible for family work and that men should "help out" (Szinovacz, 1984), and wives typically do much more family work than husbands (Warner, 1986). Even though most wives do two to three times more

"You have no idea how nice it is to have someone to talk to."

Copyright © 1964 Don Orehek. Reprinted by permission.

family work than their husbands, most wives report they are satisfied with the small amount their husbands do (Kamo, 1988; Peplau & Gordon, 1985). In one study, 10 percent of the husbands did as much family work as their wives (Berk, 1985); most of these "exceptional" men had many, usually young, children and wives who worked full time.

The nature of women's involvement in family work is often different from men's. Besides the fact that women do more, what women do and how they experience family work differs from men. The family work most women do is unrelenting, repetitive, and routine, often involving cleaning, cooking, child care, shopping, laundry, and straightening up. The family work most men do is infrequent, irregular, and nonroutine, often involving household repairs, taking out the garbage, and yard work. Women often report having to do several tasks at once, which may explain why they find domestic work less relaxing and more stressful than men do (Shaw, 1988).

Because family work is intertwined with love and embedded in family relations, it has complex and contradictory meanings (DeVault, 1987). Most women feel that family tasks are mindless but essential. They usually enjoy tending to the needs of their loved ones and keeping the family going, even if they do not find the activities themselves enjoyable and fulfilling. Family work is both positive and negative for women. They are unsupervised and rarely criticized, they plan and control their own work, and they have only their own standards to meet. However, women's family work is often worrisome, tiresome, menial, repetitive, isolating, unfinished, inescapable, and often unappreciated. It is not surprising that men report that they are more satisfied with their marriage than women do (Flowers, 1991).

Divorce. The stress of separation and divorce places both men and women at risk for psychological and physical difficulties (Amato & Keith, 1991; Chase-Lansdale & Hetherington, 1990; Coombs, 1991). Separated and divorced men and women

have higher rates of psychiatric disturbance, admission to psychiatric hospitals, clinical depression, alcoholism, and psychosomatic problems, such as sleep disturbances, than do married adults. There is increasing evidence that stressful events of many types—including marital separation—reduce the immune system's capabilities, rendering separated and divorced men and women vulnerable to disease and infection. In one recent study, the most recently separated women (1 year or less) were more likely to show impaired immunological functioning than women whose separations had occurred 1 to 6 years earlier (Kiecolt-Glaser & Glaser, 1988). In addition, the unhappily married individuals had poorer immune function than the happily married individuals.

Single Adults. Many myths are associated with being single, ranging from "the swinging single" to the "desperately lonely, suicidal single." Most singles are somewhere between these two extremes. The pluses of being single include time to make decisions about one's life, time to develop personal resources to meet goals, freedom to make autonomous decisions and pursue one's own schedule and interests, opportunities to explore new places and try new things, and privacy. Some common problems of single adults include a lack of intimate relationships with others, loneliness, and trouble finding a niche in a marriage-oriented society. Some single adults would rather remain single; others would rather be married.

Stage Theories of Adult Personality Development. Psychologists have proposed several theories about adult development. Most theories address the themes of work and love, career and intimacy. One set of theories proposes that adult development unfolds in stages.

Erikson's eight stages of the life cycle include one stage for early adulthood and one stage for middle adulthood. Erikson believes that only after identity has been well developed can true intimacy occur. **Intimacy versus isolation** *is Erikson's sixth stage of development, occurring mainly in early adulthood. Intimacy is the ability to develop close, loving relationships.* Intimacy helps us form our identity because, in Erikson's words, "We are what we love." If intimacy does not develop, Erikson argues, a deep sense of isolation and impersonal feelings overcome the individual. **Generativity versus stagnation** *is Erikson's seventh stage of development, occurring mainly in middle adulthood. Middle-aged adults need to assist the younger generation in leading useful lives.* Competent childrearing is one way to achieve generativity. However, adults can also satisfy this need through guardianship or a close relationship with the children of friends and relatives. The positive side of this stage—generativity—reflects an ability to positively shape the next generation. The negative side—stagnation—leaves the individual with a feeling of having done nothing for the next generation. As Erikson (1968) put it, "Generations will depend on the ability of all procreating individuals to face their children."

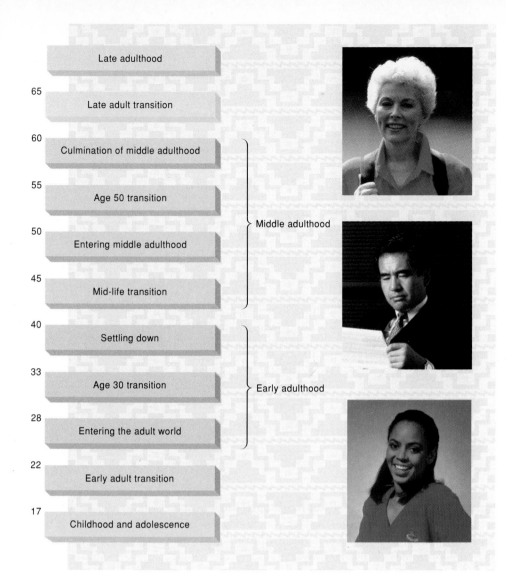

FIGURE 9.8

Levinson's periods of adult development.

In *Seasons of a Man's Life* (1978), Daniel Levinson also described adult development as a series of stages. He extensively interviewed middle-aged male hourly workers, academic biologists, business executives, and novelists and concluded that developmental tasks must be mastered at a number of points in adulthood (see figure 9.8).

In early adulthood, the two major tasks are exploring the possibilities for adult living and developing a stable life structure. The twenties represent the novice phase of adult development. By the end of a boy's teens, according to Levinson, a transition from dependence to independence should occur. This transition is marked by a dream—an image of the kind of life the young man wants, especially in terms of marriage and a career. The novice phase is a time of experimenting and testing the dream in the real world.

Men actually determine their goals by the age of 28 to 33. During his thirties, a man usually works to develop his family life and career. In the late thirties, he enters a phase of becoming his own man (or BOOM, "becoming one's own man," as Levinson calls it). By age 40, he reaches a stable point in his career, outgrows his earlier, more tenuous status as an adult, and looks forward to the kind of life he will lead as a middle-aged adult.

In Levinson's view, the change to middle adulthood lasts about 5 years and requires that men come to grips with four major conflicts that have existed since adolescence: (1) being young versus being old, (2) being destructive versus being constructive, (3) being masculine versus being feminine, and (4) being attached to others versus being separated from them. The success of the midlife transition depends on how effectively they can reduce these polarities and accept each of them as a part of their being. Levinson's original subjects were all males, but more recently he reported that these midlife issues hold for females as well (Levinson, 1987).

Erikson and Levinson emphasize that we go through a number of adult stages of development. In evaluating these stage theories, several points need to be kept in mind. First, the research on which they are based is not empirically sound—much of it involves clinical observations rather than rigorous, controlled observations. Second, the perspectives tend to describe the stages as crises, especially in the case of the midlife stage. Research on middle-aged adults reveals that few adults experience midlife in the tumultuous way described by the stage-crisis views: individuals vary extensively in how they cope with and perceive midlife (Vaillant, 1977).

Activity/event	Appropriate age range	% who agree (late '50s study)		% who agree (late '70s study)	
		Men	Women	Men	Women
Best age for a man to marry	20–25	80	90	42	42
Best age for a woman to marry	19–24	85	90	44	36
When most people should become grandparents	45–50	84	79	64	57
Best age for most people to finish school and go to work	20–22	86	82	36	38
When most men should be settled on a career	24–26	74	64	24	26
When most men hold their top jobs	45–50	71	58	38	31
When most people should be ready to retire	60–65	83	86	66	41
When a man has the most responsibilities	35–50	79	75	49	50
When a man accomplishes most	40–50	82	71	46	41
The prime of life for a man	35–50	86	80	59	66
When a woman has the most responsibilities	25–40	93	91	59	53
When a woman accomplishes most	30–45	94	92	57	48

FIGURE 9.9

Individuals' conceptions of the right age for major life events and achievements: late 1950s and late 1970s.

Life Events, Cohort Effects, and Social Clocks. Life events rather than stages may be responsible for changes in our adult lives. Such events as marriage, divorce, the death of a spouse, a job promotion, and being fired from a job involve varying degrees of stress and influence our development as adults (Holmes & Rahe, 1967). However, we also need to know about the many factors that mediate the influence of life events on adult development—for example, physical health, intelligence, personality, family support, and income (Hansell, 1991; Hultsch & Plemons, 1979). In addition, we need to know how people perceive the life events and how they cope with the stress involved. For instance, one person may perceive a divorce as highly stressful, whereas another person may perceive the same life event as a challenge. We also need to consider the person's life stage and circumstances. Divorce may be more stressful for an individual in his fifties who has been married for many years, for example, than for someone in her twenties who has been married only a few years (Chiriboga, 1982). Similarly, people may cope with divorce more effectively in the 1990s than in the 1890s because divorce is more commonplace and accepted today.

An increasing number of developmental psychologists believe that changing social expectations influence how different cohorts—groups of individuals born in the same year or time

period—move through the life cycle. For example, people born during the Depression may have a different outlook on life than those born during the optimistic 1950s (Rossi, 1989; Stewart & Healy, 1989).

Bernice Neugarten (1986) believes that the social environment of a particular age group can alter its "social clock"— the timetable according to which individuals are expected to accomplish life's tasks, such as getting married, having children, and establishing themselves in a career. Social clocks act as guides for our lives. People who are somehow out of sync with these social clocks find their lives more stressful than those who are on schedule, says Neugarten. One study found that, between the late 1950s and the late 1970s, there was a dramatic decline in adults' beliefs that there is a "right age" for major life events and achievements (Passuth, Maines, & Neugarten, 1984) (see figure 9.9).

Gender, Culture, and Middle Age. Stage theorists have tried to chart how our lives generally unfold over the years. Critics say that, when it comes to the middle years, these blueprints focus on career choice and work achievement, issues that have traditionally dominated men's lives more than women's (Deutsch, 1991; Fodor & Franks, 1990). They also assert that stage theories do not adequately address women's concerns about relationships,

Critics say the stage theories of adult development have a male bias by emphasizing career choice and achievement. The stage theories do not adequately address women's concerns about relationships, interdependence, and caring. The stage theories assume a normative sequence of development, but, as women's roles have become more varied and complex, determining what is normative is difficult.

interdependence, and caring and that they give short shrift to the importance of childbearing and childrearing (Gilligan, 1982). As mentioned earlier, women bear the burden of family work; men seldom experience the same demands of balancing career and family roles that women do.

One problem of comparing men and women according to stage theory is the assumption that most people encounter a given developmental stage at more or less the same time—graduating from high school and college, starting a family, and retiring, for example. As Neugarten points out, however, today people adhere less to social clocks. Many women return to college and begin careers, for example, after spending a number of years starting a family. Many other women delay marriage and childbearing until after they have successfully established a career. As a result of women's increasingly complex and varied roles, defining *what* women should be doing *when* has become difficult, if not impossible.

Although middle age may be a time of fewer options for many women in Western cultures, it carries many advantages in some nonindustrialized societies. Anthropologist Judith Brown (1985) argues that, as women in many nonindustrialized societies reach middle age, three changes take place that improve their status. First, they are often freed from cumbersome restrictions that were placed on them as younger women. For example, in middle age they are freer to travel. Middle-aged women can visit distant relatives, go on religious pilgrimages, and venture from

their villages to seek money-making opportunities. The second major change is that their work tends to be administrative; they can delegate tasks to younger women. Middle-aged women also make some important family decisions, such as what a grandchild is to be named, who is ready to be initiated, and who is eligible to marry whom. The third major change for middle-aged women is the opportunity to step into venerated functions, such as midwife, curer, holy woman, and matchmaker, roles that bring recognition beyond the household.

We have already seen that midlife crises are less pervasive in the United States than is commonly believed (Chiriboga, 1982). There has been little cross-cultural research on middle adulthood; adult stage theories, such as Levinson's, have not been tested in other cultures. In some cultures, especially those in nonindustrialized countries, the concept of middle age is ambiguous or absent. For example, a person may be described as young or old, but not as middle-aged (Foner, 1984). Some cultures have no words for *adolescent, young adult,* or *middle-aged adult.*

The Gusii culture of Kenya in Africa describes the flow of life differently for females than for males (LeVine, 1979):

Females	Males
1. Infant	1. Infant
2. Uncircumcised girl	2. Uncircumcised boy
3. Circumcised girl	3. Circumcised boy warrior
4. Married woman	4. Male elder
5. Female elder	

Life events, not age, determine a person's status in the Gusii culture. Although the Gusii do not clearly label midlife, around the age of 40 some individuals reassess their lives and examine the limited time that remains. Recognizing that their physical strength is decreasing and that they cannot farm their land forever, some Gusii become spiritual practitioners or healers. As is true for Americans, a midlife crisis among the Gusii is the exception rather than the rule.

The concept of a midlife crisis implies that middle adulthood involves considerable change. Let's explore further the issue of change in adult development.

Continuity and Discontinuity. Richard Alpert, an achievement-oriented, hard-working college professor in the 1960s became Ram Dass, a free-spirited guru in search of an expanded state of consciousness in the 1970s. It would seem as though Richard Alpert and Ram Dass were two very different people. However, Harvard psychologist David McClelland, who knows Ram Dass well, says that he is the same old Richard—still charming, still concerned with inner experience, and still power hungry. Jerry Rubin viewed his own transformation from yippie to Wall Street businessman in a way that under-

Gusii dancers perform on habitat day, Nairobi, Kenya. Movement from one status to another in the Gusii culture is due primarily to life events, not age. The Gusii do not have a clearly labeled midlife transition.

scores continuity in personality. Rubin said that he discovered his identity in a typical Jerry Rubin fashion—trying out anything and everything, behaving in a wild and crazy manner. Whether yippie or Wall Street yuppie, Rubin approached life with enthusiasm and curiosity.

William James (1890) said that our basic personality is like plaster, set by the time we are 30. James believed that our bodies and attitudes may change through the adult years—as did Richard Alpert's and Jerry Rubin's—but the basic core of our personality remains the same. Some modern researchers, such as Paul Costa, also believe that such traits as how extraverted we are, how well-adjusted we are, and how open we are to new experiences do not change much during our adult lives (Costa, 1988; Costa & others, 1987). Costa says that a person who is shy and quiet at age 25 will be basically that same shy, quiet person at age 50. Still other psychologists are enthusiastic about our capacity for change as adults, arguing that too much importance is attached to personality change in childhood and not enough to change in adulthood.

A more moderate view of the stability-change issue comes from the architects of the California Longitudinal Study, which now spans more than 50 years (Eichorn & others, 1981). These

a.   b.

How much does personality change and how much does it stay the same through adulthood? In the early 1970s, Jerry Rubin was (a) a yippie demonstrator, but in the 1980s Rubin became (b) a Wall Street businessman. Rubin said that his transformation underscored continuity in personality: whether yippie or Wall Street yuppie, he approached life with curiosity and enthusiasm.

Ageism is one of our society's ugliest words. Older adults may be shunned socially because they are perceived as senile or boring. Their children may edge them out of their lives. In these circumstances, a social network of friendships becomes an important support system for older adults. Researchers have found that close attachment to one or more individuals, whether friends or family, is associated with greater life satisfaction.

researchers believe that some stability exists over the long course of adult development but that adults are more capable of changing than Costa thinks. For example, a person who is shy and introverted at age 25 may not be completely extraverted at age 50, but she may be less introverted than at 25. This person may have married someone who encouraged her to be more outgoing and supported her efforts to socialize; perhaps she changed jobs at age 30 and became a salesperson, placing her in a situation in which she was required to develop her social skills.

Humans are adaptive beings. We are resilient throughout our adult lives, but we do not acquire entirely new personalities. In a sense, we change but remain the same—underlying the change is coherence and stability.

Late Adulthood

In the past, the image of an older adult was of a person sitting in a rocking chair, watching the world go by. Now we know that the most well-adjusted and satisfied older adults are active, not passive.

Activity Theory. **Activity theory** *states that the more active and involved older people are, the more satisfied they are and the more likely it is they will stay healthy.* Researchers have found that older people who go to church, attend meetings, take trips, and exercise are happier than those who simply sit at home. Predictably, the better the health and the higher the income, the more likely it is that an older person will be satisfied with life as well.

Ageism. The elderly often face painful discrimination. A new word in our vocabulary is **ageism,** *which is prejudice against older people.* Older adults may be branded by a number of stereotypes—such as feebleminded, boring, ugly, parasitic. As a result, they may be treated like children and described as cute and adorable. Far worse, they often are not hired for new jobs or are forced out of existing ones, they may be shunned, or they may even be edged out of their own families. The elderly who are poor or from ethnic minority backgrounds face special hardships.

Ethnicity and Gender. Of special concern are the ethnic minority elderly, especially Black Americans and Hispanic Americans, who are overrepresented in the elderly poor (Atchley, 1989; Hernandez, 1991; Krause, Jay, & Liang, 1991; Stanford, 1990; Watson, 1990). Nearly one-third of all elderly Black Americans live on less than $5,300 per year. Among Black American women living alone, the figure is 55 percent. Almost one-fourth of all elderly Hispanic Americans are below the poverty line. Only 10 percent of elderly White Americans fall below the poverty line (Bahr, 1989).

Comparative information about Black Americans, Hispanic Americans, and White Americans indicates a possible double jeopardy for elderly ethnic minority individuals, who face problems related to *both* ageism and racism (Dowd & Bengston, 1978; Kart, 1990; Milligan, 1990; Tran, Wright, & Chatters, 1991). Both the wealth and health of the ethnic minority elderly decrease more rapidly than that of elderly White Americans. Ethnic minority elderly are more likely to become ill but less likely to receive treatment. They are also more likely to have a history of less education, unemployment, worse housing conditions, and shorter life expectancies than their elderly White American counterparts. Also, many ethnic minority workers never enjoy the Social Security and Medicare benefits to which their earnings contribute, because they die before reaching the age of eligibility for benefits (Gelfand, 1982; Skinner, 1990; Williams, 1990).

A possible double jeopardy also faces many women—the burden of *both* ageism and sexism (Datan, 1989; Gerlach, 1991; Harrison, 1991; Kite, Deaux, & Miele, 1991; Macdonald, 1989). The poverty rate for elderly women is almost double that of elderly men. According to Congresswoman Mary Rose Oakar, the number one priority for midlife and older women should be economic security. She predicts that 25 percent of all women working today can expect to be poor in old age (Porcino, 1983). Only recently has scientific and political interest in aging women developed. For many years, aging women were virtually invisible in aging research and in protests involving rights for the elderly. An important research and political agenda for the 1990s is increased interest in the aging and rights of elderly women.

Not only is it important to be concerned about the double jeopardy of ageism and sexism involving older women, but special attention also needs to be devoted to the elderly who are female ethnic minority individuals. They face what could be described as triple jeopardy—ageism, sexism, and racism (Edmonds, 1990). Income is a special problem for these women. For example, more than one-third of all older Black American women have incomes below the poverty level (compared to less than one-fourth of all older Black American men and approximately 13 percent of older White American women). One-fourth of all older Hispanic American women have incomes below the poverty level (compared to 19 percent of Hispanic American men) (U.S. Bureau of the Census, 1990). More information about being female, ethnic, and old appears in Sociocultural Worlds 9.4.

Cultural Comparisons. For many generations, the elderly in China and Japan experienced higher status than the elderly in the United States (Ikels, 1989; Palmore, 1975). In Japan the

As Japan has become more urbanized and Westernized, fewer elderly adults have lived with their children and more elderly adults have returned to work. Today respect for the elderly in Japan is greater than in the United States but not as strong as the idealized images we sometimes have.

elderly are more integrated into their families than the elderly in most industrialized countries. More than 75 percent live with their children; few single older adults live alone. Respect for the elderly surfaces in many circumstances: the best seats may be reserved for the elderly, cooking caters to their tastes, and individuals bow to them.

However, the image of elderly Japanese who are spared the heartbreak associated with aging in the United States by the respect and devotion they receive from children, grandchildren, and society is probably idealized and overexaggerated (Tobin, 1987). Americans' images of the elderly in other cultures may be idealized, too—we imagine elderly Eskimos adrift on blocks of ice and 120-year-old Russian yogurt eaters, in addition to the honored elders of Japan. For example, Japan has become more urbanized and Westernized; fewer elderly live with their children and more elderly adults return to work, usually in a lower-status job, with lower pay, a loss of fringe benefits, and a loss of union membership. The Japanese culture has acted as a powerful brake in slowing the decline in the respect for the elderly—today respect for the elderly is greater in Japan than in the United States, but not as strong as the idealized images we sometimes have (Usui, 1989).

Seven factors are most likely to predict high status for the elderly in a culture (Cogwill, 1974; Sangree, 1989; Sokolovsky, 1983):

1. Older persons have valuable knowledge.
2. Older persons control key family/community resources.
3. Older persons are permitted to engage in useful and valued functions as long as possible.
4. There is role continuity throughout the life span.
5. Age-related role changes involve greater responsibility, authority, and advisory capacity.

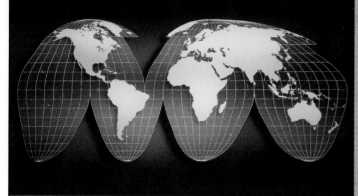

Being Female, Ethnic, and Old

A special concern is the stress faced by Black elderly women, many of whom view religion as a source of strength to help them cope with stress.

Part of the unfortunate history of ethnic minority groups in the United States has been the negative stereotypes against members of their groups. Many have also been hampered by their immigrant origins in that they are not fluent or literate in English, may not be aware of the values and norms involved in American social interaction, and may have life-styles that differ from mainstream America. Often included in these cultural differences is the role of women in the family and in society. Many, but not all, immigrant ethnic groups traditionally have relegated the woman's role to family maintenance. Many important decisions may be made by a woman's husband or parents, and she is often not expected to seek an independent career or enter the workforce except in the case of dire financial need.

Some ethnic minority groups may define an older woman's role as unimportant, especially if she is unable to contribute financially. However, in some ethnic minority groups, an older woman's social status improves. For example, older Black American women can express their own needs and can be given status and power in the community. Despite their positive status in the Black family and the Black culture, Black women over the age of 70 are the poorest population group in the United States. Three of five elderly Black women live alone; most of them are widowed. The low incomes of elderly Black women translate into less than adequate access to health care. Substantially lower incomes for Black American elderly women are related to the kinds of jobs they hold, which either are not covered by Social Security or, in the case of domestic service, are not reported even when legally required.

A portrayal of older Black women in cities reveals some of their survival strategies. They highly value the family as a system of mutual support and aid, adhere to the American work ethic, and view religion as a source of strength. The use of religion as a

way of coping with stress has a long history in the Black culture, with roots in the slave experience. The Black church came to fulfill needs and functions once met by religious-based tribal and community organizations that Blacks brought from Africa (McAdoo, 1979). In one investigation, the elderly Black women valued church organizations more than their male counterparts did, especially valuing the church's group activities and organizations (Taylor, 1982).

In sum, Black elderly women have faced considerable stress in their lives (Edmonds, 1990). In the face of this stress, they have shown remarkable adaptiveness, resilience, responsibility, and coping skills.

Erikson's stages

Periods of the life cycle	1	2	3	4	5	6	7	8
Late adulthood								Integrity vs. despair
Middle adulthood							Generativity vs. stagnation	
Young adulthood						Intimacy vs. isolation		
Adolescence					Identity vs. identity confusion			
Middle and late childhood				Industry vs. inferiority				
Early childhood			Initiative vs. guilt					
Infancy		Autonomy vs. shame, doubt						
	Trust vs. mistrust							

FIGURE 9.10

Erikson's eight stages of the human life cycle.

6. The extended family is a common family arrangement in the culture, and the older person is integrated into the extended family.

7. The culture is more collectivistic than individualistic.

Life Review and Integrity. "Life is lived forward, but understood backwards," said Danish philosopher Søren Kierkegaard. This is truer of late adulthood than of any other life period. Kierkegaard's words reflect Erikson's final stage of development through the life span. Erikson called this eighth stage **integrity versus despair;** *occurring mainly in late adulthood, it is a time of looking back at what we have done with our lives. If an older person has developed a positive outlook in each of the preceding periods of development, the retrospective glances and reminiscences will reveal a life well spent, and the individual will feel satisfied (integrity). However, if the older adult has a negative outlook on life, the retrospective glances may produce doubt, gloom, and despair about the value of one's life.* (For an overview of Erikson's eight stages of development, see figure 9.10.) As Erikson (1968) put it, "To whatever abyss ultimate concerns may lead individual men, man as a psychosocial creature will

In late adulthood, we review our lives, looking backward and examining our journey through the human life cycle. The words of Sarah Teasdale in *Dark of the Moon* (1926) capture our search for meaning in late adulthood:

When I look life in the eyes
Grown calm and very coldly wise,
Life will have given me the truth,
And taken in exchange—my youth.

face, toward the end of his life, a new edition of the identity crisis, which we may state in the words, 'I am what survives me.' "

Death and Dying

"I'd like to know what this show is all about before it's out," wrote the twentieth-century Dutch poet and inventor Piet Hein. Death may come at any time, but it is during late adulthood that we realize that our days are literally numbered. Societies throughout history have had philosophical or religious beliefs about death, and most have rituals to mark the passing from life to death. Some cultures hold a ceremonial meal accompanied by festivities. In others, mourners wear a black armband. Figure 9.11 shows two rituals that deal with death.

In most cultures, death is not viewed as the end of existence—although the biological body dies, the spirit lives on. This belief is held by many Americans. Reincarnation, the belief that the soul is reborn in a new human body, is an important aspect of Hindu and Buddhist religions. Cultures often differ in their perception of and reaction to death. In the Gond culture of India, death is believed to be caused by magic and demons; Gonds react to death with anger. In the Tanala culture of Madagascar, death is thought to be caused by natural forces. The members of the Tanala culture react peacefully to death.

Elisabeth Kübler-Ross (1974) says that we go through five stages in facing death: denial and isolation, anger, bargaining, depression, and acceptance. Initially a dying individual responds, "No, it can't be me. It's not possible." However, denial is only a temporary defense. When the individual recognizes that denial can no longer be maintained, she often becomes angry and resentful; the individual's question becomes, "Why me?" Anger often is displaced onto physicians, nurses, family members, and even God. In the third stage, the dying person develops the hope that death can somehow be postponed or delayed. The individual says, "Yes, me, but . . ." The dying person bargains and negotiates, often with God, offering a reformed life dedicated to God and the service of others for a few more months of life.

a.

b.

FIGURE 9.11

Cultural variations in death. (a) A New Orleans street funeral is in progress. (b) A deceased person's belongings are left on a mountainside in Tibet.

As a dying individual comes to accept the certainty of her death, she often enters a period of preparatory grief, becoming silent, refusing visitors, and spending much of the time crying or grieving. This behavior is a normal effort to disconnect the self from all love objects. Kübler-Ross describes the final stage, characterized by peace and acceptance of one's fate, as the end of the struggle, the final resting stage before death. Not everyone goes through the stages in the sequence Kübler-Ross proposed. Indeed, Kübler-Ross says she has been misread, pointing out that she never believed every individual copes with death in a specific sequence. She does maintain, however, that the optimal way to cope with death is through the stages she has outlined.

Some individuals struggle until the very end, angrily hanging onto their lives. They follow the encouragement of Dylan Thomas: "Do not go gentle into that good night. Old age should burn and rave at close of day. . . . rage, rage against the dying of the light." In these instances, acceptance of death never comes. People die in different ways and experience different feelings and emotions in the process: hope, fear, curiosity, envy, apathy, relief, even anticipation. They often move rapidly from one mood to another and, in some instances, two moods may be present simultaneously.

Those left behind after the death of an intimate partner suffer profound grief and often endure financial loss, loneliness, increased physical illness, and psychological disorders, including depression. How they cope with the crisis varies considerably. Widows outnumber widowers by the ratio of 5 to 1, because women live longer than men, because women tend to marry men older than themselves, and because a widowed man is more likely to remarry. Widowed women are probably the poorest group in America, despite the myth of huge insurance settlements. Many are also lonely, and the poorer and less educated they are, the lonelier they tend to be. The bereaved are also at increased risk for many health problems, including death.

Optimal adjustment after a death depends on several factors. Women do better than men largely because, in our society, women are responsible for the emotional life of a couple, whereas men usually manage the finances and material goods. Thus, women have better networks of friends, closer relationships with relatives, and experience in taking care of themselves psychologically. Older widows do better than younger widows, perhaps because the death of a partner is more expected for older women. For their part, widowers usually have more money than widows do, and they are much more likely to remarry (DiGiulio, 1989; Lopata, 1979).

For either widows or widowers, social support helps them adjust to the death of a spouse (Bass, Bowman, & Noelker, 1991; LaGrand, 1991; Sankar, 1991). Such programs as Widow-to-Widow, begun in the 1960s, provide support for newly widowed people. Its objective is to prevent the potentially negative effects of the loss. Volunteer widows reach out to other widows, intro-

ducing them to others who may have similar problems, leading group discussions, and organizing social activities. The program has been adopted by the American Association of Retired Persons and disseminated throughout the United States as the Widowed Person's Service. The model has since been adopted by numerous community organizations to provide support for those going through a difficult life transition that will confront the vast majority of us (Silverman, 1988).

By now you can appreciate that much development takes place in adolescence and adulthood, just as in infancy and childhood. In the next chapter, you will read about the nature of gender roles and sexuality, a discussion that includes information about how our gender roles develop and issues of sexuality at various points in the life cycle.

REVIEW

Social Development in Adulthood and Death and Dying

Special concerns in early and middle adulthood are careers and work, life-styles, theories of adult personality development, cohort effects, gender, culture, and the issue of continuity-discontinuity. Among the important aspects of careers and work are the increasing number of females in the workforce. Adults must choose the life-style they want to follow—single, married, or divorced, for example. One set of adult personality development theories proposes that adult development unfolds in stages (Erikson, Levinson). Other theories emphasize life events, social clocks, and cohort effects. The stage theorists have overexaggerated the prevalence of a midlife crisis. Critics say the adult stage theories have a male bias by emphasizing career choice and achievement. The stage theories do not adequately address women's concerns about relationships. The stage theories assume a normative sequence, but, as

women's roles have become more varied and complex, determining what is normative is difficult. In many nonindustrialized societies, a woman's status often improves in middle age. In many cultures, the concept of middle age is not clear, although most cultures distinguish between young and old adults. There is both continuity and discontinuity in adult personality development. Everything we know about late adulthood suggests that an active older life is preferred to disengagement. Special concerns are ageism and the ethnic minority elderly. Cross-cultural comparisons reveal greater respect for the elderly in some cultures, such as Japan, than in the United States. Erikson believes that the final issue in the life cycle is integrity versus despair, which involves a life review.

Death may come at any point in the life cycle but in late adulthood we know it is near. Most societies have rituals that deal with death, although cultures vary in their orientation toward it. Kübler-Ross proposed five stages of coping with death. A special concern is the coping skills of widows and widowers.

Summary

I. Historical Beginnings and the Nature of Adolescence

G. Stanley Hall is the father of the scientific study of adolescence. In the early 1900s, he proposed the storm and stress view. Adolescence is a transition between childhood and adulthood that involves biological, cognitive, and social development. In most cultures, adolescence begins at approximately 10 to 13 years of age and

ends at approximately 18 to 21 years of age. Adolescence is more appropriately viewed as a time of decision making and commitment than a time of rebellion, crisis, and pathology. Different portrayals of adolescence emerge, depending on the particular group of adolescents being described. Adults' idealized images and ambivalent messages may contribute to adolescent problems.

II. Physical Development in Adolescence

Puberty is a rapid change to maturation that usually occurs in early adolescence. It has arrived earlier in recent years. Hormone changes are prominent. Puberty occurs roughly 2 years later in boys than in girls, although its normal range is large. Early maturation generally favors boys but has mixed effects for girls. Some experts believe that puberty's effects are overstated.

III. Cognitive Development in Adolescence

Piaget argued that formal operational thought appears between 11 and 15 years of age. Thought is abstract and idealistic but includes planning and logical analysis. Some of Piaget's ideas on formal operational thought are being challenged. Egocentrism also characterizes adolescent thought.

IV. Social and Personality Development in Adolescence

The old model of parent-adolescent relationships emphasized autonomy and detachment from parents, as well as intense, stressful conflict throughout adolescence. The new model emphasizes both attachment and autonomy, with parents acting as important support systems and attachment figures for adolescents; the new model also emphasizes that moderate, rather than severe, conflict is common and can serve a positive developmental function. Conflict with parents is greater in early adolescence, especially during the apex of pubertal change, than in late adolescence. The developmental trajectories of parent-adolescent relationships are changing. Adolescents spend increased time with peers. Conformity to antisocial peer standards peaks around the eighth and ninth grades. A special concern is the peer relations of ethnic minority adolescents. The functions of secondary schools continue to be debated. Some maintain that the function should be to promote intellectual development; others argue for more comprehensive functions. Successful schools for young adolescents take individual differences in development seriously, show a deep concern for what is known about early adolescence, and emphasize social and emotional development as much as intellectual development. Dropping out of school has been a serious problem for decades. Many dropouts have serious educational deficiencies that curtail their economic and social well-being for most of their adult lives. Some progress has been made; dropout rates for most ethnic minority groups have declined in recent decades, although dropout rates for inner-city, low-income minorities are still precariously high. Students drop out of school for school-related, economic, and personal reasons. To reduce the dropout rate, community institutions, especially schools, need to break down the barriers between work and school. Erikson believes that identity versus identity confusion, the fifth stage of the human life cycle, characterizes adolescence. Adolescents enter a psychological moratorium between childhood dependency and adult independence, seeking to discover who they are and where they are going in life. Erikson shows a special concern for the role of culture and ethnicity in identity development. Adolescence is often a special juncture in the identity development of ethnic minority adolescents because, for the first time, they consciously confront their ethnic identity. Helms amended Cross' model of minority identity development to include four stages: preencounter, encounter, immersion/emersion, and internalization/commitment. Helms also proposed a model of White racial identity. Kohlberg proposed three levels (each with two stages) of moral development, which vary in the degree to which moral development is internalized—preconventional, conventional, and postconventional. Among his critics are Gilligan, who believes he underrepresented the care perspective. Rites of passage are ceremonies that mark an individual's transition from one status to another, especially into adulthood. In some cultures, rites of passage are well defined. In contemporary America, rites of passage are ill defined.

V. Physical Development in Middle and Late Adulthood

The peak of our physical skills and health usually comes in early adulthood, a time when it is easy to develop bad health habits. In middle adulthood, most individuals experience a decline in physical fitness, some deterioration in health, and an increased interest in health-related matters.

VI. Physical Development in Late Adulthood and Aging

Everything we know about older adults suggests they are healthier and happier the more physically active they are, and they live longer. Life expectancy has increased dramatically but the life span has remained virtually unchanged for centuries. Longevity is influenced by such factors as heredity, family, health, education, personality, and life-style. Virtually all biological theories of aging assign an important role to genes. Based on the rate at which cells divide, biologists place the upper limit on the human life cycle at 115 to 120 years. As we age through late adulthood, our chance of developing an impairment increases. Alzheimer's disease is a degenerative brain disorder that impairs memory and social behavior.

VII. Cognitive Development in Early and Middle Adulthood

Some psychologists argue that cognition is more pragmatic in early adulthood. Cognitive skills are strong in early adulthood. In middle adulthood, memory may decline, but such strategies as organization can reduce the decline.

VIII. Cognitive Development in Late Adulthood

There is extensive debate over the issue of whether intelligence declines in late adulthood. We have many forms of intelligence, and the overall question of intellectual decline is a global one. As we age, speed of processing declines, but wisdom increases.

IX. Social Development in Early and Middle Adulthood

Special concerns are careers and work, life-styles, theories of adult personality development, cohort effects, gender, culture, and continuity-discontinuity. Among the important aspects of careers and work is the increasing number of females in the workforce. Adults face the task of choosing which adult life-style they want to follow—single, married, or divorced, for example. One set of adult personality development theories proposes that adult development unfolds in stages (Erikson, Levinson). Other theories emphasize life events, social clocks, and cohort effects. The stage theorists have overexaggerated the prevalence of a midlife crisis. Critics say the adult stage theories have a male bias by emphasizing career choice and achievement. The stage theories do not adequately address women's concerns about relationships. The stage theories assume a normative sequence, but, as women's roles have become more varied and complex, determining what is normative is difficult. In many nonindustrialized societies, a woman's status often improves in middle age. In many cultures, the concept of middle age is not clear, although most cultures distinguish between the young and the old. There is both continuity and discontinuity in adult personality development.

X. Social Development in Late Adulthood

Everything we know about late adulthood suggests that an active older life is preferred to disengagement. Special concerns are ageism and the ethnic minority elderly. Cross-cultural comparisons reveal greater respect for the elderly in some cultures, such as Japan, than in the United Sates. Erikson believes that the final issue in the life cycle to be negotiated is integrity versus despair, which involves a life review.

XI. Death and Dying

Death may come at any point in the life cycle but in late adulthood we know it is near. Most societies have rituals that deal with death, although many cultures vary in their orientation toward it. Kübler-Ross proposed five stages of coping with death. A special concern is the coping skills of widows and widowers.

Key Terms

adolescence 258
storm and stress view 258
puberty 261
testosterone 261
estradiol 261
formal operational thought 262
hypothetical-deductive reasoning 263
adolescent egocentrism 263

identity versus identity confusion 268
internalization 271
preconventional level 271
conventional level 271
postconventional level 271
justice perspective 273
care perspective 273
rites of passage 274
early adulthood 276

middle adulthood 276
late adulthood 276
Alzheimer's disease 279
intimacy versus isolation 284
generativity versus stagnation 284
activity theory 289
ageism 289
integrity versus despair 292

Suggested Readings

Erikson, E. H. (1968). *Identity: Youth and crisis*. New York: W. W. Norton. This is Erikson's masterpiece, in which he outlined his insightful ideas about our search for who we are, what we are all about, and where we are headed during the adolescent years.

Levinson, D. J. (1978). *The seasons of a man's life*. New York: Knopf. In this best-selling book, Levinson outlines his view of the stages males go through as adults. It includes a number of biographies.

Maddox, G. (Ed.). (1987). *The encyclopedia of aging*. New York: Springer. This book covers a number of topics pertaining to the social, personality, and mental health needs of the elderly; contemporary information on the cultural and social worlds of older adults is provided.

Miller, J. B. (1986). *Toward a new psychology of women*. Boston: Beacon. A leading feminist scholar, Jean Baker Miller, describes the increased interest in studying the nature of women's experiences and development.

Santrock, J. W. (1992). *Life-span development* (4th ed.). Dubuque, IA: Wm. C. Brown. This book describes development through the entire human life cycle. It includes extensive overviews of what is known about adolescent development and adult development and aging.

William T. Grant Committee. (1988). *The forgotten half: Non-college youth in America today*. New York: William T. Grant Foundation. This special evaluation calls attention to one of our nation's greatest needs, helping noncollege youths adjust and develop into competent adults.

Answers to the Marriage Quiz

1. False
2. True
3. False
4. False
5. True

6. True
7. False
8. False
9. False
10. False

11. False
12. True
13. False
14. False
15. False

CHAPTER

10

ontroversial currents swirl around today's women and men. Women increasingly struggle to gain influence and change the worlds of business, politics, and relationships with men. The changes are far from complete, but social reformers hope that, a generation from now, the struggles of the last decades of the twentieth century will have generated more freedom, influence, and flexibility for women. Possibly in the next generation, such issues as equal pay, child care, abortion, rape, and domestic violence will no longer be discussed as "women's issues" but, rather, as economic issues, family issues, and ethical issues—reflecting the equal concern of men and women. Possibly a woman heading a large corporation will not make headlines by virtue of her gender. Half the presidential candidates may be women and nobody will notice.

What would it take to get from here to there? The choices are not simple ones. When Barbara Bush recently went to Wellesley College to celebrate motherhood and wifely virtues, she stimulated a national debate on what it means to be a successful woman. The debate was further fueled by TV anchorwoman Connie Chung's announcement that she would abandon the fast track at CBS in a final drive to become a mother at age 44. At the same time, male role models are also in flux. Wall Street star Peter Lynch, the head of Fidelity Investment's leading mutual fund, resigned to have more time with his family and to pursue humanitarian projects (Gibbs, 1990).

When asked to sketch their futures, many of today's college students say they want good careers, good marriages, and two or three children, but they don't want their children to be raised by strangers (Spade & Reese, 1991). Idealistic? Maybe. Some will reach these goals; some will make other choices as they move through their adult years. Some women will choose to remain single as they pursue their career goals; others will become married but not have children, and yet others will balance the demands of family and work. In a word, not all women have the same goals; neither do all men. What is important is to develop a society free of barriers and discrimination, one that allows women and men to choose freely, to meet their expectations, and to realize their potential.

This chapter is about gender and sexuality, our worlds as female or male. You may remember from our discussion in chapter 1 that many psychologists today prefer to distinguish between sex and gender, using the term *sex* only when referring to such biological factors as sex chromosomes or sexual anatomy and using the term *gender* only when describing the social, cultural, and psychological facets of being female or male. Let's now look more closely at the concept of gender.

Gender

Few aspects of our lives are more central to our identity and social relationships than our gender. We'll define gender and discuss its biological, cognitive, and social roots. We'll also explore such

questions as the following: How many true gender differences are there? What apparent differences are actually cultural stereotypes? How can gender roles be classified? What is the feminist perspective on gender? What is the relationship between ethnicity and gender?

What Is Gender?

What exactly is meant by gender? **Gender** *refers to the sociocultural dimension of being female or male.* Two aspects of gender bear special mention: gender identity and gender role. **Gender identity** *is the sense of being female or male, which most children acquire by the time they are 3 years old.* A **gender role** *is a set of expectations that prescribe how females and males should think, act, and feel.*

Biological Influences

As mentioned in chapter 2, it was not until the 1920s that researchers confirmed the existence of human sex chromosomes, the genetic material that determines our sex. Humans normally have 46 chromosomes arranged in pairs. The 23rd pair may have two X-shaped chromosomes to produce a female, or it may have an X-shaped and a Y-shaped chromosome to produce a male (see figure 10.1).

In the first few weeks of gestation, female and male embryos look alike. Male sex organs start to differ from female sex organs when XY chromosomes in the male embryo trigger the secretion of **androgen,** *the main class of male sex hormones.* Low levels of androgen in a female embryo allow the normal development of female sex organs.

Although rare, an imbalance in this system of hormone secretion can occur during fetal development. If there is insufficient androgen in a male embryo or an excess of androgen in a female embryo, the result is an individual with both male and female sex organs, a hermaphrodite. When genetically female (XX chromosomes) infants are born with masculine-looking genitals, surgery at birth can achieve a genital/genetic match. **Estrogen** *is the main class of female sex hormones.* At puberty, the production of estrogen begins to influence both physical development and behavior, but before then these females often behave in a "tomboyish" manner, acting more aggressively than most girls. They also dress and play in ways that are more characteristic of boys than girls (Ehrhardt, 1987; Money, 1987).

Is the behavior of these surgically corrected girls due to their prenatal hormones, or is it the result of their social experiences? Experiments with various animal species reveal that, when male hormones are injected into female embryos, the females develop masculine physical traits and behave more aggressively (Hines, 1982). However, in humans, hormones exert less control over behavior. Perhaps, because these girls look more masculine, they are treated more like boys and so adopt their boyish ways.

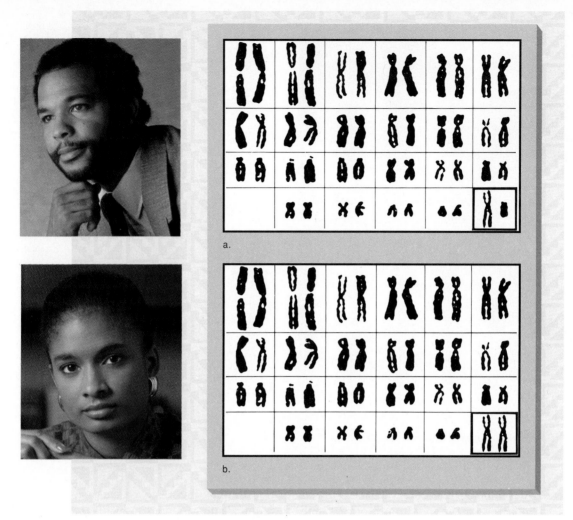

FIGURE 10.1

The genetic difference between males and females. In (a) is the chromosome structure of a male, and in (b) is the chromosome structure of a female. The 23rd pair is shown in the bottom right box of each figure; notice that the Y chromosome of the male is smaller. To obtain this chromosomal picture, a cell is removed from the individual's body, usually from the inside of the mouth. The chromosomes are magnified extensively and then photographed.

Although prenatal hormones may or may not influence gender behavior, psychoanalytic theorists, such as Sigmund Freud and Erik Erikson, have argued that an individual's genitals do play a pivotal role. Freud argued that human behavior and history are directly influenced by sexual drives and suggested that gender and sexual behavior are essentially unlearned and instinctual. Erikson went even further: he argued that, because of genital structure, males are more intrusive and aggressive, females more inclusive and passive. Erikson's critics contend that he has not given enough credit to experience and they argue that women and men are more free to choose their behavior than Erikson allowed. In response, Erikson has clarified his view, pointing out that he never said that biology is the sole determinant of differences between the sexes. Biology, he said, interacts with both cultural and psychological factors to produce behaviors. Today researchers acknowledge that biology is an important influence, but we also know that hormones and sexual anatomy are less important than social and cultural expectations when it comes to behavior.

Social Influences

In our culture, adults discriminate between the sexes shortly after an infant's birth. The "pink and blue" treatment may be applied to girls and boys before they leave the hospital. Soon afterward, differences in hairstyles, clothes, and toys become obvious. Adults and peers reward these differences throughout development, and boys and girls learn gender roles through imitation or observational learning by watching what other people say and do. In recent years, however, the idea that parents are the critical

Theory	Processes	Outcome
Freud's identification theory	Sexual attraction to opposite-sex parent at 3–5 years of age; anxiety about sexual attraction and subsequent identification with same-sex parent at 5–6 years of age	Gender behavior similar to same-sex parent
Social learning theory	Rewards and punishments of gender-appropriate and inappropriate behavior by adults and peers; observation and imitation of models' masculine and feminine behavior	Gender behavior

FIGURE 10.2

A comparison of identification and social learning views of gender development.

agents in gender role development has come under fire (Huston, 1983). Culture, schools, peers, the media, and other family members also influence gender behavior, yet it is important to guard against swinging too far in this direction, because—especially in the early years of development—parents are important influences on gender development.

Two prominent theories address the way children acquire masculine and feminine attitudes and behaviors from their parents: identification theory and social learning theory of gender. **Identification theory** *stems from Freud's view that a preschool child develops a sexual attraction to the parent of the opposite sex. At about the age of 5 or 6, Freud theorized, the child renounces this attraction because of anxious feelings and identifies with the same-sex parent, unconsciously adopting this parent's behavior.* Today, however, many experts do not believe that sexual attraction is involved in gender development. Children become feminine or masculine much earlier than 5 or 6 years of age, even when the same-sex parent is absent from the family. The **social learning theory of gender** *emphasizes that children learn maleness and femaleness by observing and imitating masculine and feminine behavior, as well as through rewards and punishments for what is considered appropriate and inappropriate gender behavior.* For example, parents teach gender behavior when they praise their daughters for playing with

dolls or when they reproach their sons for crying. (A comparison of the identification and social learning theories is presented in figure 10.2.)

Although parents provide children with the first models of gender roles, children also learn from observing other adults in the neighborhood and on television. As children get older, peers also become increasingly important influences. For example, when children play in ways that our culture says are gender-appropriate, they tend to be rewarded by their peers. Those who engage in activities that are considered inappropriate tend to be criticized or abandoned by their peers. Also, children show a clear preference for same-sex peers (Maccoby, 1990; Maccoby & Jacklin, in press). After watching elementary school children repeatedly play in same-sex groups, two researchers characterized the playground as a "gender school" (Luria & Herzog, 1985). Critics of the social learning view argue that gender roles are not as passively acquired as the theory suggests. Another view, known as cognitive developmental theory, argues that individuals actively construct their gender world.

Cognitive Influences

Two prominent theories have addressed the role of cognitive influences on gender: cognitive developmental theory and gender schema theory.

Theory	Processes	Outcome
Cognitive developmental theory	Development of gender constancy, especially around 6–7 years of age, when conservation skills develop; after children develop ability to consistently conceive of themselves as male or female, children often organize their world on the basis of gender, such as selecting same-sex models to imitate	Gender-typed behavior
Gender schema theory	Sociocultural emphasis on gender-based standards and stereotypes; children's attention and behavior are guided by an internal motivation to conform to these gender-based standards and stereotypes, allowing children to interpret the world through a network of gender-organized thoughts	Gender-typed behavior

FIGURE 10.3

A comparison of cognitive developmental and gender schema theories of gender development.

Cognitive Developmental Theory

In the **cognitive developmental theory of gender,** *children's gender typing occurs after they have developed a concept of gender. Once they consistently conceive of themselves as male or female, children often organize their world on the basis of gender.* Initially developed by psychologist Lawrence Kohlberg (1966), this theory argues that gender development proceeds in the following way: a child realizes, "I am a girl; I want to do girl things; therefore, the opportunity to do girl things is rewarding." Having acquired the ability to categorize, children then strive toward consistency in the use of categories and behavior. Kohlberg based his ideas on Piaget's cognitive developmental theory. As children's cognitive development matures, so does their understanding of gender. Although 2-year-olds can apply the labels of *boy* and *girl* correctly to themselves and others, their concept of gender is simple and concrete. Preschool children rely on physical features, such as dress and hairstyle, to decide who falls into which category. Girls are people with long hair, they think, whereas boys are people who never wear dresses. Many preschool children believe that people can change their own gender at will by getting a haircut or a new outfit. They do not yet have the cognitive machinery to think of gender as adults do. According to Kohlberg, all the reinforcement in the world won't modify that fact. However, by the concrete operational stage (the third stage in Piaget's theory, entered at about 6 or 7 years of age), children understand gender constancy—that a male is still a male regardless of whether he wears pants or a skirt, or his hair is short or long (Tavris & Wade, 1984). When their concept of gender constancy is clearly established, children are then motivated to become a competent, or "proper," girl or boy. Consequently, she or he finds female or male activities rewarding and imitates the behavior of same-sex models.

Gender Schema Theory

In our discussion of memory in chapter 6, we indicated that a *schema* is a mental framework that organizes and guides an individual's perceptions. A **gender schema** *organizes the world in terms of female and male.* **Gender schema theory** *states that an individual's attention and behavior are guided by an internal motivation to conform to gender-based sociocultural standards and stereotypes* (Bem, 1981; Levy, 1991; Levy & Carter, 1989; Liben & Signorella, 1987; Martin, 1989; Martin & Halverson, 1987; Martin & Rose, 1991). Gender schema theory suggests that "gender typing" occurs when individuals are ready to encode and organize information along the lines of what is considered appropriate or typical for males and females in a society. Whereas Kohlberg's cognitive developmental theory argues that a particular cognitive prerequisite—gender constancy—is necessary for gender typing, gender schema theory states that a general readiness to respond to and categorize information on the basis of culturally defined gender roles fuels children's gender-typing activities. A comparison of the cognitive developmental and gender schema theories is presented in figure 10.3.

Some researchers have found that children develop a sense of gender as they mature mentally (Serbin & Sprafkin, 1986), but other research shows that young children often have a better understanding of gender than cognitive developmental theory would predict (Carter & Levy, 1988; Carter & Taylor, in press). Psychologists today are more apt to acknowledge the importance of both gender constancy and gender schemas (Levy & Carter, 1989). That is, children actively construct mental concepts of gender, though society determines to a large extent the concepts of gender that are most important.

Gender Stereotypes, Similarities, and Differences

How pervasive is gender role stereotyping? What are the real differences in gender behavior? We will consider each of these questions in turn.

Gender Role Stereotyping

Gender role stereotypes *are broad categories that reflect our impressions and beliefs about females and males.* All stereotypes, whether they are based on gender, ethnicity, or something else, are images of the typical member of a particular social category. The world is extremely complex, and the use of stereotypes is one way we simplify this complexity. If we assign a label, such as "soft," to someone, we then have much less to consider when we think about that person. However, once labels are assigned, they are remarkably difficult to abandon—even in the face of contradictory evidence.

Many stereotypes are so general that they are very ambiguous— "masculine" and "feminine," for instance. Diverse behaviors can be called on to support each stereotype, such as scoring a touchdown and growing facial hair for "masculine" and playing with dolls and wearing lipstick for "feminine."

Stereotypes are often modified in the face of cultural change: during the reign of Louis XIV, for example, French noblemen wore satin breeches, cosmetics, and high heels; in contrast, as our country expanded westward, men were rugged, clothed in leather, and often dirty. Stereotypes also fluctuate according to socioeconomic circumstances. For example, a lower socioeconomic group might be more likely than higher socioeconomic groups to include "rough and tough" as part of a masculine stereotype.

Even though stereotypes are often inaccurate, the label itself can have significant consequences. A man who becomes labeled "feminine," for instance, can experience significant social difficulty in both work and social situations (Mischel, 1970). A woman labeled "masculine" might be excluded from social events, not asked to parties, or passed over for certain jobs, such as teaching young children, that are seen as requiring "feminine" skills.

Stereotyping of females and males is pervasive, according to a far-ranging study of college students in 30 countries (Williams & Best, 1982). Men are widely believed to be dominant, independent, aggressive, achievement-oriented, and enduring, whereas women are widely believed to be nurturant, affiliative, less confident than men, and more helpful than men in times of distress.

A more recent investigation shows that women and men in developed countries perceive themselves as more similar to one another than do women and men who live in less well developed countries (Williams & Best, 1989). This makes sense. In the more highly developed countries, women are more likely to attend college and have careers, and, as sexual equality increases, stereotypes of women and men probably diminish. Women are more likely than men to perceive similarity between the sexes (Williams & Best, 1989).

Gender Similarities and Differences

There is a growing consensus in gender research that differences between the sexes have often been exaggerated (Benbow, 1992; Hyde, 1981; Linn & Hyde, 1991). You might remember our discussion of reducing sexist research in psychology in chapter 1. In the research, it is not unusual to find such statements as the following: "While only 32 percent of the women were found to . . . fully 37 percent of the men were . . ." This difference of 5 percent is a small difference and may not even be statistically significant or capable of being replicated (Denmark & others, 1988). Also, when statements are made about female-male comparisons, such as "males outperform females in math," this does not mean all females versus all males. Rather, it usually means the average math achievement scores for males at certain ages are higher than the average math achievement scores for females. The math achievement scores of females and males overlap considerably, so that, although an average difference may favor males, many females have higher math achievement than many males. Further, there is a tendency to think of differences between females and males as biologically based. Remember that, when differences occur, they may be influenced by society and culture.

Let's now examine some of the differences between the sexes, keeping in mind that (a) the differences are averages; (b) even when differences are reported, there is considerable overlap between the sexes; and (c) the differences may be due primarily to biological factors, sociocultural factors, or both. First, we will examine physical and biological differences, then turn to cognitive and social differences.

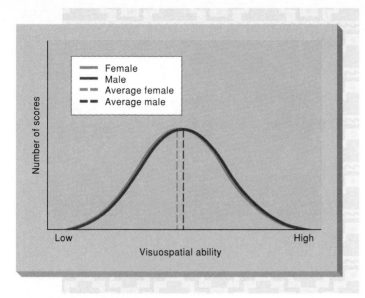

FIGURE 10.4

Visuospatial ability of males and females. Notice that, although an average male's visuospatial ability is higher than an average female's, the overlap between the sexes is substantial. Not all males have better visuospatial ability than all females—the substantial overlap indicates that, although the average score of males is higher, many females outperform many males on such tasks.

Females, on average, live longer than males. Females are also less likely than males to develop physical disorders. Estrogen strengthens the immune system, making females more resistant to infection, for example, and female hormones signal the liver to produce more "good" cholesterol, which makes the blood vessels more "elastic." Testosterone triggers the production of low-density lipoprotein, which clogs blood vessels; as a result, males have twice the risk of coronary disease. Higher levels of stress hormones cause faster blood clotting in males, but also higher blood pressure. Women have about twice the body fat of their male counterparts, most of it concentrated around breasts and hips; in males, fat is more likely to go to the abdomen. Males grow about 10 percent taller than females on average—male hormones promote the growth of long bones; female hormones stop such growth at puberty. In sum, there are many physical differences between females and males. Are there as many cognitive differences?

In a classic review of gender differences in 1974, Eleanor Maccoby and Carol Jacklin concluded that males have better math skills and better visual and spatial ability (the kind of skills an architect would need to design a building's angles and dimensions), whereas females have better verbal abilities. Recently Maccoby (1987) revised her conclusion about several gender dimensions. Verbal differences between the sexes have virtually disappeared, she now says, though the math and spatial differences still exist.

A number of researchers believe there are more cognitive similarities than differences between females and males. They also believe that the differences that exist, such as the math and visuospatial differences, have been exaggerated. Males do outperform females in math, but only for a certain portion of the population—the gifted (Hyde & Frost, in press). Further, males do not always outperform females on all visuospatial tasks; consistent differences occur only in the ability to rotate objects mentally (Linn & Petersen, 1986). Also keep in mind the considerable overlap between females and males. Figure 10.4 shows the small average difference in visuospatial ability that favors males, but it also clearly reveals the substantial overlap in the visuospatial abilities of females and males. In light of this overlap and the fact that females no longer have higher scores on the verbal section of the SAT, we can conclude that cognitive differences between females and males do not exist in many areas, are disappearing in other areas, and are small when they do exist.

Most males are more active and aggressive than most females (Maccoby, 1987; Maccoby & Jacklin, 1974). The consistent difference in aggression often appears in children's development as early as 2 years of age. Although males and females do not experience different emotions, they frequently differ in the emotions they feel free to express in public and in the way in which they express those emotions (Doyle & Paludi, 1991), and females tend to be better at "reading" emotions (Malatesta, 1990). With regard to helping behavior, social psychologists Alice Eagly and Maureen Crowley (1986) argue that the female gender role fosters helping that is nurturant and caring, whereas the male gender role promotes helping that is chivalrous. They found that males are more likely to help in situations in which there is a perceived danger and in which males feel most competent to help. For example, males are more likely than females to help when a person is standing by the roadside with a flat tire, a situation involving some danger and a circumstance in which many males feel a sense of competence—automobile problems. In contrast, if the situation involves volunteering time to help a disturbed child, most researchers have found more helping by females, because there is little danger present for the helper and because females feel more competent in nurturing (Hyde, 1990). As early as elementary school, girls show more caregiving behavior (Zahn-Waxler, 1990). However, in cultures where boys and girls both care for younger siblings, boys and girls are more similar in their nuturant behavior (Whiting, 1989).

Might the way females and males are socialized as they grow up produce differences in the way they talk with each other? Sociolinguist Deborah Tannen (1990) thinks so. To read about her provocative ideas on women and men in conversation, turn to Sociocultural Worlds 10.1.

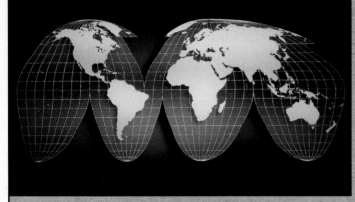

SOCIOCULTURAL WORLDS 10.1

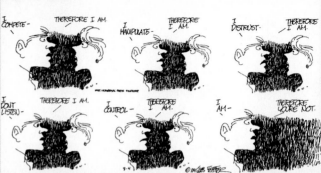

You Just Don't Understand: Women and Men in Conversation

Deborah Tannen (1990) analyzed the talk of women and men. She reported that a common complaint that wives have about their husbands is "He doesn't listen to me anymore." Another is "He doesn't talk to me anymore." Lack of communication, although high on women's lists of reasons for divorce, is much less often mentioned by men.

Tannen makes a distinction between rapport talk and report talk. *Rapport talk* is the language of conversation and a way of establishing connections and negotiating relationships. *Report talk* is public speaking, which men feel more comfortable doing. Men hold center stage through such verbal performances as story telling, joking, and imparting information. Men learn to use talking as a way of getting and keeping attention. By contrast, women enjoy private speaking more, talk that involves discussing similarities and matching experiences. It is men's lack of interest in rapport talk that bothers many women.

Women's dissatisfaction with men's silence at home is captured in a typical cartoon setting of a breakfast table at which a husband and wife are sitting: he's reading the newspaper, while she's glaring at the back of the newspaper. Another cartoon shows a husband opening a newspaper and asking his wife, "Is there anything you want to say to me before I begin reading the newspaper?" The reader knows there isn't but that, as soon as he starts reading the paper, she will think of something. The cartoon highlights the difference between what women and men think talk is for: *to him, talk is for information*, so, when his wife interrupts his reading, it must be to inform him of something he needs to know. Since this is the case, she might as well tell him what she thinks he needs to know before he starts reading. *For her, however, talk is for interaction.* She believes saying things is a way to show involvement; listening is a way to show caring and interest.

Tannen says that the difference between public speaking (report talk) and private speaking (rapport talk) can be understood in terms of status and connection. It is not surprising that women are more comfortable talking when they feel safe and close, among friends and equals, whereas men feel comfortable talking when there is a need to establish and maintain their status in a group. However, the situation is complex. What seems like a bid for status could be intended as a display of closeness, and what seems like distancing may have been intended to avoid the appearance of pulling rank. Harmful and unjustified misinterpretations might be avoided by understanding the conversational styles of the other gender.

When men do all of the talking at a meeting, many women perceive that they are trying to dominate the meeting and are intentionally preventing women from participating, publicly flexing their higher-status muscles. In many instances, even though men do most of the talking in public, it does not mean they want to prevent women from talking. Thus, in such circumstances, women should recognize their lack of participation in meetings and speak up more often instead of blaming men for locking them out, says Tannen.

The problem, then, may not be an individual man, or even men's styles alone, but the difference between women's and men's styles. If so, both men and women can make adjustments. A woman can push herself to speak up without being invited, or she can begin to speak even at the slightest pause in talk. The adjustment should not be one-sided, however; men can learn that women who are not accustomed to speaking up in groups are not as free as they are to do so. By understanding this reluctance on the part of women, men can make them feel more comfortable by warmly encouraging and allowing them to speak rather than hogging public talk.

What about private talk—the rapport talk Tannen describes? Understanding women's and men's different views of rapport talk can help detoxify the situation. Recognizing that women and men have different assumptions about the place of talk in relationships, a woman can observe a man's motivation for reading the morning newspaper at the breakfast table and not interpret it as a rejection of her or a failure in their relationship. At the same time, a man can understand a woman's motivation for talk without interpreting it as an unreasonable demand or a manipulative attempt to prevent him from doing what he wants to do.

REVIEW

The Nature of Gender; Biological, Cognitive, and Social Influences on Gender; and Gender Stereotypes, Similarities, and Differences

Gender refers to the sociocultural dimension of being female or male. Gender identity is the sense of being male or female. Gender role is a set of expectations that prescribes how females and males should think, act, and feel.

The 23rd pair of chromosomes determines our sex. Ordinarily females have two X chromosomes; males have an X and a Y. Chromosomes determine anatomical sex differences, but gender behavior is strongly influenced by society and culture. Freud's and Erikson's theories promote the thesis that anatomy determines behavior. Hormones from the testes (androgen) determine whether an organism will have male genitals (if androgen is secreted) or female genitals (if no androgen is secreted). Androgen in males and estrogen in females are the dominant sexual hormones. Hermaphrodites are individuals whose genitals become intermediate between male and female because of a hormonal imbalance.

Adults and peers reward and model gender-appropriate behavior. Parents—as well as culture, schools, peers, the media, and other family members—influence the development of children's gender behavior. Two prominent theories address the way children acquire masculine and feminine attitudes and behavior from their parents—identification theory and social learning theory.

Two theories address cognitive influences on gender—cognitive developmental theory and gender schema theory. In the cognitive developmental theory, children's gender typing occurs after children have developed a concept of gender, which is achieved in concert with the development of conservation skills at about 6 or 7 years of age. Gender schema theory states that an individual's attention and behavior are guided by an internal motivation to conform to gender-based, sociocultural standards and stereotypes. Gender schema theorists point out that very young children have more gender role knowledge than cognitive developmental theory predicts.

Gender role stereotypes are broad categories that reflect our impressions and beliefs about males and females. These stereotypes are widespread around the world, especially emphasizing the male's power and the female's nurturance. However, in more highly developed countries, females and males are more likely to be perceived as similar. Many gender researchers believe that a number of differences between females and males have been exaggerated. In considering differences, it is important to recognize that they are averages; there is considerable overlap between the sexes; and the differences may be due primarily to biological factors, sociocultural factors, or both. There are a number of physical differences between the sexes, but cognitive differences are either small or nonexistent. At the level of the gifted, the average male outperforms the average female in math achievement. In terms of social behavior, most males are more aggressive and active than most females, but females are usually more adept at "reading" emotions. Females also show more nurturant helping behavior than males. Overall, though, there are more similarities than differences between females and males.

Gender Role Classification

How have gender roles been viewed historically? What is androgyny, and is it the best gender role to adopt? Might adolescent males who identify with a traditional masculine role be prone to problem behaviors? What is gender role transcendence? We will consider each of these questions in turn.

Gender Roles in Historical Perspective

Not too long ago, it was accepted that boys are made of "snips and snails and puppy dogs' tails" and that girls are made of "sugar and spice and all that's nice." Today our culture allows far more diversity. Although a girl's mother might promote traditional femininity, the girl might also be close friends with a tomboy, and her teachers at school might encourage her to be assertive.

In the past, a well-adjusted male was expected to be independent, aggressive, and power-oriented. A well-adjusted female was expected to be dependent, nurturant, and uninterested in power. Further, masculine characteristics were considered to be healthy and good by society; female characteristics were considered undesirable. A classic study in the early 1970s summarized the traits and behaviors that college students believed were characteristic of males and those they believed were characteristic of females (Broverman & others, 1972). The traits clustered into two groups that were labeled "instrumental" and "expressive." The instrumental traits paralleled the male's purposeful, competent entry into the outside world to gain goods for his family; the expressive traits paralleled the female's responsibility to be warm and emotional in the home. Such stereotypes are more harmful to females than to males because the charac-

TABLE 10.1
The Bem Sex-Role Inventory: Are You Androgynous?

The following items are from the Bem Sex-Role Inventory. To find out whether you score as androgynous, first rate yourself on each item, on a scale from 1 (never or almost never true) to 7 (always or almost always true).

1. self-reliant	16. strong personality	31. makes decisions easily	46. aggressive
2. yielding	17. loyal	32. compassionate	47. gullible
3. helpful	18. unpredictable	33. sincere	48. inefficient
4. defends own beliefs	19. forceful	34. self-sufficient	49. acts as a leader
5. cheerful	20. feminine	35. eager to soothe hurt feelings	50. childlike
6. moody	21. reliable	36. conceited	51. adaptable
7. independent	22. analytical	37. dominant	52. individualistic
8. shy	23. sympathetic	38. soft-spoken	53. does not use harsh language
9. conscientious	24. jealous	39. likable	54. unsystematic
10. athletic	25. has leadership abilities	40. masculine	55. competitive
11. affectionate	26. sensitive to the needs of others	41. warm	56. loves children
12. theatrical	27. truthful	42. solemn	57. tactful
13. assertive	28. willing to take risks	43. willing to take a stand	58. ambitious
14. flatterable	29. understanding	44. tender	59. gentle
15. happy	30. secretive	45. friendly	60. conventional

SCORING

(a) Add up your ratings for items 1, 4, 7, 10, 13, 16, 19, 22, 25, 28, 31, 34, 37, 40, 43, 46, 49, 55, and 58. Divide the total by 20. That is your masculinity score.

(b) Add up your ratings for items 2, 5, 8, 11, 14, 17, 20, 23, 26, 29, 32, 35, 38, 41, 44, 47, 50, 53, 56, and 59. Divide the total by 20. That is your femininity score.

(c) If your masculinity score is above 4.9 (the approximate median for the masculinity scale) and your femininity score is above 4.9 (the approximate femininity median) then you would be classified as androgynous on Bem's scale.

From Janet S. Hyde, *Half the Human Experience: The Psychology of Women*, 3d ed. Copyright © 1985 D. C. Heath and Company, Lexington, MA. Reprinted by permission.

teristics assigned to males are more valued by society than those assigned to females. The beliefs and stereotypes have led to the negative treatment of women because of their sex, or what is called *sexism*. Females receive less attention in school, are less visible in leading roles on television, are rarely depicted as competent, dominant characters in children's books, are paid less than males even when they have more education, and are underrepresented in decision-making roles throughout our society, from corporate executive suites to Congress.

Androgyny

In the 1970s, as both females and males became dissatisfied with the burdens imposed by their strictly stereotyped roles, alternatives to "masculinity" and "femininity" were explored. Instead of thinking of masculinity and femininity as a continuum, with more of one meaning less of the other, some psychologists argued that people could show both *expressive* and *instrumental* traits. This thinking led to the concept of **androgyny,** *the presence of desirable masculine and feminine characteristics in the same individual* (Bem, 1977; Spence & Helmreich, 1978). An androgynous individual might be a male who is assertive (masculine) and nurturant (feminine) or a female who is dominant (masculine) and sensitive to others' feelings (feminine).

Psychological measures have been developed to assess androgyny. One of the most widely used gender measures is the Bem Sex-Role Inventory, developed by a leading early proponent of androgyny, Sandra Bem. To see what the items on Bem's measure are like, turn to table 10.1. Based on their responses to the items in the Bem Sex-Role Inventory, individuals are classified as having one of four gender role orientations: masculine, feminine, androgynous, or undifferentiated (see figure 10.5). An androgynous individual is simply a female or male who has a high degree of both feminine (expressive) and masculine (instrumental) traits. An undifferentiated individual is high on neither feminine nor masculine traits. Androgynous males and females, according to Bem, are described as more flexible and more mentally healthy than either masculine or feminine individuals, whereas undifferentiated individuals are the least competent. To a degree, though, context influences which gender role is most adaptive. In close relationships, a feminine or an androgynous gender role may be more desirable because of the expressive nature of close relationships. However, a masculine or an androgynous gender role may be more desirable in academic and work settings because of their demands for action and assertiveness. Also, the culture in which individuals live plays an important role in determining what is adaptive. On the one

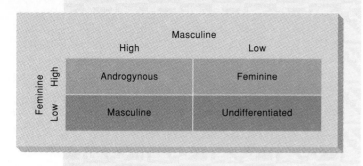

FIGURE 10.5

Gender role classification.

hand, increasing numbers of children in the United States and other modern countries, such as Sweden, are being raised to behave in androgynous ways. On the other hand, traditional gender roles continue to dominate many cultures around the world. To read abut the traditional gender roles in Egypt and China, turn to Sociocultural Worlds 10.2.

Traditional Masculinity and Problem Behaviors in Adolescent Males

In our discussion of masculinity so far, we have discussed how the masculine role has been accorded a prominent status in the United States, as well as in most other cultures. However, might there be a negative side to traditional masculinity, especially in adolescence? An increasing number of gender theorists and researchers believe there is.

Joseph Pleck and his colleagues (Pleck, 1983; Pleck, Sonnenstein, & Ku, in press) believe that what defines traditional masculinity in many Western societies includes engaging in certain behaviors that, although officially socially disapproved, validate masculinity. That is, in the male adolescent culture, male adolescents perceive that they are more masculine, and that others will perceive them as more masculine, if they engage in premarital sex, drink alcohol and take drugs, and participate in delinquent activities.

In one recent investigation, the gender role orientation and problem behaviors of 1,680 15-to-19-year-old males were assessed (Pleck, Sonnenstein, & Ku, in press). In this study—referred to as the National Survey of Adolescent Males—there was strong evidence that problem behaviors in adolescent males are associated with their attitudes toward masculinity. The adolescent males who reported traditional beliefs about masculinity (for example, endorsing such items as "A young man should be tough, even if he's not big," "It is essential for a guy to get respect from others," and "Men are always ready for sex") also were likely to say that they had school difficulties, engaged in alcohol and drug use, participated in delinquent activities, and were sexually active.

The idea that male problem behaviors have something to do with "masculinity" has recently gotten the attention of policy makers. U.S. Department of Health and Human Services Secretary Louis Sullivan (1991) called for action to address a generation whose manhood is measured by the caliber of gun he carries or the number of children he fathers. In a similar vein, Virginia Governor Douglas Wilder (1991) urged policy makers to get across the message that, contrary to what many of today's youths think, making babies is no act of manhood. Addressing and challenging traditional beliefs about masculinity in adolescent males may have the positive outcome of helping reduce their problem behaviors.

Gender Role Transcendence

Although the concept of androgyny was an improvement over exclusive notions of femininity and masculinity, it has turned out to be less of a panacea than many of its early proponents envisioned (Doyle & Paludi, 1991). Some theorists, such as Pleck (1981), believe that the idea of androgyny should be replaced with **gender role transcendence**, *the belief that, when an individual's competence is at issue, it should not be conceptualized on the basis of masculinity, femininity, or androgyny, but rather on a personal basis.* Thus, rather than merging gender roles or stereotyping people as "masculine" or "feminine," Pleck believes we should begin to think about people as people. However, both the concepts of androgyny and gender role transcendence draw attention away from women's unique needs and the power imbalance between women and men in most cultures (Hare-Muston & Maracek, 1988). As we will see next, a major focus of the feminist agenda is to reduce that imbalance of power.

The Feminist Perspective on Gender

Many feminist scholars believe that, historically, psychology has portrayed human behavior with a "male dominant theme" (DeFour & Paludi, in press; Denmark & Paludi, in press; Paludi, 1992). They also believe that sexism is still rampant in society. As leading feminist scholar Jean Baker Miller (1986) wrote in *Toward a New Psychology of Women,*

> In the last decade it has become clearer that if women are trying to define and create a full personhood, we are engaged in a huge undertaking. We see that this attempt means building a new way of living which encompasses all realms of life, from global economic, social and political levels to the most intimate personal relationships. (p. xi)

Feminist scholars are putting greater emphasis on women's life experiences and development, including girls and women as authorities about their own experiences, or as Harvard psychologist Carol Gilligan (1990, 1992) advocates, listening to women's

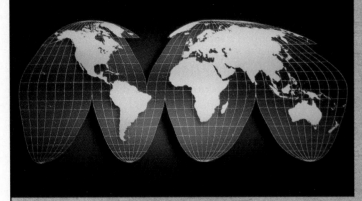

Gender Roles in Egypt and China

In recent decades, male and female roles in the United States have become increasingly similar—that is, androgynous. In many countries, though, gender roles have remained gender specific. In Egypt, for example, the division of labor between males and females is dramatic. Egyptian males are socialized to work in the public sphere, females in the private world of home and childrearing. The Islamic religion dictates that a man's duty is to provide for his family, a woman's to care for her family and household; any deviations from these traditional gender roles are severely disapproved of (Dickersheid & others, 1988).

In many Islamic countries, women do not have the same legal rights as men, and in recent years some of their rights have eroded further. In Egypt, for example, the Supreme Court in 1985 struck down a 1979 law that gave a woman the right to divorce her husband should he take a second wife. In Sudan, the military regime, which seized power in 1989, refused to allow women who are not accompanied by a father, husband, or brother to leave the country without permission from one of the three. The Family Code adopted by Algeria in 1984 gave a husband the right to divorce his wife for almost any reason and eject her from the family home. During debate over the code, one legislator actually proposed specifying the length of the stick that a husband might use to beat his wife.

Similarly, in the People's Republic of China, the teachings of fifth-century B.C. Chinese philosopher Confucius have been used to enforce female inferiority. Beginning with the revolution in 1949, however, women have gained economic freedom and greater equality in marriage, but even the socialist government has not completely uprooted the old patriarchal traditions of male supremacy. Chinese women still make considerably less money than Chinese men in comparable positions, and in rural China a tradition of male supremacy still governs many women's lives.

In Egypt, near the Aswan Dam, women are returning from the Nile River, where they have filled their water jugs. How might gender role socialization for girls in Egypt compare with that in the United States?

The old patriarchal tradition of male supremacy in China is still present in many Chinese families, especially in rural areas. When women do have a career outside the home in China, they earn considerably less money than men do.

voices; on women's ways of knowing (Belenky & others, 1986); on women's career and family roles (Baruch, Biener, & Barnett, 1987); on the abuse of women and rape (McBride, 1990; Russo, 1990); and on women's experiences of connectedness and self-determination (Brown & Gilligan, 1990; Chodorow, 1989; Gilligan, Brown, & Rogers, 1990; Josselson, 1987; Lerner, 1989; Miller, 1986).

Miller (1976, 1986) has been an important voice in stimulating the examination of psychological issues from a female perspective. She believes that the study of women's psychological development opens up paths to a better understanding of all psychological development, male or female. She also concludes that, when researchers examine what women have been doing in life, they find that a large part of it is active participation in the development of others. In Miller's view, women often try to interact with others in ways that foster the others' development along many dimensions—emotionally, intellectually, and socially.

Many feminist thinkers believe that it is important for women not only to maintain their competency in relationships but to be self-motivated too. Miller believes that, through increased self-determination and already developed relationship skills, many women will gain greater power in the American culture. As feminist scholar Harriet Lerner (1989) concludes in her book *The Dance of Intimacy*, it is important for women to bring to their relationships nothing less than a strong, assertive, independent, and authentic self. She believes that competent relationships are those in which the separate "I-ness" of both persons can be appreciated and enhanced while staying emotionally connected to each other.

Not only is a distinct female voice an important dimension of the feminist perspective on gender, but so is the effort to reduce and eventually end prejudice and discrimination against women (Paludi, 1992; Yentsch & Sindermann, 1992). Although women have broken through many male bastions in the past several decades, feminists argue that much work is left to be done. Feminists today believe that too many people passively accept traditional gender roles and believe that discrimination no longer exists in politics, work, the family, and education. They encourage individuals to question these

Jean Baker Miller, a leading feminist scholar, believes it is important for women not only to maintain their competency in relationships but to balance this other-oriented competence with an increased motivation for self-determination.

assumptions, and especially strive to get females to evaluate the gender circumstances of their lives. For example, if you are a female, you may remember situations in which you were discriminated against because of your sex. If derogatory comments are made to you because you are a female, you may ask yourself why you have allowed these comments to go unchallenged or why they made you so angry. Feminists hope that, if you are a male, you will become more conscious of gender issues, of female and male roles, and of fairness and sensitivity in female-male interactions and relationships. To read about some of the inequities that women around the world continue to experience in the 1990s, turn to Sociocultural Worlds 10.3.

Ethnicity and Gender

Are gender-related attitudes and behavior similar across ethnic groups? All ethnic minority women are women and all ethnic minority men are men, so there are many similarities in the gender-related attitudes of women and of men across ethnic minority groups. Nevertheless, the different ethnic and cultural experiences of Black American, Hispanic American, Asian American, and Native American women and men need to be considered in understanding their gender-related attitudes and behavior, because in some instances even small differences can be important (Swanson & Cunningham, 1991; Walsh, Katz, & Downey, 1991). For example, the socialization of males and females in other cultures who subsequently migrate to America often reflects a wider gap between men and women than in America. Let's first examine the concept of women of color, then turn to information about men and women from specific ethnic minority groups.

Women of Color

The term *women of color* has gained considerable popularity in recent years, to the extent that it, too, has become a stereotype (DeFour & Paludi, in press). However, women of color are as varied and differ as much among themselves as White women (Hall, 1991; Hooks, 1991; Kimmel & Garco, 1991).

The term *women of color* has become popular among Asian, Latin, African, and Native American women living in the United States (Bandarage, 1986). The term is especially

Shown here are women attending an International Women's Conference in Mexico City. Although many cultures around the world remain male-dominant, the feminist viewpoint is becoming an important voice.

popular among those who are feminists but who fundamentally disagree with the White, middle-class women's movement. For women who are oppressed by both patriarchy and White supremacy, women of color—*mujeres de color*—is a concept that underscores the pride and power of individuals as women and as people of color.

Ethnic Minority Females

Let's now consider the behavior and psychological orientations of females from specific ethnic minority groups, beginning with Black females and then, in turn, Asian Americans, Hispanic Americans, and Native Americans.

Psychologists have begun to focus only recently on the behavior of Black females. For too long, Black females served only as a comparison group for White females or as the subjects in studies of poverty, unwed motherhood, and other topics related to the underclass (Hall, Evans, & Selice, 1989). The nature and focus of psychological research on Black females have begun to change—to an extent paralleling societal changes

Fortunately, in the past decade, psychologists have begun to study the positive traits of Black females, such as self-esteem, achievement, motivation, and self-control. As with White women, connectedness in close relationships is an important concern of Black women.

Women's Struggle for Equality: An International Journey

What are the political, economic, educational, and psychosocial conditions of women around the world? Frances Culbertson (1991), president of the section of the American Psychological Association on the Clinical Psychology of Women, recently summarized these conditions.

Women and Politics

In politics, too often women are treated like burdens rather than assets. Especially in developing countries, women marry early and have many children quickly, in many cases before their undernourished bodies have an opportunity to mature. In such developing countries, women need greater access to education, work, health care, and especially family planning. Some experts on women's issues believe that these needs would have a better chance of being met if women were more strongly represented at the decision-making and managerial levels of governments and international organizations. For example, in 1990, less than 10 percent of the members of national legislatures were women and, for every 100 ministerial-level positions around the world, only 5 were filled by women (Sadik, 1990).

Women and Employment

Women's work around the world is more limiting and narrower than that of men (Monagle, 1990). Bank tellers and secretaries are most often women. Domestic workers in North America and in Central and South America are most often women. Around the world, jobs defined as women's work too often carry low pay, low status, and little security. Two authors described many of these circumstances as "job ghettos" (Seager & Olson, 1985). In 1990 the only countries in the world that had maternity leave and guaranteed jobs on the basis of national law were Brazil, Chile, Mexico, Finland, Switzerland, Germany, Italy, Egypt, Syria, Russia, Japan, and Thailand. Among the major countries without these provisions were the United States, England, and France.

Women and Education

The countries with the fewest women being educated are in Africa, where in some areas the education of women is completely absent. Canada, the United States, and Russia have the highest percentage of educated women (Seager & Olson, 1985). In developing countries, 67 percent of the women and 50 percent of the men over the age of 25 have never been to school. In 1985, 80 million more boys than girls were in primary and secondary educational settings around the world.

Women and Psychosocial Issues

Women around the world, in every country, experience violence, often by someone close to them. In Canada 10 percent of the women report that they have been beaten in their homes by the man they live with, and in the United States almost 2 million women are beaten in their homes each year (Seager & Olson, 1986). In a recent survey, "The New Woman Ethics Report," wife abuse was listed as number one among 15 of the most pressing concerns facing society today (Johnson, 1990). Although most countries around the world now have battered women's shelters, there are some countries where beating women continues to be accepted and expected.

In a recent investigation of depression in high-income countries, the women were twice as likely as the men to be diagnosed as being in depression (Nolen-Hoeksema, 1990). In the United States, from adolescence through adulthood, females are more likely to be depressed than males (McGrath & others, 1990). There are many sociocultural inequities and experiences that have contributed to the greater incidence of depression in females than males. We will discuss the nature of depression in women in greater detail in chapter 14, Abnormal Psychology.

(Thomas, 1991). In the past decade, psychologists have studied the more positive traits of Black females, such as self-esteem, achievement, motivation, and self-control.

Ethnic minority women have experienced both racism and sexism. As indicated in chapter 1, Black women are underrepresented in all areas of psychology and other academic disciplines. However, these women have shown remarkable ingenuity and perseverance. For example, in 1986, 499 Black women earned doctoral degrees. This represents only 2 percent of the Ph.D.'s awarded (compared with 6.4 percent of the general population represented by Black females), yet it also represents a 16 percent increase over the number earned in 1977. Despite such gains, our society needs to make a strong commitment to providing ethnic minority women with the opportunities they deserve.

Asian women are often expected to carry on domestic duties, to marry, to become obedient helpers of their mothers-in-law, and to bear children, especially males (Sue, 1989). These expectations are deep-rooted. In China, for instance, a mother's responsibility for the emotional nurturance and well-being of her family derives from Confucian ethics (Huang & Ying, 1989). However, as China has become modernized, these roles have become less rigid. Similarly, in acculturated Chinese families in the United States, only derivatives of these rigidly defined roles remain. For example, Chinese American females are not entirely relegated to subservient roles.

In Mexican families, women traditionally have assumed the role of homemaker and caretaker of children. This continues to be the norm, although less so than in the past (Ramirez, 1989). Historically, the Mexican female's role has been one of self-denial; her needs have been subordinate to those of other family members. However, Mexican American families have recently achieved greater equality between males and females (Ramirez & Arce, 1981). Of special significance is the increased frequency of Mexican American women's employment outside the home, which in many instances has enhanced a wife's status in the family and in decision making (Baca Zinn, 1980; Marín & Marín, 1991).

For Native Americans, the amount of social and governing control exhibited by women and men depends on the tribe (LaFromboise & Low, 1989). For example, in the traditional

Traditionally, in Mexicans, machismo has required men to be forceful and strong and to withhold affection. How is the feeling of machismo being transformed in today's Mexican American families?

matriarchal Navajo family, an older woman might live with her husband, her unmarried children, her married daughter, and the daughter's husband and children (Ryan, 1980). In patriarchal tribes, women function as the "core" of the family, maintaining primary responsibility for the welfare of children. Grandmothers and aunts often provide child care. As with other ethnic minority females, Native American females who have moved to urban areas experience the cultural conflict of traditional ethnic values and the values of the American society (Ferron, 1991).

Ethnic Minority Males

Ethnic minority males have also experienced considerable discrimination and have had to develop coping strategies in the face of adversity. Again, let's consider Blacks, Asian Americans, Hispanic Americans, and Native Americans.

Statistics portray the difficulties many Black males have faced. Black American males of all ages are three times as likely as White American males to live below the poverty line. Black males are also twice as likely as White males to die between the ages of 20 and 44. Black male heads of households earn 70 percent of the income of their White male counterparts. Although they make up only 6.3 percent of the U.S. population, Black males comprise 42 percent of all jail inmates and more than 50 percent of all men executed for any reason in the past 50 years.

The sociocultural contexts of discrimination must be taken into account to understand these statistics (Evans & Whitfield, 1988). Just as with Black females, researchers are beginning to focus on some of the more positive dimensions of Black males. Researchers are finding, for example, that Black males are especially good at the use of body language in communication, the decoding of nonverbal cues, multilingual/multicultural expression, and improvised problem solving.

Asian cultural values are reflected in traditional patriarchal Chinese and Japanese families (Evans, 1992; Sue, 1989). Fathers are typically dignified, authoritative, remote, and aloof. Sons are generally valued over daughters, and first-born sons have an especially high status. As with Asian American females, the acculturation experienced by Asian American males has eroded some of the rigid gender roles that characterized Asian families in the past. Fathers still are often the figurative heads of families, especially when dealing with the public, but in private they have relinquished some of their decision-making power to their wives (Huang & Ying, 1989).

In Mexican families, men have traditionally assumed the instrumental role of provider and protector of the family (Ramirez, 1989). The concept of machismo—being a strong, forceful man—continues to influence men and the patriarchal nature of Mexican families, though less so than in the past. Traditionally machismo has required men to withhold affection. It has involved a strong sense of personal honor, family, loyalty, and care for children, but it also has involved exaggerated masculinity and aggression (Trankina, 1983). The concepts of machismo and absolute patriarchy currently are diminishing in influence, although adolescent males are still given much more freedom than adolescent females in Mexican American families.

Some Native American tribes are also patriarchal, with the male being the head of the family and the primary decision maker. In some tribes, though, child care is shared by men. For example, Mescalero Apache men take responsibility for children when not working away from the family (Ryan, 1980). Autonomy is highly valued among the male children in many Native American tribes, with the males operating semi-independently at an early age (LaFromboise & Low, 1989). As with Native American females, increased movement to urban areas has led to modifications in the values and traditions of some Native American males.

REVIEW

Gender Role Classification, the Feminist Perspective, and Ethnicity and Gender

In the past, a well-adjusted female was supposed to show expressive traits, a well-adjusted male instrumental traits. Masculine traits were more valued by society. Sexism was widespread. In the 1970s, alternatives to traditional masculinity and femininity were explored. It was proposed that individuals could show both expressive and instrumental traits. This thinking led to the development of the concept of androgyny—the presence of desirable feminine and masculine traits in the same individual. Gender role measures often categorize individuals as masculine, feminine, androgynous, or undifferentiated. Androgynous individuals are often more flexible and mentally healthy, although the particular context and the individual's culture also determine the adaptiveness of a gender role orientation. What defines traditional masculinity in many Western societies includes engaging in certain behaviors that, although officially socially disapproved of, validate masculinity. Researchers have found that problem behaviors in adolescent males—school difficulties, drug use, and delinquency, for example—are associated with traditional beliefs about masculinity. One alternative to androgyny is gender role transcendence but, like androgyny, it diverts attention away from the imbalance of power between women and men.

Feminist scholars are developing new perspectives that focus on girls' and women's experiences and development. Girls' and women's strengths have been especially important in relationships and connections with others. A special emphasis is that, while staying emotionally connected to significant others, females can enhance their psychological well-being by developing stronger self-determination. The feminist perspective emphasizes the importance of reducing, and eventually ending, prejudice and discrimination against women.

There are many similarities among women in different ethnic minority groups and among men in different ethnic minority groups, but even small differences can sometimes be important. The term women of color has gained considerable popularity in recent years. However, it is important to recognize the diversity that exists among women of color. Women who adopt the label women of color believe that it underscores their pride and power as women and as people of color. Researchers in psychology have only begun to focus on female behavior in specific ethnic groups in a positive way. Many ethnic minority females have experienced the double jeopardy of racism and sexism. In many instances, Asian American, Hispanic American, and Native American females have lived in patriarchal, male-dominated families, although gender roles have become less rigid in these ethnic groups in recent years. Just as ethnic minority females have experienced considerable discrimination and have had to develop coping strategies in the face of adversity, so have ethnic minority males. Just as with Black females, researchers are beginning to focus more on the positive dimensions of Black males. A patriarchal, male-dominant orientation has characterized many ethnic minority groups, such as Asian American, Hispanic American, and Native American, although women are gaining greater decision-making power in these cultures, especially women who develop careers and work outside of the home.

Sexuality

The importance of sex in our lives was vividly captured by Woody Allen's observation: "Sex without love is an empty experience. Yes, but as empty experiences go, it is one of the best." We do not need sex for everyday survival the way we need food and water, but we do need it for the survival of the species. Following are some of the fascinating inquiries about our sexual lives that we will examine: What is the nature of the human sexual response? What are our sexual attitudes and behavior like? What kind of psychosexual disorders can individuals develop? How do sexual violence and pornography influence our lives? What kinds of sexually transmitted diseases can people get? How sexually literate are Americans?

The Human Sexual Response

The first time you experienced a tingling sensation in the genital area, you may have been reading a book, thinking about a boy or a girl you were attracted to, or even sleeping, dreaming about a pleasurable encounter. If you wondered what that tingling sensation was about you were not alone. Most of us became sexual beings before we had any idea what sex is all about. What causes us to get sexually aroused?

Sexual Arousal

Both biological and psychological factors are involved in sexual arousal. Human sexual behavior is influenced by the presence of hormones in the bloodstream. Remember from an earlier discussion that sex hormones are among the most powerful and subtle chemicals in nature. Also recall that these hormones are controlled by the master gland in the brain, the pituitary, and that in females estrogen is the main class of sex hormones, whereas in males androgen is the main hormone. In males the testes secrete androgen from puberty on in amounts that do not vary over a short period of time (see figure 10.6 for a diagram of the male genital system, including the testes). Males, then, are hormonally ready to be stimulated to engage in sexual behavior at any time.

At puberty females' ovaries begin to produce the female sex hormone, estrogen (see figure 10.7 for a diagram of the female genital system). Unlike androgen, however, estrogen is not constantly produced. Rather, estrogen levels vary over an approximate monthly cycle. The levels of estrogen are highest when a female is ovulating (releasing an egg from one of her ovaries), which is midway through the menstrual cycle, the time when the female is most likely to become pregnant. The high levels of estrogen increase the probability the egg will be fertilized. In lower animals, this is the only time that females are receptive to male sexual overtures. In humans, although the strength of sexual interest varies with estrogen levels, women are receptive to sexual involvement throughout the menstrual cycle. Thus, in humans, although hormonal control over behavior is

Sexuality plays an important role in our lives. For most of us, sex has had its pleasurable and its unpleasurable moments. In thinking about the nature of sexuality, take a few moments and examine your own sexual history. What would you have changed? What would you like to be the same?

less dominant, hormones still play an important part in sexual arousal. However, as we will see next, sociocultural and cognitive factors also play important roles.

What turns people on is influenced by their sociocultural background, their individual preferences, and their cognitive interpretations. Some cultures consider certain sexual pleasures as normal, whereas others may see them as weird and abnormal. Consider the people who live on the small island of Ines Beag off the coast of Ireland. They are among the most sexually repressed people in the world. They know nothing about French kissing or hand stimulation of the penis, nudity is detested, and premarital sex is out of the question. Men believe that sexual intercourse reduces their energy level. Sexual intercourse takes place as quickly as possible and only at night, when the husband opens his nightclothes under the covers and the wife raises her nightgown. Female orgasm is rare (Messinger, 1971).

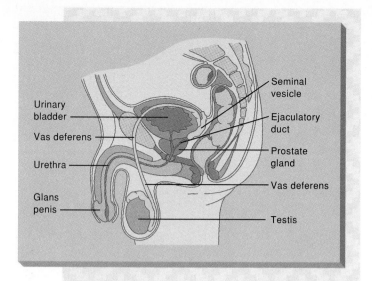

FIGURE 10.6

Male reproductive organs. The testes are the male gonads that produce sperm cells and manufacture the male androgen called testosterone. The glans penis is the head of the penis. The vas deferens is the duct through which stored sperm is passed. It is the vas deferens that is cut or blocked in a vasectomy. The seminal vesicles are the two sacs of the male internal genitalia, which secrete nutrients to help sperm become motile. The prostrate gland is a structure of the internal male genitalia that secretes a fluid into the semen prior to ejaculation to aid sperm motility and elongate sperm life. The urethra is the tube through which the bladder empties urine outside the body and through which the male sperm exits.

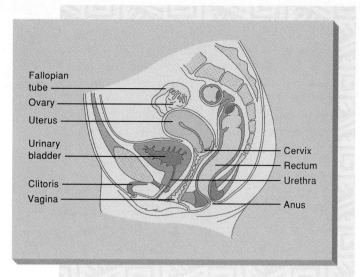

FIGURE 10.7

Female reproductive organs. The uterus is a pear-shaped, hollow structure of the female genitalia, in which the embryo and fetus develop prior to birth. The thick, muscular wall of the uterus expands and contracts during pregnancy. The cervix is the mouth of the uterus, through which the vagina extends. The vagina is the hollow, tunneled structure of the female internal genitalia; its reproductive functions are to receive the penis and its ejaculate, to be a route of exit for the newborn, and to provide an exit for menstrual flow. The clitoris is a part of the female genitalia that is very sensitive to stimulation. The ovary houses ova prior to their maturation and discharge; it also produces estrogen. The fallopian tubes are the routes through which eggs leave the ovaries on their way to the uterus. It is in the fallopian tubes that fertilization usually takes place.

By contrast, consider the Mangaian culture in the South Pacific. Boys learn about masturbation as early as 6 or 7 and, at 13, boys undergo a ritual that introduces them to sexual manhood. They are instructed about sexual strategies, such as how to help their partner achieve orgasm before they do. Two weeks after the ceremony, each 13-year-old boy has intercourse with an experienced woman. She helps him hold back ejaculation so she can achieve orgasm with him. By the end of adolescence, Mangaians have sex virtually every day, and Mangaian women report a high frequency of orgasm.

Ours is a culture more liberal than the Ines Beag, but we do not come close to matching the sexual practices of the Mangaians. The cultural diversity in sexual behavior around the world is a testimony to the importance of environmental experiences in determining sexual arousal. For humans, however, experience takes on a more powerful role in sexuality. Although we cannot mate in midair, as bees do, or display our plumage as magnificently as peacocks, humans can talk about sex with each other, read about it in magazines, and watch it on television or at the movies.

Touch, visual cues, certain words written or heard, and smells can all be sexually arousing. However, there are individual differences in what turns people on. One woman may thrill to having her ears nibbled; another may find it annoying. Most of us think of kissing as highly stimulating, but, in a vast majority of tribal societies, kissing is either unknown or thought to be disgusting (Rice, 1989).

Sexual fantasies are also a common sexual stimulant for both men and women. In one investigation, 60 percent of the college men and women said they engaged in fantasy during intercourse (Sue, 1979). Oral-genital sex and being found irresistible by others were the most common fantasies of both males and females. Sex with an imaginary lover was a much more common fantasy of the males than of the females.

Fantasizing can be a healthy way of fulfilling sexual desires, a way of imagining ourselves the way we would like to be, or even a way of rehearsing actions that we plan to perform. As long as the fantasies do not become obsessive, fantasy can enhance rather than hinder the development of an intimate sexual relationship.

Gender and Sexuality   **317**

The Human Sexual Response Cycle

How do humans respond physiologically during sexual activity? To answer this question, gynecologist William Masters and his colleague Virginia Johnson (1966) carefully observed and measured the physiological responses of 382 female and 312 male volunteers as they masturbated or had sexual intercourse. The **human sexual response cycle** *consists of four phases—excitement, plateau, orgasm, and resolution—identified by Masters and Johnson* (see figure 10.8).

The *excitement phase* begins erotic responsiveness; it lasts from several minutes to several hours, depending on the nature of the sex play involved. Two processes characterize this phase: engorgement of blood vessels and increased blood flow in genital areas, and muscle tension. The most obvious signs of response in this phase are partial erection of the penis and lubrication of the vagina.

The second phase of the human sexual response is called the *plateau phase*; it is a continuation and heightening of the arousal begun in the excitement phase. The increases in breathing, pulse rate, and blood pressure that occurred during the excitement phase become more intense, penile erection is more complete, and orgasm is closer.

Sexual behavior has its magnificent moments throughout the animal kingdom. Insects mate in midair, peacocks display their plumage, and male elephant seals have prolific sex lives. Experience plays a more important role in human sexual behavior. We can talk about sex with each other, read about it in magazines, and watch it on television and the movie screen.

The third phase of the human sexual response cycle is *orgasm*. How long does orgasm last? Some individuals sense that time is standing still when it takes place, but orgasm lasts only for about 3 to 15 seconds. For both sexes, orgasm involves an explosive discharge of neuromuscular tension and an intense pleasurable feeling.

Following the 3 to 15 seconds of orgasm, the individual enters the final phase, *resolution*. In this phase, arousal diminishes and engorged blood vessels return to their normal state. One difference between males and females in this phase is that males enter a refractory period, lasting from several minutes to an entire day, in which they cannot have another orgasm. Females have no refractory period and may repeatedly experience orgasm.

Sexual Attitudes and Behavior

Gathering information about sexual attitudes and behavior has not always been a straightforward task. Consider how you would respond if someone asked you how often you have intercourse or how many different sexual partners you have had. When sexual surveys are conducted, the people most likely to respond are those with liberal sexual attitudes who engage in liberal sexual behaviors. Thus, what researchers know is limited by the reluctance of individuals to answer questions candidly about ex-

tremely personal matters and by an inability to get any answer, candid or otherwise, from individuals who believe that talking about sex with strangers should not be done. With these cautions in mind, we will now examine a number of surveys of sexual attitudes and behavior at different points in the twentieth century, considering heterosexual and homosexual attitudes and behavior.

Heterosexual Attitudes and Behavior

Had you been a college student in 1940, you probably would have had a very different attitude toward many aspects of sexuality than you do today, especially if you are female. A review of college students' sexual practices and attitudes from 1900 to 1980 reveals two important trends (Darling, Kallon, & Van Duesen, 1984). First, the percentage of young people reporting intercourse has dramatically increased, and, second, the proportion of females reporting sexual intercourse has increased more rapidly than in the case of males, although males started off having intercourse more frequently. Prior to the 1970s, about twice as many college males as females reported they engaged in sexual intercourse, but since 1970 the number of males and females has become about equal. These changes suggest that major shifts in the standards governing sexual behavior have taken place—that is, movement away from a double standard in which it is more appropriate for males than females to have intercourse (Robinson & others, 1991).

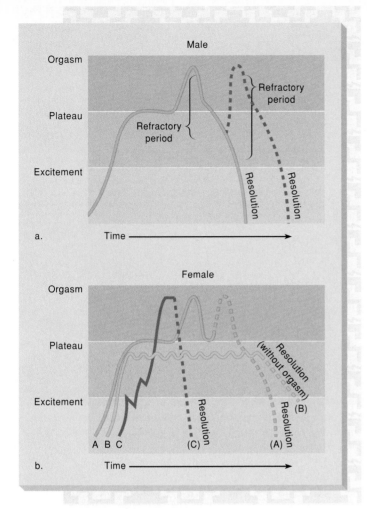

FIGURE 10.8

Male and female human sexual response patterns. (a) This diagram shows the excitement, plateau, orgasm, and resolution phases of the human male sexual response pattern. Notice that males enter a refractory period, which lasts from several minutes up to a day, in which they cannot have another orgasm. (b) This diagram shows the excitement, plateau, orgasm, and resolution phases of the human female sexual response pattern. Notice that female sexual responses follow one of three basic patterns. Pattern A somewhat resembles the male pattern, except that pattern A includes the possibility of multiple orgasm (the second peak in pattern A) without falling below the plateau level. Pattern B represents nonorgasmic arousal. Pattern C represents intense female orgasm, which resembles the male pattern in its intensity and rapid resolution.

Two surveys that included wider age ranges of adults verified these trends. Morton Hunt's survey of more than 2,000 adults in the 1970s revealed more permissiveness toward sexuality than Alfred Kinsey's inquiries in the 1940s (Hunt, 1974; Kinsey, Pomeroy, & Martin, 1948). Hunt's survey, however, may have overestimated sexual permissiveness be-

cause it was based on a sample of *Playboy* magazine readers. Kinsey found that foreplay consisted of a kiss or two, but, by the 1970s, Hunt discovered that foreplay had lengthened, averaging 15 minutes. Hunt also found that individuals in the 1970s were using more varied sexual techniques in their lovemaking. Oral-genital sex, virtually taboo at the time of Kinsey's survey, was more accepted in the 1970s.

Two more things about heterosexual attitudes and behavior are important to consider: the double standard mentioned earlier and the nature of extramarital sex. Although it has recently become more appropriate for females to engage in premarital sex, some vestiges of the double standard still exist (Erickson & Rapkin, 1991). As one male adolescent remarked, "I feel a lot of pressure from my buddies to go for the score." Further evidence of physical and emotional exploitation of females was found in a survey of 432 14-to-18-year-old adolescents (Goodchilds & Zellman, 1984). Both male and female adolescents accepted the right of the male adolescent to be sexually aggressive but left matters up to the female to set the limits for the male's overtures. Yet another manifestation of the double standard is the mistaken belief that it is wrong for females to plan ahead to have sexual intercourse (by taking contraceptive precautions), but it is somewhat permissible for them to be swept away by the passion of the moment.

The double standard is also at work in extramarital relations, although not as extensively as in earlier years. In Kinsey's research, about half of the husbands and one-fourth of the wives had engaged in sexual intercourse with someone other than their spouse during their marriage. In Hunt's survey in the 1970s, the figure was still about the same for men but had increased for women, especially for younger women—24 percent of wives under the age of 25 had experienced extramarital affairs, whereas only 8 percent had in the 1940s. The majority of men and women still disapprove of extramarital sex; in the Hunt survey, more than 80 percent said it is wrong.

Homosexual Attitudes and Behavior

Most individuals think that heterosexual and homosexual behavior are distinct patterns of behavior that can be easily defined. In fact, preference for a sexual partner of the same or opposite sex is not always a fixed decision, made once in life and adhered to forever. For example, it is not unusual for an individual, especially a male, to engage in homosexual experimentation in adolescence but not as an adult. Some individuals engage in heterosexual behavior during adolescence, then turn to homosexual behavior as adults. Homosexual behavior is common among prisoners and others with no alternative sexual partners. Sexual researchers report that lesbians are more likely to be involved in intimate, enduring relationships, have fewer sexual partners, and have fewer "one night stands" than are homosexual men (Bell & Weinberg, 1978).

Both the early (Kinsey) and the more recent (Hunt) surveys indicated that about 4 percent of the males and 3 percent of the females surveyed were exclusively homosexual. Although the incidence of homosexual behavior does not seem to have increased, attitudes toward homosexuality appeared to have become more permissive, at least until recently. In 1986 the Gallup Poll began to detect a shift in attitudes brought about by public awareness of acquired immune deficiency syndrome (AIDS). For example, in 1985 slightly more than 40 percent of all Americans believed that "homosexual relations between consenting adults should be legal"; by 1986 the figure had dropped to just about 30 percent (Gallup Report, 1987). Individuals who have negative attitudes toward homosexuals also are likely to favor severe controls for AIDS, such as excluding AIDS carriers from the workplace and schools (Fish & Rye, 1991; Pryor & others, 1989).

Why are some individuals homosexual and others heterosexual? Speculation about this question has been extensive, but no firm answers are available (Rowlett, Patel, & Greydanus, 1992). Homosexual and heterosexual males and females have similar physiological responses during sexual arousal and are aroused by the same types of tactile stimulation. Investigators find no differences between homosexuals and heterosexuals for a wide range of attitudes, behaviors, and adjustments (Bell, Weinberg, & Mammersmith, 1981). Recognizing that homosexuality is not a form of mental illness, the American Psychiatric Association has discontinued its classification of homosexuality as a disorder, except in cases in which the individuals themselves consider the sexual orientation to be abnormal.

An individual's sexual orientation—heterosexual or homosexual—is most likely determined by a combination of genetic, hormonal, cognitive, and environmental factors (McWhirter, Reinisch, & Sanders, 1989; Money, 1987; Remafedi, 1991). Most experts on homosexuality believe that no one factor alone causes homosexuality and that the relative weight of each factor may vary from one individual to the next. In effect, no one knows exactly what causes an individual to become a homosexual. Scientists have a clearer picture of what *does not* cause homosexuality. For example, children raised by gay or lesbian parents or couples are no more likely to be homosexual than are children raised by heterosexual parents. There also is no evidence that male homosexuality is caused by a dominant mother or a weak father, or that female homosexuality is caused by girls choosing male role models. One of the biological factors believed to be involved in homosexuality is prenatal hormone conditions (Ellis & Ames, 1987). In the second to fifth months after conception, the exposure of the fetus to hormone levels characteristic of females may cause the individual (male or female) to become attracted to males. If this "critical prenatal period hypothesis" turns out to be correct, it would explain why researchers and clinicians have found that a homosexual orientation is difficult to modify.

An individual's sexual preference—heterosexual or homosexual—is most likely determined by a mix of genetic, hormonal, cognitive, and environmental factors.

How can gays and lesbians adapt to a world in which they are a minority? According to psychologist Laura Brown (1989), gays and lesbians experience life as a minority in a dominant, majority culture. For lesbian women and gay men, developing a *bicultural identity* creates new ways of defining themselves. Brown believes that gays and lesbians adapt best when they don't define themselves in polarities, such as trying to live in an encapsulated gay or lesbian world completely divorced from the majority culture or completely accepting the dictates and bias of the majority culture. Balancing the demands of the two cultures—the minority gay/lesbian culture and the majority heterosexual culture—can often lead to more effective coping for homosexuals, says Brown.

A special concern in the lives of gays and lesbians is the bias and discrimination they face. In some instances, the bias has led to violence against homosexuals, not only violence toward them but toward their children as well. Becoming a more gentle, humane society requires that we not only reduce bias, discrimination, and prejudice against ethnic minority groups and women, but also against other minority groups, such as lesbians and gays. To become such a culture, each of us needs to be willing to ask how viewing certain human experiences through the lens of lesbian and gay realities might alter our understanding of those experiences (Brown, 1992).

Now that we have considered a number of ideas about the human sexual response and about heterosexual and homosexual attitudes and behaviors, we will turn our attention to the kinds of psychosexual disorders individuals can develop.

Psychosexual Disorders

Psychosexual disorders *are sexual problems caused mainly by psychological factors.* The psychosexual disorders we will discuss are psychosexual dysfunctions, incest, and paraphilias.

Psychosexual Dysfunctions

Myths about males and females would have us believe that many women are "frigid" and uninterested in sexual pleasure, whereas most men can hardly get enough. Both myths conceal the facts, revealed through the accumulating experience of sex therapy clinics. The facts are that men and women have similar desires for sexual pleasure, but both sexes may experience psychological problems that interfere with the attainment of pleasure. **Psychosexual dysfunctions** *are disorders that involve impairments in the sexual response cycle, either in the desire for gratification or the inability to achieve it.* In disorders associated with the desire phase, both men and women show little or no sexual drive or interest. In disorders associated with the excitement phase, men may not be able to maintain an erection. In disorders associated with the orgasmic phase, both men and women reach orgasm too quickly or not at all. Premature ejaculation in men occurs when the time between the beginning of sexual stimulation and ejaculation is unsatisfactorily brief. Many women do not routinely experience orgasm in sexual intercourse, a pattern so common it can hardly be called dysfunctional. Inhibited male orgasm does occur, but it is much less common than inhibited female orgasm.

The treatment of psychosexual dysfunctions has undergone nothing short of a revolution in recent years. Once thought of as an extremely difficult therapeutic challenge, most cases of psychosexual dysfunction now yield to techniques tailored to improve sexual functioning.

Attempts to treat psychosexual dysfunctions through traditional forms of psychotherapy, as if the dysfunctions were personality disorders, have not been very successful; however, new treatments that focus directly on each sexual dysfunction have reached success rates of 90 percent or more. For example, the success rate of a treatment that encourages women to enjoy their bodies and engage in self-stimulation to orgasm, with a vibrator if necessary, approaches 100 percent (Anderson, 1983). Some of these women subsequently transfer their newly developed sexual responsiveness to interactions with partners. Success rates also approach 100 percent in the treatment of premature ejaculation, but considerably lower success rates occur in the treatment of males who cannot maintain an erection.

Cross-cultural researchers have found that compliance with directed sex therapy techniques are more common among middle-class, Western clients than among clients from other cultural backgrounds. One study, for example, looked at males referred for sex therapy in Istanbul, Turkey (Basoglu & others, 1986). Turkish males with erectile problems were more likely to drop out of the sex therapy program than their counterparts with ejaculation problems. In the Turkish culture, especially in lower-income and rural areas, more importance is attached to a male's ability to achieve an erection and penetrate the vagina than to his ability to control his ejaculation. This might be explained by the fact that sex is viewed largely as a procreative rather than a pleasurable act. Many cultures also do not value a woman's orgasm. Given these values, it is understandable that a treatment emphasizing open communication and pleasure for both partners would be incomprehensible to males in many cultures. The success of sex therapies based on middle-class, Western values in other cultures hinges on the therapist's ability to reformulate these therapies into culturally relevant terms. Next, we will examine a psychosexual disorder that is frowned upon in most cultures.

Incest

Incest *is a sexual relationship between two relatives, which is virtually a universal taboo.* By far the most common form of incest is a brother-sister sexual relationship, followed by a father-daughter sexual relationship. Mother-son incest is rare. Same-sex incest, usually father-son, is also rare. Incest is psychologically harmful, not only for immediate family relationships, but also for the future relationships of a child involved in incest. A biological hazard of incest is that an offspring that results from incest has very high chances of mental retardation.

Paraphilias

Paraphilias *are psychosexual disorders in which the source of an individual's sexual satisfaction is an unusual object, ritual, or situation.* Many sexual patterns deviate from what we consider to be normal. These abnormal patterns of sexual arousal from unusual sources include fetishism, transvestism, transsexualism, exhibitionism, voyeurism, sadism, masochism, and pedophilia.

Fetishism *is a psychosexual disorder in which an individual relies on inanimate objects or a specific body part for sexual gratification.* Even though an individual may have a sexual preference—for example, a man's preference for women with long legs or a woman's preference for men with beards—most of us are attracted to someone because of a wide range of personal factors. Some individuals are obsessed with certain objects—fur, women's underpants, stockings—that arouse them. Most fetishists are male.

Transvestism *is a psychosexual disorder in which an individual obtains sexual gratification by dressing up as a member of the opposite sex.* Most transvestites view themselves as heterosexual and lead quiet, conventional lives, cross-dressing usually only in the privacy of their homes. A transvestite may cross-dress only during sex with his or her spouse (Brown & Collier, 1989).

Transsexualism *is a psychosexual disorder in which an individual has an overwhelming desire to become a member of the opposite sex.* The individual's gender identity is at odds with the anatomical facts, and he or she may undergo surgery to change sex. Transsexuals often say that, as far back as they can remember, they have felt they belonged to the wrong sex. Psychologists are uncertain why people become transsexual. Can transsexuals lead full sex lives? In the female-to-male transformation, the male sex organs are cosmetic and the clitoris retains its sensations; male sex hormones intensify orgasm. Males-to-females describe a diffuse, intense body glow. They enjoy functioning as females, especially in terms of body closeness, skin responsiveness, and breast sensations (Prior, Vigna, & Watson, 1989).

Exhibitionism and voyeurism are the two sex practices that often come to the attention of the police. **Exhibitionism** *is a psychosexual disorder in which individuals expose their sexual anatomy to others to obtain sexual gratification.* **Voyeurism** *is a psychosexual disorder in which individuals derive sexual gratification by observing the sex organs or sex acts of others, often from a secret vantage point.* Both exhibitionism and voyeurism provide substitute gratification and a sense of power to otherwise sexually anxious individuals, especially males. In many instances, voyeurs are sexually inhibited.

Aggressive sexual fantasies are not uncommon, and, in the course of sexual activity, a slight amount of force can be involved; however, in normal sexual activity, force is not extensive and does not harm the sexual partner or oneself. In contrast, **sadism** *is a psychosexual disorder in which individuals derive sexual gratification from inflicting pain on others.* The word *sadism* comes from the novels of the Marquis de Sade (1740-1814), who wrote about erotic scenes in which women were whipped. **Masochism** *is a psychosexual disorder in which individuals derive sexual gratification from being subjected to physical pain inflicted by others or themselves.* The word *masochism* comes from the novels of Austrian writer Leopold von Sacher-Masoch (1836-1895), whose male characters became sexually excited and gratified when they were physically abused by women. It is not unusual for a sadist and a masochist to pair up to satisfy each other's sexual wishes; such relationships are called sadomasochistic, or S & M.

Pedophilia *is a psychosexual disorder in which the sex object is a child and the intimacy usually involves manipulation of the child's genitals.* A pedophile covertly or overtly masturbates while talking to children, manipulates the child's sex organs, or has the child engage in sexual behavior. Most pedophiles are men, usually in their thirties or forties (Feierman, 1990). Like exhibitionists, they often have puritanical ideas about sex. The target of a male pedophile often is a girl he knows well, such as a relative, neighbor, or family friend.

Now that we have considered a number of ideas about the human sexual response, sexual attitudes and behavior, and psychosexual disorders, we will turn our attention to an aspect of sexual behavior that has been increasingly discussed and condemned—forcible sexual behavior.

REVIEW

The Human Sexual Response, Sexual Attitudes and Behavior, and Psychosexual Disorders

Both biological and psychological factors are involved in sexual arousal. Hormones are important biological factors, with estrogen being the dominant sex hormone in females, androgen in males. From puberty on, the level of male androgen does not vary over a short period of time, as the production of estrogen does in females. In humans, hormonal control over sexual behavior is less dominant, although hormones still play an important role in sexual arousal. In humans, sexual arousal is also influenced by sociocultural standards, individual preferences, and cognitive interpretation. Sexual fantasies are a common sexual stimulant. Masters and Johnson mapped out the nature of the human sexual response cycle, which consists of four phases—excitement, plateau, orgasm, and resolution.

Heterosexual attitudes and behavior have become more liberal in the twentieth century. However, some dimensions of the sexual double standard still exist. Preference for a sexual partner of the same sex is not always a fixed decision. Rates of homosexual behavior have remained constant in the twentieth century. Until recently acceptance of homosexuality had been increasing, but, in concert with the AIDS epidemic, acceptance of homosexuality has decreased. An individual's sexual orientation—heterosexual or homosexual—is likely to be determined by a combination of genetic, hormonal, cognitive, and environmental factors. A special concern is the bicultural adjustment of lesbians and gays, as well as bias and discrimination against homosexuals.

Psychosexual dysfunctions involve impairments of the sexual response cycle, either in the desire for sexual gratification or in the ability to achieve it. Significant advances in the treatment of psychosexual dysfunctions have been made in recent years. Incest is a sexual relationship between two relatives, virtually a universal taboo. The most common form is brother-sister, followed by father-daughter. Incest can cause extensive psychological harm for children. Paraphilias are psychosexual disorders in which the source of an individual's sexual satisfaction is an unusual object, ritual, or situation. Many sexual patterns deviate from what we consider to be normal. These abnormal patterns of sexual arousal from unusual sources include fetishism, transvestism, transsexualism, exhibitionism, voyeurism, sadism, masochism, and pedophilia.

Forcible Sexual Behavior

Most people choose to engage in sexual intercourse or other sexual activities, but, unfortunately, some people force others to engage in sex. **Rape** *is forcible sexual intercourse with a person who does not give consent.* Legal definitions of rape differ from state to state. For example, in some states, husbands are not prohibited from forcing their wives to have intercourse, although this law has been challenged in several states (Greenberg & others, 1989). Because of the difficulties involved in reporting rape, the actual incidence is not easily determined. It appears that rape occurs most often in large cities, where it has been reported that 8 of every 10,000 women 12 years and older are raped each year. Nearly 200,000 rapes are reported each year in the United States.

Why is rape so pervasive in the American culture? Feminist writers believe that males are socialized to be sexually aggressive, to regard women as inferior beings, and to view their own pleasure as the most important objective. Researchers have found the following characteristics common among rapists: aggression enhances the offender's sense of power or masculinity; rapists are angry at women generally; and they want to hurt their victims (Donat & D'Emilio, 1992; Knight, Rosenberg, & Schneider, 1985).

An increasing concern is **date, or acquaintance, rape,** *which is coercive sexual activity directed at someone with whom the individual is at least casually acquainted.* Date rape is an increasing problem on college campuses (Lloyd, 1991). In one investigation, 15 percent of a sample of college men admitted that they had obtained sexual intercourse against their date's will (Rapaport & Burkhart, 1984). A survey of college women found that 24 percent had experienced unwanted attempts at intercourse, and 31 percent had been subjected to unwanted fondling of their genitals (Kavin & Parcell, 1977).

Rape is a traumatic experience for the victim and those close to her or him (Sorenson & White, 1992). The rape victim initially feels shock and numbness, and is often acutely disorganized. Some victims show their distress through words and tears; others show more internalized suffering. As victims strive to get their lives back to normal, they may experience depression, fear, and anxiety for months or years. Sexual dysfunctions, such as reduced sexual desire and the inability to reach orgasm, occur in 50 percent of all rape victims (Sprei & Courtoi, 1988). Many rape victims make changes in their life-style, moving to a new apartment or refusing to go out at night. A victim's recovery depends on both her coping abilities and her psychological adjustment prior to the assault. Social support from parents, spouse, and others close to her are important factors in recovery, as is the availability of professional counseling, which sometimes is obtained through a rape crisis center (Koss, 1990).

Most victims of rape are women (Sorenson & Siegel, 1992). Male rape does occur, however. Men in prisons are especially vulnerable to rape, usually by heterosexuals who use rape as a means of establishing their domination and power.

Anita Hill's testimony before the Senate Committee on the Judiciary focussed attention on harassment of women in the workplace. Fifteen percent of the letters she received after the hearings recounted experience with sexual harassment.

Though it might seem impossible for a man to be raped by a woman, a man's erection is not completely under his voluntary control, and some cases of male rape by women have been reported (Sarrel & Masters, 1982). Although male victims account for fewer than 5 percent of all rapes, the trauma that males suffer is just as great as that experienced by females.

Sexual Harassment

Women and men encounter sexual harassment in many different forms—from sexist remarks and covert physical contact (patting, brushing against their bodies) to blatant propositions and sexual assaults (DeFour & Paludi, 1991; Doyle & Paludi, 1991; Paludi, 1992). Literally millions of women experience such sexual harassment each year in work and educational settings. In one investigation of Harvard University students, 17 percent of the women said they had received verbal sexual advances, 14 percent were given sexual invitations, 6 percent

Feminists organized campaigns against pornography in the late 1970s. When sexual content is combined with violence, increased male aggression toward females may occur. However, there is no evidence that sexual content without aggression stimulates negative feelings toward women.

had been subjected to physical advances, and 2 percent received direct sexual bribes. In the same study, 13 percent of the women said they had avoided taking a class or working with certain professors because of the risk of being subjected to sexual advances. Sexual harassment can result in serious psychological consequences for the victim. Sexual harassment is a manifestation of power and domination of one person over another. The elimination of such exploitation requires the development of work and academic environments that are compatible with the needs of women workers and students, providing them with equal opportunities to develop a career and obtain an education in a climate free of sexual harassment.

Pornography and Violence Against Women

Feminist campaigns against pornography began in the late 1970s. The objections to pornography are twofold. First, pornography demeans women, depicting them as sex slaves in male fantasies, for instance. Second, much of pornography glorifies violence against women, perpetuating the myth that women who say no to sex really want to be overpowered.

Sexual researchers have found that erotic films or slides provide visual cues that influence sexual behavior, but only for a brief period of time. Both men and women show increased sexual activity within 24 hours of exposure to sexually explicit material. Both viewing sexual violence and reading sexually violent material increase male acceptance of sexual and other aggression toward females. However, sex researcher Edward Donnerstein (1987) argues that it is the violence against women in some erotic films, not the erotic material itself, that causes viewers to have negative attitudes toward women and is related to forcible sexual behavior.

In one investigation, Donnerstein (1980) studied college males in a three-part experiment. First, they were either provoked or treated neutrally by an accomplice of the experimenter. Next, they were shown one of three types of films—neutral; erotic; or aggressive-erotic, depicting rape. Third, the subjects were given a chance to shock the accomplice with any level of intensity they wanted. Men who had been provoked and who had seen the aggressive-erotic film showed the highest levels of aggression.

Rapists themselves report less exposure to erotic magazines and movies during their adolescent years than do those who are not sex offenders. When the censorship of pornographic materials was removed in the 1960s in Denmark, sex-related crimes actually decreased. In short, when sexual content is combined with violence, increased male aggression toward females may occur (Malamuth & Donnerstein, 1983), but there is no evidence that sexual content without aggression stimulates negative feelings or behavior toward women.

We have covered a number of topics in the vast, complex territory of sexuality. Another topic that has captured our attention and concern, especially in recent years, is sexually transmitted diseases.

Sexually Transmitted Diseases

Sexually transmitted diseases (STDs) *are diseases that are contracted primarily through sex—intercourse as well as oral-genital and anal-genital sex.* You may be more familiar with the term *venereal disease,* or VD, an older term that has been increasingly replaced with the term *STDs.* STDs are an increasing health problem in the United States, especially for men and women in their late teens and early twenties. For example, in 1988, 720,000 new cases of gonorrhea were reported by the National Center for Health Statistics. At greatest risk are 20-to-24-year-olds (32 percent of cases, compared with their 8 percent of the population). Those 15 to 19 years old have the second highest level of risk (27 percent of reported cases versus 7 percent of the population).

The information presented in this section should encourage you to protect yourself and your sexual partner(s) from these highly contagious sexually transmitted diseases. We will begin our discussion with two STDs caused by bacterial infections—gonorrhea and syphilis.

Gonorrhea

Gonorrhea *is a sexually transmitted disease that is commonly called the "drip" or the "clap." It is reported to be the most common STD in the United States and is caused by a bacterium called gonococcus, which thrives in the moist mucous membranes lining the mouth, throat, vagina, cervix, urethra, and anal tract.* The bacterium is spread by contact between the infected moist membranes of one individual and the moist membranes of another. Thus, virtually all forms of sexual contact can spread the gonococcus, although transfer does not necessarily occur with every contact. Males have a 10 percent chance of becoming infected with each exposure to gonococcus. Females have more than a 40 percent chance of infection with each exposure because of the large surface area of the vaginal mucous membrane (Greenberg & others, 1989).

Symptoms of gonorrhea appear in males from 3 days to a month after contact. The symptoms include discharge from the penis, burning during urination, blood in the urine, aching pain or pressure in the genitals, and swollen and tender lymph glands in the groin. Gonorrhea can be successfully treated in its early stages with penicillin or other antibiotics. Unfortunately, 80 percent of the infected females show no symptoms in the early stages of the disease, although pelvic inflammation is common at this early point. Untreated, the disease causes infection in the reproductive area and pelvic region within 2 months. Scarring of the fallopian tubes and infertility may result.

Despite reporting laws, many gonorrhea cases go unreported. Public health experts estimate that approximately 1.6 to 2.0 million cases of gonorrhea occur annually in the United States (Greenberg & others, 1989).

Syphilis

Syphilis *is a sexually transmitted disease caused by the bacterium Treponema pallidum, also called a spirochete.* The spirochete needs a warm, moist environment to survive, and it is transmitted by vaginal, oral-genital, or anal contact. It can also be transmitted from a pregnant woman to her unborn child after the fourth month of pregnancy. If the mother is treated with penicillin before this time, the syphilis will not be transmitted to the child.

Syphilis occurs in four stages: primary, secondary, latent, and tertiary. In the primary stage, a sore, or chancre, appears at the site of the infection. The sore heals after 4 to 6 weeks, giving the impression that the problem has gone away; however, untreated it moves into the secondary stage. A number of symptoms occur at this stage, including a rash, fever, sore throat, headache, swollen glands, joint pain, poor appetite, and hair loss. Treatment with penicillin can be successful if begun at this stage or earlier; however, without treatment, symptoms of the secondary stage go away after 6 weeks and the disease enters a latent stage. The spirochetes spread throughout the body and, in 50 to 70 percent of those affected, remain there for years in the same stage. After 1 or 2 years, the disease is no longer transmitted through sexual contact, but it can be passed from a pregnant woman to her unborn child. For 30 to 50 percent of those who reach the latent stage, a final, tertiary stage follows. In this advanced stage, syphilis can cause paralysis, insanity, or even death. In 1988, 103,000 cases of syphilis were reported to the Public Health Service, and syphilis is on the rise in many areas of the United States.

We will now turn to two STDs that are caused by viruses—herpes genitalis and acquired immune deficiency syndrome (AIDS).

Herpes Genitalis

Herpes *is a sexually transmitted disease caused by a large family of viruses with many different strains. These strains produce such diseases as chicken pox and mononucleosis, as well as herpes simplex, an STD that has two variations.* Type 1 is characterized by cold sores and fever blisters. Type 2 includes painful sores on the lower body—genitals, thighs, and buttocks. Type 1 infections can be transmitted to the lower body, and type 2 infections can be transmitted to the mouth through oral-genital contact. Approximately 75 percent of the individuals exposed to an infected partner will develop herpes. Three to five days after contact, itching and tingling can occur, followed by an eruption of sores and blisters. The attacks can last up to 3 weeks and may recur in a few weeks or a few years. The blisters and sores in subsequent attacks are usually milder, but while the virus is dormant in the body it can travel to the brain and other parts of the nervous system. Although rare, this transmission through the nervous system can cause such disorders as encephalitis and blindness.

Herpes infections can also be transmitted from a pregnant woman to her offspring at birth, leading to brain damage or even death for the infant. A cesarean section can prevent infection, which occurs as the baby moves through the birth canal. Women with herpes are also eight times more likely to develop cervical cancer than are unaffected women (Harvard Medical School Newsletter, 1981).

In 1986, the Center for Disease Control estimated that 98 million Americans were infected with type 1 herpes and 9 million with type 2. Up to 600,000 new cases of type 2 herpes appeared annually in the United States during the 1980s. There is no known cure for herpes, although such drugs as acyclovir can be used to alleviate symptoms. People infected with herpes often experience severe emotional distress in addition to the considerable physical discomfort. The virus can be transmitted through condoms and foams, making infected individuals reluctant about sex, angry about the unpredictability of their lives, and fearful that they won't be able to cope with the pain of the next attack. For these reasons, support groups for victims of herpes have been established. If you or someone you know would like more information about dealing with herpes, The Information Center on Herpes Disease (15 Park Row, New York, NY 10038) is a good resource.

AIDS

No single STD has had a greater impact on sexual behavior, or created more public fear in the past decade, than AIDS. **AIDS** *is a sexually transmitted disease that is caused by a virus, human immunodeficiency virus (HIV) that destroys the body's immune system* (see figure 10.9). Following exposure to HIV, an individual is vulnerable to germs that a normal immune system could destroy. In 1981, when AIDS was first recognized in the United States, there were fewer than 60 reported cases. Beginning in 1990, according to Dr. Frank Press, president of the

FIGURE 10.9

AIDS. The virus destroys the body's immune system. This individual with AIDS is one of more than 60,000 Americans who die every year from AIDS.

National Academy of Sciences, we started losing as many Americans each year to AIDS as the total number killed in the Vietnam War, almost 60,000 Americans. According to federal health officials, 1 to 1.5 million Americans are now asymptomatic carriers of AIDS—those who are infected with the virus and presumably capable of infecting others but who show no clinical symptoms of AIDS. The incidence of AIDS is especially high among ethnic minorities in the United States (Mays, 1991). Although Blacks and Hispanics represented 12.3 percent and 8 percent of the United States population in 1988, 30 percent of the reported AIDS cases were Blacks and 14 percent were Hispanics. Much of the AIDS prevention literature, as well as the instructions included with condoms, require a high school reading proficiency. It is estimated that approximately 40 percent of adult Hispanics lack this proficiency.

In 1989 the first attempt to assess AIDS among college students was made. Tests of 16,861 students found 30 infected with the virus (American College Health Association, 1989). If the 12.5 million students attending college that year were infected in the same proportion, 25,000 students would have the AIDS virus.

Experts say that AIDS can be transmitted only by sexual contact, the sharing of needles, or blood transfusions. Although 90 percent of all AIDS cases continue to occur among homosexual males and intravenous drug users, a disproportionate increase among females who are heterosexual partners of bisexual males or of intravenous drug users has been noted recently (Cantor & others, 1991; Smith, 1991). This increase suggests that the risk of AIDS may be increasing among heterosexual individuals who have multiple sex partners (Boyer & Hein, 1991; Corless & Pittman-Lindemann, 1989; Fisher & Fisher, 1992).

Remember that it is not who you are, but what you do that puts you at risk for getting HIV. *Anyone* who is sexually active or uses intravenous drugs is at risk. No one is immune. Once an individual is infected, the prognosis is likely to be illness and death. The only *safe* behavior is abstinence from sex, which is not perceived as an option by most individuals. Beyond abstinence, there is only *safer* behavior, such as sex with a condom.

Just asking a date about his or her sexual behavior does not guarantee protection from AIDS and other sexually transmitted diseases. For example, in one recent investigation, 655 college students were asked to answer questions about lying and sexual behavior (Cochran & Mays, 1990). Of the 442 respondents who said they were sexually active, 34 percent of the males and 10 percent of the females said they had lied so their partner would have sex with them. Much higher percentages—47 percent of the men and 60 percent of the women—said they had been lied to by a potential sexual partner. When asked what aspects of their past they would be most likely to lie about, more than 40 percent of the men and women said they would understate the number of their sexual partners. Twenty percent of the men, but only 4 percent of the women, said they would lie about their results from an AIDS blood test. Let's now examine the course of AIDS.

In the first stage of the disease, referred to as *HIV+ and asymptomatic*, individuals do not show the characteristics of AIDS but can transmit the disease. It is estimated that 20 to 30 percent of those in Stage 1 will develop AIDS within 5 years. In Stage 2—*HIV+ and symptomatic*—an unknown number of those who had the silent infection develop symptoms, including swelling of the lymph glands, fatigue, weight loss, diarrhea, fever, and sweats. Many who are HIV+ and symptomatic continue to the final stage—*AIDS*. A person with AIDS has the symptoms of AIDS plus one or more diseases, such as pneumonia, which is fatal to AIDS patients because of their vulnerable immune systems. Although there is no known cure for AIDS, several drugs are being tested, including AZT or zidovudine, approved by the FDA for treatment of the symptoms of AIDS in 1987.

Because it is possible, and even probable among high-risk groups, to have more than one STD at a time, efforts to prevent one disease can help reduce the prevalence of other diseases. Efforts to prevent AIDS can also help prevent adolescent pregnancy and other sex-related problems.

The AIDS epidemic has generated an increased interest in sex education, especially when, in November 1991, basketball legend Magic Johnson of the Los Angeles Lakers announced that he was HIV-positive. The Monday morning after Johnson told the nation he has HIV, adolescents' conversations were buzzing with comments and questions about Johnson and AIDS. Within several weeks, condom sales increased and AIDS awareness programs were attracting more people. Sex education instructors reported a dramatic increase in AIDS-related questions from their students. The first question many students asked was, "How did Magic get it?"

Educators continue to debate how best to answer that question and how best to handle other questions raised by students since Johnson's announcement (Marklein & DeRosa, 1991). Schools also report a dramatic increase in calls from parents in the months following Johnson's revelation; they wanted to know what the schools were teaching their children and adolescents about AIDS. Some experts on sexuality hope that Johnson's announcement will prompt more school systems to require sex education and provide more explicit information about contraception. Most states now require AIDS education. However, the nature of the AIDS education programs vary considerably. In Michigan, Minnesota, and Nevada, school districts are required to develop an HIV education program, but students do not have to take it, and most states allow parents the option of taking their children and adolescents out of such courses.

Furthermore, there are clear differences of opinion about what is appropriate for class discussion, and the range of responses to Johnson's announcement underscores the complexity of the issue. Some educators dismiss Johnson's usefulness as a teaching aid. Others fear that the rush to embrace him as a role model is misguided. Still others believe that the well-known superstar can have a special influence on children and adolescents. Yet even others believe that, although Johnson can play an important role in AIDS awareness, his message that "safe sex" is the way to go was the wrong thing to say. They argue that he should be communicating abstinence rather than safe sex.

The AIDS epidemic has led an increasing number of school systems to distribute condoms to students, and since the Johnson announcement others are considering the distribution. New York City and San Francisco school districts already have condom programs, and Massachusetts is encouraging its districts to adopt them. Los Angeles officials are considering a proposal to make condoms available to 135,000 students in 49 schools. At the same time, critics of the condom distribution programs argue that abstinence education, not condoms for safe sex, should be the focus of sex education programs in the nation's schools. Given the moral issues that become wrapped up in sexuality, it is likely that such opposing views will continue to be voiced.

If you or someone you know would like more information about AIDS, you can call the National AIDS Hot Line at 1-800-342-7432, 8 A.M.-2 A.M. EST, 7 days a week. Given the increasing incidence of AIDS and other sexually transmitted diseases, it's crucial that both teenagers and adults understand these diseases and other aspects of sexuality; however, how much do Americans really know about sex?

Sexual Knowledge

According to June Reinisch (1990), director of the Kinsey Institute for Sex, Gender, and Reproduction, the United States is a nation whose citizens know more about how their automobiles function than how their bodies function sexually. Reinisch directed a recent national assessment of basic sexual knowledge, given to 1,974 adults. Among the results of the assessment were the following:

Sixty-five percent of the respondents did not know that most erection difficulties begin with physical problems.
Seventy-five percent did not know that approximately 40 percent of all American men have had an extramarital affair (some experts believe that the rate of male infidelity is 60 percent or more).
Fifty percent did not know that oil-based lubricants should not be used with condoms or diaphragms, since some can produce holes in less than 60 seconds.

American adolescents also have woefully inadequate sexual knowledge. In one investigation, a majority of the adolescents believed that pregnancy risk is greatest during menstruation (Zelnik & Kantner, 1977).

Of course, it's not that American adolescents and adults are sheltered from sexual messages. Sexual information is abundant, but much of it is misinformation. In some cases, even sex education teachers display sexual ignorance. One high school sex education teacher referred to erogenous zones as "erroneous zones," possibly causing the students to wonder if their sexually sensitive zones were characterized by error.

We get very little sex education from our parents. A large majority of American adolescents say they cannot talk freely about sex with their parents (Thornburg, 1981). Because parents so inadequately handle sex education, it is not surprising that a majority of parents prefer to let the schools do the job. In a national poll conducted by *Time* magazine, 78 percent of the parents wanted schools to teach sex education, including information about birth control (Wallis, 1985). Despite the majority opinion, sex education remains swirled in controversy. On one side are such groups as Planned Parenthood, which argue that sex education should be more open and birth control more available, as in European countries. (See Sociocultural Worlds 10.4 to read about the sex education and attitudes of adolescents in Holland and Sweden.) On the other side are individuals who believe sex education should be provided only by parents. They usually believe that teaching adolescents about birth control is giving them a license to have sex and be promiscuous. The controversy has led to clashes at school board meetings throughout the nation. New York City, for example, initiated a program to

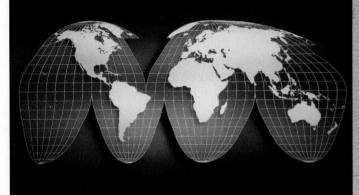

SOCIOCULTURAL WORLDS 10.4

Sex Education and Attitudes Among Adolescents in Holland and Sweden

Sex is much more demystified and dedramatized in Sweden than in the United States, and adolescent pregnancy rates are much lower in Sweden than in the United States.

In Holland and Sweden, sex does not carry the mystery and conflict it does in American society. Holland does not have a mandated sex education program, but adolescents can obtain contraceptive counseling at government-sponsored clinics for a small fee. The Dutch media also have played an important role in educating the public about sex through frequent broadcasts focused on birth control, abortion, and related matters. Most Dutch adolescents do not consider having sex without birth control.

Swedish adolescents are sexually active at an earlier age than are American adolescents, and they are exposed to even more explicit sex on television. However, the Swedish National Board of Education has developed a curriculum that ensures that every child in the country, beginning at age 7, will experience a thorough grounding in reproductive biology and, by the age of 10 or 12, will have been introduced to information about various forms of contraception. Teachers are expected to handle the subject of sex whenever it becomes relevant, regardless of the subject they are teaching. The idea is to dedramatize and demystify sex so that familiarity will make students less vulnerable to unwanted pregnancy and sexually transmitted diseases (Wallis, 1985). American society is not nearly so open about sex education.

combat its runaway adolescent pregnancy problem. Religious groups showed up at a school board meeting with a list of 56 objections. In San Juan Capistrano, California, conservative opponents of sex education in the schools appeared at a school board meeting dressed in Revolutionary War clothes. They even brought a cannon with them.

Sex education programs in schools may not, by themselves, prevent adolescent pregnancy and sexually transmitted diseases. Researchers have found that sex education classes improve adolescents' knowledge about human sexuality but do not always change their sexual behavior. When sex education classes are combined with readily available contraceptives, teen pregnancy rates are more likely to drop (Wallis, 1985). Such findings have led to the development of school-linked, rather than school-based, approaches to sex education and pregnancy prevention. In one program pioneered by some Baltimore public schools in cooperation with Johns Hopkins University, family-planning clinics were located adjacent to the schools (Zabin,

1986). They sent a nurse and a social worker into the schools to make formal presentations about sexuality and the services available from the clinics. They also made themselves available to the students for counseling several hours each day. The same personnel also conducted after-school sessions at the clinics, which consisted of further counseling, films, and family planning information. The results were very positive. Students who participated in the school-linked programs delayed their first intercourse longer than students in a control group. After 28 months, the pregnancy rate had declined to 30 percent in the school-linked programs, whereas it rose to 60 percent in the control group. Thus, the support services provided by the community-based, school-linked family-planning clinic were effective in reducing adolescent pregnancy.

Sexual motivation is one of many aspects of our motivational life. In the next chapter, we will examine the concept of motivation in general and will study different areas of motivation, as well as emotion.

REVIEW

Forcible Sexual Behavior, Sexual Harassment, Pornography and Violence Against Women, Sexually Transmitted Diseases, and Sexual Knowledge

Some individuals force others to engage in sexual activity. Rape is forcible sexual intercourse with a person who does not give consent. Legal definitions of rape vary from state to state. An increasing concern is date, or acquaintance, rape. Rape is a traumatic experience and a woman's recovery depends on her coping resources, as well as on how well she was adjusted prior to the assault. Male rape occurs in about 5 percent of all rape cases. Sexual harassment is a consequence of the power of one individual over another.

Feminists and others organized the first campaigns against pornography in the late 1970s. When sexual content is combined with violence, increased male aggression toward females may occur. However, there is no evidence that sexual content without aggression stimulates negative feelings toward women.

Sexually transmitted disease (also called STDs) are diseases that are contracted primarily through sexual con-

tact. Gonorrhea is commonly called the "drip" or the "clap." It is reported to be the most common STD in the United States. Gonorrhea is caused by a tiny bacterium called gonococcus. It can be treated with penicillin and other antibiotics. Syphilis is caused by the bacterium Treponema pallidum, also called a spirochete. Syphilis occurs in four phases—primary, secondary, latent, and tertiary. If detected in the first two phases, it can be successfully treated with penicillin. Herpes is caused by a family of viruses with different strains. Herpes simplex has two variations. Type 1 is characterized by cold sores and fever blisters. Type 2 includes sores on the lower body—genitals, thighs, and buttocks. There is no known cure for herpes. AIDS is caused by a virus, HIV (human immunodeficiency virus), that destroys the body's immune system. AIDS can only be transmitted through sexual contact, the sharing of needles, or blood transfusions. There is no known cure for AIDS.

According to a recent national survey, Americans are not very knowledgeable about sex. Many American adults and adolescents have misconceptions about sex. A majority of parents favor letting schools handle sex education, although school-based sex education has been controversial. School-linked, community-based family-planning clinics have reduced adolescent pregnancy rates. In many European countries, such as Holland and Sweden, sex does not carry the mystery and conflict it does in America.

Summary

I. What Is Gender?

Gender refers to the sociocultural dimension of being female or male. Gender identity is the sense of being male or female. A gender role is a set of expectations that prescribes how females or males should think, act, and feel.

II. Biological Influences on Gender

The 23rd pair of chromosomes determines our sex. Ordinarily, females have two X chromosomes, males an X and a Y. Chromosomes determine anatomical sex differences, but gender behavior is strongly influenced by societally and culturally determined factors. Freud's and Erikson's theories promote the thesis that anatomy determines behavior. The hormones from the testes (androgen) determine whether the organism will have male genitals (if androgen is secreted) or female genitals (if no androgen is secreted). Androgen in males and estrogen in females are the dominant sexual hormones. Hermaphrodites are individuals whose genitals become intermediate between male and female because of a hormonal imbalance.

III. Social and Cognitive Influences on Gender

Adults and peers reward and model gender-appropriate behavior. Parents, schools, peers, the media, and other family members influence the development of children's gender behavior. Two prominent theories address the way children acquire masculine and feminine attitudes and behavior from their parents—identification theory and social learning theory. Two theories address the role of cognition in gender—cognitive developmental theory and gender schema theory. In cognitive developmental theory, children's gender typing occurs after children have developed a concept of gender, which is achieved in concert with the development of conservation skills at about 6 or 7 years of age. Gender schema theory states that an individual's attention and behavior are guided by an internal motivation to conform to gender-based, sociocultural standards and stereotypes. Gender schema theorists point out that young children have more gender role knowledge than cognitive developmental theory predicts.

IV. Gender Stereotypes, Similarities, and Differences

Gender role stereotypes are broad categories that reflect our impressions and beliefs about females and males. These stereotypes are widespread around the world, especially emphasizing male power and female nurturance. However, in more highly developed countries, females and males are more likely to be perceived as similar. Many gender researchers believe that a number of differences between females and males have been exaggerated. In considering differences, it is important to recognize that the differences are averages; there is considerable overlap between the sexes; and the differences may be due primarily to biological factors, sociocultural factors, or both. There are a number of physical differences between females and males, but cognitive differences are either small or nonexistent. The average gifted male outperforms the average gifted female in math achievement. In terms of social behavior, males are more aggressive and active than females, but females are usually more adept at "reading" emotions, and they show more nurturant helping behavior than males. Overall, though, there are more similarities than differences between females and males.

V. Gender Role Classification

In the past, a well-adjusted male was supposed to show instrumental traits, a well-adjusted female expressive traits. Masculine traits were more valued by society. Sexism was widespread. In the 1970s, alternatives to traditional masculinity and femininity were explored. It was proposed that individuals could show both expressive and instrumental traits. This thinking led to the development of the concept of androgyny, the presence of desirable masculine and feminine traits in the same individual. Gender role measures often categorize individuals as masculine, feminine, androgynous, or undifferentiated. Androgynous individuals are often flexible and mentally healthy, although the particular context and the individual's culture also determine the adaptiveness of a gender role orientation. One alternative to androgyny is gender role transcendence, but like androgyny it draws attention from the imbalance of power between women and men.

VI. The Feminist Perspective on Gender

Feminist scholars are developing new perspectives that focus on girls' and women's experiences and development. Girls' and women's strengths have been especially important in relationships and connections with others. A special emphasis is that, while staying emotionally connected to significant others, females can enhance their psychological well-being by becoming more self-reliant. The feminist perspective also emphasizes the importance of reducing, and eventually ending, prejudice and discrimination against women.

VII. Gender and Ethnicity

What defines traditional masculinity in many Western societies includes engaging in certain behaviors that, although officially socially disapproved of, validate masculinity. Researchers have found that problem behaviors in adolescent males—school difficulties, drug use, and delinquency, for example—are associated with traditional beliefs about masculinity. There are many similarities between women in different ethnic minority groups and between men in different ethnic minority groups, but even small differences are sometimes significant. The term *women of color* has gained considerable popularity in recent years, but it is important to recognize that women of color are a diverse group. Women who adopt the label women of color believe that it underscores their pride and power as women and as people of color. Researchers in psychology have only begun to focus on female behavior in specific ethnic groups in a positive way. Many ethnic minority females have experienced the double jeopardy of racism and sexism. In many instances, Asian American, Hispanic American, and Native American females have lived in patriarchal, male-dominated families, although gender roles have become less rigid in these ethnic groups in recent years. Just as ethnic minority females have experienced considerable discrimination and have had to develop coping strategies in the face of adversity, so have ethnic minority males. As with Black females, researchers are beginning to focus more on the positive dimensions of Black males. A patriarchal, male-dominant orientation has characterized many ethnic minority groups, such as Asian American, Hispanic American, and Native American, although females are gaining greater decision-making power in these cultures, especially when they develop careers and work outside of the home.

VIII. The Human Sexual Response
Both biological and psychological factors are involved in sexual arousal. Hormones are important biological factors, with estrogen being the dominant sex hormone in females, androgen in males. From puberty on, the level of male androgen remains steady, unlike the production of estrogen in females. From the lower to the higher animals, hormonal control over behavior is less dominant, although hormones still play an important role in human sexual arousal. In humans sexual arousal is also influenced by sociocultural standards, individual preferences, and cognitive interpretation. Sexual fantasies are a common sexual stimulant. Masters and Johnson mapped out the nature of the human sexual response cycle, which consists of four phases—excitement, plateau, orgasm, and resolution.

IX. Sexual Attitudes and Behavior
Heterosexual attitudes and behavior have become more liberal in the twentieth century, but some vestiges of the sexual double standard remain. Preference for a sexual partner of the same sex is not always a fixed decision. Rates of homosexual behavior have remained constant during the twentieth century. Until recently acceptance of homosexuality had been increasing, but the AIDS epidemic has reversed that trend. An individual's sexual orientation—whether heterosexual or homosexual—is likely to be determined by a mix of genetic, hormonal, cognitive, and environmental factors. A special concern is the bicultural adjustment of lesbians and gays, as well as bias and discrimination against homosexuals.

X. Psychosexual Disorders
Psychosexual dysfunctions involve impairments of the sexual response cycle, either in the desire for sexual gratification or in the ability to achieve it. Significant advances in the treatment of psychosexual dysfunctions have been made in recent years. Incest, a sexual relationship between two relatives, is virtually a universal taboo. The most common form is brother-sister, followed by father-daughter. Incest can cause extensive psychological harm to children. Paraphilias are psychosexual disorders in which the source of an individual's sexual satisfaction is an unusual object, ritual, or situation. Many sexual patterns deviate from what is considered normal. These abnormal patterns of sexual arousal from unusual sources include fetishism, transvestism, transsexualism, exhibitionism, voyeurism, sadism, masochism, and pedophilia.

XI. Forcible Sexual Behavior, Sexual Harassment, Pornography, and Violence Against Women
Some individuals force others to engage in sexual activity. Rape is forcible sexual intercourse with a person who does not give consent. Legal definitions of rape vary from state to state. An increasing concern is date, or acquaintance, rape. Rape is a traumatic experience; a woman's recovery depends on her coping resources and how well adjusted she was prior to the assault. Male rape occurs in about 5 percent of all rape cases. Sexual harassment is a conse-

quence of the power of one individual over another. Feminists and others organized the first campaigns against pornography in the late 1970s. When sexual content is combined with violence, increased male aggression toward females may occur. However, there is no evidence that sexual content without aggression stimulates negative feelings toward women.

XII. Sexually Transmitted Diseases
Sexually transmitted diseases (also called STDs) are diseases that are contracted primarily through sexual contact. Gonorrhea, commonly called the "drip" or the "clap," is reported to be the most common STD in the United States. Gonorrhea is caused by a bacterium called gonococcus. It can be treated with penicillin and other antibiotics. Syphilis is caused by the bacterium Treponema pallidum, also called a spirochete. Syphilis occurs in four phases—primary, secondary, latent, and tertiary. If detected in the first two phases, it can be successfully treated with penicillin. Herpes is caused by a family of viruses with different strains. Herpes simplex has two variations. Type 1 is characterized by cold sores and fever blisters. Type 2 includes sores on the lower body—genitals, thighs, and buttocks. There is no known cure for herpes. AIDS is caused by a virus, HIV (human immunodeficiency virus), that destroys the body's immune system. AIDS can only be transmitted through sexual contact, the sharing of needles, or blood transfusions. There is no known cure for AIDS.

XIII. Sexual Knowledge
According to a recent national survey, Americans are not very knowledgeable about sex. Many American adults and adolescents have misconceptions about sex. A majority of parents favor letting schools handle sex education, although school-based sex education has been controversial. School-linked, community-based family-planning clinics have reduced adolescent pregnancy rates. In many European countries, such as Holland and Sweden, sex does not carry the mystery and conflict it does in America.

Key Terms

gender 300
gender identity 300
gender role 300
androgen 300
estrogen 300
identification theory 302
social learning theory of gender 302
cognitive developmental theory
   of gender 303
gender schema 303
gender schema theory 303

gender role stereotypes 304
androgyny 308
gender role transcendence 309
human sexual response cycle 318
psychosexual disorders 321
psychosexual dysfunctions 321
incest 321
paraphilias 321
fetishism 321
transvestism 321
transsexualism 322
exhibitionism 322

voyeurism 322
sadism 322
masochism 322
pedophilia 322
rape 323
date, or acquaintance, rape 323
sexually transmitted diseases (STDs) 325
gonorrhea 325
syphilis 325
herpes 325
AIDS 326

Suggested Readings

Doyle, J., & Paludi, M. (1991). *Sex and gender: The human experience*. Dubuque, IA: Wm. C. Brown. In this up-to-date discussion, the authors examine a number of issues pertaining to gender. It includes chapters on how different power bases affect women's and men's relationships, psychological perspectives on gender, and anthropological perspectives on gender.

Greenberg, J. S., Bruess, C. E., Mullen, K. D., & Sands, D. W. (1989). *Sexuality* (2nd ed.). Dubuque, IA: Wm. C. Brown. This broad-based text covers many areas of sexuality. Separate chapters are devoted to such topics as sexual response and arousal, sexual diseases, fertility control, and sexual dysfunctions.

McWhirter, D. P., Reinisch, J. M., & Sanders, S. A. (1989). *Homosexuality/heterosexuality*. New York: Oxford University Press.
Extensive information is presented about the biological, psychological, and social dimensions of homosexuality and hetero-sexuality.

Miller, J. B. (1986). *Toward a new psychology of women* (2nd ed.). Boston: Beacon. A leader in the feminist movement in psychology, Jean Baker Miller describes the male bias of society, females' connectionist strengths, and the future of women's roles.

MOTIVATION AND EMOTION

CHAPTER 11

omic John Belushi and Russian master-mind and manipulator Rasputin were high-profile people motivated to take risks, seek adventure, and thrive on excitement. Belushi excelled at making audiences laugh and sought emotional highs through cocaine. Rasputin gained a reputation early in the twentieth century as a mystic. The giant, uncouth Russian monk was an unruly man who delighted in keeping the aristocracy in an uproar with his embarrassing and outlandish comments and behavior.

Psychologist Frank Farley (1986) believes that motivation to seek thrills, like Belushi's and Rasputin's, can be either destructive or constructive and that people can seek thrills in either the physical or the cognitive domain. Sir Francis Crick, Nobel Prize winner for codiscovering DNA's cellular structure, sought thrills in the cognitive domain. Evel Knievel, a daredevil entertainer, has pursued physical highs. Both Crick and Knievel turned their thrill-seeking motivation into constructive accomplishments. However, Rasputin became destructive in the cognitive domain. Belushi's motivation to seek thrills led to both constructive and destructive consequences: the ability to make millions of people laugh and a drug-induced death. The motivation to seek thrills is just one of many reasons behind human behavior. Let's explore other "whys" of our behavior.

Some Ideas Behind the "Whys" of Behavior

Sam Walton, the founder of Walmart stores, made about $6 billion in 1988. What motivated him to do this? "Every why hath a wherefore," said Shakespeare. Why are you so hungry? Why are you so interested in having sex? Why do you want to get an A in this class? Why do you want a change in your life? The answer is because you are motivated. **Motivation** *involves the question of "why" people behave, think, and feel the way they do.*

If you are hungry, you will probably put this book down and go to the refrigerator. If you are sexually motivated, you may go to a party and flirt with someone you think is attractive. If you are motivated to achieve, you may study in the library until midnight. When you are motivated, your behavior is energized and directed; you go to the refrigerator, to a party, to the library.

Motivation differs not only in kind, such as an individual being motivated to eat rather than have sex, but also in intensity. We can speak of an individual being more or less hungry or more or less motivated to have sex. Let's now turn our attention to the ways in which psychologists conceptualize motivation, beginning with instincts.

Instincts

An **instinct** *is an innate, biological determinant of behavior.* Did Sam Walton have an instinct for acquisitiveness? Early in this century, interest in instincts flourished. Influenced by Darwin's evolutionary theory, American psychologist William McDougall (1908) argued that all behavior is determined by instincts. He said we have instincts for acquisitiveness, curiosity, gregariousness, pugnacity, and self-assertion. At about the same time, Sigmund Freud (1917) argued that behavior is instinctually based. He believed that sex and aggression are especially powerful in motivating behavior.

It was not long before a number of psychologists had created copious lists of instincts. Psychologists thought that perhaps we have one instinct for physical aggression, one for assertive behavior, and yet another for competitive behavior. Instinct theory, though, did not really explain anything; the wherefore behind Shakespeare's why was not adequately explored. An instinct was invariably inferred from the behavior it was intended to explain. For example, if a person was aggressive, he had an instinct for aggression. If another person was sociable, she had an instinct for sociability. However, instinct theory did call attention to the idea that some of our motivation is unlearned and involves physiological factors.

a.   b.

c.

(a) John Belushi, comic; (b) Evel Knievel, daredevil stuntman; (c) Rasputin, Russian mastermind and manipulator—all these high-profile individuals took risks, sought adventure, and thrived on excitement. All would score high on the trait of sensation seeking.

This idea is important in our understanding of motivation today, but instinct theory itself landed in psychology's dustheap many years ago.

Needs and Drives

If you do not have an instinct for sex, maybe you have a need or a drive for it. A **drive** *is an aroused state that occurs because of a physiological need.* A **need** *is a deprivation that energizes the drive to eliminate or reduce the deprivation.* You might have a need for water, for food, or for sex. The need for food, for example, arouses your hunger drive. This motivates you to do something—to go to McDonald's for a Big Mac, for example—to reduce the drive and satisfy the need. As a drive becomes stronger, we are motivated to reduce it. This explanation is known as drive-reduction theory.

Usually needs and drives are closely associated in time. For example, when your body needs food, your hunger drive will probably be aroused. An hour after you have eaten a Big Mac, you might still be hungry (thus, you need food), but your hunger drive might have subsided. From this example, you can sense that drive pertains to a psychological state; need involves a physiological state.

The goal of drive reduction is **homeostasis,** *the body's tendency to maintain an equilibrium, or steady state.* Hundreds of biological states in the body must be maintained within a certain range: temperature, blood sugar level, potassium and sodium levels, oxygen level, and so on. When you dive into an icy swimming pool, your body heats up. When you walk out of an air-conditioned room into the heat of a summer day, your body cools down. These changes occur automatically in an attempt to restore your body to its optimal state of functioning.

Homeostasis is achieved in the body much like a thermostat in a house keeps the temperature constant. For example, assume the thermostat in your house is set at 68 degrees. The furnace heats the house until a temperature of 68 degrees is reached, then the furnace shuts off. Without a source of heat, the temperature in the house eventually falls below 68 degrees. The thermostat detects this and turns the furnace back on again. The cycle is repeated so that the temperature is maintained within narrow limits.

Incentives

"If a man runs after money, he's money mad; if he keeps it, he's a capitalist; if he spends it, he's a playboy; if he doesn't try to get it, he lacks ambition; and if he accumulated it after a lifetime of hard work, people call him a fool who never got anything out of life." These words of Vic Oliver suggest that something more than internal drives can sometimes motivate our behavior—something external. Money is an example of an external stimulus that is a powerful motivator of behavior.

Incentives *are positive or negative external stimuli or events that motivate an individual's behavior.* For example, a lucrative income of $100,000+ is a positive incentive for becoming a physician; the threat of an intruder is a negative incentive for purchasing a security system for your home. By identifying the concept of incentives, psychologists expanded their definition of the "why" of behavior to include both internal factors (physiological needs and psychological drives) and external factors (incentives).

Hierarchy of Motives

Is getting an A in this class more important to you than eating? If the person of your dreams were to tell you that you are marvelous, would that motivate you to throw yourself in front of a car for her safety? According to Abraham Maslow (1954, 1971), our "basic" needs must be satisfied before our "higher" needs. The **hierarchy of motives** *is Maslow's concept that all individuals have five main needs, which must be satisfied in the following sequence: physiological, safety, love and belongingness, self-esteem, and self-actualization* (see figure 11.1). According to Maslow's hierarchy of motives, people need to eat before they can achieve, and they must satisfy their needs for safety before their needs for love.

It is the need for self-actualization that Maslow has described in the greatest detail. **Self-actualization,** *the highest and most elusive of Maslow's needs, is the motivation to develop one's full potential as a human being.* According to Maslow, self-actualization is possible only after the other needs in the hierarchy are met. Maslow cautions that most people stop maturing after they have developed a high level of self-esteem and, thus, do not become self-actualized. Many of Maslow's writings focus on how people can reach the elusive motivational state of self-actualization. We will discuss much more about Maslow's theory in chapter 12, Personality.

The idea that human motives are hierarchically arranged is an appealing one. Maslow's theory stimulates us to think about the ordering of motives in our own lives. However, the ordering of needs is somewhat subjective. Some people seek greatness in a career to achieve self-esteem, for example, while putting their needs for love and belongingness on hold.

Motivation's Biological, Cognitive, and Sociocultural Dimensions

At this point, we have discussed a number of approaches to understanding motivation. As we near the twenty-first century, what has had staying power in understanding motivation and what is being added today? Above all else, most psychologists today recognize that behavior is energized and directed by a complex mix of biological, cognitive, and sociocultural processes (Ford, 1992).

FIGURE 11.1

Maslow's hierarchy of motives. Abraham Maslow developed the hierarchy of human motives to show how we have to satisfy certain basic needs before we can satisfy higher needs. The diagram shows lower-level needs toward the base of the pyramid, higher-level needs toward the peak. The lowest needs (those that must be satisfied first) are physiological—hunger, thirst, and sleep, for example. The next needs that must be satisfied are safety needs, which ensure our survival—we have to protect ourselves from crime and war, for example. Then we must satisfy love and belongingness needs—we need the security, affection, and attention of others, for example. Near the top of Maslow's hierarchy are self-esteem needs—we need to feel good about ourselves as we learn skills, pursue a profession, and deal with people, for example. Finally, at the top of the pyramid and the highest of Maslow's needs are self-actualization needs—reaching our full potential as human beings. Included among self-actualization needs are the motivations for truth, goodness, beauty, wholeness, and justice.

Self-actualization

Self-esteem

Love and belongingness

Safety

Physiological

Biological Processes

Although psychologists rejected the biological concept of instinct many years ago, biology's role in motivation continues to be strong. You might remember our discussion of Konrad Lorenz's classic study of imprinting in chapter 9. Recall how the goslings became attached to Lorenz because he was the first moving object they saw shortly after they were born. Lorenz interpreted the goslings' behavior as evidence of rapid, innate learning within a critical time period. Lorenz's field is **ethology,** *the study of the biological basis of behavior in natural habitats*. Ethology is sometimes referred to as modern instinct theory, although Lorenz and other ethologists have carefully avoided using the term "instinct" because of the tainted name it got earlier in psychology's history. Ethology emerged as an important field because of the work of European zoologists, such as Lorenz, in the 1930s, who argued that behaviorism had gone too far in promoting the role of environmental experiences in motivation.

Like behaviorists, ethologists are careful observers of behavior. Unlike many behaviorists, though, ethologists believe that laboratories are not good settings for observing behavior. They observe behavior in its natural surroundings instead, believing that behavior cannot be completely understood unless it is examined in the context in which it evolved. For example, ethologists have observed many species of animals in the wild, discovering their powerful motivation to stake out their own territory and band together to fight off any intruders (Lorenz, 1966).

Ethological theory reminds us of our biological origins and raises the issue of how strongly we are motivated by our biological makeup versus our experiences in life. Are we motivated to hurt someone else because we were born that way or because of our interactions with people who hit and yell, for example? As you can see, even though classical instinct theory bit the dust, the issue regarding whether motivation is innate or learned, biologically or experientially based, is still alive.

The body's physiological makeup—brain structures, body organs, and hormones—also plays an important role in contemporary views of motivation. We'll discuss these physiological mechanisms in our discussion of hunger, but first we'll look at how thought influences motivation.

Cognitive Processes

The contemporary view of motivation also emphasizes the importance of cognitive factors. Consider your motivation to do well in this class. Your confidence in your ability to do well and your expectation for success may help you relax, concentrate better, and study more effectively. If you think too much about not doing well in the class and fear that you will fail, you may become too anxious and not perform as well. Your ability to consciously control your behavior and resist the temptation to party too much and to avoid studying will improve your achievement, too. So will your ability to use your information-processing abilities of attention, memory, and problem solving as you study for and take tests.

Psychologists continue to debate the role of conscious versus unconscious thought in understanding motivation. Freud's legacy to contemporary psychoanalytic theory is the belief that we are largely unaware of why we behave the way we do (Kurzweil, 1990; Yorke, Wiseberg, & Freeman, 1989). Psychoanalytic theorists argue that few of us know why we love someone, why we eat so much, why we are so aggressive, or why we are so shy. (Much more detail about psychoanalytic theory appears in the next chapter.) Cognitive psychologists, in contrast, emphasize that people are rational and aware of their motivation. Humanistic theorists, such as Maslow, also stress our ability to examine our lives and become aware of what motivates us. (Much more about humanistic theory also appears in the next chapter.)

Sociocultural Processes

As is true of so much human behavior, environmental and sociocultural influences play an important role in motivation (D'Andrade & Strauss, 1992; de Rivera, 1989). Even "biological" motives have environmental and sociocultural underpinnings. Why does the same meal—say, steak, baked potato, and salad—satisfy our hunger so much more when we are seated near someone we love in a candle-lit room than in a noisy school cafeteria, for example? Consider also the social motive of achievement. To fully understand achievement, we need to examine how parents and children interact, how peers compare one another, and which people we look up to as models of success, along with the standards for achievement in various cultures.

The role of sociocultural and environmental factors raises another important issue regarding motivation: are we internally motivated or externally motivated? Do we study hard because we have an internal standard that motivates us to do well or because of external factors, such as wanting to get good grades so we can get into a doctoral program in psychology or medical school? As a rule, the study of biological and cognitive factors stresses the role of internal motivation, and the study of sociocultural and environmental factors stresses the role of external motivation. We'll get back to the internal-external issue in motivation later in the chapter in our discussion of achievement motivation.

In our description of motivation's biological, cognitive, and sociocultural underpinnings, we have encountered three important questions. (1) To what degree are we motivated by innate, unlearned, biological factors as opposed to learned, sociocultural, experientially based factors? (2) To what degree are we aware of what motivates us—that is, to what extent is our motivation conscious? (3) To what degree are we internally or externally motivated? These are issues that researchers continue to wrangle with and debate. Not only will these issues reappear in this chapter, but they also will resurface in our discussion of personality in the next chapter. Now we will turn our attention to an important dimension of motivation—hunger.

Hunger

Imagine that you live in the Bayambang area of the Philippines. You are very poor and have little food to eat. Hunger continuously gnaws at everyone in your village. Now imagine yourself as the typical American, eating not only breakfast, lunch, and dinner, but snacking along the way—and maybe even raiding the refrigerator at midnight.

Food is an important aspect of life in any culture. Whether we have very little or large amounts of food available to us, hunger influences our behavior. What mechanisms explain why we get hungry?

Physiological Factors

You are sitting in class and it is 2 P.M. You were so busy today that you skipped lunch. As the professor lectures, your stomach starts to growl. For many of us, a growling stomach is one of the main signs that we are hungry. Psychologists have wondered for many years about the role of peripheral factors—such as the stomach, liver, and blood chemistry—in hunger.

Peripheral Factors

In 1912 Walter Cannon and A. L. Washburn conducted an experiment that revealed a close association between stomach contractions and hunger (see figure 11.2). As part of the procedure, a partially inflated balloon was passed through a tube inserted in Washburn's mouth and pushed down into his stomach. A machine that measures air pressure was connected to the balloon to monitor Washburn's stomach contractions. Every time Washburn reported hunger pangs, his stomach was also contracting. This finding, which was confirmed in subsequent experiments with other volunteers, led the two to believe that gastric activity is *the* basis for hunger.

Stomach signals are not the only factors that affect hunger, however. People who have had their stomachs surgically removed still get hunger pangs. Stomach contractions can be a signal for hunger, but the stomach also can send signals that stop hunger. We all know that a full stomach can decrease our appetite. In fact, the stomach actually tells the brain not only how full it is, but also how much nutrient is in the stomach load. That is why a stomach full of rich food stops your hunger faster than a stomach full of water (Deutsch & Gonzales, 1980). The same stomach hormone that helps start the digestion of food (called cholecystokinin, or CCK) reaches your brain through the bloodstream and signals you to stop eating.

Blood sugar (or glucose) is an important factor in hunger, probably because the brain is critically dependent on sugar for energy. One set of sugar receptors is located in the brain itself, and these receptors trigger hunger when sugar levels get too low. Another set of sugar receptors is in the liver, which is the organ that stores excess sugar and releases it into the blood when needed. The sugar receptors in the liver signal the brain via the vagus

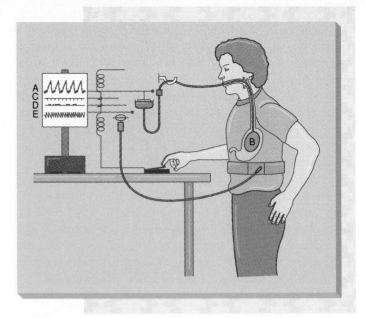

FIGURE 11.2

Cannon and Washburn's classic experiment on hunger. Notice the letters A, B, C, D, and E in the drawing. A is the record of the increases and decreases in the volume of the balloon in the subject's stomach, B. Number of minutes elapsed is shown in C. The subject's indication of feeling hungry is recorded at D. E is a reading of the movements of the abdominal wall to ensure that such movements are not the cause of changes in stomach volume.

nerve; this signal can also make you hungry (Novlin & others, 1983). Another important factor in blood sugar control is the hormone insulin, which causes excess sugar in the blood to be stored in the cells as fats and carbohydrates. Insulin injections cause profound hunger because they drastically lower blood sugar.

Psychologist Judith Rodin (1984) has further clarified the role of insulin and glucose in understanding hunger and eating behavior. She points out that, when we eat complex carbohydrates, such as cereals, bread, and pasta, insulin levels go up but then fall off gradually. When we consume simple sugars, such as candy bars and soft drinks, insulin levels rise and then fall off sharply—the familiar "sugar low." Glucose levels in the blood are affected by these complex carbohydrates and simple sugars in similar ways. The consequence is that we are more likely to eat again within several hours of eating simple sugars than complex carbohydrates. Also, the food we eat at one meal often influences how much we will eat at our next meal. Thus, consuming doughnuts and candy bars, in addition to providing no nutritional value, sets up an ongoing sequence of what and how much we probably will crave the next time we eat.

Brain Processes

So far we have been talking about peripheral factors in hunger. However, the brain is also involved in hunger. The brain's **ventromedial hypothalamus (VMH)** *is a region of the hypothala-*

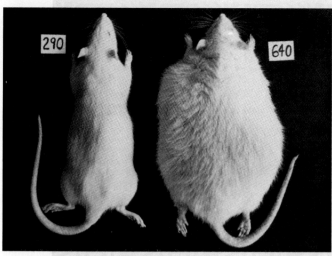

a.

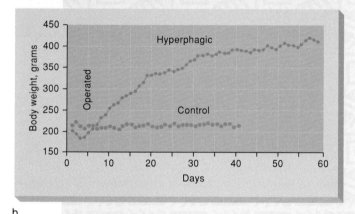

b.

FIGURE 11.3

The role of the ventromedial hypothalamus (VMH) in the obesity of rats. (a) A hyperphagic rat gained three times its body weight after a lesion (surgical destruction) had been made in its VMH. (b) This graph displays the weight gain by a group of rats in which lesions had been made in the VMH (hyperphagic) and by a group of rats in which no lesions had been made (control). Notice how quickly the hyperphagic rats gained weight, but that after about 1 month they virtually stopped gaining weight. This suggests that hormones and body cells control the body's overall set point for body weight.

mus that plays an important role in controlling hunger. When a rat's VMH is surgically destroyed, it immediately becomes hyperphagic (that is, it eats too much) and rapidly becomes obese (Brobeck, Tepperman, & Long, 1943). Researchers thought that the VMH was a "satiety center," and its destruction left animals unable to fully satisfy their hunger. The picture now emerging, however, suggests that the destruction causes a hormonal disorder (remember that the hypothalamus is the master control center for many hormones). After the VMH is destroyed, a rat's body cells act as if they are starving, constantly converting all nutrients from the blood into fat and never releasing them. That is the main reason the animals become obese (see figure 11.3). One of

"Let's just go in and see what happens."

Drawing by Booth; © 1986 The New Yorker Magazine, Inc.

the fascinating aspects of this condition is that the animals stop gaining weight once they reach a certain weight, suggesting that hormones and body cells control the body's overall "set point" for body weight. **Set point** *refers to the weight maintained when no effort is made to gain or lose weight.*

To summarize, the brain monitors both blood sugar levels and the condition of the stomach, then integrates this information (and probably other information as well) in the process of regulating hunger. Hypothalamic regions, especially the VMH, are involved in integrating information about hunger.

Your internal physiological world is very much involved in your feelings of hunger. In addition to the physiological processes, some external and cognitive factors are involved.

External Cues

Psychologists are interested in how environmental cues might stimulate hunger. You may know someone who seems incapable of walking past an ice cream shop without stopping to eat a huge hot fudge sundae.

Stanley Schachter (1971) believes that one of the main differences between obese and normal-weight individuals is their attention to environmental cues. From his perspective, people of normal weight attend to internal cues for signals of when to eat—for example, when blood sugar level is low or hunger pangs are sensed in the stomach. In contrast, an obese person responds to such external cues as signals of when to eat—how food tastes, looks, and smells, for example.

Self-control and Exercise

Rodin (1984) points out that, not too long ago, we believed that obesity was caused by such factors as unhappiness or responses to external food cues. According to Rodin, a number of biological, cognitive, and social factors are more important. We already discussed the important biological factors, including the roles of complex carbohydrates and simple sugars in insulin and glucose levels. In regard to external cues, Rodin says that, although obese persons are more responsive to external food cues than are normal-weight persons, there are individuals at all weight levels who respond more to external than internal stimuli. Many persons who respond to external cues also have the conscious ability to control their behavior and keep environmental food cues from externally controlling their eating patterns (Stunkard, 1989).

Rodin believes that, not only is conscious self-control of eating patterns important in weight control, but so is exercise. No matter what your genetic background, aerobic exercise increases your metabolic rate, which helps you burn calories. Much more information about dieting, eating behavior, and exercise appears in our discussion of health in chapter 15.

At this point, we have discussed a number of ideas about the overall nature of motivation and about hunger. Next, we will consider two other important dimensions of motivation—competence and achievement.

REVIEW

Principles of Motivation and Hunger

Motivation involves the question of "why" people behave, think, and feel the way they do. Motivation varies not only in kind but also in intensity. Instinct theory flourished early in the twentieth century, but instincts do not adequately explain motivation. Drive-reduction theory emphasizes a drive as an aroused state brought about by a physiological need. Reducing the drive satisfies the need. Homeostasis is an important motivational process promoted by drive-reduction theory. Incentives are based on the belief that external factors are important in motivation. Maslow believed that some motives need to be satisfied before others; self-actualization is given considerable importance in Maslow's hierarchy of motives. The contemporary view of motivation includes a focus on biological (especially physiological) factors, conscious thoughts and understanding, and sociocultural processes. Three important issues are the degree to which motivation is innate versus learned, conscious versus unconscious, and internal versus external.

In hunger the brain monitors both blood sugar level and the condition of the stomach (interest in the stomach was stimulated by Cannon's research), then integrates this information. Hypothalamic regions are important in hunger, especially VMH. Schachter stressed that environmental cues are involved in the control of eating, but Rodin argues that conscious self-control and exercise are more important than external cues in understanding hunger and eating behavior.

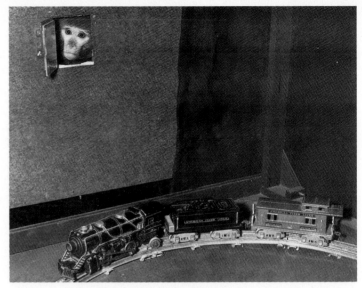

FIGURE 11.4

Motivation for novel stimulation. This monkey showed a motivation for novel stimulation and was willing to work just so he could unlock the window and watch a toy train go around in a circle.

Competence and Achievement

We are a species motivated to gain mastery over our world, to explore unknown environments with enthusiasm and curiosity, and to achieve greatness. Unlike the motives of hunger and sex (which were discussed in chapter 10), the social motives of competence and achievement are less likely to involve the reduction of a drive or the satisfaction of a need.

Competence Motivation

In the 1950s, psychologists recognized that motivation involves much more than the reduction of biological needs. **Competence motivation** *describes our motivation to deal effectively with the environment, to be adept at what we attempt, to process information efficiently, and to make the world a better place.* R. W. White (1959) said we do these things not because they serve biological needs, but because we have an internal motivation to effectively interact with our environment.

Among the research White used to support his concept of competence motivation were experiments that showed that organisms are motivated to seek stimulation rather than to reduce a need. For example, monkeys solved simple problems just for the opportunity to watch a toy train (Butler, 1953) (see figure 11.4). Rats consistently chose a complex maze with a number of pathways over a simple maze with few pathways. A series of experiments suggested that college students could not tolerate sensory deprivation for more than 2 to 3 days (Bexton, Heron, & Scott, 1954). These students developed a strong

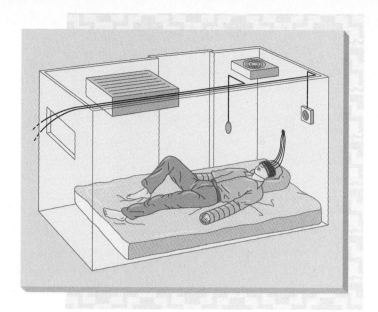

FIGURE 11.5

Isolation chamber used in Heron's sensory deprivation study. College students were paid $20 a day to remain in this isolation chamber ($20 was a reasonably good sum of money in the 1950s, especially since the students were getting paid to do as little as possible). Their sensory input was drastically reduced. Outside noises were masked by fans, the subjects wore goggles that kept them from seeing, and they were prevented from touching objects by having their arms wrapped in cotton. How did the students react to this situation? Initially they slept most of the time. After 2 to 3 days, though, they quit the experiment, which they were free to do at any time. The students said they became very bored and restless, and, after several days, they felt so uncomfortable they couldn't wait to get out of the situation, even though it meant losing $20 a day.

Adapted from "The Pathology of Boredom" by Woodburn Heron. Copyright © 1957 by Scientific American, Inc. All rights reserved.

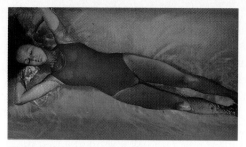

FIGURE 11.6

Restricted environmental stimulation therapy (REST). The woman shown here is lying in a water immersion tank during a Restricted Environmental Stimulation Therapy (REST) session. This virtual absence of environmental stimuli for approximately 1 hour at a time during the "float" has been effective in improving such conditions as hypertension.

motivation to quit the experiment, even though they were getting paid to participate in it. They became bored, restless, and irritable (figure 11.5 shows the isolation chamber of the sensory deprivation experiment).

Psychologists have investigated how shorter periods of sensory deprivation—such as spending time in a water immersion tank—can reduce stress (Suedfeld & Coren, 1989). Imagine that you have just stepped into a shallow pool of densely salted water. You close the hatch, then lie on your back and float (see figure 11.6). The tank is totally dark. The only sound is your own breathing, which is barely audible. Feeling suspended, you have no sense of temperature and little sense of time. Gradually your muscles relax. After 55 minutes, music is piped into the tank to signal the end of the session. The flotation tank experience is called Restricted Environmental Stimulation Therapy (REST). Researchers have documented that a series of about 20 REST sessions can significantly lower the blood pressure of many

individuals with hypertension (Fine & Turner, 1987). REST also has been found to improve athletic performance and creative thinking and to reduce chronic pain (Fine & Turner, 1985; Suedfeld, Metcalfe, & Bluck, 1987). Researchers suspect that REST is effective because our fast-paced lives have become overstimulating and demanding. REST allows us to "get away from it all" in a dramatic way. In summary, sensory deprivation can both harm and help. It's harmful when we are deprived of sensory input for too long; it's helpful in short spurts.

Achievement Motivation

"Winning isn't everything, it is the *only* thing," exhorted Vince Lombardi, the former coach of the Green Bay Packers. We live in an achievement-oriented world, with standards that tell us success is important. Some psychologists believe that our world is too achievement-oriented. David Elkind (1981) said we are a nation of hurried, wired people who are too uptight about success and failure and far too worried about what we accomplish in comparison with others.

Some people are highly motivated to succeed and expend a lot of effort striving to excel. Other people are not as motivated to succeed and don't work as hard to achieve. These two types of individuals vary in their **achievement motivation (need for achievement)**, *the desire to accomplish something, to reach a standard of excellence, to expend effort to excel.* Borrowing from Henry Murray's (1938) theory and measurement of personality, psychologist David McClelland (1955) assessed achievement by showing individuals ambiguous pictures that were likely to stimulate achievement-related responses. The individuals were asked to tell a story about the pictures, and their comments were scored according to how strongly they reflected achievement. Researchers have found that individuals whose stories reflect high achievement motivation have a stronger hope for success than fear of failure, are moderate rather than high or low risk takers, and persist with effort when tasks become difficult (Atkinson & Raynor, 1974).

McClelland also wondered if you could boost achievement behavior by increasing achievement motivation. To find out, he trained the businessmen in a village in India to become more achievement-oriented, encouraging them to increase their hope for success, reduce their fear of failure, take moderate risks, and persist with a great deal of effort when tasks become difficult (McClelland, 1978). Compared with village businessmen in a nearby town, the village businessmen who were trained by McClelland started more new businesses and employed more new people in the 2 years after the training.

Matina Horner (1968) wondered if there were any differences in achievement motivation between men and women. She was struck by the fact that much of the research on achievement motivation was based on male experiences. She found that, when women had lower achievement motivation, it was not fear of failure that held women back but just the opposite—**fear of success,** *individuals' worry that they might be rejected if they are successful.* Years later researchers came to realize that some men also fear success, but for different reasons. Women worry about social rejection; men worry that they might misspend their life chasing a goal that will leave them wondering, "Is that all there is?" (Williams, 1987).

Today social theorists argue about the merit of Horner's concept. Fear of success doesn't really explain, for instance, why there are so few women in the Senate or conducting symphony orchestras. The final explanation probably involves the complex interaction between achievement motivation and gender role socialization (discussed in chapter 10.) Black women are less likely than White women to have been socialized into traditionally female roles, for example, and tend to have less fear of success (Weston & Mednick, 1970). Women may have come a long way since the 1960s, but they still report feeling caught between roles that call for traditional femininity and those that demand hard-nosed competitiveness.

Intrinsic and Extrinsic Motivation

Parents have always wanted their children to do their best. In the 1950s, McClelland argued that parents who wanted their children to be achievers should train them to become more independent. More recently researchers have found that, to increase their children's achievement motivation, parents need to set high standards for achievement and model achievement-oriented behavior.

Achievement motivation—whether in school, at work, or in sports—can be divided into two main types: **intrinsic motivation,** *the internal desire to be competent and to do something for its own sake,* and **extrinsic motivation,** *which is influenced by external rewards and punishments.* If you work hard in college because a personal standard of excellence is important to you, intrinsic motivation is involved, but, if you work hard in college because you know it will bring you a higher-paying job when you graduate, extrinsic motivation is at work.

FIGURE 11.7

Intrinsic motivation and drawing activity. Students spent more time in art activity when no reward was mentioned than when a reward was expected for their participation (Lepper, Greene, & Nisbett, 1973).

Almost every boss, parent, and teacher has wondered whether to offer a reward to someone who does well (extrinsic motivation) or to let his or her internal, self-determined motivation operate (intrinsic motivation). If someone is producing shoddy work, seems bored, or has a negative attitude, offering incentives may improve his or her motivation. However, there are times when external rewards can get in the way of achievement motivation. In one study of students who already had a strong interest in art, students who didn't expect a reward spent more time drawing than did their counterparts who knew they would be rewarded (Lepper, Greene, & Nisbett, 1973) (see figure 11.7).

Some of the most achievement-oriented people are those who have a high personal standard for achievement (internal) and who also are highly competitive (external). In one study, students who had poor math skills but who set their own goals (internal) and received information about their peers' achievement (external) worked more math problems and got more of them correct than their counterparts who experienced either situation alone (Schunk, 1983). Other research suggests that social comparison by itself is not a wise strategy (Ames & Ames, 1989). The argument is that social comparison puts an individual in an ego-involved, threatening, self-focused state rather than a task-involved, effortful, strategy-focused state. Next, we will examine another important area of motivation and achievement—sports psychology.

Motivation and Sports Psychology

The Chicago Bulls trail the Detroit Pistons 102 to 101, with 10 seconds left in the game. Michael Jordan dribbles the ball until 4 seconds are left in the game. He drives to the basket and is fouled, with 1 second remaining. Calmly, confidently, he sinks both free throws and the Bulls win 103 to 102. Nancy Lopez is tied for the lead in the Ladies' Professional Golf Championship. On the 18th hole of the final round, she sinks a birdie putt to win the championship. What psychological and motivational characteristics allow such athletes as Jordan and Lopez to perform so well under pressure?

One of psychology's newest and most rapidly growing fields is sports psychology. Whether it is Little League Baseball or Olympic competition, sports are an integral part of our society. Do athletes become stars because they are internally or externally motivated? Just as with other areas of life, both internal and external factors are involved. Most star athletes have had the backing of a remarkable set of teachers, parents, and other external supports throughout their long careers. In addition, many are motivated by the desire for fame and fortune or by a competitive spirit. However, most top athletes also have a deep, burning desire to do their best, to reach a personal standard of excellence.

One study showed that elite athletes—the stars in 23 sports—differ from lesser athletes in several important ways (Mahoney, Gabriel, & Perkins, 1987). Although all professional athletes have innate physical gifts, the way elite athletes handle psychological matters—self-confidence, anxiety, concentration, and motivation—is what tips the balance and makes them great.

Self-confidence is a tricky area to study, partly because it is not simply the absence of self-doubt, and, although confidence is a uniquely personal experience, there are also some characteristics common to all self-confident athletes (Mahoney, 1989). They show a willingness, sometimes even an eagerness, to be under pressure and the ability to remain focused on immediate demands. With 2 seconds to go in the game and down one point, Michael Jordan, Larry Bird, and Isaiah Thomas all want the ball.

Star athletes generally report that they have set reasonable and personally meaningful goals in training but that sometimes pushing themselves too hard can harm their performance or lead to "burn out." Athletes who seek a balanced life, for example, tend to do better than those who spend all their time in training.

What psychological and motivational characteristics help basketball player Michael Jordan and golfer Nancy Lopez perform well under pressure?

Top athletes also have the ability to control their emotions. In particular, they are able to control their anxiety. For many years, sports psychologists thought that very low and very high levels of anxiety produce lower performances. That view is now seen as too simplistic. Top athletes say that what is more important is what anxiety means to them and what they do with it (Mahoney, 1989). Many get the jitters before a game—maybe a week before, maybe just minutes before. Sometimes their anxiety even spills over into the first few minutes of the game. However, once they are into the heat of competition, they are able to get past their anxiety and become totally absorbed in the moment. When athletes let their anxiety get the upper hand, however, their muscles tense, their minds race, and they may "choke."

Ever since Jackie Robinson broke the racial barrier in major league baseball, sports have been one of the careers most accessible to Blacks. As a result, Black families are four times more likely than White families to try to increase their teenagers' motivation to participate in sports, often to the neglect of their intellectual and personal development. Tragically, only 5 percent of Black high school athletes go on to compete at the college level. Of those who attend 4-year colleges on athletic scholarships, approximately 70 percent never graduate, and less than 2 percent ever make the roster on a professional team. Among the chosen few, 60 percent are out of professional sports in 3 to 4 years. More often than not, these Black athletes find themselves financially destitute and without the credentials or the skills to start a new career. According to sociologist Harry Edwards (1990), this does not mean that Blacks should abandon sports but that young Black athletes need to understand the realities of a sports career and give more attention to academic achievement.

Cultural, Ethnic, and Social-Class Variations in Achievement

People in the United States are often more achievement-oriented than people in many other countries. One study of 104 societies revealed that the parents in nonindustrialized countries placed a lower value on their children's achievement and independence and a higher value on obedience and cooperation than did the parents in industrialized countries (Barry, Child, & Bacon, 1959). In comparisons between Anglo American children and Mexican and Hispanic American children, the Anglo American children were more competitive and less cooperative. For example, one study found that Anglo American children are more likely to keep other children from gaining when they could not realize those gains themselves (Kagan & Madsen, 1972). Another study showed that Mexican children are more family-oriented, whereas Anglo American children tend to be more concerned about themselves (Holtzmann, 1982).

Until recently, researchers studying achievement focused almost exclusively on White males, and, when achievement in ethnic minority groups has been studied, the cultural differences have too often been viewed against standards of achievements for White males. As a result, many researchers have reached the conclusion that ethnic minorities are somehow deficient when it comes to achievement (Gibbs & Huang, 1989; Trimble, 1989).

UCLA psychologist Sandra Graham is shown here talking with a group of young boys about motivation. Dr. Graham has conducted important research showing that middle-class Black children—like their White counterparts—have high achievement expectations and understand that their failure is often due to lack of effort rather than to lack of luck.

In addition, most studies on ethnic minorities do not take into account socioeconomic status. Socioeconomic status (also called SES) is determined by a combination of occupation, education, and income. When both ethnicity and social class are taken into account in the same study, social class tends to be a far better predictor of achievement than is ethnicity (Graham, 1986). For example, middle-class individuals, regardless of their ethnic background, have higher aspirations and expectations for success, and they recognize the importance of effort more than their lower-class counterparts (Gibbs, 1989).

Psychologist Sandra Graham (1986, 1987, 1990), for example, has found that middle-class Black children do not fit the stereotypes of either deviant or special populations. They, like their middle-class White counterparts, have high expectations for their own achievement and understand that failure is often due to lack of effort, rather than to luck.

It's also an indisputable fact that many people from ethnic minority backgrounds face educational, career, and social barriers (Huang & Gibbs, 1989). The Civil Rights Act of 1964 has made some progress in chipping away at these barriers, but much more needs to be done. We do not have all of the answers to the problems of poverty and racism in this country, but, as the Reverend Jesse Jackson commented, perhaps we have begun to ask some of the right questions. As you will see in Sociocultural Worlds 11.1, some of the right questions are finally being asked, and answered, at least in regard to Black and Hispanic American math and science students.

Just as psychologists are concerned about the fact that Black and Hispanic American students tend to underachieve in math, they are intrigued by a group of superachievers—Japanese, Chinese, and Asian American students. Japanese eighth graders, for example, have the highest average math scores of all eighth graders from 20 countries. Also, Japanese seniors are second only to Chinese seniors in Hong Kong (Garden, 1987; McKnight & others, 1987). In contrast, American 8th- and 12th-grade students have among the lowest scores in problem solving, geometry, algebra, and calculus. In another recent cross-national investigation of the math and science achievement of 9-to-13-year-olds, Korean and Taiwanese students placed first and second, respectively (Educational Testing Service, 1992). In this study, 9-to-13-year old students in the United States finished 13th (out of 15) in science and 15th (out of 16) in math achievement. Critics of the cross-national studies say that such comparisons are flawed because countries, the percentage of children and adolescents who go to school, and the curricula vary so widely. Even in the face of such criticisms, most education experts agree that many U.S. students are achieving far below their potential in math.

Developmental psychologist Harold Stevenson and his colleagues (1990) wanted to find out why Japanese students are such superlative math students. They examined Japanese and American children's math achievement in the first and fifth grades and found some striking differences: Japanese students spent 62 more days a year in school; first-grade teachers in Japan

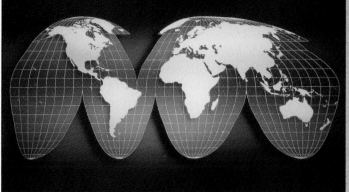

Professor Treisman confers with students in a math study group at the University of California–Berkeley. Treisman's research revealed the importance of collaborative learning in helping Black students succeed in math and science courses.

Modifying the Math/Science Study Strategies of Black American College Students

In 1986 Black and Hispanic Americans received just 8 of the more than 600 doctoral degrees in math in the United States. At every level of education, a comparatively small percentage of Black and Hispanic American students enroll in math and science courses. More alarming, the enrollment rate, especially for Black students, actually declined in the 1980s. With more than one-fourth of America's college-age population expected to be Black or Hispanic in 1995, educators need to find ways to entice Black and Hispanic Americans into math and the sciences.

Mathematician Philip Treisman, who teaches at the University of California, Berkeley, wanted to find out why the success rate in math is so low for Black and Hispanic American students. He realized that the most successful math students at UC–Berkeley, as is true of universities throughout the country, are Asian Americans. Thus, Treisman extensively compared 20 Black students with 20 Chinese American students who were enrolled in freshman calculus.

Treisman observed the students in the library, in their dormitory rooms, and in their homes, where he even interviewed their families. He found that the differences between the Black and Chinese American students were not the result of motivation, income, family support, or academic preparation. For example, even Black students who entered UC with the best test scores and other positive predictors tended to do poorly in math.

The most striking difference was that the Black students virtually isolated themselves when they studied. Eighteen of the 20 Black students always studied alone—the two who studied together eventually dropped out to marry each other. Treisman suggests that the self-reliance these students had developed to buffer themselves from the distractions of the inner city—and that gave them the academic edge to get into a top university—became their downfall at Berkeley. In their isolation, these students had to "learn the ropes" at UC–Berkeley alone, and

they had no way to make sure they understood the material in their math and science courses.

In contrast, within 4 weeks after arriving at Berkeley, 13 of the 20 Chinese American students had found partners to study with, and several others were still searching for partners. The study groups got together only after each student had spent a great deal of time studying on his or her own. Group study was a final, but very important, step. Together, the students were able to solve problems that stumped them when they worked on their own. When their collective effort failed to solve a particular problem, they realized the problem was an especially knotty one, so they didn't fall prey to self-criticism. In addition to studying together, these students discussed such things as what professors expected, what the university requirements were, and how many hours they should be studying. They shared tips for handling the bureaucratic mazes of financial aid and housing, and they talked about their feelings and experiences with the White community.

Based on his observations of the Black and Chinese American students, Treisman developed a math workshop, with three overriding goals: (1) help ethnic minority students excel, not just avoid failure, (2) emphasize collaborative learning and small-group teaching methods, (3) and require faculty sponsorship. After 7 years, the track record for the math workshop speaks for itself: 55 percent of the workshop's 231 Black students (compared with 21 percent of the 234 Black students not in the workshop) have earned a grade of B– or better in first-year calculus. Black students in the workshop have consistently scored a full grade higher than Black students who have not participated. In addition, 44 percent of the Black students who entered Berkeley in 1978 or 1979 and who participated in the workshop graduated in math and science majors, whereas only 10 percent of the Black students who not did take the workshop graduated in these fields.

Freshman mathematics and science courses too often have been the burial ground for the aspirations of Black and Hispanic American students who entered college with the goal of majoring in math or science. Such programs as Philip Treisman's reveal how the underachievement of Black and Hispanic American students can be turned into accomplishment (Charles A. Dana Foundation Report, 1988).

Japanese children consistently outperform American children in math. What reasons are likely to be responsible for the superior performance by Japanese children?

devoted about a quarter of classroom time in math instruction, whereas American teachers spent only one-tenth; and Japanese children spent far more time doing homework on weekends than American children—66 minutes versus 18 minutes (Chen & Stevenson, 1989; Stevenson, Stigler, & Lee, 1986; Stevenson & others, 1990). In another study, the researchers also found that Chinese and Japanese children have a much more positive attitude about homework than American children (Chen & Stevenson, 1989).

In his most recent research, Stevenson and his colleagues (1990, 1991) focused on the family's role in children's academic achievement in Japan, China, and the United States. The researchers found that Japanese and Chinese families place far more emphasis on education than American parents. Chinese and Japanese parents invest more time helping their elementary school children with homework and studying for tests than American parents. Chinese and Japanese mothers simply expect and demand more of their children; these mothers stress hard work as the basis for achievement. American mothers, on the other hand, are more likely to point to their children's innate abilities as the reason for their level of achievement.

In summary, a number of related cultural factors play a part in American children's poor math scores. Stevenson and his colleagues believe that good teachers, interested parents, and hard work would go a long way toward boosting American children's math achievement.

In addition to Chinese and Japanese children, many Asian American children fit into the "whiz kid, superachiever" image. This is especially true of second- and third-generation Japanese and Chinese students, as well as the children of Asian families who arrived in the United States in the late 1960s and early 1970s. Many of these more recent immigrants came from Hong Kong, South Korea, India, the Philippines, and Indochina. Most of these families had professional, well-educated backgrounds, and they passed along a strong interest in education and a strong work ethic to their children.

Remember, though, that diversity exists within any ethnic or cultural group (Phinney, 1991; Slaughter-DeFoe & others, 1990; Spencer, 1991). For thousands of Asian Americans, including a high percentage of the 600,000 Indochinese refugees who fled Vietnam, Laos, and Cambodia in the late 1970s, the problems are legion. Many in this wave of refugees are poor and have few skills and little education. They speak little English and have a difficult time finding a decent job. Housing is often crowded, shared with many relatives. Many of these Asian American children struggle in school; some drop out, and others are attracted to gangs and drugs. Only a few schools have a range of culturally focused academic programs and social services to help these children adapt more effectively to life in America.

Achievement and Gender

The motivation for work and achievement is the same for both sexes; however, women and men often make different career choices because of the way they have been socialized and the opportunities available to them. Because women have been socialized to adopt nurturing roles rather than career or achieving roles, traditionally they have not seriously planned careers, have not extensively explored career options, and have restricted their choices to gender-stereotyped careers (Baumrind, 1989; Diamond, 1988).

For some areas of achievement, gender differences are so large they can best be described as nonoverlapping. For example, no major league baseball players are female, and 96 percent of all registered nurses are female. In contrast, many measures of achievement-related behaviors do not reveal gender differences. For example, girls show just as much persistence at tasks as boys. The question of whether males and females differ in their expectations for success at various achievement tasks is not yet settled (Eccles, 1987).

Because females are often stereotyped as less competent than males, the incorporation of gender-role stereotypes into a person's self-concept could lead females to have less confidence than males in their general intellectual abilities. This could lead females to have lower expectations for success at difficult academic and vocational activities. It could also lead females to expect to have to work harder to achieve success at these activities than males expect to have to work. Evidence supports these predictions (Eccles, Harold-Goldsmith, & Miller, 1989). Either of these beliefs could keep females from selecting demanding educational or vocational options, especially if these options are not perceived as important or interesting.

Gender roles could also produce different expectations of success depending on the gender stereotyping of the activity. Both educational programs and vocational options are gender stereotyped in our culture. Many high-level professions, especially those that are math-related and scientific/technical, are thought to be male activities. In contrast, teaching below the

Some of the brightest and most gifted girls do not have achievement and career aspirations that match their talents. Gender researchers hope that gender-role stereotypes that prevent girls from developing a more positive orientation toward math and science can be eliminated.

college level, working in clerical and related support jobs, and excelling in language-related courses are thought to be female activities by both children and adults (Eccles, 1987; Eccles & Hoffman, 1984; Huston, 1983). Incorporating these beliefs into their self-concepts could cause females to have lower expectations for success in male-typed activities and higher expectations for success in female-typed activities. This pattern could lead females to select female-typed activities over male-typed activities. Some support for this perspective has been found (Eccles, 1987). At times, though, researchers have found no gender differences in achievement expectations.

A special concern is that some of the brightest and most gifted girls do not have achievement and career aspirations that match their talents. In one investigation, high-achieving girls had much lower expectations for success than high-achieving boys (Stipek & Hoffman, 1980). In the gifted research program at Johns Hopkins University, many mathematically precocious girls selected scientific and medical careers, although only 46 percent aspired to a full-time career, compared with 98 percent of the boys (Fox, Brody, & Tobin, 1979).

To help talented female youths redirect their paths, some high schools are using programs developed by colleges and universities. Project CHOICE (Creating Her Options In Career Education) was designed by Case Western University to detect barriers in reaching one's potential. Gifted 11th-grade females received individualized counseling that included interviews with female role models, referral to the appropriate occupational groups, and information about career workshops. A program at the University of Nebraska (Kerr, 1983) was successful in encouraging talented female high school students to pursue more prestigious careers. This was accomplished by individualized counseling and participation in a "Perfect Future Day," in which girls shared career fantasies and discussed barriers that might impede their fantasies. Internal and external constraints were evaluated, gender-role stereotypes were discouraged, and high aspirations were applauded. Although these programs have shown short-term success in redirecting the career paths of high-ability females, in some instances the benefits fade over time—6 months or more, for example. It is important to be concerned about improving the awareness of career alternatives for all female youths, however, and not just those of high ability.

Parents also play an important role in their sons' and daughters' career development. In one recent study, 1,500 mothers and their young adolescent sons and daughters were studied to determine the role of maternal expectations, advice, and the provision of opportunities in their sons' and daughters' occupational aspirations (Harold & Eccles, 1990). Mothers were more likely to encourage their sons to consider the military, to expect their sons to go into the military right after high school, and to discuss with their sons the education needed for and likely income of various jobs. Expecting marriage right after high school and discussing the problems of combining work and family were more common to daughters. Also, mothers were more worried that their daughters would not have a happy marriage, and they were more likely to want their sons to have a job that would support a family. This study also indicated that the mothers worked more with the boys on computers; they also more often provided the boys with computers, software, and programs. The mothers also bought more math or science books and games for the boys and more often enrolled the boys in computer classes. The boys were provided more sports opportunities, whereas the girls were given more opportunities in music, art, and dance. The mothers said the boys had more talent in math and were better suited for careers involving math, although they believed that the girls had more talent in English and were better suited for English-related careers. In sum, there were differences in the kinds of advice and opportunities the mothers provided and in their expectations for and ability assessments of their sons and daughters.

The maternal advice, provision of opportunities, expectations, and ability assessments were associated with adolescents' occupational aspirations in the previous study. More often, these mothers tended to provide math or science books to daughters who aspired to male-typed occupations (nontraditional girls) than to daughters who aspired to female-typed jobs (traditional girls). The mothers talked more about the importance of looking good to their daughters who aspired to more female-typed occupations than to their daughters who aspired to male-typed jobs. They also expected their daughters who aspired to more female-typed occupations to be more likely to get married right after high school than their nontraditional counterparts. Further, several of the mothers' and adolescent daughters' family/work role values were related. For example, the mothers' belief that it was better for a man to be a breadwinner and a woman to take care of the family was related to the adolescents' belief. The mothers' belief that working mothers can establish just as warm and secure a relationship with their children as nonworking mothers was related to their adolescents' belief that it is all right for mothers to have full-time careers. The nontraditional girls were more likely to endorse the belief that women are better wives and mothers if they have paid jobs. In sum, this research study documented that parental socialization practices in the form of provision of opportunities, expectations, and beliefs are important sources of adolescent females' and males' occupational aspirations (Harold & Eccles, 1990).

It also is important to consider that girls' and women's abilities are underutilized (Doyle & Paludi, 1991). The underutilization occurs because of the American culture's value-laden definition of achievement. The areas that are perceived as successful often have a masculine bias—prestigious occupations, academic excellence, and other accomplishments that are associated with masculine values. Accomplishments associated with traditional feminine values are rarely given attention. Many women manage a household and children, yet this accomplishment is rarely categorized as achievement motivation and work (Betz, 1992; Betz &

Jacqueline Eccles has conducted extensive research on the nature of gender roles in the development of achievement. In her recent research, she has shown how parents influence their sons' and daughters' career choices.

Fitzgerald, 1987). Some psychologists believe that, when achievement is studied, greater consideration of women's lives and realities needs to be made (Doyle & Paludi, 1991).

At this point, we have discussed a number of ideas about motivation. Next, we will turn our attention to emotion.

REVIEW

Competence and Achievement

Competence motivation is the motivation to deal effectively with the environment, to be adept at what is attempted, to process information efficiently, and to make the world a better place. This concept recognizes that motivation is much more than simply reducing physiological needs.

Achievement motivation (need for achievement) is the desire to accomplish something and to reach a standard of excellence. McClelland studied variations of achievement motivation by getting individuals to tell stories about achievement-related themes. Horner developed the concept of fear of success. Intrinsic motivation is the internal desire to be competent and to do something for its own sake. Extrinsic motivation is externally determined by rewards and punishments. In many instances, individuals' achievement motivation is influenced by both internal and external factors. Sports psychology is one of psychology's most rapidly growing fields. Both external and internal factors are involved in whether an athlete becomes a star. Top athletes are self-confident, set reasonable and personally meaningful goals, and have the ability to control their emotions.

Individuals in the United States are more achievement motivated than individuals in most cultures. A special concern is the achievement of individuals from various ethnic groups. Too often ethnic differences are interpreted as "deficits" by middle-class White standards. When ethnicity and social class are considered in the same investigation, social class is often a much better predictor of achievement. Middle-class individuals fare better than their lower-class counterparts in a variety of achievement situations. Psychologists are especially interested in the high achievement levels of Japanese and Asian American individuals. Japanese schools and parents place a much stronger emphasis on education and achievement, especially math achievement, than their American counterparts. It is important to remember that there is diversity in the achievement of any ethnic or cultural group. The motivation for achievement and work is the same for both sexes; however, females and males often make different career choices because of the way they have been socialized and the opportunities available to them.

Emotion

Motivation and emotion are closely linked. Think about sex, which often is associated with joy; about aggression, which usually is associated with anger; and about achievement, which is associated with pride, joy, and anxiety. The terms *motivation* and *emotion* both come from the Latin word *movere*, which means "to move." Both motivation and emotion spur us into action.

Just as with motivation, there are different kinds and intensities of emotions (Brehm & Self, 1989). Not only can a person be motivated to eat rather than have sex but be more or less hungry and more or less interested in having sex. Similarly a person can be happy or angry and can be fairly happy or ecstatic, annoyed or fuming.

Defining emotion is difficult because it is not easy to tell when a person is in an emotional state. Are you in an emotional state when your heart beats fast, your palms sweat, and your stomach churns? Are you in an emotional state when you think about how much you are in love with someone, or when you smile or grimace? The body, the mind, and the face play important roles in understanding emotion. Psychologists debate how critical each is in determining whether we are in an emotional state (Evans, 1989). For our purposes, we will define **emotion** as *feeling or affect, that involves a mixture of physiological arousal (fast heart beat, for example), conscious experience (thinking about being in love with someone, for example), and overt behavior (a smile or grimace, for example).*

Range and Classification of Emotions

When we think about emotions, a few dramatic feelings, such as rage, fear, and glorious joy, usually spring to mind. However, emotions can be subtle as well—the feeling a mother has when she holds her baby, the mild irritation of boredom, the uneasiness of living in the nuclear age (Whissell, 1989). The kinds of emotions we can experience are legion. There are more than 200 words for emotions in the English language.

Psychologists have classified our many different emotions. Robert Plutchik (1980, 1989), for example, believes that emotions have four dimensions: (1) they are positive or negative, (2) they are primary or mixed, (3) many are polar opposites, and (4) they vary in intensity. Ecstasy and enthusiasm are positive emotions; grief and anger are negative emotions. For example, think about your ecstasy when you get an unexpected A on a test or your enthusiasm about the football game this weekend—these are positive emotions. In contrast, think about negative emotions, such as your grief when someone close to you dies or your anger when someone verbally attacks you. Positive emotions enhance our self-esteem; negative emotions lower our self-esteem. Positive emotions improve our relationships with others; negative emotions depress the quality of those relationships.

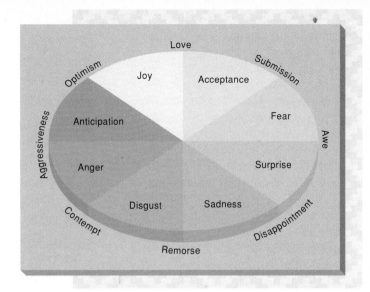

FIGURE 11.8

Plutchik's wheel of emotions. This diagram shows the eight primary emotions and "dyads" that result from mixtures of adjacent primaries. For example, a combination of the primary emotions of fear and surprise produces awe. Joy mixed with acceptance leads to love.
REPRINTED WITH PERMISSION FROM *PSYCHOLOGY TODAY* MAGAZINE. Copyright © 1980 (Sussex Publishing, Inc.).

Plutchik also believes that emotions are like colors. Every color of the spectrum can be produced by mixing the primary colors. Possibly some emotions are primary, and they can be combined to form all other emotions. Happiness, disgust, surprise, sadness, anger, and fear are candidates for primary emotions. For example, combining sadness and surprise gives disappointment. Jealousy is composed of love and anger. Plutchik developed an emotion wheel (shown in figure 11.8) to show how primary emotions work. Mixtures of primary emotions adjacent to each other combine to produce other emotions. Some emotions are opposites—love and remorse, optimism and disappointment. Plutchik believes we cannot simultaneously experience emotions that are polar opposites. You cannot feel sad at the same time you feel happy, he says. Imagine getting a test back in this class. As you scan the paper for the grade, your emotional response is happy or sad, not both.

Happiness is an emotion we all seek. Like other emotions, its intensity varies. Sometimes we are incredibly happy, at others just a bit happy. You might be overwhelmed with happiness if you get the highest A on the next test in this class but only slightly happy if you get a B or a low A.

It was not until 1973 that *Psychological Abstracts*, the major source of psychological research summaries, included happiness as an index term. The recent interest in happiness focuses on positive ways we experience our lives, including cognitive judgments of our well-being. That is, psychologists want to know what makes you happy and how you perceive your happiness.

Many years ago, French philosopher Jean-Jacques Rousseau described the subjective nature of happiness in this way: "Happiness is a good bank account, a good cook, and a good digestion." In a review of research on happiness, "a good cook" and "good digestion" were not on the list of factors that contribute to our happiness, but self-esteem, a good marriage or love relationship, social contacts, regular exercise, the ability to sleep well, and meaningful religious faith were (Diener, 1984). Age, gender, race, education, intelligence, and children were not related to happiness.

What about Rousseau's "good bank account"? Can we buy happiness? One study tried to find out if lottery winners are happier than people who have not received a landslide of money (Brickman, Coates, & Janoff-Bulman, 1978). Twenty-two major lottery winners were compared with 22 people living in the same area of the city. The general happiness of the two groups did not differ when they were asked about the past, present, and the future. The people who hadn't won a lottery actually were happier doing life's mundane things, such as watching television, buying clothes, and talking with a friend. Winning a lottery does not appear to be the key to happiness. What is important, though, is having enough money to buy life's necessities. Extremely wealthy people are not happier than people who can purchase the necessities. People in wealthy countries are not happier than people in poor countries. The message is clear: if you believe money buys happiness, think again (Diener, 1984).

Psychologist Ed Diener agrees that intense positive emotions—such as winning a lottery or getting a date with the person of your dreams—do not add much to a person's general sense of well-being in part because they are rare, and because they can decrease the positive emotion and increase the negative emotion we feel in other circumstances. According to Diener, happiness boils down to the frequency of positive emotions and the infrequency of negative emotions. Diener's view flies in the face of common sense; you would think that frequent, intense positive emotions and minimal, nonintense negative emotions produce the most happiness. However, the commonsense view fails to consider that intense positive moments can diminish the sensation of future positive events. For example, if you shoot par in a round of golf, you will be overwhelmed with happiness at the time you perform this feat, but, if you play golf a week later and do well but not great, the previous emotional high can diminish your positive emotion the next week. It is the rare, if nonexistent, human being who experiences intense positive emotions and infrequent negative emotions week after week after week.

"My life is O.K., but it's no jeans ad."

Drawing by Cline; © 1988 The New Yorker Magazine, Inc.

When you are happy, are you aroused? What about when you are sad? Do you have to be aroused when you experience these and other emotions?

Physiological Arousal and Brain Processes in Emotion

Remember from our definition of emotion that it includes physiological arousal. What is the nature of that arousal?

The Nature of Arousal

As you drive down a highway, the fog thickens. Suddenly you see a pile of cars in front of you. Your mind temporarily freezes, your muscles tighten, your stomach becomes queasy, and your heart feels like it is going to pound out of your chest. You immediately slam on the brakes and try to veer away from the pile of cars. Tires screech, windshield glass flies, and metal smashes. Then all is quiet. After a few short seconds, you realize you are alive. You find that you can walk out of the car. Your fear turns to joy, as you sense your luck in not being hurt. In a couple of seconds, the joy turns to anger. You loudly ask who caused the accident.

As you moved through the emotions of fear, joy, and anger, your body changed. During intense arousal, your sympathetic nervous system was working. At the time of the accident, your arousal decreased as the parasympathetic nervous system became more dominant: your heart rate, breathing rate, and blood sugar level decreased; your pupils constricted; and your stomach secretion and salivation increased. The sympathetic and parasympathetic nervous systems, the two divisions of the autonomic nervous system, were described in chapter 2—you may want to review that discussion now.

Early in this century, two psychologists described the role of arousal in performance. What is now known as the **Yerkes-Dodson law** *states that performance is best under conditions of moderate rather than low or high arousal.* At the low end of arousal, you might be too lethargic to perform tasks well; at the high end, you may not be able to concentrate. Think about how aroused you were the last time you took a test. If your arousal was too high, your performance probably suffered.

Moderate arousal often serves us best in tackling life's tasks, but there are times when low or high arousal produces optimal performance. For well-learned or simple tasks (signing your name, pushing a button on request), optimal arousal can be quite high. By contrast, when learning a task (such as how to play tennis) or doing something complex (such as solving an algebraic equation) much lower arousal is preferred. Figure 11.9 projects how arousal might influence easy,

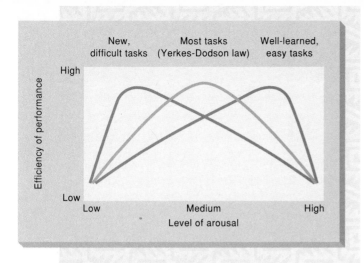

FIGURE 11.9

Arousal and performance: the Yerkes-Dodson law. The Yerkes-Dodson law states that optimal performance occurs under moderate arousal. However, for new or difficult tasks, low arousal may be best; for well-learned, easy tasks, high arousal can facilitate performance.

moderate, and difficult tasks. As tasks become more difficult, the ability to be alert and attentive, but relaxed, is critical to optimal performance.

The Polygraph

You have been asked to think about your emotional states in the face of an automobile crash and a college exam. Now put yourself in the situation of lying to someone. Because bodily changes predictably accompany emotional states, it was reasoned that a machine might be able to determine if a person is lying. A **polygraph** *is a machine that tries to determine if someone is lying by monitoring changes in the body—heart rate, breathing, and electrodermal response (an index detecting skin resistance to a weak electric current)—thought to be influenced by emotional states.* In a typical polygraph test, an individual is asked a number of neutral questions and several key, not so neutral questions. If an individual's heart rate, breathing, and electrodermal response increase substantially when the key questions are asked, the individual is assumed to be lying (see figure 11.10 to observe a polygraph testing situation).

The polygraph has been widely used, especially in business to screen new employees for honesty and to reveal employee theft. Following President Reagan's directive in 1983, the government increased its use of the polygraph to discover which individuals were leaking information to the media. Congressional hearings followed, and psychologists were called to testify about the polygraph's effectiveness (Saxe, Dougherty, & Cross, 1985). Testimony focused on how a "standard" lie detector situation does not exist. Inferring truth or deception based on

FIGURE 11.10

The polygraph. The polygraph tries to tell whether someone is lying by monitoring changes in the body believed to be influenced by emotional states. Controversy has swirled about the polygraph's use. Because of the polygraph's inaccuracy, Congress passed the Employee Polygraph Protection Act of 1988, restricting the use of the polygraph in nongovernment settings.

physiological assessment of emotions requires a number of strategies. The complexity of the lie detector situation was brought out in testimony. Although the degree of arousal to a series of questions is measured through simple physiological changes, no unique physiological response to deception has been revealed (Lykken, 1987). Heart rate and breathing can increase for reasons other than lying, making interpretation of the physiological indicators of arousal complex.

Accurately identifying truth or deception by using a polygraph rests on the skill of the examiner and the skill of the individual being examined. There are simple things people can do to avoid being detected when lying, such as moving the body, taking drugs, and using various cognitive strategies or biofeedback techniques. Tensing your muscles, biting your tongue, squeezing your toes, and shifting your position in the chair can affect the polygraph's accuracy—examiners detect only about 80 percent of the countermeasures. Drugs, such as tranquilizers that have a calming effect on the individual, are more difficult to detect unless a test is conducted to reveal their use. Sometimes, though, the mere presence of the polygraph and the subject's belief it is accurate at detecting deception triggers confession. Police may use the polygraph in this way to get a criminal to confess. In such cases, the polygraph has served a positive purpose, but in too many instances it has been misused and misrepresented. Experts argue that the polygraph errs about one-third of time, especially because it cannot distinguish between such feelings as anxiety and guilt (Lykken, 1985). The testimony of psychologists that lie detectors are not always accurate led to the Employee Polygraph Protection Act of 1988, which restricts most nongovernment polygraph testing.

James-Lange and Cannon-Bard Theories

Psychologists have developed a number of theories about the role of arousal in emotion. Imagine that you and your date are enjoying a picnic in the country. As you prepare to eat, a bull runs across the field toward you. Why are you afraid? Two well-known theories of emotion provide answers to this question: the James-Lange theory and the Cannon-Bard theory.

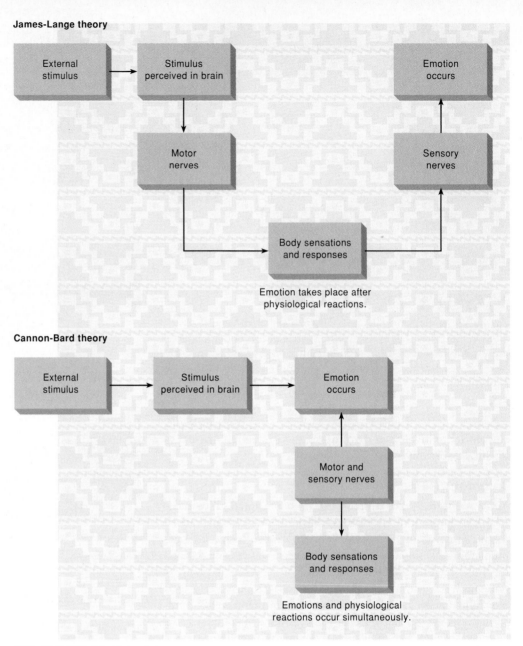

FIGURE 11.11

James-Lange and Cannon-Bard theories of emotion.

Common sense tells you that you are trembling and running away from the bull because you are afraid. However, William James (1890) and Carl Lange (1922) said that emotion works in the opposite way. The **James-Lange theory** *suggests that emotion results from physiological states triggered by stimuli in the environment. Emotion occurs after physiological reactions.* You see the bull scratching its hoof and you begin to run away. The aroused body then sends sensory messages to the brain, at which point emotion is perceived. According to this theory, you do not run away because you are afraid; rather, you are afraid because you are running away. In other words, you perceive a stimulus in

the environment, your body responds, and you interpret the body's reaction as emotion. In one of James' examples, you perceive you have lost your fortune, you cry, and then you interpret the crying as feeling sad. This goes against the commonsense sequence of losing your fortune, feeling sorry, and then crying.

Walter Cannon (1927) objected to the James-Lange theory. To understand his objection, imagine the bull and the picnic once again. Seeing the bull scratching its hooves causes the hypothalamus of your brain to do two things simultaneously: it stimulates your autonomic nervous system to produce the physi-

FIGURE 11.12

Opponent processes of emotions in parachute jumping. How is parachute jumping an example of the way in which the opponent-process theory works? Parachute jumpers feel euphoric after a jump. The euphoria opposes the high level of fear that existed before the jump. After several jumps, the fear diminishes, but the euphoria remains strong, so the individual continues to jump. Fear is the primary process and euphoria is the secondary process.

ological changes involved in emotion (increased heart rate, rapid breathing) and it sends messages to your cerebral cortex, where the experience of emotion is perceived. Philip Bard (1934) supported this view, and so it became known as the **Cannon-Bard theory,** *the theory that emotion and physiological reactions occur simultaneously.* In the Cannon-Bard theory, the body plays a less important role than it does in the James-Lange theory. Figure 11.11 shows other differences between the James-Lange and Cannon-Bard theories.

As psychologists probed the elusive nature of emotion, they revealed the brain's important role (Adelmann & Zajonc, 1989; Carlson & Hatfield, 1989). Next, we will examine a theory that opponent processes in the central nervous system are involved in emotion.

The Opponent-Process Theory

Richard Solomon (1980) developed a provocative view of the brain's role in emotion. He assumed the brain always seeks to maintain a state of equilibrium, just as in the concept of homeostasis discussed earlier in the chapter. **Opponent-process theory** *is Solomon's theory of emotion that pleasant or unpleasant stimuli can cause both a primary and a secondary process to occur in the brain. The secondary process is the central nervous system's reaction to the primary process of the autonomic nervous system. The secondary process reduces the intensity of a feeling.*

Parachute jumping and drug addiction provide examples of how the opponent-process theory works. Parachute jumpers experience a euphoric feeling after their jump. The euphoria

opposes the high level of fear before the jump. After several jumps, the initial fear diminishes, but the euphoria remains strong, so the person continues to jump. In this example, fear is the primary process and euphoria the secondary process (see figure 11.12). When a person takes opium, an intense rush occurs, followed by a less intense but pleasurable feeling. When the drug effects wear off, the user experiences discomfort and craves the drug, which leads to another dose, but the next dose produces a less intense rush and diminished pleasure. The aftereffects are more unpleasant—abstinence can cause sheer agony. The rush and pleasurable feelings represent the primary process of emotion, the unpleasant feelings and craving the secondary process.

Much of what we have said about emotion has focused on its physiological basis. Although physiological factors play important roles in emotion, cognitive processes are at work as well.

REVIEW

The Nature of Emotion, Arousal, and Physiological Processes

Emotions are feeling, or affect, that involves a mixture of physiological arousal, conscious experience, and overt behavior. We experience a wide range of emotions. Plutchik believes emotions are positive or negative, primary or mixed, bipolar opposites, and variable in intensity. We all are especially interested in the emotion of happiness.

The sympathetic nervous system is involved in arousal; the parasympathetic nervous system is involved when arousal decreases. Many aspects of the body are influenced by arousal. The Yerkes-Dodson law addresses the issue of arousal and performance. The polygraph rests on the principle of arousal in emotion. The polygraph situation is complex, and psychologists remain skeptical about its validity.

In the James-Lange view of emotion, we initially perceive a stimulus, our body responds, then we experience the emotion. By contrast, the Cannon-Bard theory plays down the body's role in emotion, saying we simultaneously experience an emotion and bodily changes. Dispute about whether the same bodily changes underlie all emotions continues. In Solomon's opponent-process theory, every emotion has a primary process and a secondary process. The secondary process is the central nervous system's reaction to the primary process of the autonomic nervous system. The secondary process reduces the intensity of an emotion and increases equilibrium; it strengthens with repeated stimulation.

Cognition and Emotion

Does emotion depend on the tides of the mind? Are we happy only when we think we are happy? Cognitive theories of emotion share an important point: emotion always has a cognitive component. Thinking is said to be responsible for feelings of love and hate, joy and sadness. While giving cognitive processes the main credit for emotion, the cognitive theories also recognize the role of the brain and body in emotion (Mandler, 1984). That is, the hypothalamus and the autonomic nervous system make connections with the peripheral areas of the body when emotion is experienced. According to cognitive theorists, body and thought are involved in emotion.

Schachter and Singer's View

Stanley Schachter and Jerome Singer (1962) developed a theory of emotion that gives cognition a strong role. They agree that emotional events produce internal physiological arousal. As we sense the arousal, we look to the external world for an explanation of why we are aroused. We interpret the external cues present and then label the emotion. For example, if you feel good after someone has made a pleasant comment to you, you might label the emotion happiness. If you feel bad after you have done something wrong, you may label the feeling guilt. Schachter and Singer believe that much of our arousal is diffuse and not tied to specific emotions. Because the arousal is not instinctive, its meaning is easily misinterpreted.

To test their theory of emotion, Schachter and Singer (1962) injected volunteer subjects with epinephrine, a drug that produces high arousal. After the subjects were given the drug, they observed someone else behave in either a euphoric way (shooting papers at a wastebasket) or an angry way (stomping out of the room). As predicted, the euphoric and angry behavior influenced the subjects' cognitive interpretation of their own arousal. When they were with a happy person, they rated themselves as happy; when they were with an angry person, they said they were angry. However, this effect was found only when the subjects were not told about the true effects of the injection. When subjects were told that the drug would increase their heart rate and make them jittery, they said the reason for their arousal was the drug, not the other person's behavior.

Psychologists have had difficulty replicating the Schachter and Singer experiment, but, in general, research supports the belief that misinterpreted arousal intensifies emotional experiences (Leventhal & Tomarken, 1986). An intriguing study substantiates this belief. In British Columbia, an attractive woman approached men while they were crossing the Capilano River Bridge, which sways precariously more than 200 feet above

FIGURE 11.13

Capilano River Bridge experiment: misinterpreted arousal intensifies emotional experiences. The precarious Capilano River Bridge in British Columbia is shown at left; the experiment is shown in progress at right. An attractive woman approached men while they were crossing the 200-foot-high bridge; she asked them to make up a story to help her out. She also made the same request on a lower, much safer bridge. The men on the Capilano River Bridge told sexier stories, probably because they were aroused by the fear or excitement of being up so high on a swaying bridge. Apparently they interpreted their arousal as sexual attraction for the female interviewer.

rapids and rocks. Only those without a female companion were approached. The woman asked the men to make up a brief story for a project she was doing on creativity (Dutton & Aron, 1974) (see figure 11.13). The female interviewer made the same request of other men crossing a lower, much safer bridge. The men on the Capilano River Bridge told more sexually oriented stories and rated the female interviewer more attractive than did the men on the lower, less frightening bridge. Apparently the men on the Capilano River Bridge misinterpreted their arousal as sexual attraction for the female interviewer.

The Primacy Debate: Cognition or Emotion?

Richard Lazarus (1984, 1991) believes that cognitive activity is a precondition for emotion. He says we cognitively appraise ourselves and our social circumstances. These appraisals, which include values, goals, commitments, beliefs, and expectations, determine our emotions. People may feel happy because they have a deep religious commitment, angry because they did not get the raise they anticipated, or fearful because they expect to fail an exam.

Robert Zajonc (1984) disagrees with Lazarus. Emotions are primary, he says, and our thoughts are a result of them. Who is right? Both likely are correct. Lazarus refers mainly to a cluster of related events that occur over a period of time, whereas Zajonc describes single events or a simple preference for one stimulus over another. Lazarus speaks about love over the course of months and years, a sense of value to the community, and plans

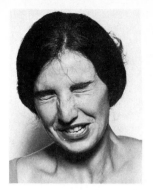

FIGURE 11.14

Emotional expressions in the United States and New Guinea. At left is a woman from the United States and, on the right, two men from the Fore tribe in New Guinea. Notice the similarity in the expression of disgust and happiness. Psychologists believe that the facial expression of emotion is virtually the same in all cultures.

for retirement; Zajonc talks about a car accident, an encounter with a snake, and a preference for ice cream over spinach. Some of our emotional reactions are virtually instantaneous and probably don't involve cognitive appraisal, such as a shriek on detecting a snake. Other emotional circumstances, especially those that occur over a long period of time, such as a depressed mood or anger toward a friend, are more likely to involve cognitive appraisal.

Sociocultural Influences on Emotion

The complete experience of emotion depends not only on the body's responses and the mind's perceptions but also on the nature of social relationships and society's customs. How do social factors influence our emotional experiences? How does culture affect emotions? How is gender related to emotion?

Social Factors

Think once again about the bull and the picnic in the field. Perhaps you decided to show your courage to your date and went through a toreador sequence that left you with feelings of pride. Had you not been with someone you liked, you might have ignored the bull and walked away disinterested.

Emotions often involve someone else: your enthusiasm for going to the beach or skiing with *friends*, your love for the *person* of your dreams, your surprise when your *parents* tell you that your younger *brother* is coming to your college next year, your fear of giving a speech in front of your *classmates* and *professor*, and your sadness when you discover that your *roommate* lost her job (Bronstein & Paludi, 1988; Sarbin, 1989).

Culture and the Expression of Emotions

In *The Expression of the Emotions in Man and Animals*, Charles Darwin (1872/1965) argued that the facial expressions of human beings are innate, are the same in all cultures around the world,

and evolved from the emotions of animals. Darwin compared the similarity of human snarls of anger with the growls of dogs and the hisses of cats. He compared the giggling of chimpanzees, when they are tickled under their arms, with human laughter.

Today psychologists still believe that emotions, especially facial expressions of emotion, have strong biological ties. For example, children who are blind from birth and have never observed the smile or frown on another person's face, still smile or frown in the same way that children with normal vision do.

The universality of facial expressions and the ability of people from different cultures to label accurately the emotion that lies behind a facial expression has been extensively researched (Matsumoto, 1989). Psychologist Paul Ekman's (1980, 1985) careful observations revealed that our many faces of emotion do not vary significantly from one culture to another. For example, Ekman and his colleague photographed people expressing such emotions as happiness, fear, surprise, disgust, and grief. When they showed the photographs to people from the United States, Chile, Japan, Brazil, and Borneo (an Indonesian island in the western Pacific Ocean), each person tended to label the faces with the same emotions (Ekman & Friesen, 1968). Another study focused on the way the Fore tribe, an isolated, Stone Age culture in New Guinea, matched descriptions of emotions with facial expressions (Ekman & Friesen, 1971). Before Ekman's visit, most of the Fore had never seen a Caucasian face. Ekman showed them photographs of American faces expressing such emotions as fear, happiness, anger, and surprise. Then he read stories about people in emotional situations. The Fore were able to match the descriptions of emotions to the facial expressions in the photographs. The similarity of facial expressions of emotions between people in New Guinea and people in the United States is shown in figure 11.14.

Whereas facial expressions of basic emotions appear to be universal across cultures, display rules for emotion are not culturally universal. **Display rules** *are sociocultural standards that*

In the Middle Eastern country of Yemen, male-to-male kissing is commonplace, but in the United States, it is very uncommon.

determine when, where, and how emotions should be expressed. For example, although happiness is a universally expressed emotion, when, where, and how it is displayed may vary from one culture to another. The same is true for other emotions, such as fear, sadness, and anger. For example, members of the Utku culture in Alaska discourage anger by cultivating acceptance and by dissociating themselves from any display of anger (Briggs, 1970). If a trip is hampered by an unexpected snowstorm, the Utku do not become frustrated but accept the presence of the snowstorm and build an igloo. Most of us would not act as mildly in the face of subzero weather and barriers to our travel.

In addition to facial expressions, emotions are also expressed in many other nonverbal signals of body movement, posture, and gesture (DePaulo, 1992). Some basic nonverbal signals appear to be universal indicators of certain emotions, just as facial expressions are. For example, when people are depressed, it shows not only in their sad facial expression, but also in their slow body movement, downturned head, and slumped posture (Blanck, Buck, & Rosenthal, 1986). Many nonverbal signals of emotion, though, vary from one culture to another. For example, male-to-male kissing is commonplace in some cultures, such as Yemen (in the Middle East), but uncommon in other cultures, such as the United States. The "thumb up" sign, which means either everything is "OK" or the desire to hitch a ride in most cultures, is an insult in Greece, similar to a raised third finger in the United States (Morris & others, 1979). More information about cultural determinants of emotion appears in Sociocultural Worlds 11.2, where we will discuss the nature of emotional experiences in Japan, Europe, and the United States.

In this chapter, we have seen the many faces of motivation and emotion. In the next chapter, we will see the many faces of personality and discover that motivation and emotion play important roles in understanding personality.

Gender and Emotion

Unless you've been isolated on a mountaintop away from people, television, magazines, and newspapers, you probably know the

Our emotional reactions are influenced by the culture in which we live. The Utku Eskimos, for example, discourage anger by cultivating acceptance and by dissociating themselves from any expression of anger.

master stereotype about gender and emotion: she is emotional; he is not. This stereotype is a powerful and pervasive image in our culture (Shields, 1991a).

Is this stereotype born out when researchers study the nature of emotional experiences in females and males? Researchers have found that females and males are often more alike in the way they experience emotion than the master stereotype would lead us to believe. Females and males often use the same facial expressions, adopt the same language, and describe their emotional experiences similarly when they keep diaries about their life experiences. Thus, the master stereotype about females being emotional and males not is simply that—a stereotype. Given the complexity and vast territory of emotion, we should not be surprised that this stereotype is not supported when actual emotional experiences are examined. Thus, for many emotional experiences, researchers do not find

Culture and Emotion: Comparisons of Japan, Europe, and the United States

One cross-cultural study examined the cultural differences in *when* people express emotions and *how* they do it. The researchers found that university students in Europe and the United States tend to express emotions more similarly than do Japanese students (Scherer & others, 1988). The researchers asked the students questions about situations or events that led them to feel joy/happiness, sadness/grief, fear/anxiety, or anger/rage. The Japanese students showed fewer physical signs of joy, gave fewer sad responses to separation and death, were fearful of but quicker to get angry at strangers, and were less likely to get angry in the face of injustice than their American and European counterparts. These differences in the expression of emotion probably are the result of cultural differences in values, customs, and the way people interact.

The researchers also found that the way these students, especially the Japanese and American students, expressed their emotions differed. The Americans reported a high intensity of emotional expressiveness and a frequent use of nonverbal expressions to show emotion—that is, the Americans were more likely to literally jump for joy, whereas the Japanese were much more circumspect. One reason for these differences may be that the Japanese culture values physical restraint—which may be interpreted as stoicism—as an essential part of everyday decorum. In the study, the American and Japanese students attempted to control their emotions more than their European counterparts.

Some cross-cultural psychologists caution about the difficulty of interpreting nonverbal behaviors across cultures. For example, the Japanese may have very subtle nonverbal behaviors that they learn to interpret within their own culture—such as a slight blankness of the face to indicate disinterest, pauses between sentences, and subtle movements of the eyes. When asked to describe these nonverbal behaviors, they may not have these in mind but, rather, report about the larger, less subtle body movements they see among Americans (either face-to-face or on American television shows they watch).

Also, despite the differences revealed in the cross-cultural study involving Americans, Japanese, and Europeans, the researchers also found the following similarities in emotion across the cultures:

- People tend to recall situations that elicit anger and joy more readily than ones that elicited sadness and fear.
- There were clear differences in the average duration of different emotions: fear < anger < joy < sadness.
- People try to control the three negative emotions (fear, anger, and sadness) more than joy.

---

differences between females and males—both sexes are equally likely to experience love, jealousy, anxiety in new social situations, anger when they are insulted, grief when close relationships end, and embarrassment when they make mistakes in public (Tavris & Wade, 1984).

When we go beyond the master stereotype and consider some specific emotional experiences, the context in which emotion is displayed, and certain beliefs about emotion, gender does matter in understanding emotion (Shields, 1991a,b). Consider anger. Men are more likely to show anger toward strangers, especially other men, when they feel they have been challenged, and men are more likely to turn their anger into aggressive action than females are (Tavris, 1989).

Female-male differences in emotion are more likely to occur in contexts that highlight social roles and relationships. For example, females are more likely than males to give accounts of emotion that include interpersonal relationships (Saarni, 1988). Females are more likely to express fear and sadness than males, especially when communicating with their friends and family.

Beliefs about emotion play an important role in understanding how gender and emotion work in our culture. We often use beliefs about emotion to define the difference between what is masculine and what is feminine (Shields, 1991a). For example, men are more likely to agree with the belief that men should conceal their feelings, but when reporting their own behavior more women than men report greater inhibition of emotional expression. Sex differences in self-reports tend to be consistent with emotion stereotypes, as if individuals compare themselves to a cultural standard when generating a response—"I must be emotional; after all, I'm a woman," or "I must be inexpressive; after all, I'm a man" (Shields, 1991b).

REVIEW

Emotion, Cognition, and Sociocultural Influences

Cognitive views argue that emotion always has a cognitive component and that, in most instances, cognition directs emotion. The Schachter-Singer view argues that emotional events produce arousal, which is often diffuse, so we look to the external world to interpret it. Then we label the emotion based on environmental cues. Lazarus believes that cognition always directs emotion. Zajonc says emotion is dominant. Both probably are right.

Emotions often involve social contexts and relationships. Most psychologists believe that the facial expression of basic emotions is universal across all cultures. Whereas facial expressions of emotions are thought to be universal, display rules for emotion often vary from one culture to another. These display rules include nonverbal signals of body movement, posture, and gesture.

The master stereotype of gender and emotion is that females are emotional and males are not. This is a stereotype; understanding emotion and gender is much more complex. When we go beyond the master stereotype and consider some specific aspects of emotional experiences, the context in which emotion is displayed, and certain beliefs about emotion, gender does matter in understanding emotion. Female-male differences in emotion are more likely to occur in contexts that highlight social roles and relationships.

Summary

I. The "Whys" of Behavior

Motivation involves the question of "why" people behave, think, and feel the way they do. Motivation varies not only in kind but also in intensity. Instinct theory flourished early in the twentieth century, but instincts do not adequately explain motivation. Drive-reduction theory provides a combination of psychological and physical factors to account for motivation. Drives are aroused states brought about by physiological needs. Reducing the drive satisfies the need. Drive-reduction theory stimulated an interest in homeostasis, an important motivational concept. Believing that external factors also are important in motivation, psychologists turned to incentives. Maslow developed the concept of hierarchy of motives. The contemporary view of motivation includes an emphasis on biological (especially physiological), cognitive, and social factors. Three important issues are the degree to which motivation is innate or learned, conscious or unconscious, and internal or external.

II. Hunger

The brain monitors both blood sugar level and the condition of the stomach (interest in the stomach was generated by Cannon's research), then integrates this information. Hypothalamic regions are very important in the integration process, especially VMH; the dopamine system helps activate actual feeding behavior. Schachter stressed that environmental cues are involved in the control of eating behavior. Rodin argues that conscious self-control and exercise are more important than external cues in understanding hunger and eating behavior.

III. Competence Motivation

Competence motivation is the motivation to deal effectively with the environment, to become competent at what is attempted, to process information efficiently, and to make the world a better place. The concept of competence motivation recognizes that motivation is much more than simply reducing physiological needs.

IV. Achievement Motivation, Intrinsic/Extrinsic Motivation, and Sports Psychology

Achievement motivation (need for achievement) is the desire to accomplish something, to reach a standard of excellence, to expend effort to excel. McClelland studied variations of achievement motivation by getting individuals to tell stories involving achievement-related themes. Horner developed the concept of fear of success. Intrinsic motivation is the internal desire to be competent and to do something for its own sake. Extrinsic motivation is externally determined by rewards and punishments. In many instances, individuals' achievement motivation is influenced by both internal and external factors. Sports psychology is one of psychology's most rapidly growing fields. Both external and internal factors are involved in whether an athlete becomes a star. Top athletes are self-confident, set reasonable and personally meaningful goals, and have the ability to control their emotions.

V. Achievement, Culture, Social Class, Ethnicity, and Gender

Individuals in the United States are more achievement-oriented than individuals in most cultures. A special concern is the achievement of individuals from various ethnic groups. Too often ethnic differences are interpreted as "deficits" by middle-class, White standards. When researchers examine both ethnicity and social class in the same study, social class is often a much better predictor of achievement. Middle-class individuals fare better than their lower-class counterparts in a variety of achievement situations. Psychologists have shown a special interest in the high achievement levels of Japanese and Asian American individuals. Japanese schools and parents place a much stronger emphasis on education and achievement, especially math achievement, than their American counterparts. It is important to remember that there is diversity in the achievement of any ethnic or cultural group. The motivation for achievement and work is the same for both sexes; however, females and males often make different career choices because of the way they have been socialized and the opportunities available to them.

VI. Definition, Range, and Classification of Emotions
Emotions are feelings, or affect, that involves a mixture of physiological arousal, conscious experience, and overt behavior. We experience a wide range of emotions. Plutchik believes that emotions are positive or negative, primary or mixed, bipolar opposites, and variable in intensity. One emotion of special interest is happiness.

VII. Emotional Arousal
The sympathetic nervous system is involved in arousal; the parasympathetic system is involved when arousal decreases. Many aspects of the body are influenced by arousal. The Yerkes-Dodson law addresses the issue of arousal and performance. The polygraph rests on the principle of arousal

in emotion. The polygraph testing situation is complex, and psychologists remain skeptical about its validity.

VIII. James-Lange, Cannon-Bard, and Opponent-Process Theories of Emotion
In the James-Lange view, we initially perceive a stimulus, our body responds, then we experience emotion. By contrast, the Cannon-Bard theory plays down the body's role in emotion, saying we simultaneously experience an emotion and bodily changes. Dispute about whether the same bodily changes underlie all emotions continues. In Solomon's opponent-process theory, every emotion has a primary and secondary process. The secondary process is the central nervous system's reaction to the primary process of the autonomic nervous system. The secondary process reduces the intensity of an emotion and increases equilibrium. With repeated stimulation, the secondary process strengthens.

IX. Emotion and Cognition
Cognitive views argue that emotion always has a cognitive component and that, in most instances, cognition directs emotion. In the Schachter-Singer view, emotional events produce emotional arousal. Arousal often is diffuse, so we look to the external world to interpret the arousal and then

label the emotion based on environmental cues. Lazarus and Zajonc have debated the issue of whether cognition or emotion dominates. Lazarus says cognition always directs emotion; Zajonc says it is the other way around. Both probably are right.

X. Sociocultural Influences on Emotion
Emotions often involve social contexts and relationships. Most psychologists believe that the facial expression of basic emotions is universal across all cultures. Whereas facial expressions of emotions are thought to be universal, display rules for emotions often vary from one culture to another. These display rules include nonverbal signals of body movement, posture, and gesture. The master stereotype of gender and emotion is that females are emotional and males are not. This is a stereotype; understanding emotion and gender is much more complex. When we go beyond the master stereotype and consider some specific aspects of emotional experiences, the context in which emotion is displayed, and certain beliefs about emotion, gender does matter in understanding emotion. Female-male differences in emotion are more likely to occur in contexts that highlight social roles and relationships.

Key Terms

Suggested Readings

Carlson, J. G., & Hatfield, E. (1989). *Psychology of emotion*. Belmont, CA: Wadsworth. This well-written, interesting account of emotion includes detailed information about many emotions.

Ekman, P. (1985). *Telling lies: Clues to deceit in the marketplace, politics, and marriage*. New York: W. W. Norton. Ekman tells how we can read facial expressions and gestures to determine whether people are lying.

Mook, D. G. (1987). *Motivation: The organization of action*. New York: W. W. Norton. This comprehensive text on the nature of

motivation includes considerable detail on many of the topics on motivation covered in our discussion.

Scherer, K. R. (Ed.). (1988). *Facets of emotion: Recent research*. Hillsdale, NJ: Erlbaum. Several articles on cross-cultural comparisons of emotions are included.

PERSONALITY

CHAPTER

12

"She has a great personality."
"He has no personality."
"She is a personality."
"She has her mother's personality."

hese statements reflect our everyday use of the term *personality*. You probably have used similar statements to describe someone you have known or known about (Peterson, 1988). Let's look further at each of these statements.

"She has a great personality." This statement is a positive evaluation. When you say this about a woman, it means you like something about her that goes beyond looks, possessions, intelligence, or status. There is something about her that makes you feel good when you are around her. Maybe it's the way she behaves, her attitude, her flair, her values, or even some of her quirks.

"He has no personality." This statement also is an evaluation, but it is a negative one. You do not really like this guy, but you may not dislike him either, unless you happen to be his college roommate or he is your boss. He makes your day boring. He has nothing unique that stamps him as different from others: no passion, no weird hobby or unusual ability, and not much desire except just to walk through life unnoticed. He can take or leave Mexican food or Geraldo Rivera, and he has no mismatched socks. He is almost like a piece of furniture.

"She is a personality." Andy Warhol once said that, in the future, everyone will be famous for 15 minutes. Then it will be someone else's turn. Some of us make *People* magazine; most of us don't. People write about celebrities so noncelebrities can read about them. Roseanne Arnold, Whoopi Goldberg, Lee Trevino, Jackie Kennedy Onassis, Eddie Murphy, and Lee Iaccoca are celebrities we think of as "personalities." They are well known not just for what they do but for how they do it. They play a role in our culture that becomes identified with the personality they bring to the role.

"She has her mother's personality." Many statements about personality focus on distinctive characteristics, what makes us different from others. Personality is also used to make comparisons among individuals, describing common characteristics and similarities. Most of us have talked about the way certain people remind us of someone else we have known. They may have similar mannerisms. She holds grudges just as her mother does, for example. They may have similar temperaments. She is the life of the party and loves to be around people, just like her father. Many people look at their family members and see certain similar personality characteristics. For example, someone may say, "My brother is an introvert just like my cousin Robert," or "My sister has my grandmother's personality—she has a stubborn streak a mile long."

Many celebrities, such as Whoopi Goldberg, are called "personalities." They are well known, not just for what they do, but also for how they do it. Whoopi Goldberg's outgoing personality is a property of Whoopi Goldberg and is related to how she functions in the world. Of course, it is not just celebrities who have a personality. Each of us has a personality that is our property and is related to how we function in the world.

How do the images of personality we use in our everyday conversations about people correspond to the way psychologists describe personality? The images suggest that personality is a property of the individual that is related to how he or she functions in the world. In our next topic of discussion—what is personality?—you will see that psychologists agree personality is a property of the individual but that some disagreement exists about the exact nature of personality.

What Is Personality?

Think about yourself for a moment. What are you *really* like? Are you outgoing or shy, aggressive or calm, intellectual or nonintellectual, considerate or uncaring? Try to come up with seven or eight of these traits that reflect the way you respond to your world. In compiling this list, you are choosing personality characteristics that you probably feel are an enduring part of your makeup as a person. For example, if you say that you are an outgoing person, wouldn't you also say that you were outgoing a year ago and that you will probably be an outgoing person 1 year, 5 years, and 10 years from now? Most of us believe that we have some enduring personality characteristics. Psychologists define **personality** *as enduring, distinctive thoughts, emotions, and behaviors that characterize the way an individual adapts to the world.*

Some personality theorists ask why individuals respond to a situation in different ways. For example, *why* is Sam so talkative and gregarious and Al so shy and quiet when they meet someone for the first time? *Why* is Gretchen so confident and Mary so insecure about their upcoming job interviews? Some theorists believe that biological and genetic factors are responsible; others argue that life experiences are more important. Some theorists claim that the way we think about ourselves is the key to understanding personality, whereas others stress that the way we behave toward each other is more important.

The diversity of theories makes understanding personality a challenge. Just when you think one theory has the correct explanation of personality, another theory will make you rethink your earlier conclusion. To keep from getting frustrated, remember that personality is a complex, multifaceted topic and no single theory has been able to account for all its aspects; each theory has contributed an important piece to the personality puzzle. In fact, many pieces of information in different personality theories are *complementary* rather than contradictory. Together they let us see the total landscape of personality in all its richness.

Psychoanalytic Perspectives

For psychoanalytic theorists, personality is unconscious—that is, beyond awareness—and heavily colored by emotion. Psychoanalytic theorists believe that behavior is merely a surface characteristic and that, to truly understand someone's personality, we have to look at the symbolic meanings of behavior and the deep inner workings of the mind. Psychoanalytic theorists also believe that early experiences with our parents extensively shape our personalities. These characteristics of personality were described by the original psychoanalytic theorist, Sigmund Freud.

Sigmund Freud

Freud's Theory

Loved and hated, respected and despised—Sigmund Freud, whether right or wrong in his views, has been one of the most influential thinkers of the twentieth century. Freud was a medical doctor who specialized in neurology. He developed his ideas about psychoanalytic theory from his work with psychiatric patients. He was born in Austria in 1856, and he died in London at the age of 83. Freud spent most of his life in Vienna, but he left the city near the end of his career to escape Nazi anti-Semitism.

As the eldest child, Freud was regarded as a genius by his brothers and sisters and doted on by his mother. Later we will see that one aspect of Freud's theory emphasizes a young boy's sexual attraction for his mother; it is possible that this belief was derived from his own romantic attachment to his mother, who was beautiful and about 20 years younger than Freud's father.

In Freud's view, much more of the mind is unconscious than conscious. He envisioned the mind as a huge iceberg, with the massive part below the surface of the water being the unconscious part. Freud said that each of our lives is filled with tension and conflict; to reduce this tension and conflict, we keep information locked in the unconscious mind. For Freud, the unconscious mind holds the key to understanding behavior. Freud believed that even trivial behaviors have special significance when the unconscious forces behind them are revealed. A twitch, a doodle, a joke, a smile, each may have an unconscious reason for appearing. They often slip into our lives without our awareness. For example, Barbara is kissing and hugging Tom, whom she is to marry in several weeks. She says, "Oh, *Jeff,* I love you so much." Tom pushes her away and says, "Why did you call me Jeff? I thought you didn't think about him anymore. We need to have a talk!" You probably can think of times when such *Freudian slips* have tumbled out of your own mouth.

The Structure of Personality

Freud (1917) believed that personality has three structures: the id, the ego, and the superego. One way to understand the three structures is to consider them as three rulers of a country (Singer, 1984). The id is king or queen, the ego is prime minister, and the superego is high priest. The id is an absolute monarch, owed complete obedience; it is spoiled, willful, and self-centered. The id wants what it wants right now, not later. The ego, as prime minister, has the job of getting things done; it is tuned into reality and is responsive to society's demands. The superego, as high priest, is concerned with right and wrong; the id may be greedy and needs to be told that nobler purposes should be pursued.

The **id** *is the Freudian structure of personality that consists of instincts, which are the individual's reservoir of psychic energy.* In Freud's view, the id is unconscious; it has no contact with reality. The id works according to the **pleasure principle,** *the Freudian concept that the id always seeks pleasure and avoids pain.*

It would be a dangerous and scary world if our personalities were all id. As young children mature, for example, they learn they cannot slug other children in the face. They also learn they have to use the toilet instead of their diaper. As children experience the demands and constraints of reality, a new structure of personality is formed—the **ego,** *the Freudian structure of personality that deals with the demands of reality. The ego is called the executive branch of personality because it makes rational decisions.* Whereas the id is completely unconscious, the ego is partly conscious. It houses our higher mental functions—reasoning, problem solving, and decision making, for example. The ego abides by the **reality principle,** *the Freudian concept by which the ego tries to bring the individual pleasure within the norms of society.* Few of us are cold-blooded killers or wild wheeler-dealers; we take into account the obstacles to our satisfaction that exist in our world. We recognize that our sexual and aggressive impulses cannot go unrestrained. The ego helps us test reality, to see how far we can go without getting into trouble and hurting ourselves.

The id and ego have no morality. They do not take into account whether something is right or wrong. In contrast, the **superego** *is the Freudian structure of personality that is the moral branch of personality. The superego takes into account whether something is right or wrong.* The superego is what we often refer to as the "conscience." Like the id, the superego does not consider reality; it doesn't deal with what is realistic, only with whether the id's sexual and aggressive impulses can be satisfied in moral terms. You probably are beginning to sense that both the id and the superego make life rough for the ego. Your ego might say, "I will have sex only occasionally and be sure to use an effective form of protection against pregnancy and sexually transmitted diseases." However, your id is saying, "I want to be satisfied; sex feels so good." Your superego is also at work: "I feel guilty about having sex."

Remember that Freud considered personality to be like an iceberg; most of our personality exists below the level of awareness, just as the massive part of an iceberg is beneath the surface of the water. Figure 12.1 illustrates this analogy and the extent of the unconscious part of our mind, in Freud's view.

Defense Mechanisms

The ego calls on a number of strategies to resolve the conflict among its demands for reality, the wishes of the id, and the constraints of the superego. Through **defense mechanisms,** *the psychoanalytic term for unconscious methods of dealing with conflict, the ego distorts reality, thereby protecting itself from anxiety.* In Freud's view, the conflicting demands of the personality structures produce anxiety. For example, when a person's ego blocks the pleasurable pursuits of the id, that person feels inner anxiety.

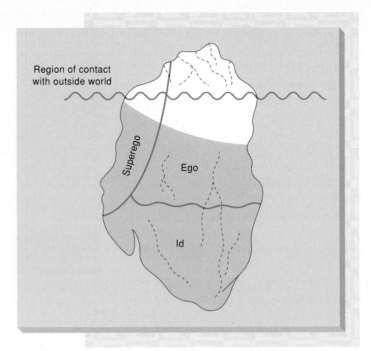

FIGURE 12.1

Conscious and unconscious processes: the iceberg analogy. This rather odd-looking diagram illustrates Freud's belief that most of the important personality processes occur below the level of conscious awareness. In examining people's conscious thoughts and their behaviors, we can see some reflections of the ego and the superego. Whereas the ego and superego are partly conscious and partly unconscious, the primitive id is the unconscious, totally submerged part of the iceberg.

This diffuse, distressed state develops when the ego senses that the id is going to cause harm. The anxiety alerts the ego to resolve the conflict by means of defense mechanisms.

Repression *is the most powerful and pervasive defense mechanism, according to Freud; it works to push unacceptable id impulses out of awareness and back into the unconscious mind.* Repression is the foundation from which all other defense mechanisms work; the goal of every psychological defense is to *repress* threatening impulses, or push them out of awareness. Freud said that our early childhood experiences, many of which he believed are sexually laden, are too threatening and stressful for us to deal with consciously. We reduce the anxiety of this conflict through repression.

Among the other defense mechanisms we use to protect the ego and reduce anxiety are rationalization, displacement, sublimation, projection, reaction formation, and regression. **Rationalization** *is the psychoanalytic defense mechanism that occurs when the real motive for an individual's behavior is not accepted by the ego and is replaced by a sort of cover motive.* For example, you are studying hard for tomorrow's exam. You are really getting into the material when a friend calls and says he is having a party in an hour. He tells you that a certain person you find attractive will be there. You know that, if you don't stay in your room and study, you will do poorly on tomorrow's exam, but you tell yourself, "I did well on the first test in this class and I have been studying hard all semester; it's time I have some fun," so you go to the party. The real motive is wanting to go to the party, to have fun, and to see the attractive person. However, that reason wouldn't justify doing poorly on the exam, so you think you should stay home and study. Your ego now steps in and comes up with a better motive. Your ego says that you have worked hard all semester and you need to unwind, and that you will probably do better on the exam if you relax a little—a rationale that is more acceptable than just going to have fun and meet the desirable other person.

Displacement *is the psychoanalytic defense mechanism that occurs when an individual shifts unacceptable feelings from one object to another, more acceptable object.* For example, a woman is harassed by her boss. She gets angry but she doesn't feel she can take the anger out on the boss because she might get fired. When she gets home that evening, she yells at her husband, thus transferring her feelings toward her boss to her husband.

Sublimation *is the psychoanalytic defense mechanism that occurs when a useful course of action replaces a distasteful one.* Sublimation is actually a type of displacement. For example, an individual with strong sexual urges may turn them into socially approved behavior by becoming an artist who paints nudes.

Projection *is the psychoanalytic defense mechanism that occurs when we attribute our own shortcomings, problems, and faults to others.* For example, a man who has a strong desire to have an extramarital affair keeps accusing his wife of flirting with other men. A manipulative businesswoman who takes advantage of everyone to shove her way up the corporate ladder tells her associate, "Everybody around here is so manipulative; they never consider my feelings." When we can't face our own unwanted feelings, we *project* them onto others and see others as having the undesirable traits.

Reaction formation *is the psychoanalytic defense mechanism that occurs when we express an unacceptable impulse by transforming it into its opposite.* For example, an individual who is attracted to the brutality of war becomes a peace activist, or a person who fears his sexual urges becomes a religious zealot.

Regression *is the psychoanalytic defense mechanism that occurs when we behave in a way characteristic of a previous developmental level.* When anxiety becomes too great for us, we revert to an earlier behavior that gave us pleasure. For example, a woman may run home to her mother every time she and her husband have a big argument.

THE FAR SIDE By GARY LARSON

"So, Mr. Fenton. . .Let's begin with your mother."

THE FAR SIDE cartoon by Gary Larson is reprinted by permission of Chronicle Features, San Francisco, CA.

Two final points about defense mechanisms need to be understood. First, defense mechanisms are unconscious; we are not aware we are calling on them to protect our ego and reduce anxiety. Second, when used in moderation or on a temporary basis, defense mechanisms are not necessarily unhealthy. For example, defense mechanisms, such as denial, can help a person cope with impending death. For the most part, though, we should not let defense mechanisms dominate our behavior and prevent us from facing life's demands.

The Development of Personality

As Freud listened to, probed, and analyzed his patients, he became convinced that their problems were the result of experiences early in life. Freud believed that we go through five stages of psychosexual development and that, at each stage of development, we experience pleasure in one part of the body more than others. **Erogenous zones** *refer to Freud's concept that, at each stage of development, one part of the body has especially strong pleasure-giving qualities.*

Freud thought that our adult personality is determined by the way we resolve conflicts among these early sources of pleasure—the mouth, the anus, and then the genitals—and the demands of reality. When these conflicts are not resolved, the individual may become fixated at a particular stage of development. **Fixation** *is the psychoanalytic defense mechanism that occurs when the individual remains locked in an earlier developmental stage because needs are under- or overgratified.* For example, a parent may wean a child too early, be too strict in toilet training, punish the child for masturbation, or "smother" the child with too much attention. We will return to the idea of fixation and how it may show up in an adult's personality, but first we need to learn more about the early stages of personality development.

The **oral stage** *is the term Freud used to describe development during the first 18 months of life, in which the infant's pleasure centers on the mouth.* Chewing, sucking, and biting are chief sources of pleasure, and they help reduce tension.

The **anal stage** *is Freud's second stage of development, occurring between 1½ and 3 years of age, in which the child's greatest pleasure involves the anus or the elimination functions associated with it.* In Freud's view, the exercise of anal muscles reduces tension.

The **phallic stage,** *Freud's third stage of development, occurs between the ages of 3 and 6: its name comes from the Latin word* phallus, *which means penis. During the phallic stage, pleasure focuses on the genitals as the child discovers that self-stimulation is enjoyable.* In Freud's view, the phallic stage has a special importance in personality development because this period triggers the Oedipus complex. This name comes from Greek mythology, in which Oedipus, the son of the King of Thebes,

TABLE 12.1
Possible Links Between Adult Personality Characteristics and Fixation at Oral, Anal, and Phallic Stages

Stage	Adult extensions	Sublimations	Reaction formations
Oral	Smoking, eating, kissing, oral hygiene, drinking, chewing gum	Seeking knowledge, humor, wit, sarcasm, being a food or wine expert	Speech purist, food faddist, prohibitionist, dislike of milk
Anal	Notable interest in one's bowel movements, love of bathroom humor, extreme messiness	Interest in painting or sculpture, being overly giving, great interest in statistics	Extreme disgust with feces, fear of dirt, prudishness, irritability
Phallic	Heavy reliance on masturbation, flirtatiousness, expressions of virility	Interest in poetry, love of love, interest in acting, striving for success	Puritanical attitude toward sex, excessive modesty

From *Introduction to Personality* by E. Jerry Phares. Copyright © 1984 by Scott, Foresman and Company. Reprinted by permission of HarperCollins Publishers.

unwittingly kills his father and marries his mother. The **Oedipus complex** *is Freud's idea that the young child develops an intense desire to replace the parent of the same sex and to enjoy the affections of the opposite-sexed parent.* As discussed in Sociocultural Worlds 12.1, Freud's concept of the Oedipus complex was not as universal as he believed, being heavily influenced by the sociohistorical, cultural setting of turn-of-the-century Vienna.

At about 5 to 6 years of age, children recognize that their same-sex parent might punish them for their incestuous wishes. To reduce this conflict, the child identifies with the same-sex parent, striving to be like him or her. If the conflict is not resolved, though, the individual may become fixated at the phallic stage. Table 12.1 reveals some possible links among adult personality characteristics and fixation, sublimation, and reaction formation involving the phallic stage, as well as the oral and anal stages.

The **latency stage** *is the fourth Freudian stage of development, occurring approximately between 6 years of age and puberty; the child represses all interest in sexuality and develops social and intellectual skills.* This activity channels much of the child's energy into emotionally safe areas and aids the child in forgetting the highly stressful conflicts of the phallic stage.

The **genital stage** *is the fifth and final Freudian stage of development, occurring from puberty on. The genital stage is the time of sexual reawakening; the source of sexual pleasure now becomes someone outside of the family.* Freud believed that unresolved conflicts with parents reemerge during adolescence. Once the conflicts are resolved, Freud believed, the individual becomes capable of developing a mature love relationship and of functioning independently as an adult. Figure 12.2 summarizes Freud's psychosexual stages.

Psychoanalytic Dissenters and Revisionists

Because Freud was among the first theorists to explore many new and uncharted regions of personality, some of his ideas have needed to be updated, others have been revised, and some have been tossed out altogether. In particular, Freud's critics have said his ideas about sexuality, early experience, social factors, and the unconscious mind were misguided (Adler, 1927; Erikson, 1968; Fromm, 1947; Horney, 1945; Jung, 1917; Kohut, 1977; Rapaport, 1967; Sullivan, 1953). The critics stressed that

- Sexuality is not the pervasive underlying force behind personality that Freud believed it to be.
- The first 5 years of life are not as powerful in shaping adult personality as Freud thought; later experiences deserve more attention.
- The ego and conscious thought processes play more dominant roles in our personality than Freud gave them credit for; we are not wed forever to the id and its instinctual, unconscious clutches. The ego has a line of development separate from the id; viewed in this way, achievement, thinking, and reasoning are not always tied to sexual impulses, as Freud thought.
- Sociocultural factors are much more important than Freud believed. Freud placed more emphasis on the biological basis of personality by stressing the id's dominance.

Let's examine three theories by dissenters and revisionists of Freud's theory in greater detail—Horney's, Jung's, and Adler's.

Horney's Sociocultural Approach

Karen Horney (1885-1952) rejected the classical psychoanalytic concept that anatomy determines behavior in favor of an approach that emphasizes the importance of sociocultural

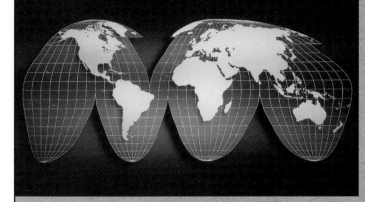

Freud's Oedipus Complex: Culturally and Gender Biased

The Oedipus complex is one of Freud's most influential concepts pertaining to the importance of early psychosexual relationships for later personality development. Freud developed his theory during the Victorian era of the late 1800s, when sexual interests, especially those of females, were repressed. According to Freud, the phallic stage begins for a girl when she realizes she has no penis. He also believed that she recognizes the superiority of the penis to her anatomy and, thus, develops *penis envy*. Blaming her mother for her lack of a penis, the girl renounces her love for her mother and becomes intensely attached to her father. Since her desire for having a penis can never be satisfied directly, Freud speculated that the young girl

yearns for a penis substitute, a baby. This version of the Oedipus complex is sometimes referred to as the *Electra complex*. Freud believed that the Electra complex is never fully resolved but merely dissipates over time as the girl begins to identify with—to take on the values and feminine behavior of—her mother. As a result, Freud assumed that women do not develop as strong a conscience (superego) as men.

Many psychologists believe that Freud placed far too much emphasis on biology's role in personality development. Freud concluded, for example, that boys are likely to develop a dominant, powerful personality because they have a penis; without a penis, girls are predisposed to become submissive and weak. In basing his view of male/female differences in personality development on anatomical differences, Freud ignored the enormous impact of culture and experience.

More than half a century ago, English anthropologist Bronislaw Malinowski (1927) observed the family dynamics of the Trobriand Islanders of the Western Pacific and found that the Oedipus complex is not universal. In the Trobriand Islands, the biological father is not the head of the household; that role is reserved for the mother's brother, who acts as a disciplinarian. In Freud's view, this family constellation should make no difference in the Oedipus complex; the young boy should still vie for his mother's love and perceive his father as a hated rival. However, Malinowski found no such conflict between fathers and sons in the Trobriand Islanders. However, he did observe that the young boys feared and directed negative feelings toward their maternal uncles, the authoritarian figures. Malinowski's finding undermined Freud's Oedipus complex theory, because it showed that the sexual relations within the family do not create conflict and fear for a child.

Freud called a young girl's desire for her father the Electra complex. What are some of the criticisms that have been directed at the Electra complex?

In the Trobriand Islands, the authoritarian figure in a young boy's life is his maternal uncle, not his father. Young boys in this culture fear their maternal uncles, not their fathers. Thus, it is not sexual relations in a family that create conflict and fear—a damaging finding for Freud's Oedipus complex theory.

Oral stage

Anal stage

Phallic stage

Latency stage

Genital stage

FIGURE 12.2

Freudian psychosexual stages. Freud said we go through five stages of psychosexual development. In the oral stage, pleasure centers around the mouth. In the anal stage, pleasure focuses on the anus—the nature of toilet training is important here. In the phallic stage, pleasure involves the genitals—the opposite-sex parent becomes a love object. In the latency stage, a child represses sexual urges—same-sex friendship is prominent. In the genital stage, sexual reawakening takes place—the source of pleasure now becomes someone outside the family.

factors in development. She cautioned that such ideas as penis envy are only hypotheses. She insisted that these hypotheses should be supported with observable data before they are accepted as fact.

Horney pointed out that previous research about how women function was limited by the fact that those who described women, who influenced and represented the culture, and who determined the standards for suitable growth and development were men. She countered the notion of penis envy with the hypothesis that both sexes envy the attributes of the other, with men coveting women's reproductive capacities. She also argued that women who feel penis envy are desirous only of the status that men have in most societies (Westkott, 1986).

Horney also believed that the need for security, not for sex or aggression, is the prime motive in human existence. Horney reasoned that, when an individual's needs for security are met,

a.

b.

(a) Karen Horney developed the first feminist-based criticism of Freud's theory, creating a model of women with positive qualities and self-valuation. (b) Nancy Chodorow has developed an important contemporary feminist revision of psychoanalysis theory that emphasizes the meaningfulness of emotions for women.

the person should be able to develop his or her capacities to the fullest extent. She also suggested that people usually develop one of three strategies in their effort to cope with anxiety. First, individuals may *move toward* people, seeking love and support. Second, individuals may *move away* from people, becoming more independent. Third, individuals may *move against* people, becoming competitive and domineering. A secure individual uses these three ways of coping in moderation and balance, whereas an insecure individual often uses one or more of these strategies in an exaggerated fashion, becoming too dependent, too independent, or too aggressive.

Psychologists are still revamping psychoanalytic theory. Nancy Chodorow's (1978, 1989) feminist revision of psychoanalytic theory, for example, emphasizes that many more women than men define themselves in terms of their relationships, that many men use denial as a defense mechanism in regard to their relationships with others, and that emotions tend to be more salient to women's lives.

Jung's Depth Psychology

Freud's contemporary, Carl Jung (1875-1961), shared an interest in the unconscious; however, he believed that Freud underplayed the unconscious mind's role in personality. Jung suspected that the roots of personality go back to the dawn of human existence. The **collective unconscious** *is the impersonal, deepest layer of the unconscious mind, which is shared by all human beings because of their common ancestral past.* These common experiences have made a deep, permanent impression on the human mind. **Archetypes** *are the primordial images in every individual's collective unconscious. Jung's psychoanalytic theory is often referred to as "depth psychology" because archetypes reside deep within the unconscious mind, far deeper than Freud's concept of our personal unconscious.*

Two common archetypes are *anima* (woman) and *animus* (man). Jung believed that each of us has a passive, "feminine" side and an assertive, "masculine" side. We also have an arche-

FIGURE 12.3

Mandalas. Carl Jung believed that mandalas were so widely used to represent the self at different points in history that they were an archetype for the self.

Swiss psychoanalytic theorist Carl Jung developed the concepts for the collective unconscious and archetypes.

type for self, which often is expressed in art. For example, the mandala, a figure within a circle, has been used so often that Jung took it to represent the self (see figure 12.3). Another archetype is the shadow, our darker self, which is evil and immoral. The shadow appears in many evil and immoral figures—Satan, Dracula, Mr. Hyde (of Jekyll and Hyde), Darth Vader (of the *Star Wars* films), even J. R. Ewing (of the television show "Dallas") (Peterson, 1988).

Adler's Individual Psychology

Alfred Adler (1870-1937) was another contemporary of Freud. **Individual psychology** *is the name Adler gave to his theory of psychology to emphasize the uniqueness of every individual.* Unlike Freud's belief in the power of the unconscious mind, Adler argued that we have the conscious ability to monitor and direct our lives; he also believed that social factors are more important in shaping our personality than is sexual motivation (Silverman & Corsini, 1984).

Adler thought that everyone strives for superiority. Adler's concept of **striving for superiority** *emphasizes the human motivation to adapt, improve, and master the environment.* Striving for superiority is our response to the feelings of inferiority that we all experience as infants and young children when we interact with people who are bigger and more powerful. We strive to overcome these feelings of inferiority because they are uncomfortable. **Compensation** *is Adler's term for the individual's attempt to overcome imagined or real inferiorities or weaknesses by developing one's abilities.* Adler believed that compensation is normal, and he said we often make up for a weakness in one ability by excelling in a different ability. For example, one person may be a mediocre student but compensate for this by excelling in athletics. **Overcompensation** *is Adler's term for the individual's attempt to deny rather than acknowledge a real situation or the individual's exaggerated effort to conceal a weakness.* Adler described two patterns of overcompensation. **Inferiority complex** *is the name Adler gave to exaggerated feelings of inadequacy.* **Superiority complex** *is his concept of exaggerated self-importance to mask feelings of inferiority.*

In summary, Adler's theory emphasizes that people are striving toward a positive being and that they create their own goals. Their adaptation is enhanced by developing social interests and reducing feelings of inferiority. Like Jung, Adler has a number of disciples today.

Evaluating the Psychoanalytic Perspectives

Although psychoanalytic theories have diverged, they do share some core principles. Psychoanalytic theorists assert that personality is determined both by current experiences and by those from early in life. Two basic principles of psychoanalytic theory have withstood the test of time: early experiences do shape our personality to a degree, and personality can be better understood by examining it developmentally (Horowitz, 1989).

Another belief that continues to receive considerable attention is that we mentally transform environmental experiences. Psychologists also recognize that the mind is not all consciousness; unconscious motives lie behind some of our puzzling behavior. Psychoanalytic theorists' emphasis on conflict and anxiety leads us to consider the dark side of our existence, not just its bright side. Adjustment is not always an easy task, and the individual's inner world often conflicts with the outer demands of reality. Finally, psychoanalytic theories continue to force psychologists to study more than the experimental, laboratory topics of sensation, perception, and learning; personality and adjustment are rightful and important topics of psychological inquiry as well.

However, the main concepts of psychoanalytic theories have been difficult to test; they are largely matters of inference and interpretation. Researchers have not, for example, successfully investigated such key concepts as repression in the laboratory.

Much of the data used to support psychoanalytic theories have come from clinicians' subjective evaluations of clients; in such cases, it is easy for each clinician to see what she expects because of the theory she holds. Other data come from patients' recollections of the distant past (especially those from early childhood) and are of doubtful accuracy. Also, psychoanalytic theories place too much weight on the ability of these early experiences within the family to shape personality. We retain the capacity for change and adaptation throughout our lives.

Some psychologists object that Freud overemphasized the importance of sexuality in understanding personality and that Freud and Jung placed too much faith in the unconscious mind's ability to control behavior. Others object that the psychoanalytic perspectives provide a model of a person that is too negative and pessimistic. We are not born into the world with only a bundle of sexual and aggressive instincts. The demands of reality do not always conflict with our biological needs.

Many psychoanalytic theories of personality have a male bias, especially Freud's. Although Horney's theory helped correct this bias, psychoanalytic theory continues to be revised today.

At this point, you should have a sense of what personality is and a basic understanding of the themes of psychoanalytic theories. Next, we will explore two views of personality that are very different from the psychoanalytic theories.

REVIEW

The Nature of Personality and Psychoanalytic Theories

Personality refers to our enduring thoughts, emotions, and behaviors that characterize the way we adapt. A key question is why individuals respond to a situation in different ways.

Freud was one of the most influential thinkers in the twentieth century. He was a medical doctor who believed that most of the mind is unconscious. Freud said that personality has three structures: id, ego, and superego. The id is the reservoir of psychic energy that tries to satisfy our basic needs; it is unconscious and operates according to the pleasure principle. The ego tries to provide pleasure by operating within the boundaries of reality. The superego is the moral branch of personality. The conflicting demands of personality structures produce anxiety; defense mechanisms protect the ego and reduce this anxiety. Repression, the most pervasive defense mechanism, pushes unacceptable id impulses back into the unconscious mind. Other defense mechanisms include rationalization, displacement, sublimation, projection, reaction formation, and regression. Freud was convinced that problems develop because of childhood experiences. He said we go through five psychosexual stages of development: oral, anal, phallic, latency, and genital. He believed that, if our needs are under- or overgratified at a particular stage, we can become fixated at that stage. During the phallic stage, the Oedipus complex is a major source of conflict.

The psychoanalytic dissenters and revisionists have argued that Freud placed too much emphasis on sexuality and the first

Behavioral and Social Learning Perspectives

Tom is engaged to marry Ann. Both have warm, friendly personalities and they enjoy being with each other. Psychoanalytic theorists would say that their personalities are derived from long-standing relationships with their parents, especially their early childhood experiences. They also would argue that the reason for their attraction is unconscious; they are unaware of how their biological heritage and early life experiences have been carried forward to influence their adult personalities.

Behaviorists and social learning theorists would observe Tom and Ann and see something quite different. They would examine their experiences, especially their most recent ones, to understand the reason for Tom and Ann's attraction to one another. The theorists would describe Tom as rewarding Ann's

5 years of life and too little emphasis on the ego and conscious thought processes, as well as sociocultural factors. Karen Horney rejected the classical psychoanalytic concept that anatomy determines behavior, advocated by Freud, in favor of a sociocultural approach. She especially emphasized that Freud's theory is male biased. Horney said that the need for security, not sex or aggression, is the prime motive in human existence. She also theorized that individuals usually develop one of three strategies to cope with anxiety—moving toward people, moving away from people, or moving against people. The rectification of male bias in psychoanalytic theory continues today through the efforts of such individuals as Nancy Chodorow. Jung thought Freud underplayed the role of the unconscious mind. He developed the concept of the collective unconscious, and his theory is often called depth psychology. Alfred Adler's theory is called individual psychology; it stresses every individual's uniqueness. Adler said people are striving toward a positive being and that they create their own goals. Their adaptation is enhanced by developing social interests and reducing feelings of inferiority.

The strengths of the psychoanalytic perspectives include an emphasis on the past, the developmental course of personality, mental representations of the environment, the concept of the unconscious mind, an emphasis on conflict, and their influence on psychology as a discipline. Their weaknesses include the difficulty in testing the main concepts, a lack of empirical data and an overreliance on reports of the past, too much emphasis on sexuality and the unconscious mind, a negative view of human nature, too much power given to early experience, and a male bias.

behavior and vice versa, for example. No reference would be made to unconscious thoughts, the Oedipus complex, defense mechanisms, and so on.

Remember from chapters 1 and 5 that behaviorists believe that psychology should examine only what can be directly observed and measured. At approximately the same time Freud was interpreting his patients' unconscious minds through their recollections of early childhood experiences, such behaviorists as Ivan Pavlov and John B. Watson were conducting detailed observations of behavior under controlled laboratory conditions. Out of the behavioral tradition grew the belief that personality is observable behavior, learned through experiences with the environment. The two current versions of the behavioral approach are the behavioral view of B. F. Skinner and social learning theory.

Skinner's Behaviorism

B. F. Skinner (1904-1990) concluded that personality is an individual's *behavior,* which is determined by the *external environment.* Skinner believed that psychologists do not have to resort to biological or cognitive processes to explain personality (behavior). Some psychologists say that including Skinner among personality theorists is like inviting a wolf to a party of lambs because he took the "person" out of personality (Phares, 1984).

Behaviorists counter that you cannot pinpoint where personality is or how it is determined. In Skinner's view, personality simply consists of a collection of a person's observed, overt behaviors; it does not include internal traits or thoughts. For example, observations of Sam reveal that his behavior is shy, achievement-oriented, and caring. In short, these behaviors *are* his personality. According to Skinner, Sam is this way because the rewards and punishments in Sam's environment have shaped him into a shy, achievement-oriented, and caring person. Because of interactions with family members, friends, teachers, and others, Sam has *learned* to behave in this fashion.

Behaviorists who support Skinner's view would say that Sam's shy, achievement-oriented, and caring behavior may not be consistent and enduring. For example, Sam is uninhibited on Saturday night with friends at a bar, unmotivated to excel in English class, and occasionally nasty to his sister. In addition, Skinnerians believe that consistency in behavior comes from consistency in environmental experiences. If Sam's shy, achievement-oriented, and caring behavior is consistently rewarded, his pattern of behavior is likely to be consistent. However, Skinner stressed that our behavior always has the capacity for change if new experiences are encountered. The issue of consistency in personality is an important one. We will return to it on several occasions later in the chapter.

Since behaviorists believe that personality is learned and changes according to environmental experiences and situations, it follows that, by rearranging experiences and situations, an individual's personality can be changed. For a behaviorist, shy behavior can be changed into outgoing behavior; aggressive behavior can be shaped into docile behavior; lethargic, boring behavior can be shaped into enthusiastic, interesting behavior. Much more about the behavioral techniques used to accomplish these changes in personality are discussed in chapter 14.

Social Learning Theory

Some psychologists believe that the behaviorists basically are right when they say that personality is learned and influenced strongly by environmental experiences. However, they believe that Skinner went too far in declaring that cognition is unimportant in understanding the nature of personality. The psychologists who emphasize behavior, environment, *and* cognition as the key factors in personality are called *social learning theorists*.

The social learning theorists say we are not mindless robots, responding mechanically to others in our environment, and we are not like weather vanes, behaving like a Communist in the presence of a Communist or like a John Bircher in the presence of a John Bircher. Rather, we think, reason, imagine, plan, expect, interpret, believe, value, and compare. When others try to control us, our values and beliefs allow us to resist their control.

Albert Bandura (1977, 1986, 1989) and Walter Mischel (1973, 1987) are the architects of social learning theory's contemporary version, which Mischel labeled *cognitive* social learning theory. Recall from chapter 5 that Bandura believes that much of our learning occurs by observing what others do. Through observational learning, we form ideas about the behavior of others and then possibly adopt this behavior ourselves. For example, a young boy may observe his father's aggressive outbursts and hostile exchanges with people; when the boy is with his peers, he interacts in a highly aggressive way, showing the same characteristics as his father. A young executive may adopt the dominant and sarcastic style of her boss. When this young woman interacts with one of her subordinates, she says, "I need this work immediately if not sooner; you are so far behind you think you are ahead!" Social learning theorists believe we acquire a wide range of such behaviors, thoughts, and feelings through observing others' behavior; these observations form an important part of our personality.

Social learning theorists also differ from Skinner's behavioral view by emphasizing that we can regulate our own behavior, despite our changing environment. For example, another young executive who observes her boss behave in a dominant and sarcastic manner toward employees may find the behavior distasteful and go out of her way to be encouraging and supportive

Albert Bandura was one of the pioneers in the development of social learning theory.

of her subordinates. Someone tries to persuade you to join a particular social club on campus and makes you an enticing offer. You reflect about the offer, consider your interests and beliefs, and make the decision not to join. Your *cognition* (your thoughts) leads you to control your behavior and resist environmental influence in this instance.

Like Skinner's behavioral approach, the social learning view emphasizes the importance of empirical research in studying personality. This research has focused on the processes that explain personality—the social and cognitive factors that influence what we are like as people. One process Mischel believes is important in understanding an individual's personality is delay of gratification, which is the ability to defer immediate satisfaction for a more desirable future outcome. For example, when you are in school, you resist the temptation to slack off and have a good time now so you will be rewarded with good grades later. Again, the point is that we are capable of controlling our behavior rather than always being influenced by others.

Evaluating the Behavioral and Social Learning Perspectives

The behavioral and social learning theories emphasize that environmental experiences and situational influences determine personality. These approaches have fostered a scientific climate for understanding personality that highlights the observation of behavior. Social learning theory emphasizes both environmental influences and the "black box" of the human mind to explain personality; this theory also suggests that people have the ability to control their environment.

Critics of both the behavioral and social learning perspectives take issue with several aspects of both theories. The behavioral view is criticized for ignoring the importance of cognition in personality and placing too much importance on the role of environmental experiences. Both approaches have been described as being too concerned with change and situational influences on personality and not paying adequate tribute to the enduring qualities of personality. Both views are said to ignore the role biology plays in personality. Both are labeled reductionistic, which means they try to explain the complex concept of personality in terms of one or two factors. The critics charge that the behavioral and social learning views are too mechanical, missing the exciting, rich dimensions of personality. This latter criticism—that the creative, spontaneous, human dimensions of personality are missing from the behavioral and social learning perspectives—has been made on numerous occasions by humanists, whose perspective we will consider next.

The Phenomenological and Humanistic Perspectives

Remember our example of the engaged couple, Tom and Ann, who were described as having warm, friendly personalities. Phenomenological and humanistic psychologists would say that Tom and Ann's warm, friendly personalities are a reflection of their inner selves; these psychologists would emphasize that a key to understanding Tom and Ann's attraction is their positive perceptions of each other. Tom and Ann are not viewed as controlling each other or each other's behavior; rather, each has determined a course of action and has freely chosen to marry. No recourse to biological instincts or unconscious thoughts as reasons for their attraction occurs in the phenomenological and humanistic perspectives.

The **phenomenological perspective** *stresses the importance of our perceptions of ourselves and our world in understanding personality; this perspective emphasizes that, for each individual, reality is what is perceived.* The **humanistic perspective** *is the most widely known phenomenological approach to personality. The humanistic perspective stresses a person's capacity for personal growth, freedom to choose one's own destiny, and positive qualities.* Humanistic psychologists believe that each of us has the ability to cope with stress, to control our lives, and to achieve what we desire. Each of us has the ability to break through and understand ourselves and our world; we can burst the cocoon and become a butterfly, say the humanists.

You probably sense that the phenomenological and humanistic perspectives provide stark contrasts to the psychoanalytic perspective, which is based on conflict, destructive drives, and little faith in human nature, and to the behavioral perspective, which, at worst, seems to reduce human beings to mere puppets on the strings of rewards and punishments. Carl Rogers and Abraham Maslow were two of the leading architects of the humanistic perspective.

Carl Rogers' Approach

Like Freud, Carl Rogers (1902-1987) began his inquiry into human nature with people who were troubled. In the knotted, anxious, defensive verbal stream of his clients, Rogers (1961) examined the conditioned, controlling world that kept them from having positive self-concepts and reaching their full potential as human beings.

Our Conditioned, Controlling World

Rogers believed that most people have considerable difficulty accepting their own feelings, which are innately positive. As we grow

Carl Rogers was a pioneer in the development of the humanistic perspective.

up, people who are central to our lives condition us to move away from these positive feelings. Our parents, siblings, teachers, and peers place constraints and contingencies on our behavior; too often we hear such phrases as "Don't do that," "You didn't do that right," and "How can you be so stupid?" When we don't do something right, we often get punished, and parents may even threaten to take away their love. **Conditional positive regard** *is Rogers' term for the concept that love and praise often are not given unless an individual conforms to parental or social standards.* The result is low self-esteem.

These constraints and negative feedback continue during our adult lives. The result tends to be that our relationships either carry the dark cloud of conflict or we conform to what others want. As we struggle to live up to society's standards, we distort and devalue our true self. We may even completely lose our sense of self by mirroring what others want us to be.

The Self

Through an individual's experiences with the world, a self emerges—the "I" or "me" of our existence. Rogers did not believe that all aspects of the self are conscious, but he did believe they are all accessible to consciousness. The self is a whole, consisting of one's self-perceptions (how attractive I am, how well I get along with others, how good an athlete I am) and the values we attach to these perceptions (good-bad, worthy-unworthy, for example). **Self-concept,** *a central theme in Rogers' and other humanists' views, refers to individuals' overall perceptions of their abilities, behavior, and personality.* In Rogers' view, a person who has a poor self-concept is likely to think, feel, and act negatively. Some psychologists are turning their interest to the differences and similarities among the self-concepts of individuals from different ethnic backgrounds (see Sociocultural Worlds 12.2).

In discussing self-concept, Rogers distinguished between the real self—that is, the self as it really is as a result of our experiences—and the ideal self, which is the self we would like to be. The greater the discrepancy between the real self and the ideal self, said Rogers, the more maladjusted we will be. To improve our adjustment, we can develop more positive perceptions of our real self, not worry so much about what others want, and increase our positive experiences in the world.

Unconditional Positive Regard, Empathy, and Genuineness

Rogers stressed that we can help a person develop a more positive self-concept through unconditional positive regard, empathy, and genuineness. Rogers said that we need to be accepted by others, regardless of what we do. **Unconditional positive regard** *is Rogers'*

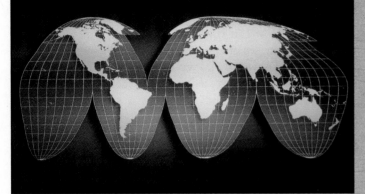

Ethnicity, Self, and Self-concept

Many of the early attempts to assess the nature of self and self-concept in various ethnic groups compared Black and White individuals (Clark & Clark, 1939; Coopersmith, 1967; Deutsch, 1967). These reports indicated that Blacks, especially Black children, have a more negative self-concept than Whites. However, more recent research suggests that Blacks, Mexican Americans, and Puerto Ricans have equally positive self-concepts and perhaps even higher self-esteem than Anglo Americans (Allen & Majidi-Ahi, 1989; Powell & Fuller, 1972).

"Ethnic pride" was one of the positive movements to spring out of the social turmoil of the sixties. Its emphasis on the richness and diversity of various cultures appears to have improved the self-esteem of ethnic minority groups (Garbarino, 1985). However, ethnic pride has both benefits and costs. One obvious benefit is a sense of cultural identity (such as being Black, Mexican American, or Native American), with clearly defined cultural roles as to what is expected of a competent person. Also, ethnic neighborhoods are often tight-knit and supportive. It's somewhat easier for a person to develop a positive sense of self in neighborhoods such as these, where people lend one another a hand and offer strategies for coping with problems. In addition, minority members who live in their ethnic neighborhoods can gain a sense of rootedness and acceptance.

However, there is no indication that acceptance within an ethnic group translates into prestige within mainstream American society (Rosenberg, 1965). Even though a person may have a secure sense of self as a member of an ethnic minority, he or she may still need to come to terms with prejudice beyond the ethnic neighborhood. When the values, morals, and behaviors of the ethnic neighborhood differ from society as a whole, an ethnic minority member may find it difficult to develop a sense of competence in mainstream society. At the same time, belonging to a group in which one is highly valued can serve as a buffer against racial prejudice.

Discussions of ethnicity, self, and self-concept still boil down to a fundamental issue: "What kind of people does the world need?" (Garbarino, 1980, 1985). If the quality of life on this planet

A generation of ethnic awareness and pride appears to have advanced the self-esteem of ethnic minority group members. A discussion of ethnicity and self-esteem raises the question of what kind of people the world needs. There is a growing need for a world of individuals who develop more harmonious, cooperative relationships.

is to be enhanced, people need to develop more harmonious, cooperative relationships. Society needs to foster individuals who define themselves in new ways that deemphasize competition, achievement, and materialism in favor of cooperation, connectedness with others, empathy, and spiritual development. We need to ask whether we are socializing children to develop the kind of self-concept that encourages a competent, caring, sustainable society.

term *for accepting, valuing, and being positive toward another person regardless of the person's behavior.* Rogers recognized that, when a person's behavior is below acceptable standards, inappropriate, or even obnoxious, the person still needs the respect, comfort, and love of others. Rogers strongly believed that unconditional positive regard elevates a person's self-worth. However, Rogers (1974) distinguished between unconditional positive regard directed at an individual as a person of worth and dignity and unconditional positive regard directed at the individual's behavior. For example, a therapist who takes Rogers' view of human behavior might say, "I don't like your behavior, but I accept you, value you, and care about you as a person."

Rogers also said we can help other people develop a more positive self-concept if we are *empathic* and *genuine.* Being empathic means being a sensitive listener and understanding another's true feelings. Being genuine means being open with our feelings and dropping our pretenses and facades. For Rogers, unconditional positive regard, empathy, and genuineness are three key ingredients of human relations. We can use these techniques to get other people to feel good about themselves, and the techniques also help us get along better with others.

The Fully Functioning Person

Rogers (1980) stressed the importance of becoming a fully functioning person—someone who is open to experience, is not very defensive, is aware of and sensitive to the self and the external world, and for the most part has a harmonious relationship with others. A discrepancy between our real self and our ideal self may occur, others may try to control us, and our world may have too little unconditional positive regard. However, Rogers believed that we are highly resilient and capable of becoming a fully functioning person. He believed that you can't keep a good man or woman down.

Our self-actualizing tendency is reflected in Rogers' comparison of a person with a plant he once observed on the coastline of northern California. As Rogers looked out at the waves beating furiously against the jagged rocks and shooting mountains of spray into the air, he noticed the breakers pounding a sea palm (a kind of seaweed that looks like a 2-to-3-foot-high palm tree). The plant seemed fragile and top-heavy. The waves crashed against the plant, bending its slender trunk almost flat and whipping its leaves in a torrent of spray, yet the moment the wave passed the plant was erect, tough, and resilient again. It was incredible that the plant could take this incessant pounding hour after hour, week after week, possibly even year after year, all the time nourishing itself, maintaining its position, and growing. In this palmlike seaweed, Rogers saw the tenacity and forward thrust of life and the ability of a living thing to push into a hostile environment and not only hold its own but adapt, develop, and become itself. So it is with each of us, in Rogers' view (Rogers, 1963).

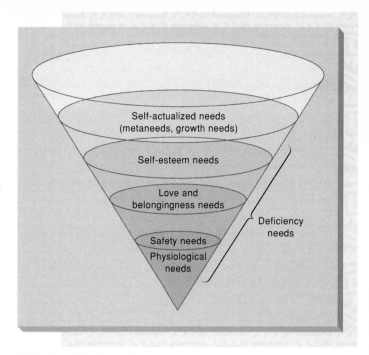

FIGURE 12.4

Maslow's hierarchy of needs. Only when the needs in the lower four circles are reasonably satisfied (the deficiency needs) can the self-actualized needs (metaneeds, growth needs) be satisfied. The deficiency needs are arranged hierarchically: the metaneeds are not.

Abraham Maslow's Approach

Another theorist who made self-actualization the centerpiece of his humanistic philosophy was Abraham Maslow (1908-1970). Maslow was one of the most powerful forces behind the humanistic movement in psychology. He called the humanistic approach the "third force" in psychology—that is, an important alternative to the psychoanalytic and behavioral forces. Maslow pointed out that psychoanalytic theories place too much emphasis on disturbed individuals and their conflicts. Behaviorists ignore the person all together, he said.

Remember from chapter 11 that Maslow (1954) said we have a hierarchy of needs in which certain basic needs (physiological, safety, love and belongingness, and self-esteem) have to be satisfied before we can satisfy the highest need of self-actualization. Remember also that Maslow described *self-actualization* as a motivation to develop one's full potential as a human being. Maslow (1971) charted the human potential of creative, talented, and healthy people.

He believed that needs come in two forms: deficiency needs and metaneeds (also called growth or self-actualization needs) (see figure 12.4). **Deficiency needs** *refers to Maslow's term for essential requirements—physiological (such as food, shelter, comfort) and psychological (such as affection, security, self-esteem)—*

that must be met; otherwise, individuals will try to make up for their absence. **Metaneeds,** *or growth needs, refers to Maslow's concept of higher, self-actualized needs; they include truth, goodness, beauty, wholeness, vitality, uniqueness, perfection, justice, inner wealth, and playfulness.* The metaneeds cannot be satisfied until all the lower needs are met. The metaneeds themselves, however, are not hierarchically arranged in Maslow's model. For example, although we have to satisfy our need for belongingness before our need for self-esteem, we do not have to satisfy our need for goodness before our need for vitality. When our metaneeds are not fulfilled, Maslow cautioned, we may become maladjusted. For example, unfulfilled metaneeds may cause individuals to become alienated, weak, or cynical.

Maslow developed psychological profiles of famous people and concluded that such individuals as Eleanor Roosevelt, Albert Einstein, Abraham Lincoln, Walt Whitman, William James, and Ludwig van Beethoven were self-actualized. Table 12.2 lists Maslow's descriptions of the characteristics of self-actualized individuals.

TABLE 12.2
Maslow's Characteristics of Self-actualized Individuals

Realistic orientation

Self-acceptance and acceptance of others and the natural world as they are

Spontaneity

Problem-centered rather than self-centered

Air of detachment and need for privacy

Autonomous and independent

Fresh rather than stereotyped appreciation of people and things

Generally have had profound mystical or spiritual, though not necessarily religious, experiences

Identification with humankind and a strong social interest

Tendency to have strong intimate relationships with a few special, loved people rather than superficial relationships with many people

Democratic values and attitudes

No confusion of means with ends

Philosophical rather than hostile sense of humor

High degree of creativity

Resistance to cultural conformity

Transcendence of environment rather than always coping with it

Source: A. H. Maslow, *The Farther Reaches of Nature*, pages 153–174. Copyright © 1971 Viking Press, New York, NY.

Evaluating the Phenomenological and Humanistic Perspectives

The phenomenological and humanistic perspectives have made psychologists aware that the way we perceive ourselves and the world around us is a key element of personality. Humanistic psychologists also have reminded us that we need to consider the whole person and the positive bent of human nature. Their emphasis on conscious experience has given us the view that personality contains a "well of potential" that can be developed to its fullest.

A weakness of the humanistic perspective is that it is difficult to test. Self-actualization, for example, is not clearly defined. Psychologists are not certain how to study this concept empirically. Some humanists even scorn the experimental approach, preferring clinical interpretation as a data base. Verification of humanistic concepts has come mainly from clinical experiences rather than controlled, experimental studies. Some critics also believe that humanistic psychologists are too optimistic about human nature, overestimating the freedom and rationality of humans. Some critics say the humanists encourage self-love and narcissism.

We have seen that the psychoanalytic, behavioral/social learning, and phenomenological/humanistic perspectives take different paths to understanding personality. Yet another important view of personality remains to be discussed—trait theory.

REVIEW
The Behavioral, Social Learning, Phenomenological, and Humanistic Perspectives

In Skinner's behaviorism, cognition is unimportant in understanding personality. Rather, personality is observed behavior, which is influenced by the rewards and punishments in the environment. Personality varies according to the situation, in the behavioral view. In social learning theory, the environment is an important determinant of personality, but so are cognitive processes. Social learning theorists believe that we are capable of controlling our own behavior through thoughts, beliefs, and values. Bandura and Mischel crafted the contemporary version of social learning theory, known as cognitive social learning theory. Strengths of both the behavioral and social learning perspectives include emphases on environmental determinants of behavior and a scientific climate for investigating personality, as well as the focus on cognitive processes and self-control in the social learning approach. The behavioral view has been criticized for taking the person out of personality and for ignoring

Trait Theory and Trait-Situation Interaction

Through the ages, we have used an infinite variety of traits to describe ourselves and one another. More than 2,000 years ago, Theophrastus described the stingy man, the liar, and the flatterer. More recently, a magazine article took a modern swipe at the stingy man:

> Could a miser be lurking beneath sensuous flesh and persuasive charm? Well, don't expect sapphires from him, dear, if he
> —itemizes who owes what when you're out Dutch-treat rather than splitting the bill
> —washes plastic party cups to reuse them
> —steams uncanceled stamps from letters
> —reshapes bent paper clips
> —has a dozen recipes for chicken wings
> —cuts his own hair
> —wants rolls and butter included in his doggie bag
>
> (*Cosmopolitan*, September 1976, p. 148)

Think about yourself and your friends. How would you describe yourself? You might say that you're outgoing and sociable and that, in contrast, one of your friends is shy and quiet. You might refer to yourself as emotionally stable and

cognition. These approaches have not given adequate attention to enduring individual differences, to biological factors, and to personality as a whole.

The phenomenological approach emphasizes our perceptions of ourselves and our world and centers on the belief that reality is what is perceived. The humanistic approach is the most widely known phenomenological approach. In Carl Rogers' approach, each of us is a victim of conditional positive regard. The result is that our real self is not valued. The self is the core of personality; it includes both the real and the ideal self. Rogers said we can help others develop a more positive self-concept in three ways: unconditional positive regard, empathy, and genuineness. Rogers also stressed that each of us has the innate, inner capacity to become a fully functioning person. Maslow called the humanistic movement the "third force" in psychology. Each of us has a self-actualizing tendency, according to Maslow. He distinguishes between deficiency needs and self-actualization needs, or metaneeds. The phenomenological and humanistic approaches sensitized psychologists to the importance of subjective experience, consciousness, self-concept, the whole person, and our innate, positive nature. Their weaknesses are the absence of an empirical orientation, a tendency to be too optimistic, and an inclination to encourage self-love.

describe one of your other friends as a bit skittish. Part of our everyday existence involves describing ourselves and others in terms of traits.

Personality Type Theory

As early as 400 B.C., Hippocrates classified people's personalities according to their body type. Hippocrates thought that people with more yellow bile than others, for example, were "choleric"—easily angered—whereas others, with an excess of blood, were more "sanguine"—cheerful and buoyant. More recently, William Sheldon (1954) proposed a theory of body types and personality. **Somatotype theory** *was Sheldon's theory stating that precise charts reveal distinct body types, which in turn are associated with certain personality characteristics.* He concluded that individuals basically are one of three types. **Endomorph** *was Sheldon's term for a soft, round, large-stomached person who is relaxed, gregarious, and food loving.* **Mesomorph** *was Sheldon's term for a strong, athletic, and muscular person who is energetic, assertive, and courageous.* **Ectomorph** *was Sheldon's term for a tall, thin, fragile person who is fearful, introverted, and restrained.*

Appealing as it was, somatotyping ran aground. For starters, research revealed that there is no significant relation between body type and personality (Cortes & Gatti, 1970). Many people simply do not fit into a neatly packaged category. In addition, using one, two, or three categories to describe individuals ignores the rich diversity and complexity of human characteristics. Thus, the somatotype theory is not popular today.

Trait Theories

Trait theories *state that personality consists of broad dispositions, called traits, that tend to lead to characteristic responses. In other words, people can be described in terms of the basic ways they behave, such as whether they are outgoing and friendly or whether they are dominant and assertive.* People who have a strong tendency to behave in certain ways are described as high on the traits; those who have a weak tendency to behave in these ways are described as low on the traits. Although trait theorists sometimes differ on which traits make up personality, they all agree that traits are the fundamental building blocks of personality (Pervin, 1989).

Trying to pigeonhole the traits that make up personality is a herculean task. Gordon Allport (1937), for example, combed the dictionary and counted almost 18,000 words that could be used to describe people. Allport said that several overarching categories could be used to reduce the vast number of words used to describe traits. One of Allport's trait categories was *individual traits*, which refers to an individual's unique way of dealing with the world.

Hans Eysenck (1967) also tackled the task of determining the basic traits of personality. He gave personality tests to large numbers of people and analyzed each person's response. Eysenck consistently found the traits of stability-instability and introversion-extraversion when the personalities of large numbers of individuals were assessed (see figure 12.5). A person with an unstable personality is moody, anxious, restless, and touchy; a person with a stable personality is calm, even-tempered, and carefree and has leadership qualities. A person with an introverted personality is quiet, unsociable, passive, and careful; a person with an extraverted personality is active, optimistic, sociable, and outgoing.

Recent Developments in Trait Psychology

Researchers continue to ferret out the basic traits of personality. Two areas of interest are known as the "basic five-factor structure of personality" and the "traits of individualism and collectivism."

Five Basic Factors

A number of trait psychologists are encouraged by evidence from a number of studies that reveal five basic dimensions of personality (Hogan, 1987; McCrae & Costa, 1989; Paunon & others, 1992), called the *big five factors in personality:*

- Extraversion-introversion
- Friendly compliance versus hostile noncompliance
- Neuroticism
- Will to achieve
- Intellect

Extraversion-introversion focuses on assertiveness, gregariousness, and shyness; friendly compliance versus hostile noncompliance involves love and friendship at one end of the spectrum and enduring problems of aggression and lawlessness at the other end; neuroticism refers to emotional stability or instability; the will to achieve emphasizes achievement motivation; and intellect includes intelligence and creativity.

Individualism and Collectivism

A small Texas corporation trying to improve productivity told its employees to look in the mirror and say, "I am beautiful" 100 times before coming to work each day. Employees of a Japanese supermarket that was recently opened in New Jersey were told to begin the day by holding hands, telling each other that "he" or "she" is beautiful. In America "the squeaky wheel gets the grease." In Japan "the nail that stands out gets pounded down." Such anecdotes suggest that people in Japan and America have different views of the self and others (Markus & Kitayama, 1991).

In cross-cultural research, the search for basic traits has even extended to characteristics common to whole nations. In recent years, the most elaborate search for traits common to the inhabitants of a particular country has focused on the dichotomy of individualism-collectivism (Gudykunst & others, 1992; Hamilton, 1992; Hofstede, 1980; Hui & Triandis, 1986; Kagitcibasi & Berry, 1989; Kilpatrick & White, 1985; Trafimow, Triandis, & Goto, 1991; Triandis, 1980; Triandis, Brislin, &

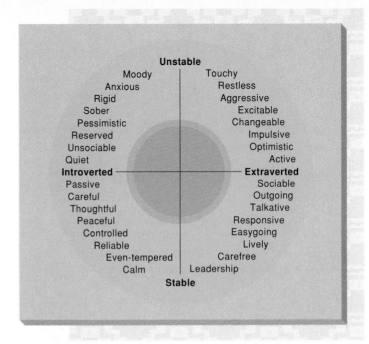

FIGURE 12.5

Eysenck's dimensions of personality. On the basis of his factor analytic studies, Eysenck concluded that personality consists of two basic dimensions: (1) stability-instability and (2) introversion-extraversion.

Hui, 1988). **Individualism** *involves giving priority to personal goals rather than to group goals; it emphasizes values that serve the self, such as feeling good, personal distinction, and independence.* **Collectivism** *emphasizes values that serve the group by subordinating personal goals to preserve group integrity, interdependence of the members, and harmonious relationships.*

As is true of a great deal of psychology's basic tenets, many of the assumptions about personality were developed in Western cultures, such as the United States, that emphasize the individual or self. Psychological terms about personality often include the word *self*—for example, self-actualization, self-awareness, self-concept, self-efficacy, self-reinforcement, self-criticism, self-serving, selfishness, and self-doubt (Lonner, 1988; Rumpel, 1988). Cross-cultural psychologists describe the cultures in many non-Western countries, such as Japan and India, as more collectivistic than individualistic (Kagitcibasi, 1988; Triandis, 1985, 1989).

Critics of the Western notion of personality point out that human beings have always lived in groups, whether large or small, and have always needed one another for survival. They argue that the Western emphasis on individualism may undermine our species' basic need for relatedness (Kagitcibasi, 1988). Some social scientists believe that many of our problems, such as anxiety, depression, and shyness, are intensified by the emphasis on the self and independence in American culture (Munroe & Munroe, 1975). As was mentioned in previous chapters, the

Some social scientists believe that many of Americans' problems, such as anxiety, depression, and shyness, are intensified by the emphasis on the self and independence in the American culture. In many Eastern cultures, such as China, there is a much stronger emphasis on connectedness with others and group behavior.

pendulum may have swung too far toward individualism in Western cultures. People, regardless of their cultural background, need a positive sense of self *and* connectedness to others to develop fully as human beings. To read about ways to improve intercultural communication between persons from individualist and collectivist cultures, turn to Sociocultural Worlds 12.3.

As with other attempts to explain personality, the individualism-collectivism dichotomy has its detractors as well. They argue that describing entire nations of people as having a basic personality obscures the extensive diversity and individual variation that characterizes a nation's people. Also, certain values serve both individual and collective interests, such as wisdom, mature love, and tolerance (Schwartz, 1990).

The Attack on Traits

In his landmark book, *Personality and Assessment,* Walter Mischel (1968) criticized the trait view of personality, as well as the psychoanalytic approach, both of which emphasize the internal organization of personality. Rather than viewing personality as consisting of broad, internal traits that are consistent across situations and time, Mischel said that personality often changes according to a given situation.

Mischel reviewed an array of studies and concluded that trait measures do a poor job of predicting behavior. For example, let's say Anne is described as an aggressive person. However, when we observe her behavior, we find that she is more or less aggressive depending on the situation—she may be aggressive with her boyfriend but almost submissive with her new boss. Mischel's view was called **situationism,** *which means that personality often varies considerably from one context to another.* Mischel's argument was an important one, but, as we will see next many psychologists were not willing to abandon the trait concept.

Trait-Situation Interaction

Today most psychologists in the field of personality are interactionists, including Mischel. They believe that both trait (person) and situation variables are necessary to understand personality. They also agree that the degree of consistency in personality depends on the kind of persons, situations, and behaviors sampled (Carson, 1989; Epstein & Meier, 1989; Pervin, 1989; Rodriguez, Mischel, & Shoda, 1989).

Suppose you want to assess the happiness of Jane, an introvert, and Bob, an extravert. According to trait-situation interaction theory, we cannot predict who will be happier unless

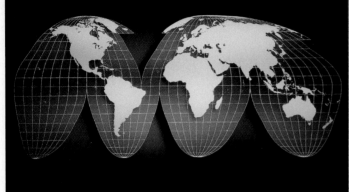

How Collectivists and Individualists Can Interact More Effectively

I f you come from a collectivist culture and you are about to interact with someone from an individualist culture, are there ways you can communicate with the other person more effectively? Similarly, if you are from an individualist culture and are about to interact with someone from a collectivist culture, are there ways you can communicate with the person more effectively? Cross-cultural psychologists Harry Triandis, Richard Brislin, and C. Harry Hui (1988) think so. Some of their recommendations follow. First are the suggestions for collectivists interacting with individualists:

1. Do not expect the individualists' compliance with group norms to be as high as it is in a collectivist culture.
2. A person from an individualist culture is likely to be very proud of his or her accomplishments. Compliment the individualist more than you are used to in your collectivist culture.
3. Expect individualists to be more emotionally detached from events that occur in their ingroup than is likely in your collectivist culture.
4. Do not feel threatened if individualists act competitively; learn to expect individualists to be more competitive than collectivists.

5. It is all right for you, as a collectivist, to talk about your accomplishments. You do not have to be modest but, at the same time, do not boast.
6. Expect a person from an individualist culture to be less strongly attached to the extended family than is the case in your collectivist culture. For example, family obligations are less likely to be accepted by an individualist as an excuse for failing to complete an assignment.
7. If you try to change an individualist's opinions, do not expect that you will be as persuasive as you are in your own collectivist culture when you use arguments that stress cooperation, harmony, or avoidance of confrontation.
8. A person from an individualist culture is more likely to define status in terms of individual accomplishments rather than on the basis of ascribed attributes (sex, age, family name, and so on) than is the case in a collectivist culture.

Following are some suggestions for individualists interacting with collectivists:

1. Learn to pay attention to group memberships. Collectivists' behavior often depends on the norms of the ingroups that are important in their lives.
2. Take into account the attitudes of a collectivist person's ingroup authorities. A collectivist person's attitudes and behaviors will probably reflect them.
3. When a collectivist person's group membership changes, his or her attitudes and even personality probably will change to reflect the different group.
4. Spend some time finding out about a collectivist person's ingroups. What events occur in them? What duties are specified? A collectivist person is more likely to do what these norms specify than an individualist is used to seeing.
5. Do not use yourself as a yardstick of involvement in activities that involve ingroups. A collectivist is much more likely to be involved with groups than is an individualist.
6. A collectivist will probably be less comfortable in competitive circumstances than an individualist will be.
7. If you have to criticize, do so carefully and only in private. In your collectivist culture, people usually do not say no or criticize.
8. Cultivate long-term relationships. Be patient. People in collectivist cultures value dealing with "old friends."

we know something about the situations they are in. Imagine you get the opportunity to observe them in two situations, at a party and in a library. As described in figure 12.6, considering both the traits of the individuals and the settings they are in improves our ability to predict their happiness.

One outcome of the trait-situation controversy is that the link between traits and situations has been more precisely

specified. For example, researchers have found that (1) the more narrow and limited a trait is, the more likely it is that it will predict behavior; (2) some people are consistent on some traits and other people are consistent on other traits; and (3) personality traits exert a stronger influence on an individual's behavior when situational influences are less powerful (Baron & Byrne, 1987; Koestner, Bernieri, & Zuckerman, 1989).

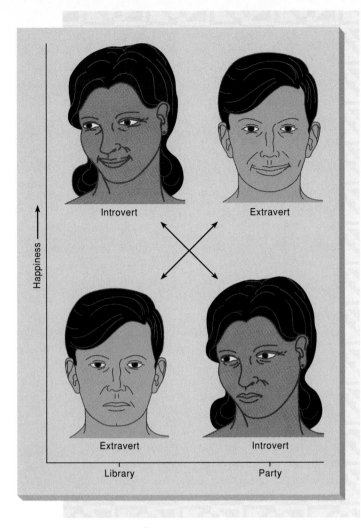

FIGURE 12.6

Trait-situation interaction. Who is happier, an introvert or an extravert? According to the concept of trait-situation interaction, we have to know the nature of the situation in which the introvert and extravert are behaving. At a party, the extravert probably will be happier than the introvert; at a library, the introvert probably will be happier than the extravert (Peterson, 1988).

Cross-cultural psychologists go several steps further. They believe that taking into account both the immediate setting *and* the broader cultural context leads to a better understanding of the situation's role in the way personality is expressed. For example, cross-cultural psychologists investigating certain aspects of personality and religion would observe a person's behavior in a chapel and put it in the context of social conventions regarding who should be in church, when, with whom, and how the person is expected to behave.

So far our discussion of personality has focused on a number of theories and viewpoints. As we will see next, assessment is also an extremely important aspect of personality.

REVIEW

Trait Theory and Trait-Situation Interaction

Personality-type theory involves classifying an individual according to a particular type; Sheldon's somatotype theory is an example. This view is heavily criticized. Trait theories emphasize that personality involves the organization of traits within the individual; these traits are believed to be enduring. Allport stressed the individuality of traits; Eysenck sought the traits common to all of us. The search for trait dimensions continues; one contemporary view stresses that we have five basic traits. A contemporary interest of cross-cultural psychologists is the individualism-collectivism dichotomy.

Mischel's *Personality and Assessment* ushered in an attack on trait theory; basically he argued that personality varies according to the situation more than trait theorists acknowledge. Today most psychologists are interactionists; they believe personality is determined by a combination of both traits or person variables and the situation. Cross-cultural psychologists believe that the situation involves both the immediate setting and the broader cultural context.

Personality Assessment

"This line running this way indicates that you are a gregarious person, someone who really enjoys being around people. This division over here suggests that you are a risk taker; I bet you like to do things that are adventurous sometimes." These are the words you might hear from a palmist. Palmistry purports to "read" an individual's personality by interpreting precisely the irregularities and folds in the skin of the hand. For example, a large mound of Saturn, the portion of the palm directly below the third joint of the middle finger, ostensibly relates to wisdom, good fortune, and prudence.

Although palmists claim to provide a complete assessment of personality through reading lines in the hand, researchers debunk palmistry as quackery (Lanyon & Goodstein, 1982). Researchers argue that palmists give no reasonable explanation for their inferences about personality and point out that the hand's characteristics can change through age and even through exercise.

Even so, palmists manage to stay in business. They do so, in part, because they are keen observers—they respond to such cues as voice, general demeanor, and dress, which are more relevant signs of personality than the lines and folds on a person's palm. Palmists also are experts at offering general, trivial statements, such as "Although you usually are affectionate with others, sometimes you don't get along with people." This statement falls into the category of the **Barnum effect:** *if you make your observations broad enough, any person can fit the description.* The effect was named after circus owner P. T. Barnum.

In contrast, psychologists use a number of scientifically developed tests and methods to evaluate personality, and they each assess personality for different reasons. Clinical and school psychologists assess personality to better understand an individual's psychological problems; they hope the assessment will improve their diagnosis and treatment of the individual. Industrial psychologists and vocational counselors assess personality to aid the individual's selection of a career. Research psychologists assess personality to investigate the theories and dimensions of personality discussed so far in this chapter. For example, if a psychologist wants to investigate self-concept, a measure of self-concept is needed.

Before we explore some specific personality tests, two more important points need to be made about the nature of personality assessment. First, the kinds of tests chosen by psychologists frequently depend on the psychologist's theoretical bent. Second, most personality tests are designed to assess stable, enduring characteristics, free of situational influence (Betz, 1989).

Projective Tests

A **projective test** *presents individuals with an ambiguous stimulus and then asks them to describe it or tell a story about it. Projective tests are based on the assumption that the ambiguity of the stimulus allows individuals to project into it their feelings, desires, needs, and attitudes. The test is especially designed to elicit an individual's unconscious feelings and conflicts, providing an assessment that goes deeper than the surface of personality.* Projective tests attempt to get *inside* your mind to discover how you *really* feel and think, going beyond the way you overtly present yourself.

The Rorschach Inkblot Test

The **Rorschach Inkblot Test,** *developed in 1921 by Swiss psychiatrist Hermann Rorschach, is the most well-known projective test; it uses an individual's perception of inkblots to determine his or her personality.* The test consists of 10 cards, half in black and white and half in color, which are shown to the individual one at a time (see figure 12.7). The person taking the Rorschach test is asked to describe what he or she sees in each of the inkblots. For

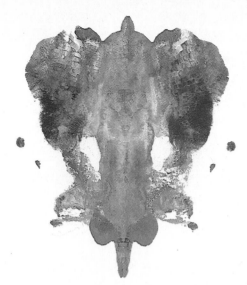

FIGURE 12.7

Type of stimulus used in the Rorschach inkblot test.

example, an individual may say, "That looks like two people fighting." After the individual has responded to all 10 inkblots, the examiner presents each of the inkblots again and inquires about the individual's earlier response. For example, the examiner might ask, "*Where* did you see the two people fighting?" and "*What* about the inkblot made the two people look like they were fighting?" Besides recording the responses, the examiner notes the individual's mannerisms, gestures, and attitudes.

How useful is the Rorschach in assessing personality? The answer to this question depends on one's perspective. From a scientific perspective, researchers are skeptical about the Rorschach (Feshbach & Wiener, 1986). Their disenchantment stems from the failure of the Rorschach to meet the criteria of reliability and validity, described in chapter 7. If the Rorschach were reliable, two different scorers should agree on the personality characteristics of the individual. If the Rorschach were valid, the individual's personality should predict behavior outside of the testing situation; that is, it should predict whether an individual will attempt suicide, become severely depressed, cope successfully with stress, or get along well with others. Conclusions based on research evidence suggest that the Rorschach does not meet these criteria of reliability and validity. This has led to serious reservations about the Rorschach's use in diagnosis and clinical practice.

However, the Rorschach continues to enjoy widespread use in clinical circles; some clinicians swear by the Rorschach, saying it is better than any other measure at getting at the true core of an individual's personality. They are not especially bothered by the Rorschach's low reliability and validity, pointing out that this is so because of the extensive freedom of response encouraged by the test. It is this freedom of response that makes the Rorschach such a rich clinical tool, say its advocates (Lerner & Lerner, 1989).

The Rorschach controversy continues, and it probably will not subside in the near future. Research psychologists will continue to criticize its low reliability and validity; many clinicians will continue to say that the Rorschach is a valuable clinical tool, providing insights about the unconscious mind that no other personality test can.

Other Projective Tests

The **Thematic Apperception Test (TAT),** *which was developed by Henry Murray in the 1930s, is an ambiguous projective test designed to elicit stories that reveal something about an individual's personality.* The TAT consists of a series of pictures, each on an

FIGURE 12.8

A picture from the Thematic Apperception Test (TAT).

individual card (see figure 12.8). A person taking the TAT is asked to tell a story about each of the pictures, including the events leading up to the situation described, the characters' thoughts and feelings, and how the situation turns out. It is assumed that the person projects her own unconscious feelings and thoughts into the story she tells. In addition to being used as a projective test in clinical practice, the TAT is used in the research of achievement motivation. Several of the TAT cards stimulate the telling of achievement-related stories, which enables the researcher to determine the person's need for achievement (McClelland & others, 1953).

Many other projective tests are used in clinical assessment. One test asks individuals to complete a sentence (for example, "I often feel . . ." "I would like to . . ."); another test asks the individual to draw a person; and another test presents a word, such as *fear* or *happy*, and asks the individual to say the first thing that comes to mind. Like the Rorschach, these projective tests have their detractors and advocates; the detractors often criticize the tests' low reliability and validity, and the advocates describe the tests' ability to reveal the underlying nature of the individual's personality better than more straightforward tests.

All projective tests share an important, often ignored characteristic. Although a person's responses may reflect the individual's personality, they also may be influenced by other factors, such as culture, social class, and gender. If the test interpreter does not share the same set of experiences as the test taker, how can the interpreter sensitively score the person's responses? Few people would recommend giving the Rorschach to someone who speaks another language, then trying to organize the syllables into acceptable responses. However, it may be just as presumptuous to assume that we can interpret another person's experiences when his or her background differs sharply from our own.

Self-report Tests

Self-report tests *assess personality traits by asking what they are; these tests are not designed to reveal unconscious personality characteristics.* For example, self-report tests of personality include such items as the following:

I am easily embarrassed.
I love to go to parties.
I like to watch cartoons on TV.

Self-report tests are questionnaires that include a large number of such statements or questions. You respond with a limited number of choices (yes or no, true or false, agree or disagree). How do psychologists construct self-report tests of personality?

Constructing Self-report Tests

Many of the early personality tests were based on **face validity,** *which is an assumption that the content of the test items is a good indicator of what an individual's personality is like.* For example, if I developed a test item that asks you to respond whether or not you are introverted and you answer, "I enjoy being with people," I accept your response as a straightforward indication that you are not introverted. Tests based on face validity assume that you are responding honestly and nondefensively, giving the examiner an accurate portrayal of your personality.

Not everyone is honest, however, especially when it concerns his or her own personality. Even if the individual is basically honest, he or she may be giving socially desirable answers. **Social desirability** *refers to a response in which an individual answers according to what he or she thinks the examiner wants to hear or in a way that makes the individual look better.* For example, if someone is basically a lazy person, she may not want you to know this and she may try to present herself in a more positive way; therefore, she would respond negatively to the following item: "I fritter away time too much." Because of such responses, psychologists realized they needed to go beyond face validity in constructing personality tests; they accomplished this by developing empirically keyed tests.

Empirically keyed tests *rely on the tests' items to predict a particular criterion. Unlike tests based on face validity, in which the content of the items is supposed to be a good indicator of what a tested individual's personality is like, empirically keyed tests make no assumptions about the nature of the items.* Imagine we want to develop a test that will determine whether or not applicants for the position of police officer are likely to be competent at the job. We might ask a large number of questions of police officers, some of whom have excellent job records, others who have not performed as well. We would then use the questions that differentiate competent and incompetent police officers on our test to screen job applicants. If the item "I enjoy reading poetry" predicts success as a police officer, then we would include it on the test, even though it seems unrelated to police work. Next we will examine the most widely used empirically keyed personality test.

The Minnesota Multiphasic Personality Inventory

The **Minnesota Multiphasic Personality Inventory (MMPI)** *is the most widely used and researched self-report personality test.* The MMPI was originally developed to improve the process of diagnosing individuals with mental disorders. A thousand statements were given to both people with mental disorders and apparently normal people. How often individuals agreed with each item was calculated; only the items that clearly differentiated the individuals with mental disorders from the normal individuals were retained. For example, a statement might be included on the depression scale of the MMPI if people diagnosed with a depressive disorder agreed with the statement significantly more than did normal individuals. For example, a statement with little face validity, such as "I sometimes tease animals," might be included on the depression scale, or any other scale, of the MMPI.

The MMPI eventually was streamlined to 550 items, each of which can be answered true, false, or cannot say. The items vary widely in content and include such statements as the following:

I like to read magazines.
I never have trouble falling asleep.
People are out to get me.

A person's answers are grouped according to 10 clinical categories, or scales, that measure such problems as depression, psychopathic deviation, schizophrenia, and social introversion.

The MMPI includes four validity scales in addition to the 10 clinical scales. The validity scales were designed to indicate whether an individual is dishonest, careless, defensive, or evasive when answering the test items. For example, if an individual responds "false" to a number of items, such as "I get angry sometimes," it would be interpreted that she is trying to make herself look better than she really is. The

rationale for the lie scale is that each of us gets angry at least some of the time, so the individual who responds "false" to many such items is faking her responses.

For the first time in its approximately 40-year history, the MMPI was revised in 1989 (Ben Porath & Butcher, in press; Butcher & others, 1989, 1990). The revision added new content scales and deleted some statements, including all items pertaining to religion and most of the questions about sexual practices. The revised MMPI has 567 items. Its basic clinical scales have not changed; however, content scales that relate to the broader interests of some clinicians and employers were added. The new content scales focus on substance abuse, eating disorders, Type A behavior, repression, anger, cynicism, low self-esteem, family problems, and inability to function in a job.

Thousands of research studies and many books have documented the ability of the MMPI to improve the diagnosis of mentally disturbed individuals (Duckworth, 1989; Friedman, Webb, & Lewak, 1989). The MMPI has been used in more than 50 countries, and more than 125 translations of the test are available. Increasingly, the MMPI has been used to assess normal rather than abnormal aspects of personality.

Despite its popularity and widespread use, critics believe that the MMPI has a number of problems. For one, critics say the MMPI is biased in terms of culture, ethnicity, and gender. Cross-cultural psychologist Walter Lonner (1990) points out that the MMPI was developed by American psychologists and follows a Western view of mental health. Because it was standardized on a group of people in Minnesota, he recommends considerable caution when using the MMPI, as well as other personality tests, on people from other cultures. The MMPI also contains some outdated stereotypes regarding gender. For example, if a woman responds on the MMPI that she likes hunting and fishing, she might be labeled abnormally masculine simply because more men report enjoying hunting and fishing. Critics also believe that the MMPI is less effective in diagnosing differences among normal than abnormal individuals. They believe that the MMPI is now being misused in business and education to predict which individual will make the best job candidate or which career an individual should pursue. Also, persons who are inadequately trained in psychological testing and diagnosis sometimes both give and interpret the MMPI. In these cases, the MMPI is often used beyond its intent.

Evaluating Self-report Tests

Adherents of the trait approach have strong faith in the utility of self-report tests. They point out that self-report tests have produced an improved understanding of the nature of personality traits than can be derived from, for example, projective tests. However, some critics (especially psychoanalysts) believe that self-report measures do not get at the core of

Type of behavior	Item
Shared activities	We sat and read together.
	We took a walk.
Pleasing interactive events	My spouse asked how my day was.
	We talked about personal feelings.
	My spouse showed interest in what I said by agreeing or asking relevant questions.
Displeasing interactive events	My spouse commanded me to do something.
	My spouse complained about something I did.
	My spouse interrupted me.
Pleasing affectionate behavior	We held each other.
	My spouse hugged and kissed me.
Displeasing affectionate behavior	My spouse rushed into intercourse without taking time for foreplay.
	My spouse rejected my sexual advances.
Pleasing events	My spouse did the dishes.
	My spouse picked up around the house.
Displeasing events	My spouse talked too much about work.
	My spouse yelled at the children.

FIGURE 12.9

Items from the Spouse Observation Checklist. Couples are instructed to complete a more extensive checklist for 15 consecutive evenings. Each spouse records the behavior of his or her partner, and they make daily ratings of their overall satisfaction with the spouse's behavior.

From N. S. Jacobson, et al., "Toward a Behavioral Profile of Marital Distress" in *Journal of Consulting and Clinical Psychology*, 48:696-703. Copyright 1980 by the American Psychological Association. Adapted by permission.

personality and its unconscious determinants. Other critics (especially behaviorists) believe that self-report tests do not adequately capture the situational variations in personality and the ways in which personality changes as individuals interact with the environment.

Behavioral Assessment

Behavioral assessment attempts to obtain more objective information about an individual's personality by directly observing the individual's behavior. Instead of removing situational influences from personality, as projective tests and self-report measures do, behavioral assessment assumes that personality cannot be evaluated apart from the environment.

Recall from chapter 5 that behavior modification is an attempt to apply learning principles to change maladaptive behavior. Behavioral assessment of personality emerged from this tradition. For example, recall that an observer often will make baseline observations of the frequency of the individual's behaviors. This might be accomplished under controlled laboratory conditions or in natural circumstances. The therapist then modifies one aspect of the environment, such as getting parents and the child's teacher to stop giving the child

attention when he engages in aggressive behavior. After a specified period of time, the therapist observes the child again to determine if the changes in the environment were effective in reducing the child's maladaptive behavior.

Sometimes, though, direct observations are impractical. What does a psychologist with a behavioral orientation do to assess personality? She might ask individuals to make their own assessments of behavior, encouraging them to be sensitive to the circumstances that produced the behavior and the outcomes or consequences of the behavior. For example, a therapist might want to know the course of marital conflict in the everyday experiences of a couple. Figure 12.9 shows a "spouse observation checklist" that couples can use to record their partner's behavior.

The influence of social learning theory has increased the use of cognitive assessment in personality evaluation. The strategy is to discover what thoughts underlie behavior; that is, how do individuals think about their problems? What kinds of thoughts precede maladaptive behavior, occur during its manifestation, and follow it? Such cognitive processes as expectations, planning, and memory are assessed, possibly through interviews or questionnaires. For example, an interview might include questions that ask whether an individual overexaggerates his faults and condemns himself more than is warranted. A questionnaire might ask a person what her thoughts are after an upsetting event or assess the way she thinks during tension-filled moments (Bellack & Hersen, 1988).

More information about behavioral and cognitive assessment appears in chapter 14, where we will discuss psychotherapies. Many of the behavioral and cognitive assessments of personality are recent developments and are just beginning to find their way into the evaluation of personality. Increasingly psychologists who use projective and self-report tests to measure personality are evaluating the individual's behavior and thoughts in the testing situation to provide important additional information.

It has been some time since we considered the different theoretical approaches to personality. Next, to conclude the chapter, we will return to those theories and compare their orientation on a number of important issues involving personality.

Comparing Personality Theories

In the course of our discussion, we have seen that personality theories have many faces. One reason so many personality theories exist is that personality is a broad, complex concept. Psychologist R. W. White (1976) recognized this complexity, saying it is not a surface illusion, but a fact. You learned in chapter 11 that three important issues in motivation are the degree to which it is innate or learned (biologically or experientially based), the degree to which it is conscious or unconscious, and the degree to which it is internally or externally determined. The personality theories we discussed in this chapter also address these three important issues.

1. *Innate versus learned.* Is personality due more to heredity and biological factors or to learning and environmental experiences? Are individuals conceited and self-centered because they inherited the tendency to be conceited and self-centered from their parents, or did they learn to be that way through experiences with other conceited, self-centered individuals? Freud's theory has a strong biogenetic foundation, although many psychoanalytic revisionists argued that he underestimated the power of environmental experiences and culture in determining personality. Behaviorism and humanism both endorse environment as a powerful determinant of personality, Skinner being the strongest advocate of environment's influence. Trait theorists vary in their emphasis on heredity and environment;

Eysenck stressed the biological basis of personality, whereas Allport weighted biology and environment more equally.

2. *Conscious versus unconscious.* Is personality due more to conscious factors or to unconscious factors? How aware are individuals that they are conceited and self-centered? How aware are they of the reasons they became conceited and self-centered? Freud and Jung were the strongest advocates of the unconscious mind's role in personality. Freud stressed that our deeply repressed experiences in infancy and early childhood determine what our personality is like as an adult, for example. Most psychoanalytic theorists argue that we are largely unaware of how individual personalities develop. Skinner argues that neither unconscious nor conscious thoughts are important in determining personality, although cognitive social learning theorists Bandura and Mischel stress that cognitive factors mediate the environment's influence on personality. The humanists, such as Rogers and Maslow, stress the conscious aspects of personality, especially in the form of self-perception. Trait theorists pay little attention to the conscious-unconscious issue.

3. *Internal versus external determinants.* Is personality due more to an inner disposition or to outer situations? Are individuals conceited and self-centered because of something inside themselves, a characteristic they have and carry around with them, or are they conceited and self-centered because of the situations they are in and the way they are influenced by people around them? Psychoanalytic theorists emphasize the internal dimensions of personality (Freud's internal structures of id, ego, and superego, for example). Trait theorists also stress internal, trait variables in personality. Humanists, likewise, emphasize internal determinants in the forms of self-concept and self-determination. By contrast, behaviorists emphasize personality's external, situational determinants, although cognitive social learning theorists examine both external and internal determinants.

A summary of personality theory comparisons on these three important issues—innate versus learned, conscious versus unconscious, and internal versus external determination—is presented in figure 12.10, along with a comparison of the methods advocated by the theories.

By now you should have a better understanding of personality and *your* personality. In this chapter, we have focused primarily on the normal aspects of personality. In the next chapter, we will turn our attention to abnormal behavior, where our discussion of personality includes its abnormal aspects.

Issue	Personality theory			
	Psychoanalytic theory	Behavioral, social learning theory	Humanistic, phenomenological theory	Trait theory
Innate versus learned	Strong emphasis on biological foundations by Freud. Adler, Sullivan, and Erikson gave social experiences and culture more importance than Freud.	Skinner said personality is behavior that is environmentally determined. Social learning theorists also emphasize environmental experiences.	Humanistic theorists emphasize that personality is influenced by experience and can be changed.	Eysenck and Cattell stress personality's biological basis; Allport gave attention to both heredity and environment.
Conscious versus unconscious	Strong emphasis on unconscious thought, especially Freud and Jung	Skinner didn't think conscious or unconscious thought was important in personality. Bandura and Mischel emphasize cognitive process.	Stress conscious aspects of personality, especially self-concept, self-perception	Pay little attention to this issue
Internal versus external determinants	Emphasize internal determinants, personality structures	Emphasize external situational determinants of personality. Bandura and Mischel emphasize internal and external determinants, especially self-control.	Emphasize internal determinants of self-concept and self-determination	Stress internal, person variables
Personality measurement	Clinical interviews, unstructured personality tests, and psychohistorical analysis of lives	Observation, especially laboratory observation	Self-report measures and interviews. Clinical judgment more important than scientific measurement is view of many humanists.	Self-report tests such as MMPI

Sigmund Freud

B. F. Skinner

Carl Rogers

Gordon Allport

FIGURE 12.10
Comparing personality theories.

REVIEW

Personality Assessment and Comparison of Personality Theories

Psychologists use a number of tests and measures to assess personality. These measures are often tied to a psychologist's theoretical orientation. Personality tests were basically designed to measure stable, enduring aspects of personality. Projective tests use ambiguous stimuli to encourage individuals to project their personality into the stimuli. They are designed to assess the unconscious aspects of personality. The Rorschach is the most widely used projective test; its effectiveness is controversial. Self-report measures are designed to assess an individual's traits; the most widely used self-report measure is the MMPI, an empirically keyed test. Behavioral assessment tries to obtain more objective information about personality through the observation of behavior and its environmental ties. Cognitive assessment increasingly is being used as part of behavioral assessment.

Three important issues addressed by personality theories are the degree to which personality is innate versus learned, conscious versus unconscious, and internally versus externally determined. Disagreements and agreements about these issues are found in the psychoanalytic, behavioral/social learning, phenomenological/humanistic, and trait theories.

Summary

I. The Nature of Personality

Personality refers to our enduring thoughts, emotions, and behaviors that characterize the way we adapt to our world. A key question in personality is why individuals respond to a situation in different ways.

II. Freud's Personality Theory

Sigmund Freud has been one of the most influential thinkers in the twentieth century. Freud was a medical doctor who believed that most of the mind is comprised of unconscious thoughts. Freud said that personality has three structures: id, ego, and superego. The id houses biological instincts, is completely unconscious, and operates according to the pleasure principle; the ego tries to provide pleasure by operating according to the reality principle; the superego is the moral branch of personality. The conflicting demands of personality structures produce anxiety; defense mechanisms protect the ego and reduce this anxiety. Freud said that repression is the most pervasive defense mechanism; others include rationalization, displacement, sublimation, projection, reaction formation, and regression. In moderation, defense mechanisms can be healthy; however, they should not be allowed to dominate our lives. Freud was convinced that our problems develop primarily because of early childhood experiences. He said we go through five psychosexual stages: oral, anal, phallic, latency, and genital. We can become fixated at each stage if our needs are under- or overgratified. During the phallic stage, the Oedipus complex is a major source of conflict.

III. Psychoanalytic Dissenters and Revisionists

Critics argue that Freud placed too much emphasis on the first 5 years of life; he also failed to recognize the power of the ego and conscious thought processes, as well as sociocultural influences. Karen Horney proposed a sociocultural approach, in which she rejected Freud's theory that anatomy determines behavior. She especially emphasized that Freud's theory was male biased. Horney said that the need for security, not sex or aggression, is the prime motive in human existence. She also suggested the theory that individuals usually develop one of three strategies to cope with anxiety—moving toward people, moving away from people, and moving against people. Nancy Chodorow is among the psychologists working to correct male bias in psychoanalytic theory today. Jung thought Freud underplayed the role of the unconscious mind. He developed the concept of the collective unconscious; his theory is called depth psychology. Alfred Adler's theory is called individual psychology; it stresses every individual's uniqueness. Adler said people strive toward a positive being and that they create their own goals. Their adaptation is enhanced by developing social interests and reducing feelings of inferiority.

IV. Evaluating the Psychoanalytic Perspectives

The strengths are an emphasis on the past, the developmental course of personality, mental representation of the environment, unconscious mind, emphasis on conflict, and influence on psychology as a discipline. Weaknesses of psychoanalytic theories are the difficulty in testing main concepts, a lack of empirical data and overreliance on clients' reports of the past, too much emphasis on sexuality and the unconscious mind, a negative view of human nature, too much power given to early experience, and a male bias.

V. The Behavioral and Social Learning Perspectives

Skinner's behavioral approach emphasizes that cognition is unimportant in understanding personality; personality is observed behavior, which is influenced by rewards and punishments in the environment. This approach stresses that personality varies according to the situation. Social learning theorists believe that the environment is an important determinant of personality, but so are cognitive processes.

We can control our own behavior through thoughts, beliefs, and values, for example. Bandura and Mischel crafted the contemporary version of social learning theory, known as cognitive social learning theory. The strengths of these approaches involve their emphasis on environmental determinants and a scientific climate for investigating personality; the focus on cognitive processes and self-control in the social learning approach also is a strength. The behavioral view has been criticized for taking the person out of personality and for ignoring cognition. These approaches do not give adequate attention to enduring individual differences, to biological factors, and to personality as a whole.

VI. The Phenomenological and Humanistic Perspectives

The phenomenological approach emphasizes our perceptions of ourselves and our world; the approach centers on the belief that reality is what is perceived. The humanistic approach is the most widely known phenomenological approach. Carl Rogers' approach emphasizes that each of us is a victim of conditional positive regard—that is, conditions are placed on our worth. The result is that our real self is not valued as positively as it should be. The self is the core of personality; it includes the real and the ideal selves. Rogers said we can help others develop a more positive self-concept in three ways: unconditional positive regard, empathy, and genuineness. Rogers stressed that each of us has the innate, inner capability of becoming a fully functioning person. Abraham Maslow was a powerful figure in the humanistic movement, calling it the "third force" in psychology. He believed that each of us has a self-actualizing capability. Maslow distinguished between deficiency needs and self-actualized needs, or metaneeds. These approaches have sensitized psychologists to the importance of subjective experience, consciousness, self-conception, the whole person, and our innate, positive nature. Their weaknesses focus on the absence of empirical data, a tendency to be too optimistic, and an inclination to encourage self-love.

VII. Trait Theory and Trait-Situation Interaction

Personality-type theory involves classifying an individual according to a particular type; Sheldon's somatotype theory is an example. This view is heavily criticized. Trait theories emphasize that personality involves the organization of traits within the individual; these traits are believed to be essentially enduring. Allport stressed the individuality of traits; Cattell and Eysenck sought the traits common to all of us. The search for basic trait dimensions continues; one contemporary view stresses that we have five basic traits. A contemporary interest in cross-cultural psychology is the individualism-collectivism dichotomy. Mischel's *Personality and Assessment* ushered in an attack on trait theory; basically he argued that personality varies according to the situation more than the trait theorists acknowledge. Today most psychologists are interactionists; they believe personality is determined by a combination of both traits or person variables and the situation. Cross-cultural psychologists believe that the situation involves both the immediate setting and the broader cultural context.

VIII. Personality Assessment

Psychologists use a number of tests and measures to assess personality; these measures often are tied to the psychologist's theoretical orientation. Personality tests basically were designed to measure stable, enduring aspects of personality. Projective tests use ambiguous stimuli to get an individual to project her personality into the stimuli; they try to discover unconscious aspects of personality. The Rorschach is the most widely used projective test; its effectiveness has been controversial. Self-report measures are designed to assess an individual's traits; the most widely used self-report test is the MMPI, which is an empirically keyed test. Behavioral assessment tries to obtain objective information about personality through observation of behavior and its environmental ties. Cognitive assessment increasingly is being used as part of the behavioral assessment process.

IX. Comparing Personality Theories

Three important issues addressed by personality theories are the degree to which personality is innate versus learned, conscious versus unconscious, and internally versus externally determined. Disagreements and agreements about these issues are found in psychoanalytic, behavioral, humanistic, and trait theories.

Key Terms

personality 365
id 366
pleasure principle 366
ego 366
reality principle 366
superego 366
defense mechanisms 366
repression 366
rationalization 366
displacement 367
sublimation 367
projection 367
reaction formation 367
regression 367

erogenous zones 367
fixation 367
oral stage 367
anal stage 367
phallic stage 367
Oedipus complex 368
latency stage 368
genital stage 368
collective unconscious 371
archetypes 371
individual psychology 371
striving for superiority 371
compensation 371
overcompensation 372

inferiority complex 372
superiority complex 372
phenomenological perspective 375
humanistic perspective 375
conditional positive regard 375
self-concept 375
unconditional positive regard 375
deficiency needs 377
metaneeds 378
somatotype theory 379
endomorph 379
mesomorph 379
ectomorph 379
trait theories 379

Suggested Readings

Allen, L., & Majidi-Ahi, S. (1989). Black American children. In J. T. Gibbs & L. N. Huang (Eds.), *Children of color*. San Francisco: Jossey-Bass. This chapter includes insightful information about the nature of Black children's personality development, including self-concept and assessment.

Journal of Personality and Social Psychology. This journal is rated as one of the best sources of information about current research on personality. Look through the issues of the past several years to obtain a glimpse of current research interests and the ways personality is assessed.

Jung, C. G. (1964). *Man and his symbols*. Garden City, NY: Doubleday. This book includes the writings of Jung and four of his disciples; Jung's ideas are applied to anthropology, literature, art, and dreams.

Peterson, C. (1988). *Personality*. San Diego: Harcourt Brace Jovanovich. This well-written, up-to-date overview of personality includes information about personality theory, research, and assessment.

Shostrum, E. L. (1972). *Man, the manipulator*. New York: Bantam. This paperback presents humanistic ideas about the route from manipulation to self-actualization. It is fascinating reading and provides many examples and case studies.

White, G. M., & Kirkpatrick, J. (Eds.). (1985). *Person, self, and experience*. Berkeley: University of California Press. This book provides a number of ideas about how personality is socially constructed, with an emphasis on the role of culture in personality.

ABNORMAL PSYCHOLOGY

CHAPTER

13

Even before his father's suicide, American author Ernest Hemingway seemed obsessed by the theme of self-destruction. As a young boy, he enjoyed reading Stevenson's *The Suicide Club*. At one point in his adult life, Hemingway said he would rather go out in a blaze of light than have his body worn out by age and his illusions shattered.

Hemingway's suicidal thoughts sometimes coincided with his marital crises. Just before marrying his first wife, Hadley, Hemingway became apprehensive about his new responsibilities and alarmed her by the mention of suicide. Five years later, during a crisis with his second wife, Pauline, he calmly told her he would have committed suicide if their love affair had not been resolved happily. Hemingway was strangely comforted by morbid thoughts of death. When he was feeling down and out, Hemingway would think about death and various ways of dying; the best way, he thought, unless he could arrange to die in his sleep, would be to go off an ocean liner at night.

Hemingway committed suicide in his sixties. His suicide made people wonder why a man with such good looks, sporting skills, friends, women, wealth, fame, genius, and a Nobel Prize would kill himself. Hemingway had developed a combination of physical and mental disorders. He had neglected his health for years, suffering from weight loss, skin disease, alcoholism, diabetes, hypertension, and impotence. His body in a shambles, he dreaded becoming an invalid and the slow death this would bring. At this point, the severely depressed Hemingway was losing his memory and no longer could write. One month before his suicide, Hemingway said, "Staying healthy. Working good. Eating and drinking with friends. Enjoying myself in bed. I haven't any of them" (Meyers, 1985, p. 559).

Mental disorders know no social and economic boundaries. They find their way into the lives of the rich and famous and the poor and unknown. In this chapter, we will study a number of mental disturbances, including depression and suicide, which troubled the life of Hemingway. Before we study these disorders, however, let's examine some questions about the nature of abnormal behavior.

Abnormal Behavior: What Is It? What Causes It? How Can It Be Classified?

Was Hemingway's depression and suicide abnormal behavior? If so, what made them abnormal? What causes abnormal behavior? How can we classify abnormal behavior? We will consider each of these important questions about abnormal behavior.

What Is Abnormal Behavior?

Defining what is normal and what is abnormal is not an easy task. Is behavior abnormal when it is *atypical?* Consider Albert Einstein, John McEnroe, and Barbara Walters, each of whom we think of as atypical. However, we don't think Einstein was abnormal because he was a genius, that McEnroe is abnormal because he is a masterful tennis player (although some might consider his temperamental outbursts a sign of abnormal behavior), or that Walters is abnormal because she is one of television's most talented interviewers.

Simply labeling atypical behavior as abnormal ignores the fact that what is atypical behavior at one point in history may be considered thoroughly acceptable at another, and that what is considered atypical behavior also varies from culture to culture. Early in this century, for example, many Americans believed that masturbation was sinful and caused everything from warts to insanity. Today only a few people think of masturbation as wicked and most people accept it as part of normal sexuality. Women of the Mangaian culture in the South Sea Islands, for instance, initiate adolescent males in sexual techniques. These young males are then encouraged to practice their skills with adolescent females. However, in the United States, such behavior probably would be looked upon askance. In some cultures, people go about their daily activities with few or no clothes on. If we were to see someone naked walking down a city street in the United States, we probably would consider such behavior inappropriate; we also might think that such behavior signaled that the person was in mental distress.

If being atypical does not make an individual abnormal, what does? **Abnormal behavior** *is behavior that is maladaptive and harmful.* Hemingway's suicide was maladaptive and harmful and, thus, abnormal behavior. Behavior that is *maladaptive* and *harmful* fails to promote the well-being, growth, and fulfillment of the person and, ultimately, of others. The maladaptive and harmful behavior takes many forms—such as depression; suicide; bizarre, irrational beliefs; assaults on others; and drug addiction. These abnormal behaviors interfere with the ability to function effectively in the world and can harm the well-being of others.

Shortly we will discuss how mental health professionals classify psychological disorders. You will learn that, in the latest classification, some disorders were added and some dropped, indicating changing standards of acceptable behavior over time.

What Causes Abnormal Behavior?

What causes people to become abnormal, to behave in maladaptive and harmful ways? The causes include biological, psychological, and sociocultural factors.

TABLE 13.1
Unusual Culture-Bound Disorders

Disorder	Culture	Description/characteristics
Amok	Malaysia, Philippines, Africa	This disorder involves sudden, uncontrolled outbursts of anger in which the person may injure or kill someone. Amok is often found in males who are withdrawn before the onset of the disorder. After an attack on someone, the individual feels exhausted and depressed and does not remember the rage and attack.
Anorexia nervosa	Western cultures, especially the United States	This eating disorder involves a relentless pursuit of thinness through starvation and can eventually lead to death. More about this disorder appears in chapter 15.
Windigo	Algonquin Indian hunters	This disorder involves a fear of being bewitched. The hunter becomes anxious and agitated, worrying he will be turned into a cannibal, with a craving for human flesh.

The Biological Approach

Proponents of the biological approach believe that abnormal behavior is due to a physical malfunction in the body, especially the brain. If an individual behaves in an uncontrollable manner, is out of touch with reality, or is severely depressed, biological factors are the culprits. Today scientists and researchers who adopt the biological approach often focus on brain processes and genetic factors as the causes of abnormal behavior. In the biological approach, drug therapy is frequently used to treat abnormal behavior.

The **medical model,** *also called the disease model, was the forerunner of the biological approach; the medical model states that abnormality is a disease or illness precipitated by internal physical causes.* Within this perspective, abnormalities are called mental *illnesses* and the individuals afflicted are *patients* in *hospitals*, who are treated by *doctors*.

The Psychological and Sociocultural Approaches

Although the biological approach provides an important perspective for understanding abnormal behavior, many psychologists believe that it underestimates the importance of psychological and sociocultural factors, such as emotional turmoil, inappropriate learning, distorted thoughts, and inadequate relationships. The theories of personality described in chapter 12—psychoanalytic, behavioral and social learning, and humanistic—provide insight into the nature of abnormal as well as normal behavior. Much more about the approaches to the treatment of abnormal behavior appears in the next chapter.

Advocates of the psychological and sociocultural approaches also criticize the medical model because they believe that it encourages the labeling of mental disturbances. When individuals are labeled "mentally ill," they may begin to perceive themselves as "sick" and avoid assuming responsibility for coping with their problems (Scheff, 1966; Szasz, 1977).

Most experts on abnormal behavior agree that many psychological disturbances are universal, appearing in most cultures (Al-Issa, 1982a; World Health Organization, 1975). However, the frequency and intensity of abnormal behavior vary across cultures (Draguns, 1980). Variations in disorders are related to social, economic, technological, religious, and other features of cultures (Costin & Draguns, 1989). Some disorders appear to be especially culture-bound. To learn about several of the more unusual culture-bound disorders, turn to table 13.1.

How prevalent are mental disturbances in the United States today? In a recent survey of 18,571 people randomly selected from five U.S. cities—New Haven, Connecticut; Baltimore, Maryland; St. Louis, Missouri; Piedmont, North Carolina; and Los Angeles, California—more than 15 percent of the respondents had suffered from a mental disturbance during the previous month (Regier & others, 1988; Robins & Regier, 1990). For the 1-month incidence of mental disorders, the data were also analyzed separately for men and women. The women had a slightly higher overall rate of mental disturbances than the men (16.6 percent versus 15.4 percent). The women had higher rates of mood disorders (for example, depression) (9.7 percent versus 4.7 percent); the men had higher rates of substance-use disorders (6.3 percent versus 1.6 percent) and antisocial personality disorders (.8 percent versus .2 percent). Surprisingly, only one-third of the individuals reporting mental disorders had received treatment in the previous 6 months. The frequency of many mental disorders was much higher than anticipated because such a large percentage of individuals with a mental disorder had never gone for treatment (Robins & Regier, 1990).

Women tend to be diagnosed as having disorders that typify traditional stereotypes of females. In particular, women are more likely than men to suffer from anxiety disorders and depression, disorders with symptoms that are internalized, or turned inward. Conversely, men are socialized to direct their energy toward the outside world—that is, to externalize their feelings and thoughts—and are more likely to show disturbances involving aggression and substance abuse.

Several explanations have been given as to why women are diagnosed and treated for mental disorders at a higher rate than men (Doyle & Paludi, 1991). One possibility is that women do not have more mental disorders than men do, but that women are simply more likely to behave in ways that others label as mental disorders. For example, women have been taught to express their emotions, whereas men have been trained to control them. If women express feelings of sorrow and sadness, some individuals may conclude that women are more mentally disturbed than men are. Thus, the difference between the rates of mental disorders could involve the possibility that women more freely display and discuss their emotional problems than men do. A second explanation of the gender difference in the diagnosis of mental disorders focuses on women's inferior social position and the greater discrimination against women. Many women are also more likely to experience certain trauma-inducing circumstances, such as incest, sexual harassment, rape, and marital abuse. Such abuse may increase women's emotional problems. A third explanation of the gender difference in the diagnosis of mental disorders is that women are often placed in a "double-bind" situation in our society. For example, women can be labeled as mentally disturbed for either overconforming or underconforming to feminine gender-role stereotypes. That is, a woman who is overdependent, overly emotional, and irrational is overconforming to the traditional feminine gender-role stereotype. On the other hand, a woman who is independent, who values her career as much as or more than her family, who doesn't express emotions, and who acts in a worldly and self-confident manner is underconforming to feminine gender-role stereotypes. In either case, the woman may be labeled emotionally disturbed. In sum, even though statistics show that women are more likely than men to have mental disorders, this gender difference may be the result of antifemale bias in American society.

In the United States, variations in mental disorders involve not only gender, but such factors as socioeconomic status, urbanization, neighborhood, and ethnicity (Bell, 1990). For example, people who live closest to the center of a city have the greatest risk of developing a mental disturbance (Suinn, 1984). Ethnic minority status also heightens the risk of mental distress (Huang & Gibbs, 1989; Mortisugu & Sue, 1983). For example, in one study on hospitalization rates, persons with Spanish surnames were more likely to be admitted for mental health

Nancy Felipe Russo (at left) has been instrumental in calling attention to the sociocultural factors involved in women's depression. She is the chair of the National Coalition of Women's Mental Health.

problems when they were in the minority than when they were the majority (Bloom, 1975). In another study, conducted in New York City, this finding was supported: the fewer the number of ethnic members in one area—whether they were White, Black, or Puerto Rican—the higher their rate of mental health hospitalization (Rabkin, 1979). In yet another study, Whites living in Black areas had more than a 300 percent higher rate of severe mental disturbance than Whites living in White neighborhoods. Similarly, Blacks living in predominately White areas have a 32 percent higher rate than Blacks living in Black neighborhoods (Mintz & Schwartz, 1964). All of these studies, however, are correlational; they do not determine cause-and-effect. It is possible that people who are mentally disturbed, or those predisposed to mental disorders, tend to choose communities in which they are the minority, or it may be that minority-group status produces stress and its related disorders.

However, knowing that people from poor minority neighborhoods have high rates of disorder does not reveal *why* they have such rates. Does poverty cause pathology, or is poverty a form of pathology for middle-class diagnosticians who are

a.   b.

(a) People living in poor minority neighborhoods have high rates of mental disorders, but knowing this does not tell us why they have such high rates. Does poverty cause pathology, or is poverty a form of pathology for middle-class diagnosticians who are unaware of what behaviors and self-protective beliefs are necessary to survive in harsh contexts? Does racial oppression cause individuals to develop mental disorders? (b) Effective therapy can take place when the client and therapist are from different sociocultural backgrounds. However, barriers to communication, which can develop in such circumstances, can destroy and undermine the effectiveness of therapy. Among the barriers are language differences, class-bound values, and culture-bound values.

unaware of what behaviors and self-protective beliefs are necessary to survive in harsh circumstances? Does racial oppression cause individuals to become mentally disturbed, or does it make members of the oppressor group label the oppressed as mentally disturbed in order to feel less guilty about oppressing them? Researchers who are sensitive to, and comfortable with, these cultural dynamics are vital to the search for answers to these questions. To read further about the mental health of ethnic minority groups, turn to Sociocultural Worlds 13.1, where information about Hispanic women's mental health is presented.

An Interactionist Approach

When considering an individual's behavior, whether abnormal or normal, it is important to remember the complexity of human nature and the multiple influences on behavior. Neither the biological nor the psychological and sociocultural approaches independently capture this complexity. Abnormal behavior is influenced by biological factors (brain processes and heredity, for example), by psychological factors (emotional turmoil and distorted thoughts, for example), and by social factors (inadequate relationships and poverty, for example). These factors often interact to produce abnormal behavior.

How Can Abnormal Behavior Be Classified?

Ever since human history began, people have suffered from diseases, sadness, and bizarre behavior. For almost as long, healers have tried to treat and cure them. The classification of

mental disorders goes back to the ancient Egyptians and Greeks and has its roots in biology and medicine.

Before we discuss the most widely used system to classify mental disturbances, the *Diagnostic and Statistical Manual of Mental Disorders,* we will explore some of the drawbacks in using such tools to diagnose members of ethnic minority groups. In particular, studies have found that a client's ethnicity may adversely influence the assessment and diagnosis of mental disorders (Allen & Majidi-Ahi, 1989; LaFromboise & Low, 1989; Nagata, 1989; Ramirez, 1989). For example, during diagnostic interviews, Native Americans may behave in ways that signal mental distress to a clinician unfamiliar with the Native American culture: they may be nonassertive, hesitant, and soft-spoken; they may exchange only limited eye contact; they may show discomfort and decreased performance on timed tasks; they may be reluctant to provide details about their personal lives; and they may have a group orientation rather than a self orientation (Hynd & Garcia, 1979). In addition, the historical difficulties between ethnic groups make it extremely difficult for many Native American, Hispanic, and Black individuals to trust a White person, or even a middle-class member of their own ethnic group, in the course of psychological assessment (Allen & Majidi-Ahi, 1989). For example, one study revealed that Black clients tend to defend themselves by uttering essentially meaningless phrases or by telling clinicians what they want to hear (Jones & Seagull, 1977).

Cultural misunderstanding can work the other way too. Clinicians who are unfamiliar with their clients' cultural background may fail to pick up on cues that signal mental distress. Japanese Americans, for instance, often view mental disturbances as inappropriate behavior or malingering (pretending to be mentally disturbed to avoid work or responsibility) (Kitano, 1970). Consequently, even when Japanese Americans are in the throes of mental problems, they may be unwilling to acknowledge them (Okano, 1977). When Japanese Americans do admit to having a problem, they often recast it as a physical ailment rather than as a psychological problem. Thus, it is especially important for clinicians with Japanese American clients to thoroughly assess both psychological *and* physical factors (Nagata, 1989).

Assessing mental disturbance in ethnic minority individuals is further complicated by the well-documented findings of ethnic and social class biases in diagnosis (Russo, 1990; Snowden & Cheung, 1990). One well-known study revealed that clinicians find fewer psychological disturbances among

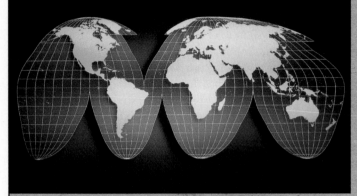

Hispanic Women and Mental Health

Mental health policymakers have begun to recognize the importance of developing culturally sensitive mental health services for the rapidly growing Hispanic population (Amaro & Russo, 1987). However, the gender bias that characterizes mental health theory, research, and practice is too often mirrored in mental health services designed to reach Hispanic populations (Russo, 1990). Any policy regarding the mental health of Hispanic women must recognize the importance of the diversity in the Hispanic population, in addition to gender bias. For example, in one study, the Cuban Americans and Puerto Ricans made more visits to physicians than either the Whites or the Blacks, whereas the Mexican Americans made fewer visits than any other group (Trevino, 1986).

To understand the mental health issues of Hispanic women, the social and economic contexts that shape their lives need to be considered. The stress of dislocation, loss of familiar people, and difficulties in starting life in a new land that accompany the experiences of migration and immigration also have mental health implications. The majority of Mexican Americans (75 percent) are born on the United States mainland; in contrast, most Puerto Ricans (55 percent), Cubans (75 percent), and Central or South Americans (64 percent) are not.

Hispanic American women, with the exception of Cuban Americans, often have lower incomes and less education, as well as higher fertility rates, than Anglo American women. However, 13 percent of all Hispanic women work in professional or managerial roles. In this group of Hispanic American women, identity and personal satisfaction are not derived solely from roles as mother and wife. Shown at the right is Hispanic American Lena Guerrero, the head of the Texas Railroad Commission.

Hispanic women, with the exception of Cubans, are likely to have lower incomes and less education, as well as higher fertility rates, than Anglo American women. Puerto Rican families are the poorest (earning 46 percent of non-Hispanics), followed by Mexican American (71 percent) and Cuban (85 percent) families. Such poverty and its related woes—crowded housing, poor nutrition, boredom from lack of a job, frustration in getting adequate health care for children—is destructive to mental health.

Most discussions of Hispanic mental health portray an individual who is pressured and harassed by the problems of poverty, slum life, and a lack of acculturation into the American society (Rogler & others, 1987). However, 13 percent of all Hispanic women work in professional or managerial roles. In this group of Hispanic women, identity and personal life satisfaction are not derived solely from the roles of mother and wife (Amaro, Russo, & Johnson, 1987). Thus, these professional Hispanic women do not fit the cultural stereotype of the Hispanic woman who derives all of her identity from the roles of mother and wife. In understanding the mental health of Hispanic women, such diversity needs to be taken into account.

people from affluent backgrounds than among poor people; in fact, people from the lowest socioeconomic backgrounds are diagnosed as having mental disturbances at twice the expected rate and are labeled with the most severe diagnoses (Hollingshead & Redlich, 1958). However, poverty and racial oppression are risk factors for mental disturbance. For example, one study found that the highest rate of mental disturbance is in poor, Black, urban communities (Gould, Wunsch-Hitzig, & Dohrenwend, 1981).

Despite the drawbacks, there are benefits of classifying mental disorders. First, a classification system provides professionals with a shorthand system for communicating with each other. For example, if one psychologist mentions that her client has a panic disorder and another psychologist says that her client has a generalized anxiety disorder, the two psychologists understand what these disturbances are like. Second, a classification system permits psychologists to construct theories about the causes of particular disturbances and design treatments for them. Third, a classification system can help psychologists predict disturbances; it provides information about the likelihood of a disorder occurring, which individuals are most susceptible to the disturbance, the progress of the disorder once it appears, and the prognosis for effective treatment (Meehl, 1986).

The DSM Classification

The first classification of mental disorders in the United States was based on the census data of 1840. One category for all mental disorders was used. Both the mentally retarded and the insane were placed in this one inclusive category.

In the twentieth century, the American Psychiatric Association is responsible for the major classification of mental disturbances in the United States. DSM-I was published in 1952. As was mentioned earlier, **DSM** *stands for* Diagnostic and Statistical Manual of Mental Disorders. DSM-I included better definitions of mental disorders than previous classification efforts. A revised edition, DSM-II, with more systematic input from expert diagnosticians, appeared in 1968. A third edition, DSM-III, was published in 1980, and the most recent version, DSM-III-R, was published in 1987.

Changes in the DSM system reflect advancements in knowledge about the classification of mental disorders. Based on research and clinical experience, some categories of mental disturbance have been added, dropped, or revised. For example, two important categories in DSM-II that were dropped from DSM-III deserve mention: neurotic and psychotic. The term **neurotic** *describes relatively mild mental disorders in which an individual has not lost contact with reality. For example, individuals who are extremely anxious, troubled, and unhappy may still be able to carry out their everyday functions and have a clear perception of reality; these individuals would be classified as neurotic.* The term **psychotic** *describes severe mental disturbances; for example, psychotic individuals have lost contact with reality. The thinking and perception of psychotic individuals are so distorted that they live in a world far removed from others.* Psychotic individuals might hear voices that are not present or think they are famous individuals, such as Jesus Christ or Napoleon.

The terms *neurotic* and *psychotic* were dropped from the DSM classification system because they were too broad and ill defined to be diagnostic labels. DSM-III replaced *neurotic* with more specific categories, such as anxiety disorders, somatoform disorders, and dissociative disorders, all of which we will discuss shortly. Rather than the general *psychotic* category, DSM-III used more precise labels, such as schizophrenia and bipolar disorder, which we also will discuss shortly. Although the labels *neurotic* and *psychotic* were dropped from the DSM classification, clinicians still sometimes use the labels as a convenient way of referring to relatively mild or relatively severe mental disorders, respectively.

DSM-III-R, *which stands for* Diagnostic and Statistical Manual of Mental Disorders, *Third Edition, Revised, is the most recent major classification of mental disorders; it contains 18 major classifications and more than 200 specific disorders.* Among the advantages of DSM-III and DSM-III-R over DSM-II are improved diagnostic criteria (vague descriptions were replaced with more specific guidelines), a redefinition of major categories in line with research findings (schizophrenia is defined more narrowly, for example), new categories (malingering, for instance), and a multiaxial system. The **multiaxial system** *is DSM-III and DSM-III-R's system of classifying individuals on the basis of five dimensions, or "axes," that include the individual's history and highest level of competent functioning in the past year. This system ensures that the individual will not merely be assigned to a mental disturbance category but, instead, will be characterized in terms of a number of clinical factors.* Following is a description of each of the axes:

Axis I: The primary classification or diagnosis of the disturbance (for example, fear of people)

Axis II: Developmental or personality disorders that begin in childhood or adolescence and often continue into adulthood (for example, mental retardation or certain personality disorders)

Axis III: Physical disorders that might be relevant in understanding the disturbances (for example, an individual's history of disease, such as a cardiovascular problem)

Axis IV: Psychosocial stressors in the individual's recent past that might have contributed to the mental problem (for example, divorce, death of a parent, or loss of a job)

Axis V: An individual's highest level of functioning in the past year. For example, does the individual have a history of poor work and relationship patterns, or have there been times when the individual performed effectively at work and enjoyed positive interpersonal relationships? If functioning has been high at a point in the past, prognosis for recovery is enhanced.

The Controversy Surrounding DSM-III and DSM-III-R

The DSM-III and DSM-III-R classifications were developed primarily by psychiatrists, who endorse the medical model more often than clinical psychologists do. Classifying individuals based on their symptoms and using medical terminology continue the tradition of thinking about mental disorders in terms of illness and disease. DSM-III and DSM-III-R also are controversial because they label some everyday problems as mental disorders. For example, DSM-III-R includes the categories of academic underachievement disorder, which involves not performing up to one's ability in school, and caffeine intoxication, which involves overactive, restless behavior from drinking too much caffeine (Hughes & others, 1992). We don't usually think of these problems as mental disturbances. Including them as mental disorders implied that such "normal" behavior should be treated as disturbed behavior and/or mental illness. However, the developers of DSM-III-R argued that mental health providers were treating many problems not included in DSM-II and that the classification system should be more comprehensive. One practical reason that everyday problems in living were included in DSM-III-R was so that more individuals could get their insurance companies to pay for professional help. Most health insurance companies reimburse their clients only for disorders listed in the DSM-III-R system.

This concession to the politics of health insurance points to another problem identified with DSM-III-R—categories of disorders are not based on empirical information about what kinds of symptoms most often occur together but, rather, on a theoretical assumption that symptoms by themselves stand for underlying pathology (Salzinger, 1986). The result is cultural bias when behaviors do not have the same meaning in different cultures. For example, aggression is more tolerated in lower-class than in middle-class homes in the United States. Does this mean that all lower-class individuals are pathologically aggressive, or that all middle-class people are pathologically passive? Of course not, but the DSM-III underpinnings do not allow for syndromes to be defined by different behaviors in different groups.

The deletion of homosexuality from DSM-III-R provides another illustration of the degree to which sociocultural forces shape this classification system. In DSM-II, homosexuality was classified as a disorder (a mental disease). Despite voluminous research indicating that homosexuals are no more poorly adjusted than heterosexuals, the diagnosis remained, mirroring the homophobia (fear of homosexuality) in our culture. Only after gay activists in the sixties and seventies advocated the end of discrimination against gays was homosexuality removed from the DSM-II. This modification did not occur because of additional information about the mental health of homosexuals but because of a change in the cultural attitudes of the mainstream group with whom the psychiatric establishment identified.

Another controversial aspect of the DSM-III classification system is the category "self-defeating personality," commonly known as "masochism." Too often women have been diagnosed as having a self-defeating personality; the implication is that their problems rest in their neurotic needs. Critics argue that, when women remain in relationships that are harmful to them, they do so because of economic and situational factors, not because they are compelled to remain in harmful relationships because of neurotic needs. Critics also emphasize that this category encourages blaming the victim rather than blaming the perpetrator, the abusive man (Koss & Harvey, 1987). In response to such criticisms, the psychiatrists who developed DSM-III-R placed the "self-defeating personality" disorder in an appendix for disorders that require further study.

Another criticism of the DSM-III, and of this type of classification system in general, is that the system focuses strictly on pathology and problems, with a bias toward finding something wrong with anyone who becomes the object of diagnostic study. A classic study by David Rosenhan (1973) demonstrated how strong the bias is toward attaching a label of mental disturbance to someone. Rosenhan asked eight "normal" individuals to go to the admissions desk of a psychiatric hospital and complain that they heard an unidentified voice saying, "Empty," "Thud," and "Hollow." The psychiatric staff interviewed the eight individuals, who were honest about their life histories. All eight of the individuals were immediately admitted. They behaved normally while in the psychiatric ward. Seven of the eight were diagnosed as schizophrenic, listed as such on their records, and labeled as schizophrenics in remission when they were discharged. Rosenhan concluded that normal people are not noticeably sane. This "blind spot" is likely to be due to the absence of a satisfying "sane" option in current mental health classification systems, which define sanity only as the absence of insanity (Rothblum, Solomon, & Albee, 1986).

Because labels can become self-fulfilling prophecies, emphasizing strengths as well as weaknesses might help destigmatize such labels as "borderline schizophrenic" or "ex-mental patient." It would also help provide clues to treatment that promotes mental competence rather than merely the reduction of mental distress. More information about the importance of emphasizing strengths as well as weaknesses in various treatments appears in the next chapter.

Although psychologists usually go along with the DSM-III-R, psychiatrists are more satisfied with it. Even though DSM-III-R has its critics, it still is the best classification system available. However, expert diagnosticians are working on the DSM-IV, which is slated to appear in 1993 (Andreasen, 1991; Frances, Widiger, & Pincus, 1989; Stoudemire & Hales, 1991).

The DSM classifications were developed by American psychiatrists (Goldman & Grebb, 1992). Most mental health professionals in other countries adopt the International Classification of Disease (ICD) guidelines established by the World Health Organization (WHO) (1977). The decision by the American Psychiatric Association to develop the DSM-III classifications separate from the ICD created considerable tension (Klerman, 1986). One of the major differences between the most recent DSM and ICD classifications of mental disturbances is that the ICD still includes neuroses and psychoses as major categories. Also, the ICD guidelines make the distinction that psychoses have a biological or constitutional base, whereas the neuroses do not. A new International Classification of Disease (ICD-10) is also scheduled to appear in 1993.

Now that we have seen what abnormal behavior is, what causes it, and how it is classified, we will turn our attention to the diagnostic categories themselves and the main types of mental disturbances, beginning with the anxiety disorders.

Abnormal Behavior: What Is It, What Causes It, and How Can It Be Classified?

Abnormal behavior is maladaptive and harmful. Atypical behavior is not always abnormal. In the biological approach, mental disorders are thought to have biological causes. The forerunner of this approach was the medical model, which describes individuals as "patients" with "mental diseases" in hospitals, where they are treated by doctors. Today's biological approach emphasizes the role of brain processes and heredity in mental disorders. Many psychologists believe that the biological approach understates the importance of psychological and sociocultural factors. They also emphasize that the medical model encourages the "labeling" of mental disorders. Although many disturbances are universal, the frequency of abnormal behavior varies across and within cultures. Such variations are related to socioeconomic status, ethnicity, technology, religion, gender, and urbanization.

DSM stands for *Diagnostic and Statistical Manual of Mental Disorders*. DSM-II included the categories of neurotic and psychotic behavior. Some mental health workers still use these terms, but they have been dropped from the DSM classification system. DSM-III, and its revision, DSM-III-R, have improved diagnostic criteria, redefined disturbances that are more in line with research findings, and contain a multiaxial approach. Psychiatrists were mainly responsible for developing the DSM classifications. Many psychologists believe that the classification still has too many characteristics of the medical model and includes problems in living that should not be classified as mental disorders. Mental health categories are often culturally biased. DSM-III and other mental health classification systems are invariably based on pathology and problems. Critics argue that competent mental health classification systems should reflect positive as well as negative characteristics.

Anxiety Disorders

Anxiety is a diffuse, vague, highly unpleasant feeling of fear and apprehension. People with high levels of anxiety worry a lot. **Anxiety disorders** *are psychological disorders that include the following main features: motor tension (jumpiness, trembling, inability to relax), hyperactivity (dizziness, a racing heart, or perspiration), and apprehensive expectations and thoughts. Five*

important types of anxiety disorders are generalized anxiety disorder, panic disorder, phobic disorders, obsessive-compulsive disorders, and post-traumatic stress disorder.

Generalized Anxiety Disorder

Anna, who is 27 years old, had just arrived for her visit with the psychologist. She seemed very nervous and was wringing her hands, crossing and uncrossing her legs, and playing nervously with strands of her hair. She said her stomach felt like it was in knots, that her hands were cold, and that her neck muscles were so tight they hurt. She said that, lately, arguments with her husband had escalated. In recent weeks, Anna indicated, she had felt more and more nervous throughout the day, as if something bad were about to happen. If the doorbell sounded or the phone rang, her heart beat rapidly and her breathing quickened. When she was around people, she had a difficult time speaking. She began to isolate herself. Her husband became impatient with her, so she decided to see a psychologist (Goodstein & Calhoun, 1982).

Anna has a **generalized anxiety disorder,** *an anxiety disorder that consists of persistent anxiety for at least 1 month; an individual with a generalized anxiety disorder is unable to specify the reasons for the anxiety.* One study found that people with generalized anxiety disorder have higher degrees of muscle tension and hyperactivity than people with other types of anxiety disorders (Barlow & others, 1986). These individuals say they have been tense and anxious for over half their lives.

Panic Disorder

Panic disorder *is a recurrent anxiety disorder marked by the sudden onset of intense apprehension or terror.* The individual often has a feeling of impending doom but may not feel anxious all the time. Anxiety attacks often strike without warning and produce severe palpitations, extreme shortness of breath, chest pains, trembling, sweating, dizziness, and a feeling of helplessness. Victims are seized by the fear that they will die, go crazy, or do something they cannot control (Baker, 1992).

What are some of the psychosocial and biological factors involved in panic disorder? As shown in figure 13.1, the majority of panic attacks are spontaneous; those that are not spontaneous are triggered by a variety of events (Breier, Charney, & Heninger, 1986). In many instances, a stressful life event has occurred in the past 6 months, most often a threatened or actual separation from a loved one or a change in job. Only recently have biological factors in panic disorder been explored (Gorman & others, 1989).

Phobic Disorders

Agnes is an unmarried 30-year-old who has been unable to go higher than the second floor of any building for more than a year. When she tries to overcome her fear of heights by going up to the

Onset of attack	No. (%) of patients
Spontaneous	47 (78%)
Nonspontaneous, precipitated by:	13 (22%)
Public speaking	3
Stimulant drug use	3
Family argument	2
Leaving home	2
Exercise (while pregnant)	1
Being frightened by a stranger	1
Fear of fainting	1

Stressful life events associated with attack	No. (%) of patients
No stressful life event within 6 months	22 (37%)
Stressful life event within 6 months*	38 (63%)
Threatened or actual separation from important person	11
Change in job, causing increased pressure	8
Pregnancy	7
Move	5
Marriage	3
Graduation	3
Death of close person	3
Physical illness	2

*Four patients had two concomitant stressful life events.

FIGURE 13.1

Nature of first panic attack and associated life events. At left is the nature of first panic attacks and associated life events, and at right is Edvard Munch's painting *The Scream.* Experts often interpret Munch's painting as reflecting the terror brought on by a panic attack.

third, fourth, or fifth floor, she becomes overwhelmed by anxiety. She remembers how it all began. One evening she was working alone and was seized by an urge to jump out of an eighth-story window. She was so frightened by her impulse that she hid behind a file cabinet for more than 2 hours until she calmed down enough to gather her belongings and go home. As she reached the first floor of the building, her heart was pounding and she was perspiring heavily. After several months, she gave up her position and became a lower-paid salesperson so she could work on the bottom floor of the store (Cameron, 1963).

A **phobic disorder,** *commonly called a phobia, is an anxiety disorder in which an individual has an irrational, overwhelming, persistent fear of a particular object or situation.* Individuals with generalized anxiety disorder cannot pinpoint the cause of their nervous feelings; individuals with phobias can. A fear becomes a phobia when a situation is so dreaded that an individual goes to almost any length to avoid it; for example, Agnes quit her job to avoid being in high places. Some phobias are more debilitating than others. An individual with a fear of automobiles has a more difficult time functioning in our society than a person with a fear of snakes, for example.

Phobias come in many forms. Some of the most common phobias involve height, open spaces, people, close spaces, dogs, dirt, the dark, and snakes (Himle & others, 1989) (see table 13.2 to read about a number of phobias and their names). **Agoraphobia,** *the fear of entering unfamiliar situations, especially open or public spaces, is the most common type of phobic disorder.* It accounts for 50 to 80 percent of the phobic population, according to some estimates (Foa, Steketze, & Young, 1984). Women are far more likely than men to suffer from agoraphobia. One study found that 84 percent of the individuals being treated for agoraphobia are women, and almost 90 percent of those women are married (Al-Issa, 1982b).

Psychologists have become increasingly interested in *social phobia,* the fear of social situations. Bashful or timid people often suffer from this phobia (Heimberg, 1989; Turner & Beidel, 1989). Social phobia affects as many as 2 of every 100 Americans and tends to be evenly distributed between the sexes (Robins & others, 1984).

Why do people develop phobias? The answer often depends on the researcher's perspective. Psychoanalytic theorists, for example, say phobias develop as defense mechanisms to ward

TABLE 13.2
Types of Phobias

Acrophobia	Fear of high places
Aereophobia	Fear of flying
Agoraphobia	Fear of open places
Ailurophobia	Fear of cats
Algophobia	Fear of pain
Amaxophobia	Fear of vehicles, driving
Arachnophobia	Fear of spiders
Astrapophobia	Fear of lightning
Claustrophobia	Fear of closed places
Cynophobia	Fear of dogs
Gamophobia	Fear of marriage
Gynephobia	Fear of women
Hydrophobia	Fear of water
Melissophobia	Fear of bees
Mysophobia	Fear of dirt
Nyctophobia	Fear of darkness
Ophidiophobia	Fear of nonpoisonous snakes
Thanatophobia	Fear of death
Xenophobia	Fear of strangers

This partial listing reveals the variety of circumstances that can cause an individual to develop a phobia.

off threatening or unacceptable impulses—Agnes hid behind a file cabinet because she feared she would jump out of an eighth-story window. Learning theorists, however, explain phobias differently; they say phobias are learned fears. In Agnes' case, she may have fallen out of a window when she was a little girl. As a result, she associates falling with pain and now fears high places. On the other hand, she may have heard about or seen other people who were afraid of high places. These last two examples are classical conditioning and observational learning explanations for Agnes' phobia. Cross-cultural psychologists point out that phobias also are influenced by cultural factors. Agoraphobia, for example, is much more common in the United States and Europe than in other areas of the world (Kleinman, 1988).

Agoraphobia is the fear of entering unfamiliar situations, especially open or public places. Individuals with agoraphobia try to avoid crowded situations. They fear that escape would be difficult or impossible if they become highly anxious in such crowded situations. Agoraphobic individuals also usually avoid standing in line and riding in transportation vehicles.

Neuroscientists are finding that biological factors, such as greater blood flow and metabolism in the right hemisphere of the brain than in the left, may also be involved in phobias. First-generation relatives of individuals suffering from agoraphobia and panic attacks have high rates of these disorders themselves, suggesting a possible genetic predisposition for phobias (d'Ansia, 1989). Others have found that identical twins reared apart sometimes develop the same phobias; one pair independently became claustrophobic, for example (Eckert, Heston, & Bouchard, 1981).

Obsessive-Compulsive Disorders

Bob is 27 years old and lives in a well-kept apartment. He has few friends and little social life. He was raised by a demanding mother and an aloof father. Bob is an accountant who spends long hours at work. He is a perfectionist. His demanding mother always nagged at him to improve himself, to keep the house spotless, and to be clean and neat, and she made Bob wash his hands whenever he touched his genitals. As a young adult, Bob finds himself ensnared in an exacting ritual in which he removes his clothes in a prearranged sequence and then endlessly scrubs every inch of his body from head to toe. He dresses himself in precisely the opposite way from which he takes off his clothes. If he deviates from this order, he *has* to start the sequence all over again. Sometimes Bob performs the cleansing ritual four or five times an evening. Even though he is aware that this ritual is absurd, he simply cannot stop (Meyer & Osborne, 1982).

Obsessive-compulsive disorder (OCD) *is an anxiety disorder in which an individual has anxiety-provoking thoughts that will not go away (obsession) and/or urges to perform repetitive, ritualistic* behaviors to prevent or produce a future situation (compulsion). Obsessive-compulsives repeat and rehearse normal doubts and daily routines, sometimes hundreds of times a day. The basic difference between obsessives and compulsives is the difference between thought and action. Obsessives may be immobilized by horrifying yet irresistible thoughts of killing someone in a traffic accident, for instance, whereas some compulsives bloody their hands after 16 hours of washing away imaginary germs. Although obsessions and compulsions are different, a person afflicted with OCD may be caught in the relentless grip of both problems.

The most common compulsions are excessive checking, cleansing, and counting. For example, a young man feels he has to check his apartment for gas leaks and make sure the windows are locked. His behavior is not compulsive if he does this once, but, if he goes back to check five or six times and then constantly worries that he may not have checked carefully enough once he has left the house, his behavior is compulsive. Most individuals do not enjoy their ritualistic behavior but feel anxious when they do not carry it out (Kozak, Foa, & McCarthy, 1987; Roy-Byrne, 1989).

Positron emission tomography (PET) and other brain-imaging techniques indicate a neurological basis for OCD. Irregularities in neurotransmitter systems, especially serotonin and dopamine, seem to be involved. There also may be a genetic basis for the disorder; OCD runs in families.

Post-Traumatic Stress Disorder

Post-traumatic stress disorder *is a mental disturbance that develops through exposure to a traumatic event (such as war), a severely oppressive situation (such as the holocaust), severe abuse (as in rape), a natural disaster (such as a flood or tornado), or an accidental disaster (such as a plane crash). The disorder is characterized by anxiety symptoms that either immediately follow the trauma or are delayed by months or even years.* The symptoms vary but can include the following:

- "Flashbacks" in which the individual relives the event in nightmares, or in an awake but dissociative-like state
- Constricted ability to feel emotions, often reported as feeling numb, resulting in an inability to experience happiness, sexual desire, enjoyable interpersonal relationships
- Excessive arousal, resulting in an exaggerated startle response or an inability to sleep
- Difficulties with memory and concentration

"But that's what you said yesterday—'Just one more cord?!'"

Drawing by Woodman; © 1986 The New Yorker Magazine, Inc.

- Feelings of apprehension, including nervous tremors
- Impulsive outbursts of behavior, such as aggressiveness, or sudden changes in life-style (Suinn, 1984)

Not every individual exposed to the same disaster develops post-traumatic stress disorder, which overloads the individual's usual coping abilities (Engdahl & others, 1991). For example, it is estimated that 15 to 20 percent of all Vietnam veterans have experienced post-traumatic stress disorder. Vietnam veterans who had some autonomy and decision-making authority during the war, such as Green Berets, are less likely to develop the disorder than soldiers who had no control over where they would be sent or when and who had no option but to follow orders. Preparation for a trauma also makes a difference in whether an individual will develop the disorder. For example, emergency workers who are trained to cope with traumatic circumstances usually do not develop post-traumatic stress disorder. Some experts consider female sexual abuse and assault victims to be the single largest group of post-traumatic stress disorder sufferers (Foa, Olasov, & Steketze, 1987; Koss, 1990).

Somatoform Disorders

"Look, I am having trouble breathing. You don't believe me. Nobody believes me. There are times when I can't stop coughing. I'm losing weight. I know I have cancer. My father died of cancer when I was 12." Herb has been to six cancer specialists in the past 2 years; none can find anything wrong with him. Each doctor has taken X rays and conducted excessive laboratory tests, but Herb's test results do not indicate any illnesses. Might some psychological factors be responsible for Herb's sense that he is physically ailing?

Somatoform disorders *are mental disturbances in which psychological symptoms take a physical, or somatic, form, even though no physical causes can be found.* Although these symptoms are not caused physically, they are highly distressing for the sufferer; the symptoms are real, not faked. Two types of somatoform disorders are hypochondriasis and conversion disorder.

Hypochondriasis

Hypochondriacs seem to overreact to a missed heart beat, shortness of breath, or a slight chest pain, fearing that something is wrong with them. **Hypochondriasis** *is a somatoform disorder in which an individual has a pervasive fear of illness and* *disease*. At the first indication of something amiss in their bodies, hypochondriacs call a doctor. When a physical examination reveals no problems, hypochondriacs usually do not believe the doctor. They often change doctors, moving from one to another, searching for a diagnosis that matches their own. Most hypochondriacs are pill enthusiasts; their medicine chests spill over with bottles of drugs they hope will cure their imagined maladies.

Hypochondriasis is a difficult category to diagnose accurately. It is quite rare for it to occur without other mental disturbances—for example, hypochondriacs often are depressed.

Conversion Disorder

Conversion disorder *is a somatoform disorder in which an individual experiences genuine physical symptoms, even though no physiological problems can be found. Conversion disorder received its name from psychoanalytic theory, which stressed that anxiety is "converted" into a physical symptom.* A hypochondriac has no physical disability; an individual with a conversion disorder does have some loss of motor or sensory ability. Individuals with a conversion disorder may be unable to speak, may faint, or may even be deaf or blind.

Conversion disorder was more common in Freud's time than today. Freud was especially interested in this disorder, in which physical symptoms made no neurological sense. For example, individuals with *glove anesthesia* report that their entire hand is numb from the tip of their fingers to a cutoff point at the wrist. As shown in figure 13.2, if these individuals were experiencing true physiological numbness, their symptoms would be very different. Like hypochondriasis, conversion disorder often appears in conjunction with other mental disturbances. During long-term evaluation, conversion disorder often turns out to be another mental or physical disorder.

Dissociative Disorders

Dissociative disorders *are psychological disorders that involve a sudden loss of memory or change in identity. Under extreme stress or shock, an individual's conscious awareness becomes dissociated (separated or split) from previous memories and thoughts.* Three kinds of dissociative disorders are amnesia, fugue, and multiple personality.

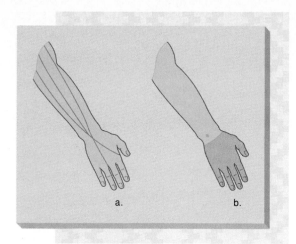

FIGURE 13.2

Glove anesthesia. A patient who complains of numbness in the hand might be diagnosed as suffering from conversion disorder if the area of the hand affected showed that a disorder of the nervous system was not responsible. The skin areas served by nerves in the arm are shown in (a). The glove anesthesia shown in (b) could not result from damage to these nerves.

From Bootzin, et al., *Abnormal Psychology*. Copyright © 1972 McGraw-Hill, Inc. Reprinted by permission of McGraw-Hill, Inc.

Amnesia and Fugue

In chapter 6, amnesia was described as the inability to recall important events. Amnesia can be caused by an injury to the head, for example. However, **psychogenic amnesia** *is a dissociative disorder involving memory loss caused by extensive psychological stress.* For example, an individual showed up at a hospital and said he did not know who he was. After several days in the hospital, he awoke one morning and demanded to be released. Eventually he remembered that he had been involved in an automobile accident in which a pedestrian had been killed. The extreme stress of the accident and the fear that he might be held responsible had triggered the amnesia.

Fugue, *which means "flight," is a dissociative disorder in which an individual not only develops amnesia but also unexpectedly travels away from home and assumes a new identity.* For example, one day a woman named Barbara vanished without a trace. Two weeks later, looking more like a teenager than a 31-year-old woman, with her hair in a ponytail and wearing bobby socks, Barbara was picked up by police in a nearby city. When her husband came to see her, Barbara asked, "Who are you?" She could not remember anything about the past 2 weeks of her life. During psychotherapy, she gradually began to recall her past. She had left home with enough money to buy a bus ticket to the town where she grew up as a child. She had spent days walking the streets and standing near a building where her father had worked. Later she had gone to a motel with a man; according to the motel manager, she had entertained a series of men over a 3-day period (Goldstein & Palmer, 1975).

Multiple Personality

Multiple personality *is the most dramatic but least common dissociative disorder; individuals suffering from this disorder have two or more distinct personalities, or selves, like the fictional Dr. Jekyll and Mr. Hyde of Robert Louis Stevenson's short story. Each personality has its own memories, behaviors, and relationships; one personality dominates the individual at one point; another personality takes over at another time. The personalities are not aware of each other, and the shift from one to the other usually occurs suddenly under distress.*

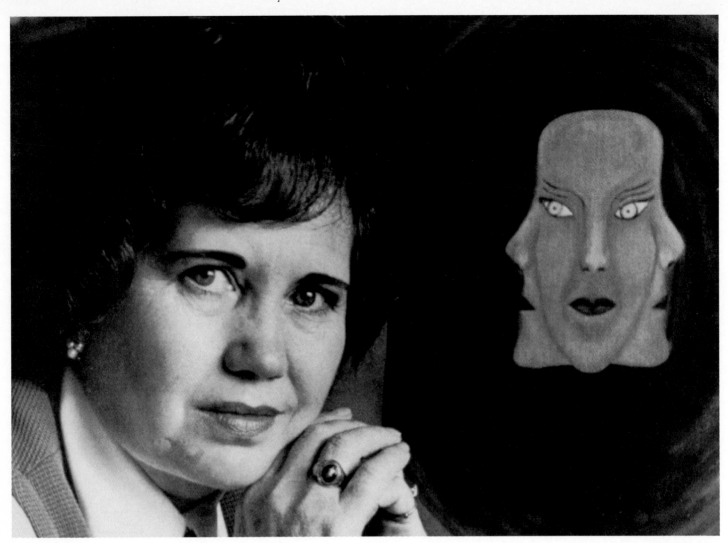

FIGURE 13.3

Multiple personality: the three faces of Eve. Chris Sizemore, the subject of the book *Three Faces of Eve*, is shown with the work she painted and entitled *Three Faces in One*.

One of the most famous cases of multiple personality involves the "three faces of Eve" (Thigpen & Cleckly, 1957). Eve White was the original, dominant personality. She had no knowledge of her second personality, Eve Black, although Eve Black had been alternating with Eve White for a number of years. Eve White was bland, quiet, and serious—a rather dull personality. Eve Black, by contrast, was carefree, mischievous, and uninhibited. She "came out" at the most inappropriate times, leaving Eve White with hangovers, bills, and a reputation in local bars that she could not explain. During treatment, a third personality, Jane, emerged. More mature than the other two, Jane seemed to have developed as a result of therapy (see figure 13.3 for a portrayal of the three faces of Eve).

A summary of the research literature on multiple personality suggests that the most striking feature related to the disorder is an inordinately high rate of sexual or physical abuse during early childhood (Ludolph, 1982). Sexual abuse occurred in 56 percent of the reported cases, for example. Their mothers had been rejecting and depressed and their fathers distant, alcoholic, and abusive. Remember that, although fascinating, multiple personality disorder is rare. Until the 1980s, only about 300 cases had been reported (Suinn, 1984). In the past decade, however, hundreds more cases have been labeled "multiple personality disorder," although some argue that the increase represents a diagnostic fad. Others believe that it is not so rare but has been frequently misdiagnosed as schizophrenia. Improved techniques for assessing the physiological changes that occur when individuals change personalities increase the likelihood that more accurate rates can be determined (Braun, 1988).

Now that we have considered three major types of mental disorders—anxiety, somatoform, and dissociative—we will turn to a set of widespread disorders—the mood disorders.

Mood Disorders

The **mood disorders** *are psychological disorders characterized by wide emotional swings, ranging from deeply depressed to highly euphoric and agitated. Depression can occur alone, as in major depression, or it can alternate with mania, as in bipolar disorder.* Depression is linked to the increasing rate of suicide. We will consider each of these disturbances in turn and then examine the causes of the mood disorders.

Major Depression

Major depression *is a mood disorder in which an individual is deeply unhappy, demoralized, self-derogatory, and bored. An individual with major depression does not feel well, loses stamina easily, has a poor appetite, and is listless and unmotivated.* For example, Peter had been depressed for several months. Nothing cheered him up. His depression began when the girl he wanted to marry decided marriage was not for her, at least not with Peter. Peter's emotional state deteriorated to the point where he didn't leave his room for days at a time, he kept the shades drawn and the room dark, and he could hardly get out of bed in the morning. When he managed to leave his room, he had trouble maintaining a conversation and he usually felt exhausted. By the time Peter finally contacted his college counseling center, he had gone from being mildly depressed to being in the grips of major depression.

Although most people don't spiral into major depression, as Peter did, everyone feels "blue" sometimes. In our stress-filled world, people often use the term *depression* to describe brief bouts of normal sadness or discontent over life's problems. Perhaps you haven't done well in a class or things aren't working out in your love life. You feel down in the dumps and say you are depressed. In most instances, though, your depression won't last as long or be as intense as Peter's; after a few hours, days, or weeks, you snap out of your gloomy state and begin to cope more effectively with your problems. Nonetheless, depression is so widespread that it has been called the "common cold" of mental disorders; more than 250,000 individuals are hospitalized every year for the disorder. Students, professors, corporate executives, laborers—no one is immune to depression, not even Ernest Hemingway, F. Scott Fitzgerald, Abraham Lincoln, or Winston Churchill, each of whom experienced major depression.

Women and Depression

A round the world, depression occurs more frequently among women than among men. The female-male ratio ranges from 2:1 to 3:1 in most industrialized countries (Depression Awareness, Recognition, and Treatment Program, 1987; Nolen-Hoeksema, 1990). Three explanations of the sex difference in depression are the following: (1) women are more willing to seek help and, therefore, are more likely to be categorized as having depression; (2) biological differences may exist between females and males that predispose females to become more depressed than males; and (3) psychosocial factors—different rearing environments, different social roles, and less favorable economic and achievement opportunities, for example—may produce greater depression in women than men. Some psychologists have also theorized that alcoholism may mask, or act as a cover for, depression in men (Culbertson, 1991).

Among the psychosocial factors in women's depression that were proposed by the American Psychological Association's National Task Force on Women and Depression (McGrath & others, 1990) were the following:

- Women's depression is related to avoidant, passive, dependent behavior patterns; it is also related to focusing too much on depressed feelings instead of on action and mastery strategies.
- The rate of sexual and physical abuse of women is much higher than previously thought and is a major factor in women's depression. Depressive symptoms may be long-standing effects of posttraumatic stress syndrome for many women.
- Marriage often confers a greater protective buffer against stress for men than for women. In unhappy marriages, women are three times as likely as men to be depressed. Mothers of young children are especially vulnerable to stress and depression; the more children in the house, the more depression women report.
- Poverty is a pathway to depression and three out of every four people in poverty in the United States are women and children. Minority women, elderly women, chemically dependent women, lesbians, and professional women are also high-risk groups for depression and merit special attention and support.

Careful diagnosis is critical in the treatment of women's depression. Diagnostic assessment for women, in particular, should include taking a history of sexual and physical violence; exploring prescription drug use; discovering past and current medical conditions; and doing a reproductive life history to determine how menstruation, birth control, pregnancy, childbirth, abortion, and menopause may have contributed to women's depression. According to the Women's Task Force, depression is misdiagnosed at least 30 to 50 percent of the time in women. Approximately 70 percent of the prescriptions for antidepressants are given to women, often with improper diagnosis and monitoring. Prescription drug misuse is a danger for many women.

Understanding the nature of women's depression is a complex undertaking and merits more attention. Perhaps the current effort to better understand women's depression will be successful and reduce women's pain and suffering from depression.

A man's lifetime risk of developing major depression is approximately 10 percent. The risk is much greater for a woman—almost 25 percent. In fact, depression is the most common psychiatric diagnosis for Black and White women (Russo, 1985). To read further about women's depression, turn to Sociocultural Worlds 13.2.

In May 1988, the National Institute of Mental Health (NIMH) launched the public education phase of the first major program to communicate information about mood disorders (Regier & others, 1988). The inadequate care that results from a lack of understanding or a misunderstanding of depression is expensive and tragic. The annual cost of major depression to the nation is more than $16 billion. Given the existing range of psychological and pharmacological treatments, many individuals who go untreated suffer needlessly.

Bipolar Disorder

Bipolar disorder *is a mood disorder characterized by extreme mood swings; an individual with this disorder might be depressed, manic, or both.* We have described the symptoms of depression. In contrast, someone who is manic experiences elation, exuberance, and tireless stamina. He or she may be humorous, scheming, restless, and irritable; have a tendency for excess; and be in almost constant motion (Depue & others, 1989). The type of

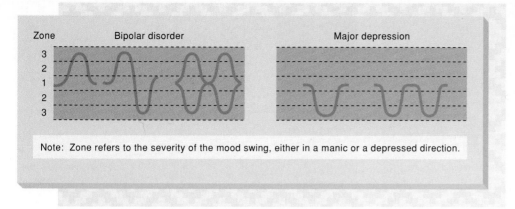

Zone	Bipolar disorder	Major depression
3		
2		
1		
2		
3		

Note: Zone refers to the severity of the mood swing, either in a manic or a depressed direction.

FIGURE 13.4

Comparison of mood swings in bipolar and major depression.

mood swings that might occur in bipolar disorder are shown in figure 13.4, where they are contrasted with the mood swings of major depression.

Consider Mrs. M. Although she had experienced extreme mood swings since she was a child, she was first admitted to a mental hospital at the age of 38. At 33, shortly before the birth of her first child, she became very depressed. One month after the baby was born, she became agitated and euphoric. Mrs. M. signed a year's lease on an apartment, bought furniture, and piled up debts. Several years later, other manic and depressive mood swings occurred. In one of her excitatory moods, Mrs. M. swore loudly and created a disturbance at a club where she was not a member. Several days later, she began divorce proceedings. On the day prior to her admission to the mental hospital, she went on a spending spree and bought 57 hats. Several weeks later, she became despondent, saying, "I have no energy. My brain doesn't work right. I have let my family down. I don't have anything to live for." In a subsequent manic bout, Mrs. M. pursued a romantic relationship with her doctor (Kolb, 1973).

The lifetime risk of bipolar disorder is estimated at approximately 1 percent for both men and women (Weissman & Boyd, 1985). It is more common among divorced persons, although, in such cases, bipolar disorder may be a cause rather than a consequence of the divorce. Bipolar disorder also occurs more frequently in the close relatives of individuals with bipolar disorder than in the close relatives of depressed but non-bipolar disordered individuals.

Suicide

The rate of suicide has tripled since the 1950s in the United States (Lann & Moscicki, 1989; Lester, 1989). Each year about 25,000 people take their own lives. At about the age of 15, the suicide rate begins to rise rapidly. Suicide accounts for 12 percent of the mortality in the adolescent and young adult age group (Brent, 1989). Men are about three times more likely than women to succeed at committing suicide. This may be due to their more active methods for attempting it—shooting themselves, for example. By contrast, females more often use passive methods, such as sleeping pills, which do not immediately cause death. Although males successfully commit suicide more frequently, females attempt it more often (Jack, 1992).

Estimates indicate that 6 to 10 suicide attempts occur for every successful suicide in the general population. For adolescents, the figure is as high as 50 attempts for every life taken. As many as 2 in every 3 college students have thought about suicide on at least one occasion. Their methods range from using drugs to crashing into the White House in an airplane.

There is no simple answer to why people commit suicide. Biological factors appear to be involved. Suicide, as with major depression, tends to run in families. Immediate and highly stressful circumstances, such as the loss of a spouse or a job, flunking out of school, or an unwanted pregnancy, can lead people, especially those who are genetically predisposed, to attempt suicide. Also, drug-related suicide attempts are more common now than in the past.

However, earlier experiences, such as a long-standing history of family instability and unhappiness, can also play a role in attempted suicides (Rubenstein & others, 1989). Studies of gifted men and women found several predictors of suicide, such as anxiety, conspicuous instability in work and relationships, depression, and alcoholism (Schneidman, 1971; Tomlinson-Keasey, Warren, & Elliot, 1986).

In high-pressure cultures, such as Japan and the United States, suicide rates are much higher than in less achievement oriented cultures. Also, as we will see next, in some cultures, religion plays an important role in deterring suicide.

Over many centuries, the majority of Hispanics have maintained their spiritual belief in Catholicism (Pacheco & Valdez, 1989). However, Hispanic subcultures interpret Catholicism differently from one another. A comparison of Mexican Americans with Puerto Ricans illustrates how different beliefs in Catholicism affect the suicide rates of various Hispanic American subcultures. For example, one study found that many depressed Mexican Americans control their suicidal impulses because Catholicism asserts that suicide is an unpardonable sin that carries church sanctions against those who attempt suicide, as well as eternal damnation in hell for those who succeed (Bach y Rita, 1982).

Over many centuries, the majority of Hispanics have maintained their spiritual belief in Catholicism. However, Catholicism does not always mean the same thing to all Hispanics. What are some variations in the meaning of Catholicism to Hispanics from different ethnic backgrounds?

TABLE 13.3

What to Do and What Not to Do When You Suspect Someone Is Likely to Commit Suicide

What to do

1. Ask direct, straightforward questions in a calm manner: "Are you thinking about hurting yourself?"

2. Assess the seriousness of the suicidal intent by asking questions about feelings, important relationships, who else the person has talked with, and the amount of thought given to the means to be used. If a gun, pills, rope, or other means has been obtained and a precise plan developed, clearly the situation is dangerous. Stay with the person until help arrives.

3. Be a good listener and be very supportive without being falsely reassuring.

4. Try to persuade the person to obtain professional help and assist him or her in getting this help.

What not to do

1. Do not ignore the warning signs.

2. Do not refuse to talk about suicide if a person approaches you about it.

3. Do not react with horror, disapproval, or repulsion.

4. Do not give false reassurances by saying such things as "Everything is going to be OK." Also do not give out simple answers or platitudes, such as "You have everything to be thankful for."

5. Do not abandon the individual after the crisis has passed or after professional help has commenced.

Reprinted from *Living with 10- to 15-Year-Olds: A Parent Education Curriculum.* Copyright by the Center for Early Adolescence, University of North Carolina at Chapel Hill, NC, rev. ed. 1991. Used with permission.

Even though Puerto Ricans tend to be Catholic, they also integrate Indian folk beliefs with their Catholicism. Overall, Puerto Ricans do not adopt organized religion, only minimally adhering to the Catholic doctrine. Many Puerto Ricans believe that spirits communicate with people through mediums, or people who act as channels of communication between the earthly world and a world of spirits (Kardec, 1957). This belief, combined with the conviction that "unsolvable" conflicts can be handled by committing suicide, promotes a much higher rate of suicide among Puerto Ricans than among Mexican Americans.

Clinicians who have Hispanic clients need to be aware of such cultural differences. If a clinician erroneously thinks of Hispanics as a homogeneous group, he or she might incorrectly evaluate the client's risk of suicide. For example, if the clinician reasons that Hispanics are Catholics and Catholics do not believe in suicide because it is an unpardonable sin against God, the clinician may assess the risk of suicide for a Puerto Rican client as low, in which case the clinician might be very wrong (Pacheco & Valdez, 1989).

Psychologists do not have the complete answers for detecting suicidal impulses or for preventing them. However, the advice offered in table 13.3 provides some valuable suggestions for communicating with someone you think may be contemplating suicide.

Causes of Mood Disorders

Explanations for mood disorders, such as Peter's depression and Mrs. M.'s bipolar disorder, come from psychoanalytic theory, cognitive and learning theories, biogenetic theories, and sociocultural theories.

Psychoanalytic Explanations

In 1917 Sigmund Freud published a paper called "Mourning and Melancholia," in which he described his view of depression. Freud believed that depression is a turning inward of aggressive instincts. He theorized that a child's early attachment to a love object (usually the mother) contains a mixture of love and hate. When the child loses the love object or her dependency needs are frustrated, feelings of loss coexist with anger. Since the child cannot openly accept such angry feelings toward the individual she loves, the hostility is turned inward and experienced as depression. The unresolved mixture of anger and love is carried forward to adolescence and adulthood, where loss can bring back these early feelings of abandonment.

British psychiatrist John Bowlby (1980, 1989) agrees with Freud that childhood experiences are an important determinant of depression in adulthood. He believes that a combination of an insecure attachment to the mother, a lack of love and affection as a child, and the actual loss of a parent during childhood give rise to a negative cognitive set, or schema. The schema built up during childhood causes the individual to interpret later losses as yet other failures in one's effort to establish enduring and close positive relationships.

One longitudinal study of depression found that parents' lack of affection, high control, and aggressive achievement orientation in their children's early childhood are associated with depression among adolescent girls but not boys (Gjerde, 1985). This difference may be because depression generally occurs more often in girls than boys.

Cognitive and Learning Explanations

Individuals who are depressed rarely think positive thoughts. They interpret their lives in self-defeating ways and have negative expectations about the future. Psychotherapist Aaron Beck believes that such negative thoughts reflect schemas that shape the depressed individual's experiences (Beck, 1967; Clark & Beck, 1989). These habitual negative thoughts magnify and expand a depressed person's negative experiences. The depressed person may overgeneralize about a minor occurrence and think that he is worthless because a work assignment was turned in late, his son was arrested for shoplifting, or a friend made a negative comment about his hair. Beck believes that depressed people blame themselves far more than is warranted. For example, an athlete may accept complete blame for a team's loss when five or six other teammates, the opposing team, and other factors were involved.

Self-defeating and sad thoughts fit the clinical picture of the depressed individual. Whether these thoughts are the cause or the consequence of the depression, however, is controversial (Rehm, 1989). Critics say that self-defeating thoughts are an outgrowth of biological and environmental conditions that produce depression.

Some years ago, in the interest of science, a researcher drowned two rats (Richter, 1957). The first rat was dropped into a tank of warm water; it swam around for 60 hours before it drowned. The second rat was handled differently. The researcher held the rat tightly in his hand until it quit struggling to get loose. Then the rat was dropped into the tank; it swam around for several minutes before it drowned. The researcher concluded that the second rat drowned more quickly because its previous experiences told it to give up hope; the rat had developed a sense of helplessness.

Learned helplessness *occurs when animals or humans are exposed to aversive stimulation, such as prolonged stress or pain, over which they have no control. The inability to avoid such aversive stimulation produces an apathetic state of helplessness.* Martin Seligman (1975) argued that learned helplessness is one reason many individuals become depressed. When individuals encounter stress and pain over which they have no control, they eventually feel helpless and depressed. Some researchers believe that the hopelessness characteristic of learned helplessness is often the result of a person's extremely negative, self-blaming attributions (Abramson, Metalsky, & Alloy, 1989).

Biogenetic Explanations

Biological explanations of depression involve genetic inheritance and chemical changes in the brain (Shelton & others, 1991). In a large twin study conducted in Denmark, the identical twins were more likely to suffer from mood disorders than were the fraternal twins (Bertelson, 1979). If one identical twin developed a mood disorder, the other had a 70 percent chance of developing the disorder; a fraternal twin ran only a 13 percent risk. Another study revealed that biological relatives of an individual with a mood disorder are more likely to suffer from the disorder than are adopted relatives (Wender & others, 1986).

Remember from chapter 2 that neurotransmitters are chemical messengers that carry information from one neuron to the next. Two neurotransmitters involved in depression are norepinephrine and serotonin. Depressed individuals have decreased levels of norepinephrine, whereas individuals in a manic state have increased levels. Patients with unusually low serotonin levels are 10 times as likely to commit suicide than individuals with normal levels (Stanley & Stanley, 1989). The endocrine system also may be involved in depression—excessive secretion of cortisol from the adrenal gland occurs in depressed individuals, for example (Joyce, Donald, & Elder, 1987). More about the biological aspects of depression appears in the next chapter, where we will discuss the use of drugs to alleviate depression.

Sociocultural Explanations

Seligman (1989) recently speculated that the reason so many young American adults are prone to depression is that our society's emphasis on self, independence, and individualism, coupled with an erosion of connectedness to others, family, and religion, has spawned a widespread sense of hopelessness. Depressive disorders are found in virtually all cultures in the world, but their incidence, intensity, and components vary across cultures (Marsella, 1980). A major difference in depression between Western and many non-Western cultures is the absence of guilt and self-deprecation in the non-Western cultures (Draguns, 1990; El-Islam, 1969; Singer, 1984).

Some cross-cultural psychologists believe that mourning rituals in many non-Western cultures reduce the risks of depression. For example, low depression rates in Taiwan may be related to the overt expression of grief that occurs in Chinese funeral celebrations (Tseng & Hsu, 1969). Ancestor worship in Japan also may act against depression because love objects are not considered to be lost through death (Yamamoto & others, 1969). The mourning practices of Black Americans also may reduce depression by providing an opportunity for adequate grieving and by providing the bereaved with support rather than having to cope with death in isolation (Vitols, 1967).

Earlier in this chapter, you learned that women run a far greater risk of depression than men—at a ratio of 2:1. Researchers have shown that depression is especially high among single women who are the head of household and among young married women who work at unsatisfying, dead-end jobs (McBride, 1990; Russo, 1985, 1990). Such stressful circumstances, as well as others involving sexual abuse, sexual harassment, unwanted pregnancy, and powerlessness disproportionately affect women. These sociocultural factors may interact with biological and cognitive factors to increase women's rate of depression. A second possibility may be that men in mainstream American society obscure their depression with aggressive behavior that "acts-out," or externalizes, their sad feelings. In cultures where alcohol abuse and aggression are rare, such as the culturally homogeneous Amish community (a religious sect in Pennsylvania), the rates of depression for women and men are virtually equal.

Separating the environmental, cognitive, biological, and sociocultural causes of depression is not easy. Whether neurotransmitters, cognitive factors, environmental factors, or cross-cultural factors are cause or effect is still unknown. Like most behaviors we have discussed, depression is best viewed as complex and multiply determined (Kendall & Watson, 1989).

Schizophrenic Disorders

Schizophrenia produces a bizarre set of symptoms and wreaks havoc on an individual's personality. **Schizophrenic disorders** *are severe psychological disorders characterized by distorted thoughts and perceptions, odd communication, inappropriate emotion, abnormal motor behavior, and social withdrawal. The term schizophrenia comes from the Latin words* schizo, *meaning "split," and* phrenia, *meaning "mind." The individual's mind is split from reality, and personality loses its unity.* Schizophrenia is not the same as multiple personality, which sometimes is called a "split personality." Schizophrenia involves the split of *one* personality from reality, not the coexistence of several personalities within one individual.

Characteristics of Schizophrenic Disorders

Bob began to miss work. He spent his time watching his house from a rental car parked inconspicuously down the street and following his fellow employees as they left work to see where they went and what they did. He kept a little black book, in which he scribbled cryptic notes. When he went to the water cooler at work, he pretended to drink but, instead, looked carefully around the room to observe if anyone seemed guilty or frightened.

Bob's world seemed to be closing in on him. After an explosive scene at the office one day, he became very agitated. He left and never returned. By the time Bob arrived at home, he was in a rage. He could not sleep that night, and the next day he kept his children home from school; all day he kept the shades pulled on every window. The next night, he maintained his vigil. At 4 A.M., he armed himself and burst out of the house, firing shots in the air while daring his enemies to come out (McNeil, 1967).

Bob is a paranoid schizophrenic. About 1 in every 100 Americans will be classified as schizophrenic in their lifetime (Gottesman, 1989). Schizophrenic disorders are serious, debilitating mental disturbances; about one-half of all mental hospital patients in the United States are schizophrenics. More now than in the past, schizophrenics live in society and periodically return for treatment at mental hospitals. Drug therapy, which will be discussed in the next chapter, is primarily responsible for fewer schizophrenics being hospitalized. About one-third of all schizophrenics get better, about one-third get worse, and another third stay about the same once they develop this severe mental disorder. What are the symptoms of these individuals?

Many schizophrenics have *delusions,* or false beliefs—one individual may think he is Jesus Christ, another Napoleon, for example. The delusions are utterly implausible. One individual may think her thoughts are being broadcast over the radio; another may think that a double agent is controlling her every move. Schizophrenics also may hear, see, feel, smell, and taste things that are not there. These *hallucinations* often take the form of voices. The schizophrenic might think he hears two people talking about him, for example. On another occasion, he might say, "Hear that rumbling in the pipe? That is one of my men in there watching out for me."

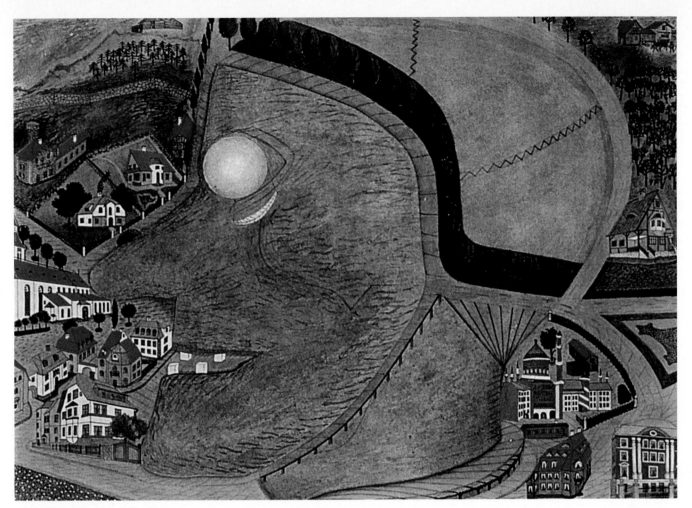

FIGURE 13.5

A painting by a schizophrenic. This painting is named *Landscape* and it is by August Neter, a successful nineteenth-century electrical engineer until he became schizophrenic in 1907. He lost interest in his work as an engineer as his mind became disorganized.

Often schizophrenics do not make sense when they talk or write. Their language does not follow any rules. For example, one schizophrenic might say, "Well, Rocky, babe, help is out, happening, but where, when, up, top, side, over, you know, out of the way, that's it. Sign off." Such speech has no meaning. These incoherent, loose word associations are called *word salad*. As shown in figure 13.5, schizophrenics' paintings also have a bizarre quality.

A schizophrenic's motor behavior may be bizarre, sometimes taking the form of an odd appearance, pacing, statuelike postures, or strange mannerisms. Some schizophrenics withdraw from their social world; they become so insulated from others that they seem totally absorbed in interior images and thoughts (Straube & Oades, 1992).

Forms of Schizophrenic Disorders

Schizophrenic disorders appear in four main forms: disorganized, catatonic, paranoid, and undifferentiated schizophrenia.

Disorganized schizophrenia *is a schizophrenic disorder in which an individual has delusions and hallucinations that have little or no recognizable meaning—hence, the label* disorganized. A disorganized schizophrenic withdraws from human contact and may regress to silly, childlike gestures and behavior. Many of these individuals were isolated or maladjusted during adolescence.

Catatonic schizophrenia *is a schizophrenic disorder characterized by bizarre motor behavior, which sometimes takes the form of a completely immobile stupor* (see figure 13.6). Even in this stupor, catatonic schizophrenics are completely conscious of what is happening around them. An individual in a catatonic state sometimes shows *waxy flexibility*; for example, if the person's arm is raised and then allowed to fall, the arm stays in the new position.

Paranoid schizophrenia *is a schizophrenic disorder characterized by delusions of reference, grandeur, and persecution.* The delusions usually form a complex, elaborate system based on a complete misinterpretation of actual events. It is not unusual for schizophrenics to develop all three delusions in the following order. First, they sense they are special and have been singled out for attention (delusions of reference). Individuals with delusions of reference misinterpret chance events as being directly relevant to their own lives—a thunderstorm, for example, might be perceived as a personal message from God. Second, they believe that this special attention is the result of their admirable and special characteristics (delusions of grandeur). Individuals with delusions of grandeur think of themselves as exalted beings— the pope or the president, for example. Third, they think that others are so jealous and threatened by these characteristics that they spy and plot against them (delusions of persecution). Individuals with delusions of persecution feel they are the target of a conspiracy— for example, recall Bob's situation described earlier.

Undifferentiated schizophrenia *is a schizophrenic disorder characterized by disorganized behavior, hallucinations, delusions, and incoherence.* This category of schizophrenia is used when an individual's symptoms either don't meet the criteria for the other types or they meet the criteria for more than one of the other types.

Causes of Schizophrenia

Schizophrenic disorders may be caused by genetic and biological factors, as well as environmental and sociocultural factors.

Genetic Factors

If you have a relative with schizophrenia, what are the chances you will develop schizophrenia? It depends on how closely you are related. As genetic similarity increases, so does your risk of becoming schizophrenic. As shown in figure 13.7, an identical twin of a schizophrenic has a 46 percent chance of developing the disorder, a fraternal twin 14 percent, a sibling 10 percent, a nephew or niece 3 percent, and an unrelated individual in the general population 1 percent (Gottesman & Shields, 1982). Such data strongly suggest that genetic factors are involved in schizophrenia, although the precise nature of the genetic influence is unknown.

FIGURE 13.6

A catatonic schizophrenic. Disturbances in motor behavior are prominent symptoms in catatonic schizophrenia. Individuals may cease to move altogether, sometimes taking on bizarre postures.

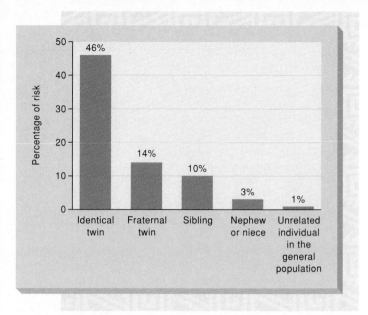

FIGURE 13.7

Lifetime risk of becoming schizophrenic according to genetic relatedness. As your genetic relatedness to an individual with schizophrenia increases, so does your risk of becoming schizophrenic.

Neurobiological Factors

Many neuroscientists believe that imbalances in brain chemistry, including deficits in brain metabolism, a malfunctioning dopamine system, and distorted cerebral blood flow, cause schizophrenia. Imaging techniques, such as the PET scan, clearly show deficits in brain metabolism. Do these deficits cause the disorder or are they simply symptoms of a disorder whose true origin lies deeper in the brain, in the genes, or in the environment? Whether the neurobiological factors are the cause or the effect, information about them improves our knowledge of schizophrenia's nature. We do know that schizophrenics produce too much of the neurotransmitter dopamine. More about the dopamine system appears in the next chapter, where we will discuss the use of drugs to block excess dopamine production. Schizophrenics also have a reduced blood flow in the prefrontal cortex. For example, when scientists monitored the brains of schizophrenics as they performed a card-sorting task, blood did not adequately flow into the prefrontal region, where much of our advanced thinking takes place (Weinberger, Berman, & Zec, 1986).

Environmental Factors

As scientists learn about schizophrenia's neurobiological basis, they may lose sight of the fact that schizophrenia, like all other behavior, does not occur in an environmental vacuum. Some researchers believe that environmental factors are important in schizophrenia (Goldstein, 1986); others believe that genetic factors outweigh environmental factors (Gottesman & Shields, 1982).

Stress is the environmental factor given the most attention in understanding schizophrenia. The **diathesis-stress view** *argues that a combination of environmental stress and biogenetic disposition causes schizophrenia* (Fowles, 1992; Meehl, 1962). A defective gene makeup may produce schizophrenia only when an individual lives in a stressful environment. Advocates of the diathesis-stress view emphasize the importance of stress reduction and family support in treating schizophrenia.

Sociocultural Factors

Disorders of thought and emotion are common to schizophrenia in all cultures, but the type and incidence of schizophrenic disorders may vary from culture to culture. For example, one of the more puzzling results is that the admission rates to mental health facilities for schizophrenia are very high for Irish Catholics in the Republic of Ireland (Torrey & others, 1984) but not for Irish Catholics living elsewhere (Murphy, 1978). One reason for this difference could be that the diagnostic criteria used in the Republic of Ireland are different from those used elsewhere, but this is not likely to be the complete answer. There are many areas of the world where the incidence of schizophrenia is considerably higher or lower than the worldwide incidence of just under 1 percent.

Rates of schizophrenia may also vary for different groups within a culture (Cohen, 1992; Sartorius, 1992). For example, one study revealed that Blacks have higher rates of schizophrenia than Whites in both the United States and Great Britain (Bagley, 1984). In that study, the Blacks had a significantly greater number of life crises that may have precipitated schizophrenic episodes. Also, the Black Americans and Black Britons who became schizophrenic had higher aspirations than those who did not. One explanation may be that the Blacks' efforts to become assimilated into and to achieve parity within a mainstream society that is oppressively racist created considerable stress.

In addition, the conditions of lower-class existence often restrict a person's ability to cope with many of life's stressors. Nonetheless, there are some individuals from lower-class backgrounds who develop considerable resourcefulness and resilience. When supposed ethnic differences in schizophrenia are examined in the context of socioeconomic status—comparing Blacks, Hispanics, and Whites, for example—the ethnic differences tend to vanish. Thus, it seems that poverty and the living conditions it engenders are much more likely to be associated with schizophrenia than is ethnicity.

We have seen that the mood disorders and the schizophrenic disorders are complex and often debilitating. Next you will read about an intriguing set of disorders involving personality.

REVIEW

Mood Disorders and Schizophrenic Disorders

The mood disorders are characterized by wide emotional swings, ranging from deeply depressed to highly euphoric and agitated. Depression can occur alone, as in major depression, or it can alternate with mania, as in bipolar disorder. Individuals with major depression are sad, demoralized, bored, and self-derogatory. They often do not feel well, lose stamina easily, have a poor appetite, and are listless and unmotivated. Depression is so widespread that it is called the "common cold" of mental disturbances.

Bipolar disorder is characterized by extreme mood swings; an individual with this disorder might be depressed, manic, or both. In the manic phase, individuals are exuberant, have tireless stamina, and have a tendency for excess. They also are restless, irritable, and in almost constant motion. The rate of suicide has increased dramatically in the United States. There is no simple answer to why individuals attempt suicide—immediate, earlier, biological, and cultural factors may be involved. Explanations of mood disorders come from psychoanalytic theory, cognitive and learning theories, biogenetic theories, and sociocultural theories.

Schizophrenic disorders are severe mental disorders characterized by distorted thoughts and perceptions, odd communication, inappropriate emotion, abnormal motor behavior, and social withdrawal. The individual's mind splits from reality, and the personality loses its unity. About 1 in 100 Americans becomes schizophrenic, and schizophrenia accounts for approximately one-half of all individuals in mental hospitals. Many schizophrenics have delusions, or false beliefs, and hallucinations. They often do not make sense when they talk or write. The schizophrenic's motor behavior may be bizarre, and the schizophrenic may withdraw from social relationships.

Schizophrenia appears in four main forms: disorganized, catatonic, paranoid, and undifferentiated. Proposed causes of schizophrenia include genetic and biological factors, as well as environmental factors. Many neuroscientists believe that imbalances in brain chemistry cause schizophrenia. The diathesis-stress model emphasizes both biogenetic and environmental stress. Cognitive and emotional disorders of thought are common in schizophrenia in all cultures, but the type and incidence of schizophrenic disorders may vary cross-culturally and across social classes.

Personality Disorders

Personality disorders *are psychological disorders that develop when personality traits become inflexible and, thus, maladaptive.* Individuals with these maladaptive traits often do not recognize that they have a problem and may show little interest in changing. Personality disorders involve odd or eccentric behaviors; dramatic, emotional, or erratic behavior; or fearful or anxious behavior.

The **antisocial personality disorder** *is the most problematic personality disorder for society. Individuals with antisocial personality disorder often resort to crime, violence, and delinquency. These individuals (who used to be called psychopaths or sociopaths) regularly violate the rights of others.* This disorder begins before the age of 15 and continues into adulthood; it is much more typical of males than females. Truancy, school suspension, running away from home, stealing, vandalism, drug use, and violation of rules at home and school are commonplace among adolescents afflicted with antisocial personality disorder. As adults, individuals are not able to maintain a consistent work record; they continue to engage in antisocial acts, such as stealing, vandalism, and harassing others; they fail to uphold financial obligations and rarely plan ahead; they repeatedly get into fights; and they show no remorse when harming someone.

Substance-Use Disorders

In chapter 4, we discussed a number of drugs and their effects on individuals. A problem associated with drug use is called a **substance-use disorder,** *which is characterized by one or more of the following features: (1) a pattern of pathological use that involves frequent intoxication, a need for daily use, and an inability to control use—in a sense, psychological dependence; (2) a significant impairment of social or occupational functioning attributed to the drug use; and (3) physical dependence that involves serious withdrawal problems.*

The use of many of the drugs described in chapter 4 can lead to a substance-use disorder. Alcohol, barbiturates, and opium derivatives all are capable of producing either physical or psychological dependence. Alcoholism is an especially widespread substance-use disorder; it has been estimated that 6 to 8 million Americans are alcoholics. Although substantial numbers of women abuse alcohol, more men than women are alcoholics. Among Black Americans, the male-female alcoholic ratio is 3:2; among White Americans, the ratio is approximately 4:1 (Russo, 1985, 1990).

Many individuals are surprised to learn that substantial numbers of women are alcoholics or abusers of other drugs. Although most of the research on drug abuse has been directed toward males, studies have found that females are just as likely to be treated for drug-related problems in emergency rooms. Without a more intense research effort directed at female drug abusers,

John Hinckley attempted to assassinate President Reagan in 1981. What was the jury's decision about Hinckley's sanity?

the unique facets of their drug abuse will go uncharted (Russo, 1990). For both male and female drug abusers, biogenetic, psychological, and sociocultural factors may all be involved.

Legal Aspects of Mental Disorders

The legal status of individuals with mental disorders raises a number of controversial issues: What is involved in committing disordered and dangerous individuals to mental institutions? What is the status of using the insanity defense for capital crimes? We will consider each of these issues in turn.

Commitment and Dangerousness

Having a mental disorder in itself is not adequate grounds for placing individuals in a mental institution against their will. However, the behavior of some mentally disordered individuals is so severe that they are a threat to themselves and/or to others, and they may need protective confinement. Although procedures vary somewhat from state to state, certain conditions usually need to be met before a person can be formally committed to a mental institution: individuals must be dangerous either to themselves or to other people. Determining whether a mentally disordered individual is dangerous is not easy, even for mental health professionals. Nonetheless, there are times when professionals have to make "dangerousness" judgments. Recent court decisions have held mental health professionals liable when unconfined clients they were treating have caused harm to others, and therapists are required to warn potential victims if their patients threaten to kill someone (Faulkner, McFarland, & Bloom, 1989; Lidz & others, 1989; Segal, 1989).

The Insanity Defense

Insanity *is a legal term, not a psychological term, which implies that individuals are mentally disordered and incapable of being responsible for their actions.* The **insanity defense** *is a plea of "innocent by reason of insanity" used as a legal defense in criminal trials.* In our culture, guilt implies responsibility and intent—to be guilty of a crime, an individual has to have knowingly and intentionally committed it. The jury determines whether the defendant is guilty, based on such legally defined criteria. Controversy swirls about the concept of insanity because of concerns that criminals will unfairly use this plea to avoid prosecution.

In recent years, the most publicized case of the use of the insanity defense is that of John Hinckley, who attempted to assassinate President Reagan in 1981. The prosecution was unable to convince the jury that Hinckley was sane—that he had the capacity to know his act was wrong—so he was placed in a mental institution. The public was outraged at this decision, especially because Hinckley will be released if he is ever judged to be sane and no longer dangerous.

The appropriateness of the insanity plea remains highly controversial. Some experts recommend changes in the defense, arguing that whether or not the defendant actually committed the crime should be determined independently of the defendant's sanity status (Steadman & others, 1989).

In this chapter, we saw that individuals engage in many behaviors that are harmful and maladaptive. In the next chapter, Therapies, we will examine ways to improve the lives of individuals with mental disorders.

REVIEW

Personality Disorders, Substance-Use Disorders, and Legal Aspects of Mental Disorders

Personality disorders develop when traits become inflexible and maladaptive. Types of personality disorders include odd or eccentric behavior; dramatic, emotional, or erratic behavior; and fear or anxious behavior. Individuals with antisocial disorder live a life of crime, violence, and delinquency.

Substance-use disorders focus on individuals with problems associated with drug use. The disorder may involve psychological dependence, physical dependence, and impairment of social or occupational functioning. Alcoholism is an especially widespread substance-use disorder.

Mentally disordered individuals must be dangerous either to themselves or to others for formal commitment to a mental institution. Judgments about "dangerousness" are not easy. Mental health professionals have been held accountable when their clients have caused harm to others. Insanity is a legal term, not a psychological term, which implies that individuals are mentally disordered and incapable of being responsible for their actions. The insanity defense is a plea of "innocent by reason of insanity" used as a legal defense in criminal trials. Controversy swirls around the insanity defense.

Summary

I. What Is Abnormal Behavior? What Causes Abnormal Behavior?

Abnormal behavior is behavior that is maladaptive and harmful. Atypical behavior is not always abnormal. Mental disorders have biological, as well as psychological and sociocultural, causes. The forerunner of the biological approach was the medical model. Today's biological approach emphasizes the roles of brain processes and heredity in mental disorders. Many psychologists believe that the biological approach understates the importance of psychological and sociocultural factors. They also emphasize that the medical model encourages the labeling of mental disorders. Although many disorders are universal, the frequency of abnormal behavior varies across and within cultures.

Such variations are related to socioeconomic status, ethnicity, technology, religion, gender, and urbanization. Biological, psychological, and social factors often interact to produce abnormal behavior.

II. How Can Abnormal Behavior Be Classified?

DSM stands for *Diagnostic and Statistical Manual of Mental Disorders*. DSM-II included the categories of neurotic and psychotic behavior. Some mental health workers still use these terms, but they have been dropped from the DSM classification system. DSM-III and its revision, DSM-III-R, have improved diagnostic criteria, have redefined mental disorders that are more in line with research findings, and contain a multiaxial approach. Psychiatrists were

mainly responsible for the DSM classifications. Many psychologists believe that the classification still has too many characteristics of the medical model and includes problems of living that should not be classified as mental disorders. Mental categories are often culturally biased. DSM-III and other mental health classification systems are invariably based on problems and pathology. Critics argue that competent mental health classification systems should reflect positive as well as negative attributes.

III. Anxiety Disorders

Anxiety is a diffuse, vague, highly unpleasant feeling of fear and apprehension. The main features of anxiety disorders are motor tension, hyperactivity, and apprehensive expectations and thoughts. Generalized anxiety disorder consists of persistent anxiety for at least 1 month without being able to specify the reason for the anxiety. Panic disorder involves recurrent panic attacks marked by the sudden onset of intense apprehension or terror. Phobic disorders, commonly called phobias, involve an irrational, overwhelming, persistent fear of a particular object or situation. Phobias come in many forms; the most common is agoraphobia. Post-traumatic stress disorder is an anxiety disorder that develops through exposure to a traumatic event, a severely oppressive situation, severe abuse, a natural disaster, or an accidental disaster. Anxiety symptoms may immediately follow the trauma or may be delayed months or even years.

IV. Somatoform Disorders
They occur when psychological symptoms take a physical, or somatic, form, even though no physical cause can be found. Hypochondriasis is a pervasive fear of illness and disease. It rarely occurs alone; it is commonly accompanied by depression. Conversion disorder is when an individual experiences genuine symptoms, even though no physiological problems can be found. Conversion disorder received its name from psychoanalytic theory, which stresses that anxiety is "converted" into a physical symptom. Some loss of motor or sensory ability occurs. The disorder was more common in Freud's time than today.

V. Dissociative Disorders
They occur when an individual has a sudden loss of memory or a change of identity. Under extreme stress, the individual's conscious awareness becomes dissociated (separated or split) from previous memories and thoughts. Psychogenic amnesia involves memory loss caused by extensive psychological stress. Fugue also involves a loss of memory, but individuals unexpectedly travel away from home or work, assume a new identity, and do not remember their old one. Multiple personality consists of the presence of two or more distinct personalities in the same individual. The disorder is rare.

VI. Mood Disorders
Mood disorders involve wide emotional swings, ranging from deeply depressed to highly euphoric and agitated. Depression can occur alone, as in major depression, or it can alternate with mania, as in bipolar disorder. Individuals with major depression are sad, demoralized, bored, and self-derogatory. They often do not feel well, lose stamina easily, have a poor appetite, and are listless and unmotivated. Depression is so widespread that it is called the "common cold" of mental disorders. Major depression sometimes leads to suicide. Bipolar disorder consists of extreme mood swings; an individual with this disorder might be depressed, manic, or both. In the manic phase, the individual's moods are elated, humorous, and scheming. Manic individuals are exuberant, have tireless stamina, and have a tendency for excess. They also are restless, irritable, and in almost constant motion. The rate of suicide has increased dramatically in the United States. There is no simple answer to why individuals attempt suicide—immediate, earlier, biological, and cultural factors may be involved. Explanations of mood disorders come from psychoanalytic theory, cognitive and social learning theories, biogenetic theories, and sociocultural theories.

VII. Schizophrenic Disorders
They are severe mental disorders characterized by distorted thoughts and perceptions, odd communication, inappropriate emotion, abnormal motor behavior, and social withdrawal. The individual's mind splits from reality, and the personality loses its unity. About 1 in 100 Americans becomes schizophrenic; schizophrenia accounts for about one-half of all mental hospital patients. Many schizophrenics have delusions, or false beliefs, and hallucinations. They often do not make sense when they talk or write. The schizophrenic's motor behavior may be bizarre, and the schizophrenic may withdraw from social relationships. Schizophrenia appears in four main forms: disorganized, catatonic, paranoid, and undifferentiated. Proposed causes of schizophrenia include genetic and biological factors, as well as environmental and sociocultural factors.

VIII. Personality Disorders
Personality disorders develop when traits become inflexible and maladaptive. The types of personality disorders include odd or eccentric behavior; dramatic, emotional, or erratic behavior; and fear or anxious behavior. Individuals with antisocial personality disorder live a life of crime, violence, and delinquency.

IX. Substance-Use Disorders
Drug-use disorders involve psychological dependence, physical dependence, and impairment of social or occupational functioning. Alcoholism is an especially widespread substance-use disorder.

X. Legal Aspects of Mental Disorders
Mentally disordered individuals must be dangerous to themselves or to others for formal commitment to a mental institution. Judgments about "dangerousness" are not easy. Mental health professionals have been held responsible when their clients have caused harm to others. Insanity is a legal term, not a psychological term, which implies that individuals are not responsible for their actions. The insanity defense is a plea of "innocent by reason of insanity" used as a legal defense in criminal trials. Controversy swirls around the insanity defense.

Key Terms

Suggested Readings

Archives of General Psychiatry. This journal has extensive coverage of many disorders and their classification according to DSM-III-R. Go to the library at your college or university or to a nearby library and leaf through issues from the past several years to get a feel for the symptoms of mental disturbances and the way they are classified.

Carson, R. C., Butcher, J. N., & Coleman, J. C. (1988). *Abnormal psychology and modern life* (8th ed.). Glenview, IL: Scott, Foresman. This is one of the leading textbooks in abnormal psychology. It provides a detailed look at many of the psychological disorders discussed in this chapter.

Diagnostic and statistical manual of mental disorders (3rd ed., revised). (1987). Washington, DC: American Psychiatric Association. Detailed descriptions of the many categories of mental disorders are provided.

Meyer, R. G., & Osborne, Y. V. H. (1982). *Case studies in abnormal behavior.* Boston: Allyn & Bacon. This book contains a series of fascinating case studies of abnormal behavior, including all of the DSM-III categories described in this chapter. The background and treatment of the abnormal behaviors are also included.

Mezzich, J. E., & Berganza, C. E. (Eds.). (1984). *Culture and psychopathology.* New York: Columbia University Press. This book includes chapters on many aspects of culture and psychopathology, such as the labeling of disorders in different cultures, ethnic groups within communities, and the role of sociocultural change.

THERAPIES

CHAPTER 14

Barbara and Tom married right after they graduated from college. She worked to help put him through graduate school. When their first child was born, she stayed home to be a full-time mother. After two more children and 15 years of being a chauffeur and cook for the family, she felt inadequate and unhappy. She decided to seek psychotherapy.

In the first several months of therapy, Barbara talked mainly about herself. As therapy continued, she increasingly talked about Tom, often with emotional intensity. After 6 months of therapy, Barbara concluded that, although she had created many of her problems, Tom had often made them worse; he treated her only as a housewife and mother, not as someone with a separate identity. Tom felt that Barbara's place was in the home. When she talked about working again or going back to school, he made derogatory comments.

As a result of therapy, Barbara developed enough self-confidence to finally confront Tom about his demeaning remarks and unwillingness to approve of her efforts to do something that would make her feel good about herself. After several months of working through her difficulties with her psychotherapist and trying to get Tom to be more flexible about her interests, Barbara asked Tom to move out. She got a job and eventually divorced Tom. She felt considerable pain and guilt over the decision, mainly because of her fear that it might have a negative impact on the children. Barbara hoped eventually to meet a man who would both love her *and* value her as an individual with her own identity (Sarason & Sarason, 1987).

Was the outcome of Barbara's therapy positive or negative? The answer obviously depends on your own values. Some people might insist that Barbara had an obligation to her husband and should not have confronted him. Others would vehemently disagree; they would say that therapy was positive because it allowed Barbara to understand herself and develop her own identity, even though it led to divorce.

Many people today seek therapy. Some, like Barbara, want to gain insight into themselves and improve their lives. Others may need help overcoming trauma, such as physical or sexual abuse in childhood. Others may find themselves in the immobilizing grip of fears, such as agoraphobia, or the delusions of schizophrenia, both of which were described in chapter 13. Whatever the reason that people seek therapy, there are many different therapeutic approaches to help them—at last count, more than 450 (Karasu, 1986). We will explore the most widely practiced therapies and give you a feel for what it would be like to go to a therapist with a particular orientation. However, before we study today's therapies, let's go back in time to discover how the mentally disabled were dealt with at different points in history.

FIGURE 14.1

Trephining. The technique of trephining involved chipping a hole in the skull through which an evil spirit, believed to be the source of the person's abnormal behavior, might escape. The fact that some people actually survived the operation is shown by this skull. The bone had had time to heal considerably before the individual died.

Historical Perspective

In primitive societies, abnormal behavior was thought to be caused by evil spirits residing within the afflicted person. *Trephining,* which involved chipping a hole in the skull, was one early method of letting the evil spirit escape (see figure 14.1). Greek physician Hippocrates believed that mental problems and abnormal behavior were the result of brain damage or an imbalance of body chemicals. In the fourth century B.C., Hippocrates prescribed rest, exercise, a bland diet, and abstinence from sex and alcohol as cures for depression.

Over time Hippocrates' ideas were lost. In the Middle Ages, theories of "possession" by evil spirits or the devil again became popular. People who simply were "different" or who suffered from neurological disorders, such as Tourette's syndrome or epilepsy, were thought to be possessed or witches. *Exorcism,* a religious rite that involved prayer, starvation, beatings, and various forms of torture, was used to cast out evil spirits. The notion behind exorcism was to make the disturbed people so physically uncomfortable that no devil would want to stay in their bodies. If that didn't work, the only "cure" left was to get rid of the body altogether. Between the fourteenth and seventeenth centuries, 200,000 to 500,000 people thought to be witches were either hanged or burned at the stake.

FIGURE 14.2

Pinel unchaining mentally disabled individuals. In this painting, Pinel is shown unchaining the inmates at La Bicetre Hospital. Pinel's efforts led to widespread reform and more humane treatment of mentally disabled individuals.

During the Renaissance, *asylums*, which means "sanctuaries," were built to house the mentally disabled. Disturbed people were placed in an asylum to protect them from the exploitation they experienced on the streets. However, the asylums were not much better; the mentally disabled often were chained to walls, caged, or fed sparingly.

Fortunately, Philippe Pinel (1745–1826), the head physician at a large asylum in Paris, initiated a significant change in the treatment of the mentally disabled, whom Pinel described as ordinary people who could not reason well because of their serious personal problems. He believed that treating the mentally disabled like animals not only was inhumane but also hindered their recovery. Pinel convinced the French government to unchain large numbers of patients, some of whom had not been outside of the asylum for 30 to 40 years (see figure 14.2). He replaced the dungeons with bright rooms and spent long hours talking with patients, listening to their problems, and giving advice.

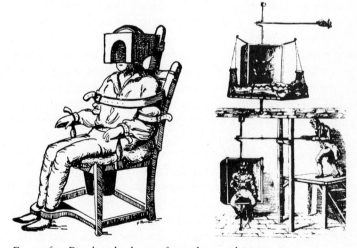

Even after Pinel and others reformed mental institutions, some rather strange techniques were invented to control the most difficult mentally disabled individuals. The tranquilizing chair (left) and circulating swing (right) were used to calm mentally disabled individuals at the beginning of the nineteenth century. Fortunately, their use was soon abandoned.

Although Pinel's efforts led to reform, it was slow. Even as late as the nineteenth century in the United States, the mentally disabled were kept alongside criminals in prisons. Dorothea Dix, a nurse who had taken a position at a prison in the middle of the nineteenth century, was instrumental in getting the mentally disabled separated from criminals. She embarked on a state-to-state campaign to upgrade prisons and persuaded officials to use better judgment in deciding which individuals should be placed in prisons. State governments began building large asylums for the mentally disabled because of Dix's efforts, although the conditions in the asylums often were no better than in the prisons.

In the twentieth century, significant advances in the ways in which we view and treat the mentally disabled have taken place. The importance of humane treatment, a concern for preventing mental disturbances, and improved methods of therapy characterize the modern view.

The Nature of Psychotherapy

Psychotherapy *is the process of working with individuals to reduce their problems and improve their adjustment.* Mental health professionals help individuals recognize, define, and overcome personal and interpersonal difficulties. Psychotherapists use a number of strategies to accomplish these goals: talking, interpreting, listening, rewarding, and modeling, for example. Psychotherapy *does not* include biomedical treatment, such as drugs or surgery.

The theories of personality discussed in chapter 12 are the basis for a number of important approaches to psychotherapy. The psychoanalytic theories of Freud, as well as those of his dissenters and revisionists, underlie the psychodynamic therapies. The humanistic theories of Rogers and Maslow provide an important foundation for the humanistic therapies. The term **insight therapy** *characterizes both the psychodynamic and humanistic therapies because their goal is to encourage insight into and awareness of one's self.* The behavioral and social learning theories of Skinner and Bandura, respectively, stimulated the development of the behavioral therapies. Other important approaches to therapy include cognitive therapies, couple and family therapy, group therapy, and the community psychology approach. We will consider each of these therapies, as well as biomedical treatment, later in the chapter.

Most contemporary therapists do not use one form of therapy exclusively with their clients. The majority of today's therapists are *eclectic*. That is, they use a variety of approaches to therapy. Often therapists tailor the therapeutic approach to their clients' needs. Even a therapist with a psychodynamic orientation might use humanistic approaches or a family therapist might use behavioral techniques, for example.

Psychotherapy is practiced by a variety of mental health professionals, including clinical psychologists, psychiatrists, and counselors. Remember from chapter 1 that psychiatrists have a medical degree and can prescribe drugs for mental disabilities. Clinical psychologists, by contrast, are trained in graduate programs of psychology and use psychotherapy rather than drugs to treat mental problems. Table 14.1 describes the main types of mental health professionals, their degrees, the years of education required for the degrees, and the nature of the training.

Just as there is a variety of mental health professionals, there is a variety of settings in which therapy takes place. During the first half of this century, psychotherapists primarily practiced in mental hospitals, where individuals remained for months and even years. During the past several decades, psychologists have recognized that psychotherapy is not just for those who are so mentally disabled that they cannot live in society. Today people who seek counseling and psychotherapy may go to a community health center, to the outpatient facility of a hospital, or to the private office of a mental health practitioner.

Psychotherapy can be expensive. Even though reduced fees, and occasionally free services, can be arranged in public hospitals for those who are poor, many of the people who are most in need of psychotherapy do not get it. Psychotherapists have been criticized for preferring to work with "young, attractive, verbal, intelligent, and successful" clients (called

REVIEW

Historical Background and the Nature of Psychotherapy

Many early treatments of mental disabilities were inhumane. Asylums were built during the Renaissance. Pinel's efforts led to extensive reform. Dix's efforts helped separate the mentally disabled from prisoners.

Psychotherapy is a process to reduce individuals' problems and improve their adjustment. The term *insight therapy* is used to describe both the psychodynamic and the humanistic therapies. Many therapists take an eclectic approach to therapy. Practitioners include clinical psychologists, counseling psychologists, psychiatrists, and social workers. Psychotherapy takes place in a greater variety of settings today than in the past. Lower socioeconomic status individuals are less likely to receive therapy than higher socioeconomic status individuals.

TABLE 14.1
Main Types of Mental Health Professionals

Professional type	Degree	Experience beyond bachelor's degree	Nature of training
Clinical psychologist and counseling psychologist	Ph.D.	5–7 years	Includes both clinical and research training. Involves a 1-year internship in a psychiatric hospital or mental health facility. Recently some universities have developed Psy.D. programs, which lead to a professional degree with stronger clinical than research emphasis. The Psy.D. training program takes about the same number of years as the clinical psychology Ph.D. program and also requires a 1-year internship.
Psychiatrist	M.D.	7–9 years	Four years of medical school, plus an internship and residency in psychiatry, are required. A psychiatry residency involves supervision in therapies, including psychotherapy and biomedical therapy.
Social worker	M.S.W. or Ph.D.	2–5 years	Graduate work in a school of social work that includes specialized clinical training in mental health facilities
Psychiatric nurse	R.N., M.A., or Ph.D.	0–5 years	Graduate work in school of nursing, with special emphasis on care of mentally disabled individuals in hospital settings and mental health facilities
Occupational therapist	B.S., M.A., or Ph.D.	0–5 years	Emphasis on occupational training, with focus on physically or psychologically handicapped individuals. Stresses getting individuals back into the mainstream of work.
Pastoral counselor	None to Ph.D. or D.D. (Doctor of Divinity)	0–5 years	Requires ministerial background and training in psychology. An internship in a mental health facility as a chaplain is recommended.
Counselor	M.A.	2 years	Graduate work in department of psychology or department of education, with specialized training in counseling techniques

Note: The above listing refers to the mental health professionals who go through formal training at recognized academic and medical institutions. The government commonly licenses these professionals and certifies their skills. Professional organizations regulate their activities.

YAVISes) rather than "quiet, ugly, old, institutionalized, and different" clients (called QUOIDs). Mental health professionals have become increasingly sensitive to such problems, but a recent national sample of clinical psychologists concluded that (a) the poorest and least-educated clients have poor prognoses for successful therapy and (b) psychologists are much less interested in treating this type of client than people from higher socioeconomic classes (Sutton & Kessler, 1986).

So far we have glimpsed the history and basic nature of psychotherapy. Contemporary psychotherapies include a number of diverse approaches to working with people to reduce their problems and improve their adjustment. We begin our survey of psychotherapies with the insight therapies, first describing psychodynamic therapies and then turning to the humanistic therapies.

Psychodynamic Therapies

The **psychodynamic therapies** *stress the importance of the unconscious mind, extensive interpretation by the therapist, and the role of infant and early childhood experiences.* Many psychodynamic approaches have grown out of Freud's psychoanalytic theory of personality. Today some therapists with a psychodynamic perspective show allegiance to Freud; others do not.

Freud's Psychoanalysis

Psychoanalysis *is Freud's therapeutic technique for analyzing an individual's unconscious thought.* Freud believed that clients' current problems could be traced to childhood experiences, many of which involved conflicts about sexuality. He also recognized that the early experiences were not readily available to the individual's conscious mind. Only through extensive questioning, probing, and analyzing was Freud able to put the pieces of the individual's personality together and help the individual become aware of how these early experiences were affecting present adult behavior. To reach the shadowy world of the unconscious, psychoanalytic therapists often use the following therapeutic techniques: free association, catharsis, interpretation, dream analysis, transference, and resistance.

In psychoanalysis the therapist uses **free association,** *the technique of encouraging individuals to say aloud whatever comes to mind, no matter how trivial or embarrassing.* When Freud detected a person resisting the spontaneous flow of thoughts, he probed further. He believed that the crux of the person's emotional problem probably lurked below this point of resistance. Freud thought that, when clients talked freely, their emotional feelings emerged. **Catharsis** *is the psychoanalytic term for clients' release of emotional tension when they relive an emotionally charged and conflicted experience.*

Interpretation plays an important role in psychoanalysis. As the therapist interprets free association and dreams, the client's statements and behavior are not taken at face value. To understand what is truly causing the client's conflicts, the therapist constantly searches for symbolic, hidden meanings in what the individual says and does. From time to time, the therapist suggests possible meanings of the client's statements and behavior.

Dream analysis *is the psychotherapeutic technique psychoanalysts use to interpret a client's dream.* Psychoanalysts believe that dreams contain information about the individual's unconscious thoughts and conflicts. Freud distinguished between the dream's manifest and latent content. **Manifest content** *is the psychoanalytic term for the conscious, remembered aspects of a dream.* **Latent content** *is the psychoanalytic term for the unconscious, unremembered, symbolic aspects of a dream.* A psychoanalyst interprets a dream by analyzing its manifest content for disguised unconscious wishes and needs, especially those that are sexual and aggressive. For some examples of the sexual symbols psychoanalysts use to interpret dreams, turn to figure 14.3. Freud cautioned against over-interpreting, however. As he once quipped, "Sometimes a cigar is just a cigar."

Freud also believed that transference was an inevitable and essential aspect of the analyst-client relationship. **Transference** *is the psychoanalytic term that describes when a client relates to an analyst in ways that reproduce or relive important relationships in the client's life.* A client might interact with an analyst as if the analyst were a parent or lover, for example. When transference dominates therapy, the client's comments may become directed toward the analyst's personal life. Transference is often difficult to overcome in psychotherapy. However, transference can be used therapeutically as a model of how clients relate to important people in their lives (Bauer & Mills, 1989; Luborksky & Crits-Christoph, 1990).

To encourage his patients to relax, Freud had them recline on the couch in his study while he sat in the chair on the left, out of their view.

Resistance *is the psychoanalytic term for a client's unconscious defense strategies that prevent the analyst from understanding the client's problems.* Resistance occurs because it is painful to bring conflicts into conscious awareness. By resisting therapy, individuals do not have to face their problems. Showing up late or missing sessions, arguing with the psychoanalyst, or faking free associations are examples of resistance. Some clients go on endlessly about a trivial matter to avoid facing their conflicts. A major goal of the analyst is to break through this resistance.

Contemporary Psychodynamic Therapies

Although the face of psychodynamic therapy has changed extensively since its inception almost a century ago, many contemporary psychodynamic therapists still probe clients' unconscious thoughts about their earliest childhood experiences to provide clues to their clients' current problems (Wallerstein, 1992). Many contemporary psychodynamic therapists also try to help clients gain insight into their emotionally laden, repressed conflicts (Strupp, 1992).

However, only a small percentage of contemporary psychodynamic therapists rigorously follow Freud's guidelines. Although many psychodynamic therapists still emphasize the importance of unconscious thought and early family experiences, they also accord more power to the conscious mind and current relationships in understanding a client's problems. Clients rarely lie on a couch or see their therapist several times a week. Now clients usually have weekly appointments and sit in a comfortable chair, facing their therapist.

Contemporary psychodynamic approaches emphasize the development of the self in social contexts (Erikson, 1968; Kohut, 1977; Mahler, 1979). In Heinz Kohut's view, early relationships with attachment figures, such as one's parents, are critical. As we

Sexual theme	Objects or activities in dreams that symbolize sexual themes
Male genitals, especially penis	Umbrellas, knives, poles, swords, airplanes, guns, serpents, neckties, tree trunks, hoses
Female genitals, especially vagina	Boxes, caves, pockets, pouches, the mouth, jewel cases, ovens, closets
Sexual intercourse	Climbing, swimming, flying, riding (a horse, an elevator, a roller coaster)
Parents	King, queen, emperor, empress
Siblings	Little animals

FIGURE 14.3

The psychoanalyst's interpretation of sexual symbolism in dreams.

develop, we do not relinquish these attachments; we continue to need them. Kohut's prescription for therapy involves getting the patient to identify and seek out appropriate relationships with others. He also wants patients to develop more realistic appraisals of relationships. Kohut believes that therapists need to interact with their clients in ways that are empathic and understanding. As we will see next, empathy and understanding are absolute cornerstones for humanistic therapists as they encourage their clients to further their sense of self.

Humanistic Therapies

In the **humanistic psychotherapies,** *clients are encouraged to understand themselves and to grow personally. In contrast to psychodynamic therapies, humanistic therapies emphasize conscious thoughts rather than unconscious thoughts, the present rather than the past, and growth and fulfillment rather than curing illness.* Two main forms of the humanistic psychotherapies are person-centered therapy and Gestalt therapy.

Person-Centered Therapy

Person-centered therapy *is a form of humanistic therapy developed by Carl Rogers (1961, 1980), in which the therapist provides a warm, supportive atmosphere to improve the client's self-concept and encourage the client to gain insight about problems.* Rogers' therapy was initially called client-centered therapy, but he rechristened it person-centered therapy to underscore his deep belief that

everyone has the ability to grow. The relationship between the therapist and the person is an important aspect of Rogers' therapy. The therapist must enter into an intensely personal relationship with the client, not as a physician diagnosing a disease but as one human being to another. Notice that Rogers referred to the "client" and then the "person" rather than the "patient."

Recall from chapter 12 that Rogers believed that each of us grows up in a world filled with *conditions of worth;* the positive regard we receive from others has strings attached. We usually do not receive love and praise unless we conform to the standards and demands of others. This causes us to be unhappy and have low self-esteem as adults; rarely do we feel that we measure up to such standards or feel that we are as good as others expect us to be.

To free the person from worry about the demands of society, the therapist creates a warm and caring environment. A Rogerian therapist never disapproves of what a client says or does. Recall from chapter 12 that Rogers believed this *unconditional positive regard* improved the person's self-esteem. The therapist's role is "nondirective"—that is, he or she does not try to lead the client to any particular revelation. The therapist is there to listen sympathetically to the client's problems and to encourage greater self-regard, independent self-appraisal, and decision making.

Rogers advocated other techniques in addition to using unconditional positive regard. **Genuineness** *is the Rogerian concept of the importance of the therapist being genuine and not hiding behind a facade. Therapists must let clients know their feelings.* **Accurate empathy** *is Rogers' term for the therapist's ability to identify with the client.* Rogers believed that therapists must sense what it is like to be the client at any moment in the client-therapist relationship. **Active listening** *is Rogers' term for the ability to listen to another person, with total attention to what that person says and means.* One way therapists improve active listening is by restating and supporting what the client has said and done.

Gestalt Therapy

Gestalt therapy *is a humanistic therapy, developed by Frederick (Fritz) Perls (1893-1970), in which the therapist questions and challenges clients, to help them become more aware of their feelings and face their problems.* Perls was trained in Europe as a Freudian psychoanalyst, but as his career developed his ideas became noticeably different from Freud's. Perls agreed with Freud that psychological problems originate in unresolved past conflicts

Fritz Perls was the founder of Gestalt therapy.

and that these conflicts need to be acknowledged and worked through. Also like Freud, Perls (1969) stressed that interpretation of dreams is an important aspect of therapy.

In other ways, however, Perls and Freud were miles apart. Perls believed that unresolved conflicts should be brought to bear on the here and now of the individual's life. The therapist *pushes* clients into deciding whether they will continue to allow the past to control their future or whether they will choose *right now* what they want to be in the future. To this end, Perls *confronted* individuals and encouraged them to actively control their lives and to be open about their feelings.

Gestalt therapists use a number of techniques to encourage individuals to be open about their feelings, to develop self-awareness, and to actively control their lives. The therapist sets examples, encourages congruence between verbal and nonverbal behavior, and uses role playing. To demonstrate an important point to a client, a Gestalt therapist might exaggerate a client's characteristic. To stimulate change, the therapist might openly confront the client.

Another technique of Gestalt therapy is role playing, either by the client, the therapist, or both. For example, if an individual is bothered by conflict with her mother, the therapist might play the role of the mother and reopen the quarrel. The therapist may encourage the individual to act out her hostile feelings toward her mother by yelling, swearing, or kicking the couch, for example. In this way, Gestalt therapists hope to help individuals better manage their feelings instead of letting their feelings control them.

As you probably noticed, a Gestalt therapist is much more directive than a person-centered therapist. By being more directive, the Gestalt therapist provides more interpretation and feedback. Nonetheless, both of these humanistic therapies encourage individuals to take responsibility for their feelings and actions, to truly be themselves, to understand themselves, to develop a sense of freedom, and to look at what they are doing with their lives.

Now that we have studied the insight therapies, we will turn our attention to therapies that take a very different approach to working with individuals to reduce their problems and improve their adjustment—the behavior therapies.

REVIEW

Psychodynamic and Humanistic Therapies

Psychodynamic therapies stress the importance of the unconscious mind, early family experiences, and extensive interpretation by the therapist. Psychoanalysis is Freud's technique for analyzing an individual's unconscious thought. Free association, catharsis, interpretation, dream analysis, transference, and resistance are techniques used in psychoanalytic therapy. Although psychodynamic therapy has changed, many contemporary psychodynamic therapists still probe the unconscious mind for early family experiences that might provide clues to the client's current problems. The development of the self in social contexts is an important theme in Kohut's contemporary approach.

In the humanistic therapies, clients are encouraged to understand themselves and to grow personally. The humanistic therapies emphasize conscious thoughts, the present, and growth and fulfillment. Person-centered therapy, developed by Rogers, emphasizes that the therapist should provide a warm and supportive atmosphere to improve the client's self-image and to encourage the client to gain insight into problems. The therapist replaces conditions of worth with unconditional positive regard and uses genuineness, accurate empathy, and active listening to raise the client's self-esteem. Gestalt therapy, developed by Fritz Perls, emphasizes that the therapist should question and challenge clients in order to help them become more aware of their feelings and face their problems. Gestalt therapy is more directive than is the nondirective approach of person-centered therapy.

Behavior Therapies

Behavior therapies *use principles of learning to reduce or eliminate maladaptive behavior*. Behavior therapies are based on the behavioral and social learning theories of learning and personality described in chapters 5 and 12. Behavior therapists do not search for unconscious conflicts, like psychodynamic therapists, or encourage individuals to develop accurate perceptions of their feelings and self, like humanistic therapists. Insight and self-awareness are not the keys to helping individuals develop more adaptive behavior patterns, say the behavior therapists. The insight therapies—psychodynamic and humanistic—treat maladaptive symptoms as signs of underlying, internal problems. Behavior therapists, however, assume that the overt maladaptive symptoms are the problem. Individuals can become aware of why they are depressed and still be depressed, say the behavior therapists. A behavior therapist tries to eliminate the depressed symptoms or behaviors themselves rather than trying to get individuals to gain insight or awareness of why they are depressed (Wilson & Agras, 1992).

The behavior therapies were initially based almost exclusively on the learning principles of classical and operant conditioning, but behavior therapies have become more diverse in recent years (Houts & Follette, 1992). As social learning theory grew in popularity and the cognitive approach became more prominent in psychology, behavior therapists increasingly included cognitive factors in their therapy. First we will discuss the classical and operant conditioning approaches; then we will turn to the cognitive behavior therapies.

Classical Conditioning Approaches

In chapter 5, you learned how some behaviors, especially fears, are acquired, or learned, through classical conditioning and that these behaviors can be unlearned, or extinguished. If an individual has learned to fear snakes or heights through classical conditioning, perhaps the individual could unlearn the fear. Two procedures based on classical conditioning that are used in behavior therapy are systematic desensitization and aversive conditioning.

Systematic Desensitization

Systematic desensitization *is a method of behavior therapy that treats anxiety by associating deep relaxation with successive visualizations of increasingly intense anxiety-producing situations; this technique is based on classical conditioning* (Wolpe, 1963). Consider the common fear of taking a test. Using systematic desensitization, a behavior therapist first asks the client which aspects of the fearful situation—in this case, taking a test—are the most and least frightening. Then, the behavior therapist arranges these circumstances in order from most to least frightening. An example of this type of desensitization hierarchy is shown in figure 14.4.

The next step is to teach individuals to relax. Clients are taught to recognize the presence of muscular contractions, or tensions, in various parts of their bodies and then how to contract and relax different muscles. Once individuals are relaxed, the therapist asks them to imagine the least fearful stimulus in the hierarchy. Subsequently the therapist moves up the list of items from least to most fearful while the clients remain relaxed. Eventually individuals are able to imagine the most fearful circumstance without being afraid—in our ex-

1. On the way to the university on the day of an examination
2. In the process of answering an examination paper
3. Before the unopened doors of the examination room
4. Awaiting the distribution of examination papers
5. The examination paper lies face down before her
6. The night before an examination
7. One day before an examination
8. Two days before an examination
9. Three days before an examination
10. Four days before an examination
11. Five days before an examination
12. A week before an examination
13. Two weeks before an examination
14. A month before an examination

FIGURE 14.4

A desensitization hierarchy from most to least fearful circumstances.

ample, on the way to the university the day of an exam. In this manner, individuals learn to relax while thinking about the exam instead of feeling anxious.

Researchers have found that systematic desensitization is often an effective treatment for a number of phobias, such as fear of giving a speech, fear of heights, fear of flying, fear of dogs, and fear of snakes. If you were afraid of snakes, for instance, the therapist might initially have you watch someone handle a snake. Then the therapist would ask you to engage in increasingly more fearful behaviors—you might first just go into the same room with the snake, next you would approach the snake, subsequently you would touch the snake, and eventually you would play with the snake (Bandura, Blanchard, & Ritter, 1969).

Aversive Conditioning

Aversive conditioning *is an approach to behavior therapy that involves repeated pairings of an undesirable behavior with aversive stimuli to decrease the behavior's rewards so the individual will stop doing it; this technique is based on classical conditioning.* Aversive conditioning is used to teach people to avoid such behaviors as smoking, over-eating, and drinking. Electric shocks, nausea-inducing substances, and verbal insults are some of the noxious stimuli used in aversive conditioning (Bernstein, 1991).

How would aversive conditioning be used to reduce a person's alcohol consumption? Every time a person drank an alcoholic beverage, he or she also would consume a mixture that induced nausea. In classical conditioning terminology, the alcoholic beverage is the conditioned stimulus and the nausea-inducing agent is the unconditioned stimulus. By repeatedly pairing alcohol with the nausea-inducing agent, alcohol becomes the conditioned stimulus that elicits nausea, the conditioned response. As a consequence, alcohol is no longer associated with something pleasant but, rather, something highly unpleasant.

Operant Conditioning Approaches

Andy is a college student who has difficulty studying. He complains that he always starts to fall sleep when he goes to his desk to study. He has decided to see a therapist about how he might improve his studying because his grades are deteriorating. The behavior therapist's first recommendation is to replace his desk lamp's 40-watt bulb with a brighter one. The second recommendation is to turn his desk away from his bed. The third recommendation is to do only schoolwork at his desk; he is not allowed to write a letter, read a magazine, or daydream while at the desk. If he wants to do any of these other things, he must leave his desk.

To help Andy improve his study habits, the behavior therapist first evaluated Andy's responses to the stimuli in his room. Then the therapist gave Andy direct and precise suggestions about what to do. The therapist did not spend time analyzing his unconscious conflicts or encouraging him to "get in touch with his feelings." Rather, the therapist wanted to change Andy's responses to the environmental stimuli that were causing the problem.

THE FAR SIDE   By GARY LARSON

"Now relax.... Just like last week, I'm going to hold the cape up for the count of 10. ... When you start getting angry, I'll put it down."

'LEAVE US ALONE! I AM A BEHAVIOR THERAPIST! I AM HELPING MY PATIENT OVERCOME A FEAR OF HEIGHTS!"

When we discussed operant conditioning in chapter 5, we examined how an individual's behavior is controlled by its consequences. We also discussed *behavior modification*, which is often used by behavior therapists. The idea behind behavior modification is to replace unacceptable, maladaptive responses with acceptable, adaptive ones. Consequences are set up to ensure that acceptable responses are reinforced and unacceptable ones are not (Foa, Rothbaum, & Kozak, 1989; Safran & Greenberg, 1989).

A **token economy** *is a behavior modification system in which behaviors are reinforced with tokens (such as poker chips) that can be exchanged later for desired rewards (such as candy, money, or going to a movie).* Token economies have been established in a number of classrooms, institutions for the mentally retarded, homes for delinquents, and mental hospitals with schizophrenics.

In some instances, behavior modification works; in others it does not. One person may become so wedded to the tokens that, when they are removed, the positive behavior associated with the tokens disappears. Yet another person might continue the positive behavior after the tokens are removed. Some critics object to behavior modification because they believe such extensive control of another person's behavior unethically infringes on the individual's rights. However, as with the college student who could not study, maladaptive responses can be turned into adaptive ones through behavior modification.

The behavior therapies you have just read about do not include cognitive processes in their effort to modify the behavior of individuals with problems. As we will see next, cognitive behavior therapy gives thought processes a more prominent role in helping individuals reduce their problems and improve their adjustment.

Cognitive Behavior Therapy

Cognitive behavior therapy *is an approach to behavior therapy that tries to help individuals behave more adaptively by modifying their thoughts.* Cognitive behavior therapy stems from both cognitive psychology, with its emphasis on the effect of thoughts on behavior, and behaviorism, with its emphasis on behavior-change techniques. Cognitive behavior therapists strive to change clients' misconceptions, strengthen their coping skills, increase their self-control, and encourage constructive self-reflection.

Self-efficacy—*the belief that one can master a situation and produce positive outcomes*—*is especially important in developing adaptive behavior, according to social learning theorist Albert Bandura.* Moreover, Bandura (1986, 1989) believes that self-efficacy is the key to successful therapy. At each step of the therapy process, people need to bolster their confidence by telling themselves, "I can do this," "I'm going to make it," "I'm getting very good," and so on. As people gain confidence and engage in more adaptive behavior, the successes become intrinsically rewarding. Before long individuals will persist with considerable effort in solving their problems because of the pleasurable outcomes that were set in motion by self-efficacy.

Self-instructional methods *are cognitive behavior techniques aimed at teaching individuals to modify their own behavior* (Meichenbaum, 1977). Using self-instructional methods, cognitive behavior therapists try to get clients to change what they say to themselves. The therapist gives the client examples of constructive statements, known as "reinforcing self-statements," that the client can repeat in order to take positive steps to handle stress or meet a goal. The therapist also encourages the client to practice the statements through role playing and strengthens the client's newly acquired skills through reinforcements. Following is a series of examples of constructive statements that can be used to cope with stressful situations (Meichenbaum, Turk, & Burstein, 1975):

Preparing for anxiety or stress

What do I have to do?
I'm going to map out a plan to deal with it.
I'll just think about what I have to do.
I won't worry; doesn't help anything.
I have a lot of different strategies to call on.

Confronting and handling the anxiety or stress

I can meet the challenge.
I'll keep on taking just one step at a time.
I can handle it. I'll just relax, breathe deeply, and use one of the strategies.
I won't think about the pain; I'll think about what I have to do.

Coping with feelings at critical moments

What is it I have to do?
I was supposed to expect the pain to increase; I just have to keep myself in control.
When the pain comes, I'll just pause and keep focusing on what I have to do.

Reinforcing self-statements

Good, I did it.
I handled it well.
I knew I could do it.
Wait until I tell other people how I did it!

The cognitive behavior therapists are not the only therapists to emphasize thought processes. As we will see next, the cognitive therapists also believe that changing the way people think about their problems is a key to helping people reduce their difficulties and adjust better to life's demands.

Cognitive Therapies

D., a 21-year-old single undergraduate student has delusions that he is evil. He perceives himself as a failure in school and a failure to his parents. He is preoccupied with negative thoughts, dwells on his problems, and exaggerates his faults. Such thinking is common among depressed individuals and suggests that cognitive therapy might be a viable approach to treating D.'s depression. The **cognitive therapies** *emphasize that an individual's cognitions, or thoughts, are the main source of abnormal behavior. Cognitive therapies attempt to change the individual's feelings and behaviors by changing cognitions.* Cognitive therapies differ from psychoanalytic therapies by focusing more on overt symptoms instead of deep-seated unconscious thoughts, by providing more structure to an individual's thoughts, and by being less concerned about the origin of the problem (Beck & Haaga, 1992). However, the cognitive therapies are less likely than the cognitive behavior therapies to use structured training sessions that require individuals to practice prescribed exercises. Instead, the cognitive therapies are more likely to adhere to a conversational format. Cognitive therapists also are less interested than the cognitive behavior therapists in manipulating the environment to increase adaptive behavior (Dryden & Trower, 1989).

In recent years, many therapists have focused more strongly on the cognitive perspective in their practices. Two of the most important cognitive therapies are Albert Ellis' rational emotive therapy and Aaron Beck's cognitive therapy.

Rational Emotive Therapy

Rational emotive therapy *is based on Albert Ellis' assertion that individuals become psychologically disturbed because of their beliefs, especially those that are irrational and self-defeating* (Ellis, 1962, 1974, 1992; Ellis & Yeager, 1989). Ellis says that we usually talk to ourselves when we experience stress; too often the statements are irrational, making them more harmful than helpful.

Ellis abbreviated the therapy process into the letters *A, B, C, D,* and *E.* Therapy usually starts at *C,* the individual's upsetting emotional Consequence; this might involve depression, anxiety, or a feeling of worthlessness. The individual

Topic	Approach			
	Psychodynamic	Humanistic	Behavior	Cognitive
Cause of problem	Client's problems are symptoms of deep-seated, unresolved unconscious conflicts.	Client is not functioning at an optimal level of development.	Client has learned maladaptive behavior patterns.	Client has developed inappropriate thoughts.
Therapy emphasis	Discover underlying unconscious conflicts and work with client to develop insight.	Develop awareness of inherent potential for growth.	Learn adaptive behavior patterns through changes in the environment or cognitive processes.	Change feelings and behaviors by changing cognitions.
Nature of therapy and techniques	Psychoanalysis, including free association, dream analysis, resistance, and transference; therapist interprets heavily.	Person-centered therapy, including unconditional positive regard, genuineness, accurate empathy, and active listening: Gestalt therapy including confrontation to encourage honest expression of feelings; self-appreciation emphasized.	Observation of behavior and its controlling conditions; specific advice given about what should be done; therapies based on classical conditioning, operant conditioning; therapies emphasizing self-efficacy and self-instruction.	Conversation with client designed to get him or her to change irrational and self-defeating beliefs.

FIGURE 14.5

Comparison of psychotherapies.

usually says that C was caused by A, the Activating Experience, such as a blowup in marital relations, the loss of a job, or failure in school. The therapist works with the individual to show that an intervening factor, B, the individual's Belief System, is actually responsible for why she moved from A to C. Then the therapist goes on to D, which stands for Disputation; at this point, the individual's irrational beliefs are disputed, or contested, by the therapist. Finally, E is reached, which stands for Effects, or outcomes, of the rational emotive therapy, as when individuals put their changed beliefs to work.

Beck's Cognitive Therapy

Aaron Beck (1976) developed a form of cognitive therapy to treat psychological dysfunctions, especially depression. He believes that the most effective therapy with depressed individuals involves four phases: (1) the depressed clients are shown how to identify self-labels—that is, how they view themselves, (2) they are taught to notice when they are thinking distorted or irrational thoughts, (3) they learn how to substitute appropriate

thoughts for inappropriate ones, and (4) they are given feedback and motivating comments from the therapist to stimulate their use of these techniques.

Results from a large-scale study by the National Institute of Mental Health (NIMH) support the belief that Beck's cognitive therapy is an effective treatment for depression (Mervis, 1986). Beck and his colleagues conducted this therapy with moderately to severely depressed individuals for 16 weeks at three sites. The symptoms of depression were eliminated completely in more than 50 percent of the individuals receiving Beck's cognitive therapy, as compared to only 29 percent in a comparison group (Clark & Beck, 1989).

A comparison group is an important feature in most psychological research. Without a comparison group, the researchers in the NIMH study would have had no way of knowing if the symptoms of depression in the experimental group would have disappeared even without therapy. That is, it is possible that, in any random sample of depressed individuals, more than 50 percent show a remission of symptoms over a 16-week period, regardless of whether or not they receive therapy. Because only 29 percent of the depressed individuals in the comparison group became free of their symptoms, the researchers had good reason to believe that the cognitive therapy—which produced more than a 50 percent remission of symptoms—was effective.

At this point, we have discussed four major approaches to therapy—psychodynamic, humanistic, behavior, and cognitive. Figure 14.5 will help you keep the approaches straight in your mind.

Group Therapies and Community Psychology

A major issue in therapy is how it can be structured to reach more people and at less cost. One way to address this problem is for therapists to see clients in a group rather than individually. A second way is through community psychology approaches.

Group Therapies

Nine people make their way into a room, each looking tentatively at the others. Although each person has met the therapist during a diagnostic interview, no one knows any of the other clients. Some of the people seem reluctant, others enthusiastic. All are willing to follow the therapist's recommendation that group therapy might help each of them learn to cope better with their problems. As they sit down and wait for the session to begin, one thinks, "Will they really understand me?" Another wonders, "Do the others have problems like mine?" Yet another thinks, "Can I stick my neck out with these people?"

Individual therapy is often expensive and time consuming. Freud believed that therapy is a long process and saw clients as often as three to five times a week for a number of years. Advocates of group therapy stress that individual therapy is limited because the client is seen outside the normal context of relationships, relationships that may hold the key to successful therapy. Many psychological problems develop in the context of interpersonal relationships—within one's family,

Since many psychological problems develop in the context of interpersonal relationships and group experiences—within one's family, marriage, or peer group—group therapy can be an important context for learning how to cope more effectively with these problems.

marriage, or peer group, for example. By seeing individuals in the context of these important groups, therapy may be more successful (Dies, 1992; MacKenzie, 1992; Rose, 1989).

Group therapy is diversified. Some therapists practice psychodynamic, humanistic, behavior, or cognitive therapy. Others use group approaches that are not based on the major psychotherapeutic perspectives. Six features make group therapy an attractive format (Yalom, 1975):

1. *Information.* Individuals receive information about their problems from either the group leader or other group members.
2. *Universality.* Many individuals develop the sense that they are the only persons who have such frightening and unacceptable impulses. In the group, individuals observe that others also feel anguish and suffering.
3. *Altruism.* Group members support one another with advice and sympathy and learn that they have something to offer others.
4. *Corrective recapitulation of the family group.* A therapy group often resembles a family (and, in family therapy, the group *is* a family), with the leaders representing parents and the other members siblings. In this "new" family, old wounds may be healed and new, more positive "family" ties made.
5. *Development of social skills.* Corrective feedback from peers may correct flaws in an individual's interpersonal skills. A self-centered individual may see that he is self-centered if five other group members inform him about his self-centeredness; in individual therapy, he may not believe the therapist.
6. *Interpersonal learning.* The group can serve as a training ground for practicing new behaviors and relationships. For example, a hostile woman may learn that she can get along better with others by not behaving so aggressively.

Family and Couple Therapy

"A friend loves you for your intelligence, a mistress for your charm, but your family's love is unreasoning; you were born into it and are of its flesh and blood. Nevertheless, it can irritate you more than any group of people in the world," commented French biographer André Maurois. His statement suggests that the family may be the source of an individual's problems. **Family therapy** *is group therapy with family members.* **Couple therapy** *is group therapy with married or unmarried couples whose major problem is their relationship.* These approaches stress that, although one person may have some abnormal symptoms, the symptoms are a function of family or couple relationships (Gurman & Kniskern, 1992). Psychodynamic, humanistic, or behavior therapies may be used in family or couple therapy, but the main form of family therapy is family systems therapy.

Family systems therapy *is a form of therapy based on the assumption that psychological adjustment is related to patterns of interaction within the family unit.* Families who do not function well foster abnormal behavior on the part of one or more of their members (Haley, 1976; Minuchin, 1985; Satir, 1964; Searight & Merkel, 1991; Snyder, 1989). Four of the most widely used family systems therapy techniques follow:

1. *Validation.* The therapist expresses an understanding and acceptance of each family member's feelings and beliefs and, thus, validates the person. When the therapist talks with each family member, she finds something positive to say.
2. *Reframing.* The therapist teaches families to reframe problems; problems are cast as a family problem, not an individual's problem. For example, a delinquent adolescent boy's problems are reframed in terms of how each family member contributed to the situation. The father's lack of attention to his son and marital conflict may be involved.
3. *Structural change.* The family systems therapist tries to *restructure* the coalitions in a family. In a mother-son coalition, the therapist might suggest that the father take a stronger disciplinarian role to relieve the mother of some of the burden. Restructuring might be as simple as suggesting that parents explore satisfying ways to be together; the therapist may recommend that, once a week, the parents go out for a quiet dinner together, for example.
4. *Detriangulation.* In some families, one member is the scapegoat for two other members who are in conflict but pretend not to be. For example, in the triangle of two parents and one child, the parents may insist that their marriage is fine but find themselves in subtle conflict over how to handle the child. The therapist tries to disentangle, or *detriangulate*, this situation by shifting attention away from the child and toward the conflict between the parents.

Although many of the principles of family therapy can be applied to most families, increasingly psychologists agree that the unique sociohistorical, cultural circumstances experienced by different ethnic minority groups require certain considerations. To read about some of the considerations regarding family therapy in Black families, turn to Sociocultural Worlds 14.1.

Couples therapy proceeds in much the same way as family therapy. Conflict in marriages and in relationships between unmarried individuals frequently involves poor com-

Family systems therapy has become increasingly popular in recent years. In family systems therapy, the assumption is that psychological adjustment is related to patterns of interaction within the family unit.

munication. In some instances, communication has broken down entirely. The therapist tries to improve the communication between the partners, in some cases focusing on the roles partners play: one may be "strong" and the other "weak" or one may be "responsible" and the other "spoiled," for example. Couples therapy addresses diverse problems, such as jealousy, sexual messages, delayed childbearing, infidelity, gender roles, two-career families, divorce, and remarriage (Jacobson, Holtzworth-Munroe, & Schmaling, 1989).

Now we will turn our attention to other forms of group therapy—personal growth and self-help groups.

Personal Growth and Self-help Groups

A number of group therapies in recent years have focused on people whose lives are lacking in intimacy, intensity, and accomplishment. **Personal growth groups** *have their roots in the humanistic therapies; they emphasize personal growth and increased openness and honesty in interpersonal relations.*

An **encounter group** *is a personal growth group designed to promote self-understanding through candid group interaction.* For example, one member of an assembled group thinks he is better than everyone else. After several minutes of listening to the guy's insufferable bragging, one group member says, "Look, jerk, nobody here likes you; I would like to sell you for what you think you are worth and buy you for what you are actually worth!" Other members of the group might also criticize the braggart. Outside of an encounter group, most people probably would not confront someone about bragging; in an encounter group, they may feel free to express their true feelings about each other.

Encounter groups improve the psychological adjustment of some individuals, but not others. For example, in one study, the majority of college students who were members of an

Black Families in Therapy

Family therapists who work with Black families are often called on to fulfill various roles, such as educator, director, advocate, problem solver, and role model (Grevious, 1985). As a therapist takes on these roles, he or she must recognize that the clients are members of a community, as well as individuals or members of families (Aponte, 1979). The following case study illustrates some of the multiple roles and the community orientation that a therapist must be aware of in working with Black families (Grevious, 1985).

Mrs. B. entered family therapy because her 11-year-old son Todd was disruptive in school and falling behind in his work. She complained of feeling overwhelmed and not being able to cope with the situation. The therapist conducted a home visit and observed that the family lived in a run-down building in a poor neighborhood. Even so, the therapist found that Mrs. B.'s apartment was immaculate, work and sleep space had been set aside for Todd, and it was obvious from the well-worn Bible on the coffee table and the religious paintings and calendars on the walls that Mrs. B. had strong religious convictions. The therapist discovered that Mrs. B.'s strong-willed mother recently had moved into the apartment after an incapacitating leg operation. The grandmother's diabetes created additional stress in the home. Despite her illness, the grandmother tried to exercise considerable control over Mrs. B. and Todd, causing a power struggle in the family. The therapist also learned that Mrs. B. had recently stopped attending church. After the therapist encouraged her to attend church again, Mrs. B.'s spirits improved considerably. In addition, the grandmother joined a senior citizens program, which transported her to the center three times a week and to church two Sundays a month. These increased community activities for the grandmother had a positive impact on the family.

Family therapists who see Black clients also believe that it is important to provide concrete advice or assistance (Foley, 1975). If the problem is a parent-child relationship, for example, a family therapist might recommend that the parents participate in a parent training program, rather than conduct insight therapy. Also, therapists may occasionally need to educate Black families about social service programs and the difficulties they might encounter in gaining access to those programs (Pinderhughes, 1982).

A family therapist who works with Black families also needs to emphasize their strengths, such as pride in being Black, the extended family, and religion, as well as take into consideration their vulnerabilities, such as the impact of racism, discrimination, and victimization (Boyd-Franklin, 1989). More about therapy with Black individuals and other ethnic minorities appears later in the chapter.

---

encounter group felt better about themselves and got along better with others than did their counterparts, who were not involved in an encounter group (Lieberman, Yalom, & Miles, 1973). However, 8 percent of the participants in the encounter group felt that the experience was harmful. For the most part, they blamed the group leader for intensifying their problems; they said the leader's remarks were so personally devastating that they could not handle them.

Although encounter groups are not as popular today as they were in the 1970s, they were the forerunners of today's self-help groups. **Self-help groups** *are voluntary organizations of individuals who get together on a regular basis to discuss topics of common interest. The group leader and members give support to help individuals with their problems. Self-help groups are so-called because they are conducted without a professional therapist.* Self-help groups play an important role in our nation's mental health—approximately 6.25 million people participate in such groups each year (Jacobs & Goodman, 1989).

In addition to reaching so many people in need of help, these groups are important because they use community resources and are relatively inexpensive. They also serve people who are less likely to receive help otherwise, such as less-educated middle-aged adults, homemakers, and blue-collar workers (Knight & others, 1980).

Founded in 1930 by a reformed alcoholic, Alcoholics Anonymous (AA) is one of the best-known self-help groups. Mental health professionals often recommend AA for their alcoholic clients. Weight Watchers and TOPS (Take Off Pounds Sensibly) are also self-help groups. There are myriad self-help groups, such as Parents Without Partners, lesbian and gay support groups, cocaine abuse support groups, and child abuse support groups. Table 14.2 provides a sampling of the wide variety of self-groups available in one city.

You may be wondering how a group of people with the same problem can come together and do one another any good. You might be asking yourself why they don't just help themselves

TABLE 14.2
A Potpourri of Self-help Groups

A recent listing of self-help groups in a Tulsa, Oklahoma, Sunday newspaper included more than 200 entries. Among the wide variety listed were the following self-help groups.

Social concerns

Tulsa Society for Depressed Women
Love Without Shame
Gamblers Anonymous
Phobia Society of Tulsa
Relocated Corporate Wives
Rebuilders: For Divorcés
Sex Addicts: Anonymous
Rap Group and Caring and Coping Partners of Vietnam Veterans

Eating/weight disorders

Movers and Shapers
Overeaters Anonymous
TOPS (Take Off Pounds Sensibly)

Alcohol/substance abuse

Students Against Drugs and Alcohol
Alcoholics Victorious
How to Cope with a Dependent Person
Adult Children of Alcoholic Parents
Alcoholics Anonymous
Teen Awareness Group
Cocaine Anonymous

Parenting

Single Working Mothers
Tulsa Adoptive Parents
Parents Without Partners
After Baby Comes
Happier Home Parents
Stepparents Group
Sooner Parents of Twins

Health

Resolve of Tulsa (an infertility group)
Mended Hearts (for those who have had open-heart surgery)
Group for Alzheimer's Caregivers
AIDS Support Program
ENCORE (for breast cancer patients)
SHHH (Self-Help for the Hard of Hearing)
LITHIUM Group (for those with bipolar disorder)
Families of Children with Diabetes
Indian Health Care Resource Center
Families of Nursing Home Residents

and eliminate the need for the group. In fact, seeing that others share the same burden makes people feel less isolated, less like freaks of nature; it increases a psychological sense of community or belonging; and it can give hope where there might have been none before (Levine & Perkins, 1987).

Self-help groups also provide an ideology, or set of beliefs, that members can use as a guide. These groups provide members with a sympathetic audience for confession, sharing, and emotional release. The social support, role modeling, and sharing of concrete strategies for solving problems that unfold in self-help groups add to their effectiveness. For instance, a woman who has been raped may not believe a male counselor who tells her that, with time, she will be able to put back together the pieces of her life and work through much of the psychological pain. However, the same message from another rape survivor—someone who has had to work through the same feelings of rage, fear, and violation—may be more believable.

Community Psychology

The community psychology movement was born in the early 1960s, when it became apparent to mental health practitioners, including clinical psychologists, that our mental health care system was woefully inadequate. The system was not reaching the poor, and many of those who could afford help often did not seek therapy because of its social stigma. As a result, deinstitutionalization became a major thrust of the community psychology movement. **Deinstitutionalization** *is the movement to transfer the treatment of mental disabilities from inpatient mental institutions to community-based facilities that stress outpatient care.* New drugs for treating the severely mentally disabled, such as schizophrenics, meant that large numbers of people could be released from mental institutions and treated in community-based centers.

In 1963 Congress passed the Community Mental Health Center Act, which provided funds for establishing one facility for every 50,000 individuals in the nation. The centers were designed to meet two basic goals—to provide community-based mental health services and to commit resources that help *prevent* disorders as well as treat them. Outpatient care is one of the important services that community mental health centers provide. Individuals can attend therapy sessions at a center and still keep their jobs and live with their families. Another important innovation that grew out of the community psychology movement is called outreach services. Rather than expecting people with mental or emotional problems to make an appointment at a mental health center, mental health care workers in this program go to community locations, such as storefront clinics, where they are accessible and needed most. Community-based mental health services stay open 24 hours a day, often handling such emergencies as suicide attempts and drug overdoses.

Coinciding with the increased use of drug therapy in mental institutions was the transfer of many mental patients back to the community. It was believed that these individuals could be given medication to keep them stabilized until they could find continuing care. However, many residents of mental health institutions have no families or homes to go to and community mental health facilities are not adequately equipped to deal with the severe cases. Many individuals who are discharged from state mental hospitals join the ranks of "the homeless." Of course, though, not all homeless people are former mental patients. Controversy continues about whether individuals should be discharged so readily from state mental institutions.

The philosophy of community-based services also includes training teachers, ministers, family physicians, and others who directly interact with community members to offer lay counseling and various workshops, such as assertive training or coping with stress. This broadens mental health resources, allowing more people to receive help in settings where they are more likely to be comfortable than in traditional mental health centers (Orford, 1992).

Borrowing from the field of public health, community psychology adopted the belief that the best way to treat a mental disorder is to prevent it from happening in the first place. Prevention takes one of three courses: primary prevention, secondary prevention, and tertiary prevention, each of which we will discuss.

Primary prevention *is a community psychology concept, borrowed from the public health field, that describes efforts to reduce the number of new cases of mental disorders.* By definition, primary prevention programs are offered to populations completely free of a disorder. Like immunization in public health, primary prevention programs try to identify and "inoculate" people against the development of mental disorders. Primary prevention programs tend to follow one of three strategies: community-wide, milestone, or high-risk (Bloom, 1985).

In the community-wide approach, programs are available to everyone in a given geographic area. Washington, DC's program "Beautiful Babies Right from the Start," for example, provides free prenatal care and well-baby care for the baby's first 18 months to women and their infants in the poorest communities. This program attempts to prevent pregnant women from engaging in harmful behaviors, such as substance abuse or poor nutrition, that put infants at risk for premature birth, low birthweight, and such disorders as hyperactivity, impaired memory, and disorganized thinking. In the milestone approach, the target group is every person in a population who reaches a certain hurdle, or critical life transition, such as being fired, becoming a parent for the first time, or going away to college. Counseling for fired employees and orientation programs for college students are two examples of milestone programs. In a high-risk program, the focus is on specific groups of people whose chances of developing mental disorders are extremely high, such as children of alcoholics, children with chronic illnesses, and ethnic minority children.

Secondary prevention *is a community psychology concept in which screening for early detection of problems, as well as early intervention, is carried out.* A major goal of secondary prevention programs is to reach large numbers of potential clients. These programs often use *paraprofessionals*, volunteers without formal mental health training who work closely with psychologists, to meet this goal. One approach to secondary prevention involves teaching coping skills to people under high levels of stress, the bereaved, the newly employed, and prospective parents. Another type involves screening groups of individuals, such as school children, to find those who show early signs of problems and provide them with mental health services.

Tertiary prevention *is a community psychology concept that describes efforts to reduce the long-term consequences of mental health disorders that were not prevented or arrested early in the course of the disorders.* Tertiary prevention programs are geared toward people who once required long-term care or hospitalization and provide services that can reduce the probability they will become so debilitated again. Halfway houses (community residences for individuals who no longer require institutionalization but who still need some support in readjusting to the community) are an example of tertiary prevention. Such programs seek to increase individuals' coping skills by reducing their social isolation, by increasing their social skills, and by developing educational strategies tailored to their needs.

Community psychology has successfully reached large numbers of mentally and emotionally distressed people, not only through prevention but also through intervention. Unfortunately, strong cutbacks in federal funding of community mental health centers in the 1980s have diminished their effectiveness and stalled their expansion.

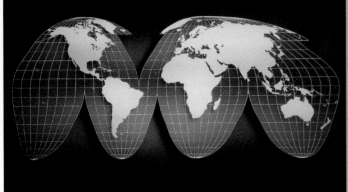

Development of Community Psychology Approaches for Hispanic Americans

According to psychologists Amado Padilla, Rene Ruiz, and Rodolfo Alvarez (1975, 1989), a wide range of innovative programs are needed to improve the lives of Hispanic Americans and to help them cope with problems. These programs include remedial education, vocational guidance and retraining, drug abuse and crime prevention programs, and college counseling.

The researchers recommend that community mental health centers, for example, serve as a hub for many activities. In addition to providing treatment for a wide range of human problems, the facilities could be used for youth activities, such as sports and dances, and for cultural events, such as Spanish-language films and fiestas. Most mental health experts believe that it makes sense to involve community members in a neighborhood center that ostensibly is there to serve their needs. Also, people from the community should be part of the center's administration, and the advertising media, in both Spanish and English, can be used to inform the community about the facility, its services, and its activities.

For example, one community mental health facility in east Los Angeles was designed to attract local Mexican Americans (Karno & Morales, 1971). The facility was located in the heart of

One community mental health facility in east Los Angeles was located in the heart of the community, convenient to transportation, comfortable, and inviting. The facility was successful in attracting local Mexican Americans to come in and discuss their problems with professionals and paraprofessionals.

the community, convenient to transportation, comfortable, and inviting. In 2½ years, the director of the facility hired 22 full-time professional, paraprofessional, and clerical personnel. Of these 22, 15 were fluent in Spanish. Ten were natives and/or residents of the area. Twelve were of Mexican American descent, one was Cuban, and another was Peruvian. The treatment program was based on a philosophy of prevention, and it helped people gain access to a wide variety of community mental health agencies. As a backup, the center offered short-term crisis-oriented treatment that included individual, family, and drug therapy. The center seemed to fulfill the objective of providing appropriate treatment for Mexican Americans. More such centers are badly needed in areas in which Hispanic Americans live.

El Centro de la Causa, on Chicago's west side, is another example of a successful community mental health center (Schensul, 1974). A group of young Chicanos started this youth center by organizing a community fiesta that raised enough money to cover the original operating budget of $1800. Within months the group had convinced a church organization to provide $40,000 for staff and services. Within 3 years, the operating budget was more than $400,000. Funding was used to train community residents as paraprofessionals in mental health, reading improvement programs, English classes, recreation and youth activities, and drug abuse programs.

Because such programs as outreach services may be the only mental health care available to those who are poor or from ethnic minority backgrounds, community psychology approaches are especially important. Remember from our earlier discussion that psychotherapy has been more available to the wealthy. An explicit value of community psychology is

that it assists people who are disenfranchised from society to lead happier, more productive lives. **Empowerment** *is a concept that refers to the importance of assisting individuals to develop skills they need to control their own lives.* To read about how community psychology is involved in empowering Hispanic Americans, turn to Sociocultural Worlds 14.2.

Behavior Therapies, Cognitive Therapies, Group Therapies, and Community Psychology

Behavior therapies use principles of learning to reduce or eliminate maladaptive behavior. Behavior therapies are based on behavioral and social learning theories of learning and personality. Behavior therapists try to eliminate symptoms or behaviors rather than trying to get individuals to gain insight into their problems. Two classical conditioning procedures used in behavior therapy are systematic desensitization and aversive conditioning. Operant conditioning approaches emphasize modifying an individual's maladaptive responses to the environment. The idea behind behavior modification is to replace unacceptable, maladaptive responses with acceptable, adaptive ones. Consequences are set up to ensure that acceptable responses are reinforced; unacceptable ones are not. A token economy is an example of behavior modification. Cognitive behavior therapy is behavior therapy that tries to help individuals behave more adaptively by modifying their thoughts. Cognitive behavior therapists strive to change misconceptions, strengthen coping skills, increase self-control, and encourage constructive self-talk.

Cognitive therapies emphasize that an individual's thoughts, or cognitions, are the main source of abnormal behavior. Cognitive therapies attempt to change the individual's feelings and behaviors by changing cognitions. Rational emotive therapy is a cognitive therapy developed by Albert Ellis. It is based on the idea that individuals become psychologically disabled because of their beliefs, especially those that are irrational and self-defeating; therapy is designed to change these beliefs. Aaron Beck developed a form of cognitive therapy to treat psychological disorders, especially depression. The therapy involves identifying self-labels, detecting irrational thoughts, substituting appropriate for inappropriate thoughts, and receiving feedback from the therapist to stimulate these cognitive changes.

Group therapies emphasize that social relationships hold the key to successful therapy; therefore, therapy involving group interactions may be more beneficial than individual therapy. Family therapy and couple therapy, as well as personal growth groups, are common. Community psychology was born in the early 1960s. Deinstitutionalization, in which the treatment of mental disorders is transferred from inpatient mental institutions to outpatient community mental health facilities, has been especially important in community psychology. As a result, mental health services are more accessible to individuals from low-income and ethnic minority backgrounds. Three community psychology approaches are primary prevention, secondary prevention, and tertiary prevention. Empowerment—providing assistance so that individuals can gain more control over their lives—is a key concept in community psychology.

Is Psychotherapy Effective?

Do individuals who go through therapy get better? Are some approaches more effective than others, or is the situation similar to that of the Dodo in *Alice's Adventures in Wonderland?* Dodo was asked to judge the winner of a race; he decided, "Everybody has won and all must have prizes." How would we evaluate the effectiveness of psychotherapy? Would we take the client's word, or the therapist's word? What would be our criteria for effectiveness? Would it be "feeling good," "adaptive behavior," "improved interpersonal relationships," "autonomous decision making," or "more positive self-concept," for example? During the past several decades, an extensive amount of thought and research has addressed these questions.

Research on the Effectiveness of Psychotherapy

Almost 4 decades ago, Hans Eysenck (1952) shocked the pundits in the field of psychotherapy by concluding that treatment is ineffective. Eysenck analyzed 24 studies of psychotherapy and found that approximately two-thirds of the individuals with neurotic symptoms improved. That sounds impressive so far; however, Eysenck also found that a similar percentage of neurotic individuals on waiting lists to see a psychotherapist also showed marked improvement, even though they were not given any psychotherapy at all.

Eysenck's pronouncement prompted a flurry of research on psychotherapy's effectiveness. Hundreds of studies on the outcome of psychotherapy have now been conducted. One strategy for analyzing these diverse studies is called **meta-analysis,** *in which a researcher statistically combines the results of many different studies.* In one meta-analysis of psychotherapy research, 475 studies were statistically combined (Smith, Glass, & Miller, 1980). Only those studies in which a therapy group had been compared with an untreated control group were compared. The results were much kinder to psychotherapy effectiveness than Eysenck's earlier results: on 88 percent of the measures, individuals who received therapy improved more than those who did not. This meta-analysis documents that psychotherapy is effective in general, but it does not inform us about the specific ways in which different therapies are effective.

People who are thinking about seeing a psychotherapist not only want to know whether psychotherapy in general is effective, but they would especially like to know which form of psychotherapy is effective for their particular problem. In the meta-analysis conducted by Mary Lee Smith and her colleagues (1980), comparisons of different types of psychotherapy were made. For example, behavior therapies were compared with insight therapies (psychodynamic, humanistic). Both the behavior and insight therapies were superior to no treatment at all, but they did not differ from each other in effectiveness. Although no particular therapy was the best in the study by Smith and her colleagues, some therapies do seem to be more effective than others in treating some disorders. For instance, the behavior therapies have been most successful in treating specific behavioral problems, such as phobias and sexual dysfunctions (Bowers & Clum, 1988), and the cognitive therapies have been most successful in treating depression (Butler & others, 1991; Clark & Beck, 1989). Also, many therapies have their maximum benefit early in treatment, with less improvement occurring as the individual remains in therapy (Karasu, 1986).

Informed consumers also need to be aware of the evidence that, in certain cases, psychotherapy can actually be harmful. For example, people who have a low tolerance for anxiety, low motivation, and strong signs of psychological deterioration may worsen as therapy progresses. The therapist's characteristics also have been related to a worsening of the client's status as therapy progresses. Therapists who are aggressive, who try to get clients to disclose personal information too quickly, and who are impatient with the process of change may exacerbate their clients' problems (Suinn, 1984). Therapist bias can also be harmful, when the therapist does not understand ethnic, religious, gender, or other cultural differences yet he or she pressures such clients to conform to White, middle-class norms. Finally, therapists who engage in sex with a client harm the client; such behavior is unethical.

Although incompetent and unethical therapists do exist, there are many competent therapists who successfully help their clients. Like jazz musicians, psychotherapists must be capable of improvising, gracefully. As psychologist Jerome Frank put it, "Successful therapy is not just a scientific process, it is a healing art as well."

Common Themes and Specificity in Psychotherapy

After carefully studying the nature of psychotherapy for more than 25 years, Jerome Frank (1982) concluded that effective psychotherapies have the common elements of expectations, mastery, and emotional arousal. By inspiring an expectation of help, a therapist motivates a client to continue coming to therapy. These expectations are powerful morale builders and symptom relievers. The therapist also increases the client's sense of mastery and competence. For example, clients begin to feel that they can cope effectively with their world. Therapy also arouses the individual's emotions, essential to motivating behavioral change, according to Frank.

The therapeutic relationship is another important ingredient in successful psychotherapy (Strupp, 1989). A relationship in which the client has confidence and trust in the therapist is essential to effective psychotherapy. One recent study revealed that the most common ingredient in the success of different psychotherapies is the therapist's supportiveness of the client (Wallerstein, 1989). The client and therapist engage in a "healing ritual," which requires the active participation of both the client and the therapist. As part of this ritual, the client gains hope and becomes less alienated (Beitman, Goldfried, & Norcross, 1989).

Although psychotherapies have common themes, some therapists worry about carrying this commonality too far. Specificity in psychotherapy still needs careful attention—therapists need to understand "*what* treatment is most effective for *this* individual with *that* specific problem, and under *which* set of circumstances" (Paul, 1967). At this time, however, it is unclear which approach works best in which situation with which therapist. Some therapists are better trained than others, some are more sensitive to a person's feelings, some are more introverted, and some are more conservative. Because of the myriad ways human beings differ from one another, the ideal "fit" of therapist and client is difficult to pinpoint scientifically.

Culture and Ethnicity

Only in the past 2 decades have psychologists become sensitive to the concerns of culture and ethnicity in psychotherapy. For too long, psychotherapists were concerned almost exclusively with helping middle- and upper-class individuals cope with their problems, while ignoring the needs of people who were poor or from ethnic minority backgrounds (Atkinson, Morten, & Sue, 1989; Comas-Díaz, 1992; Fabrega, 1989; Gibbs & Huang, 1989; Jones, 1989).

a.

b.   c.

d.

How might therapy proceed differently in the following contexts: (a) an ethnic minority client with a White, middle-class therapist, (b) a White male client from impoverished circumstances in rural Appalachia, (c) an Asian American client who is a recent immigrant to the United States, and (d) a Black female client with a Black female therapist?

Orientation of Ethnic Minority and Low-Income Individuals to Therapy

As part of their history of being ignored by psychotherapists, ethnic minority individuals have developed a preference for discussing problems with parents, friends, and relatives rather than mental health professionals. Another reason they turn to family and friends when they are in emotional or mental distress is that there are so few ethnic minority psychotherapists (Boyd-Franklin, 1989; Hess & Street, 1991; Russo & others, 1981). For example, one study found that Black college students are more likely to use their college's mental health facilities if a Black clinician or counselor is available than if only White counselors are available (Thompson & Cimbolic, 1978). However, therapy can be effective when the therapist and client are from different cultural backgrounds if the therapist has excellent clinical skills and is culturally sensitive (Gim, Atkinson, & Kim, 1991; Sue, 1990; Wade & Bernstein, 1991). Researchers have also found that Asian Americans, African Americans, Hispanic Americans, and Native Americans terminate psychotherapy after an initial session at a much higher rate than do Anglo Americans (Sue, Allen, & Conaway, 1978). The social stigma of being a "mental patient," the fear of hospitalization, the conflict between their own belief system and the beliefs of modern mental health practitioners, and the availability of an alternate healer are additional reasons ethnic minority individuals terminate therapy early (Lefley, 1984).

Psychotherapy involves interpersonal interaction and communication. Verbal and nonverbal messages need to be accurately sent and received. Very effective therapy can take place when the client and therapist are from different sociocultural backgrounds. However, when the psychotherapist and client come from different cultural backgrounds, barriers to communication can develop, which can lead to misunderstandings that destroy rapport and undermine the effectiveness of psychotherapy (Atkinson, Morten, & Sue, 1989). Among the barriers that can impede psychotherapy's effectiveness with individuals from ethnic minority groups are (1) language differences, (2) class-bound values, and (3) culture-bound values.

Language Differences. A psychotherapist's reliance on verbal interaction to establish rapport with a client presupposes that the psychotherapist and the client can understand each other. However, many psychotherapists fail to recognize that there may be a language barrier between them and ethnic minority individuals that restricts the development of rapport. Also, many educationally and economically impoverished clients may not have the verbal skills required to benefit from the psychotherapist's advice, interpretation, and counseling, especially if the psychotherapist communicates complex concepts to the client. Psychotherapists may also misinterpret the body language—gestures and postures, for example—of individuals from ethnic minority groups. For example, Black clients often avoid eye contact in conversation, whereas White clients usually maintain eye contact. A psychotherapist may inappropriately interpret a Black client's lack of eye contact as inattentiveness, lack of interest, or anger.

Class-Bound Values. One of the most frequently encountered issues involving middle-class psychotherapists and lower-class clients is the willingness to make and keep psychotherapy appointments. Lower-class clients may be concerned with "survival" or "making it through the day." Appointments made for 2 weeks in the future or 50-minute sessions may not be appropriate for the needs of a lower-class client who requires immediate help. One clinician described poor Appalachian Whites as refusing to live by the clock and not only refusing to adhere to the values of promptness, planning, and protocol but also suspecting people who do adhere to these values (Vontress, 1973). The clients' socioeconomic status also affects the kind of treatment they receive. For example, one study revealed that students from upper socioeconomic backgrounds are given more exploratory counseling interviews than students from lower socioeconomic backgrounds (Ryan & Gaier, 1968).

Culture-Bound Values. Psychotherapists often impose their own values on clients from a different cultural background. Referring to clients from other cultures, especially those from ethnic minority groups, as "culturally deprived" exemplifies this imposition. Cultural misunderstandings can lead to difficulties in communication, expectations, the quality of care given, and the client's motivation to continue psychotherapy (Cayleff, 1986). For instance, many psychotherapists believe that self-disclosure is an important condition for effective psychotherapy. However, clients are less likely to disclose private, sensitive information about themselves to someone who has a different cultural background. Also, self-disclosure may be contrary to the basic cultural values of individuals from some cultures. For example, Chinese Americans are taught at an early age to refrain from emotional expression; they may find psychotherapists' demands to disclose personal information as threatening (Sue & Sue, 1972). Similar conflicts have been reported for Chicanos (Cross & Maldonado, 1971) and Native Americans (Trimble, 1976).

Further Considerations in the Roles of Culture and Ethnicity in Therapy

Another obstacle in psychotherapy is that not all cultures share the Western mainstream views about the causes and appropriate treatment of disorders. In one investigation, six ethnic minority groups viewed maladaptive behavior more broadly than did the mainstream mental health professionals (Flaskerud, 1984). For example, the ethnic minority groups described maladaptive behavior in spiritual, moral, somatic (bodily), psychological, and metaphysical terms. The ethnic minority groups also had different ideas about therapy than the mental health professionals.

The ethnic groups said the management of abnormal behavior could include social, spiritual, economic, vocational, recreational, personal, physical, and psychological strategies, whereas the mental health professionals said it should involve traditional psychotherapy and psychopharmaceutical approaches.

An example of a broad, culturally sensitive approach to therapy is the recent interest in integrating folk healers into Western therapy when certain ethnic groups are involved. For example, the University of Miami's (Fla.) Community Mental Health Center uses folk healers, including Afrocuban *santeros*, Haitian *houngans* or *mambos*, Hispanic *espiritistas*, and Black American root doctors as consultants, trainers, and referral sources. Such collaboration allows clients in need of therapy to derive whatever benefit they can from Western methods without turning their backs on the methods of their culture (Lefley, 1984).

In response to demands for more concrete recommendations on how to conduct therapy, some clinicians have attempted to devise culturally responsive treatments (Sue, 1990). For example, in working with Asian Americans, a number of therapists recommend a directive and structured approach because Asian Americans are used to being guided. In working with Hispanic Americans, some therapists recommend a reframing of problems as medical rather than psychological to reduce resistance. The assumption is that Hispanic Americans will be more receptive to a medical rather than a psychological orientation. In working with Black Americans, some therapists recommend externally focused, action-oriented therapy rather than internally focused, intrapsychic therapy.

Such recommendations, however, raise some important questions. For example, isn't it impossible for therapists to effectively change their therapy orientation to work with ethnic minority groups? Thus, a psychoanalytic therapist might find it difficult to use the externally focused, action-oriented therapy recommended for Black Americans. By using a specific approach, supposedly based on the client's cultural background, how does a therapist deal with diversity and individual differences in an ethnic or cultural group? Because of the problems raised by such questions, one cannot just say, "Know the cultural background of the client," or "Use this approach with that particular ethnic or cultural group."

According to Stanley Sue (1990), what we can say is that, when they see ethnic minority clients, therapists should emphasize two processes, at least in initial therapy sessions: (1) credibility and (2) giving. **Credibility** *refers to the fact that the therapist is believable.* **Giving** *refers to the fact that clients receive a benefit from treatment early in the therapy process.* Two factors are important in increasing credibility: ascribed status and achieved status. Ascribed status is one's position or role, as defined by others or by cultural norms. In some cultures, the young are subordinate to the old, those who are naive abide by those in authority, and females have less power than males. Credibility must also be achieved. A therapist can achieve credibility by doing something the client perceives as helpful or competent. A therapist's lack of ascribed status may be the main reason ethnic minority individuals tend to steer clear of therapy; a therapist's lack of achieved credibility may be the main reason ethnic minority individuals terminate therapy once it has begun.

In terms of giving, clients may wonder how talking to a therapist will alleviate their problems. Therapists need to help ethnic minority clients see the relation of therapy and its benefits. It is important for the therapist to make this association in the first session. Many ethnic minority clients do not understand Western psychotherapy. The first session should not be just an assessment session; rather, the therapist should find out about the client, give some recommendations for treatment, and say something concrete to the client so the client will leave the first session saying, "I got something out of that meeting that I think will help me and I want to come back again."

In addition to culture and ethnicity, gender also plays a role in psychotherapy. As we will see next, concern about gender bias in psychotherapy has increased dramatically in the past 2 decades.

Gender

One of the by-products of changing gender roles for women and men is a rethinking of the approaches to psychotherapy (Doyle & Paludi, 1991; Goldberg & Pepitone-Arreola-Rockwell, 1986; Goodheart & Markham, 1992; Maracek, 1990; Travis, 1988; Worrell & Remer, 1992). Our discussion of gender and therapy focuses on three areas: autonomy and relatedness in therapy, consciousness-raising groups, and feminist therapies, each of which we will examine.

Autonomy and Relatedness in Therapy

Autonomy and relatedness, or independence and connectedness to others, are issues central to an understanding of gender conditioning. For many years, autonomy was championed as an important characteristic of maturity. As a result, autonomy was the unquestioned goal of many psychotherapies; relatedness was not. Thomas Szasz (1965), for example, claimed that the basic goal of psychotherapy is to foster autonomy, independence, and freedom. The humanistic therapies—of Rogers, Maslow, and Perls—argued that to become psychologically healthy an individual has to become self-actualized through self-determination and the fulfillment of needs independent of social constraints or personal commitments.

However, therapists are taking a new look at autonomy as the ideal goal of therapy for females. Should therapy with females focus more on the way most females have been socialized and place more emphasis on relationships? Can females, even with psychotherapy, achieve autonomy in a male-dominated society? Are conventional ways of thinking about autonomy and relatedness appropriate for capturing the

Increased interest has focused on gender roles in psychotherapy. Might female psychotherapists be more likely to encourage autonomy and relatedness as psychotherapy goals rather than autonomy alone?

Rachel Hare-Mustin (left) and Jeanne Maracek (right) have made important contributions to understanding the role of gender in psychotherapy. They have been especially concerned about the inclusion of strategies in psychotherapy to help women break free from gender stereotypes and male bias.

complexity of human experience? Would psychotherapy for females, as well as for males, be improved if its goals were more androgynous, stressing better psychological functioning in *both* autonomy and relatedness?

Because traditional therapy often has not adequately addressed the specific concerns of women in a sexist society, several nontraditional approaches have arisen. These nontraditional therapies emphasize the importance of helping people break free from traditional gender roles and stereotypes. The nontraditional therapies avoid language that labels one gender as more socially desirable or valuable than the other (Worrell, 1989). Let's now consider two such nontraditional therapies: consciousness-raising groups and feminist therapy.

Consciousness-Raising Groups

Consciousness-raising groups *are believed by some feminists to be important alternatives or adjuncts to traditional therapies; they often involve several people meeting in one member's home, are frequently leaderless (or members take turns facilitating the discussion), and focus on the members' feelings and self-perceptions.* Instead of seeking and accepting male-biased therapy, women may meet in consciousness-raising groups to define their own experiences using their own criteria (Kirsh, 1974; Travis, 1988).

Some men have followed suit and formed all-male consciousness-raising groups, in which they discuss what it means to be male in our society (Rabinowitz & Cochran, 1987; Wong, 1978). Several colleges and universities have rape-awareness programs, a form of consciousness-raising group for men. Going even further, the University of Wisconsin group "Men Stopping Rape" offers a version of its program to junior high and high school students (Doyle & Paludi, 1991).

Feminist Therapies

Feminist therapies *are usually based on a critique of a society wherein women are perceived to have less political and economic power than men. Also, feminist therapies assume that the reasons for women's problems are social, not personal.* Many individuals assume that feminist therapies and nonsexist therapies are identical. However, some feminists distinguish between the two. For example, **nonsexist therapy** *is therapy practiced by a therapist who has become aware of and has primarily overcome his or her own sexist attitudes and behavior.* Thus, a nonsexist therapist would not perceive a dependent man or an independent woman to be showing emotional problems just because he or she is acting in a counterstereotypic way. Nonsexist therapists also do not view marriage as any better for women or men, and they encourage women and men to adopt androgynous gender roles rather than stereotypic masculine or feminine ones (Doyle & Paludi, 1991; Paludi, 1992).

Feminist therapists, both male and female, believe that traditional psychotherapy continues to carry considerable gender bias and that female clients cannot realize their full potential without becoming aware of society's sexism (Brown & Brodsky, 1992). The goals of feminist therapists are no different than those of other therapists. Feminist therapists make no effort to turn clients into feminists but want female clients to be fully aware of how the nature of the female role in American society can contribute to the development of a mental disorder. Feminist therapists believe that women must become aware of the effects of social oppression on their own lives if they are to achieve their mental health goals.

In one feminist approach to therapy, women go through three phases en route to mental health (Williams, 1987). First, in *harmful adaptation*, women accept dependency and the rules of a patriarchal society. In this phase, women harm themselves because they subordinate their own desires and needs to the values of the system. Once women realize what harmful adaptation has done to them, they take *corrective action* to develop their own identity and to articulate personal goals. Third, in *health maintenance*, women develop pride in their new identity and form alliances with other women to work toward better conditions for all women. In this model of feminist therapy, women move from accepting an oppressive society to taking pride in a new, positive status and helping other women achieve the same.

So far we have discussed a wide variety of psychotherapies that can help individuals cope more effectively with stress and develop more adaptive, less harmful behavior. In recent years, considerable progress has also been made in biomedical therapies, which we will now discuss.

Biomedical Therapies

Biomedical therapies *are treatments to reduce or eliminate the symptoms of psychological disorders by altering the way an individual's body functions. Drug therapy is the most common form of biomedical therapy. Much less widely used biomedical therapies are electroconvulsive therapy and psychosurgery.* Psychologists and other mental health professionals may provide psychotherapy in conjunction with the biomedical therapy administered by psychiatrists and other medical doctors.

Drug Therapy

Psychotherapeutic drugs are used to treat many mental disorders—anxiety, depression, and schizophrenia, for example. In some instances, these drugs are effective when other forms of therapy are not. Drug therapy has substantially reduced the amount of time schizophrenics must spend in hospitals, for example. Three main types of psychotherapeutic drugs are antianxiety drugs, antipsychotic drugs, and antidepressant drugs.

Antianxiety Drugs

Antianxiety drugs *are commonly known as tranquilizers; these drugs reduce anxiety by making individuals less excitable and more tranquil.* Why are antianxiety drugs so widely used? Many individuals experience stress, anxiety, or an inability to sleep well; family physicians and psychiatrists prescribe these drugs to improve our abilities to cope with these situations more effectively. The most widely used antianxiety drugs are Xanax and Valium.

The relaxed feelings brought on by antianxiety drugs are a welcome relief to individuals experiencing anxiety and stress in their lives. However, these drugs often cause fatigue and drowsiness; motor abilities can be impaired and work productivity reduced; and extended use can produce dependency. In some instances, the combination of antianxiety drugs and alcohol has caused death. When an individual feels anxious, it may be best to face the problems creating the anxiety rather than relying on antianxiety drugs to avoid the problems.

Antipsychotic Drugs

Antipsychotic drugs *are powerful drugs that diminish agitated behavior, reduce tension, decrease hallucinations and delusions, improve social behavior, and produce better sleep patterns in severely mentally disabled individuals, especially schizophrenics.* Neuroleptics are the most widely used antipsychotic drugs.

The main value of antipsychotic drugs is their ability to block the dopamine system's action in the brain. Recall from our discussion in chapter 13 that schizophrenics have too much of the neurochemical messenger dopamine. Numerous well-controlled investigations have revealed that, when used in sufficient doses, the neuroleptics reduce a variety of schizophrenic symptoms, at least in the short term (Kirkpatrick & others, 1989; Wolkowitz & Pickar, 1991). The neuroleptics do not cure schizophrenia, however, and they may have severe side effects. The neuroleptics treat the symptoms of schizophrenia, not its causes. If an individual stops taking the drugs, the symptoms return.

Neuroleptic drugs have substantially reduced the lengths of hospital stays for schizophrenics. Although schizophrenics often are able to return to the community because drug therapy keeps their symptoms from reappearing, most have difficulty coping with the demands of society and most are chronically unemployed (Rosenstein, Milazzo-Sayre, & Manderscheid, 1989).

Tardive dyskinesia *is a major side effect of the neuroleptic drugs; it is a neurological disorder characterized by grotesque, involuntary movements of the facial muscles and mouth, as well as extensive twitching of the neck, arms, and legs.* As many as 20 percent of all schizophrenics taking neuroleptics develop this disorder, and elderly women are especially vulnerable (Wolf & Mosnaim, 1989).

Long-term neuroleptic therapy also is associated with increased depression and anxiety. For example, schizophrenics who have taken neuroleptics for many years report that they feel miserable most of the time. Nonetheless, for the majority of schizophrenics, the benefits of neuroleptic treatment outweigh its risks and discomforts.

Some strategies used to increase the effectiveness of the neuroleptics involve (1) administering lower dosages over time rather than giving a large initial dose and (2) combining drug therapy with psychotherapy. The small percentage of schizophrenics who are able to hold jobs suggests that drugs alone will not make them contributing members of society. Vocational, family, and social-skills training are needed in conjunction with drug therapy to facilitate improved psychological functioning and adaptation to society (Bellack, Morrison, & Mueser, 1989; Fisher & Greenberg, 1989).

Antidepressant Drugs

Antidepressant drugs *regulate mood. The two main classes of antidepressant drugs are tricyclics, such as Elavil, and MAO inhibitors, such as Nardil.* The tricyclics, so-called because of their three-ringed molecular structure, probably work because they increase the level of certain neurotransmitters, especially norepinephrine and serotonin. The tricyclics reduce the symptoms of depression in approximately 60 to 70 percent of all cases. The tricyclics are not effective in improving mood until 2 to 4 weeks after the individual begins taking them, and they sometimes have adverse side effects—such as restlessness, faintness, and trembling (Berwish & Amsterdam, 1989). The MAO inhibitors are not as widely used as the tricyclics because they are more toxic, they require more dietary restrictions, and they usually have less potent therapeutic effects. Nonetheless, some severely depressed individuals who do not respond to the tricyclics do respond to the MAO inhibitors.

Lithium *is a drug that is widely used to treat bipolar disorder* (recall that this disorder involves wide mood swings of depression and mania). The amount of lithium that circulates in the bloodstream needs to be monitored carefully because its effective dosage is precariously close to toxic levels. Memory impairment is also associated with lithium use (Schou, 1989).

As with schizophrenia, the treatment of affective disorders might also involve a combination of drug therapy and psychotherapy. In one study, the combination of tricyclics and interpersonal psychotherapy produced a lower than normal relapse rate for depressed clients (10 percent versus 22 percent) (Frank & Kupfer, 1986). The interpersonal therapy focused on the clients' ability to develop and maintain positive interpersonal relationships and included an educational workshop for the clients and their families.

The use of psychotherapeutic drugs is the most widely practiced biomedical therapy. However, as we will see next, in extreme circumstances electroconvulsive therapy and even psychosurgery may be used.

Electroconvulsive Therapy

"Then something bent down and took hold of me and shook me like the end of the world. Wee-ee-ee-ee-ee, it shrilled, through an air crackling with blue light, and with each flash a great jolt drubbed me until I thought my bones would break and the sap fly out of me like a split plant." Such images as this description from Sylvia Plath's (1971) autobiographic novel, *The Bell Jar*, have shaped the public's view of **electroconvulsive therapy (ECT).** *Commonly called "shock treatment," ECT is sometimes used to treat severely depressed individuals. The goal of ECT is to cause a seizure in the brain much like what happens spontaneously in some forms of epilepsy.* A small electric current, lasting for 1 second or less, passes through two electrodes placed on the individual's head. The current excites neural tissue, stimulating a seizure that lasts for approximately 1 minute.

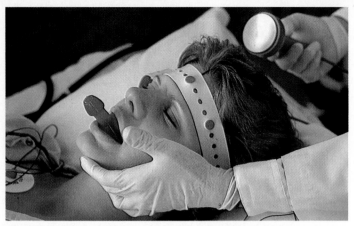

Electroconvulsive therapy (ECT), commonly called "shock therapy," causes a seizure in the brain. ECT is still given to as many as 60,000 people a year, mainly to treat major depression.

ECT has been used for more than 40 years. In earlier years, it often was used indiscriminately, sometimes even as a punishment for patients. ECT is still used on as many as 60,000 individuals a year, mainly to treat major depression. Adverse side effects may include memory loss or other cognitive impairment. Today ECT is given mainly to individuals who have not responded to drug therapy or psychotherapy.

ECT sounds as if it would entail intolerable pain, but the manner in which it is administered today involves little discomfort. The patient is given anesthesia and muscle relaxants before the current is applied; this allows the individual to sleep through the procedure, it minimizes convulsions, and it reduces the risk of physical injury. The individual awakens shortly afterward with no conscious memory of the treatment.

The following example reveals how ECT, used as a last resort, can be effective in reducing depression (Sackheim, 1985). Ann is a 36-year-old teacher and mother. She has been in psychotherapy for several years. Prior to entering the hospital, she had taken tricyclics with unsuccessful results. In the first 6 months of her hospital stay, doctors tried various drugs to reduce her depression; none worked. She slept poorly, lost her appetite, and showed no interest even in reading newspaper headlines. Obsessed with the idea that she had ruined her children's lives, she repeatedly threatened suicide. With her consent, doctors began ECT; after five treatments, Ann returned to her family and job several days later. Not all cases of ECT turn out as positively, however, and even when ECT works no one knows why it works (Kramer, 1987).

Psychosurgery

One biomedical treatment is even more extreme than ECT. **Psychosurgery** *is a biomedical therapy that involves the removal or destruction of brain tissue to improve the individual's psychological adjustment.* The effects of psychosurgery are irreversible.

In the 1930s, Portuguese physician Egas Moniz developed a procedure known as a *prefrontal lobotomy*. In this procedure, a surgical instrument is inserted into the brain and rotated, severing fibers that connect the frontal lobe, important in higher thought processes, and the thalamus, important in emotion. Moniz theorized that, by severing the connections between these brain structures, the symptoms of severe mental disorders could be alleviated. Prefrontal lobotomies were conducted on thousands of patients from the 1930s through the 1950s. Moniz was even awarded the Nobel Prize for his work. However, although some patients may have benefited from the lobotomies, many were left in vegetablelike states because of the massive assaults on their brains.

These crude lobotomies are no longer performed. Since the 1960s, psychosurgery has become more precise. When psychosurgery is now performed, a small lesion is made in the amygdala or another part of the limbic system. Today only several hundred patients per year undergo psychosurgery; it is used as a last resort and with extreme caution.

Our coverage of therapies has taken us through many diverse psychotherapies and biomedical therapies. In closing this chapter, we will now consider several basic guidelines that can be followed in seeking psychotherapy.

Guidelines for Seeking Psychotherapy

At a certain point in our lives, many of us will consider seeking psychotherapy. The problems we encounter vary enormously, so no absolute guidelines for seeking psychotherapy can guarantee that it will be of benefit. For most of us, if we accept our feelings, know our faults, work on developing our talents and interests, and create a network of friends as a support system, we are probably psychologically healthy. Nonetheless, sometimes our ability to adjust psychologically is limited.

If problems overwhelm you, it may be time to think about seeing a mental health professional. If you find that your problems or difficulties disrupt your daily life and you decide to seek psychotherapy, do not consider it an indication that you are a weak human being. On the contrary, commend yourself—it takes emotional maturity to seek psychotherapy.

If you decide to work with a mental health professional, the following guidelines may help (Weiten, 1983):

1. Do not jump into a particular therapeutic situation too quickly. Ask the therapist what type of therapy he or she practices. Try to read about the type of therapy, talk with the individuals involved, and converse with others who have gone through or are in this type of therapy.

2. Don't forget that improvement and adjustment take considerable effort on your part. Old patterns of behavior and thought do not go away overnight.

3. When you choose a therapist and a therapy, give the therapy time to work, and, even if you find you are improving, remember that temporary setbacks are common.

In this chapter, we have explored the promises and challenges of many different therapy forms. In the next chapter, we will turn our attention to one of psychology's fastest-growing fields—health psychology, which addresses issues related to improving both our mental health and our physical health.

REVIEW

The Effectiveness of Psychotherapy, Biomedical Therapies, and Guidelines for Seeking Psychotherapy

Psychotherapy in general is effective, but no single treatment is more effective than others. Behavioral therapies are often most successful in treating specific behavioral problems, such as phobias; cognitive therapy is often most successful in treating depression. Common themes in successful therapies include expectations, a sense of mastery, emotional arousal, and a confiding relationship. We still need to examine further which therapy works best with which individual in which setting with which therapist. For too long, the needs of people from poor and ethnic minority backgrounds were ignored by psychotherapists. Among the barriers that impede psychotherapy's effectiveness with ethnic minority individuals are language differences, class-bound values, and culture-bound values. Credibility and giving are two important therapy processes with ethnic minority clients. Historically the goal of therapy has been autonomy, but questions are raised about this as an ideal goal of therapy, especially for females. The goals of psycho-therapy should include more attention to relatedness. Two nontraditional, gender-related forms of therapy are consciousness-raising groups and feminist therapy. Some feminist therapists distinguish between feminist therapy and nonsexist therapy.

Biomedical therapies are designed to reduce or eliminate the symptoms of psychological disorders by altering the way an individual's body functions. Drug therapy is the most common biomedical therapy. Drug therapy may be effective when other therapies have failed, as in reducing the symptoms of schizophrenia. Three major classes of psychotherapeutic drugs are antianxiety, antipsychotic, and antidepressant. Electroconvulsive therapy, commonly called "shock treatment," creates a seizure in the brain; its most common use is as a last resort in treating severe depression. Psychosurgery is an irreversible procedure; brain tissue is destroyed in an effort to improve psychological adjustment. Today's psychosurgery is more precise than the early prefrontal lobotomies. Psychosurgery is used only as a last resort.

Seeking therapy should not be seen as a sign of weakness. Although no absolute guidelines can be given, if individuals seek therapy, they should learn about the approach and the therapist, remember that improvement takes effort, and give the therapy time to work.

Summary

I. Historical Perspective
Many early treatments of mental disabilities were inhumane. Asylums were built during the Renaissance. Pinel's efforts led to extensive reform. Dix's efforts helped separate the mentally disabled from prisoners.

II. The Nature of Psychotherapy
Psychotherapy is a process used to reduce individuals' problems and improve their adjustment. Psychotherapy approaches include psychodynamic, humanistic, and behavioral and social learning perspectives. The term *insight therapy* is used to describe both the psychodynamic and the humanistic therapies. Many therapists take an eclectic approach to therapy. Practitioners include clinical psychologists, counseling psychologists, psychiatrists, and social workers. Psychotherapy takes place in a greater variety of settings today than in the past. Mentally and emotionally distressed people from lower socioeconomic backgrounds are less likely to receive therapy than their more well-to-do counterparts.

III. Psychodynamic Therapies
Psychodynamic therapies stress the importance of the unconscious mind, early family experiences, and extensive interpretation by the therapist. Psychoanalysis is a therapeutic technique developed by Freud for analyzing an individual's unconscious thought. Free association, catharsis, interpretation, dream analysis, transference, and resistance are techniques used in psychoanalytic therapy. Although psychodynamic therapy has changed, many contemporary psychodynamic therapies

still probe the unconscious mind for early family experiences that might give clues to a client's current problems. The development of the self in social contexts is an important theme of Kohut's contemporary approach.

IV. Humanistic Therapies

In the humanistic therapies, clients are encouraged to understand themselves and to grow personally. The humanistic therapies emphasize conscious thought, the present, and growth and fulfillment. In Carl Rogers' person-centered therapy, the therapist provides a warm, supportive atmosphere to improve the client's self-concept and to encourage the client to gain insight into problems. The therapist replaces conditions of worth with unconditional positive regard and uses genuineness, accurate empathy, and active listening to raise the client's self-esteem. In Fritz Perls' Gestalt therapy, the therapist questions and challenges clients to help them become more aware of their feelings and face their problems. Gestalt therapy is more directive than the nondirective approach of person-centered therapy.

V. Behavior Therapies

Behavior therapies use principles of learning to reduce or eliminate maladaptive behavior. Behavior therapies are based on behavioral and social learning theories of learning and personality. Behavior therapists try to eliminate the symptoms or behaviors themselves rather than trying to get individuals to gain insight into their problems. Classical conditioning approaches include systematic desensitization and aversive conditioning. Operant conditioning approaches emphasize the modification of an individual's maladaptive responses to the environment. The idea behind behavior modification is to replace unacceptable, maladaptive responses with acceptable, adaptive ones. Consequences are set up to ensure that acceptable responses are reinforced but unacceptable ones are not. A token economy is an example of behavior modification. Cognitive behavior therapy is behavior therapy that tries to help individuals behave more adaptively by modifying their thoughts. Cognitive behavior therapists strive to change clients' misconceptions, strengthen their coping skills, increase their

self-control, and encourage constructive self-talk. Although behavior therapy has become less popular, it is still widely used in treating a number of psychological disorders, including the severe disorders of schizophrenia and major depression.

VI. Cognitive Therapies

Cognitive therapies emphasize that an individual's thoughts, or cognitions, are the main sources of abnormal behavior. Cognitive therapies attempt to change an individual's feelings and behaviors by changing cognitions. Rational emotive therapy is a cognitive therapy developed by Albert Ellis; it is based on the idea that individuals become psychologically disabled because of their beliefs, especially those that are irrational and self-defeating. Rational emotive therapy is designed to change these beliefs. Aaron Beck developed a form of cognitive therapy to treat psychological disorders, especially depression. The therapy involves identifying self-labels, detecting irrational thoughts, substituting appropriate for inappropriate thoughts, and receiving feedback from the therapist to stimulate these cognitive changes.

VII. Group Therapies and Community Psychology

Social relationships hold the key to successful group therapy; therefore, therapy involving group interaction may be more beneficial than individual therapy. Family therapy and couple therapy, as well as personal growth and self-help groups, are common. Community psychology was born in the early 1960s. Deinstitutionalization, in which the treatment of mental disabilities is transferred from inpatient mental hospitals to outpatient community mental health facilities, has been especially important in the community psychology movement. Community psychology has made mental health services more accessible for individuals from low-income and ethnic minority backgrounds. Three community psychology approaches are primary prevention, secondary prevention, and tertiary prevention. Empowerment—providing assistance so that individuals can gain more control over their lives—is a key concept in community psychology.

VIII. The Effectiveness of Psychotherapy

Psychotherapy in general is effective, but no single treatment is more effective than others. Behavioral therapies are often most successful in treating specific behavioral problems, such as phobias; cognitive therapy is often most successful in treating depression. Common themes in successful therapies include expectations, a sense of mastery, emotional arousal, and a confiding relationship. We still need to examine further which therapy works best with which individual in which setting with which therapist.

IX. Culture, Ethnicity, Gender, and Psychotherapy

For too long, the needs of people from poor and ethnic minority backgrounds were ignored by psychotherapists. Among the barriers that impede psychotherapy's effectiveness with individuals from ethnic minority groups are language differences, class-bound values, and culture-bound values. Credibility and giving are two important therapy processes with ethnic minority clients. Historically the goal of therapy has been autonomy, but questions are raised about this as an ideal goal of therapy, especially for females. The goals of psychotherapy should include more attention to relatedness. Two nontraditional, gender-related forms of therapy are consciousness-raising groups and feminist therapy. Some feminist therapists distinguish between feminist therapy and nonsexist therapy.

X. Biomedical Therapies

Biomedical therapies are treatments designed to reduce or eliminate the symptoms of psychological disorders by altering the way an individual's body functions. Drug therapy is the most common biomedical therapy. Drug therapy may be effective when other therapies have failed, as in reducing the symptoms of schizophrenia. Three major classes of psychotherapeutic drugs are antianxiety, antipsychotic, and antidepressant. Commonly called "shock treatment," electroconvulsive therapy creates a seizure in the brain; its most common use is as a last resort in treating severe depression. Psychosurgery is an irreversible procedure

in which brain tissue is destroyed in an attempt to improve psychological adjustment. Today's psychosurgery is more precise than the early prefrontal lobotomies. Psychosurgery is rarely used.

XI. Guidelines for Seeking Psychotherapy
Seeking therapy should not be seen as a sign of weakness. Although no absolute guidelines can be given, if individuals seek therapy they should learn about the approach and the therapist, remember that improvement takes effort, and give the therapy time to work.

Key Terms

psychotherapy 426
insight therapy 426
psychodynamic therapies 427
psychoanalysis 427
free association 428
catharsis 428
dream analysis 428
manifest content 428
latent content 428
transference 428
resistance 428
humanistic psychotherapies 429
person-centered therapy 429
genuineness 429
accurate empathy 429
active listening 429
Gestalt therapy 429

behavior therapies 430
systematic desensitization 431
aversive conditioning 431
token economy 432
cognitive behavior therapy 432
self-efficacy 433
self-instructional methods 433
cognitive therapies 433
rational emotive therapy 433
family therapy 435
couple therapy 435
family systems therapy 436
personal growth groups 436
encounter group 436
self-help groups 437
deinstitutionalization 438
primary prevention 439

secondary prevention 439
tertiary prevention 439
empowerment 440
meta-analysis 442
credibility 444
giving 444
consciousness-raising groups 446
feminist therapies 446
nonsexist therapy 446
biomedical therapies 446
antianxiety drugs 446
antipsychotic drugs 447
tardive dyskinesia 447
antidepressant drugs 447
lithium 447
electroconvulsive therapy (ECT) 447
psychosurgery 448

Suggested Readings

Atkinson, D. R., Morten, G., & Sue, D. W. (1989). *Counseling American minorities* (3rd ed.). Dubuque, IA: Wm. C. Brown. This book provides valuable information about counseling and psychotherapy with individuals from ethnic minority backgrounds. It includes sections on Native American clients, Asian American clients, Black clients, and Latino clients.

Behavior Therapy. This journal publishes a wide-ranging set of behavior therapy strategies and a number of fascinating case studies. Look through recent issues to see how behavior therapy is conducted.

Corsini, R. J. (Ed.). (1989). *Current psychotherapies* (4th ed.). Itasca, IL: Peacock. Therapists from different schools of psychotherapy describe their approaches.

Perls, F. S. (1969). *Gestalt therapy verbatim*. Lafayette, CA: Real People. Fritz Perls, the founder of Gestalt therapy, lays out the main ideas of his approach in vivid detail.

Travis, C. B. (1988). *Women and health psychology: Mental health issues*. Hillsdale, NJ: Erlbaum. Feminist therapy and women's issues in mental health are examined.

Wedding, D., & Corsini, R. J. (1979). *Great cases in psychotherapy*. Itasca, IL: Peacock. A complete description of a number of well-known cases and transcripts of cases involving Fritz Perls, Eric Berne, Sigmund Freud, Alfred Adler, Carl Jung, and Carl Rogers is presented.

CHAPTER

15

Mort, age 52, has worked as an air-traffic controller for the past 15 years. An excitable person, he compares the job to being in a cage. During peak air traffic, the tension is almost unbearable. In these frenzied moments, Mort's emotions are a mixture of rage, fear, and anxiety, and the tension spills over into his family life. In his own words, "When I go home, my nerves are hopping. I take it out on the nearest person." Two years ago, Mort's wife, Sally, told him that, if he could not calm his emotions and handle stress more effectively, she would leave him. She suggested he change to a less upsetting job, but he ignored her advice. His intense emotional behavior continued and she left him.

Last week the roof fell in on Mort. That Sunday evening, the computer that monitors air traffic temporarily went down and Mort had a heart attack. Quadruple bypass surgery saved his life. Yesterday his doctor talked with him about the stress in his life and what could be done to reduce it. The doctor gave Mort a test to reveal his vulnerability to stress. Mort was told to score each test item from 1 (almost always) to 5 (never), according to how much each statement applied to him. Table 15.1 shows the stress test given to Mort.

You probably fared better than Mort on the test. Mort rarely gets enough sleep, frequently skips meals, has not dated steadily since his divorce, has no relatives living within 50 miles, never exercises, smokes two packs of cigarettes a day, drinks two to three scotches on the rocks every evening (more on weekends), is overweight, and has no religious interests. He has only one friend and does not feel very close to him. Mort says he never has enough time to do the things he wants to do, he has fun only about once every 2 weeks, and he rarely has quiet time to himself during the day. Mort scored 68 on the stress test, indicating he is seriously vulnerable to stress and close to the extremely vulnerable range.

Stress is inevitable in our lives, so it is important to understand it and cope with it effectively.

TABLE 15.1
Stress Test

Rate yourself on each item, using a scale of 1 (almost always) to 5 (never).

1. I eat at least one hot, balanced meal a day.

2. I get 7 to 8 hours of sleep at least four nights a week.

3. I give and receive affection regularly.

4. I have at least one relative within 50 miles whom I can rely on.

5. I exercise to the point of perspiration at least twice a week.

6. I smoke less than half a pack of cigarettes a day.

7. I take fewer than five alcoholic drinks a week.

8. I am the appropriate weight for my height.

9. I have an income adequate to meet my basic expenses.

10. I get strength from my religious beliefs.

11. I regularly attend church.

12. I have a network of friends and acquaintances.

13. I have one or more friends to confide in about personal matters.

14. I am in good health (including eyesight, hearing, teeth).

15. I am able to speak openly about my feelings when angry or worried.

16. I have regular conversations with the people I live with about domestic problems (e.g., chores, money, and daily living issues).

17. I do something for fun at least once a week.

18. I am able to organize my time effectively.

19. I drink fewer than three cups of coffee (or tea or cola drinks) a day.

20. I take quiet time for myself during the day.

Total:

To get your total score, add up the figures and subtract 20. Any number over 30 indicates a vulnerability to stress. You are seriously vulnerable if your score is between 50 and 75 and extremely vulnerable if it is over 75.

"Vulnerability Scale" from *The Stress Audit*, developed by Lyle H. Miller and Alma Dale Smith. Copyright © 1983, Biobehavioral Associates, Brookline, MA, reprinted with permission.

a.

(a) Members of the Masai tribe in Kenya, Africa, can stay on a treadmill for a long time because of their very active life. Heart disease is extremely low in the Masai tribe, which also can be attributed to their energetic life-style. (b) Americans are increasingly recognizing the health benefits of exercise and an active lifestyle. The role of exercise in health is one of health psychology's many interests.

b.

By the end of his conversation with the doctor, Mort had promised to look into another career and to slow down. He also vowed to increase his social network and to reduce his smoking and drinking.

Mort is a classic example of someone whose life is filled with stress and poor health habits. This chapter is about stress, health, and the ways people like Mort can cope with stress and live more healthily.

The Scope of Health Psychology

Around 2600 B.C., Asian physicians and, around 500 B.C., Greek physicians recognized that good habits are essential for good health. They did not blame the gods for illness and think that

magic would cure it. They realized that people have some control over their health. A physician's role was as guide, assisting patients in restoring a natural and emotional balance.

As we approach the twenty-first century, once again we recognize the power of life-styles and psychological states in promoting health. We are returning to the ancient view that the ultimate responsibility for influencing health rests with the individuals themselves.

Health psychology *is a multidimensional approach to health that emphasizes psychological factors, life-style, and the nature of the health care delivery system.* To underscore the increasing interest in psychology's role in health, a new division of the American Psychological Association called *health psychology* was formed in 1978 (Matarazzo, 1979). **Behavioral medicine** *is a field closely related to health psychology; it attempts to combine medical and behavioral knowledge to reduce illness and to promote* *health*. The interest of health psychologists and behavioral medicine researchers are broad; they include the reasons patients do or do not comply with medical advice, the effectiveness of media campaigns in reducing smoking, the psychological factors involved in losing weight, and the role of exercise in reducing stress (Bakai, 1992; Bruess & Richardson, 1992; Feist & Brannon, 1989; Garrick & Lowenstein, 1989; Meyers, 1991).

One of the main areas of research in health psychology and behavioral medicine is the link between stress and illness. Both our psychological and physical well-being are related to stress and how we cope with it. Because stress is an inevitable part of our lives, we need to understand it better and learn how to handle it more effectively.

Stress

We live in a world that includes many stressful circumstances. According to the American Academy of Family Physicians, two-thirds of all office visits to family doctors are for stress-related symptoms. Stress is also believed to be a major contributor to coronary heart disease, cancer, lung problems, accidental injuries, cirrhosis of the liver, and suicide, six of the leading causes of death in the United States. In 1989 two of the five best-selling drugs in the United States were an antianxiety drug (Xanax) and an ulcer medication (Zantac).

Stress is a sign of the times. Everywhere you look, people are jogging, going to health clubs, and following diets designed to reduce tension. Even corporations have developed elaborate stress management programs. No one really knows whether we experience more stress than our parents or grandparents did, but it seems as if we do.

How can we define stress? Stress is one of those terms that is not easy to define. Initially the word *stress* was loosely borrowed from physics. Humans, it was thought, are in some ways similar to physical objects, such as metals, that resist moderate outside forces but lose their resiliency at a point of greater pressure. However, unlike metal, human beings can think, reason, and experience a myriad of social and environmental circumstances that make defining stress more complex in psychology than in physics (Hobfoll, 1989). In humans is stress the threats and

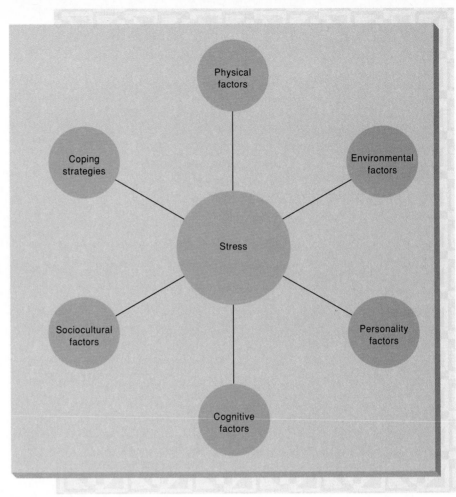

FIGURE 15.1

Factors involved in stress. Among the most important factors involved in understanding stress are physical factors (such as our body's response to stress), environmental factors (such as the frustrating stressors we experience in our world), personality factors (such as how we handle anger and whether we trust others), cognitive factors (such as whether we perceive and appraise an event as threatening or challenging), sociocultural factors (such as oppressive contacts with the mainstream society), and coping strategies (such as how we use our skills and abilities to manage stress).

challenges that our environment places on us, as when we say, "Sally's world is so stressful that it is overwhelming her"? Is stress our responses to such threats and challenges, as when we say, "Bob is not coping well with the problems in his life; he is experiencing a lot of stress, and his body is falling apart"? Although psychologists debate whether stress is the threatening events in our world or our response to those demands, we will define stress broadly. **Stress** *is the response of individuals to the circumstances and events, called stressors, that threaten them and tax their coping abilities.* To understand stress, we need to know about the following factors: physical, personality, cognitive, environmental, sociocultural, and coping skills (see figure 15.1).

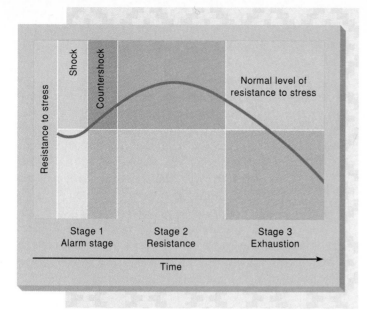

FIGURE 15.2

Selye's general adaptation syndrome. The general adaptation syndrome (GAS) describes an individual's general response to stress. In the first stage (alarm), the body enters a temporary state of shock, a time when resistance to stress is below normal. Then a rebound called "countershock" occurs, in which resistance to stress begins to pick up. Not much later, the individual moves into the second state (resistance), during which resistance to stress is intensified in an all-out effort to combat stress. If the effort fails and stress persists, the individual moves into the third and final stage (exhaustion), when wear and tear on the body worsens, the person may collapse in a state of exhaustion, and vulnerability to disease increases.

From H. Selye, *The Stress of Life.* Copyright © 1976 McGraw-Hill, Inc. Reprinted by permission of McGraw-Hill, Inc.

The Body's Response to Stress

According to the Austrian-born founder of stress research, Hans Selye (1974, 1983), stress simply is the wear and tear on the body due to the demands placed on it. Any number of environmental events, or stimuli, will produce the same stress response in the body. Selye observed patients with various problems: the death of someone close, a loss of income, arrest for embezzlement. Regardless of which problem the patient had, similar symptoms appeared: loss of appetite, muscular weakness, and decreased interest in the world.

The **general adaptation syndrome (GAS)** *is Selye's concept to describe the common effects on the body when demands are placed on it. The GAS consists of three stages: alarm, resistance, and exhaustion.* First, in the *alarm stage,* the body enters a temporary state of shock, a time when resistance to stress is below normal. The body detects the stress and tries to elimi-

nate it. The body loses muscle tone, temperature decreases, and blood pressure drops. Then, a rebound called "countershock" occurs, in which resistance to stress begins to pick up; the adrenal cortex enlarges and hormone release increases. Soon after the alarm stage, which is short, the individual moves into the *resistance stage,* a no-holds-barred effort to combat stress. Stress hormones flood the body; blood pressure, heart rate, temperature, and respiration rate all skyrocket. If the all-out effort to combat stress fails and the stress persists, the individual moves into the *exhaustion stage.* The wear and tear on the body takes its toll—the person may collapse in a state of exhaustion and vulnerability to disease increases. Figure 15.2 illustrates Selye's general adaptation syndrome.

Not all stress is bad, though. **Eustress** *is Selye's concept to describe the positive features of stress.* Competing in an athletic event, writing an essay, or pursuing someone who is attractive requires the body to expend energy. Selye does not say we should avoid these fulfilling experiences in life, but he does emphasize that we should minimize their wear and tear on our bodies.

One of the main criticisms of Selye's view is that human beings do not always react to stress in the uniform way he proposed. There is much more to understanding stress in humans than knowing their physical reactions to it. We also need to know about their personality, their physical makeup, their perceptions, and the context in which the stressors occur (Hobfoll, 1989).

Psychoneuroimmunology *is the field that explores the connections among psychological factors, such as attitudes and emotions, the nervous system, and the immune system.* The immune system keeps us healthy by recognizing foreign materials, such as bacteria, viruses, and tumors, and then destroying them (Camara & Danao, 1989). Its machinery consists of billions of white blood cells located in the lymph system.

Researchers are beginning to uncover connections between psychological factors and the immune system (Levenson & Bemis, 1991; Weisse, 1992). Sandra Levy (1985) explored the immune system's activity when cancer spreads to the lymph nodes of women treated for breast cancer. Levy found that women who become angry and agitated about their disease have stronger immune systems than women who passively accept the disease and their condition. Levy believes that accepting the disease reflects a feeling of helplessness; in contrast, anger indicates that patients think they can fight the disease. Beliefs about control, she says, may affect the immune system. Psychologists believe that directly confronting problems, seeking solutions, getting answers, sharing concerns, and taking an active role in treatment are wise strategies that help cancer patients cope more effectively, and they may have physical benefits (Weisman, 1989).

AIDS is another disease that may be affected by psychoneuroimmunological factors. Often when individuals are told they have been exposed to AIDS, they go into a deep depression. Since depression is thought to adversely affect the immune system, an AIDS patient may end up with an even greater suppression of the immune system. Although researchers suspect this may be true, no research has documented this phenomenon.

Much of what psychologists know about psychoneuroimmunology needs to be further clarified, verified, and explained. Over the next several decades, research in this field should expand. Researchers hope to tease apart the precise links among psychological factors, the brain, and the immune system (Cohen & Williamson, 1991; Levenson & Bemis, 1991). These research findings may provide clues to more successful treatments for some of the most baffling diseases, cancer and AIDS among them. As we will see next, more than biological factors are involved in understanding stress.

Personality Factors in Stress

Do you have certain personality characteristics that help you cope more effectively with stress? Do other characteristics make you more vulnerable to stress? Two important characteristics are the Type A behavior pattern and hardiness.

Type A Behavior Pattern

In the late 1950s, a secretary for two California cardiologists, Meyer Friedman and Ray Rosenman, observed that the chairs in their waiting rooms were tattered and worn, but only on the front edge. The doctors had also noticed the impatience of their cardiac patients, who often arrived exactly on time for an appointment and were in a great hurry to leave. Subsequently they conducted a study of 3,000 healthy men between the ages of 35 and 59 over a period of 8 years (Friedman & Rosenman, 1974). During the 8 years, one group of men had twice as many heart attacks or other forms of heart disease as anyone else, and autopsies of the men who died revealed that this same group had coronary arteries that were more obstructed than the other men. Friedman and Rosenman described the coronary disease group as characterized by a **Type A behavior pattern,** *a cluster of characteristics—excessively competitive, hard-driven, impatient, and hostile—thought to be related to the incidence of heart disease.*

Further research on the link between Type A behavior and coronary disease indicates that the association is not as strong as Friedman and Rosenman believed (Edwards & Baglioni, 1991; Siegman & Dembrowski, 1989; Williams, 1989b). Re-

TYPE Z BEHAVIOR

Drawing by D. Reilly; © 1987 The New Yorker Magazine, Inc.

searchers have examined the components of Type A behavior, such as hostility, to determine a more precise link with coronary risk. It turns out that people who are hostile or who consistently turn anger inward are more likely to develop heart disease (Siegman, 1989; Williams, 1989a,b). Such people have been labeled "hot reactors," meaning they have intense physiological reactions to stress—their hearts race, their breathing quickens, and their muscles tense—which could lead to heart disease. Redford Williams, a leading researcher in charting the behavioral and psychological dimensions of heart disease, says that we have the ability to control our anger and develop more trust in others, which he believes will reduce the risk for heart disease.

Hardiness

Hardiness *is a personality style characterized by a sense of commitment (rather than alienation), control (rather than powerlessness), and a perception of problems as challenges (rather than threats).* In the Chicago Stress Project, male business managers 32 to 65 years of age were studied over a 5-year period. During the 5 years, most of the managers experienced stressful events, such as divorce, job transfers, the death of a close friend, inferior performance evaluations at work, and an unpleasant boss. One study compared the managers who developed an illness (ranging from the flu to a heart attack) with those who did not (Kobasa, Maddi, & Kahn, 1982). More men in the latter group had a hardy personality. Another study evaluated whether or not hardiness, along with exercise and social support, buffers stress and reduces illness in executives' lives. When all three factors were present in an executive's life, the level of illness dropped dramatically. This suggests the power of multiple buffers of stress, rather than a single buffer, in maintaining health in managerial men (Allred & Smith, 1989; Dienstbier, 1989; Hogan, 1989; Wiebe, 1991).

Cognitive Factors in Stress

Most of us think of stressors as environmental events that place demands on our lives, such as losing our notes from a class, being yelled at by a friend, failing a test, or being in a car wreck. Although there are some common ways we all experience stress, not everyone perceives the same events as stressful. For example, one person may perceive an upcoming job interview as threatening, whereas another person may perceive it as challenging. One person may perceive a *D* grade on a paper as threatening; another person may perceive the same grade as challenging. To a degree, then, what is stressful depends on how people cognitively appraise and interpret events. This view has been most clearly presented by Richard Lazarus (1966; Lazarus & Folkman, 1984). **Cognitive appraisal** *is Lazarus' term to describe individuals' interpretation of events in their lives as harmful, threatening, or challenging and their determination of whether they have the resources to cope effectively with the event.*

In Lazarus' view, events are appraised in two steps: primary appraisal and secondary appraisal. In *primary appraisal,* individuals interpret whether an event involves *harm* (loss that has already occurred), a *threat* of future danger, or a *challenge* to be overcome. *Harm* is an individual's appraisal of the damage the event has already inflicted. For example, if you overslept yesterday and missed an exam, the harm has already been done. *Threat* is an individual's appraisal of potential damage an event may bring. For example, missing the exam may lower the instructor's opinion of you and increase the probability you will get a low grade in the course at the end of the semester. *Challenge* is an individual's appraisal of the potential to overcome the adverse circumstances of an event and, ultimately, to profit from it. For example, a student may use missing the exam as an opportunity to become acquainted with the instructor and actually benefit from what initially appeared to be a hopelessly bad circumstance.

Lazarus says that, after individuals cognitively appraise an event for its harm, threat, or challenge, they engage in secondary appraisal. In *secondary appraisal,* individuals evaluate their resources and determine how effectively they can be used to cope with the event. This appraisal is called *secondary* because it comes after primary appraisal and depends on the degree to which the event has been appraised as harmful, threatening, or challenging. Coping involves a wide range of potential strategies, skills, and abilities for effectively managing stressful events. In the example of missing an exam, if you learn that a makeup exam will be given 2 days later, you may not experience much stress, since you have already studied for the exam and have several additional days to study. However, if the instructor says that you have to write a lengthy paper for missing the test, you may cognitively appraise your situation and determine that this additional requirement places considerable demands on your time and you wonder whether you will be able to meet the requirement. In this case, your secondary appraisal indicates a more stressful situation than simply having to take a makeup test several days later (Sears & others, 1988).

Lazarus believes an individual's experience of stress is a balance of primary and secondary appraisal. When harm and threat are high and challenge and resources are low, stress is likely to be high; when harm and threat are low and challenge and resources are high, stress is more likely to be low.

At this point, we have discussed the biological, personality, and cognitive factors that are involved in stress. Next, we will study the important role of environmental and sociocultural factors.

REVIEW

Health Psychology, Defining Stress, the Body's Response to Stress, Personality Factors, and Cognitive Factors

Health psychology is a multidimensional approach to health that emphasizes psychological factors, life-style, and the nature of the health care delivery system. Closely aligned with health psychology is behavioral medicine, which combines medical and behavioral knowledge to reduce illness and promote health.

Stress is the way we respond to circumstances that threaten us and tax our coping abilities. Selye's general adaptation syndrome (GAS) describes the common effects of stress on the body. Stress is described as the wear and tear on the body due to the demands placed on it, according to Selye. This involves three stages—alarm, resistance, and exhaustion. Not all stress is bad; Selye calls good stress eustress. Critics argue that humans do not always respond as uniformly as Selye envisioned and that we also need to know about such factors as an individual's coping strategies. Psychoneuroimmunology explores the connections among psychological factors, the nervous system, and the immune system. Exploratory research suggests that our emotions and attitudes are connected to our immune system.

Personality factors that are related to stress include Type A behavior and hardiness. The Type A behavior pattern refers to a cluster of characteristics—excessively competitive, hard-driven, impatient, and hostile—thought to be related to heart disease. The Type A pattern is controversial, with some researchers arguing that only specific components of the cluster, such as hostility, are associated with heart disease. Hardiness is a personality style characterized by commitment, control, and a perception of problems as challenges rather than threats. Hardiness buffers stress and is related to reduced illness.

Lazarus believes that stress depends on how individuals cognitively appraise and interpret events. Cognitive appraisal is Lazarus' term for individuals' interpretation of events in their lives as harmful, threatening, or challenging (primary appraisal) and their determination of whether they have the resources to cope effectively with the event (secondary appraisal).

Economic factors can produce stress. In one recent investigation, economic hardship in Iowa brought on by crisis in the agricultural industry was associated with inconsistent parenting, as well as increased drug use by adolescents (Lempers, Clarke-Lempers, & Simons, 1989).

Sometimes stimuli become so intense that we become overloaded and can cope no longer. In today's information age, we are especially faced with information overload. It is easy to develop the overwhelming feeling that we don't know as much about a topic as we should, a circumstance that produces what has been dubbed "information anxiety."

Environmental Factors in Stress

Many circumstances, large and small, can produce stress in our lives. In some instances, cataclysmic events, such as war, an automobile accident, a fire, or the death of a loved one, produce stress. In others the everyday pounding of being overloaded with work, of being frustrated in an unhappy relationship, or of living in poverty produces stress. What makes some situations stressful and others less so?

Overload, Conflict, and Frustration

Sometimes stimuli become so intense that we can no longer cope with them. For example, persistent high levels of noise overload our adaptability. Overload can occur with work as well. How often have you said to yourself, "There are not enough hours in the day to do all I have to do." In today's computer age, we are especially faced with information overload. It is easy to develop the stressful feeling that we don't know as much about a topic as we should, even if we are a so-called expert.

Today the buzzword for overload is **burnout,** *a hopeless, helpless feeling brought on by relentless, work-related stress. Burnout leaves its sufferers in a state of physical and emotional exhaustion that includes chronic fatigue and low energy.* Burnout usually does not occur because of one or two traumatic events but because of a gradual accumulation of heavy, work-related stress (Pines & Aronson, 1988).

On a number of college campuses, reaching a rate of 25 percent at some schools, burnout is the most frequent reason students leave school before earning their degrees. Dropping out of college for a semester or two used to be considered a sign of weakness. Now sometimes called "stopping out" because stu-

dents fully intend to return, counselors may actually encourage some students who feel overwhelmed with stress to take a break from college. Before recommending "stopping out," though, most counselors first suggest that students examine ways to reduce overload and consider some possible coping strategies that would allow them to remain in school. The simple strategy of taking a reduced or better-balanced class load sometimes works, for example. Most college counseling services have professionals who can work effectively with students to alleviate their sense of being overloaded and overwhelmed by life (Leafgren, 1989; Rayman & Garis, 1989).

Stimuli not only overload us, but they also can be a source of conflict. Conflict occurs when we must decide between two or more incompatible stimuli. Three major types of conflict are approach/approach, avoidance/avoidance, and approach/avoidance. The **approach/approach conflict** *is a conflict in which an individual must choose between two attractive stimuli or circumstances.* Should you go out with the attractive blond or with the attractive brunette? Do you buy a Corvette or a Porsche? The approach/approach conflict is the least stressful of the three types of conflict because either choice leads to a positive result.

The **avoidance/avoidance conflict** *is a conflict in which an individual must choose between two unattractive stimuli or circumstances.* Will you go to the dentist for a root canal or endure the toothache? Do you go through the stress of giving an oral presentation in class or not show up and get a zero? You want to avoid both but, in each case, you must choose one. Obviously these conflicts are more stressful than having the luxury of choosing between two enticing alternatives. In many instances, we delay our decision in an avoidance/avoidance conflict until the last possible moment.

The **approach/avoidance conflict** *is a conflict involving a single stimulus or circumstance that has both positive and negative characteristics.* Let's say you really like the person you are going with and are thinking about getting married. On the one hand, you are attracted by the steady affection and love marriage might bring but, on the other hand, marriage is a commitment you might not feel ready to make. In another example, you look at a menu and face a dilemma—the double chocolate delight would be sumptuous, but is it worth the extra pound of weight? Our world is full of approach/avoidance conflicts and they can be highly stressful. Often in these circumstances, we vacillate before deciding (Miller, 1959).

Frustration is another circumstance that produces stress. **Frustration** *occurs in any situation in which a person cannot reach a desired goal.* If we want something and cannot have it, we feel frustrated. Our world is full of frustrations that build up to make our life more stressful—not having enough money to buy the car we want, not getting promoted at work, not getting an A average, being delayed for an important appointment by traffic, and being rejected by a friend. Failures and losses are especially frustrating—not getting grades that are high enough to get into medical school or losing a loved one through death, for example. Sometimes the frustrations we experience are major life events, as in the cases of divorce and death. At other times, the accumulation of daily hassles may make us very frustrated.

Life Events and Daily Hassles

Think about your life. What events have created the most stress for you? A change in financial status, the loss of a job, a divorce, the death of someone you loved, a personal injury? What about the everyday circumstances of your life? What hassles you the most? Not having enough time to study, arguing with your girlfriend or boyfriend, not getting enough credit for your work on the job?

Researchers have proposed that significant life events are a major source of stress and have linked such life events with illnesses. The effects of individual life events, such as a tornado or volcano eruption, can be evaluated, or the effects of *clusters* of events can be studied. Thomas Holmes and Richard Rahe (1967) devised a scale to measure clusters of life events and their possible impact on illness. Their widely used Social Readjustment Rating Scale includes events ranging from the death of a spouse (100 stress points) to minor violations of the law (11 stress points).

People who experience clusters of life events in a short period of time, such as divorce, loss of a job, and sexual difficulties, are more likely to become ill (Maddi, 1986). However, the ability to predict illness from life events alone is modest. Total scores on life events scales, such as the Social Readjustment Rating Scale, are frequently ineffective at predicting future health problems. A life-events checklist tells us nothing about a person's physiological makeup, constitutional strengths and weaknesses, ability to cope with stressful circumstances, and support systems or about the nature of the social relationships involved, all of which are important in understanding how stress is related to illness. A divorce, for example, might be less stressful than a marriage filled with day-to-day tension. In addition the Holmes-Rahe scale includes positive events, such as marital reconciliation and gaining a new family member, which can also create stressors that must be faced. However, the changes that result from positive events are not as difficult to cope with as the changes that result from negative events.

Increasingly psychologists are considering the nature of daily hassles and uplifts to gain more insight into the nature of stress (Kanner & Feldman, 1991; Lazarus & Folkman, 1984). It may not be life's major events, but rather our daily experiences, that are the primary sources of stress. Enduring a boring but tense job or marriage and living in poverty do not show up on scales of major life events, yet the everyday tension involved in these living conditions adds up to a highly stressful life and, in some cases, psychological disturbance or illness (Compas, 1989). One study revealed that people who experience the most daily hassles have the most negative self-images (Tolan, Miller, & Thomas, 1988).

How about your own life? What are the biggest hassles? One study showed that the most frequent daily hassles of college students are wasting time, being lonely, and worrying about meeting high achievement standards (Kanner & others, 1981). In fact, the fear of failing in our success-oriented world often plays a role in college students' depression. College students also find that the small things in life—having fun, laughing, going to movies, getting along well with friends, and completing tasks—are their main sources of feeling uplifted.

Critics of the daily hassles approach argue that some of the same problems with life-events scales occur when assessing daily hassles (Dohrenwend & Shrout, 1985). For example, knowing about a person's daily hassles tells us nothing about the body's resiliency to stress, the person's coping ability or strategies, or the person's perceptions of stress. Supporters of the daily hassles concept contend that information about daily hassles can be used in concert with information about physiological reactions, coping, and perceptions of stress to provide a more complete picture of the causes and consequences of stress.

Sociocultural Factors in Stress

Sociocultural factors influence the stressors individuals are likely to encounter, their perceptions of events as stressful or not, and their expectations about how stressors should be confronted (Revenson, in press). Among the sociocultural factors that influence stress are acculturation, socioeconomic status, and gender, each of which we will consider.

Canadian cross-cultural psychologist John Berry (second from left) has been an important pioneer in developing theoretical ideas and conducting research pertaining to how various dimensions of culture influence stress and coping. For example, he has described how a person facing acculturation can adapt to the pressures of change in four ways—assimilation, integration, separation, and marginalization.

Acculturation and Acculturative Stress

Cultural subgroups in the United States can find contacts with mainstream society stressful. **Acculturation** *refers to cultural change that results from continuous, first-hand contact between two distinctive cultural groups.* **Acculturative stress** *is the negative consequences of acculturation.*

Acculturation takes place over time in a series of phases (Berry & Kim, 1988). In the *precontact phase*, two cultural groups remain distinct, each with its own set of customs. The people within each culture represent a "normal" mix of people who range, by cultural definition, from mentally well adjusted to maladjusted. In the *contact phase*, the groups meet and interact, and new stressors appear. The impetus toward contact may be the result of stressors (such as overpopulation, war, or famine) in one of the cultures. In the contact phase, cultural and behavioral changes begin to take place. The concept of acculturation allows for cultural exchange in both directions. In practice the balance of flow is usually from the larger, more dominant culture to the smaller, less dominant group. As a result, more stress is placed on the smaller, more acculturating group. Often, but not inevitably, a *conflict phase* develops, in which tension builds up and the smaller cultural group is pressured to change its way of life.

Conflict can involve intergroup or psychological conflict. Intergroup conflict creates threats to person and property, whereas psychological (intrapsychic) conflict creates confusion and uncertainty. If conflict and tension do occur, a highly stressful *crisis phase* may evolve, in which the conflict comes to a head, and a resolution is required. The crisis phase is often associated with increased homicide, suicide, family abuse, and substance abuse in acculturating peoples. Finally an *adaptation phase* may occur, in which the cultural relations are stabilized. The kind of adaptation achieved has consequences for mental and physical health.

Canadian cross-cultural psychologist John Berry (1980) believes that a person facing acculturation can adapt to the pressures of change in four ways—assimilation, integration, separation, and marginalization. These four outcomes depend on how the individual answers two important questions: (1) Is my cultural identity of value and should I retain it? and (2) Do I want to seek positive relations with the larger, dominant culture?

Assimilation *occurs when individuals relinquish their cultural identity and move into the larger society.* The nondominant group may be absorbed into an established "mainstream," or many groups may merge to form a new society (often called a "melting pot"). By contrast, **integration** *implies the maintenance of cultural integrity as well as the movement to become an integral part of the larger culture*. In this circumstance, a number of ethnic groups all cooperate within a larger social system ("a mosaic"). **Separation** *refers to self-imposed withdrawal from the larger culture*. However, if imposed by the larger society, separation becomes *segregation*. People may maintain their traditional way of life because they desire an independent existence (as in "separatist" movements), or the dominant culture may exercise its power to exclude the other culture (as in slavery and apartheid).

Sociologist Deborah Belle, shown here interviewing a young girl, has documented how poverty imposes considerable stress on children. Chronic life conditions, such as inadequate housing, dangerous neighborhoods, burdensome responsibilities, and economic uncertainties are potent stressors in the lives of the poor.

There also is an option that involves a considerable amount of confusion and anxiety because the essential features of one's culture are lost but are not replaced by those of the larger society. **Marginalization** *refers to the process in which groups are out of cultural and psychological contact with both their traditional society and the larger, dominant society*. Marginalization often involves feelings of alienation and a loss of identity. Marginalization does not mean that a group has no culture but indicates that this culture may be disorganized and unsupportive of acculturating individuals.

As you can see, separation and marginalization are the least adaptive responses to acculturation. Although separation can have benefits under certain circumstances, it may be especially stressful for individuals who seek separation while most members of their group are seeking assimilation. Integration and assimilation are healthier adaptations to acculturative pressures. However, assimilation means some cultural loss, so it may be more stressful than integration, in which selective involvement in the two cultural systems may provide the supportive base for effective coping. More about the acculturative stress of ethnic minority individuals appears in Sociocultural Worlds 15.1.

Socioeconomic Status

Poverty imposes considerable stress on individuals and families (Belle, 1990). Chronic conditions, such as inadequate housing, dangerous neighborhoods, burdensome responsibilities, and economic uncertainties, are potent stressors in the lives of the poor. Ethnic minority families are disproportionately among the poor. For example, Puerto Rican families headed by women are 15 times more likely to live in poverty than are families headed by White men. Similarly families headed by Black women are 10 times more likely to live in poverty than are families headed by White men (National Advisory Council on Economic Opportu-

nity, 1980). Many people who become poor during their lives remain so for only 1 or 2 years. However, Blacks and female heads of household are especially at risk for persistent poverty. The average poor Black child experiences poverty that will last almost 20 years (Wilson & Neckerman, 1986).

Poverty is also related to threatening and uncontrollable life events (Belle, 1990; Russo, 1990). For example, poor women are more likely to experience crime and violence than middle-class women (Belle & others, 1981). Poverty also undermines the sources of social support that play a role in buffering the effects of stress. Poverty is related to marital unhappiness and to having spouses who are unlikely to serve as confidants (Brown, Bhrolchain, & Harris, 1975). Further, poverty means having to depend on many overburdened and unresponsive bureaucratic systems for financial, housing, and health assistance, which may contribute to a poor person's perception of powerlessness (Belle, 1988, 1990).

Gender

Another sociocultural factor that plays a role in stress is gender. As more and more women go to work outside of the home and take on demanding careers, researchers are especially interested in how these changes influence women's stress and health (Rodin & Ickovics, 1990). In almost all studies, the employed women are healthier than the nonemployed women (LaCroix & Haynes, 1987). Researchers have found that women who stay at home and who perceive their lives as stressful and unhappy, who feel extremely vulnerable, and who engage in little physical activity or exercise are especially at risk for health problems (Verbrugge, 1989). However, figuring out the causality in these associations of low employment and high stress is like the old chicken and egg question. It may be that employment directly promotes health and reduces risk for women, or it may be that women in poor health are unable to obtain or keep jobs.

Women and men have always had multiple roles, but researchers have found that women experience more conflict between roles and overload than men do (McBride, 1990; Wortman, Bernat, & Lang, in press). An important difference seems to be women's family responsibilities, discussed in chapter 9. Remember that, even when both spouses work, wives perform a disproportionate share of child care and household tasks (Scarr, Phillips, & McCartney, 1989). In spite of all the strain, however, the more roles a woman juggles, the healthier she seems to be (Baruch, Biener, & Barnett, 1987). Women who take on varied

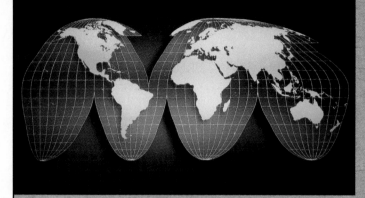

The Acculturative Stress of Ethnic Minority Individuals

A s upwardly mobile ethnic minority families have attempted to penetrate historically all-White neighborhoods, interracial tensions have mounted (Huang & Gibbs, 1989). Although many Americans have thought of racial tensions and prejudice largely as Black/White issues, this is no longer the case. Racial tensions and hostility often emerge among the various ethnic minorities as each struggles for housing and employment opportunities, seeking its fair share in these limited markets. Clashes become inevitable as Hispanic family markets spring up in Black urban neighborhoods, as Vietnamese extended families displace Puerto Rican apartment dwellers, and as the increasing enrollment of Asian students on college campuses is perceived as a threat to affirmative action policies by other ethnic minority students.

Although the dominant White society has, on many occasions, tried to enslave or dispossess entire populations, these ethnic minority groups have survived and flourished. In the face of severe stress and oppression, these groups have shown remarkable resilience and adaptation by developing their own communities and social structures—such as Black churches, Vietnamese mutual assistance associations, Chinese American family associations, Japanese language schools, Indian "bands" and tribal associations, and Mexican American kin systems. In addition, they have learned to negotiate with the dominant White culture. Essentially they have mastered two cultures and have developed impressive strategies for adapting to life in America. The resilience and adaptation of ethnic minority groups can teach us much about coping and survival in the face of overwhelming adversity (Prillerman, Myers, & Smedley, 1989; Saldaña, 1989).

To help buffer the stress in their lives, many ethnic minority groups have developed their own social structures, which include Mexican American kin systems, Black churches, Chinese American family associations, and Native American tribal associations.

roles benefit from new sources of self-esteem, control, and social support, which in turn may improve both their mental and physical health (Rodin & Ickovics, 1990).

The nature and quality of a woman's experiences within a role are also important considerations in understanding stress and health. For example, roles with time constraints, irregular schedules, and little autonomy, such as factory worker, may jeopardize health. Women clerical workers, in particular, are more prone to health problems, such as eye strain and back pains, than other working women (Haynes & Feinleib, 1980). However, contrary to the belief that a high-powered career is more stressful to a woman's well-being, the more authority and autonomy a woman has on the job, the greater her sense of well-being (Baruch, Barnett, & Rivers, 1985; Verbrugge, 1987).

Earlier in our discussion of social class and stress, we found that poverty is associated with increased stress and poor health. Women are disproportionately among the poor. What's more, poor women face the double jeopardy of poverty and sexism. For example, women are paid less than men and, at the same time, may be denied opportunities to work because of their sex. The term **feminization of poverty** *refers to the fact that far more women than men live in poverty. Women's low income, divorce, and the resolution of divorce cases by the judicial system, which leaves women with less money than they and their children need to survive, are the likely causes of the feminization of poverty.* Approximately one of every two marriages will end in a divorce, meaning that far more women today than in the past must support themselves and, in many cases, one or more children as well. Further, women today are far less likely to receive alimony, or spousal support, than in the past. Even when alimony or child-support payments are awarded to a woman, they are poorly enforced.

As we saw in our discussion of socioeconomic status, ethnic minority women have especially high rates of poverty. These women face the extremely stressful triple jeopardy of poverty, racism, and sexism. It is important for researchers to turn their attention to the mental health risks that accompany poverty and to ways that poor people, especially women, can cope more effectively with stress.

At this point, we have discussed the biological, personality, cognitive, environmental, and sociocultural factors involved in stress. Next, we will see that it also is extremely important to understand how to cope with stress.

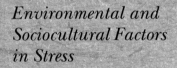

REVIEW

Environmental and Sociocultural Factors in Stress

Overload, conflict, and frustration can lead to stress. Stress can be produced because stimuli become so intense and prolonged that we cannot cope. Three types of conflict are approach/approach, avoidance/avoidance, and approach/avoidance. Frustration occurs when we cannot reach a goal. Stress also may be produced by major life events or daily hassles. Life-events lists tell us nothing about how individuals cope with stress, their body strengths and weaknesses, and other important dimensions of stress. Daily hassles provide a more focused look, but their evaluation should include information about a person's coping ability and physical characteristics.

Acculturation is cultural change that results from continuous, first-hand contact between two cultural groups. Acculturative stress is the negative consequences of acculturation. Acculturation takes place over time in a series of phases: precontact, contact, conflict, crisis, and adaptation. Four outcomes characterize an acculturating individual: assimilation, integration, segregation, and marginalization. The resilience and adaptation of ethnic minority groups can teach us much about coping and survival in the face of overwhelming adversity. Poverty imposes considerable stress on individuals. Chronic conditions, such as inadequate housing, dangerous neighborhoods, burdensome responsibilities, and economic uncertainties, are potent stressors in the lives of the poor. The incidence of poverty is especially high in ethnic minority families.

Gender is also a sociocultural determinant of stress. Of special interest is how the increased participation by women in the workforce has influenced their stress and health. Employment is associated with increased health among women. Even though women experience more conflict between roles and overload than men, women who engage in multiple roles are healthier because multiple roles expand potential resources and rewards. However, stressful roles with little autonomy and authority, such as being a clerical worker, often decrease women's health. Special concerns are the feminization of poverty and poverty among ethnic minority women.

Coping with Stress

If you think back to the first weeks of this class, you may remember students who used to sit next to you, or in front of you, whom you don't see in class anymore. Every semester several students stop showing up for classes, often after the first exam. They never talk to their professors about their performance in class, and they don't go through the proper procedures for dropping a class. The result of their immediate stress avoidance is having to face the delayed stressful circumstance of getting an *F* on their record at the end of the semester. Students also sometimes strike out with anger when faced with stress. For example, one student who flunked an introductory psychology class went to the instructor's office and delivered a few choice epithets after receiving his grade. The next day, he returned to apologize, saying he deserved the *F* and that he had also failed two other classes. The behavior of these two types of students, in one case avoiding stress and in the other discharging anger, illustrates two of many ways we deal with stress. Let's explore some ways to cope with stress that will serve us better than the strategies used by the two students.

Stress Removal, Problem-Focused Coping, and Defense Mechanisms

Stress is so abundant in our society that many of us are confronted with more than one stressor at the same time. A college student might be taking an extra course load, not have enough money to eat regularly, and have problems in a close relationship. Researchers have found that, when several stressors are experienced simultaneously, the effects are often compounded (Rutter & Garmezy, 1983). For example, one study found that people who feel besieged by two chronic life stressors are four times more likely to need psychological services eventually than are those who cope with only one chronic stressor (Rutter, 1979). The student facing the triple whammy of school, financial, and relationship difficulties probably would benefit from removing one of the stressors, such as dropping one class and taking a normal course load.

Richard Lazarus (1984) believes that coping takes one of two forms. **Problem-focused coping** *is Lazarus' term for the cognitive strategy of squarely facing one's troubles and trying to solve them.* For example, if you are having trouble with a class, you might go to the study skills center at your college or university and enter a training program to learn how to study more effectively. You have faced your problem and attempted to do something about it. **Emotion-focused coping** *is Lazarus' term for responding to stress in an emotional manner, especially using defensive appraisal.* Emotion-focused coping involves using the defense mechanisms described in chapter 12. In emotion-focused coping, you might avoid something, rationalize what has happened to you, deny it is occurring, laugh it off, or call on your religious faith for support. If you use emotion-

focused coping, you might avoid going to a class you're having trouble in. You might say the class doesn't matter, deny that you are having a problem, laugh and joke about it with your friends, or pray that you will do better. One recent study revealed that depressed people tend to use coping strategies that avoid facing their problems more than people who are not depressed (Ebata & Moos, 1989).

However, there are times when emotion-focused coping is adaptive. For example, denial is one of the main protective psychological mechanisms that enable people to cope with the flood of feelings that occurs when the reality of death or dying becomes too great. In other circumstances, emotion-focused coping is maladaptive. Denying that the person you were dating doesn't love you any more when that person has become engaged to someone else is not adaptive, for example. However, denial can be used to avoid the destructive impact of shock by postponing having to deal with stress. Over the long term, though, individuals should use problem-focused rather than emotion-focused coping (Blanchard-Fields & Robinson, 1987). Would thinking positively also help us cope with stress?

Positive Thinking and Self-efficacy

"Don't worry, be happy" are the words of a popular tune by Bobby McFerrin, "Cause when you worry, your face will frown, and that will bring everybody down." Is McFerrin's cheerful optimism a good coping strategy? It is, in fact, a good strategy to avoid negative thinking when handling stress. A positive mood improves our ability to process information efficiently, makes us more altruistic, and gives us higher self-esteem. In most cases, an optimistic attitude is superior to a pessimistic one. It gives us a sense that we are controlling our environment, or what Albert Bandura (1986, 1989) calls self-efficacy. For example, in 1989 sports psychologist Jim Loehr pieced together videotaped segments of 17-year-old Michael Chang's most outstanding tennis matches during that year. Chang periodically watched the videotape—he always saw himself winning, he never saw himself making mistakes, and he always saw himself in a positive mood. Several months later, Chang became the youngest male to win the French Open Tennis Championship.

For a number of years, mental health professionals believed that seeing reality as accurately as possible was the best path to health. Recently, though, researchers have found increasing evidence that maintaining some positive illusions about one's self and the world is healthy. Happy people often have falsely high opinions of themselves, give self-serving explanations for events, and have exaggerated beliefs about their ability to control the world around them (Snyder, 1988; Taylor & others, 1988).

Illusions, whether positive or negative, are related to one's sense of self-esteem. Having too grandiose an idea of yourself or thinking too negatively about yourself both have negative con-

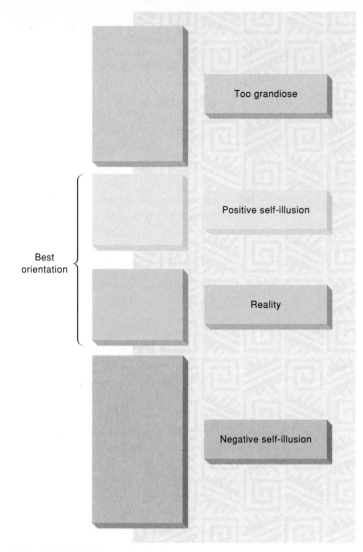

Best
orientation

Too grandiose

Positive self-illusion

Reality

Negative self-illusion

FIGURE 15.3

Reality and self-illusion. In Baumeister's model of self-illusion, the most healthy individuals often have self-illusions that are slightly above their current level of functioning and ability. Having too grandiose an opinion of yourself or thinking negatively about yourself can have negative consequences. For some individuals, seeing things too accurately can be depressing. Overall, in most contexts, a reality orientation or a slightly above average self-illusion may be most effective.

sequences. Rather, the ideal overall orientation may be an optimal margin of illusion in which individuals see themselves as slightly above their current level of functioning and ability (Baumeister, 1989) (see figure 15.3).

A negative outlook can increase our chances of getting angry, feeling guilty, and magnifying our mistakes. For some people, seeing things too accurately can lead to depression. Seeing one's suffering as meaningless and random does not help a person cope and move forward, even if the suffering *is* random

and meaningless. An absence of illusions may also thwart individuals from undertaking the risky and ambitious projects that may yield the greatest rewards (Baumeister, 1989).

In some cases, though, a strategy of defensive pessimism may actually work best in handling stress. By imagining negative outcomes, people can prepare for stressful circumstances (Norem & Cantor, 1986). Think about an honors student who is worried that she will flunk the next test or a nervous host who is afraid his lavish dinner party will fall apart. For these two people, thoughts of failure may not be paralyzing but, instead, may motivate them to do everything necessary to ensure that things go smoothly. By imagining potential problems, they may develop relevant strategies for dealing with or preventing negative outcomes. One study found that negative thinking spurs constructive thinking and feelings, such as evaluating negative possibilities, wondering what the future holds, psyching up for future experiences so they would be positive, feeling good about being prepared to cope with the worst, and forming positive expectations (Showers, 1986). Positive *and* negative thinking, then, are involved in coping with stress.

At this point, we have discussed the roles of stress removal, problem-focused coping, defense mechanisms, positive thinking, and self-efficacy in coping with stress. In the next two sections, we will discuss some techniques for coping with stress that have been increasingly used in recent years—biofeedback, meditation, and relaxation.

Biofeedback

For many years, operant conditioning was believed to be the only effective means of dealing with voluntary behaviors, such as aggression, shyness, and achievement. Behavior modification helped people reduce their aggression, be more assertive and outgoing, and get better grades, for example. Involuntary behaviors, such as blood pressure, muscle tension, and pulse rate, were thought to be outside the boundaries of operant conditioning and more appropriate for classical conditioning. Beginning in the 1960s, though, Neal Miller (1969) and others began to demonstrate that people can control internal behaviors. **Biofeedback** *is the process in which individuals' muscular or visceral activities are monitored by instruments, and information from the instruments is given (fed back) to the individuals so they can learn to voluntarily control their physiological activities.*

How does biofeedback work? Let's consider the problem of reducing muscle tension. An individual's muscle tension is monitored and the level of tension is fed back, often in the form of an audible tone. As muscle tension rises, the tone becomes louder; as it drops, the tone becomes softer. The reinforcement in biofeedback is the rising and lowering of the tone (or, in some cases, seeing a dot move up or down on a television screen) as the individual learns to control muscle tension. Figure 15.4 shows how biofeedback was used to repair nerve damage in a young boy's arm after an automobile accident.

When biofeedback was developed, some overzealous individuals exaggerated its success and potential for helping people with such problems as high blood pressure and migraine headaches. However, findings from carefully designed research have replaced the wildly enthusiastic early claims with a more realistic appraisal of biofeedback's effectiveness. For example, although it is easier to raise blood pressure through biofeedback, there has been some success in lowering it. Relaxation training and stress management are as effective as biofeedback in reducing blood pressure (Achmon & others, 1989).

Meditation and Relaxation

At one time, meditation was believed to have more in common with mysticism than with science. Although meditation has become popular in the United States only in recent years, it has been an important part of life in Asia for centuries (West, 1988).

Meditation *is the system of thought that incorporates exercises to attain bodily or mental control and well-being, as well as enlightenment.* The strategies of meditation vary but usually take one of two forms: either cleansing the mind to have new experiences or increasing concentration. **Transcendental meditation (TM)** *is the most popular form of meditation in the United States; it is derived from an ancient Indian technique and involves using a mantra, which is a resonant sound or phrase repeated mentally or aloud to focus attention.* One widely used TM mantra is the phrase "Om Mani Padme Hum." Through concentration, an individual substitutes this phrase for other, random thoughts. In transcendental meditation, the individual learns to associate a mantra with a special meaning, such as beauty, peace, or tranquility.

As a physiological state, meditation shows qualities of both sleep and wakefulness, yet it is distinct from them. It resembles the hypnagogic state, which is the transition from wakefulness to sleep, but at the very least it is a prolongation of that state.

Early research on meditation's effects on the body revealed that oxygen consumption is lowered, heart rate slows down, blood flow increases in the arms and forehead, and EEG patterns are predominantly of the alpha variety, being regular and rhythmic (Wallace & Benson, 1972). Other research supports these findings but questions whether meditation is more effective than relaxation in reducing body arousal (Garrick & Lowenstein, 1989). For example, in the research of David Holmes and his colleagues, trained and experienced meditators were asked to relax for 5 minutes, then to meditate for 20 minutes, and finally

FIGURE 15.4

Biofeedback. A therapist used biofeedback to train a young boy to relearn the use of a nerve-damaged hand that had been impaired because of an automobile accident. A television monitor was attached to electrodes on individual muscles in the boy's arm. The electrodes measure motor signals from the brain to those muscles, signaling them when to contract. When the signal gets through to the correct muscles, dots on the TV screen move toward the top of the screen.

to relax for 5 minutes (1988; Holmes & others, 1983). Ten other volunteers who had no training or experience in meditation were asked to follow the same regimen, with one exception—during the 20 minutes the meditators meditated, the nonmeditators were simply told to rest. Body arousal—in heart rate, skin resistance, respiration, and blood pressure—was measured throughout the experiment. Meditation lowered body arousal, but no more than relaxation did.

You can feel the peaceful, tranquil feeling of the "relaxation response," as it is called by health psychologists and behavioral medicine specialists, by following some simple instructions. Sit quietly and upright in a comfortable chair. Let your chin rest comfortably on your chest, your arms in your lap. Close your eyes. Then pay attention to your breathing. Notice every time you inhale and every time you exhale and pay attention to the sensations of air flowing through your body, the feeling of your lungs filling and emptying. After you have done this for several breaths, begin to repeat a single word silently to yourself every time you breathe out. The word you choose does not have to mean anything. You can make up the word; you can use the word *one*; or you can try a word that is associated with the emotion you want to produce, such as *trust*, *love*, *patience*, or *happy*. Try several different words to see which one works best for you. At first you will find that thoughts intrude and you are no longer attending to your breathing. Just return to your breathing and say the word each time you exhale. After you have practiced this exercise for 10 to 15 minutes, twice a day, every day for 2 weeks, you will be ready for a shortened version. If you notice stressful thoughts or circumstances appearing, simply engage in the relaxation response on the spot for several minutes. If you are in public, you don't have to close your eyes, just fix your gaze on a nearby object, attend to your breathing, and say your word silently every time you exhale. Audiotapes that induce the relaxation response are available in most bookstores. They usually include soothing background music, along with instructions on doing the relaxation response. These audiotapes can especially help induce a more relaxed state before you go to bed at night.

At this point, we have found that such factors as removing stress, increasing problem-focused coping, reducing the use of defense mechanisms, thinking positively, following a self-efficacy strategy, practicing biofeedback, and engaging in meditation or the relaxation response can help us cope with

Meditation has been an important dimension of Asians' lives for centuries.

stress. As we will see next, increasingly psychologists believe that support systems are also extremely beneficial in coping with stress.

Social Support

Our crowded, polluted, noisy, and achievement-oriented world can make us feel overwhelmed and isolated. Now, more than ever, we may need support systems, such as family members, friends, and co-workers to buffer stress. **Social support** *is information and feedback from others that one is loved and cared for, esteemed and valued, and included in a network of communication and mutual obligation.*

The benefits of social support can be grouped into three categories: tangible assistance, information, and emotional support (Taylor, 1991). Family and friends can provide *tangible assistance* by giving individuals actual goods and services in stressful circumstances. For example, gifts of food are often given after a death in the family occurs, meaning that bereaved family members won't have to cook for themselves and for visiting relatives in a time when their energy and motivation is low. Individuals who provide support can also give *information* by recommending specific actions and plans to help the person under stress cope more effectively. Friends may notice that a co-worker is overloaded with work and suggest ways for him or her to manage time more efficiently or delegate tasks more effectively. In stressful situations, individuals often suffer emotionally and may develop depression, anxiety, and loss of self-esteem. Friends and family can provide *emotional support* by reassuring

the person under stress that he or she is a valuable individual who is loved by others. Knowing that others care allows a person to approach and cope with stress with greater assurance.

Researchers consistently have found that social support helps individuals cope with stress. For example, in one study, depressed persons had fewer and less supportive relationships with family members, friends, and co-workers than people who were not depressed (Billings, Cronkite, & Moos, 1983). In another study, the prognosticators of cancer, mental illness, and suicide included a lack of closeness to one's parents and a negative attitude toward one's family (Cohen, 1979). Widows die at a rate that is 3 to 13 times higher than married women for every known cause of death. Close, positive attachments to others, both family and friends, consistently show up as important buffers against stress (Kessler & others, 1992).

Consider Robert, who had been laid off by an automobile manufacturer when it was about to fold, then a decade later by a truck manufacturer, and more recently by yet another automobile manufacturer. By all accounts, you would expect Robert to be down in the dumps or possibly feel that life had given him a bum deal, yet he is one of the most well-adjusted individuals in his community. When asked his secret in the face of adversity and stress, he attributes his ability to cope to a wonderful family and some great friends. Far more important than Robert's trials and tribulations is the support he receives from others, which helps him handle stress.

In thinking about ways to improve your coping, it is important for you to recognize the potential sources of social support in your own environment and learn how to effectively draw on these resources in times of stress (Taylor, 1991). Sometimes your coping can also be improved by joining community groups, interest groups, or informal social groups that meet regularly. As we will see next, some individuals can learn to cope more effectively through assertiveness training.

Assertiveness Training

Assertiveness training *involves teaching individuals to act in their own best interests, to stand up for their legitimate rights, and to express their views directly and openly.* Although individuals of both sexes may have trouble asserting themselves, the problem has often been more acute for females because they have more frequently been socialized to be passive and dependent. Thus, assertiveness training has been especially effective in helping females stand up for their rights and express themselves more openly. However, assertiveness training can benefit virtually anyone who has a tendency to let people walk all over them and can hardly ever say no.

It is important to distinguish among nonassertive behavior, aggressive behavior, and assertive behavior. **Nonassertive behavior** *is submissive, self-denying, inhibited and allows others to choose.* **Aggressive behavior** *is hostile, often involves anger, is self-enhancing at the expense of others, depreciates others, and achieves desired goals by hurting others.* **Assertive behavior** *involves acting* *in one's own best interests, standing up for one's legitimate rights, expressing one's views directly and openly, is self-enhancing, and involves self-choice.* Based on these definitions, it is clear that assertive behavior is a desirable coping strategy.

Behavior therapist Joseph Wolpe (1968) commented that there are essentially three possible broad approaches to the conduct of interpersonal relations. The first is to consider one's self only and ride roughshod over others. The second is to always put others before one's self and let others run roughshod over you. The third approach is the golden mean—placing yourself first but taking others into account. The third approach reflects an assertive orientation to human encounters.

In most cultures around the world, women have been more likely to be nonassertive and men aggressive. However, as part of the changing gender roles in the United States and many other Western countries, some women have become more assertive, stressing that they are persons who have rights, who deserve equal recognition/status/pay, and who are not inherently "weaker" than men (Alberti & Emmons, 1986). Assertive women demonstrate that they are capable of choosing their own life-style, free of the dictates of tradition, husband, children, and bosses (Phelps & Austin, 1987). They may *choose* to become a homemaker, *elect* to enter a male-dominated occupation, or *opt* to have only one child. In their sexual relationships, women can be comfortable taking the initiative, or they can say no firmly and make it stick.

Just as an increasing number of women are stepping up their efforts to move from being a nonassertive to an assertive person, more men are making the choice to move away from being aggressive to being assertive. Assertive men feel comfortable with themselves and don't have to put others down to enhance themselves. In contrast, aggressive men often try to demonstrate their manhood by being *macho* and dominating, showing little concern for others' feelings. Our society would benefit by increasingly valuing the assertive woman and the assertive man.

If you feel that you are either too nonassertive or too aggressive in your relationships with others, you might consider signing up for a stress management workshop that focuses on assertiveness training. You might also read a book on assertiveness training. Two recommendations are *Your Perfect Right* by Robert Alberti and Michael Emmons (1986) and *The Assertive Woman* by Stanlee Phelps and Nancy Austin (1987).

Multiple Coping Strategies

There are many ways to cope effectively with stress, just as there are many ways to cope ineffectively with stress. We have just highlighted a number of these effective and ineffective strategies. An important point about coping strategies is that we can call on more than one to help us deal with stress. For example, heart attack victims are usually advised to change more than one aspect of their lives. The advice might include these guidelines: develop a more trusting attitude, reduce your anger, take vaca-

tions on a regular basis, practice relaxation, make sure you have one or more friends in whom you can confide, quit smoking, lose weight, and exercise vigorously at least several times a week. One of these alone may not be able to turn the tide against stress, but a combination may be effective. You will read about smoking, weight, and exercise later in this chapter.

REVIEW

Coping with Stress

Most of us are confronted with more than one stressor. Removing one stressor can sometimes be very beneficial. In most cases, problem-focused coping is better than emotion-focused coping and the use of defense mechanisms, especially in coping with stress over the long term. Most of the time, we should think positively and avoid negative thinking. An optimistic attitude produces a sense of self-efficacy. Positive self-illusions can improve some individuals' lives, but it is important to guard against unrealistic expectations. A strategy of defensive pessimism helps some individuals cope more effectively.

Biofeedback is the process in which individuals' muscular or visceral activities are monitored by instruments, and information from the instruments is given (fed back) to the individuals so they can learn to voluntarily control the physiological activities. Biofeedback has been successful in reducing muscle tension and blood pressure. Meditation is the system of thought that incorporates exercises to attain bodily or mental control and well-being, as well as enlightenment. Transcendental meditation is the most popular form of meditation in the United States. Researchers have found that meditation reduces body arousal but usually no more than relaxation does. The "relaxation response" can be especially helpful in reducing arousal and calming the individual.

Social support is information and feedback from others that one is loved and cared for, esteemed and valued, and included in a network of communication and mutual obligation. Three important benefits of social support are tangible assistance, information, and emotional support. Researchers have consistently found that social support helps individuals cope more effectively with stress. Assertiveness training involves teaching individuals to act in their own best interests, to stand up for their legitimate rights, and to express their views directly and openly. Distinctions are made between nonassertive behavior, aggressive behavior, and assertive behavior, with assertive behavior favored as the best coping strategy. We can and should use more than one coping strategy to deal with stress.

Coping with Illness

Even if we manage stress effectively and practice good health habits, we cannot always prevent illness. How do we recognize, interpret, and seek treatment for the symptoms of an illness? What is a patient's role? How good are we at complying with medical advice and treatment? We will consider each of these questions in turn.

Recognizing, Interpreting, and Seeking Treatment for Symptoms

How do you know if you are sick? Each of us diagnoses how we feel and interprets the meaning of symptoms to decide whether we have a cold, the flu, a sexually transmitted disease, an ulcer, heart disease, and so on. However, many of us are not very accurate at recognizing the symptoms of an illness. For example, most people believe that they can tell when their blood pressure is elevated. The facts say otherwise. The majority of heart attack victims have never sought medical attention for cardiac problems. Many of us do not go to the doctor when the early warning signs of cancers, such as a lump or cyst, appear. Also, we are better at recognizing the symptoms of illnesses we are more familiar with, such as a cold or the flu, than illnesses we are less familiar with, such as diabetes.

As you learned in chapter 6, on memory, we use schemas to interpret information about ourselves in our world. Our prior experiences with a particular symptom may lead us to interpret it based on the schema we have for that symptom. For example, an individual with a long record of sprained ankles may dispel a swollen ankle as simply another sprain, not recognizing that she has a more serous injury—a fracture. By contrast, an individual who has never had a sprained ankle may perceive the swelling as serious and seek treatment.

Whether or not we seek treatment for symptoms depends on our perception of their severity and the likelihood medical treatment will relieve or eliminate them. If a person's ankle is fractured so badly he cannot walk without assistance, he is more likely to seek treatment than if the fracture produces only a slight limp. Also, someone may not seek treatment for a viral infection if she perceives that no drug is available to combat it effectively. By contrast, a person is more likely to seek treatment if she believes that a fungus infection on her foot can be remedied by antibiotics.

When people direct their attention outward, they are less likely to notice symptoms than when they direct their attention inward. For example, a woman whose life is extremely busy and full of distracting activities is less likely to notice a lump on her breast than a woman who has a much less active life. People who have boring jobs, who are socially inactive, and who live alone are more likely to report symptoms than people who have interesting jobs, who have active social lives, and who live with others (Pennebaker, 1983). Perhaps people who lead more active lives have more distractions and focus their attention less on themselves than do people with quieter lives. Even for people who have active lives, situational factors influence whether they will be attentive to symptoms. In one experiment, joggers were more likely to experience fatigue and be aware of their running-related aches and pains when they ran on a boring course than on a more interesting and varied course (Pennebaker & Lightner, 1980). The boring course likely increased the joggers' tendency to turn their attention inward and, thus, recognize their fatigue and pain.

The Patient's Role

Shelley Taylor (1979) identified two general types of patient roles. According to her analysis, some hospitalized individuals take on a "good patient" role, others a "bad patient" role. In the **"good patient" role,** *a patient is passive and unquestioning and behaves "properly."* The positive consequences of this role include being well-liked by the hospital staff, who in turn respond quickly to the good patient's emergencies. Like many roles, however, the good patient is somewhat superficial, and Taylor believes that, behind the facade, the patient may feel helpless, powerless, anxious, and depressed. In the **"bad patient" role,** *a patient complains to the staff, demands attention, disobeys staff orders, and generally misbehaves.* The refusal to become helpless, and the accompanying anger, may actually have some positive consequences, because bad patients take an *active* role in their own health care. The negative side of bad patient behavior, however, may aggravate such conditions as hypertension and angina, and such behavior may stimulate staff members to ignore, overmedicate, or prematurely discharge a bad patient.

How can the stress of hospitalization be relieved? Realistic expectations about the experience, predictable events, and social support reduce the stress of hospitalization (Spacapan, 1988). When doctors communicate clearly to their patients about the nature of the treatment procedures and what to expect when they are hospitalized, patients' confidence in the medical treatment also increases, and, as you learned in the discussion of stress, a social network of individuals who deeply care about us goes a long way toward reducing stress. Visits, phone calls, cards, and flowers from family members and friends lift patients' spirits and improve their recovery from illness.

Compliance with Medical Advice and Treatment

An estimated one-third of all patients fail to follow recommended treatments. Compliance depends on the disorder and the recommendation. Only about 15 percent of all patients do not follow doctors' orders for tablets and ointments, but more than 90 percent of patients do not heed life-style advice, such as to stop smoking, to lose weight, or to stop drinking (DiNicola & DiMatteo, 1984).

Why do we pay money to doctors and then not follow their advice? We may not comply with a doctor's orders because we are not satisfied with the quality of the care we are receiving and because we have our own theories about our health and do not completely trust the doctor's advice. This mistrust is exacerbated when doctors use jargon and highly technical descriptions to inform patients about a treatment. Sometimes doctors do not give patients clear information or fully explain the risks of ignoring their orders. To be motivated to stop smoking, to eat more nutritionally, or to stop drinking, patients need a clear understanding of the dangers involved in noncompliance with the doctor's recommendations. Success or failure in treatment may depend on whether the doctor can convince patients that a valid, believable danger exists and can offer an effective, concrete strategy for coping with the problem (Lau, 1988).

REVIEW

Coping with Illness

Many of us are not very accurate at diagnosing the symptoms of illness. When our attention is directed outward, we are less likely to detect symptoms than when our attention is directed inward. We use schemas developed through prior experience to interpret symptoms. Seeking treatment depends on our perception of the severity of the symptoms and the likelihood that medical treatment will reduce or eliminate the symptoms.

In the "good patient" role, individuals are passive and unquestioning and behave properly. In the "bad patient" role, individuals complain to the staff, demand attention, disobey staff orders, and generally misbehave. Realistic prior expectations, predictable events, and social support reduce the stress of hospitalization.

Approximately one-third of all patients do not follow treatment recommendations. Compliance varies with the disorder and the treatment recommendation, with our level of satisfaction with the quality of care we are receiving, and with our own theories about why we are sick and how we can get well. Clearer doctor-patient communication is needed for improved compliance.

Promoting Health

In our earlier discussion of stress, we explored a number of coping strategies that people can adopt to deal with stress and that can also improve their health. Our nation's health profile can also be improved by reducing behaviors that impair health, such as smoking and overeating, and by engaging in healthier behaviors that include good nutrition and exercise.

Smoking

The year 1988 marked the 75th anniversary of the introduction of Camel cigarettes. Some magazines surprised readers with elaborate pop-up advertisements for Camels. Camel's ad theme was "75 years and still smokin'." Coincidentally 1988 was also the 75th anniversary of the American Cancer Society.

In 1989 the Surgeon General and his advisory committee issued a report, *Reducing the Health Consequences of Smoking: 25 Years of Progress*. It was released 25 years after the original warnings that cigarettes are responsible for major health problems, especially lung cancer. New evidence was presented to show that smoking is even more harmful than previously thought. For example, the report indicated that in 1985 cigarette smoking accounted for more than one-fifth of all deaths in the United States—20 percent higher than previously believed. Thirty percent of all cancer deaths were attributed to smoking, as were 21 percent of all coronary heart disease deaths and 82 percent of chronic pulmonary disease deaths.

Researchers are also increasingly finding that passive smoke (environmental smoke inhaled by nonsmokers who live or work around smokers) carries health risks (Sandler & others, 1989). Passive smoke is estimated to be the culprit in as many as 8,000 lung cancer deaths a year in the United States. Children of smokers are at special risk for respiratory and middle-ear diseases. For children under the age of 5, the risk of upper respiratory tract infection is doubled if their mothers smoke.

The Surgeon General's 1989 report contains some good news, however. Fewer people smoke today and almost half of all living adults who ever smoked have quit. In particular the prevalence of smoking among men fell from over 50 percent in 1965 to about 30 percent in 1989. As a consequence, a half-century's uninterrupted escalation in the rate of death due to lung cancer among males has ceased, and the incidence of lung cancer among White males has fallen. Although approximately 56 million Americans 15 to 84 years of age were smokers in 1985, the Surgeon General's report estimates that 91 million would have been smoking had there been no changes in smoking and health knowledge, norms, and policy over the past quarter century (Warner, 1989).

However, the bad news is that over 50 million Americans *continue* to smoke, most having failed at attempts to quit. Why, in the face of the damaging figure that more than one-fifth of all deaths are due to smoking, do so many people still smoke?

Smoking Is Addictive and Reinforcing

Most adult smokers would like to quit, but their addiction to nicotine often turns their efforts into dismal failure. Nicotine, the active drug in cigarettes, is a stimulant that increases a smoker's energy and alertness, a pleasurable experience that is positively reinforcing. Nicotine also causes the release of acetylcholine and endorphin neurotransmitters, which have a calming and pain-reducing effect. However, smoking not only works as a positive reinforcer; it also works as a negative reinforcer by ending a smoker's painful craving for nicotine. A smoker gets relief from this painful aversive state simply by smoking another cigarette.

We are rational, cognitive beings. Can't we develop enough self-control to overcome these pleasurable, immediate, reinforcing circumstances by thinking about the delayed, long-term, damaging consequences of smoking? As indicated earlier, many adults have quit smoking because they recognize that it is "suicide in slow motion," but the immediate pleasurable effects of smoking are extremely difficult to overcome. In chapter 5, Learning, we described self-control programs that are effective in helping individuals quit smoking.

Preventing Smoking

Smoking usually begins during childhood and adolescence. Adolescent smoking reached its peak in the mid-1970s, when 29 percent of all high school seniors smoked on a daily basis. By 1991 this rate had dropped only 1 percent—to 28 percent (Johnston, O'Malley, & Bachman, 1992). The smoking rate is at a level that will cut short the lives of many adolescents. Despite the growing awareness that it is important to keep children from starting to smoke in the first place, there are fewer restrictions on children's access to cigarettes today than there were in 1964, and the existing restrictions are rarely reinforced (U.S. Department of Health and Human Services, 1989).

Traditional school health programs appear to have succeeded in educating adolescents about the long-term health consequences of smoking, but they have had little effect on adolescent smoking *behavior*. That is, teens who smoke know many of the facts about the health risks, such as lung cancer, emphysema, and suicide in slow motion, but they go ahead and smoke just as much anyway (Miller & Slap, 1989). As a result of this gap between what teens know and what they do in regard to smoking, researchers are focusing on the factors that place teens at high risk for future smoking, especially social pressures from peers, family members, and the media. The tobacco industry preys on young people's desire to feel grown up by advertising "cool" people who smoke—successful young women smoking Virginia Slims and rugged, handsome men smoking Marlboros, for example. The advertisements encourage adolescents to asso-

THE FAR SIDE   By GARY LARSON

The real reason dinosaurs became extinct

THE FAR SIDE cartoon by Gary Larson is reprinted by permission of Chronicle Features, San Francisco, CA.

ciate cigarette smoking with a successful and, ironically, athletic/active life-style. Legislators are trying to introduce more stringent laws to further regulate the tobacco industry.

In recent years, American health concerns have focused not only on smoking, but on eating as well. Next we will discuss some of the eating habits that cause people problems.

Eating Problems

Even after a challenging workout, a tall, slender woman goes into the locker room of the fitness center, hurls her towel across the bench, looks squarely in the mirror and says, "You fat pig. You are nothing but a fat pig." Across town, the alarm goes off and 35-year-old Robert jumps out of bed, throws on his jogging shorts and begins his daily predawn 3-mile run. Returning to shower and dress, he observes his body in the mirror, tugging at the flabby overhang and commenting, "Why did you eat that bowl of ice cream last night?" In another instance, the Chicago Bears' William "the Refrigerator" Perry ballooned to 350 pounds and coach Mike Ditka suspended him, requiring him to enroll in a 28-day eating-disorder program.

We are a nation obsessed with food, spending an extraordinary amount of time thinking about, gobbling, and avoiding food. In chapter 11, Motivation and Emotion, we discussed the nature of hunger. In this chapter, we will focus on the problem of our increasingly heavy population, weight-loss programs, anorexia nervosa, and bulimia.

An Increasingly Heavy Population

The human gustatory system and taste preferences developed at a time when reliable sources of food were scarce. Our earliest ancestors probably developed a preference for sweets, since ripe fruit, which is a concentrated source of sugar (and thus, calories), was so accessible. Today we still have a "sweet tooth." However, unlike our ancestors' ripe fruit, which contained sugar *plus* vitamins and minerals, the soft drinks and candy bars we often snack on fill us with empty calories.

In the United States, approximately 50 percent of all those who are middle-aged and 25 percent of all adolescents are estimated to be overweight (Andres, 1989). Further, the number of American children who are overweight increased more than 50 percent from the 1960s to the 1980s (Dietz, 1986). Medical and mental health professionals have become increasingly concerned about getting children and teens to establish good eating habits early. Eating patterns in childhood and adolescence are

Ethnicity and Nutrition

I n the late 1960s, and again in the 1980s, national attention focused on the relationship between poverty and malnutrition for millions of Americans, a disproportionate percentage of whom are members of ethnic minority groups. In response to grim evidence from a 10-state survey of more than 40,000 individuals, Congress expanded the existing food assistance programs and created new ones, such as the special Supplemental Food Program for Women, Infants, and Children (WIC). Despite these programs, which largely survived the budget-cutting fever of the 1980s, malnutrition, obesity, and other dietary problems remain a national problem (Allen & Mitchell, in press).

Black women are much less likely than White women to develop eating disorders that reflect an obsession with thinness;

Black women seem more comfortable with larger body sizes. However, Black women who do become anorexic, like their White counterparts, are usually members of the middle class. A high rate of obesity among Black women is often due to both low rates of exercise and diets high in fat and sodium, a legacy of the Southern roots of most Black Americans. Haitian Americans believe that a fat person is healthy and happy but a thin person is the opposite (LaGuerre, 1981).

Both economic and cultural factors affect the nutritional intake of Native Americans (Walter, 1974). Many Navaho Indians have a lactose intolerance, making it difficult for them to consume dairy products. Further, because they have strong ethnic food preferences, surplus foods supplied by the Department of Agriculture are often discarded, even when their normal supply of food is disrupted (Kunitz & Levy, 1981). Mexican Americans also have high rates of lactose intolerance, contributing to high rates of malnutrition among pregnant, lactating Mexican American women and their children under the age of 6 (Schrieber & Homiack, 1981).

Chinese Americans have an elaborate system of classifying foods and herbs into *hot* and *cold*, which must be balanced to achieve health. Chinese Americans consume a wide variety of foods, so, unless they are poor, they usually eat nutritionally balanced meals. The elderly Chinese American poor tend to eat a lot of salt despite their high rates of hypertension. Salt is present in soy sauce, which is used liberally by most Chinese Americans (Gould-Martin & Ngin, 1981).

In short, ethnic background is related to a person's preferences for certain foods and to his or her nutritional health.

strongly associated with obesity in adulthood—80 percent of all obese adolescents become obese adults, for example (Brone & Fisher, 1988).

The percentage of people who are overweight also varies by sex and ethnic group. For example, among 35-to-44-year-olds, 28.2 percent of the White men, 24.8 percent of the White women, 40.9 percent of the Black men, and 40.8 percent of the Black women are overweight (National Center for Health Statistics, 1989). To read further about the nutritional health of ethnic minorities in the United States, turn to Sociocultural Worlds 15.2.

Ever since fashion model Twiggy redefined the ideal feminine physique in the 1960s, losing weight has become a national obsession. The number of dollars spent on diet foods, books, and programs nearly doubled in the 1980s—to close to $30 billion (Brownell, 1991). Next we will take a look at the world of dieting.

Weight-Loss Programs

Even ancient Roman women were known to starve themselves. However, never before have women spent so much time, energy, and money on their weight. Since its inception in 1963, Weight Watchers alone has enrolled more than 15 million members. Although men *and* women have gained weight and both sexes show concern about losing weight, the obsession with dieting seems to be more intense among women.

A myriad of ways to lose weight exists: bypass surgery, exercise, diets, and psychotherapy. Which ones work? Does one work better than the rest? Do any of them work at all?

The most dramatic form of losing weight involves intestinal or gastric bypass surgery, which has been successful in reducing overeating. One study of more than 700 patients followed for 1 year or longer found that 55 percent of the excess pounds were lost (Halmi, 1980). In some instances, though, bypass operations have serious side effects, among them liver

Everything we know about weight loss suggests that a combination of eating healthy foods and exercising works best.

disease, and the procedure is recommended only for people who are 100 pounds or more overweight, in which case the obesity may be life threatening. For extremely obese people, though, the benefits may be greater than the adverse side effects; for example, in addition to eating less, many of these people find that they are in better moods and they exercise more.

People also take drugs to help them lose weight. Amphetamines are widely used because they diminish appetite. Weight loss with amphetamines usually is short-lived, and the drugs often have adverse side effects, such as increased blood pressure and possible addiction. No drug currently available has been proven successful in long-term weight reduction (Logue, 1986). The ineffective drugs include over-the-counter drugs, such as Dexatrim.

Exercise is a much more attractive alternative than weight-loss drugs. Exercise not only burns up calories but it continues to raise a person's metabolic rate for several hours *after* the activity. Exercise actually lowers your body's set point for weight, making it much easier to maintain a lower weight (Bennett & Gurin, 1982). Nonetheless, it is difficult to convince obese individuals

to exercise. One problem is that moderate exercise does not reduce calorie consumption, and in many cases individuals who exercise take in more calories than their sedentary counterparts (Stern, 1984). Still, exercise combined with conscious self-control of eating habits can produce a viable weight-loss program (Polivy & Herman, 1991; Stotland & Zuroff, 1991). When exercise is a component of weight-loss programs, individuals keep weight off longer than when calorie reduction alone is followed.

Anorexia Nervosa and Bulimia

Eighteen-year-old Jane gradually eliminated foods from her diet to the point at which she subsisted by eating *only* applesauce and eggnog. She spent hours observing her body, wrapping her fingers around her waist to see if it was getting any thinner. She fantasized about becoming a beautiful fashion model and wearing designer bathing suits. However, even when she dropped to 85 pounds, Jane still felt fat. She continued to lose weight, eventually emaciating herself. She was hospitalized and treated for **anorexia nervosa,** *an eating disorder that involves the relentless* *pursuit of thinness through starvation.* Anorexia nervosa can eventually lead to death, as it did for pop singer Karen Carpenter (Casper, 1989).

Anorexia nervosa primarily afflicts females during adolescence and the early adulthood years (only about 5 percent of all anorexics are male). Most adolescents with this disorder are White and from well-educated, middle- and upper-income families. Although anorexics avoid eating, they have an intense interest in food. They cook for others, they talk about food, and they insist on watching others eat. Anorexics have a distorted body image, perceiving themselves as overweight even when they become skeletal. As self-starvation continues and the fat content of their body drops to a bare minimum, menstruation usually stops and their behavior often becomes hyperactive.

Numerous causes of anorexia nervosa have been proposed, including societal, psychological, and physiological factors (Brumberg, 1988; Fisher & Brone, 1991; Litti, 1991; Pike & Rodin, 1991; Sigman & Flanery, 1992). The societal factor most often held responsible is the current fashion image of thinness. Psychological factors include motivation for attention, desire for individuality, denial of sexuality, and a way of coping with overcontrolling parents. Anorexics sometimes have families that place high demands for achievement on them. Unable to meet their parents' high standards, they feel unable to control their own lives. By limiting their food intake, anorexics gain a sense of self-control. Physiological causes involve the hypothalamus, which is abnormal in a number of ways in an anorexic adolescent. However, the bottom line is that, at this time, the cause of anorexia nervosa is unknown.

Bulimia *is an eating disorder in which an individual consistently follows a binge-and-purge eating pattern.* A bulimic goes on an eating binge and then purges by self-induced vomiting or by using a laxative. Sometimes the binges alternate with fasting and at other times with normal eating, producing gastric and chemical imbalances in the body. Whereas anorexics can control their eating, bulimics cannot, and depression is a common characteristic of bulimics (Levy, Dixon, & Stern, 1989). Like anorexia nervosa, bulimia is primarily a female disorder; it is especially prevalent among college women. Some estimates suggest that one in two college women binge and purge at least some of the time. However, estimates suggest that true bulimics—those who binge and purge on a regular basis—make up less than 2 percent of the college female population (Stunkard, 1987). In one survey of 1,500 high school and university students, 4 percent of the high school students and 5 percent of the university students were bulimic (Howat & Saxton, 1988). Many of the causes proposed for anorexia nervosa are also offered for bulimia.

At this point, we have discussed the importance of reducing smoking and coping with eating problems as ways to improve health. Next we will consider another very important factor that can improve health—exercise.

This exhausted runner at the end of a grueling marathon endorses the "no pain, no gain" philosophy of exercise's role in health. An alternative philosophy is that, for most individuals, moderate exercise is more pleasurable and easier to participate in over the long term. For some of us, intense exercise may be best, for others moderate exercise is best, but a sedentary life with little exercise at all should be avoided.

Exercise

In 1961 President John F. Kennedy offered the following message: "We are underexercised as a nation. We look instead of play. We ride instead of walk. Our existence deprives us of the minimum of physical activity essential for healthy living." Without question, people are jogging, cycling, and aerobically exercising more today than in 1961, but far too many of us are still couch potatoes. **Aerobic exercise** *is sustained exercise—jogging, swimming, or cycling, for example—that stimulates heart and lung activity* (Cooper, 1970).

Effects of Exercise on Physical and Mental Health

The main focus of research on exercise's role in health has been on preventing heart disease. Most health experts recommend that you should try to raise your heart rate to 60 percent of your maximum heart rate during exercise. Your maximum heart rate is calculated as 220 minus your age; if you are 20, you should aim for an exercise heart rate of 120 ($220 - 20 = 200 \times .60 = 120$). People in some occupations get more vigorous exercise than those in others. For example, longshoremen have about half the risk of fatal heart attacks of their co-workers, such as crane drivers and clerks, who have less physically demanding jobs. Further, in an elaborate study of 17,000 male alumni of Harvard University, those who played strenuous sports regularly had a lower risk of heart disease and were more likely to still be alive at the time of the study (Paffenbarger & others, 1986). Based on such findings, some health experts conclude that, regardless of other risk factors (smoking, high blood pressure, overweight, heredity), if you exercise enough to burn more than 2,000 calories a week, you can cut your risk of heart attack by an impressive two-thirds (Sherwood, Light, & Blumenthal, 1989). However, burning 2,000 calories a week through exercise requires a lot of effort, far more than most of us are willing to expend. To burn 300 calories a day through exercise, you would have to do one of the following: swim or run for about 25 minutes, walk for 45 minutes at about 4 miles an hour, or participate in aerobic dancing for 30 minutes.

The risk of heart attack can also be cut by as much as one-third over a 7-year period with such moderate exercise as rapid walking and gardening. The catch is that you have to spend an hour a day in these activities for them to pay off. Health experts uniformly recommend that, if you are unaccustomed to exercise, start any exercise program slowly (Morgan & Goldston, 1987).

Robert Ornstein and David Sobel (1989) go against the grain of the "no pain, no gain" philosophy and believe that exercise should be pleasurable, not painful. They point out that 20 percent of all joggers running 10 miles a week suffer significant injuries, such as torn knee cartilage and pulled hamstring muscles. Ornstein and Sobel argue that most people can stay healthy by participating in exercise that burns only 500 calories a week. They believe it is overkill to run 8-minute miles, 3 miles at a time, 5 days a week, for example. Not only are fast walking and gardening on their recommended list of exercises, so are 20 minutes of sex (110 calories), 20 minutes of playing with children (106 calories), and 45 minutes of dancing (324 calories).

Researchers have found that exercise benefits not only physical health but mental health as well. In particular, exercise improves self-concept and reduces anxiety and depression (Doyne

In one recent experiment, the self-concept of depressed women was improved by either weight lifting or running (Ossip-Klein & others, 1989).

& others, 1987; Lobstein, Ismail, & Rasmussen, 1989; Ossip-Klein & others, 1989). In one recent study, 109 nonexercising volunteers were randomly assigned to one of four groups: high-intensity aerobic training, moderate-intensity aerobic training, low-intensity nonaerobic training, and a waiting list (Moses & others, 1989). In the high-intensity aerobic group, participants engaged in a continuous walk-jog program that elevated their heart rate to 70 to 75 percent of maximum. In the moderate-intensity aerobic group, participants engaged in walking or jogging that elevated their heart rate to 60 percent of maximum. In the low-intensity nonaerobic group, participants engaged in strength, mobility, and flexibility exercises in a slow, discontinuous manner for approximately 30 minutes. Those who were assigned to exercise programs worked out three to five times a week. Those who were on the waiting list did not exercise. The programs lasted for 10 weeks. As expected, the group assigned to the high-intensity aerobic program showed the greatest aerobic fitness on a 12-minute walk-run. Fitness also improved for those assigned to moderate- and low-intensity exercise programs. However, only the people assigned to the moderate-intensity aerobic training programs showed psychological benefits. These benefits appeared immediately in the form of reduced tension and anxiety and, after 3 months, improved ability to cope with stress.

Why were the psychological benefits superior in the moderate-intensity aerobic condition? Perhaps the participants in the high-intensity program found the training too demanding; this is not surprising since these people were nonexercisers prior to the study. The superiority of the moderate-intensity aerobic training program over the nonaerobic low-intensity exercise program suggests that a minimum level of aerobic conditioning may be required to obtain important psychological benefits.

Research on the benefits of exercise suggests that both moderate and intense activities produce important physical and psychological gains (Brown, 1991; Plante & Rodin, 1990). Some people enjoy rigorous, intense exercise. Others enjoy more moderate exercise routines. The enjoyment and pleasure we derive from exercise added to its aerobic benefits make exercise one of life's most important activities.

Exercise in Children and Adolescents

Many of our health patterns, both good and bad, are longstanding. Our experiences as children and adolescents contribute to our health practices as adults. Are today's children getting enough exercise? In 1980 and 1989, a national assessment compared 6-to-17-year-olds' physical fitness on a test that included sprints, situps, pushups, and longjumps. The overall rating of "satisfactory" dropped from 43 percent in 1980 to 32 percent in 1989 (Updyke, 1989).

Some health experts blame television for the poor physical condition of our nation's children. One study revealed that children who watch little television are much more physically fit than their heavy television-viewing counterparts (Tucker, 1987). The more children watch television, the more they are likely to be overweight. No one is quite sure whether this is because children spend their leisure time in front of a television set, whether they tend to eat a lot of junk food they see advertised on television, or whether less physically fit children find physical activity less reinforcing than watching television.

The family plays an important role in a child's exercise program. A wise strategy for families is to take up vigorous physical activities that parents and children can enjoy together. Running, swimming, cycling, and hiking are especially recommended. In encouraging children to exercise more, parents should not push them beyond their physical limits or expose them to intense competitive pressures that take the fun out of sports and exercise. For example, long-distance running may be too strenuous for young children and can result in bone injuries. Recently there has been an increase in the number of children participating in strenuous events, such as marathons and triathalons. Doctors are beginning to see injuries in children they previously saw only in adults, such as stress fractures and tendonitis (Risser, 1989). If left to their own devices, how many 8-year-old children would want to prepare for a marathon?

Is there evidence that exercise might buffer children's and adolescents' stress? In one study of 364 girls in grades 7 through 11 in Los Angeles, the negative impact of stressful events on health declined as the girls' exercise levels increased, suggesting that exercise can be a valuable resource for combating adolescents' stress (Brown & Siegel, 1988). In another study, adolescents who exercised a lot coped more effectively with stress and had more positive identities than adolescents who engaged in little exercise (Grimes & Mattimore, 1989).

In the fourth century B.C., Aristotle commented that the quality of life is determined by its activities. In today's world, we know that exercise is one of the principal activities that improve the quality of life, both children's and adults'.

Toward Healthier Lives

In this chapter, we have seen that being healthy involves far more than simply going to a doctor when you get sick and being treated for disease. We are becoming increasingly aware that our

a.

b.

(a) Children who watch little television are more physically fit than their counterparts who watch a lot of television. The more television children watch, the more likely they are to be overweight. (b) The family plays an important role in a child's exercise program. A wise strategy is for families to take up vigorous physical activities that parents and children can enjoy together, such as running, swimming, hiking, or cycling.

behavior determines whether we will develop a serious illness and when we will die (Erben, 1991; Minkler, 1989; Stanhope & Lancaster, 1991). Seven of the 10 leading causes of death in the United States are associated with the *absence* of health behaviors. Such diseases as influenza, polio, and rubella are no longer major causes of death. More deaths now are caused by heart disease (36 percent of all deaths in 1986), cancer (22 percent), and stroke (17 percent).

Gender and ethnicity play roles in life expectancy and health. According to psychologist Bonnie Strickland (1989), males are at greater risk than females for death at every age in the life span. The cause of death also varies for men and women. For example, four times more men than women die as a result of homicide, and twice as many men than women die as a result of respiratory cancer, suicide, pulmonary disease, accidents, cirrhosis of the liver, and heart disease.

In general Blacks have a higher mortality rate than Whites for 13 of the 15 leading causes of death (Winett, King, & Altman, 1989). Also, of all ethnic minority women, Black women are the most vulnerable to health problems, reports the Public Health Service Task Force on Women's Health Issues (1985). For example, Black American women, compared with White American women, are three times more likely to have high blood pressure, are twice as likely to die from cardiovascular disease, have a 35 percent higher death rate for diabetes, and are four times more likely to be a victim of homicide. More information about the health and health care of individuals from ethnic minority backgrounds appears in Sociocultural Worlds 15.3.

As we have seen repeatedly in this chapter, personal habits and life-style play key roles in disease. These findings lead health psychologists, behavioral medicine specialists, and public health professionals to predict that the next major step in improving the general health of the American population will be primarily behavioral, not medical. The federal government and the Society for Public Health Education have set health objectives for the year 2000 (Schwartz & Eriksen, 1989). Among them are the following:

- To develop preventive services targeting diseases and such problems as cancer, heart disease, stroke, unintended pregnancy (especially among adolescents), and AIDS
- To promote health, including behavior modification and health education; stronger programs are urged for dealing with smoking, alcohol and drug abuse, nutrition, physical fitness, and mental health
- To work toward cleaner air and water and to improve workplace safety, including reducing exposure to toxic chemicals
- To meet the health needs of special populations, such as gaining a better understanding of disease prevention in Black and Hispanic populations (Klonoff, 1991); ethnic minority groups suffer disproportionately from cancer, heart disease, diabetes, and other major diseases

America's health care costs have soared and are moving toward the $1 trillion mark annually. Health experts hope to make a dent in these costs by encouraging people to live healthier lives. Many corporations have begun to recognize that health promotion for their employees is cost effective. Businesses are increasingly examining their employees' health behavior and the workplace environment as they recognize the role health plays in productive work. Smoke-free work environments, on-site exercise programs, bonuses to quit smoking and lose weight, and company-sponsored athletic events are increasingly found in American businesses.

Culture and Health

We have seen that, in the United States, a person's health varies according to his or her sex and ethnicity. Earlier in the chapter, we found that acculturation can also cause stress. In this section, we will further consider the role culture plays in health beliefs and behavior. In turn we will discuss cultural factors in coronary problems, cultural factors in cancer, and government interventions and preventive health care.

Cultural Factors in Coronary Problems

Cross-cultural psychologists believe that studies of migrant ethnic groups help shed light on the role culture plays in health. As ethnic groups migrate, the health practices dictated by their culture change while their genetic predisposition to certain disorders remains constant (Ilola, 1990). The Ni-Hon-San Study (Nipon-Honolulu-San Francisco), part of the Honolulu Heart Study, is an ongoing study of approximately 12,000 Japanese men in Hiroshima and Nagasaki (Japan), Honolulu, and San Francisco. In the study, the Japanese men living in Japan have had the lowest rate of coronary heart disease, those living in Honolulu have had an intermediate rate, and those living in San Francisco have had the highest rate. John Berry's concept of acculturation—discussed earlier in the chapter—provides a valuable framework for understanding why the Japanese men's cholesterol level, glucose level, and weight all increased as they migrated and acculturated. As the Japanese men migrated farther away from Japan, their health practices, such as diet, changed. The Japanese men in California, for example, ate 40 percent more fat than the men in Japan.

Conversely Japanese men in California have much lower rates of cerebrovascular disease (stroke) than Japanese men living in Japan. Businessmen in Japan tend to consume vast quantities of alcohol and chain smoke, two high-risk factors for stroke. As a result, stroke was the leading cause of death in Japan until it was surpassed by cancer in 1981. However, death rates from stroke for Japanese American men are at the same level as that of Anglo American men. Researchers suspect that this level is related to a change in behavior. That is, Japanese American men consume less

a.

b.

In the cross-cultural Honolulu Heart Study, (a) the Japanese men living in Japan had the lowest rate of coronary heart disease, those living in Honolulu had an intermediate rate, and (b) those living in San Francisco had the highest rate. The Japanese men in California ate 40 percent more fat than the men in Japan.

alcohol and smoke less than their counterparts in Japan. Next we will see that culture appears to play an important role in cancer as well.

Cultural Factors in Cancer

Researchers have found that mice fed on a high-fat diet are more likely to develop breast cancer than mice fed on a low-fat diet, and a cross-national study involving women also found a strong positive correlation between fat consumption and death rates from breast cancer (Cohen, 1987) (see figure 15.5 on page 482).

SOCIOCULTURAL WORLDS 15.3

Health Promotion in Black Americans, Hispanic Americans, Asian Americans, and Native Americans

A s mentioned before, there are differences within ethnic groups as well as among them. This is just as true of health among ethnic groups as it is of, say, family structure. The spectrum of living conditions and life-styles within an ethnic group are influenced by social class, immigrant status, social and language skills, occupational opportunities, and such social resources as the availability of meaningful support networks—all of which can play a role in an ethnic minority member's health. Psychologists Felipe Castro and Delia Magaña (1988) developed a course in health promotion in ethnic minority communities, which they teach at UCLA. A summary of some of the issues they discuss in the course follows.

Prejudice and racial segregation are the historical underpinnings for the chronic stress of discrimination and poverty that adversely affects the health of many Black Americans. Support systems, such as an extended family network, may be especially important resources to improve the health of Black Americans and help them cope with stress (Boyd-Franklin, 1989; McAdoo, 1988).

Some of the same stressors mentioned for Black Americans are associated with migration to the United States by Puerto Ricans, Mexicans, and Latin Americans. Language is often a

One of the most telling comparisons to link fat intake and cancer is between the United States and Japan. Both countries have similar levels of industrialization and education, as well as high medical standards. Although the overall cancer rates of the two countries are similar, cancers of the breast, colon, and prostrate are common in the United States but rare in Japan. By contrast, cancer of the stomach is common in Japan but rare in the United States. Within two generations, Japanese immigrants to Hawaii and California have breast cancer rates that are significantly higher than those in Japan and that approach those of Ameri-cans. Many researchers believe that the high fat intake of Americans and the low fat intake of the Japanese are implicated in the countries' different cancer rates.

The general good health, low cancer rates, and longevity of Seventh Day Adventists, an evangelical Protestant sect, further support the link between cultural factors, especially diet, and cancer. Strict Seventh Day Adventists adhere to biblical precepts that determine diet and other life-style behaviors. Their well-balanced diet includes generous portions of unrefined foods, grains, vegetable protein, fruits, and vegetables. Smoking is

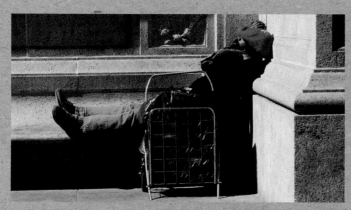

Prejudice and racial segregation provide historical underpinnings for the chronic stress of discrimination and poverty that adversely affect the health of many Black Americans.

Herbalists and folk healers continue to play an important role in the health care of Chinese Americans. For example, there are Chinese herbalists and folk healers in every Chinatown in the United States.

barrier for unacculturated Hispanics in doctor-patient communica-tions. In addition, there is increasing evidence that diabetes occurs at an above average rate in Hispanics, making this disease a major health problem that parallels the above average rate of high blood pressure among Blacks (Gardner & others, 1984).

Asian Americans are characterized by their broad diversity in national backgrounds and life-styles. They range from highly accul-turated Japanese Americans who may be better educated than many Anglo Americans and have excellent access to health care, to the many Indochinese refugees who have few economic resources and may be in poor health.

Cultural barriers to adequate health care include a lack of financial resources and poor language skills. In addition, members of ethnic minority groups are often unfamiliar with how the medical system operates, confused about the need to see numerous people, and uncertain about why they have to wait so long for service (Snowden & Cheung, 1990).

Other barriers may be specific to certain cultures, reflecting differing ideas regarding what causes disease and how it should be treated. For example, there are Chinese herbalists and folk healers in every Chinatown in the United States. Depending on their degree of acculturation to Western society, Chinese Americans may go to either a folk healer or a Western doctor first, but generally they will consult a folk healer for follow-up care. Chinese medicines are usually used for home care. These include ginseng

tea, boiled centipede soup for cancer, and eucalyptus oil for dizziness resulting from hypertension.

Native Americans view Western medicine as a source of crisis intervention, quick fixes for broken legs, or cures for other symp-toms. They do not view Western medicine as a source for treating the causes of disease or for preventing disease. For example, they are unlikely to attend a seminar on preventing alcohol abuse. They also are reluctant to become involved in care that requires long-term hospitalization or surgery.

Both Navaho Indians and Mexican Americans rely on family members to make decisions about treatment. Doctors who expect such patients to decide on the spot whether or not to undergo treatment will likely embarrass the patient or force the patient to give an answer that may lead to canceled appointments. Mexican Americans also believe that some illnesses are due to natural causes whereas others are due to supernatural causes. Depending on their level of acculturation, Mexican Americans may be disappointed and confused by doctors who do not show an awareness of how to treat diseases with supposed supernatural origins.

Health care professionals can increase their effectiveness with ethnic minority patients by improving their knowledge of patients' attitudes, beliefs, and folk practices regarding health and disease (Anderson, 1991; Martin, 1991). Such information should be integrated into Western treatment rather than ignored at the risk of alienating patients.

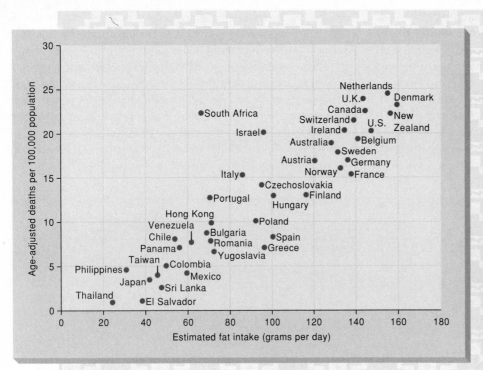

FIGURE 15.5

Cross-cultural comparisons of diet and cancer. In countries in which individuals have a low daily intake of fat, the rate of breast cancer is low (in Thailand, for example). In countries in which individuals have a high daily intake of fat, the rate of breast cancer is high (in the Netherlands, for example).

From "Diet and Cancer" by Leonard A. Cohen. Copyright © 1987 by Scientific American, Inc. All rights reserved.

prohibited. As a result, there is a very low incidence of lung cancer among Seventh Day Adventists. In addition, fewer Seventh Day Adventists have cancer of any type—including breast, pancreas, and colorectal cancer—than other cultural groups in the United States.

As is the case with any cultural group, some Seventh Day Adventists adhere more strictly to the sect's life-style than do others. In one study of religiously inactive Norwegian Seventh Day Adventists, their risk of disease was similar to Norwegians who were not Seventh Day Adventists (Fonnebo, 1985). Similarly Seventh Day Adventists in the United States who marginally adhere to the sect's guidelines for physical, mental, and spiritual health have an increased risk of disease (Phillips & others, 1980).

Government Interventions and Preventive Health Care

The Seventh Day Adventists have strong convictions about behavior and health. Could a government be as successful as the Seventh Day Adventists in promoting behavior that ensures the health of its citizens? Several governments have tried various measures, with mixed success. The government of Finland, for example, has placed more restrictions on tobacco advertise-

ments and liquor sales than most countries, resulting in improved health for Finnish citizens. However, in the United States, both citizen and industry lobbying groups have made it difficult for health-related legislation to be approved. Cross-cultural psychologist Lisa Ilola (1990) points to seat belt use and mandatory helmets for motorcycle riders as an example of how many Americans, instead of accepting these reasonable protections for health and safety, bridle at what they believe is government intrusion into freedom of choice. The degree of respect for the government and the appropriateness of the government action, it appears, are important factors in whether or not people will abide by legal constraints to promote their health and safety (Brislin, 1990).

Cross-cultural psychologist Richard Brislin (1990) emphasizes that, to ensure the success of a social service program, the people who introduce or maintain it should be highly respected members of the community. For example, Hawaii has a highly successful program to encourage citizens to receive free blood pressure checkups. Firefighters volunteer to oversee the program. Anyone in Hawaii can have their blood pressure checked free of charge simply by going to a fire station. Residents take advantage of this program in large part because firefighters

Richard Brislin has made numerous contributions to our understanding of how culture influences human behavior, feelings, and thought. He has been especially sensitive to the ways in which knowledge about cultural contexts can be used to improve health, develop more effective ways of coping with stress, and develop better relations between people from different cultures.

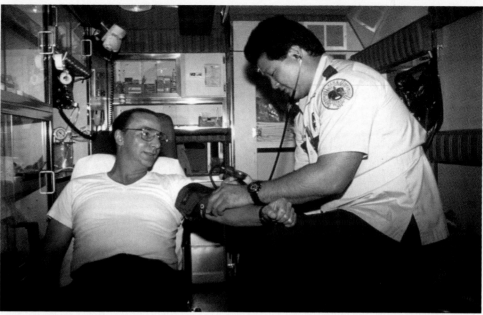

Cross-cultural psychologists, such as Richard Brislin, believe that, to ensure the success of social service programs, the people who introduce or maintain them should be highly respected members of the community. In Hawaii, for example, firefighters—highly respected and visible in Hawaiian communities—have been successful in getting Hawaiian residents to have their blood pressure checked.

are highly respected and visible in Hawaiian communities—they have an active program in presenting safety information to schools, they entertain school children on field trips to fire stations, they are active in community service, and many are members of native Hawaiian families that go back five or six generations.

Women's Health Issues

Not only are there cross-cultural and ethnic variations in health, but women and men experience health and the health care system differently (Paludi, 1992). Special concerns about women's health today focus on unintended and unwanted childbirth, abuse and violence, AIDS, the role of poverty in women's health, eating disorders, drug abuse, breast diseases, reproductive health, and the discrimination of the medical establishment against women.

The women's health movement in the United States rejected an assumption that was all too often made by the male medical profession: that women lose control of their bodies out of ignorance. Consciousness-raising groups and self-help groups were formed throughout the country to instruct women about their bodies, reproductive rights, nutrition, and health care. Information was also given on how to conduct breast and pelvic examinations. The Boston Women's Health Book Collective, which was formed in 1969, has, as one of its goals, to

teach women about their physical and mental health. It published *Our Bodies, Ourselves* (1984) and *Ourselves Getting Older* (1987), which are excellent resources for information about women's health.

Although females are increasingly becoming physicians, medicine continues to be a male-dominated profession. All too often in this male-dominated world, women's physical complaints are devalued, interpreted as "emotional" rather than physical in origin, and dismissed as trivial. In one investigation, physicians described their men and women patients differently: the men were characterized as very direct, very logical, good decision makers, and rarely emotional, whereas the women were characterized as very excitable in minor crises, more easily influenced, less adventurous, less independent, very illogical, and even very sneaky (Broverman & others, 1970).

The issue of sex and gender bias has also recently been raised in selecting participants in medical research studies (Rabinowitz & Sechzur, in press). Most medical research has been conducted with men, and frequently the results are generalized to women without apparent justification. For example, in a large-scale study involving 22,000 physicians that demonstrated the beneficial effect of an aspirin every other day on coronary heart disease, not a single woman was included in the study. Women's health advocates continue to press for greater inclusion of women in medical studies to reduce the bias that has characterized research on health, and they hope that the medical establishment will give increased attention to women's health concerns and treat women in less prejudiced and biased ways (Strickland, 1988).

In this chapter and others, we have seen that sociocultural factors—culture, ethnicity, and gender—are important determinants of behavior. Culture, ethnicity, and gender provide *contexts* for the way in which health and the treatment of illness are perceived. In addition, these sociocultural factors are involved in the actual biological processes of health and illness. We have studied many aspects of stress and health. In the next chapter, we will turn our attention to social psychology's fascinating world of how we relate to one another.

REVIEW

Promoting Health

In 1989 the Surgeon General released extensive new evidence that smoking is more harmful than previously believed, accounting for one-fifth of all deaths in the United States. Researchers are increasingly finding that passive smoke also carries health risks. Smoking is both addictive and reinforcing. Stronger educational and policy efforts regarding smoking are needed. Current prevention programs with young people focus on social pressures from family, peers, and the media.

The population is increasingly heavy and weight-loss programs abound. Cognitive strategies, especially self-control techniques, and exercise are helpful in weight reduction. Two increasingly common eating disorders, especially among females, are anorexia nervosa and bulimia. Both moderate and intense exercise produce important physical and psychological gains, such as lowered risk of heart disease and reduced anxiety. Experts increasingly recommend that the level of exercise you participate in should be pleasurable. Every indication suggests our nation's children are not getting enough exercise.

Seven of the 10 leading causes of death—heart disease, cancer, and stroke, for example—are associated with the absence of healthy behaviors. The next major improvements in general health may be behavioral, not medical. A number of health goals for the year 2000 have been proposed and businesses are increasingly interested in improving the health of their employees. Cultural factors influence coronary problems, as the study of migrant ethnic groups shows. Cross-national studies also show that cultural factors influence cancer. Government interventions and preventions in health care require consideration of the degree of respect for the government and the appropriateness of the intervention and prevention.

Women and men often experience health and the health care system differently. The medical profession has been male-dominated, and female patients have frequently been treated in inferior ways to male patients. The issue of sex and gender bias has also recently been raised in selecting participants for medical research studies.

Summary

I. Health Psychology
Health psychology, like the holistic orientation, emphasizes psychology's role in understanding health behavior. Closely aligned with health psychology and the holistic orientation is behavioral medicine, which combines medical and behavioral knowledge to reduce illness and promote health.

II. Defining Stress and the Body's Response to Stress
Stress is the way we respond to circumstances that threaten us and tax our coping abilities. Selye's general adaptation syndrome (GAS) describes the common effects of stress on the body. Stress is described as the wear and tear on the body due to the demands placed on it. This involves three stages: alarm, resistance, and exhaustion. Not all stress is bad—Selye called good stress eustress. Critics argue that humans do not always respond as uniformly to stress as Selye envisioned and that we also need to know about such factors as an individual's coping strategies. Psychoneuroimmunology explores the connections between psychological factors, the nervous system, and the immune system. Exploratory research suggests that our emotions and attitudes are connected to our immune system.

III. Personality Factors in Stress
The Type A behavior pattern refers to a cluster of characteristics—excessively competitive, hard-driven, impatient, and hostile—thought to be related to heart disease. The Type A behavior pattern is controversial, with some researchers arguing that only specific components of the cluster, such as hostility, are associated with heart disease. Hardiness is a personality style characterized by a sense of commitment, control, and a perception of problems as challenges rather than threats. Hardiness buffers stress and is related to reduced illness.

IV. Cognitive Factors in Stress
Lazarus believes that stress depends on how individuals cognitively appraise and interpret events. Cognitive appraisal is Lazarus' term to describe individuals'

interpretation of events in their lives as harmful, threatening, or challenging (primary appraisal) and their determination of whether they have the resources to cope effectively with the event (secondary appraisal).

V. Environmental Factors in Stress

Stress overload occurs when stimuli become so intense and prolonged that we cannot cope. Three types of conflict are approach/approach, approach/avoidance, and avoidance/avoidance. Frustration occurs when we cannot reach a goal. Stress may be produced by major life events or daily hassles. Life-events lists tell us nothing about how people cope with stress, body strengths and weaknesses, and other important dimensions of stress. Daily hassles provide a more focused look, but their evaluation should include information about coping and body characteristics.

VI. Sociocultural Factors in Stress

Acculturation refers to cultural change that results from continuous first-hand contact between two distinct cultural groups. Acculturative stress refers to the negative consequences of acculturation. Acculturation takes place over time in a series of phases: precontact, contact, conflict, crisis, and adaptation. Four outcomes can characterize an acculturating individual: assimilation, integration, segregation, and marginalization. The resilience and adaptation of ethnic minority groups can teach us much about coping and survival in the face of overwhelming adversity. Poverty imposes considerable stress on individuals. Chronic conditions, such as inadequate housing, dangerous neighborhoods, burdensome responsibilities, and economic uncertainties, are potent stressors in the lives of the poor. The incidence of poverty is especially high in ethnic minority families. Gender is also a sociocultural determinant of stress. Of special interest is how women's increased participation in the workforce has affected their stress and health. Employment is associated with increased health among women. Even though women experience more conflict among roles and overload than men, women who engage in multiple roles are healthier than women who do not because multiple roles expand potential resources and rewards. However, roles with little

autonomy and authority, such as being a clerical worker, decrease women's health. Special concerns are the feminization of poverty and poverty among ethnic minority women.

VII. Coping with Stress

Most of us are confronted with more than one stressor. Removing one stressor can sometimes be very beneficial. In most cases, problem-focused coping is better than emotion-focused coping and the use of defense mechanisms, especially in coping with long-term stress. Most of the time, we want to think positively and avoid negative thinking. An optimistic attitude produces a sense of self-efficacy. Positive self-illusions can improve some individuals' lives, but it is important to guard against unrealistic expectations. A strategy of defensive pessimism helps some individuals cope effectively. Biofeedback is the process in which individuals' muscular or visceral activities are monitored by instruments, and information from the instruments is given to the individuals so they can learn to voluntarily control the physiological activities. Biofeedback has been successful in reducing muscle tension and blood pressure. Meditation is the system of thought that incorporates exercises to attain bodily or mental control and well-being, as well as enlightenment. Transcendental meditation is the most popular form of meditation in the United States. Researchers have found that meditation reduces body arousal but usually no more than relaxation does. The "relaxation response" can be especially helpful in reducing body arousal and calming individuals. Social support is information and feedback from others that one is loved and cared for, esteemed and valued, and included in a network of communication and obligation. Three important benefits of social support are assistance, information, and emotional support. Researchers have consistently found that social support helps individuals cope more effectively with stress. Assertiveness training involves teaching individuals to act in their own best interests, to stand up for their legitimate rights, and to express their views directly and openly. Distinctions are made among nonassertive behavior, aggressive behavior, and assertive behavior, with assertive behavior favored as the best

coping strategy. We can and should use more than one coping strategy to deal with stress.

VIII. Coping with Illness

Many of us are not very accurate at diagnosing the symptoms of an illness. When our attention is directed outward, we are less likely to detect symptoms than when our attention is directed inward. We use schemas developed through prior experience to interpret symptoms. Seeking treatment depends on our perception of the severity of the symptoms and the likelihood that medical treatment will reduce or eliminate the symptoms. In the "good patient" role, individuals are passive and unquestioning and behave properly. In the "bad patient" role, individuals complain to the medical staff, demand attention, disobey staff orders, and generally misbehave. Realistic prior expectations, predictable events, and social support reduce the stress of hospitalization. Approximately one-third of all patients do not follow treatment recommendations. Compliance varies with the disorder and the recommended treatment, with patients' satisfaction with the quality of the care they are receiving, and with their own theories about why they are sick and how they can get well. Clearer doctor-patient communication is needed for improved compliance.

IX. Smoking, Eating Problems, and Exercise

In 1989 the Surgeon General released an extensive report with new evidence that smoking is more harmful than previously believed, accounting for one-fifth of all deaths in the United States. Researchers are increasingly finding that passive smoke also carries health risks. Smoking is both addictive and reinforcing. Stronger educational and policy efforts regarding smoking are needed. Current prevention programs with young people focus on social pressures from family, peers, and the media. The population is increasingly heavy and weight-loss programs abound. Cognitive strategies, especially self-control techniques, and exercise are helpful in weight reduction. Two increasingly common eating disorders, especially among women, are anorexia nervosa and bulimia. Both moderate and intense exercise produce important physical and psychological gains, such as lowered risk of heart disease and reduced anxiety. Experts have increasingly recommended that the level of exercise you participate in should be pleasurable. Every indication suggests that our nation's children are not getting enough exercise.

X. Toward Healthier Lives, Culture, and Health

Seven of the 10 leading causes of death—heart disease, cancer, and stroke, for example—are associated with the absence of health behaviors. The next major improvement in general health may be behavioral, not medical. A number of health goals for the year 2000 have been proposed, and businesses have increasingly become interested in improving the health of their employees. Cultural factors influence coronary problems, as evidenced by the study of migrant ethnic groups, such as the Japanese who have moved to the United States. Cross-national studies show that cultural factors also influence cancer. Government interventions and preventions in health care require consideration of the degree of respect for the government and the appropriateness of the intervention and prevention.

XI. Women's Health Issues

Women and men often experience health and the health care system differently. The medical profession has been male-dominated, and female patients have frequently been treated in inferior ways to male patients. The issue of sex and gender bias also has been raised recently in selecting participants for medical research studies.

Key Terms

health psychology 455
behavioral medicine 455
stress 456
general adaptation syndrome (GAS) 457
eustress 457
psychoneuroimmunology 457
Type A behavior pattern 458
hardiness 458
cognitive appraisal 459
burnout 460
approach/approach conflict 460
avoidance/avoidance conflict 460

approach/avoidance conflict 461
frustration 461
acculturation 462
acculturative stress 462
assimilation 462
integration 463
separation 463
marginalization 463
feminization of poverty 465
problem-focused coping 466
emotion-focused coping 466
biofeedback 467

meditation 468
transcendental meditation (TM) 468
social support 469
assertiveness training 469
nonassertive behavior 469
aggressive behavior 469
assertive behavior 469
"good patient" role 471
"bad patient" role 471
anorexia nervosa 475
bulimia 476
aerobic exercise 476

Suggested Readings

American Psychologist (1990), *45*, 368-389. This issue of the American Psychological Association's journal includes an entire section on women's mental health. The articles focus on such topics as research priorities for women's mental health, the mental health effects of women's multiple roles, and the role of poverty in women's mental health.

Burns, D. D. (1980). *The new mood therapy.* New York: Morrow. This best-selling paperback is by a member of the cognitive therapy team at the University of Pennsyl-vania. It is an excellent choice if you are searching for an easy-to-read, competent discussion of how to use cognitive therapy to reduce stress.

Dasen, P. R., Berry, J. W., & Sartorius, N. (Eds.). (1988). *Health and cross-cultural psychology: Toward applications.* Newbury Park, CA: Sage. This book includes a number of chapters by cross-cultural psychology experts that focus on the role of culture in understanding health. An especially insightful chapter is Berry and Kim's discussion of acculturation and health.

Logue, A. W. (1986). *Eating and drinking.* New York: W. H. Freeman. This is a thorough overview of eating and drinking behavior, including a detailed examination of the pluses and minuses of various diets.

Ornstein, R., & Sobel, D. (1989). *Healthy pleasures.* Reading, MA: Addison-Wesley. In this fascinating look at the role of pleasure in health, Ornstein and Sobel argue that we should engage in health practices that are enjoyable for us.

Taylor, S. E. (1991). *Health psychology* (2nd ed.). New York: McGraw-Hill. This leading textbook in the field of health psychology includes details about health promotion, health education, and a wide variety of other health-related topics.

SOCIAL PSYCHOLOGY

CHAPTER

16

With the noble intent of eliminating social injustice and improving interracial harmony, James W. Jones established a small church in Indiana in 1953. His congregation included a number of Blacks. He and his wife adopted seven children, including a Black, a Chinese, and a Korean. As a missionary for 2 years, Jones lived in Brazil, where he founded an orphanage and a mission. When he returned to the United States, he changed the name of his church to the People's Temple Full Gospel.

Jones moved his church to northern California, where he increased his money-raising efforts and community work. By the early 1970s, Jones had developed churches in the Black areas of San Francisco and Los Angeles. He was showered with accolades, and his social programs were rated among the best in the country.

However, Reverend Jones' dark side began to surface. As he stepped-up fundraising, he at first asked his congregation to make modest donations in the name of universal brotherhood and peace. Eventually he induced people to sell their homes and turn over all their money as a testament to their faith and loyalty. Rumors leaked that physical abuse, death threats, and attempts to gain the guardianship of children were meted out to members who were disobedient or tried to leave Jones' church. Jones was able to deflect public investigations through his tight reign on information and his respectability in the community.

During the early 1970s, Jones increasingly saw parallels between himself and Christ. He portrayed himself as a messiah and required his congregation to call him Father. Jones declared that everything he said was law. Jones was a charismatic leader and a master at getting members to conform to his wishes.

In 1977, shortly before an article exposing Jones' megalomania and repressive cruelty appeared in *New West* magazine, Jones' "flock" migrated en masse to Jonestown, Guyana, South America. In Jonestown the members of the People's Temple were isolated from their families and the world. They had been stripped of their possessions and individuality, and they were utterly obedient.

On November 17, 1978, U.S. Representative Leo Ryan and four of his aides, who were in Guyana to evaluate charges of abuse in the People's Temple, were gunned down by Jones' henchmen as they boarded a plane to leave the country. Jones

then convinced his congregation that hostile intruders were on their way to exterminate them in retaliation for the deaths at the airstrip.

The next day Jones gathered before him more than 900 members of the People's Temple. It was time, he said, for them to die. Their death, the "martyr," Jones claimed, would be a revolutionary and positive act. Amid few protests or acts of resistance, parents gave their children cyanide-laced Kool-Aid, drank it themselves, then lay down and waited to die.

How could such a gruesome event as the mass suicide at Jonestown happen? What forces could compel parents to poison their children? The Jonestown massacre, as it is known, is an example of the macabre side of social thinking and influence; it shows the power of obedience and conformity and how such power can be abused. **Social psychology** *is the field of psychology that studies individuals' social interactions, relationships, perceptions, and attitudes.* In this chapter, we will begin by studying attitudes, then turn our attention to a number of other topics: social perception and attribution, conformity, altruism, close relationships, group relations, and organizational behavior.

The Jonestown massacre, elaborately planned by People's Temple leader James Jones, reveals the macabre side of social thinking and influence.

Attitudes and Persuasion

As Mark Twain said, "It is a difference of opinion that makes horses race." **Attitudes** *are beliefs and opinions that can predispose individuals to behave in certain ways.* We have attitudes about all sorts of things, and we live in a world in which we try to influence the attitudes of each other.

Attitudes and Behavior

Think about your attitudes toward religion, politics, and sex. Now think about your behavior in these areas. Consider sex, for example. How liberal or conservative are your sexual attitudes? Does your behavior match your attitudes? Researchers have found that we have more accepting attitudes toward sexual practices than our behavior actually shows (Dreyer, 1982). As we study the relation of attitudes to behavior, two questions arise: How strongly do attitudes influence behavior? How strongly does behavior influence attitudes?

Predicting Behavior from Attitudes

More than 50 years ago, Richard LaPiere (1934) toured the United States with a Chinese couple. LaPiere expected to encounter prejudice against the Asians. He thought they would be banned from restaurants and hotels, for example. Surprisingly, in more than 10,000 miles of travel, the threesome was rejected only once. It appeared, LaPiere thought, that there were few negative attitudes toward Asians in the United States. To see if this actually was the case, LaPiere wrote a letter to all 251 places he and his Asian friends had visited, asking the proprietors if they would provide food or lodging to Asians. More than half responded; of those, a resounding 90 percent said they absolutely would not allow Asians in their restaurant or motel. LaPiere's study documented a powerful lesson in understanding human behavior: what we *say* may be different from what we *do*.

The connection between attitudes and behaviors may vary with the situation. In the study of attitudes toward Asians in the 1930s, the Chinese who accompanied LaPiere were well dressed and carried expensive luggage; they may have inspired different attitudes if they had appeared in cheaper attire. To consider further situational influences on attitude-behavior connections, imagine asking someone about his attitude toward people who drive pickup trucks. Let's say he responds, "Totally classless." A month later the guy stops for a cup of coffee in a small west Texas town. A burly man in the next booth is talking with his buddies about the merits of pickup trucks. He turns to our friend and asks, "How do you like that green pickup truck sitting outside?" Needless to say, his response is not "totally classless." This example suggests that the demands of the situation can be powerful even when we hold strong beliefs.

Behavior's Influence on Attitudes

"The actions of men are the best interpreters of their thoughts," asserted seventeenth-century English philosopher John Locke. Does doing change your believing? If you quit drinking, will you have a more negative attitude toward drinking? If you take up an exercise program, are you more likely to extol the benefits of cardiovascular fitness when someone asks your attitude about exercise?

Changes in behavior can precede changes in attitudes (Bandura, 1989). Social psychologists offer two main explanations of behavior's influence on attitudes. The first view is that we have a strong need for cognitive consistency; consequently, we change our attitudes to make them more consistent with our behavior. The second view is that often our attitudes are not completely clear, so we observe our behavior and make inferences about it to determine what our attitudes should be. Let's consider these two views in more detail.

Cognitive dissonance *is a concept developed by social psychologist Leon Festinger (1957); it refers to an individual's motivation toward consistency and away from inconsistency.* For example, we might feel uneasy about the discrepancy between our attitudes and our behavior, which often leads us to justify our actions. Imagine the circumstance in which you do something you do not feel good about—flunking a test or losing your temper, for example. We often justify our behavior, as George Bernard Shaw did with his father's alcoholism: "If you cannot get rid of the family skeleton, you may as well make it dance." Shaw's justifi-

cation helped him reduce the tension between his attitude about his father's drinking problem and its occurrence. Cognitive dissonance is about making our skeletons dance, about trying to reduce tension by cognitively justifying things that are unpleasant (Aronson, 1992).

Not all social psychologists, however, are satisfied with cognitive dissonance as an explanation for the influence of behavior on attitudes. Daryl Bem, for example, believes that the cognitive dissonance view relies too heavily on internal factors, which are difficult to measure. Bem (1967) argues that we should move away from such nebulous concepts as "cognitions" and "psychological discomfort" and replace them with more behavioral terminology. **Self-perception theory** *is Bem's theory of the attitude-behavior connection; it stresses that individuals make inferences about their attitudes by perceiving their behavior.* For example, consider the remark "I am spending all of my time thinking about the test I have next week; I must be anxious," or "This is the third time I have gone to the student union in 2 days; I must be lonely." Bem believes we look to our own behavior when our attitudes are not completely clear. This means that, when we have clear ideas about something, we are less likely to look to our behavior for clues about our attitudes; however, if we feel ambivalent about something or someone, our behavior is a good place to look to determine our attitude. Figure 16.1 compares cognitive dissonance and self-perception theories.

Understanding the nature of attitudes not only involves the relation of attitudes to behavior, but also the nature of persuasion and attitude change. We form many attitudes as we go through our lives, attitudes that are often under pressure to be changed (Greenwald, 1989; McGuire, 1989).

Persuasion and Attitude Change

We spend many hours trying to persuade people to do certain things. For example, the words from the song *Emotion in Motion* go like this: "I would do anything just to hold on to you. Just about anything that you want me to do." One person is trying to *persuade* another of the intensity of his or her love. Politicians and corporations are also heavily involved in the persuasion process. Politicians, for example, have full arsenals of speech writers and image consultants to ensure that their words and behavior are as persuasive as possible.

Advertisers also go to great lengths to persuade people to buy their products. Consider trying to persuade someone to buy raisins. How would you make raisins appeal to consumers? An imaginative advertisement had a chorus line of animated raisins dancing to the tune of "I Heard It Through the Grapevine." What is it about this advertisement that persuades us to buy raisins? Social psychologists believe that persuasion involves four key components: who conveys the message (the source), what the message is (the communication), what medium is used (the channel), and for whom the message is intended (the target, or audience).

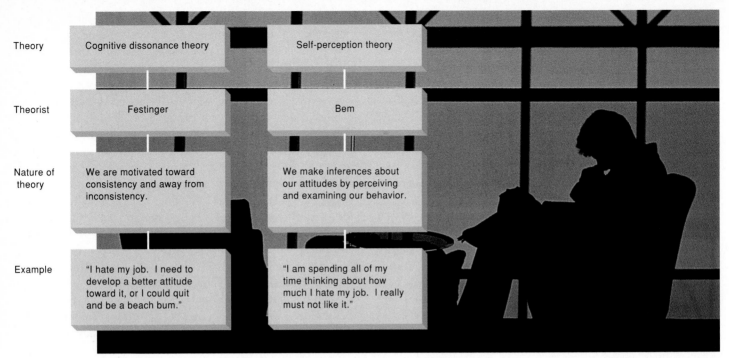

Theory	Cognitive dissonance theory	Self-perception theory
Theorist	Festinger	Bem
Nature of theory	We are motivated toward consistency and away from inconsistency.	We make inferences about our attitudes by perceiving and examining our behavior.
Example	"I hate my job. I need to develop a better attitude toward it, or I could quit and be a beach bum."	"I am spending all of my time thinking about how much I hate my job. I really must not like it."

FIGURE 16.1

Two views of behavior's influence on attitudes.

The Communicator (Source)

Suppose you are running for president of the student body. You tell students you are going to make life at your college better. Would they believe you? That would depend on several factors, which we will examine in turn.

One factor involved in whether or not we believe someone is the *expertise* and *credibility* of the communicator. Expertise depends on qualifications. If you had held other elective offices, students would be more likely to believe that you have the expertise to be their president. We attribute competence to experts, believing they are knowledgeable about the topics they address.

In addition to expertise and credibility, trustworthiness is an important quality of an effective communicator. This factor depends on whether your words and how you say them are perceived as honest or dishonest. It was in Abraham Lincoln's best interest, then, to be called "Honest Abe"; being perceived as honest increased the power of his communication.

"First off, by way of establishing some credibility, I'd like to note that twenty years ago I was living in a fur-lined van."

Drawing by D. Reilly; © 1989 The New Yorker Magazine, Inc.

Jesse Jackson is shown here campaigning for President in 1988. Whether a candidate is running for President of the United States or president of a college's student body, expertise, credibility, trustworthiness, power, attraction, and similarity are important characteristics.

Social psychologists believe that power, attractiveness, likableness, and similarity to the message receivers are four important characteristics that add to a communicator's ability to change people's attitudes. In running for student body president, you will probably have more clout with students if you have been on the university president's student issues committee. Power may be an important characteristic for a communicator because it is associated with the ability to impose sanctions or control rewards and punishments (Kelley & Thibaut, 1978). In running for student body president, you are more likely to get votes if students perceive you as attractive and similar to themselves. That's why you often see presidential candidates putting on miners' helmets in West Virginia, speaking a Spanish phrase in San Antonio, or riding a tractor in Iowa. The candidates are striving to show that they share common interests and an identity with their audience.

Similarity is also widely used in advertising. In commercials we might see a homemaker scrubbing the floor while advertising a new cleaner or a laborer laughing with his

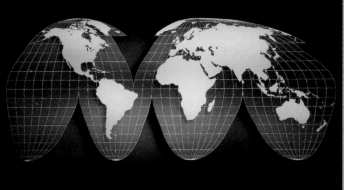
Gender and Politics—from Ferraro to County Clerk

Geraldine Ferraro campaigned as a vice-presidential candidate on the Mondale-Ferraro Democratic ticket in 1984. What is gender's role in political attitudes?

I t is the summer of 1984. The November presidential election is only months away; the Democrats are far behind in the polls. The economy is looking better, and Republican incumbent Ronald Reagan's lead seems insurmountable. What could the Democratic party do to persuade the American population to switch their allegiance? It would have to be something bold, something never tried before in the history of American politics.

One of the areas in which Reagan seemed vulnerable was women's rights; the National Organization for Women (NOW) called Reagan insensitive to women, for example. For the first time in history, a woman—Geraldine Ferraro—was selected to fill the vice-presidential slot on the Democratic ticket. Although the Democrats did not win the 1984 presidential election, Ferraro's selection was an important step for women in their effort to achieve equality.

As more women have sought political office, the issue of gender has assumed a more important role in attitude change. Surveys reveal that, in today's political climate, we are more likely to vote for qualified female candidates, especially if they are running for lower political offices (Gallup, 1984). Discrimination still exists, though, especially in gubernatorial campaigns (Yankelovich, Skelly, & White, 1984).

The challenge is to determine for whom and under what circumstances gender makes the most difference. Social psychologist Carol Sigelman and her colleagues (1986) wanted to find out to what extent voters are influenced by a candidate's gender, physical attractiveness, and prestige in relation to the responsibility of the office being sought. The researchers gave college students information about six challengers to an incumbent in either a mayoral or county clerk's race. The challengers were men and women of high, moderate, or low physical attractiveness. The researchers found that the male, but not the female, voters discriminated against the female candidates. In addition, the men saw the women as less qualified, fewer of the men voted for the women, and the men rated the women lower overall. The males' antifemale bias was not offset by a preference for the women candidates by the female voters, however. The female voters tended to choose evenly between the male and female candidates. Also, attractiveness was less consistently an asset for the female candidates than it was for the males. Although it appears that less discrimination against female candidates occurs today than in past years, this research suggests that equality has not yet been reached.

buddies at a bar while drinking beer. The creators of these commercials hope you will relate to these people because you perceive them as similar to yourself. Of course, many products are promoted by appealing to our personal ideals. To do this, attractive or famous individuals are used in advertisements. Cher tries to persuade us to buy cologne and Michael Jordan tries to persuade us to buy athletic shoes, for example.

Other factors that influence attitudes are the sex of the communicator and gender roles. To learn more about how gender might be a factor in attitudes about political candidates, turn to Sociocultural Worlds 16.1. As we will see next, the content of the message also is an important factor in influencing attitudes.

The Message

What should the content of a persuasive message be? Should appeals be more positive than negative? Should a rational or an emotional strategy be used?

How often have we seen politicians vow to run a clean campaign but, as soon as the bell sounds, come out swinging below the belt? In the 1988 presidential campaign, negative advertising became a big issue, and it proved to be effective. George Bush succeeded in branding Michael Dukakis with the "L" word (liberal) in the campaign. Some negative appeals play on our emotions, whereas many positive appeals are directed at our rational, logical thinking. The less informed we are, the more likely we will respond to an emotional appeal. For example, if we do not know anything about nuclear waste, an emotional appeal to keep a hazardous waste dump from being built near our home may influence our attitude about the project more than an appeal based on reasoning. Bush's criticism of Dukakis was probably a wise strategy for influencing people who did not know much about Dukakis' political background.

All other things being equal, the more frightened we are, the more we will change our attitude. The day after the telecast of a vivid nuclear war film, *The Day After,* negative attitudes about the United States massive nuclear arsenal surfaced (Schofield & Pavelchak, 1985, 1989). Also, advertisers sometimes take advantage of our fears to stimulate attitude change. For example, you may have seen a life insurance company ad showing a widow and her young children moving out of their home, which they lost because they did not have enough insurance.

Not all emotional appeals are negative, though. Music is widely used to make us feel good about messages. Think about how few television commercials you have seen without music either in the background or as a prominent part of the message. When we watch commercials, we may associate the pleasant feelings of the music with the product, even though the music itself does not provide information about the product.

The Medium (Channel)

Although there are many factors to consider in regard to the message itself, a communicator also needs to be concerned about which medium to use to get a message across. Consider the difference between watching a presidential debate on television and reading about it in a newspaper. Television lets us see how the candidates deliver their message, what their appearance and mannerisms are like, and so on. Because it presents live images, television is considered the most powerful medium for changing attitudes. In one study, the winners of various political primaries were predicted by the amount of media exposure they had (Grush, 1980).

Television's power of persuasion is staggering. By the time the average American adolescent graduates from high school, he or she has watched 20,000 hours of television, far more than the number of hours spent in the classroom. Social scientists have studied television's influence on such matters as the impact of commercials on purchases, of mass media political campaigning on voting, of public service announcements on health, of broad-based ideological campaigns on life-styles, and of television violence on aggression.

How strong is television's influence on an individual's attitudes and behavior? Some reviews of research conclude that there are few effects (Zeigler & Harmon, 1989). Other reviews conclude that television has a more formidable effect (Condry, 1989).

The Target (Audience)

What are some audience characteristics that determine whether a message will be effective? Age, gender, and self-esteem are three such factors. Younger people are more likely to change their attitudes than older ones, females are more susceptible to persuasion than males, and self-esteem is believed to be important but does not have a predictable pattern. Another factor is the strength of the audience's attitude. If the audience is not strongly committed to a particular attitude, change is more likely; if commitment is strong, the communicator will have more difficulty.

REVIEW

Attitudes and Persuasion

Attitudes are beliefs and opinions. Social psychologists are interested in how strongly attitudes predict behavior. Today it is believed that, when situational influences are weak, the attitude-behavior connection is strengthened. Cognitive dissonance theory, developed by Festinger, argues that, because we have a strong need for cognitive consistency, we change our attitudes to make them more consistent with our behavior so that dissonance is reduced. Bem developed a more behavioral approach, called self-perception theory; it stresses the importance of making inferences about our own behavior, especially when our attitudes are not clear.

Social Perception and Attribution

As we interact with our world, we are both actors and spectators, doing and perceiving, acting and thinking. Social psychologists are interested in how we perceive our social world and how we try to make sense of it.

Social Perception

Social perception *is our judgment about the qualities of individuals, which involves how we form impressions of others, how we gain self-knowledge from our perception of others, and how we present ourselves to others to influence their perceptions of us.* We will examine each of these topics in turn.

Developing Impressions of Others

Our evaluations of people often fall into broad categories—good or bad, happy or sad, introverted or extraverted, for example. If someone asks for your impression of your psychology professor, you might respond, "She is great." Then you might go on to describe your perception of her characteristics, for example, "She is charming, intelligent, witty, and sociable." From this description, we can infer that you have a positive impression of her.

Understanding persuasion and attitude focuses on the communicator (source), the message (communication), the medium (channel), and the target (audience). Communicators are most influential when they have expertise and credibility, trustworthiness, and power; attractiveness and similarity also are important. The less informed we are, the better emotional appeals work; the more frightened we are, the more we will be influenced. Positive emotional appeals can be persuasive, especially through the use of music. Because it delivers live images, television may be the most powerful medium; its persuasive capabilities are staggering, given the frequency of viewing. Experts debate television's influence. Younger individuals are more likely to change their attitudes than older individuals and females are more readily persuaded than males. Self-esteem is thought to be important, but a predictable effect for it has not been found. If an audience is not strongly committed to a preexisting attitude, change is more likely.

As we form impressions of others, they are *unified*. A person's traits, actions, and appearance and all of the other information we obtain about that individual are closely connected in our memory, even though we may have obtained the information in an interrupted or random fashion. We might obtain some information today, more next week, and some more in 2 months. During those 2 months, we interact with many other people and develop impressions of them as well. Nonetheless, we usually perceive the information about a particular person as unified, as a continuous block of information (Brown, 1986).

Our first encounter with someone also contributes to the impression we form. First impressions are often enduring. **Primacy effect** *is the term used to describe the enduring quality of initial impressions.* One reason for the primacy effect is that we pay less attention to subsequent information about the individual (Anderson, 1965). Next time you want to impress someone, make sure you put your best foot forward in your first encounter.

Gaining Self-knowledge from Our Perceptions of Others: Social Comparison

How many times have you asked yourself such questions as "Am I as smart as Jill?" "Is Bob better looking than I am?" "Is my taste as good as Carmen's?" We gain self-knowledge from our own behavior; we also gain it from others through **social comparison,** *the process in which individuals evaluate their thoughts, feelings, behaviors, and abilities in relation to other people. Social comparison helps individuals evaluate themselves, tells them what their distinctive characteristics are, and aids them in building an identity.*

Some years ago, Leon Festinger (1954) proposed a theory of social comparison. He stressed that, when no objective means is available to evaluate our opinions and abilities, we compare ourselves with others. Festinger believed that we are more likely to compare ourselves with others who are similar to us than with those who are dissimilar to us. He reasoned that, if we compare ourselves with someone who is very different from us, we will not be able to obtain an accurate appraisal of our own behavior and thoughts. This means that we will develop more accurate self-perceptions if we compare ourselves with people in communities similar to those in which we grew up and live, with people who have similar family backgrounds, and with people of the same sex, for example. Social comparison theory has been extended and modified over the years and continues to provide an important rationale for why we affiliate with others and how we come to know ourselves (Major & Testa, 1989; Masters & Smith, 1987; Smith, Diener, & Wedell, 1989; Wheeler & Miyake, 1992).

Presenting Ourselves to Others to Influence Their Social Perceptions

How do you present yourself to others? Do you try to act naturally and be yourself, or do you deliberately change your behavior to get other people to have a more favorable impression of you? **Impression management** *is the process by which individuals strive to present themselves in a favorable light.* When we present ourselves to others, we usually try to make ourselves look better than we really are. We spend billions of dollars rearranging our faces, our bodies, our minds, and our social skills. Sometimes we spend the money so we will feel good about ourselves regardless of what others think and sometimes so that others will form a more favorable impression of us.

How can you influence the impressions you make on others? The following are four recommended "impression management" strategies:

1. *Use behavioral matching.* This simply means do what the other person is doing. When you are with a modest person, behave in a modest way. When you are with a carefree person, behave in a carefree way.
2. *Conform to situational norms.* For example, don't show up barefooted in your professor's office—save that look for the beach or frat house. Don't play a radio in the library, and don't read at a party.
3. *Show appreciation of others and flatter them.* People like to be complimented. Look for something good to say about the person you are communicating with, such as "I really like your sweater. It looks great on you."
4. *Use positive nonverbal cues.* We can influence what others think of us not only by our words but also by a number of nonverbal cues—smile more than you frown when you are with people, for example.

Keep in mind, though, that impression management techniques that work in one cultural setting may not work in another. In particular, appreciation and flattery are often culture bound. For example, in some Eastern European countries, if one person expresses great admiration for another's watch, courtesy dictates that the watch be given to the admirer. In the Native American culture of the Sioux, it's considered courteous to open a conversation with a compliment. Nonverbal cues also vary considerably from culture to culture. For example, as was mentioned in chapter 10 in discussing display rules, the "thumbs up" sign, which means everything is OK or the desire to hitch a ride in most cultures, means something very different in Greece—an insult similar to a raised third finger in the United States.

In seeking better ways to present ourselves to others, it helps to know the causes of an individual's behavior. In our effort to find out the causes of people's behavior, we make attributions about the behavior.

Attribution

Attribution theorists argue that we want to know why people do the things they do because the knowledge will enable us to cope more effectively with the situations that confront us. **Attribution theory** *states that individuals are motivated to discover the underlying causes of behavior as part of their interest in making sense out of the behavior.* In a way, attribution theorists say, people are much like intuitive scientists, seeking the reason something happens (McClure & others, 1989).

We can classify the reasons individuals behave the way they do in a number of ways, but one basic distinction stands out above all the others: the distinction between internal causes, such as the individual's personality traits or motives, and external causes, which are environmental, situational factors (Heider, 1958). If you don't do well on a test, do you attribute it to the fact that the professor plotted against you and made the test too difficult (external cause) or to the fact that you did not study hard enough (internal cause)? Your answer to such a question influences how you feel about yourself. If you believe your poor performance is the professor's fault (he gives unfair tests, for example), you don't feel as bad as when you do not spend enough time studying.

Our attributions are not always accurate. In a given situation, the person who acts, the actor, produces the behavior to be explained. Then the onlooker, the observer, offers a causal explanation of the actor's behavior or experience. Actors often explain their own behavior with external causes, whereas observers often explain actors' behavior with internal causes. Either the actor or the observer must be wrong. The **fundamental attribution error** *states that observers overestimate the importance of traits and underestimate the importance of situations when they seek explanations of an actor's behavior* (Ross, 1977). Based on the fundamental attribution error, observers are more likely than actors to be wrong when explaining actors' behavior (see figure 16.2). For example, a classmate is giving an oral report and you think, "Isn't she cool? She must be the calmest, most confident person I've ever seen." At the podium, your classmate is thinking, "What in the world am I doing here? I'm terrified of speaking in public. If my roommate hadn't practiced with me so many times, I would surely have passed out by now."

Since actors and observers often have different ideas about what causes behavior, many attributions are biased. Behavior is determined by a number of factors, so it is not surprising that our lives are full of arguments about the causes of behavior. Attribution theory provides us with a more informed perspective on disagreements in marriages, the courts, the Senate, and many other social arenas (Weary, Stanley, & Harvey, 1989).

Our social world not only involves making attributions, it also involves our tendency to conform or not conform to the attitudes and behavior of others. As we will see next, conformity can occur in a variety of circumstances.

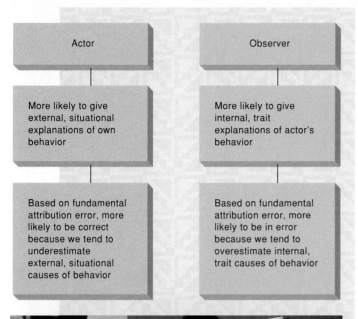

Actor	Observer
More likely to give external, situational explanations of own behavior	More likely to give internal, trait explanations of actor's behavior
Based on fundamental attribution error, more likely to be correct because we tend to underestimate external, situational causes of behavior	Based on fundamental attribution error, more likely to be in error because we tend to overestimate internal, trait causes of behavior

FIGURE 16.2

Actor-observer context and the accuracy of attributions. In this situation, the two supervisors are the observers and the employee is the actor (top middle of the photograph). If the employee has made an error in her work, how are the employee and her supervisors likely to give different explanations of her behavior, based on your knowledge of actor-observer differences and the fundamental attribution error?

Conformity

"Each of you, individually, walketh with the tread of a fox, but collectively, ye are geese," Greek philosopher Solon reflected on the importance of conformity in our lives.

Conforming in a Variety of Circumstances

Conformity comes in many forms and affects many areas of our lives. Do you take up jogging because everyone else is doing it? Does fashion dictate that you let your hair grow long this year and cut it short the next? Would you take cocaine if pressured by others or would you resist? **Conformity** *occurs when individuals adopt the attitudes or behavior of others because of real or imagined pressure from others.*

Put yourself in the following situation. You are taken into a room, where you see five other people seated around a table. A person in a white lab coat enters the room and announces that you are about to participate in an experiment on perceptual accuracy. The group is shown two cards, the first having only a single vertical line on it, the second card with three vertical lines of varying length. You are told that the task is to determine which of the three lines on the second card is the same length as the line on the first card. You look at the cards and think, "What a snap. It's so obvious which is longest." The other people in the room are actually associates of the experimenter (researchers often call them "confederates" of the experimenter); they've been hired to perform in ways the experimenter dictates (of course, you are not aware of this). On the first several trials, everyone agrees about which line matches the standard. Then, on the fourth trial, each of the others picks an incorrect line; you have a puzzled look on your face. As the last person to make a choice, you're in the dilemma of responding as your eyes tell you or conforming to what the others have said. How do you think you would answer?

Solomon Asch conducted this classic experiment on conformity in 1951 (see figure 16.3). He believed there would be little yielding to group pressure. To find out if this was so, Asch instructed his accomplices to respond incorrectly on 12 of the 18 trials. To Asch's surprise, the volunteer participants conformed to the incorrect answers 35 percent of the time. The pressure to conform is strong. Even in a clear-cut situation, such as in the Asch experiment, we often conform to what others say and do. We don't want to be laughed at or have others be angry with us.

Put yourself in another situation. You have volunteered to participate in a psychology experiment. By the flip of a coin, half of the volunteers are designated as prisoners and half as guards in a mock prison; you are one of the fortunate ones because you will be a guard. How much would you and your fellow volunteers conform to the social roles of "guard" and "prisoner"? You are instructed to maintain law and order—to do a guard's job. You will make a fine guard, you think, because you are kind and respect the rights and dignity of others. In just a few hours, however, you find that your behavior, and that of the other "guards" and "prisoners," has changed; each of you has begun to conform to what you think are the expected social roles for guards and prisoners. Over the course of 6 days, you and the other guards begin to make the prisoners obey petty, meaningless rules and force them to perform tedious, useless work. What's more, you find yourself insulting the prisoners and keeping them "in line" with night sticks. Many of the prisoners begin acting like robots. They develop an intense hatred for you and the other guards and constantly think about ways to escape.

You may be thinking that this scenario stretches credibility. No one you know, and certainly not you, would behave in such an abusive way. However, psychologist Philip Zimbardo and his colleagues (1972) conducted just such an experiment with a group of normal, mature, stable, intelligent young men at Stanford University. In fact, the prison study was scheduled to last 2 weeks, but the behavior of the "guards" and "prisoners" changed so drastically that the experiment had to be stopped after 6 days. Although many of the prisoners resisted the guards and asked questions initially, after a while they gave up and virtually stopped reacting. Five of the prisoners had to be released, four because of severe depression or anxiety and the fifth because he broke out in a rash all over his body; several of the guards became brutal with the prisoners. Figure 16.4 shows some of the circumstances in the prison study.

Cross-cultural psychologists wondered if this tendency to conform in such dramatic ways is an American phenomenon or if the same behavior occurs in other cultures. Using the Asch experiment, researchers have found that research participants in Lebanon, Hong Kong, Brazil, and Fiji conform at about the same rate, 35 percent (Mann, 1980). However, they found conformity lower in Germany (22 percent) and higher among the Bantu of Rhodesia (51 percent). Surprisingly, conformity in Japan was found to be relatively low—25 percent (Frager, 1970). The results of the Japanese study were counterintuitive—that is, contrary to what the researchers expected. Because of strong social pressures to conform in Japan, the researchers expected a much higher rate. Perhaps the Japanese feel strong loyalty to their own social groups but not to groups created in the laboratory. We cannot conclude that the Japanese are nonconforming; it may be that they simply do not conform to the wishes of strangers.

Other cross-cultural research on conformity suggests that people in agricultural societies have a tendency to conform more than people in hunter-gatherer groups (Berry, 1967). Agricultural societies rely on the cooperation of their residents to cultivate, plant, and harvest their food supply. This high degree of interdependence makes it vital that members conform to societal norms. More complex societies sometimes reward nonconformity, encouraging members to exploit the diverse opportunities for career and self-expression offered in the multifaceted dimensions of the societies.

FIGURE 16.3

Asch's conformity experiment. The figures show the stimulus materials for the Asch conformity experiment on group influence. The photograph shows the dilemma for the subject (seated in the middle) after five confederates of the experimenter chose the incorrect line.

Obedience

Obedience *is behavior that complies with the explicit demands of an individual in authority.* In Zimbardo's prison experiment, the prisoners and guards were obedient. Obedient behavior sometimes can be destructive; it rapidly became so with the prison guards. The mass suicide at Jonestown described at the beginning of the chapter, the massacre of Vietnamese civilians at My Lai, and the Nazi crimes against Jews in World War II are other examples of destructive obedience. Adolph Eichmann, for example, has been described as an ambitious functionary who believed that it was his duty to obey Hitler's orders. An average middle-class man with no identifiable criminal tendencies, Eichmann ordered the killing of 6 million Jews. The following experiment, first performed by Stanley Milgram, provides insight into such obedience.

As part of an experiment in psychology, you are asked to deliver a series of painful electric shocks to another person. You are told that the purpose of the study is to determine the effects of punishment on memory. Your role is to be the "teacher" and punish the mistakes made by a "learner"; each time the learner makes a mistake, your job is to increase the intensity of the shock by a certain amount. You are given a 75-volt shock to show you

a.

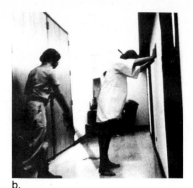
b.

FIGURE 16.4

Zimbardo's prison experiment. (a) A volunteer for a psychology experiment is picked up on campus—he had lost a coin flip and was designated a prisoner. (b) A student conforms to the hostile, abusive role of prison guard.

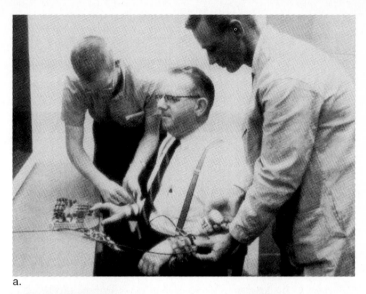
a.

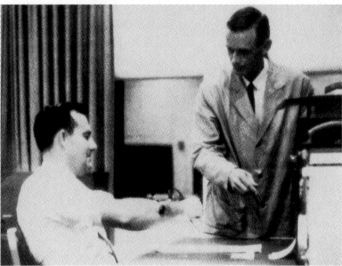
b.

FIGURE 16.5

Milgram obedience study. (a) A 50-year-old man ("learner") is strapped into a chair. The experimenter makes it look as if a shock generator is being connected to his body through a number of electrodes. (b) The subject ("teacher") is given a sample 75-volt shock.

how it feels. You are then introduced to the "learner," a nice 50-year-old man who mumbles something about having a heart condition. He is strapped to a chair in the next room and communicates with you through an intercom. As the trials proceed, the "learner" quickly runs into trouble and is unable to give the correct answers. Should you shock him? The apparatus in front of you has 30 switches, ranging from 15 volts (light) to 450 volts (marked as "dangerous, severe shock XXX"). As you raise the intensity of the shock, the "learner" says he's in pain. At 150 volts, he demands to have the experiment stopped. At 180 volts, he cries out that he can't stand it anymore. At 300 volts, he yells about his heart condition and pleads to be released. If you hesitate in shocking the learner, however, the experimenter tells you that you have no choice; the experiment must continue.

As you might imagine, in Milgram's study the "teachers" were uneasy about shocking the "learner." At 240 volts, one "teacher" responded, "Two hundred forty volts delivered: Aw, no. You mean I've got to keep going with that scale? No sir, I'm not going to kill that man—I'm not going to give him 450 volts!" (Milgram, 1965, p. 67). At the very high voltage, the "learner" quit responding. When the "teacher" asked the experimenter what to do, he simply instructed the "teacher" to continue the experiment and told him that it was his obligation to complete the job. Figure 16.5 shows the setting of the experiment. The 50-year-old "learner" was a confederate of the experimenter. He was not being shocked at all. Of course, the "teachers" were unaware of this.

Forty psychiatrists were asked how they thought individuals would respond in this situation. The psychiatrists predicted that most would go no further than 150 volts, that fewer than 1 in 25 would go as far as 300 volts, and that only 1 in 1,000 would deliver the full 450 volts. The psychiatrists, it turns out, were way off the mark. The majority of the individuals obeyed the experimenter. In fact, almost two of every three delivered the full 450 volts.

In subsequent studies, Milgram set up a storefront in Bridgeport, Connecticut, and recruited volunteers through newspaper ads. Milgram wanted to create a more natural environment for the experiment and to use a wider cross-section of volunteers. In these additional studies, close to two-thirds of the individuals still selected the highest level of shock for the "learner." In variations of the experiment, Milgram discovered some circumstances that encouraged disobedience: when an opportunity was given to see others disobey, when the authority figure was not perceived to be legitimate and was not close by, and when the victim was made to seem more human.

In 1989 Chinese students led a massive demonstration against the Chinese government in Beijing. The students resisted the government's social influence by putting together resources to challenge the Chinese authorities; however, the government eventually eliminated the protests.

We're going to sidetrack for a moment and explore an important point about the Milgram experiments: how *ethical* were they? The volunteers in Milgram's experiment clearly felt anguish, and some were very disturbed about harming another individual. After the experiment was completed, they were told that the "learner" was not actually shocked. Even though they were debriefed and told that they really had not shocked anyone, was it ethical to impose such anguish on them?

Milgram argues that we have learned a great deal about human nature from the experiments. He claims that they tell us how far individuals will go in their obedience, even if it means being cruel to someone. The volunteers were interviewed later and more than four of every five said that they were glad they had participated in the study; none said they were sorry they had participated. When Milgram conducted his studies on obedience, the ethical guidelines for research were not as stringent as they are today. The current ethical guidelines of the American Psychological Association stress that researchers should obtain informed consent from their volunteers. Deception should be used only for very important purposes. Individuals are supposed to feel as good about themselves when the experiment is over as they did when it began. Under today's guidelines, it is unlikely that the Milgram experiment would be conducted.

Resisting Social Influence

"If a man does not keep pace with his companions, perhaps it is because he hears a different drummer. Let him step to the music which he hears, however measured or far away." Thoreau's words suggest that some of us resist social influence. Most of us would prefer to think of ourselves as stepping to our own music, maybe even setting the rhythms for others, rather than trying to keep pace with our companions. However, a certain degree of conformity is required if society is to function at all. As we go through our lives, we are both conformists and nonconformists. Sometimes we are overwhelmed by the persuasion and influence of others; in other circumstances, we resist and gain personal control over our lives. It is important to remember that our relation to the social world is reciprocal. Individuals may be trying to control us, but we can exert personal control over our actions and influence others in turn (Bandura, 1986, 1989).

If you believe someone in a position of authority is making an unjust request or is asking you to do something wrong, what choice of action do you have?

• You can comply.
• You can give the appearance of complying but secretly do otherwise.
• You can publicly dissent by showing doubts and disenchantment but still follow directives.
• You can openly disregard the orders and refuse to comply.
• You can challenge or confront the authority.

REVIEW

Social Perception and Attribution

Three important dimensions of social perception are developing impressions of others, making social comparisons, and presenting ourselves to others to influence their social perceptions. Our impressions are unified. First impressions are important and influence impressions at a later point. We evaluate ourselves by comparison with others. Festinger stressed that social comparison provides an important source of self-knowledge, especially when no other objective means is available; we are more likely to compare ourselves with others who are similar. We usually try to make ourselves look better than we really are. Four recommended impression management strategies are (1) use behavioral matching, (2) conform to situational norms, (3) show appreciation of others and flatter them, and (4) use positive nonverbal cues.

Attribution focuses on the motivation to infer causes of behavior in order to make sense out of the world. One of the most frequent and important ways we classify the causes

• You can get higher authorities to intervene or organize a group of people who agree with you to show the strength of your view.

At this point, we have discussed a number of ideas about attitudes and persuasion, social perception and attribution, and conformity. Next we will explore altruism, or helping others without thought of personal gain.

Altruism

Altruism *is an unselfish interest in helping someone*. We often hear or read about acts of generosity and courage, such as rock concerts and fund raisers to help AIDS victims, a taxi driver who risks his life to save a woman being attacked in a dark alley, and volunteers who pull a baby from an abandoned well. You probably have placed some of your hard-earned cash in the palm of a homeless person or perhaps cared for a wounded cat. How do psychologists account for such acts of human altruism?

Reciprocity and exchange are important aspects of altruism. Humans everywhere give to and receive from others. Reciprocity is a fundamental tenet of every widely practiced religion in the world—Judaism, Christianity, Buddhism, and Islam, for example. Reciprocity encourages us to do unto others as we would have them do unto us. Certain human sentiments

"*All I'm saying is, giving a little something to the arts might help our image.*"

Drawing by P. Steiner; © 1989 The New Yorker Magazine, Inc.

are involved in reciprocity: trust is probably the most important principle over the long run, guilt occurs if we do not reciprocate, and anger results if someone else does not reciprocate.

Social exchange theory *states that individuals should benefit those who benefit them or that, for a benefit received, an equivalent benefit should be returned*. Many examples of altruism involve social exchanges. We exchange gifts, cards, and tips for competent service, for example. It may sound cold and calculating to describe altruism in terms of costs and benefits, but that is exactly what social exchange theory does.

Not all altruism is motivated by reciprocity and social exchange, but this view alerts us to the importance of considering interactions between oneself and others to understand altruism. At the same time, not all seemingly altruistic behavior is unselfish. Some psychologists even argue that true altruism has never been demonstrated; others argue that a distinction between altruism and egoism is possible (Batson & others, 1986; Cialdini & others, 1987). **Egoism** *is involved when person A gives to person B to ensure reciprocity; to gain self-esteem; to present oneself as powerful, competent, or caring; or to avoid social and self-censure for failing to live up to normative expectations*. By contrast, altruism occurs when person A gives to person B with the ultimate goal of benefiting person B. Any benefits that come to person A are unintended.

Describing individuals as having altruistic or egoistic motives implies that person variables are important in understanding altruistic behavior (McClintock & Allison, 1989). Recall from chapter 12 that behavior is determined by both person and situational variables. A person's ability to empathize with the

of behavior is in terms of internal and external causes. Our attributions are not always accurate; the human mind has a built-in bias in making causal judgments. The fundamental attribution error involves overestimating the importance of traits and internal causes while underestimating the importance of situations and external causes. Actors are more likely to choose external causes, observers internal causes. The observer may be in greater error.

Conformity is change in an individual's behavior because of real or imagined pressure. Two experiments demonstrated conformity's power in our lives: Asch's study on judgments of line length and Zimbardo's study on social roles in a mock prison. Obedience is behavior that complies with the explicit demands of an authority. Milgram's classic experiment demonstrated the power of obedience. The subjects followed the experimenter's directions even though they perceived they were hurting someone. Milgram's experiments raise the question of ethics in psychological experimentation. As we go through our lives, we are both conformists and nonconformists. Sometimes we are overwhelmed by the power of persuasion; at other times, we exert personal control and resist such influence.

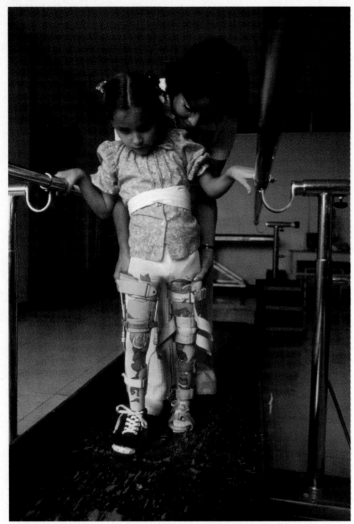

Examples of human altruism are plentiful. Here a young woman assists a handicapped child.

needy or to feel a sense of responsibility for another's welfare affect altruistic motivations. The stronger these dispositions, the less we would expect situational variables to influence whether giving, kindness, or helping occur.

As with any human behavior, however, characteristics of the situation influence the strength of altruistic motivation. Some of these characteristics include the degree of need shown by the other individual, the needy person's responsibility for his or her plight, the cost of assisting the needy person, and the extent to which the altruistic person expects reciprocity.

One of the most widely studied aspects of altruism is bystander intervention. Why does one person help a stranger in distress, whereas another won't lift a finger? It often depends on the circumstances. More than 20 years ago, a young woman named Kitty Genovese cried out repeatedly as she was brutally murdered at about 3 A.M. in a respectable area of New York City. The murderer left three times; he finally put an end to Kitty's life as she crawled to her apartment door and screamed for help. It took the slayer about 30 minutes to kill Kitty. Thirty-eight neighbors watched the gory scene and heard Kitty's screams. No one helped or even called the police.

The **bystander effect** *states that individuals who observe an emergency are less likely to help when someone else is present than when they are alone.* The bystander effect helps explain the apparent cold-blooded indifference to Kitty Genovese's murder. Social psychologists John Darley and Bibb Latané (1968) documented the bystander effect in a number of criminal and medical emergencies. Most of the bystander intervention studies show that, when alone, a person will help 75 percent of the time but, when another bystander is present, the figure drops to 50 percent. Apparently the difference is due to the diffusion of responsibility among witnesses and our tendency to look to the behavior of others for clues about what to do. People may think that someone else will call the police or that, since no one is helping, possibly the person does not need help.

Many other aspects of the situation influence whether an individual will intervene and come to the aid of a person in distress. Bystander intervention is less likely to occur in the following situations (Shotland, 1985):

- When the intervention might lead to personal harm, retaliation by the criminal, or days in court testifying
- When helping takes time
- When a situation is ambiguous
- When the individuals struggling or fighting are married or related
- When a victim is drunk rather than disabled or of a different ethnic group
- When bystanders have no prior history of victimization themselves; have witnessed few crimes and intervention efforts; or have not had training in first aid, rescue, or police tactics

Helping others improves our ability to get along in the world. As we will see next, in our discussion of close relationships, liking others and loving others are also important dimensions of our social relationships.

Close Relationships

What attracts us to others and motivates us to spend more time with them? What is love? Is it lustful and passionate, or should we be more cautious in our pursuit of love, as a Czech proverb advises, "Do not choose your wife at a dance, but in the fields among the harvesters." Of equal importance is why relationships dissolve. Many of us know all too well that someone we thought was a marvelous human being may not turn out to be so marvelous after all. However, there is an old saying that it is better to have loved and lost than never to have loved at all. Loneliness is a cloud that darkens many people's lives. As we explore close relationships, we will examine their beginnings, the faces of love, and loneliness.

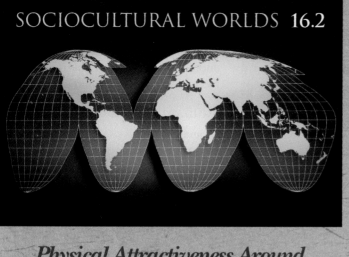

Physical Attractiveness Around the World

A re there universal criteria for physical attractiveness? Two social psychologists recently reviewed the research on physical attractiveness and concluded that "today, scholars have admitted defeat in their search for universal beauty. . . . Anthropologists have ended where they began—able to do no more than point to the dazzling array of characteristics that various people in various places at various times, have idealized" (Hatfield & Sprecher, 1986, p. 12). Even within a culture, the criteria for beauty may change over time. In the United States in the 1940s and 1950s, Marilyn Monroe (with a well-rounded, shapely appearance) was the ideal beauty. In the early 1970s, women aspired to look like fashion model Twiggy and other virtually anorexic females. In the 1980s and 1990s, the ideal physique for women has been neither pleasingly plump nor anorexic. Many Americans are preoccupied with health; as a result, a tall, toned body has become the ideal physique.

Exotic definitions of beauty notwithstanding, some cross-cultural psychologists believe that some aspects of attractiveness are consistent across cultures (Zebrowitz & McArthur, 1988). One study found that health, feminine plumpness, and cleanliness are criteria for attractiveness in a wide range of cultures (Ford & Beach, 1951). Although plumpness is no longer an indicator of health in economically developed countries, extreme emaciation continues to indicate ill health in modern as well as more traditional cultures. Another study found that both Kenyan and British individuals regard extremely thin physiques as unattractive but that Kenyans find fatter bodies more attractive than do the British (Furnham & Alibbai, 1983). In sum, there likely are both similarities and differences in criteria for physical attractiveness across cultures.

What Attracts Us to Others in the First Place?

Does just being around someone increase the likelihood a relationship will develop? Do birds of a feather flock together? That is, are we likely to associate with those who are similar to us? How important is the attractiveness of the other person?

Physical proximity does not guarantee a positive relationship will develop. Familiarity can breed contempt, but familiarity is also a necessary condition for any close relationship to develop. For the most part, friends and lovers have been around each other for a long time; they may have grown up together, gone to high school or college together, worked together, or gone to the same social events. Once we have been exposed to someone for a period of time, what is it that makes the relationship breed friendship and even love?

Birds of a feather do indeed flock together. One of the strongest lessons from studies of close relationships is that we generally like to associate with people who are similar to us. Usually our friends, as well as our lovers, are much more like us than unlike us. We share similar attitudes, behaviors, and characteristics with whom we are closely involved—clothes, intelligence, personality, political attitudes, other friends, values, attitudes, life-style, physical attractiveness, and so on. Some-times opposites are attracted to one another, however. An introvert may wish to be with an extravert, or someone with little money may wish to associate with someone who has a lot of money, for example. Overall, though, we are attracted to individuals with similar rather than opposite characteristics (Berndt & Perry, 1990). In one study, for example, the old adage "misery loves company" was supported as depressed college students preferred to meet other unhappy people, whereas college students who felt good about life preferred to meet other happy people (Wenzlaff & Prohaska, 1989).

Heterosexual men and women differ on the importance they place on good looks when they seek an intimate partner. Women tend to rate as most important such traits as considerateness, honesty, dependability, kindness, and understanding; men prefer good looks, cooking skills, and frugality (Buss & Barnes, 1986). Attractive men tend to initiate contacts with women more than less attractive men do. Women's physical attractiveness is not related to their involvement with men, both because men are likely to pursue women who they feel will accept them and because attractive women, who may worry that men want them only for their looks, are less trusting of men (Lips, 1988). To read about the criteria for physical attractiveness in different cultures, turn to Sociocultural Worlds 16.2.

Consensual validation *explains why people are attracted to others who are similar to them. Our own attitudes and behavior are supported when someone else's attitudes and behavior are similar to ours—their attitudes and behavior validate ours.* People tend to shy away from the unknown. We may tend, instead, to prefer people whose attitudes and behavior we can predict. Similarity also implies that we will enjoy doing things with the other person, which often requires a partner who likes the same things and has similar attitudes. As we will see next, our close relationships may go beyond simply liking someone.

The Faces of Love

Love is a vast and complex territory of human behavior. A common classification of love involves four types: altruism, friendship, romantic (passionate) love, and affectionate (companionate) love (Berscheid, 1988). We have discussed altruism. Let's examine friendship, romantic (passionate) love, and affectionate (companionate) love.

Friendship

True friendship is hard to come by. As American historian Henry Adams succinctly put it, "One friend in life is much, two are many, and three hardly possible." **Friendship** *is a form of close relationship that involves enjoyment (we like to spend time with our friends), acceptance (we take our friends as they are without trying to change them), trust (we assume our friends will act in our best interest), respect (we think our friends make good judgments), mutual assistance (we help and support our friends and they us), openness (we share experiences and deeply personal matters with friends), understanding (we feel that friends know us well and understand what we like), and spontaneity (we feel free to be ourselves around friends)* (Davis, 1985). One study of more than 40,000 individuals revealed that many of these characteristics are considered to be the qualities of a best friend (Parlee, 1979).

Friends and lovers are similar in some ways. Keith Davis (1985) has found that friends and romantic partners share the characteristics of acceptance, trust, respect, openness, understanding, spontaneity, mutual assistance, and happiness. How-

Friendships are an important dimension of our close relationships. What characteristics describe friendship?

In a study in 1967, the men said they would not get married unless they were in love with a woman, but the women were either undecided or said they would get married even if they did not love the man. However, in the 1980s, women had changed their opinions to the point they were almost identical to men, no longer maintaining they would get married if they were not in love.

ever, he found that relationships with spouses or lovers are more likely to also involve fascination and exclusiveness. Relationships with friends are perceived as more stable, especially more than relationships between unmarried lovers.

Romantic (Passionate) Love

Romantic love *is also called passionate love or Eros; it has strong components of sexuality and infatuation, and it often predominates in the early part of a love relationship.* Poets, playwrights, and musicians through the ages have lauded the fiery passion of romantic love—and lamented the searing pain when it fails. Think for a moment about songs and books that hit the top of the charts. Chances are, many of them are about love. Well-known love researcher Ellen Berscheid (1988) says that it is romantic love we mean when we say we are "in love" with someone. She believes that it is romantic love we need to learn more about if we are to discover what love really is.

Romantic love is the main reason we get married. In a famous study in 1967, men maintained that they would not get married if they were not "in love" (Kephart, 1967). The women in the study either were undecided or said they would get married even if they did not love their prospective husband. In the 1980s, women and men tend to agree that they would not get married unless they were "in love," and more than half of today's men and women say that not being "in love" is sufficient reason to dissolve a marriage (Berscheid, Snyder, & Omoto, 1989).

Romantic love is especially important to college students. One study of unattached college men and women found that more than half identify a romantic partner as their closest relationship rather than naming a parent, sibling, or friend (Berscheid, Snyder, & Omoto, 1989). We are referring to romantic love when we say, "I am *in love*," not just "I *love*."

Romantic love includes a complex intermingling of emotions—fear, anger, sexual desire, joy, and jealousy, for example. Obviously, some of these emotions are a source of anguish. One study found that romantic loves are more likely to be the cause of depression than are friends (Berscheid & Fei, 1977).

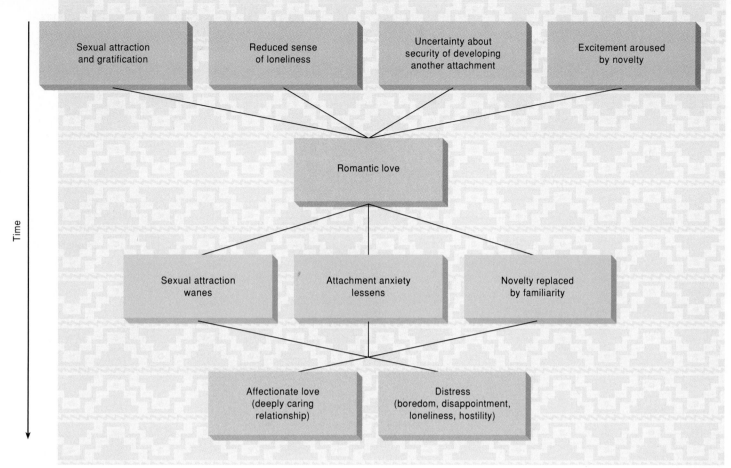

FIGURE 16.6

Shaver's developmental model of love.

Berscheid has concluded that romantic love is about 90 percent sexual desire. She believes that sexual desire is vastly neglected in the study of romantic love (1988; Berscheid, Snyder, & Omoto, 1989). As she puts it, "To discuss romantic love without also prominently mentioning the role sexual arousal and desire plays in it is very much like printing a recipe for tiger soup that leaves out the main ingredient."

Affectionate (Companionate) Love

Love is more than just passion. **Affectionate love,** *also called companionate love, is the type of love that occurs when an individual desires to have another person near and has a deep, caring affection for that person.*

There is a growing belief that the early stages of love have more romantic ingredients but that, as love matures, passion tends to give way to affection. Phillip Shaver (1986) describes the initial phase of romantic love as a time fueled by a mixture of sexual attraction and gratification, a reduced sense of loneliness, uncertainty about the security of developing attachment, and excitement from exploring the novelty of another human

being. With time, he says, sexual attraction wanes, attachment anxieties either lessen or produce conflict and withdrawal, novelty is replaced with familiarity, and lovers either find themselves securely attached in a deeply caring relationship or distressed—feeling bored, disappointed, lonely, or hostile, for example. In the latter case, one or both partners may eventually seek another close relationship.

When two lovers go beyond their preoccupation with novelty, unpredictability, and the urgency of sexual attraction, they are likely to detect deficiencies in each other's caring (Vannoy-Hiller & Philliber, 1989). This may be the point in a relationship when women, who often are better caregivers than men, sense that the relationship has problems. Wives are almost twice as likely as husbands to initiate a divorce, for example (National Center for Health Statistics, 1989). Figure 16.6 shows Shaver's developmental model of love.

So far we have discussed two forms of love: romantic (passionate) and affectionate (companionate). Robert J. Sternberg (1988) believes that affectionate love actually consists of two components: intimacy and commitment. The

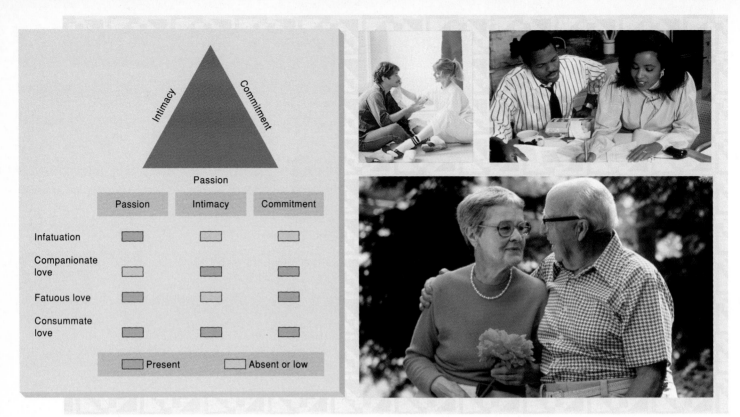

FIGURE 16.7

Sternberg's triangle of love.

triangular theory of love *is Sternberg's belief that love has three main forms: passion, intimacy, and commitment.* Passion, as described earlier, is physical and sexual attraction to a lover. Intimacy is the emotional feelings of warmth, closeness, and sharing in a relationship. Commitment is our cognitive appraisal of the relationship and our intent to maintain the relationship even in the face of problems. If passion is the only ingredient (with intimacy and commitment low or absent), *infatuation* occurs. This might happen in an affair or a fling in which there is little intimacy and even less commitment. A relationship marked by intimacy and commitment but with a lack of passion is called *affectionate love*, a pattern often found among couples who have been married for many years. If passion and commitment are present but intimacy is not, Sternberg calls the relationship *fatuous love,* as when one person worships another from a distance. Couples must share all three components—passion, intimacy, and commitment— to experience the strongest, fullest type of love. Sternberg calls this *consummate love* (see figure 16.7).

Not all of us experience the passion, intimacy, and commitment of love, and not all of us have many, or even one, close friend in whom we can confide. Understanding our social relationships also involves exploring feelings of loneliness.

Loneliness

Some of us are lonely. We may feel that no one knows us very well. We may feel isolated and sense that we do not have anyone we can turn to in times of need or stress. Our society's emphasis on self-fulfillment and achievement, the importance we attach to commitment in relationships, and a decline in stable close relationships are among the reasons loneliness is common today (de Jong-Gierveld, 1987).

Loneliness is associated with a person's gender, attachment history, self-esteem, and social skills (Lau & Gruen, 1992). Both men and women who lack female companions have a greater risk of being lonely, and lonely people often have a history of poor relationships with their parents. Early experiences of rejection and loss (as when a parent dies) can cause a lasting feeling of being alone. Lonely people often have a low self-esteem and tend to blame themselves more than they deserve for their inadequacies. Also, lonely people usually have poor social skills (Jones, Hobbs, & Hockenbury, 1982). For example, they show inappropriate self-disclosure, self-attention at the expense of attention to a partner, or an inability to develop comfortable intimacy.

It is important to distinguish being alone from being lonely. Most of us cherish the moments we can be left alone for a while. Aloneness can heal, but loneliness can hurt.

When students leave the familiar world of their hometown and family to enter college, they may feel especially lonely. Many college freshmen feel anxious about meeting new people and developing a new social life. One student commented:

> My first year here at the university has been pretty lonely. I wasn't lonely at all in high school. I lived in a fairly small town—I knew everyone and everyone knew me. I was a member of several clubs and played on the basketball team. It's not that way at the university. It is a big place and I've felt like a stranger on so many occasions. I'm starting to get used to my life here and in the past few months I've been making myself meet people and get to know them, but it has not been easy.

As this comment illustrates, freshmen rarely take their high school popularity and social standing into the college environment. There may be a dozen high school basketball stars, National Merit scholars, and former student council presidents in a single dormitory wing. Especially if students attend college away from home, they face the task of forming new social relationships.

In one study, 2 weeks after the school year began, 75 percent of 354 college freshmen felt lonely at least part of the time since arriving on campus (Cutrona, 1982). More than 40 percent said their loneliness was moderate to severe in intensity. Students who were the most optimistic and had the highest self-esteem were more likely to overcome their loneliness by the end of their freshman year. Loneliness is not reserved only for college freshmen, though. Upperclassmen are often lonely as well.

Lonely males and females attribute their loneliness to different sources, with men more likely to blame themselves and women more likely to blame external factors. Men are socialized to initiate relationships, whereas women are traditionally socialized to wait, then respond. Perhaps men blame themselves because they feel they should do something about their loneliness, whereas women wonder why no one calls (Lips, 1988).

How do you determine if you are lonely? Scales of loneliness ask you to respond to such questions as the following:

I don't feel in tune with the people around me.
I can find companionship when I want it.

If you consistently respond that you never or rarely feel in tune with people around you and rarely or never can find companionship when you want it, you are likely to fall into the category of people who are moderately or intensely lonely.

How can lonely people reduce their loneliness? Two recommendations are (1) change your actual social relations and (2) change your social need and desires (Peplau & Perlman, 1982). Probably the most direct and satisfying way to become less lonely is to improve your social relations. You can do this by forming new relationships; by using your existing social network more competently; by volunteering in such community activities as food banks; or by creating "surrogate" relationships with pets, television personalities, and the like. A second way to reduce loneliness is to reduce your desire for social contact. Over the short run, you might do this by choosing activities you can enjoy alone rather than activities that require someone's company. Over the long run, though, you should make an effort to form new relationships. A third, unfortunate coping strategy some people adopt is to distract themselves from their painful feelings by drinking to "drown their sorrows" or by becoming a workaholic. Some of the negative health consequences of loneliness may be the product of such maladaptive coping strategies. If you think of yourself as a lonely person, you might consider contacting the counseling center at your college for advice on ways to reduce your loneliness and improve your social skills.

At this point, we have discussed many aspects of social relationships, including helping others, liking others, loving others, and feeling lonely. Earlier we also discussed the power of conformity to group influence. Next we will further discuss the role of group relations in our lives.

REVIEW

Altruism and Close Relationships

Examples of human altruism are plentiful. Reciprocity and social exchange are often, but not always, involved. Motivation can be altruistic or egoistic. Psychologists have studied both the person and the situation variables involved in altruism. Extensive research has been conducted on bystander intervention.

Familiarity precedes a close relationship. We like to associate with individuals who are similar to us. Berscheid believes that love has four forms: altruism, friendship, romantic (passionate) love, and affectionate (companionate) love. Friends and lovers have similar and dissimilar characteristics. Romantic love is involved when we say we are "in love"; it includes passion, sexuality, and a mixture of emotions, some of which may be negative. Affectionate love is more important as relationships mature. Sternberg believes that affectionate love is made up of intimacy and commitment, which, along with romantic love, constitute the three faces of love in his triangular theory. Loneliness is associated with an individual's gender, attachment history, self-esteem, and social skills. The transition to college is a time when loneliness often surfaces.

Group Relations

A student joining a fraternity, a jury deciding a criminal case, a company president delegating authority, a prejudiced remark against a minority group, conflict among nations, and attempts to reach peace—all of these circumstances reflect our lives as members of groups. Each of us belongs to many groups. Some we choose; others we do not. We choose to belong to a club, but we are born into a particular ethnic group, for example. Some of the important questions about group relations include the following: Why do we join groups? What is the structure of groups? How do we perform and make decisions in groups? Why are some people leaders and others followers? How do groups deal with each other, especially ethnic groups and nations?

Motivation for Group Behavior and the Structure of Groups

Why does one student join a study group, a church, an athletic team, or a company? Groups satisfy our personal needs, reward us, provide information, raise our self-esteem, and give us an identity. We might join a group because we think it will be enjoyable and exciting and satisfy our need for affiliation and companionship. We might join a group because we will receive rewards, either material or psychological. By taking a job with a company, we get paid to work for a group, but we also reap prestige and recognition. Groups are an important source of information. For example, as we listen to other members talk in a Weight Watchers group, we learn about their strategies for losing weight. As we sit in the audience at a real estate seminar, we learn how to buy property with no money down. The groups in which you are a member—

your family, a college, a club, a team—make you feel good, raise your self-esteem, and provide you with an identity.

Any group to which you belong has certain things in common with all other groups. All groups have their own **norms,** *rules that apply to all members of a group.* A sorority may require all of its members to maintain a 3.0 grade point average. This is a norm. The city government requires each of its workers to wear socks, Mensa requires individuals to have a high IQ, Polar Bear Club members must complete a 15-minute swim in below-freezing temperatures. These, too, are norms.

Roles *are rules and expectations that govern certain positions in a group. Roles define how people should behave in a particular position in the group.* In a family, parents have certain roles, siblings have other roles, and a grandparent has yet another role. On a football team, many roles must be filled: center, guard, tackle, end, quarterback, halfback, and fullback, for example, and that only covers the offense. Roles and norms, then, tell us what is expected of the members of a group.

Deindividuation

Our behavior in groups can become deindividuated. **Deindividuation** *is the loss of identity as an individual and the development of group identity in group situations that promote arousal and anonymity.* As early as 1895, Gustav LeBon observed that a group can foster uninhibited behavior, ranging from wild celebrations to mob behavior. Ku Klux Klan violence, Mardi Gras wild times, and "good ol' boys" rolling a car on spring break in Fort Lauderdale might be due to deindividuated behavior. One explanation of deindividuation is that the group gives us anonymity. We may act in an uninhibited way because we believe authority figures and victims are less likely to discover that we are the culprits (Rogers, 1989).

Groupthink

Sometimes groups make rational decisions and come up with the best solution to a problem. Not always. Group members, especially leaders, often want to develop or

a.

b.

c.

Our behavior in groups can become deindividuated. Examples of situations in which people can lose their individual identity include (a) at Ku Klux Klan rallies, (b) at Mardi Gras, and (c) in national patriotism crowds.

maintain unanimity among group members. **Groupthink** *is the motivation of group members to maintain harmony and unanimity in decision making, suffocating differences of opinion in the process* (Janis, 1972). Groupthink evolves because members often boost each other's egos and increase each other's self-esteem by seeking conformity, especially in stressful circumstances. This motivation for harmony and unanimity may result in disastrous decisions and policy recommendations. Examples of groupthink include the United States invasion of Cuba (the Bay of Pigs), the escalation of the Vietnam war, the failure to prepare for the invasion of Pearl Harbor, the Watergate cover-up, and Irangate.

Leaders often favor a solution and promote it within the group. Members of the group also tend to be cohesive and isolate themselves from qualified outsiders who could influence their decisions. Leaders can avoid groupthink by encouraging dissident opinions, by not presenting a favored plan at the outset, and by having several independent groups work on the same problem.

Leadership

"I am certainly not one of those who need to be prodded. In fact, if anything, I am the prod," British Prime Minister Winston Churchill said of himself. What made Churchill a great leader? Was it a set of personality traits, the situation into which he was thrust, or a combination of the two?

The **great person theory** *says that individuals have certain traits that are best suited for leadership positions.* Leaders are commonly thought to be assertive, cooperative, decisive, dominant, energetic, self-confident, tolerant of stress, willing to assume responsibility, diplomatic and tactful, and persuasive. Although we can list traits and skills possessed by leaders, a large number of research studies conclude that we cannot predict who will become a leader solely from an individual's personality characteristics. Is it the situation, then, that produces leaders? The situational view of leadership argues that the needs of a group change from time to time. A person who emerges as a leader in one circumstance will not necessarily be the person who becomes a leader in another circumstance. Many psychologists believe that a combination of personality characteristics and skills and situational influences determines who will become a leader.

At this point, our discussion of group relations has focused on why we join groups, how groups are structured, how we perform and make decisions in groups, and why some individuals are leaders and others are followers. Next we will discuss how groups deal with each other, especially ethnic groups and nations.

Majority-Minority Influence

Think about the groups in which you have been a member. Who had the most influence, the majority or the minority? In most groups—whether a jury, family, or corporate meeting—the majority holds sway over the minority. The majority exerts both normative and informational pressure on the group. Its adherents set the group's norms; those who do not go along may be rejected or even given the boot. The majority also has a greater opportunity to provide information that will influence decision making.

In most cases, the majority wins, but there are occasions when the minority has its day. How can the minority swing the majority? The minority cannot win through normative influence because it is outnumbered. It must do its work through *informational pressure*. If the minority presents its views consistently and confidently, then the majority is more likely to listen to the minority's views.

Certain individuals in a minority may play a crucial role. Individuals with a history of taking minority stands may trigger others to dissent, showing them that disagreement is possible and the minority stand may be the best course. Such is the ground of some of history's greatest moments—when Lincoln spoke out against slavery, racism dominated and tore at the country, and, when Corazon Aquino became a candidate for president of the Philippines, few people thought Ferdinand Marcos could be beaten.

a.

b.

Certain individuals in the minority have played important roles in history. (a) Martin Luther King, Jr., helped Black Americans gain important rights. (b) Corazon Aquino, who became president of the Philippines after defeating Ferdinand Marcos, toppled a corrupt political regime and reduced the suffering of many Philippine citizens.

Intergroup Relations

On refusing to serve in Vietnam in 1966, Muhammed Ali said, "No Viet Cong ever called me a nigger." In response to the power of the United States in 1956, Nikita Kruschev said, "Whether you like it or not, history is on our side. We will bury you." In seeking to reduce conflict in 1963, John Kennedy said, "Peace is a daily, a weekly, a monthly process, gradually changing opinions, slowly eroding old barriers, quietly building new structures." These are the themes of our study of intergroup relations. First we will discuss prejudice, ethnocentrism, and conflict. Then we will evaluate ways to reduce conflict and find peace.

Prejudice, Ethnocentrism, and Conflict

You probably think you know what prejudice means and, like most people, you probably don't think of yourself as prejudiced. In fact, each of us has prejudices and stereotypes. **Prejudice** *is an unjustified negative attitude toward an individual based on the individual's membership in a group.* The group against which the individual is prejudiced can be made up of people of a particular race, ethnic group, sex, age, religion, nation, or other detectable characteristic (Aboud, 1988; Devine, 1989; Schaller & Maass, 1989).

A **stereotype** *is a generalization about a group's characteristics that does not take into account any variation from one individual to the next.* Think about your image of a dedicated accountant. Most of us would probably describe such a person as "quiet," "boring," and "unsociable." Rarely would we come up with a mental image of this person as extraverted, the life of the party, or artistic. Characterizing all accountants as boring is a clear example of a stereotype. Another stereotype is that all Italians are excitable. Researchers have found that we are less likely to detect variations among individuals who belong to "other" groups than among those who belong to "our" group. For example, Whites are more likely to stereotype Blacks than other Whites during eyewitness identification (Brigham, 1986).

How do prejudices develop? We can learn something about prejudice by examining the concept of **ethnocentrism,** *the tendency to favor one's own group over other groups*. Ethnocentrism's positive side is that it fosters a sense of pride in our group that fulfills the human urge to attain and maintain a positive self-image. As we approach the end of the twentieth century, group pride has mushroomed. There's Black Pride and Gay Pride. The Scots grow more Scottish, the Irish more Irish.

There is something paradoxical, though, about such pride. Most members of a group will attest that the group does not discriminate against others. As American radical Stokeley Carmichael said in 1966, "I'm for the Negro. I'm not against anything." Too often members of groups stress differences between them and others rather than pride in their own group. More information about recent changes in stereotypes and prejudice appears in Sociocultural Worlds 16.3.

Henry Tajfel (1978) has proposed **social identity theory,** *which states that, when individuals are assigned to a group, they invariably think of the group as an in-group for them. This occurs because individuals want to have a positive self-image. Social identity theory helps explain prejudice and conflict among groups.* Tajfel is one of an increasingly small group of European Jews who survived World War II. His goal is to explain the extreme violence and prejudice his group experienced.

Self-image consists of both a personal identity and many social identities. Tajfel argues that individuals can improve their self-image by enhancing either their personal or social identity. Tajfel believes that social identity is especially important. When we compare the social identity of our group with the social identity of another group, we often maximize the distinctiveness of each group. Think about your social identity with your hometown, or imagine two professional basketball fans, one who lives in Detroit and is a Detroit Pistons fan, the other who lives in Chicago and is a Chicago Bulls fan. When the Pistons won the 1989 and 1990 NBA championships, the Detroit fan's self-image was enhanced; when the Bulls won the 1991 NBA championship, the Chicago fan's self-image was enhanced. As these two fans talk with each other, they argue about the virtues of their teams, reinforcing the distinctiveness of their social identities within the two groups. As they strive to promote their social identities, it is not long before they intersperse proud, self-congratulatory remarks with nasty comments about the opposing team. In a capsule, the theme of the conversation becomes, "My team is good and I am good. Your team is bad and you are bad." So it goes with the sexes, ethnic groups, nations, social classes, religions, sororities, fraternities, and countless other groups. These comparisons often lead to competition and even to "legitimizing" discrimination against other groups.

a.

b.

c.

d.

Group members often show considerable pride in their group identity, as reflected in (a) African Americans' celebration of Martin Luther King Day, (b) Mexican Americans' celebration of Cinco de Mayo, (c) Native Americans' celebration of their heritage, and (d) Polish Americans' celebration of their cultural background.

The Changing Forms of Prejudice

We live in a society that has discriminated against virtually every ethnic minority group—Asians, Hispanics, eastern and southern Europeans, for example—as it arrived at these shores. However, the oppression of slavery and the system of segregation that followed it are unique to Blacks. Some psychologists argue that, as a result, Black Americans have had more difficulty achieving equality than any other ethnic minority group (Sears & others, 1988).

Today Whites show a much more accepting attitude toward Blacks than even 2 decades ago. The vast majority of Whites support Black Americans' rights to public office, access to public accommodations, fair housing, and so on, and violence by Whites toward Blacks has diminished considerably. However, occasional incidents still spark conflict and hatred between Blacks and Whites—a Black person is abused or even murdered by a White police officer when the circumstances did not seem to warrant such violence, for example. Also, there still is strong resistance to programs that would help Black Americans reach full equality—affirmative action and school desegregation, for example (Taylor, Sheatsley, & Greeley, 1978).

Some social scientists are engaged in a lively controversy about whether White society will continue to move toward liberal racial attitudes or resist further change (Sears & others, 1988). For example, although most Whites ostensibly support integration, it may just be *lip service*. That is, on the surface, many Whites make socially correct comments about Blacks but underneath may harbor racist feelings. Whites' support for general principles of equality may be *superficial*. It is easy to espouse equality in the abstract, but supporting its implementation has costly implications. It may also be that White Americans have a genuine *ambivalence* about Black Americans, in which White Americans sympathize with the problems Black Americans have faced and continue to face but also feel that Black Americans have contributed to their plight by their lack of ambition and failure to take advantage of opportunities (Katz, Wackenhut, & Hass, 1986).

Another possibility is that old-fashioned racism has been replaced by a new form called *aversive racism*, which describes the conflict White Americans experience between their genuinely egalitarian values and their own negative feelings toward Black Americans (Dovidio & Gaertner, 1986). White Americans may be ashamed of their negative feelings and do not want them to be exposed, so they simply avoid Black Americans. In old-fashioned racism, Whites felt hostility and hatred toward Blacks; in aversive racism, they feel discomfort, uneasiness, and fear.

Yet another possibility is that old-fashioned racism has been replaced by another version, called *symbolic racism*, which consists of a combination of anti-Black feelings and traditional values, such as those of the Protestant ethic (Sears & McConahay, 1973). Symbolic racism is the attitude that Black Americans are pushing too hard and too fast for equality, making unfair demands and getting undeserved special attention, such as jobs and college admissions (Sears, 1987).

In short, although old-fashioned racial prejudice has diminished in recent years, other forms of racial prejudice seem to have replaced it.

Tajfel showed that it doesn't take much for us to think in terms of "we" and "they." For example, he assigned one person to a particular group because she overestimated the number of dots on a screen. He assigned another person to a different group because he underestimated the number. Once assigned to the two groups, the members were asked to award money to other participants. Those eligible to receive the money were distinguished only by their membership in one of the two groups. Invariably individuals acted favorably toward (awarded money to) a member of their own group. It is no wonder, then, that if we favor our own group based on such trivial criteria that we will show intense in-group favoritism when differences are not as trivial (LaLonde, Taylor, & Moghaddam, 1992; Rappaport, Bornstein, & Erev, 1989). However, aren't there ways we can reduce conflict and live more peacefully?

Reducing Conflict and Seeking Peace

Martin Luther King, Jr., said, "I have a dream—that my four little children will one day live in a nation where they will not be judged by the color of their skin but by the content of their character." Carl Sandburg commented, "Sometime they will give a war and nobody will come." How might we possibly reach the world Martin Luther King, Jr., and Carl Sandburg envisioned—a world without prejudice and war?

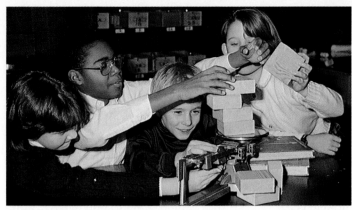

Eliot Aronson developed the concept of the jigsaw classroom to reduce ethnic conflict. How does the jigsaw classroom work?

Years ago social psychologist Muzafer Sherif fueled "we-they" competition between two groups of 11-year-old boys at a summer camp called Robbers Cave in Oklahoma (Sherif & others, 1961). In the first week, one group hardly knew the other group existed. One group became known as the Rattlers (a tough and cussing group whose shirts were emblazoned with a snake insignia), and the other was known as the Eagles.

Near the end of the first week, each group learned of the other's existence. It took little time for "we-they" talk to surface ("They had better not be on our ball field." "Did you see the way one of them was sneaking around?"). Sherif, who disguised himself as a janitor so he could unobtrusively observe the Rattlers and Eagles, had the two groups compete in baseball, touch football, and tug-of-war. Counselors manipulated and judged events so the teams were close. Each team perceived the other to be unfair. Raids, the burning of the other group's flag, and fights resulted. The Rattlers and Eagles further derided one another, holding their noses in the air as they passed each other. Rattlers described all Rattlers as brave, tough, and friendly and called all Eagles sneaks and smart alecks. The Eagles reciprocated by labeling the Rattlers crybabies.

After "we-they" competition transformed the Rattlers and Eagles into opposing "armies," Sherif devised ways to reduce hatred between the groups. He tried noncompetitive contact but that didn't work. Only when both groups were required to work cooperatively to solve a problem did the Rattlers and Eagles develop a positive relationship. Sherif created three superordinate tasks that required the efforts of both groups: working together to repair the only water supply to the camp, pooling their money to rent a movie, and cooperating to pull the camp truck out of a ditch.

Might Sherif's idea—that of creating cooperation between groups rather than competition—be applied to ethnic groups? When the schools of Austin, Texas, were desegregated through extensive busing, increased racial tension among Blacks, Mexi-

can Americans, and Whites resulted in violence in the schools. The superintendent consulted Eliot Aronson, a prominent social psychologist who was at the University of Texas in Austin at the time. Aronson thought it was more important to prevent racial hostility than to control it. This led him to observe a number of elementary school classrooms in Austin. What he saw was fierce competition among children of unequal status.

Aronson stressed that the reward structure of the elementary school classrooms needed to be changed from a setting of unequal competition to one of cooperation among equals, without making any curriculum changes. To accomplish this, he put together the *jigsaw classroom*. The jigsaw classroom works by creating a situation in which all the students have to pull together to "get the big picture." Let's say we have a class of 30 students, some White, some Black, some Hispanic. The academic goal is to learn about the life of Joseph Pulitzer. The class might be broken up into five study groups of six students each, with the groups as equal as possible in terms of ethnic composition and academic achievement level. Learning about Pulitzer's life becomes a class project divided into six parts, with one part given to each member of each six-person group. The components might be paragraphs from Pulitzer's biography, such as how the Pulitzer family came to the United States, Pulitzer's childhood, his early work, and so on. The parts are like the pieces of a jigsaw puzzle. They have to be put together to form the complete puzzle.

Each student has an allotted amount of time to study her or his part. Then the group meets and each member tries to teach that part to the group. After an hour or so, each student is tested on the life of Pulitzer. Each student must learn the entire lesson; learning depends on the cooperation and effort of all members. Aronson (1986) believes that this type of learning increases students' interdependence through cooperatively reaching a common goal.

The strategy of emphasizing cooperation rather than competition and the jigsaw approach have been widely used in classrooms in the United States. A number of studies reveal that this type of cooperative learning is associated with increased self-esteem, better academic performance, friendships among classmates, and improved interethnic perceptions (Slavin, 1989).

It is not easy to get groups who do not like each other to cooperate. The air of distrust and hostility is difficult to overcome. Creating superordinate goals that require the cooperation of both groups is one viable strategy, as evidenced by Sherif's and Aronson's work. Other strategies include disseminating positive information about the "other" and reducing the potential threat of each group (Worschel, 1986).

As social psychologists search for ways to decrease tension among nations, they are turning their attention to reducing potential threat. The **GRIT strategy,** *which stands for Graduated and Reciprocated Initiatives in Tension-Reduction, is a* strategy to decrease tension and mistrust among nations so that disarmament and regular negotiation, trade, and international diplomacy can proceed. *The GRIT strategy begins when one nation makes unilateral reductions in its threat capability* (Lindskold & Han, 1988; Osgood, 1962).

In the GRIT strategy, the escalating arms race is seen as one of distorted perceptions, stress, mistrust, and stereotyping. The cognitive dynamics involved produce a mirror-image phenomenon; that is, the citizens of each nation see each other as the aggressor. The Soviet Union accused the United States of being the aggressor in Vietnam; the United States accused the Soviet Union of being the aggressor in Afghanistan. Each side says its missiles are defensive and the other side's are offensive. Such distrust and tension make negotiation extremely difficult. Virtually any stance a nation takes is perceived as trickery by the other side. Each side perceives the other as totally self-interested and inflexible.

The strategy calls for one party to make unilateral reductions in threat capability, to be announced in advance. After the reduction, the other group is requested to make a similar reduction. The eventual goal of the GRIT plan is to reach a point at which each group has dramatically lowered its threat potential and, therefore, the source of conflict. In GRIT, one group must take the initiative for threat reduction.

In 1991 the United States and Russia signed a treaty that reduced the strength of both sides' missiles. The recent improvement in U.S.-Russian relations raises hope that further mutual conciliation will occur. The power to end the human species rests in the hands of American and Russian leaders (Wagner, 1988). We should not underestimate the complexity of the delicate power balance that exists in today's world, but, as twentieth-century Dutch inventor and poet Piet Hien wrote, "The noble art of losing face may one day save the human race and turn into eternal merit what weaker minds would call disgrace."

At this point in our discussion of social psychology, we have examined the nature of our thoughts, behavior, and group relations in many social contexts. Next we will explore the social world of work.

Organizational Behavior

Not only does work provide us with a means of earning a living, but we also hope it will give us a sense of purpose and fulfillment in life. Because work is such a fundamental part of most people's lives, psychologists are becoming increasingly interested in understanding what makes the workplace a good environment. We will discuss industrial/organizational psychology, workers' functions in groups, the roles of gender and ethnicity in the workplace, and the changing faces and places of organizations.

Industrial/Organizational Psychology

Industrial/organizational psychology *is the branch of psychology that focuses on the workplace, both its workers and the organizations that employ them.* Industrial/organizational psychologists are concerned with personnel selection and development; with employee attitudes, motivation, and morale; and with the many facets of understanding and predicting behavior in organizations. Every individual brings to an organization a unique set of personal characteristics, experiences from other organizations, and a personal background (Moorhead & Griffin, 1989). Organizational psychologists take into account each employee's unique perspective as they explore ways to improve the workplace. For example, an organizational psychologist studying employee turnover at IBM might analyze the kind of people IBM hires. The goal of this analysis would be to learn as much as possible about the company's workforce as individuals—their expectations, motivations, and so on.

Most individuals, though, do not work in isolation. They interact with other people and the organization in many ways. Workers are affected by managers, co-workers, the organization's formal policies and procedures, and various changes made by the organization. Clearly, then, organizational psychologists need to study the way individuals and organizations interact. In addition to understanding the kind of people IBM hires, an organizational psychologist might examine the company's orientation procedures for new employees. The goal would be to understand the psychological dimensions of how new employees interact within the broader organizational context.

Workers in Groups

Organizations consist of both formal and informal groups. **Formal groups** *are established by management to do the organization's work.* Formal groups include such departments as quality assurance, electrical engineering, cost accounting, and personnel. Organizations are increasingly using formal groups known as work teams (Sundstrom, De Meuse, & Futrell, 1990). Work teams are often established for subsections of manufacturing and assembly processes. For example, General Motors recently reorganized its assembly lines into work teams of 5 to 20 workers. In the work team approach, the team members decide among themselves who will do each task. This approach is derived from the Japanese style of management, which is discussed in greater detail in Sociocultural Worlds 16.4.

Informal groups *are clusters of workers formed by the group's members.* Informal groups develop because of the interests and needs of the individuals who work in the organization. They consist of both friendship groups, arising from relationships that develop among members of the organization, and interest groups, which are organized around a common activity or interest, such as sports, the arts, or politics. Among the interest groups that have developed in recent years are networks of working women

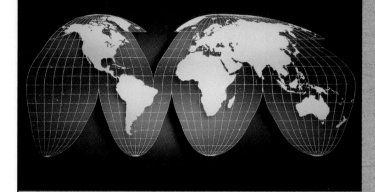

SOCIOCULTURAL WORLDS 16.4

Japanese Management Style

In the past several decades, Americans have become very interested in the Japanese style of management, which emphasizes group and consensual decision making. The Japanese management style consists of three basic strategies: view the organization as an internal labor market, articulate a unique company philosophy, and engage employees in extensive socialization (Hatvany & Pucik, 1981).

With regard to viewing the organization as an internal labor market, employees are hired soon after they graduate and generally are expected to remain in the organization throughout their career. With regard to articulating a unique company philosophy, Japanese companies go to great lengths to establish a "family" atmosphere. Employees not only work together, they often live together in company housing, vacation at company resorts, and socialize at company centers. With regard to engaging employees in extensive socialization, young employees are selected not only on the basis of their technical qualifications but also on the ease with which they can be assimilated into the organization. As part of their socialization, employees are expected to dedicate their service and loyalty to the company. In their first several years of work, employees are also rotated into different jobs at the same level in an organization so they can learn various aspects of the business and get to know their co-workers. This strategy helps socialize employees to the company's culture and philosophy.

Japanese organizations use a number of specific techniques to support their three basic strategies (Hatvany & Pucik, 1981). Work teams have an important function in Japanese organizations. Tasks are usually assigned to teams, not to individuals, and managers evaluate group performance rather than individual performance. Not surprisingly, Japanese workers usually have a strong group identity. Employees are subtly pressured to develop team spirit and to seek friendships in the organization. Managers spend considerable time talking with employees about everyday matters, providing housing assistance, suggesting recreational activities, and so on. Such strategies help a Japanese firm's management convey its concern for the employees' welfare; in return, employees become committed to the organization.

In Japan—a collectivist culture—the management style emphasizes group and consensual decision making, and Japanese management engages employees in extensive socialization.

Advocates of the Japanese management approach argue that its basic strategies can help American organizations improve their performance. The approach has been successfully applied in some American firms, such as Rockwell International, an aerospace firm, and Eli Lilly, a pharmaceutical company. However, the Japanese approach has its critics. For example, this approach blatantly discriminates against women, who are considered only temporary employees. Also, the management approach just described is found only in the major Japanese firms; many small companies cannot afford the luxury of hiring employees for life. Critics also point out that the Japanese management approach may not be the actual cause of Japan's recent economic success. They argue that Japan's meteoric economic rise also has been fueled by postwar reconstruction; a close alliance between government and business; a strong sense of nationalism, which promotes high levels of motivation among workers; and a strong cultural tradition of duty, obedience, and discipline (Steers, 1988). The Japanese management style also has been heavily criticized for promoting conformity at the expense of individual creativity. Despite such criticisms, the approach does have considerable value for certain firms, although others may function more effectively with different management approaches (Lincoln & Kalleberg, 1990).

Among interest groups that have developed in recent years are networks of working women. Many of these groups began as informal gatherings of women in male-dominated organizations who wanted the support of other women.

The corporate board rooms of American business are male dominated and in many instances are filled exclusively with males. Only one Black heads a Fortune 1000 company and, in one survey of 1,700 senior executives, only 8 were women, all of them White.

(Moorhead & Griffin, 1989). Many of these groups began in male-dominated organizations as informal gatherings of women who wanted the support of other women. Soon, however, they developed far beyond their initial social purposes. The interest groups became sources of counseling, job placement, and management training. Some of the interest groups were established as formal, permanent associations, whereas others remained informal groups.

Informal groups can be as influential as formal groups in determining behavior in an organization. One classic study demonstrated the sensitivity of workers to the behavior of others in their group and the importance of informal norms of behavior at the Hawthorne Plant of the Western Electric Company in Chicago (Mayo, 1933; Roethlisberger & Dickson, 1939). Management set a goal for each worker to wire a certain number of telephone switchboards per day. However, the work group as a whole established an acceptable level of output for its members. Workers who were above or below this informally established norm were criticized by other members of the work group. Workers who failed to meet the acceptable level were called "chiselers," whereas those who exceeded the norm were labeled "rate busters" or "speed kings." A worker who wanted to be accepted by the group could not produce at too low or too high a level. Thus, as a worker approached the accepted level for each day, he or she slowed down rather than overproduce. Even though the individual workers could have made more money by producing more switchboards, they adhered to the informal work group's norm.

Gender and Ethnicity in the Workplace

In the Japanese workplace, most women have inferior roles as temporary workers. Although women and ethnic minorities in the American workplace are considered permanent employees,

organizational psychologists Ann Morrison and Mary Ann Von Glinow (1990) assert that White women and people of color experience a "glass ceiling" in management. The glass ceiling concept was popularized in the 1980s to describe a subtle barrier that is virtually transparent yet so strong that it prevents women and ethnic minorities from moving up in the management hierarchy. Today women fill nearly one-third of all management positions, an improvement from 19 percent in 1972, but most are in jobs with little authority and low pay. Only 2 percent of all senior executives are women, and only 1.7 percent of the corporate officers of all Fortune 500 companies are women. The picture for ethnic minority executives is even more dismal. Only one Black heads a Fortune 1000 company (Leinster, 1988). Of more than 1,700 senior executives surveyed in 1979, 3 were Black, 2 were Asian, and 2 were Hispanic; only 8 were women, all of them White.

A number of reasons have been proposed for these gender and ethnic disparities in management (Morrison & Von Glinow, 1990). One explanation points to inadequacies in women and ethnic minorities themselves. For example, women's fear of success or their unwillingness to take risks have been proposed as reasons for their lack of management positions (Riger & Galligan, 1980). However, female and male managers are much more similar than dissimilar on many personality, motivational, and intellectual factors. Ethnic minority managers have shown special strengths in interpersonal relations and stability of performance. A second explanation is that the dominant group is biased. Many employers, customers, and employees believe that women and people of color are less suited for management positions, even when they are perfect candidates. Another belief that handicaps women in particular is that the "good manager" is still described as masculine rather than androgynous in most organizations. A third explanation is that the racist underpinnings of society permeate organizations. Intergroup theory states

As we move into the twenty-first century, the workforce will be increasingly diverse. However, many barriers still prevent women and ethnic minorities from reaching the high levels of management. One training strategy of some corporations is to provide support groups for recruiting women and ethnic minorities and socializing them about the culture of the organization.

that two types of groups exist in organizations—identity groups (based on ethnicity, family, gender, and age) and organization groups (based on common work tasks, work experience, and positions in the hierarchy). Tension results when the composition of an organization's group membership changes but the mix in identity group membership does not (Aldefer, 1986; Thomas & Aldefer, 1989). An organization's demographics often mirror the pattern in society as a whole, as when Whites fill most of the high-status positions and Blacks the low-status positions. As a result, managers may evaluate women and people of color through the distorted lens of prejudice.

Many organizational psychologists believe that the workplace needs to adjust to accommodate women and ethnic minorities. Eastman Kodak and Dupont are two companies that have implemented programs designed to help managers work together within a diverse workforce and to reduce discrimination. The value of such programs is that issues are brought out into the open, allowing individuals to discuss their beliefs.

A special concern for women and ethnic minorities in organizations is **tokenism,** *which means being treated as a representative of a group rather than as an individual.* The token position places enormous pressure on women and ethnic minority indi-

viduals. Organizational psychologists believe that, when women and ethnic minority individuals face tokenism, they need to perfect certain skills, such as the ability to negotiate and resolve conflict (Morrison & Von Glinow, 1990).

Support groups may help increase the number of women and ethnic minority members in management. For example, Security Pacific National Bank developed a program titled Black Officers Support System (BOSS) to recruit Blacks and reduce their turnover (Irons & Moore, 1985). In Washington, DC, the Executive Leadership Council is made up of 50 Black managers from major industries who recruit and hire ethnic minorities (Leinster, 1988). Such groups provide career guidance and psychological support for women and ethnic minority individuals seeking managerial positions.

The Changing Faces and Places of Organizations

As we move into the twenty-first century, what will the workplace be like? Changes are expected in both the workers and the work environment. In the year 2000, workers will be more culturally diverse—one-third of all new entrants into the labor force are anticipated to be ethnic minority members. Larger numbers of women will enter the labor force, putting greater pressure on society to help balance the demands of work and family (Ickovics, 1991; Offermann & Gowing, 1990).

Organizations themselves also will change. Corporations are failing at a noticeable rate, whereas others are scaling down the size of their operations to survive. Mergers and acquisitions displace workers with increasing regularity. The types of jobs available continue to shift from the manufacturing sector to the service sector, which accounted for 71 percent of the nation's jobs in 1990. In addition, businesses are increasingly becoming international organizations. As a result, many companies' success may rest on the ability to relate to workers and companies in other countries (Offermann & Gowing, 1990).

Many jobs are becoming more complex and more cognitively demanding. As knowledge increases exponentially, technically trained workers, such as engineers, face a "half life" of 5 years; that is, half of what engineers know in any given year is obsolete 5 years later because of rapid technological advances (Goldstein & Gilliam, 1990). In the future, such demands will require considerable continuing education and training programs for workers.

Millions of workers center a great deal of their lives on the workplace. As a result, the heads of organizations are realizing that the workplace is an important setting for promoting an individual's health and welfare (Offermann & Gowing, 1990). Many organizations have programs to help workers balance work and family and promote health through stress-management courses and fitness centers.

This is the last of *Psychology*'s 16 chapters. Perhaps you can look back and say you learned a lot about yourself and other human beings. Many unanswered questions about human behavior remain, but psychology does provide clues to make life more enjoyable and humane. What could be more important to us all than psychology's mission to describe, explain, and predict human behavior? One of the most important themes of *Psychology* has been sociocultural issues. Following this chapter, you will find an Epilogue that focuses on critical thinking about sociocultural issues.

REVIEW

Group Relations, Intergroup Relations, and Organizational Behavior

Groups satisfy our personal needs, reward us, provide us with information, raise our self-esteem, and enhance our identity. Every group has norms and roles. Deindividuation is the loss of identity as an individual and the development of group identity in group situations, which promote arousal and anonymity. Groupthink is the motivation of group members to maintain harmony and unanimity in decision making, suffocating differences of opinion in the process. Both the great person theory, which emphasizes personality traits and skills, and situational factors have been proposed to explain why certain people become leaders. Personality and situational factors likely combine to determine who will become a leader. The majority usually has the most influence, but at times the minority has its day, being most effective through informational pressure.

Prejudice is an unjustified attitude toward an individual because of the individual's group identity. A stereotype is a generalization about a group's characteristics. Ethnocentrism is the tendency to favor one's group over other groups. Ethnocentrism has a positive side—in-group pride—and a negative side—emphasis on differences between groups. One theory devised to explain both prejudice and conflict is Tajfel's social identity theory, which states that, when individuals are assigned to a group, they invariably think of the group as an in-

group for them. This occurs because we want to have a positive self-image. Contact between groups does not reduce conflict. The most effective strategy is to develop a superordinate goal requiring the cooperation of both groups. The jigsaw classroom uses the cooperative strategy to reduce racial tension in schools. GRIT is another strategy used, especially to reduce tension among nations. GRIT involves reducing the potential threat of each group.

Industrial/organizational psychology focuses on the workplace, both its workers and the organizations that employ them. Groups in organizations include both formal groups—established by management to do the organization's work—and informal groups—formed by the group's members. Informal groups include friendships and interest groups. Some organizational psychologists believe that women and ethnic minority individuals face a number of barriers in their efforts to move up the management hierarchy. There are very few women in the top levels of management and even fewer ethnic minorities. A reason for these low numbers is based on differences that handicap women and ethnic minorities, as well as discrimination. However, there are more similarities than differences between White males and their female and ethnic minority counterparts. A special concern is tokenism. Changes are expected in both workers and the environment of the workplace. The workplace will increasingly become diverse, service oriented, and internationally linked. Many jobs are becoming more complex and cognitively demanding. Increased interest in the workplace as a setting for promoting individuals' health and welfare is occurring.

Summary

I. Attitudes and Behavior

Attitudes are beliefs and opinions. Social psychologists are interested in how strongly attitudes predict behavior. Today it is believed that, when situational influences are weak, the attitude-behavior connection is strengthened. In studying behavior's influence on attitudes, two theories have been proposed. Cognitive dissonance theory, developed by Festinger, argues that we have a strong need for cognitive consistency; we change our attitudes to make them more consistent with our behavior. Bem developed a more behavioral approach, called self-perception theory; it stresses the importance of making inferences about our own behavior, especially when our attitudes are not clear.

II. Persuasion and Attitude Change

Understanding persuasion and attitude change requires information about the communicator, the message, the medium, and the target. Communicators are most effective when they have expertise and credibility, trustworthiness, and power; attractiveness and similarity also are important. With regard to the message, the less informed we are, the more emotional appeals work; the more frightened we are, the more we will be influenced too. Positive emotional appeals can also be persuasive, especially through music. Because it delivers live images, television is the most powerful medium. Its persuasive capabilities are staggering, although experts debate its influence. With regard to the target, or audience, younger individuals are more likely to change their attitudes than older individuals, and females are more readily persuaded than males. Self-esteem is thought to be important, but a consistent effect has not been found. If the audience is not strongly committed to a preexisting attitude, change is more likely.

III. Social Perception

Our impressions are unified. First impressions are important and influence impressions at a later point. We evaluate ourselves by comparison with others. Festinger stressed that social comparison provides an important source of self-knowledge, especially when no other objective means is available. We are more likely to compare ourselves with similar rather than dissimilar others. We usually try to make ourselves look better than we really are when we present ourselves to others. Four recommended impression management strategies are to use behavioral matching, to conform to situational norms, to show appreciation of others and flatter them, and to use positive nonverbal cues.

IV. Attribution

Attribution theory focuses on the motivation to infer causes of behavior in order to make sense out of the world. One of the most frequent and important ways in which we classify the causes of behavior is in terms of internal and external causes. Our attributions are not always accurate. Humans have a built-in bias in making causal judgments. The fundamental attribution error involves overestimating the importance of traits and internal causes and underestimating the importance of situations and external causes. Actors are more likely to choose external causes, observers internal causes. The observer may be in greater error.

V. Conformity

Conformity is change in an individual's behavior because of real or imagined pressure. Two experiments demonstrated conformity's power in our lives: Asch's study on judgments of line length and Zimbardo's study of social roles in a mock prison. Obedience is behavior that complies with the explicit demands of an individual in authority. Milgram's classic experiment demonstrated obedience's power. Milgram's experiments raise the question of ethics in psychological experimentation. As we go through our lives, we are both conformists and nonconformists.

VI. Altruism

Examples of human altruism are plentiful. Reciprocity and social exchange often are involved, although not always. Motivation can be altruistic or egoistic. Psychologists have studied both person and situation variables involved in altruism. Extensive research has been conducted on bystander intervention.

VII. Close Relationships

Familiarity precedes a close relationship. We like to associate with individuals who are similar to us. Berscheid believes that love has four faces: altruism, friendship, romantic (passionate) love, and affectionate (companionate) love. Friends and lovers have similar and dissimilar characteristics. Romantic love is involved when we say we are "in love"; it includes passion, sexuality, and a mixture of emotions, some of which may be negative. Affectionate love is more important as relationships age. Sternberg believes that affectionate love is made up of intimacy and commitment, which, along with passionate love, constitute the three faces of love in his triangular theory. Loneliness is associated with an individual's sex, attachment history, self-esteem, and social skills. The transition to college is a time when loneliness often surfaces.

VIII. Group Relations

Groups satisfy our personal needs, reward us, provide us with information, raise our self-esteem, and enhance our identity. Every group has norms and roles. Deindividuation is the loss of identity as an individual and the development of group identity in group situations that promote arousal and anonymity. Groupthink is the motivation of group members to maintain harmony and unanimity in decision making, in the process suffocating differences of opinion. Both the great person theory, which emphasizes personality traits and skills, and situational factors have been proposed to explain why certain people become leaders. Personality and situational factors likely combine to determine who will become a leader. In a group, the majority usually has the most influence, but at times the minority has its day, being the most effective through informational pressure.

IX. Prejudice, Ethnocentrism, and Conflict

Prejudice is an unjustified attitude toward an individual because of the individual's group identity. A stereotype is a generalization about a group's characteristics. Ethnocentrism is the tendency to favor one's group over other groups. Ethnocentrism has a positive side—in-group pride—and a negative side—emphasis on differences between groups. One theory to explain both prejudice and conflict is Tajfel's social identity theory, which states that, when individuals are assigned to a group, they invariably think of the group as an in-group because they want to have a positive self-image.

X. Reducing Conflict and Seeking Peace

Contact between groups does not reduce conflict. The most effective strategy is to develop a superordinate goal requiring the cooperation of both groups. The jigsaw classroom uses the cooperative strategy to reduce racial tension in schools. GRIT is another strategy, used especially to reduce tension among nations. GRIT involves reducing the potential threat of each group.

XI. Organizational Behavior

Industrial/organizational psychology focuses on the workplace, both its workers and the organizations that employ them. Groups in organizations include both formal groups—established by management to do the organization's work—and informal groups—formed by the group's members. Informal groups include friendships and interest groups. Some organizational psychologists believe that women and ethnic minority members face a number of barriers in their efforts to move up the management hierarchy. There are very few women in top management positions and even fewer ethnic minority individuals. A reason for these low numbers is the differences that handicap women and ethnic minorities, as well as discrimination. However, there are more similarities between White males and their ethnic minority and female counterparts than there are differences. A special concern is tokenism. Changes are expected in both the workers and the workplace environment. The workforce will become increasingly diverse, service oriented, and internationally linked. Many jobs are becoming more complex and cognitively demanding. There is increased interest in the workplace as a setting for promoting individuals' health and welfare.

Key Terms

social psychology 490
attitudes 490
cognitive dissonance 491
self-perception theory 491
social perception 495
primacy effect 495
social comparison 495
impression management 496
attribution theory 496
fundamental attribution error 496
conformity 497

obedience 498
altruism 501
social exchange theory 501
egoism 501
bystander effect 502
consensual validation 504
friendship 504
romantic love 504
affectionate love 505
triangular theory of love 506
norms 509
roles 509

deindividuation 509
groupthink 509
great person theory 509
prejudice 510
stereotype 510
ethnocentrism 511
social identity theory 511
GRIT strategy 513
industrial/organizational psychology 514
formal groups 514
informal groups 514
tokenism 517

Suggested Readings

American Psychologist. (1990, February), 45. This special issue is devoted to organizational psychology. Articles include ideas about the changing face and place of work, the development and maintenance of competitiveness, and women and minorities in management.

Aronson, E. (1992). The social animal (6th ed.). New York: W. H. Freeman. This highly enjoyable presentation of research and thinking in social psychology was written by Eliot Aronson, who has conducted a number of important research studies. Included are interesting chapters on conformity, mass communication, persuasion, and self-justification.

Bond, M. H. (Ed.). (1988). The cross-cultural challenge to social psychology. Newbury Park, CA: Sage. A number of experts in cross-cultural psychology examine the extent to which theories and concepts in social psychology can be generalized across cultures.

Pettigrew, T. F. (1984). A profile of the Negro American. New York: Greenwood. Thomas Pettigrew's fascination with race relations began as a young boy growing up in Richmond, Virginia, in the 1930s. For more than 30 years, he has been one of the leading authorities on race relations. This book details his belief that race relations can be improved and provides strategies for accomplishing this.

Powell, J. (1969). Why am I afraid to tell you who I am? Niles, IL: Argus. This easy-to-read book focuses on self-awareness and interpersonal relationships. Its main theme is that we often do not open up to others and that there are many barriers to communication. The author uses a number of catchy phrases, such as "the braggart," "the clown," and "the egghead," to describe some of the many masks we use.

Sternberg, R. J. (1988). The triangle of love. New York: Basic. Sternberg outlines his theory that love is based on passion, intimacy, and commitment. He includes valuable information on the components of a successful love relationship, as well as the causes of problems in love.

EPILOGUE

Critical Thinking About Sociocultural Issues

Much of the knowledge we are exposed to in the course of our education passes through our minds like tiny grains of sand washed through a sieve. We need to do more than just memorize or passively absorb new information; we need to learn how to think critically. It is the ability to *think* that you should carry beyond this course, an ability that will enable you to acquire new knowledge about mind, behavior, and sociocultural issues and to recognize what types of knowledge about mind, behavior, and sociocultural issues are worth acquiring in the first place. First, we will explore some basic ideas about how to think critically and, second, we will examine some basic sociocultural issues, including some ways in which to think critically about them.

The Nature of Critical Thinking

According to leading cognitive psychologist Robert J. Sternberg (1987), to think critically we need to use the right thinking processes, develop problem-solving strategies, expand our knowledge base, and become motivated to use our newly learned thinking skills. We will consider each of these ideas in turn.

Using the Right Thinking Processes

What are the right thinking processes? To think critically, or to solve any problem or learn any new knowledge, you need to take an active role in the learning process. This means that you must call on a variety of active thinking methods, such as the following:

- Listening carefully
- Identifying or formulating questions
- Identifying or formulating criteria for judging possible answers
- Organizing your thoughts
- Noting similarities and differences
- Deducing
- Distinguishing between logically valid and invalid inferences
- Making value judgments
- Asking and answering questions of clarification, such as "What is the main point?" "What did the author or researcher mean by that?" and "Why?"

As you read this textbook, you were asked many questions, often at the beginning of a topic, encouraging you to think about that topic. As you made your way through the book, you should not have uncritically accepted all of the information that was presented. Psychology is a changing discipline—we are acquiring new information about behavior and sociocultural issues at a rapid pace, replacing old knowledge with new information. Have an inquiring mind. As you encounter information about behavior and sociocultural issues in the future, remember to ask such questions as the following: "If the researchers had conducted their study this way instead of that way, what would they have discovered?" "Do the results of this study generalize to all ethnic groups and is the information culturally universal, or is it culture specific?" "How much concern did the researcher have for individual variation within an ethnic group?" Do not be afraid to think, "The research study does not make sense to me. I think the conclusion fails to take into account the changing roles of females in today's society," for example. It is through such critical thinking that psychology has advanced as a science.

Strategies

Good thinkers use more than just the right thinking processes—they also know how to combine them into workable strategies for solving problems. It is the rare problem that can be solved by a single type of thought process used in isolation. We need to learn to *combine* thinking processes to master new tasks.

For example, Robert Ennis (1987), who has developed a well-known set of critical thinking skills, described the importance of multiple thinking processes in his experience as a juror serving on a murder trial. Ennis did not study "juries" or "murder" in college, but he and his fellow jurors were called on to *judge* the credibility of the witnesses; *interpret* a complicated set of legal criteria for murder and manslaughter; *draw* conclusions about the intentions, beliefs, and truthfulness of the defendant; and *determine* how the victim might have been stabbed. Critical thinking involves combining such complex thought processes in a way that makes sense and that produces concrete conclusions.

Knowledge Base

It is important for you to keep in mind that thinking does not occur in the absence of knowledge: you need to have something to think about. However, it is a mistake to concentrate only on information, to the exclusion of thinking skills, because you simply would become a person who has a lot of knowledge but does not know how to evaluate and apply it. It is equally a mistake to concentrate only on improving your thinking skills, because you would become a person who knows how to think but has nothing to think about. The information in this book and your psychology instructor's lectures are the beginning of a sound knowledge base about behavior and sociocultural issues. Continue to build your knowledge of psychology and sociocultural issues by taking more courses in psychology and by reading psychological journals. Four journals that will help you increase your knowledge and encourage you to think critically about these topics are the following: *American Psychologist, Journal of Social Issues, Journal of Cross-Cultural Psychology,* and *Sex Roles*.

Motivation to Use Thinking Skills

All of the thinking skills you could possibly master would be irrelevant if they were not put to use. Use critical thinking skills as you continue your college career and as you go about your everyday activities. Critical thinking is both a matter for academic study *and* a part of living. Using the right thought processes, combining them into workable strategies, and having access to psychology's knowledge base can help you think critically about issues and problems as you go through the course of your daily life.

Sociocultural Issues

One of this book's most important themes is that the sociocultural approach provides a valuable perspective for understanding behavior. We live in a complex, rapidly changing, multicultural world. There is a special sense of urgency in addressing sociocultural issues because of the changes in the ethnic composition of the population. From 1980 to 2000, the Asian American population is expected to increase by 97 percent, the Hispanic American population by 71 percent, and the Black American population by 24 percent, whereas the Anglo American population is only expected to increase by 11 percent. At a point early in the twenty-first century, one-third of the population in the United States will be composed of ethnic minority groups. Three important tasks for psychologists involve these rapid changes in population (Sue, 1990):

1. To intensify research and knowledge development related to ethnic minority groups
2. To develop appropriate conceptualizations of behavior that apply to diverse groups
3. To promote the welfare of all human beings through education, teaching, and psychological intervention

What are the important sociocultural issues that require critical thinking? They include the following:

1. Understanding diversity within an ethnic, cultural, or gender group
2. Recognizing and respecting legitimate differences among ethnic, cultural, and gender groups
3. Searching for similarities among ethnic, cultural, and gender groups when differences have been incorrectly assumed
4. Reducing discrimination and prejudice
5. Comprehending that value conflicts are often important factors in understanding ethnic and cultural issues
6. Globalizing psychology and understanding American psychology's ethnocentrism

7. Recognizing that the behavior of every individual from every ethnic, cultural, and gender group is multiply determined
8. Considering different sides of sensitive ethnic, cultural, and gender issues
9. Using the field of psychology to improve understanding of sociocultural issues and to promote the welfare of all human beings through education, teaching, research, and psychological prevention or intervention

Understanding Diversity Within an Ethnic, Cultural, or Gender Group

An especially important fact is that there is diversity within every ethnic, cultural, and gender group (Kavanaugh & Kennedy, 1992; Paludi, 1992). For example, no cultural characteristic is common to all or nearly all Black Americans or Hispanic Americans and absent in Anglo Americans, unless it is the experience of being Black or being Hispanic and the beliefs that develop from that experience. Consider also Native Americans. The federal government now recognizes the existence of 511 Native American tribes, each having a unique ancestral background with its own values and characteristics. Consider Asian Americans, who include the Chinese, Japanese, Filipinos, Koreans, and Southeast Asians; each group has a distinct ancestry and language. Within each of these groups, there is considerable individual variation.

Sometimes well-meaning individuals fail to recognize the diversity within an ethnic group. Consider the circumstance of an elementary school teacher in a human relations workshop, who is shown the necessity of incorporating more ethnicity into her instructional planning. Since she has two Mexican American children in her class, she asks them to demonstrate to the class how they dance at home. The teacher expects both of the children to perform Mexican folk dances, reflecting their ethnic heritage. The first child gets up in front of the class and begins dancing in a typical American fashion. The teacher says, "No, I want you to dance as you and your family do at home, as you do when you have Mexican American celebrations." The child informs the teacher that her family doesn't dance that way. The second child does demonstrate a Mexican folk dance to the class. The first student has been highly assimilated into the American culture and does not know how to dance Mexican folk dances. The second child has been less assimilated and comes from a Mexican American family that has retained more of its ethnic heritage.

This example illustrates the strong diversity and individual differences that exist within any ethnic group. Failure to recognize diversity and individual variation results in the stereotyping of any ethnic, cultural, or gender group.

As a group, Asian Americans show exceptional achievement patterns. However, Asian Americans represent a heterogeneous group with marked variations in characteristics. There is considerable diversity in every ethnic group. For example, Asian Americans show high educational attainments but many Asian Americans have very little education (Sue & Padilla, 1986). Although the "whiz kid" image fits many Asian Americans, for thousands of other Asian Americans, including a high percentage of the 600,000 Indochinese refugees who fled Vietnam, Laos, and Cambodia in the late 1970s, the problems are legion. Many in this wave of refugees lived in poor surroundings in their homelands. They came to the United States with little education and few skills. They speak little English and have a difficult time finding a decent job. They often share housing with relatives. Adjusting to school is difficult for their children. Better school systems use a range of social services to help the Indochinese refugees adapt.

Recognizing and Respecting Legitimate Differences Among Ethnic, Cultural, and Gender Groups

There are some legitimate differences among ethnic and cultural groups, and between males and females. Recognizing and respecting these differences are important aspects of getting along with others in a diverse, multicultural world. In cross-cultural psychologist Harry Triandis' (1990) view, historical, economic, and social experiences produce differences among ethnic, cultural, and gender groups. Individuals living in a particular culture adapt to the values, attitudes, and stresses of that culture. Their behavior, although possibly different from ours, is, nonetheless, often functional for them. It is important for each of us to take the perspective of individuals from ethnic and cultural groups that are different from ours, and the perspective of individuals from the opposite sex, and think, "If I were in their shoes, what kind of experiences might I have had? How would I feel if I were a member of their ethnic, cultural, or gender group? How would I think and behave if I had grown up in their world?" Such perspective taking often increases our empathy and understanding of individuals from ethnic, cultural, and gender groups different from ours.

For too long, differences between females and males were thought of as deficits or inferior characteristics on the part of females, both by society and by psychology. Fortunately, today some of the bias against females has diminished, and there is recognition of the strengths of females. Among those strengths are the ability to read emotions, caregiving and helping behavior, and connectedness in relationships.

Unfortunately, the differences among ethnic and cultural groups and between males and females that society and, too often, psychology have emphasized have been damaging to ethnic minority individuals and females. Ethnicity has defined who will enjoy the privileges of citizenship, to what degree, and in what ways (Jones, 1990b). An individual's ethnic background determines whether the individual will be alienated, oppressed, or disadvantaged, all too often humiliating and embarrassing ethnic minority individuals. Being female has also meant exposure to a world of restrictions, barriers, and unfair treatment.

Psychology's current emphasis on searching for differences among ethnic groups, which underscores the strengths of particular ethnic minority groups and females, is long overdue. For example, the extended family support system that is more likely to characterize some ethnic minority groups, such as Black American, Hispanic American, and Asian American, is now recognized as a positive, valuable factor in an individual's coping ability. Also, researchers are finding that Black males are better than White males at the use of body language in communication, the decoding of nonverbal cues, multilingual/multicultural expression, and improvised problem solving (Evans & Whitfield, 1988).

For too long, differences between virtually any ethnic minority group and Whites were conceptualized as deficits or inferior characteristics on the part of the ethnic minority group. Indeed, much research on many ethnic minority groups focused only on negative, stressful aspects of the ethnic group. For example, research on Black American females invariably examined such topics as poverty, unwed motherhood, and school dropout rates. These topics continue to be important and much needed research areas of psychology, but research on the positive aspects of Black women in a pluralistic society are also necessary and have been sorely neglected. The self-esteem, achievement, motivation, and self-control of individuals from various ethnic minority groups deserve considerable study.

For too long, differences between females and males were conceptualized as deficits or inferior characteristics on the part of females, both by society and by psychologists. For example, in relationships, females were negatively characterized as more dependent and passive than males. Fortunately, today, some of the bias against females is being corrected through an emphasis on female strengths in relation to males, such as the ability to read emotions, caregiving and helping behavior, and connectedness in relationships. Thus, what were once labeled weaknesses in relation to males—being dependent and passive—are currently being examined as strengths in relation to males—having positive connectedness in relationships.

Searching for Similarities Among Ethnic, Cultural, and Gender Groups When Differences Have Been Incorrectly Assumed

Through much of their history, American society and American psychology have had a White, middle-class, male bias. White, middle-class, male Americans have functioned as the dominant, controlling majority in both society and psychology. Because of society's and psychology's dominance by White, middle-class males, ethnic minority individuals and females have not had adequate opportunities to contribute their ideas and values. The result has been that many differences that have been emphasized among White Americans and ethnic minority Americans, and between females and males, may have been incorrectly assumed. As ethnic minority individuals and females have begun to have a stronger voice in society and in American psychology, what once were considered differences are now sometimes found to be similarities. The search for legitimate similarities among White Americans and ethnic minority Americans, and between females and males, is important because incorrectly assumed differences involve stereotyping and can lead to prejudice.

Feminist psychologists have especially emphasized that there are far more similarities between females and males than differences (Doyle & Paludi, 1991). For example, in the area of math skills, differences favoring males have been widely reported. However, in recent years, a number of gender researchers have pointed out that the differences in math skills that do exist have been exaggerated (Hyde, in press; Tavris, 1990). They exist only in the gifted portion of the population and may be due to cultural bias against females. Recently researchers also have found that a verbal ability difference that once favored females has now disappeared (Jacklin, 1989).

An important aspect of thinking about sociocultural issues is to examine similarities and differences among ethnic groups, among cultures, and between females and males. However, it is important not just to stop at the point of *describing* similarities and differences. The next important step in critical thinking is to ask *why* these similarities and differences exist and then to *explain* them. For example, when gender researchers have discovered that talented females have not achieved as well in math as talented males, they seek to explain why. They examine such important factors as society's cultural bias against females in the math curriculum and many parents' negative expectations for their daughters' math achievement.

Reducing Prejudice and Discrimination

In a recent Gallup poll, Americans stated that they believe that the United States is ethnically tolerant and that overt racism is basically unacceptable (*Asian Week*, 1990). However, many ethnic minority individuals continue to see persistent forms of discrimination and prejudice (Edelman, 1992; Sue, 1990; White

& Parham, 1990). Discrimination and prejudice continue to be present in many domains of American life—in the media, in interpersonal interactions, and in daily conversations, for example. Crimes, strangeness, poverty, mistakes, and deterioration are wrongly attributed to foreigners or ethnic minority individuals in many instances (van Dijk, 1987). Also, as discussed in chapter 16, prejudice and racism are now often expressed in a more indirect way (Sears & others, 1988).

As sociocultural researcher Stanley Sue (1990) points out, there are opposing views about discrimination and prejudice. On one side are individuals who value and praise the significant strides made in civil rights in recent years, pointing to affirmative action programs as proof of these civil rights advances. On the other side are individuals who criticize American institutions, such as education, because they believe many forms of discrimination and prejudice continue to characterize these institutions. Progress has been made in ethnic minority and race relations, but discrimination and prejudice still exist and equality has not been achieved. In thinking about discrimination and prejudice, it is important to recognize that positive changes have occurred, yet much still needs to be accomplished.

Discrimination, of course, is not confined to ethnic groups. Through much of our culture's history, women have faced almost insurmountable odds when they have strived to be heard. As Charlotte Whitton (1990), former mayor of Ottawa, Canada, recently commented, "Whatever women do, they must do twice as well as men to be thought half as good." Coping with the challenge of living in a male-dominated world has not been easy for many women, and, although their efforts to revolutionize society into a world where women and men are treated equally have met with some success, the revolution is far from complete.

Comprehending That Value Conflicts Are Often Important Factors in Understanding Ethnic Minority Issues

Stanley Sue (1989, 1990) argues that value conflicts are often involved when individuals respond to ethnic issues. These value conflicts have been a source of considerable controversy. According to Sue, without properly identifying the assumptions and effects of the conflicting values, it is difficult to resolve ethnic minority issues. Let's examine a value conflict Sue (1990) describes and see how it might influence an individual's responses to an ethnic minority issue: assimilation versus pluralism.

One faculty member commented that he was glad his psychology department was interested in teaching students about ethnic and cultural issues. He felt that, by becoming aware of various cultures, students would improve their understanding of their own and other cultures. However, another faculty member disagreed. She felt that students' knowledge of ethnic minority issues and various cultures is a relevant concern but that the department's scarce resources should not be devoted to ethnic and cultural issues. She also believed that, if too much attention is given to ethnic and cultural issues, it might actually increase the segregation of students, and even cause friction among ethnic and cultural groups. She commented that we all live in this society and, therefore, we must all learn the same skills to succeed. In Sue's (1990) perspective, a value conflict involving assimilation and pluralism underlies these opposing views about whether a psychology department should devote any or increased funds to teaching students about ethnicity and culture.

Assimilation refers to the absorption of ethnic minority groups into the dominant group, which often means the loss of some or virtually all of the behavior and values of the ethnic minority group. Individuals who adopt an assimilation stance usually advocate that ethnic minority groups become more American. By contrast, pluralism refers to the coexistence of distinct ethnic and cultural groups in the same society. Individuals who adopt a pluralism stance usually advocate that cultural differences be maintained and appreciated.

For many years, an assimilation approach was thought to be the best course for American society because it was believed that the mainstream was superior in many ways. Even though today many people reject the notion that the mainstream culture is intrinsically superior to ethnic minority cultures, the assimilation approach is currently resurfacing with a more complex face. Advocates of the assimilation approach now use practical and functional arguments rather than intrinsic superiority arguments to buttress their point of view. For example, assimilation advocates stress that educational programs for immigrant children (Mexican, Chinese, and so on) should stress the learning of English as early as possible in education rather than bilingual education. Their argument is that spending time on any language other than English may be a handicap, both in schools and in mainstream society (where English proficiency is required for competence). By contrast, the advocates of pluralism argue that an English-only approach reasserts the mainstream-is-right-and-best belief. Thus, responses to the ethnic minority issue of bilingual education involve a clash of fundamental values. As Sue (1990) asks, how can one argue against the development of functional skills and, to a degree, the support of Americanization? Similarly how can one doubt that pluralism, diversity, and respect for various cultures are valid principles? Sue believes that the one-sidedness of the issue is the main problem. Advocates of assimilation often overlook the fact that a consensus may be lacking on what constitutes functional skills, or that a particular context may alter what skills are useful. For example, with an increasing immigrant population, the ability to speak Spanish or Japanese may be an asset, as is the ability to interact with and collaborate with diverse ethnic groups.

Sue (1990) believes that one way to resolve value conflicts about sociocultural issues is to conceptualize or redefine them in innovative ways. For example, in the assimilation/pluralism conflict, rather than deal with the assumption that assimilation is necessary for the development of functional skills, one strategy is to focus on the fluctuating criteria for functional skills or on the possibility that developing functional skills does not prevent the existence of pluralism. For instance, a classroom instructor might teach social studies using multicultural examples while discussing culturally universal (etic) and culturally specific (emic) approaches to American and other cultures.

Globalizing Psychology and Understanding American Psychology's Ethnocentrism

For the most part, American psychology has been ethnocentric, emphasizing American values, especially middle-class, White values. Cross-cultural psychologists point out that many of the assumptions about contemporary ideas in psychology were developed in Western cultures (Lonner, 1988; Rumpel, 1988). One example of American psychology's ethnocentrism—the tendency to favor one's own group over other groups—is the American emphasis on the individual or self. Self-oriented terms dominate thinking about personality in Western cultures—self-actualization, self-awareness, self-concept, self-efficacy, self-reinforcement, self-criticism, self-serving, selfishness, self-doubt—and were generated by American psychologists. However, remember from our discussion in chapter 12 on personality that many Eastern countries, such as China, Japan, and India, are collectivistic or group oriented. So is the Mexican culture. Indeed, the pendulum may have swung too far in the individualistic direction in Western cultures. However, to develop in a healthy, optimal way, all people in all cultures need to develop a positive sense of self *and* a positive connectedness to others. Competent individuals are not characterized by a single positive trait, such as individualism or collectivism; it is important to develop multiple competent characteristics, such as a positive sense of self and a concern for the welfare of others.

Global interdependence is no longer a matter of belief or preference. It is an inescapable reality. We are not just citizens of the United States or Canada. We are citizens of the world, a world that has become increasingly interactive through technological and transportational advances. By increasing our understanding of the behavior and values of cultures around the world, we hope that we can interact with people from other cultures more effectively and make this planet a more hospitable, peaceful place in which to live. Consider how knowledge of the following cultural differences might benefit you if you were conducting business with the culture in question (Harris & Moran, 1987):

• In Japan a strong sense of group identity is promoted. Creating ambiguity is almost a social obligation that often leads Americans to draw false conclusions based on Japanese appearances.

We are not just citizens of the United States or Canada. We are citizens of the world. By increasing our understanding of the behavior and values of cultures around the world, we hope that we interact with people from other cultures more effectively and make this planet a more hospitable, peaceful place in which to live.

- In Saudi Arabia the protocol is to use the first meeting for social acquaintance, warm-up, or trust building, not for conducting serious business.
- In Indonesia handshaking with either sex in business is perfectly acceptable but it has to be done with the right hand only; using only the left hand for handshaking is strictly taboo. In some cultures, handshakes are avoided altogether, and in some cultures a bow is preferred.

Recognizing That the Behavior of Every Individual from Every Ethnic, Cultural, and Gender Group Is Multiply Determined

An important aspect of thinking about the behavior of any individual, regardless of his or her ethnic, cultural, or gender group, is that the individual's behavior is multiply determined. When we think about what causes an individual's behavior, it is not unusual to lean toward explaining it in terms of a single cause. For example, a friend might tell you, "Our marriage did not work because he could not let go of his mother." The husband's inability to relinquish his strong attachment to his mother may have been one cause for the divorce, but there were probably others as well—perhaps economic problems, sexual difficulties, or personality conflicts. One of psychology's great lessons is that behavior is not singly determined; behavior is multiply determined. Understanding and applying this principle can help you think critically about behavior—others' and your own.

Consider another example—a 7-year-old Black American child named Bobby. His teacher says that he is having trouble in school because he is from a father-absent home. The implication is that not having a father present in the home causes Bobby's poor academic performance. Not having a father present may be one factor in Bobby's poor performance in school, but many others influence his behavior as well. These factors include his genetic heritage and a host of environmental and sociocultural experiences, both in the past and in the present. On closer inspection of Bobby's circumstances, we learn that not only has he been father-absent all of his life, never knowing his father, but that his extended family support system has also been weak. We also learn that he lives in a low-income area with little community support for recreation, libraries, and youth facilities. The school system in which Bobby is enrolled has a poor record of helping low-achieving children and has little interest in developing programs for ethnic minority children from disadvantaged circumstances. We could find other reasons that help explain Bobby's poor school achievement, but these examples illustrate the importance of going beyond accepting a single cause as *the* reason for an individual's behavior. As with each of us, Bobby's behavior is multiply determined.

Considering Different Sides of Sensitive Ethnic, Cultural, and Gender Issues

When thinking about sensitive ethnic, cultural, and gender issues, it is important to consider different sides of the issues in a contemplative, analytical way. We need to see things from many points of view. Unless we can mentally represent information about sociocultural issues from more than one point of view, we may rely on inadequate information to draw conclusions. If we do not seek alternative explanations and interpretations of problems and issues, our conclusions may be based solely on our own expectations, prejudices, stereotypes, and personal experience.

Stanley Sue (1990) described the importance of considering different sides of the sociocultural issues of equal opportunity and equality of outcomes. For example, in discussing his stance on ethnic issues, a university administrator commented that he believes in equality and does not discriminate against any group. He commented that in hiring teachers his university is ethnic- and color-blind, focusing only on the applicants' qualifications. By contrast, an administrator at a small college said that his college follows an affirmative action course and recruits faculty from various ethnic groups. He further commented that hiring practices at his college are designed to reflect the ethnic composition of the community. The administrators' statements illustrate a clash of values over the appropriate course of action to follow in addressing ethnic minority concerns. The position of the university administrator ensures that all members of society will have the same opportunity. That is, all individuals are treated the same with regard to education, employment, and housing. By contrast, the position of the college administrator advocates achieving equality of outcomes through affirmative action procedures. Such procedures might involve increasing the ethnic pool of applicants, selecting applicants by taking ethnicity into account, and using different criteria for selecting various groups.

According to Sue, proponents of equal opportunity want to eliminate discrimination. Their goal is to abolish racial or ethnic bias, intentional patterns of segregation, and discriminatory admissions or selection criteria. However, even if discrimination is eliminated, there is no guarantee that equal outcomes will be achieved. Realizing this, advocates of equal outcomes believe it is important to have special programs and affirmative action to narrow the gap between ethnic minority groups and Whites. In their view, color-blind policies that are applied to ethnic groups already showing negative disparities with Whites only maintain those differences. In Sue's view, the dilemma is apparent—advocates of equal opportunity run the risk of perpetuating unequal outcomes. The controversy has unfortunately been turned into one of discrimination. That is, if it is unfair to discriminate against ethnic minority groups, should we now discriminate in reverse against the majority group? A more meaningful question is, What kind of society do we want? According to Sue, the goal of our society should be to maximize the potential of every individual, irrespective of color, ethnic group, or sex.

Using Psychology to Improve Understanding of Sociocultural Issues and to Promote the Welfare of All Human Beings Through Education, Teaching, Research, and Psychological Prevention or Intervention

The knowledge base of information about sociocultural issues in psychology is increasing, but a lot of blank spaces remain in the study of ethnicity, culture, and gender. It is very important for psychologists to devote increased effort toward expanding the knowledge base of information about ethnicity, culture, and gender (Graham, 1992; Sue, in press). We need to know more about how diverse socialization experiences and adaptations to changing environments, especially those that present competing demands, can be integrated to produce a more competent human being (Jones, 1990). We need to know more about why Hispanic and Native American children drop out of school at such high rates. We especially need to know more about ways to prevent such high dropout rates, or how to intervene and help high school dropouts lead more competent, satisfying lives. Also, ethnicity, culture, and gender should be increasingly included on the agendas at all levels of education—from preschool through graduate school.

Through much of its history, psychology has not had an admirable record when ethnicity, culture, and gender have been the topics of inquiry or when student recruitment or faculty hiring is involved. The 1990s represent an outstanding opportunity for individuals to make important contributions to our understanding of sociocultural issues. Psychology not only needs to improve its knowledge base about sociocultural issues but, as indicated in chapter 1, psychology also needs more ethnic minority psychologists. Use psychology to improve your understanding of sociocultural issues and consider a career in psychology in which you can help improve the lives of all human beings through education, teaching, research, and psychological prevention or intervention.

APPENDIX

Analyzing the Data
Statistics in Psychology and Everyday Life

Don H. Hockenbury
Tulsa Junior College

Whether or not you realize it, you are exposed to statistics every day. For example, the federal government releases reports showing the number of homeless people per 1,000 by regions of the country, the dramatic increase in the number of women in prisons, and so on. Advertisers use statistics to try to persuade you to buy their products by showing you how consumers prefer their products over the competition by five to one. High schools, colleges, and universities use statistics to track student demographics, such as the number of students attending, the number of students in particular programs, and student grade point averages. Statistics are also widely used in sports, such as football, baseball, and basketball. Statistics also are used in psychology and the other sciences to analyze data that have been collected. In short, statistics are so much a part of our lives that an understanding of basic statistics is essential if you want to be an informed member of society. Thus, the purpose of this Appendix is to help you make sense out of some basic statistical concepts that are used in everyday life as well as in scientific research.

Statistics *are mathematical methods used to describe, summarize, and draw conclusions about data.* There are two basic categories of statistics: (1) descriptive and (2) inferential.

Descriptive Statistics

Descriptive statistics *are mathematical procedures used to describe and summarize samples of data in a meaningful fashion.* More specifically, descriptive statistics can be used to describe the characteristics of either a single variable or an interaction between two variables. This is important in most psychological studies because, if we were to simply report all the individual scores, it would be virtually impossible to summarize the results. Descriptive statistics allow us to avoid this situation by providing numerous measures that reveal the overall characteristics of the data. Let's look at some of those measures.

Descriptive Statistics for One Variable

The descriptive statistics for one variable include frequency distributions, histograms, and frequency polygons; measures of central tendency; measures of variability; and normal distribution.

Frequency Distributions, Histograms, and Frequency Polygons

Recently some educational researchers found a connection between how many siblings a student has and her academic performance. Let's assume your introductory psychology class is dubious about this finding, but your classmates want to see if a connection between number of siblings and academic perfor-

"Tonight, we're going to let the statistics speak for themselves."

Drawing by Koren; © 1974 The New Yorker Magazine, Inc.

mance applies to them. All 20 students in your psychology class answer a short questionnaire, indicating the number of brothers and sisters they have, if any, and their cumulative high school grade point average. For now let's focus on the variable of number of siblings. Following are the number of siblings each member of your class indicated:

6	4	3	8
6	2	0	2
1	2	3	0
2	3	2	1
3	2	2	8

It is difficult to draw any general conclusions about the overall tendencies of the group just by looking at the raw data (that is, the number of brothers and sisters each person reported). It would be even more difficult if our sample size were 500 or 1,000 students instead of just 20. In any case, the first thing we need to do is to organize the data in a more meaningful way, such as in a frequency distribution. A **frequency distribution** *is simply a listing of scores from lowest to highest, with the number of times each score appears in a sample.* Figure A.1a shows the frequency distribution for our data on number of siblings. The column on the left lists the possible responses (number of siblings), and the column on the right shows how often that response was given.

Another way to present the data is visually through the use of either a histogram or a frequency polygon. A **histogram** *is a frequency distribution in graphic form, in which vertical bars represent the frequency of scores per category or class.* Figure A.1b shows a histogram for our data on the category of number of siblings. A histogram is often called a *bar graph* or, occasionally, a *block diagram*.

A **frequency polygon** *is basically the same as a histogram except that the data are represented with lines rather than bars.* Figure A.1c shows a frequency polygon for the data on number of siblings. Notice that, in both the histogram and the frequency polygon, the horizontal axis (the y-axis) indicates the possible scores, and the vertical axis (the x-axis) indicates how often each score occurs in the set of data points.

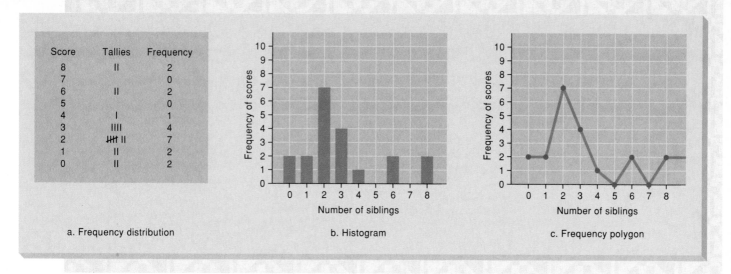

Score	Tallies	Frequency
8	II	2
7		0
6	II	2
5		0
4	I	1
3	IIII	4
2	HHt II	7
1	II	2
0	II	2

a. Frequency distribution

b. Histogram

c. Frequency polygon

FIGURE A.1

Frequency distribution, histogram, and frequency polygon. These data are from a hypothetical survey on number of siblings reported by 20 students in your psychology class. (a) A frequency distribution lists the scores from lowest to highest, with the number of times each score appears. (b) A histogram depicts the frequency distribution in graphic form, with vertical bars representing the frequency of scores. (c) A frequency polygon is basically the same as a histogram except that the data are represented with lines rather than bars.

Although frequency distributions, histograms, and frequency polygons can help *graphically* represent a group of scores, you may want to represent a group of scores *numerically* by providing a measure of central tendency, a measure of variability, or both. Let's look at these two measures.

Measures of Central Tendency

If you want to describe an "average" value for a set of scores, you would use one of the measures of central tendency. In essence, a **measure of central tendency** *is a single number that tells you the overall characteristics of a set of data.* There are three measures of central tendency: the mean, the median, and the mode.

The **mean** *is the numerical average for a group of scores or values.* The mean is calculated by adding all the scores and then dividing by the number of scores. To compute the mean for the data collected on number of siblings, we add all the scores, equaling 60, then divide by the total number of scores, 20. This gives us a mean of 3 siblings. This procedure is shown on the left side of figure A.2 on page 536.

In general the mean is a good indicator of the central tendency for a group of scores; it is the measure of central tendency that is used most often. One exception to this general rule is when a group of scores contains one or a couple of extreme scores. For example, consider the annual earnings for the two groups of five people in the table that follows. Group 1 lists the earnings of five relatively average people. Group 2 is composed of the earnings of four average people plus the approximate earnings of movie director Steven Spielberg. The vast difference between the mean earnings for the two groups is due to the one extreme score. In such a situation, one of the other two measures of central tendency would more accurately describe the data's overall characteristics.

Group 1	Group 2
$17,000	$17,000
21,000	21,000
23,000	23,000
24,000	24,000
25,000	45,000,000
Mean = $22,000	*Mean* = $9,017,000
Median = $23,000	*Median* = $23,000
Mode = N/A	*Mode* = N/A

The **median** *is the score that falls exactly in the middle of a distribution of scores after they have been arranged (or ranked) from highest to lowest.* When you have an odd number of scores (say, five or seven scores), the median is the score with the same number of scores above it as below it after they have been ranked. Thus, in our example comparing earnings, each group had a median income of $23,000. When you have an even number of scores (8, 10, or 20 scores, for example), you simply add the middle 2 scores and divide by 2 to arrive at the median. In our example using number of siblings, we have an even number of scores (20), so the median is the 10th and 11th scores added together and divided by 2, or (2 + 2)/2. Thus, the median number of siblings for our set of 20 responses is 2, as shown in the middle panel of figure A.2.

Mean	Median			Mode	
	Ranking	Scores in order		Score	Frequency
6	1	0		8	2
6	2	0		7	0
1	3	1		6	2
2	4	1		5	0
3	5	2		4	1
4	6	2		3	4
2	7	2		2	7 ← Most frequent score
2	8	2		1	2
3	9	2		0	2
2	10	2	Middle of rankings		
3	11	2		Mode = 2	
0	12	3			
3	13	3			
2	14	3			
2	15	3			
8	16	4			
2	17	6			
0	18	6			
1	19	8			
8	20	8			

60/20 = 3

Because there is an even set of scores, median equals middle two scores added together, then divided by 2. Thus, $\frac{2+2}{2} = 2$.

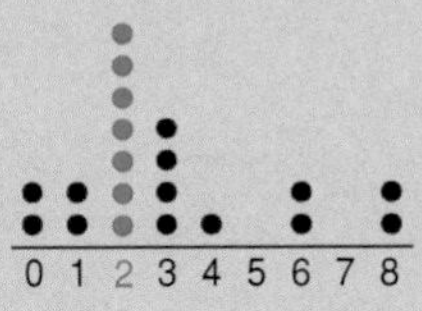

FIGURE A.2

Mean, median, and mode. These data are from a hypothetical survey on number of siblings reported by 20 students in your psychology class. The mean is the numerical average for a group of scores; it is calculated by adding all the scores and then dividing by the number of scores. The median is the score that falls exactly in the middle of a distribution of scores after they have been ranked from highest to lowest. When there is an even number of scores, as there is here, you add the middle two scores and divide by 2 to calculate the median. The mode is the score that appears most often.

Notice that, unlike the mean, the median is unaffected by one or a few extreme scores. Look again at the earnings of the two groups. The medians are the same for both groups ($23,000), but their means are extremely different ($22,000 versus $9,017,000).

The **mode** *is the score that occurs most often*. The mode can be determined very easily by looking at a frequency distribution, histogram, or frequency polygon. In our present example, the mode is 2, which is the number of siblings indicated most often by the members of your psychology class. Although the mode is the least used measure of central tendency, it has descriptive value because, unlike the mean and the median, there can be two or more modes. Consider the following 15 scores on a 10-point surprise quiz: 9, 3, 8, 5, 9, 3, 6, 9, 4, 10, 2, 3, 3, 9, 7. The quiz scores 9 and 3 each appear four times. No other score in this example appears as often or more often. Thus, this set of scores has two modes, or a *bimodal distribution*. It is, in fact, possible to have several modes, or a *multimodal distribution*. It also is possible to have no mode at all, which was the case when we compared the earnings of the two groups of five people. Depending on the research question being investigated, the mode may actually provide more meaningful information than either the mean or the median. For example, developers of a program to help people stop smoking would benefit more from knowing that the "modal" age of the greatest number of people who smoke is either 22 *or* 58 than from knowing that the mean age of smokers is 37. By knowing that smoking behavior is distributed bimodally in the population, they can more appropriately target their program to young adults and older adults rather than to middle-aged adults.

Measures of Variability

Consider the following example. You are the owner of three clothing stores that all have the same mean annual earnings of $1,000,000. These three stores fluctuate widely in their monthly earnings, however. Store #1 consistently produces a monthly income of about $100,000. Store #2 generates no income some months but produces $250,000 of income other months. Store

Scores	Score minus mean (x)	Difference squared (x²)
0	−3	9
0	−3	9
1	−2	4
1	−2	4
2	−1	1
2	−1	1
2	−1	1
2	−1	1
2	−1	1
2	−1	1
2	−1	1
3	0	0
3	0	0
3	0	0
3	0	0
4	1	1
6	3	9
6	3	9
8	5	25
8	5	25
Mean = 60/20 = 3		$\Sigma x^2 = 102$

$$\text{Standard deviation} = \sqrt{\frac{\Sigma x^2}{N}} = \sqrt{\frac{102}{20}} = \sqrt{5.1} = 2.26$$

FIGURE A.3

Computing the standard deviation. The standard deviation is a measure of how much the scores vary on the average around the mean of a sample. In this figure, you can see how the standard deviation was calculated for the data gathered from a hypothetical survey on number of siblings reported by 20 students in your psychology class.

#3 loses money the first 9 months of every year but makes enormous profits during October, November, and December. It would be to your advantage to be able to represent the individual fluctuations of your three stores. Measures of variability can be very useful in this regard.

Along with obtaining the overall or central characteristics for a sample, *we can also ask how much the scores in a sample vary from one another. These measures are called* **measures of variability** *or* **measures of dispersion.** The two measures of variability are called the range and the standard deviation.

The **range** *is the distance between the highest and the lowest scores.* The range for our data on number of siblings would be 8 (high score) minus 0 (low score), for a range of 8. Generally speaking, the range is a rather simplistic estimate of variability, or dispersion, for a group of scores. More important, because the range involves only two scores, it can produce a misleading index of variability; thus, the range is rarely used as a measure of variability. The most commonly used measure of variability is the standard deviation.

The **standard deviation** *is a measure of how much the scores vary on the average around the mean of a sample.* It indicates how closely scores are clustered around the mean. The smaller the standard deviation, the less variability from the mean and vice versa. A simple example will illustrate how this measure of variability works. Consider the following four race scores for each of three joggers:

	Jogger #1	Jogger #2	Jogger #3
Race #1	44 minutes	40 minutes	32 minutes
Race #2	36 minutes	40 minutes	48 minutes
Race #3	44 minutes	40 minutes	32 minutes
Race #4	36 minutes	40 minutes	48 minutes
Mean time	40 minutes	40 minutes	40 minutes
Standard deviation	4 minutes	0 minutes	8 minutes

Notice that all three joggers had the same mean race time of 40 minutes, but Jogger #1 and Jogger #3 each had race times that varied from race to race, whereas Jogger #2 had exactly the same time for each of the four races. This variability from race to race, or the lack of it, is expressed by the three different standard deviations. Because Jogger #2 had no variability from race to race, that person's standard deviation is 0. Jogger #1's race time varied 4 minutes on the average from his mean of 40 minutes. In other words, Jogger #1 had a standard deviation of 4 minutes for his race times. Jogger #3's race times varied 8 minutes on the average from her mean time of 40 minutes. Thus, Jogger #3 had a standard deviation of 8 minutes for her race times. The different standard deviations tell you that Jogger #2 had no variability among his race scores, Jogger #1 had some variability among his race scores, and Jogger #3 had even more variability among her race scores.

Calculating a standard deviation is not very difficult if you use a calculator capable of doing square roots. To compute a standard deviation, follow these four steps:

1. Calculate the mean of the scores.
2. From each score, subtract the mean and then square that difference. (Squaring the scores will eliminate any negative signs that result from subtracting the mean.)
3. Add the squares and then divide by the number of scores.
4. Calculate the square root of the value obtained in Step 3. This is the standard deviation.

The formula for these four steps is

$$\text{Standard deviation} = \sqrt{\frac{\Sigma x^2}{N}}$$

where x = the individual score minus the mean, N = the number of scores, and Σ = the sum of. The application of these four steps to our example of number of siblings is illustrated in figure A.3. As you can see, when all the calculations are completed, the standard deviation equals 2.26.

The Normal Distribution

As we saw earlier, the scores for any distribution can be plotted on a frequency polygon and can take a variety of shapes. One shape in particular has been of considerable interest to psychologists—the **normal distribution,** or **bell-shaped curve.** *In this type of frequency polygon, most of the scores cluster around the mean. The farther above or below the mean a score appears, the less frequently it occurs.* Many naturally occurring phenomena, such as human intelligence, height, weight, and athletic abilities, follow or closely approximate a normal distribution. For example, the normal distribution of IQ scores as measured by the Wechsler Adult Intelligence Scale is shown in figure A.4. Notice that the mean IQ is 100 and the standard deviation is 15 IQ points. We will come back to these numbers in a moment.

Figure A.5 illustrates several important characteristics of the normal distribution. First, it is perfectly symmetrical. There is the same number of scores above the mean as below it. Because of this perfect symmetry, the mean, median, and mode are identical in a normal distribution. Second, its bell shape illustrates that the most common scores are near the middle. The scores become less frequent and more extreme the farther away from the middle they appear. Third, the normal distribution incorporates information about both the mean and the standard deviation, as shown in figure A.5. The area on the normal curve that is one standard deviation above the mean and one standard deviation below the mean represents 68.26 percent of the scores. At two standard deviations above and below the mean, 95.42 percent of the scores are represented. Finally, at three standard deviations above and below the mean, 99.74 percent of the scores are contained. If we apply this information to figure A.4, which shows the normal distribution of IQ scores in the population, we can readily see that 68 percent of the population has an IQ between 85 and 115, 95 percent of the population has an IQ between 70 and 130, and 99 percent of the population has an IQ between 55 and 145.

Descriptive Statistics for Two Variables

Descriptive statistics for two variables include scatter plots and the correlation coefficient.

Scatter Plots

Up to this point, we've focused on descriptive statistics used to describe only one variable. Often the goal of research is to describe the relationship between two variables. In our example, we collected information from the 20 members of your psychology class on their number of siblings and their high school grade point average. The raw data we collected are shown on the left side of figure A.6. Also shown is a scatter plot of those scores. A **scatter plot** *is a graph on which pairs of scores are represented.* In this case, we are looking at the possible relationship between number of siblings and academic performance. The possible scores for

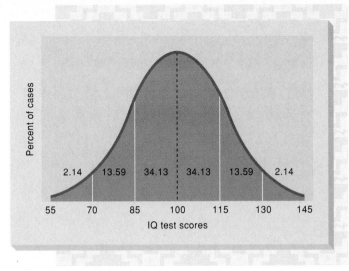

FIGURE A.4

Normal distribution, or bell-shaped curve. This graph shows the normal distribution of IQ scores as measured by the Wechsler Adult Intelligence Scale. The normal distribution is a type of frequency polygon in which most of the scores are clustered around the mean. The scores become less frequent the farther they appear above or below the mean.

one variable—number of siblings—are indicated on the *x*-axis, and the scores for the second variable—grade point average—are indicated on the *y*-axis. Each dot on the scatter plot represents one pair of scores as reported by each member of your class. As you can see, there seems to be a distinct pattern to our scatter plot—that is, as the number of siblings increases, high school GPA decreases. Tentatively, at least, there appears to be an association between these two variables. Just how related are these two factors? It's difficult to go beyond a broad generalization from simply viewing a scatter plot.

The Correlation Coefficient

Just as we found measures of central tendency and measures of variability to be more precise than frequency distributions or histograms in describing one variable, it would be helpful if we had a type of measurement that is more precise than a scatter plot to describe the relationship between two variables. In such cases, we could compute a correlation coefficient.

A **correlation coefficient** *is a numerical value that expresses the degree of relationship between two variables.* For example, let's assume that we have calculated the correlation coefficient for the relationship between how long your instructor lectures (the *X* variable) and the number of times students yawn (the *Y* variable). For the sake of this example, let's assume these data produce a correlation coefficient (represented by the letter *r*) of +.70. Remember this number, as we will use it to illustrate what a correlation coefficient tells you.

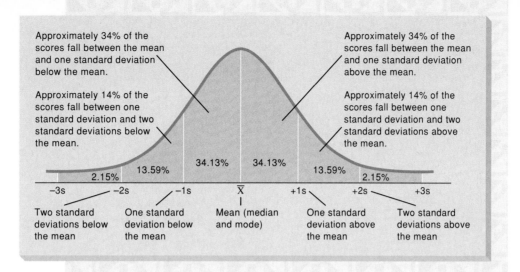

FIGURE A.5

The normal distribution.

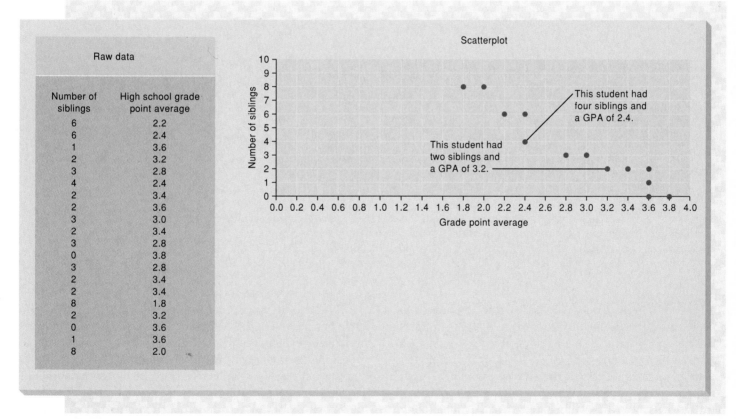

FIGURE A.6

Descriptive measures for two variables. This scatter plot depicts the possible relationship between number of siblings and grade point average. Each dot on the scatter plot represents one pair of scores as reported by each member of your class in a hypothetical survey. The raw data from that survey are shown on the left.

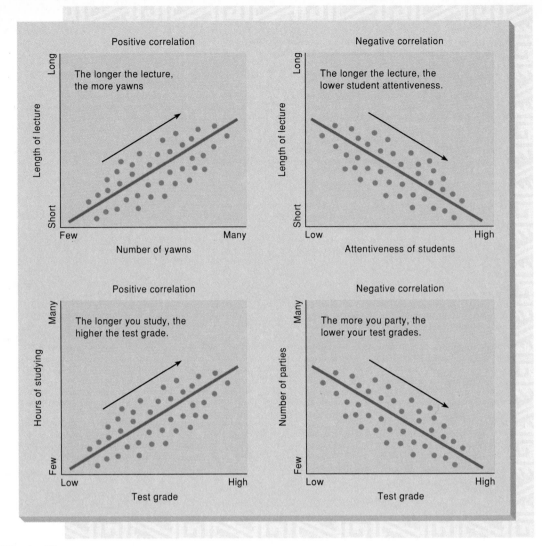

FIGURE A.7

Scatter plots showing positive and negative correlations. A positive correlation is a relationship in which two factors vary in the same direction, as shown in the two scatter plots on the left. A negative correlation is a relationship in which two factors vary in opposite directions, as shown in the two scatter plots on the right.

The numeric value of a correlation coefficient falls within the range from +1.00 to −1.00. This is simply an arbitrary range that does *not* parallel an integer number line (for example, . . . −3, −2, 1, 0, 1, 2, 3, . . .). In other words, negative numbers are *not* less than positive numbers. A correlation of +.65 is just as strong as a correlation of −.65. The plus or minus sign has a different meaning when applied to correlation coefficients, which we will discuss in a moment. Also, avoid the temptation to attach value judgments to correlational signs. A positive correlation is not "good" or "desirable" and a negative correlation is not "bad" or "undesirable."

There are two parts to a correlation coefficient: the number and the sign. The number tells you the strength of the relationship between the two factors. The rule is simple: regardless of the sign, the closer the number is to 1.00, the stronger the correlation; conversely, the closer the number is to .00, the weaker the correlation. Remember that the plus or minus sign tells you nothing about the strength of the correlation; thus, a correlation of −.87 is stronger than a correlation of +.45. The following table offers guidelines for interpreting correlational numbers.

Student number	Number of siblings (X variable)	Score minus mean (3.0)	Difference squared	High school GPA (Y variable)	Score minus mean (3.0)	Difference squared	x multiplied by y
N	X	x	x^2	Y	y	y^2	xy
1	6	3	9	2.2	−.8	.64	−2.4
2	6	3	9	2.4	−.6	.36	−1.8
3	1	−2	4	3.6	.6	.36	−1.2
4	2	−1	1	3.2	.2	.04	−0.2
5	3	0	0	2.8	−.2	.04	0.0
6	4	1	1	2.4	−.6	.36	−0.6
7	2	−1	1	3.4	.4	.16	−0.4
8	2	−1	1	3.6	.6	.36	−0.6
9	3	0	0	3.0	0.0	.00	0.0
10	2	−1	1	3.4	.4	.16	−0.4
11	3	0	0	2.8	−.2	.04	0.0
12	0	−3	9	3.8	.8	.64	−2.4
13	3	0	0	2.8	−.2	.04	0.0
14	2	−1	1	3.4	.4	.16	−0.4
15	2	−1	1	3.4	.4	.16	−0.4
16	8	5	25	1.8	−1.2	1.44	−6.0
17	2	−1	1	3.2	.2	.04	−0.2
18	0	−3	9	3.6	.6	.36	−1.8
19	1	−2	4	3.6	.6	.36	−1.2
20	8	5	25	2.0	−1.0	1.00	−5.0
	N = 20	Mean = 3.0	$\Sigma x^2 = 102$	Mean = 3.0		$\Sigma y^2 = 6.72$	$\Sigma xy = -25.00$

$$r = \frac{\Sigma xy}{\sqrt{\Sigma x^2 \times \Sigma y^2}} = \frac{-25.00}{\sqrt{(102)(6.72)}} = \frac{-25.00}{\sqrt{685.44}} = \frac{-25.00}{26.18} = -.95$$

FIGURE A.8

Computation of a correlation coefficient. These data are from a hypothetical survey on number of siblings and high school GPA reported by 20 students in your psychology class. The correlation coefficient of −.95 indicates a very strong negative relationship between number of siblings and high school GPA.

1.00	Perfect relationship; the two factors always occur together
.76–.99	Very strong relationship; the two factors occur together very often
.51–.75	Strong relationship; the two factors occur together frequently
.26–.50	Moderate relationship; the two factors occur together occasionally
.01–.25	Weak relationship; the two factors seldom occur together
.00	No relationship; the two factors never occur together

The plus or minus sign tells you the direction of the relationship between the two variables. A **positive correlation** *is a relationship in which the two factors vary in the same direction.*

Both factors tend to go up together *or* both factors tend to go down together. Either relationship represents a positive correlation. A **negative correlation** *is a relationship in which the two factors vary in opposite directions.* As one factor increases, the other factor decreases. Thus, a correlation of +.15 indicates a weak positive correlation, and a −.74 indicates a strong negative correlation. Examples of scatter plots showing positive and negative correlations appear in figure A.7.

Let's return to our example about how long your professor lectures and the number of times students yawn. Those two factors produced a correlation coefficient of +.70. The number .70 tells us that these two factors happen together frequently. We also know from the preceding discussion that the positive sign indicates the two factors vary in the same direction. As the amount of time your professor lectures increases, the number of yawns increases. An example of a negative correlation in this situation might be the relationship between how long your instructor lectures and the level of student attentiveness. As the length of time your instructor lectures increases, the level of student attentiveness decreases—these two factors vary in opposite directions.

The following formula is used to calculate a correlation coefficient:

$$r = \frac{\Sigma xy}{\sqrt{\Sigma x^2 \times \Sigma y^2}}$$

where x is the difference between each X variable minus the mean; y is the difference between each Y variable minus the mean; Σxy is the sum of the cross products (each x score multiplied by its corresponding y score); Σx^2 is the sum of the squares of the x scores; and Σy^2 is the sum of the squares of the y scores.

Let's return to our original example examining the relationship between number of siblings and high school grade point average. Figure A.8 contains the calculation of the correlation coefficient of –.95. From our previous discussion, we know that this is a very strong association indicating that, as number of siblings increases, grade point average decreases. What exactly does this mean? How are we supposed to interpret this hypothetical finding? Does this mean that, if you are an only child, you will have a 4.0 GPA? Does this mean that, if you grew up in a large family, you are destined to make poor grades?

Although researchers frequently use correlation coefficients to analyze the relationship between two variables, they are almost as frequently misinterpreted by the general public. The problem is that *correlation does not necessarily indicate causality*. Causality means that one factor makes, produces, or creates change in a second factor. Correlation means that two factors *seem* to be related, associated, or connected such that, as one factor changes, the other factor seems to change. Correlation implies potential causality that may or may not actually be there. Even though two factors are strongly or even perfectly correlated, in reality a third factor may be responsible for the changes observed. Thus, in our hypothetical example showing a very strong negative correlation between number of siblings and GPA, the changes observed in these two variables could be due to a third factor. For example, perhaps children who grow up in larger families have a greater tendency to hold part-time jobs after school, thereby limiting the amount of time they can study, or children who grow up in small families may be more likely to have their own room, with a desk, thereby allowing them more uninterrupted study time. In any case, the point remains the same: correlation only potentially indicates a causal relationship.

Look at the terms in bold type in the following headlines:

Researchers **Link** Coffee Consumption to Cancer of Pancreas
Scientists Find **Connection** Between Ear Hair and Heart
   Attacks

Sometimes experiments can't be conducted because the factors are beyond control by experimental manipulation. Such would be the case in studying the psychological effects of natural disasters, such as the San Francisco earthquake on October 17, 1989. In these instances, psychologists frequently use the correlational method and collect data through systematic observation.

Psychologists Discover **Relationship** Between Marital Status
   and Health
Researchers Identify **Association** Between Loneliness and
   Social Skills
Parental Discipline **Tied** to Personality Disorders in Children

All of the words in bold type are synonymous with correlation, not causality. The general public, however, tends to equate such terms as "connection" or "association" with causality. As you read about the findings of psychological studies, or findings in other sciences, guard against making the same interpretation. Remember, correlation means only that two factors seem to occur together.

How, then, can a researcher provide compelling evidence of a causal relationship between two variables? By using the experimental method, a research strategy that was described in chapter 1. As you may recall, in the experimental method, researchers try to hold all variables constant, then systematically manipulate the factor that they think produces change (the independent variable); finally, they measure the variable believed to be affected by these manipulations (the dependent variable). If the researchers have held all factors constant except for their manipulation of the independent variable, then any changes observed in the dependent variable can be attributed to the independent variable; changes in the independent variable *caused* changes to occur in the dependent variable. This is the most compelling evidence of causality that science can provide, assuming that the experiment was carefully designed and controlled to avoid such experimental pitfalls as experimenter bias, subject bias, situational bias, or invalid scores. Furthermore, experimental evidence of causality is even more compelling if the research can be *replicated*, or repeated, by other researchers using different subjects.

Why do researchers even bother doing correlational studies if they only potentially indicate causality? Why don't researchers simply conduct experiments all the time, since experiments provide the most compelling evidence of causality? There are several reasons. One, it is not always ethically possible to conduct an experiment on the research question at hand. It may be unethical to conduct an experiment because it poses either physical or psychological danger to the subjects. For instance, it would be unethical to carry out an experiment in which expectant mothers are directed to smoke varying numbers of cigarettes (the independent variable) to see how cigarette smoke affects birthweight and fetal activity level (the dependent variables). Two, the issue under investigation may be post hoc (after the fact) or historical, such as studying the childhood backgrounds of people who are abusive parents. Three, sometimes the factors simply cannot be manipulated experimentally, such as the effects of the October 1989 earthquake on the residents of San Francisco. Fourth, experiments can be incredibly costly to conduct. Correlational studies, on the other hand, are often less expensive. These are some of the limitations associated with the experimental method.

What do researchers do in the situations in which formal experiments are inappropriate or impossible? They use the correlational method and collect data based on *systematic observation* of subjects rather than *systematic manipulation* of the subjects. Systematic observation techniques, which were described in chapter 1, include case studies, naturalistic observation, interviews, questionnaires, and standardized tests.

Thus, the correlation coefficient is a very useful and important statistical tool for psychological as well as for other kinds of research. By understanding how to interpret the number and sign of a correlation coefficient, you can judge how closely two factors are related and in what direction they vary. By understanding the difference between "correlation" and "causation," you are more likely to interpret correctly the research findings described in newspapers, magazines, and journals. Every time the words *association*, *link*, *tie*, *connection*, and *relationship* are used to explain research findings, a correlational study is being described, because all of those words imply correlation, not causation.

Although descriptive statistics can help us summarize and characterize a sample of data, they have limitations. For instance, descriptive statistics cannot tell us whether data are meaningful or significant. A different category of statistics is necessary to accomplish this—inferential statistics.

Inferential Statistics

Assume you have conducted a naturalistic observation investigating whether boys play more aggressively than girls. Assume further that you have followed all the procedures for a good research design to eliminate or minimize any bias or other factors that might distort the data you have collected. When you calculate the descriptive statistics comparing the aggressive behavior of boys with that of girls, it appears that there are large differences between the two groups. How large do those differ-

ences have to be before you are willing to conclude confidently that the differences are significant? Inferential statistics can help answer that question.

Inferential statistics *are complex mathematical methods used to draw conclusions about data that have been collected.* More specifically, inferential statistics are used to indicate whether or not data sufficiently support or confirm a research hypothesis. To accomplish this, inferential statistics rely on statements of probability and statistical significance, two important concepts that we will examine briefly.

There are many kinds of inferential statistics. Depending on the characteristics of the data and the number of groups being compared, different tests are applied. Some examples of inferential statistical measures include the *t*-test, chi-square, analysis of variance, and the Mann-Whitney *U* Test. Although it's beyond the scope of this Appendix to look at these different measures of inferential statistics in detail, the logic behind inferential statistics is relatively simple. Measures of inferential statistics yield a statement of probability about the differences observed between two or more groups; this probability statement tells what the odds are that the observed differences were due simply to chance. If an inferential statistical measure tells you that the odds are less than 5 out of 100 (or .05) that the differences are due to chance, the results are considered statistically significant. In statistical terminology, this is referred to as the *.05 level of statistical significance*, or the *.05 confidence level*. Put another way, **statistical significance** *means that the differences observed between two groups are so large that it is highly unlikely those differences are due merely to chance.*

The .05 level of statistical significance is considered the minimum level of probability that scientists will accept for concluding that the differences observed are real, thereby supporting a hypothesis. Some researchers prefer to use more rigorous levels of statistical significance, such as the .01 level of statistical significance (1 out of 100) or the .001 level of statistical significance (1 out of 1,000). Regardless of which level of statistical significance used, by knowing that a research result is statistically significant, you can be reasonably confident that the finding is not due simply to chance. Of course, replication of the study, with similar significant results, can increase your confidence in the finding even further.

However, a statistically significant difference does not always translate into a difference that has meaning in everyday life. Before assuming that a finding is significant both statistically and in everyday terms, it's wise to look at the actual differences involved. Sometimes the differences are so small as to be inconsequential. For example, in comparisons of average scores for males and females on the math section of the Scholastic Aptitude Test, the difference is statistically significant, with males performing better than females (Benbow & Stanley, 1983). In reality, however, the average difference is only a few points. Caution, therefore, should be exercised in the practical interpretation of statistically significant findings.

Summary

I. Introduction to Statistics

Statistics are very much a part of everyday living. As such, an understanding of basic statistics is necessary to be an informed participant in today's society. Statistics are mathematical methods used to describe, summarize, and infer conclusions about data. There are two basic categories of statistics: (1) descriptive and (2) inferential. Descriptive statistics are used to describe and summarize scores pertaining to one or two variables. Inferential statistics are used to draw conclusions about whether data support a hypothesis.

II. Descriptive Statistics

Descriptive statistics used to describe the characteristics of one variable include frequency distributions, histograms, frequency polygons, measures of central tendency, and measures of variability. The most commonly used descriptive statistics are measures of central tendency and measures of variability. Measures of central tendency describe the overall or average characteristics of a group of scores. Measures of central tendency include the mean, median, and mode. Measures of variability describe how much scores differ from one another. The standard deviation is the most commonly used measure of variability.

III. The Normal Distribution

The normal distribution, or bell-shaped curve, is a frequency polygon of special interest to psychologists. A perfect normal distribution is completely symmetrical; thus, the mean, median, and mode are identical. By knowing the mean and the standard deviation for a normally distributed variable, you can determine what percentage of the population has a particular score.

IV. Scatter Plot and Correlation Coefficient

Descriptive statistics examining the relationship between two variables include the scatter plot and the correlation coefficient. Whereas a scatter plot provides a graphic illustration of the relationship between two variables, correlation coefficients provide a numeric summary of the association between two variables. Although correlational research is widely used, many people confuse correlation and causality. Correlation simply means that two variables seem to occur together in a systematic fashion. Correlation, however, does not necessarily indicate causality. Causality means that one factor makes, produces, or creates change in a second factor. The most compelling evidence to demonstrate that one variable causes change to occur in a second variable comes from experiments. Formal experiments, however, cannot always be conducted for a variety of reasons; thus, scientists frequently rely on correlational research to demonstrate a potential relationship between two variables.

V. Inferential Statistics

Inferential statistics are complex mathematical methods used to draw conclusions based on data. Inferential statistical measures yield a statement of probability about the differences observed between two or more groups. This probability statement tells you what the odds are that the observed differences were due simply to chance. If an inferential statistical measure tells you that the odds are less than 5 out of 100 (or .05) that the observed differences are due to chance, the results are considered statistically significant. Although research results may be statistically significant, they may actually have little or no implication in everyday terms. Thus, caution should be exercised in the practical interpretation of statistically significant findings.

Key Terms

Suggested Readings

Comrey, A., Bott, P., & Lee, H. (1989). *Elementary statistics: A problem-solving approach* (2nd ed.). Dubuque, IA: Wm. C. Brown. This excellent introductory statistics text uses a step-by-step problem-solving approach to understanding statistics.

Huff, D. (1954). *How to lie with statistics*. New York: W. W. Norton. This delightful book is the classic primer on how statistics are frequently used to mislead or deceive people. Originally published in 1954, the examples are not only humorous and effective, but they also provide a wonderful glimpse of everyday life in America almost 4 decades ago. Currently in its 37th printing, this book is must reading for every college student.

GLOSSARY

A

abnormal behavior This is behavior that is maladaptive and harmful. 396

absolute threshold This is the minimum amount of energy an individual can detect 50 percent of the time. 66

accommodation This occurs when individuals adjust to new information. 226

acculturation This term refers to cultural change that results from continuous, first-hand contact between two distinctive cultural groups. 462

acculturative stress This term refers to the negative consequences of cultural change. 462

accurate empathy This is Rogers' term for the therapist's ability to identify with the client. 429

acetylcholine (ACh) This neurotransmitter produces contractions of skeletal muscles by acting on motor nerves. 49

achievement motivation (need for achievement) This is the desire to accomplish something, to reach a standard of excellence, to expend effort to excel. 343

action potential This is the brief wave of electrical charge that sweeps down the axon. 47

activation-synthesis view This view states that dreams reflect the brain's efforts to make sense out of or find meaning in the neural activity that takes place during REM sleep. 110

active listening This is Rogers' term for the ability to listen to another person, with total attention to what the person says and means. 429

activity theory This theory states that, the more active and involved older people are, the more satisfied they are and the more likely it is they will stay healthy. 289

acupuncture This is a technique in which thin needles are inserted at specific points in the body to relieve specific symptoms. 79

addiction This is a physical dependence on a drug. 115

additive mixture This term refers to mixing beams of light from different parts of the color spectrum. 73

adolescence This is the transition from childhood to adulthood, which involves physical, cognitive, and social changes. 258

adolescent egocentrism This is the belief that others are as preoccupied with the adolescent as she herself is, that one is unique and indestructible. 263

adrenal glands Each of these glands secretes epinephrine and norepinephrine and is involved in our moods, energy level, and ability to cope with stress. 60

aerobic exercise This is sustained exercise that stimulates heart and lung activity. 476

affectionate love Also called companionate love, this type of love occurs when an individual desires to have another person near and has a deep, caring affection for that person. 505

afferent nerves These nerves carry information to the brain. 45

afterimages These are sensations that remain after a stimulus is removed. 74

ageism This is prejudice against older people. 289

aggressive behavior This is characterized by hostility, self-enhancement at the expense of others, deprecation of others, and the achievement of goals by hurting others. 469

agoraphobia This is the fear of entering unfamiliar situations, especially open or public spaces. 404

AIDS This is a sexually transmitted disease that is caused by a virus, the human immunodeficiency virus (HIV), that destroys the body's immune system. 326

algorithms These are procedures that guarantee an answer to a problem. 182

all-or-none principle Once the electrical impulse reaches a certain level of intensity, it fires and moves all the way down the axon, remaining at the same strength throughout its travel. 47

alpha waves These waves make up the EEG pattern of individuals who are in a relaxed or drowsy state. 103

altered state of consciousness This is a mental state that noticeably differs from normal awareness. 103

altruism This is an unselfish interest in helping someone. 501

Alzheimer's disease This degenerative, irreversible brain disorder impairs memory and social behavior. 279

amnesia This is the loss of memory. 164

amphetamines These stimulants are widely prescribed. 116

amplitude This is the change in pressure created by sound waves. 77

anal stage This is Freud's second stage of development, occurring between 1½ and 3 years of age, in which the child's greatest pleasure involves the anus or the elimination functions associated with it. 367

analogy This type of formal reasoning is always made up of four parts, and the relation between the first two parts is the same as the relation between the last two. 185

androgen This is the main class of male sex hormones. 300

androgyny This is the presence of desirable masculine and feminine characteristics in the same individual. 308

anorexia nervosa This is an eating disorder that involves the relentless pursuit of thinness through starvation. 475

anterograde amnesia This memory disorder affects the retention of new information or events. 165

antianxiety drugs Commonly known as tranquilizers, these drugs reduce anxiety by making individuals less excitable and more tranquil. 446

antidepressant drugs These drugs regulate mood. 447

antipsychotic drugs These powerful drugs diminish agitated behavior, reduce tension, decrease hallucinations and delusions, improve social behavior, and produce better sleep patterns in severely mentally disabled individuals, especially schizophrenics. 447

antisocial personality disorder Individuals with this disorder often resort to crime, violence, and delinquency and regularly violate the rights of others. 418

anxiety disorders These psychological disorders include the following main features: motor tension, hyperactivity, and apprehensive expectations and thoughts. 403

approach/approach conflict This is a conflict in which an individual must choose between two attractive stimuli or circumstances. 460

approach/avoidance conflict This is a conflict involving a single stimulus or circumstance that has both positive and negative characteristics. 461

archetypes These are the primordial images in every individual's collective unconscious. 371

assertive behavior This involves acting in one's own best interest, standing up for one's legitimate rights, and expressing one's views directly and openly; it is self-enhancing and involves self-choice. 469

assertiveness training This involves teaching individuals to act in their own best interests, to stand up for their legitimate rights, and to express their views directly and openly. 469

assimilation (chapter 1) This term refers to the absorption of an ethnic minority group into the dominant group, which often means the loss of some or all of the behaviors and values of the ethnic minority group. 16

assimilation This occurs when individuals incorporate new information into their existing knowledge. 226, 462

association cortex This area of the brain is involved in the highest intellectual functions, such as problem solving and thinking. 55

attachment This is the close emotional bond between an infant and its caregiver. 236

attitudes These are beliefs and opinions that can predispose individuals to behave in certain ways. 490

attribution theory This theory states that individuals are motivated to discover the underlying causes of behavior as part of their interest in making sense out of the behavior. 496

authoritarian parenting This is a restrictive, punitive style that exhorts a child to follow the parent's directions and to respect work and effort. 240

authoritative parenting This style encourages children to be independent but places limits and controls on their behavior. 241

automatic processes These are a form of consciousness that requires minimal attention and does not interfere with other ongoing activities. 103

automatic processing This does not require capacity, resources, or effort to encode information in memory. 158

autonomic nervous system This system takes messages to and from the body's internal organs, monitoring such processes as breathing, heart rate, and digestion. 45

autonomy versus shame and doubt At approximately 1 to 3 years of age, infants begin to discover that their behavior is their own. They start to assert their sense of independence in Erikson's second stage of development. 235

aversive conditioning This approach to behavior therapy involves repeated pairings of an undesirable behavior with aversive stimuli to decrease the behavior's rewards so the individual will stop doing it. 431

avoidance/avoidance conflict This is a conflict in which an individual must choose between two unattractive stimuli or circumstances. 460

axon This is the part of the neuron that carries information away from the cell body to other cells. 46

B

"bad patient" role In this role, a patient complains to the staff, demands attention, disobeys staff orders, and generally misbehaves. 471

barbiturates These are depressant drugs that induce sleep or reduce anxiety. 116

Barnum effect If you make your observations broad enough, any person can fit the description. 384

behavior This is everything we can do that can be directly observed. 5

behavioral approach This approach emphasizes the scientific study of observable behavioral responses and their environmental determinants. 8

behavioral medicine This field, closely related to health psychology, attempts to combine medical and behavioral knowledge to reduce illness and to promote health. 455

behavior modification This is the application of operant conditioning principles to changing human behavior. 136

behavior therapies These therapies use principles of learning to reduce or eliminate maladaptive behavior. 430

biofeedback This is the process in which individuals' muscular or visceral activities are monitored by instruments, and information from the instruments is given to the individuals so they can learn to voluntarily control their physiological activities. 467

biological processes These involve changes in an individual's physical nature. 216

binocular cues These are depth cues that are based on both eyes working together. 86

biomedical therapies These are treatments to reduce or eliminate the symptoms of psychological disorders by altering the way an individual's body functions. 446

bipolar disorder This is a mood disorder characterized by extreme mood swings; an individual with this disorder might be depressed, manic, or both. 410

brightness This measure of color is based on the color's intensity. 73

brightness constancy An object retains the same degree of brightness even though different amounts of light fall on it. 89

bulimia This is an eating disorder in which an individual consistently follows a binge-and-purge eating pattern. 476

burnout This is a hopeless, helpless feeling brought on by relentless, work-related stress. 460

bystander effect This theory states that individuals who observe an emergency are less likely to help when someone else is present than when they are alone. 502

C

Cannon-Bard theory This is the theory that emotion and physiological reactions occur simultaneously. 355

care perspective Carol Gilligan's theory of moral development sees people in terms of their connectedness with others and focuses on interpersonal communication, relationships with others, and concern for others. 273

carpentered-world hypothesis This hypothesis states that people who live in cultures in which straight lines, right angles, and rectangles predominate learn to interpret nonrectangular figures as rectangular, to perceive the figures in perspective, and to interpret them as two-dimensional representations of three-dimensional objects. 92

case study This is an in-depth look at one individual; it is used mainly by clinical psychologists when the unique aspects of an individual's life cannot be duplicated for study, for either practical or ethical reasons. 23

catatonic schizophrenia This is a schizophrenic disorder characterized by bizarre motor behavior, which sometimes takes the form of a completely immobile stupor. 415

catharsis This is the psychoanalytic term for clients' release of emotional tension when they relive an emotionally charged and conflicted experience. 428

cell body This structure contains the nucleus, which directs the manufacture of the substances the neuron uses for its growth and maintenance. 46

central nervous system (CNS) This is made up of the brain and spinal cord. 44

cerebellum Extended from the rear of the hindbrain and located just above the medulla, this structure consists of two rounded structures thought to play important roles in motor control. 51

chaining This is an operant conditioning technique used to teach a complex sequence, or chain, of behaviors by shaping the final response in the sequence, then working backward until a chain of behaviors is learned. 133

chromosomes These are threadlike structures that come in 23 pairs, one member of each pair coming from each parent. 39

chunking The grouping, or packing, of information into higher-order units expands short-term memory by making large amounts of information more manageable. 154

circadian rhythm This is a daily behavioral or physiological cycle. 107

clairvoyance This involves the ability to perceive remote events that are not in sight. 95

classical conditioning This is a learning process in which a neutral stimulus acquires the ability to produce a response originally produced by another stimulus. 125

clinical and counseling psychology Psychologists who practice this type of psychology diagnose and treat people with psychological problems. 30

cochlea This is a snail-shaped, fluid-filled structure that contains the receptors for hearing. 78

cognition This term refers to the mental processes—perception, memory, thought, and language—that together produce knowledge. 178

cognitive appraisal Lazarus' term describes individuals' interpretation of events in their lives as harmful, threatening, or challenging and their determination of whether they have the resources to cope effectively with the event. 459

cognitive approach This approach to psychology emphasizes the mental processes involved in knowing. 9

cognitive behavior therapy This approach to behavior therapy tries to help individuals behave more adaptively by modifying their thoughts. 432

cognitive developmental theory of gender Children's gender typing occurs after they have developed a concept of gender. 303

cognitive dissonance Festinger's concept refers to an individual's motivation toward consistency and away from inconsistency. 491

cognitive map This is an organism's mental representation of the structure of physical space. 142

cognitive processes These processes involve changes in an individual's thought, intelligence, and language. 216

cognitive therapies These therapies emphasize that an individual's cognitions, or thoughts, are the main source of abnormal behavior. 433

collective unconscious This is the impersonal, deepest layer of the unconscious mind, which is shared by all human beings because of their common ancestral past. 371

collectivism This emphasizes values that serve the group by subordinating personal goals to preserve group integrity, interdependence of the members, and harmonious relationships. 380

community psychology This branch of psychology focuses on providing accessible care for people with psychological problems and on preventing those problems through individual and ecological interventions. 31

compensation This is Adler's term for an individual's attempt to overcome imagined or real inferiorities or weaknesses by developing his or her abilities. 371

competence motivation This term describes the motivation to deal effectively with the environment, to be adept at what we attempt, to process information efficiently, and to make the world a better place. 342

complexity This term refers to the numerous frequencies of sound blending together, which is sensed as the sound's timbre. 78

computer-assisted axial tomography (CAT scan) This is a three-dimensional imaging technique obtained by passing X rays through the head; then a computer assembles the individual pictures into a composite image. 59

concept This is a category used to group objects, events, and characteristics on the basis of common properties. 179

conception Also called fertilization, this occurs when a single sperm cell from the male penetrates the female's ovum (egg). 219

concrete operational thought This is the term Piaget gave to the 7-to-11-year-old child's understanding of the world. At this stage, logical reasoning replaces intuitive thought as long as the principles are applied to concrete examples. 230

conditional positive regard This is Rogers' term for the concept that love and praise often are not given unless an individual conforms to parental or social standards. 375

conditioned response (CR) This is the learned response to the conditioned stimulus that occurs after CS-UCS pairing. 125

conditioned stimulus (CS) This is a previously neutral stimulus that eventually elicits the conditioned response after being paired with the unconditioned stimulus. 125

cones These receptors in the retina are sensitive to color. 69

conformity This occurs when individuals adopt attitudes or behavior of others because of real or imagined pressure from others. 497

consciousness This is the awareness of both external and internal stimuli or events. 102

consciousness-raising groups These groups often involve several people meeting in one member's home, are frequently leaderless, and focus on the members' feelings and self-perceptions. 446

consensual validation This term states that our own attitudes and behavior are supported when someone else's attitudes and behavior are similar to ours. 504

conservation This principle states that a substance's quantity stays the same even though its shape changes. 229

content validity This term refers to a test's ability to give a broad picture of what is to be measured. 197

contexts This term refers to the historical, economic, social, and cultural factors that influence mental processes and behavior. 6

continuity of development This is the view that development involves gradual, cumulative change from conception to death. 217

contour This is a location at which a sudden change of brightness occurs. 85

control group This is the comparison group. It is treated like the experimental group except for the manipulated factor. 27

controlled processes These represent the most alert mental state of consciousness, in which individuals actively focus their effort toward a goal. 102

conventional level Individuals at Kohlberg's intermediate level of internalization abide by certain standards (internal), but they are the standards of others (external), such as the standards of parents (Stage 3) or the laws of society (Stage 4). 271

convergence This is a binocular cue for depth perception in which the eyes turn more inward as an object gets closer. 87

convergent thinking This type of thinking produces one correct answer. 209

conversion disorder This is a somatoform disorder in which an individual experiences genuine physical symptoms even though no physiological problems can be found. 407

cooperative learning This is an approach to teaching in which children from various ethnic backgrounds or ability levels are assigned to groups. Each member works on problems at his or her skill level and pace but is also encouraged to perform as part of a group. 251

cornea This is a clear membrane in front of the iris that bends light rays as they enter the eye. 69

corpus callosum This is a large bundle of axons that connects the brain's hemispheres. 56

correlational strategy The goal is to describe the strength of the relation between two or more events or characteristics. 25

correlation coefficient This is a numerical value that expresses the degree of relationship between two variables. 538

counterconditioning This is a classical conditioning procedure for weakening a CR by associating the stimuli with a response that is incompatible with the CR. 128

couple therapy This is group therapy with married or unmarried couples whose major problem is their relationship. 435

creativity This is the ability to think about something in novel and unusual ways and to come up with unique solutions to problems. 209

credibility This term refers to the fact that a therapist is believable. 444

criterion validity This term refers to a test's ability to predict other measures, or criteria, of an attribute. 197

cross-cultural psychology This branch of psychology examines the role of culture in understanding behavior, thought, and emotion. 31

cue-dependent forgetting This form of forgetting is due to a failure to use effective retrieval cues. 162

cultural-familial retardation This is a mental deficit in which no evidence of organic brain damage can be found; individuals' IQs range from 50 to 70. 208

culture This term refers to the behavior patterns, beliefs, and other products of a particular group of people, such as the values, work patterns, music, dress, diet, and ceremonies that are passed on from one generation to the next. 9

culture-fair tests These are intelligence tests that attempt to reduce cultural bias. 203

culture specificity hypothesis This theory states that cultural experiences determine what is socially relevant in a person's life and, therefore, what the person is most likely to remember. 170

D

date, or acquaintance, rape This is coercive sexual activity directed at someone with whom the individual is at least casually acquainted. 323

daydreaming This is a form of consciousness that involves a low level of conscious effort. 103

decay theory When something new is learned, a neurochemical "memory trace" is formed, but over time this trace tends to disintegrate. 164

decibels (dB) This is the amount of pressure produced by a sound wave relative to a standard. 77

declarative memory This is the conscious recollection of information that can be communicated verbally. 155

deductive reasoning This is reasoning from the general to the specific. 184

defense mechanisms This psychoanalytic term for unconscious methods of dealing with conflict states that the ego distorts reality, thereby protecting itself from anxiety. 366

deficiency needs This is Maslow's term for essential requirements—physiological and psychological—that must be met. 377

deindividuation This is the loss of identity as an individual and the development of group identity in a group situation that promotes arousal and anonymity. 509

deinstitutionalization This term refers to the movement to transfer the treatment of mental disabilities from inpatient mental institutions to community-based facilities that stress outpatient care. 438

delta waves These large, slow EEG waves last up to 30 minutes in Stage 4 sleep. 103

dendrite This is the receiving part of the neuron, serving the important function of collecting information and orienting it toward the cell body. 46

deoxyribonucleic acid (DNA) This is a complex molecule that contains genetic information. 39

dependent variable This is the factor that is measured in an experiment. 27

depressants These are psychoactive drugs that slow the central nervous system, body functions, and behaviors. 115

depth perception This is the ability to perceive objects three-dimensionally. 86

descriptive statistics These are mathematical procedures used to describe and summarize samples of data in a meaningful fashion. 534

development This is a pattern of movement or change that begins at conception and continues throughout the life cycle. 216

developmentally appropriate practice This approach to teaching is based on knowledge of the typical development of children with an age span, as well as the uniqueness of the child. 246

developmental psychology This branch of psychology is concerned with how we become who we are from birth to death. 31

diathesis-stress view This view argues that a combination of environmental stress and biogenetic disposition causes schizophrenia. 417

difference threshold This is the smallest difference in stimulation required to discriminate one stimulus from another 50 percent of the time. 68

discontinuity of development This view of development involves distinct stages in the life span. Each of us is described as passing through a sequence of stages in which change is qualitatively rather than quantitatively different. 217

discrimination (classical conditioning) This is the process of learning to respond to certain stimuli and not to others. 126

discrimination (operant conditioning) This is the process of responding in the presence of a stimulus that is not reinforced. 135

discriminative stimuli These signal that a response will be reinforced. 135

disorganized schizophrenia This is a schizophrenic disorder in which an individual has delusions and hallucinations that have little or no recognizable meaning. 415

displacement This psychoanalytic defense mechanism occurs when an individual shifts unacceptable feelings from one object to another, more acceptable object. 367

display rules These are sociocultural standards that determine when, where, and how emotions should be expressed. 357

dissociative disorders These are psychological disorders that involve a sudden loss of memory or change in identity. 407

divergent thinking Characteristic of creativity, this type of thinking produces many answers to the same question. 209

dominant-recessive genes principle If one gene of a pair is dominant and one is recessive, the dominant gene exerts its effect, overriding the potential influence of the recessive gene. A recessive gene exerts its influence only if both genes of a pair are recessive. 40

dopamine This neurotransmitter is related to mental health—too much dopamine in the brain's synapses is associated with schizophrenia. 50

dream analysis This is the psychotherapeutic technique psychoanalysts use to interpret a client's dream. 428

drive This is an aroused state that occurs because of a physiological need. 337

DSM Diagnostic and Statistical Manual of Mental Disorders is a system of classification of mental disturbances in the United States. 401

DSM-III-R This, the most recent classification of mental disorders, contains 18 major classifications and more than 200 specific disorders. 401

E

early adulthood This is a time, which begins in the late teens or early twenties and ends in the late thirties to early forties, when individuals establish personal and economic independence, intensely pursue a career, and seek intimacy with one or more individuals. 276

echoic memory This is the name given to the auditory sensory registers, in which information is retained up to several seconds. 153

ecological theory This evolution-based approach argues that the main purpose of sleep is to prevent animals from wasting their energy and harming themselves during parts of the day or night to which they have not adapted. 108

ectomorph This is Sheldon's term for a tall, thin, fragile person who is fearful, introverted, and restrained. 379

efferent nerves These nerves carry the brain's output. 45

effortful processing This process requires capacity or resources to encode information in memory. 158

ego This is the Freudian structure of personality that deals with the demands of reality. 366

egoism This concept is involved when person A gives to person B to ensure reciprocity; to gain self-esteem; to present oneself as powerful, competent, or caring; or to avoid social and self-censure for failing to live up to normative expectations. 501

elaboration This is the term used to describe the extensiveness of processing at any given depth in memory. 159

electroconvulsive therapy (ECT) Commonly called "shock treatment," this therapy is sometimes used to treat severely depressed individuals by causing a seizure in the brain, much like what happens spontaneously in some forms of epilepsy. 447

electroencephalograph This instrument records the electrical activity of the brain; electrodes placed on an individual's scalp record brain-wave activity, which is reproduced on a chart known as an electroencephalogram. 59

embryonic period This is the time from 2 to 8 weeks after conception. 219

emic approach The goal is to describe behavior in one culture or ethnic group in terms that are meaningful and important to the people in that culture or ethnic group, without regard to other cultures or ethnic groups. 23

emotion This is the feeling, or affect, that involves a mixture of physiological arousal, conscious experience, and overt behavior. 351

emotion-focused coping This is Lazarus' term for responding to stress in an emotional manner, especially using defensive appraisal. 466

empirically keyed tests These tests rely on the tests' items to predict a particular criterion. 386

empowerment This concept refers to the importance of assisting individuals to develop skills they need to control their own lives. 440

encoding This term refers to transforming and/or transferring information into a memory system. 157

encounter group This is a personal growth group designed to promote self-understanding through candid group interactions. 436

endocrine glands These glands release their chemical products directly into the bloodstream. 60

endomorph This is Sheldon's term for a soft, round, large-stomached person who is relaxed, gregarious, and food loving. 379

endorphins These natural opiates are neurotransmitters that are involved in pleasure and the control of pain. 50

environment This term refers to all of the surrounding conditions and influences that affect the development of living things. 41

epigenetic principle Erikson's principle states that human beings unfold according to a blueprint, with each stage of development coming at a predictable time. 234

episodic memory This is a declarative memory system that involves the retention of information about the where and when of life's happenings. 155

erogenous zones This term refers to Freud's concept that, at each stage of development, one part of the body has especially strong pleasure-giving qualities. 367

estradiol This hormone is associated with breast, uterine, and skeletal development in girls. 261

estrogen This is the main class of female sex hormones. 300

ethnic identity This term refers to a sense of membership based on the shared language, religion, customs, values, history, and race of an ethnic group. 9

ethnicity This concept is based on cultural heritage, nationality, characteristics, race, religion, and language and involves descent from common ancestors. 9

ethnocentrism This is the tendency to favor one's own group over other groups. 16, 511

ethology This is the study of the biological basis of behavior in natural habitats. 339

etic approach The goal is to describe behavior so that generalizations can be made across cultures. 23

eustress This is Selye's concept to describe the positive features of stress. 457

exhibitionism This is a psychosexual disorder in which individuals expose their sexual anatomy to others to obtain sexual gratification. 322

experiment This is a carefully regulated procedure in which one or more of the factors believed to influence the behavior being studied are manipulated and all others are held constant. 26

experimental and physiological psychology These areas often involve pure research. 31

experimental group This is the group whose experience is manipulated. 27

experimental strategy This approach allows psychologists to precisely determine behavior's causes. 26

extinction (classical conditioning) This is the weakening of the CS's tendency to elicit the CR as a result of unreinforced presentations of the CS. 127

extinction (operant conditioning) This is a decrease in the tendency to perform the response. 134

extrasensory perception (ESP) This is perception that occurs outside of the use of known sensory processes. 94

extrinsic motivation This motivation is influenced by external rewards and punishments. 344

F

face validity This is an assumption that the content of the test items is a good indicator of what an individual's personality is like. 385

family systems therapy This form of therapy is based on the assumption that psychological adjustment is related to patterns of interaction within the family unit. 436

family therapy This is group therapy with family members. 435

fear of success This term refers to individuals' worry that they might be rejected if they are successful. 344

feminist therapies These therapies are usually based on a critique of a society wherein women are perceived to have less political and economic power than men. 446

feminization of poverty This term refers to the fact that far more women than men live in poverty. 465

fetal alcohol syndrome (FAS) This cluster of characteristics describes children born to mothers who are heavy drinkers. 220

fetal period This period begins 2 months after conception and lasts, on average, for 7 months. 219

fetishism Individuals with this psychosexual disorder rely on inanimate objects or a specific body part for sexual gratification. 321

figure-ground relationship This is the principle by which we organize the perceptual field into stimuli that stand out and those that are leftover. 85

fixation This is the psychoanalytic defense mechanism that occurs when an individual remains locked in an earlier developmental stage. 367

fixed-interval schedule The first appropriate response after a fixed amount of time has elapsed is reinforced. 134

fixed-ratio schedule Behavior is reinforced after a set number of responses. 134

forebrain This is the highest region of the human brain; among its most important structures are the thalamus, hypothalamus, and neocortex. 53

formal groups These groups are established by management to do an organization's work. 514

formal operational thought Coined by Piaget, this term refers to the fourth stage of cognitive development, which appears between 11 and 15 years of age. 262

fovea This is a minute area in the center of the retina where the optic nerve leaves the eye on its way to the brain. 69

free association This is the psychological technique of encouraging individuals to say aloud whatever comes to mind, no matter how trivial or embarrassing. 428

frequency This is the number of cycles that pass through a point in a given time. 77

frequency distribution This term refers to a listing of scores from lowest to highest, with the number of times each score appears in a sample. 534

frequency polygon This is basically the same as a histogram except that the data are represented with lines rather than bars. 534

frequency theory This theory states that perception of sound is due to how often the auditory nerve fires. 78

friendship This form of close relationship involves enjoyment, acceptance, trust, respect, mutual assistance, openness, understanding, and spontaneity. 504

frontal lobe The portion of the neocortex behind the forehead is involved in the control of voluntary muscles and in intelligence. 54

frustration This occurs in any situation in which a person cannot reach a desired goal. 461

fugue This is a dissociative disorder in which an individual not only develops amnesia but also unexpectedly travels away from home and assumes a new identity. 407

functional fixedness This is the inability to solve a problem because it is viewed only in terms of its usual functions. 183

fundamental attribution error This theory states that observers overestimate the importance of traits and underestimate the importance of situations when they seek explanations of an actor's behavior. 496

G

GABA Gamma aminobutyric acid is a neurotransmitter that inhibits the firing of neurons. 48

gate-control theory This is Melzach and Wall's theory that the spinal column contains a neural "gate" that can be opened and closed. 79

gender This term refers to everything people learn about and think of their sex in different cultures. 11, 300

gender identity This is the sense of being male or female, which most children acquire by the time they are 3 years old. 300

gender role This is a set of expectations that prescribes how females and males should think, act, and feel. 300

gender role stereotypes These are broad categories that reflect our impressions and beliefs about females and males. 304

gender role transcendence This is the belief that, when an individual's competence is at issue, it should not be conceptualized on the basis of masculinity, femininity, or androgyny but, rather, on a personal basis. 309

gender schema This schema organizes the world in terms of female and male. 303

gender schema theory An individual's attention and behavior are guided by an internal motivation to conform to gender-based sociocultural standards and stereotypes. 303

general adaptation syndrome (GAS) Selye's concept describes the common effects on the body when demands are placed on it: alarm, resistance, and exhaustion. 457

generalization (classical conditioning) This is the tendency of a stimulus similar to the original conditioned stimulus to produce a response that is similar to the conditioned response. 126

generalization (operant conditioning) This term refers to giving the same response to similar stimuli. 135

generalized anxiety disorder This is an anxiety disorder that consists of persistent anxiety for at least 1 month. 403

generativity versus stagnation Erikson's seventh stage of development occurs mainly in middle adulthood. Middle-aged adults need to assist the younger generation in leading useful lives. 284

genes These are the units of hereditary information. 39

genital stage This is the final Freudian stage of development, occurring from puberty on. The source of sexual pleasure becomes someone outside the family. 368

genuineness This is the Rogerian concept of the importance of the therapist being genuine and not hiding behind a facade. 429

germinal period This is the first 2 weeks after conception. 219

Gestalt psychology This is an approach which states that people naturally organize their perceptions according to certain patterns. 85

Gestalt therapy In this humanistic therapy, therapists question and challenge clients in order to help them become more aware of their feelings and face their problems. 429

gifted This term refers to people who have above-average intelligence (an IQ of 120 or higher) and/or superior talent for something. 208

giving This term refers to the fact that clients receive a benefit from treatment early in the therapy process. 444

gonorrhea Commonly called the "drip" or the "clap," this is the most common STD in the United States and is caused by a bacterium called gonococcus, which thrives in the moist mucous membranes lining the mouth, throat, vagina, cervix, urethra, and anal tract. 325

"good patient" role This patient is passive and unquestioning and behaves "properly." 471

great person theory This theory states that individuals have certain traits that are best suited for leadership positions. 509

GRIT strategy The Graduated and Reciprocated Initiatives in Tension-Reduction is a strategy to decrease tension and mistrust among nations so that disarmament and regular negotiation, trade, and international diplomacy can proceed. 513

groupthink This is the motivation of group members to maintain harmony and unanimity in decision making, suffocating differences of opinion in the process. 509

H

hallucinogens These psychoactive drugs modify a person's perceptual experiences and produce visual images that are not real. 118

hardiness This personality style is characterized by a sense of commitment, control, and a perception of problems as challenges. 458

health psychology This multidimensional approach to health emphasizes psychological factors, life-style, and the nature of the health care delivery system. 455

herpes This is a sexually transmitted disease caused by a large family of viruses with many different strains. These strains produce such diseases as chicken pox and mononucleosis, as well as herpes simplex, an STD that has two variations. 325

heuristics These rules of thumb suggest a solution to a problem but do not ensure that it will work. 182

hidden observer Used by Hilgard, this term explains how part of a hypnotized individual's mind is completely unaware of what is happening: the individual remains a passive, or hidden, observer until called on to comment. 113

hierarchy of motives This is Maslow's concept that all individuals have five main needs, which must be satisfied in the following sequence: physiological, safety, love and belongingness, self-esteem, and self-actualization. 337

hindbrain Located at the skull's rear, this is the lowest portion of the brain. 51

histogram This is a frequency distribution in graphic form, in which vertical bars represent the frequency of scores per category class. 534

holophrase hypothesis This concept, characterizing an infant's first words, states that a single word is used to imply a complete sentence. 192

homeostasis This is the body's tendency to maintain an equilibrium, or steady state. 337

hormones These are chemical messengers manufactured by the endocrine glands. 60

hue This measure of color is based on the color's intensity. 73

humanistic approach This approach to psychology emphasizes a person's capacity for personal growth, freedom to choose one's own destiny, and positive qualities. 9, 375

humanistic psychotherapies Clients are encouraged to understand themselves and to grow personally. 429

human sexual response cycle This consists of four phases—excitement, plateau, orgasm, and resolution. 318

hypnosis This is a psychological state of altered attention and awareness in which an individual is unusually receptive to suggestions. 113

hypochondriasis This is a somatoform disorder in which an individual has a pervasive fear of illness and disease. 406

hypothalamus Much smaller than and located just below the thalamus, this structure monitors eating, drinking, and sex and is involved in emotion, stress, and reward. 53

hypothetical-deductive reasoning Coined by Piaget, this term refers to adolescents' cognitive ability to develop hypotheses, or best guesses, about ways to solve problems, such as an algebraic equation. They then systematically deduce, or conclude, which is the best path to follow to solve the equation. 263

I

iconic memory This is the name given to the visual sensory registers, in which information is retained only for about one-quarter of a second. 153

id This is the Freudian structure of personality that consists of instincts, which are an individual's reservoir of psychic energy. 366

identification theory At about the age of 5 or 6, Freud theorized, the child renounces an attraction for the parent of the opposite sex because of anxious feelings and identifies with the same-sex parent, unconsciously adopting this parent's behavior. 302

identity versus identity confusion The fifth stage of Erikson's stages of human development occurs primarily during the adolescent years. The development of identity involves finding out who we are, what we are all about, and where we are headed in life. 268

impression management This is the process by which individuals strive to present themselves in a favorable light. 496

imprinting Infant animals have a tendency to form an attachment to the first moving objects they see and/or hear. 236

incentives These positive or negative external stimuli or events motivate an individual's behavior. 337

incest This is a sexual relationship between two relatives. 321

independent variable This is the manipulated, influential, experimental factor in an experiment. 27

individual differences These are the consistent, stable ways people are different from each other. 195

individualism This involves giving priority to personal goals rather than to group goals; it emphasizes values that serve the self, such as feeling good, personal distinction, and independence. 380

individual psychology This is the name Adler gave to his theory of psychology to emphasize the uniqueness of every individual. 371

inductive reasoning This is reasoning from the specific to the general—that is, drawing conclusions about all members of a category based on observing only some of the members. 184

industrial/organizational psychology This branch of psychology deals with the workplace, focusing on both the workers and the organizations that employ them. 31, 514

industry versus inferiority As children move into middle and late childhood, Erikson's fourth developmental stage, they direct their energy toward mastering knowledge and intellectual skills. 236

inferential statistics These are complex mathematical methods used to draw conclusions about data that have been collected. 543

inferiority complex This is the name Adler gave to exaggerated feelings of inadequacy. 372

infinite generativity People have the ability to produce an endless number of meaningful sentences using a finite set of words and rules. 187

informal groups These are clusters of workers formed by a group's members. 514

initiative versus guilt During Erikson's third stage of development, which occurs during the preschool years, children develop an increased sense of responsibility, which increases initiative. 236

inner ear This part of the ear consists of the oval window, the cochlea, and the organ of Corti. 78

insanity This legal term implies that individuals are mentally disordered and incapable of being responsible for their actions. 419

insanity defense The plea of "innocent by reason of insanity" is used as a legal defense in criminal trials. 419

insight learning In this form of problem solving, an organism develops a sudden insight into or understanding of a problem's solution. 143

insight therapy This term characterizes both the psychodynamic and humanistic therapies because their goal is to encourage insight into and awareness of one's self. 426

insomnia This is the inability to sleep. 109

instinct This is an innate, biological determinant of behavior. 336

instinctive drift This is the tendency of animals to revert to instinctive behavior that interferes with learning. 144

integration This term implies the maintenance of cultural integrity as well as the movement to become an integral part of the larger culture. 463

integrity versus despair Erikson's final stage of development is a time of looking back at what we have done with our lives. 292

intelligence This term refers to verbal ability, problem-solving skills, and the ability to learn from and adapt to the experiences of everyday life. 195

intelligence quotient (IQ) Devised in 1912 by William Stern, this consists of a person's mental age divided by chronological age, multiplied by 100. 198

interference theory This theory states that we forget not because memories are actually lost from storage but because other information gets in the way of what we want to remember. 162

internalization In moral development, this is the developmental change from behavior that is externally controlled to behavior that is controlled by internal standards and principles. 271

interneurons These are central nervous system neurons that go between sensory input and motor output. 45

intimacy versus isolation Erikson's sixth stage of development occurs mainly in early adulthood. Intimacy is the ability to develop close, loving relationships. 284

intrinsic motivation This is the internal desire to be competent and to do something for its own sake. 344

introspection This is a process of turning inward in search of the mind's nature. 7

ions These are electrically charged particles. 47

iris This ring of muscles in the eye ranges in color from light blue to dark brown. 69

J

James-Lange theory This theory suggests that emotion results from physiological states triggered by stimuli in the environment. 354

justice perspective This theory of moral development focuses on the rights of the individual; individuals independently make moral decisions. 273

K

kinesthetic senses These senses provide information about movement, posture, and orientation. 82

L

laboratory This is a controlled setting, with many of the complex factors of the "real world" removed. 20

language This is a system of symbols used to communicate with others. 187

late adulthood Beginning around the age 60 to 70 and ending when an individual dies, this is a time of adjustment to decreased strength and health, retirement, reduced income, and new social roles. 276

latency stage This is the fourth Freudian stage of development, occurring approximately between 6 years of age and puberty; the child represses all interest in sexuality and develops social and intellectual skills. 368

latent content This is the psychoanalytic term for the unconscious, unremembered, symbolic aspects of a dream. 428

law of effect Developed by Thorndike, this law states that behaviors followed by positive outcomes are strengthened, whereas behaviors followed by negative outcomes are weakened. 130

learned helplessness Animals that are exposed to aversive stimulation over which they have no control enter an apathetic state of helplessness. 413

learning This is a relatively permanent change in behavior that occurs through experience. 124

learning set This is the tendency to solve all problems using the same strategy. 183

lens This is the part of the eye that changes shape to bring objects into focus. 69

levels of processing Craik and Lockhart's theory states that memory is on a continuum from shallow to deep; in this theory, deeper processing produces better memory. 159

light This is a form of electromagnetic energy that can be described in terms of wavelength. 69

linguistic relativity hypothesis This hypothesis states that language determines the structure of thinking and shapes our basic ideas. 192

lithium This drug is widely used to treat bipolar disorder. 447

long-term memory This relatively permanent memory system holds huge amounts of information for a long period of time. 155

LSD This hallucinogen produces striking perceptual changes, even in low doses. 118

lucid dreams These are dreams in which a person "wakes up" mentally but remains in the sensory landscape of the dream world. 112

M

maintenance rehearsal This conscious repetition of information increases the length of time the information stays in short-term memory. 154

major depression This is a mood disorder in which an individual is deeply unhappy, demoralized, self-derogatory, and bored. 409

manifest content This is the psychoanalytic term for the conscious, remembered aspects of a dream. 428

marginalization This term refers to the process in which groups are out of cultural and psychological contact with both their traditional society and the larger, dominant society. 463

marijuana This hallucinogen is milder than LSD. 118

masochism This is a psychosexual disorder in which individuals derive sexual gratification from being subjected to physical pain inflicted by others or themselves. 322

maturation This orderly sequence of changes is dictated by genetic code. 216

mean This is the numerical average of a group of scores or values. 535

measure of central tendency This is a single number that tells the overall characteristics of a set of data. 535

measures of variability (measures of dispersion) This term refers to how much the scores in a sample vary from one another. 537

median This is the score that falls exactly in the middle of a distribution of scores after the scores have been arranged from highest to lowest. 535

medical model Also called the disease model, this model states that abnormality is a disease or illness precipitated by internal physical causes. 397

meditation This is the system of thought that incorporates exercises to attain bodily or mental control and well-being, as well as enlightenment. 468

medulla Beginning where the spinal cord enters the skull, this structure helps control breathing and regulates a portion of the reflexes that allow us to maintain an upright posture. 51

memory This term refers to the retention of information over time. 152

memory processes This term refers to the encoding of new information into memory and the retrieval of information that was previously stored. 157

memory span This is the number of digits an individual can report back in order after a single presentation. 154

mental age (MA) This is an individual's level of mental development relative to others. 197

mental processes This term describes the thoughts, feelings, and motives that each of us experiences privately but that cannot be observed directly. 5

mental retardation This is a condition of limited mental ability in which an individual has a low IQ, usually below 70 on a traditional intelligence test, and has difficulty adapting to everyday life. 207

mesomorph This is Sheldon's term for a strong, athletic, and muscular person who is energetic, assertive, and courageous. 379

meta-analysis In this strategy for analyzing diverse studies, a researcher statistically combines the results of many different studies. 442

metaneeds This is Maslow's concept of higher, self-actualized needs; they include truth, goodness, beauty, wholeness, vitality, uniqueness, perfection, justice, inner wealth, and playfulness. 378

midbrain Located between the hindbrain and forebrain, this is an area where many nerve fiber systems ascend and descend to connect the higher and lower portions of the brain. 52

middle adulthood Beginning at about 35 to 45 years of age and ending at 55 to 60 years of age, this is a time of expanding personal and social involvement, increased responsibility, adjustment to physical decline, and career satisfaction. 276

middle ear This part of the ear consists of four main structures: eardrum, hammer, anvil, and stirrup. 78

Minnesota Multiphasic Personality Inventory (MMPI) This is the most widely used and researched self-report personality test. 386

mnemonics This is the term used to describe the techniques designed to make memory more efficient. 172

mode This is the score that occurs most often. 536

monocular cues These are depth cues based on each eye working independently. 86

mood disorders These psychological disorders are characterized by wide emotional swings, ranging from deeply depressed to highly euphoric and agitated. 409

morphology This term refers to the rules for combining morphemes, the smallest string of sounds that gives meaning to what we say and hear. 187

motherese Parents and other adults often talk to babies in a higher-than-normal frequency, in a greater-than-normal pitch, and in simple words and sentences. 190

motivation This term involves the question of why people behave, think, and feel the way they do. 336

multiaxial system This is DSM-III and DSM-III-R's system of classifying individuals on the basis of five dimensions that include an individual's history and highest level of competent functioning in the past year. 401

multiple-factor theory Thurston's theory states that intelligence consists of seven primary mental abilities: verbal comprehension, number ability, word fluency, spatial visualization, associative memory, reasoning, and perceptual speed. 200

multiple personality This is the most dramatic but least common dissociative disorder; individuals suffering from this disorder have two or more distinct personalities, or selves. 407

myelin sheath This layer of fat cells encases most axons. 46

N

narcolepsy This is the overpowering urge to fall asleep. 109

naturalistic observation Psychologists observe behavior in real-world settings and make no effort to manipulate or control the situation. 20

natural selection This is the evolutionary process that favors individuals within a species that are best adapted to survive and reproduce in a particular environment. 40

nature This term is often used to describe an organism's biological inheritance. 41

need This is a deprivation that energizes the drive to eliminate or reduce the deprivation. 337

negative correlation This is a relationship in which the two factors vary in opposite directions. 541

negative reinforcement The frequency of a response increases because the response either removes an unpleasant stimulus or lets an individual avoid the stimulus. 131

neocortex This is the largest part of the brain, making up about 80 percent of its volume. 53

neurobiological approach This approach to psychology emphasizes that the brain and nervous system play central roles in understanding behavior, thought, and emotion. 9

neurons These are the basic units of the nervous system. 44

neurotic This term describes relatively mild mental disorders in which an individual has not lost contact with reality. 401

neurotransmitters These are chemical substances that carry information across the synaptic gap to the next neuron. 48

nightmare This is a frightening dream that awakens the sleeper from REM sleep. 109

night terror This is characterized by sudden arousal from sleep and intense fear, usually accompanied by a number of physiological reactions, such as rapid heart rate and breathing, loud screams, heavy perspiration, and physical movement. 102

noise This is the term given to irrelevant and competing sound. 67

nonassertive behavior This is characterized by submissiveness, self-denial, inhibition, and the allowing of others to choose. 469

nonsexist therapy This is therapy practiced by a therapist who has become aware of and has primarily overcome his or her own sexist attitudes and behavior. 446

nonstate view This view states that hypnotic behavior is similar to other forms of social behavior and can be explained without resorting to special processes. 114

norepinephrine This neurotransmitter usually inhibits the firing of neurons in the brain and spinal cord but excites the heart muscles, intestines, and urogenital tract. 49

normal distribution This distribution is symmetrical, with a majority of cases falling in the middle of the possible range of scores and few scores appearing toward the extremes of the range. 198, 538

norms (chapter 7) These are the established standards of performance for a test. 197

norms (chapter 16) These are rules that apply to all members of a group. 509

nuclear magnetic resonance (NMR) Also known as MRI, this involves placing a magnetic field around a person's body and using radio waves to construct images of brain tissues and biochemical activity. 59

nurture This term is often used to describe an organism's environmental experiences. 41

O

obedience This is behavior that complies with the explicit demands of an individual in authority. 498

object permanence This is Piaget's term for one of an infant's most important accomplishments: understanding that objects and events continue to exist even when they cannot directly be seen, heard, or touched. 227

observational learning This is learning that occurs when a person observes and imitates someone's behavior. 139

obsessive-compulsive disorder (OCD) This is an anxiety disorder in which an individual has anxiety-provoking thoughts that will not go away and/or urges to perform repetitive, ritualistic behaviors to prevent or produce a future situation. 405

occipital lobe This is the portion of the neocortex at the back of the head. 54

Oedipus complex This is Freud's idea that the young child develops an intense desire to replace the parent of the same sex and to enjoy the affections of the opposite-sex parent. 368

olfactory epithelium Located at the top of the nasal cavity, this is the sheet of receptor cells for smell. 82

operant conditioning (instrumental conditioning) In this form of learning, a behavior produces changes in the probability of a behavior's occurrence. 129

operations In Piaget's theory, these are mental representations that are reversible. 228

opiates Consisting of opium and its derivatives, these drugs depress the central nervous system's activity. 116

opponent-process theory (chapter 11) This is Solomon's theory of emotion that pleasant or unpleasant stimuli can cause both a primary and a secondary process to occur in the brain. 355

opponent-process theory This theory states that cells in the retina respond to red-green and blue-yellow colors—with a given cell, for example, being excited by red and inhibited by green and another cell excited by yellow and inhibited by blue. 74

optic chiasm This is the point at which approximately two-thirds of the fibers that make up the optic nerve cross over the midline of the brain. 72

optic nerve Leading out of the eye toward the brain, this nerve carries information about light. 72

oral stage This is the term Freud used to describe development during the first 18 months of life, in which the infant's pleasure centers on the mouth. 367

organic retardation This term refers to mental retardation caused by a genetic disorder or by brain damage. 208

outer ear This is made up of the pinna and external auditory canal. 78

overcompensation This is Adler's term for an individual's attempt to deny rather than acknowledge a real situation or the individual's exaggerated effort to conceal a weakness. 372

P

pain threshold This is the stimulation level at which pain is first perceived. 79

panic disorder This is a recurrent anxiety disorder marked by the sudden onset of intense apprehension or terror. 403

papillae These are bumps on the tongue that contain taste buds. 81

paranoid schizophrenia This is a schizophrenic disorder characterized by delusions of reference, grandeur, and persecution. 415

paraphilias In this psychosexual disorder, an individual's sexual satisfaction is an unusual object, ritual, or situation. 321

parasympathetic nervous system This is the division of the autonomic nervous system that calms the body. 45

parietal lobe The portion of the neocortex at the top of the head and toward the rear is involved in body sensations. 54

partial reinforcement Responses are not reinforced each time they occur. 134

pedophilia This is a psychosexual disorder in which the sex object is a child and the intimacy usually involves manipulation of the child's genitals. 322

perception This is the process of organizing and interpreting sensory information to give it meaning. 66

peripheral nervous system This is a network of nerves that connects the brain and spinal cord to other parts of the body. 44

permissive-indifferent Parents who use this style of parenting are very removed from their child's life; this style is associated with children's social incompetence. 241

permissive-indulgent Parents who use this style of parenting are highly involved with their children but place few demands or controls on them. 241

personal growth groups These groups, whose roots are in humanistic therapies, emphasize personal growth, increased openness, and honesty in interpersonal relations. 436

personality This term refers to enduring, distinctive thoughts, emotions, and behaviors that characterize the way an individual adapts to the world. 365

personality disorders These psychological disorders develop when personality traits become inflexible and, thus, maladaptive. 418

personality psychology This branch of psychology focuses on the relatively enduring traits and characteristics of individuals. 31

person-centered therapy In this form of humanistic therapy, the therapist provides a warm, supportive atmosphere to improve the client's self-concept and encourage the client to gain insight about problems. 429

phallic stage This is Freud's third stage of development, occurring between the ages of 3 and 6, in which pleasure focuses on the genitals as the child discovers that self-stimulation is enjoyable. 367

phenomenological perspective This psychological perspective stresses the importance of our perceptions of ourselves and our world in understanding personality; this perspective emphasizes that, for each individual, reality is perceived. 375

phobias These are irrational fears. 128

phobic disorder This is an anxiety disorder in which an individual has an irrational, overwhelming, persistent fear of a particular object or situation. 404

phonology This is the study of language's sound system. 187

pitch This is the ear's detection of a sound wave's frequency. 77

pituitary gland This pea-sized endocrine gland, seated at the base of the skull, controls growth and regulates other glands. 60

place theory This is a theory of hearing which states that each frequency produces vibrations at a particular spot on the basilar membrane. 78

pleasure principle This is the Freudian concept that the id always seeks pleasure and avoids pain. 366

pluralism This term refers to the coexistence of distinct ethnic and cultural groups in the same society. 16

polygraph This is a machine that tries to determine if someone is lying by monitoring changes in the body—heart rate, breathing, and electrodermal response—thought to be influenced by emotional states. 353

pons This is a bridge in the hindbrain that contains several clusters of fibers involved in sleep and arousal. 52

positive correlation This is a relationship in which the two factors vary in the same direction. 541

positive reinforcement The frequency of a response increases because it is followed by a pleasant stimulus. 131

positron-emission tomography (PET scan) This procedure measures the amount of specially treated glucose in various areas of the brain. 59

postconventional level Individuals at Kohlberg's highest level of moral thinking have completely internalized their own moral code. The code is among the principles generally accepted by the community (Stage 5) or it is more individualized (Stage 6). 271

posthypnotic amnesia Induced by the hypnotist's suggestion, this is the subject's inability to remember what took place during hypnosis. 113

posthypnotic suggestion This is a suggestion, made by the hypnotist while the subject is in a hypnotic state, that the subject carries out after emerging from the hypnotic state. 113

post-traumatic stress disorder This is a mental disturbance that develops through exposure to a traumatic event, a severely oppressive situation, severe abuse, a natural disaster, or an accidental disaster. The disorder is characterized by anxiety symptoms that either immediately follow the trauma or are delayed by months or even years. 406

precognition This involves "knowing" events before they happen. 95

preconventional level Individuals at Kohlberg's lowest level of moral thinking, in which an individual shows no internalization of moral values, base their moral thinking on punishments (Stage 1) or rewards (Stage 2) that come from the external world. 271

prejudice This is an unjustified negative attitude toward an individual based on the individual's membership in a group. 510

preoperational thought This is Piaget's term for a 2-to-7-year-old child's understanding of the world. Children at this stage of reasoning cannot understand such logical operations as the reversibility of mental representations. 228

preparedness This is the species-specific biological predisposition to learn in certain ways but not in others. 144

preterm infant This is an infant born prior to 38 weeks after conception. 221

primacy effect (chapter 16) This term is used to describe the enduring quality of initial impressions. 495

primacy effect This term refers to superior recall for items at the beginning of a list. 161

primary prevention This community psychology concept describes efforts to reduce the number of new cases of mental disorders. 439

primary reinforcement In this type of reinforcement, reinforcers that are innately satisfying are used. 134

proactive interference This occurs when material that was learned earlier disrupts the recall of material learned later. 162

problem-focused coping This is Lazarus' term for the cognitive strategy of squarely facing one's troubles and trying to solve them. 466

problem solving This is an attempt to find an appropriate way of attaining a goal when the goal is not readily available. 181

procedural memory This is knowledge of skills and cognitive operations of how to do something. 155

Project Head Start This compensatory education program is designed to provide children from low-income families with an opportunity to acquire the skills and experiences needed to succeed in school. 247

projection This psychoanalytic defense mechanism occurs when we attribute our own shortcomings, problems, and faults to others. 367

projective test These tests present individuals with ambiguous stimuli and then ask them to describe the stimuli or tell a story about them. These tests are especially designed to elicit an individual's unconscious feelings and conflicts, providing an assessment that goes deeper than the surface of personality. 384

psychiatry This is a branch of medicine practiced by physicians who subsequently specialize in abnormal behavior and psychotherapy. 31

psychoactive drugs These drugs act on the nervous system to alter state of consciousness, modify perceptions, and change moods. 115

psychoanalysis This is Freud's therapeutic technique for analyzing an individual's unconscious thought. 427

psychoanalytic approach This approach to psychology emphasizes the unconscious aspects of the mind, conflict between biological instincts and society's demands, and early family experiences. 8

psychodynamic therapies These therapies stress the importance of the unconscious mind, extensive interpretation by the therapist, and the role of infant and early childhood experiences. 427

psychogenic amnesia This is a dissociative disorder involving memory loss caused by extensive psychological stress. 407

psychokinesis Closely associated with ESP, this is the mind-over-matter phenomenon of being able to move objects without touching them. 95

psychological dependence This is the need to take a drug to cope with problems and stress. 115

psychology This is the scientific study of behavior and mental processes in contexts. 5

psychology of women This branch of psychology emphasizes the importance of promoting the research and study of women, integrating this information about women with current psychological knowledge and beliefs, and applying the information to society and its institutions. 31

psychoneuroimmunology This field explores the connections among psychological factors, such as attitudes and emotion, the nervous system, and the immune system. 457

psychosexual disorders These are sexual problems caused mainly by psychological factors. 321

psychosexual dysfunctions These are disorders that involve impairments in the sexual response cycle, either in the desire for gratification or the inability to achieve it. 321

psychosurgery This biomedical therapy involves the removal or destruction of brain tissue to improve an individual's psychological adjustment. 448

psychotherapy This is the process by which psychologists work with individuals to reduce their problems and improve their adjustment. 426

psychotic This term describes severe mental disturbances; psychotic individuals have lost contact with reality. 401

puberty This is a period of rapid skeletal and sexual maturation that occurs mainly in early adolescence. 261

punishment This is a consequence that decreases the probability a behavior will occur. 130

pupil This is the opening in the center of the iris; its primary function is to reduce glare in high illumination. 69

Q

questionnaire This is similar to a highly structured interview except that respondents read the questions and mark their answers on paper rather than respond verbally to their interviewer. 22

R

race This term refers to a system for classifying plants and animals into subcategories according to specific physical and structural characteristics. 41

random assignment Psychologists assign subjects to experimental and control conditions by chance, thus reducing the likelihood that the results of the experiment will be due to preexisting differences between the two groups. 26

random sample Every member of a population or group has an equal chance of being selected. 22

range This is the distance between the highest and the lowest score. 537

rape This is forcible sexual intercourse with a person who does not give consent. 323

rational emotive therapy This is based on Ellis' assertion that individuals become psychologically disturbed because of their beliefs, especially those that are irrational and self-defeating. 433

rationalization This is the psychoanalytic defense mechanism that occurs when the real motive for an individual's behavior is not accepted by the ego and is replaced by a sort of cover motive. 366

reaction formation This psychoanalytic defense mechanism occurs when we express an unacceptable impulse by transforming it into its opposite. 367

reality principle This is the Freudian concept by which the ego tries to bring the individual pleasure within the norms of society. 366

reasoning This is the mental activity of transforming information to reach conclusions. 184

recall In this memory measure, an individual must retrieve previously learned information, as on an essay test. 162

recency effect This term refers to superior recall for items at the end of a list. 161

reciprocal socialization This is the process by which children socialize parents, just as parents socialize children. 241

recognition In this memory measure, an individual only has to identify learned items, as on a multiple-choice test. 162

reflexes These are automatic stimulus-response connections. 125

regression This psychoanalytic defense mechanism occurs when we behave in a way characteristic of a previous developmental level. 367

reinforcement (reward) This is a consequence that increases the probability a behavior will occur. 130

reliability This term refers to how consistently a person performs on a test. 197

REM sleep This is a periodic stage of sleep during which daydreaming occurs. 107

repair theory Sleep restores, replenishes, and rebuilds our brains and bodies, which somehow are worn out or used up by the day's waking activities. 108

repression This is the most powerful and pervasive defense mechanism, according to Freud; it works to push unacceptable id impulses out of awareness and back into the unconscious mind. 366

resistance This is the psychoanalytic term for a client's unconscious defense strategies that prevent the analyst from understanding the client's problems. 428

resting potential This is the stable, negative charge of an inactive neuron. 47

retina This is the light-sensitive surface in the back of the eye; it consists of light receptors and various kind of neurons. 69

retinal or binocular disparity This is the perception in which an individual sees a single scene, even though the images on the eyes are slightly different. 87

retroactive interference This is a phenomenon that occurs when material learned later disrupts retrieval of information learned earlier. 164

retrograde amnesia This is memory loss for a segment of the past but not for new events. 165

rites of passage These are ceremonies or rituals that mark an individual's transition from one status to another. 274

rods These receptors in the retina are sensitive to black, white, and gray. 69

roles These are rules and expectations that govern certain positions in a group. 509

romantic love This type of love has strong components of sexuality and infatuation, and it often predominates in the early part of a love relationship. 504

Rorschach Inkblot Test The most well-known projective test, this test uses an individual's perception of inkblots to determine his or her personality. 384

S

sadism This is a psychosexual disorder in which individuals derive sexual gratification from inflicting pain on others. 322

saturation This measure of color is based on the color's purity. 73

scatter plot This is a graph on which pairs of scores are represented. 538

schedules of reinforcement These are timetables that determine when a response will be reinforced. 134

schema This is already existing information, concepts, and events in an individual's memory that influences how the individual interprets new information and knowledge. 166

schizophrenic disorders These are severe psychological disorders characterized by distorted thoughts and perceptions, odd communication, inappropriate emotion, abnormal motor behavior, and social withdrawal. 414

school and educational psychology Those who practice this type of psychology are concerned with children's learning and adjustment in school. They counsel children and parents when children have problems in school and often give psychological tests. 31

science This is a discipline that uses systematic methods to observe, describe, explain, and predict behavior. 5

scientific method This approach to discovering accurate information about mind and behavior includes the following steps: identify and analyze the problem, collect data, draw conclusions, and revise theories. 19

sclera This is the white part of the eye; it helps maintain the shape of the eye and protect it from injury. 69

script This is a schema for an event. 168

secondary prevention In this community psychology concept, screening for early detection of problems, as well as early intervention, is carried out. 439

secondary reinforcement This form of reinforcement acquires its positive value through experience; secondary reinforcers are learned, or conditional, reinforcers. 134

secure attachment Infants use a caregiver as a secure base from which to explore the environment. 237

selective attention This is the focusing of attention on a narrow band of information. 157

self-actualization The highest and most elusive of Maslow's needs, this is the motivation to develop one's full potential as a human being. 337

self-concept A central theme in Rogers' and other humanist views, this refers to individuals' overall perceptions of their abilities, behavior, and personality. 375

self-efficacy This is the belief that one can master a situation and produce positive outcomes. 433

self-help groups These are voluntary organizations of individuals who get together on a regular basis to discuss topics of common interest. 437

self-instructional methods These are cognitive behavior techniques aimed at teaching individuals to modify their own behavior. 433

self-perception theory This theory stresses that individuals make inferences about their attitudes by perceiving their behavior. 491

self-report tests These tests assess personality traits by asking what they are; these tests are not designed to reveal unconscious personality characteristics. 385

semantic memory This is a declarative memory system that describes a person's world knowledge; it appears to be independent of the individual's personal identity with the past. 155

semantics This term refers to the meaning of words and sentences. 188

semicircular canals Located in the inner ear, these canals contain sensory receptors that detect body motion, such as tilting the head or body. 83

sensation This is the process of detecting and encoding stimulus energy in the world. 66

sensorimotor thought Coined by Piaget, this term corresponds to the period of infancy during which an infant constructs an understanding of the world by coordinating sensory experiences with physical actions. 227

sensory adaptation This is a weakened sensitivity to prolonged stimulation. 69

sensory registers These are the initial part of the memory system, in which information from the world is retained in its original sensory form for only an instant, not much longer than the brief time it is exposed to the visual, auditory, and other senses. 153

separation This term refers to self-imposed withdrawal from the larger culture. 463

serial position effect This states that recall is superior for the items at the beginning and at the end of a list. 161

serotonin This neurotransmitter is involved in the regulation of sleep and seems to play a role in depression. 50

set point This term refers to the weight maintained when no effort is made to gain or lose weight. 341

sexually transmitted diseases (STDs) These are diseases that are contracted primarily through sex—intercourse as well as oral-genital and anal-genital sex. 325

shape constancy This is the recognition that an object remains the same even though its orientation changes. 89

shaping This is the process of rewarding approximations of desired behavior. 133

short-term memory This is a limited-capacity memory system in which information is retained for as long as 30 seconds unless the information is rehearsed. 154

situationism This is a view that states that personality often varies considerably from one context to another. 381

size constancy This is the recognition that an object is the same size even though the retinal image of the object changes. 89

sleep apnea This is a sleep disorder in which individuals stop breathing while they are asleep because their windpipe fails to open or brain processes involved in respiration fail to work properly. 109

sleep spindles These brief bursts of higher-frequency waves periodically occur during Stage 2 sleep. 103

social comparison This is the process in which individuals evaluate their thoughts, feelings, behaviors, and abilities in relation to other people. 495

social desirability This term refers to a response in which an individual answers according to what he or she thinks the examiner wants to hear or in a way that makes the individual look better. 385

social exchange theory This theory states that individuals should benefit those who benefit them or that for a benefit received an equivalent benefit should be returned. 501

social identity theory This theory states that, when individuals are assigned to a group, they invariably think of the group as an in-group for them. 511

social learning theory of gender This theory emphasizes that children learn maleness and femaleness by observing and imitating masculine and feminine behavior, as well as through reward and punishments for what is considered appropriate and inappropriate gender behavior. 302

social perception This term refers to our judgment about the qualities of individuals, which involves how we form impressions of others, how we gain self-knowledge from our perception of others, and how we present ourselves to others to influence their perceptions of us. 495

social policy This is the national government's course of action designed to influence the welfare of its citizens. 217

social processes These processes involve changes in an individual's relationship with other people, changes in emotions, and changes in personality. 216

social psychology This branch of psychology deals with people's social interactions, relationships, perceptions, and attitudes. 31, 490

social support This is information and feedback from others that one is loved and cared for, esteemed and valued, and included in a network of communication and mutual obligation. 469

sociobiology This is a contemporary evolutionary view in psychology that states that all behavior is motivated by the desire to contribute one's genetic heritage to the greatest number of descendants. 40

sociocultural approach This approach to psychology emphasizes that culture, ethnicity, and gender are essential to understanding behavior, thought, and emotion. 9

somatic nervous system This consists of sensory nerves that convey information from the skin and muscles to the CNS about such matters as pain and temperature and motor nerves, which inform muscles when to act. 45

somatoform disorders These are mental disturbances in which psychological symptoms take a physical, or somatic, form, even though no physical causes can be found. 406

somatotype theory This is Sheldon's theory stating that precise charts reveal distinct body types, which in turn are associated with certain personality characteristics. 379

somnambulism This is the formal term for sleepwalking. 109

S-O-R model Short for stimulus, organism, response, this model of learning gives some importance to cognitive factors. 140

sound This term refers to vibrations in the air that are processed by our auditory system. 77

special process theory In this theory, hypnotic behavior is different from nonhypnotic behavior. Hypnotic responses elicited by suggestions are involuntary reactions. Dissociations in cognitive systems take place and amnesic barriers are formed. 113

spontaneous recovery (classical conditioning) This is the process by which a conditioned response can recur without further conditioning. 127

standard deviation This is a measure of how much the scores vary on the average around the mean of a sample. 537

standardization This process involves developing uniform procedures for administering and scoring a test, and it also involves developing norms for the test. 197

standardized tests These tests require people to answer a series of written and oral questions. Psychologists then total an individual's scores to yield a single score that reflects something about the individual and can be used to determine how the individual responded relative to others. 23

statistical significance These are the differences observed between two groups that are so large that it is highly unlikely those differences are due merely to chance. 543

statistics These are mathematical methods used to describe, summarize, and draw conclusions about data. 534

stereotype This is a generalization about a group's characteristics that does not take into account any variation from one individual to the next. 510

stimulants These psychoactive drugs increase the central nervous system's activity. 116

storm and stress view This concept, coined by G. Stanley Hall, states that adolescence is a turbulent time charged with conflict and mood swings. 258

stream of consciousness This is a continuous flow of changing sensations, images, thoughts, and feelings. 102

stress This is the response of individuals to the circumstances and events, called stressors, that threaten them and tax their coping abilities. 456

striving for superiority This term emphasizes the human motivation to adapt, improve, and master the environment. 371

subliminal perception This is the perception of stimuli below the threshold of awareness. 68

sublimination This psychoanalytic defense mechanism occurs when a useful course of action replaces a distasteful one. 367

substance-use disorder This disorder is characterized by one or more of the following: psychological dependence, significant impairment of social or occupational functioning attributed to the drug use, and physical dependence that involves serious withdrawal problems. 418

subtractive mixture This term refers to mixing pigments rather than beams of light. 73

superego This is the Freudian structure of personality that is the moral branch of personality. 366

superiority complex This is Adler's concept of exaggerated self-importance to mask feelings of inferiority. 372

syllogism This deductive reasoning task consists of a major premise, a minor premise, and a conclusion. 186

sympathetic nervous system This is the division of the autonomic nervous system that arouses the body. 45

synapses These are tiny gaps between neurons. 48

synchrony This term refers to the carefully coordinated interaction between parent and child in which, often unknowingly, they are attuned to each other's behavior. 241

syntax This involves the way words are combined to form acceptable phrases and sentences. 188

syphilis This is a sexually transmitted disease caused by the bacterium Treponema pallidum. 325

systematic desensitization Based on classical conditioning, this is a method of behavior therapy that treats anxiety by associating deep relaxation with successive visualizations of increasingly intense anxiety-producing situations. 431

T

tardive dyskinesia This neurological disorder is characterized by grotesque, involuntary movements of the facial muscles and mouth, as well as extensive twitching of the neck, arms, and legs. 447

telegraphic speech Characteristic of young children's two- or three-word combinations, this is the use of short and precise words to communicate. 192

telepathy This involves the transfer of thought from one person to another. 95

temporal lobe This portion of the neocortex, just above the ears, is involved in hearing. 54

teratogen This is any agent that causes a birth defect. 220

tertiary prevention This community psychology concept describes efforts to reduce mental health disorders that were not prevented or arrested early in the course of the disorders. 439

testosterone This hormone is associated with the development of genitals, an increase in height, and a change in voice in boys. 261

test-retest reliability A method of assessing reliability, this involves giving the same person the same test on two different occasions. 197

thalamus Seated at the top of the brain stem in the central core of the brain, this structure serves as a relay station. 53

Thematic Apperception Test (TAT) This is an ambiguous projective test designed to elicit stories that reveal something about an individual's personality. 384

theory This is a coherent set of ideas that helps explain data and make predictions. 19

timbres Otherwise known as tone colors, these are what we experience as different qualities of sound. 78

tip-of-the-tongue phenomenon (TOT state) This is a type of effortful retrieval that occurs when people are confident they know something but just can't quite seem to pull it out of memory. 161

token economy In this behavior modification system, behaviors are reinforced with tokens that can be exchanged later for desired rewards. 432

tokenism This term refers to being treated as a representative of a group rather than as an individual. 517

tolerance A greater amount of a drug is needed to produce the same effect. 115

trait theories This theory states that personality consists of broad dispositions, called traits, that tend to lead to characteristic responses. 379

tranquilizers These depressant drugs reduce anxiety and induce relaxation. 116

transcendental meditation (TM) This, the most popular form of meditation in the United States, is derived from an ancient Indian technique and involves using a mantra, which is a resonant sound or phrase repeated mentally or aloud to focus attention. 468

transference This psychoanalytic term describes when a client relates to an analyst in ways that reproduce or relive important relationships in the client's life. 428

transsexualism This is a psychosexual disorder in which an individual has an overwhelming desire to become a member of the opposite sex. 322

transvestism This is a psychosexual disorder in which an individual obtains sexual gratification by dressing up as a member of the opposite sex. 321

triangular theory of love This is Sternberg's belief that love has three main forms: passion, intimacy, and commitment. 506

triarchic theory Sternberg's theory states that intelligence consists of componential intelligence, experiential intelligence, and contextual intelligence. 200

trust versus mistrust Occurring during an infant's first year, this is Erikson's first psychosocial stage. Trust is built when an infant's basic needs are met. 235

two-factor theory Spearman's theory states that individuals have both general intelligence and specific intelligence. 200

Type A behavior pattern This cluster of characteristics—excessively competitive, hard-driven, impatient, and hostile—is thought to be related to the incidence of heart disease. 458

U

unconditional positive regard This is Rogers' term for accepting, valuing, and being positive toward another person regardless of the person's behavior. 375

unconditioned response (UCR) This is an unlearned response that is automatically associated with the UCS. 125

unconditioned stimulus (UCS) This is a stimulus that produces a response without prior learning. 125

unconscious thought (Freudian) This is Freud's concept of a reservoir of unacceptable wishes, feelings, and thoughts that are beyond conscious awareness. 102

undifferentiated schizophrenia This schizophrenic disorder is characterized by disorganized behavior, hallucinations, delusions, and incoherence. 416

V

validity This is the extent to which a test measures what it is intended to measure. 197

variable-interval schedule A response is reinforced after a variable amount of time has elapsed. 134

variable-ratio schedule This is a timetable in which responses are rewarded an average number of times, but on an unpredictable basis. 134

ventromedial hypothalamus (VMH) This is a region of the hypothalamus that plays an important role in controlling hunger. 340

vestibular sense This sense provides information about balance and movement. 82

visual illusion This occurs when two objects produce exactly the same retinal image but are perceived as different images. 90

volley theory This theory accounts for high-frequency tones by arguing that there are teams of neurons, with each neuron on the team firing at a different time. 78

voyeurism This is a psychosexual disorder in which individuals derive sexual gratification by observing the sex organs or sex acts of others, often from a secret vantage point. 322

W

wavelength This is the distance from the peak of one wave to the peak of the next. 69

Weber's law The difference threshold is a constant percentage rather than a constant amount. 68

withdrawal This is the undesirable intense pain and craving of an addictive drug. 115

working memory This concept is used to describe short-term memory as a place for mental work. 154

working memory model In this, the most widely accepted explanation of how sensory registers, short-term memory, and long-term memory interact, long-term comes before short-term, and short-term uses long-term in a variety of flexible ways. 156

Y

Yerkes-Dodson law Performance is best under conditions of moderate arousal. 352

Young-Helmholtz trichromatic theory This is a theory of color vision which states that the retina's cones are sensitive to one of three colors—red, green, or blue. 74

Z

zone of proximal development (ZPD) These are tasks that are too difficult for children to master alone but that can be mastered with the guidance and assistance of adults or more highly skilled children. 223

zygote This is a fertilized egg. 219

REFERENCES

Abel, E. L. (1984). *Fetal alcohol syndrome and fetal alcohol effects*. New York: Plenum.

Aber, L., Allen, L., Mitchell, C., & Seidman, E. (1992, March). *Neighborhood social isolation and adolescent academic achievement: Gender and race-specific patterns and processes*. Paper presented at the meeting of the Society for Research on Adolescence, Washington, DC.

Aboud, F. (1988). *Children and prejudice*. New York: Basil Blackwell.

Abramson, L. Y., Metalsky, G. I., & Alloy, L. B. (1989). Hopelessness depression: A theory-based subtype of depression. *Psychology Review, 96*, 358–372.

Achmon, J., Granek, M., Golomb, M., & Hart, J. (1989). Behavioral treatment of essential hypertension: A comparison between cognitive therapy and biofeedback of heart rate. *Psychosomatic Medicine, 51*, 152–164.

Adelmann, P. K., & Zajonc, R. B. (1989). Facial efference and the experience of emotion. *Annual Review of Psychology, 40*. Palo Alto, CA: Annual Reviews.

Adler, A. (1927). *The theory and practice of individual psychology*. New York: Harcourt Brace and World.

Adler, T. (1991, January). Seeing double? Controversial twins study is widely reported, debated. *APA Monitor, 22*, 1, 8.

Ahlstrom, P. A., Richmond, D., Townsend, C., & D'Angelo, L. (1992, March). *The course of HIV infection in adolescence*. Paper presented at the meeting of the Society for Adolescent Medicine, Washington, DC.

Ainsworth, M. D. S. (1967). *Infancy in Uganda: Infancy care and the growth of love*. Baltimore: Johns Hopkins University Press.

Ainsworth, M. D. S. (1979). Infant-mother attachment. *American Psychologist, 34*, 932–937.

Ainsworth, M. D. S. (1988, August). *Attachments beyond infancy*. Paper presented at the meeting of the American Psychological Association, Atlanta.

Alan Guttmacher Institute. (1981). *Teenage pregnancy: The problem that hasn't gone away*. New York: Alan Guttmacher Institute.

Albee, G. W. (1988). Foreword. In P. A. Bronstein & K. Quina (Eds.), *Teaching a psychology of people: Resources for gender and sociocultural awareness*. Washington, DC: American Psychological Association.

Albert, R. D. (1988). The place of culture in modern psychology. In P. A. Bronstein & K. Quina (Eds.), *Teaching a psychology of people: Resources for gender and sociocultural awareness*. Washington, DC: American Psychological Association.

Albert, R. D., & Triandis, H. C. (1985). Intercultural education for multicultural societies: Critical issues. *International Journal of Intercultural Relations, 9*, 319–337.

Alberti, R. E., & Emmons, M. L. (1986). *Your perfect right* (5th ed.). San Luis Obispo, CA: Impact.

Alcock, J. E. (1989). *Science and supernature: A critical appraisal of parapsychology*. Buffalo, NY: Prometheus.

Aldefer, C. P. (1986). An intergroup perspective on group dynamics. In J. Lorsch (Ed.), *Handbook of organizational behavior*. Englewood Cliffs, NJ: Prentice-Hall.

Aldrich, M. S. (1989). Cardinal manifestations of sleep disorders. In M. H. Dryger, T. Roth, & W. C. Dement (Eds.), *Principles and practice of sleep medicine*. San Diego: Harcourt Brace Jovanovich.

Al-Issa, I. (1982a). Does culture make a difference in psychopathology? In I. Al-Issa (Ed.), *Culture and psychopathology*. Baltimore: University Park Press.

Al-Issa, I. (1982b). Sex differences in psychopathology. In I. Al-Issa (Ed.), *Culture and psychopathology*. Baltimore: University Park Press.

Allen, L., & Majidi-Ahi, S. (1989). Black American children. In J. T. Gibbs & L. N. Huang (Eds.), *Children of color*. San Francisco: Jossey-Bass.

Allen, L., & Mitchell, C. M. (in press). *Poverty and adolescent health*. Paper prepared for the U.S. Congress, Office of Technology Assessment.

Allport, G. W. (1937). *Personality: A psychological interpretation*. New York: Holt.

Allred, K. D., & Smith, T. W. (1989). The hardy personality: Cognitive and physiological responses to evaluative threat. *Journal of Personality and Social Psychology, 56*, 257–266.

Amaro, H., & Russo, N. F. (1987). Hispanic women and mental health: An overview of contemporary issues in research and practice. *Psychology of Women Quarterly, 11*, 393–407.

Amaro, H., Russo, N. F., & Johnson, J. (1987). Family and work predictors of psychological well-being among Hispanic women professionals. *Psychology of Women Quarterly, 11*, 505–521.

Amato, P. R., & Keith, B. (1991). Parental divorce and adult well-being: A meta-analysis. *Journal of Marriage and the Family, 53*, 43–58.

American College Health Association. (1989, May). *Survey of AIDS on American college and university campuses*. Washington, DC: American College Health Association.

Ames, C., & Ames, R. (Eds.). (1989). *Research on motivation in education* (Vol. 3). San Diego: Academic Press.

Amoore, J. E. (1970). *Molecular basis of odor*. Springfield, IL: Charles C Thomas.

Anastasi, A. (1988). *Psychological testing* (6th ed.). New York: Macmillan.

Anderson, B. L. (1983). Primary orgasmic dysfunction: Diagnostic considerations and a review of treatment. *Psychological Bulletin, 93,* 105–136.

Anderson, E. A., & Leslie, L. A. (1991). Coping with employment and family stress: Employment arrangement and gender differences. *Sex Roles, 24,* 223–237.

Anderson, J. R. (1990). *Cognitive psychology and its implications* (3rd ed.). New York: W. H. Freeman.

Anderson, N. (1991, August). *Sociodemographic aspects of hypertension in African Americans: A research agenda for health psychology.* Paper presented at the meeting of the American Psychological Association, San Francisco.

Anderson, N. H. (1965). Primacy effects in personality impression formation using a generalized order effect paradigm. *Journal of Personality and Social Psychology, 2,* 1–9.

Andreasen, N. C. (1991). Schizophrenia and related disorders in DSM-IV. *Schizophrenia Bulletin, 17,* 25–26.

Andres, R. (1989). Does the "best" body weight change with age? In A. J. Stunkard & A. Baum (Eds.), *Perspectives in behavioral medicine.* Hillsdale, NJ: Erlbaum.

Anson, C. A. (1988). *Atlanta's adopt-a-student project.* William T. Grant Foundation Annual Report, New York.

Aponte, H. (1979). Family therapy and the community. In M. S. Gibbs, J. R. Lachenmeyer, & J. Sigel (Eds.), *Community psychology: Theoretical and empirical approaches.* New York: Gardner.

Armsden, G. G., & Greenberg, M. T. (1984). *The inventory of parent and peer attachment: Individual differences and their relationship to psychological well-being in adolescence.* Unpublished manuscript, University of Washington.

Aronson, E. (1986, August). *Teaching students things they think they already know all about: The case of prejudice and desegregation.* Paper presented at the meeting of the American Psychological Association, Washington, DC.

Aronson, E. (1992). *The social animal* (6th ed.). New York: W. H. Freeman.

Asher, J., & Garcia, R. (1969). The optimal age to learn a foreign language. *Modern Language Journal, 53,* 334–341.

Asher, S. R., & Parker, J. G. (in press). The significance of peer relationship problems in childhood. In B. H. Schneider, G. Attili, J. Nadel, & R. P. Weisberg (Eds.), *Social competence in developmental perspective.* Amsterdam: Kluwer.

Asian Week. (1990, June 29). *Poll finds racial tension decreasing,* p. 4.

Atchley, R. C. (1989). Demographic factors and adult psychological development. In K. W. Schaie & C. Schooler (Eds.), *Social structure and aging.* Hillsdale, NJ: Erlbaum.

Atkinson, D. R., Morten, G., & Sue, D. W. (1989). *Counseling American minorities: A cross-cultural perspective* (3rd ed.). Dubuque, IA: Wm. C. Brown.

Atkinson, J. W., & Raynor, I. O. (1974). *Motivation and achievement.* Washington, DC: V. H. Winston & Sons.

Atkinson, R. C., & Shiffrin, R. M. (1968). Human memory: A proposed system and its control processes. In K. W. Spence (Eds.), *The psychology of learning and motivation* (Vol. 2). New York: Academic Press.

Avis, H. (1990). *Drugs and life.* Dubuque, IA: Wm. C. Brown.

Baars, B. J. (1989). *A cognitive theory of consciousness.* New York: Cambridge University Press.

Baca Zinn, M. (1980). Employment and education of Mexican-American women: The interplay of modernity and ethnicity in eight families. *Harvard Educational Review, 50,* 47–62.

Bachman, J., O'Malley, P., & Johnston, L. (1978). *Youth in transition. Vol. VI, Adolescence to adulthood—Change and stability of the lives of young men.* Ann Arbor: Institute of Social Research, University of Michigan.

Bachman, J. G. (1991). Dropouts, school. In R. M. Lerner, A. C. Petersen, & J. Brooks-Gunn (Eds.), *Encyclopedia of adolescence* (Vol. 1). New York: Garland.

Bach y Rita, G. (1982). The Mexican-American religion and cultural influences. In R. M. Bacera, M. Karno, & J. Escobar (Eds.), *Mental health and Hispanic Americans: Clinical perspectives.* New York: Grune & Stratton.

Baddeley, A. D. (1986). *Working memory.* Oxford, England: Clarendon.

Baddeley, A. D. (1990). *Human memory: Theory and research.* Boston: Allyn & Bacon.

Baddeley, A. D. (1992). Working memory. *Science, 255,* 556–560.

Baddeley, A. D., Bressi, S., Della Sala, S., Logie, R., & Spinnler, H. (in press). Working memory. *Brain.*

Bagley, C. (1984). The social aetiology of schizophrenia in immigrant groups. In J. E. Mezzich & C. E. Berganza (Eds.), *Culture and psychopathology.* New York: Columbia University Press.

Bahr, S. J. (1989). Prologue: A developmental overview of the aging family. In S. J. Bahr & E. T. Peterson (Eds.), *Aging and the family.* Lexington, MA: Lexington.

Bahrick, H. P., Bahrick, P. O., & Wittlinger, R. P. (1975). Fifty years of memory for names and faces: A cross-sectional approach. *Journal of Experimental Psychology: General, 104,* 54–75.

Bakai, D. A. (1992). *Psychology and health* (2nd ed.). New York: Springer.

Baker, R. (Ed.). (1992). *Panic disorder.* New York: John Wiley.

Ball, W., & Tronick, E. (1971). Infant responses to impending collision: Optical and real. *Science, 171,* 818–820.

Baltes, P. B., & Baltes, M. M. (Eds.). (in press). *Successful aging.* New York: Cambridge University Press.

Bandarage, A. (1986). Women of color: Toward a celebration of power. *Women of Power, 4,* 8–14.

Bandura, A. (1965). Influence of models' reinforcement contingencies on the acquisition of imitative responses. *Journal of Personality and Social Psychology, 1,* 589–595.

Bandura, A. (1971). *Social learning theory.* New York: General Learning.

Bandura, A. (1977). *Social learning theory.* Englewood Cliffs, NJ: Prentice-Hall.

Bandura, A. (1986). *Social foundations of thought and action: A social cognitive theory.* Englewood Cliffs, NJ: Prentice-Hall.

Bandura, A. (1989). Social cognitive theory. In R. Vasta (Ed.), *Six theories of child development.* Greenwich, CT: JAI.

Bandura, A., Blanchard, E. B., & Ritter, B. (1969). Relative efficacy of desensitization of modeling approaches for inducing behavioral, affective, and attitudinal changes. *Journal of Personality and Social Psychology, 13,* 173–199.

Barber, B. L., & Eccles, J. S. (1992). Long-term influence of divorce and single parenting on adolescent family- and work-related values, behaviors, and aspirations. *Psychological Bulletin, 111,* 108–126.

Barber, T. X., & Wilson, S. C. (1977). Hypnosis suggestions, and altered states of consciousness: Experimental evaluation of a new cognitive behavioral theory and the traditional trance-state theory of "hypnosis." *Annals of the New York Academy of Sciences, 296,* 34–47.

Bard, P. (1934). Emotion. In C. Murchison (Ed.), *Handbook of general experimental psychology.* Worcester, MA: Clark University Press.

Barlow, D. H., Blaachard, E. B., Vermilyea, J. A., Vermilyea, B. B., & Dimardo, P. A. (1986). Generalized anxiety and generalized anxiety disorder: Description and reconceptualization. *American Journal of Psychiatry, 143,* 40–44.

Barnard, E. A., & Darlison, M. G. (1989). Neurotransmitter-activated ionic channels. *Annual Review of Physiology, 50.* Palo Alto, CA: Annual Reviews.

Barnard, C., & Lentz, G. (1992). Making diversity a reality within our profession. *Journal of Career Planning and Employment, 27,* 30–35.

Barnouw, V. (1963). *Culture and personality.* Homewood, IL: Dorsey.

Baron, R. A., & Byrne, D. (1987). *Social psychology* (5th ed.). Boston: Allyn & Bacon.

Barron, F. (1989, April). The birth of a notion: Exercises to tap your creative potential. *Omni,* pp. 112–119.

Barry, H., Child, I. L., & Bacon, M. K. (1959). Relation of child training to subsistence economy. *American Anthropologist, 61,* 51–63.

Bartlett, F. C. (1932). *Remembering.* Cambridge, England: Cambridge University Press.

Bartley, S. H. (1969). *Principles of perception.* New York: Harper & Row.

Baruch, C. (1991, April). *The influence of the mother-child relationship on the emergence of symbolic play.* Paper presented at the biennial meeting of the Society for Research in Child Development, Seattle.

Baruch, G. K., Barnett, R. C., & Rivers, C. (1985). *Lifeprints: New patterns of love and work for today's women.* New York: Signet.

Baruch, G. K., Biener, L., & Barnett, R. C. (1987). Women and gender in research on work and family. *American Psychologist, 42,* 130–136.

Basoglu, M., Yetkin, N., Sercan, M., & Karaduman, B. (1986). Patterns of attrition for psychological and pharmacological treatment of male sexual dysfunction: Implications for sex therapy and cross-cultural perspectives. *Sexual and Marital Therapy, 1,* 179–189.

Bass, D. M., Bowman, K., & Noelker, L. S. (1991). The influence of caregiving and bereavement support on adjusting to an older relative's death. *The Gerontologist, 31,* 31, 32–41.

Batson, C. D., Bolen, M. H., Cross, J. A., & Jeuringer-Benefiel, H. E. (1986). Where is the altruism in the altruistic personality? *Journal of Personality and Social Psychology, 50,* 212–220.

Bauer, G. P., & Mills, J. A. (1989). Use of transference in the here and now: Patient and therapist resistance. *Psychotherapy, 26,* 112–119.

Baumeister, R. F. (1989). *Masochism and the self.* Hillsdale, NJ: Erlbaum.

Baumrind, D. (1971). Current patterns of parental authority. *Developmental Psychology Monographs, 4* (1, Pt. 2).

Baumrind, D. (1989a). Parenting styles and adolescent development. In J. Brooks-Gunn, R. Lerner, & A. C. Petersen (Eds.), *The encyclopedia of adolescence.* New York: Garland.

Baumrind, D. (1989b, April). *Sex-differentiated socialization effects in childhood and adolescence.* Paper presented at the biennial meeting of the Society for Research in Child Development, Kansas City, MO.

Baumrind, D. (in press). Effective parenting during the early adolescent transition. In P. A. Cowan & E. M. Hetherington (Eds.), *Advances in family research* (Vol. 2). Hillsdale, NJ: Erlbaum.

Beals, D. E., & De Temple, J. (1991, April). *Reading, reporting, and repast: Three R's for co-constructing language and literacy skills.* Paper presented at the Society for Research in Child Development meeting, Seattle.

Beck, A. (1976). *Cognitive therapies and the emotional disorders.* New York: International Universities Press.

Beck, A. T. (1967). *Depression.* New York: Harper & Row.

Beck, A. T., & Haaga, D. A. F. (1992). The future of cognitive therapy. *Psychotherapy, 29,* 34–38.

Beckwith, L., & Howard, J. (1991, April). *Development of toddlers exposed prenatally to PCP and cocaine.* Paper presented at the Society for Research in Child Development meeting, Seattle.

Beilin, H. (1989). Piagetian theory. In R. Vasta (Ed.), *Six theories of child development: Revised formulations and current issues.* Greenwich, CT: JAI.

Beitman, B. D., Goldfried, M. R., & Norcross, J. C. (1989). The movement toward integrating the psychotherapies: An overview. *American Journal of Psychiatry, 146,* 138–147.

Belenky, M. F., Clinchy, B. M., Goldberger, N. R., & Tarule, J. M. (1986). *Women's ways of knowing.* New York: Basic.

Bell, A. P., & Weinberg, M. S. (1978). *Homosexualities.* New York: Simon & Schuster.

Bell, A. P., Weinberg, M. S., & Mammersmith, S. K. (1981). *Sexual preference: Its development in men and women.* New York: Simon & Schuster.

Bell, D. (1990). Poverty and women's mental health. *American Psychologist, 45,* 385–389.

Bellack, A. S., & Hersen, M. (Eds.). (1988). *Behavioral assessment.* Elmsford, NY: Pergamon.

Bellack, A. S., Morrison, R. L., & Meuser, K. T. (1989). Social problem-solving in schizophrenia. *Schizophrenia Bulletin, 15,* 101–116.

Belle, D. (1987). Gender differences in the social moderators of stress. In R. C. Barnett, L. Biener, & G. K. Barusch (Eds.), *Gender and stress.* New York: Free Press.

Belle, D. (1988). *Women's mental health research agenda: Poverty.* Rockville, MD: National Institute of Mental Health.

Belle, D. (1990). Poverty and women's mental health. *American Psychologist, 45,* 385–389.

Belle, D., & Burr, R. (1992, March). *The afterschool experiences of young people: A contextual and longitudinal analysis.* Paper presented at the meeting of the Society for Research on Adolescence, Washington, DC.

Belle, D., Burr, R., Shadmon, O., Woodbury, A., Heffernan, M., & Ozer, D. (1991, April). *Unsupervised after-school time, social support, and children's well-being.* Paper presented at the Society for Research in Child Development meeting, Seattle.

Belle, D., Longfellow, C., Makosky, V., Saunder, E., & Zelkowitz, P. (1981). Income, mothers' mental health, and family functioning in a low-income population. In American Academy of Nursing, *The impact of changing resources on health policy.* Kansas City, MO: American Nurses' Association.

Bell-Scott, P., & Taylor, R. L. (1989). Introduction: The multiple ecologies of Black adolescent development. *Journal of Adolescent Research, 4,* 119–124.

Belmont, J. M. (1989). Cognitive strategies and strategic learning: The socio-instructional approach. *American Psychologist, 44,* 142–148.

Belsky, J. (1989a, April 2). *Conversation hour: Day care research today.* Biennial meeting of the Society for Research in Child Development, Kansas City, MO.

Belsky, J. (1989b). Infant-parent attachment and day care: In defense of the strange situation. In J. S. Lande, S. Scarr, & N. Gunzenhauser (Eds.), *Caring for children: Challenge to America.* Hillsdale, NJ: Erlbaum.

Bem, D. J. (1967). Self-perception: An alternative interpretation of cognitive dissonance phenomena. *Psychological Review, 74,* 183–200.

Bem, S. L. (1977). On the utility of alternative procedures for assessing psychological androgyny. *Journal of Consulting and Clinical Psychology, 45,* 196–205.

Bem, S. L. (1981). Gender schema theory: A cognitive account of sex-typing. *Psychological Review, 88,* 354–364.

Benbow, C. P. (1990). Sex differences in mathematical reasoning among the intellectually talented: Further thoughts. *Behavioral and Brain Sciences, 13,* 196–198.

Benbow, C. P. (1992). Academic achievement in mathematics and science of students between ages 13 and 23: Are there differences in the top one percent of mathematical ability? *Journal of Educational Psychology, 84,* 51–61.

Benbow, C. P., & Stanley, J. C. (1983). Sex differences in mathematical reasoning ability: More facts. *Science, 222,* 1029–1031.

Benet, S. (1976). *How to live to be 100.* New York: Dial.

Bennett, W. I., & Gurin, J. (1982). *The dieter's dilemma: Eating less and weighing more.* New York: Basic.

Ben Porath, Y. S., & Butcher, J. N. (in press). The psychometric stability of rewritten MMPI items. *Journal of Personality Assessment.*

Berk, S. F. (1985). *The gender factory: The apportionment of work in American households.* New York: Plenum.

Berndt, T. J. (1979). Developmental changes in conformity to peers and parents. *Developmental Psychology, 15,* 608–616.

Berndt, T. J., & Perry, T. B. (1990). Distinctive features and effects of early adolescent friendships. In R. Montemayor (Ed.), *Advances in adolescent research.* Greenwich, CT: JAI.

Bernstein, I. L. (1991). Aversion conditioning in response to cancer and cancer treatment. *Clinical Psychology Review, 11,* 185–191.

Berry, J. (1969). On cross-cultural comparability. *International Journal of Psychology, 4,* 119–128.

Berry, J. W. (1967). Independence and conformity in subsistence level societies. *Journal of Personality and Social Psychology, 7,* 415–418.

Berry, J. W. (1971). Ecological and cultural factors in spatial perceptual development. *Canadian Journal of Behavioral Science, 3,* 324–336.

Berry, J. W. (1980). Introduction to methodology. In H. C. Triandis & J. W. Berry (Eds.), *Handbook of cross-cultural psychology: Methodology* (Vol. 2). Boston: Allyn & Bacon.

Berry, J. W. (1983). Textured contexts: Systems and situations in cross-cultural psychology. In S. H. Irvine & J. W. Berry (Eds.), *Human assessment and cultural factors.* New York: Plenum.

Berry, J. W. (1990). Psychology of acculturation: Understanding individuals moving between cultures. In R. W. Brislin (Eds.), *Applied cross-cultural psychology.* Newbury Park, CA: Sage.

Berry, J. W., & Bennett, J. A. (1992). Cree conceptions of cognitive competence. *International Journal of Psychology, 27,* 73–88.

Berry, J. W., & Kim, U. (1988). Acculturation and mental health. In P. R. Dasen, J. W. Berry, & N. Sartorius (Eds.), *Health and cross-cultural psychology: Toward applications.* Newbury Park, CA: Sage.

Berry, J. W., Poortinga, Y. H., Segall, M. H., & Dasen, P. R. (in press). *Cross-cultural psychology: Theory, method, and applications.* Cambridge, England: Cambridge University Press.

Berscheid, E. (1988). Some comments on love's anatomy: Or, whatever happened to old-fashioned lust? In R. J. Sternberg & M. L. Barnes (Eds.), *Anatomy of love.* New Haven: Yale University Press.

Berscheid, E., & Fei, J. (1977). Sexual jealousy and romantic love. In G. Clinton & G. Smith (Eds.), *Sexual jealousy.* Englewood Cliffs, NJ: Prentice-Hall.

Berscheid, E., Snyder, M., & Omoto, A. M. (1989). Issues in studying close relationships: Conceptualizing and measuring closeness. In C. Hendrick (Ed.), *Close relationships.* Newbury Park, CA: Sage.

Bertelson, A. (1979). A Danish twin study of manic-depressive disorders. In M. Schous & E. Stromgren (Eds.), *Origin, prevention, and treatment of affective disorders.* Orlando, FL: Academic Press.

Berwish, N. J., & Amsterdam, J. D. (1989). An overview of investigational antidepressants. *Psychosomatics, 30,* 1–14.

Betz, N. (1992). Career development. In F. L. Denmark & M. A. Paludi (Eds.), *Handbook on the psychology of women.* Westport, CT: Greenwood.

Betz, N., & Fitzgerald, L. F. (1987). *The career psychology of women.* New York: Academic Press.

Betz, N. E. (1989). Contemporary issues in testing use. In C. E. Watkins & V. L. Campbell (Eds.), *Testing in counseling practice.* Hillsdale, NJ: Erlbaum.

Bexton, W. H., Heron, W., & Scott, T. H. (1954). Effects of decreased variation in the sensory environment. *Canadian Journal of Psychology, 8,* 70–76.

Bianchi, S. M., & Spani, D. (1986). *American women in transition.* New York: Russell Sage Foundation.

Billings, A. G., Cronkite, R. C., & Moos, R. H. (1983). Social environment factors in unipolar depression. *Journal of Abnormal Psychology, 92,* 119–133.

Blackmore, S. (1987). A report of a visit to Carl Sargent's laboratory. *Journal of the Society for Psychical Research, 54,* 186–198.

Blair, S. N. (1989, February). [Personal communication.] Dallas, TX: The Aerobics Institute.

Blair, S. N. (1990, January). [Personal communication.] Dallas, TX: The Aerobics Institute.

Blanchard-Fields, F., & Robinson, S. (1987, April). *Controllability and adaptive coping from adolescence through older adulthood.* Paper presented at the biennial meeting of the Society for Research in Child Development, Baltimore.

Blanck, P. D., Buck, R., & Rosenthal, R. (Eds.). (1986). *Nonverbal communication in the clinical context.* University Park: Pennsylvania State University Press.

Block, R. W. (1992). Chemical dependency in the adolescent. In D. E. Greydanus & M. L. Wolraich (Eds.), *Behavioral pediatrics.* New York: Springer-Verlag.

Bloom, B. (1975). *Changing patterns of psychiatric care.* New York: Human Science.

Bloom, B. L. (1985). *Community mental health: A general introduction* (2nd ed.). Monterey, CA: Brooks/Cole.

Bloom, F. E., Lazerson, A., & Hofstadter, L. (1985). *Brain, mind, and behavior.* New York: W. H. Freeman.

Bloome, C. (1989). *Classrooms and literacy.* Norwood, NJ: Ablex.

Bloor, C., & White, F. (1983). Unpublished manuscript, University of California at San Diego.

Blos, P. (1989). The inner world of the adolescent. In A. H. Esman (Ed.), *International annals of adolescent psychiatry.* Chicago: University of Chicago Press.

Blount, B. G. (1982). Culture and the language of socialization: Parental speech. In D. A. Wagner & H. W. Stevenson (Eds.), *Cultural perspectives on child development.* San Francisco: W. H. Freeman.

Blount, W. R., & Dembo, R. (1984). Personal drug use and attitudes toward prevention among youth living in a high risk environment. *Journal of Drug Education, 14,* 207–224.

Blumstein, P., & Schwartz, P. (1983). *American couples: Money, work, sex.* New York: William Morrow.

Bogatz, G., & Ball, S. (1972). *Reading with television: An evaluation of the Electric Company.* Princeton, NJ: Educational Testing Service.

Bohannon, J. N. III, & Stanowicz, L. (1988). The issue of negative evidence: Adult responses to children's language errors. *Developmental Psychology, 24,* 684–689.

Bornstein, M. H., & Krasnegor, N. A. (1989). *Stability and continuity in mental development.* Hillsdale, NJ: Erlbaum.

Boston Women's Health Book Collective. (1984). *The new our bodies, ourselves.* New York: Simon & Schuster.

Boston Women's Health Book Collective. (1987). *Ourselves growing older.* New York: Simon & Schuster.

Bouchard, T. J., Heston, L., Eckert, E., Keyes, M., & Resnick, S. (1981). The Minnesota Study of Twins Reared Apart: Project description and sample results in the developmental domain. *Twin Research, 3,* 227–233.

Bower, G. H., Clark, M., Winzenz, D., & Lesgold, A. (1969). Hierarchical retrieval schemes in recall of categorized word lists. *Journal of Verbal Learning and Verbal Behavior, 3*, 323–343.

Bowers, T. G., & Clum, G. A. (1988). Relative contribution of specific and nonspecific treatment effects: Meta-analysis of placebo-controlled behavior therapy research. *Psychological Bulletin, 103*, 315–323.

Bowlby, J. (1969). *Attachment and loss* (Vol. 1). London: Hogarth.

Bowlby, J. (1980). *Attachment and loss. Vol. 3. Loss, sadness, and depression.* New York: Basic.

Bowlby, J. (1988). *Secure attachment.* New York: Basic.

Bowlby, J. (1989). *Secure attachment.* New York: Basic.

Boyd-Franklin, N. (1989). *Black families in therapy: A multisystems approach.* New York: Guilford.

Boyer, C. B., & Hein, K. (1991). AIDS and HIV infection in adolescents: The role of education and antibody testing. In R. M. Lerner, A. C. Petersen, & J. Brooks-Gunn (Eds.), *Encyclopedia of adolescence* (Vol. 1). New York: Garland.

Boynton, R. M. (1989). Color vision. *Annual Review of Psychology, 39*. Palo Alto, CA: Annual Reviews.

Bransford, J. D., Franks, J. J., Vye, N. J., & Sherwood, R. D. (1989). Multiple analogies for complex concepts. In S. Vosniadou & A. Ortony (Eds.), *Similarity and analogical reasoning.* New York: Cambridge University Press.

Bransford, J. D., & Stein, B. S. (1984). *The ideal problem solver.* New York: W. H. Freeman.

Braun, B. G. (1988). *The treatment of multiple personality disorder.* Washington, DC: American Psychiatric Press.

Brean, H. (1958, March 31). What hidden sell is all about. *Life*, pp. 104–114.

Bredekamp, S. (1987). Developmentally appropriate practice in early childhood programs for 4- and 5-year-olds. *Young Children, 41*, 20–29.

Brehm, J. W., & Self, E. A. (1989). The intensity of motivation. *Annual Review of Psychology, 40*. Palo Alto, CA: Annual Reviews.

Breier, A., Charney, D. S., & Heninger, G. R. (1986). Agoraphobia with panic attacks. *Archives of General Psychiatry, 43*, 1029–1036.

Breland, K., & Breland, M. (1961). The misbehavior of organisms. *Psychologist, 16*, 681–684.

Brent, D. A. (1989). Suicide and suicidal behavior in children and adolescents. *Pediatrics in Review, 10*, 269–275.

Brewer, M. B., & Campbell, D. T. (1976). *Ethnocentrism and intergroup attitudes.* New York: Wiley.

Brickman, P., Coates, D., & Janoff-Bulman, R. J. (1978). Lottery winners and accident victims: Is happiness relative? *Journal of Personality and Social Psychology, 36*, 917–927.

Briggs, J. L. (1970). *Never in anger.* Cambridge, MA: Harvard University Press.

Brigham, J. C. (1986). Race and eyewitness identifications. In S. Worschel & W. G. Austin (Eds.), *Psychology of intergroup relations.* Chicago: Nelson-Hall.

Brigham, J. C. (1989, August). *Assessing the fairness of police lineups.* Paper presented at the meeting of the American Psychological Association, New Orleans.

Brigham, J. C., Maas, A., Snyder, L. D., & Spaulding, K. (1982). Accuracy of eyewitness identification in a field setting. *Journal of Personality and Social Psychology, 41*, 683–691.

Brislin, R. W. (1981). *Cross-cultural encounters.* New York: Pergamon.

Brislin, R. W. (1987). Increasing awareness of class, ethnicity, culture, and race by expanding on students' own experiences. In *The G. Stanley Hall Lecture Series* (Vol. 8). Washington, DC: American Psychological Association.

Brislin, R. W. (1990). Applied cross-cultural psychology: An introduction. In R. W. Brislin (Ed.), *Applied cross-cultural psychology.* Newbury Park, CA: Sage.

Brislin, R. W. (1991, August). *Directions in cross-cultural psychology.* Paper presented at the meeting of the American Psychological Association, San Francisco.

Brobeck, J. R., Tepperman, T., & Long, C. N. (1943). Experimental hypothalamic hyperphagia in the albino rat. *Yale Journal of Biological Medicine, 15*, 831–853.

Brody, N. (1992). *Intelligence* (2nd ed.). San Diego: Academic Press.

Brone, R. J., & Fisher, C. B. (1988). Determinants of adolescent obesity: A comparison with anorexia nervosa. *Adolescence, 23*, 155–169.

Bronfenbrenner, U. (1989, April). *The developing ecology of human development.* Paper presented at the biennial meeting of the Society for Research in Child Development, Kansas City.

Bronstein, P. (1988). Marital and parenting roles in transition: An overview. In P. Bronstein & C. P. Cowan (Eds.), *Fatherhood today.* New York: Wiley.

Bronstein, P. A., & Paludi, M. (1988a). The introductory course from a broader perspective. In P. A. Bronstein & M. Paludi (Eds.), *Teaching a psychology of people.* Washington, DC: American Psychological Association.

Bronstein, P. A., & Paludi, M. (1988b). *The introductory psychology course from a broader perspective.* Washington, DC: American Psychological Association.

Bronstein, P. A., & Quina, K. (1988). Perspectives on gender balance and cultural diversity in the teaching of psychology. In P. A. Bronstein & K. Quina (Eds.), *Teaching a psychology of people: Resources for gender and sociocultural awareness.* Washington, DC: American Psychological Association.

Brooks-Gunn, J. (1991). Maturational timing variations in adolescent girls, antecedents of. In R. M. Lerner, A. C. Petersen, & J. Brooks-Gunn (Eds.), *Encyclopedia of adolescence.* New York: Garland.

Brooks-Gunn, J. (1992, March). *Revisiting theories of "storm and stress": The role of biology.* Paper presented at the meeting of the Society for Research on Adolescence, Washington, DC.

Broverman, I., Broverman, D., Clarkson, F., Rosenkrantz, P., & Vogel, S. (1970). Sex-role stereotypes and clinical judgements of mental health. *Journal of Consulting and Clinical Psychology, 34*, 1–7.

Broverman, I., Vogel, S., Broverman, D., Clarkson, F., & Rosenkranz, P. (1972). Sex-role stereotypes: A current appraisal. *Journal of Social Issues, 28*, 59–78.

Brown, D. R., & Gary, L. E. (1985). Social support network differentials among married and nonmarried black females. *Psychology of Women Quarterly, 9*, 229–241.

Brown, E., Deffenbacher, K., & Sturgill, W. (1977). Memory for faces and the circumstances of encounter. *Journal of Applied Psychology, 6*, 311–318.

Brown, G., Bhrolchain, M., & Harris, T. (1975). Social class and psychiatric disturbance among women in an urban population. *Sociology, 9*, 225–254.

Brown, G. R., & Collier, L. (1989). Transvestites' women revisited: A nonpatient sample. *Archives of Sexual Behavior, 18*, 73–84.

Brown, J. D. (1991). Staying fit and staying well: Physical fitness as a moderator of life stress. *Journal of Personality and Social Psychology, 60*, 555–561.

Brown, J. D., & Siegel, J. D. (1988). Exercise as a buffer of life stress: A prospective study of adolescent health. *Health Psychology, 7*, 341–353.

Brown, J. K. (1985). Introduction. In J. K. Brown & V. Kerns (Eds.), *In her prime: A new view of middle-aged women.* South Hadley, MA: Bergin & Garvey.

Brown, L. (1989). New voice, new visions. Toward a lesbian/gay paradigm for psychology. *Psychology of Women Quarterly, 13*, 445–458.

Brown, L. (1992). [Interview]. In M. A. Paludi, *The psychology of women*. Dubuque, IA: Wm. C. Brown.

Brown, L. M., & Gilligan, C. (1990, March). *The psychology of women and the development of girls*. Paper presented at the meeting of the Society for Research on Adolescence, Atlanta.

Brown, L. S., & Brodsky, A. M. (1992). The future of feminist therapy. *Psychotherapy, 29,* 51–57.

Brown, R. (1973). *Language: The early stage*. Cambridge, MA: Harvard University Press.

Brown, R. (1986). *Social psychology* (2nd ed.). New York: Free Press.

Brown, R. (1988). Development of a first language in the human species. In M. B. Franklin & S. S. Barten (Eds.), *Child language: A reader*. New York: Oxford University Press.

Brownell, K. D. (1991). Dieting and the search for the perfect body: Where physiology and culture collide. *Behavior Therapy, 22,* 1–12.

Bruess, C. E., & Richardson, G. E. (1992). *Decisions for health* (3rd ed.). Dubuque, IA: Wm. C. Brown.

Brumberg, J. J. (1988). *Fasting girls: The emergence of anorexia nervosa as a modern disease*. Cambridge, MA: Harvard University Press.

Buenker, J. D., & Ratner, L. (Eds.). (1992). *Multiculturalism in the United States: A comparative guide to acculturation and ethnicity*. Westport, CT: Greenwood.

Burgess, K. (1968). The behavior and training of a killer whale (Orcinus orca) at San Diego Sea World. *International Zoo Yearbook, 8,* 202–205.

Burgio, L. D., & Burgio, K. L. (1986). Behavioral gerontology: Application of behavioral methods to the problem of older adults. *Journal of Applied Behavior Analysis, 19,* 321–328.

Burts, D. C., Charlesworth, R., & Fleege, P. O. (1991, April). *Achievement of kindergarten children in developmentally appropriate and developmentally inappropriate classrooms*. Paper presented at the Society for Research in Child Development meeting, Seattle.

Buss, D. M., & Barnes, M. (1986). Preferences in human mate selection. *Journal of Personality and Social Psychology, 50,* 559–570.

Buss, D. M., & others. (1990). International preferences in selecting mates: A study of 37 cultures. *Journal of Cross-Cultural Psychology, 21,* 5–47.

Butcher, J. N., Dahlstrom, W. G., Graham, J. R., Tellegen, A., & Kaemmer, B. (1989). *Manual for the restandardized Minnesota Multiphasic Personality Inventory (MMPI-2): An administrative and interpretive guide*. Minneapolis: University of Minnesota Press.

Butcher, J. N., Graham, J. R., Williams, C. L., & Ben Porath, Y. S. (1990). *Innovations in MMPI interpretation and research: Development and use of the MMPI-2 content scales*. Minneapolis: University of Minnesota.

Butler, G., Fennell, M., Robson, P., & Gelder, M. (1991). Comparison of behavior therapy and cognitive behavior therapy in the treatment of generalized anxiety disorder. *Journal of Consulting and Clinical Psychology, 59,* 167–175.

Butler, R. A. (1953). Discrimination learning by rhesus monkeys to visual-exploration motivation. *Journal of Comparative and Physiological Psychology, 46,* 95–98.

Byrnes, J. P. (1988a). Formal operations: A systematic reformulation. *Developmental Review, 8,* 66–87.

Caldwell, B. (1964). The effects of infant care. In M. Hoffman & L. Hoffman (Eds.), *Review of child development research* (Vol. 1). New York: Russell Sage.

Caldwell, B. (1991, October). *Impact on the child*. Paper presented at the symposium on day care for children, Arlington.

Camara, E. G., & Danao, T. C. (1989). The brain and immune system: A psychosomatic network. *Psychosomatics, 30,* 140–146.

Cameron, N. (1963). *Personality development and psychopathology*. Boston: Houghton Mifflin.

Campbell, D. T., & LeVine, R. A. (1968). Ethnocentrism and intergroup relations. In R. Abelson & others (Eds.), *Theories of cognitive consistency: A sourcebook*. Chicago: Rand McNally.

Cannon, W. B. (1927). The James-Lange theory of emotions: A critical examination and an alternative theory. *American Journal of Psychology, 39,* 106–124.

Cantor, K. P., Weiss, S. H., Goedert, J. J., & Battjes, R. J. (1991). HTLV-I/II seroprevalence and HIV/HTLV coinfection among U.S. intravenous drug users. *Journal of Acquired Immune Deficiency Syndromes, 4,* 460–467.

Carlson, J. G., & Hatfield, E. (1989). *Psychology of emotion*. Belmont, CA: Wadsworth.

Carnegie Corporation. (1989). *Turning points: Preparing youth for the 21st century*. New York: Carnegie Corporation.

Carpenter, P. A., & Just, M. A. (1981). Cognitive processes in reading: Models based on readers' eye fixations. In A. M. Lesgold & C. A. Perfetti (Eds.), *Interactive processes in reading*. Hillsdale, NJ: Erlbaum.

Carraher, T. H., & Carraher, D. W. (1981). Do Piagetian stages describe the reasoning of the unschooled adults? *Quarterly Newsletter of the Laboratory of Comparative Human Cognition, 3,* 61–68.

Carrasquillo, A. L. (1991). *Hispanic children and youth in the United States*. New York: Garland.

Carson, R. C. (1989). Personality. *Annual Review of Psychology, 40*. Palo Alto, CA: Annual Reviews.

Carter, D. B., & Levy, G. D. (1988). Cognitive aspects of children's early sex-role development: The influence of gender schemas on preschoolers' memories and preference for sex-typed toys and activities. *Child Development, 59,* 782–793.

Carter, D. B., & Taylor, R. D. (in press). The development of children's awareness and understanding of flexibility in sex-role stereotypes: Implications for preferences, attitude, and behavior. *Sex Roles*.

Cartwright, R. D. (1978). *A primer on sleep and dreaming*. Reading, MA: Addison-Wesley.

Cartwright, R. D. (1989). Dreams and their meaning. In M. H. Dryger, T. Roth, & W. C. Dement (Eds.), *Principles and practice of sleep medicine*. San Diego: Harcourt Brace Jovanovich.

Case, R. (1991). Advantages and disadvantages of the neo-Piagetian position. In R. Case (Ed.), *The mind's staircase*. Hillsdale, NJ: Erlbaum.

Casper, R. C. (1989). Psychodynamic psychotherapy in acute anorexia nervosa and acute bulimia nervosa. In A. H. Esman (Ed.), *International annals of adolescent psychiatry*. Chicago: University of Chicago Press.

Castro, F. G., & Magaña, D. (1988). A course in health promotion in ethnic minority populations. In P. A. Bronstein & K. Quina (Eds.), *Teaching a psychology of people*. Washington, DC: American Psychological Association.

Catania, A. C. (1990, March). *The significance of nonhuman research in the analysis of human behavior*. Paper presented at the Eastern Psychological Association, Philadelphia.

Cayleff, S. E. (1986). Ethical issues in counseling gender, races, and culturally distinct groups. *Journal of Counseling and Development, 64,* 345–347.

Cervantes, R. C. (1987). Hispanics in psychology. In P. J. Woods & C. S. Wilkinson (Eds.), *Is psychology the major for you?* Washington, DC: American Psychological Association.

Chance, P. (1979). *Learning and behavior*. Belmont, CA: Wadsworth.

Charles A. Dana Foundation Report. (1988, Spring). *Dana award winner's innovations in educating minority students in math and science attract nationwide attention*. New York: The Charles A. Dana Foundation.

Charlesworth, R., Hart, C. H., Burts, D. C., & Hernandez, S. (in press). Kindergarten teachers' beliefs and practices. *Early Child Development and Care*.

Chase-Lansdale, P. L., & Hetherington, E. M. (1990). The impact of divorce on life-span development: Short- and long-term effects. In P. B. Baltes, D. L. Featherman, & R. M. Lerner (Eds.), *Life-span development and behavior*. Hillsdale, NJ: Erlbaum.

Chen, C., & Stevenson, H. W. (1989). Homework: A cross-cultural comparison. *Child Development, 60*, 551–561.

Children's Defense Fund. (1990). *Children 1990*. Washington, DC: Children's Defense Fund.

Chiriboga, D. A. (1982). Adaptation to marital separation in later and earlier life. *Journal of Gerontology, 37*, 109–114.

Chodorow, N. J. (1978). *The reproduction of mothering*. Berkeley: University of California Press.

Chodorow, N. J. (1989). *Feminism and psychoanalytic theory*. New Haven, CT: Yale University Press.

Chomsky, N. (1957). *Syntactic structure*. The Hague: Mouton.

Cialdini, R. B., Schaller, M., Houlihan, D., Arps, K., Pultz, J., & Beaman, A. L. (1987). Empathy based helping: Is it selflessly or selfishly motivated? *Journal of Personality and Social Psychology, 52*, 749–758.

Clark, D. A., & Beck, A. T. (1989). Cognitive theory and therapy of anxiety and depression. In P. C. Kendall & D. Watson (Eds.), *Anxiety and depression*. San Diego: Academic Press.

Clark, E. V. (1983). Meanings and concepts. In P. H. Mussen (Ed.), *Handbook of child psychology* (4th ed., Vol. 3). New York: Wiley.

Clark, J. M., & Paivio, A. (1989). Observational and theoretical terms in psychology: A cognitive perspective on scientific language. *American Psychologist, 44*, 513–524.

Clark, K. (1965). *Dark ghetto*. New York: Harper.

Clark, K. B. (1991, August). *Brown versus Board of Education: Then and now*. Paper presented at the meeting of the American Psychological Association, San Francisco.

Clark, K. B., & Clark, M. P. (1939). The development of self and the emergence of racial identification in Negro preschool children. *Journal of Social Psychology, 10*, 591–599.

Clarke-Stewart, K. A. (1989). Infant day care: Maligned or malignant? *American Psychologist, 44*, 266–273.

Coe, W. C. (1989, August). *Perspectives on psychological hypnosis*. Conversation hour at the meeting of the American Psychological Association, New Orleans.

Cogwill, D. O. (1974). Aging and modernization: A revision of theory. In J. Gubrium (Ed.), *Late life*. Springfield, IL: Charles C Thomas.

Cohen, A. (1992). Prognosis for schizophrenia in the third world: A reevaluation of cross-cultural research. *Culture, Medicine, and Psychiatry, 16*, 53–75.

Cohen, F. (1979). Personality, stress, and development of physical illness. In G. S. Stone, F. Cohen, & N. E. Adler (Eds.), *Health psychology*. San Francisco: Jossey-Bass.

Cohen, G. (1989). *Memory in the real world*. Hillsdale, NJ: Erlbaum.

Cohen, L. A. (1987, November). Diet and cancer. *Scientific American*, pp. 128–137.

Cohen, S., & Williamson, G. M. (1991). Stress and infectuous disease in humans. *Psychological Bulletin, 109*, 5–24.

Colby, A., Kohlberg, L., Gibbs, J., & Lieberman, M. (1983). A longitudinal study of moral judgment. *Monographs of the Society for Research in Child Development* (Serial No. 201).

Cole, M. (1992). Culture and cognitive development: From cross-cultural comparisons to model systems of cultural mediation. In A. F. Healy, S. M. Kosslyn, & E. M. Shiffrin (Eds.), *From learning processes to cognitive processes*. Hillsdale, NJ: Erlbaum.

Cole, M., & Cole, S. R. (1989). *The development of children*. New York: W. H. Freeman.

Coles, C. D., Platzman, K. A., & Smith, I. E. (1991, April). *Substance abuse and neonates: Alcohol and cocaine effects*. Paper presented at the Society for Research in Child Development meeting, Seattle.

Coles, R. (1986). *The political life of children*. Boston: Little, Brown.

Comas-Díaz, L. (1992). The future of psychotherapy with ethnic minorities. *Psychotherapy, 29*, 88–94.

Comer, J. P. (1988). Educating poor minority children. *Scientific American, 259*, 42–48.

Committee for Economic Development. (1987). *Children in need: Investment strategies for the educationally disadvantaged*. Washington, DC: Committee for Economic Development.

Compas, B. (1989, April). *Vulnerability and stress in childhood and adolescence*. Paper presented at the biennial meeting of the Society for Research in Child Development, Kansas City.

Condry, J. C. (1989). *The psychology of television*. Hillsdale, NJ: Erlbaum.

Conti-Ramsden, G., & Snow, C. E. (Eds.). (1991). *Children's language* (Vol. 7). Hillsdale, NJ: Erlbaum.

Coombs, R. H. (1991). Marital status and personal well-being: A literature review. *Family Relations, 40*, 97–102.

Cooper, C. R., & Ayers-Lopez, S. (1985). Family and peer systems in early adolescence: New models of the role of relationships in development. *Journal of Early Adolescence, 5*, 9–22.

Cooper, C. R., Baker, H., Polichar, D., & Welsh, M. (1992, March). *Ethnic perspectives on individuality and connectedness in adolescents' relationships with families and peers*. Paper presented at the meeting of the Society for Research on Adolescence, Washington, DC.

Cooper, C. R., & Grotevant, H. D. (1989, April). *Individuality and connectedness in the family and adolescents' self and relational competence*. Paper presented at the biennial meeting of the Society for Research in Child Development, Kansas City.

Cooper, C. R., Grotevant, H. D., Moore, M. S., & Condon, S. M. (1982, August). *Family support and conflict: Both foster adolescent identity and role taking*. Paper presented at the meeting of the American Psychological Association, Washington, DC.

Cooper, K. (1970). *The new aerobics*. New York: Bantam.

Coopersmith, S. (1967). *The antecedents of self-esteem*. New York: W. H. Freeman.

Coren, S., & Girus, J. S. (1972). Illusion decrement in interacting lines and figures. *Psychonomic Science, 26*, 108–110.

Coren, S., & Ward, I. M. (1989). *Sensation and perception*. San Diego: Harcourt, Brace, Jovanovich.

Corless, I. B., & Pittman-Lindemann, M. (1989). *AIDS: Principles, practices, and politics*. New York: Hemisphere.

Cortes, J. B., & Gatti, F. M. (1970, April). Physique and propensity. *Psychology Today*, pp. 42–44.

Costa, P. T. (1988, August). *Personality, continuity and the changes of adult life*. Paper presented at the American Psychological Association, Atlanta.

Costa, P. T., Zonderman, A. B., McCrea, R. R., Cormon-Humtely, J., Locke, B. Z., & Barbeno, H. E. (1987). Longitudinal analyses of psychological well-being in a national sample: Stability and mean levels. *Journal of Gerontology, 42*, 50–55.

Costin, F., & Draguns, J. G. (1989). *Abnormal psychology*. New York: Wiley.

Cowan, P. A. (1988). Becoming a father: A time of change, an opportunity for development. In P. Bronstein & C. P. Cowan (Eds.), *Fatherhood today*. New York: Wiley.

Cowley, G. (1988, May 23). The wisdom of animals. *Newsweek*, pp. 52–58.

Craighead, L. W., & Blum, M. D. (1989). Supervised exercise in behavioral treatment for moderate obesity. *Behavior Therapy, 20*, 49–59.

Craik, F. I. M. (1989). On the making of episodes. In H. L. Roediger & F. I. M. Craik (Eds.), *Varieties of memory and consciousness.* Hillsdale, NJ: Erlbaum.

Craik, F. I. M., & Lockhart, R. S. (1972). Levels of processing: A framework for memory research. *Journal of Verbal Learning and Verbal Behavior, 11,* 671–684.

Craik, F. I. M., & Tulving, E. (1975). Depth of processing and retention of words in episodic memory. *Journal of Experimental Psychology: General, 104,* 268–294.

Crick, M. (1977). *Explorations in language and meaning: Toward a scientific anthropology.* New York: Halstead.

Crisafi, M. A., & Driscoll, J. M. (1991, April). *Developmental outcome in very low birth-weight infants at three years of age.* Paper presented at the Society for Research in Child Development meeting, Seattle.

Crosby, F. (1991). *Juggling: The unexpected advantages of balancing career and home for women and their families.* New York: Free Press.

Cross, W. C., & Maldonado, B. (1971). The counselor, the Mexican American, and the stereotype. *Elementary School Guidance and Counseling, 6,* 27–31.

Cross, W. E. (1972). The Negro-to-Black conversion experience. *Black World, 20,* 13–27.

Culbertson, F. M. (1991, August). *Mental health of women: An international journey.* Paper presented at the meeting of the American Psychological Association, San Francisco, CA.

Cummins, J. (1983). Bilingualism and special education: Program and pedagogical issues. *Learning Disability Quarterly, 6,* 373–386.

Curtiss, S. (1977). *Genie.* New York: Academic Press.

Cushner, K. (1990). Cross-cultural psychology and the formal classroom. In R. W. Brislin (Ed.), *Applied cross-cultural psychology.* Newbury Park: CA: Sage.

Cutrona, C. E. (1982). Transition to college: Loneliness and the process of social adjustment. In L. A. Peplau & D. Perlman (Eds.), *Loneliness: A sourcebook of current theory, research and therapy.* New York: Wiley.

Dallenbach, K. M. (1927). The temperature spots and end-organs. *American Journal of Psychology, 52,* 331–347.

D'Andrade, R. G., & Strauss, C. (1992). *Human motives and cultural models.* New York: Cambridge University Press.

d'Ansia, G. I. D. (1989). Familial analysis of panic disorder and agoraphobia. *Journal of Affective Disorders, 17,* 1–8.

Darley, J. M., & Latané, B. (1968). Bystander intervention in emergencies: Diffusion of responsibility. *Journal of Personality and Social Psychology, 8,* 377–383.

Darling, C. A., Kallon, D. J., & Van Duesen, J. E. (1984). Sex in transition, 1900–1984. *Journal of Youth and Adolescence, 13,* 385–399.

Darwin, C. (1859). *On the origin of species.* London: John Murray.

Darwin, C. (1872/1965). *The expression of the emotions in man and animals.* Chicago: University of Chicago Press.

Dasen, P. R. (1977). Are cognitive processes universal? A contribution to cross-cultural Piagetian psychology. In N. Warran (Ed.), *Studies in cross-cultural psychology* (Vol. 1). London: Academic Press.

Dasen, P. R., Ngini, L., & Lavalée, M. (1979). Cross-cultural training studies of concrete operations. In L. H. Eckenberger, W. J. Lonner, & Y. H. Poortinga (Eds.), *Cross-cultural contributions to psychology.* Boston: Allyn & Bacon.

Datan, N. (1989). Aging women: The silent majority. *Women's Studies Quarterly,* 12–19.

Davis, K. E. (1985, February). Near and dear: Friendship and love compared. *Psychology Today,* pp. 22–29.

Dawkins, M. S. (1990). From an animal's point of view. *Behavioral and Brain Sciences, 13,* 1–8.

DeAngelis, T. (1990, June). House child-care bill ignores quality issue. *APA Monitor,* p. 21.

DeFour, D. C., & Paludi, M. (1991, August). *Ethnicity, sex, and sexual harassment.* Paper presented at the meeting of the American Psychological Association, San Francisco.

DeFour, D. C., & Paludi, M. A. (in press). Integrating scholarship on ethnicity into the psychology of women course. *Teaching of Psychology.*

de Jong-Gierveld, J. (1987). Developing and testing a model of loneliness. *Journal of Personality and Social Psychology, 53,* 119–128.

Dement, W. C. (1976). *Some must watch while some must sleep.* New York: Doubleday.

Denmark, F. L. (1991, August). *The psychology of women: Examining the past—predicting the future.* Paper presented at the meeting of the American Psychological Association, San Francisco.

Denmark, F. L., & Paludi, M. A. (Eds.). (in press). *Handbook on the psychology of women.* Westport, CT: Greenwood.

Denmark, F. L., Russo, N. F., Frieze, I. H., & Sechzur, J. (1988). Guidelines for avoiding sexism in psychological research: A report of the Ad Hoc Committee on nonsexist research. *American Psychologist, 43,* 582–585.

Denton, R. K. (1988). Lucidity, sex, and horror in Senoi dreamwork. In J. Gackenbach & S. P. LaBerge (Eds.), *Conscious mind, sleeping brain: Perspectives on lucid dreaming.* New York: Plenum.

DePaulo, B. M. (1992). Nonverbal behavior and self-presentation. *Psychological Bulletin, 111,* 203–243.

Depression/Awareness, Recognition, and Treatment (D/ART) Publication Series. (1987). *Sex differences in depressive disorders.* Washington, DC: U.S. Dept. of Health and Human Services, NIMH.

Depue, R. A., Krauss, S., Spoont, M. R., & Arbisi, P. (1989). General behavior inventory identification of unipolar and bipolar affective conditions in a nonclinical university population. *Journal of Abnormal Psychology, 98,* 117–126.

Deregowski, J. (1980). *Illusions, patterns, and pictures: A cross-cultural perspective.* London: Academic Press.

Deregowski, J. B. (1970). Effect of cultural value of time upon recall. *British Journal of Social and Clinical Psychology, 9,* 37–41.

de Rivera, J. (1989). Choice of emotion and ideal development. In L. Cirillo, B. Kaplan, & S. Wapner (Eds.), *Emotions in ideal human development.* Hillsdale, NJ: Erlbaum.

Deutsch, F. M. (1991). Women's lives: The story not told by theories of development. *Contemporary Psychology, 36,* 237–238.

Deutsch, J. A., & Gonzales, M. F. (1980). Gastric nutrient content signals satiety. *Behavioral and Neural Biology, 30,* 113–116.

Deutsch, M. (Ed.). (1967). *The disadvantaged child: Selected papers of Martin Deutsch and his associates.* New York: Basic.

DeVault, M. L. (1987). Doing housework: Feeding and family life. In N. Gerstel & H. E. Gross (Eds.), *Families and work.* Philadelphia: Temple University Press.

Devine, P. G. (1989). Stereotypes and prejudice: Their automatic and controlled components. *Journal of Personality and Social Psychology, 56,* 5–18.

Diamond, E. E. (1988). Women's occupational plans and decisions: An introduction. *Applied Psychology: An International Review, 37,* 97–102.

Dickerscheid, J. D., Schwarz, P. M., Noir, S., & El-Taliawy, T. (1988). Gender concept development of preschool-aged children in the United States and Egypt. *Sex Roles, 18,* 669–677.

Dickinson, D. K., & Moreton, Jr. (1991, April). *Predicting specific kindergarten literacy skills from three-year-olds' preschool experiences.* Paper presented at the Society for Research in Child Development meeting, Seattle.

Diener, E. (1984). Subjective well-being. *Psychological Bulletin, 95,* 542–575.

Dienstbier, R. A. (1989). Arousal and physiological toughness: Implications for mental health. *Psychological Review, 96,* 84–100.

Dies, R. R. (1992). The future of group therapy. *Psychotherapy, 29,* 58–64.

Dietz, W. (1986, March). *Comments at the workshop on childhood obesity.* Washington, DC: National Institutes of Health.

DiGiulio, R. C. (1989). *Beyond widowhood.* New York: Free Press.

Dinges, D. F. (1989). The influence of the human circadian timekeeping system on sleep. In M. H. Dryger, T. Roth, & W. C. Dement (Eds.), *Principles and practice of sleep medicine.* San Diego: Harcourt Brace Jovanovich.

DiNicola, D. D., & DiMatteo, M. R. (1984). Practitioners, patients, and compliance with medical regimens: A social psychological perspective. In A. Baum, S. E. Taylor, & J. E. Singer (Eds.), *Handbook of psychology and health* (Vol. 4). Hillsdale, NJ: Erlbaum.

Dixon, S. D. (1991, April). *Infants exposed perinatally to cocaine or methaamphetamine demonstrate behavioral and neurophysiologic changes.* Paper presented at the Society for Research in Child Development meeting, Seattle.

Dohrenwend, B. S., & Shrout, P. E. (1985). "Hassles" in the conceptualization and measurement of life stress variables. *American Psychologist, 40,* 780–785.

Dolnick, E. (1988, December). The right (left) stuff. *Omni,* p. 45.

Domhoff, G. W. (1985). *The mystique of dreams.* Berkeley: University of California Press.

Donat, P. L. N., & D'Emilio, J. D. (1992). A feminist redefinition of rape and sexual assault: Historical foundations and change. *Journal of Social Issues, 48,* 9–22.

Donnerstein, E. (1980). Aggressive erotica and violence against women. *Journal of Personality and Social Psychology, 39,* 269–277.

Donnerstein, E. (1987, May). *Pornography, sex, and violence.* Invited presentation, University of Texas at Dallas.

Dornbusch, S. M., Carlsmith, J. M., Bushwall, S. J., Ritter, P. I., Leidman, P. H., Hastorf, A. H., & Gross, R. T. (1985). Single parents, extended households, and the control of adolescents. *Child Development, 56,* 326–341.

Dovidio, J. F., & Gaertner, S. L. (Eds.). (1986). *Prejudice, discrimination, and racism.* New York: Academic Press.

Dowd, J. J., & Bengston, V. L. (1978). Aging in minority populations: An examination of the double jeopardy hypothesis. *Journal of Gerontology, 30,* 584–593.

Doyle, J. A., & Paludi, M. A. (1991). *Sex and gender: The human experience* (2nd ed.). Dubuque, IA: Wm. C. Brown.

Doyne, E. J., Ossip-Klein, D. J., Bowman, E. D., Osborne, K. M., McDougall-Wilson, I. B., & Neimeyer, R. A. (1987). Running versus weight lifting in the treatment of depression. *Journal of Consulting and Clinical Psychology, 55,* 748–754.

Draguns, J. G. (1980). Psychological disorders of clinical severity. In H. C. Triandis & J. G. Draguns (Eds.), *Handbook of cross-cultural psychology* (Vol. 6). Boston: Allyn & Bacon.

Draguns, J. G. (1990). Applications of cross-cultural psychology in the field of mental health. In R. W. Brislin (Ed.), *Applied cross-cultural psychology.* Newbury Park, CA: Sage.

Dreyer, P. H. (1982). Sexuality during adolescence. In B. B. Wolman (Ed.), *Handbook of developmental psychology.* Englewood Cliffs, NJ: Prentice-Hall.

Driscoll, J. W., & Bateson, P. (1988). Animals in behavioral research. *Animal Behavior, 36,* 1569–1574.

Dryden, W., & Trower, P. (Eds.). (1989). *Cognitive psychotherapy.* New York: Springer.

Dryfoos, J. G. (1992, March). *Integrating services for adolescents: The community schools.* Paper presented at the meeting of the Society for Research on Adolescence, Washington, DC.

Duckworth, J. C. (1989). The Minnesota Multiphasic Personality Inventory. In C. E. Watkins & V. L. Campbell (Eds.), *Testing in counseling practice.* Hillsdale, NJ: Erlbaum.

Duke, D. L., & Canady, R. L. (1991). *School policy.* New York: McGraw-Hill.

Dutton, D., & Aron, A. (1974). Some evidence for heightened sexual attraction under conditions of high anxiety. *Journal of Personality and Social Psychology, 30,* 510–517.

Eagly, A. H., & Crowley, M. (1986). Gender and helping behavior: A meta-analytic review of the social psychological literature. *Psychological Bulletin, 100,* 283–308.

Ebata, A. T., & Moos, R. H. (1989, April). *Coping and adjustment in four groups of adolescents.* Paper presented at the biennial meeting of the Society for Research in Child Development, Kansas City.

Eccles, J. S. (1987). Gender roles and achievement patterns: An expectancy value perspective. In J. M. Reinisch, L. A. Rosenblum, & S. A. Sanders (Eds.), *Masculinity/femininity: Basic perspectives.* New York: Oxford University Press.

Eccles, J. S. (1991). Academic achievement. In R. M. Lerner, A. C. Petersen, & J. Brooks-Gunn (Eds.), *Encyclopedia of adolescence* (Vol. 1). New York: Garland.

Eccles, J. S., Harold-Goldsmith, R., & Miller, C. R. (1989, April). *Parents' stereotyping beliefs about gender differences in adolescence.* Paper presented at the biennial meeting of the Society for Research in Child Development, Kansas City, MO.

Eccles, J. S., & Harold, R. (1991, April). *Influences on, and consequences of, parents' beliefs regarding their children's abilities and interests.* Paper presented at the Society for Research in Child Development meeting, Seattle.

Eccles, J. S., & Hoffman, L. W. (1984). Sex roles, socialization, and occupational behavior. In H. W. Stevenson & A. E. Siegel (Eds.), *Research in child development and public policy* (Vol. 1). Chicago: University of Chicago Press.

Eckert, E. D., Heston, L. L., & Bouchard, T. J. (1981). MZ twins reared apart: Preliminary findings of psychiatric disturbances and traits. In L. Gedda, P. Paris, & W. D. Nance (Eds.), *Twin research* (Vol. 1). New York: Alan Liss.

Edelman, M. W. (1987). *Families in peril.* Cambridge, MA: Harvard University Press.

Edelman, M. W. (1992). *The measure of our success: A letter to my children and yours.* Boston: Beacon.

Edmonds, M. Mc. (1990). The health of the black aged female. In Z. Harel, E. A. McKinney, & M. Williams (Eds.), *Black aged.* Newbury Park, CA: Sage.

Edwards, B. (1979). *Drawing on the right side of the brain.* Los Angeles: J. P. Farcher.

Edwards, H. (1990). The sociology of sport. In J. E. Farley (Ed.), *Sociology.* Englewood Cliffs, NJ: Prentice-Hall.

Edwards, J. R., & Baglioni, A. J. (1991). Relation between Type A behavior pattern and mental and physical symptoms: A comparison of global and component measures. *Journal of Applied Psychology, 76,* 276–290.

Efron, R. (in press). *The decline and fall of hemispheric specialization.* Hillsdale, NJ: Erlbaum.

Egeland, B., & Farber, E. (1984). Infant-mother attachment: Factors related to its development and changes over time. *Child Development, 55,* 753–771.

Ehrhardt, A. A. (1987). A transactional perspective on the development of gender differences. In J. M. Reinisch, L. A. Rosenblum, & S. A. Sanders (Eds.), *Masculinity/femininity: Basic perspectives.* New York: Oxford University Press.

Eich, E. (1989). Theoretical issues in state-dependent memory. In H. L. Roediger & F. I. M. Craik (Eds.), *Varieties of memory and consciousness.* Hillsdale, NJ: Erlbaum.

Eich, E. (1990, June). *Searching for mood dependent memory.* Paper presented at the meeting of the American Psychological Society, Dallas.

Eichorn, D. H., Clausen, J. A., Hass, N., Honzik, M. P., & Messen, P. H. (Eds.). (1981). *Present and past in middle life.* New York: Academic Press.

Ekman, P. (1980). *The face of man.* New York: Garland STPM.

Ekman, P. (1985). *Telling lies: Clues to deceit in the marketplace, politics, and marriage.* New York: W. W. Norton.

Ekman, P., & Friesen, W. V. (1968). The repertoire of nonverbal behavior—Categories, origins, usage and coding. *Semiotica, 1*, 49–98.

Ekman, P., & Friesen, W. V. (1971). Constants across cultures in the face and emotion. *Journal of Personality and Social Psychology, 17*, 124–129.

El-Islam, F. (1969). Depression and guilt: A study at an Arab psychiatric centre. *Social Psychiatry, 4*, 56–58.

Elkind, D. (1978). Understanding the young adolescent. *Adolescence, 13*, 127–134.

Elkind, D. (1981). *The hurried child.* Reading, MA: Addison-Wesley.

Ellis, A. (1962). *Reason and emotion in psychotherapy.* New York: Lyle Stuart.

Ellis, A. (1974). *Growth through reason.* Hollywood: Wilshire.

Ellis, A. (1992). My early experiences in developing the practice of psychology. *Professional Psychology, 23*, 7–10.

Ellis, A., & Yeager, R. J. (1989). *Why some therapies don't work.* Buffalo, NY: Prometheus.

Ellis, H. C. (1987). Recent developments in human memory. In V. P. Maksosky (Ed.), *The G. Stanley Hall Lecture Series.* Washington, DC: American Psychological Association.

Ellis, H. C., Thomas, R. L., & Rodriguez, I. A. (1984). Emotional mood states and memory: Elaborative encoding, semantic processing, and cognitive effort. *Journal of Experimental Psychology: Learning, Memory, and Cognition, 10*, 470–482.

Ellis, L., & Ames, M. A. (1987). Neurohormonal functioning and sexual orientation: A theory of homosexuality-heterosexuality. *Psychological Bulletin, 101*, 233–258.

Emmerich, W., Goldman, K. S., Kirsch, B., & Sharabany, R. (1977). Evidence for a transitional phase in the development of gender constancy. *Child Development, 48*, 930–936.

Engdahl, B. E., Speed, N., Eberly, R. E., & Schwartz, J. (1991). Comorbidity of psychiatric disorders and personality profiles of American World War II prisoners of war. *The Journal of Nervous and Mental Disease, 179*, 181–187.

Engel, J. W. (1984). Marriage in the People's Republic of China: Analysis of a new law. *Journal of Marriage and the Family, 46*, 947–954.

Ennis, R. H. (1987). Critical thinking skills. In J. B. Baron & R. J. Sternberg (Eds.), *Teaching thinking skills: Theory and practice.* New York: W. H. Freeman.

Entwisle, D. R. (1990). Schools and the adolescent. In S. S. Feldman & G. R. Elliott (Eds.), *At the threshold: The developing adolescent.* Cambridge, MA: Harvard University Press.

Epstein, C. F. (1987). Multiple demands and multiple roles: The conditions of successful management. In F. J. Crosby (Ed.), *Spouse, parent, worker: On gender and multiple roles.* New Haven, CT: Yale University Press.

Epstein, S., & Meier, P. (1989). Constructive thinking: A broad coping variable with specific components. *Journal of Personality and Social Psychology, 57*, 332–350.

Erben, R. (1991). Health challenges for the year 2000: Health promotion and AIDS. *Health Education Quarterly, 18*, 29–37.

Erickson, P. I., & Rapkin, A. J. (1991). Unwanted sexual experiences among middle and high school youth. *Journal of Adolescent Health, 12*, 319–325.

Erikson, E. H. (1950). *Childhood and society.* New York: W. W. Norton.

Erikson, E. H. (1968). *Identity: Youth and crisis.* New York: W. W. Norton.

Essed, P. (1992). *Understanding everyday racism.* Newbury Park, CA: Sage.

Evans, B. J., & Whitfield, J. R. (Eds.). (1988). *Black males in the United States: An annotated bibliography from 1967 to 1987.* Washington, DC: American Psychological Association.

Evans, M. E. (1992, March). *Achievement and achievement-related beliefs in Asian and Western contexts: Cultural and gender differences.* Paper presented at the meeting of the Society for Research on Adolescence, Washington, DC.

Evans, P. (1989). *Motivation and emotion.* New York: Routledge.

Eysenck, H. J. (1952). The effects of psychotherapy: An evaluation. *Journal of Consulting Psychology, 16*, 319–324.

Eysenck, H. J. (1967). *The biological basis of personality.* Springfield, IL: Charles C Thomas.

Fabrega, H. (1989). An ethnomedical perspective of Anglo-American psychiatry. *American Journal of Psychiatry, 146*, 588–596.

Farley, F. (1986, August). *Assessment of Type T personality: Implications for intervention and wellness.* Paper presented at the meeting of the American Psychological Association, Washington, DC.

Fasick, F. A. (1988). Patterns of formal education in high school as rites of passage. *Adolescence, 23*, 457–468.

Faulkner, L. R., McFarland, B. H., & Bloom, J. D. (1989). An empirical study of emergency commitment. *American Journal of Psychiatry, 146*, 182–186.

Feierman, J. R. (1990). *Pedophilia: Biosocial dimensions.* New York: Springer-Verlag.

Feingold, A. (1988). Cognitive gender differences are disappearing. *American Psychologist, 43*, 95–103.

Feist, J., & Brannon, L. (1989). *An introduction to behavior and health.* Belmont, CA: Wadsworth.

Feldman, S. S., & Elliott, G. R. (1990). Progress and promise of research on normal adolescent development. In S. S. Feldman & G. Elliott (Eds.), *At the threshold: The developing adolescent.* Cambridge, MA: Harvard University Press.

Ferguson, C. A. (1977). Baby talk as a simplified register. In C. E. Snow & C. A. Ferguson (Eds.), *Talking to children.* New York: Cambridge University Press.

Ferguson, D. M., Harwood, L. J., & Shannon, F. T. (1987). Breast feeding and subsequent social adjustment in six to eight year old children. *Journal of Child Psychology and Psychiatry, 28*, 378–386.

Ferrini, A. F. (1989). *Health in the later years.* Dubuque, IA: Wm. C. Brown.

Ferron, R. (1991, August). *Current issues in the lives of American Indian women.* Paper presented at the meeting of the American Psychological Association, San Francisco.

Feshbach, S., & Weiner, B. (1986). *Personality* (2nd ed.). Lexington, MA: D. C. Heath.

Festinger, L. (1954). A theory of social comparison processes. *Human Relations, 7*, 117–140.

Festinger, L. (1957). *A theory of cognitive dissonance.* Evanston, IL: Row Peterson.

Fine, T. H., & Turner, J. S. (1985). REST-assisted relaxation and chronic pain. In J. J. Sanchez-Sosa (Ed.), *Health and clinical psychology.* New York: Elsevier.

Fine, T. H., & Turner, J. W. (1987). *Proceedings of the Second International Conference on REST.* Toledo, OH: IRIS.

Fischer, J., & Gochros, H. L. (1975). *Planned behavior change.* New York: Free Press.

Fish, T. A., & Rye, B. J. (1991). Attitudes toward a homosexual or heterosexual person with AIDS. *Journal of Applied Psychology, 21*, 651–667.

Fisher, C. B., & Brone, R. J. (1991). Eating disorders in adolescence. In R. M. Lerner, A. C. Petersen, & J. Brooks-Gunn (Eds.), *Encyclopedia of adolescence* (Vol. 1). New York: Garland.

Fisher, J. D., & Fisher, W. A. (1992). Changing AIDS-risk behavior. *Psychological Bulletin, 111*, 455–474.

Fisher, R. P., & Quigley, K. L. (1989, August). *The cognitive interview, person description, and person recognition.* Paper presented at the meeting of the American Psychological Association, New Orleans.

Fisher, S., & Greenberg, R. P. (Eds.). (1989). *The limits of biological treatments for psychological distress.* Hillsdale, NJ: Erlbaum.

Flaskerud, J. (1984). A comparison of perceptions of problematic behavior by six minority groups and mental health professionals. *Nursing Research, 33,* 190–228.

Flavell, J. H. (1985). *Cognitive development* (2nd ed.). Englewood Cliffs, NJ: Prentice-Hall.

Foa, E. B., Olasov, B., & Steketze, G. S. (1987, September). *Treatment of rape victims.* Paper presented at the conference, State of the Art in Sexual Assault, Charleston.

Foa, E. B., Rothbaum, B. O., & Kozak, M. J. (1989). Behavioral treatments for anxiety and depression. In P. C. Kendall & D. Watson (Eds.), *Anxiety and depression.* San Diego: Academic Press.

Foa, E. B., Steketze, G., & Young, M. C. (1984). Agoraphobia. *Clinical Psychology Review, 4,* 431–457.

Fodor, I. G., & Franks, V. (1990). Women in midlife and beyond: The new prime of life? *Psychology of Women Quarterly, 14,* 445–449.

Foley, V. (1975). Family therapy with black disadvantaged families: Some observations on roles, communications, and techniques. *Journal of Marriage and Family Counseling, 1,* 29–38.

Foner, N. (1984). *Ages in conflict.* New York: Columbia University Press.

Fonnebo, V. (1985). The Tormso heart study: Coronary risk factors in Seventh-Day Adventists. *American Journal of Epidemiology, 112,* 789–793.

Ford, C., & Beach, F. (1951). *Patterns of sexual behavior.* New York: Harper.

Ford, M. E. (1992). *Motivating humans.* Newbury Park, CA: Sage.

Forsyth, B. W. C., Leventhal, J. M., & McCarthy, P. L. (1985). Mothers' perceptions of feeding and crying behaviors. *American Journal of Diseases of Children, 139,* 269–272.

Fowers, B. J. (1991). His and her marriage: A multivariate study of gender and marital satisfaction. *Sex Roles, 24,* 209–222.

Fowler, C. A., Wolford, G., Slade, R., & Tassinary, L. (1981). Lexical access with and without awareness. *Journal of Experimental Psychology: General, 110,* 341–362.

Fowles, D. C. (1992). Schizophrenia: Diathesis-stress revisited. *Annual Review of Psychology, 43.* Palo Alto, CA: Annual Reviews.

Fox, L. H., Brody, L., & Tobin, D. (1979). *Women and mathematics.* Baltimore: Intellectually Gifted Study Group, Johns Hopkins University.

Frager, R. (1970). Conformity and anti-conformity in Japan. *Journal of Personality and Social Psychology, 15,* 203–210.

Frances, A. J., Widiger, T. A., & Pincus, H. A. (1989). The development of DSM-IV. *Archives of General Psychiatry, 46,* 373–375.

Frank, E., & Kupfer, D. J. (1986). Psychotherapeutic approaches to treatment of recurrent unipolar depression: Work in progress. *Psychopharmacology Bulletin, 22,* 558–565.

Frank, J. D. (1982). Therapeutic components shared by all psychotherapies. In J. H. Harvey & M. M. Parks (Eds.), *Psychotherapy research and behavior change.* Washington, DC: American Psychological Association.

Freud, S. (1900/1953). The interpretation of dreams. In J. Strachey (Ed.), *The standard edition of the complete psychological works of Sigmund Freud.* London: Hogarth.

Freud, S. (1917). *A general introduction to psychoanalysis.* New York: Washington Square Press.

Friedman, A. F., Webb, J. T., & Lewak, R. (1989). *Psychological assessment with the MMPI.* Hillsdale, NJ: Erlbaum.

Friedman, M., & Rosenman, R. (1974). *Type A behavior and your heart.* New York: Knopf.

Fromm, E. (1947). *Man for himself.* New York: Holt Rinehart.

Fujino, D. (1991, August). *An alternative theoretical and empirical approach to the examination of the acculturation process: The case of Asian Americans.* Paper presented at the meeting of the American Psychological Association, San Francisco.

Furnham, A., & Alibbai, N. (1983). Cross-cultural differences in the perception of female body shapes. *Psychological Medicine, 13,* 829–837.

Furrow, D., & Moore, C. (1991, April). *Mothers' feedback to children's utterances: The role of context.* Paper presented at the Society for Research in Child Development meeting, Seattle.

Furth, H. G., & Wachs, H. (1975). *Thinking goes to school.* New York: Oxford University Press.

Furumoto, L. (1989). The new history of psychology. In I. S. Cohen (Ed.), *The G. Stanley Hall Lecture Series* (Vol. 9). Washington, DC: American Psychological Association.

Furumoto, L., & Scarborough, E. (1986). Placing women in the history of psychology. *American Psychologist, 41,* 35–42.

Gallup, G. (1984, August-September). *The Gallup Report,* Nos. 228 and 229, 2–9.

Gallup Report. (1987). Legalized gay relations. *Gallup Report, 254,* 25.

Galotti, K. M. (1989). Approaches to studying formal and everyday reasoning. *Psychological Bulletin, 105,* 331–351.

Gannon, L., Luchetta, T., Rhodes, K., Pardie, L., & Segrist, D. (1992). Sex bias in psychological research: Progress or complacency? *American Psychologist, 47,* 389–396.

Garbarino, J. (1980). The issue is human quality: In praise of children. *Children and Youth Services Review, 1,* 353–377.

Garbarino, J. (1985). *Adolescent development: An ecological perspective.* Columbus, OH: Merrill.

Garden, R. A. (1987). The second IEA mathematics study. *Comparative Education Review, 31,* 47–68.

Gardner, B. T., & Gardner, R. A. (1971). Two-way communication with an infant chimpanzee. In A. Schrier & F. Stollnitz (Eds.), *Behavior of nonhuman primates* (Vol. 4). New York: Academic Press.

Gardner, H. (1985). *The mind's new science.* New York: Basic.

Gardner, L. I., Stern, M. P., Haffner, S. M., Gaskill, S. P., Hazuda, H. P., Relethford, J. H., & Eifter, C. W. (1984). Prevalence of diabetes in Mexican Americans: Relationships to percent of gene pool derived from Native American sources. *Diabetes, 33,* 86–92.

Garrick, T. R., & Loewenstein, R. J. (1989). Behavioral medicine in the general hospital. *Psychosomatics, 30,* 123–134.

Garwood, S. G., Phillips, D., Hartman, A., & Zigler, E. F. (1989). As the pendulum swings: Federal agency programs for children. *American Psychologist, 44,* 434–440.

Gazzaniga, M. S. (1983). Right hemisphere language following brain bisection: A 20-year perspective. *American Psychologist, 38,* 525–537.

Gazzaniga, M. S. (1986). *The social brain.* New York: Plenum.

Gelfand, D. E. (1982). *Aging: The ethnic factor.* Boston: Little, Brown.

Gelman, R. (1991). Epigenetic foundations of knowledge structures: Initial and transcendent constructions. In S. Carey & R. Gelman (Eds.), *The epigenesis of mind: Essays on biology and cognition.* Hillsdale, NJ: Erlbaum.

George, R. L. (1990). *Counseling the chemically dependent.* Englewood Cliffs, NJ: Prentice-Hall.

Gerlach, J. (1991). Introduction: Women, education, and aging. *Educational Gerontology, 17,* iii.

Gibbs, J. T. (1989). Black American adolescents. In J. T. Gibbs & L. N. Huang (Eds.), *Children of color.* San Francisco: Jossey-Bass.

Gibbs, J. T., & Huang, L. N. (1989a). A conceptual framework for assessing and treating minority youth. In J. T. Gibbs & L. N. Huang (Eds.), *Children of color.* San Francisco: Jossey-Bass.

Gibbs, J. T., & Huang, L. N. (Eds.). (1989b). *Children of color.* San Francisco: Jossey-Bass.

Gibbs, N. (1990, Fall). The dreams of youth. *Time,* pp. 10–14.

Gibson, E. J., & Walk, R. D. (1960). The "visual cliff." *Scientific American, 202*, 64–71.

Gilligan, C. (1982). *In a different voice.* Cambridge, MA: Harvard University Press.

Gilligan, C. (1990). Teaching Shakespeare's sister. In C. Gilligan, N. Lyons, & T. Hanmer (Eds.), *Making connections: The relational worlds of adolescent girls at Emma Willard School.* Cambridge, MA: Harvard University Press.

Gilligan, C. (1992, May). *Joining the resistance: Girls' development in adolescence.* Paper presented at the symposium on development and vulnerability in close relationships, Montreal, Quebec.

Gilligan, C., Brown, L. M., & Rogers, A. G. (1990). Psyche embedded: A place for body, relationships, and culture in personality theory. In A. I. Rabin, R. A. Zucker, R. A. Emmons, & S. Frank (Eds.), *Studying persons and lives.* New York: Springer.

Gim, R. H., Atkinson, D. R., & Kim, S. J. (1991). Asian-American acculturation, counselor ethnicity and cultural sensitivity, and ratings of counselors. *Journal of Counseling Psychology, 38*, 57–62.

Gjerde, P. (1985, April). *Adolescent depression and parental socialization patterns: A prospective study.* Paper presented at the biennial meeting of the Society for Research in Child Development, Toronto.

Glasser, W. (1990). The quality school. *Phi Delta Kappan.*

Glick, J. (1975). Cognitive development in cross-cultural perspective. In F. Horowitz (Ed.), *Review of child development research* (Vol. 4). Chicago: University of Chicago Press.

Glisky, E. L., & Schacter, D. L. (1987). Acquisition of domain-specific knowledge in organic amnesia: Training for computer-related work. *Neuropsychologica, 25*, 893–906.

Godden, D. R., & Baddeley, A. D. (1975). Context-dependent memory in two natural environments: On land and under water. *British Journal of Psychology, 66*, 325–331.

Goldberg, H., & Pepitone-Arreola-Rockwell, F. (Eds.). (1986, Summer). Forward. *Psychotherapy, 23*, IV.

Goldman, H. H., & Grebb, J. A. (1992). Classifying mental disorders: DSM-III-R. In H. E. Goldman (Ed.), *Review of general psychiatry.* Hillsdale, NJ: Erlbaum.

Goldstein, I. R., & Gilliam, P. (1990). Training system issues in the year 2000. *American Psychologist, 45*, 134–143.

Goldstein, J. H. (Ed.). (1989). *Sports, games, and play.* Hillsdale, NJ: Erlbaum.

Goldstein, M. J. (1986, August). *Psychosocial factors in the course and onset of schizophrenia.* Paper presented at the meeting of the American Psychological Association, Washington, DC.

Goldstein, M. J., & Palmer, J. O. (1975). *The experience of anxiety.* New York: Oxford University Press.

Goodchilds, J. D., & Zellman, G. L. (1984). Sexual signaling and sexual aggression in adolescent relationships. In N. M. Malamuth & E. D. Donnerstein (Eds.), *Pornography and sexual aggression.* New York: Academic Press.

Goodheart, C. D., & Markham, B. (1992). The feminization of psychology: Implications for psychotherapy. *Psychotherapy, 29*, 130–138.

Goodlad, J. (1983). *A place called school.* New York: McGraw-Hill.

Goodstein, L. D., & Calhoun, J. F. (1982). *Understanding abnormal behavior.* Reading, MA: Addison-Wesley.

Gorman, J. M., Liebowitz, M. R., Fyer, A. J., & Stein, J. (1989). A neuroanatomical hypothesis for panic disorder. *American Journal of Psychiatry, 146*, 148–161.

Gottesman, I. I. (1989). Vital statistics, demography, and schizophrenia. *Schizophrenia Bulletin, 15*, 5–8.

Gottesman, K. I., & Shields, J. (1982). *The schizophrenic puzzle.* New York: Cambridge University Press.

Gould, M., Wunsch-Hitzig, R., & Dohrenwend, B. S. (1981). Estimating the prevalence of childhood psychopathology. *Journal of American Academy of Child Psychiatry, 20*, 462–476.

Gould, S. J. (1981). *The mismeasure of man.* New York: W. W. Norton.

Gould-Martin, K., & Ngin, C. (1981). Chinese Americans. In A. Harwood (Ed.), *Ethnicity and medical care.* Cambridge, MA: Harvard University Press.

Graham, S. (1986, August). *Can attribution theory tell us something about motivation in blacks?* Paper presented at the meeting of the American Psychological Association, Washington, DC.

Graham, S. (1987, August). *Developing relations between attributions, affect, and intended social behavior.* Paper presented at the meeting of the American Psychological Association, New York.

Graham, S. (1990). Motivation in Afro-Americans. In G. L. Berry & J. K. Asamen (Eds.), *Black students: Psychosocial issues and academic achievement.* Newbury Park, CA: Sage.

Graham, S. (1992). "Most of the subjects were White and middle class." Trends in published research on African Americans in selected APA journals, 1970–1989. *American Psychologist, 47*, 629–639.

Grambs, J. D. (1989). *Women over forty* (rev. ed.). New York: Springer.

Grant, J. P. (1989). *The state of the world's children.* New York: UNICEF.

Greenberg, J. S., Bruess, C. E., Mullen, K. D., & Sands, D. W. (1989). *Sexuality* (2nd ed.). Dubuque, IA: Wm. C. Brown.

Greenfield, P. M. (1966). On culture and conservation. In J. S. Bruner, R. P. Olver, & P. M. Greenfield (Eds.), *Studies in cognitive growth.* New York: Wiley.

Greenwald, A. G. (1989). Why are attitudes so important? In A. R. Pratkanis, S. J. Breckler, & A. G. Greenwald (Eds.), *Attitude structure and function.* Hillsdale, NJ: Erlbaum.

Gregory, R. (1992). *Psychological testing.* Needham Heights, MA: Allyn & Bacon.

Gregory, R. L. (1978). *Eye and brain: The psychology of seeing* (3rd ed.). New York: McGraw-Hill.

Grevious, C. (1985). The role of the family therapist with low-income black families. *Family Therapy, 12*, 115–122.

Grimes, B., & Mattimore, E. (1989, April). *The effects of stress and exercise on identity formation in adolescence.* Paper presented at the biennial meeting of the Society for Research in Child Development, Kansas City.

Grush, J. E. (1980). Impact of candidate expenditures, regionality, and prior outcomes on the 1976 Democratic presidential primaries. *Journal of Personality and Social Psychology, 38*, 337–347.

Gudykunst, W. B., Gao, G., Schmidt, K. L., Nishida, T., Bond, M. H., Leung, K., & Barraclugh, R. A. (1992). The influence of individualism—Collectivism, self-monitoring, and predicted-outcome value on communication in ingroup and outgroup relationships. *Journal of Cross-Cultural Psychology, 23*, 196–213.

Guilford, J. P. (1967). *The structure of intellect.* New York: McGraw-Hill.

Guilleminault, C. (1989). Narcolepsy syndrome. In M. H. Dryger, T. Roth, & W. C. Dement (Eds.), *Principles and practice of sleep medicine.* San Diego: Harcourt Brace Jovanovich.

Gurman, A. S., & Kniskern, D. P. (1992). The future of marital and family therapy. *Psychotherapy, 29*, 65–71.

Gustafson, S. B., & Magnusson, D. (1991). *Female life careers: A pattern approach.* Hillsdale, NJ: Erlbaum.

Guthrie, R. (1976). *Even the rat was white: A historical view of psychology.* New York: Harper & Row.

Guttman, N., & Kalish, H. L. (1956). Discriminability and stimulus generalization. *Journal of Experimental Psychology, 51*, 79–88.

Hahn, A. (1987, December). Reaching out to America's dropouts: What to do? *Phi Delta Kappan*, pp. 256–263.

Hakuta, K., & Garcia, E. E. (1989). Bilingualism and education. *American Psychologist, 44*, 374–379.

Haley, J. (1976). *Problem-solving therapy*. San Francisco: Jossey-Bass.

Hall, C. C. I. (1991, August). *Work with me: Priorities for Black women*. Paper presented at the American Psychological Association, San Francisco.

Hall, C. C. I., Evans, B. J., & Selice, S. (Eds.). (1989). *Black females in the United States: A bibliography from 1967 to 1987*. Washington, DC: American Psychological Association.

Halmi, D. (1980). Gastric bypass for massive obesity. In A. J. Stunkard (Ed.), *Obesity*. Philadelphia: W. B. Saunders.

Hamilton, V. L. (1992). Introduction to social psychological approaches to responsibility and justice: The view across cultures. *International Journal of Psychology, 27*, 137–141.

Hansell, S. (1991). The meaning of stress. *Contemporary Psychology, 36*, 112–114.

Hare-Muston, R., & Marecek, J. (1988). The meaning of difference: Gender theory, postmodernism, and psychology. *American Psychologist, 43*, 455–464.

Harlow, H. F., & Zimmerman, R. R. (1959). Affectional responses in the infant monkey. *Science, 130*, 421–432.

Harold, R. D., & Eccles, J. S. (1990, March). *Maternal expectations, advice, and provision of opportunities: Their relationships to boys' and girls' occupational aspirations*. Paper presented at the meeting of the Society for Research in Adolescence, Atlanta.

Harris, P. R., & Moran, R. T. (1987). *Managing cultural differences* (2nd ed.). Houston, TX: Gulf.

Harris, R. A., & Buck, K. J. (1991). The process of alcohol tolerance and dependence. *Alcohol World, 14*, 105–111.

Harris, R. F., Wolf, N. M., & Baer, D. M. (1964). Effects of adult social reinforcement on child behavior. *Young Children, 20*, 8–17.

Harris, R. J., Schoen, L. M., & Hensley, D. L. (1992). A cross-cultural study of story memory. *Journal of Cross-Cultural Psychology, 23*, 133–147.

Harrison, C. A. (1991). Older women in our society: America's silent, invisible majority. *Educational Gerontology, 17*, 111–122.

Harter, S. (1990a). Processes underlying adolescent self-concept formation. In R. Montemayor, G. R. Adams, & T. P. Gullotta (Eds.), *From childhood to adolescence: A transitional period?* Newbury Park, CA: Sage.

Harter, S. (1990b). Self and identity development. In S. S. Feldman & G. R. Elliott (Eds.), *At the threshold: The developing adolescent*. Cambridge, MA: Harvard University Press.

Hartmann, E. (1989). Normal and abnormal dreams. In M. H. Dryger, T. Roth, & W. C. Dement (Eds.), *Principles and practice of sleep medicine*. San Diego: Harcourt Brace Jovanovich.

Hartup, W. W. (1983). Peer relations. In P. H. Mussen (Ed.), *Handbook of child psychology* (4th ed., Vol. 4). New York: Wiley.

Harvard Medical School Newsletter. (1981). Cambridge, MA: Harvard Medical School, Dept. of Continuing Education.

Hasher, L., & Zacks, R. T. (1979). Automatic and effortful processes in memory. *Journal of Experimental Psychology: General, 108*, 356–388.

Haskins, R. (1989). Beyond metaphor: The efficacy of early childhood education. *American Psychologist, 44*, 274–282.

Hatfield, E., & Sprecher, S. (1986). *Mirror, mirror . . . The importance of looks in everyday life*. Albany: State University of New York Press.

Hatvany, N., & Pucik, V. (1981). An integrated management system: Lessons from the Japanese experience. *Academy of Management Review, 6*, 469–480.

Hayflick, L. (1975, September). Why grow old? *Stanford Magazine*, pp. 36–43.

Hayflick, L. (1977). The cellular basis for biological aging. In C. E. Finch & L. Hayflick (Eds.), *Handbook of the biology of aging*. New York: Van Nostrand.

Haynes, G. S., & Feinleib, M. (1980). Women, work and coronary heart disease: Prospective findings from the Framingham Heart Study. *American Journal of Public Health, 70*, 130–141.

Heath, D. (1987). A decade of development in the anthropological study of alcohol use, 1970–1980. In M. Douglas (Ed.), *Constructive drinking: Perspectives on drink from anthropology*. New York: Cambridge University Press.

Heath, S. B. (1983). *Ways with words*. New York: Cambridge University Press.

Heath, S. B. (1989). Oral and literate traditions among black Americans living in poverty. *American Psychologist, 44*, 367–373.

Heider, F. (1958). *The psychology of interpersonal relations*. New York: Wiley.

Heimberg, R. G. (1989a). Cognitive and behavioral treatments for social phobia: A critical analysis. *Clinical Psychology Review, 9*, 107–128.

Heimberg, R. G. (1989b). Social phobia: No longer neglected. *Clinical Psychology Review, 9*, 1–2.

Heinicke, C. M., Beckwith, L., & Thompson, A. (1988). Early intervention in the family system: A framework and review. *Infant Mental Health Journal, 9*, 2.

Hellige, J. B. (1990). Hemispheric asymmetry. *Annual Review of Psychology, 41*. Palo Alto, CA: Annual Reviews.

Helms, J. E. (1985). Cultural identity in the treatment process. In P. Pedersen (Ed.), *Handbook of cross-cultural counseling and therapy*. Westport, CT: Greenwood.

Helms, J. E. (1990, August). *Black and White racial identity theory and professional interracial collaboration*. Paper presented at the meeting of the American Psychological Association, Boston.

Hendry, J. (1986). *Becoming Japanese: The world of the preschool child*. Honolulu: University of Hawaii Press.

Herbert, J. (1989). The physiology of aggression. In J. Groebel & R. A. Hinde (Eds.), *Aggression and war*. New York: Cambridge University Press.

Hernandez, D. J. (1988). Demographic trends and the living arrangements of children. In E. M. Hetherington & J. D. Arasteh (Eds.), *Impact of divorce, single-parenting, and stepparenting on children*. Hillsdale, NJ: Erlbaum.

Hernandez, G. G. (1991). Not so benign neglect: Researchers ignore ethnicity in defining family caregiver burden and recommending services. *The Gerontologist, 31*, 271.

Hershenson, M. (1989). The most puzzling illusion. In M. Hershenson (Ed.), *The moon: An anomaly of visual space*. Hillsdale, NJ: Erlbaum.

Hess, R. S., & Street, E. M. (1991). The effect of acculturation on the relationship of counselor ethnicity and client ratings. *Journal of Counseling Psychology, 38*, 71–75.

Hetherington, E. M. (1989). Coping with family transitions: Winners, losers, and survivors. *Child Development, 60*, 1–14.

Hetherington, E. M. (1991). The role of individual differences and family relationships in coping with divorce and remarriage. In P. A. Cowan & E. M. Hetherington (Eds.), *Family transitions*. Hillsdale, NJ: Erlbaum.

Hetherington, E. M., & Clingempeel, W. G. (in press). Coping with marital transitions: A family systems perspective. *Society for Research in Child Development Monographs*.

Hetherington, E. M., Hagan, M. S., & Anderson, E. R. (1989). Marital transitions: A child's perspective. *American Psychologist, 44*, 303–312.

Heyns, B. (1982). The influence of parents' work on children's school achievement. In S. B. Kamerman & C. D. Hayes (Eds.), *Families that work: Children in a changing world.* Panel on Work, Family and Community, Committee on Child Development Research and Public Policy, Commission on Behavioral and Social Sciences and Education, National Research Council. Washington, DC: National Academy Press.

Hilgard, E. R. (1965). *Hypnotic suggestibility.* New York: Harcourt Brace.

Hilgard, E. R. (1977). *Divided consciousness: Multiple controls in human thought and action.* New York: Wiley.

Hill, J. P., & Holmbeck, G. (1986). Attachment and autonomy in adolescence. In G. Whitehurst (Eds.), *Annals of child development.* Greenwich: JAI.

Himle, J. A., McPhee, K., Cameron, O. G., & Curtis, G. C. (1989). Simple phobia: Evidence for heterogeneity. *Psychiatry Research, 28,* 25–30.

Hinde, R. A. (1984). Why do the sexes behave differently in close relationships? *Journal of Social and Personal Relationships, 1,* 471–501.

Hinde, R. A. (1992). Commentary: Can biology explain human development? *Human Development, 35,* 34–39.

Hines, M. (1982). Prenatal gonadal hormones and sex differences in human behavior. *Psychological Bulletin, 92,* 56–80.

Hines, T. M. (1988). *Pseudoscience and the paranormal.* Buffalo, NY: Prometheus.

Hines, T. M., & Dennison, T. (1989). A reaction-time test of ESP and precognition. *The Skeptical Inquirer, 14,* 161–170.

Hirsch, E. D. (1987). *Cultural literacy: What every American needs to know.* Boston: Houghton Mifflin.

Ho, D. Y. F. (1987). Fatherhood in Chinese culture. In M. E. Lamb (Ed.), *The father's role: Cross-cultural perspectives.* Hillsdale, NJ: Erlbaum.

Ho, M. K. (1992). *Minority children and adolescents in therapy.* Newbury Park, CA: Sage.

Hobfoll, S. E. (1986). *Stress, social support, and women.* Washington, DC: Hemisphere.

Hobfoll, S. E. (1989). Conservation of resources: A new attempt at conceptualizing stress. *American Psychologist, 44,* 513–524.

Hobson, J. A. (1992). A new model of brain-mind state: Activation level, input source, and mode of processing. In J. S. Antrobus & M. Bertini (Eds.), *The neuropsychology of sleep and dreaming.* Hillsdale, NJ: Erlbaum.

Hobson, J. A., Lydic, R., & Baghdoyan, H. A. (1986). Evolving concepts of sleep cycle generation: From brain centers to neuronal populations. *Behavioral and Brain Sciences, 9,* 371–448.

Hobson, J. A., & McCarley, R. W. (1977). The brain as a dream state generator. An activation-synthesis hypothesis of the dream process. *American Journal of Psychiatry, 134,* 1335–1348.

Hodapp, R. M., Burack, J. A., & Zigler, E. (Eds.). (in press). *Issues in the developmental approach to mental retardation.* New York: Cambridge University Press.

Hofferth, S. L., & Phillips, D. A. (1991). Child care policy research. *Journal of Social Issues, 47,* 1–13.

Hofstede, G. (1980). *Culture's consequences.* Newbury Park, CA: Sage.

Hogan, J. (1989). Personality correlates of physical fitness. *Journal of Personality and Social Psychology, 56,* 284–288.

Hogan, R. (1987, August). *Conceptions of personality and the prediction of job performance.* Paper presented at the meeting of the American Psychological Association, New York.

Hollingshead, A. B., & Redlich, F. C. (1958). *Social class and mental illness.* New York: Wiley.

Holmes, D. S. (1988). The influence of meditation versus rest on physiological considerations. In M. West (Ed.), *The psychology of meditation.* New York: Oxford University Press.

Holmes, D. S., Solomon, S., Cappo, B. M., & Greenberg, J. L. (1983). Effects of transcendental meditation versus resting on physiological and subjective arousal. *Journal of Personality and Social Psychology, 44,* 1244–1252.

Holmes, T. H., & Rahe, R. H. (1967). The social readjustment rating scale. *Journal of Psychosomatic Research, 11,* 213–218.

Holtzmann, W. (1982). Cross-cultural comparisons of personality development in Mexico and the United States. In D. Wagner & H. W. Stevenson (Eds.), *Cultural perspectives on child development.* San Francisco: W. H. Freeman.

Hooks, B. (1991, August). *Gender, class, and ethnicity.* Paper presented at the meeting of the American Psychological Association, San Francisco.

Hooper, F. H., & Hooper, J. O. (in press). The family as a system of reciprocal relations: Searching for a developmental life-span perspective. In G. Brody & I. E. Siegel (Eds.), *Family research journeys* (Vol. 1). Hillsdale, NJ: Erlbaum.

Horner, M. (1968). *Sex differences in achievement motivation and performance in competitive and non-competitive situations.* Unpublished doctoral dissertation, University of Michigan.

Horney, K. (1945). *Our inner conflicts.* New York: W. W. Norton.

Horowitz, F. D., & O'Brien, M. (1989). In the interest of the nation: A reflective essay on the state of knowledge and the challenges before us. *American Psychologist, 44,* 441–445.

Horowitz, M. J. (1989). *Introduction to psychoanalysis.* New York: Basic.

Houts, A. C., & Follette, W. C. (1992). Philosophical and theoretical issues in behavioral therapy. *Behavior Therapy, 23,* 145–150.

Howat, P. M., & Saxton, A. M. (1988). The incidence of bulimic behavior in a secondary and university school population. *Journal of Youth and Adolescence, 17,* 221–231.

Huang, L. N., & Gibbs, J. T. (1989). Future directions: Implications for research, training, and practice. In J. T. Gibbs & L. N. Huang (Eds.), *Children of color.* San Francisco: Jossey-Bass.

Huang, L. N., & Ying, Y. (1989). Japanese children and adolescents. In J. T. Gibbs & L. N. Huang (Eds.), *Children of color.* San Francisco: Jossey-Bass.

Hubel, D. H., & Wiesel, T. N. (1965). Receptive fields and functional architecture into nonstriated visual areas (18 and 19) of the cat. *Journal of Neurophysiology, 28,* 229–289.

Hudson, W. (1960). Pictorial depth perception in subcultural groups in Africa. *Journal of Social Psychology, 52,* 183–208.

Hughes, J. R., Liveto, A. H., Helzer, J. E., Higgins, S. T., & Bickel, W. K. (1992). Should caffeine abuse, dependence, or withdrawal be added to DSM-IV and ICD-10? *American Journal of Psychiatry, 149,* 33–40.

Hughes, S. O., Power, T. G., & Francis, D. J. (1992, March). *Attachment, autonomy, and adolescent drinking: Differentiating abstainers, experimenters, and heavy users.* Paper presented at the meeting of the Society for Research on Adolescence, Washington, DC.

Hui, C. H., & Triandis, H. C. (1986). Individualism-collectivism: A study of cross-cultural researchers. *Journal of Cross-Cultural Psychology, 17,* 222–248.

Hultsch, D. F., & Plemons, J. K. (1979). Life events and life-span development. In P. B. Baltes & O. G. Brim (Eds.), *Life-span development and behavior.* New York: Academic Press.

Hunt, E. (1989). Cognitive science: Definition, status, and questions. *Annual Review of Psychology, 40.* Palo Alto, CA: Annual Reviews.

Hunt, M. (1974). *Sexual behavior in the 1970s.* Chicago: Playboy.

Hurvich, L. M., & Jameson, D. (1969). Human color perception. *American Scientists, 57,* 143–166.

Huston, A. C. (1983). Sex-typing. In P. H. Mussen (Ed.), *Handbook of child psychology* (4th ed., Vol. 4). New York: Wiley.

Hyde, J. S. (1981). How large are cognitive gender differences? A meta-analysis using w^2 and *d. American Psychologist, 36,* 892–901.

Hyde, J. S. (1990). Meta-analysis and the psychology of gender differences. *Signs: Journal of Women in Culture and Society, 16,* 55–69.

Hyde, J. S. (1991, August). *Gender and sex: So what has meta-analysis done for me?* Paper presented at the meeting of the American Psychological Association, San Francisco.

Hyde, J. S. (in press). Meta-analysis and the psychology of women. In F. L. Denmark & M. A. Paludi (Eds.), *Handbook on the psychology of women.* Dubuque, IA: Wm. C. Brown.

Hyde, T. S., & Jenkins, J. J. (1969). Differential effects of incidental tasks on the organiza-tion of recall of lists of highly associated words. *Journal of Experimental Psychology, 82,* 472–481.

Hynd, G. W., & Garcia, W. I. (1979). Intellectual assessment of the Native American student. *School Psychology Digest, 8,* 446–454.

Ickovics, J. R. (1991, August). *Labor force diversity: A challenge to psychology.* Paper presented at the meeting of the American Psychological Association, San Francisco.

Ikels, C. (1989). Becoming a human being in theory and practice: Chinese views of human development. In D. I. Kertzer & K. W. Schaie (Eds.), *Age structuring in comparative perspective.* Hillsdale, NJ: Erlbaum.

Ilola, L. M. (1990). Culture and health. In R. W. Brislin (Ed.), *Applied cross-cultural psychology.* Newbury Park, CA: Sage.

Inclan, J. E., & Herron, D. G. (1989). Puerto Rican adolescents. In J. T. Gibbs & L. N. Huang (Eds.), *Children of color.* San Francisco: Jossey-Bass.

Irons, E. E., & Moore, G. W. (1985). *Black managers: The case of the banking industry.* New York: Praeger.

Irvine, M. J., Johnston, D. W., Jenner, D. A., & Marie, G. V. (1986). Relaxation and stress management in the treatment of essential hypertension. *Journal of Psychosomatic Research, 30,* 437–450.

Irvine, S. H., & Berry, J. W. (1988). The abilities of mankind: A reevaluation. In S. H. Irvine & J. W. Berry (Eds.), *Human abilities in cultural context.* New York: Cambridge University Press.

Jack, R. (1992). *Women and attempted suicide.* Hillsdale, NJ: Erlbaum.

Jacklin, C. N. (1989). Female and male: Issues of gender. *American Psychologist, 44,* 127–133.

Jackson, J. H. (1992). Trials, tribulations, and triumphs of minorities in psychology: Reflections at century's end. *Professional Psychology, 23,* 80–86.

Jackson, J. S. (Ed.). (1991). *Life in Black America.* Newbury Park, CA: Sage.

Jackson, J. S., McCullough, W. R., Gurin, G., & Broman, C. L. (1991). Race identity. In J. S. Jackson (Ed.), *Life in Black America.* Newbury Park, CA: Sage.

Jacobs, M. K., & Goodman, G. (1989). Psychology and self-help groups. *American Psychologist, 44,* 536–545.

Jacobson, N. S., Holtzworth-Munroe, A., & Schmaling, K. B. (1989). Marital therapy and spouse involvement in the treatment of depression, agoraphobia, and alcoholism. *Journal of Consulting and Clinical Psychology, 57,* 5–10.

Jahoda, G. (1980). Theoretical and systematic approaches in cross-cultural psychology. In H. C. Triandis & J. G. Draguns (Eds.), *Handbook of cross-cultural psychology* (Vol. 1.). Boston: Allyn & Bacon.

James, W. (1890). *The principles of psychology.* New York: Dover.

Jameson, D., & Hurvich, L. M. (1989). Essay concerning color constancy. *Annual Review of Psychology, 40.* Palo Alto, CA: Annual Reviews.

Janis, I. (1972). *Victims of groupthink, psychologi-cal study of foreign-policy decisions and.* Boston: Houghton Mifflin.

Janos, P. M., & Robinson, N. N. (1985). Psychosocial development in intellectually gifted children. In F. D. Horowitz & M. O'Brien (Eds.), *The gifted and the talented.* Washington, DC: American Psychological Association.

Jensen, A. R. (1969). How much can we boost IQ and scholastic achievement? *Harvard Educational Review, 39,* 1–123.

Johnson, C. (1990, May). The new woman's ethics report. *New Woman,* p. 6.

Johnson-Laird, P. N. (1989). *The computer and the mind.* Cambridge, MA: Harvard University Press.

Johnston, L., Bachman, J., & O'Malley, P. (1989, February 24). [News Release.] *Teen Drug Use.* Ann Arbor: Institute for Social Research, University of Michigan.

Johnston, L. D., O'Malley, P. M., & Bachman, J. G. (1991, January 23). *News release on national drug use by young Americans.* Ann Arbor, MI: Institute for Social Research, University of Michigan.

Johnston, L. D., O'Malley, P. M., & Bachman, J. G. (1992). *The 1991 survey of drug use by American high school and college students.* Ann Arbor, MI: Institute of Social Research.

Jones, A., & Seagull, A. (1977). Dimensions of the relationship between the Black client and the White therapist. *American Psychologist, 32,* 850–856.

Jones, B. E. (1989). Basic mechanisms of sleep-wake states. In M. H. Dryger, T. Roth, & W. C. Dement (Eds.), *Principles and practice of sleep medicine.* San Diego: Harcourt Brace Jovanovich.

Jones, J. (1989, August). *How does ethnicity influence behavior?* Paper presented at the meeting of the American Psychological Association, New Orleans.

Jones, J. M. (1987). Blacks in psychology. In P. J. Woods & C. S. Wilkinson (Eds.), *Is psychology the major for you?* Washington, DC: American Psychological Association.

Jones, J. M. (1990a, August). Invitational address: Who is training our ethnic minority psychologists, and are they doing it right? In G. Stricker & others (Eds.), *Toward ethnic diversification in psychology, education, and training.* Washington, DC: American Psychological Association.

Jones, J. M. (1990b, August). *Psychological approaches to race: What have they been and what should they be?* Paper presented at the meeting of the American Psychological Association, Boston.

Jones, J. M. (1991). Psychological models of race: What have they been and what should they be? In J. D. Goodchilds (Ed.), *Psychological perspectives on human diversity in America.* Washington, DC: American Psychological Association.

Jones, M. C. (1924). A laboratory study of fear: The case of Peter. *Journal of Genetic Psychology, 31,* 308–315.

Jones, M. C. (1965). Psychological correlates of somatic development. *Child Development, 36,* 899–911.

Jones, W. H., Hobbs, S.A., & Hockenbury, D. (1982). Loneliness and social skills deficits. *Journal of Personality and Social Psychology, 42,* 682–689.

Josselson, R. (1987). *Finding herself.* San Francisco: Jossey-Bass.

Joyce, P. R., Donald, R. N., & Elder, P. N. (1987). Individual differences in plasma cortisol changes during manta and depres-sion. *Journal of Affective Disorders, 12,* 1–6.

Jung, C. G. (1917). *Analytic psychology.* New York: Moffat, Yard.

Kagan, J. (1988, August). *The idea of tempera-ment categories.* Paper presented at the meeting of the American Psychological Association, Atlanta.

Kagan, J. (1989). *Unstable ideas: Temperament, cognition, and self.* Cambridge, MA: Harvard University Press.

Kagan, J., Kearsley, R. B., & Zetazo, P. R. (1978). *Infancy.* Cambridge, MA: Harvard University Press.

Kagan, S., & Madsen, M. C. (1972). Experi-mental analysis of cooperation and competition of Anglo-American and Mexican children. *Developmental Psychology, 6,* 49–59.

Kagan, S. L. (1988, January). Current reforms in early childhood education: Are we addressing the issues? *Young Children, 43,* 27–38.

Kagitcibasi, C. (1988). Diversity of socialization and social change. In P. R. Dasen, J. W. Berry, & N. Sartorious (Eds.), *Health and cross-cultural psychology: Toward applications.* Newbury Park, CA: Sage.

Kagitcibasi, C., & Berry, J. W. (1989). Cross-cultural psychology: Current research and trends. *Annual Review of Psychology, 40.* Palo Alto, CA: Annual Reviews.

Kail, R., & Pellegrino, J. W. (1985). *Human intelligence.* New York: W. H. Freeman.

Kamo, Y. (1988). Determinants of the household division of labor: Resources, power, and ideology. *Journal of Family Issues, 9,* 177–200.

Kandel, E. R., & Schwartz, J. H. (1982). Molecular biology of learning: Modulation of transmitter release. *Science, 218,* 433–443.

Kanner, A. D., Coyne, J. C., Schaefer, C., & Lazarus, R. S. (1981). Comparisons of two modes of stress measurement: Daily hassles and uplifts versus major life events. *Journal of Behavioral Medicine, 4,* 1–39.

Kanner, A. D., & Feldman, S. S. (1991). Control over uplifts and hassles and its relationship to adaptational outcomes. *Journal of Behavioral Medicine, 14,* 187–198.

Kantrowitz, B., & Wingert, P. (1989, April 17). How kids learn. *Newsweek,* pp. 4–10.

Karasu, T. B. (1986). The psychotherapies: Benefits and limitations. *American Journal of Psychotherapy, 15,* 324–342.

Kardec, A. (1957). *El libro de los espiritus.* Mexico: Editorial Diana.

Karno, M., & Morales, A. (1971). A community mental health service for Mexican Americans in a metropolis. *Comprehensive Psychiatry, 12,* 115–121.

Kart, C. S. (1990). *Diversity among aged black males.* In Z. Harel, E. A. McKinney, & M. Williams (Eds.), *Black aged.* Newbury Park, CA: Sage.

Katz, I., Wackenhut, J., & Hass, R. G. (1986). Racial ambivalence, value duality, and behavior. In J. F. Dovidio & S. L. Gaertner (Eds.), *Prejudice, discrimination, and racism.* New York: Academic Press.

Katz, L., & Chard, S. (1989). *Engaging the minds of young children: The project approach.* Norwood, NJ: Ablex.

Kaufman, A. S., & Kaufman, N. L. (1983). *Kaufman Assessment Battery for Children.* Circle Pines, MN: American Guidance Service.

Kavanaugh, K. H., & Kennedy, F. M. (1992). *Promoting cultural diversity.* Newbury Park, CA: Sage.

Kavin, E. J., & Parcell, S. R. (1977). Sexual aggression: A second look at the offended female. *Archives of Sexual Behavior, 6,* 67–76.

Kearns, D. T. (1988, April). An education recovery plan for America. *Phi Delta Kappan,* pp. 565–570.

Keating, D. P. (in press). Structuralism, deconstruction, reconstruction: The limits of reasoning. In W. F. Overton (Ed.), *Reasoning, necessity, and logic. Developmental perspectives.* Hillsdale, NJ: Erlbaum.

Keefe, S. E., & Padilla, A. M. (1987). *Chicano ethnicity.* Albuquerque: University of New Mexico Press.

Keil, F. C. (1989). *Concepts, kinds, and cognitive development.* Cambridge, MA: MIT Press.

Kelley, H. H., & Thibaut, J. (1978). *Interpersonal relations: A theory of interdependence.* New York: Wiley.

Kendall, P. C., & Watson, D. (Eds.). (1989). *Anxiety and depression.* San Diego: Academic Press.

Kephart, W. M. (1967). Some correlates of romantic love. *Journal of Marriage and the Family, 29,* 470–474.

Kerr, B. A. (1983). Raising the career aspirations of gifted girls. *Vocational Guidance Quarterly, 32,* 37–43.

Kessler, R. C., Kendler, K. S., Heath, A., Neale, M. C., & Eaves, L. J. (1992). Social support, depressed mood, and adjustment to stress: A genetic epidemiologic investigation. *Journal of Personality and Social Psychology, 62,* 257–272.

Kiecolt-Glaser, J. K., Fisher, L. D., Ogrocki, P., Sout, J. C., Speicher, B. S., & Glaser, R. (1987). Marital quality, marital disruption, and immune function. *Psychosomatic Medicine, 40,* 13–34.

Kiecolt-Glaser, J. K., & Glaser, R. (1988). Behavioral influences on immune function. In T. Field, P. McCabe, & N. Schneiderman (Eds.), *Stress and coping across development.* Hillsdale, NJ: Erlbaum.

Kilpatrick, A. C. (1992). *Long-range effects of childhood and adolescent sexual experiences: Myths, mores, and menaces.* Hillsdale, NJ: Erlbaum.

Kilpatrick, J., & White, G. M. (1985). Exploring ethnopsychologies. In G. M. White & J. Kilpatrick (Eds.), *Person, self, and experience.* Berkeley: University of California Press.

Kimble, G. A. (1961). *Hilgard and Marquis's conditioning and learning.* New York: Appleton-Century-Crofts.

Kimmel, E. B. (1992). Women's contributions to psychology. *Contemporary Psychology, 37,* 201–202.

Kimmel, E. B., & Garco, M. G. (1991, August). *The experience of feminism by women of color.* Paper presented at the meeting of the American Psychological Association, San Francisco.

Kimmel, H. D. (1989). The importance of classical conditioning. *Behavioral and Brain Sciences, 12,* 147.

Kinsey, A. C., Pomeroy, W. B., & Martin, E. E. (1948). *Sexual behavior in the human male.* Philadelphia: W. B. Saunders.

Kirkpatrick, B., Buchanan, R. W., Waltrip, R. W., Jauch, D., & Carpenter, W. T. (1989). Diazepam treatment of early symptoms of schizophrenic relapse. *Journal of Nervous and Mental Disease, 177,* 52–53.

Kirsh, B. (1974). Consciousness-raising groups as a therapy for women. In V. Franks & V. Burtle (Eds.), *Women in therapy.* New York: Brunner/Mazel.

Kitano, H. H. L. (1970). Mental illness in four cultures. *Journal of Social Psychology, 80,* 121–134.

Kite, M. E., Deaux, K., & Miele, M. (1991). Stereotypes of young and old: Does age outweigh gender? *Psychology and Aging, 6,* 19–27.

Klass, D. (1988). *Parental grief.* New York: Springer.

Klatzky, R. S. (1984). *Memory and awareness.* New York: W. H. Freeman.

Klein, S. B., Loftus, J., & Burton, H. A. (1989). Two self-reference effects: The importance of distinguishing between self-descriptiveness judgments and autobiographical retrieval in self-referent encoding. *Journal of Personality and Social Psychology, 56,* 853–865.

Kleinman, A. (1988). *Rethinking psychiatry.* New York: Macmillan.

Kleinman, J. C. (1992). The epidemiology of low birthweight. In S. L. Friedman & M. D. Sigman (Eds.), *The psychological development of low birthweight children.* Norwood, NJ: Ablex.

Klerman, G. L. (1986). Historical perspectives on contemporary schools of psychopathology. In T. Millon & G. L. Klerman (Eds.), *Contemporary directions in psychopathology: Toward the DSM-IV.* New York: Guilford.

Klinger, E. (1987, October). The power of daydreams. *Psychology Today,* pp. 36–45.

Klonoff, E. A. (1991, August). *Ethnicity and women's health: The neglected women.* Paper presented at the meeting of the American Psychological Association, San Francisco.

Knight, B., Wollert, R. W., Levy, L. H., Frame, C. L., & Padgett, V. P. (1980). Self help groups: The members' perspectives. *American Journal of Community Psychology, 8,* 53–65.

Knight, R. A., Rosenberg, R., & Schneider, B. (1985). Classification of sexual offenders: Perspectives, methods, and validation. In A. W. Burgess (Ed.), *Rape and sexual assault.* New York: Garland.

Kobasa, N., Maddi, S., & Kahn, S. (1982). Hardiness and health: A prospective study. *Journal of Personality and Social Psychology, 42*, 168–177.

Koestner, R., Bernieri, F., & Zuckerman, M. (1989). Trait-specific versus person-specific moderators of cross-situational consistency. *Journal of Personality, 56*, 1–16.

Kohlberg, L. (1966). A cognitive-developmental analysis of children's sex-role concepts and attitudes. In E. E. Maccoby (Ed.), *The development of sex differences*. Palo Alto, CA: Stanford University Press.

Kohlberg, L. (1969). Stage and sequence: The cognitive-developmental approach to socialization. In D. A. Goslin (Ed.), *Handbook of socialization theory and research*. Chicago: Rand McNally.

Kohlberg, L. (1976). Moral stages and moralization: The cognitive-developmental approach. In T. Lickona (Ed.), *Moral development and behavior*. New York: Holt, Rinehart & Winston.

Kohlberg, L. (1986). A current statement on some theoretical issues. In S. Modgil & C. Modgil (Eds.), *Lawrence Kohlberg*. Philadelphia: Falmer.

Kohler, W. (1925). *The mentality of apes*. New York: Harcourt Brace Jovanovich.

Kohn, M. L. (1977). *Class and conformity: A study in values* (2nd ed.). Chicago: University of Chicago Press.

Kohut, H. (1977). *The restoration of the self*. New York: International Universities Press.

Kolb, L. (1973). *Modern clinical psychiatry* (8th ed.). Philadelphia: W. B. Saunders.

Kopp, C. B. (1987). Developmental risk: Historical reflections. In J. D. Osofsky (Ed.), *Handbook of infant development* (2nd ed.). New York: Wiley.

Kopp, C. B., & Kaler, S. R. (1989). Risk in infancy: Origins and implications. *American Psychologist, 44*, 224–230.

Kornetsky, C. (1986, August). *Effects of opiates and stimulants on brain stimulation: Implications for abuse*. Paper presented at the meeting of the American Psychological Association, Washington, DC.

Koss, M. P. (1990). The women's mental health research agenda: Violence against women. *American Psychologist, 45*, 374–380.

Koss, M. P., & Harvey, M. (1987). *The rape victim: Clinical and community approaches to treatment*. Lexington, MA: Stephen Greene.

Kozak, M. J., Foa, E. B., & McCarthy, P. R. (1987). Obsessive-compulsive disorder. In C. G. Last & M. Hersen (Eds.), *Handbook of anxiety disorders*. Elmsford, NY: Pergamon.

Kramer, B. A. (1987). Electroconvulsive therapy use in geriatric depression. *Journal of Nervous and Mental Disease, 175*, 233–235.

Krause, N., Jay, G., & Liang, J. (1991). Financial strain and psychological well-being among the American and Japanese elderly. *Psychology and Aging, 6*, 17–181.

Kübler-Ross, E. (1974). *Questions and answers on death and dying*. New York: Macmillan.

Kunitz, S. J., & Levy, J. E. (1981). In A. Harwood (Ed.), *Ethnicity and medical care*. Cambridge, MA: Harvard University Press.

Kunitz, S. J., Levy, J. E., Odoroff, C. L., & Bollinger, J. (1971). The epidemiology of alcoholic cirrhosis in two southwestern Indian tribes. *Quarterly Journal of Studies on Alcoholism, 32*, 706–720.

Kurtines, W. M., & Gewirtz, J. (Eds.). (1991). *Moral behavior and development* (Vol. 2). Hillsdale, NJ: Erlbaum.

Kurzweil, E. (1990). *The Freudians*. New Haven: Yale University Press.

LaBerge, S. P. (1985). *Lucid dreaming*. Los Angeles: Tarcher.

LaBerge, S. P. (1988). The psychophysiology of lucid dreaming. In J. Gackenbach & S. P. LaBerge (Eds.), *Conscious mind, sleeping brain: Perspectives on lucid dreaming*. New York: Plenum.

LaBerge, S. P. (1992). *Physiological studies of lucid dreaming*. Hillsdale, NJ: Erlbaum.

Labouvie-Vief, G. (1986, August). *Modes of knowing and life-span cognition*. Paper presented at the annual meeting of the American Psychological Association, Washington, DC.

LaCroix, A. Z., & Haynes, S. G. (1987). Gender differences in the health effects of workplace roles. In R. C. Barnett, L. Biener, & G. K. Baruch (Eds.), *Gender and stress*. New York: Free Press.

LaFromboise, T. D., & Low, K. G. (1989). American Indian children and adolescents. In J. T. Gibbs & L. N. Huang (Eds.), *Children of color*. San Francisco: Jossey-Bass.

LaGrand, L. E. (1991). United we cope: Support groups for the dying and bereaved. *Death Studies, 15*, 207–230.

LaGuerre, M. S. (1981). Haitian Americans. In A. Harwood (Ed.), *Ethnicity and medical care*. Cambridge, MA: Harvard University Press.

LaLonde, R. N., Taylor, D. M., & Moghaddam, F. M. (1992). The process of social identification for visible immigrant women in a multicultural context. *Journal of Cross-Cultural Psychology, 23*, 25–39.

Lamb, M. E. (1986). *The father's role. Applied perspectives*. New York: Wiley.

Lamb, M. E., Fredi, A. M., Hwang, C. P., Frodi, M., & Steinberg, J. (1982). Mother- and father-infant interaction involving play and holding in traditional and nontraditional Swedish families. *Developmental Psychology, 18*, 215–221.

Lane, H. (1976). *The wild boy of Aveyron*. Cambridge, MA: Harvard University Press.

Lange, C. G. (1922). *The emotions*. Baltimore: Williams and Wilkins.

Lange, M. D. (1991, August). *Gender and multicultural issues in textbooks: An editor and publisher's perspectives*. Paper presented at the meeting of the American Psychological Association, San Francisco.

Lann, I. S., & Moscicki, E. K. (1989). Introduction. *Suicide and Life-threatening Behavior, 19*, xi–xiii.

Lanyon, R. I., & Goodstein, L. D. (1982). *Personality and assessment* (2nd ed.). New York: Wiley.

LaPiere, R. (1934). Attitudes versus actions. *Social Forces, 13*, 230–237.

Lapsley, D. G. (1989). Continuity and discontinuity in adolescent social cognitive development. In R. Montemayor, G. Adams, & T. Gullotta (Eds.), *Advances in adolescence research* (Vol. 2). Orlando, FL: Academic Press.

Larson, J. H. (1988). The marriage quiz: College students' beliefs in selected myths about marriage. *Family Relations, 37*, 3–11.

Lashley, K. S. (1950). In search of the engram. In *Symposium of the society for experimental biology* (Vol. 4). New York: Cambridge University Press.

Lau, R. R. (1988). Beliefs about control and health behavior. In D. S. Gochman (Ed.), *Health behavior: Emerging perspectives*. New York: Plenum.

Lau, S., & Gruen, G. E. (1992). The social stigma of loneliness: Effect of target person's and perceiver's sex. *Personality and Social Psychology Bulletin, 18*, 182–189.

Lazar, I., Darlington, R., & collaborators. (1982). Lasting effects of early education: A report from the consortium for longitudinal studies. *Monographs of the Society for Research in Child Development, 47*.

Lazarus, R. S. (1966). *Psychological stress and the coping process*. New York: McGraw-Hill.

Lazarus, R. S. (1984). On the primacy of cognition. *American Psychologist, 39*, 124–129.

Lazarus, R. S. (1991). *Emotion and adaptation*. New York: Oxford University Press.

Lazarus, R. S., & Folkman, N. (1984). *Stress appraisal and coping*. New York: Springer.

Leafgren, A. (1989). Health and wellness programs. In M. L. Upcraft & J. N. Gardner (Eds.), *The freshman year experience*. San Francisco: Jossey-Bass.

Leahey, T. H., & Harris, R. J. (1989). *Human learning* (2nd ed.). Englewood Cliffs, NJ: Prentice-Hall.

Lefley, H. P. (1984). Delivering mental health services across cultures. In P. B. Pedersen, N. Sartorius, & A. J. Marsella (Eds.), *Mental health services: The cross-cultural context*. Beverly Hills: Sage.

Leinster, C. (1988, January 18). Black executives: How they're doing. *Fortune*, pp. 109–120.

Lempers, J. D., Clarke-Lempers, D., & Simons, R. L. (1989). Economic hardship, parenting, and distress in adolescence. *Child Development*, 60, 25–39.

Lenneberg, E. H., Rebelsky, F. G., & Nichols, I. A. (1965). The vocalization of infants born to deaf and hearing parents. *Human Development*, 8, 23–37.

Lepper, M., Greene, D., & Nisbett, R. E. (1973). Undermining children's intrinsic interest with extrinsic rewards. *Journal of Personality and Social Psychology*, 28, 129–137.

Lerner, H. G. (1989). *The dance of intimacy*. New York: Harper & Row.

Lerner, P., & Lerner, H. (1989). Rorschach measures of psychoanalytic theories of defense. In J. N. Butcher & C. D. Spielberger (Eds.), *Advances in personality assessment* (Vol. 8). Hillsdale, NJ: Erlbaum.

Lerner, R. M., Petersen, A. C., & Brooks-Gunn, J. (Eds.). (1991). *Encyclopedia of adolescence*. New York: Garland.

Lerner, R. M., & von Eye, A. (1992). Sociobiology and human development: Arguments and evidence. *Human Development*, 35, 12–33.

Lesser, G., Fifer, G., & Clark, D. (1965). Mental abilities of children from different social classes and cultural groups. *Monographs of the Society for Research in Child Development*, 304 (4, Whole No. 102).

Lester, D. (1989). *Can we prevent suicide?* New York: AMS.

Levenson, J. L., & Bemis, C. (1991). The role of psychological factors in cancer onset and progression. *Psychosomatics*, 32, 124–132.

Leventhal, H., & Tomarken, A. J. (1986). Emotion: Today's problems. *Annual Review of Psychology*, 37, 565–610.

Levine, M., & Perkins, D. V. (1987). *Principles of community psychology*. New York: Oxford University Press.

LeVine, S. (1979). *Mothers and wives: Gusii women of East Africa*. Chicago: University of Chicago Press.

Levinson, D. (1978). *The seasons of a man's life*. New York: Knopf.

Levinson, D. J. (1987, August). *The seasons of a woman's life*. Paper presented at the meeting of the American Psychological Association, New York.

Levitan, I. B., & Kaczmarek, L. K. (1991). *The neuron*. New York: Oxford University Press.

Levy, G. D. (1991, April). *Effects of gender constancy, figure's sex and size on preschoolers' gender constancy: Sometimes big girls do cry*. Paper presented at the Society for Research in Child Development meeting, Seattle.

Levy, G. D., & Carter, D. B. (1989). Gender schema, gender constancy, and gender-role knowledge: The roles of cognitive factors in preschoolers' gender-role stereotype attributions. *Developmental Psychology*, 25, 444–449.

Levy, A. B., Dixon, K. N., & Stern, S. O. (1989). How are depression and bulimia related? *American Journal of Psychiatry*, 146, 162–169.

Levy, S. M. (1985). *Behavior and cancer*. San Francisco: Jossey-Bass.

Lewinsohn, P. M., Antonuccio, D. O., Steinmetz, J., & Teri, L. (1984). *The coping with depression course: A psychoeducational intervention for unipolar depression*. Eugene, OR: Castalia.

Lewinsohn, P. M. (1987). The Coping with Depression course. In R. F. Munoz (Ed.), *Depression prevention*. New York: Hemisphere.

Lewis, M., Feiring, C., McGuffog, C., & Jaskir, J. (1984). Predicting psychopathology in six-year-olds from early social relations. *Child Development*, 55, 123–136.

Liben, L. S., & Signorella, M. L. (Eds.). (1987). *Children's gender schemata: New directions in child development*. San Francisco: Jossey-Bass.

Lidz, C. W., Mulvey, E. P., Appelbaum, P. S., & Cleveland, S. (1989). Commitment: The consistency of clinicians and the use of legal standards. *American Journal of Psychiatry*, 146, 176–181.

Lieberman, M. A., Yalom, I. D., & Miles, M. B. (1973). *Encounter groups: First facts*. New York: Basic.

Liebert, R. J., & Sprafkin, J. (1988). *The early window: Effects of television on children and youth* (2nd ed.). New York: Pergamon.

Lifshitz, F., Pugliese, M. T., Moses, N., & Weyman-Daum, M. (1987). Parental health beliefs as a cause of non-organic failure to thrive. *Pediatrics*, 80, 175–182.

Lincoln, J. R., & Kalleberg, A. L. (1990). *Culture, control, and commitment: A study of work organization and work attitudes in the United States and Japan*. New York: Cambridge University Press.

Lindskold, S., & Han, G. (1988). GRIT as a foundation for integrative bargaining. *Personality and Social Psychology Bulletin*, 14, 335–345.

Linn, M. C., & Hyde, J. S. (1991). Cognitive and psychosocial gender differences, trends in. In R. M. Lerner, A. C. Petersen, & J. Brooks-Gunn (Eds.), *Encyclopedia of adolescence* (Vol. 1). New York: Garland.

Linn, M. C., & Peterson, A. C. (1986). A meta-analysis of gender differences in spatial ability: Implications for mathematics and science achievement. In J. S. Hyde & M. C. Linn (Eds.), *The psychology of gender: Advances through meta-analysis*. Baltimore: Johns Hopkins University Press.

Lips, H. M. (1988). *Sex and gender*. Mountain View, CA: Mayfield.

Lipsitz, J. (1984). *Successful schools for young adolescents*. New Brunswick, NJ: Transaction.

Litt, I. F. (1991). Eating disorders, medical complications of. In R. M. Lerner, A. C. Petersen, & J. Brooks-Gunn (Eds.), *Encyclopedia of adolescence* (Vol. 1). New York: Garland.

Lloyd, S. A. (1991). The darkside of courtship: Violence and sexual exploitation. *Family Relations*, 40, 14–20.

Lobstein, D. D., Ismail, A. H., & Rasmussen, C. L. (1989). Beta-endorphin and components of emotionality discriminate between physically active and sedentary men. *Biological Psychiatry*, 26, 3–14.

Locke, J. L., Bekken, K. E., Wein, D., & Ruzecki, V. (1991, April). *Neuropsychology of babbling: Laterality effects in the production of rhythmic manual activity*. Paper presented at the Society for Research in Child Development meeting, Seattle.

Loehlin, J. C. (1992). *Genes and environment in personality development*. Newbury Park, CA: Sage.

Loehr, J. (1989, May). [Personal communication.] United States Tennis Association Training Camp, Saddlebrook, FL.

Loftus, E. F. (1975). Spreading activation within semantic categories: Comments on Rosch's "Cognitive representations of semantic categories." *Journal of Experimental Psychology*, 104, 234–240.

Loftus, E. F. (1979). *Eyewitness testimony*. Cambridge, MA: Harvard University Press.

Logue, A. W. (1986). *Eating and drinking*. New York: W. H. Freeman.

Long, P. (1986, January). Medical mesmerism. *Psychology Today*, pp. 28–29.

Long, T., & Long, L. (1984). *The handbook for latchkey children and their parents*. New York: Berkley.

Longabaugh, R. (1980). The systematic observation of behavior in naturalistic settings. In H. C. Triandis & J. W. Berry (Eds.), *Handbook of cross-cultural psychology: Methodology* (Vol. 2). Boston: Allyn & Bacon.

Lonner, W. J. (1980). The search for psychological universals. In H. C. Triandis & W. E. Lambert (Eds.), *Handbook of cross-cultural psychology* (Vol. 1). Boston: Allyn & Bacon.

Lonner, W. J. (1988, October). *The introductory psychology text and cross-cultural psychology: A survey of cross-cultural psychologists*. Bellingham, WA: Center for Cross-Cultural Research, Western Washington University.

Lonner, W. J. (1990). An overview of cross-cultural testing and assessment. In R. W. Brislin (Ed.), *Applied cross-cultural psychology*. Newbury Park, CA: Sage.

Lopata, H. (1979). *Women as widows*. New York: Elsevier.

Lorenz, K. (1966). *On aggression*. San Diego: Harcourt Brace Jovanovich.

Lorion, R., & Allen, L. (1989). Preventive services in mental health. In D. A. Rochefort (Ed.), *Handbook on mental health policy in the United States*. New York: Greenwood.

Lozoff, B. (1989). Nutrition and behavior. *American Psychologist, 44*, 231–236.

Luborsky, L., & Crits-Christoph, P. (1990). *Understanding transference*. New York: Basic.

Ludolph, P. (1982, August). *A reanalysis of the literature on multiple personality*. Paper presented at the American Psychological Association, Washington, DC.

Luria, A., & Herzog, E. (1985, April). *Gender segregation across and within settings*. Paper presented at the biennial meeting of the Society for Research in Child Development, Toronto.

Lykken, D. T. (1985). The probity of the polygraph. In S. M. Kassin & L. S. Wrightsman (Eds.), *The psychology of evidence and trial procedure*. Beverly Hills: Sage.

Lykken, D. T. (1987, Spring). The validity of tests: Caveat emptor. *Jurimetrics Journal*, 263–270.

Lynch, G. (1990, June). *The many shapes of memory and the several forms of synaptic plasticity*. Paper presented at the meeting of the American Psychological Society, Dallas.

Maccoby, E. E. (1980). *Social development*. San Diego: Harcourt Brace Jovanovich.

Maccoby, E. E. (1987, November). Interview with Elizabeth Hall: All in the family. *Psychology Today*, pp. 54–60.

Maccoby, E. E. (1990, June). *Gender differentiations*. Paper presented at the meeting of the American Psychological Society, Dallas.

Maccoby, E. E., & Jacklin, C. N. (1974). *The psychology of sex differences*. Palo Alto, CA: Stanford University Press.

Maccoby, E. E., & Jacklin, C. N. (in press). Gender segregation in childhood. In H. Reese (Ed.), *Advances in child development and behavior* (Vol. 20). New York: Academic Press.

Maccoby, E. E., & Martin, J. A. (1983). Socialization in the context of the family: Parent-child interaction. In P. H. Mussen (Ed.), *Handbook of child psychology* (4th ed., Vol. 4). New York: Wiley.

Macdonald, B. (1989). Outside the sisterhood: Ageism in women's studies. *Women's Studies Quarterly*, 6–11.

MacDonald, K. (1987). Parent-child physical play with rejected, neglected and popular boys. *Developmental Psychology, 23*, 705–711.

MacIver, D., Urdan, T., Beck, J., Midgley, C., Reuman, D., Tasko, A., Fenzel, L. M., Arhar, J., & Kramer, L. (1992, March). *Changing schools and classrooms in the middle grades: Research on new partnerships, processes, practices, and programs*. Paper presented at the meeting of the Society for Research on Adolescence, Washington, DC.

MacKenzie, R. (Ed.). (1992). *Classics in group psychotherapy*. New York: Guilford.

Maddi, S. (1986, August). *The great stress-illness controversy*. Paper presented at the meeting of the American Psychological Association, Washington, DC.

Mader, S. S. (1991). *Human biology* (2nd ed.). Dubuque, IA: Wm. C. Brown.

Madsen, W. (1964). The alcoholic agringado. *American Anthropologist, 66*, 355–361.

Mager, R. F. (1972). *Goal analysis*. Belmont, CA: Fearon.

Mahler, M. (1979). *Separation-individuation*. New York: Jason Aronson.

Mahoney, M. J. (1989). Sport psychology. In *The G. Stanley Hall Lecture Series* (Vol. 9). Washington, DC: American Psychological Association.

Mahoney, M. J., Gabriel, T. J., & Perkins, T. S. (1987). Psychological skills and exceptional athletic performance. *The Sport Psychologist, 1*, 181–199.

Maier, N. R. F. (1931). Reasoning in humans. *Journal of Comparative Psychology, 12*, 181–194.

Major, B., & Testa, M. (1989). Social comparison processes and judgments of entitlement and satisfaction. *Journal of Experimental Social Psychology, 25*, 101–120.

Malamuth, N. M., & Donnerstein, E. (Eds.). (1983). *Pornography and sexual aggression*. New York: Academic Press.

Malatesta, C. (1990, May 28). Commentary. *Newsweek*, p. 61.

Malinowski, B. (1927). *Sex and repression in savage society*. New York: Humanities.

Mandler, G. (1980). Recognizing: The judgment of previous occurrences. *Psychological Review, 87*, 252–271.

Mandler, G. (1984). *Mind and body*. New York: W. W. Norton.

Manley, A., Lin-Fu, J. S., Miranda, M., Noonan, A., & Parker T. (1985). Special health concerns of ethnic minority women. In U.S. Department of Health and Human Services, *Women's health: Report of the Public Health Service Task Force on Women's Health Issues*. Washington, DC: U.S. Public Health Service.

Mann, L. (1980). Cross-cultural study of small groups. In H. C. Triandis & R. W. Brislin (Eds.), *Handbook of cross-cultural psychology* (Vol. 5). Boston: Allyn & Bacon.

Manning, A. (1989). The genetic bases of aggression. In J. Groebel & R. A. Hinde (Eds.), *Aggression and war*. New York: Cambridge University Press.

Maraceck, J. (1990, August). *Towards a feminist post-structural psychology*. Paper presented at the meeting of the American Psychological Association, Boston.

Maratsos, M. (1989). Innateness and plasticity in language acquisition. In M. L. Rice (Ed.), *The teachability of language*. Baltimore, MD: Brookes.

Maratsos, M. P. (1991). How the acquisition of nouns may be different from that of verbs. In N. A. Krasnegor, D. M. Rumbaugh, M. Studdert-Kennedy, & R. L. Schiefelbusch (Eds.), *Biological and behavioral determinants of language development*. Hillsdale, NJ: Erlbaum.

Marek, G. J., & Seiden, L. S. (1991). Neurotransmitters in affective disorders. In T. Archer & S. Hansen (Eds.), *Behavioral biology: Neuroendocrine axis*. Hillsdale, NJ: Erlbaum.

Marín, G., & Marín, B. V. (1991). *Research with Hispanic populations*. Newbury Park, CA: Sage.

Markein, M. B., & DeRosa, R. (1991, November 19). Magic's HIV affects health educators' game plans. *USA Today*, p. 80.

Markus, H. R., & Kitayama, S. (1991). Culture and the self: Implications for cognition, emotion, and motivation. *Psychological Review, 98*, 224–253.

Marlatt, G. A., Baer, J. S., Donovan, M. A., & Kirlahan, D. R. (1989). Addictive behavior: Etiology. *Review of Physiology, 39*. Palo Alto, CA: Annual Reviews.

Marsella, A. J. (1980). Depressive experience and disorder across cultures. In H. C. Triandis & J. G. Draguns (Eds.), *Handbook of cross-cultural psychology: Psychopathology* (Vol. 6). Boston: Allyn & Bacon.

Martin, B. (1991, August). *Challenges of using the theory of reasoned action in Hispanic health research*. Paper presented at the meeting of the American Psychological Association, San Francisco.

Martin, C. L. (1989, April). *Beyond knowledge-based conceptions of gender schematic processing*. Paper presented at the biennial meeting of the Society for Research in Child Development, Kansas City.

Martin, C. L., & Halverson, C. F. (1987). The role of cognition in sex role acquisition. In D. B. Carter (Ed.), *Current conceptions of sex roles and sex typing: Theory and research*. New York: Praeger.

Martin, C. L., & Rose, H. A. (1991, April). *Children's gender-based distinctive theories*. Paper presented at the Society for Research in Child Development, Seattle.

Martin, G., & Pear, J. (1988). *Behavior modification: What it is and how to do it* (3rd ed.). Englewood Cliffs, NJ: Prentice-Hall.

Maslow, A. H. (1954). *Motivation and personality*. New York: Harper & Row.

Maslow, A. H. (1971). *The farther reaches of human nature*. New York: Viking.

Masters, J. C., & Smith, W. P. (1987). *Social comparison, social justice, and relative deprivation*. Hillsdale, NJ: Erlbaum.

Masters, W. H., & Johnson, V. E. (1966). *Human sexual response*. Boston: Little, Brown.

Matarazzo, J. D. (1979). Health psychology: APA's newest division. *The Health Psychologist I*.

Matas, L., Arend, R. A., & Sroufe, L. A. (1978). Continuity in adaptation: Quality of attachment and later competence. *Child Development, 49*, 547–556.

Matlin, M. W. (1983). *Cognition*. New York: Holt, Rinehart & Winston.

Matlin, M. W. (1988). *Perception*. Needham Heights, MA: Allyn & Bacon.

Matsumoto, D. (1989). Cultural influences on the perception of emotion. *Journal of Cross-Cultural Psychology, 20*, 92–105.

Mayo, E. (1933). *The human problems of industrial civilization*. New York: Macmillan.

Mays, V. M. (1991a, August). *Social policy implications of the definition of race*. Paper presented at the meeting of the American Psychological Association, San Francisco.

Mays, V. M. (1991b, August). *The role of sexual orientation and ethnic identification in HIV health risk*. Paper presented at the meeting of the American Psychological Association, San Francisco.

McAdoo, H. P. (Ed.). (1988). *Black families* (2nd ed.). Newbury Park, CA: Sage.

McAdoo, J. L. (1979). Well-being and fear of crime among the Black elderly. In D. E. Gelfand & A. J. Kuztik (Eds.), *Ethnicity and aging*. New York: Springer.

McBride, A. B. (1990). Mental health effects of women's multiple roles. *American Psychologist, 45*, 381–384.

McCall, R. B. (1991). Underachievers and dropouts. In R. M. Lerner, A. C. Petersen, & J. Brooks-Gunn (Eds.), *Encyclopedia of adolescence* (Vol. 2). New York: Garland.

McCandless, B. R., & Trotter, R. J. (1977). *Children* (3rd ed.). New York: Holt, Rinehart & Winston.

McCarley, R. W. (1989). The biology of dreaming sleep. In M. H. Dryger, T. Roth, & W. C. Dement (Eds.), *Principles and practice of sleep medicine*. San Diego: Harcourt Brace Jovanovich.

McClelland, D. C. (1955). Some social consequences of achievement motivation. In M. R. Jones (Ed.), *Nebraska symposium on motivation*. Lincoln: University of Nebraska Press.

McClelland, D. C. (1978). Managing motivation to expand human freedom. *American Psychologist, 33*, 201–210.

McClelland, D. C., Atkinson, J. W., Clark, R., & Lowell, E. L. (1953). *The achievement motive*. New York: Appleton-Century-Crofts.

McClintock, C. G., & Allison, S. T. (1989). Social value orientation and helping behavior. *Journal of Applied Social Psychology, 19*, 353–362.

McClure, J., Lalljee, M., Jaspers, J., & Abelson, R. P. (1989). Conjunctive explanations of success and failure: The effect of different types of causes. *Journal of Personality and Social Psychology, 56*, 19–26.

McCrae, R. R., & Costa, P. T. (1989). The structure of interpersonal traits: Wiggins' circumplex and the five-factor model. *Journal of Personality and Social Psychology, 56*, 586–595.

McDaniel, M. A., & Pressly, M. (1987). *Imagery and related mnemonic processes*. New York: Springer-Verlag.

McDougall, W. (1908). *Social psychology*. New York: G. Putnam & Sons.

McGaugh, J. L., Weinberger, N. M., & Lynch, G. (Eds.). (1990). *Brain organization and memory*. New York: Oxford University Press.

McGrath, E., Keita, G. P., Strickland, B., & Russo, N. F. (1990). *Women and depression: Risk factors and treatment issues*. Washington, DC: American Psychological Association.

McGue, M., & Bouchard, T. J. (1989). Genetic and environmental determinants of information processing and special mental abilities. In R. J. Sternberg (Ed.), *Advances in the psychology of human intelligence*. Hillsdale, NJ: Erlbaum.

McGuire, W. J. (1989). The structure of individual attitudes and of attitude systems. In A. R. Pratkanis, S. J. Breckler, & A. G. Greenwald (Eds.), *Attitude structure and function*. Hillsdale, NJ: Erlbaum.

McHugh, M., Koeske, R., & Frieze, I. H. (1986). Issues to consider in conducting nonsexist psychological research: A guide for researchers. *American Psychologist, 41*, 879–890.

McIver, T. (1988). Backward masking and other backward thoughts about music. *The Skeptical Inquirer, 13*, 50–63.

McKnight, C. C., Crosswhite, F. J., Dossey, J. A., Kifer, E., Swafford, J. O., Travers, K. J., & Cooney, T. J. (1987). *The underachieving curriculum: Assessing U.S. school mathematics from an international perspective*. Champaign, IL: Stipes.

McLaughlin, B. (1987). *Theories of second language learning*. London: Edward Arnold.

McLoyd, V. C. (in press). The declining fortunes of Black children: Psychological distress, parenting, and socioemotional development in the context of economic hardship. *Child Development*.

McNeil, E. B. (1967). *The quiet furies*. Englewood Cliffs, NJ: Prentice-Hall.

McShane, D. A. (1987). American Indians and Alaska natives in psychology. In P. J. Woods & C. S. Wilkinson (Eds.), *Is psychology the major for you?* Washington, DC: American Psychological Association.

McWhirter, D. P., Reinisch, J. M., & Sanders, S. A. (1989). *Homosexuality/heterosexuality*. New York: Oxford University Press.

Mead, M. (1928). *Coming of age in Samoa*. New York: Morrow.

Medvedev, A. A. (1974). The nucleic acids in the development of aging. In B. L. Strehler (Ed.), *Advances in gerontological research* (Vol. 1). San Diego: Academic Press.

Meehl, P. E. (1962). Schizotama, schizotypy, schizophrenia. *American Psychologist, 17*, 827–838.

Meehl, P. E. (1986). Diagnostic taxa as open concepts. In T. Millon & G. I. Klerman (Eds.), *Contemporary directions in psychopathology*. New York: Guilford.

Meichenbaum, D. (1977). *Cognitive-behavior modification. An integrative approach*. New York: Plenum.

Meichenbaum, D. (1986). Cognitive behavior modification. In F. H. Kanfer & A. P. Goldstein (Eds.), *Helping people change: A textbook of methods*. New York: Pergamon.

Meichenbaum, D., Turk, D., & Burstein, S. (1975). The nature of coping with stress. In I. Sarason & C. Spielberger (Eds.), *Stress and anxiety*. Washington, DC: Hemisphere.

Melzack, R., & Wall, P. D. (1965). Pain mechanisms: A new theory. *Science, 150*, 971–979.

Melzack, R., & Wall, P. D. (1983). *The challenge of pain*. New York: Basic.

Mercer, J. R., & Lewis, J. F. (1978). *System of multicultural pluralistic assessment*. New York: Psychological Corporation.

Mervis, J. (1986, July). NIMH data point way to effective treatment. *APA Monitor, 17*, 1, 13.

Messinger, J. C. (1971). Sex and repression in an Irish folk community. In D. S. Marshall & R. C. Suggs (Eds.), *Human sexual behavior: Variations in the ethnic spectrum*. New York: Basic.

Meyer, R. G., & Osborne, Y. V. H. (1982). *Case studies in abnormal behavior*. Boston: Allyn & Bacon.

Meyers, A. W. (1991). Biobehavioral interactions in behavioral medicine. *Behavior Therapy, 22*, 129–131.

Meyers, J. (1985). *Hemingway.* New York: Harper & Row.

Midgeley, J. (1971). Drinking and attitudes toward drinking in the Muslim community. *Quarterly Journal of Studies on Alcoholism, 32,* 148–158.

Milgram, S. (1965). Some conditions of obedience and disobedience to authority. *Human Relations, 18,* 56–76.

Milgram, S. (1974). *Obedience to authority.* New York: Harper & Row.

Miller, G. A. (1956). The magical number seven, plus or minus two: Some limits on our capacity for information processing. *Psychological Review, 48,* 337–442.

Miller, G. A. (1981). *Language and speech.* New York: W. H. Freeman.

Miller, J. B. (1976). *Toward a new psychology of women.* Boston: Beacon.

Miller, J. B. (1986). *Toward a new psychology of women* (2nd ed.). Boston: Beacon.

Miller, J. G., & Bersoff, D. M. (in press). Culture and moral judgment: How are conflicts between justice and interpersonal responsibilities resolved? *Journal of Personality and Social Psychology.*

Miller, N. E. (1959). Liberalization of basic S-R concepts: Extension to conflict behavior, motivation, and social learning. In S. Koch (Ed.), *Psychology: A study of science.* New York: McGraw-Hill.

Miller, N. E. (1985). The value of behavioral research on animals. *American Psychologist, 40,* 432–440.

Miller, N. W. (1969). Learning of visceral and glandular responses. *Science, 161,* 434–445.

Miller, S. K., & Slap, G. B. (1989). Adolescent smoking: A review of prevalence and prevention. *Journal of Adolescent Health Care, 10,* 129–135.

Miller-Jones, D. (1989). Culture and testing. *American Psychologist, 44,* 360–366.

Milligan, S. E. (1990). Understanding diversity of the urban black aged: Historical perspectives. In Z. Harel, E. A. McKinney, & M. Williams (Eds.), *Black aged.* Newbury Park, CA: Sage.

Minkler, M. (1989). Health education, health promotion and the open society: An historical perspective. *Health Education Quarterly, 16,* 17–30.

Mintz, N., & Schwartz, D. (1964). Urban ecology and psychosis: Community factors in the incidence of schizophrenia and manic-depression among Italians in Greater Boston. *International Journal of Social Psychiatry, 10,* 101–118.

Minuchin, P. (1985). Families and individual development: Provocations from the field of family therapy. *Child Development, 56,* 289–302.

Mischel, W. (1968). *Personality and assessment.* New York: Wiley.

Mischel, W. (1970). Sex-typing and socialization. In P. H. Mussen (Ed.), *Manual of child psychology* (3rd ed., Vol. 2). New York: Wiley.

Mischel, W. (1973). Toward a cognitive social learning reconceptualization of personality. *Psychological Review, 80,* 252–283.

Mischel, W. (1987). *Personality* (4th ed.). New York: Holt, Rinehart & Winston.

Mistleberger, R. E., & Rusak, B. (1989). Mechanisms and models of the circadian timekeeping system. In M. H. Dryger, T. Roth, & W. C. Dement (Eds.), *Principles and practice of sleep medicine.* San Diego: Harcourt Brace Jovanovich.

Moates, D. R., & Schumacher, G. M. (1980). *An introduction to cognitive psychology.* Belmont, CA: Wadsworth.

Monagle, K. (1990, October). Women around the world. *New Woman,* 195–197.

Money, J. (1987). Sin, sickness, or status? Homosexual gender identity and psychoneuroendocrinology. *American Psychologist, 42,* 384–399.

Monk, T. H. (1989). Circadian rhythms in subjective activation, mood, and performance efficiency. In M. H. Dryger, T. Roth, & W. C. Dement (Eds.), *Principles and practice of sleep medicine.* San Diego: Harcourt Brace Jovanovich.

Monnier, M., & Hosli, L. (1965). Humoral regulation of sleep and wakefulness by hypnogenic and activating dialyzable factors. *Progress in Brain Research, 18,* 118–123.

Montemayor, R., Adams, G. R., & Gulotta, T. P. (Eds.). (1990). *From childhood to adolescence: A transitional period.* Newbury Park, CA: Sage.

Montemayor, R., & Flannery, D. J. (1991). Parent-adolescent relations in middle and late adolescence. In R. M. Lerner, A. C. Petersen, & J. Brooks-Gunn (Eds.), *Encyclopedia of adolescence* (Vol. 2). New York: Garland.

Montemayor, R., & Hanson, E. (1985). A naturalistic view of conflict between adolescents and their parents and siblings. *Journal of Early Adolescence, 5,* 23–30.

Moorhead, G., & Griffin, R. W. (1989). *Organizational behavior.* Boston: Houghton Mifflin.

Morgan, W. P., & Goldston, S. E. (1987). *Exercise and mental health.* Washington, DC: Hemisphere.

Morris, D., Collett, P., Marsh, P., & O'Shaugnessy, M. (1979). *Gestures.* New York: Stein & Day.

Morrison, A. M., & Von Glinow, M. A. (1990). Women and minorities in management. *American Psychologist, 45,* 200–209.

Morrow, L. (1988, August 6). Through the eyes of children. *Time,* pp. 32–33.

Mortisugu, J., & Sue, S. (1983). Minority status as a stressor. In R. Felner, L. Jason, J. Mortisugu, & S. Farber (Eds.), *Preventive psychology: Theory, research, and practice.* Elmsford, NY: Pergamon.

Moses, J., Steptoe, A., Mathews, A., & Edwards, D. (1989). The effects of exercise training on mental well-being in the normal population: A controlled trial. *Journal of Psychosomatic Research, 33,* 47–61.

Munroe, R. L., & Munroe, R. H. (1975). *Cross-cultural human development.* Monterey, CA: Brooks/Cole.

Murphy, H. B. (1978). Cultural factors in the genesis of schizophrenia. In D. Rosenthal & S. S. Kety (Eds.), *The transmission of schizophrenia.* Elmsford, NY: Pergamon.

Murray, H. A. (1938). *Explorations in personality.* New York: Oxford University Press.

Muuss, R. E. (1988). Carol Gilligan's theory of sex differences in the development of moral reasoning during adolescence. *Adolescence, 23,* 229–241.

Nagata, D. K. (1989). Japanese American children and adolescents. In J. T. Gibbs & L. N. Huang (Eds.), *Children of color.* San Francisco: Jossey-Bass.

Nathan, P. (1985). Prevention of alcoholism. *Prevention is health psychology.* Hanover, NH: University Press of New England.

Nathans, J., Thomas, D., & Hogness, D. S. (1986). Molecular genetics of human color vision: The genes encoding blue, green, and red pigments. *Science, 232,* 193–202.

National Advisory Council on Economic Opportunity. (1980). *Critical choices for the '80s.* Washington, DC: U.S. Government Printing Office.

National Association for the Education of Young Children. (1988). NAEYC position statement on developmentally appropriate practices in the primary grades, serving 5-through 8-year-olds. *Young Children, 43,* 64–83.

National Center for Health Statistics. (1989a). *Health, United States, 1988.* DHHS Pub. No. (PHS) 89–1232, Public Health Service. Washington, DC: U.S. Government Printing Office.

National Center for Health Statistics. (1989b, June). *Statistics on marriage and divorce.* Washington, DC: U.S. Government Printing Office.

National Institute on Drug Abuse. (1989, July). *Survey of drug use in the United States.* Washington, DC: U.S. Government Printing Office.

Neisser, U. (1991). The development of consciousness and the acquisition of skill. In F. Kessel, P. Cole, & D. Johnson (Eds.), *Self and consciousness: Multiple perspectives.* Hillsdale, NJ: Erlbaum.

Neugarten, B. L. (1986). The aging society. In A. Pifer & L. Bronte (Eds.), *Our aging society: Paradox and promise*. New York: W. W. Norton.

Nicholson, A. N., Bradley, C. M., & Pasco, P. A. (1989). Medications: Effect on sleep and wakefulness. In M. H. Dryger, T. Roth, & W. C. Dement (Eds.), *Principles and practice of sleep medicine*. San Diego: Harcourt Brace Jovanovich.

Nolen-Hoeksema, S. (1990). *Sex differences in depression*. Stanford, CA: Stanford University Press.

Norem, J. K., & Cantor, N. (1986). Anticipatory and post-hoc cushioning strategies: Optimism and defensive pessimism in "risky" situations. *Cognitive Therapy Research, 10*, 347–362.

Nottelman, E. D., Susman, E. J., Blue, J. H., Inoff-Germain, G., Dorn, L. D., Loriaux, D. L., Cutler, G. B., & Chrousos, G. P. (1987). Gonadal and adrenal hormone correlates of adjustment in early adolescence. In R. M. Lerner & T. T. Foch (Eds.), *Biological-psychological interactions in early adolescence*. Hillsdale, NJ: Erlbaum.

Novak, C. A. (1977). Does youthfulness equal attractiveness? In L. E. Troll, J. Israel, & K. Israel (Eds.), *Looking ahead: A woman's guide to the problems and joys of growing older*. Englewood Cliffs, NJ: Prentice-Hall.

Novlin, D., Robinson, B. A., Culbreth, L. A., & Tordoff, M. G. (1983). Is there a role for the liver in the control of food intake? *American Journal of Clinical Nutrition, i*, 233–246.

Nyiti, R. M. (1982). The validity of "cultural differences explanations" for cross-cultural variation in the rate of Piagetian cognitive development. In D. Wagner & H. Stevenson (Eds.), *Cultural perspectives on child development*. New York: W. H. Freeman.

O'Brien, E. J., & Myers, J. L. (1985). When comprehension difficulty improves memory for text. *Journal of Experimental Psychology: Learning, Memory, and Cognition, 11*, 12–21.

Offer, D., & Church, R. B. (1991). Turmoil, adolescent. In R. M. Lerner, A. C. Petersen, & J. Brooks-Gunn (Eds.), *Encyclopedia of adolescence* (Vol. 2). New York: Garland.

Offer, D., Ostrov, E., Howard, K. I., & Atkinson, R. (1988). *The teenage world: Adolescents' self-image in ten countries*. New York: Plenum.

Offerman, L. R., & Gowing, M. K. (1990). Organizations of the future: Changes and challenges. *American Psychologist, 45*, 95–108.

Ogbu, J. U. (1974). *The next generation: An ethnography of education in an urban neighborhood*. New York: Academic Press.

Ogbu, J. U. (1986). The consequences of the American caste system. In U. Neisser (Ed.), *The school achievement of minority children: New perspectives*. Hillsdale, NJ: Erlbaum.

Ogbu, J. U. (1989, April). *Academic socialization of Black children: An inoculation against future failure?* Paper presented at the Society for Research in Child Development meeting, Kansas City.

Okano, Y. (1977). *Japanese Americans and mental health*. Los Angeles: Coalition for Mental Health.

Olds, J. M. (1958). Self-stimulation experiments and differentiated rewards systems. In H. H. Jasper, L. D. Proctor, R. S. Knighton, W. C. Noshay, & R. T. Costello (Eds.), *Reticular formation of the brain*. Boston: Little, Brown.

Olds, J. M., & Milner P. M. (1954). Positive reinforcement produced by electrical stimulation of the septal area and other areas of the rat brain. *Journal of Comparative and Physiological Psychology, 47*, 419–427.

Orford, J. (1992). *Community psychology: Theory and practice*. New York: John Wiley.

Ornstein, R., & Sobel, D. (1989). *Healthy pleasures*. Reading, MA: Addison-Wesley.

Osgood, C. E. (1962). *An alternative to war or surrender*. Urbana: University of Illinois Press.

Ossip-Klein, D. J., Doyne, E. J., Bowman, E. D., Osborn, K. M., McDougall-Wilson, I. B., & Neimeyer, R. A. (1989). Effects of running or weight lifting on self-concept in clinically depressed women. *Journal of Consulting and Clinical Psychology, 57*, 158–161.

Overton, W. F., & Byrnes, J. P. (1991). Cognitive development. In R. M. Lerner, A. C. Petersen, & J. Brooks-Gunn (Eds.), *Encyclopedia of adolescence* (Vol. 1). New York: Garland.

Pacheco, S. L., & Valdez, L. F. (1989, August). *The present state and future direction of Hispanic psychology*. Paper presented at the meeting of the American Psychological Association, New Orleans.

Padilla, A. M., & Ruiz, R. A. (1975). Community mental health services for the Spanish speaking/surnamed population. *American Psychologist, 30*, 392–405.

Padilla, A. M., Ruiz, R. A., & Alvarez, R. (1989). Community mental health services for the Spanish speaking/surnamed population. In D. R. Atkinson, G. Morten, & D. W. Sue (Eds.), *Counseling American minorities*. Dubuque, IA: Wm. C. Brown.

Paffenbarger, R. S., Hyde, R. T., Wing, A. L., & Hsieh, C. (1986). Physical activity, all-cause mortality, and longevity of college alumni. *New England Journal of Medicine, 314*, 605–612.

Paivio, A. (1971). *Imagery and verbal processes*. New York: Holt, Rinehart & Winston.

Paivio, A. (1986). *Mental representation: A dual coding approach*. New York: Oxford University Press.

Palaca, J. (1990). Women left out at NIH. *Science, 248*, 1601–1602.

Palmore, E. B. (1975). *The honorable elders: A cross-cultural analysis of aging in Japan*. Durham, NC: Duke University Press.

Paludi, M. A. (1992). *The psychology of women*. Dubuque, IA: Wm. C. Brown.

Parke, R. (1988). Families in life-span perspective: A multilevel developmental approach. In E. M. Hetherington & M. Perlmutter (Eds.), *Child development in life-span perspective*. Hillsdale, NJ: Erlbaum.

Parker, J. G., & Asher, S. R. (1987). Peer relations and later personal adjustment: Are low accepted children at risk? *Psychological Bulletin, 102*, 357–389.

Parker, J. G., & Gottman, J. M. (1989). Social and emotional development in a relational context: Friendship interaction from early childhood to adolescence. In T. J. Berndt & G. W. Ladd (Eds.), *Peer relations in child development*. New York: Wiley.

Parkin, A. J. (1984). Levels of processing, context, and facilitation of pronunciation. *Acta Psychologica, 55*, 19–29.

Parlee, M. B. (1979, April). The friendship bond: *PT*'s survey report on friendship in America. *Psychology Today*, pp. 43–54, 113.

Passuth, P. M., Maines, D. R., & Neugarten, B. L. (1984). *Age norms and age constraints twenty years later*. Paper presented at the annual meeting of the Midwest Sociological Society, Chicago.

Patterson, G. R. (1991, April). *Which parenting skills are necessary for what?* Paper presented at the biennial meeting of the Society for Research in Child Development, Seattle.

Patterson, K., Vargha-Khadem, F., & Polkey, C. E. (1989). Reading with one hemisphere. *Brain, 112*, 39–63.

Paul, G. L. (1967). Strategy of outcome research in psychotherapy. *Journal of Consulting Psychology, 31*, 109–119.

Paunonen, S. V., Jackson, D. N., Trzebinski, J., & Forsterling, F. (1992). Personality structure across cultures: A multimethod evaluation. *Journal of Personality and Social Psychology, 62*, 447–456.

Pavlov, I. P. (1927). *Conditioned reflexes* (F. V. Anrep, Trans. and Ed.). New York: Dover.

Pellegrini, A. D., Perlmutter, J. C., Galda, L., & Brody, G. H. (1990). Joint reading between Black Head Start children and their mothers. *Child Development, 61*, 443–453.

Penfield, W. (1947). Some observations in the cerebral cortex of man. *Proceedings of the Royal Society, 134*, 349.

Pennebaker, J. W. (1983). *The psychology of physical symptoms*. New York: Springer-Verlag.

Pennebaker, J. W., & Lightner, J. M. (1980). Competition of internal and external information in an exercise setting. *Journal of Personality and Social Psychology, 39,* 165–174.

Penner, S. G. (1987). Parental responses to grammatical and ungrammatical child utterances. *Child Development, 58,* 376–384.

Peplau, L. A., & Gordon, A. L. (1985). Women and men in love: Gender differences in close heterosexual relationships. In V. E. O'Leary, R. K. Unger, & B. S. Wallston (Eds.), *Women, gender, and social psychology.* Hillsdale, NJ: Erlbaum.

Peplau, L. A., & Perlman, D. (Eds.). (1982). *Loneliness: A sourcebook of current theory, research and therapy.* New York: Wiley.

Perlmutter, M. (Ed.). (in press). *Late-life potential.* Washington, DC: Gerontological Association of America.

Perls, F. S. (1969). *Gestalt therapy verbatim.* Lafayette, CA: Real People.

Persinger, M. A., & Krippner, S. (in press). Experimental dream telepathy-clairvoyance and geomagnetic activity. *Journal of the American Society for Psychical Research.*

Pert, A. B., & Snyder, S. H. (1973). Opiate receptor: Demonstration in a nervous tissue. *Science, 179,* 1011–1104.

Pervin, L. (1989). *Personality: Theory and research* (5th ed.). New York: Wiley.

Peskin, H. (1967). Pubertal onset and ego functioning. *Journal of Abnormal Psychology, 72,* 1–15.

Petersen, A. C. (1979, January). Can puberty come any faster? *Psychology Today,* pp. 45–56.

Peterson, C. (1988). *Personality.* San Diego: Harcourt Brace Jovanovich.

Peterson, S. B. (1991, August). *Development of a general coding manual for evaluating gender and race bias in texts.* Paper presented at the meeting of the American Psychological Association, San Francisco.

Phares, E. J. (1984). *Personality.* Columbus, OH: Merrill.

Phelps, R. E., Spreight, S. L., Pepinsky, H., Baker, M., & Cox, C. (1991, August). *Implementing our knowledge of cross-cultural interaction: The African and American case.* Paper presented at the meeting of the American Psychological Association, San Francisco.

Phelps, S., & Austin, N. (1987). *The assertive woman.* San Luis Obispo, CA: Impact.

Phillips, D. (1989). Future directions and needs for child care in the United States. In J. Lande, S. Scarr, & N. Gunzenhauser (Eds.), *Caring for children: Challenge to America.* Hillsdale, NJ: Erlbaum.

Phillips, R. L., & others. (1980). Influence of selection versus lifestyle on risk of fatal cancer and cardiovascular disease among Seventh-Day Adventists. *American Journal of Epidemiology, 112,* 296–314.

Phinney, J. (1991, April). *Research with ethnic minority adolescents.* Paper presented at the Society for Research in Child Development meeting, Seattle.

Phinney, J. S. (1989). Stages of ethnic identity development in minority group adolescents. *Journal of Early Adolescence, 9,* 34–49.

Phinney, J. S., & Alipura, L. L. (1990). Ethnic identity in college students from four ethnic groups. *Journal of Adolescence, 13,* 171–183.

Phinney, J. S., Chavira, V., & Williamson, L. (1992). Acculturation attitudes and self-esteem among high school and college students. *Youth and Society, 25,* 299–312.

Phinney, J. S., Espinoza, C., & Onwughalu, M. N. (1992, March). *Accommodation and conflict: The relationship of ethnic identity and American identity among Asian American, Black, and Hispanic adolescents.* Paper presented at the meeting of the Society for Research on Adolescence, Washington, DC.

Piaget, J. (1960). *The child's conception of the world.* Totowa, NJ: Littlefield.

Piccione, C., Hilgard, E. R., & Zimbardo, P. G. (1989). On the degree of stability in measured hypnotizability over a 25-year period. *Journal of Personality and Social Psychology, 56,* 289–295.

Pike, K. M., & Rodin, J. (1991). Mothers, daughters, and disordered eating. *Journal of Abnormal Psychology, 100,* 198–204.

Pinderhughes, E. (1982). Afro-American families and the victim system. In M. McGoldrick, M. J. Pearce, & J. Giordano (Eds.), *Ethnicity and family therapy.* New York: Guilford.

Pines, A., & Aronson, E. (1988). *Career burnout: Causes and cures.* New York: Free Press.

Pipes, P. (1988). Nutrition during infancy. In S. R. Williams & B. S. Worthington-Roberts (Eds.), *Nutrition through the life cycle.* St. Louis: Times Mirror/Mosby.

Pirsig, R. (1974). *Zen and the art of motorcycle maintenance.* New York: Morrow.

Plante, T. G., & Rodin, J. (1990). Physical fitness and enhanced psychological health. *Current psychology research and reviews, 9,* 3–24.

Plath, S. (1971). *The bell jar.* New York: Harper & Row.

Pleck, J. (1981). *Three conceptual issues in research on male roles.* Working paper no. 98, Wellesley College Center for Research on Women, Wellesley, MA.

Pleck, J. H. (1983). The theory of male sex role identity: Its rise and fall, 1936–present. In M. Lewin (Ed.), *In the shadow of the past: Psychology portrays the sexes.* New York: Columbia University Press.

Pleck, J. H., Sonnenstein, F. L., & Ku, L. C. (in press). Problem behaviors and masculine ideology in adolescent males. In R. Ketterlinus & M. E. Lamb (Eds.), *Adolescent problem behaviors.* Hillsdale, NJ: Erlbaum.

Plomin, R. (1989). Environment and genes: Determinants of behavior. *American Psychologist, 44,* 105–111.

Plomin, R. (1991, April). *The nature of nurture: Genetic influence on "environmental" measures.* Paper presented at the meeting of the Society for Research in Child Development, Seattle.

Plomin, R., DeFries, J. C., & McClearn, G. E. (1990). *Behavioral genetics: A primer* (2nd ed.). New York: W. H. Freeman.

Plomin, R., DeFries, J. C., & McClearn, G. E. (in press). *Behavioral genetics: A primer.* New York: W. H. Freeman.

Plotnick, A. B., Payne, P. A., & O'Grady, D. J. (1991). Correlates of hypnotizability in children: Absorption, vividness of imagery, fantasy play, and social desirability. *American Journal of Clinical Hypnosis, 34,* 51–58.

Plutchik, R. (1980). *Emotion: A psychoevolutionary synthesis.* New York: Harper & Row.

Plutchik, R. (1989). Measuring emotions. In R. Plutchik & H. Kellerman (Eds.), *The measurement of emotions* (Vol. 5). San Diego: Academic Press.

Polivy, J., & Herman, C. P. (1991). Good and bad dieters: Self-perception and reaction to a dietary challenge. *International Journal of Eating Disorders, 10,* 91–99.

Porcino, J. (1983). *Growing older, getting better: A handbook for women in the second half of life.* Reading, MA: Addison-Wesley.

Posner, M., & Rothbart, M. (1989, August). *Attention: Normal and pathological development.* Paper presented at the meeting of the American Psychological Association, New Orleans.

Pouissant, A. F. (1972, February). Blaxploitation movies—Cheap thrills that degrade Blacks. *Psychology Today,* pp. 22–33.

Powell, G. J., & Fuller, M. (1972). The variables for positive self-concept among young Southern Black adolescents. *Journal of the National Medical Association, 43,* 72–79.

Premack, D. (1986). *Gavagai! The future history of the ape language controversy.* Cambridge, MA: MIT Press.

Price, J. M., & Dodge, K. A. (in press). Reactive and proactive aggression among young children: Relations to peer status and social context dimensions. *Journal of Abnormal Child Psychology.*

Price-Williams, D., Gordon, W., & Ramirez, M. (1969). Skill and conservation: A study of pottery-making children. *Developmental Psychology, 1,* 796.

Prillerman, S. L., Myers, H. F., & Smedley, B. D. (1989). Psychosocial stress, academic achievement and psychological well-being of Afro-American college students. In G. L. Berry & J. K. Asamen (Eds.), *Black students: Psychological issues and academic achievement.* Newbury Park, CA: Sage.

Prior, J., Vigna, Y. M., & Watson, D. (1989). Spironolactone with physiological female steroids for presurgical therapy of male-female transsexualism. *Archives of Sexual Behavior, 18,* 49–58.

Proust, M. (1928). *Swanns' way* (C. K. Scott Moncrieff, trans.). New York: Modern Library.

Pryor, J. B., Reeder, G. D., Vinacco, R., & Kott, T. L. (1989). The instrumental and symbolic functions of attitudes toward persons with AIDS. *Journal of Applied Social Psychology, 19,* 377–404.

Pylyshyn, Z. W. (1973). What the mind's eye tells the mind's brain: A critique of mental imagery. *Psychological Bulletin, 80,* 1–24.

Quina, K. (1986). *Teaching research methods: A multidimensional feminist curricular transformation plan.* Wellesley College Center for Research on Women. Working Paper No. 164.

Rabin, D. S., & Chrousos, G. P. (1991). Androgens, gonadal. In R. M. Lerner, A. C. Petersen, & J. Brooks-Gunn (Eds.), *Encyclopedia of adolescence* (Vol. 1). New York: Garland.

Rabinowitz, F. E., & Cochran, S. V. (1987). Counseling men in groups. In M. Scher, M. Stevens, G. Good, & G. A. Eichenfield (Eds.), *Handbook of counseling and psychotherapy with men.* Newbury Park, CA: Sage.

Rabinowitz, V. C., & Sechzur, J. (in press). Feminist methodologies. In F. L. Denmark & M. A. Paludi (Eds.), *Handbook on the psychology of women.* Westport, CT: Greenwood.

Rabkin, J. (1979). Ethnic density and psychiatric hospitalization: Hazards of minority status. *American Journal of Psychiatry, 136,* 1562–1566.

Ramey, C. (1989, April). *Parent-child intellectual similarities in natural and altered ecologies.* Paper presented at the biennial meeting of the Society for Research in Child Development, Kansas City.

Ramirez, M. (1990). *Psychotherapy and counseling with minorities.* Riverside, NJ: Pergamon.

Ramirez, O. (1989). Mexican American children and adolescents. In J. T. Gibbs & L. N. Huang (Eds.), *Children of color.* San Francisco: Jossey-Bass.

Ramirez, O., & Arce, C. Y. (1981). The contemporary Chicano family: An empirically based review. In A. Baron (Ed.), *Explorations in Chicano psychology.* New York: Praeger.

Randi, J. (1980). *Flim-flam!* New York: Lippincott.

Rapaport, D. (1967). On the psychoanalytic theory of thinking. In M. M. Gill (Ed.), *The collected papers of David Rapaport.* New York: Basic.

Rapaport, K., & Burkhart, B. (1984). Personality and attitudes characteristic of sexually coercive college males. *Journal of Abnormal Psychology, 93,* 216–221.

Rappaport, A., Bornstein, G., & Erev, I. (1989). Intergroup competition for public goods: Effects of unequal resources and relative group size. *Journal of Personality and Social Psychology, 5,* 748–756.

Rawlins, W. K. (1992). *Friendship matters.* Hawthorne, NY: Aldine.

Rayman, J. R., & Garis, J. W. (1989). Counseling. In M. L. Upcraft & J. N. Gardner (Eds.), *The freshman year experience.* San Francisco: Jossey-Bass.

Regier, D. A., Hirschfeld, R. M. A., Goodwin, F. K., Burke, J. D., Lazar, J. B., & Judd, L. L. (1988). The NIMH depression awareness, recognition, and treatment program: Structure, aims, and scientific basis. *The American Journal of Psychiatry, 145,* 1351–1357.

Rehm, L. P. (1989). Behavioral models of anxiety and depression. In P. K. Kendall & D. Watson (Eds.), *Anxiety and depression.* San Diego: Academic Press.

Reinisch, J. M. (1990). *The Kinsey Institute new report on sex: What you must know to be sexually literate.* New York: St. Martin's.

Remafedi, G. (1991). Homosexuality, adolescent. In R. M. Lerner, A. C. Petersen, & J. Brooks-Gunn (Eds.), *Encyclopedia of adolescence* (Vol. 1). New York: Garland.

Restak, R. M. (1988). *The mind.* New York: Bantam.

Revenson, T. A. (in press). All other things are not equal: An ecological approach to personality and disease. In H. S. Friedman (Ed.), *The disease-prone personality.* New York: Wiley.

Revitch, E., & Schlesinger, L. B. (1978). Murder: Evaluation, classification, and prediction. In I. L. Kutash, S. B. Kutash, & L. B. Schlesinger (Eds.), *Violence.* San Francisco: Jossey-Bass.

Reynolds, C. R., & Kamphaus, R. W. (Eds.). (1990). *Handbook of psychological and educational assessment of children: Intelligence and achievement.* New York: Guilford.

Rice, F. P. (1989). *Human sexuality.* Dubuque, IA: Wm. C. Brown.

Richter, C. P. (1957). On the phenomenon of sudden death in animals and man. *Psychosomatic Medicine, 19,* 191–198.

Rickel, A. U., & Allen, L. (1987). *Preventing maladjustment from infancy through adolescence.* Newbury Park: Sage.

Riger, S., & Galligan, P. (1980). An exploration of competing paradigms. *American Psychologist, 35,* 902–910.

Risser, W. L. (1989). Exercise for children. *Pediatrics in Review, 10,* 131–140.

Robins, L., & Regier, D. A. (Eds.). (1990). *Psychiatric disorders in America.* New York: Macmillan.

Robins, L. N., Helzer, J. R., Weissman, M. M., Orvasheel, H., Gruenberg, F., Burke, J. D., & Regier, D. A. (1984). Lifetime prevalence of specific psychiatric disorders in three sites. *Archives of General Psychiatry, 41,* 949–958.

Robinson, F. P. (1961). *Effective study.* New York: Harper & Row.

Robinson, I., Ziss, K., Ganza, B., Katz, S., & Robinson, E. (1991). Twenty years of the sexual revolution, 1965–1985: An update. *Journal of Marriage and the Family, 53,* 216–220.

Rodin, J. (1984, December). Interview: A sense of control. *Psychology Today,* pp. 38–45.

Rodin, J., & Ickovics, J. R. (1990). Women's health: Review and research agenda as we approach the 21st century. *American Psychologist, 45,* 1018–1034.

Rodriguez, M. L., Mischel, W., & Shoda, Y. (1989). Cognitive person variables in the delay of gratification of older children at risk. *Journal of Personality and Social Psychology, 57,* 358–366.

Roethlisberger, F., & Dickson, W. J. (1939). *Management and the worker.* Cambridge, MA: Harvard University Press.

Rogers, C. R. (1961). *On becoming a person.* Boston: Houghton Mifflin.

Rogers, C. R. (1963). The actualizing tendency in relation to "motives" and consciousness. In M. R. Jones (Ed.), *Nebraska Symposium on Motivation.* Lincoln: University of Nebraska Press.

Rogers, C. R. (1974). In retrospect: Forty-six years. *American Psychologist, 29,* 115–123.

Rogers, C. R. (1980). *A way of being.* Boston: Houghton Mifflin.

Rogers, R. W. (1989). Deindividuation and the self-regulation of behavior. In P. B. Paulus (Ed.), *Psychology of group influence.* Hillside, NJ: Erlbaum.

Roghmann, K. J. (1981). The health of school-aged children. In L. V. Klemman (Ed.), *Research priorities in maternal and child health.* Waltham, MA: Brandeis University, Office of Maternal and Child Health.

Rogler, L. H., Cortes, D. E., & Malgady, R. G. (1991). Acculturation and mental health status among Hispanics: Convergence and new directions for research. *American Psychologist, 46,* 585–597.

Rogler, L. H., Malgady, R. G., Costantino, G., & Blumenthal, R. (1987). What do culturally sensitive mental health services mean? *American Psychologist, 42,* 565–570.

Rogoff, B. (1990). *Apprenticeship in thinking: Cognitive development in social context.* New York: Oxford University Press.

Rogoff, B. (in press). Peer influences on cognitive development: Piagetian versus Vygotskian perspectives. In M. H. Bornstein & J. S. Bruner (Eds.), *Interaction in human development.* Hillsdale, NJ: Erlbaum.

Rogoff, B., & Morelli, G. (1989). Perspectives on children's development from cultural psychology. *American Psychologist, 44,* 343–348.

Rohner, R. P., & Rohner, E. C. (1981). Parental acceptance-rejection and parental control: Cross-cultural codes. *Ethnology, 20,* 245–260.

Roll, S., Hinton, R., & Glazer, M. (1974). Dreams and death: Mexican Americans vs. Anglo-Americans. *Interamerican Journal of Psychology, 8,* 111–115.

Roopnarine, J. L., & Carter, D. B. (Eds.). (1992). *Parent-child socialization in diverse cultures.* Norwood, NJ: Ablex.

Root, M. P. (Ed.). (1992). *Racially mixed people in America.* Newbury Park, CA: Sage.

Rosch, E. H. (1973). On the internal structure of perceptual and semantic categories. In T. E. Moore (Ed.), *Cognition and the acquisition of language.* New York: Academic Press.

Rose, S. D. (1989). Coping skill training in groups. *International Journal of Group Psychotherapy, 39,* 59–78.

Rosenberg, M. (1965). *Society and the adolescent self-image.* Princeton, NJ: Princeton University Press.

Rosenhan, D. L. (1973). On being sane in insane places. *Science, 179,* 250–258.

Rosenstein, M. J., Milazzo-Sayre, L. J., & Manderscheid, R. W. (1989). Care of persons with schizophrenia: A statistical profile. *Schizophrenia Bulletin, 15,* 45–58.

Rosenthal, R., & Jacobsen, L. (1968). *Pygmalian in the classroom.* New York: Holt, Rinehart & Winston.

Ross, L. (1977). The intuitive psychologist and his shortcomings: Distortions in the attribution process. In L. Berkowitz (Ed.), *Advances in experimental psychology* (Vol. 10). New York: Academic Press.

Ross, M. (1989). Relation of implicit theories to the construction of personal histories. *Psychological Review, 96,* 341–357.

Rossi, A. S. (1989). A life-course approach to gender, aging, and intergenerational relations. In K. W. Schaie & C. Schooler (Eds.), *Social structure and aging.* Hillsdale, NJ: Erlbaum.

Rothblum, E. D., Soloman, L. J., & Albee, G. W. (1986). The sociopolitical perspective of DSM-III. In T. Millon & G. L. Klerman (Eds.), *Contemporary directions in psychopathology: Toward the DSM-IV.* New York: Guilford.

Rowlett, J. D., Patel, D., & Greydanus, D. E. (1992). Homosexuality. In D. E. Greydanus & M. L. Wolraich (Eds.), *Behavioral pediatrics.* New York: Springer-Verlag.

Roy-Byrne, P. P. (Ed.). (1989). *Anxiety: New findings for the clinician.* Washington, DC: American Psychiatric Press.

Rubenstein, J., Heeren, T., Housman, D., Rubin, C., & Stechler, G. (1989). Suicidal behavior in "normal" adolescents: Risk and protective factors. *American Journal of Orthopsychiatry, 59,* 59–71.

Rubin, L. B. (1984). *Intimate strangers: Men and women working together.* New York: Harper & Row.

Rubin, Z., & Mitchell, C. (1976). Couples research as couples counseling. *American Psychologist, 31,* 17–25.

Rumbaugh, D. M., Hopkins, W. D., Washburn, D. A., & Savage-Rumbaugh, E. S. (1991). Comparative perspectives of brain, cognition, and language. In N. A. Krasnegor, D. M. Rumbaugh, M. Studdert-Kennedy, & R. L. Schiefelbusch (Eds.), *Biological and behavioral determinants of language development.* Hillsdale, NJ: Erlbaum.

Rumbaugh, D. M., & Rumbaugh, E. S. (1990, June). *Chimpanzees: Language, speech, counting and video tasks.* Paper presented at the meeting of the American Psychological Society, Dallas.

Rumberger, R. W. (1983). Dropping out of high school: The influence of race, sex, and family background. *American Educational Research Journal, 20,* 199–220.

Rumberger, R. W. (1987). High school dropouts: A review of the issues and evidence. *Review of Educational Research, 57,* 101–121.

Rumpel, E. (1988, August). *A systematic analysis of the cultural content of introductory psychology textbooks.* Unpublished master's thesis, Western Washington University.

Rushton, J. P. (1985). Differential K theory: The sociobiology of individual and group differences. *Journal of Personality and Individual Differences, 9,* 1009–1024.

Rushton, J. P. (1988). Race differences in behavior: A review and evolutionary analysis. *Journal of Personality and Individual Differences, 9,* 1035–1040.

Russo, N. F. (1984). *Women in the American Psychological Association.* Washington, DC: Women's Program Office, American Psychological Association.

Russo, N. F. (1985). *A women's mental health agenda.* Washington, DC: American Psychological Association.

Russo, N. F. (1990). Overview: Forging research priorities for women's mental health. *American Psychologist, 45,* 368–374.

Russo, N. F. (1991, August). Discussant. *Symposium on implications of demographic shifts for curriculum content in psychology.* Meeting of the American Psychological Association, San Francisco.

Russo, N. R., Olmedo, E. L., Stapp, J., & Fulcher, R. (1981). Women and minorities in psychology. *American Psychologist, 36,* 1315–1363.

Rutter, M. (1979). Protective factors in children's response to stress and disadvantage. In M. W. Kent & J. E. Rolf (Eds.), *Primary prevention in psychopathology* (Vol. 3). Hanover, NH: University Press of New England.

Rutter, M., & Garmezy, N. (1983). Developmental psychopathology. In P. H. Mussen (Eds.), *Handbook of child psychology* (4th ed., Vol. 4). New York: Wiley.

Ryan, D. W., & Gaier, E. L. (1968). Student socio-economic status and counselor contact in junior high school. *Personnel and Guidance Journal, 46,* 466–472.

Ryan, R. A. (1980). Strengths of the American Indian family: State of the art. In F. Hoffman (Ed.), *The American Indian family: Strengths and stresses.* Isleta, NM: American Indian Social Research and Development Association.

Rybash, J., Roodin, P., & Santrock, J. W. (1991). *Adult development and aging* (2nd ed.). Dubuque, IA: Wm. C. Brown.

Saarni, C. (1988). Children's understanding of the interpersonal consequences of dissemblance of nonverbal emotional-expressive behavior. *Journal of Nonverbal Behavior, 12,* 275–294.

Sackheim, H. A. (1985, June). The case for ECT. *Psychology Today,* pp. 37–40.

Sadik, N. (1991, March-April). Success in development depends on women. *Popline.* New York: World Population News Service.

Safran, J. D., & Greenberg, L. S. (1989). The treatment of anxiety and depression: The process of affective change. In P. C. Kendall & D. Watson (Eds.), *Anxiety and depression.* San Diego: Academic Press.

Sagan, C. (1980). *Cosmos.* New York: Random House.

Saldaña, D. H. (1989, August). *Acculturative stress: Hispanics face where to belong.* Paper presented at the meeting of the American Psychological Association, New Orleans.

Salzinger, K. (1986). Diagnosis: Distinguishing among behaviors. In T. Millon & G. L. Klerman (Eds.), *Contemporary directions in psychopathology: Toward the DSM-IV*. New York: Guilford.

Sandler, D. P., Comstock, G. W., Helsing, K. J., & Shore, D. L. (1989). Death from all causes in non-smokers who lived with smokers. *American Journal of Public Health, 79*, 163–167.

Sangree, W. H. (1989). Age and power: Life-course trajectories and age structuring of power relations in East and West Africa. In D. I. Kertzer & K. W. Schaie (Eds.), *Age structuring in comparative perspective*. Hillsdale, NJ: Erlbaum.

Sankar, A. (1991). Ritual and dying: A cultural analysis of social support for caregivers. *The Gerontologist, 31*, 43–50.

Santrock, J. W. (1993a). *Adolescence* (5th ed.). Dubuque, IA: Wm. C. Brown.

Santrock, J. W. (1993b). *Children* (3rd ed.). Dubuque, IA: Wm. C. Brown.

Santrock, J. W., & Warshak, R. A. (1986). Development, relationships, and legal/clinical considerations in father custody families. In M. E. Lamb (Ed.), *The father's role: Applied perspectives*. New York: Wiley.

Sarason, I. G., & Sarason, B. R. (1987). *Abnormal psychology* (5th ed.). Englewood Cliffs, NJ: Prentice-Hall.

Sarbin, T. R. (1989). Emotions as situated actions. In L. Cirillo, B. Kaplan, & S. Wapner (Eds.), *Emotions in ideal human development*. Hillsdale, NJ: Erlbaum.

Sargent, C. (1987). Skeptical fairytales from Bristol. *Journal of the Society for Psychical Research, 54*, 261–265.

Sarrel, P., & Masters, W. (1982). Sexual molestation of men by women. *Archives of Human Sexuality, 11*, 117–131.

Sartorius, N. (1992). Commentary on prognosis for schizophrenia in the third world. *Culture, Medicine, and Psychiatry, 16*, 81–84.

Saslow, C. (1982). *Basic research methods*. Reading, MA: Addison-Wesley.

Satir, V. (1964). *Conjoint family therapy*. Palo Alto, CA: Science and Behavior Books.

Sattler, J. (1988). *Assessment of children* (3rd ed.). San Diego: Jerome Sattler.

Savage-Rumbaugh, E. S. (1991). Language learning in the Bonobo: How and why they learn. In N. A. Krasnegor, D. M. Rumbaugh, M. Studdert-Kennedy, & R. L. Schiefelbusch (Eds.), *Biological and behavioral determinants of language development*. Hillsdale, NJ: Erlbaum.

Sax, G. (1989). *Principles of educational and psychological measurement* (3rd ed.). Belmont, CA: Wadsworth.

Saxe, G. B. (1981). Body parts as numerals: A developmental analysis of numeration among the Oksapmin in Papua, New Guinea. *Child Development, 52*, 306–316.

Saxe, L., Dougherty, D., & Cross, T. (1985). The validity of polygraph testing: Scientific analysis and public controversy. *American Psychologist, 40*, 355–366.

Scales, P. C. (1992). *A portrait of young adolescents in the 1990s: Implications for promoting healthy growth and development*. Carrboro, NC: Center for Early Adolescence.

Scarr, S. (1984a, May). [Interview.] *Psychology Today*, pp. 59–63.

Scarr, S. (1984b). *Mother care/other care*. New York: Basic.

Scarr, S. (1989, April). *Transracial adoption: A unique social experiment to address normative questions in human development*. Discussion at the biennial meeting of the Society for Research in Child Development, Kansas City.

Scarr, S. (1991, April). *Developmental theories for the 1990s*. Presidential address, biennial meeting of the Society for Research in Child Development, Seattle.

Scarr, S., Lande, J., & McCartney, K. (1989). Child care and the family: Complements and interactions. In J. Lande, S. Scarr, & N. Gunzenhauser (Eds.), *Caring for children: Challenge to America*. Hillsdale, NJ: Erlbaum.

Scarr, S., Phillips, D., & McCartney, K. (1989). Working mothers and their families. *American Psychologist, 44*, 1402–1409.

Scarr, S., & Weinberg, R. A. (1976). IQ test performance of black children adopted by white families. *American Psychologist, 31*, 726–739.

Schacter, S. (1971). Some extraordinary facts about obese humans and rats. *American Psychologist, 26*, 129–144.

Schachter, S., & Singer, J. E. (1962). Cognitive, social, and physiological determinants of emotional state. *Psychological Review, 69*, 379–399.

Schacter, D. L., & McGlynn, S. M. (1989). Implicit memory: Efforts of elaboration depend on unitization. *American Journal of Psychology, 102*, 151–181.

Schaffer, H. R., & Emerson, P. E. (1964). The development of social attachments in infancy. *Monographs of the Society for Research in Child Development* 2913 Serial No. 941.

Schaller, M., & Maass, A. (1989). Illusory correlation and social categorization: Toward an integration of motivational and cognitive factors in stereotype formation. *Journal of Personality and Social Psychology, 56*, 709–721.

Schank, R., & Abelson, R. (1977). *Scripts, plans, goals, and understanding*. Hillsdale, NJ: Erlbaum.

Scheff, T. J. (1966). *Being mentally ill: A sociological theory*. Chicago: Aldine.

Schensul, S. L. (1974). Commentary: Skills needed in action anthropology: Lessons from El Centro de la Causa. *Human Organization, 33*, 203–209.

Scherer, K. R., Wallbott, H. G., Matsumoto, D., & Kudoh, T. (1988). Emotional experience in cultural context: A comparison between Europe, Japan, and the United States. In K. R. Scherer (Ed.), *Facets of emotion: Recent research*. Hillsdale, NJ: Erlbaum.

Schneidman, E. S. (1971). Suicide among the gifted. *Suicide and Life-threatening Behavior, 1*, 23–45.

Schofield, J., & Pavelchak, M. (1985). The day after: The impact of a media event. *American Psychologist, 40*, 542–548.

Schofield, J. W., & Pavelchak, M. A. (1989). Fallout from *The Day After*: Impact of the TV film on attitudes related to nuclear war. *Journal of Applied Social Psychology, 19*, 433–448.

Schou, M. (1989). Lithium prophylaxis: Myths and realities. *The American Journal of Psychiatry, 146*, 573–576.

Schreiber, J. M., & Homiak, J. P. (1981). Mexican Americans. In A. Harwood (Ed.), *Ethnicity and medical care*. Cambridge, MA: Harvard University Press.

Schulz, R., & Curnow, C. (1988). Peak performance and age among superathletes: Track and field, swimming, baseball, tennis, and golf. *Journal of Gerontology, 43*, 113–120.

Schunk, D. H. (1983). Developing children's self-efficacy and skills: The roles of social comparative information and goal-setting. *Contemporary Educational Psychology, 8*, 76–86.

Schuster, C. S., & Ashburn, S. S. (1986). *The process of human development* (2nd ed.). Boston: Little, Brown.

Schwartz, R., & Eriksen, M. (1989). Statement of the Society for Public Health Education on the national health promotion disease prevention objectives for the year 2000. *Health Education Quarterly, 16*, 3–7.

Schwartz, S. H. (1990). Individualism-collectivism. *Journal of Cross-Cultural Psychology, 21*, 139–157.

Scribner, S. (1977). Modes of thinking and ways of speaking: Culture and logic reconsidered. In P. N. Johnson-Laird & P. C. Watson (Eds.), *Thinking: Readings in cognitive science*. New York: Cambridge University Press.

Seager, J., & Olson, A. (Eds.). (1986). *Women of the world: An international atlas*. New York: Simon & Schuster.

Searight, H. R., & Merkel, W. T. (1991). Systems theory and its discontents: Clinical and ethical issues. *The American Journal of Family Therapy, 19*, 19–29.

Sears, D. O. (1987). Symbolic racism. In P. Katz & D. Taylor (Eds.), *Towards the elimination of racism: Profile in controversy*. New York: Plenum.

Sears, D. O., & McConahay, J. B. (1973). *The politics of violence: The new urban Blacks and the Watts riot*. Boston: Houghton Mifflin.

Sears, D. O., Peplau, L. A., Freedman, J. L., & Taylor, S. E. (1988). *Social psychology* (6th ed.). Englewood Cliffs, NJ: Prentice-Hall.

Segal, S. P. (1989). Civil commitment standards and patient mix in England/Wales, Italy, and the United States. *American Journal of Psychiatry, 146*, 187–193.

Segall, M. H., Campbell, D. T., & Herskovits, M. J. (1963). Cultural differences in the perception of geometric illusions. *Science, 139*, 769–771.

Segall, M. H., Dasen, P. R., Berry, J. W., & Poortinga, Y. H. (1990). *Human behavior in global perspective*. New York: Pergamon.

Seligman, M. E. P. (1970). On the generality of the laws of learning. *Psychological Review, 77*, 406–418.

Seligman, M. E. P. (1975). *Helplessness. On depression development and death*. San Francisco: W. H. Freeman.

Seligman, M. E. P. (1989). Why is there so much depression today? The waxing of the individual and the waning of the common. In *The G. Stanley Hall Lecture Series*. Washington, DC: American Psychological Association.

Selye, H. (1974). *Stress without distress*. Philadelphia: W. B. Saunders.

Selye, H. (1983). The stress concept: Past, present, and future. In C. I. Cooper (Ed.), *Stress research*. New York: Wiley.

Semaj, L. T. (1985). Afrikanity, cognition, and extended self-identity. In M. B. Spencer, G. K. Brookins, & W. R. Allen (Eds.), *Beginnings: The social and affective development of Black children*. Hillsdale, NJ: Erlbaum.

Serbin, L. A., & Sprafkin, C. (1986). The salience of gender: The process of sex-typing in three- to seven-year-old children. *Child Development, 57*, 1188–1209.

Shanks, D. R. (1991). Categorization by a connectionist network. *Journal of Experimental Psychology: Learning, Memory, and Cognition, 17*, 433–443.

Shaver, P. (1986, August). *Being lonely, falling in love: Perspectives from attachment theory*. Paper presented at the meeting of the American Psychological Association, Washington, DC.

Shaw, S. M. (1988). Gender differences in the definition and perception of household labor. *Family Relations, 37*, 333–337.

Sheldon, W. H. (1954). *Atlas of men*. New York: Harper & Brothers.

Shelton, R. C., Hollon, S. D., Purdon, S. E., & Loosen, P. T. (1991). Biological and psychological aspects of depression. *Behavior Therapy, 22*, 201–228.

Shepard, R. (1967). Recognition memory for words, sentences, and pictures. *Journal of Verbal Learning and Verbal Behavior, 6*, 156–163.

Sheridan, C. L., & Radmacher, S. A. (1992). *Health psychology*. New York: Wiley.

Sherif, C. W. (1982). Needed concepts in the study of gender identity. *Psychology of Women's Quarterly, 6*, 375–398.

Sherif, M., Harvey, O. J., White, B. J., Hood, W. R., & Sherif, C. W. (1961). *Intergroup cooperation and competition: The Robbers Cave experiment*. Norman: University of Oklahoma Press.

Sherwood, A., Light, K. C., & Blumenthal, J. A. (1989). Effects of aerobic exercise training on hemodynamic responses during psychosocial stress in normotensive and borderline hypertensive Type A men: A preliminary report. *Psychosomatic Medicine, 51*, 123–136.

Shields, S. A. (1991a, August). *Doing emotion/doing gender*. Paper presented at the meeting of the American Psychological Association, San Francisco.

Shields, S. A. (1991b). Gender in the psychology of emotion: A selective research review. In K. T. Strongman (Ed.), *International review of studies on emotion* (Vol. I). New York: John Wiley.

Shotland, R. L. (1985, June). When bystanders just stand by. *Psychology Today*, pp. 50–55.

Showers, C. (1986, August). *The motivational consequences of negative thinking: Those who imagine the worst try harder*. Paper presented at the annual meeting of the American Psychological Association, Washington, DC.

Siegel, J. M. (1989). Brainstem mechanisms generating REM sleep. In M. H. Dryger, T. Roth, & W. C. Dement (Eds.), *Principles and practice of sleep medicine*. San Diego: Harcourt Brace Jovanovich.

Siegman, A. W. (1989). The role of hostility, neuroticism, and speech style in coronary-artery disease. In A. W. Siegman & T. Dembrowski (Eds.), *In search of coronary-prone behavior: Beyond Type A*. Hillsdale, NJ: Erlbaum.

Siegman, A. W., & Dembrowski, T. (Eds.). (1989). *In search of coronary-prone behavior: Beyond Type A*. Hillsdale, NJ: Erlbaum.

Siffre, M. (1975). Six months alone in a cave. *National Geographic*, pp. 426–435.

Sigelman, C. K., Thomas, D. B., Sigelman, L., & Ribich, F. D. (1986). Gender, physical attractiveness, and electability: An experimental investigation of vote biases. *Journal of Applied Social Psychology, 16*, 229–248.

Sigman, G. S., & Flanery, R. C. (1992). Eating disorders. In D. E. Greydanus & M. L. Wolraich (Eds.), *Behavioral pediatrics*. New York: Springer-Verlag.

Silverman, N. N., & Corsini, R. J. (1984). Is it true what they say about Adler's individual psychology? *Teaching of Psychology, 11*, 188–189.

Silverman, P. (1988). *Widow-to-widow: A mutual help program for the widowed*. Washington, DC: American Psychological Association.

Simmons, R. G., & Blyth, D. A. (1987). *Moving into adolescence*. Hawthorne, NY: Aldine.

Simon, H. A. (1990). Invariants of human behavior. *Annual Review of Psychology, 41*. Palo Alto, CA: Annual Reviews.

Singer, J. L. (1984). *The human personality*. San Diego: Harcourt Brace Jovanovich.

Singer, K. (1984). Depressive disorders from a transcultural perspective. In J. E. Mezzich & C. E. Berganza (Eds.), *Culture and psychopathology*. New York: Columbia University Press.

Sizer, T. R. (1984). *Horace's compromise: The dilemma of the American high school today*. Boston: Houghton Mifflin.

Skinner, B. F. (1938). *The behavior of organisms: An experimental analysis*. New York: Appleton-Century-Crofts.

Skinner, B. F. (1948). *Walden two*. New York: Macmillan.

Skinner, B. F. (1961). Teaching machines. *Scientific American, 205*, 90–102.

Skinner, J. H. (1990). Targeting benefits for the black elderly: The Older Americans Act. In Z. Harel, E. A. McKinney, & M. Williams (Eds.), *Black aged*. Newbury Park, CA: Sage.

Slaughter-Defoe, D. T., Nakagawa, K., Takanishi, R., & Johnson, D. J. (1990). Toward cultural/ecological perspectives on schooling and achievement in African- and Asian-American children. *Child Development, 61*, 363–383.

Slavin, R. E. (1987). Developmental and motivational perspectives on cooperative learning: A reconciliation. *Child Development, 58*, 1161–1167.

Slavin, R. E. (1989). Cooperative learning and student achievement. In R. E. Slavin (Ed.), *School and classroom organization*. Hillsdale, NJ: Erlbaum.

Sloan, T. S. (1990). Psychology for the third world? *Journal of Social Issues, 46*, 1–20.

Slobin, D. (1972, July). Children and language: They learn the same all around the world. *Psychology Today*, pp. 71–76.

Smith, M. L., Glass, G. N., & Miller, R. L. (1980). *The benefit of psychotherapy*. Baltimore: Johns Hopkins Press.

Smith, R. H., Diener, E., & Wedell, D. H. (1989). Intrapersonal and social comparison determinants of happiness: A range-frequency analysis. *Journal of Personality and Social Psychology, 56*, 317–325.

Smith, T. W. (1991). Adult sexual behavior in 1989: Number of partners, frequence of intercourse, and risk of AIDS. *Family Planning Perspectives, 23*, 102–107.

Snarey, R. (1987, June). A question of morality. *Psychology Today*, pp. 6–8.

Snow, C. E. (1989a, April). *Imitation as one path to language acquisition*. Paper presented at the biennial meeting of the Society for Research in Child Development, Kansas City.

Snow, C. E. (1989b). Understanding social interaction in language interaction: Sentences are not enough. In M. H. Bornstein & J. S. Bruner (Eds.), *Interaction in human development*. Hillsdale, NJ: Erlbaum.

Snowden, L. R., & Cheung, F. K. (1990). Use of inpatient mental health services by members of ethnic minority groups. *American Psychologist, 45*, 347–355.

Snyder, C. R. (1988, August). *Reality negotiation: From excuses to hope*. Paper presented at the meeting of the American Psychological Association, Atlanta.

Snyder, D. K. (1989). Introduction to special series on treatment of marital and family disorders. *Journal of Consulting and Clinical Psychology, 57*, 3–4.

Sokolovsky, J. (1983). *Growing old in different societies: Cross-cultural perspectives*. Belmont, CA: Wadsworth.

Solantaus, T. (1992, March). *The global world: A challenge to young people's development and well-being?* Paper presented at the meeting of the Society for Research on Adolescence, Washington, DC.

Solomon, R. L. (1980). The opponent-process theory of acquired motivation: The costs of pleasure and the benefits of pain. *American Psychologist, 35*, 691–712.

Sorenson, S. B., & Siegel, J. M. (1992). Gender, ethnicity, and sexual assault: Findings from a Los Angeles study. *Journal of Social Issues, 48*, 93–104.

Sorenson, S. B., & White, J. W. (1992). Adult sexual assault: Overview of research. *Journal of Social Issues, 48*, 1–8.

Spacapan, S. (1988). Social psychology and health. In S. Spacapan & S. Oskamp (Eds.), *The social psychology of health*. Newbury Park, CA: Sage.

Spade, J. Z., & Reese, C. A. (1991). We've come a long way, maybe: College students' plans for work and family. *Sex Roles, 24*, 309–322.

Spanos, N. P., Burgess, C. A., Cross, P. A., & MacLeod, G. (1992). Hypnosis, reporting bias, and suggested negative hallucinations. *Journal of Abnormal Psychology, 101*, 192–199.

Spearman, C. E. (1927). *The abilities of man*. New York: Macmillan.

Spence, J. T., & Helmreich, R. (1978). *Masculinity and femininity: Their psychological dimensions*. Austin: University of Texas Press.

Spence, M., & DeCasper, A. J. (1982). *Human fetuses perceive human speech*. Paper presented at the International Conference of Infant Studies, Austin.

Spencer, M. B. (1991). Identity, minority development of. In R. M. Lerner, A. C. Petersen, & J. Brooks-Gunn (Eds.), *Encyclopedia of adolescence* (Vol. 1). New York: Garland.

Spencer, M. B., & Dornbusch, S. M. (1990). Challenges in studying minority youth. In S. S. Feldman & G. R. Elliott (Eds.), *At the threshold: The developing adolescent*. Cambridge, MA: Harvard University Press.

Sperling, G. (1960). The information available in brief visual presentations. *Psychological Monographs, 74* (Whole No. 11).

Sperling, G. (1989, August). *Toward a computational theory of attention*. Paper presented at the meeting of the American Psychological Association, New Orleans.

Sperry, R. W. (1968). Hemisphere deconnection and unity in conscious awareness. *American Psychologist, 23*, 723–733.

Sperry, R. W. (1974). Lateral specialization in surgically separated hemispheres. In F. O. Schmitt & F. G. Worden (Eds.), *The neurosciences: Third study program*. Cambridge, MA: MIT Press.

Sperry, R. W., & Gazzaniga, M. S. (1967). Language following surgical disconnection of the hemispheres. In C. H. Milikan & F. L. Darley (Eds.), *Brain mechanisms underlying speech and language*. New York: Grune & Stratton.

Sprei, J. E., & Courtois, C. A. (1988). The treatment of women's sexual dysfunctions arising from sexual assault. In R. A. Brown & J. R. Field (Eds.), *Treatment of sexual problems in individual and couples therapy*. Great Neck, NY: PMA.

Squire, L. (1987). *Memory and brain*. New York: Oxford University Press.

Squire, L. (1990, June). *Memory and brain systems*. Paper presented at the meeting of the American Psychological Society, Dallas.

Squire, L. R. (1992). Memory and the hippocampus: A synthesis from findings with rats, monkeys, and humans. *Psychological Review, 99*, 195–231.

Sroufe, L. A. (1985). Attachment classification from the perspective of infant-caregiver relationships and infant temperament. *Child Development, 56*, 1–14.

Sroufe, L. A. (in press). Pathways to adaptation and maladaptation: Psychopathology as developmental deviation. In D. Cicchetti (Ed.), *Developmental psychopathology: Past, present, and future*. Hillsdale, NJ: Erlbaum.

Stanford, E. P. (1990). Diverse Black aged. In Z. Harel, E. A. McKinney, & M. Williams (Eds.), *Black aged*. Newbury Park, CA: Sage.

Stanhope, M., & Lancaster, J. (1991). Toward a healthy tomorrow. *Family and Community Health, 14*, 1–7.

Stanley, M., & Stanley, B. (1989). Biochemical studies in suicide victims: Current findings and future implications. *Suicide and Life-Threatening Behavior, 19*, 30–42.

Steadman, H. J., Callahan, L. A., Robbins, P. C., & Morrissey, J. P. (1989). Maintenance of an insanity defense under Montana's "abolition" of the insanity defense. *American Journal of Psychiatry, 146*, 357–360.

Steers, R. M. (1988). *Introduction to organizational behavior* (2nd ed.). Glenview, IL: Scott, Foresman.

Steil, J. M., & Weltman, K. (1991). Marital inequality: The importance of resources, personal attributes, and social norms on career valuing and the allocation of domestic responsibilities. *Sex Roles, 24*, 161–180.

Steinberg, L. D. (1986). Latchkey children and susceptibility to peer pressure. An ecological analysis. *Developmental Psychology, 22*, 433–439.

Steinberg, L. D. (1988). Simple solutions to a complex problem: A response to Rodman, Pratto, & Nelson. *Developmental Psychology, 24*, 295–296.

Steinberg, L. D. (1989). *Adolescence* (2nd ed.). New York: Knopf.

Steinberg, L. D. (1991). Parent-adolescent relations. In R. M. Lerner, A. C. Petersen, & J. Brooks-Gunn (Eds.), *Encyclopedia of adolescence*. New York: Garland.

Stern, J. S. (1984). Is obesity a disease of inactivity? In A. J. Stunkard & F. Stellar (Eds.), *Eating and its disorders*. New York: Raven.

Sternberg, R. J. (1986). *Intelligence applied*. San Diego: Harcourt Brace Jovanovich.

Sternberg, R. J. (1987). Teaching intelligence: The application of cognitive psychology of intellectual skills. In J. B. Baron & R. J. Sternberg (Eds.), *Teaching thinking skills: Theory and practice*. New York: W. H. Freeman.

Sternberg, R. J. (1988a). A triarchic view of intelligence in cross-cultural perspective. In S. H. Irvine & J. W. Berry (Eds.), *Human abilities in cultural context*. Cambridge: Cambridge University Press.

Sternberg, R. J. (1988b). *The triangle of love*. New York: Basic.

Stevens-Simon, C., & McAnarney, E. R. (1992). Adolescent pregnancy: Continuing challenges. In D. E. Greydanus & M. L. Wolraich (Eds.), *Behavioral pediatrics*. New York: Springer-Verlag.

Stevenson, H. W., Chen, C., Lee, S., & Fulgni, A. J. (1991). Schooling, culture, and cognitive development. In L. Okagaki & R. J. Sternberg (Eds.), *Directors of development: Influences on the development of children's thinking*. Hillsdale, NJ: Erlbaum.

Stevenson, H. W., Lee, S., Chen, C., Stigler, J., Hsu, C., & Kitamura, G. (1990). Contexts of achievement. *Monograph of the Society for Research in Child Development* (Serial No. 221, Vol. 55, Nos. 1–2).

Stevenson, H. W., Stigler, J. W., & Lee, S. (1986). Achievement in mathematics. In H. W. Stevenson, H. Azuma, & K. Hakuta (Eds.), *Child development and education in Japan*. San Francisco: W. H. Freeman.

Stewart, A. J., & Healy, J. M. (1989). Linking individual development and social change. *American Psychologist, 44*, 30–42.

Stewart, K. R. (1953). Culture and personality in two primitive groups. *Complex, 9*, 3–23.

Stewart, K. R. (1972). Dream theory in Malaya. In C. Tart (Ed.), *Altered states of consciousness*. New York: Anchor.

Stipek, D. J., & Hoffman, J. M. (1980). Children's achievement-related expectancies as a function of academic performance histories and sex. *Journal of Educational Psychology, 72*, 861–865.

Stotland, S., & Zuroff, D. C. (1991). Relations between multiple measures of dieting, self-efficacy, and weight change in a behavioral weight control program. *Behavior Therapy, 22*, 47–59.

Stoudemire, A., & Hales, R. E. (1991). Psychological and behavioral factors affecting medical conditions and DSM-IV: An overview. *Psychosomatics, 32*, 5–13.

Straube, E. R., & Oades, R. D. (1992). *Schizophrenia*. San Diego: Academic Press.

Streissguth, A. P., Martin, D. C., Sandman, B. M., Kirchner, G. L., & Darby, B. L. (1984). Intrauterine alcohol and nicotine exposure: Attention and reaction time in four-year-old children. *Developmental Psychology, 20*, 533–543.

Stricker, G., Davis-Russell, E., Bourg, E., Duran, E., Hammond, W. R., McHolland, J., Polite, K., & Vaughn, B. E. (1990). *Toward ethnic diversification in psychology, education, and training*. Washington, DC: American Psychological Association.

Strickland, B. (1988). Sex-related differences in health and illness. *Psychology of Women Quarterly, 12*, 381–399.

Strickland, B. (1989). Sex-related differences in health and illness. *Psychology of Women Quarterly, 12*, 382–399.

Strupp, H. H. (1989). Psychotherapy. *American Psychologist, 44*, 717–724.

Strupp, H. H. (1992). The future of psychodynamic psychotherapy. *Psychotherapy, 29*, 21–28.

Studdert-Kennedy, M. (1991). Language development from an evolutionary perspective. In N. A. Krasnegor, D. M. Rumbaugh, M. Studdert-Kennedy, & R. L. Schiefelbusch (Eds.), *Biological and behavioral determinants of language development*. Hillsdale, NJ: Erlbaum.

Stunkard, A. J. (1987). The regulation of body weight and the treatment of obesity. In H. Weiner & A. Baum (Eds.), *Eating regulation and discontrol*. Hillsdale, NJ: Erlbaum.

Stunkard, A. J. (1989). Perspectives on human obesity. In A. J. Stunkard & A. Baum (Eds.), *Perspectives on behavioral medicine: Eating, sleeping, and sex*. Hillsdale, NJ: Erlbaum.

Sue, D. (1979). Erotic fantasies of college students during coitus. *Journal of Sex Research, 15*, 299–305.

Sue, D. W. (1989). Ethnic identity: The impact of two cultures on the psychological development of Asians in America. In D. R. Atkinson, G. Morten, & D. W. Sue (Eds.), *Counseling American minorities: A cross-cultural perspective*. Dubuque, IA: Wm. C. Brown.

Sue, D. W., & Sue, D. (1972). *Counseling the culturally different: Theory and practice*. New York: Wiley.

Sue, D. W., & Sue, S. (1972). Counseling Chinese-Americans. *Personnel and Guidance Journal, 50*, 637–644.

Sue, S. (1989). Foreword. In J. T. Gibbs & L. N. Huang (Eds.), *Children of color*. San Francisco: Jossey-Bass.

Sue, S. (1990, August). *Ethnicity and culture in psychological research and practice*. Paper presented at the meeting of the American Psychological Association, Boston.

Sue, S. (1991, August). *Ethnicity and mental health: Research and policy issues*. Paper presented at the meeting of the American Psychological Association, San Francisco.

Sue, S. (in press). Ethnicity and mental health: Research and policy issues. *Journal of Social Issues*.

Sue, S., Allen, D., & Conaway, L. (1978). The responsiveness and equality of mental health care to Chicanos and Native Americans. *American Journal of Community Psychology, 6*, 137–146.

Sue, S., & Ikazaki, S. (1990). Asian-American educational achievements: A phenomenon in search of an explanation. *American Psychologist, 45*, 913–920.

Sue, S., & Padilla, A. (1986). Ethnic minority issues in the United States: Challenges for the educational system. In California State Department of Education (Ed.), *Beyond language: Social and cultural factors in school language minority students*. Los Angeles: California State Department of Education, Evaluation, Dissemination, and Assessment Center.

Suedfeld, P., & Coren, S. (1989). Perceptual isolation, sensory deprivation, and rest: Moving introductory psychology texts out of the 1950s. *Canadian Psychology, 30*, 17–29.

Suedfeld, P., Metcalfe, J., & Bluck, S. (1987). Enhancement of scientific creativity by flotation REST (Restricted Environmental Stimulation Technique). *Journal of Environmental Psychology, 7*, 219–231.

Suinn, R. M. (1984). *Fundamentals of abnormal psychology*. Chicago: Nelson-Hall.

Suinn, R. M. (1987). Asian Americans in psychology. In P. J. Woods & C. S. Wilkinson (Eds.), *Is psychology the major for you?* Washington, DC: American Psychological Association.

Sullivan, H. S. (1953). *The interpersonal theory of psychiatry*. New York: W. W. Norton.

Sullivan, L. (1991, May 25). US secretary urges TV to restrict "irresponsible sex and reckless violence." *Boston Globe*, p. A1.

Sullivan, R. M., Henke, P. G., Ray, A., Hebert, M. A., & Trimper, J. M. (1989). The GABA/benzodiazepine receptor complex in the central amygdalar nucleus and stress ulcers in rats. *Behavioral and Neural Biology, ·51*, 262–269.

Suls, J. (1989). Self-awareness and self-identity. In J. Worrell & F. Danner (Eds.), *The adolescent as decision maker*. New York: Academic Press.

Sundstrom, E., De Meuse, K. P., & Futrell, D. (1990). Work teams: Applications and effectiveness. *American Psychologist, 45*, 120–133.

Super, C. M. (1980). Cross-cultural research on infancy. In H. C. Triandis & A. Heron (Eds.), *Handbook of cross-cultural psychology, developmental psychology* (Vol. 4). Boston: Allyn & Bacon.

Super, C. M. (1981). Behavioral development in infancy. In R. H. Munroe, R. L. Munroe, & B. B. Whiting (Eds.), *Handbook of cross-cultural human development*. New York: Garland STPM.

Super, C. M., & Harkness, S. (1982). The development of affect in infancy and early childhood. In D. A. Wagner & H. W. Stevenson (Eds.), *Cultural perspectives on child development*. San Francisco: W. H. Freeman.

Susman, E. J., & Dorn, L. (1991). Hormones and behavior in adolescence. In R. M. Lerner, A. C. Petersen, & J. Brooks-Gunn (Eds.), *Encyclopedia of adolescence* (Vol. 1). New York: Garland.

Sutton, R. G., & Kessler, M. (1986). National study on the effects of clients' socioeconomic status on clinical psychologists' professional judgments. *Journal of Consulting and Clinical Psychology, 54*, 275–276.

Swanson, D. P., & Cunningham, M. (1991, April). *Issues in gender and racial socialization of African American children*. Paper presented at the Society for Research in Child Development meeting, Seattle.

Syvalahti, E. K. (1985). Drug treatment of insomnia. *Annals of Clinical Research, 17*, 265–272.

Szasz, I. (1977). *Psychiatric slavers: When confinement and coercion masquerade as cure*. New York: Free Press.

Szasz, T. (1965). *The ethics of psychoanalysis*. New York: Basic.

Szinovacz, M. E. (1984). Changing family roles and interactions. In B. B. Hess & M. B. Sussman (Eds.), *Women and the family: Two decades of change*. New York: Haworth.

Tajfel, H. (1978). The achievement of group differentiation. In H. Tajfel (Ed.), *Differentiation between social groups: Studies in the social psychology of intergroup relations*. London: Academic Press.

Tannen, D. (1990). *You just don't understand: Women and men in conversation*. New York: Ballantine.

Tavris, C. (1989). *Anger: The misunderstood emotion* (2nd ed.). New York: Touchstone.

Tavris, C. (1990, August). *The mismeasure of woman: Paradoxes and perspectives in the study of gender*. Paper presented at the meeting of the American Psychological Association, Boston.

Tavris, C., & Wade, C. (1984). *The longest war: Sex differences in perspective* (2nd ed.). San Diego: Harcourt Brace Jovanovich.

Taylor, D. G., Sheatsley, P. B., & Greeley, A. M. (1978). Attitudes toward racial integration. *Scientific American*, pp. 42–49.

Taylor, S. E. (1979). Hospital patient behavior: Reactance, helplessness, or control? *Journal of Social Issues, 35*, 156–184.

Taylor, S. E. (1991). *Health psychology* (2nd ed.). New York: McGraw-Hill.

Taylor, S. E., Collins, R., Skokan, L., & Aspinwall, L. (1988, August). *Illusions, reality, and adjustment in coping with victimizing events*. Paper presented at the meeting of the American Psychological Association, Atlanta.

Taylor, S. P. (1982). Mental health and successful coping among aged Black women. In R. C. Manuel (Ed.), *Minority aging*. Westport, CT: Greenwood.

Teachman, J. D., & Polonko, K. A. (1990). Cohabitation and marital stability in the United States. *Social Forces, 69*, 207–220.

Teasdale, S. (1926). *Dark of the moon*. New York: Macmillan.

Terman, L. (1925). *Genetic studies of genius: Vol. l. Mental and physical traits of a thousand gifted children*. Stanford, CA: Stanford University Press.

Thigpen, C. H., & Cleckley, H. M. (1957). *Three faces of Eve*. New York: McGraw-Hill.

Thomas, D. A., & Aldefer, C. P. (1989). The influence of race on career dynamics: Theory and research on minority career experiences. In M. Arthur, D. Hall, & B. Lawrence (Eds.), *Handbook of career theory*. Cambridge, England: Cambridge University Press.

Thomas, R. (1991, August). *From affirmative action to affirming diversity*. Paper presented at the meeting of the American Psychological Association, San Francisco.

Thomas, V. G. (1991, August). *The psychology of Black women: Past, present, future*. Paper presented at the meeting of the American Psychological Association, San Francisco.

Thompson, E. T., & Hughes, E. C. (1958). *Race: Individual and collective behavior*. Glencoe, IL: Free Press.

Thompson, L., & Walker, A. J. (1989). Gender in families: Women and men in marriage, work, and parenthood. *Journal of Marriage and the Family, 51*, 845–871.

Thompson, R. A. (1991). Construction and reconstruction of early attachments: Taking perspective on attachment theory and research. In D. P. Keating & H. G. Rosen (Eds.), *Constructivist perspectives on atypical development*. Hillsdale, NJ: Erlbaum.

Thompson, R. A., & Cimbolic, P. (1978). Black students' counselor preference and attitudes toward counseling center use. *Journal of Counseling Psychology, 25*, 570–575.

Thornburg, H. D. (1981). Sources of sex education among early adolescents. *Journal of Early Adolescence, 1*, 171–184.

Thurstone, L. L. (1938). *Primary mental abilities*. Chicago: University of Chicago Press.

Tobin, J. J. (1987). The American idealization of old age in Japan. *The Gerontologist, 27*, 53–58.

Tobin, J. J., Wu, D. Y. H., & Davidson, D. H. (1989). *Preschool in three cultures*. New Haven, CT: Yale University Press.

Tolan, P., Miller, L., & Thomas, P. (1988). Perception and experience of types of social stress and self-image among adolescents. *Journal of Youth and Adolescence, 17*, 147–163.

Tolman, E. C. (1948). Cognitive maps in rats and men. *Psychological Review, 55*, 189–208.

Tomlinson-Keasey, C., Warren, L. W., & Elliott, J. E. (1986). Suicide among gifted women: A prospective study. *Journal of Abnormal Psychology, 95*, 123–130.

Torrey, E. F., & others. (1984). Endemic psychosis in western Ireland. *American Journal of Psychiatry, 141*, 966–970.

Trafimow, D., Triandis, H. C., & Goto, S. G. (1991). Some tests of the distinction between the private self and the collective self. *Journal of Personality and Social Psychology, 60*, 649–655.

Tran, T. V., Wright, R., & Chatters, L. (1991). Health, stress, psychological resources, and subjective well-being among older Blacks. *Psychology and Aging, 6*, 100–108.

Trankina, F. (1983). Clinical issues and techniques in working with Hispanic children and their families. In G. J. Powell, J. Yamamoto, A. Romero, & A. Morales (Eds.), *The psychosocial development of minority group children*. New York: Brunner/Mazel.

Travis, C. B. (1988). *Women and health psychology: Mental health issues*. Hillsdale, NJ: Erlbaum.

Trevino, R. (1986). National statistical data systems and the Hispanic population. In *Task force on Black and minority health, report of the secretary's task force on Black and minority health. Vol. VIII: Hispanic health issues*, pp. 45–54. Washington, DC: U.S. Department of Health and Human Services.

Triandis, H. (1985). Collectivism vs. individualism: A reconceptualization of a basic concept in cross-cultural social psychology. In C. Bagley & G. K. Verman (Eds.), *Personality, cognition, and values*. London: Macmillan.

Triandis, H. C. (1980). *Introduction. Handbook of cross-cultural psychology* (Vol. 1). Boston: Allyn & Bacon.

Triandis, H. C. (1989, March). *Cross-cultural studies of individualism and collectivism*. Paper presented at the Nebraska Symposium on Motivation, Lincoln.

Triandis, H. C. (1990). Theoretical concepts that are applicable to the analysis of ethnocentrism. In R. W. Brislin (Ed.), *Applied cross-cultural psychology*. Newbury Park, CA: Sage.

Triandis, H. C. (1991, August). *Training for diversity*. Paper presented at the meeting of the American Psychological Association, San Francisco.

Triandis, H. C., Brislin, R., & Hui, C. H. (1988). Cross-cultural training across the individualism divide. *International Journal of Intercultural Relations, 12*, 269–288.

Trimble, J. E. (1976). Value differences among American Indians: Concern for the concerned counselor. In P. Pedersen, W. J. Lonner, J. G. Draguns (Eds.), *Counseling across cultures*. Honolulu: The University of Hawaii Press.

Trimble, J. E. (1989). *The enculturation of contemporary psychology*. Paper presented at the meeting of the American Psychological Association, New Orleans.

Trimble, J. E. (in press). Ethnic specification, validation prospects and the future of drug use research. *International Journal of Addiction*.

Trimble, J. E., & Fleming, C. (1989). Client, counselor, and community characteristics. In P. Pedersen, J. Draguns, W. Lonner, & J. Trimble (Eds.), *Counseling across cultures* (3rd ed.). Honolulu: The University of Hawaii Press.

Trimble, J. F. (1991, August). *Cognitive-behavioral skills enhancement and deterring drug abuse among American-Indian youth*. Paper presented at the meeting of the American Psychological Association, San Francisco.

Tseng, W., & Hsu, J. (1969). Chinese culture, personality formation, and mental illness. *International Journal of Social Psychiatry, 16*, 5–14.

Tucker, L. A. (1987). Television, teenagers, and health. *Journal of Youth and Adolescence, 16*, 415–425.

Tulving, E. (1972). Episodic and semantic memory. In E. Tulving & W. Donaldson (Eds.), *Origins of memory*. New York: Academic Press.

Turkkan, J. S. (1989). Classical conditioning: The new hegemony. *Behavioral and Brain Sciences, 12*, 121–136.

Turnbull, C. (1961). Some observations regarding the experiences and behavior of Bambuti pygmies. *American Journal of Psychology, 74*, 304–308.

Turner, S. M., & Beidel, D. C. (1989). Social phobia: Clinical syndrome, diagnosis, and comorbidity. *Clinical Psychology Review, 9*, 3–18.

Ulbrich, P. M. (1988). The determinants of depression in two-income marriages. *Journal of Marriage and the Family, 50*, 121–131.

Unger, R. K. (1990, August). *Sources of variability: A feminist analysis*. Paper presented at the meeting of the American Psychological Association, Boston.

Unger, R. K., & Crawford, M. (1992). *The psychology of sex and gender*. New York: McGraw-Hill.

United States Department of Health and Human Services, Public Health Service. (1989). *Reducing the health consequences of smoking: 25 years of progress*. Washington, DC: U.S. Government Printing Office.

Updyke, W. F. (1989, September 15). [News conference.] Washington, DC: The Crysler Fund/AAU Physical Fitness Program.

U.S. Bureau of the Census. (1990). *Statistical abstracts of the United States, 1990*. Washington, DC: U.S. Department of Commerce.

U.S. Department of Justice, Bureau of Justice Statistics. (1983, October). *Report to the nation on crime and violence* (NJC-87068). Washington, DC: U.S. Government Printing Office.

Vaillant, G. E. (1977). *Adaptation to life*. Boston: Little, Brown.

Vandell, D. L., & Corasiniti, M. A. (1988). Variations in early child care: Do they predict subsequent social, emotional, and cognitive differences? *Child Development, 59*, 176–186.

Van den Berghe, P. L. (1978). *Race and racism: A comparative perspective*. New York: John Wiley & Sons.

Van Deusen-Henkel, J., & Argondizza, M. (1987). Early elementary education: Curriculum planning for the primary grades. In *A framework for curriculum design*. Augusta, ME: Division of Curriculum, Maine, Department of Educational and Cultural Services.

van Dijk, T. A. (1987). *Communicating racism*. Newbury Park, CA: Sage.

Vannoy-Hiller, D., & Philliber, W. W. (1989). *Equal partners: Successful women in marriage*. Newbury Park, CA: Sage.

Verbrugge, L. M. (1987). Role responsibilities, role burdens, and physical health. *Journal of Community Health, 7*, 262–283.

Verbrugge, L. M. (1989). The twain meet: Empirical explanations of sex differences in health and mortality. *Journal of Health and Social Behavior, 30*, 282–304.

Vitols, M. (1967). *Patterns of mental disturbance in the Negro*. Unpublished manuscript, Cherry Hospital, Goldsboro, NC.

Von Bekesy, G. (1960). Vibratory patterns of the basilar membrane. In E. G. Wever (Ed.), *Experiments in hearing*. New York: McGraw-Hill.

Vontress, C. E. (1973). Counseling: Racial and ethnic factors. *Focus on Guidance, 5*, 1–10.

Vosniadou, S., & Ortony, A. (Eds.). (1989). *Similarity and analogical reasoning*. New York: Cambridge University Press.

Vygotsky, L. S. (1962). *Thought and language*. Cambridge, MA: MIT Press.

Wachs, T. D. (1992). *The nature of nurture*. Newbury Park, CA: Sage.

Wade, P., & Bernstein, B. L. (1991). Culture sensitivity training and counselor's race: Effects on black female clients' perceptions and attrition. *Journal of Counseling Psychology, 38*, 9–15.

Wagner, D. (1980). Culture and memory development. In H. Triandis & A. Heron (Eds.), *Handbook of cross-cultural psychology, Vol. 4, developmental psychology*. Boston: Allyn & Bacon.

Wagner, R. V. (1988). Distinguishing between positive and negative approaches to peace. *Journal of Social Issues, 44*, 1–15.

Wallace, R. K., & Benson, H. (1972). The physiology of meditation. *Scientific American, 226*, 85–90.

Wallerstein, J. S. (1989). Effects of maternal employment in the two-parent family. *American Psychologist, 44*, 283–292.

Wallerstein, R. (1992). *The common ground of psychoanalysis*. Northvale, NJ: Jason Aronson.

Wallerstein, R. S. (1989). The psychotherapy research project of the Menninger Foundation: An overview. *Journal of Consulting and Clinical Psychology, 57*, 195–205.

Wallis, C. (1985, December 9). Children having children. *Time*, pp. 78–88.

Walsh, P. V., Katz, P. A., & Downey, E. P. (1991, April). *A longitudinal perspective on race and gender socialization in infants and toddlers*. Paper presented at the Society for Research in Child Development meeting, Seattle.

Walter, J. P. (1974). Two poverties equal many hungry Indians: An economic and social study of nutrition. *American Journal of Economics and Sociology, 33*, 33–44.

Warner, K. E. (1989). Smoking and health: A 25-year perspective. *American Journal of Public Health, 79*, 141–143.

Warner, R. L. (1986). Alternative strategies for measuring household division of labor: A comparison. *Journal of Family Issues, 7*, 179–185.

Wasserman, G. S. (1978). *Color vision: An historical introduction*. New York: Wiley.

Waterman, A. S., & Archer, S. I. (in press). A life-span perspective on identity formation. In P. B. Baltes, D. L. Featherman, & R. M. Lerner (Eds.), *Life-span development and behavior* (Vol. 10). Hillsdale, NJ: Erlbaum.

Waters, E. (1991). Individual differences in infant-mother attachment. In J. Columbo & J. W. Fagen (Eds.), *Individual differences in infancy*. Hillsdale, NJ: Erlbaum.

Watson, J. B. (1928). *Psychological care of the infant and child*. New York: W. W. Norton.

Watson, J. B., & Raynor, R. (1920). Emotional reactions. *Journal of Experimental Psychology, 3*, 1–14.

Watson, W. H. (1990). Family care, economics, and health. In Z. Harel, E. A. McKinney, & M. Williams (Eds.), *Black aged*. Newbury Park, CA: Sage.

Watts, T. D., & Lewis, R. G. (1988). Alcoholism and Native American youth: An overview. *Journal of Drug Issues, 18*, 69–86.

Weary, G., Stanley, M. A., & Harvey, J. H. (1989). *Attribution*. New York: Springer-Verlag.

Webb, W. B. (1978). Sleep and dreams. *Annual Review of Psychology*. Palo Alto, CA: Annual Reviews.

Wechsler, D. (1949). *Wechsler Intelligence Scale for Children*. New York: Psychological Corporation.

Wechsler, D. (1955). *Wechsler Adult Intelligence Scale manual*. New York: Psychological Corporation.

Wechsler, D. (1967). *Wechsler Preschool and Primary Scale of Intelligence*. New York: Psychological Corporation.

Wechsler, D. (1972). "Hold" and "Don't Hold" Test. In S. M. Chown (Ed.), *Human aging*. New York: Penguin.

Wechsler, D. (1974). *Wechsler Intelligence Scale for Children-Revised*. New York: Psychological Corporation.

Wechsler, D. (1981). *Wechsler Adult Intelligence Scale-Revised*. New York: Psychological Corporation.

Weil, A. (1972). *The natural mind*. Boston: Houghton Mifflin.

Weinberg, R. A. (1989). Intelligence and IQ: Landmark issues and great debates. *American Psychologist, 44*, 98–104.

Weinberger, D. R., Berman, K. F., & Zec, R. F. (1986). Physiological dysfunction of the dorsolateral prefrontal cortex in schizophrenia. *Archives of General Psychiatry, 43*, 114–124.

Weinstein, S. (1968). Intensive and extensive aspects of tactile sensitivity as a function of body part, sex, and laterality. In D. R. Kenshalo (Ed.), *The skin senses*. Springfield, IL: Charles C Thomas.

Weisenberg, M. (1982). Cultural and ethnic factors in reaction to pain. In I. Al-Issa (Ed.), *Culture and psychopathology*. Baltimore, MD: University Park Press.

Weisman, A. D. (1989). Vulnerability and the psychological disturbances of cancer patients. *Psychosomatics, 30*, 80–85.

Weisse, C. S. (1992). Depression and immunocompetence: A review of the literature. *Psychological Bulletin, 111*, 475–489.

Weissman, M. M., & Boyd, J. H. (1985). Affective disorders: Epidemiology. In H. I. Kaplan & B. J. Sadock (Eds.), *Comprehensive textbook of psychiatry/IV*. Baltimore: Williams & Wilkins.

Weiten, W. (1983). *Psychology applied to modern life*. Monterey, CA: Brooks/Cole.

Weizmann, F., Wiener, N. I., Wiesenthal, D. L., & Ziegler, M. (1990). Differential K theory and racial hierarchies. *Canadian Psychology, 31*, 1–13.

Wender, P. H., Kety, S. S., Rosenthal, D., Schulsinger, E., Ortmann, J., & Lunde, I. (1986). Psychiatric disorders in the biological and adoptive families of adopted individuals with affective disorders. *Archives of General Psychiatry, 43*, 923–939.

Wenzlaff, R. M., & Prohaska, M. L. (1989). When misery loves company: Depression, attributions, and responses to others' moods. *Journal of Experimental Social Psychology, 25*, 220–223.

West, L. J. (1972). A cross-cultural approach to alcoholism. *Annals of the New York Academy of Sciences, 197*, 214–216.

West, M. (Ed.). (1988). *The psychology of meditation*. New York: Oxford University Press.

Westkott, M. (1986). *The feminist legacy of Karen Horney*. New Haven, CT: Yale University Press.

Weston, P. J., & Mednick, M. T. (1970). Race, social class, and the motive to avoid success in women. *Journal of Cross-Cultural Psychology, 1*, 284–291.

Wheeler, L., & Miyake, K. (1992). Social comparison in everyday life. *Journal of Personality and Social Psychology, 62*, 760–773.

Whissell, C. M. (1989). The dictionary of affect in language. In R. Plutchik & H. Kellerman (Eds.), *The measurement of emotions*. San Diego: Academic Press.

White, B. L. (1988). Nutrition during infancy. In S. R. Williams & B. S. Worthington-Roberts (Eds.), *Nutrition through the life cycle*. St. Louis: Times Mirror/Mosby.

White, D. P. (1989). Central sleep apnea. In M. H. Dryger, T. Roth, & W. C. Dement (Eds.), *Principles and practice of sleep medicine*. San Diego: Harcourt Brace Jovanovich.

White, J. L., & Parham, T. A. (Eds.). (1990). *Psychology of Blacks* (2nd ed.). Englewood Cliffs, NJ: Prentice-Hall.

White, R. W. (1959). Motivation reconsidered: The concept of competence. *Psychological Review, 66*, 297–333.

White, R. W. (1976). *The enterprise of living* (2nd ed.). New York: Holt, Rinehart & Winston.

Whiting, B. B. (1989, April). *Culture and interpersonal behavior*. Paper presented at the biennial meeting of the Society for Research in Child Development, Kansas City.

Whiting, B. B., & Whiting, J. W. M. (1975). *Children of six cultures*. Cambridge, MA: Harvard University Press.

Whitton, C. (1990, Fall). Commentary. The road to equality. *Time*, p. 12.

Whorf, B. (1956). *Language, thought, and creativity*. New York: John Wiley.

Wiebe, D. J. (1991). Hardiness and stress moderation: A test of proposed mechanisms. *Journal of Personality and Social Psychology, 60*, 89–99.

Wilcox, B. L., & Naimark, H. (1991). The rights of the child: Progress toward human dignity. *American Psychologist, 46*, 49.

Wilder, D. (1991, March 28). To save the Black family, the young must abstain. *Wall Street Journal*, p. A14.

Wilkinson, R. T., & Allison, S. (1989). Age and simple reaction time: Decade differences for 5,325 subjects. *Journal of Gerontology, 44*, 29–35.

Williams, J. (1987). *Psychology of women: Behavior in a biosocial context* (3rd ed). New York: W. W. Norton.

Williams, J. E., & Best, D. L. (1982). *Measuring sex stereotypes: A thirty nation study*. Newbury Park, CA: Sage.

Williams, J. E., & Best, D. L. (1989). *Sex and psyche: Self-concept viewed cross-culturally*. Newbury Park: CA: Sage.

Williams, M. (1990). African American elderly experiences with Title II: Program assumptions and economic well-being. In Z. Harel, E. A. McKinney, & M. Williams (Eds.), *Black aged*. Newbury Park, CA: Sage.

Williams, M. E., & Condry, J. (1989, April). *Minority portrayals and cross-racial interaction television*. Paper presented at the biennial meeting of the Society for Research in Child Development, Kansas City.

Williams, R. B. (1989a). Biological mechanisms mediating the relationship between behavior and coronary prone behavior. In A. W. Siegman & T. Dembrowski (Eds.), *In search of coronary-prone behavior: Beyond Type A*. Hillsdale, NJ: Erlbaum.

Williams, R. B. (1989b). *The trusting heart: Great news about Type A behavior*. New York: Random House.

William T. Grant Foundation Commission. (1988). *The forgotten half: Non-college bound youth in America*. New York: William T. Grant Foundation.

William T. Grant Foundation. (1989). *American youth: A statistical snapshot*. Washington, DC: William T. Grant Foundation.

Willis, C. E., & Wrightsman, L. S. (1989, August). *Cognitive heuristic in eyewitness identification*. Paper presented at the biennial meeting of the American Psychological Association, New Orleans.

Wilson, E. O. (1975). *Sociobiology: The new synthesis*. Cambridge, MA: Harvard University Press.

Wilson, G. T., & Agras, W. S. (1992). The future of behavior therapy. *Psychotherapy, 29*, 39–43.

Wilson, M. (1989). Child development in the context of the extended family. *American Psychologist, 44*, 380–385.

Wilson, M., Kohn, L., Hinton, I., Underwood, A., & Do, L. (1991, April). *The context of socialization in diverse Black families*. Paper presented at the Society for Research in Child Development meeting, Seattle.

Wilson, W. J., & Neckerman, K. M. (1986). Poverty and family structure: The widening gap between evidence and public policy issues. In S. Danziger & D. Weinberg (Eds.), *Fighting poverty*. Cambridge, MA: Harvard University Press.

Winett, R. A., King, A. C., & Altman, D. G. (1989). *Health psychology and public health: An integrative approach*. New York: Pergamon.

Winner, E. (1986, August). Where pelicans kiss seals. *Psychology Today*, pp. 24–35.

Winner, E. (1989). Development in the visual arts. In W. Damon (Ed.), *Child development today and tomorrow*. San Francisco: W. H. Freeman.

Wise, R. A., & Rompre, P. P. (1989). Brain dopamine and reward. *Annual Review of Psychology, 40*. Palo Alto, CA: Annual Reviews.

Wober, M. (1966). Sensotypes. *Journal of Social Psychology, 70*, 181–189.

Wober, M. (1974). Towards an understanding of the Kiganda concept of intelligence. In J. W. Berry & P. R. Dasen (Eds.), *Culture and cognition*. London: Methuen.

Wolfe, M. E., & Mosnaim, A. D. (1989). *Tardive dyskinesia: Biological mechanisms and clinical aspects*. Washington, DC: American Psychiatric Press.

Wolkowitz, O. M., & Pickar, D. (1991). Benzodiazepines in the treatment of schizophrenia: A review and reappraisal. *American Journal of Psychiatry, 148*, 714–726.

Wolpe, J. (1963). Behavior therapy in complex neurotic states. *British Journal of Psychiatry, 110*, 28–34.

Wolpe, J. (1968). *Psychotherapy by reciprocal inhibition*. Stanford, CA: Stanford University Press.

Wong, H. Z. (1982). Asian and Pacific Americans. In L. Snowden (Ed.), *Reaching the undeserved: Mental health needs of neglected populations*. Beverly Hills, CA: Sage.

Wong, M. (1978). Males in transition and the self-help group. *The Counseling Psychologist, 7*, 46–50.

Woods, P. J., & Wilkinson, C. S. (1987). *Is psychology the major for you?* Washington, DC: American Psychological Association.

World Health Organization. (1975). *Schizophrenia: A multi-national study*. Geneva: World Health Organization.

World Health Organization. (1977). *International classification of diseases* (9th rev.). Geneva: World Health Organization.

Worrell, J. (1989). Images of women in psychology. In M. A. Paludi & G. A. Steuernagel (Eds.), *Foundations for a feminist restructuring of the academic disciplines*. New York: Haworth.

Worrell, J., & Remer, P. (1992). *Feminist perspectives in therapy*. New York: John Wiley.

Worschel, S. (1986). The role of cooperation in reducing intergroup conflict. In S. Worschel & W. G. Austin (Eds.), *Psychology of intergroup relations*. Chicago: Nelson-Hall.

Worthington-Roberts, B. S. (1988). Lactation and human milk. In S. R. Williams & B. S. Worthington-Roberts (Eds.), *Nutrition through the life cycle*. St. Louis: Times Mirror/Mosby.

Wortman, C., Bernat, M., & Lang, E. (in press). Coping with overload. In M. Frankenhaeuser, M. Chesney, & V. Lundberg (Eds.), *Women, work, and stress*. New York: Plenum.

Yalom, I. D. (1975). *The therapy and practice of group psychotherapy*. New York: Basic.

Yamamoto, J., Okonogi, K., Iwasaki, T., & Yoshimura, S. (1969). Mourning in Japan. *American Journal of Psychiatry, 125*, 1660–1665.

Yankelovich, D., Skelly, F., & White, A. (1984). *Sex stereotypes and candidacy for high level political office*. New York: Yankelovich, Skelly, & White.

Yarmey, A. D. (1973). I recognize your face but I can't remember your name: Further evidence on the tip of the tongue phenomenon. *Memory and Cognition, 1*, 287–290.

Yates, B. (1985). *Self-management: The science and art of helping yourself*. Belmont, CA: Wadsworth.

Yentsch, C. M., & Sindermann, C. J. (1992). *The woman scientist: Meeting the challenges for a successful career*. New York: Plenum.

Yorke, C., Wiseberg, S., & Freeman, T. (1989). *Development and psychopathology*. New Haven: Yale University Press.

Young, K. T. (1990). American conceptions of infant development from 1955 to 1984: What the experts are telling parents. *Child Development, 61*, 17–28.

Zabin, L. S. (1986, May/June). Evaluation of a pregnancy prevention program for urban teenagers. *Family Planning Perspectives*, p. 119.

Zahn-Waxler, C. (1990, May 28). Commentary. *Newsweek*, p. 61.

Zajonc, R. B. (1984). On the primacy of affect. *American Psychologist, 39*, 117–123.

Zarcone, V. P. (1989). Sleep hygiene. In M. H. Dryger, T. Roth, & W. C. Dement (Eds.), *Principles and practice of sleep medicine*. San Diego: Harcourt Brace Jovanovich.

Zebrowitz-McArthur, L. (1988). Person perception in cross-cultural perspective. In M. H. Bond (Ed.), *The cross-cultural challenge to social psychology*. Newbury Park, CA: Sage.

Zeigler, L. H., & Harom, W. (1989). More bad news about the news. *Public Opinion, 12*, 50–52.

Zelnik, M., & Kantner, J. F. (1977). Sexual and contraceptive experiences of young unmarried women in the United States, 1976 and 1971. *Family Planning Perspectives, 9*, 55–71.

Ziegert, K. A. (1983). The Wedesih prohibition of corporal punishment: A preliminary report. *Journal of Marriage and the Family, 45*, 917–926.

Zigler, E. (1989, April). *Discussion, symposium of effects of caregiving quality on children and families*. Presentation at the biennial meeting of the Society for Research in Child Development, Kansas City.

Zigler, E. (1991, October). *Day care in America: What is needed*. Paper presented at the symposium on day care for children, Arlington.

Zigler, E., & Frank, M. (Eds.). (1988). *The parental leave crisis: Toward a national policy*. New Haven, CT: Yale University Press.

Zimbardo, P., Haney, C., Banks, W., & Jaffe, D. (1972). *The psychology of imprisonment: Privation, power, and pathology*. Unpublished manuscript, Stanford University.

Zorick, F. (1989). Overview of insomnia. In M. H. Dryger, T. Roth, & W. C. Dement (Eds.), *Principles and practice of sleep medicine*. San Diego: Harcourt Brace Jovanovich.

Zorumski, C. F., & Isenberg, K. E. (1991). Insights into the structure and function of GABA-benzodiazepine receptors: Ion channels and psychiatry. *American Journal of Psychiatry, 148*, 162–171.

CREDITS

Photographs

by permission of the Publishers from Henry A. Murray, "Thematic Apperception Test," Cambridge, MA: Harvard University Press, Copyright © 1943 by the President and Fellows of Harvard College, © 1971 by Henry A. Murray.; 12.9B: © Spencer Grant/Marilyn Gartman Agency; 12.10B: The Bettmann Archive; C: © Joe McNally/Sygma; D: Center for the Study of the Person; E: The Bettmann Archive

Chapter 13

Opener: © Alain Choisnet/The Image Bank; Page 398: Courtesy of Nancy Felipe Russo; p. 399A: Adam Tannen/Comstock; B: Stephen Marks/The Image Bank; p. 400 left: © Jim Shaffer; right: © Bob Daemmrich/Stock Boston; Figure 13.1B: Scala/Art Resource; p. 405: © Richard Laird/FPG; 13.3: © Gerald Martineau/The Washington Post; p. 412: © Bob Daemmrich/Stock Boston; 13.5A: August Natterer, Inv. Nr. 184, "Hexenkopf," date unknown, mixed media, 259 X 342mm, Prinhorn-Collection of the Psychiatric Clinic, University of Heidelberg, Jugeborg Klinger; 13.6: Grunnitus/Monkmeyer Press; p. 418: AP/Wide World Photos

Chapter 14

Opener: Stacy Pickerell/Tony Stone World Wide; Figure 14.1: National Museum of Denmark; 14.2, Page 428: Historical Pictures/Stock Montage, Inc.; 14.3B: © Bosch/Art Resource; p. 430: © Deke Simon/Real People Press; 14.4B: David Frazier Photolibrary; 14.5B: DPI; p. 435: © Bohdan Heynewch/Southern Lights Photography; p. 436: © Bob Daemmrich/Stock Boston; p. 439: © Jay Lurie Photography; p. 440: © Buzz Lawrence Photography; p. 443A: Comstock; B: © J. Y. Rabeuf/The Image Works, Inc.; C: © Peter Menzel/Stock Boston; D: © Robert Houser/Comstock; p. 445 top: © Russ Kinne/Comstock; bottom: Courtesy of Rachel Hare-Mustin & Jeanne Maracek; p. 448: © Will McIntyre/Photo Researchers, Inc.

Chapter 15

Opener: © John P. Kelly/The Image Bank; Page 454: © Tom Tracey/After Images; p. 455A: © George V. Mann, Sc.D., M.D.; B: © David Stoecklein/The Stock Market; p. 460 left: © William Steve Burr/The Image Bank; right: © Ted Kawalerski/The Image Bank; p. 462: Courtesy of John Berry; p. 463: Courtesy of Deborah Belle; p. 464 top left: © Bob Daemmrich/The Image Works, Inc.; top right: © Luis Villota/The Stock Market; bottom left & right: © Catherine Gehm; Figure 15.4: "Sussex Publishers, Inc. © 1985, Roe Di Bona."; p. 469: © Cary Wolkinsky/Stock Boston; p. 475 top: © Jamie Villasseca/The Image Bank; background: © David Frazier Photolibrary; p. 476: © William Hopkins; p. 477 top: Douglas J. Fischer/The Image Bank; bottom: Four by Five; p. 478A: © David Frazier Photolibrary; B: © 1992 Lawrence Migdale; p. 480A: Obremski/The Image Bank; B:

© David Frazier Photolibrary; p. 481 left: Roy Morsch/The Stock Market; right: Comstock; 15.5B: © John Elk, III; p. 483 left: Courtesy Dr. Richard Brislin; right: © John Bowen

Chapter 16

Opener: © Four by Five; Page 490: AP/Wide World Photos; Figure 16.1B: © Stephen Wilkes/The Image Bank; p. 492 bottom: © Paul Miller/Light Images; p. 493: © Arthur Grace/Stock Boston; 16.2B: © Jeff Smith/The Image Bank; 16.3B: William Vandivert and Scientific American; 16.4A&B: Courtesy of Philip Zimbardo, Stanford University; 16.5A&B: © 1965 by Stanley Milgram. From the film "Obedience" distributed by the Pennsylvania State University, PCR; p. 500: AP/Wide World Photos; p. 502: © Merrell Wood/The Image Bank; p. 504 top: © Joel Gordon; bottom: © Miguel/The Image Bank; 16.7B: © Robert Farber/The Image Bank; C: © Elyse Lewin/The Image Bank; D: © Benn Mitchell/The Image Bank; p. 507: © Brett Froomer/The Image Bank; p. 509 top: © Michael Edrington/The Image Works, Inc.; middle: © Andrea Pistolesi/The Image Bank; bottom: © J. Marc/Loubat-Vandystadt/Photo Researchers, Inc.; p. 510 top: AP/Wide World Photos; bottom: © Alberto Garcia/Gamma Liaison; p. 511A: © Larry Kolvoord/The Image Works, Inc.; B: © Bob Daemmrich/The Image Works, Inc.; C: © Bill Gillette/Stock Boston; D: © Ellis Herwig/The Picture Cube; p. 513: © Cleo Freelance Photography; p. 515: Andy Levine/Photo Researchers, Inc.; p. 516 left: David Frazier Photolibrary; right: Four by Five; p. 517: © Janeart, LTD/The Image Bank

Epilogue

Opener: © Marc Romanelli/The Image Bank; Page 526 top: © Superstock; bottom: Bruce Coleman; p. 527: © Ellis Herwig/Stock Boston; p. 530 top left: © Fuji Fotos/The Image Works, Inc.; top right: © Derek Berwin/The Image Bank; bottom left: Superstock; bottom right: © Cameramann/The Image Works, Inc.

Appendix

Page 542: © Francois Gohier/Photo Researchers, Inc.

Line Art/Text

Prologue

Page xxiv: From Pauk, Walter, *How to Study in College*, Fourth Edition. Copyright © 1989 by Houghton Mifflin Company. Used with permission.

Chapter 2

Figure 2.13: Figure from *Functional Neuroscience* by Michael S. Gazzaniga et al. Copyright © 1979 by Harper & Row, Publishers, Inc. Reprinted by permission of HarperCollins Publishers. 2.16: Adapted from John W. Hole, Jr., *Human Anatomy and Physiology*, 5th ed. Copyright ©

1990 Wm. C. Brown Publishers, Dubuque, Iowa. All Rights Reserved. Reprinted by permission. 2.23: From *The Neurosciences: A Third Study Program*, edited by Schmitt and Worden. Copyright © 1974 MIT Press, Cambridge, MA. Reprinted by permission.

Chapter 3

Figure 3.10: Figure from *Introduction to Psychology*, Seventh Edition, by Ernest R. Hilgard, Rita L. Atkinson and Richard C. Atkinson, copyright © 1979 by Harcourt Brace Jovanovich, Inc., reprinted by permission of the publisher. 3.15A: Adapted from John W. Hole, Jr., *Human Anatomy and Physiology*, 5th ed. Copyright © 1990 Wm. C. Brown Publishers, Dubuque, Iowa. All Rights Reserved. Reprinted by permission. 3.17: From Dodge L. Fernald and Peter S. Fernald, *Introduction to Psychology*, 5th ed. Copyright © 1985 Wm. C. Brown Publishers, Dubuque, Iowa. All Rights Reserved. Reprinted by permission. 3.20: Figures from *Fundamentals of Child Development*, Second Edition, by Harry Munsinger, copyright © 1975 by Holt, Rinehart and Winston, Inc., reprinted by permission of the publisher. 3.24: From Gibson, James J., *The Perception of the Visual World*. Copyright © 1977, 1950 by Houghton Mifflin Company. Used with permission. 3.31: From R. L. Gregory and J. C. Wallace, "Recovery from Early Blindness," *Experimental Psychological Society Monograph*, No. 2. Copyright © 1963 Cambridge University Press. Reprinted by permission.

Chapter 4

Figure 4.4: From R. J. Berger, "The Sleep and Dream Cycle," in A. Kales, *Sleep: Physiology and Pathology*, pp. 17–32. Copyright © 1969 J.B. Lippincott Company. Reprinted by permission of Anthony Kales, MD.

Chapter 5

Figure 5.1B: Adapted from Benjamin B. Lahey, *Psychology: An Introduction*, 3d ed. Copyright © 1989 Wm. C. Brown Publishers, Dubuque, Iowa. All Rights Reserved. Reprinted by permission. 5.6: From W. N. Dember, J. J. Jenkins, and T. Teyler, *General Psychology*, 2d ed. Copyright © 1984 Lawrence Erlbaum Associates, Inc. Reprinted by permission. 5.7: Source: E. L. Thorndike (1898), "Animal Intelligence: An Experimental Study of the Associative Process in Animals," in *Psychological Review Monograph Supplement*, 2(4, Whole No. 8). 5.10: Source: B. F. Skinner, "Pigeons in a Pelican," *American Psychologist* 5:28–37. Copyright © 1960 American Psychological Association. 5.12: From P. Chance, *Learning and Behavior*. Copyright © 1979 Wadsworth Publishing Company. Used by permission. TA 5.15A: Source: Figure based on data from Paul Chance, *Learning and Behavior*, p. 24. Copyright © 1979 Wadsworth Publishing Company. 5.18: From Albert Bandura, "Influence of Model's Reinforcement Contingencies on the Acquisition of Imitative Response," in *Journal of Personality and Social Psychology* 1:589–595.

Copyright © 1965 by the American Psychological Association. Reprinted by permission. 5.21A&B: Source: E. C. Tolman, et al., "Studies in Spacial Learning I: Orientation and Short-cut" in *Journal of Experimental Psychology*, 36:13–24. Copyright © 1946 by the American Psychological Association. 5.A: From G. B. Saxe, "Body Parts as Numerals: A Developmental Analysis of Numeration Among the Oksapmin in Papua, New Guinea," in *Child Development* 52:306–316. Copyright © 1981 Society for Research in Child Development. Reprinted by permission. 5.B (left): From *Child Development and Education in Japan*, ed. H. W. Stevenson, et al. Copyright © 1986 by W.H. Freeman and Company. Reprinted by permission.

Chapter 6

Figure 6.8: From Gordon H. Bower, "Organizational Factors in Memory," in *Cognitive Psychology* 1:18–46. Copyright © 1970 Academic Press, Orlando, FL. Reprinted by permission of the publisher and author. 6.9: From Bennett B. Murdock, *Human Memory: Theory and Data*. Copyright © 1974 Lawrence Erlbaum Associates, Inc. Reprinted by permission. 6.12: From A. M. Collins and M. R. Quillan, "Retrieval Time from Semantic Memory," in *Journal of Verbal Learning and Verbal Behavior* 3L240-248. Copyright © 1969 Academic Press. Reprinted with permission. 6.13: From Roy Lachman, et al., *Cognitive Psychology and Information Processing: An Introduction*. Copyright © 1979 Lawrence Erlbaum Associates, Inc. Reprinted by permission. 6.14 (left): From Roger C. Schank and Robert P. Abelson, *Scripts, Plans, Goals and Understanding*. Copyright © 1976 Lawrence Erlbaum Associates, Inc. Reprinted by permission.

Chapter 7

Figure 7.2: From Danny R. Moates and Gary M. Schumacher, *An Introduction to Cognitive Psychology*. Copyright © 1980 Wadsworth Publishing Company. Used by permission. 7.16: Reprinted by permission of J. W. Berry. 7.18: Figure A5 from the Raven *Standard Progressive Matrices*. Copyright © J. C. Raven Limited. Reprinted by permission.

Chapter 8

Figure 8.12A: Joshua Nove/Dennie Palmer Wolf. Used by permission. 8.12B: Reprinted with permission of Ellen Winner.

Chapter 9

Lyrics on p. 258: "Time in a Bottle" by Jim Croce © 1971, 1972 Denjac Music Co. USED BY PERMISSION ALL RIGHTS RESERVED. Figure 9.1A (top): From A. F. Roche, "Secular Trends in Human Growth, Maturation and Development," in *Monographs of the Society for Research in Child Development*, Series 179, 44:20. Copyright © 1979 The Society for Research in Child Development, Inc. Reprinted by permission. 9.2 (top): From J. M. Tanner, et al., "Standards from Birth to Maturity for Height, Weight, Height Velocity and Weight Velocity: British Children, 1965," in *Archives of Disease in Childhood*, vol. 41, fig. 10.2. Copyright © 1966 the British Medical Journal. Used by permission. 9.3: From D. Blythe et al., "The Impact of Puberty on Adolescence: A Longitudinal Study," in *Girls at Puberty* edited by Jeanne Brooks-Gunn and A. Peterson. Copyright © 1981 Plenum Publishing Corporation. Used by permission. 9.7: Sources: U.S. Census data; Social Security Administration: *The Statistical History of the United States*, 1976. 9.8A (left): From *The Seasons of a Man's Life* by Daniel J. Levinson et al. Copyright © 1978 by Daniel J. Levinson. Reprinted by permission of Alfred A. Knopf, Inc. 9.9A (right): From P. M. Passuth, D. R. Maines, and B. L. Neugarten, "Age Norms and Age Constraints Twenty Years Later," paper presented at annual meeting of Midwest Sociological Society, Chicago, April 1984. Used by permission.

Chapter 10

Figure 10.4: From Janet S. Hyde et al., "Gender Differences in Mathematics Performance," in *Psychological Bulletin* 107:139–155. Copyright © 1990 by the American Psychological Association. Reprinted by permission. 10.8: From W. H. Masters and V. E. Johnson, *Human Sexual Response*. Copyright © 1966. Reprinted by permission of Masters and Johnson.

Chapter 11

Figure 11.1: Source: Abraham Maslow, *Motivation and Personality*, 2d ed. Copyright © 1970 by Abraham H. Maslow. 11.2: From W. B. Cannon, "Hunger and Thirst," in *The Foundations of Experimental Psychology*, edited by C. Murchison. Copyright © 1928 Clark University Press. Reprinted by permission. 11.3B: Reprinted from the 1961 *Nebraska Symposium on Motivation*, by permission of University of Nebraska Press. Copyright © 1961 by the University of Nebraska Press. 11.7: From M. R. Lepper, D. Greene, and R. E. Nisbett, "Undermining Children's Intrinsic Interest with Extrinsic Rewards," in *Journal of Personality and Social Psychology* 28:134. Copyright © 1973 by the American Psychological Association. Reprinted by permission.

Chapter 12

Figure 12.1: From *Psychology: A Scientific Study of Human Behavior*, 5th Ed. by L. S. Wrightsman and C. K. Sigelman. © 1979 by Wadsworth, Inc. Reprinted by permission of Brooks/Cole Publishing Company, Pacific Grove, CA 93950. 12.4: Source: Abraham Maslow, "A Theory of Human Motivation" in *Motivation and Personality*, 2d ed. Copyright © 1970 by Abraham H. Maslow. Text on p. 379: *Cosmopolitan*, September 1976. Used by permission. 12.5: Reprinted by courtesy of Dr. Hans J. Eysenck, London, England. 12.9: From Neil S. Jacobson, et al., "Toward a Behavioral Profile of Marital Distress," in *Journal of Consulting and Clinical Psychology* 48:696–703. Copyright © 1980 by the American Psychological Association. Adapted by permission.

Chapter 13

Figure 13.4: Reprinted with permission from *DSM-III Training Guide*, edited by Linda J. Webb, et al. Copyright © 1981 Brunner/Mazel, Inc., New York, NY. 13.7: From I. I. Gottesman and J. Shields, *The Schizophrenic Puzzle*. Copyright © 1982 Cambridge University Press. Used by permission.

Chapter 14

Illustration on p. 425: Source: National Library of Medicine.

Chapter 16

Figure 16.3A: Source: S. E. Asch, "Studies of Independence and Conformity: A Minority of One Against a Unanimous Majority" in *Psychological Monographs*, 90, Whole no. 416. Copyright © 1956 by the American Psychological Association. 16.7: Source: Data from R. J. Sternberg, *The Triangle of Love*. Copyright © 1988 Basic Books Inc.

Appendix

Figure A.1: Source: Data from Wayne Weiten, *Psychology Applied to Modern Life: Adjustment in the 1980's*, 2d ed. Copyright © 1983 Wadsworth Publishing Company.

Illustrator

Illustrious, Inc.

P.1, 1.2, 1.3, 1.4, 1.5, 1.7, 1.8, 1.9, 2.2, 2.3, 2.4, 2.5, 2.6, 2.7, 2.8, 2.11, 2.12, 2.13, 2.14, 2.16, 2.17, 2.18, 2.23, 3.1, 3.2, 3.3, 3.5, 3.6, 3.A, 3.11, 3.12, 3.13, 3.15, 3.20, 3.24, 3.25, 3.26, 3.27, 3.29, 4.1, 4.2, 4.4, 5.1, 5.2, 5.3, 5.4, 5.5, 5.6, 5.7, 5.8, 5.9, 5.A, 5.B, 5.10, 5.12, 5.13, 5.14, 5.15, 5.16, 5.18, 5.19, 5.20, 5.21, 6.1, 6.2, 6.3, 6.4, 6.5, 6.6, 6.7, 6.8, 6.9, 6.10, 6.11, 6.12, 6.13, 6.14, 7.1, 7.2, 7.3, 7.4, 7.5, 7.6, 7.7, 7.8, 7.9, 7.13, 7.14, 7.16, 7.18, TA 7.11, 8.1, 8.11, 8.13, 8.14, 8.15, 8.16, 8.17, 8.18, 8.19, 8.22, 8.23, 8.24, 9.1, 9.2, 9.3, 9.4, 9.5, 9.7, 9.8, 9.9, 9.10, 10.1, 10.2, 10.3, 10.4, 10.5, 10.6, 10.7, 10.8, 11.1, 11.2, 11.3, 11.5, 11.7, 11.8, 11.9, 11.11, 12.1, 12.4, 12.5, 12.6, 12.9, 12.10, 13.1, 13.2, 13.4, 13.7, 14.3, 14.4, 14.5, 15.1, 15.2, 15.3, 15.5, 16.1, 16.2, 16.3, 16.6, 16.7, A.1, A.2, A.3, A.4, A.5, A.6, A.7, A.8

NAME INDEX

A

Abel, E. L., 220
Abelson, R., 168–169
Aber, L., 259–260
Aboud, F., 510
Abramson, L. Y., 413
Achmon, J., 468
Adams, G. R., 262
Adelmann, P. K., 355
Adler, A., 368, 371–372, 389
Adler, T., 38
Agras, W. S., 431
Ahlstrom, P. A., 259
Ainsworth, M. D. S., 236, 237
Alan Guttmacher Institute, 274
Albee, G. W., 33, 402
Albert, R. D., 5, 6, 14
Alberti, R. E., 470
Alcock, J. E., 96
Aldrich, M. S., 109
Ali, M., 510
Alibbai, N., 503
Alipura, L. L., 270
Al-Issa, I., 397, 404
Allen, D., 443
Allen, L., 117, 244, 260, 274, 376, 399, 474
Allison, S., 280
Allison, S. T., 501
Alloy, L. B., 413
Allport, G. W., 13, 379, 388, 389
Allred, K. D., 458
Alpert, R., 287
Altman, D. G., 479
Alvarez, R., 440
Amaro, H., 400
Amato, P. R., 284
American College Health Association, 326
Ames, C., 344
Ames, M. A., 320
Ames, R., 344
Amoore, J. E., 82
Amsterdam, J. D., 447

Anastasi, A., 201, 207
Anderson, B. L., 321
Anderson, E. A., 281
Anderson, E. R., 244
Anderson, J. R., 9
Anderson, N., 481
Anderson, N. H., 495
Andreasen, N. C., 402
Andres, R., 473
Anson, C. A., 141
Aponte, H., 437
Aquino, C., 510
Arce, C. Y., 314
Archer, S. I., 269
Arend, R. A., 237
Argondizza, M., 249
Aristotle, 7, 40, 108, 146
Armsden, G. G., 265
Arnold, R., 364
Aron, A., 356
Aronson, E., 460, 491, 513
Asch, S., 497
Ashburn, S. S., 225
Asher, J., 189
Asher, S. R., 245
Asian Week, 16, 524
Atchley, R. C., 289
Atkinson, D. R., 24, 41, 442, 443
Atkinson, J. W., 343
Atkinson, R. C., 161
Austin, N., 470
Avis, H., 115
Ayers-Lopez, S., 265

B

Baars, B. J., 102
Baca Zinn, M., 314
Bachman, J., 118, 277
Bachman, J. G., 116, 118, 268, 473
Bach y Rita, G., 411
Bacon, M. K., 346
Baddeley, A. D., 154, 162, 163
Baer, D. M., 136

Baghdoyan, H. A., 109
Bagley, C., 417
Baglioni, A. J., 458
Bahr, S. J., 290
Bahrick, H. P., 155
Bahrick, P. O., 155
Bakai, D. A., 456
Baker, R., 403
Ball, S., 124
Baller, W., 91
Baltes, M. M., 280
Baltes, P. B., 280
Bandura, A., 13, 20, 138, 139, 142, 311, 374, 388, 389, 426, 431, 433, 466, 491, 500
Barber, B. L., 244
Barber, T. X., 114
Bard, P., 355
Barlow, D. H., 403
Barnard, C., 17
Barnard, E. A., 48
Barnes, M., 503
Barnett, R. C., 311, 463, 465
Barnouw, V., 110
Barnum, P. T., 384
Baron, R. A., 382
Barron, F., 209
Barry, H., 346
Bartlett, F. C., 166–167
Baruch, C., 237
Baruch, G. K., 311, 463, 465
Basoglu, M., 321
Bass, D. M., 294
Bateson, P., 29
Batson, C. D., 501
Bauer, G. P., 428
Baumeister, R. F., 467
Baumrind, D., 240, 348
Beach, F., 503
Beals, D. E., 194
Beck, A. T., 413, 433, 434, 442
Beckwith, L., 201, 221
Beethoven, L. van, 378
Beidel, D. C., 404
Beilin, H., 231

H

Hagan, M. S., 244
Hahn, A., 268
Hakuta, K., 194
Haley, J., 436
Hall, C. C. I., 311, 312
Hall, G. S., 258, 265
Halmi, D., 474
Halverson, C. F., 303
Hamilton, V. L., 9, 380
Han, G., 514
Hansell, S., 286
Hanson, E., 265
Hare-Muston, R., 309, 445
Harkness, S., 241
Harlow, H. F., 236
Harold, R. D., 349, 350
Harold-Goldsmith, R., 348
Harom, W., 494
Harris, P. R., 525
Harris, R. A., 115
Harris, R. F., 136
Harris, R. J., 124, 170
Harris, T., 463
Harrison, C. A., 290
Harter, S., 270
Hartmann, E., 109
Hartup, W. W., 245
Harvey, J. H., 496
Harvey, M., 402
Harwood, L. J., 224
Hasher, L., 158
Haskins, R., 247, 249
Hass, R. G., 512
Hatfield, E., 355, 503
Hatvany, N., 515
Hayflick, L., 278
Haynes, G. S., 465
Haynes, S. G., 463
Healy, J. M., 286
Heath, D., 117
Heath, S. B., 191, 243
Heider, F., 496
Heimberg, R. G., 136, 404
Hein, K., 326
Heinicke, C. M., 201
Hellige, J. B., 57
Helmreich, R., 308
Helms, J. E., 269, 270
Hemingway, E., 396, 409
Hemingway, H., 396
Hemingway, P., 396
Hendry, J., 248
Heninger, G. R., 403
Hensley, D. L., 170
Herbert, J., 24
Hering, E., 74
Herman, C. P., 475
Hernandez, D. J., 281
Hernandez, G. G., 289
Heron, W., 342, 343
Herron, D. G., 244
Hersen, M., 388
Hershenson, M., 90

Herskovits, M. J., 92
Herzog, E., 302
Hess, R. S., 443
Heston, L. L., 405
Hetherington, E. M., 5, 244
Heyns, B., 244
Hilgard, E. R., 113–114
Hill, A., 323
Hill, J. P., 265
Himle, J. A., 404
Hinckley, J., 419
Hinde, R. A., 41
Hines, M., 300
Hines, T. M., 96
Hinton, R., 111
Hippocrates, 379, 424
Hirsch, E. D., 171
Ho, M. K., 11
Hobbs, S. A., 506
Hobfoll, S. E., 456, 457
Hobson, J. A., 109, 110
Hockenbury, D., 506
Hodapp, R. M., 208
Hofferth, S. L., 239
Hoffman, J. M., 349
Hoffman, L. W., 349
Hofstadter, L., 66
Hofstede, G., 5, 380
Hogan, J., 458
Hogan, R., 380
Hogness, D. S., 74
Hollingshead, A. B., 400
Holmbeck, G., 265
Holmes, D. S., 468
Holmes, T. H., 286, 461
Holtzmann, W., 346
Homiak, J. P., 474
Hooks, B., 311
Hooper, F. H., 241
Hooper, J. O., 241
Horner, M., 344
Horney, K., 13, 368, 370–371
Horowitz, F. D., 217, 252
Horowitz, M. J., 372
Hosli, L., 108
Houts, A. C., 431
Howard, J., 221
Howard, R., 13, 33
Howat, P. M., 476
Howe, E., 110
Hsu, J., 414
Huang, L. N., 203, 250, 266, 314, 315, 346, 398, 442, 464
Hubel, D. H., 72
Hudson, W., 94
Hughes, E. C., 44
Hughes, S. O., 265, 401
Hui, C. H., 380, 382
Hultsch, D. F., 286
Hunt, E., 178
Hunt, M., 319, 320
Hurvich, L. M., 76
Huston, A. C., 302, 349
Hyde, J. S., 5, 17, 304, 305, 308, 524
Hyde, T. S., 159
Hynd, G. W., 399

I

Iacocca, L., 364
Ickovics, J. R., 11, 463, 465, 518
Ikels, C., 290
Ilola, L. M., 479, 482
Inclan, J. E., 244
Irons, E. E., 517
Irvine, M. J., 27
Irvine, S. H., 94, 202
Isenberg, K. E., 49
Ismail, A. H., 477

J

Jack, R., 411
Jacklin, C., 13
Jacklin, C. N., 5, 302, 305, 524
Jackson, J., 492
Jackson, J. S., 44, 270
Jacobs, M. K., 437
Jacobsen, L., 207
Jacobson, N. S., 387, 436
Jahoda, G., 263
James, W., 7, 13, 102, 223, 288, 354, 378
Jameson, D., 76
Janis, I., 509
Janoff-Bulman, R. J., 352
Janos, P. M., 208
Jay, G., 289
Jenkins, J. J., 159
Jensen, A. R., 200–201
Johnson, C., 313
Johnson, J., 400
Johnson, M., 327
Johnson, V., 318
Johnson-Laird, P. N., 178
Johnston, L., 118, 277
Johnston, L. D., 116, 473
Jones, A., 399
Jones, B. E., 108
Jones, G., 33
Jones, J., 442
Jones, J. M., 11, 15, 17, 33, 44, 243, 523, 528
Jones, J. W., 490
Jones, M. C., 128, 261
Jones, W. H., 506
Jordan, M., 344–345, 493
Josselson, R., 311
Joyce, P. R., 413
Joyner, F. G., 277
Jung, C., 388, 389
Jung, C. G., 368
Just, M. A., 157

K

Kaczmarek, L. K., 46
Kagan, J., 237, 239
Kagan, S., 346
Kagan, S. L., 2, 247, 249
Kagitcibasi, C., 7, 94, 202, 380
Kahn, S., 458
Kail, R., 195
Kaler, S. R., 220, 221

SUBJECT INDEX

A

Abnormal behavior, 395–420
  anxiety disorders and, 403–406
  causes of, 396–399
  classification of, 399–402
  culture-bound, 397
  definition of, 396
  dissociative disorders, 407–408
  legal aspects of, 418–419
  mood disorders, 409–414
  personality disorders, 418
  schizophrenic disorders, 414–417
  somatoform disorders, 406–407
  substance-use disorders, 418
Absolute threshold, 66–67
Accommodation, 226
Acculturation, 462–463, 464
Acculturative stress, 462–463, 464
Accurate empathy, 429
Acetylcholine (ACh), 49, 50
Achievement. See Competence and achievement
Achievement motivation, 343–344
  intrinsic and extrinsic, 344
Acquaintance rape, 323
Acquired immunodeficiency syndrome (AIDS), 320, 326–327
  neuroimmunological factors and, 458
Acrophobia, 405
Action potential, 47
Activating system, sleep and, 108
Activation-synthesis view of dreams, 110
Activity, in late adulthood, 277–278
Activity theory, 289
Acupuncture, 79, 82
Adaptation
  culture and intelligence and, 202–203
  sensory, 69
Adaptation phase of acculturation, 462
Addiction
  to drugs, 115
  to smoking, 472–473
Additive mixture of color, 73
Adolescence, 258–275

cognitive development during, 262–264
culture and, 274–275
early- and late-maturing adolescents, 261–262
exercise in, 478
historical beginnings and nature of, 358–360
identity development during, 268–271, 272
moral development during, 271, 273–274
parent-adolescent relationships during, 265, 266
peer relationships during, 365–366
physical development during, 260–262
pregnancy during, 274–275
problem behaviors in males during, 309
school and, 266–268
social development during, 264–275
storm and stress view of, 258
Adolescent egocentrism, 263
Adrenal glands, 60–61
Adrenaline (epinephrine), 60
Adulthood, 276–293. See also Aging; Early adulthood; Late adulthood; Middle adulthood
  personality development in, 284–285
Aereophobia, 405
Aerobic exercise, 476
Affectionate love, 505–506
Afferent nerves, 45
African Americans, 10, 11
  acculturative stress of, 464
  achievement and, 346, 347
  athletes, 345
  birth of, 221
  childrearing and, 243, 244
  dropout rates among, 268
  education of, 250
  health of, 479, 480–481
  identity development among, 271
  intelligence comparisons and, 201, 202
  language tradition of, 191
  in late adulthood, 289–290, 291
  male, 314
  mental disorders and, 399
  nutrition and, 474
  observational learning and, 141
  population of, 525

· prejudice and, 512
  psychotherapy and, 437, 443–444
  schizophrenia among, 417
  self-concept and, 376
  stress and, 463
  in workplace, 516, 517
African culture
  abnormal behavior and, 397
  infant motor development and, 222–223
Afterimages, 74, 75
Ageism, 289, 290
Aggressive behavior, 469
  cultural influences on, 24, 25
Aging
  biological theories of, 278
  death and dying and, 293–294
  longevity and, 278, 279
Agoraphobia, 404, 405
Agringado culture, alcohol abuse and, 117
Ailurophobia, 405
Alarm stage, of general adaptation syndrome, 457
Alcohol, 115–116, 117
  abuse of, 117, 418
  during pregnancy, 220–221, 222
Alcoholics Anonymous (AA), 437
Algophobia, 405
Algorithms, 182, 183
All-or-none principle, 47–48
Alpha waves, 103
Altered state of consciousness, 103. See also Psychoactive drugs
  religions and, 104
Altruism, 501–502
  group therapies and, 435
Alzheimer's disease, 279
Amaxophobia, 405
American Psychiatric Association, position on homosexuality, 320
American Psychological Association (APA), 455
  Committee on Ethnic Minority Affairs of, 33
  ethical guidelines of, 28–29, 500
American Psychologist, 520
Amnesia, 164–165

Critical thinking, 524–525
  knowledge base for, 524
  motivation to use thinking skills and, 525
  strategies for, 524
  using the right thinking process and, 524
Cross-cultural psychology, 31
Cross-cultural research, 23–24
Cue-dependent forgetting, 162
Cultural bias, intelligence tests and, 203
Cultural evolution, 42
  language and, 188
Cultural-familial retardation, 208
Cultural groups. *See also* Culture; Ethnicity;
      Ethnic minorities; Sociocultural
      approach; Sociocultural factors;
      Sociocultural issues; *specific groups*
  discrimination and prejudice and, 16
  diversity among, 14526
  diversity within, 14–15, 525–527
  pain perception and, 80
  similarities among, 15, 528
Cultural literacy, 171
Culture. *See also* Culture; Ethnicity; Ethnic
      minorities; Sociocultural approach;
      Sociocultural factors; Sociocultural
      issues; *specific groups*
  abnormal behavior and, 397, 399–400
  acculturative stress, 462–463, 464
  achievement and, 345–348
  adaptation and, 202, 203
  adolescents and, 274–275
  aggression and, 24, 25
  assimilation and, 462–463
  cancer and, 480–482
  changing pattern in United States, 11
  coronary problems and, 479–480
  definition of, 9
  dreams and, 110–111
  emotion and, 357–358, 359
  Freudian psychoanalytic theory and, 369
  gender roles and, 310, 314
  integration and, 463
  intelligence and, 201–206
  language and, 192–194
  late adulthood and, 290, 292
  learning and, 144–147
  marginalization and, 463
  marriage and, 282
  memory and, 170–172
  middle adulthood and, 287
  perception and, 92–94
  psychotherapy and, 442–445
  separation and, 463
  synchrony and, 241
Culture-fair tests, 203, 206, 207
Culture specificity hypothesis of memory, 170
Curare, 49
Cynophobia, 405

D

Daily hassles, 461
Dangerousness, commitment and, 418
Dani culture, language and color perception
      and, 194

Date rape, 323
Day care, 238–240
Daydreaming, 103
Death and dying, 293–294
Decay theory, 164–165
Deception, in research, 29
Decibels (dB), 77
Declarative memory, 155
Deductive reasoning, 184–185, 186
  during adolescence, 263
Defense mechanisms, 366–367
Deficiency needs, 377–378
Deindividuation, 509
Deinstitutionalization, 438
Delta waves, 103
Dendrite, 46
Deoxyribonucleic acid (DNA), 39, 44
Dependent variable, 27
Depressants, 115–116, 117
Depression
  major, 409–410
  treatment of, 447
  women and, 410
Depth perception, 86–88
Depth psychology, 371
Descriptive statistics, 534–543
  for one variable, 534–538
  for two variables, 538–543
Desensitization, systematic, 431
Detriangulation, family systems therapy and, 436
Development, 215–254. *See also* Cognitive
      development; Identity development;
      Personality development; Physical
      development; Social development
  continuity and discontinuity in, 216–217,
      287–289
  definition of, 216–219
  of language, 192
  maturation and experience, 216
  moral, 271, 273–274
  physical, 221–226
  prenatal, 219–221, 222
  social policy and, 217–219
  of social skills, group therapies and, 435
Developmentally appropriate practice, 246, 247
Developmental psychology, 31
Devil's tuning fork, 90, 91, 94
*Diagnostic and Statistical Manual of Mental
      Disorders (DSM)*, 399
  controversy surrounding, 401–402
  DSM-I, 401
  DSM-II, 401
  DSM-III, 401–402
  DSM-III-R, 401–402
Diathesis-stress view of schizophrenia, 417
Difference threshold, 68–69
Discontinuity of development, 217
  personality and, 287–289
Discrimination, 126
  in operant conditioning, 135–136
  reducing, 16, 528
Discriminative stimuli, 135–136
Disease model, 397
Disintegration stage of minority identity
      development, 270

Disorganized schizophrenia, 415
Dispersion measures, 536–537
Displacement, 367
Dissociative disorders, 407–408
Divergent thinking, 209
Divorce, 281, 284
DNA (deoxyribonucleic acid), 39, 44
Dominant-recessive genes principle, 40
Dopamine, 50
Dream analysis, 428
Dreams, 107, 110–112
  culture and, 110–111
  daydreaming and, 103
  interpretation of, 110
  lucid, 112
  manifest content of, 428
Drives, 337. *See also* Motivation; Needs
Dropouts, 268
Drugs
  antianxiety, 456
  in biomedical therapies, 446–447
  during pregnancy, 220–221, 222
  psychoactive, 114–119
  for weight loss, 475
DSM. *See Diagnostic and Statistical Manual of
      Mental Disorders*

E

Each One/Reach One Program, 141
Ear, 77, 78
  inner, 78
  middle, 78
  outer, 78
  semicircular canals of, 83, 84
Early adulthood, 276
  cognitive development in, 279–280
  physical development in, 277
  social development in, 280–289
Eating problems, 473–476
  anorexia nervosa and bulimia, 475–476
  ethnicity and, 474
  overweight and, 473–474
  weight-loss programs and, 474–475
Echoic memory, 153
Eclectic approaches to psychotherapy, 426
Ecological theory, 108
Ectomorph, 379
Education. *See also* School(s)
  Project Head Start and, 247, 249
  social development and, 245–251
  women and, 313
  of young children, 246–247, 248
Educational psychology, 31
Efferent nerves, 45
Effortful processing, 158–159
Ego, 366
Egocentrism, adolescent, 263–264
Eidetic memory, 154
Elaboration, 159
Elavil, 447
Electra complex, 369
Electroconvulsive therapy (ECT), 447–448
Electroencephalograph, 59
  sleep and, 103, 107

death and, 292–293
definition of, 300
emotion and, 358–359
ethnicity and, 311–312, 314–315
feminist perspective on, 309, 311, 313
Freudian psychoanalytic theory and, 369
gender role classification and, 307–309, 310
gender role stereotyping and, 304, 348–349
identification theory and, 302
intimacy and family work and, 283–284
late adulthood and, 290, 291
life expectancy and, 479
mental disorders and, 398, 400
middle adulthood and, 286–287
politics and, 493
psychotherapy and, 445–446
similarities and differences between sexes, 304–306
social influences on, 301–302
social learning theory of, 302
stress and, 463, 465
traditional masculinity and problem behaviors in adolescent males, 309
in workplace, 516–517
Gender bias
in medical care, 483–484
in research, 28
Gender groups. *See also* Gender; Males; Women
discrimination and prejudice and, 16
diversity among, 14–15, 526–527
diversity within, 14, 525
similarities among, 15, 528
Gender identity, 300
Gender roles, 300, 307–309
androgyny and, 308–309, 310
culture and, 310, 314
historical perspective on, 307–308
stereotypes and, 304, 348–349
transcendence of, 309
Gender schema, 303
Gender schema theory, 303–304
General adaptation syndrome (GAS), 457
Generalization, 126
in operant conditioning, 135
Generalized anxiety disorder, 403
Generativity versus stagnation, 284
Genes, 39–40, 44
dominant-recessive genes principle, 40
Genetic factors
in mood disorders, 413
in schizophrenia, 416
Genetics, 38, 39–40. *See also* Heredity-environment controversy
Genital stage, 368, 370
Genuineness, 377
Gestalt psychology, 85–86, 87
Gestalt therapy, 429–430
Giftedness, 208–209
Giving, psychotherapy and, 444, 445
Glove anesthesia, 407
Gonorrhea, 325
"Good patient" role, 471
Government interventions, preventive health care and, 482–483
Great person theory, 509–510
Grey matter. *See* Neocortex

GRIT (Graduated and Reciprocated Initiatives in Tension-Reduction) strategy, 513–514
Group(s). *See also* Group relations; Group therapies; Intergroup relations
informal, 514, 516
workers in, 514–516
Group relations, 508–510
deindividuation and, 509
groupthink and, 509
leadership and, 509–510
majority-minority influence and, 510
motivation for group behavior and structure of groups, 508–509
Group therapies, 435–438
family and couple therapy, 435–436 437
personal growth and self-help groups, 436–438
Groupthink, 509
Growth hormone (GH), 60
Gusii culture, life events in, 287
Gustatory sense, 80, 81
Gynephobia, 405

H

Haitian Americans
nutrition and, 474
pain perception and, 80
Hallucinogens, 118
Happiness, 351–352
Hardiness, 458
Harmful adaptation, in feminist therapy, 446
Health
culture and, 479–483
effects of exercise on, 476–477
in middle adulthood, 277
Health insurance, classification of mental disorders, 402
Health maintenance, in feminist therapy, 446
Health promotion, 472–483
culture and, 479–483
eating problems and, 473–476
ethnic minorities and, 480–481
exercise and, 476–479
government interventions and, 482–483
smoking and, 472–473
Health psychology, 453–486. *See also* Health promotion; Stress
coping with illness, 471–472
scope of, 455–456
women's health issues, 483–484
Hearing. *See* Auditory system
Helplessness, learned, 413
Hemispheres, 54
split-brain research and, 56–58
Heredity-environment controversy, 41, 42
intelligence and, 200–201
Herpes genitalis, 325–326
Heterosexual attitudes and behavior, 318–319
Heuristics, 182–183
Hidden observer, 113–114
Hierarchy
memory and, 160
of motives, 337, 338
of needs, 377–378
Hindbrain, 51

Hispanic Americans, 11, 525
acculturative stress of, 464
achievement and, 346, 347
childrearing and, 243
community psychology approaches for, 440
dreams and, 111
dropout rates among, 268
education of, 250
female, 314
health promotion and, 480–481
identity development among, 271
intelligence comparisons and, 201, 202
in late adulthood, 289–290
male, 315
mental disorders and, 399, 400
nutrition and, 474
observational learning and, 141
population of, 525
psychotherapy and, 443, 444
stress and, 463
suicide among, 411–412
Hispanic Journal of Behavioral Science, 33
Histogram, 534, 535
Holland, sex education and attitudes in, 328
Holmes-Rahe scale, 461
Holophrase hypothesis of language development, 192
Homeostasis, 337
Homosexuality
homosexual attitudes and behavior, 319–321
as mental disorder, 320, 402
Honolulu Heart Study, 479
Horizontal-vertical illusion, 90
Hormones, 60–61
Hue, 73
Humanistic perspective, 9
on personality, 375–378, 389
Humanistic therapies, 429–430, 434, 445
Gestalt, 429–430
person-centered, 429
Human sexual response, 316–318
cycle of, 318, 319
sexual arousal and, 316–317
Hunger, 340–342
external cues and, 341
physiological factors and, 340–341
self-control and exercise and, 341–342
Huntington's chorea, 48–49
Hydrophobia, 405
Hypnosis, 113–114
applications of, 114
features of , 113
individual differences in, 113
theories of, 113–114
Hypochondriasis, 406–407
Hypothalamus, 53, 60
ventromedial, 340–341
Hypothetical-deductive reasoning, 263

I

Iatmul culture, intelligence and, 203
Iconic memory, 153
Id, 366
Identification theory, 302

Nerve impulses, 46–48
Nervous system, 44–50
  autonomic, 45
  central, 44, 53. *See also* Brain
  neurons and, 45–50
  organization of, 44–45
  parasympathetic, 45
  peripheral, 44–45
  somatic, 45
  sympathetic, 45
Network theories of memory, 165–166 167
Neurobiological approach, 9
Neurobiological factors, in schizophrenia, 416
Neuroleptic drugs, 447
Neurons, 44, 45–50
  afferent (sensory), 45
  efferent (motor), 45
  interneurons and, 46
  memory and, 169–170
  nerve impulses and, 46–48
  structure of, 46
  synapses and neurotransmitters, 48–50
Neuroticism, 401
Neurotransmitters, 48–50
  mood disorders and, 413, 447
Newborn, 221
Nicotine. *See also* Smoking
  during pregnancy, 222
  sleep and, 109
Nightmares, 109
Night terrors, 102, 109
Noise, perception and, 67
Nonassertive behavior, 469
Nonsexist therapy, 446
Nonstate view of hypnosis, 114
Norepinephrine (noradrenaline), 49–50, 60–61
  mood disorders and, 413
Norm(s)
  of group, 509
  for tests, 197
Normal distribution, 198, 538, 539
Nuclear magnetic resonance (NMR), 59
Nurture, 41
Nutrition
  ethnic minorities and, 474
  during infancy, 223–225
Nyctophobia, 405

O

Obedience, 498–500
Object permanence, 227–228
Observation, 20, 22
  naturalistic, 20, 22
  systematic, 543
Observational learning, 124, 138–140, 141
Obsessive-compulsive disorder (OCD), 405–406
Occipital lobe, 54
Oedipus complex, 368, 369
Oksapmin culture, learning math and, 146, 147
Olfactory epithelium, 82
Olfactory sense, 80, 81–82, 83
Operant conditioning, 129–138
  applications of, 136–138
  behavior therapies based on, 432

classical conditioning compared with, 129
  principles of, 132–136
  Skinnerian behaviorism and, 130–132 133
  Thorndike's law of effect and, 130
Operations, 228
Opiates, 116
Opium, 50, 116
Opponent-process theory
  of color vision, 74, 76
  of emotion, 355
Optic chiasm, 72
Optic nerve, 72
Oral stage, 367, 368, 370
Organic retardation, 208
Organizational behavior, 514–518
  changing faces and places of organizations and, 517–518
  gender and ethnicity and, 516–517
  industrial/organizational psychology and, 514
  Japanese management style and, 515
  workers in groups and, 514–516
Organ of Corti, 78
Orgasm, 318
Outer ear, 78
Oval window, 78
Ovaries, 60
Overcompensation, 372
Overweight, 473–474
  weight-loss programs and, 437, 474–475, 508

P

Pain, perception of, 79, 80, 81, 82
Pain threshold, 79
Palmistry, 383–384
Pancreas, 60
Panic disorder, 403
Papillae, 81
Paranoid schizophrenia, 415–416
Paraphilias, 321–322
Parasympathetic nervous system, 45
Parathyroid glands, 60
Parent(s), achievement and, 349–350
Parent-child relationships, 240–242
  adolescents and, 265, 266
  father's role and, 242
  parenting styles and, 240–242
Parents Without Partners, 437
Parietal lobe, 54
Parkinson's disease, 51
Partial reinforcement, 134
Passionate love, 504–505, 506
Patient's role, 471
Pedophilia, 322
Peer relationships, 345
  during adolescence, 265–266
Peg method, 172
Penis envy, 369
Perception, 85–96
  culture and, 92–94
  definition of, 66
  of depth, 86–88
  extrasensory, 94–96
  illusions and, 90, 91
  during infancy, 223

innate versus learned nature of, 90–94
  perceptual constancy and, 88–90
  of shape, 85–86, 87
  social, 495–496
  subliminal, 68
Perceptual constancy, 88–90
Performance, learning compared with, 139
Peripheral cues, hunger and, 341
Peripheral nervous system, 44–45
Permissive-indifferent parenting, 241
Permissive-indulgent parenting, 241
Personal growth groups, 436–437
Personality, 363–391. *See also* Personality assessment; Personality development
  Adler's individual psychology of, 371–372
  behaviorist approach to, 373–374
  comparison of theories of, 388–389
  definition of, 364–365
  Freudian theory of, 365–368, 369–370
  hardiness and, 458
  Horney's sociocultural approach to, 369, 370–371
  Jung's depth psychology of, 371
  Maslow's approach to, 377–378
  multiple, 407–408
  personality type theory of, 379
  phenomenological and humanistic perspectives on, 375–378
  psychoanalytic perspectives on, 365–372
  Rogers' approach to, 375–377
  self-defeating, 402
  social learning theory and, 374
  stress and, 458
  structure of, 365–366
  trait theories of, 379–383
  type A, 458
Personality assessment, 383–388
  behavioral, 387–388
  Minnesota Multiphasic Personality Inventory, 386
  projective tests and, 384
  Rorschach Inkblot Test and, 384
  self-report tests and, 385–387
  Thematic Apperception Test and, 384–385
Personality development, 367–368, 369–370
  in adulthood, 284–285
  continuity and discontinuity in, 287–289
Personality disorders, 418
Personality psychology, 31
Personality type theory, 379
Person-centered therapy, 429
Persuasion, 491–494
  communicator and, 492–493
  medium and, 494
  message and, 494
  target and, 494
PET scan (positron-emission tomography), 59
Phallic stage, 367–368, 369, 370
Phenomenological theories of personality, 375–378, 389
Philippine culture, abnormal behavior and, 397
Phobic disorders (phobias), 403–405
  classical conditioning and, 128
Phonology, 187
Physical development, 216, 221–226

addictiveness and reinforcing nature of, 472–473

preventing, 473

Social class

achievement and, 346

childrearing and, 243

mental disorders and, 398

pain perception and, 80

poverty and, 463, 465

psychotherapy and, 443–444

in schools, 250–251

stress and, 463

Social clocks, 286

Social comparison, 495

Social desirability, self-report tests and, 385

Social development, 216, 234–251

during adolescence, 264–275

attachment and, 236–238

changing American family and, 244

cultural, social class, and ethnic variations among families and, 242–244

day care and, 238–240

in early and middle adulthood, 280–289

Erikson's theory of, 234–236

in late adulthood, 289–293

parent-child relationships and, 240–242

peers and play and, 245

schools and, 245–251

Social exchange theory, 501

Social factors

in development, 216

in emotion, 357

gender and, 301–302

Social identity theory, 511

Socialization, reciprocal, 241

Social learning theory

of gender, 302

of personality, 389

personality and, 374

Social perception, 495–496

developing impressions and, 495

influencing, 496

social comparison and, 495

Social phobia, 404

Social policy, development and, 217–219

Social psychology, 31, 489–520

altruism and, 501–502

attitudes and persuasion and, 490–494

attribution and, 496, 497

close relationships and, 502–508

conformity and, 497–501

group relations and, 508–510

intergroup relations and, 510–514

organizational behavior and, 514–518

social perception and, 495–496

Social Readjustment Rating Scale, 461

Social skill development, group therapies and, 435

Social support, coping with stress and, 469

Sociobiology, 40–41

Sociocultural approach, 9–12

to abnormal behavior, 397–399, 400

to personality, 369, 370–371

Sociocultural factors. See also Cultural groups; Culture; Ethnicity; Ethnic minorities

alcohol abuse and, 117

mood disorders and, 414

motivation and, 339

schizophrenia and, 417

in stress, 461–465

Sociocultural issues, 12, 14–17, 523–532

critical thinking and, 524–525

diversity within ethnic, cultural, and gender groups, 14–15, 525–527

globalizing psychology and ethnocentrism of psychology, 16–17, 529–531

improving understanding of, 17, 532

journals to increase knowledge about, 524

multiple determination of behavior and, 17, 531

reducing discrimination and prejudice, 16, 528

sensitive ethnic, cultural, and gender issues, 17, 531

similarities among ethnic, cultural, and gender groups, 15, 528

value conflicts and, 16, 528–529

Socioeconomic status (SES). See Social class

Somatic nervous system, 45

Somatoform disorders, 406–407

Somatotype theory, 379

Somnambulism, 109

SOMPA (System of Multicultural Pluralistic Assessment), 203, 206

S-O-R model, 140, 142

Sound, 76–78

amplitude of, 77

complexity of, 78

frequency of, 77

Special process theory of hypnosis, 113–114

Split-brain research, 56–58

Spontaneous recovery, 127

Sports psychology, motivation and, 344–345

SQ3R, 172

S-R theory, 130

Standard deviation, 537

Standardization, of tests, 197

Standardized tests, 23, 197. See also Intelligence tests; Personality assessment

Stanford-Binet tests, 198

Statistical significance, 543

Statistics, 533–544

descriptive, 534–543

inferential, 543

Stereotypes

gender role, 304

intergroup relations and, 510–511

Stimulants, 116, 118

Stimulus

conditioned, 125

unconditioned, 125

Stirrup, 78

Stomach, hunger and, 341

Storm and stress view, of adolescence, 258

Stream of consciousness, 102

Stress, 456–470

body's response to, 457–458

cognitive factors in, 458–459

coping with, 466–470

environmental factors in, 460–461

personality factors in, 458

sociocultural factors in, 461–465

Striving for superiority, 371

Structural change, family systems therapy and, 436

Study strategies, 172

Sublimation, 367

Subliminal perception, 68

Substance-use disorders, 117, 418

Subtractive mixture of color, 73

Success, fear of, 344

Suicide, 396, 411–412

Superego, 366

Superiority, striving for, 371

Superiority complex, 372

Sweden, sex education and attitudes in, 328

Syllogism, 186

Symbolic racism, 512

Symbolism, in dreams, 110

Sympathetic nervous system, 45

Synapses, 48, 49

Synchrony, 241

Syntax, 188

Syphilis, 325

Systematic desensitization, 431

Systematic manipulation, 543

Systematic observation, 543

T

Tanala culture, death and dying in, 292

Tangible assistance, coping with stress and, 469

Tarahumara culture, alcohol abuse and, 117

Tardive dyskinesia, 447

Target, persuasion and, 494

Taste buds, 81

Taste sense, 80, 81

Telegraphic speech, 192

Telepathy, 95

Television

observational learning and, 141

persuasion and, 494

Temperature sense, 79

Temporal lobe, 54

Teratogen, 220

Tertiary prevention, 439

Testes, 60

Testosterone, 261

Test-retest reliability, 197

Tests, standardized, 23. See also Intelligence tests; Personality assessment

Texture gradient, 88

Thalamus, 52

Thalidomide, 220

Thanatophobia, 405

THC (delta-9-tetrahydrocannabinol), 118

Thematic Apperception Test (TAT), 384–385

Theory, 19

revising, 20

Thought, 178–186. See also Critical thinking

concept formation and, 178–181

concrete operational, 230–231, 232, 233

convergent and divergent, 209

formal operational, 262–263

positive, coping with stress and, 466–467

preoperational, 228–229, 230